AN ANALYTICAL APPROACH TO EVIDENCE

How to use your Connected Casebook

Step 1: Go to **www.CasebookConnect.com** and redeem your access code to get started.

Access Code:

STXT84388677327

Step 2: Go to your **BOOKSHELF** and select your Connected Casebook to start reading, highlighting, and taking notes in the margins of your e-book.

Step 3: Select the **STUDY** tab in your toolbar to access a variety of practice materials designed to help you master the course material. These materials may include explanations, videos, multiple-choice questions, flashcards, short answer, essays, and issue spotting.

Step 4: Select the **OUTLINE** tab in your toolbar to access chapter outlines that automatically incorporate your highlights and annotations from the e-book. Use the My Notes area for copying, pasting, and editing your book notes or creating new notes.

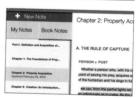

Step 5: If your professor has enrolled your class, you can select the **CLASS INSIGHTS** tab and compare your own study center results against the average of your classmates.

Is this a used casebook? Access code already scratched off?

You can purchase the Digital Version and still access all of the powerful tools listed above. Please visit CasebookConnect.com and select Catalog to learn more.

PIN: 10050801-0001 AlEvD6

AN ANALYTICAL APPROACH TO EVIDENCE

TEXT, PROBLEMS, AND CASES

Sixth Edition

RONALD J. ALLEN
John Henry Wigmore Professor of Law
Northwestern University School of Law

ELEANOR SWIFT
Professor of Law Emerita
University of California at Berkeley School of Law

DAVID S. SCHWARTZ
Foley & Lardner-Bascom Professor of Law
University of Wisconsin Law School

MICHAEL S. PARDO
Henry Upson Sims Professor of Law
University of Alabama School of Law

ALEX STEIN
Professor of Law
Benjamin N. Cardozo School of Law

Wolters Kluwer

Published by Wolters Kluwer in New York.

Wolters Kluwer Legal & Regulatory Solutions U.S. serves customers worldwide with CCH, Aspen Publishers, and Kluwer Law International products. (www.WKLegaledu.com)

To contact Customer Service, e-mail customer.service@wolterskluwer.com, call 1-800-234-1660, fax 1-800-901-9075, or mail correspondence to:

> Wolters Kluwer
> Attn: Order Department
> PO Box 990
> Frederick, MD 21705

Printed in the United States of America.

4 5 6 7 8 9 0

ISBN 978-1-4548-6298-7

Library of Congress Cataloging-in-Publication Data

Names: Allen, Ronald J. (Ronald Jay), 1948- author.
Title: An analytical approach to evidence: text, problems, and cases /
Ronald J. Allen, John Henry Wigmore Professor of Law, Northwestern
University School of Law, Eleanor Swift, Professor of Law Emerita, University of
California at Berkeley School of Law, David S. Schwartz, Foley &
Lardner-Bascom Professor of Law, University of Wisconsin Law School,
Michael S. Pardo, Henry Upson Sims Professor of Law, University of Alabama
School of Law, Alex Stein, Professor of Law, Benjamin N. Cardozo School of
  Law.
Description: Sixth edition. | New York: Wolters Kluwer, [2016]
Identifiers: LCCN 2016000011 | ISBN 9781454862987
Subjects: LCSH: Evidence (Law)—United States. | LCGFT: Casebooks.
Classification: LCC KF8935 .A53 2016 | DDC 347.73/6—dc23
LC record available at http://lccn.loc.gov/2016000011

About Wolters Kluwer Legal & Regulatory Solutions U.S.

Wolters Kluwer Legal & Regulatory Solutions U.S. delivers expert content and solutions in the areas of law, corporate compliance, health compliance, reimbursement, and legal education. Its practical solutions help customers successfully navigate the demands of a changing environment to drive their daily activities, enhance decision quality and inspire confident outcomes.

Serving customers worldwide, its legal and regulatory solutions portfolio includes products under the Aspen Publishers, CCH Incorporated, Kluwer Law International, ftwilliam.com and MediRegs names. They are regarded as exceptional and trusted resources for general legal and practice-specific knowledge, compliance and risk management, dynamic workflow solutions, and expert commentary.

SUMMARY OF CONTENTS

CONTENTS

CHAPTER NINE
LAY OPINIONS AND EXPERT WITNESSES   699

CHAPTER TEN

THE PROCESS OF PROOF IN CIVIL AND CRIMINAL CASES: BURDENS OF PROOF, JUDICIAL SUMMARY AND COMMENT, AND PRESUMPTIONS   803

Contents

PREFACE

In this sixth edition of our book, we maintain our focus on the study of evidence law through the text of the Federal Rules of Evidence and the ideas and principles that underlie those rules. The book presents the rules in a systematic format that is used consistently throughout. This format provides students with the text of the rules, interpretations and illustrations of the rules' terms, an elaboration of principles and policies used to explain and interpret the rules, illustrations from recent case law, and problems that call for the application of each significant rule in its most basic as well as its most challenging contexts.

We have returned to the book's former name, *An Analytical Approach to Evidence*, because we believe it captures one of the unique contributions of this book. This is a problem-based casebook designed to elicit a critical examination of the Federal Rules of Evidence in context and to illuminate the Rules' underlying theories and perspectives. Analysis is encouraged through explanatory text, excerpted materials, case summaries, and problems. Lively discussion and interesting problems engage students in discovering the principles, policies, and debates that surround evidence law. In every instance, although we begin with the basics, we deepen the analysis to the conceptual foundations of the particular aspects of evidence under consideration, and indeed to the conceptual foundations of the entire field.

Although the casebook text has been edited throughout, adding new excerpts from judicial opinions and scholarly work, updating the case citations that illustrate application of the rules, and adding new problems, much remains familiar. As always, we have sought throughout to present each set of problems in ascending order of difficulty—easy, medium, and difficult. This edition still includes ongoing "saga" problems that build, in successive chapters, on each developing "saga" fact pattern. These unique problems demonstrate how the rules of evidence actually apply to individual items of evidence in "layers" as students' knowledge of those rules increases.

New to this edition are:

- probing discussions of fundamental moral questions (e.g., sexual politics rules);
- enhanced focus on the way in which evidence law serves not just an epistemological function but also involves critically important allocations of authority between trial and appellate courts, between the trial judges and the parties, and others;

- emphasis on another increasingly important aspect of the law of evidence in its effects on both non-litigation ("primary") and litigation behavior;
- economic justifications for different rules of evidence;
- self-assessment questions, accompanied with answers and explanations, in each chapter;
- additional pedagogical elements, redesigned formatting, and softened notes/ questions to make the discussion less austere (without sacrificing intellectual sophistication).

As in previous editions, we have not been content to present a mass of doctrines and cases. We have endeavored instead to show, through discursive text and problems, the relationship between the theories underlying the rules and the rules themselves. This emphasis on the underlying theories reflects our view that the study of any field of law should not consist primarily of ingesting enormous amounts of doctrinal "stew." Rather, the pursuit should be gaining an understanding of the conditions that give rise to the forms of regulation of decision making that are contained in the rules of evidence.

From its inception, another factor has heavily influenced this book. We believe that the field of evidence is in large measure a coherent whole rather than an amalgam of virtually unrelated parts. Unlike traditional works on evidence, we present an analytic theme in our text that attempts to show the underlying relationships between the various common law categories of evidence. This theme is relevancy and the assumptions about decision making that inhere in a system of proof based on relevancy. With this theme in mind, we explore all of the major federal rules of evidence, requiring students to develop a systematic approach to the admission of evidence that begins with the relationship of evidentiary facts to the essential elements of the case. Only with such a beginning can one properly understand the principles governing the selection of evidence and their judicial interpretation.

We also emphasize the process by which facts are established in court, and the roles played by each of the participants in the courtroom. Chapter One begins with the study of a transcript from a real case. This introduces students to the process of analyzing evidence in terms of the essential elements of a legal dispute, as well as experiencing what is at stake in run-of-the-mill trials. We believe that the transcript serves as an effective introduction to much of the course to follow. Although accurate fact finding is the dominant goal of trial, the rules of evidence also regulate with other goals in mind, such as efficiency, fairness and incentives to out-of-court behavior. The transcript usefully illustrates these matters, and we return to it at relevant points throughout the text. We have also generated a series of problems on the transcript so that student investment in reading it pays off with a deeper understanding of the context within which isolated evidence issues arise and are resolved.

Chapter Two provides additional background information on trial process and strategy that brings the evidence course alive. After a brief introduction advising students on how to incorporate the book into their study of evidence, the chapter describes how trials are structured, how witnesses are examined, and it begins our exploration of the relationship between inferential reasoning as used by the factfinder and the process of presenting proof at trial.

Chapter Three examines the single most important concept in the study of evidence — relevance — and introduces students to the trial judge's discretion to exclude even relevant, and probative, evidence. Some judicial opinions, including the U.S.

Supreme Court's majority opinion in Old Chief v. United States, give students a more concrete understanding of how the context of the whole "case" can influence the judge's exercise of discretion.

Chapter Four discusses the foundation principle underlying evidence law: that no evidence is admissible until it is first shown to be what its proponent claims that it is. The chapter analyzes and elaborates the complex of rules from which this principle is derived, and applies the principle specifically to testimony and exhibits in various forms. Because of its close connection to documentary evidence, Chapter Four also covers the Best Evidence Rule.

Chapter Five focuses on the character and propensity rules. We start by introducing the primary rule of exclusion, the policies that justify exclusion, and the policing of the borderline between forbidden "character" and permitted "non-character" uses of specific acts. We then turn to instances in which character is a permissible topic of proof.

Chapter Six contains other relevancy rules. These rules determine the admissibility of subsequent remedial measures evidence, settlement and plea bargain discussions, availability of insurance and offers to pay an opponent's medical expenses. Our analysis of these rules separates between permissible and impermissible uses of the evidence and explains how it affects the parties' litigation conduct and primary behavior.

Chapter Seven presents the doctrines of impeaching and rehabilitating witnesses, prior to the study of the hearsay rule. The attention paid to examining witnesses, we believe, helps students better understand the hearsay rules, which we discuss in Chapter Eight.

Chapter Eight unfolds a comprehensive analysis of hearsay dangers and the hearsay doctrine. This chapter contains revised text on the problem of "implied assertions" that we think streamlines presentation without sacrificing accuracy. It also provides an up-to-date discussion of the U.S. Supreme Court's recent jurisprudence on the Confrontation Clause.

Chapter Nine, focuses on the rules governing lay and expert witness opinion testimony, and includes principal Supreme Court cases on rule 702 and the 2000 amendments to the Federal Rules. The chapter proceeds to elaborate on both practical and theoretical issues arising out of expert testimony, concluding with a substantial reflection section that features excerpts from the National Academy of Science Report in 2009 largely critiquing the current state of the forensic sciences.

Chapter Ten has reorganized the presentation of the burdens of proof and presumptions by focusing separately on civil and criminal law.

Chapter Eleven has streamlined the study of judicial notice.

The book concludes, as before, with an examination of rules of privilege in Chapter Twelve, which we thoroughly updated. This discussion includes material on the recent Federal Rule 502 concerning waiver of the attorney-client privilege.

Despite the substantial amount of text, this book is not a treatise on the law of evidence. We have not attempted to cover everything. Rather, we have put together materials that we believe will contribute to the effective teaching and learning of the law of evidence. Our selection of materials has been driven by one criterion alone. We have selected materials that in our judgment are the most effective pedagogical tools.

Perhaps the most important change in this edition has been the addition of our new co-author Alex Stein (Cardozo). Professor Stein is an eminent authority in evidence, torts, medical malpractice, criminal law, and legal theory, and brings a wealth of expertise to the sixth edition. We are very pleased to have him on board. Professor Swift unfortunately has retired and did not contribute to this revision. We are very sorry to see her go. Because her immense contribution to the previous editions continues in the current edition, Professor Swift's name has been retained among the authors. Her calm and erudite influence will be sorely missed, and we wish her well in her new endeavors.

Ronald J. Allen
David S. Schwartz
Michael S. Pardo
Alex Stein

January 2016

ACKNOWLEDGMENTS

The authors gratefully acknowledge permission to reprint excerpts from the following:

Allen, Ronald J., The Evolution of the Hearsay Rule to a Rule of Admission, 76 Minn. L. Rev. 797 (1992). Reprinted with permission.

Allen, Ronald J. et al., A Positive Theory of the Attorney-Client Privilege and the Work Product Doctrine, 19 J. Legal Stud. 359 (1990). Reprinted with permission.

Blakely, Newell H., Article IV: Relevancy and Its Limits, 30 Hous. L. Rev. 281 (1993). Reprinted with permission.

Chayes, Abram, The Role of the Judge in Public Law Litigation, 89 Harv. L. Rev. 1281 (1976). Reprinted with permission of Harvard Law Review; permission conveyed through Copyright Clearance Center, Inc.

Gross, Samuel R., Expert Evidence, 1991 Wis. L. Rev. 1113 (1991). Copyright © 1991 by The Board of Regents of the University of Wisconsin System. Reprinted by permission of the Wisconsin Law Review.

Krafka, Carol et al., Judge and Attorney Experiences, Practices, and Concerns Regarding Expert Testimony in Federal Civil Trials. Federal Judicial Center (2002).

McCormick, Charles Tilford et al., McCormick on Evidence (Kenneth S. Broun ed., 6th ed. 2006). Reprinted with permission of the West Group.

Park, Roger C., A Subject Matter Approach to Hearsay Reform, 86 Mich. L. Rev. 51 (1987). Reprinted with permission.

Posner, Richard A., The Law and Economics of the Economic Expert Witness, 13 J. Econ. Perspectives 91 (1999). Reprinted with permission.

Pennington, Nancy, and Reid Hastie, Juror Decision-Making Models: The Generalization Gap, 89 Psychol. Bull. 246 (1981). Reprinted with permission.

Seigel, Michael L., Rationalizing Hearsay: A Proposal for a Best Evidence Hearsay Rule, 72 B.U. L. Rev. 893 (1992). Reprinted with permission. Copyright © 1992 by Boston University Law Review, Boston University. Forum of original publication. Boston University bears no responsibility for any errors which have occurred in reprinting, translation, or editing.

WHY STUDY EVIDENCE?
A STUDENT'S PREFACE

Evidence law is, in one sense, one of the most practical courses that you will take in law school. It is the study of rules in action, rules that are interpreted and applied in the often heated context of adversarial litigation over matters of life and death, personal rights (and obligations), property rights, human relationships, and even such matters as the structure of government and the meaning of the Constitution. As you read the text, the judicial opinions, and the problems in this book, you will be analyzing and evaluating the impact that evidence law has on the litigants and the outcomes of their cases. One of the most significant manifestations of evidence law is the rules of evidence. We concentrate in this book on the Federal Rules of Evidence. The Federal Rules were adopted by Congress in 1975, and since then more than 40 states have revised their rules of evidence more or less adopting the Federal Rules, in many instances virtually verbatim. When you first read the Federal Rules of Evidence you many think them to be cold and sterile doctrines written in abstract conceptual terms, but you will soon find them imbued with the human drama of the courtroom. Behind the formalities of the law there are real people who are called on to testify concerning matter of great personal and social import, as well as parties whose cases rest on that testimony.

The study of evidence, however, is not just the study of the rules of evidence. It is the study of the vast complex of ideas, principles, customs, and values underlying the process of litigation. The rules of evidence give form and content to this process—they determine the admissibility of evidence, define the roles of all the participants at trial (judge, jury, advocates, and witnesses), and structure the relationships among these various actors. They reflect our society's views on many issues, among them: (1) the appropriate means of resolving disputes; (2) the nature of knowledge, what it means to "know" something, and how knowledge is transmitted to others; (3) the dynamics of small group decision-making, and the confidence that we invest in the common person to reach wise and informed judgments that affect the lives of fellow citizens; (4) moral and ethical concerns, such as how difficult it should be for the prosecution to obtain a conviction in a criminal case, or whether certain individuals (spouses, children, friends) should have a privilege not to testify against those close to them; and (5) the relationship between the ideal of justice and the value of efficiency. The rules of evidence rest on and are a crystallization of these various, often conflicting, views. To understand the rules requires an understanding of the compromises they make between competing beliefs and interests; thus, to study the rules one must engage with the foundation of beliefs that underlies them.

The study of evidence will serve any lawyer well, no matter what specialization that person pursues. Obviously litigators must know and understand the rules of evidence in order to use them effectively. Do not overlook that while litigation is virtually always the worst-case scenario of any legal transaction, competent lawyers must always be prepared for it no matter what the nature of the relevant legal enterprise happens to be. If a contractual relationship fails or a merger is not consummated and litigation results, what will matter is how well the parties will be able to defend their respective positions. That will be determined in significant measure by the application of the rules of evidence in the trial itself, and by their implications throughout pretrial procedures, including negotiations leading to settlement.

To use the rules effectively, one must understand their meaning, source, and purpose. To do so requires that one see the rules in relationship to the assumptions, values, and concerns that give rise to them. Even if—indeed, especially if—one intends to become a litigator, it will not do to be content with a cursory grasp of the language of the various rules. One must be in a position to work with the rules, and to argue for one's position from the perspective of the purposes that underlie the relevant provisions.

Whatever legal path the student may be planning to follow, a thorough grasp of the law of evidence and its conceptual foundations is a critical component in the education of a responsible attorney. The value of the inquiry lies not just in some future utility but instead in its enlightenment of our shared vision of how disputes should be resolved in a civilized society. With that enlightenment may come—indeed, we hope *will* come—disagreement. You may not like all that you see; and if you do not, you will be in a better position to work for change through the legislative and rule-making processes.

We attempt in these materials to facilitate an inquiry into the meaning and use of the rules of evidence and all that underlies them. At times we focus extensively—in fact, almost exclusively—on the rules themselves, while at other times we deal quite explicitly with the assumptions and values from which the rules originate. On completion of this inquiry, you should have a thorough understanding of the rules of evidence, as well as considerable appreciation for the concerns that give rise to them.

SPECIAL NOTICE ON CITATIONS

In general, some citations and footnotes have been omitted from quoted material without indication. Footnotes are numbered consecutively in each chapter; that is, the original footnote numbers in quoted material have not been retained. Footnotes in quoted material that are written by the casebook authors are marked "—Eds." In addition, throughout the text we quote from the Federal Rules of Evidence and from the Federal Rules' legislative history without giving specific citations. The Federal Rules quoted in the text are the restyled Rules that became effective on December 1, 2011. These Rules are available at http://www.supremecourt.gov/orders/courtorders/frev11.pdf and https://www.law.cornell.edu/rules/fre.

The Notes of the Advisory Committee appointed by the Supreme Court to draft the rules remain applicable to the restyled Rules. The Advisory Committee Notes are set forth at 56 F.R.D. 183. The judiciary committees of both the House of Representatives and the Senate held hearings on the Federal Rules. The report of the House Committee is H.R. Rep. No. 650, 93d Cong., 1 Sess. (1973), appearing at 1974 U.S.C.C.A.N. 7075; and the report of the Senate is S. Rep. No. 1277, 93d Cong., 2d Sess. (1974), appearing at 1974 U.S.C.C.A.N. 7051. The Conference Committee report is H.R. Rep. No. 1597, 93d Cong., 2d Sess. (1974), and appears at 1974 U.S.C.C.A.N. 7098.

We have deleted *cert. denied* references throughout the book.

AN ANALYTICAL APPROACH
TO EVIDENCE

CHAPTER ONE

THE CASE OF
PEOPLE v. JOHNSON

We start with an edited transcript of a real trial, People v. Johnson.[1] A trial transcript is a good place to start for a number of reasons. Most of you have not experienced litigation, and the transcript allows you to study a complete trial, to get a sense of its structure and dynamic, that is, a sense of how it is put together and how it unfolds. The transcript introduces you to the principal stages of trial process so that you can begin to appreciate the organization of a case, who is doing what to whom, and why. The transcript also introduces you to the Federal Rules of Evidence[2] and gives an overview of much that is to follow in succeeding chapters. We hope that you will get a sense of the rules of evidence in action, and an awareness of the distinction between the rules in real life and their theoretical justifications.

Another reason we begin with a transcript is to increase your understanding of the human element at work in the law of evidence. The *Johnson* case involves serious issues of real people in a dangerous environment with a lot at stake. The case concerns criminal charges of battery brought against an inmate at a California state prison. But Pelican Bay is not just any prison; rather, it was designed as a high-tech "state of the art" facility to house the state's most violence-prone inmates. The Security Housing Unit (SHU) at Pelican Bay was designed for control of prison gang members, not for rehabilitation. A class action lawsuit brought under the federal civil rights act alleged that the isolation conditions in the SHU amounted to cruel and unusual punishment. Prisoners housed in the general population areas of the prison also complained of the use of excessive force by guards and the denial of basic medical attention and access to legal counsel. In January of 1995, U.S. District Court Judge Thelton Henderson found that Pelican Bay staff routinely used unwarranted violence on inmates (based

---

1. The names of all the participants have been changed to provide some anonymity to the parties involved. In addition, we have added footnotes, made very minor editorial changes, and eliminated essentially repetitious testimony.

2. The *Johnson* case was tried in California state court and was governed by the California Evidence Code. The California Code, enacted in 1965, was extremely influential in the drafting of the Federal Rules of Evidence seven years later and there are only a few substantive differences between the Code and the Rules. We refer to the applicable Federal Rules in the footnotes to the transcript.

on 105 pages of documented violent incidents including assaults, beatings, and naked cagings in inclement weather, and an unusually high number of lethal shootings). He also found that Pelican Bay operated a medical and mental health care program that was significantly deficient. The judge ordered prison officials to stop housing mentally ill inmates in the SHU, but refused to hold that incarceration there constituted cruel and unusual punishment for all prisoners. Judge Henderson's opinion is reported as Madrid v. Gomez, 889 F. Supp. 1146 (N.D. Cal. 1995).

As you begin reading the transcript, remember that much has already occurred in the *Johnson* case. The parties have selected a jury and have participated in a preliminary hearing, mutual discovery, and motions in limine. These pretrial events shape issues of proof, as you will see. In addition, they shape the understanding of the participants: Judges are informed, and perhaps influenced, by what they learn in the pretrial stage; jurors are educated in the voir dire process; and the lawyers learn more about the respective strengths and weaknesses of their own case and that of their opponent. Indeed, this last point cannot be overemphasized. The single most important variable in success at litigation is preparation. If you take away one "rule" of evidence from this course, let it be "prepare, prepare, prepare." As you read the transcript, try to get an insight into how well these lawyers prepared.

THE PEOPLE OF THE STATE OF CALIFORNIA v. JAMES JOHNSON

SUPERIOR COURT, DEL NORTE COUNTY, CALIFORNIA
DATE: Monday, July 27, 1992, 1:45 P.M.

1   **APPEARANCES**

For the People: William Cummings, II, ESQ., District Attorney
For the Defendant: Mark Deemer, ESQ., Attorney at Law

The Court: In the People versus Johnson let the record reflect that all jurors,
5   counsel and the defendant are present. I am going to read to you now the charge that has been filed against the defendant, again reminding you that the information is not evidence but is charged as follows:[3] "Superior Court of Del Norte, State of California. The People of the State of California, plaintiff, versus James Johnson, C-66125, defendant, No. 92-190-X. Information.
10   "The District Attorney of the County of Del Norte, State of California, hereby charges James Johnson (C-66125) with having committed, in the County of Del Norte, the crime of:
         "Count 1. Battery on a correctional officer, in violation of Section 4501.5 of the Penal Code, a felony.

---

3. The role of the judge includes informing the jury of the substantive law that will govern the jury's verdict. In California, an information is the pleading filed in Superior Court for the prosecution of a felony. Is there any reason why the judge read the information to the jury rather than simply reading the Code section that the defendant allegedly violated? Is there any reason why the judge did not try to translate the legalese into English?

1   "On or about March 28, 1992, the defendant did willfully and unlawfully being a person confined in a State Prison of this state, commit a battery upon the person of any individual who is not himself a person confined therein to wit, Officer Huston.

5   "Count 2. Battery on correctional officer, in violation of Section 4501.5 of the Penal Code, a felony.

           "On or about March 28th 1992, the defendant did willfully and unlawfully being a person confined in a State Prison of this state, commit a battery upon the person of any individual who is not himself a person confined therein to

10   wit, Officer Van Berg.

           "Dated June 23rd, 1992, William Cummings, II, District Attorney.

           Signed Wm. Cummings for Richard Davis Deputy District Attorney."[4]

    Mr. Deemer: At this time there is a motion to exclude witnesses. I see two are in the courtroom.

15 *The Court:*   All persons who are present as witnesses in the matter will have to remain outside the courtroom and not discuss their testimony with any other witnesses until the hearing is concluded.[5] Counsel are responsible for enforcing this order as to their own witnesses.

           Now, before we get under way with the evidence there are also a few other

20   things. One is an instruction that I will read to you that will cover how you are to handle certain things that may come up during the course of the trial. Because you must determine the facts in this case solely from the evidence, you must be guided by the following principles.[6] One, you must not consider as evidence any statement or arguments of counsel, meaning the attorneys,

25   except that if counsel agree or stipulate to any fact you must regard such fact as being conclusively proved.

           Second, you must not consider as evidence any off the record evidence that was rejected or any evidence that is stricken out by me.

           Third, as to any question to which an objection is sustained, you must not

30   speculate as to what the answer might have been or as to the reason for the objection.

           And fourth, since a question is not evidence you must not suspect that any insinuation suggested by a question is true. In other words, you can consider the questions only as they supply meaning to the answer. Because, for

35   instance, an answer of "yes" or an answer of "no" doesn't mean anything unless

---

4. Substantive law provides the essential elements that the prosecution will have to prove to obtain a conviction. What are the essential elements of the crimes with which defendant Johnson is charged? *Battery* is not defined in the information but an instruction on the elements of a battery is given at page 64 *infra*. In a civil case, the essential elements of the plaintiff's case are derived from the common or statutory law that governs the dispute.

5. FRE 615 permits the court to exclude witnesses from the courtroom while another witness is testifying to safeguard against the possibility of "contaminating" a witness. The objective is to preclude a witness from altering or modifying testimony to explain or dovetail with the testimony of another witness.

6. When you have finished reading the instructions, consider how well they communicate the salient aspects of the role that the jurors are about to undertake. Note in particular that the judge provides very little illumination concerning the legal standards relevant to this trial. Why do you suppose that is?

1 you know what the question was. But the question is not evidence. Only the evidence that comes from the witness is evidence. So nothing that is said in a question should be assumed by you to be true or considered by you to be fact.

It may also happen during the course of the trial, in fact it has happened
5 a couple times already, that you have seen we'll have what are called bench conferences, and this is where the attorneys come up here to the bench and we discuss matters out of your hearing. The reason for this is from time to time things come up in the course of the trial. Sometimes it has to do with objections to the admissibility of evidence. Sometimes it has to do with motions the
10 attorneys are making before the court or other matters that should be heard out of the presence of the jury. If it is going to be something lengthy we'll probably give you a recess and have you step out of the court room. But if it is something very brief, to save the time of doing that, we come up here to the bench and we try and speak in tones of voice that are low enough and for that
15 very reason you should try not to overhear what we are saying. If it would help you, certainly feel free to converse among yourselves as long as it is not about the case. If you would like to stand up in place and stretch and generally make yourself comfortable, feel free to do that and we can get back to you shortly if that happens.[7]
20 If there is anyone in the jury that feels they need a recess for any reason, please do not hesitate or feel embarrassed. If you need to use the rest room or whatever it is, I would rather take care of it, just take a few minutes and break the proceedings and have you take care of it and then you won't be distracted
25 and thinking about something else when you are listening to the evidence when we are here in court.

Also, if any of you would like to take notes you may do so. Usually it's not necessary. I expect in this case where it's going to be a fairly short trial lasting a couple days or so that you will probably be able to hold most everything in
30 your memory. We do have the court reporter taking everything down on a word for word basis. So during your deliberations if you need to know exactly what some witness said that will be available to you and that testimony can be read back to you by the reporter. A few juries like to take notes and you may if you wish.[8]

---

7. A "bench conference" or a "sidebar" may be initiated by either side or by the judge when a point of contention or procedure arises that requires resolution for the smooth functioning of the proceeding. Most bench conferences are on the record—that is, they are recorded by the court reporter—but they occur outside the jury's hearing, in order to keep the jury from overhearing what is discussed. Longer hearings on the admissibility of evidence may also be held without the jury present. See FRE 104.

8. What might be the advantages and disadvantages of note taking by jurors? A classic study has concluded that note taking has neither strong benefits nor strong disadvantages. Larry Heuer & Steven Penrod, Increasing Jurors' Participation in Trials: A Field Experiment with Juror Note Taking and Question Asking, 12 Law & Human Behavior 231 (1988).

Heuer and Penrod also examined the implications of jurors being allowed to pose questions at trial, usually by having the judge ask their questions. Lawyers and judges tend to be wary of encouraging such behavior, but there is some reason to believe that involving the jury somewhat in the evidence production process has beneficial results. Allowing jury questions may help resolve critical ambiguity, as well as keep the attention of the jurors. In general, should lawyers be receptive or hostile to questioning from jurors?

1   The one caution is you should be very careful that your note taking does
not interfere with your ability to closely watch and observe the witnesses as
they give their testimony because it oftentimes happens in trials and it may
happen in this trial that one witness will testify to something and another will
5   testify to exactly the opposite. Just in the words that they are saying you may
not be able to figure out which one you believe. It may be necessary for you
to rely upon such things as facial expression or tone of voice or what we call
body language, the general things that we use in our day to day life when we
decide whether we believe what somebody is telling us or we don't. Don't let
10   your note taking interfere with closely watching and scrutinizing and observing the witnesses as they testify.

Also, you should not on your own undertake any investigation of this matter.[9] You should not try to interview any witnesses, not try to visit the scene
where anything may have happened. You should not consult any reference
15   works and you should not try to perform any experiments. And that is because
the evidence in this case, strictly the evidence that comes from the witnesses,
is all that should be considered in deciding what your verdict should be in this
case. So do not try to gather evidence of facts or information from any other
source except from the witnesses.[10]

20   I have already mentioned to you that you should be very careful not to—
when you encounter the attorneys or other people involved in this case during
the recesses be very careful not to fall into conversation with them.[11] We mentioned that before lunch.

One final thing and that is that you should not consider as evidence the
25   fact that the defendant is here in physical custody of officers. You should not
take into consideration as evidence either for him or against him whether
he is confined in physical restraints or the clothing that he is wearing or that
there may be additional security here in the courtroom. Those are not facts
that should be considered in any way as showing whether the defendant is
30   guilty or not guilty. Disregard those matters and decide the case strictly on the
evidence.

All right. The final thing before we get under way with the evidence is that
the attorneys have the opportunity to make opening statements to the jury and

---

9. Why shouldn't jurors learn more about the specific facts of the case by conducting their own
inquiry? Jurors bring their own background knowledge and general experience with them, and they use
this knowledge to interpret the testimony they hear. Wouldn't it be useful for them to read up on subjects
that are pertinent to the dispute as well?

10. Later in the transcript, you will see that documentary exhibits are entered into evidence, too.
Why not explain exhibits at this point? Are verbal testimony and exhibits the only sources of evidence?
The judge has just told the jury to pay close attention to the demeanor of witnesses, and to use common
sense. On the basis of common sense, jurors also draw inferences from the evidence. Is there a clear distinction between "evidence" and the "inferences" one draws from evidence? Begin to think about what it
means for something to be "evidence."

11. Why should jurors not discuss the case with anyone else, including other jurors? Jurors are undergoing a learning process. Does learning occur most effectively when the learner sits passively, as this
instruction directs these jurors to do? What are possible risks of discussion that offset its value in an educational process? Why is the court imposing this type of decisionmaking process on the jury?

1   these are very brief outlines the attorneys could give you if they wish show-
       ing what they expect the evidence in the case is going to prove. Sometimes
       it happens, of course, that the evidence comes out differently from what they
       expect. The witness may remember something differently from what one or
5   the other of the attorneys may think the witness is going to testify to. But gen-
       erally speaking the attorneys can give a fair outline of what's going to happen
       in the case and what they expect the issues are going to be. But, of course, if
       there is any difference between what they say the evidence is going to be and
       what it actually is, of course you follow the evidence.

10   Since the prosecution has the burden of proof and presents evidence first,
       the prosecutor makes the first opening statement. When he is finished defense
       counsel has a choice. He can either make his opening statement at that time
       or if he prefers he can wait until the prosecution presents their evidence and
       then make his opening statement. Mr. Cummings?[12]

15 *Mr. Cummings:*   Thank you, Your Honor.[13] Ladies and gentlemen, we are about
       to get under way and the purpose of my opening statement is basically to give
       you some idea of where I believe our witnesses are going to take us in testi-
       mony. Witnesses are the people who testify from the witness stand, nowhere
       else. In other words, as the judge told you, what the attorneys have to say is not
20   evidence, and you notice neither side here have raised their hands to tell the
       truth and nothing but the truth. So your testimony comes from the witness
       stand.

            As the prosecutor in the case I expect to call three, probably four witnesses.
       I may call more. I have an option of putting on rebuttal witnesses if I want to.
25   You will see that if it happens. Eye witnesses are going to start out with Officer
       Huston who has worked at Pelican Bay State Prison who is what we call a
       percipient witness, which means he saw, he was present when the incident
       happened in 1992 at one of the branches at Pelican Bay State Prison. They
       call it B Facility. And I will have testimony about what B Facility means and
30   what type of people are housed in B Facility.

            The defendant, Mr. Johnson, was in his cell with his cell mate, a person by
       the name of Butler and that for whatever reason they refused to give up some
       trays, food trays. That on that date, March the 28th, 1992, Butler and inmate
       Johnson were in their cell. They had been fed in their cell, and, as I indicated
35   before, for unknown reasons they weren't going to give up their trays.

---

12. What aspect of the jury's role did the judge focus on in the instructions? Do the instructions prepare the jury for its decisionmaking role? Has the judge adequately informed the jury about the role of
the court or the adversaries?

13. The primary purposes of an opening statement are to state the facts that the advocate expects to
produce at trial; to present these facts within the framework of a story or theme that is persuasive and that
will be the basis for closing argument; and to personalize the client. Argument about what inferences
should be drawn from the evidence is made in the closing arguments, not here. The opening statement is
also used to introduce the jury to weaknesses in the case. Jury surveys have shown that opening statements
are very important in jury decisionmaking, and that jurors often vote consistently with views they form
during the opening. See the discussion in Chapter Two, Section F. Reflections on Natural Reasoning and
the Adversary System.

1   At that point in time several officers were summoned to go over to the cell
        and try to talk to them to give up their trays. And it's a mainline production,
        meaning they have to feed, get back the trays, and they have a lot of people to
        take care of. Officer Huston will testify that basically there was a couple trays
5   inside the cell and that he and other officers went into his cell along with
        some other people and talked to them about giving up the trays.
               Officer Huston will tell you—and I would suspect Officer Van Berg will
        tell you basically the same story—that Mr. Johnson had possession of the trays,
        he was holding on to them, and that in the door of the cell, the actual cell
10   door, there was a little food port door. You can slide one tray at a time through
        there. And you can't slide two through and you can't slide one with a lot of
        garbage piled on top, just enough to slide one tray back and forth.
               For whatever reason, inmate Johnson, the defendant in this case, was standing
        in the cell with the trays in his hand and he had had some discussion with the
15   officers about a package. He wanted some package. And he was not going to relin-
        quish those two trays. So basically what happened in the case, as Officers Huston
        and Van Berg and Walker will testify, is that a sergeant sent some of them over
        to discuss the matter with inmate Johnson and to try to persuade them basically
        verbally to give up the tray, "we have got to get on our route, our day's business."
20   He asked at that point in time to see a sergeant. And the officers will testify
        that what they told Johnson at that point in time was, "We'll get you a sergeant;
        we'll have a sergeant drop by and talk to you, but we can't do it right now. We
        have got our work to do. We have got to finish up what we are doing."
               At that point Johnson was going to give up the trays. He was not verbally
25   abusive. He was not physically—didn't appear to be physically dangerous
        at that point. He was just standing there with his trays. So the officer—and
        he wasn't too far back from the cell door. So one of the officers, the Officer
        Smith, signaled to the gentleman who controls—the sectional officer who
        controls the doors electronically or hydraulically but they are controlled from
30   a different location—go ahead and open up the cell door.
               So the cell door was opened a substantial distance, wide enough for some-
        body to charge out. And behind the door you have Johnson hanging on to the
        two trays piled with garbage. And basically at that point with Walker in front,
        Van Berg, Smith was there and Huston was there, their testimony is going to
35   be that Johnson dropped the trays, kind of lowered his head a little bit and
        charged Officer Walker who was kind of at the head of this line where he can
        get the job done.
               At that point in time the officers met him. The approximate location was
        the doorway to the cell. Stopped him at the door as he tried to approach them
40   rapidly. He was swinging his fists, clenched right fist, that the officers basically
        pushed him back into the cell. The cells are not that large. Got him on top of
        a table and subdued him. One officer had handcuffs on one side of him and
        Mr. Johnson still was swinging, being combative. He was still trying to injure
        people and they were trying to subdue him. So four or five officers at this
45   point, trying to subdue him and get him cuffed up, handcuffed.

1   During the course of that melee two officers were injured. One ended up
with a broken bone—I think it was a bone chip in his thumb—and was off
work a period of time, suffered some injuries. Another officer went down to
Sutter Coast Hospital with a shin injury, received a small laceration on his
5   shin.
        These are the two counts of battery that I am going to ask you to consider.
The people will put on a final witness, probably an officer by the name of
Henderson who will testify about a 969B package. It's a package of documents
from the prison certified to verify that that person was lawfully in custody at
10   Pelican Bay State Prison at the time. I do have to prove that he was in custody
at the time. And it basically establishes the fact that he was in our prison system as well, which is another element that I have to prove.
        I would expect at this point in time that would be my case in chief.
Depending on how and what the defense puts on, I may call rebuttal wit-
15   nesses, probably officers or actually two lieutenants, Foster and Kurtz. I will
call those two as rebuttal. Thank you.[14]

Mr. Deemer: Reserve.[15]

The Court: First witness.

Mr. Cummings: Officer Huston I believe is outside.

20 *The Court:*   Raise your right hand.

GEORGE HUSTON

called as a witness by the People, after having been sworn to tell the truth, the
whole truth and nothing but the truth, was examined and testified as follows:

The Clerk: Be seated and state your name and address for the record.

25 *The Witness:*   George Huston, Pelican Bay State Prison.

Direct Examination

Q: by Mr. Cummings: Thank you, Your Honor. Sir, what's your occupation?[16]

A: Correctional officer.

Q: How long have you been a correctional officer?

30 A: Six years.

Q: Where are you currently employed?

---

14. Has the prosecutor fulfilled the primary purposes for opening statements discussed in note 13? Did a story or theme emerge? Could it have been done more vividly? Does vividness matter in an open- ing statement? Compare the effectiveness of the prosecutor's opening to the defense's opening statement, which follows the close of the prosecution's case.

15. Defense counsel is reserving his right to make his opening statement following the presentation of the state's case. Should he have delayed, or should he have made his statement right now? Most defense attorneys make their opening statement right after the plaintiff or prosecution in order to challenge that version of the case and to make sure that the jury hears both sides. Otherwise, there is a risk that the jury is already convinced by the time the defense begins.

16. As you read the prosecutor's direct examinations, make a note of what testimony you think tends to establish the essential elements of the prosecution's case against the defendant. For example, at what point does Officer Huston provide testimony to show that the defendant's alleged battery was committed against a person not confined in State Prison?

1 A: Pelican Bay State Prison.

    Q: How long have you worked at Pelican Bay?

    A: Since November '89.

    Q: Was that basically the opening date for the prison?

5 A: Yes.

    Q: So you are part of the original team that started out at the institution?

    A: Yes, sir.

    Q: Sir, were you working in the capacity of a correctional officer on March the 28th, 1992?

10 A: Yes.

    Q: Did you have occasion to come into contact with an inmate by the name of Johnson seated at the other end of this table?

    A: Yes.

    Q: Do you recognize him today?

15 A: Yes, I do.

    Q: What facility was he housed in, do you know?

    A: Facility B.

    Q: What is the significance of Facility B?

    A: It's a general population.

20 Q: As opposed to what, sir?

    A: Security Housing Unit.

    Q: Is there a transition of inmates from one facility like SHU, Security Housing Unit, to, say, general population?

    A: Yes.

25 *Mr. Deemer:*   Objection. I don't see the relevance.[17]

    The Court: Sustained.

    Q. by Mr. Cummings: Officer, what type of people—what type of inmates are typically housed in Facility B?

    Mr. Deemer: Again, objection. I don't see the relevance.[18]

---

17. There are two general types of objections. The first is to the form of the question. For example, the question might be leading, argumentative, assume facts not in evidence, be compound (that is ask two or more questions in the guise of one), or call for a narrative response. These issues are discussed in Chapter Two. The other type of objection goes to the answer that is likely to be obtained. The answer might be irrelevant, hearsay, violate a dead man's statute, violate the parol evidence or best evidence rules, lack a sufficient foundation, or involve privilege. In each case, the proper procedure is to interpose the objection after the question has been asked. Witnesses should allow the adversary time to interpose the objection before the answer. There will be times when such a procedure will be inadequate, such as whenever asking the question itself is as damaging as getting the answer. ("Isn't Facility B a transition facility for violent inmates coming out of SHU, before they are placed in general population?")

18. Consider FRE 103. Is Deemer's objection satisfactory to preserve the issue for appeal? The stock objection "irrelevant" or "irrelevant, incompetent, and immaterial" is just that, a stock objection that communicates virtually nothing to the trial judge except the objector's desire to exclude the proffered evidence. Unless that evidence is clearly not admissible for any purpose, the objector must state the specific ground of objection to the trial judge. FRE 103(a)(1). Evidentiary rulings admitting evidence over objection will virtually never be the basis of appellate reversal if the objector has not been clear, direct, and correct in the objection and if there is any ground on which the trial judge can be sustained. If evidence is excluded, the losing side must make sure that the substance of the evidence, and the theory of its admissibility, are apparent from the record in order to preserve the issue for appeal. FRE 103(a)(2). It is the job

1 *The Court:*   Approach the bench.

(The following bench conference was had outside the presence of the jury.[19])

The Court: Where is the relevance?
Mr. Cummings: The relevance is the fact that Facility B is a transition facility
5   from Security Housing Unit to General Population and there are more inci-
      dents of violence and reported violence in general at Facility B than there is
      in the General Population. Conversely there is less out of SHU.[20]
Mr. Deemer: Less what?
Mr. Cummings: Less reported violence and there is actually less in SHU than
10   there is in Facility B. Facility B is a transition facility where they take people
      who have been in SHU and kind of mainline them back into the way of
      General Population.
The Court: How does that help the jury?
Mr. Cummings: I think where you have an allegation of battery against the offi-
15   cers I think it's important that they understand that the facility which this
      person was housed is a facility where — it's a facility where people go, they are
      in transition. I am not going to say in transition from what to what. The fact
      of the matter is that you have already given these preliminary rulings that you
      are going to allow Mr. Deemer to go into some issues of "Do you know Officer
20   Walker's propensity" or "Do you know his reputation for violence among
      other inmates?"[21] I think when you have that kind of testimony coming out,

of the advocates to create a record that adequately reflects the objection, any response to it, and the judge's ruling. This is called "perfecting the record" and "preserving the issue for appeal."

There are tactical issues to take into account when deciding whether to object to an opponent's question. First, if a question will not elicit damaging information, there is no reason to weigh the proceedings down with trivial objections. Attorneys should also be wary of imparting the impression to the jury that they have something to hide. Moreover, an objection can often underscore the damaging aspects of an objectionable question, and wisdom may on these occasions dictate silence in the hope that the jury will miss the point. Finally, objectionable questions sometimes will be helpful to one's own case either because the specific answer will be helpful or because the question will "open the door" to one's own testimony that might not otherwise be admissible.

19. Here, the bench conference was recorded by the court reporter. If the conference were held off the record, the lawyers must remember to summarize what occurred for the record when the trial goes back on the record. Failure to "perfect the record" may result in an inability to appeal any asserted error in the trial judge's ruling.

20. If the trial judge is unable to tell whether the proffered evidence is admissible because the necessary context is lacking, the advocate has the duty to make an offer of proof. The lawyer presents to the judge what evidence is expected to be produced so that the judge can analyze the objection in that light. See FRE 103(a)(2). Offers of proof may be made in a number of different ways. The lawyer may simply describe for the trial judge what the evidence is going to be. Alternatively, the court may require that the attorney put the relevant witnesses on the stand and ask the appropriate questions of the witnesses. Again, it is the lawyer's obligation to make sure that the record is sufficiently complete so as to preserve any asserted error for appeal. A useful short description of the process of perfecting the record is Jon Waltz & John Kaplan Evidence: Making the Record (1982).

21. If an advocate knows that an evidentiary problem is likely to arise at trial, the advocate can attempt to get a pretrial resolution of that issue. Motions to suppress illegally obtained evidence are examples of this. A more general procedure involves filing a motion in limine. Motions in limine (meaning at the threshold) can be used to get pretrial rulings on virtually any evidentiary question. Here, the defense has obtained a ruling from the judge that he will admit reputation evidence about one of the officers. Whether raising an evidentiary objection in a motion in limine is sufficient to preserve that objection for appeal is discussed in Chapter Two.

1   I think it is relevant on the issue that in Facility B we have people who are in
fact more prone to violence and have proven to be more prone to violence
and are in fact in transition trying to get back into the general mainstream of
General Population.

5 *The Court:*   I will allow you to establish that this is a maximum security section,
but I think the implication that the jury is likely to get from this testimony
if you are allowed to go forward with it is in fact he has just been in trial for
something coming out of SHU. I don't think you should be allowed to do
that because it gets into impermissible character evidence.[22] So if you want to
10   describe physically what Facility B is and if you want to describe what precautions are taken in Facility B, you can do that. But you can't go into what he may
have done in prison unless it becomes otherwise relevant. At this point I don't
think it is relevant so I am going to sustain the objection.

(The following proceedings were had in open court.)

15 Q. *by Mr. Cummings:*   Officer Huston, would you tell me physically how Facility
B is set up? Are they single-celled, are they double-celled cells?
A: They are double-celled cells.
Q: Are they arranged in what sort of a format?
A: One hundred twenty-eight inmates available per housing unit, eight housing units.
20 Q: This is still a Level IV maximum security prison setting; is that correct?
A: Yes.
Q: Sir, do you work or were you working on March the 28th, 1992, in B Facility?
A: Yes, I was.
Q: What was your position or what did you do in B Facility?[23]
25 A: Yard officer.
Q: What's a yard officer?
A: Yard officer maintains safety and security on the yard, General Population
inmates. And in that first response, emergency response.
Q: When you say "first response," what do you mean by "first response"?
30 A: In an emergency I am designated to respond anywhere in the facility.
Q: So if there was an incident in B Facility, it would be expected that you would
respond; is that correct?[24]

---

22. Why is the judge going to admit reputation evidence with respect to Officer Walker, but not character evidence with respect to the defendant? The answer to this question requires analysis of why character evidence is relevant. The testimony regarding Walker's reputation for violence would be relevant
to show defendant's state of mind of fear of Walker, whereas the testimony about the defendant's violent
character would be relevant to show that he acted in conformity with his character and was the aggressor.
As you will see in Chapter Five, infra, under FRE 404 character evidence is normally not admitted to
show that a person committed an act in conformity with that character. This is one example of the general
principle that relevancy is a necessary but not a sufficient condition for admissibility.

23. Notice the form of the prosecutor's questions to Officer Huston concerning his work at B Facility
and the incident involving the defendant. The prosecutor is using "who, what, where, when, why, and
how" questions. A direct examination usually takes the form of short, nonsuggestive questions that, when
asked and answered in sequence, tell the witness's story efficiently.

24. The prosecutor here, and three questions later, is using a common form of "leading question"
that explicitly suggests the answer that the advocate is looking for. The tag "isn't that correct" or "isn't it

1 A: Yes.
   Q: Are you aware of an incident involving inmate Johnson on March 28th of this
       year?
   A: It wasn't really an incident.
   Q: What was it?
5 A: It was a simple denial of a breakfast tray. When an inmate gets fed in the
       morning they are supposed to—after breakfast they gave up their breakfast
       trays and silverware. Floor officer on that day said that inmate Johnson and his
       cellie, cell mate Butler, were holding their breakfast trays.
   Q: And at some point in time somebody summoned you; is that correct?
10 A: Yes.
   Q: Who was that, do you know
   A: I don't remember on the day. There was several of us and we were told to go
       over and see if we could get the breakfast trays.
   Q: What did you expect to do that day, did you know?
15 A: Go over and simply, "Give us the trays."
   Q: Talk to them first?
   A: Yeah.
   Q: Is that what you did?
   A: I didn't myself. The officer that ordered him to give up the trays is the one that
20   ordered—gave him the direct order.
   Q: Which officer ordered him to give up the trays?
   A: Officer Smith.
   Q: Was the order to give up the trays once or more than once if you know?
   A: More than twice.
25 Q: Could you see from where you were at inmate Johnson inside his cell?
   A: Yes.
   Q: Physically tell us how he appeared at the time that he was ordered to give up
       and relinquish those two trays.
   A: Quiet. Did not say anything except he asked to see the sergeant.
30 Q: Did he indicate why he wanted to see a sergeant?
   A: No.
   Q: Did he have anything in his hands as you remember?
   A: Not at that immediate moment. After the food port was opened, he picked up
       his trays and acted like he was going to give us the trays.
35 Q: You indicated the food port. Where is the food port located?
   A: In the middle of the door about waist high.
   Q: Can you describe it for us?
   A: It's approximately probably a four-to-five-inch opening. Has a door on it, prob-
       ably twelve inches wide.
40 Q: It's a hinged door?
   A: Yes.

---

true that" permits only a yes or no answer. Thus, the information that the jury hears is really supplied by
the lawyer's question; the witness's response simply confirms or denies it.

1 Q: And that door opens and shuts?
   A: Yes, and it is locked when it's not used.
   Q: It is locked when it's not used?
   A: When it's not used.
5 Q: Normally a person can pass how many trays through a food port opening?
   A: One.
   Q: How many trays did inmate Johnson have in his hands?
   A: He had two trays with disposable garbage on the top of them.
   Q: Would those two trays with the garbage on top pass through the food port
10   door?
   A: No.
   Q: How would a person normally pass the trays through, just slide them through?
   A: Yes. Officer would unlock the food port and it's got another lock. When you
       pull down on it and at that time they pass the food tray through and the officer
15   grabs it and takes it.
   Q: At some point in time it became clear to you that inmate Johnson was not
       going to slide the trays through the food port door.[25]
   A: No. When he picked up the trays and brought them to the food port it was not
       subtle, I guess. He didn't say anything, he was calm, walked up to the door and
20   held the tray.
   Q: At that point in time did somebody order the door be opened?
   A: Yes. Officer Smith.
   Q: And is that an appropriate method to get back the trays?
   A: Yes.
25 *Mr. Deemer:*   Excuse me. A, lack of qualifications; B, lack of foundation; and, C,
       it's leading.[26]
   The Court: Are you asking for an expert opinion, Mr. Cummings?
   Q. by Mr. Cummings: Officer Huston, you stated that you have worked as a cor-
       rectional officer at Pelican Bay for six years?
30 A: Yes.
   Q: And during those six years, did you receive special education and training for
       your job?
   A: Yes.
   Q: What was that?
35 A: There are training manuals, and training courses for correctional officers on-
       site and throughout the state that we attend.

---

25. Here is another leading question that directs the witness's attention back to what the prosecutor thinks is important.

26. The objection's references to lack of qualifications and foundation amount to the same thing. Does this witness possess the knowledge to answer the question adequately? Essentially the witness is being asked to offer an opinion concerning the proper operation of the prison system. To do so, he should be qualified as an expert, who is a specially qualified person empowered under the Rules of Evidence to offer testimony because of special competence. See FRE 702. Opinions by nonexperts are admissible in somewhat limited, but very important, circumstances. See FRE 701.

1   Q: And does this training include the handling of specific problems that inmates
          sometimes cause?
     A: Yes it does.
     Q: And based on this training, do you have an opinion on the proper means to
5   handle situations like inmate Johnson's, that is, on whether it is appropriate to
          open the cell door? Just tell us whether you have an opinion.
     A: Yes I do.
     Mr. Cummings: I would offer Officer Huston's opinion now based on his special
          experiences and training at Pelican Bay.
10   The Court: You may answer.
     Q. by Mr. Cummings: Is opening the cell door an appropriate way to get back
          the food trays?
     A: Yes, on the General Population side it is. If the inmates are General Population
          inmates so they are out of their cells a lot of the time and if they are, what we
15   say, programmed and everything else and they seem calm and everything else,
          well, we—yeah, we get the trays that way, especially when they have more
          than two trays or have two trays with garbage on the top.
     Q: I am going to draw a distinction here between the Secured Housing Unit, the
          SHU inmates, and the General Population inmates. Inmate Johnson was at
20   that point a General Population inmate?
     A: Yes, he was.
     Q: And if this incident had occurred on the Secured Housing Unit side, the other
          section of the prison, would the doors have been opened in this fashion?
     A: Absolutely not.
25   Q: So the procedure is different from your experience whether a person is in
          General Population or is in the Secured Housing Unit?
     A: Yes, it is.
     Q: For inmate Johnson, housing in General Population, this was an appropriate
          way to retrieve the trays, if necessary?
30   A: Yeah.
     Q: Was the door opened?
     A: Yes, the door was opened.
     Q: What happened when the door opened?
     A: Inmate Johnson—when the door was opened up inmate Johnson immedi-
35   ately instantly dropped the food trays. He was standing just inside the door,
          up next to the door. Dropped the food trays immediately and bowed his head,
          brought up his fists and just tried to come through the door and hit Officer
          Walker in the chest.
     Q: Where did Officer Walker make contact or where did Johnson make contact
40   with Walker?
     A: In the door. In the doorway after the door was opened. Officer Walker was on
          the outside of the cell.
     Q: Do you recall the other officers who were present?
     A: The other officers that I knew that were present were Officer Smith and
45   Officer Walker and Officer Van Berg.

1 Q: Were there other officers there that you don't recall by name?
   A: Yes, Officer White was there, but I didn't find that out until after the incident.
   Q: When officers are retrieving food items, trays, et cetera, in General Population
       are they wearing protective gear?
5 A: No.
   Q: What happened when Johnson charged the officers and made contact with
       Walker?
   A: Officer Walker immediately grabbed him and pushed him inside the cell and
       inmate Johnson fell back up against the desk area, which is approximately
10   three feet inside the cell.
   Q: What was inmate Johnson doing at that time?
   A: Combative.
   Mr. Deemer: One moment, Your Honor. I am going to object to that term. It's
       conclusionary.[27]
15 The Court: Overruled.
   Q. by Mr. Cummings: Describe for me what you mean by "combative"?
   A: Swinging his arms, not complying with orders, using his strength.
   Q: What sort of orders were being given to Johnson at that time?
   A: To cuff up.
20 Q: What's cuff up?
   A: Handcuff.
   Q: Standard procedure?
   A: Yes.
   Q: Was there a cell mate in the same cell?
25 A: Yes.
   Q: Do you recall his name?
   A: Inmate Butler.
   Q: What did inmate Butler do, if anything?
   A: Inmate Butler was immediately told to get down by Officer Smith in the cell.
30 Q: What does "get down" mean?
   A: "Get down" means hit the floor in a prone position.
   Q: Did he comply?
   A: Yes, he did comply immediately.
   Q: And he was secured, too?
35 A: Yes, Officer Smith restrained him.
   Q: Why was inmate Johnson and inmate Butler secured, handcuffed? What's the
       purpose?
   A: Because if they are combative or not complying with orders; disciplinary rea-
       sons, you know.

---

27. The objection that a question calls for a conclusion is just another way to say that it calls for an opinion. Here the opinion would be a lay opinion, not an expert opinion. But is "combative" a fact or an opinion? What is the difference? Even though the objection is overruled, note how the prosecutor develops the record by having the witness explain what "combative" means.

1 Q: Officer safety reasons?
   A: Yes, officer safety and security.
   Q: Inmate Butler basically did exactly what he was told to do?
   A: Yes, he did.
5 Q: Was there kind of a wrestling or a pushing or a shoving or some sort of an altercation inside the cell?
   A: Yes. Inmate Johnson was not complying. He was swinging, he was kicking, he was using his strength against us. In fact, after we got him pushed up against the desk area, we couldn't get him handcuffed in the cell. So we brought him out
10   of the cell, put him in the prone position outside the cell. He was in the prone position. He wouldn't give up his hands for restraint. I finally got one handcuff on the right wrist. Several orders—he wouldn't give up his left one. He kept it underneath him. When I did get it out from underneath him, he brought—and husbanding his strength he wouldn't let me have his wrists. It took me a little
15   while to get him restrained and in the left handcuff. He was resisting it.
   Q: Using both his hands and his feet?
   A: Both hands and feet.
   Q: Was he saying anything during this period of time?
   A: No.
20 Q: Sir, were you injured in that altercation?
   A: Yes, I was.
   Q: Describe your injuries for us.
   Mr. Deemer: Excuse me. May we approach the Bench at this time?

(The following proceedings were had at the bench, outside the hearing of the jury.)

25 Mr. Deemer: My understanding is that the witness is going to testify that he received a gash and yet he also testifies at the preliminary hearing—and I assume his testimony isn't going to change today—that he doesn't know how he received the injury. So I think this testimony at this point becomes irrelevant.
   Mr. Cummings: I think that's an awkward summary. What he is going to testify
30   to is he received the injuries as a result of this melee. He cannot testify that inmate Johnson slugged him, kicked him or directly caused it. But for the melee he certainly would not have been injured in that fashion. Obviously this witness can testify to what he observed on his own body. He doesn't have to be a doctor or a nurse or anything else to testify what injuries he personally
35   received on his own body, and that's all I am looking for, and whether or not he went to the hospital or went home or returned to work.
   The Court: I would possibly preclude you or limit you in some fashion if you attempted to call a doctor.
   Mr. Cummings: I have no intention of it.
40 The Court: He can testify to his own knowledge what he observed on his own body. I am not going to preclude him from that.

(The following proceedings were had in open court.)

Q. by Mr. Cummings: Officer Huston, where were you injured?
A: My left shin had a one-inch gash.

1 Q: Did you ever seek medical attention for that?
   A: Yes, they did a triage and then I was sent to Sutter Coast Hospital.
   Q: And you were treated at Sutter Coast?
   A: Yes.
5 Q: How long did this whole thing take—or how little time did it take?
   A: Everything happened real fast. I couldn't give you a time on it. Everything was
       instantaneous from the time the food trays were dropped and Mr. Johnson
       trying to get through the door and I really couldn't give you—several—
       probably several seconds. When the adrenaline is flowing you have no idea
10   how long it is.
   Q: Sir, when you are working as a yard officer as you were that day, do you carry
       a side-handled baton?
   A: Yes, I do.
   Q: In this incident involving inmate Johnson did you have to—or did you have
15   time to remove your side-handled baton?
   A: I did not. At that time I had no time to.
   Q: I take it, then, you were not expecting trouble when the door was being
       opened.
   A: Absolutely not.
20 Q: You were taken by surprise?
   A: Yes, I was.
   Mr. Cummings: Thank you sir. Nothing further.

Cross-examination

   Q. by Mr. Deemer: Officer Huston, who at that point unlocked the food port?
25 A: Officer Smith.
   Q: And then was anything done with the food port prior to the door being opened?
   A: You mean was there anything—it was opened prior to the door being—
   Q: But was it then closed again?
   A: I could not say whether it was or not.
30 Q: Now, the defendant, if he was going to pass you these trays they can be passed
       through the food port one at a time?
   A: Yes.
   Q: And that's a normal way to pass through the food port?
   A: Yes.
35 Q: Now, normally the inmates aren't fed in the cells, are they?
   A: Not all the time, no—
   Q: And they are fed in the cells on this particular instance because they are on
       lock-down?[28]
   A: I don't know what the particulars were at that time. They might have been on
40   a lock-down.

---

28. What is a lock-down? Is the lawyer adequately attending to the jury?

 1 Q: Normally you only feed them in the cell when inmates are on lock-down, don't you?
    A: Normally, except if the kitchen isn't running right, the dining room isn't running right or other—if we get some confidential information or whatever, yeah.
 5 Q: Now, did any of the other officers at the time you were all at the door—and I take it there is eight or ten officers at the door; is that correct?
    A: I have no idea if there was eight or ten. I am saying there was the four that I know of.
    Q: But there were more than four. There were some other officers—
10 A: I understand that there was, but I didn't have any identification and know who the officers are and how many others.
    Q: Hey, I am not trying to trip you. All I am trying to figure out is there were four officers there that you know including yourself?
    A: Yes.
15 Q: And there were some officers you didn't know?
    A: Yes.
    Q: You don't remember what the total number of the other officers were?
    A: No.
    Q: Could it have been as many as eight or ten?
20 A: I guess maybe, yes.
    Q: Now, did any of the officers just prior to the time the cell door was opened put on some gloves?
    A: I have no idea. I didn't put any on my myself, no.
    Q: Do you recall any officers putting on—pulling out the side-handled batons,
25   PRC 24 or something like that?
    A: No, I don't recall that.
    Q: Now, when the door was opened—first of all, there is absolutely nothing aggressive about the defendant up until the time the door is opened; is that correct?
    A: No, there wasn't anything aggressive about him until he dropped the trays.
30 Q: Okay. And when the door is opened Walker is standing in front of him?
    A: Yes.
    Q: And at that point the defendant is standing there and he has got two trays in his hands and he just drops the trays like that; is that correct?
    A: Instantly.
35 Q: And brought his hands up toward his head?
    A: He brought them up, yeah.
    Q: How were they shaped when he brought them up towards his head?
    A: In a clenched fist.
    Q: And at that point you observed Walker push him?
40 A: I, at that point—he had struck Walker in the chest.
    Q: With what?
    A: With his fist.
    Q: And then Walker pushed him back?
    A: And Walker pushed him back into the cell.
45 Q: And then the melee ensues?
    A: Yes.

1 Q: Now, you search inmates' cells frequently, don't you?

A: In my job once in a while I do.

Q: And when you search an inmate's cell, whether he is in General Population or in SHU, the first thing you do is get the inmate out of the cell; is that correct?

5 *Mr. Cummings:*   Objection. Relevance.

The Court: Overruled. You may answer.

The Witness: If you are going to search the cell, yes, you bring the inmate out and—out of the cell.

Q. *by Mr. Deemer:*   In your training except when you are forming some sort of

10 what they call a cell extraction team, you are never supposed to be in the same room like a closed room, like a cell or a sally port or something like that with an inmate, are you?[29]

A: Not in a cell with an inmate. In a sally port, yeah, you are in with the General Population inmates.

15 Q: Let's stick with a cell. The reason you don't go into a cell with an inmate is because you are afraid something might happen; is that correct?

A: It's safety and security.

Q: So wouldn't the normal procedure of removing these trays have been to order the inmates to the cell port to cuff up and remove them from the cell?

20 A: It depends on the circumstances.

Q: All right. How long have you known Officer Walker?

A: Approximately one and a half years.

Q: You weren't at Folsom with him?

A: No.

25 Q: If something is to be removed forcibly from an inmate or an inmate is to be forcibly moved, isn't the normal way to do it by means of a cell extraction team?

A: If he is to be forcibly removed from his cell?

Q: Either something is to be forcibly removed from him or he is to be forcibly

30 moved from the cell. In either instance—and he is in the cell. Isn't the cell extraction team normally the way to do that?

A: If he fails to comply with cuffing up and stuff like that, yes, it could be done.

Q: Prior to opening the cell door you never asked the inmate to cuff up, did you?

A: No, not that I—not myself, no.

35 Q: Now, when you opened the door—or excuse me. When the door was opened, did you expect that the trays were going to be handed out to you?

A: Yes. Yes, I did think he was going to give the trays to the officer.

Q: Now, in connection with this case did you prepare some sort of a report?

A: Yes, I did a 115, CDC 115 report.

40 Q: And that's a rules violation report?

A: That's a rules violation report.

Q: And that's basically what is done for disciplinary purposes; is that correct?

A: Yes.

---

29. What is an extraction team? A sally port? Again, is the lawyer attending to the jury?

1 Q: Do you have a copy of that with you?
   A: Yeah, yes, I do.
   Q: Could you look at that? Have you got it there?
   A: Yes.
5 Q: On the CDC 115—and I am asking you to go down one, two, three lines, the
      sentence that begins "The inmates were given repeated orders." Would you
      read that to yourself?
   A: "The inmates were given —"
   Q: Just read it to yourself. You don't have to read it to the jury.
10 A: Yes.
   Q: All right. And in that report basically you state that Officer Smith instructed
      the control booth officer, quote, "to open the door to the cell in order for staff
      to enter and retrieve the trays." Is that correct?
   A: What line are you reading there?
15 Q: One, two, three, four, five, six lines down. I think that is the fifth line down.
      "Officer Smith instructed the control booth officer," quote, "to open the
      door." Do you see that there?
   A: Yes.
   Q: So Smith instructed—what you thought at least at that point in time was that
20   staff was going to enter and retrieve the trays; is that correct?
   A: Well, when you say "enter," if I am handing my hand through the door I am
      entering the cell.
   Q: But earlier you testified that he was going to hand—you expected the trays to
      be handed out; is that correct?
25 A: Yes, hand them right at the door, yes.
   Q: Now, on the next line down you indicate that Johnson rushed toward
      Correctional Officer Walker; is that correct?
   A: Yes.
   Q: Attempting to strike him with clenched fists; is that correct?
30 A: Yes.
   Q: Doesn't say any place in there that he actually struck him with a clenched fist,
      does it?
   A: What line are we reading here? Yes.
   Q: It doesn't say that, does it?
35 A: No.
   Q: And it doesn't say anything in your report about an open food port, does it?
   A: No.
   Q: It doesn't say anything in your report about who opened the food port, does it?
   A: No.
40 Q: Sir, do you remember testifying at the preliminary hearing?
   A: Yes, I do.
   Q: Is it correct to state—you have had an opportunity to review your preliminary
      hearing transcript, haven't you?
   A: Yes, I did read it.
45 Q: By the way, did you discuss your testimony with some of the other officers?
   A: No.

1 *Q:* And is it correct that based on your testimony from the preliminary hearing
       transcript you don't know how you received the gash in your leg?

   A: No, I don't.

   Q: And, sir, in connection with injuries that you received on the job you get some
5   sort of Workers' Comp; is that correct?

   Mr. Cummings: Objection. Relevance.[30]

   Mr. Deemer: Want me to make my offer of proof in front of the jury or the
       bench?

   The Court: Overruled. You may answer.

10 *The Witness:*   Yes. Yes, I do get workmen's compensation.

   Q. by Mr. Deemer: And officers get a different level of Workers' Comp if they are
       injured by an inmate as opposed to some sort of accidental injury; isn't that
       correct?

   A: Yes.

15 *Q:* If you are injured by an inmate you get three-quarters of your base pay as
       Workers' Comp. If you just happened to have an ordinary injury on the job it's
       one-half; is that correct?

   A: No. If it's an assaultive by an inmate the first three days I get back on sick
       time. So in other words, if I am out on sick time because of an injury from
20   an inmate, well, then I don't lose those three days' sick time. It's taken off my
       books and it's covered. Doesn't come off my books.

   Q: But if you have been injured on an ordinary type accident, that would come
       off your books?

   A: Yes, the first three days would be on-site injury. The first three days I would
25   lose, okay, and then would be picked up by workmen's comp.

   Q: And there is also a difference in the Workers' Comp rate, too; isn't there?

   Mr. Cummings: Same objection. Relevance.

   The Court: Overruled.

   The Witness: It's two-thirds pay whether it is one injury or not, whether it's a staff
30   injury from an inmate or—

   Mr. Deemer: No further questions.

Redirect Examination[31]

   Q. by Mr. Cummings: If a person is in General Population is it to the best of
       your knowledge appropriate for food trays to be retrieved in the fashion that

---

30. Relevance refers to whether an item of evidence tends to prove the proposition it is offered to
prove, and whether that proposition is of significance—is material—to the litigation. Here, the objection
is that Workers' Compensation payments have no significance—are not "material"—to the litigation.
Relevancy is examined in Chapter Three.

31. The direct examiner may conduct a redirect examination when cross-examination has been completed. The scope of redirect is limited to matters that were raised in cross-examination; this means that the
direct examiner is usually not permitted to prove an essential element of the case that was overlooked, although
judges vary widely in how strictly they will enforce this limitation. There is no Federal Rule of Evidence that
covers this specific topic. See generally FRE 611. The two parties in this case constantly seesawed back and
forth with redirect and recross-examinations, trying to have the last word. This is quite boring for the jury, and
usually develops no new information. Much of this repetitive testimony has been edited out of this transcript.

1   they were retrieved in this case? In other words, open up the door a little
    bit.
    A: Yes.
    Q: There was nothing wrong with that?
5   A: No. I had a housing unit for a year and a half down there with General
        Population inmates. They are programmed inmates.
    Q: Tell us what "programmed" means.
    A: Program is they go to work, they are—disciplinaries are very few, they are usu-
        ally not staff assaultive. I don't know how to say this. They are calm inmates.
10   They are programmed to prison life.
    Q: Now, that is very different from somebody who is in another portion of the
        institution that is, a SHU, Security Housing Unit, inmate; is that correct?
    A: Oh, yes, it's a lot different in Security Housing Unit.
    Q: If hypothetically this same incident happened on the Secured Housing Unit
15   side of Pelican Bay, which is not where it occurred, if it happened over there
        would it be appropriate for the correctional officers to order a door opened to
        retrieve the tray?
    A: No.
    Q: Why not?
20 A: Because they are assaultive to inmates or staff. They are highly disciplinary.
    Q: Is it safe to say that if they are in the other side, the Secured Housing Unit side,
        you are basically expecting trouble all the time?
    A: Yes.
    Q: Are you expecting less trouble or hopefully none at all when they are in the
25   General Population side?
    A: Yes, hopefully, yes.
    Q: What would you have done if inmate Johnson had been in the Secured
        Housing Unit? What would have been appropriate then?
    A: I would have a vest on. I would have a partner with me before I went to the
30   cell. When I picked up the breakfast tray I would open the food port. There
        would only be one inmate up to the food port and he would pass the tray in
        and I would not be standing in front of the food port.
    Q: You take additional precautions?
    A: Oh, yes.
35 Q: It's embarrassing to even ask you this, but are you in any way financially ben-
        efitted by getting injured on the job?
    A: Heavens, no. I have got a scar to prove it, and I don't like my scar.
    Q: That scar came out of this incident?
    A: Yes, it did.
40 Mr. Cummings: Thank you sir. Nothing further.
    Mr. Deemer: Nothing.
    The Court: Thank you. You are excused. You can either leave or stay, as you
        wish. Next witness.
    Mr. Cummings: Officer Van Berg.
45 The Court: Come up to the front, please, and raise your right hand.

1   RICHARD VAN BERG

called as a witness by the People, after having been sworn to tell the truth, the whole truth and nothing but the truth, was examined and testified as follows:

The Clerk: Be seated in the witness chair and state your name and business
5   address for the record.
The Witness: Richard Van Berg.

Direct Examination

Q. by Mr. Cummings: Your business address is fine. Pelican Bay State Prison?
A: Right.
10 Q: Officer, what's your occupation?
A: Correctional officer.
Q: How long have you been so employed?
A: Six years.
Q: Where are you currently stationed?
15 A: Pardon?
Q: What's your current assignment at the prison?
A: B Facilities at Pelican Bay.
Q: How long have you been at Pelican Bay?
A: Two and a half years.
20 Q: You were there when the institution opened?
A: Yes.
Q: Sir, were you working as a correctional officer on March the 28th, 1992?
A: Yes, I was.
Q: Did you have occasion on that day to come into contact with an inmate by the
25   name of Johnson?
A: Yes, I did.
Q: Same individual seated at the end of counsel table?
A: Yes, it is.
Q: Do you recall where he was?
30 A: He was inside of his cell.
Q: Was there a cell mate?
A: Yes, there was.
Q: Do you recall his name?
A: Not offhand.
35 Q: What is your routine assignment in B Facility?
A: I am a search and escort officer.
Q: Would you tell us what a search and escort officer does?
A: Searches cells, escorts inmates, delivers 115 rules violations, assists the pro-
      gram sergeant. He has a variety of duties.
40 Q: Were you involved in attempting to retrieve some trays from inmate Johnson
      on that date?
A: Yes, I was.

1 Q: Were you assigned to that or was that your normal duty for that day? Did some-
        one tell you to assist?

    A: I was ordered to go to A block and assist in receiving the trays.

    Q: Had you had any prior contact with inmate Johnson?

5 A: No.

    Q: Do you know inmate Johnson at all?

    A: No.

    Q: What other officers were in front of inmate Johnson's cell when you got there?

    A: The only two that I recall were Officer Smith and Walker.

10 Q: Were there other officers besides those two and you don't recall the names?

    A: Yes.

    Q: Did you hear Officer Smith make any orders or any commands of inmate
        Johnson?

    A: Yes.

15 Q: What did he order him to do?

    A: He ordered him to return the food trays to him through the food port on sev-
        eral occasions.

    Q: I take it two or more?

    A: Yes.

20 Q: Could you observe what inmate Johnson was doing from your position?

    A: From what I could see he was just standing at the door holding his food trays.

    Q: Door was closed at that point?

    A: Yes.

    Q: I am referring to the full cell door now, not the food port door.

25 A: Right. The food port was open.

    Q: Do you recall if the food port door was open?

    A: Yes.

    Q: Did you have a pretty good view of the person behind that door?

    A: Fairly well, yeah.

30 Q: You can tell whether or not they are swinging their arms or they look like they
        might be combative, I take it.

    A: Yes.

    Q: Did it appear to you that inmate Johnson was going to be combative?

    A: No, he was just standing there holding those two trays and had once asked to
35   speak to a sergeant.

    Q: And did you hear anybody reply what would happen as far as getting a sergeant
        to see him?

    A: He was told that he could see a sergeant but first he had to return the food
        trays.

40 Q: Did he say anything?

    A: No.

    Q: Did he take one of the trays off the other tray and slide it on through the food
        door as ordered?

    A: No.

45 Q: He just stood there with the two trays in his hand?

    A: Yes.

1 Q: At some point in time did Officer Smith order the door be opened?

    A: Yes.

    Q: Was the door open?

    A: Yes, it was.

5 Q: Was it open wide enough so that inmate Johnson could charge through if he wanted to?

    A: Yes.

    Q: Were you expecting that to happen?

    A: No.

10 Q: Did inmate Johnson—was he verbally assaultive or verbally threatening at all?

    A: No.

    Q: Was he physically assaultive? Did he appear to be physically dangerous at all?

    A: No, not at that point.

    Q: When the cell door opened what happened?

15 A: Inmate Johnson just dropped the food trays and rushed, you know, one sudden step towards the door.

    Q: Did he do anything with his hands?

    A: I seen one hand come out through the cell door. I believe it was his right hand and it was in a clenched fist. Officer Walker was standing right up against the

20   door so when it opened he was attempting to assault Officer Walker.

    Q: Let me make this clear. Did inmate Johnson make forward motions towards Correctional Officer Walker?

    A: Yes.

    Q: Or did Officer Walker make motions towards Johnson?

25 A: No, inmate Johnson stepped towards Officer Walker.

    Q: So he moved forward?

    A: Yes.

    Q: Did he appear to be attempting to fight or strike Walker?

    A: Yes

30 *Mr. Deemer:*   One moment. That's leading.

    The Court: Overruled. You may answer.

    Q. by Mr. Cummings: Did you see inmate Johnson strike Officer Walker?

    Mr. Deemer: Same objection.

    The Court: Overruled. You may answer.

35 *The Witness:*   Actual body contact, no.

    Q. by Mr. Cummings: Is that because from your position you couldn't see it?

    A: Yes.

    Q: What did you see Officer Walker do when inmate Johnson moved toward him?

40 A: The two just came together, Officer Walker had ahold of inmate Johnson and they were going back inside the cell.

    Q: Is that appropriate? Is that what a correctional officer should do in that situation is take command of him?

    A: Yes.

1 Q: At some point in time did you come in contact with the other officers' hands on inmate Johnson?

A: Yes.

Q: Was that inside the cell or outside the cell?

5 A: That was outside the cell.

Q: And why did you get involved at that point?

A: I assisted Officers Walker and I believe Huston in trying to get inmate Johnson's arm behind him so we could place it in handcuffs.

Q: And at that point in time was inmate Johnson being combative?

10 A: Yes.

Q: Was he being resistive?

A: Yes, absolutely.

Q: Was he complying with the orders that were being given him at that point?

A: No.

15 Q: Were you injured, sir?

A: Yes, I was.

Q: Where?

A: My left thumb.

Q: How?

20 A: I'm not sure how it happened.

Q: In the course of that altercation you were injured, I take it.

A: Yes.

Q: Did you seek medical attention?

A: Yes, I did.

25 Q: Where did you go?

A: Sutter Coast Hospital.

Q: Did they tell you that something had happened to your hand?

A: Yes, I had a bone chip.

Q: One of the bones in your hand was chipped?

30 A: Yes, sir.[32]

Mr. Cummings: Thank you sir. Nothing further.

Cross-examination

Q. *by Mr. Deemer:*   I have been watching you around the court. Those cowboy boots aren't state issue, are they?

35 A: No.

Q: Sir, you wrote a report in this matter, didn't you?

A: Yes, I did.

Q: You have a copy of that report with you, don't you?

A: Not with me, no.

---

32. Does Officer Van Berg have personal knowledge of the bone chip in his thumb? He does have knowledge of what the hospital told him about his injury, but if he testified "They told me I had a bone chip," it would be hearsay under FRE 801 and would be inadmissible unless it fit within an exception under FRE 803 or 804.

1 *Mr. Deemer:*   If I could approach the witness, Your Honor.

   The Court: Yes.

   Q. by Mr. Deemer: You will have to pardon my underlining, but I would like to show you your report and see if it refreshes your recollection at all.[33]

5 *Mr. Cummings:*   I don't believe there has been a question posed that indicates he does not recall.

   Mr. Deemer: I would just appreciate it if he would review it.

   The Witness: Yes, I'm done with that.

   Q. by Mr. Deemer: There is nothing in that report that gives any indication about

10   a food port being opened, is there?

   A: No.

   Q: How high up is the food port from the floor?

   A: I'm going to guess probably three and a half feet.

   Q: And the food port is up high enough so that, for example, if you want to move

15   an inmate or have an inmate cuff up that he can basically back up to the food port and stick his hands sort of like that; is that correct?

   A: Yes.

   Q: And so basically the food port is probably just a little bit lower than waist high for most people?

20 A: Yeah, probably pretty close to waist high.

   Q: Now, who opened the food port?

   A: Officer Smith, I believe.

   Q: And how did he open the food port?

   A: Take your key and take the padlock off the food port and then open it up.

25 Q: And again your report doesn't make any mention about the defendant being— requested to pass food trays through the food port, was there?

   A: No.

   Q: Now, as a practical matter while the defendant is standing in front of the door with these—he is standing with two trays in his hand; is that correct?

30 A: Yes.

   Q: If the port is open the trays could just be slid right through; isn't that correct?

   A: One at a time, yes.

   Q: And of course also if the doors—if the food tray door is open somebody could just reach in and grab a tray fairly easily, is that correct, if somebody handed it

35   to them?

   A: If it was pushed out to you. I wouldn't advise anybody sticking their hands though there.

   Q: Would it be fair to state that most of the inmates are afraid of Officer Walker?[34]

   A: That what?

---

33. Is the report admitted into evidence? Should it be? Normally an advocate can "refresh the memory" of a witness in any fashion that the judge will allow. If one party uses a document to refresh a witness's memory, the opposing party will be permitted to inspect it, examine the witness on it, and in many cases admit it into evidence. See FRE 612.

34. How would the witness know this? What objections can be made to this question? Why was none made?

1 *Q:* That the inmates are afraid of Officer Walker?

A: No.

Q: And you don't know how you sustained the injury that you sustained?

A: No.

5 *Mr. Deemer:*   No further questions.

Mr. Cummings: Officer Walker.

BRANDON WALKER

called as a witness by the People, after having been sworn to tell the truth, the whole truth and nothing but the truth, was examined and testified as follows:

10 *The Clerk:*   Be seated in the witness box and state your name and business address for the record, and could you also spell your name, please?

The Witness: Brandon Walker and I am at Pelican Bay State Prison.

Direct Examination

Q. by Mr. Cummings: Thank you. Sir, what's your occupation?

15 *A:* Correctional officer.

Q: How long have you been a correctional officer?

A: Just over five years.

Q: What prison are you currently assigned to?

A: Pelican Bay State Prison.

20 *Q:* How long have you been at Pelican Bay?

A: Since April of '91.

Q: Where did you come from, what institution?

A: Folsom.

Q: Sir, were you a correctional officer on duty on March the 28th, 1992?

25 *A:* Yes, I was.

Q: Did you have occasion on that date to come into contact with inmate Johnson?

A: Yes.

Q: Do you recognize inmate Johnson today?

A: Yes, I do, sir. He is sitting over next to Mr. Deemer.

30 *Q:* Before March the 28th, 1992, the day of this incident, did you know inmate Johnson?

A: No, I did not.

Q: Had you had any prior contact to your knowledge with inmate Johnson at Pelican Bay?

35 *A:* Not to my knowledge.

Q: What about at Folsom?

A: Not to my knowledge.

Q: What's your assignment at Pelican Bay or what was your assignment on March the 28th?

40 *A:* B Facility, 7 block, floor.

Q: What's a floor officer do?

A: We do just cell searches. We have to take inmates to R and R for packages or for picture ID, we take them there. Basically it's an escort position.

1 Q: Is feeding part of your normal duties?
   A: Oh, yes, sir.
   Q: Actually takes up quite a bit of time?
   A: Well, for cell feeding it takes about an hour to feed both buildings. And then
5 if we are feeding in the dining room it takes anywhere from an hour and a half
   to two hours.
   Q: When you say you worked normally 7 Block, is that the same block that
   inmate Johnson is on?
   A: No, sir.
10 Q: I believe he is in 8 Block; is that correct?
   A: That is correct.
   Q: Were you sent to inmate Johnson's cell that day?
   A: Yes, I was.
   Q: Who sent you?
15 A: Sergeant Kurtz.
   Q: What were you told?
   A: I was told that he had two food trays that he would not give up and we were to
   go and relinquish those trays.
   Q: How did you expect to do that, do you know?
20 A: Well, ideally it would have been to open the food port and have him hand us
   the trays.
   Q: When you arrived on March the 28th, what other officers were present out-
   side Johnson's cell?
   A: My partner. He came. The two yard officers, Smith and Huston, they came.
25 And Officer Van Berg. So there were five of us.
   Q: Do you know whether any of those officers normally work 8 Block or were
   they all sent?
   A: They were all sent from the yard.
   Q: When you arrived did you make—did you order inmate Johnson to give up
30 the trays?
   A: No.
   Q: Did you hear somebody else do it?
   A: Yes.
   Q: Who?
35 A: Officer Smith.
   Q: How many times, roughly?
   A: Three or four. He had been sitting on his bed and then when he started telling
   him to give up the trays then he stood up and stood at the door. So three, four
   times maybe.
40 Q: Was inmate Johnson saying anything to any of the officers at that time?
   A: No, he indicated that he had a 602, which is an appeal form that the inmate
   fills out for a sergeant, and then he was requesting to see a sergeant at that
   time.
   Q: Did you hear anybody respond to his request to see a sergeant?
45 A: Yes, Officer Smith did.

1   Q: What did he say?
    A: He said that he would be permitted to see the sergeant but that we needed to
        have the food trays at that time.
    Q: Why couldn't you just stop the whole operation and get him a sergeant right
5   away?
    A: Because sergeants on the yard have got other duties and if we were to set prec-
        edents in calling a sergeant over every time there was a small problem, then
        sergeant—we wouldn't be able to operate with just one sergeant in the yard.
    Q: Somebody ordered the door to be opened?
10 A: Yes.
    Q: Who?
    A: Smith.
    Q: And when Officer Smith ordered the door be opened, you were the first one
        who would normally have contact with whoever was behind it?
15 A: Right, because of my position where the door was opening. As the door opened
        I was number one.
    Q: What were you expecting to happen?
    A: I was expecting to get the trays and then to leave.
    Q: I take it you had your own job to do that day?
20 A: Yes.
    Q: Did you carry on that day a side-handled baton?
    A: Every day, yes.
    Q: In this incident did you pull your side-handled baton?
    A: No, I did not.
25 Q: Did you use your side-handled baton in any fashion?
    A: No, sir.
    Q: If you are expecting trouble, officer, do you normally pull out your side-han-
        dled baton if you are anticipating it?
    A: If I am anticipating it, yes.
30 Q: Were you anticipating trouble on this day in this incident?
    A: No, I was not based on—he was not showing any signs of any kind of tension or
        anger or anything. He was merely standing with two trays with trash all over them.
    Q: That's what I want to go into next. Was he being verbally abusive to anybody?
    A: Not at all.
35 Q: Did he give you indications from his body language that he was going to be
        aggressive or going to be violent?
    A: None.
    Q: The door opened up. What happened next?
    A: He dropped the food trays.
40 Q: Then what happened?
    A: Then he lunged towards me.
    Q: Did he make contact with you?
    A: Yes, he did.
    Q: What part of his anatomy struck what part of your anatomy?
45 A: He attempted to strike me in the facial area with his fists, but as soon as he
        lunged towards me and basically, you know, grabbed my body, then I was able

1   to turn him back around and push him back into the cell trying to put him on
       the floor.

   Q: Is that what you are trained to do?

   A: Yes.

5 Q: Is that what you are supposed to do to take control of the situation?

   A: Yes.

   Q: And when you got your hands on him did he go backwards or what happened?

   A: No. We were kind of almost kind of like dancing. We were kind of wrestling
       standing up and trying to get him to go to the floor and the whole time he was

10   still trying to punch me. You know, he was punching me in the side.

   Q: You two were basically face to face real close together?

   A: Right, holding on to one another.

   Q: And you are doing your best to hold on to him and he is attempting to strike
       you?

15 A: Yes.

   Q: And he is striking you?

   A: Yes, he is. And kicking.

   Q: And kicking? Were there other officers behind you?

   A: Yes, there was.

20 Q: Did several of them go into the cell also?

   A: Yes.

   Q: At some point in time did you actually end up on the ground?

   A: Yes, I did.

   Q: Did somebody get a handcuff on him?

25 A: Before he left the cell he had handcuffs.

   Q: One or both, do you remember?

   A: He had both.

   Q: Before he left the cell?

   A: Uh-huh.

30 Q: Was he resisting being handcuffed?

   A: Ever since—ever since he lunged towards me. See, when we are assaulted out
       there it's our job to, you know, communicate as much as possible telling him
       what we want them to do. And in this case we were all telling him to get down
       and his cellie was possibly a problem. So one of the officers went in and told

35   him to stay back and he resisted the whole time.

   Q: When you say "he," you are referring to Johnson.

   A: Inmate Johnson, yes.

   Q: Were you injured to the point of having to receive any outside medical
       treatment?

40 A: No, I was not.

   Mr. Cummings: Thank you sir. Nothing further.

Cross-examination

Q. by Mr. Deemer: Sir, you prepared a report in this matter, did you not?

   A: *Yes, I did, sir.*

1 Q: And you got it with you?
   A: Yes.
   Q: And you got an opportunity to review it today, haven't you?
   A: Yes.
5 Q: That report doesn't mention anything about food ports, does it?
   A: Well, or cell ports.
   Q: I am talking about your report, the one you signed.
   A: Yes, sir, I am looking at that right now. No, it does not indicate.
   Q: And when the door gets open you say the defendant dropped the trays; is that
10   correct?
   A: Yes, yes, he did.
   Q: About how far from the door is he when the trays dropped?
   A: An inch. Well, the trays—we have to count for the distance that composes the
      trays was about maybe twelve inches plus a couple more. He was within a foot
15   and a half.
   Q: And the door opens and the trays drop; is that correct?
   A: That is correct.
   Q: Do you recall seeing his head drop?
   A: No, I don't recall that.
20 Q: Do you recall what he did with his head?
   A: No, I don't.
   Q: You say Johnson's hands come up; is that correct?
   A: I'm sorry?
   Q: Johnson's hands come up?
25 A: His hands come up simultaneously as he is lunging toward me, yes.
   Q: And how far out the door does he get?
   A: Just about—he wasn't all the way out of the door.
   Q: And you are telling me that Johnson is totally cuffed in the cell itself; is that
      correct?
30 A: Yes, he was.
   Q: At some point in the cell you had him—I wasn't sure exactly what you are talk-
      ing about. But you simply kind of demonstrated there to the jury.[35] You had
      him actually turned around with his hands behind his back and pushed over
      something?
35 A: Over the desk.
   Q: And at that point that's when he was cuffed?
   A: Yes.
   Q: And then he was taken outside?
   A: Yes, he was.

---

35. Suppose you were an appellate judge reading this record on appeal. Would you have any idea
what the lawyer is talking about? Indeed, reading the transcript, did you notice when the witness was demonstrating something to the jury? The examiner must always keep well in mind that the court reporter has
ears but not eyes. Whatever demonstration the witness made should have been described by the lawyer
in adequate detail.

1   *Q:* You came here from Folsom; is that correct?

    A: That is correct.

    Q: And regardless of what your beliefs are about what your behavior patterns are, isn't it fair to state that inmates are generally afraid of you?

5   *Mr. Cummings:* Objection. Lack of foundation.

    The Court: Overruled. You may answer.

    The Witness: I don't know the fact that an inmate is afraid of me. Why would they be afraid of me?[36]

    Q. by Mr. Deemer: Well, I will put it this way. Are you aware of the fact that

10   inmates are afraid of you because you tend to be, say, a little bit more physical with them than they think you should be?

    A: No, I don't think that's accurate.

    Mr. Deemer: I have no further questions.

Redirect Examination

15   *Q. by Mr. Cummings:* Sir, why did you transfer from Folsom to Pelican Bay?

    A: The area.

    Q: I take it it was your choice?

    A: Oh, yes.

    Q: Do you know what a 602 is?

20   *A:* Oh, yes.

    Q: What is it?

    A: It's an inmate appeal form.

    Q: Is that where the inmate typically could write down grievances regarding an officer?

    A: Sure.

25   *Q:* When an inmate grieves an officer on a 602 that's an actual document, correct?

    A: Yes, it is.

    Q: Are you made aware of that?

    A: I am supposedly. If it pertains to me, yes.

    Q: And by CDC policies are you required to respond to that?

30   *A:* Within five days.

    Q: To an actual written response?

    A: Yes.

    Q: To your knowledge had you had any other contact with Johnson anywhere in the CDC system or outside the CDC system before March 28th of this year?

35   *A:* Prior to the day that he refused to give up his food tray, I don't think I have ever met the man.

    Mr. Cummings: Thank you. Nothing further.

Recross-examination

    Q. by Mr. Deemer: Emotionally exciting though, isn't it?

40   *Mr. Cummings:* Objection. Relevance.

    The Court: Overruled. You may answer.

---

36. How would he know the answer to that question? Why was this allowed?

1 *Q. by Mr. Deemer:*   It's emotionally exciting, though, isn't it, when you are
   involved in an altercation?

   A: Well, is a victim emotionally excited?

   Q: Well, it's emotionally exciting when you win, isn't it?

5 *Mr. Cummings:*   Object as being argumentative.

   The Court: Sustained as argumentative.[37]

   Q. by Mr. Deemer: When you get into one of these altercations with an inmate is
   it fair to say your adrenaline gets pumped up pretty good?

   A: Oh, absolutely. And then understand this, it's not my desire to go and get
10 into a physical altercation because not only is that not my job, but I could get
   hurt. And so when I am asked by the department to go and do something that
   is going to require possibly physically taking something away or restraining
   them, I have possibilities of getting hurt and that's not what my intentions
   are.

15 Q: When you go to—when you went to the door you are not dressed the way you
   are now, are you?

   A: Oh, no.

   Q: You got a jumpsuit on of some sort. Let me rephrase it. Some sort of utility
   type fatigues on; is that correct?

20 A: I might have. If we are not on lock-down then I am not entitled to wear the
   jumpsuit-type clothing.

   Q: Do you recall whether you had a jumpsuit-type clothing on or fatigue clothing?

   A: I was not wearing fatigues, no.

   Q: What were you wearing that particular day?

25 A: I don't recall.

   Q: But regardless of what you are wearing when you go in there, your name tag
   or some sort of a name thing is on.

   A: Absolutely.

   Q: Your shirt?

30 A: That's part of the uniform, yes.

   Q: And those cell doors, they got little holes in them, don't they?

   A: Yes.

   Q: When you stand up close to the cell door you can look outside and you can
   see what's there?

35 A: I'm sure I wouldn't have to stand even right up to the cell door. You can probably see me if I was standing in the day room with my name.

   Mr. Deemer: No further questions.

(Court was adjourned at 4:05 P.M., to be resumed at 9:00 A.M., Tuesday, the 28th
day of July, 1992.)

---

37. Although all jurisdictions recognize the objection that a question is argumentative, the boundaries of the concept are difficult to define. A question is argumentative if it is essentially an argument to
the jury, eliciting no new information. Like a leading question, it simply states a conclusion and asks the
witness to agree with it. Here, the defense counsel's questions seem to be actually arguing with a witness,
calling for an argument in response, also objectionable as argumentative.

1   CRESCENT CITY, CA.,

DATE: Tuesday, July 28, 1992, 9:00 A.M.

(The following proceedings were had in camera.)

5 *The Court:*   We are in chambers out of the presence of the jury. Both attorneys are present. The defendant is not present. Do you waive his appearance for this?

Mr. Deemer: Yeah.

The Court: Mr. Cummings, you have indicated you wish to make a motion out of the presence of the jury.

10 *Mr. Cummings:*   I do, Your Honor. It regards the offer of testimony from inmate Grant which I believe has been transported and is available today for testimony. Inmate Grant was approximately one week ago, maybe ten days ago at the most, found to be 1368.

15   Actually I believe it was a stipulated 1368. And that he was not competent to stand trial in his own case and could not assist counsel and didn't know the nature of the proceedings. And I find it somewhat amazing that someone who there has been a finding of 1368 on and a pending transportation order to Atascadero is being offered as some sort of a witness. This is the same individual who wants to talk about an instance going back to December of '91 if my memory serves me. In other words, he is not claiming to offer anything as a percipient witness to this action. He is claiming that he has had previous dealings with one or two of the officers but nothing to add as far as this particular incident.

20

Mr. Deemer: The Grant testimony is going to be directed, I hope—and I agree that he is certified 1368 and I'm not sure I am going to get this out of him as a witness. He rambles all over the place. Grant's testimony is going to be directed that he has had prior instances with Officer Walker and Officer Walker has a reputation and he knows who Walker is and the reputation amongst the inmates for using force and violence to excess.

25

30 *The Court:*   Well, competent to stand trial and competent to take an oath are not the same.[38] And if anything I would say standing trial involves a good many more considerations. If Grant appears to be reasonably rational as the

---

38. Under the Federal Rules, Rule 601 states the general rule of competency that "all persons are competent to be witnesses." Under this standard, are there any grounds to exclude the testimony of Grant? What risks are identified in the ensuing discussion between counsel and the court?

   At common law, there were numerous rules of competency that would keep a person off the stand entirely. Spouses at common law were incompetent to testify for or against each other; interested persons, including parties, could not testify; atheists were incompetent, as were children and the mentally ill. The Federal Rules have largely eliminated competency as a separate limitation on the admissibility of evidence. FRE 601 provides that everyone is competent to be a witness, except as "otherwise provided in these rules." Except in diversity cases, FRE 602 is the only general competency rule left, limiting testimony to those with personal knowledge. FRE 605 and 606 provide narrow exceptions that, for obvious reasons, make judges and jurors incompetent to testify in the case before them. As we explore in Chapter Seven, there are also restrictions on the testimony of experts that are analogous to FRE 602's "competency" restriction of firsthand knowledge. In diversity cases, FRE 601 provides that state law determines competency. Apart from these matters, the word "incompetency" today simply refers to evidence excluded by a specific exclusionary rule. These matters are discussed more fully in Chapter Three.

1   questioning proceeds, he can testify. If his testimony comes out as gibberish,
     of course, we can terminate the testimony.
     Mr. Deemer: I freely admit it may well come out as gibberish because his atten-
     tion span is so short I don't think he can, you know, at this point he is not
5   capable of lying anyhow.
     Mr. Cummings: How do you know?
     Mr. Deemer: You don't. In other words, all I'm saying is his attention span is so
     short there is no way you can tell him "I want you to testify to such and such
     a thing," and he is going to get on the stand and testify to it. Admit that's a
10   problem with him and I think that's something the DA can comment on to
     the jury. I think that's for the jury to take a look at.
     Mr. Cummings: Is it a problem you can tell him what to say?
     Mr. Deemer: I assure you, you could not tell him what to say.
     The Court: Have you spoken with him this morning?
15   *Mr. Deemer:*   I have not spoken with him this morning. I tried to cut my witness
     list down substantially. I haven't looked. What I propose to do is to call the two
     inmates and one of whom observed Walker's incident with Grant in the—out-
     side the kitchen and will basically testify as to what it is and what that's based
     on, what their fear is of Walker and what it's based on and also basically what
20   took place in the cell during this incident. And I'm probably not going to
     call the other lieutenants because after some brief discussions with them it's
     obvious they are all going to support, you know—it's officer versus inmate or
     inmate versus officer so they are not going to undercut their officers. . . .

     (The following proceedings were had in open court.)

25   **CRESCENT CITY, CA.,**

     DATE: Tuesday, July 28, 1992, 9:00 A.M.
     The Court: The record will reflect that all jurors, counsel and defendant are
     present. You may call your next witness.
     Mr. Cummings: Officer Smith.

30   **STEPHEN SMITH**

     called as a witness by the People, after having been sworn to tell the truth, the
     whole truth and nothing but the truth, was examined and testified as follows:

     The Clerk: Please be seated and state your name and business address for the
     record.
35   *The Witness:*   Stephen Smith, Pelican State Prison.

                          Direct Examination

     Q. by Mr. Cummings: Sir, what's your profession?
     A: Correctional officer.
     Q: How long have you been a correctional officer?
40   A: Eight years.

1 Q: What institutions have you worked at?
   A: I worked at the Idaho State Prison for two years, San Quentin for three and a
       half years, and I have been in Pelican Bay for approximately three years.
   Q: Are you part of the start-up team up here?
5 A: Yes, sir.
   Q: Sir, were you a correctional officer employed in that capacity on March the
       28th, 1992?
   A: Yes, sir, I was.
   Q: And did you have occasion to come into contact with inmate Johnson and
10   actually Johnson's cell mate Butler on that date?
   A: Yes, I did.
   Q: Under what circumstances?
   A: I was—I'm a yard officer. I was out on a yard and my supervisor asked me,
       wanted me to go over to A block and pick up a tray. Apparently Mr. Johnson
15   didn't want to give up his food tray that morning out of his cell. So I went over
       to pick up the tray.
   Q: And where was inmate Johnson in the cell when you first saw him?
   A: He was sitting on the end of the bunk, the lower bunk.
   Q: Where were the trays if you remember?
20 A: The trays were approximately less than a foot inside the door sitting on the
       floor next to the wall.
   Q: How many were there?
   A: There was two trays with a pile of garbage on them.
   Q: Would those trays pass through the food port door if they wanted to?
25 A: If you took the tray, took the garbage off and everything one at a time they would.
   Q: If you were going to pass it through the food port door would you have to pass
       it lengthwise or could you pass them crosswise?
   A: Lengthwise.
   Q: So I take it the food port door is somewhat narrow.
30 A: I really can't tell you the exact width of it. I have never measured one, but it
       would be difficult to put a tray through sideways.
   Q: What exactly did you order inmate Johnson to do?
   A: Well, if I may, I didn't order him at first. What I did is I walked up. He was sit-
       ting on the end of the bunk. He had a piece of paper in his hand. As I arrived
35   at his cell I said, "How are you doing? What's up? Are you having a bad day?"
       Mr. Johnson at that time stood up. He said, "I need to see a sergeant, man."
       I said, "Well, you can see a sergeant later on. Right now I am here to pick up
       those trays. Sergeant asked me to get them."
           At that time he walked over towards the door. He had some paperwork in
40   his hand, a 602, a green piece of paper. Started to come towards the door and
       he never spoke again. He reached down, picked up the trays, both trays with
       a pile of garbage. He had them both in his hand like in this manner. He had
       the piece of paper underneath holding all of that in his hands. He walked over
       to the door. And it's a normal procedure—as I walked up to the door I had
45   already opened up the port—

1   Q: The food port door?
    A: Yes, sir. I had opened that up. It's a little slot about this wide, that high. I
        already opened that up as I arrived and he stood there in front of the door. He
        never spoke again, not another word.
5   Q: Did you ask him anything else?
    A: Yes, I asked him at that time, "Can I have the trays?" He stood there looking
        at me.
    Q: No response?
    A: No response, just stood there looking. I asked him a second time, "Are you
10   going to give me the trays?"
    Q: Let me show you this photograph that has been marked Exhibit 1 for identifi-
        cation. Can you tell me what that is a photograph of?
    A: It's the port door.
    Q: Do you mean the food port door like the one in inmate Johnson's cell door?
15 A: Yes.
    Q: How do you know?
    A: It looks just like the food port doors in all the cells in B facility.
    Q: Is it a fair and accurate picture of the food port door?
    A: Yes.
20 *Mr. Cummings:*   I move the admission of People's Exhibit 1.[39]
    Mr. Deemer: This photograph may be misleading, Your Honor, because it does
        not show the width of the cell door. It does not show how wide the food port
        door is, to any scale.
    Mr. Cummings: There has already been testimony that the port door is twelve
25   inches wide, wide enough for the tray. The jury knows this, so the photograph
        is not misleading.
    The Court: I'll admit it in this situation since there has been testimony about its
        width already. Exhibit 1 is received in evidence.
    Q. by Mr. Cummings: Now, Officer, if the door to this food port is open, and you
30   are standing in front of it, you can pass your trays through here just by sticking
        them through?

---

39. There is a universal principle of evidence law that no evidence is admissible until the proponent
shows that the evidence is what the proponent claims it to be. Tangible evidence, including real objects,
photographs, and documents, must be shown to be "authentic." See FRE 901, 902. Authentication usually
requires the testimony of a witness who can supply the facts necessary to satisfy these rules. In the case of a
photograph, the witness must be familiar with the subject of the photograph; identify the subject; and state
whether the photograph is a fair and accurate depiction of the subject. The process of authentication is
referred to as "laying the foundation" for admission. You will study this process again in Chapter Three. For
a very useful work on the subject of foundations, see Edward Imwinkelreid, Evidentiary Foundations (3d
ed. 1995). Generally speaking, to have an exhibit admitted into evidence the attorney must first have the
exhibit marked for identification by the court reporter. By marking an exhibit for identification and then
by referring to the identification number or letter when the exhibit is used, the attorney can ensure that the
record accurately reflects which exhibit is being discussed. The attorney must then introduce the necessary
foundational testimony to show that the exhibit is what the attorney claims it to be. Then the proponent
offers the exhibit into evidence ("Your Honor, we now offer Exhibit 1 into evidence"), and makes sure that
the trial court rules on its admissibility. The requirement of authentication is a prerequisite to the admissibility of evidence, and thus it is for the judge to decide whether the conditions of admissibility have been
satisfied under the terms of FRE 901(a). Authentication of all kinds of exhibits is discussed in Chapter Four.

1 A: One at a time. It was obvious that he had such a load in his hands that he could not pass them through the port.

Q: Did it appear to you that inmate Johnson was acting aggressively towards the correctional officers?

5 A: Well, when we first arrived no, sir. He had a very docile attitude. He was not aggressive. That's why we went with the procedure we did. There was no vulgarities, which is the normal—you usually get, "Well, I want to see so and so; you are not doing this and that." There was no argumentativeness out of him at all. When I explained to him, "You will see the sergeant after you give me the trays, 10 I will tell the sergeant to come and talk to you," he got up, walked over in a very docile manner.

Q: If an inmate had been acting violently, verbally abusive, kicking, spitting, screaming, would it then be appropriate to have the door opened?

A: No.

15 Q: What is the difference?

A: Well, if the inmate is violent, we just can't open the door up and have him attack us. So if he is already in his cell, we are not going to open the door up just to get, you know, a bunch of trouble.

Q: Do you know why inmate Johnson wanted to see a sergeant?

20 A: I found out later. I didn't know then. But apparently he had a 602, something about some property. He wanted his property right now or something and I don't work the unit so I wasn't involved in that. I found out later.

Mr. Deemer: Objection. Hearsay and not the best evidence. If there is going to be testimony about the 602 report it should be admitted on its own.

25 Mr. Cummings: The exact contents are not important here, Your Honor. He had a complaint. That's all we're testifying to.

The Court: Testimony about the complaint in general is permitted. Detail about the contents is not important.

Q. by Mr. Cummings: So, tell us in general what a 602 is.

30 A: A 602 is an appeal process that the convicts use if there is a discrepancy, any type of discrepancy. They can utilize it if they don't get enough toothpaste, if they think they want some toothpaste. If an officer is disrespectful they can utilize a 602, which is an appeal process. We have four different levels on that. It will come to you directly, which is an informal level, which you respond 35 directly to that convict. If he has a complaint against me, I file or I give him a written answer on that. It is processed through the department. We have a system where it is logged in a log and then once—if he is not satisfied with my response, he sends it on up the line. There are four separate levels.

Q: So there is a whole appeal process for inmates to air their grievances?

40 A: Yes, sir.

Q: Is the point of that to cut down on friction between correctional officer staff?

A: Absolutely. That is the main purpose of the 602 process is to alleviate any problems at a lower level.

Mr. Cummings: Thank you. Nothing further.

1   *Cross-examination*

Q. by Mr. Deemer: Sir, is it fair to state that some inmates at least have a certain
     fear of officers' use of force and violence, whether or not that is justified?

A: I'm sure they probably feel that way.

5 *Q:*   And is it also fair to state that if an officer starts into a cell with the presence of
     other officers that it would be reasonable for an inmate to assume that some
     sort of force and violence is going to be imposed upon him?

Mr. Cummings: Objection. Lack of foundation.[40]

The Court: Overruled. You may answer.

10 *The Witness:*   I don't think so. We are on a GP.

Q. by Mr. Deemer: You are what?

A: It's a General Population and many times we go in the cells with the inmates there.

Q: But basically the more officers—talking of the type of situation we are talking
     about here. The more officers that are outside the door, the more likely it is
15   for an inmate to believe that because of his refusal when that door is opened,
     what is going to happen?

A: Whenever we have a problem we always send over a lot of officers. That is not
     an unusual thing. And we do not open the door up and rush in there and do
     anything. In the three years that I have worked B Facility, I have never cell
20   extracted anyone on second watch, not one time.

Mr. Deemer: One moment. No further questions.

Mr. Cummings: Nothing.

The Court: Thank you. You are excused. You can leave or stay as you wish. Next
     witness.

25 *Mr. Cummings:*   Yes. Ruth Taylor.

The Court: Come up to the front and raise your right hand.

RUTH TAYLOR

called as a witness by the People, after having been sworn to tell the truth, the
whole truth and nothing but the truth, was examined and testified as follows:

30 *The Clerk:*   Be seated in the witness chair and state your name and business
     address for the record and could you spell your name for us, please.

The Witness: Sure. My name is Ruth Taylor and my business address is Pelican
     Bay State Prison.

The Court: You may examine.

35   *Direct Examination*

Q. by Mr. Cummings: Thank you, Your Honor. Miss Taylor, what's your
     occupation?

A: I am a correctional case records specialist.

---

40. Under FRE 701, a lay witness's opinion must be rationally based on personal knowledge. Could
Officer Smith know what is reasonable for inmates to assume? As it turns out, he does have personal
knowledge on which to base his opinion and defense counsel probably regrets asking this question.

1   *Q:* Tell us what your job basically entails.

    A: Analyzing commitments, calculating release dates, normally case work for the inmates.

    Q: Keeping track of how many days they gain or they lose and when they are due

5   out?

    A: Yes, sir.

    Q: Do you have with you today the C File—and I will ask you in a minute what a C File is. But do you have the C File of inmate Johnson?

    A: Yes, I do.

10   *Q:* What is a C File?

    A: It's a collection of all of his records during the period that he was incarcerated with the Department of Corrections under that CDC number. It is maintained by the Department of Corrections and contains all original records, except medical records, pertaining to that inmate's incarceration, including informa-

15   tion on sentencing, classification actions, disciplinary hearings and grievances, and parole. Information related to an inmate's movement in and out of the prison system is summarized on a sheet attached to the cover of the file.

    Q: I am going—do you know what a 969B package is?

    A: Yes, I do. It is a collection of certified copies of documents from the C file,

20   including abstracts of judgments and the chronological case history.

    Q: This has been marked People's Exhibit No. 2 for identification and would ask you to identify that if you could, please.

(Exhibit 2 was marked.)

25   *A:* Yes.

    Q: Does it show abstracts, court abstracts?

    A: Yes, it does.

    Q: What is an abstract?

    A: That is the document the courts provide committing an individual to the

30   Department of Corrections.

    Q: Are those true copies, certified to be true copies of the ones in the original C File?

    A: Yes, they are.

    Q: And to the best of your knowledge are they identical to the ones in the C File?

    A: Yes, they are.

35 *Mr. Cummings:* Thank you, ma'am. Move People's 2 in.

    Mr. Deemer: Objection, yes, sir, to pages—well, considering the cover letter page 1, would be pages 2 and 3, the chronological listings, in view of the fact there is great varieties of inadmissible hearsay.

    The Court: Any reason why those pages should not be included?

40 *Mr. Cummings:* It will be stipulated that in any case he is a state inmate.

    Mr. Deemer: We'll stipulate he is an inmate.

    The Court: Both sides are stipulating the defendant was a state inmate on the date of this alleged offense, which would have been March 28th, 1992?[41]

---

41. Parties can stipulate that certain facts are not subject to dispute for purposes of deciding their case. Such an agreement relieves the party with the burden of proof from having to submit evidence on

1 *Mr. Cummings:*   With that stipulation I will withdraw Exhibit 2.

The Court: Ladies and gentlemen, you should regard the fact that the defendant was confined as an inmate in the state prison on March 28th, 1992 as being conclusively true because of the stipulation without any further proof as to
5 that fact.

Mr. Cummings: Thank you. Nothing further.

Mr. Deemer: I have no questions.

The Court: You are excused. You may leave or stay as you wish.

Mr. Cummings: No further witnesses, Your Honor.

10 *The Court:*   People rest?

Mr. Cummings: I am resting.[42]

(The following proceedings were had outside the presence of the jury.)

The Court: Let the record reflect that the jury has left the court room. We still have left the attorneys and defendant.

15 *Mr. Deemer:*   Motion to dismiss at this time.[43] The information charge is battery on Huston and a battery on Van Berg. Battery is described as the unlawful application of force upon the person of another. Van Berg does not know how he got injured. Huston does not know how he got injured. There is no testimony—no testimony from anybody that any of these injuries were inflicted by the defen-
20 dant. There is no testimony about any of his feet coming in contact. There is no testimony about what he had on in the way of shoes. There is no testimony of his fists coming in contact. And frankly I never felt there was enough evidence to even bring this case past the preliminary hearing stage. Judge Schott did.

But we are at trial now and there is simply not enough evidence before the
25 jury from which the jury can conclude beyond a reasonable doubt that a battery has been committed upon these officers. They could have scraped themselves going through a door. Anything could have happened. And there is absolutely no evidence whatsoever of the defendant striking either Officer Van Berg or Officer Huston, and I don't think you can submit this case to the jury at the
30 present time. You are just asking them to totally speculate as to what took place.

---

the stipulated fact. And the opponent may be willing to stipulate to facts that are uncontrovertible or that might require evidentiary proof that is even more harmful or embarrassing to their own case. Because stipulations eliminate the need for proof, their enforcement can be justified on grounds of efficiency.

There is recent authority that a court can require the prosecution in a criminal case to accept a stipulation offered by the defendant, and thus to forego proof of the stipulated fact, when that proof is not probative of any other fact or issue in the case. But a party may not be required to forego proof when this would impair the presentation of the party's case or would be relevant to other issues. The effect of stipulations on the application of FRE 403 is discussed in Chapter Three.

42. The prosecution has now completed its case. The court will entertain various motions from defense counsel; after that the defense will present whatever case it chooses to. Before reading the remainder of the transcript, think about how the prosecution has proved its case and about what you might do were you defense counsel.

43. At the close of the prosecution's case, the defense may move for judgment of acquittal based on the insufficiency of the evidence to sustain a conviction. The test in California, which is fairly standard, is whether there is "substantial evidence"—that is, evidence that is reasonable, credible, and of solid value—such that a reasonable trier of fact could find the defendant "guilty beyond a reasonable doubt" on each element of the offense. People v. Johnson, 26 Cal. 3d 557, 606 P.2d 738 (1980). The same test is applied by an appellate court deciding an appeal that alleges insufficiency of the evidence.

1 *Mr. Cummings:* Sometimes I wonder whether Mr. Deemer and I actually sat
   through the same trial and heard the same evidence. I find it somewhat amazing when he says there is no evidence of any direct striking. There is no evidence and that is true of any direct striking. No one can testify truthfully that
5 this right blow caused injury to my left hand or et cetera. However, what the
   testimony is very clear on and is clear from multiple witnesses is that the fracas
   continued, resistance continued. He was kicking. Multiple officers testified
   he was kicking. Multiple officers testified he was swinging over and over again
   with a clenched fist.

10   A couple of officers viewed it a little differently. One saw him duck down
   as to put his head down. A couple officers did not see it that way. It's just the
   perception of different officers perceiving the same incident slightly different,
   an honest recitation of what the facts were.

        You have a person who is obviously of a stocky build, of a firm stature, and
15 he is for some reason hell-bound that he is going to go ahead and do what
   he can to make his point for whatever reasons. Drops those trays and moves
   forward at a rapid motion. Multiple officers testified in an aggressive fashion.
   Defense attorney would have you believe that Walker walks in and subdues
   him. That's not what the testimony was.

20   Walker's testimony was that "he was on top of me pushing me back for a
   while; I was on top of him pushing him back for a while." He even said it was
   "kind of like dancing" at one point and basically the whole time the order is
   to "get down," none of which are being complied with. I mean what standard
   are we going to put on correctional officers in a prison? Are we going to say,
25 "Unless you can come in and say this person kicked me in my left thumb and
   because of that I know I was injured"? These officers know they were injured
   because inmate Johnson caused a nothing incident to grow into a significant
   injury with two injuries, both of which required some hospital treatment.
   Submit it.

30 *The Court:* The motion is denied. I agree that the case is weak, particularly with
   the two counts that are charged. Had there been a charge of an assault against
   Officer Walker it would be almost a slam dunk.[44] There is plenty of evidence
   to suggest to the jury that count. But that was not charged. As to the two
   who were charged I think the jury can draw the inference because there was
35 ample testimony of the defendant striking and kicking in the course of this
   struggle. They could draw the inference that it was kicks or blows from the
   defendant causing injury to Officers Huston and Van Berg. So the motion is
   denied.[45]

---

44. So why wasn't the defendant charged with assault on Walker?

45. Consider the prosecution and defense theories of what evidence is necessary to sustain a conviction for the crime of battery. Wouldn't there likely be case law on this point that should be helpful to the
court? Why didn't either lawyer refer to any? When you read the judge's final charge to the jury, notice
whether the court gives the jury any instructions that are helpful in answering the question "what is a
battery."

1 *Mr. Cummings*: Your Honor, People have a motion at this time basically to amend and conform the information to the facts as they were deduced during the trial. That would be Count 3, Penal Code Section 4501.5, the victim being Walker.

5 *Mr. Deemer*: Your Honor, I think it's a little bit late for that motion. Number one, the district attorney has rested. Prior to that he might have made the motion. Secondly, the real problem is there really isn't any testimony to support that allegation in the 995. Motions to attend—Mr. Cummings did the preliminary hearing in this matter and he is the one that did the charging, and

10 I think that if that's the way he feels at this point in time, that—I mean he has simply charged—there is just no way that he should be allowed to add Count 3 at this point in time or to amend it.

The Court: Well, there is no showing of why that could not have been done in a timely fashion. Apparently the facts were out front in the beginning, at least at

15 the time of the hearing. So the motion to amend is denied. Anything further before we hear the defense case?

Mr. Cummings: No, Your Honor.

Mr. Deemer: No, Your Honor.

The Court: Return the jury to the courtroom, please.

20 (The jury was returned to the courtroom.)

The Court: The jury has returned to the courtroom. Both attorneys and defendant are present. It is the defense case, Mr. Deemer.

Mr. Deemer: Thank you. Ladies and gentlemen of the jury, it's my opportunity at this time to outline to you basically where I expect the defense case is going

25 to go. And again, you never know what witnesses are going to testify to sometimes so I may end up being surprised. But essentially what I believe took place is this.[46] Is that the defendant was notified that a package had arrived— that he was aware of the fact somehow or other that a package had been sent to him by his family. A substantial period of time goes by.

30 The first thing that happens is that apparently the wrong Johnson is taken down to get the package. To get the package the inmates in General Population have to go to what they call R and R, which I understand stands for release and receiving or receiving and release or something of that sort. I wonder if there is some sort of analogy with R and R in the service.

35 So apparently around the 12th of March the wrong Johnson goes down to R and R to get the package. The next day—and probably most of you remember this; it was the 13th of March—the electricity goes off and there was some delays. Now, the officer that's in charge of doing the R and R routine and escorting inmates out to get the package had to go on vacation. So he leaves a

40 note in the sergeant's office or in the office in this unit, which the defendant watches this note written and gets stuck up on one of those little post-em slips to go down and get the package.

---

46. It is actually improper for a lawyer to express a belief as to what happened. Why might that be so? Why, in any event, did the state not object at this point?

1   This officer goes on vacation and this drags on and drags on. The defendant says "I want to see a lieutenant or a sergeant I can get my package." That never happens. Finally on the 28th he withholds the tray, which I agree is disobedient. He is asked to give up the tray.

5   Now, essentially everything that you have heard up until the time that the defendant drops the trays is consistent with the defendant's recollection except one or two things. Number one, the defendant does not recall the tray slot being opened and is standing there waiting for the tray slot to be opened in order to slide the trays through the slot.

10   The second thing is that he has this recollection of Officer Walker placing gloves on just before the doors open. And the third thing is that the defendant has been incarcerated as you have heard since around 1983 or '85 and he knows Officer Walker, knows who Officer Walker is. Officer Walker came up here from Folsom and he knows what Walker's reputation is. At least among

15   the inmates Officer Walker has a reputation for pounding on inmates.

      So there he is standing with the trays in his hand. Walker is on the other side. He can obviously identify him because it says Walker on the name tag. And the door opens and instead of the tray slot opening, the door opens and he figures he is going to get pounded. He drops the trays, drops his head, puts

20   his hands up over his head, and as the officers testified, the melee ensues.

      The defense testified that to his knowledge he never, ever came in contact with Officer Huston or Officer Van Berg, which is really curious because so far they have—and I doubt that it will come back to this, but neither of them testify as to any contact by them between them and the defendant in terms

25   of force. And the only officer he comes in contact with is this Officer Walker until after he is escorted out of the cell, at which place some additional incidents take place. But it wasn't any of the officers that got battered at that time.

      There are two other inmate, possibly three other inmate witnesses. One of them is the defendant's cell mate, whose recollection of the incident is some-

30   what different from the officers and who I believe in essence is going to testify that Officer Walker came in, just piled through the door and the defendant ended up getting beaten. The other inmate is an inmate who is in an adjacent cell who could see the crowd of what they believed is eight or ten officers outside the door and see this incident take place. There is—one of these two

35   inmates, I'm not sure which, was with the defendant I believe at some point in time prior to this incident and observed Walker engaging in some, shall we call it, aggressive conduct towards another inmate outside a kitchen area and then some comments made by either Walker or Walker and Van Berg afterwards. And which goes to basically what he thinks is going to happen when

40   the door opened.

      Now, what I got to have you understand is this, is that I'm not trying to establish that Walker is a bad guy or is an aggressive officer in this case. The key thing is this, if you have reason to believe that you are going to be assaulted you can do something to defend yourself. And in essence I believe what the testimony is going to show is that the defendant had this belief that when

1   this door opens he drops—I mean he is standing there totally not aggressive,
     dropped the trays, okay, ducks his head and does the most normal thing that
     all of us would do under those circumstances, puts his hands over his head to
     avoid getting beat.[47] . . .

5   **GEORGE BUTLER**

     called as a witness by the Defendant, after having been sworn to tell the truth, the
     whole truth and nothing but the truth, was examined and testified as follows:

     The Clerk: Could you state your name for the record, please.
     The Witness: George Butler.

10   *Direct Examination*

     Q. by Mr. Deemer: Mr. Butler, you are an inmate out at Pelican Bay, right?
     A: Yes.
     Q: And the jury is going to know this anyhow. You are out there because you are
         convicted of a felony of some sort?[48]
15   A: Yes.
     Q: What kind of felonies have you been convicted of?
     A: Robbery.
     Q: Anything else?
     A: Battery.
20   Q: And do you know Mr. Johnson?
     A: Yes.
     Q: How do you know him?
     A: He was my cell mate.
     Q: How long was he your cell mate?
25   A: Three months.
     Q: And where was he your cell mate?
     A: In Pelican Bay B Facility, 8 Block.
     Q: And do you remember an incident taking place with him on or about, say,
         towards the end of March sometime?
30   A: Yes.
     Q: Where did that incident take place?
     A: In his cell.

---

47. What do you think of the style and effectiveness of this opening statement? Has defense counsel
personalized his client? Has he effectively summarized the facts concerning the defense of self-defense
and presented them as a memorable story or theme?
48. FRE 609 provides that felony convictions may be admitted to impeach the character for truthfulness of any testifying witness. Why would inmate Butler's commission of the crimes of robbery and battery
have anything to do with his truthfulness on the witness stand at this trial? The defense could make a
motion in limine seeking a ruling that Butler's convictions should not be admissible under Rule 609. If
this is not successful, the defense will often bring out the convictions on direct examination—as was done
here—to minimize the impact on the jury.

1 Q: Do you recall—I take it you got fed in the cell that day; is that correct?
  A: Yes.
  Q: Why were you fed in the cell?
  A: Because we was on institutional lock-down.
5 Q: Institutional lock-down?
  A: Yes.
  Q: What's that mean?
  A: They was having problems out off the main facilities and for institutional security reasons they felt the best to feed us in our cells.
10 Q: And did you get fed in your cells that morning?
  A: Yes.
  Q: Did somebody come around to pick up the trays?
  A: Yes.
  Q: Do you know whether or not the trays were turned over?
15 A: Yes.
  Q: They were or weren't?
  A: No.
  Q: And do you know why the trays weren't turned over?
  A: Yes.
20 Q: Can you tell the court why—or the jury why?
  A: Because we had a problem. We was having a problem with the cell in which my cell mate felt the need to talk to the sergeant, you know, a higher, you know, correctional officer other than a floor officer.
  Q: What was that problem?
25 A: My cell mate had a package up in R and R. They continuously played around with him and wouldn't give him his package and which is a known procedure is go to the higher person in the chain of command. And he continuously asks the floor officer can he speak to a sergeant, which the floor officer continually denied and ignored him.
30 Q: How long had this problem been going on about a package?
  A: About 30 days.
  Q: Would you tell the jury what R and R is?
  A: It's receiving and release. It's where if you get mail packages it comes to there and they got to inspect and everything. They will call you up there when your
35   property is ready to come get it.
  Q: And do you know—do you know how Johnson got notified there was a package of some sort?
  A: Yes. In the beginning of the month they told him that he had a package up there, but they want to send it back home because that they didn't have a
40   proper form on the top of the box. So they told him to send the address and everything back to R and R. But about 20 days later he filled the 602—that's a document that you form when you have a grievance with the correctional facility. And they wrote him back and said that they would talk to him about it. And they told him his package has been sitting up there for like 20, 30 days,
45   and they say they would give it to him and he continuously asked the correctional officers about it and they just ignored him.

1 *Q*: How often are you allowed to get packages?
   Mr. Cummings: Objection. Relevance.
   The Court: Overruled.[49]
   The Witness: I believe every 90 days, 90 days to six months, I believe.
5 *Q. by Mr. Deemer*:   Ninety days to six months?
   A: Yes.
   Q: What kind of packages? These packages come from your family?
   A: Yes.
   A: What do they send you?
10 *A*: Shoes, sweat suits and thermals, you know, little food to eat.
   Q: Little what?
   A: Food, little cookies and chips, Kool-Aid.
   Q: And on the day this incident took place was it an officer that you asked to be
        taken back out initially?
15 *A*: Yes.
   Q: What was the next thing that happened?
   A: He asked us to get our trays up. And my cell mate said, "I would like to speak
        to a sergeant." And the officer said, "Give us the trays." The officer didn't say,
        "Well, I will go get a sergeant." He said, "Give me the trays." And then my
20   cellie said, "I want to talk to a sergeant." And the officer just closed the door
        to the cell and say, "You guys will be sorry for this," and walked off.
   Q: Then did some other officers appear?
   A: Yeah, about 20 minutes later we sitting in the cell and about like—it was
        about seven to twelve officers walked inside the building with their gloves and
25   everything on, you know, and came to the door and said, "Give us the trays."
        And my cellie, he walked up to the door, they cracked the door open and ran
        up in there.
   Q: How many times do you recall when the officers were there at the front of the
        door, how many times do you recall somebody asking for the tray to be given?
30 *A*: They only said it one time.
   Q: Do you recall whether the cell port was open or closed at that time?
   A: The door to the cell?
   Q: The port.
   A: It was closed.
35 *Q*: Did you ever see the cell port open?
   A: No.

---

49. This question does probably call for irrelevant information. Why, then, does the judge allow it? The rules of evidence provide only a minimal structure for what actually occurs at trial. Natural everyday reasoning processes form the core of the event. There is a natural inclination for the jury to want to know the full details of events, even when aspects of those details may not be formally relevant or material to a litigated case. Almost always in such cases, the rules of evidence are ignored, and the parties are allowed to provide information of the event regardless of its technical admissibility. Indeed, an undefined rule of evidence, known as the res gestae rule, developed as the cover for just such activity. It is often said that the jury may be informed of the "res gestae" of the event, which means all its details, whether otherwise admissible or not.

1 Q: And when the door was open what happened?
   A: They rushed in. They just rushed in.
   Q: What did your cellie do?
   A: He was like—they had him held—like three or four held him. They rushed
5   me and pushed me to the back of the wall and told me to get down.
   Q: Did you see what happened after that?
   A: No. Then they picked me up and they said, "Let's take him out." They had
      him handcuffed and they was grabbing him by his arms and they said—I
      think he had a cut or something on the side. They said, "This must be a
10   weapon." And the MTA was laughing about it. In the sally port they was bang-
      ing him up against the wall, and he pushed my head against the wall and took
      us to the—outside in front of the program office.
   Q: All right. Where was Johnson cuffed up to the best of your recollection?
   A: In the cell.
15 Q: Now, do you know Officer Walker?
   A: Excuse me?
   Q: Do you know who Officer Walker is?
   A: No. I believe he is a tall officer. I don't really—
   Q: And when you saw—have you ever—excuse me. When you saw the number
20   of officers you saw outside the door, what did you think was going to happen?
   Mr. Cummings: Objection. Relevance. Calls for speculation.
   The Court: Overruled. You can answer.
   The Witness: I knew they was going to rush up in there.
   Q. by Mr. Deemer: That was what was in your mind?
25 A: Yes.
   Mr. Deemer: No further questions.

Cross-examination

   Q. by Mr. Cummings: Mr. Butler, how long had you lived with your cell mate,
      Mr. Johnson?
30 A: I think about three months.
   Q: Are you pretty good friends with him?
   A: Yeah, he was all right.
   Q: Do you know whether or not Mr. Johnson has any gang affiliation?
   A: No.
35 Mr. Deemer: Objection. That's irrelevant. Highly prejudicial.
   The Court: The no answer will stand. However, it's not relevant.
   Q. by Mr. Cummings: Sir, do you have any gang affiliation?
   A: Yes.
   Q: What is it?
40 A: I'm a Crip.
   Mr. Deemer: Well, again there is some case law just came down. Counsel knows
      that is clearly not admittable under these circumstances.
   Mr. Cummings: I will do it here or I will do it at the side bar.
   The Court: Approach the bench.

1 (The following proceedings were had outside the presence of the jury.)

Mr. Cummings: I believe Lieutenant Stokes is the one who can testify to the fact
that he has knowledge, I find out today, that Mr. Johnson is also a Crip. That
is also typical to put fellow gang members of the same gang in the same cells.

5 *The Court:*   How is he going to confess that he is a Crip?

Mr. Cummings: Through intelligence gathering techniques. I'm not sure exactly
how.

Mr. Deemer: You haven't provided me with any discovery on this.

Mr. Cummings: I just found out today.

10 *The Court:*   Intelligence gathering techniques other than hearsay?[50]

Mr. Cummings: Well, certainly if he asked the person and he admitted it, it
would be an admission. I would have an exception to the hearsay.[51]

Mr. Deemer: But the problem is that whether or not they are gang members at
this stage of the proceedings is really totally irrelevant and highly prejudicial.

15 *Mr. Cummings:*   No, it is not. It is not irrelevant because what a gang expert is I
believe Lieutenant Stokes will testify that gang members testify in a fashion
that is helpful to other gang members and that's also been common knowledge of the jury.[52] And probably don't even need an expert for that.

Mr. Deemer: First of all, if you were to ask my client if he were a gang member
20   he would simply deny it. Secondly, if you were a gang member based on what
other gang members—based on what I know about and they had confidential information sufficient to establish that—based on what I know about the
handling of these matters, it wouldn't be a General Population. He would be
in SHU.

25 *Mr. Cummings:*   Pure speculation.

Mr. Deemer: It's not speculation because that is their policy and I mean—

Mr. Cummings: This gentleman has an admitted gang affiliation and he is in
GP.

The Court: If you can show that this defendant has admitted to some officer that
30   he is a member of the same gang as this witness, you might be able to make
it, other than by hearsay. But certainly if it's going to be the usual way that
they determine they are gang members just by confidential informants, they
can make administrative decisions based on that, but that's not admissible in
court. So you have established this defendant is a member of the gang and the
35   defendant is—

Mr. Deemer: If he proposes to go with somebody else—other than an admission,
if it is based on some sort of confidential arrangement—

---

50. Lieutenant Stokes does not appear to have firsthand knowledge that inmate Johnson is a gang
member, as would be required by FRE 602. Therefore, he would be relating hearsay if he stated that his
"intelligence sources" had told him that Johnson was a Crip.

51. As you will see in Chapter Eight, statements made by parties, in this case by inmate Johnson,
are exempted from the general prohibition against hearsay under FRE 801. Thus if Johnson himself told
Stokes that he was a Crip, Stokes could testify about this statement to the jury.

52. Do you think the behavior of gang members is well known to the public? Why would it be well
known to this particular jury?

1 *Mr. Cummings:*   That has already been ruled on. I am clear on the rule.
   The Court: All right.

   (The following proceedings were had in open court.)

   Q. by Mr. Cummings: Mr. Butler, you already indicated that you have been or at
5   least you are a member of the Crips; is that correct?
   A: Yes.
   Q: What is the Crips?
   A: An organization in Los Angeles.
   Q: What kind of organization?
10 A: A neighborhood protecting organization.
   Q: Is "a gang" a fair term to apply to that or not?
   A: No, that's not a fair term.
   Q: Sir, when you were in your cell—do you recall what day this happened by the way?
   A: Saturday. It happened on Saturday.
15 Q: Do you know what month?
   A: It was May or March the 28th.
   Q: March the 28th is the date. And on March the 28th when this incident started
        to happen where were you in your cell?
   A: I was sitting at the desk.
20 Q: An officer earlier testified that you were sitting either—I think you testified
        you were sitting either at the desk or on a bunk. Does that sound possible?
   A: Yes, 'cause I was at the desk.
   Q: So the officer would have been truthful about that; is that correct?[53]
   A: Yes.
25 Q: The officer, one of the officers also testified that when the incident actually
        started that you stood up for a short period of time; is that correct?
   A: Yes.
   Q: So the officer would have been truthful about that; is that correct?
   A: Yes.
30 Q: The officer, one of the officers testified that you were given a command the
        same way that you said you had been to get down and the officer testified that
        you complied fully. Is that what you did, exactly what you were told?
   A: Yes.
   Q: Is that accurate?
35 A: Yes.
   Q: So the officer is being truthful about that; is that correct?
   A: Yes.
   Q: The officer testified the way they are trained in their procedures require them
        to basically secure you or handcuff you until the incident is over and then
40   release you. Is that what happened?
   A: To me, yes.

---

53. What do you think of the technique of cross-examination reflected in this question and the line
of questioning that follows? Notice how the prosecutor's use of leading questions allows him to recite the
information—to "play the tune"—that he wants the jury to hear.

1 Q: To you, correct?
    A: Yes.
    Q: So the officer was truthful in that line of questioning; is that correct?
    A: Yes.
5 Q: You indicated that you heard your cell mate request a package; is that correct?
    A: He requested to talk to the sergeant.
    Q: About a package.
    A: Yes.
    Q: And what was the response of the officers at that point?
10 A: When they came to the door they had the gloves and everything on. They came up, they said "give us the trays." And my cellie says, "Can I talk to a sergeant" "Give us the trays." I bent and my cellie bent over to the doors. And there was no talking until they rushed in there hollering "get down, get down."
    Q: Did your cell mate at some point in time drop the trays in his hands?
15 A: He didn't have time to touch them. When he bent over, the door opened up.
    Q: Did he have the trays in his hand?
    A: I don't believe so.
    Q: Is that because you were in the back of the cell and couldn't see everything?
    A: No, I was standing—the reason why I was standing up is because when they
20   say "give us the trays" I was going to attempt to give them the trays. He was in front. So when he bent over I stood and that's when the door opened up.
    Q: Did you see your cell mate raise either one of his two arms?
    A: No.
    Q: Did you see your cell mate make a fist?
25 A: No.
    Q: Did you see your cell mate swing at any of the officers?
    A: No.
    Q: Sir, from the position that you were in inside the cell did your roommate, your friend, Mr. Johnson, did he kind of duck his head down?
30 A: He bent over to grab the trays, of course.
    Q: You are saying he did not have his trays in his hands; is that correct?
    A: That's correct.
    Q: How many trays were on the floor in front of him?
    A: Two.
35 Q: Was there some garbage piled up on top of them?
    A: No, food.
    Q: Food or whatever. Was there a mound of something on top of them?
    A: No.
    Q: Can you put two food trays through the food port door in the cell door at the
40   same time?
    A: Yes.
    Q: You don't have to feed them out one at a time?
    A: No.
    Q: And if there is some garbage piled on top, some paperwork, wrappers, whatever,
45   some disposable garbage on top, can you feed them through that food port door?

1 A: Yes, you would have to compact it down a little bit.
   Mr. Cummings: Thank you sir. Nothing further.
   Mr. Deemer: No questions.
   The Court: You are excused. Thank you. Next witness.
5 *Mr. Deemer:*   Call inmate Green.

MICHAEL GREEN

called as a witness by the Defendant, after having been sworn to tell the truth, the whole truth and nothing but the truth, was examined and testified as follows:

The Clerk: Would you state your name for the record and spell it, please.
10 *The Witness:*   Michael Green.

Direct Examination

   Q. by Mr. Deemer: Mr. Green you are an inmate at Pelican Bay; is that correct?
   A: Yes.
   Q: And you are in there because you have been convicted of a felony. The jury is
15   going to know this anyhow so go ahead and tell them what the felony is.
   A: Murder.
   Q: Any others?
   A: (No audible response.)
   Q: And do you know Johnson, Mr. Johnson?
20 A: Yes.
   Q: Did you know him around the end of March 1992?
   A: Yes.
   Q: Do you recall an incident taking place either—well, excuse me. Where did
     you live in relationship to where he lived?
25 A: In the next cell.
   Q: Do you recall an incident taking place in connection with attempting to get a
     food tray from him sometime?
   A: Yes.
   Q: Do you recall what date that was?
30 A: No.
   Q: Do you recall what time of day it was?
   A: The morning.
   Q: Do you have any recollection of what day of the week it was?
   A: No.
35 Q: First of all, do you recall how many officers you could see outside his cell?
   A: About eight.
   Q: And what did you observe those officers do?
   Mr. Cummings: Objection. Vague as to time.[54]

---

54. Occasionally, advocates object to clarify the other side's question, which seems to be the case here. This may explain why no one seems to care whether the judge rules on the objection.

1 *Q. by Mr. Deemer:* Well, when you first observed the officers, what did you
      observe the officers do?

  A: Come to Johnson's cell.

  Q: In front of the cell, yes.

5 A: They was talking to him.

  Q: Do you recall what they said?

  A: No, I was in the vent.

  Q: You were what?

  A: I was listening in the vent.

10 Q: What did you hear?

  A: They had asked him to give him the tray.

  Q: And did he say anything?

  A: Yeah, he was going to give them the tray.

  Q: Then how were the officers that were outside—did you take a look to see how

15   they were dressed?

  A: They was in—

  Q: What were they wearing?

  A: Police uniforms.

  Q: After he said something about giving the tray, then what happened?

20 A: One of the police, they didn't care. They just went to get it anyway.

  Q: Now, do you know who Officer Walker is?

  A: Yeah, I know him.

  Q: Did you see him there that day?

  A: Yeah, I seen him.

25 Q: How long have you known him?

  A: Just since he has been over there.

  Q: In where, Pelican Bay?

  A: Yeah, since I have been in Pelican Bay.

  Q: Did you ever know him at Folsom?

30 A: I never been to Folsom.

  Q: Do you have a fear of Officer Walker?

  A: Yeah.

  Q: Why is that?

  A: Because I hear he is, you know, a bad cop.[55]

35 Q: When you say he is a "bad cop," you mean what?

  A: That he is no good, he sets inmates up and, you know, he don't go by the
     policy of Pelican Bay.

  Q: I am having a hard time understanding.

  A: He doesn't go by the policy of Pelican Bay.

---

55. In questioning inmate Green, is defense counsel seeking to prove that Officer Walker is, in truth,
a "bad cop" who roughs up inmates? Or, is he seeking to prove that Walker has a bad reputation and that,
whether true or not, this reputation causes inmates to fear him? The first purpose would be to prove that
Walker was aggressive and acted consistently with his character, inadmissible under FRE 404. The second would be reputation evidence used to prove effect on Johnson's state of mind. Keep this distinction
in mind as you read the testimony of inmate Johnson, and of Lieutenant Stokes later in the transcript.

1   *Q:* All right. And do you know—have you ever seen him rough anybody up?
    A: No.
    Q: What about Officer Van Berg, do you know him?
    A: Yeah.
5   *Q:* Do you know what his reputation is amongst the inmates?
    A: Same thing.
    Q: And do you recall any discussion between officers and inmate Johnson with respect to a sergeant?
    A: Yeah, he had asked—he had been trying to see the sergeant for his package
10   prior to the events several days and on that day and before all the doors came, but they kept denying him.
    Q: Then after the officers went into the cell, when they came back out again did you see anything?
    A: Yeah, they had him handcuffed, pulling his hair. They had him bent over,
15   pulling his—how they grab his hands.
    Q: Did they move him past your cell or in some other direction?
    A: Just go straight out.
    Mr. Deemer: No further questions.

Cross-examination

20 *Q. by Mr. Cummings:*   Mr. Green, you indicated that you have previously been convicted of a murder; is that true?
    A: Yeah.
    Q: First or second degree?
    A: First.
25 *Q:* You said that was your only felony conviction?
    A: Yeah, it is.
    Q: Did you go to trial or did you plead?
    A: I went to trial.
    Q: At the same time you went to trial were you charged with Count 2, an assault
30   with a deadly weapon on the person, use of a firearm.
    A: That's all in with the murder.
    Q: But you were convicted of that, too, weren't you?
    A: Yeah, everything.
    Q: Were you convicted also of burglary at first degree?
35 *A:* Yeah.
    Q: All at the same time?
    A: It's all during the same offense.
    Q: What's your term you are serving, sir?
    A: Life sentence.
40 *Q:* You indicated that you—let me go back a little bit. You indicated that you did hear the officers asking for trays; is that correct?
    A: Yes.
    Q: And how many times did they ask?
    A: I can't remember.

1 Q: Once, twice, three, four times?
   A: I don't remember.
   Q: Was it more than once?
   A: I don't remember.
5 Q: How good of a position are you in to hear when you got your ear up to that
       vent?
   A: All I got to do is jump up on the sink and put my ear to the vent and I can hear
       what goes on in the next cell.
   Q: Pretty darn well?
10 A: Pretty darn well.
   Q: You indicated that you personally expressed some concern, some fear regard-
       ing Officer Walker; is that true?
   A: Uh-huh.
   Q: What are you basing it on?
15 A: What am I basing it on?
   Q: Yeah. You testified that you never saw him rough anybody up; is that correct?
   A: Right.
   Q: So this is stuff—
   A: But I had an experience with police that do that sort of thing.
20 Q: But you are not talking about Officer Walker, are you?
   A: No.
   Q: You are talking about some other policemen.
   A: Yeah.
   Q: You basically have a fear or a concern with a lot of cops, a lot of policemen
25   about getting roughed up, don't you?
   A: With anybody?
   Q: I think the answer to that probably is how would you answer that? Do you?
   A: I mean if I hear you use unprofessional cop, of course.
   Q: Are you personally scared, concerned for your own safety around probably
30   most cops?
   A: No, not most cops.
   Q: Around a certain percentage of them?
   A: Just the ones I know don't go by the procedure.
   Q: And had you ever been roughed up by Officer Van Berg?
35 A: No, but I seen him in action.
   Q: Do you know what Van Berg looks like?
   A: No, I know what he looks like.
   Q: Tall, short?
   A: Short.
40 Mr. Cummings: Thank you, sir. Nothing further.

Redirect Examination

   Q. by Mr. Deemer: But it is common knowledge amongst black inmates that
       Officer Walker as—you people that Officer Walker is prone to beat on you; is
       that correct?

1 A: Uh-huh.

Mr. Deemer: No further questions.

Mr. Cummings: Nothing.

The Court: Anything further of this witness?

5 *Mr. Deemer:* No, sir.

The Court: You may step down. The next witness.

Mr. Deemer: Call the defendant.

JAMES JOHNSON

called as a witness by the Defendant, after having been sworn to tell the truth,
10 the whole truth and nothing but the truth, was examined and testified as follows:

The Clerk: Please state your full name for the record.

The Witness: James Johnson.

Direct Examination

Q. by Mr. Deemer: Mr. Johnson, you are an inmate at Pelican Bay State
15   Prison?

A: Yes, sir.

Q: Are you—or obviously you are there because you have been convicted of a
   felony.

A: Rape.

20 Q: How many times?

A: Once.

Mr. Cummings: Say that again.

The Defendant: Once.

Q. by Mr. Deemer: And back sometime in February or March was there a prob-
25   lem concerning a package of some sort?

A: Yes, there was.

Q: And would you explain to the jury what that problem was?

A: Well, February my family and them send me a package. The package—I
   didn't know that the package was there in the institution until the institution
30   sent me a little form and let me know that they had the package. But they say
   the package was improper to issue to me because the fact that the package
   didn't have a form on top of the package. So they wouldn't let me have the
   package. But instead the officer that was working down there, I wrote a 602
   out to the officer and he wrote me back and let me know I could come down
35   there and we can settle the difference over the package. He stated this to the
   officer that was working on floor to bring me out. But instead of bringing me
   down there they brought this other Johnson down there in my place because
   they didn't see fit to use the numbers which we go by, C numbers, D numbers
   and things like that in prison.
40   Now, by them not doing that and just going by the last name there was a
   mistake made. So they sent the wrong guy down there. When I come back I
   talked to the floor officer and floor officer let me know that my package was

58 Chapter One. The Case of People v. Johnson

1   down there and he would make an effort to get me down there on time. That
was on Friday. But on occasion they get me down there they couldn't get me
down there because there was so much going on. Friday he wrote out a note
and he stuck it on the window. I am right there in the office with him. He
5   stuck it on the window and he stated on the note for the next officer to come
on to take me down on R and R.

    I am asking all the officers that's in the building that know about the note
that he left in there, let me go down and get my package. Now, they tell me,
"We can't let you go down there now; we got the lights went out on us; we
10   can't let you go down there. So we try next Friday." And that next Friday continued on and continued on and continued on until so many Fridays.

    Now, I started asking the floor officer to see a sergeant. They wouldn't let
me see a sergeant, too. I asked them over and over again to let me see a sergeant
and the sergeant never come see me. So I found out that my package had been
15   setting down there 27 days after that. You know what I'm saying? So now nobody
is making no efforts to let me get my property. You know what I'm saying?

    So what I do is at that Friday they had an incident in the building, building
eight. They had an incident where another convict cut another convict with a
razor. That put us on lock-down. We can't go nowhere. We can't do nothing.
20   No moving or nothing.

    So now that Saturday before that incident happened I asked them about
a sergeant and he told me no. So that Saturday came along. I asked the floor
officer that morning about seeing the sergeant. He said no. I took the trays and
I hold the trays.

25 *Mr. Cummings:*   Objection, Your Honor, at this point. No question pending.[56]

  Q. by Mr. Deemer: So Saturday morning you held the trays, right?

  A: Uh-huh.

  Q: What time do you guys get fed?

  A: We got fed around seven.

30 Q: And does somebody come around to get the trays?

  A: Yeah.

  Q: Who comes around to get the trays?

  A: Floor officer.

  Q: When you are being fed how does he get the trays?

35 A: He come by and you can unlock the tray slot to receive trays.

---

56. How did you respond to this lengthy narrative by the defendant? As previously explained, a direct examination usually takes the form of short, nonsuggestive questions that, when asked and answered in sequence, tell the witness's story efficiently. A narrative response is the witness's account in his or her own words and chronology without the benefit of the examining counsel's direction. Was it an effective technique for the direct examiner to let Johnson proceed to tell his story?

Why do you think the prosecutor objected here? The advantage of a narrative form of questioning, from the point of view of the direct examiner, is that often more information is presented when a witness is given free rein to testify in a narrative. The disadvantage is that it is often less orderly, and more objectionable or inadmissible information may be transmitted. There is no evidence rule that forbids a narrative form of testimony, but the trial judge has discretion under FRE 611 to ensure that the adversary is not disadvantaged by being unable to anticipate objectionable material.

1 Q: And what did you tell him when he unlocked the tray slot?

   A: I told him I would like to see a sergeant. He said, "No, you ain't seeing no sergeants." So I say, "I am going to hold these trays until I see a sergeant."

   Q: Then what did he do with the tray slot?

5 A: He locked the tray slot back and he said I was in trouble and he walked to the next cell and picked up their trays and walked out the block. Then when he came back about 20 minutes, 30 minutes later, he came back with at least 12 officers. When they come in the building, Walker is in front of all the officers.

   Q: When they come up, where is Walker standing? Do they come up to the cell
10   door?

   A: Yeah.

   Q: Who was in the lead?

   A: Walker.

   Q: Do you know him?

15 A: Yes, I do.

   Q: How long have you known him?

   A: I been knowing him ever since Folsom.

   Q: Did you ever have contact with him there?

   A: I had contact with him and I know of other inmates that had contact with
20   him, too.

   Q: And does that—did that cause some sort of apprehension to you?

   A: Yes, it does.

   Q: Could you explain to the jury what apprehension your prior association and knowledge of Walker caused in you?

25 A: The officer as he claimed to be is not—he is not a good officer at all. He give you this one side of him. He will give you this one side of him and then the next time you see him is another side that came out in him and he is violent. He is a violent officer.[57]

   Q: What did you think would happen to you when Walker showed up?

30 A: I thought—what I thought was going to happen did happen. When he opened up that door and ran in on him, he assaulted me.

   Q: Did the officers come up to the door of the cell?

   A: Walker was the only officer. It wasn't no Smith, there wasn't no Huston. It wasn't no Van Berg. It wasn't none of them guys. Walker was the only guy
35   that came and ordered—they say Smith ordered the officer open up the door. Smith did not order officer to open up the door. It was Walker that ordered them to open up the door.

   Q: Did anybody talk to you—before they opened the cell door did anybody talk to you about giving up the trays?

40 A: Walker asked me—he asked me and my cellie—we both in the cell. He says, "Are you going to give up the trays?" I gets up off my bed and go and pick up the trays. As soon as I get ready to pick up the trays, the door come open and Walker run in on me.

---

57. Again, consider what the defense is seeking to prove: that Officer Walker is in fact a violent officer, or that inmate Johnson has reason to believe that he is, and therefore fears him?

1 Q: Was the cell port open at any time?

A: No.

Q: What do you do when Walker comes in on you?

A: There wasn't nothing I could do but cover myself up because I already knew

5   what was coming.

Q: What happened?

A: Walker come up in there socking me with the gloves that he had on.

Q: And how long did that go on?

A: That went on for about a good two seconds.

10 Q: Then what happened?

A: Then all the rest of the officers came in, they come in the cell, and they was all like grabbing me over this way, grabbing me over that way. And then when they did get me on the ground and gets me handcuffed, it wasn't I was resisting the officer. I wasn't resisting no officer at all.

15 *Mr. Cummings:*   Objection.

Q. by Mr. Deemer: At some point they got you on the ground?

A: Yes.

Q: They described you as resisting.

A: No, wasn't no resisting.

20 Q: What happened?

A: Once Walker ran into the cell on me and have me on the table, me off the table, put me on the floor, and handcuffed me right away. It can't be no more than three seconds for them to do all that.

Q: Then what happened?

25 A: They took me out the building. Van Berg had my hair behind like this, pulling my hair. Took me out the section, took me right there on the side of the section right where the entrance is to coming into the building, and Van Berg took my head and smashed it into the wall.

Q: Did he say anything?

30 A: He said he been wanting to do that for a long time.

Q: Did he use any expression which you might think is impolite in front of a jury? Do you remember that?

A: (No audible response.)

Q: It's all right if you don't. Did you ever have any contact with Officer Huston.

35 A: I never had no contact with Officer Huston.

Q: Other than Mr. Van Berg grabbing you by the head—

A: I never had no contact with Officer Van Berg.

Q: Did you ever kick Officer Van Berg?

A: No, I never touched him. I never touched Officer Huston neither.

40 Q: You indicate that you had some other—you say you have known Walker for a long time.

A: Yeah.

Q: How long had you known him at Folsom?

A: It's New Folsom. He was there up until the time he came here, which was two

45   years ago. And when he was there he had the same type of attitude that he got here.

1 *Q:* While he has been up here have you ever observed him, either he or Van
     Berg—have you ever observed him lay hands on an inmate?
   A: Yes, I have.
   Q: Where did that take place?
5 *A:* In the kitchen.
   Q: What happened then?
   A: He snatched a Hispanic guy up off the seat, took him out the kitchen, drug him
     by the hair out of the kitchen in the front by the sally port and jumped on the guy.
   Q: Then when they came back do you recall a statement being made?
10 *A:* Yes, Van Berg said that the guy that he did like that had assaulted the staff, and
     it wasn't like that.
   Q: Did that—how did that make you feel?
   A: At the time I looked at it like this: If they did him like that, who would be next?
     You know what I'm saying? And he showed—it shows in the action that any-
15   body could have been next, you know? That's not no frequent thing. It's not
     nothing that a person—a person has to be taught to treat somebody like that.
     And it had to have been in all this time to do this. This is not no "I'm going to
     do this today and tomorrow I am not going to do it." This is an everyday occa-
     sion when they can do this.
20 *Q:* Did this cause you to fear Officer Walker?
   A: Yes, it did.
   Q: Are there other inmates, for example, besides yourself and inmate Green who
     is here that have expressed to you their fear of Mr. Walker?
   A: There is plenty of guys that I ran across that have the same feeling.
25 *Q:* Is that fear more in connection with—is that by black inmates or is that all
     inmates?
   A: It's about all inmates, not just black inmates.
   Mr. Deemer: No further questions.

Cross-examination

30 *Q. by Mr. Cummings:*   Mr. Johnson, you indicated that you had been convicted,
     what, one time before of rape?
   A: Yes.
   Q: It sounds like you took real personal offense at the way Officer Walker treated
     you; is that true?
35 *A:* No, it wasn't the way he treated me.
   Q: What was it?
   A: The things I knew about him.
   Q: So it wasn't what he did, it's what you thought he was going to do.
   A: It wasn't what I thought—it wasn't what I was thinking he was going to do. It's
40   what I knew he was going to do. Once I seen him in the front of the line, I knew.
   Q: In other words, Officer Walker didn't have to do anything. As you just said,
     when you saw him in the front of that line in your mind you were sure to
     yourself, I'm positive of that, you knew what was coming.
   A: Yes.

 1 Q: Now, given that state of mind, sir, your state of mind, you were going to pro-
        tect yourself?
     A: No, I was not going to protect myself.
     Q: Why not?
 5 A: There wasn't no need to protect myself.
     Q: There wasn't any need?
     A: No, there was no need to protect myself.
     Q: Let me see if I got this straight. You are positive in your own mind that Walker,
        who you fear is at the head of the line, you see it doors go closed and you know
10   what's going to happen, don't you?
     A: Yes.
     Q: And you are not scared?
     A: I'm not going to put up no defense towards him.
     Q: So you didn't act in self-defense.
15 A: I didn't act at all.[58]
     Q: Do you respect the rights of other people?
     A: Yes, I do.
     Q: And you want them to respect your rights, too?
     A: Yes, I do.
20 Q: You had indicated earlier that you were convicted one time of rape, Sir?
     A: Yes, I was.
     Q: Does that go back to a 1981 conviction out of Long Beach, Los Angeles?
     A: No, it goes back to '85.
     Q: Let's go back a little further than that. Your rap sheet seems to indicate that
25   you were convicted in '81 of forcible rape.
     A: I wasn't—what you mean is a conviction? What do you mean by that?
     Q: Says convicted, felony conviction.
     Mr. Deemer: Excuse me, Your Honor. I am going to object to this line of ques-
        tioning, and I think counsel has agreed based on the information which he
30   provided to the Court, which I think he has offered, in that there is a convic-
        tion in 1983. I don't know what the 1981 conviction is he is talking about.
     Mr. Cummings: Counsel has seen the rap sheet the same as I have.
     Mr. Deemer: The rap sheet is obviously in error, then, because the abstract says
        1983.
35 *Mr. Cummings:*   We'll get to that one, counsel.
     The Court: You can question him. The jury is, of course, reminded that the ques-
        tions are not evidence. The answers that come from the witness are evidence.[59]

---

58. Does this testimony contradict the officers' testimony that they saw the defendant raise his fist against Officer Walker? Would the raising of the fist be justified under the theory of self-defense—a use of force reasonably necessary to prevent an injury that the defendant reasonably believes to be imminent? Given this testimony, what story of the incident, from the defendant's point of view, should defense counsel argue to the jury? Remember this point when you read the closing argument for the defense.

59. Can a juror successfully separate the implications of the questions from the answers? Can anyone?

1 *Q. by Mr. Cummings:*   Sir, are you denying you were convicted in 1981 out of Long Beach, Los Angeles court, sentenced to five years felony on a rape forcible?

  A: I could see conviction of a jury, being convicted by a jury. I thought the plea
5   bargain—

  Q: That was a plea bargain?

  A: Yes, it was.

  Q: And in your mind that's different than a conviction?

  A: Yes.

10 Q: Were you paroled out of the Department of Corrections?

  A: Yes.

  Q: Sometime in '84?

  A: August 31st, '84.

  Q: That's exactly the right date, August 31st, 1984. And went home for a while?

15 A: Yes.

  Q: Did you end up back in the criminal system?

  A: Yes.

  Q: And was that as a result of a 1985 conviction again out of Long Beach, Count 2, you were convicted of a rape by force or fear?

20 A: Yes.

  Q: Also convicted of a burglary first degree?

  A: Yes.

  Q: Sentenced to 23 years state prison?

  A: Yes.

25 Q: Sir, do you have any gang affiliations?

  A: No.

  Q: Your testimony was that at the head of that cell door that Officer Walker was there and you knew him.

  A: Yeah.

30 Q: And at least you knew of him.

  A: Yes.

  Q: Smith wasn't there?

  A: Smith was there, Smith was there, but Smith was not like Smith say he was on the side of the door. Smith was way behind. He was way behind Walker.
35   Walker is the only one in front of this door. Walker is the only one. Ain't no—I can't even imagine at that time that this happened that any other officers could have been in front of Walker. It wasn't no other officer in front of Walker. It was only Walker in front of the cell.

  Q: Now, the officers testified almost unanimously—and you heard them—that
40   actually it was unanimously that you were acting aggressive once the cell door opened and you dropped the trays.

  A: No, I was not acting aggressively at all with no officers, period.

  Q: Sir, have you ever acted aggressively?

  A: What do you mean?

45 Q: Are you an aggressive person?

  A: I think everybody have aggression in them.

1   Q: And I know you said for the defense attorney you weren't resisting, but tell us what you were doing.

    A: I wasn't doing—it wasn't too much that I could do, period.

    Q: Officer Walker testified that he was the first one through, made contact with
5   you—or actually you made contact with him close to the door. True or not true?

    A: That's not true.

    Q: Where did contact get made?

    A: Contact got made when that door came open and Walker ran up in that cell
10   on me. That's where contact got made, the only contact.

    Q: Multiple officers testified that they saw a clenched fist, probably your right fist, come swinging at the front officer. True or not true?

    A: Not true.

    Q: Officers are lying about that?
15   A: Officers are lying about that.

    Q: Officers testified they saw you kicking. True or not true?

    A: Not true.

    Q: Officers lying about that?

    A: Officers are lying about that.
20   Q: All of them?

    A: All of them.

    Q: Officers testified that you were difficult to handcuff. True or not true?

    A: Not true.

    Q: Officers are lying about that, too?
25   A: Yes, sir.

    Q: Officers testified that you ended up going from inside the cell to the outside of the cell so that they could finish up what they had to do, which was get you cuffed up and secured.

    A: I was handcuffed on the outside of the cell, yes. That's where they brought me
30   out of the cell to the outside of the cell.

    Q: And you got handcuffed.

    A: Yes.

    Q: So the officers were telling the truth about that?

    A: They had to get me handcuffed.
35   Q: How well do you know Officer Walker?

    A: I know him—I know him quite—I think I know him well enough.

    Q: How many times did you come in contact?

    A: I come in contact with Officer Walker this time here and a time when he was in New Folsom.
40   Q: So one time three years ago or more and one time up here?

    A: Yes.

    Q: Two times three years apart?

    A: Yes. But I see him do other things besides how many times I know him.

    Mr. Cummings: Nothing further.
45 *The Witness:*   Him and Van Berg, too.

1   *Redirect Examination*

Q. by Mr. Deemer: Are you right-handed or left-handed?[60]
A: I am left-handed.
Mr. Deemer: No further questions.
5 *Mr. Cummings:*   Nothing.

(There was a lunch recess taken from 12:00 P.M. to 1:38 P.M. of the same day.)

The Court: The district attorney is now present and, Mr. Deemer, you have indi-
   cated you do not intend then to call any further witnesses?
Mr. Deemer: No, sir.
10 *The Court:*   Defense rests. Prosecution, any rebuttal evidence?
Mr. Cummings: Yes, Your Honor. Lieutenant Stokes.
Mr. Deemer: Your Honor, while he is calling Lieutenant Stokes, could we have
   an offer of proof at the bench?
The Court: Yes, approach the bench.

15 (The following proceedings were had outside the presence of the jury.)

Mr. Cummings: I intend to call Stokes and ask him whether or not he is aware of
   the professional reputation of Correction Officer Walker.
Mr. Deemer: The only thing you can ask him is whether or not—what his reputation is among the inmates. What his reputation is among the staff, I don't
20   think is very relevant.
The Court: I am going to overrule the objection because although the inmates
   and the staff are not precisely the same, they are a part of the community
   within the prison and are in communication with one another on a constant
   basis. So reputation is something that is back and forth and it is the kind of
25   thing that would be known. And it's a question that goes solely to reputation
   and not to prior incidents in the officers' personnel file. I think the whole
   Pitchess issue is side stepped anyway, so you can ask strictly about reputation.
Mr. Cummings: Reputation both among the inmates and among the correctional staff?
30 *The Court:*   Yes, if he knows. Of course, foundation first.
Mr. Cummings: I just want to make it clear in the record that we are at the rebuttal stage at this point.
The Court: Right, the defense has rested.[61]
Mr. Cummings: Exactly.
35
(The following proceedings were had in open court.)

ROBERT STOKES

called as a witness by the People, after having been sworn to tell the truth, the
whole truth and nothing but the truth, was examined and testified as follows:

---

60. Why is this question asked? More importantly, pay attention to whether any further reference is
made to the answer.

61. Rebuttal evidence is put on by the prosecution after the defense has rested. It is restricted to
evidence made necessary by defendant's case—such as response to new evidence or to new grounds of
innocence—and should not include what the prosecutor should have proved in the case-in-chief.

1   *Rebuttal Examination*

Q. *by Mr. Cummings:*   Thank you, Your Honor. Lieutenant, we know that you
    are currently employed as a lieutenant and you were employed as a lieuten-
    ant, a correctional lieutenant, on March the 28th, 1992, when you were at
5   Pelican Bay State Prison, correct?
A: Yes, sir.
Q: What were your duties on the 28th of March this year?
A: I was the watch commander, second watch, six o'clock in the morning until
    two o'clock in the afternoon.
10 Q: Lieutenant, as a watch commander are you responsible for any specific busi-
    ness within the prison or as a whole on that shift?
A: I am basically in charge of the overall security of the prison. And as the watch
    commander I coordinate any problems that one facility would have that would
    need assistance from another facility.
15 Q: Are you directly responsible for B Facility when you are on duty?
A: No, sir, I am not.
Q: Do you have occasion to work with or direct the work of different correctional
    officers?
A: Yes, sir, I have.
20 Q: Sir, do you know the reputation among the inmates of certain correctional
    officers?
A: Yes, I do.
Q: Where does that information come from?
A: That comes—
25 Q: How is it you would know that?
A: Specifically, sir, are we talking about the staff, specific staff in B Facility?
Q: Yes, specific staff. Do you have occasion in your job capacity to know what the
    reputation is of certain staff members among the inmates?
A: Yes, sir, I would. Mainly through the appeal process.
30 Q: Would you explain that?
A: The appeal process is a way of airing grievances by the inmates. It is generally
    recorded on a CDC 602.
Mr. Deemer: Excuse me, Your Honor. If this is the basis of his knowledge, I don't
    think that he ought to be allowed to testify to that. Moreover, that is just hear-
35 say statements of the inmates.
The Court: Approach the bench, counsel.

(The following proceedings were had outside the presence of the jury.)

The Court: Well, I'm not going to permit Bob go into specific instances to prove
40 conduct on a particular occasion. But I will allow him to go as far as he has,
    i.e., to show that that's generally how he keeps his finger on the pulse of what's
    going on in there. But that point we are going to have to get to the bottom-line
    question of what reputation is, if there is one.
Mr. Cummings: That's fine. This is being preliminary and foundational. That's
    all.

1 *The Court:* I will note for the record that since I handle several hundred habeas corpus issues a year and almost all of that have to go through the 602 process before they go to court and usually the 602s are attached, I read hundreds of 602s myself and I am aware that they give a pretty good overview of what's—what the
5 scuttlebutt is inside the prison. So it seems to me that this is an appropriate place for his source of knowledge, but not specific instances, as to reputation generally.

Mr. Cummings: That's fine.

(The following proceedings were had in the presence of the jury.)

Q. by Mr. Cummings: Sir, in your capacity as a lieutenant in Pelican Bay State
10 Prison have you had occasion to determine what you believe is the reputation of Officer Walker among the inmates?

A: Yes, sir, I have.

Q: What would your opinion be as to what his reputation is among the inmates?

A: Among—his reputation among inmates and of staff—and as he worked for
15 me for 13 months—is he is an excellent officer; he is very fair and he is very understanding and he runs a very smooth block.[62]

Q: And what are you basing this on?

A: My 13 months of supervision of B Facility.

Q: And when you were supervising B Facility was Officer Walker one of the offi-
20 cers in your command?

A: Yes, sir, he was.

Q: And that was for a period of 13 months?

A: Approximately 11 months for Officer Walker. He left for two months and then came back.
25 *Mr. Cummings:* Thank you, sir. Nothing further.

Cross-examination

Q. by Mr. Deemer: When was the last time you discussed Officer Walker's reputation amongst inmates?
30 A: I'm sorry.

Q: Have you ever discussed Officer Walker's reputation with inmates?

A: No, sir, I have not.

Q: All right. And as a practical matter as a lieutenant you really don't have that much contact with inmates, do you?
35 A: Not as much as you do as a sergeant over an officer.

Q: And basically what you are really familiar with is reputation amongst the other correctional officers. Would that be fair to say?

A: No, I am familiar with his manner of doing his job for that time that he worked for me.

Q: Are you aware of the fact that at least one lieutenant out there has refused to
40 have Officer Walker on his or her watch because of problems?

A: I'm not familiar with that, no, sir.

---

62. Is it possible that this testimony about Officer Walker's reputation among inmates can be based solely on the 602 forms? Do the 602 forms contain such positive assertions about officers?

1 Q: Do you know Lieutenant Rodriguez?
   A: I know of Lieutenant Rodriguez, yes.
   Q: Does she have something to do with B Facility?
   A: I believe she works the evening watch from two o'clock in the afternoon till
5   ten o'clock at night.
   Q: And you are aware of the fact that she has refused to work on the watch with
       Officer Walker?
   A: I am not aware of it, no, sir.
   Q: No further questions.
10 *Mr. Cummings*: Nothing further.
   The Court: May he be excused?
   Mr. Deemer: Yes.
   Mr. Cummings: Yes.
   The Court: You can leave or stay as you wish. Any further evidence, prosecution?
15 *Mr. Cummings*: No, People would rest. People have rested.
   The Court: Defense?
   Mr. Deemer: I have one witness but she is not going to be able to be here, Your
       Honor, so I have no choice but to rest at this time.
   The Court: Both sides rest then?
20 *Mr. Cummings*: Yes.
   The Court: What remains, ladies and gentlemen, is to put their jury instructions in
       their final form. That could not be done until this point, although there has been
       some done to this point already. I am going to give you a recess for that purpose.

   (The following proceedings were had in the presence of the jury.)

25 *The Court*: Let the record reflect that all jurors, counsel, and defendant are pres-
       ent. Ladies and gentlemen of the jury, you have heard all the evidence and
       now it is my duty to instruct you on the law that applies to this case.
           The law requires that I read the instructions to you, and you will have
       these instructions in written form in the jury room to refer to during your
30   deliberations.
           You must base your decision on the facts and the law. You have two duties
       to perform. First, you must determine the facts from the evidence received in
       the trial and not from any other source. A fact is something proved directly or
       circumstantially by the evidence or by stipulation. A stipulation is an agree-
35   ment between attorneys regarding the facts. Second, you must apply the law
       that I state to you, to the facts, as you determine them, and in this way arrive
       at your verdict and any finding you are instructed to include in your verdict.
           You must accept and follow the law as I state it to you, whether or not you
       agree with the law. If anything concerning the law said by the attorneys in
40   their arguments or at any other time during the trial conflicts with my instruc-
       tions on the law, you must follow my instructions.
           You must not be influenced by pity for a defendant or by prejudice against
       him. You must not be biased against the defendant because he has been
       arrested for these offenses, charged with a crime, or brought to trial. None

of these circumstances is evidence of guilt and you must not infer or assume
from any or all of them that he is more likely to be guilty than innocent.
You must not be influenced by mere sentiment, conjecture, sympathy, passion, prejudice, public opinion, or public feeling. Both the People and the
defendant have a right to expect that you will conscientiously consider and
weigh the evidence, apply the law, and reach a just verdict regardless of the
consequences.[63]

Statements made by the attorneys during the trial are not evidence,
although if the attorneys have stipulated or agreed to a fact, you must regard
that fact as conclusively proved.

If an objection was sustained to a question do not guess what the answer
might have been and do not speculate as to the reason for the objection.

Do not assume to be true any insinuation suggested by a question asked a
witness. A question is not evidence and may be considered only as it enables
you to understand the answer.

Do not consider for any purpose any offer of evidence that was rejected, or
any evidence that was stricken by the court; treat it as though you had never
heard it.[64]

Evidence consists of testimony of witnesses, writings, material objects, or
anything presented to the senses and offered to prove the existence or nonexistence of a fact.

Evidence is either direct or circumstantial. Direct evidence is evidence
that directly proves a fact, without the necessity of an inference. It is evidence
which by itself, if found to be true, establishes that fact.

Circumstantial evidence is evidence that, if found to be true, proves a fact
from which an inference of the existence of another fact may be drawn.

An inference is a deduction of fact that may logically and reasonably be
drawn from another fact or group of facts established by the evidence.

It is not necessary that facts be proved by direct evidence. They may be
proved also by circumstantial evidence or by a combination of direct evidence and circumstantial evidence. Both direct evidence and circumstantial
evidence are acceptable as a means of proof. Neither is entitled to any greater
weight than the other.

However, a finding of guilt as to any crime may not be based on circumstantial evidence unless the proved circumstances are not only (1) consistent
with the theory that the defendant is guilty of the crime, but (2) cannot be
reconciled with any other rational conclusion. If the circumstantial evidence
permits two reasonable interpretations, one of which points to the defendant's
guilt and the other to his innocence, you must adopt that interpretation that
points to the defendant's innocence, and reject that interpretation that points
to guilt.

---

63. Why does the judge give this instruction? Does it describe the normal way an individual absorbs information? If not, why is an artificial decisionmaking process being urged upon the jury?

64. Such instructions are common in the course of a trial. Do you think jurors are influenced by rejected or stricken evidence, a judge's instruction notwithstanding?

1   Further, each fact which is essential to complete a set of circumstances necessary to establish the defendant's guilt must be proved beyond a reasonable doubt. In other words, before an inference essential to establish guilt may be found to have been proved beyond a reasonable doubt, each fact or circumstance upon which such inference necessarily rests must be proved beyond a reasonable doubt.[65]

Every person who testifies under oath is a witness. You are the sole judges of the believability of a witness and the weight to be given the testimony of each witness.

In determining the believability of a witness you may consider anything that has a tendency in reason to prove or disprove the truthfulness of the testimony of the witness, including but not limited to any of the following:[66]

The extent of the opportunity or the ability of the witness to see or hear or otherwise become aware of any matter about which the witness has testified;

The ability of the witness to remember or to communicate any matter about which the witness has testified; The character and quality of that testimony;

The demeanor and manner of the witness while testifying; The existence or nonexistence of a bias, interest, or other motive;

Evidence of the existence or nonexistence of any fact testified to by the witness;

The attitude of the witness toward this action or toward the giving of testimony;

A statement previously made by the witness that is consistent or inconsistent with the testimony of the witness or the witness's prior conviction of a felony.

Discrepancies in the witness's testimony or between his or her testimony and that of others, if there were any, do not necessarily mean that the witness should be discredited. Failure of recollection is a common experience; and innocent misrecollection is not uncommon. It is a fact, also, that two persons witnessing an incident or a transaction often will see or hear it differently. Whether a discrepancy pertains to a fact of importance or only to a trivial detail should be considered in weighing its significance.

A witness who is willfully false in one material part of his or her testimony is to be distrusted in others. You may reject the whole testimony of a witness who willfully has testified falsely as to a material point, unless, from all the evidence, you believe the probability of truth favors his or her testimony in other particulars.

---

65. What, exactly, might this instruction mean? See the discussion of "circumstantial evidence" in Chapter Three.

66. This instruction tracks the language of Cal. Evid. Code §780, which lists permissible topics of impeachment. You will study the Federal Rules governing cross-examination and impeachment in Chapter Seven.

You are not bound to decide an issue of fact in accordance with the testimony of a number of witnesses, which does not convince you, as against the testimony of a lesser number or other evidence, which appeals to your mind with more convincing force.

You may not disregard the testimony of the greater number of witnesses merely from caprice, whim, or prejudice, or from a desire to favor one side against the other. You must not decide an issue by the simple process of counting the number of witnesses who have testified on the opposing side. The final test is not in the relative number of witnesses, but in the convincing force of the evidence.

The fact that a witness has been convicted of a felony, if such be a fact, may be considered by you only for the purpose of determining the believability of that witness. The fact of such a conviction does not necessarily destroy or impair a witness's believability. It is one of the circumstances that you may take into consideration in weighing the testimony of such a witness.

A defendant in a criminal action is presumed to be innocent until the contrary is proved, and in case of a reasonable doubt whether his guilt is satisfactorily shown, he is entitled to a verdict of not guilty. This presumption places upon the People the burden of proving him guilty beyond a reasonable doubt.

Reasonable doubt is defined as follows. It is not a mere possible doubt because everything relating to human affairs and depending on moral evidence is open to some possible or imaginary doubt. It is that state of the case, which after the entire comparison and consideration of all the evidence, leaves the mind of the jurors in that condition that they cannot say that they feel an abiding conviction or a moral certainty of the truth of the charge.[67]

In the crimes charged in the information there must exist a union or joint operation of act or conduct and general criminal intent. To constitute general criminal intent it is not necessary that there should exist an intent to violate the law. When a person intentionally does that which the law declares to be a crime, he is acting with general criminal intent, even though he may not know that his act or conduct is unlawful.

Any person who, while confined in a state prison, commits a battery upon a person who is not themselves confined in a state prison, is guilty of a felony.

Every person who willfully and unlawfully uses any force or violence upon the person of another is guilty of battery.

As used in the foregoing instruction, the words "force" and "violence" are synonymous and mean any unlawful application of physical force against the person of another, even though it causes no pain or bodily harm or leaves no mark and even though only the feelings of such person are injured by the act. The slightest unlawful touching, if done in an insolent, rude, or angry manner, is sufficient.

It is not necessary that the touching be done in an actual anger or with actual malice; it is sufficient if it was unwarranted and unjustifiable.

---

67. Does either advocate make use of this reasonable-doubt instruction in closing argument?

The touching essential to a battery may be a touching of the person, of the person's clothing, or of something attached to or closely connected with the person.

It is lawful for a person who is being assaulted to defend himself from attack if, as a reasonable person, he has grounds for believing and does believe that bodily injury is about to be inflicted upon him. In doing so such person may use all force and means which he believes to be reasonably necessary and which would appear to a reasonable person in the same or similar circumstances to be necessary to prevent the injury which appears to be imminent.[68]

I have not intended by anything I have said or done, or by any questions that I have asked, or by any ruling I may have made, to intimate or suggest what you should find to be the facts, or that I believe or disbelieve any witness.

The People and the defendant are entitled to the individual opinion of each juror. Each of you must consider the evidence for the purpose of reaching a verdict if you can do so. Each of you must decide the case for yourself, but should do so only after discussing the evidence and instructions with the other jurors.

Do not hesitate to change an opinion if you are convinced it is wrong. However, do not decide any question in a particular way because a majority of the jurors, or any of them, favor such a decision.

Do not decide any issue in this case by chance, such as the drawing of lots or by any other chance determination.

The attitude and conduct of jurors at all times are very important. It is rarely helpful for a juror at the beginning of deliberations to express an emphatic opinion on the case or to announce a determination to stand for a certain verdict. When one does that at the outset, a sense of pride may be aroused, and one may hesitate to change a position even if shown it is wrong. Remember that you are not partisans or advocates in this matter. You are impartial judges of the facts.

In your deliberations do not discuss or consider the subject of penalty or punishment. That subject must not in any way affect your verdict.

At this time the attorneys will give their closing summations, and like the opening summations they are not evidence. They are a chance for the attorneys to sum up for you what they claim the evidence has shown.[69] In doing that I assume they will discuss both the testimony that you have heard and also some of the instructions I have read to you. Of course, if you notice any

---

68. Does either advocate make use of this self-defense instruction in closing argument? Which party has the burden of proof on this issue? Does the judge ever make this clear?

69. Closing argument is the final opportunity for the advocates to speak directly to the jury about the case. Many closing arguments contain summations of the evidence, meaning a recitation of the key witnesses and key testimony. But where the case is not long and complicated, and where not many witnesses have testified, the jury may not need much help keeping things straight. Summing up the evidence should be contrasted, then, with arguing the evidence, where the advocate seeks to persuade the jury about contested facts and about why his or her client is entitled to prevail. Such arguments should be simple enough to be clearly understood, and sound enough to withstand the jury's scrutiny. As you read the closing arguments of the prosecution and the defense, consider whether these two standards have been met.

1   difference between what they tell you the evidence is and what the instructions were, you must decide what the evidence is and follow my instructions that I have given to you.

     Since the prosecution has the burden of proof the prosecutor makes the
5   first closing summation followed by defense counsel, and then in order that each side will have an opportunity to reply to the other, the prosecutor is allowed a rebuttal argument.

  Mr. Cummings: Thank you, Your Honor. Ladies and gentlemen, this is my opportunity to sum up what I believe the evidence has been, which is just
10   what the judge explained to you. If anything you hear from me differs from what your own recollection was, from what your recollection of what the witnesses swore to tell you the truth about on the witness stand, you should go by your own recollection and you should go by your own notes. Neither counsel is trying intentionally to mislead you, and sometimes when we are explaining
15   our case we are thinking a witness or two ahead and sometimes we don't get exactly all the details right.

     I told you in the beginning that I expected the case to be predominantly Pelican Bay State Prison officers. It was. I told you that it was going to involve two batteries. In reality it involved three batteries. I will explain that in a little
20   bit. It involves the credibility of numerous officers. This was a scenario which I believe the very first officer, Officer Huston, almost wanted to sum up as a great big nothing originally because that's really what it was, something that the inmate himself had some control over.

     Inmates for whatever reason do things that you and I do not understand
25   and we are never going to understand because we don't think that way and we are not in that environment. But for some reason inmate Johnson chose to draw the line that day over some package that he claimed that he wasn't getting, may or may not be true. Maybe it's 100 percent true for all I know. Entirely possible. However, in any case, as the officer explained to you in
30   court and to Mr. Johnson in his cell, that wasn't the way to go about it.

     Pelican Bay State Prison and the State of California cannot stop all things and run in and get this man, a sergeant, at that point in time and run and get his parcel for him. It's just not possible. They deal with a mainline system or a mainline production and it really is. You are feeding a tremendous number of
35   inmates, got to get trays back, you have got to go on to the next one, you have got another job assignment. That's what these officers had to do.

     What is interesting is that it appears that the major thrust of the evidence in this case is not, although the defendant denies doing it, is not so much that it didn't happen—he certainly acknowledges that it happened—but it was all
40   their fault. Of course, it is never their fault. It is always somebody else's fault. But what we really have here and what the defense would like to paint the picture of is that Walker, Officer Walker, is on trial.[70] See, Officer Walker

---

70. Here the prosecutor seems to be challenging the defense theory of the case, that Officer Walker was the first aggressor. This puts the defense on the defensive, as you will see.

1   ought to be sitting over there where inmate Johnson is because what they are
     really trying to do is prosecute Officer Walker, and I urge you and the law
     urges you to stay focused on who is on trial. The person on trial in this case is
     inmate Johnson. There is no other. It is inmate Johnson that caused the fracas.
5   It is inmate Johnson that drew the line. It is inmate Johnson who decided for
     whatever reason something was going to give that day and something did give
     and of course it had nothing to do with him.

     So the People put on witnesses like Officer Huston, who when I asked him
     about "Would you describe for us what happened on March the 28th, 1992 as
10   that incident," his response was something like "I mean, it wasn't really even
     an incident originally," and it wasn't an incident. It escalated into an incident
     and it is a serious matter where two officers were injured.

     In this situation it is important to remember that basically none of the
     officers that were actually there came in and testified in court were assigned
15   to Mr. Johnson's care. They were rovers.

     They were yard officers. They were other block officers who were called by
     the sergeant and went to go and basically talk this guy out of his trays, do what
     was necessary to talk him out of his trays, get the trays back and get on with
     their own assignments, and that's exactly what they tried to do.

20   Classic situation where three officers tell you what they see and what they
     feel is exactly what happened, and I'm sure you all noticed there were some
     differences between Officer Huston's version, Officer Van Berg's version and
     Officer Walker's version. Those are the three primary ones that ended up in
     the cell at least in one point in time and there were three different versions to
25   a slight degree.[71]

     One person has the inmate holding two trays. Don't be confused. It is not
     important whether he is holding two trays in two separate hands or two trays in
     one hand. That's not important. What is important is that the officers are tell-
     ing you the truth because the three stories do not come out exactly the same.
30   These three officers or these four officers or these five officers did not get
     together and decide, "Okay, folks, this is what happened," because obviously
     you are not going to have some small discrepancies, and one of the instruc-
     tions in the jury instruction package that the judge just read to you and that
     you will see back in the jury room is that people who see and hear an event
35   often see and hear it differently and report it differently. That does not mean
     they are not being truthful. Be more suspicious of the people that take the
     stand and tell you five people in a row exactly what happened almost verba-
     tim. Common sense tells you there is probably something wrong.

     In this case they relayed that basically the officer that did most of the talk-
40   ing was Smith. Smith came in and told you what he said. He explained that
     he made a demand that basically started out as a request. It escalated into a
     demand or an order to return the trays, get the trays back. He made comments

---

71. The prosecutor is able to summarize the testimony of several officers by emphasizing the consistency in their stories. Arguing the facts involves more than reciting testimony; it requires choosing those
facts and inferences that together create the story that should win the case.

1 like, "Are you having a bad day today, guy?" and stuff to that effect, something
to try to spark the guy to just give up the trays. They have got their job to do.
These are not correctional officers who are dealing with Johnson on a regular
basis. There is no vendetta here. The only one who alleges any sort of ven-
5 detta is Johnson.

You heard Officer Walker say, "I don't know inmate Johnson." I don't
recall any officer that was there that had any prior dealings with this particular
inmate. Now, that doesn't mean that this inmate was necessarily lying to you
when he says, "There is some sort of history here between Walker and myself."
10 He may very well believe that for reasons you and I cannot understand. But
in his mind he may be telling the truth in his own mind. That happens unfortunately quite often.

So basically the way the story seemed to shake out remarkably consistently
in his point of view was the person, inmate Johnson, gets up in the cell. He is
15 holding them in front of him, he is roughly a little bit behind, foot, foot and
a half, whatever, behind the door. Smith again signals to the control booth
officer to open the door.

As soon as the door is opened wide enough for a person to get through if
he wanted to, trays are dropped instantly, denied by the defendant, but the
20 officers were all pretty consistent. And immediately—and some officers saw
him duck his head, some officers didn't, and you would have to understand
that they all had a different perspective. That's common sense. They all had a
different perspective from where they were.

The ones closer are going to see a little bit better than the ones behind.
25 One officer had to go off to the side and look through what is the equivalent
of a window so he could see whether or not Johnson had any weapons because
he is concerned for the officers. He actually left and went off to one side.

So you had a person who has just dropped the trays, who was not showing
any sign of aggression before. He is not being violent and everybody agrees
30 on this, no sign of aggression. If they were trying to make Johnson out to be
a bad guy, they would make him out to be violent, they would make him out
to be verbally abusive, they would make him out to be throwing a fit, acting
out some frustration or some anger. And they were all consistent in that there
was no hint that this guy was going to go off and unfortunately these people
35 do go off at times. Folks do blow up in prisons and that happened in this case.

So he drops his trays and the officers were not exactly the same as to
what they saw, but it was remarkably similar to what the threat was. They
saw inmate Johnson making a forward motion coming at the officer in front,
Walker. Walker happened to be in front. He of course was going to be the one
40 that came in contact with him first. It's the only logical conclusion.

Walker basically does what he is trained to do, wrestles with the guy for a
while. He even says it is even like dancing a little bit, but basically gets him
back into the cell, and the whole time he is saying, "Get down, get down,
knock it off, stop the aggression," and that's for everybody's safety, including
45 the inmates. Butler, the defendant's roommate, cell mate in his cell, does

1   exactly what he is told and he basically complies with all instructions. He gets
     cuffed up for a few minutes while they secure the situation and it's all over.
         Is that what happens with this gentleman? No, it is not. He continues to
     fight. Every officer was consistent to the extent that the aggression continued,
5   the fighting continued, kicking and fists were going. And then the officer, I
     believe it was Van Berg who was trying to handcuff him, said, "I couldn't get
     the second cuff on him." So they did what they had to do. They got him cuffed
     up. Perfectly reasonable, perfectly responsible to do when you are operating in
     a maximum-level prison. You are not operating out of the streets of Crescent
10   City. You are not operating at Del Norte High School. You are operating in a
     maximum-security prison.
         Every officer had a little bit different version, but every officer also had
     a little bit different role and a little bit different perspective as to where they
     were.
15   I started out by saying that this is a credibility issue and you should think
     of it as a credibility issue and think about, as the judge explained to you in the
     instructions, who has a motive in this case. Let's say a motive to lie. You can
     consider that. Who has a motive to be less than truthful with you?[72] Four cor-
     rectional officers who come in here and swore to tell you the whole truth and
20   they got their law enforcement career on the line. If they were caught lying
     they would lose their jobs. I am sure their whole usefulness to the California
     correction system goes right out the window.
         Or the defendant? You heard the defendant is serving 20-plus years or
     about. Some of his witnesses, one of which is serving life for murder in the
25   first degree who has nothing to lose with a few lies. Not a thing. We can't do
     anything to him and he knows that. And everybody basically admitted to one
     degree or another that they are friends. One of the inmates admitted that he
     was a Crip. The defendant denied any Crip affiliation but they were room-
     mates together. There is some degree of friendship among the whole group of
30   them. I think that's fairly obvious.
         It is fair to look at who has the motive to tell you the truth, who has got the
     motive to lie in that case. There is no motive on the part of the correctional
     officers, but coming here and telling you basically what happened as best they
     can recall. In this case one of the elements the People do have to prove—and
35   I do have to prove that he was a state prisoner at the time of the incident. It's
     a small thing, but it has been proven. That was stipulated to. It just means
     that both defense attorney and I agreed he was a state prisoner at the time
     the judge accepted the stipulation, and that is a fact that has been proven at
     this point in time. No further documentary evidence or anything else need
40   be given.
         The verdict forms in this case are basically three separate pieces of paper.
     The first one is going to have Count 1 on it and it's going to say was guilty and

---

72. How persuasive do you find the arguments that follow concerning the motives of the officers and
the inmates to lie? What could the defense argue in response? Which group do you think had the most
compelling reason to lie about the incident?

1   it will name—it will say battery and it will name Officer Huston being the
      victim of that battery. Officer Huston was the first gentleman who testified,
      who testified that as a result of this fracas, had it not been for this fracas with
      this fight, he would not have gotten a gash. He got a gash in his shin, went to
5   Sutter Coast and got medical treatment. That's an injury. That's more than a
      battery, okay? But certainly qualifies as a battery. But that's Count 1. I am ask-
      ing you to return a verdict of guilty on Count 1.

          A separate piece of paper has Count 2. Again it's a battery and it's a battery
      of, in this case, Officer Van Berg. Officer Van Berg was the second officer that
10   testified. As a result of this fracas he cannot tell you exactly what blow but
      that's not what their attention is focused on. Their attention is focused on qui-
      eting people down and breaking it up. As a direct result of this fracas and this
      fight he ended up with a bone chip knocked on his hand, basically a fracture
      of one of the bones in his hand, and ended up going to Sutter Coast and was
15   treated medically for it. Those are two batteries.

          Let's talk a little bit about how simple the section is, the section of the
      law is. Penal Code section 4501.5, which is the battery section, it says, "Any
      person who while confined in a state prison," we have stipulated to that, he is
      confined in the state prison, "commits a battery on a person who is not them-
20   selves confined in a state prison," that would be staff, correctional officers,
      civilian workers, "is guilty of a felony," period. It's one sentence. It's not a big
      complicated law. "Any person who while confined in the state prison com-
      mits a battery upon a person who is not themselves confined in a state prison
      is guilty of a felony."

25   I told you earlier I would define battery for you, too, while I am at it.
      Battery has a one-sentence definition. "Every person who willfully and unlaw-
      fully uses any force or violence upon the person of another is guilty of a bat-
      tery," period. That's it.[73]

          I told you earlier there was a third battery in the case and legally there is a
30   third battery in the case and I am not asking you to return a verdict of guilty on
      that. It is not before you for your consideration. But a battery does not require
      injuries. Legally speaking you don't have to have people actually injured.

          The relevant portion of that instruction says the slightest unlawful touch-
      ing, if done in an insolent, rude or angry manner is sufficient for a battery.
35   So no injury need result. So you really could have another battery which was
      not charged as far as the victim being Officer Walker because he was attacked
      basically when the person charged the front door. That was not charged.
      Thank you, ladies and gentlemen.

      Mr. Deemer: I don't mean to sound like I am running away. When I opened
40   that door to get something I remember one time many years ago when I was
      a deputy district attorney down in Compton with an attorney there who had
      problems and one day after going to trial he said, "Your Honor," he says, "I

---

73. Advocates often refer to the instructions during closing argument, particularly those that define
critical legal terms. Here, the prosecutor reads the definition of battery, but makes no argument that the
facts proved against the defendant satisfy the definition.

1   am going out to get the witness, going to solve my case and prove my client
innocent," and he walked out the door. We all sat around and sat around and
nothing happened. Sat around and nothing happened and finally they sent
the bailiff out to get him. He had completely forgotten about the trial and he
5   was sitting in his office talking to clients.[74]

Mr. Cummings always makes a lot of fun about my chart and I admit I use
it on a regular basis. I am supposed to stop waving my hands so I wave the stick
instead. This is basically kind of a circumstantial evidence case and I know
that there is a lot of direct testimony about what people observed, but unfortu-
10   nately one of the things you have to do when you evaluate that testimony is to
decide do people see what they really say they saw. That is, you have to evaluate some circumstances that go around that testimony because there is a lot
of things that cause people to perceive—that may cause Johnson to perceive
things one way and the officers to perceive things a different way.[75]

15   What you got to do with this is figure out what's going on in this guy's
mind, what's he doing. And one of the things—basically three rules which you
are going to get in the jury instructions. First of all, the circumstances have to
be consistent with the theory. Not only consistent with the theory of defense
guilt, but it can't be reconciled with any other rational conclusion. Each fact
20   necessary to the set of circumstances has to be proved beyond a reasonable
doubt.

And of course the other thing which I also keep on the back of this—I only
billed the court once for this by the way—is the presumption of innocence.
You got to remember that burden is on the district attorney, not on me. I don't
25   have any burden. James Johnson doesn't have any burden. And if there is a
reasonable doubt as to whether James is guilty or not, you got a moral obligation and a legal obligation to come back with a not-guilty verdict. You got to
remember that. That's very important.

So when you look at that—and part of this I will sort of backtrack over
30   Mr. Cummings's argument. You look at that and you talk about, first of all,
the motive to be truthful. All right. These officers don't have a motive to be
untruthful. Well, you know, there is something I found really interesting is
that when they got Lieutenant Stokes on the stand about how we really stress
making sure these officers write down every last important detail. What's the
35   important detail that wasn't in any of the reports by their own admission?
There isn't anybody that mentions anything about the cell port in the reports
but the witnesses were asked about it. Not a one. Not even Lieutenant Stokes.

All right. I think Lieutenant Stokes made it clear, his testimony made it
clear that these reports start out at the lower level and get passed on up to the
40   upper level, and I think it's highly unlikely that he, in the kind of environment
you are dealing with out there, that you are not going to get a certain amount

---

74. Jury attention is at its peak during the first minutes of argument. Does defense counsel accomplish anything with this opening gambit?

75. Does defense counsel argue from the facts how inmate Johnson *did* perceive things?

1   of cover your derriere. And this isn't because they are trying to protect themselves against the inmates.

      I think what you are dealing with is a suggestion where they are kind of—
they got to make it look good and I think that's a normal course of events,
5   make it look good to the higher-ups, that the lower-downs are doing the job
right. In other words, the farther up the paperwork goes, you want to make
sure there is no criticism that is going to float back down to the bottom. So
there is a motive and there is a motive to ignore things.[76]

      When I look at the circumstances in this case, the first thing that struck me
10   is that the three officers all—and demeanor of a witness is something you can
look at. The three officers that testified about the assaultive behavior all give
the appearance—I'm sorry, I don't know how to express it—of being—give
the appearance of being cowboys. There is just something about their manner, their dress, their boots, everything. They are cowboys. And I suspect that
15   they run that institution pretty much the same way. That's the first thing that
bothers me.[77]

      The second thing, a significant item is the cell port.[78] The third thing
is the defendant—by the way, the comment was made that the defendant's
motive is, "Well, I don't want to accept responsibility; it is always somebody
20   else's fault." And again I think that same issue goes with the report-writing
issue. I mean, I dare say that any of you that get in an auto accident and write
a report to your insurance company are going to try to diminish your fault
somewhat. There is very few of us that come around and say, "Yeah, I made a
left turn in front of the guy and smacked him and that's it."

25   The officers have the same motive. They want to make sure it's somebody
else's fault and that's inevitable. That affects their appreciation—excuse me,
their perception. But you go and you look at the circumstances and Johnson
obviously wanted something done about his seeing a sergeant. He listened to
a great number of people, "Well, the sergeant can't see everybody," although
30   this problem seems to have been one that had been floating around since
the first part of the month. And Mr. Cummings says Johnson chose to draw
the line. I agree. He drew the line, "I want something done; I want to see a
sergeant."

      And it's obvious from the testimony that if he just kept on drawing the
35   line at some point in time he would have seen a sergeant. That doesn't mean
Johnson made a choice to go out and start battering the officer or officers.[79]
When you look at the circumstances surrounding this whole situation,

---

76. Was this an effective argument about the officers' motive to be untruthful about the incident?
Did it respond to the prosecutor's argument about motive?

77. Does defense counsel weave in the other facts that might support the defendant's story that the
officers were the first aggressors?

78. If the cell port is significant, why doesn't defense counsel say anything about it here?

79. This appears to be a response to the prosecutor's theme that inmate Johnson chose to have this
aggressive encounter with the officers. Defense counsel does present some of the facts that tell the story
from Johnson's point of view. Notice, however, that on a few key points, he does not forcefully argue the
truth of Johnson's own testimony.

1   Johnson is calm, he is not abusive, and all the testimony is, depending on who
      perceived it correctly—and there is obviously some different perceptions—he
      is standing there. When the door opens he doesn't throw the tray at the offi-
      cers. He just drops it.[80]

5   And the general testimony is that his head drops down and I gather what-
      ever was going on with his fists, whether it was pushing towards the officer or
      whatever, there was no—I guess there is even some discrepancy amongst the
      officers' testimony as to whether there was, quote, an assault or an attempt
      to assault the officer—or Officer Walker.[81] But, you know, I am accused of
10   putting Officer Walker on trial and I apologize. But, you know, you are deal-
      ing with somebody that's in a maximum-level prison, level four, and I'm not
      concerned with really whether Walker is a bad guy or not as I told you orig-
      inally. You know, there is a lot of testimony around here brought in by the
      prosecution about Walker as a great officer, he is wonderful. I expect CDC
15   staff to stick with each other on those kind of issues. You notice none of them
      go down the inmate population and say, "Hey, have you guys had problems
      with Walker," or, "What's your opinion about Walker in terms of how he uses
      force and violence?"
      I think what's significant is that this inmate is terrified of him and at least
20   two other inmates seem to think that—or one other inmate, rather, says, "You
      know, I have seen him engage in this kind of conduct before." You are kind of
      totally at the mercy of those cops out there. It's not like being out in the street.
      So he is standing here and he is waiting for the cell port door to be opened.
      Now, possibly the cell port door was open.[82] I suspect the cell port door was
25   closed. But even if it is open you notice nobody ever says, "Pass the food tray
      through the cell port." It's, "Give us the food tray, give us the food tray."
      You know, if this cell port is, say, basically at waist high or a little below—
      some say it's a little below, it's twelve inches wide, six inches high and four
      inches deep—I can understand how in his perception even if the officers are
30   right about the cell port door being open—and I question that—I can under-
      stand from his perception how standing there he would be aware of the cell
      port door opening.
      What happened? The cell door opens and here is Walker. What goes
      through his mind? "I am going to get the you know what beat out of me." He
35   drops the trays, ducks and the melee ensues. I really think that's an honest
      interpretation of what happen. And it's obvious that in any kind of a confron-
      tation like that the officers are going to see and believe in the fact that they are
      going to assume that an assault has taken place and obviously the inmate is the
      one that's going to get blamed.[83]

---

80. The defendant testified that he bent over to pick up the trays.

81. Defense counsel does not mention that the defendant testified that he was left-handed, whereas
Officers Van Berg and Smith testified that it was Johnson's right fist that was thrust through the cell door
at Walker.

82. The defendant testified that the food port door was closed.

83. Could everybody be telling the truth? Perhaps the defendant did drop the trays, duck his head
from fear, and even raise his fist to protect himself, but perhaps his behavior was interpreted as aggressive

1   I think what really happens is the officers may well have perceived this as a battery, but what happens is Mr. Johnson figures, "I am going to get the you know what kicked out of me," he drops the trays and down he goes. Now, regardless of how you see that initial confrontation, Mr. Cummings is right.

5   The issue involving a battery against Walker ain't on trial here today. The issue that's on trial is was there a battery against Van Berg and was there a battery against Huston.

You know what? If you sit back and think about the testimony I will bet your recollection is the same as mine. There wasn't one bit of testimony about

10   this defendant striking any other officer. In fact, none of the officers—neither of those two officers testified the defendant struck him. They didn't testify that way at the preliminary hearing. They didn't testify here that way.

I assume with all these other officers, "Oh, yeah, I saw him strike Van Berg," or, "I saw him strike somebody else with his foot" or something of

15   this sort. None of—nobody has testified about the defendant striking anybody other than Walker and that issue isn't on trial here. Huston and Van Berg both stated—and I'm going to just paraphrase their testimony to my notes— but I believe that there was a question to the effect of, you know, on Officer Huston's part, "Do you know how you received the gash specifically?" "No."

20   And on Van Berg's part, "Do you know how you got hurt?" "No."

I don't know if they banged their legs on the cell door. I don't know if they banged their legs when Van Berg was banging my client's head against the wall, if he banged his thumb by accident at the same time. I don't know what happened. And you don't know what happened. The problem is that you can't

25   speculate as to what happened because without that evidence that's presented before you in some way, shape or form that my client kicked them or hit them or did something like that, the DA doesn't have a case. And there is absolutely not one bit of evidence before the court as to Van Berg and as to Huston and I think you need to go look at that and go into that jury room and come back

30   with a verdict of not guilty.

This case has absolutely no business wasting your time and your money. This is not—the defendant is entitled to a not-guilty verdict. There is absolutely no contact where the defendant is exercising force. There is lots of force being exercised on the defendant. But there is absolutely not one shred of

35   evidence that the defendant exercised any force against Huston or Van Berg.[84] Thank you.

Mr. Cummings: I would suspect Mr. Deemer has been watching the Olympics on TV the last couple of nights and he has watched how some of the referees score those boxing matches where one makes contact, okay, that's a point.

---

by the equally fearful officers. Wouldn't this be an appropriate point in the argument for the defense counsel to remind the jury of the self-defense instruction, and to argue that it applies? Or even to relate this self-defense theory to the reasonable doubt instruction?

84. Shouldn't the judge's instructions cover the question whether evidence of direct touching is required for battery? Do they? It is the advocate's responsibility to request instructions on issues of law that are raised by the facts. Then the advocate can read those instructions to the jury during closing.

1   That one didn't score, this one did score. Ladies and gentlemen, this whole
argument regarding that not one bit of evidence did either one of these officers actually testify that a blow struck them causing that injury and the DA
doesn't have a case is nonsense. It's ridiculous.

5   There is nothing in the law that requires any officer to come in here or
anybody to tell you or anybody else that "It was his third right jab that caught
my thumb that jammed it against the floor that caused the injury." It's ridiculous. Think about it logically.

There is nothing in the law that requires any officer to come in here or
What the law is trying to prevent and punish is the acts and the resulting
10   injury. Because you have officers who are honest enough to come up here and
say, "We can't tell you exactly what blow it was, I can't tell you exactly even
when it happened because professionally what we are trying to do is subdue
a person, get him down, get him quiet, get him cuffed. We are trying to do it
fast for everybody's safety, officer safety, safety of this gentleman, safety of his
15   roommate, cell mate, everybody involved," and that's what they are supposed
to be doing. That's what the State of California pays them to do.

So this idea that because they cannot truthfully tell you exactly what blow
caused the injury the People don't have a case is not true. Legally it's just a fiction, a lie. It seems like Mr. Deemer and the defense is—what they are really
20   trying to say is that Walker had it in for—at least this guy believed that Walker
had it in for him. Remember the testimony from the defendant himself. Had
two prior contacts. Walker recalls none but then again he probably deals with
thousands of people, or has in his career. It's had two prior contacts with him,
one at Folsom and one here. Based upon that and some other perceptions that
25   he has from other people he is scared to death of an officer that he doesn't
have regular contact with, scared to death.

Ladies and gentlemen, that type of an argument, if that were legally sufficient for a self-defense argument, which is what he is really saying, he is
really saying that it was perfectly appropriate for Johnson in this case to do
30   what he did. Now, the defense is trying to minimize, of course, what he did.
The defense would have you believe, "Well, you know, he was covering up
his head so of course he had to drop the trays; and because he didn't throw the
trays at the officer, which is one thing he could have done, then it couldn't
really be an assault."

35   That's ridiculous. He chose to drop the trays, maybe duck, maybe not
duck. The evidence is 50/50 on that. But in any case it was real clear about
right fist coming up clenched and moving forward, him being the aggressor. I
even asked one officer is there any way—it's almost embarrassing asking these
questions. But is there any way that you could have mistaken him for bowing
40   down, the forward motion. He said no. Did he act aggressively? Was he acting
violently? At that point he was. That's all that mattered.[85]

---

85. The theory of a self-defense claim is that the defendant has the right to respond with reasonable
force when he has reasonable fear of bodily injury. Thus, inmate Johnson's aggressive move, if it occurred,
could be viewed as a reasonable response to the aggression he feared from the assembled group of officers.
Is this ever explained to the jury?

1   Because Johnson initiated that and the officers responded in a professional and appropriate fashion and because of that two of them were injured and that's all we are asking you to return a verdict on are those two counts. Nothing more. It is real important that people realize that the burden is on the People
5   and I do have to prove my case and I have to prove my case beyond a reasonable doubt and just that, beyond a reasonable doubt.

As the law says, it is not a mere possible doubt, because everything is open to some doubt. In other words, you can have some doubt and you can still convict Mr. Johnson of Counts 1, Counts 2. You can have some doubt. I
10   could not and I cannot and no prosecutor can ever prove their case beyond any shadow of a doubt. This is not Perry Mason. Nor can we do it beyond any possible doubt. I can't do it. I don't believe anybody can because we are dealing with human fears and human people and you are always going to have different perceptions. Always do.

15   It's just gut level feelings, folks. Beyond a reasonable doubt, four correctional officers come in here and tell you what happened on March the 28th, 1992, to the point where you believe beyond a reasonable doubt that what they say happened really did happen; and if you can do that, you can find Mr. Johnson guilty of Count 1, guilty of Count 2. Thank you very much.

20   *The Court*:   You shall now retire and select one of your number to act as foreperson. He or she will preside over your deliberations. In order to reach verdicts all twelve jurors must agree to the decision, to the findings you have been instructed to include in your verdict. As soon as all of you have agreed upon a verdict so that when polled each may state truthfully that the verdict expresses
25   his or her decision, dated and signed by your foreperson and then return with them to this courtroom. Return any unsigned verdict forms.

Count 1 has to do with Officer Huston. Count 2 is identical except it applies to the allegation concerning Officer Van Berg. It is either guilty or not guilty, date and sign the verdict form.
30   (The bailiff was sworn.) . . .

(At 6:37 P.M. court was reconvened.)

The Court: Let the record reflect the defendant and both attorneys and the jury are present in court. Mr. Baker, has the jury reached a verdict?
Mr. Baker: Yes, sir.
35   *The Court*:   Hand the verdict to the bailiff, please.
The Clerk: Superior Court of the State of California, County of Del Norte, People of the State of California versus James Johnson. We the jury impaneled in the above-entitled matter find the defendant, James Johnson, guilty of battery on a correctional officer in violation of Section 4501.5 of the Penal
40   Code, Officer Huston, Count 1.

We the jury empaneled in the above-entitled matter find the defendant, James Johnson, guilty on Count 2, battery on correctional officer in violation of Section 4501.5 of the Penal Code, Officer Van Berg.

NOTES AND QUESTIONS

1. Defendant Johnson appealed his conviction to the District Court of Appeals in California. The appellate court stated that "[t]he only real dispute in appellant's case was who provoked the incident." Was this the way the case was presented to the jury in the closing arguments? Did the defense attorney even make an argument that the correctional officers started the melee? Consider the evidence in the case that would sustain such an argument, or the related argument that the various combatants misinterpreted each other's conduct to be aggressive. Think about the stories you could tell to the jury that would raise a reasonable doubt about Johnson's guilt.

2. Would evidence of other incidents at Pelican Bay have affected the outcome in *Johnson*? Here is an excerpt from Judge Henderson's opinion in the Pelican Bay class action, *Madrid v. Gomez*, 889 F. Supp. 1146, 1162, 1199-1200 (N.D. Cal. 1995):

> . . . Castillo refused to return his food tray in protest against a correctional officer who had called him and other inmates derogatory names. After leaving the tray near the front of the cell, Castillo retreated to the back and covered himself with his mattress for protection, in anticipation of a cell extraction. . . . Castillo, who is small in stature, made no verbal threats or aggressive gestures. . . .
>
> To accomplish [his] removal, two rounds from a 38 millimeter gas gun were fired into the cell. A taser gun was also fired, striking Castillo in the chest and stomach. Then, without attempting to retrieve the tray, . . . some number of officers entered the cell. . . . Castillo testified that one of the officers then hit him on the top of the head with the butt of the gas gun, knocking him unconscious. When he regained consciousness, he was on the floor with his face down. An officer was stepping on his hands and hitting him on the calves with a baton. . . . When he regained consciousness again, he was dragged out of the cell face down; his head was bleeding, and a piece of his scalp had been detached or peeled back. . . . [H]e was taken to the infirmary and then the hospital. . . .

On the basis of this and other incidents, Judge Henderson concluded:

> We agree that the extent to which force is misused at Pelican Bay, combined with the flagrant and pervasive failures in defendants' systems for controlling the use of force . . . reveal an affirmative management strategy . . . . All together, [the evidence] paints a picture of a prison that all too often uses force, not only in good faith efforts to restore and maintain order, but also for the very purpose of inflicting punishment and pain.

Why do you think the defense lawyer in *Johnson* did not put the "management strategy" of Pelican Bay on trial? If the lawyer had tried, would the judge have permitted it? How many incidents would have to be tried in such a case? How would the prosecution have responded? How long would the *Johnson* case have taken to try if other incidents were explored at trial?

CHAPTER TWO

THE PROCESS OF PROOF: HOW TRIALS ARE STRUCTURED

This chapter provides context for studying the rules of evidence in two ways. First, we briefly introduce you to our methodology and to the Federal Rules of Evidence ("FRE"), and offer some study tips. Second, we provide you an overview of the structure of the proof process in our adversarial system of trials. This is the setting in which the evidence rules operate.

A. INTRODUCTION TO THE STUDY OF EVIDENCE

How to Use This Book.   This book uses the problem method. We present the evidence rules and explain them in straightforward text, somewhat like a treatise or hornbook, rather than by requiring you to extract doctrinal points from judicial opinions. To enable you to put the rules into practice, and explore their limits and applications, we rely on realistic hypothetical problems. Our approach reflects our considered judgment that the problem method is preferable to the case method for studying evidence. Since your professor assigned this book, undoubtedly she or he agrees. We include just a handful of case excerpts in this book, doing so only where a case is critical to fully presenting a significant doctrine, or where the fact pattern is particularly useful to demonstrating a particular application of the rule.

We cover most of the Federal Rules of Evidence in this book, but have been selective, omitting some of the less important ones. Our general approach is to start by reproducing the text of the rule, and in the next section, explaining its core meaning and application. In sections after that, where the rule warrants it, we discuss more difficult applications of the rule, problems and doubts surrounding the rule, its underlying policies, and practice-related issues. These problems are interspersed throughout the book, starting in Chapter Three, after significant chunks of rule-explanation material (typically around 5 to 12 pages). At the end of each chapter (again, starting with Chapter Three), we offer "assessments," typically multiple choice or true/false questions testing a core application of the rule. Answers to all the assessment questions are found in the back of the book.

Studying Evidence.   Techniques for studying the law of evidence depend heavily on how your professor teaches the course. But we can offer some general ideas that are likely to work in most classes. Law students tend to rely heavily on course outlines as a study tool, whether commercially prepared or prepared by themselves or classmates. While commercial outlines may be helpful for casebooks, where the doctrinal take-away from a given case may be unclear, we think they are less useful in connection with this book. We don't hide the ball in presenting black letter doctrine; it's challenging enough to apply the rule to the problems.

As for an outline you prepare yourself, our suggestion is that you be strategic. If you write an outline that simply summarizes black letter evidence law, you may gain something from your efforts, but it may inefficient. You'll wind up with something that looks a lot like a slightly annotated copy of the Federal Rules of Evidence themselves. Instead, consider the following approach. For each one-hour assignment, write the number of the rule you studied (e.g., FRE 602) and a short phrase identifying its gist (e.g., "firsthand knowledge"). Copy a bullet point version of the rule if you like—we do this in the book, and the formatting of the many rules in the FRE is pretty much bullet-pointed. More important is to bullet-point any doctrinal points that are not obvious from the text of the rule—that have been added by judicial interpretation, for example.

So far, we've suggested nothing different from a normal outline. Here's where our suggestion differs, and ties in to the problem method. For each rule, you should do two additional things. First, write up a short fact pattern that captures your understanding of the core application of the rule. Then write up at least one or two fact patterns that illustrate problematic or uncertain applications of the rule. You can draw these fact patterns from the problems in the book, from problems supplied by your professor, or (even better) from problems you make up yourself. When you write up the fact pattern, the key point is that you write in your own words how the rule applies, or the arguments for and against applying the rule to the fact pattern. This approach will help your learning and your exam preparation.

Reading the "Restyled" FRE.   While the Federal Rules of Evidence are by no means perfect in the way they're written, they are more compact and well organized than many other federal codes and rules regulating some aspect of litigation. To give yourself an overview, you should try to become familiar with the FRE's table of contents. There are 11 main sections (called "Articles"), each dealing with a separate subject matter. The rules for the most part attempt to explain themselves in straightforward language, giving you a good starting point to study their applications and difficulties.

Another thing you should know is that at the end of 2011, the FRE were "restyled." That is to say, the pre-2011 version of the FRE was edited to express the rules in plainer language. In addition, some subsection numbering within each of several rules was changed around in the hope of making them clearer and more bullet-pointed. These changes necessarily had to go through the amendment process: The rules Advisory Committee proposes changes to the Supreme Court, which reviews and approves them before sending them to Congress for final approval. However, the revisions are called a "restyling" to make clear that the intention was not to make substantive changes to the meaning or interpretation of any rule, but rather to make them easier to read and understand. In a few cases, the restyling attempted to clarify a formerly ambiguous wording by conforming the rule's new wording to a dominant judicial interpretation.

In this book, we of course reproduce the FRE in their current, "restyled" form. Our explanations and discussions use the current wording and subsection numbering. The reason we bring all this up is to alert you to the fact of the change. Cases decided under the pre-2011 (that is, pre-restyled) rules may have slightly different language and subsection numbering, so we want to make sure you're not thrown off by this. And you can now understand what we mean later in the text when, on occasion, we explicitly mention the "restyling."

B. THE ADVERSARY/ JURY TRIAL SYSTEM: AN OVERVIEW

As you begin your study of the law of evidence, it can be useful to put yourself in the role of the trial lawyer trying to present a case persuasively to the jury. This necessarily requires you to imagine at the same time how the trial process appears to the jurors. It is a bewildering mixture of the familiar and the unfamiliar. To begin with, most litigated events involve conventional human affairs. Although the prison setting in the *Johnson* case is outside the personal experience of most people, the crucial question for decision is simply how a fight came about, which reduces, as is typical, to the question of whom to believe—here, the inmate or the guards. Although the issues that typify litigation are usually within general experience, the decisionmaking methodology differs radically from the manner in which an ordinary citizen makes day-to-day decisions. The trial setting is unusual, perhaps on occasion mystifying, and often intimidating for jurors. Indeed, a theme running through the trial process that you may have already detected is the insulation of the jury from much of what happens during trial. Although, historically, juries were allowed to decide issues of law as well as fact—even as late as the end of the nineteenth century in the United States—the modern jury decides only factual issues. Therefore, virtually all legal discussion—including the proper substantive and procedural law to be applied to the case, and whether evidence should be admitted or excluded—occurs outside the hearing or presence of the jury. Relatively brief legal discussions in the midst of trial may be conducted in a sidebar conference, in which the lawyers and judge talk in low voices so as not to be heard by the jurors. Longer discussions are held either in the judge's chambers, or, if in the courtroom, at times when jurors are not present.

This theme of jury insulation also runs through the evidence course, because, to a large degree, the rules of evidence focus directly on the question of what evidence the jury will be allowed to hear. The policy implications of most evidence rules are therefore based on someone's answer to the question: What is the effect on the accurate resolution of disputes of allowing a jury to consider this type of information?

1. The Adversary System.

The rules structuring litigation, including the rules of evidence, are derived from, and implement, the dominant theory of dispute resolution in this country, known as the adversary system. Adverse parties each present a self-serving version of the truth to a presumably disinterested factfinder, judge or jury, which hears the evidence the parties present and decides in a disinterested fashion what actually happened, and thus what verdict is appropriate. The adversarial process, in turn, is derived from a conception of the appropriate role of government in the resolution of disputes between private individuals and between the state and an individual. The government has the obligation to provide a fair and disinterested forum for the impartial resolution of disputes; and for the most part that is all the government has an obligation, or a right, to do. Even in criminal cases, the courts stand apart from the prosecution, treating the representatives of the sovereign as though they were representing a private party. The parties are responsible for investigating the case, preparing the case for trial, and in large measure controlling the presentation of evidence at trial. In this country, many believe that adversarial investigation and presentation of evidence is more likely to yield a verdict consistent with the truth than is a process more dominated by a tribunal.

The Roles of the Trial Participants.   Although probably quite familiar to you from fictional and real-life courtroom dramas, the well-defined roles of participants in a trial are worth briefly reviewing: **Witnesses** are people with knowledge of out-of-court events who are called on to reveal that knowledge in court, under oath, in front of the judge, jury, and litigants.

The jury (meaning each of its members) uses its senses to perceive information in the courtroom and its reasoning capacity to evaluate and make inferences about that information in order to reach a conclusion about which version of disputed events is (closer to?) the truth. Jurors are expected to come to conclusions about disputed facts in the case without bringing to bear any outside or firsthand knowledge of their own: Typically, they know nothing about the case beforehand, and (as in the *Johnson* case, Chapter One) are instructed by the judge not to investigate the facts on their own. However, jurors are not expected to disregard their own generalized background knowledge and experience, and indeed it is assumed that they will use their knowledge and experience in reasoning and making inferences about the evidence before them. As is typical, the jury instructions in the *Johnson* case did not give the jury any guidance about what its reasoning process should be, other than to define "inference" and "circumstantial evidence," and to rule out certain "irrational" factors: emotions, the number of witnesses on a side, chance, or the drawing of lots. Pages 68-72, supra.

The lawyers provide information to the jury through the use of witnesses, documents, and other exhibits.[1] Because the jury is passive, the role of the advocates is to investigate, interview, select, prepare, and present the sources of information that the

---

1. The judge in *Johnson* instructed the jury that "[e]vidence consists of testimony of witnesses, writings, material objects, or anything presented to the senses and offered to prove the existence or nonexistence of a fact." Page 69, supra.

advocates think will most advance their respective cases. This competitive process is at the heart of the adversary system of proof and it results in the presentation of competing and contradictory versions of events. The advocates also argue inferences and conclusions to the jury, but the jury is instructed that attorneys' statements are not evidence.

The judge controls the trial process by setting limits, primarily pursuant to the rules of evidence, on the advocates' proof in the interests of rationality of results, fairness between the parties, social and moral values, and efficiency. The judge has power to make all the trial participants conform to their roles in courtroom behavior and decorum. In addition, the judge may call witnesses and may question witnesses whether called by the court or not. See FRE 611 and 614. But the judge is not supposed to control the content or the overall presentation of the advocates' cases. Thus, a standard jury instruction states that neither side had to produce all witnesses who might have knowledge of the facts, or present all objects or documents that might be mentioned. Throughout this course you should ask whether the judge should have the power to keep knowledge about the disputed facts from the jury.

Jury Trials versus Bench Trials.   The rules of evidence have been created and shaped over time with the jury in mind as the factfinder. However, many trials are held without a jury. While the parties in most criminal cases and many civil claims for damages have a constitutional right to trial by jury, the parties sometimes waive that right and agree to a try the case to the judge without a jury. In addition, many civil cases—primarily, those seeking so-called equitable relief, such as injunctions—are tried before a judge without a jury. In such "bench trials," the judge acts not only as the decision maker on points of law and admission or exclusion of evidence, but also as the sole fact finder, weighing the evidence. A similar situation is presented by "evidentiary hearings": pretrial proceedings (such as a preliminary hearing in a criminal case) in which witnesses are called to testify. The rules of evidence typically apply in bench trials and evidentiary hearings, but because no jury is present, the application of the rules may be relaxed somewhat. The theory is that a judge, due to experience and professional training, can disregard inadmissible evidence far more easily and effectively than a jury. Therefore, erroneous admission or exclusion of evidence is thought to be less problematic; and the judge can couch findings in such a way as to claim that the decision would not be affected by a particular doubtful evidentiary ruling.

C. ADVERSARIAL PRESENTATION OF PROOF: THE IDEA OF COMPETING NARRATIVES AND "THEORY OF THE CASE"

In the adversary system of trials, the opposing parties each present a narrative or story of civil liability or criminal guilt, or their negations (nonliability or not guilty). As Professor Thomas Mauet says, "A jury trial is essentially a competition to see which party's theory of the case the jury will select as more probably true." Thomas A. Mauet,

Trial Techniques 62 (8th ed. 2010). Trials (1) render a final and binding decision that leads to imposition of the coercive power of the state, and (2) gather facts exclusively from the presentations of adverse parties. Consider how this differs from the many other forms of investigative factfinding inquiry. Many investigatory processes, like trials, attempt to reconstruct past events. But investigations take a different approach to facts. Investigators examine plausible hypotheses, consider "leads" that are deemed possibly true but that may not be probably true (at least at early stages). In investigations, speculation is a useful tool to generate leads and possible avenues of further inquiry. Investigations need not come to a conclusion. A congressional committee may fail to reach a conclusion or recommend legislation; a police detective may fail to identify a suspect, and leave the case classified as "unsolved."

Trials thus differ from investigations in two significant ways. First, trials must come to a conclusion. Second, evidence is presented, rather than gathered. This means that the parties are not inquiring into what the facts may be, but claiming what the facts are.

> From what may have been several plausible hypotheses in an investigatory stage, parties to a trial are required to have committed themselves to a specific version of events. It is axiomatic in our justice system that a claim is entitled to a remedy only if it is true. While our system of trial and evidence is designed to accommodate the uncertainty inherent in reconstructing past events, it does so by allowing parties to base their claims on proof of what probably happened; but it does not permit parties to assert "possibly-true" alternative claims. David S. Schwartz, A Foundation Theory of Evidence, 100 Geo. L.J. 95, 126 (2011).

To see this point, Consider an opening statement in a medical malpractice trial in the absence of such a principle:

> The defendant may have left a surgical sponge in the plaintiff's body when the incision was re-sewn—we're not sure. If he did not, it's possible that he injured the plaintiff by cutting a nerve. Or maybe it wasn't a surgery at all; maybe he prescribed unnecessary heart medication. All we know is that he was negligent in some way.

This example is extreme, but you can see the point. If a party "may rely on ways in which the litigated event could have happened . . . , the task becomes one of establishing a probability conditioned on all conceivable evidence. This is obviously a burden that neither party could bear[.]" Ronald J. Allen, The Nature of Juridical Proof, 13 Cardozo L. Rev. 373, 378 (1991). If the claiming party doesn't know what happened to him, he can't claim entitlement to a remedy.

This means that the parties must commit themselves to a specific story in order to proceed to trial. Moreover, the story has to follow a certain structure: It must contain "elements" prescribed by the substantive law. The elements of a contract claim are (1) a contract (consisting of offer, acceptance and consideration), (2) a breach, (3) causation, and (4) damages. A good way to think of elements is to think of legal claims as recurring genres or types of story. The way that you can recognize a case as a "negligence case" is analogous to the way that you can recognize a movie as a romantic comedy. A movie is a Rom Com if it has the following elements: (1) boy meets girl, (2) the couple falls in love and starts a relationship, (3) the couple has a falling out, and (4) the couple winds up together—typically after a montage set to music of their poignant together moments, followed by a scene in which the boy runs through city streets or drives at great speed to stop the girl from doing the thing that will break them up irrevocably. The details of the story differ, but the presence of those elements defines it as a romantic comedy. Same for negligence, breach of contract, or what have you.

The story told by a claiming party at trial must do two things. It must commit to a specific version of events. That doesn't necessarily mean that every last detail must be known. But the party must meet the second requirement: The story must contain facts that establish each of the elements the substantive law requires for that type of legal claim (that genre, if you will). Establishing an element in the previous sentence means meeting the burden of proof. The case-specific facts have to be weighty and detailed enough that a factfinder could be persuaded that the generic element is probably true. The degree of probability depends on the applicable burden of persuasion, as we examine in Chapter Ten.

The story told by the claiming party that meets these two criteria is called the "theory of the case." A theory of the case "is your side's version of 'what really happened.' . . . It must be logical, fit the legal requirements of the claims or defenses, be simple to understand, and be consistent with the jurors' common sense[.]" Mauet, supra, at 62. Some trial practitioners and practice manuals refer to "theory of the case" in a looser sense, referring to trial tactics and persuasive storytelling. We use it in a more rigorous sense to refer to an implicit requirement. It is a narrative containing all the facts necessary to establish the probable truth of the essential elements of the claim. Viewed this way, the theory of the case is also essential to determine relevance: A relevance argument shows how an item of evidence fits into the offering party's theory of the case.

Thus far, we've been defining "theory of the case" with a focus on the claiming party (the plaintiff or prosecution). For civil defendants, the points made about theory of the case apply equally to their affirmative defenses (because the defendants bear the burden of proof). Theory of the case differs slightly for defendants, to the extent that they can claim nonliability or nonguilt based on casting doubt on the claimant's case. For defendants in this sense, having a theory of the case may be more of a strategic imperative than a formal requirement. Nevertheless, if a defendant offers a countertheory of the case that includes facts left out of the claimants' theory of the case, the effect will be to expand the scope of what will be deemed relevant evidence in the litigation.

D. THE STRUCTURE OF A TRIAL

1. Pretrial Motions

Trials usually begin with "motions *in limine*" (pronounced "in lim-in-ay," meaning "at the threshold"). These are motions made by the parties to obtain rulings on anticipated evidentiary problems. Parties anticipating the introduction of problematic evidence by their adversaries make motions in limine to *exclude* that evidence, though motions in limine can be used to get a pretrial ruling on any evidentiary question. Motions in limine are often made in writing, with short supporting briefs, and argued outside the presence of the jury.

Tactical considerations will typically drive counsels' decisions on whether to file motions in limine. For example, a criminal defendant, such as Johnson, may want to testify only if the jury will not learn of his prior criminal convictions. In order to make an informed decision about whether to testify, the defendant could file a motion in limine asking that the prior convictions be excluded from evidence. This would eliminate uncertainty as to whether the defendant's prior felonies will come before the jury. If no motion in limine were made, defense counsel would have to wait until the prosecutor were to ask, while cross-examining the defendant, "Isn't it a fact, Mr. Johnson, that you were convicted of rape in 1981?" and then object. Even if the objection were sustained, the jury, having heard the question, might nevertheless believe the prosecutor had a good-faith basis for asserting that the defendant had such a conviction. But if defense counsel were to have made a successful motion in limine, the prosecutor would be instructed ahead of time by the judge not to ask such a question at all.

2. Jury Selection

Following motions in limine, the jury selection process begins. Jury selection varies both in the process for selection and the number of jurors empanelled, depending on the type of case and the jurisdiction; anywhere from 6 to 12 jurors may be required. In federal court, 12 jurors sit in criminal trials and six in civil trials.

The jury selection process is founded on the belief that trials are more likely to result in an accurate verdict—assigning liability or blame only where warranted by the facts—by having cognitively competent, disinterested jurors. Consequently, the process allows parties to object to potential jurors who are incompetent, who have a financial or emotional interest in the case, or who cannot put aside any preconceptions about the case they may have in order to decide it based on the evidence produced at trial.

The primary means of selecting a jury is by questioning the jury "venire"—the group from whom the jury panel will be chosen—in order to uncover any ground for dismissing them. The questioning process, called "voir dire,"[2] may be conducted by the trial judge, the lawyers, or by means of a written questionnaire, or by a combination of any of the three. (The most common practice in federal court is for the judge to do the questioning, with the lawyers' participation limited to suggesting questions to ask.) Questions may be directed to individual jurors, or to the venire as a whole. The judge can dismiss potential jurors "for cause" (such as some type of bias for or against

---

2. "Voir" is pronounced "vwahr" and "dire" is usually pronounced "deer," although the prevailing pronunciation in the South is "dire" (as in "dire straits"). The term *voir dire* applies not only to jurors in jury selection, but also to trial witnesses, when the latter are asked questions outside the presence of the jury in order to determine whether some aspect of their testimony will be admitted into evidence in front of the jury.

one of the parties) or practical reasons (such as inability to serve for the length of the trial). The lawyers can request dismissal for cause, or may make so-called peremptory challenges. Because the lawyers are not required to give reasons for exercising peremptory challenges, they may be used, as a practical matter, for any reason at all, or no reason beyond a hunch or a whim. The only constraints on peremptory challenges are that each side is given only a limited number, and that they may not be used merely because of the race or sex of the potential juror. See Batson v. Kentucky, 476 U.S. 79 (1986) (race); J.E.B. v. Alabama ex rel. T.B., 511 U.S. 127 (1994) (sex).

Properly conducted, voir dire is a sensible way to begin a trial designed to elicit a rational verdict. Even if people are generally rational, competent actors, from time to time some are also unable to put aside interests and biases that may infect their decisions (as is true of judges as well, who are disqualified for similar reasons). Investing some time and effort in removing such people from the trial makes eminent good sense. Like much of the trial process, the laudable social goal is achieved through taking advantage of the self-interest of the parties, whose respective desires to wind up with the most favorable jury possible will, it is hoped, cancel out and result in a reasonably fair-minded panel of jurors.

3. Preliminary Instructions

Once the jury is empanelled and sworn, the judge will typically issue some preliminary jury instructions. Again, practice varies from court to court, and judge to judge: These instructions may be nothing more than admonitions not to talk about the case prior to jury deliberations; or may include certain generic guidelines about considering the evidence or credibility of witnesses; or, less typically, may even include instructions about the substantive law governing the case. In *Johnson*, the court read the jury a series of generic instructions as well as the "information," the written criminal pleading setting forth the charge, which stated the statutory elements of the alleged crime.

4. Opening Statements

Now, the lawyers take turns introducing their respective cases to the jury, in the order in which they will present evidence: The plaintiff (civil) or prosecution (criminal) proceeds first, then the defendant. An opening statement is neither evidence nor argument, but is supposed to be a compact narrative of what the lawyer believes in good faith the evidence will show. The "official" purpose is to provide the jury with a coherent overview of the case to make it easier for the jurors to assimilate the testimony they will soon hear, testimony that may necessarily tell the story in a fragmented, nonchronological fashion.

Argument is not allowed in an opening statement, and can result in an objection being sustained. Generally speaking, conclusions or inferences derived from the evidence, contentions about legal rules, and comments about witness credibility are considered "argument." For example, pointing out weaknesses in your adversary's case would clearly constitute objectionable argument. However, the line between a factual statement and an argument is not always clear, much like the distinction between factual news reporting and editorializing, and is equally hard to draw. A great deal falls into a gray area between "evidence" and "argument." Consider the facts of People v. Johnson: To say in an opening statement that "the defendant violently attacked Officer Walker" is closer to "argument" than is "the defendant punched Officer Walker with his fists," yet both could be considered statements of evidence. How much leeway the lawyers get depends heavily upon the discretion of the trial judge. A good practical method to assess the evidence/argument distinction is to ask whether a witness could say it on the stand—if so, then it is probably evidence.

Notwithstanding the rule against argument, the lawyers are advocates, and they will present the facts in the light most favorable to their cases. A well-presented opening statement can, without editorializing, offer a compelling argument for one side, and many trial advocates contend that juries begin to make up their minds on hearing the opening statements. (There is empirical research to support this view.)

Trial lawyers often describe the opening statement as the lawyer's "covenant with the jury." The representations about what "the evidence will show" are best viewed as promises, because the jury may resent or mistrust the lawyer whose claims in the opening statement are not backed up by evidence admitted during trial. This means that it is risky in the opening statement to stress evidence whose admissibility is in doubt.

5. Presentation of Evidence and the Burden of Production

The evidence-presentation phase is obviously the core of the trial. The manner in which the parties introduce evidence is discussed below. (See infra, subsection D.) This section deals with the order in which the parties present their cases and with the key, related issue of the burden of production.

a. The Order of the Parties' Presentation of Cases

After opening statements, the plaintiff/prosecution presents its case-in-chief. This means calling a series of witnesses to the stand. Primarily through the direct examination of these witnesses,[3] the plaintiff/prosecution must present evidence sufficient to prove—that is, sufficient to support a finding by the jury to establish—each element of its cause of action (or of the crime charged). In the Johnson case, for example, the charge of battery (one of several charges against Johnson) required the prosecution to prove: (1) willful and unlawful (2) use of force or violence (3) upon the person of another.

After the plaintiff or prosecution "rests" its case, and any motion to dismiss is heard (and denied), defendant's case begins. Like the plaintiff, the defendant conducts direct examinations of witnesses, but the thrust of the defense case is to cast doubt on

---

3. Two important devices make it unnecessary, in many instances, to prove facts through testimony or other evidence at trial: These are known as "stipulation" (facts agreed by the parties) and "judicial notice" (see Fed. R. Evid. 201, discussed in Chapter Eleven).

the plaintiff's evidence and to present evidence sufficient to prove each element of any affirmative defenses.

When the defense rests its case, the plaintiff/prosecution has an opportunity to call witnesses in a so-called rebuttal case. (The term "case-in-chief" is used to distinguish the plaintiff's main case from its rebuttal case.) The presentation of rebuttal evidence proceeds in the same way as in the case-in-chief, except that the scope of rebuttal evidence is limited. Rebuttal evidence must respond to either (a) matters raised as part of defendant's affirmative defenses; or (b) attacks during the defense case on the credibility of the plaintiff/prosecution's evidence. Normally, a plaintiff or prosecutor will not be allowed to repeat evidence presented in its case-in-chief, or to present evidence that should have been part of its case-in-chief. A defendant may be entitled to a "sur-rebuttal" (a rebuttal to the rebuttal), but this is unusual. The rebuttal case is necessarily much shorter than the case-in-chief.

b. The Burden of Production

The "burden of production" (discussed in detail in Chapter Ten) means producing enough evidence so that a "reasonable" factfinder can make a finding for the plaintiff or prosecution on each element of the civil claim or criminal charge. The "factfinder," again, is the jury in jury trials (or the judge in bench trials). The "finding" involved is a finding of the facts necessary to establish those elements of the claim or charge, and it must meet the applicable "burden of persuasion"—"beyond a reasonable doubt" in criminal cases, and "more likely than not" (also known as "a preponderance of the evidence") in civil cases.

Thus, the plaintiff meets its burden of production in civil cases with evidence sufficient for a reasonable jury to find that the facts establishing each element of the plaintiff's claim are more likely than not true. In a tort case, for instance, the plaintiff has to present evidence sufficient for jury findings on duty, breach, causation, and damages. In a criminal case, the prosecution meets its burden of production if it offers enough admissible evidence so that a reasonable jury can find that each element of the crime charged has been established "beyond a reasonable doubt." In the *Johnson* case, for example, this meant producing evidence sufficient for the jury to find beyond a reasonable doubt that, among other things, Johnson "touched" Huston or Van Berg in the manner described in the jury instructions.

Note: In civil cases, defendants have the burden of production on their affirmative defenses. In criminal cases, however, the prosecution has the burden of production to *negate* any defenses, such as "self defense" in the *Johnson* case.

A failure by the plaintiff or prosecutor to meet the burden of production on each element of a claim can result in a judgment as a matter of law for the defense on that claim. Motions for judgment as a matter of law can be made at several different points in the litigation process. In civil cases, motions for summary judgment (before trial), nonsuit/directed verdict/dismissal (after plaintiff's case-in-chief), directed verdict (after close of evidence) or JNOV (after verdict) all argue that the moving party wins the case on facts that are not genuinely disputed. (In federal civil cases, such motions made during or after trial are now all called motions for judgment as a matter of law.

See Fed. R. Civ. P. 50.) In criminal cases, only the defendant can move for judgment as a matter of law, and may do so after the prosecution's case-in-chief, after close of evidence or after the verdict.

There is a basic similarity between all these motions seeking judgment as a matter of law on a factual record: In each, the court is supposed to refrain from usurping the jury's role. This means that the judge should not resolve conflicts in the evidence or questions of witness credibility. Moreover, if the party with the burden of production has produced enough evidence to support a finding by a reasonable jury, the court should not issue judgment based on the judge's own view of how the jury should decide the case. Put another way, the judge has to make all inferences in favor of the party opposing judgment as a matter of law.

The verbal formulae for judgment as a matter of law may sound different in sum-mary judgment as compared to a post verdict motion, and in civil as compared to criminal cases, but they are all essentially the same: whether there is evidence suffi-cient for a reasonable jury to find for the prosecutor or plaintiff (or civil defendant on an affirmative defense). A defense counsel in a civil case might argue:

> Your Honor, plaintiff's evidence is not sufficient to support a finding by a reasonable jury that its version of the facts is more likely than not true. Some of the necessary facts are just plain missing, and on others, the evidence is based on inferences that are just too weak. Plaintiff's case should not get to the jury; judgment should be granted as a matter of law.

For criminal cases, substitute "prosecution" for "plaintiff" and "beyond a reasonable doubt" for "more likely than not."

The burden of production, and the resultant prospect of losing a judgment as a matter of law, has important implications for the order in which a party will present its evidence. While evidence that arises during the defendant's case can ultimately be relied upon by the plaintiff or prosecution as proof of such elements, it is extremely unwise for a plaintiff or prosecutor to do so, because the defense can make its motion for judgment as a matter of law at the end of the plaintiff's (or prosecutor's) case-in-chief, without putting on any of its own witnesses. The defense in People v. Johnson, did just that, arguing that there was insufficient testimony to show that the alleged battery victims, Huston and Van Berg, were ever actually touched by the defendant Johnson.

6. Post-evidence Matters

After the close of evidence, the court may take up certain legal matters with the lawyers outside the presence of the jury. The defendant may make a motion for "directed verdict" on the ground that "no reasonable jury" could find for the plaintiff because the evidence, as a matter of law, fails to establish one or more elements of the plaintiff's claims; or that the plaintiff has not raised sufficient evidence to dispute an affirmative defense. Similarly, the plaintiff could move for judgment as a matter of law on the ground that the defendant has not raised sufficient evidence to dispute its claims. The prosecution cannot move for a directed verdict of guilt, because that would be deemed a violation of the criminal defendant's Sixth Amendment right to jury trial.

At this stage the parties also argue over jury instructions. Most courts require the litigants to submit proposed jury instructions. These are to assist the court, which has the ultimate responsibility to decide how the jury will be instructed; indeed, the trial court can come up with its own instructions, and need not adopt what is proposed by the parties. Many of the instructions are standard (and may be contained in books or manuals of "pattern" jury instructions). The parties typically agree quickly upon generic instructions of the sort given in every case — an instruction on the burden of persuasion, for example. Arguments usually arise over how to instruct the jury on substantive law, particularly in areas where the law is developing or unsettled. If a party disagrees with an instruction the court decides to give, it may object and argue instructional error as a basis for appeal. For that reason, some trial judges, hoping to reduce grounds for appeal, may try to pressure or cajole the parties to agree on compromise instructions on controversial points.

In order to avoid keeping the jury waiting while the final jury instructions are physically typed up, the court may hold the jury instruction conference before the close of evidence; however, most judges like to wait until the evidence phase is near an end, because some important jury instruction questions will depend upon what evidence was actually presented. Once these legal issues are resolved, the jury is called back to the courtroom for one last phase of presentations — closing argument and jury instructions.

7. Closing Arguments

Unlike opening statements, in which argument and discussion of the law are prohibited, closing argument permits both. In closing argument, the lawyers "argue" the facts. Significantly, they may only discuss facts based on evidence admitted at trial. "Arguing the facts" is not merely summarizing the evidence; rather, lawyers in closing argument should analyze the evidence, identifying and arguing for the inferences and conclusions they believe should be drawn from it. A critical feature of closing argument should be to explain to the jury the chain of inferences that connect the evidentiary facts heard by the jury with the facts of consequence in the case. If you found the closing argument of defense counsel Deemer in the *Johnson* trial to have been unsatisfactory, an important reason for this may be that he failed to establish this inferential chain as to much of his key evidence. Throughout this book, we use diagrams to illustrate this chain of inferences, which you will see is necessary not only to argue the significance of evidence to a jury, but also to determine the application of such rules as relevance and hearsay.

An effective closing presents a coherent story of the events that proves one's case, while trying to show how the most likely interpretation of every point of conflict or ambiguity in the evidence supports that story. The lawyers should stress evidence corroborating key points of their cases as well as evidence that undermines the credibility of witnesses whose testimony contradicts key points.

Finally, it is also important to weave key jury instructions into the closing argument: In this way, the lawyers can show the jury how they believe the evidence maps onto the controlling substantive law—how they have proved the elements of their case and how the other side has failed to cast doubt on the proof or to prove its own case. This aspect of the closing links the facts of consequence with the essential elements required by the substantive law, a point that we illustrate diagrammatically throughout this book.

Courts vary in their practice of whether closing argument goes before or after jury instructions. The important point is that disagreement over jury instructions has been resolved before closing argument. That way, even if closing argument goes before the jury is actually instructed, the lawyers can refer to the jury instructions in their closing.

8. Jury Instructions and the Burden of Persuasion

Because jury instructions are a fertile source of "error" for the losing litigant to raise on appeal, most trial judges instruct the jury by simply reading word-for-word the written set of instructions. While extemporizing or ad-libbing might keep the jury's attention better than a droning verbatim recitation, trial judges typically opt for the prudent (if dull) approach of sticking to the script. (An exception to this might be the type of boilerplate instructions and admonitions given to the jury before opening statements.) Jury instructions can be quite lengthy and complex, and difficult if not impossible to remember on one hearing. Thus, courts in many jurisdictions provide the jury with a written copy of the instructions to take into the jury room for their deliberations; strangely, however, many courts do not allow that, and at most will offer only verbal repetition of instructions if it occurs to the jurors to request it.

An important concept explained to the jury in every case in the form of a jury instruction (and usually by the lawyers in closing argument as well) is the burden of persuasion. Earlier, we explained the burden of production as requiring a party to produce evidence sufficient to support a finding on a particular issue. The burden of persuasion specifies the degree of certainty that the jury must have in order to make a finding on a particular issue. This concept is further explained in Chapter Ten. In civil cases, the jury must find by a preponderance of the evidence that the plaintiff's claims are true. A preponderance of the evidence means greater than a 50 percent probability, or "more likely than not." In criminal cases, the burden of persuasion is guilt "beyond a reasonable doubt."

9. Jury Deliberations and Verdict

After closing arguments and jury instructions, the jurors go into the jury room for their deliberation. Jurors are allowed to have all the exhibits—the documents and objects admitted into evidence—with them in the jury room. They can also request to have portions of testimony read back to them (and are usually instructed that they can do this). Such "read-backs" involve bringing the jurors back into the courtroom, with

the lawyers present, to hear the court-reporter reading the testimony from the steno-
graphic notes (typically in a monotone). Some courts allow jurors to take notes during
trial, and to bring their notes with them into deliberations. While jurors may ask questions about the facts or the law during deliberations (by having the bailiff bring out a
note to the judge), the answers are often very uninformative. Unless the parties agree
on a response, the judge will be loath to create grounds for appeal with an informative
but arguably erroneous response to a question.

Again, depending on the type of case, the jury verdict may or may not have to be
unanimous. While unanimity is required in federal criminal cases, many jurisdictions
permit nonunanimous verdicts in civil and even some criminal cases. Federal civil
verdicts must be unanimous unless the parties agree otherwise. Fed. R. Civ. P. 48.

In criminal cases, a verdict takes the form of a decision—guilty or not guilty—on
each crime charged. Civil verdicts present more possibilities. In some trials, the jury is
asked only for a general verdict—"we find for the plaintiff," plus an amount of money
damages—where that is the issue, or just "we find for the defendant." In many cases,
particularly where the legal issue has a more complex structure, the court may use a
"special verdict" form or "jury interrogatories." Under these latter practices, the jury
is asked for its answers to a series of questions from which a judgment can be derived.
These questions might ask for separate jury findings on each element of a claim or a
defense. Given that the burden of proof is on the plaintiff to prove each element of its
case, a special verdict form or jury interrogatories may work to the defendant's advantage, because a "wrong" answer to any one of several questions may result in a defense
judgment. On the other hand, if a general verdict is used in a legally complex case,
the jury may not have followed the correct path to its final verdict. Such mistakes in
the jury's reasoning process are not considered proper grounds for an appeal. Indeed,
the evidence rules in most jurisdictions prohibit any inquiry into the jury's mental
processes or deliberations. See, e.g., FRE 606(b). Once the jury has rendered its final
verdict, and announced it in court, the jury is dismissed.

Some trials are "bifurcated" or even "trifurcated"—conducted in two or three separate phases, each one with its own set of jury instructions and closing arguments, and
its own separate verdict. Examples of this are civil cases involving punitive damages
and criminal cases involving the death penalty. In both these examples, the logically
prior issue is liability or guilt—is the defendant liable at all?—whereas the issue of
penalty, which may be based (at least in part) on other bad conduct separate from the
tort or crime alleged in the case, calls for evidence irrelevant to liability or guilt but
that might sway the jury against the defendant. These kinds of cases are thus "bifurcated" into a "liability" or "guilt" phase—whether the defendant committed the tort
or crime—and a "penalty" phase. The penalty phase is not even reached if the jury
returns a defense verdict in the liability phase.

10. Post-trial Motions

Once the jury has rendered its verdict and been dismissed, the jury trial proper is over.
Significantly, the "verdict" is not the same as the "judgment" in a case. A verdict is

the jury's ultimate decision. A judgment is a judicial act that concludes a case. After a jury trial, the trial judge eventually enters a judgment on a jury verdict. The judgment, usually a short document of a page or two signed by the trial judge, may do nothing more than restate the jury's verdict. In some cases, however, the judgment may include further issues that are not decided by a jury—such as injunctive relief, for example. It is the judgment, rather than the verdict itself, which has such legal effects as res judicata and that is subject to appellate review. Also, the judgment may differ from the jury verdict if, for example, the court grants a post-trial motion reversing the verdict.

Post-trial motions form an important aftermath of the trial. They do not occur right away, but within periods of a few weeks (set by statute or court rule) after the jury's verdict, but before the entry of judgment in the case. There are two types of post-trial motions: motion for judgment notwithstanding the verdict, and motion for new trial. The party that loses the case (or loses at least one ultimate issue) can bring either of these motions, and typically brings both together. In essence, a post-trial motion is an "appeal" from a jury verdict, only it is made to the trial judge rather than to an appellate court. And, indeed, an appeal from a jury verdict to a court of appeal requires that these motions have been made; technically, appellate review of a jury trial is actually review of a trial court decision denying a motion for new trial or for judgment notwithstanding the verdict.

A motion for judgment notwithstanding the verdict (also known by its Latin equivalent, "judgment *non obstante veredicto*," or "JNOV" for short) seeks judgment as a matter of law, on the ground that (again, considering the evidence in the light most favorable to the nonmoving party), the court can say that no reasonable jury could have reached this particular verdict. If the motion is granted, the court reverses the jury verdict and enters a directly contrary judgment: A defense verdict is overruled and judgment entered for the plaintiff, or vice versa.

A judgment notwithstanding the verdict allows the court, in effect, to delay the type of decision put to it in a directed verdict motion. A court might be inclined to direct a verdict in favor of the defendant, for example, due to the apparent insufficiency of the plaintiff's evidence. By deferring its ruling on this question until after the jury renders its verdict, however, the court allows the jury the opportunity to find against the plaintiff and thereby possibly avoids the need itself to make an outcome-dispositive ruling that would be subject to appellate review. In federal court, a motion for judgment notwithstanding the verdict can only be made if the moving party had previously moved for a directed verdict. (Fed. R. Civ. P. 50(b).)

The parties can move for a new trial on any of several grounds: erroneous jury instructions, excessiveness or inadequacy of a jury's damage award, irregularities in the trial or the jury deliberations, or—most significant for our purposes—erroneous admission or exclusion of evidence. These new trial motions argue that significant errors undermined the trial, which, therefore, must be done over.

The losing party can also move for a new trial on the ground that the verdict is "against the weight of the evidence." This is a lower standard than that required to get a judgment as a matter of law. Put another way, while a JNOV argues, in essence that the nonmoving party has failed to meet its burden of production, a new trial motion typically argues that the nonmoving party failed to meet its burden of persuasion. In contrast to motions for judgment as a matter of law, the trial judge gets to weigh conflicting evidence and assess witness credibility in considering whether to grant a new trial. Again, granting a new trial motion results in trying the case over, rather than determining the outcome of the case.

E. EXAMINATION OF WITNESSES AND FRE 611

The questioning (or "examination") of witnesses, and the witnesses' answers—their testimony—form the core of the trial, as seen above. Most evidence in most trials takes the form of testimony. Of course, documents, photographs, demonstrative and other tangible objects are introduced into evidence. However, as we will see in this course, the rules of evidence require presentation of testimony about documentary or tangible evidence to establish its admissibility and often to explain its significance. (Documentary and tangible evidence requires a witness to provide foundation testimony unless the parties agree to forgo the formalities.) Therefore, witness testimony is generally the most crucial form of evidence.

The examination of witnesses in the evidence-presentation phases of the trial follows a pattern of taking turns. The party calling the witness conducts a direct examination. The opposing party cross-examines, with cross-examination being limited in scope to matters raised on direct examination. The party calling the witness may respond to points made on cross by conducting a redirect examination. Recross and further redirect examinations can be permitted.

The rules for presenting testimony, including the order of examinations, are not set out in the rules of evidence or any procedural code. Rather, they arise from an unwritten tradition of trial practice that has developed over the years. The only provision of the Federal Rules dealing directly with witness examinations is FRE 611, which seems to take largely for granted the established modes of presenting direct and cross-examinations, specifying only a few limitations and otherwise granting the trial judge broad discretion over "the mode and order" of examining witnesses.

1. FRE 611

RULE 611. MODE AND ORDER OF EXAMINING WITNESSES AND PRESENTING EVIDENCE

(a) Control by the Court; Purposes. The court should exercise reasonable control over the mode and order of examining witnesses and presenting evidence so as to:

(1) make those procedures effective for determining the truth;

(2) avoid wasting time; and

(3) protect witnesses from harassment or undue embarrassment.

(b) Scope of Cross-Examination. Cross-examination should not go beyond the subject matter of the direct examination and matters affecting the witness's credibility. The court may allow inquiry into additional matters as if on direct examination.

(c) Leading Questions. Leading questions should not be used on direct examination except as necessary to develop the witness's testimony. Ordinarily, the court should allow leading questions:

(1) on cross-examination; and

(2) when a party calls a hostile witness, an adverse party, or a witness identified with an adverse party.

2. Explanation of FRE 611(a) and (b)

Breadth of the Court's Power.   FRE 611(a) recognizes in broad terms the sweeping authority of the judge to control the examination of witnesses during the trial. Indeed, even the two express provisions purporting to limit the scope of cross-examination (subsection (b)) and the use of leading questions (subsection (c)) may be overridden in the discretion of the trial judge to serve the purposes outlined in Rule 611(a). This principle is reflected by the words "should" in Rule 611(b) and (c) and the Advisory Committee Note to FRE 611(a), which states:

> Spelling out detailed rules to govern the mode and order of interrogating witnesses and presenting evidence is neither desirable nor feasible. The ultimate responsibility for the effective working of the adversary system rests with the judge. The rules set forth the objectives which he should seek to attain.

Thus, the following discussion of FRE 611 and witness examination is best understood not as a summary of binding rules, but rather as a description of the common trial practice that judges tend to follow out of long-standing tradition.

Direct Examination.   Trials are usually won or lost on the strength of a party's case-in-chief rather than the weaknesses in the opponent's case. Direct examination—the questioning of witnesses you call in your case-in-chief—is the most straightforward and effective way to prove your case. Indeed, each party must plan to meet its burden of production with evidence developed through direct examination. Civil defendants, who cannot win simply by raising a reasonable doubt, must also usually rely on direct examination to put their case before the jury. It's neither feasible nor strategically prudent to depend on eliciting the needed evidence through cross-examination. Therefore, direct examination is extremely important, and probably the dominant feature of success at trial.

FRE 611 says nothing affirmatively about direct examination, but simply assumes that direct examination will be conducted. As we discuss below, FRE 611(b) states that direct examination should set a limit on the scope of cross-examination and in 611(c) provides that, with limited exceptions, leading questions should not be used on direct examination.

FRE 611(b): The Scope of Cross-examination.   Cross-examination is one of the defining features of the adversary system. "For two centuries, common law judges and lawyers have regarded the opportunity of cross-examination as an essential safeguard of the accuracy and completeness of testimony. They have insisted that the opportunity is a right, not a mere privilege."[4] Direct examination generally reflects some degree of cooperation between the examiner and the witness, and therefore raises the danger that the witness will be permitted, if not encouraged, to present a self-serving version of events. Cross-examination is an effective way to test the witness's credibility and show that there may be another side to the story. It also provides some of the more exciting moments in a trial.

FRE 611(b) establishes, as a guideline, that two general areas of inquiry are permissible for cross-examination. First, it is permissible to explore matters about which the witness has testified on direct examination. For example, in the *Johnson* case defense counsel's cross-examination of the correctional officers explored details of the altercation about which the witnesses testified on direct examination.

Second, it is always permissible to ask questions that may impeach the credibility of the witness even though there may have been no reference to these matters on direct examination. For example, the prosecutor in the *Johnson* case cross-examined Johnson's cell mate, George Butler, about Johnson's and Butler's gang affiliations even though this subject was not part of the direct examination (pages 51, 76, supra). The purpose of these questions, as the sidebar conference makes clear, was to undermine Butler's credibility by showing his bias or prejudice in favor of Johnson. Similarly, in the *Johnson* case it was appropriate for the prosecutor to ask defense witnesses about prior convictions not mentioned on direct examination because proof of prior convictions is one of the traditional ways to impeach a witness's character for truthfulness.

The same principle applies to the rehabilitation of witnesses on cross-examination. Thus, if a direct examiner impeaches a hostile witness, it would be appropriate to rehabilitate the witness on cross-examination with questions about matters relating to credibility that were not covered on direct examination.

Unless the court exercises its discretion pursuant to the last sentence of FRE 611(b), it is improper to explore on cross-examination subjects that were not mentioned on direct examination and that do not affect the credibility of a witness. Consider, for example, the testimony in the *Johnson* case of Ruth Taylor, the records specialist (page 40, supra). Her direct examination testimony was limited to questions about Johnson's criminal record. Thus, even if Taylor had been an eyewitness to the jail cell incident, it would have been inappropriate, in the absence of special permission from the court, to question her about the incident on cross-examination. If the defendant wanted to explore the matter with Taylor, the proper course of action would be to call her as a witness during the presentation of the defense.

---

4. John W. Strong, et al., McCormick on Evidence 34 (5th ed. 1999). Wigmore suggested that the "abuses and puerilities often found associated with cross-examination" were outweighed by its value. "It may be that in more than one sense it takes the place in our system which torture occupied in the mediaeval system. . . . Nevertheless, it is beyond any doubt the greatest legal engine ever invented for the discovery of truth." 2 John Henry Wigmore, A Treatise on the System of Evidence in Trials at Common Law 1697 (1904). The latter phrase is oft-repeated. See, e.g., California v. Green, 399 U.S. 149, 158 (1970).

Redirect and Recross-examination.   The direct examiner may conduct a redirect examination when cross-examination has been completed. The scope of redirect is limited to matters that were raised in cross-examination; this means that the direct examiner is usually not permitted to prove an essential element of the case that was overlooked, although judges vary widely in how strictly they will enforce this limitation.

Recross and further redirect examinations are sometimes allowed. Each such successive examination is smaller in scope since it is limited to responding to the immediately preceding redirect or recross-examination. Although the party calling the witness is theoretically entitled to the "last word," judges will not let this process go on ad nauseam. Such seesawing back and forth with redirect and recross, trying to have the last word, can irritate the judge and jury, and usually develops no new information. (This occurred frequently in the *Johnson* trial, but has been edited out of the transcript in Chapter One.)

3. FRE 611(a) and (b) and the Examination of Witnesses: Practical Applications

a. Direct Examination

On direct examination, the goal is to let the witness provide pieces of narrative, in his or her own words, that build an overall "story" to the jury. It is important to help your witness appear as credible as possible, since the witness will be supporting your case. Furthermore, most of the evidence you will introduce at trial comes in through direct examination. Although you can also introduce evidence through cross-examination, the danger in relying on cross-examination (by definition, the questioning of witnesses called by your opponent) to introduce key evidence is that you have no control over what witnesses your opponent will call; if your opponent elects not to call a witness you were counting on to introduce some vital testimony, document, or other evidence, you may find you have failed to prove some essential element of your case.

Conducting an effective direct examination can be more challenging than you might think. Generally speaking, the witness will describe one or more incidents or factual occurrences, things the witness did or perceived. Your role as questioner is generally that of a skilled, sympathetic interviewer. Imagine that you know someone who has a very interesting story to tell, and that you would like someone else to hear the story. Although you could tell the story in your own words, you believe it would be much more effective coming from the person who had the experience firsthand. The witness should be allowed to testify in a narrative format, with the lawyer's questions keeping the story moving forward, keeping the witness from digressing, and helping to vary the pace so the witness's story does not become boring.

Questions for the most part should be open-ended: "What happened next?" "What did you see?" "Why did you do that?" Witnesses should be allowed to explain their actions. One way to remind a witness to concentrate on communicating with the jury is occasionally to begin a question with an admonition: "Tell the jury . . . " As the direct examiner, you also have to pace the testimony by asking several short questions and answers followed by a question with a longer narrative answer, followed by short questions again. Consider the kind of narrative that occurs when a lawyer fails to pace the testimony with questions, such as when defendant Johnson spoke at the outset of his direct examination. Was this an effective presentation of Johnson's story? Should witnesses be allowed to testify in that manner?

As a general rule, a witness you call in your case will be cooperative enough to meet with you in advance. (There is an important exception to this. See "c. Direct Examination of 'Adverse' and 'Hostile' Witnesses," below.) This means that you can and should "prepare" the witness by giving some idea of the subject matter you plan to cover. Many attorneys rehearse the direct examination, asking the planned questions and giving tips about how to answer them. The idea of this is not to put words in the witness's mouth but to help the witness tell the story effectively and avoid pitfalls that would unduly damage credibility. Preparing the witness, while essential, also poses an additional challenge. Having rehearsed the direct testimony with a cooperative witness and become thoroughly familiar with it, you must nevertheless appear to have a genuine interest in the questions being asked and to ensure as much as possible that the witness is not merely reciting a rehearsed text, but sincerely communicating to the jury.

b. Cross-examination

FRE 611(b) embodies the "American" or "restrictive" rule of cross-examination, in contrast to the wide-open rule of cross-examination, used in the English trial system, which permits the opposing party to question witnesses about anything that is relevant to the case. The primary advantage of the American rule is that it allows the parties to control the development of their cases. For example, the plaintiff may wish to introduce a document into evidence early on in the trial and may need to call the defendant or somebody closely associated with the defendant to authenticate the document. Even if the witness has knowledge of other aspects of the case, the plaintiff, for reasons of strategy, may not want to go into those matters at this time or with this witness. If the plaintiff limits the direct examination to the question of authentication, application of the restrictive cross-examination rule will prevent the defendant on cross-examination from exploring the witness's knowledge about other aspects of the case.

The primary advantage of the English rule is that it allows the cross-examiner to go directly to any relevant fact and incentivizes parties to select their witnesses carefully. This rule also avoids the necessity of determining what the scope of direct examination was. While the English rule also avoids the necessity of recalling witnesses who may have testimony to give regarding several issues in a case, FRE 611(b) reserves for the trial judge the discretion to accomplish the same efficiency by permitting questions about matters that are beyond the scope of direct examination, in which case the examination shall be conducted "as if on direct examination." This means, in effect, that the witness has become the cross-examiner's witness and that, therefore, "leading questions should not be used . . . except as may be necessary to develop the witness' testimony." FRE 611(c).

Strategy and Goals of Cross-examination.   An important strategic goal for you as a cross-examiner is to take advantage of the subtle opportunity to argue your case. Whole lines of questioning can develop themes that you can emphasize by repetition and then argue to the jury in closing. Leading questions, which can be asked on cross-examination, also provide an opportunity to make assertions that emphasize the inferences or interpretations you want the jury to draw from the evidence.

A second goal of cross-examination is to fill in gaps in your evidence or obtain favorable admissions. Sometimes an adverse witness is the only witness who can provide admissible testimony needed to establish an element of your claim or defense, or to tell part of the story you want to convey to the jury. In many instances, you may have to call such a witness yourself as an "adverse witness." In addition to filling in gaps, some witnesses called by your opponent may make (voluntarily or otherwise) admissions favorable to your side. Helpful testimony can be particularly strong when it comes from the mouth of the adversary or his witnesses.

Finally, you can use cross-examination questions to control damage by minimizing the effect of adverse testimony by one or both of two means. Without discrediting the witness, you can try to show how the witness's version of the facts is consistent with, or at least not inconsistent with, your theory of the case. Or you can discredit the witness by attacking his or her credibility, either on specific points or overall. Typically, a witness will not have been called by your opponent to testify unless that testimony helps the opponent's case. (If it does not, you may not need to bother with cross-examination.) There are several techniques for discrediting, or attacking the credibility of, a witness. These techniques, known collectively as "impeachment," are discussed in Chapter Seven.

Cross-examination Technique.   The manner of conducting cross-examination is perhaps most easily understood by contrasting it with direct examination. Because direct examination seeks to develop the story through the witness's own words and to bolster the witness's credibility, the direct examiner wants the jury to focus on the witness. Factual information arising out of the testimony should therefore come from what the witness says, not the questioner. Questions should be shorter than the answers; and should generally be open-ended. The question "why" is often effective on direct.

On cross-examination, by contrast, the lawyer wants to provide (in effect) most of the information the jury hears, while attempting to control what the witness actually says by asking leading questions. This usually means making an assertion of fact to which the witness can fully respond by simply agreeing with a "yes" or "no" answer. Skilled cross-examiners try to formulate precise, narrow questions that don't call for explanation, keeping open-ended questions to a minimum. In particular, "how" and "why" questions are generally avoided like the plague: Such questions relinquish the cross-examiner's control over the flow of information to factfinders and give it to the witness. Asking such questions allows the witness to give a self-serving explanation of the facts and argue inferences adverse to your case. After a "why"-type question, you may be standing there while the witness goes on at length and you have no basis to shut the witness off.

An old saw about cross-examination is not to ask "one question too many." This usually means that you shouldn't ask the witness to agree to a conclusion or inference that constitutes the point you will make in closing argument, even if you feel that the conclusion follows logically from a series of propositions that the witness has agreed to. The witness will invariably disagree and attempt to give a self-serving explanation, arguing his or her own case. It can be difficult to know when.you have reached the stopping point where the next question is the "one too many." If words like "thus" and "therefore" seem to be part of the question, that is a red flag not to ask it.

c. Direct Examination of "Adverse" and "Hostile" Witnesses

FRE 611(c) sets forth two circumstances in which a direct examination may be conducted in the manner of a cross-examination, using leading questions and following the tactics of cross-examination: the direct examination of "adverse" and "hostile" witnesses.

"Adverse witness" is a term used in common legal parlance to refer to "an adverse party, or a witness identified with an adverse party" within the meaning of FRE 611(c). This concept includes not only the adverse party, but also his/her/its agents, employees, and people who, through legal or other ties, are strongly identified with the adverse party. It is not uncommon to call such an adverse witness in your case-in-chief. You would typically call an adverse witness where some item of evidence necessary to prove your case is uniquely within the knowledge of the adverse witness; or where there is reason to believe that the adverse witness will be so disliked or disbelieved by the jury that his testimony will necessarily help rather than hurt your case. An example would be calling the alleged sexual harasser to the stand to show the jury what a bad guy he is, with the goal of thereby supporting the plaintiff's credibility. If an adverse witness is necessary or strategically helpful to your case, you may not want to run the risk of waiting to cross-examine this witness. Your adversary may not call this witness; or may do so but keep the direct examination so circumscribed that you will not be able to cover the subjects you want on cross-examination. (See FRE 611(b), limiting scope of cross-examination.)

When questioning an adverse witness on direct examination, you are allowed to use leading questions and, as a tactical matter, should use all the techniques of cross-examination. Although using cross-examination techniques, you do not have a limitation on the scope of questioning as you do on an actual cross-examination. When you are finished, your adversary has the right to do a "friendly cross-examination," during which leading questions will normally be prohibited, as though that were a direct examination. See Advisory Committee Notes to FRE 611(c) (the word "Ordinarily" in "Ordinarily leading questions should be permitted on cross-examination" is designed to encourage judges to prohibit leading questions on "friendly cross-examination").

A "hostile witness" is one who is presumed friendly or neutral when called to the stand (i.e., a non-adverse witness), but who, during questioning, demonstrates an attitude sufficiently hostile to the questioner to raise an inference of opposition to the examiner's client or identification with the adverse party. The examining attorney then asks the court to declare the witness "hostile." If the court does so, the examiner can proceed with leading questions, and may want to use the other cross-examination techniques as well.

In addition to asking leading questions, the party calling an adverse or hostile witness may also impeach that witness—attack the witness's credibility using the techniques and rules discussed in Chapter Seven. According to FRE 607, "the credibility of a witness may be attacked by any party, including the party calling the witness." Indeed, the rule suggests that a party may impeach a witness on direct examination even if the witness is not formally adverse or hostile. FRE 607 abolishes the common law "voucher rule," according to which a party who called a witness was held to vouch for the credibility of that witnesses. See 3A John Henry Wigmore, Evidence §896, at 658-660 (James Chadbourne rev. 1970). Despite the unqualified language in FRE 607, some courts have held that it is impermissible to impeach one's own witness if the impeachment is a subterfuge to get otherwise inadmissible evidence before the jury. The admissibility of evidence for impeachment purposes, when that evidence is inadmissible as "substantive evidence," is discussed in Chapter Seven.

4. Explanation of FRE 611(c): Leading Questions

Leading questions are questions that suggest the answer the examiner is seeking. A classic example of a leading question takes the form of a statement with a brief interrogative tag at the beginning or end, such as "You saw defendant Johnson lunge out of his cell with his fist, didn't you?" FRE 611(c) confirms—again, in the form of a guideline to the trial judge—the common practice that leading questions are normally prohibited on direct, but allowed on cross-examination. This rule thus accounts for the most obvious difference between the mode of conducting direct and cross-examination. ("Redirect" is treated the same as direct examination, and recross the same as cross-examination for purposes of the leading question rule.) The assumption underlying FRE 611(c) is that a witness is likely to be friendly or at least cooperative with the party calling the witness, and will not be equally cooperative with the cross-examiner. This presumed bias against the cross-examiner may make leading questions essential in order to get at the truth. If counsel were not permitted to ask a very specific "Isn't it true that . . . ?" question that calls for a yes or no answer, it might be impossible adequately to explore the details and nuances of the witness's knowledge and testimonial qualities. Conversely, because of the witness's presumed willingness to cooperate with the direct examiner, there is thought to be a risk that the suggestiveness in leading questions on direct examination may cause the witness to distort the truth in the direct examiner's favor.

5. FRE 611(c) and Leading Questions: Practical Applications

a. What Is a Leading Question?

A leading question is best defined as one that suggests the answer the questioner wants the witness to give. This definition is probably overbroad; on some level, many if not most questions asked on direct suggest in some way what the questioner wants the witness to say. If they didn't, there would be no way to direct the witness's attention to the type of information the examiner is seeking. Therefore, many, perhaps most, questions that fit this definition will ultimately be allowed, because the judge (or opposing counsel) believes them to be nonleading or else to be "borderline" or close calls that do not merit the trouble of making or sustaining an objection. Ultimately, the "test" of a leading question may often come down to a matter of degree—how suggestive is the question?—that is heavily dependent on context. You have to develop an intuitive feel for when these "borderline" questions are leading or nonleading.

A common misconception is that questions calling for "yes or no" answers are leading; in actuality, some in that form are, some aren't. For example, "Do you live in Chicago?" is not leading.

Leading questions are often phrased as an assertion of fact, ending either with a tone of voice implying a question mark at the end, or with an actual verbal tag asking the witness to agree.

> You were at home the night of the murder, isn't that correct [. . . isn't that true?
>   . . . right? . . . weren't you?]?
> Weren't you at home the night of the murder?
> You were at home the night of the murder?
> Isn't it a fact that you were at home the night of the murder?

In this form, the questions are clearly leading. But questions can be leading without taking this form. It is the suggestion of the desired answer that makes a question leading. A typical leading question occurs when the questioner suggests a fact to a witness who seems to have overlooked it. Consider the following piece of direct examination of Officer Huston from the *Johnson* trial (page 15, supra).

> Q: Why was inmate Johnson and inmate Butler secured, handcuffed? What's the purpose?
> A: Because if they are combative or not complying with orders; disciplinary reasons, you know?
> Q: Officer safety reasons?
> A: Yes, officer safety and security.

The prosecutor wanted the witness to give "safety" as the reason for handcuffing the inmates, but the witness said "discipline" instead. Imagine that defense counsel had made a timely objection after "Q: Officer safety reasons?" and that the objection was sustained (as it should be). The problem with the question is its leading form, not that the answer will put inadmissible matter before the jury. (This will be further explained when we deal with the subject of "objections.") Here, the prosecutor can then simply rephrase the question.

> Q. by Mr. Cummings: Okay, Officer Huston, was "officer safety" a further reason to handcuff the inmates?
> Mr. Deemer: Objection. That's still leading.
> The Court: Sustained.

This question is phrased more like a normal question than a statement, but it is really no different from the first time it was asked: It still suggests the desired answer.

> Q. *by Mr. Cummings*:   [Huge sigh.] Did you have any reasons other than disciplinary reasons for handcuffing the inmates?

This question may be borderline. It could technically be construed as leading because, in the present context, the question suggests that Huston should say "yes." Whether a question unduly suggests the desired answer may often depend on context. But the judge would in all likelihood overrule a "leading" objection at this point; also the jury will start to think that the objecting lawyer did not want the information to come out.

> A: Yes.
> Q: What other reason or reasons?
> A: Officer safety.

To be sure, the "leading" objection did not keep the witness from supplementing his answer in the manner suggested by the questioner—an attentive witness would know what he's supposed to say from the first phrasing of the leading question. However, the objections may serve to make the point to the jury that the ultimate answer was the "lawyer's answer" more than the witness's, and—who knows—the questioner might have moved on without getting the answer after the first objection was sustained.

b. Leading Questions: Tactical Considerations

In practice, there will be considerable variation in how much leading you can "get away with" in direct examination. If the opposing counsel does not object, the court is unlikely to stop you on its own initiative. Even if objections are made, the trial judge has virtually unreviewable discretion to allow leading questions. In the *Johnson* case, the prosecutor got away with numerous leading questions that were truly objectionable because the defense counsel didn't bother to object (perhaps because he was discouraged that the judge overruled his "leading" objection when he made one). See, e.g., pages 11-12, 13, 25, supra.

There is a downside, however, to asking a lot of leading questions. Because the focus on direct examination should be on the witness, rather than on the examiner, leading questions can backfire as a direct examination technique. A witness who delivers key testimony in response to leading questions on direct examination will give the impression of saying whatever the lawyer wants, and can lose credibility. And of course, conducting a direct examination in this way makes the examiner vulnerable to objection: "Your Honor, counsel is testifying rather than the witness." On the other hand, if the witness is weak, equivocal, or otherwise has difficulties getting his testimony out in his own words, it may on balance be better to lead than not—if you can get away with it.

F. OBJECTIONS AND PRESERVATION OF ERROR FOR APPEAL: FRE 103

The substantive rules of evidence revolve most clearly around two features of the trial process that remain to be considered: trial objections, and "making a record" that preserves evidentiary issues for appellate review. These two subjects are closely inter-twined. Evidentiary rulings admitting evidence over objection will virtually never be the basis of appellate reversal without a clear, direct, and correct objection in the trial record. If evidence is excluded, the losing side must make sure that the substance of the evidence, and the theory of its admissibility, are apparent from the record in order to preserve the issue for appeal. FRE 103(a)(2). It is the job of the advocates to create a record that adequately reflects the objection, any response to it, and the judge's ruling. This is called "perfecting the record" and "preserving the issue for appeal." In this section we will first discuss the principles and mechanics of objections, and then turn to appellate review of the trial record.

1. FRE 103

RULE 103.   RULINGS ON EVIDENCE

(a) Preserving a Claim of Error. A party may claim error in a ruling to admit or exclude evidence only if the error affects a substantial right of the party and:

(1) if the ruling admits evidence, a party, on the record:

(A) timely objects or moves to strike; and

(B) states the specific ground, unless it was apparent from the context; or

(2) if the ruling excludes evidence, a party informs the court of its substance by an offer of proof, unless the substance was apparent from the context.

(b) Not Needing to Renew an Objection or Offer of Proof. Once the court rules definitively on the record—either before or at trial—a party need not renew an objection or offer of proof to preserve a claim of error for appeal.

(c) Court's Statement About the Ruling; Directing an Offer of Proof. The court may make any statement about the character or form of the evidence, the objection made, and the ruling. The court may direct that an offer of proof be made in question-and-answer form.

(d) Preventing the Jury from Hearing Inadmissible Evidence. To the extent practicable, the court must conduct a jury trial so that inadmissible evidence is not suggested to the jury by any means.

(e) Taking Notice of Plain Error. A court may take notice of a plain error affecting a substantial right, even if the claim of error was not properly preserved.

2. Explanation of FRE 103(a) and (d): Objections, Offers of Proof, and Preservation of Evidentiary Issues for Appeal

An objection is the means by which a lawyer can interrupt the trial to oppose the intro-duction of evidence. Although objections are most frequently made to questions or answers during a witness's testimony, objections can be made to any type of evidence:

real evidence, demonstrative evidence, or testimony. The purpose of an objection is twofold: (1) if the objection is sustained, to increase your chances of winning the trial by excluding harmful evidence from consideration by the trier of fact; (2) if the objection is overruled, to preserve for appeal your argument that the evidence should have been excluded, pursuant to FRE 103(a)(1).

When an objection is made, one of three things will usually happen. The court will "sustain" (agree with) the objection, "overrule" (disagree with) the objection, or ask counsel for further elaboration or argument, usually outside the hearing of the jury, such as at the sidebar. If the judge rules on the objection right away, the losing lawyer may feel it necessary to try to make further argument before the trial proceeds any further, and may ask to approach the bench to argue the point. Trial lawyers typically request such sidebar conferences when the judge's ruling will admit significantly prejudicial evidence, or will deprive the party of an opportunity to present evidence at the right moment in the trial.

Moreover, where an objection has been sustained, it may be necessary for the lawyer offering the evidence to approach the bench to make an offer of proof. FRE 103(a) (2) provides that in order to preserve an appeal of an erroneous ruling excluding evidence (an incorrectly sustained objection), the party must "[make] the substance of the evidence . . . known to the court" unless the substance "was apparent from the context in which the questions were asked." This procedure of advising the court of the substance of the excluded evidence is called an "offer of proof." Id. An offer of proof can take the form of a statement on the record by counsel summarizing what the excluded evidence would show (e.g., "Your Honor, the witness would testify that Officer Smith told him that the prison was on lockdown because Officer Walker had beaten an inmate.").

FRE 103(a) provides that an evidentiary ruling will be a ground for reversal on appeal only if two conditions are met. The error must "affect a substantial right" of a party, meaning that the ruling made some difference in the outcome of the trial. Second, the party must have made a timely objection and, where the ruling excludes evidence, an "offer of proof" alerting the court to the substance of the excluded evidence. Failure to object will probably mean that the judge's ruling, or the adversary's behavior, cannot be grounds for reversal. There is an exception to this general rule. "Plain" error, referred to in FRE 103(d), means an error so serious, and so obvious, that it can be grounds for reversal even though no objection was made to it during trial. The trial judge should have noticed it, and it is highly probable that it affected the outcome. This doctrine was originally developed in criminal cases to protect defendants from the errors of appointed counsel. Under FRE 103(d) it applies in civil cases as well.

3. FRE 103(a)(1) and (2) and Objections: Practical Applications

a. Two Types of Objections

There are two basic types of objections: an objection to the improper form of a question, and an objection to the admissibility of the answer.

An objection to admissibility of the answer is intended to exclude inadmissible evidence. Such objections are made when it appears that the question, even if properly phrased, calls for evidence barred by exclusionary rules of evidence or whose relevance or foundation has not been established. Most of the substantive law of evidence that you will study in this course concerns these questions of admissibility, and the grounds for ruling on the objections are for the most part found in the rules of evidence.

An objection to the form of the question is intended to regulate the mode of questioning and the behavior of the examiner. In contrast to objections going to admissibility, objections as to form are governed by traditional trial practice and the trial judge's inherent, discretionary authority rather than formal evidence rules.[5] Examples of objections to the form of the question include "leading," "argumentative," or "calls for a narrative response." Other examples of objections to the form of the question include "compound," "vague," "ambiguous," "mischaracterizes the testimony." (See "Trial Objection Cheat Sheet," page 120-22, infra.)

Questions objectionable as to form may be sustained even though the evidence they seek is ultimately admissible. Consider the beginning of Officer Van Berg's direct examination in People v. Johnson (page 23, supra):

Q: Did you have occasion on that day [March 28] to come into contact with an inmate by the name of Johnson?
A: Yes, I did.
Q: Same individual seated at the end of counsel table?
A: Yes.

The last question is leading, and would have been objectionable had the defendant's identity as the perpetrator been in dispute. It would be the form of the question that is objectionable, not the answer. The same information could be obtained through a proper nonleading question:

Q: Do you see that person in the courtroom today?
A: Yes.
Q: Where?
A: Seated next to the defense counsel.

A common mistake of inexperienced attorneys is to move on to the next question after an objection to the form of the question—such as "leading"—has been sustained.

Questions can violate more than one rule relating to form, and it is appropriate to mention multiple grounds for the objection.

Q: Did you see the defendant first lunge at Officer Walker and then eventually strike Officer Huston?

---

5. An arguable "source" of authority to rule on objections as to form is FRE 611(a), which directs the trial judge to "exercise reasonable control over the mode and order of interrogating witnesses and presenting evidence[.]" Courts rarely cite FRE 611(a) for these or other purposes, however. In fact the rule adds little, if anything, to what is explicit or implicit in other rules. For example, FRE 403 provides authority to exclude cumulative evidence, and FRE 102 admonishes courts to construe the rules "to secure fairness in administration, elimination of unjustifiable expense and delay, and promotion of growth and development of the law of evidence to the end that the truth may be ascertained and proceedings justly determined."

> *Defense Counsel*:   Objection: leading, compound.
> *The Court*:   Sustained.

In addition to its leading form, the question is also compound because it asks the witness to describe two logically separable facts of importance to the case. The objections can also be made one after the other, if the first one is overruled.

> *Defense Counsel*:   Objection, compound.
> *The Court*:   Overruled.
> *Defense Counsel*:   Leading.
> *The Court*:   Sustained.

It is also possible, of course, that a question can be framed in an objectionable form and seek arguably inadmissible matter. Consider the discussion of "Facility B" during the Huston direct examination in *Johnson*. Suppose the prosecutor, Cummings, had introduced this subject with the question:

> Q: Isn't Facility B a transition facility for violent inmates coming out of SHU, before they are placed in general population?

This question is not only leading (an objection to form), but it also calls for arguably inadmissible character evidence to the effect that defendant Johnson is a violent person because he was housed in Facility B. This example also illustrates how a timely objection will not always be adequate to prevent the jury from hearing inadmissible matter—here, it was embedded in the prosecutor's leading question.

b. Timing of Objections

Making timely objections is probably the most difficult trial skill to learn. In a very short time—often no longer than the second or two before the witness answers the question—you have to determine whether the question is objectionable, on what basis, whether tactically the objection is worth making, and then actually say "objection," typically while getting to your feet. This is challenging to do. But failing to make a timely objection can result in a failure of both goals of objecting at all. A failure to object—and even an untimely objection—fails to keep the evidence from the jury, and normally waives the evidentiary error on appeal. There is a narrow exception to this so-called contemporaneous-objection rule: Under FRE 103(d), an appellate court may correct "plain error" in spite of the absence of a contemporaneous objection. The plain error exception is used "sparingly," and only to correct "particularly egregious errors" that would result in a miscarriage of justice if not corrected. United States v. Young, 470 U.S. 1, 15 (1985).

A timely objection to the form of the question must be made before the question is answered. This point is easy to understand. In *Johnson*, the defense counsel was consistently late in objecting to the prosecutor's questions (see, e.g., pages 9, 25, 39):

> Q: Did he appear to you to be attempting to fight or strike Walker or any of the officers?
> A: Yes.
> *Mr. Deemer*:   One moment. That's leading.

If the answer is given before the objection, judges will often allow the answer to stand, and will either overrule the objection or simply say, "the witness already answered" or "the answer stands." But there is also an expectation that the witness should not jump the gun with his answer. If the witness answers an objectionable question after the objecting lawyer has already started speaking or before the judge rules, the judge may strike the answer and caution the witness not to answer questions while objections are being made or ruled on.

A timely objection to the inadmissibility of an answer must be made as soon as the inadmissibility becomes apparent. This can be tricky. Typically, it will be apparent that a question is likely to call for an objectionable response: "Did they tell you that something had happened to your hand?" sounds like it calls for inadmissible hearsay, for example. Or suppose a supervising correctional officer were to testify that he sent the correctional officers to Johnson's cell to retrieve the trays, but that he did not go himself. If such a witness were asked whether Johnson hit or kicked Huston or Van Berg, the question would clearly call for speculation or lack the foundational requirement of firsthand knowledge. Where a clear potential for an inadmissible answer inheres in the question, the objection should be made before the answer is given. However, in contrast to objections to the form of the question, where the judge is unlikely to strike the answer, if you did not object fast enough to an inadmissible answer, you might still object belatedly and ask the judge to strike the answer.

Sometimes, the objectionable matter cannot be anticipated from the question. "Tell us what happened next" is generally an unobjectionable question, but the witness could say all kinds of things that are not admissible testimony. Consider, for example the lengthy narrative defendant Johnson gave in response to defense counsel's question "Would you explain to the jury what that problem [concerning the package] was?" The lengthy answer that followed contained some arguably objectionable hearsay and irrelevant matter. It is fair game to cut the witness off with an objection and motion to strike as soon as the objectionable character of the answer becomes clear; most judges will be more lenient about striking inadmissible portions of an answer in this situation, even if you did not jump in at the first possible moment. For example:

Q: Tell us what happened next.
A: Well, the Sergeant told me we were on lockdown because —
Counsel: Objection. Hearsay. Move to strike.
The Court: Sustained. The answer is stricken.

When inadmissible matter has gotten in front of the jury and you failed to object (presumably because you couldn't anticipate the objectionable matter from the question) the proper response is a motion to strike the offending testimony, and perhaps a request for the judge to admonish the jury to disregard it.

Q: Tell us what happened next.
A: Well, the Sergeant told me we were on lockdown because another inmate had gotten beat up by Officer Walker.
Counsel: [Snapping belatedly to attention.] I move to strike the last answer. It's inadmissible hearsay.
The Court: The last answer is stricken. The jury will disregard it.

c.   *Stating the Objection*

An objection is not preserved for appeal unless "a timely objection or motion to strike appears of record, stating the specific ground for the objection." FRE 103(a)(1).

In practice, you will encounter and even make both specific and general objections. A general objection is an expression of an objection without stating the grounds. Where the basis for the objection seems obvious, the lawyer may say nothing more than "objection"—or the judge may rule on it without waiting for the lawyer to specify the grounds. You may hear similarly "general" objections using some boilerplate phrase that does not specify the ground, such as "Objection to the form of the question," or one that is merely vague and conclusory, such as "irrelevant, incompetent, and immaterial." It may not hurt your case if you make a general objection that is sustained, because your goal of keeping the evidence out is accomplished, and you have no basis to appeal your own successful objection. If a general objection is overruled, however, it is likely to be deemed to waive the issue on appeal for failure to state the ground. Therefore, it is better practice to specify your grounds in the objection.

It is vital to state the correct basis for the objection. The judge is required to rule only on the stated ground of the objection. If you state an invalid basis for an otherwise proper objection, your objection could be overruled even if it could have been sustained on another ground. Judges do not usually cue an attorney as to the correct objection, or make the correct objection on their own. More likely, the judge will simply overrule an incorrect objection.

Specific objections need only communicate the basic reason for the objection. "Objection, hearsay" should probably be sufficient to preserve the point for appeal; it is not necessary to spell out your theory as to how the only relevant use of the out-of-court statement is for the hearsay purpose of proving the truth of the matter asserted. Indeed, most judges frown upon so-called speaking objections—making arguments in the course of stating an objection—and may even specifically warn the lawyers at the start of the trial to refrain from doing so. The general rule of decorum, then, is to state the ground for an objection as succinctly as possible; and if extended argument is needed, the objecting lawyer is expected to request a sidebar conference.

As you can see from the "Trial Objection Cheat Sheet," which follows on pages 120-22, there are certain commonly used words or phrases to make certain routine objections. But these are not magic words; anything that gets the point across succinctly will do. "Objection, calls for inadmissible character evidence" and "Objection, Rule 404" probably would both suffice to make the same point. In addition, laundry lists of common or boilerplate objections should not obscure the fact that an objection can be based on any rule or principle that would exclude the evidence. Some of these principles may not be adequately expressed in the common boilerplate terms.

Some experienced trial practitioners suggest trying to put objections into plain language rather than using legal buzz-words. Since the objection tends to signal the jury that you want to keep them from hearing something, that impression may only be reinforced when the objection is stated in legalese. Thus, it may be preferable to say "Objection—this witness has no way of knowing who wrote the document" rather than to say "Objection—lack of foundation." On the other hand, using plain language could run afoul of a judge's warning against "speaking objections." In addition, there may be occasions when you want to obscure your reasons from the jury. You have to use your judgment.

If offending matter has already been stated by the witness, the proper procedure is to make a motion to strike. You need to specify both the grounds for the motion (which are the same kinds of points as grounds for objections) and the portion of testimony you contend should be stricken. "I move to strike the witness's answer in its entirety. It's hearsay." or "Motion to strike as nonresponsive. I move to strike the witness's answer after the word 'yes.'" Having testimony stricken is, of course, a much less effective remedy than preventing it from coming into the record before the jury. As the old saying goes, "you can't unring a bell." However, it should be done to preserve the issue for appeal. Moreover, the remedy can have a practical consequence if the jury asks for a "read-back" of the trial transcript during jury deliberations: Stricken portions of testimony are omitted from the read-back.

d. Tactical Considerations

Many objectionable questions are asked with impunity because the opposing counsel decides an objection is not worth making. Again, an objection signals to the jurors that counsel wants to keep them from hearing some information. This could create an impression of having something to hide, and this downside of objecting has to be weighed against the damage to one's case if the evidence comes in. Other downsides to objecting can include irritating the judge or jury, or (if the objection is made during your opponent's cross-examination of your witness) possibly confusing the witness. Objections to the form of a question may simply cue your adversary to phrase a clearer, more effective question. Moreover, an objection can often underscore the damaging aspects of an objectionable question, and wisdom may on these occasions dictate silence in the hope that the jury will miss the point. Finally, objectionable questions sometimes will be helpful to your case either because the specific answer will be helpful or because the question will "open the door" to helpful testimony that might not otherwise be admissible.

On the other hand, there are tactical advantages to making objections. Jurors will expect the lawyers to make some objections, which gives you some leeway to do so without reaching an irritation threshold. Moreover, by sitting mute while your witness is being flogged with seemingly unfair questions, you may send a signal that you are being lazy, inattentive, or indifferent to your case. Finally, objections—particularly if sustained—can disrupt the rhythm or flow of your opponent's examination or leave your opponent stumped as to how to ask a proper question to get in some important piece of evidence.

Of course, these tactical considerations in favor of objections—particularly those regarding disruption of one's adversary's questioning—do not justify making objections in bad faith. To be sure, some trial attorneys will cross the line and make objections purely to rattle the opposing counsel; but one hopes that bad karma will be visited upon them. You should have a good-faith, arguable basis for any objection you make.

4. FRE 103(a) and (d): Preservation of Error for Appellate Review

The appellate court reviewing the defendant's conviction in People v. Johnson ruled that the prosecutor committed prosecutorial misconduct by referring to Johnson's alleged gang membership when questioning inmates Butler and Johnson, and in closing argument to the jury. (See pages 49-51, and 76, supra). The court held this to be misconduct because no evidence was ever produced that gave the prosecutor reasonable grounds for believing that Johnson was in fact a gang member. The court held the error was harmless, however, because

> the passing mention of gangs was a peripheral matter in appellant's case. The jury knew that the defense witnesses were inmates in a maximum security prison [and that] appellant was a rapist, Butler a robber, and Green a murderer. In these circumstances, it is not reasonably probable that the jury's assessment of credibility would have been materially different if gangs had never been mentioned.

How are such issues concerning erroneous admission (or exclusion) of evidence raised and preserved for appellate review?

a. Making the Record—in General

When a judgment is rendered based on a jury or bench trial, any appeal is most likely to focus on the evidence "in the record." Appellate questions of substantive law will look at whether sufficient evidence supports the legally defined elements of the claims or defenses. Evidentiary questions will consider whether the appellant's rights were unduly harmed by excluding evidence that should have been admitted or admitting evidence that should have been excluded. Such determinations can't be made without, typically, a review of "the record" of the trial.

The phrase "the record" often is meant as a broad reference to the trial court's file on the case. It contains all the court papers filed by the parties' lawyers, transcripts of any trial or evidentiary hearing held by the court, and any evidence submitted in a trial, hearing, or motion. The trial "record" is a subset of the court's file, including the trial transcripts and exhibits. The key point is that the record serves as the universe of facts and trial court rulings within which an appellate court must operate in making its rulings on appeal. Appellate courts are not allowed to "go outside the record" by considering facts or legal arguments that have not been presented to the trial court.

At trial, therefore, it is vitally important for counsel to be attentive to the record to ensure that it is complete, both in terms of evidence and legal arguments and rulings. "Making the record" very often means nothing more or less than having what is said recorded (typically stenographically) and ultimately transcribed by the court reporter so that it becomes part of the official trial transcript. Sometimes, the judge, either inadvertently or by design, will conduct some important moments of legal argument or ruling during the trial without the court reporter present—an argument in chambers or a sidebar conference, for example, might go unrecorded, and therefore be "off the record." In such cases, it is the responsibility of the lawyer to put the matter "on the record"—that is, to summarize what occurred when the court reporter is back on duty and making the verbatim record. Otherwise the matter occurring off the record could be effectively insulated from appellate review. For example, the sidebar conference involving whether to admit evidence about "Facility B" in *Johnson* happened to be held on the record. Had it not been, an appellate court would have been no more able to review the issues raised in that discussion than you would have been as a reader of the transcript.

Likewise, lawyers have to be conscious of the record becoming garbled or confusing. There are a number of mistakes that inexperienced trial lawyers occasionally make that can be avoided by paying careful attention to what is occurring at trial. Think about the following issues: (a) overlapping—if a trial is being conducted with a court reporter, which is still typical today, the reporter cannot accurately record what happens when more than a single person talks at once. In such a circumstance, the careful attorney will be sure to go back and explain "for the record" what transpired; (b) spelling—names often cause problems because quite different spellings are often pronounced similarly (e.g., White, Whyte, Wite, Wyatt); (c) figures—when an attorney says "thirty-one-o-four," does this mean 3104, 31.04, 30,104, or what? Make sure it is clear; (d) gestures—make sure gestures are explained ("let the record show that the witness pointed at the defendant").

b. Making the Record for Appeal of Evidentiary Rulings

For purposes of appeal of evidentiary rulings, "making the record" means complying with FRE 103. The appealing party must have made ("on the record") a specific objection or an offer of proof, depending on whether the disputed item of evidence was admitted or excluded. See FRE 103(a)(1) and (2). This requirement of FRE 103(a) is a mainstay of the adversary system. The judge is not responsible for running an error-free trial. Rather, the burden is on the parties to protect their own interests through timely arguments aimed at redressing errors that significantly affect their interests. The advocates must therefore take the initiative to object to their opponents' improper use of evidence or other inappropriate courtroom behaviors. In addition, the advocates must make known the grounds for their objections, and the opponent is always given the opportunity to respond. Only then is the judge required to, and is in a better informed position to, make a ruling that affects the conduct of the trial. This requirement raises the stakes of the lawyer's tactical decisions as to when or when not to object.

Motions in limine and FRE 103 interact in important ways. Formerly in many federal courts (and still in several state court systems), if a motion in limine to exclude evidence was denied, the advocate was required to renew the objection to the evidence at trial in order to preserve the issue for appeal. Effective December 1, 2000, however, FRE 103(a) was amended to provide that any "definitive ruling on the record admitting or excluding evidence, either at or before trial" is now sufficient "to preserve a claim of error for appeal." This amendment was specifically intended to apply to "so-called *in limine* rulings." Advisory Committee Notes to FRE 103.

c. Standards of Appellate Review of Evidentiary Errors

Analytically, appellate courts proceed through two steps in considering whether a trial judgment should be reversed for an erroneous evidentiary ruling. The first analytical step asks "was there error?" Most, but not all, trial court decisions about whether to admit or exclude evidence are reviewed on appeal under an "abuse of discretion" standard. This means the appellate court will not "substitute its judgment" for that of the trial court—that is, the appellate court will not redecide the issue as though it were the original decision maker. (The latter kind of appellate review is called "independent" or "de novo" review. De novo review is applied to trial court rulings deemed "questions of law," such as whether the court selected the correct legal rule or interpreted it properly. This is discussed further in Chapter Three, Section B.3.) Under the abuse of discretion standard, to find error at all, the appellate court has to conclude that the trial court's decision was not merely wrong, but something close to an unreasonable decision.

Second, if there was error, was the error "harmless"? FRE 103(a) states that an appeal based on an erroneous ruling admitting or excluding evidence at trial cannot win a reversal unless the error affects a "substantial right" of the party. "Substantial right" has been construed by courts in most circumstances as invoking the "harmless error" standard. An error is harmless if it did not affect the outcome of the trial. Would the jury have reached the same result had the erroneously admitted evidence been excluded (or had the erroneously excluded evidence been admitted)? If so, the error is harmless. California Evidence Code §353, interpreted in the appeal of the *Johnson* case, similarly requires that the error resulted in a "miscarriage of justice." Both FRE 103 and the California Code thus require the appellate court to answer the same question—how likely is it that the error actually affected the outcome?

What degree of certainty must there be in evaluating the hypothetical state of affairs (the outcome of the trial had the error not been made)? Here, there is some variation among different courts. For example, the U.S. Court of Appeals for the Ninth Circuit formulated the "harmless error" standard as requiring the appellate court to affirm the trial court if the evidentiary error "more probably than not was harmless," or if there was a "fair assurance" that the error was harmless (e.g., United States v. Hitt, 981 F.2d 422 (9th Cir. 1992)). The Third Circuit phrased the standard differently: The trial court will be affirmed only if it is "highly probable" that the evidentiary error did not affect substantial rights (e.g., McQueeney v. Wilmington Trust Co., 779 F.2d 916 (3d Cir. 1985)). The California standard applied in the People v. Johnson appeal holds that a judgment should be reversed only if it is "reasonably probable" that the error affected the outcome.

The foregoing has assumed what might be thought of as "garden variety"—that is to say, nonconstitutional—error. Some erroneous evidentiary rulings are held to violate constitutional rights—for example, erroneous admission of hearsay might violate a criminal defendant's Sixth Amendment right to confront opposing witnesses. Where constitutional error occurs, the trial court judgment will be affirmed only if the error was "harmless beyond a reasonable doubt."

TRIAL OBJECTION CHEAT SHEET

Note: This list of objections is not intended to be exhaustive. A comma separating objections suggests interchangeable phrasing; a semicolon suggests different but closely related objections.

OBJECTIONS TO THE FORM OF THE QUESTION:

Argumentative	Question contends that the witness must agree with a disputable inference, is framed as if it were closing argument to the jury, or seeks to pick a fight with the witness or embarrass the witness. This objection is often made (and sustained) inappropriately to questions that are proper, vigorous cross-examination, as in "Objection, Your Honor, tough question!"
Asked and answered	Question has previously been asked of the same witness by the same examiner. (Does not apply to question asked by the opposing counsel.) Technically, there is nothing wrong with repeating questions, but judges may sustain this objection if they feel testimony is cumulative, or the examination is too lengthy or out of control.
Assumes facts not in evidence	Question is phrased so that to answer it, the witness would have to adopt, by implication, an asserted fact that is in dispute but that has not been proved.
Calls for narrative	Question asks the witness to describe events very broadly or generally. Technically, there is nothing wrong with a "narrative" answer, and many questions can only be phrased in open-ended fashion to avoid leading; rather the danger is that the question will permit the witness to ramble and possibly interject inadmissible evidence. The objection might also be phrased as "too general."
Compound	Question asks the witness to testify about more than one separate fact.
Leading	Question suggests the desired answer to the witness; improper during direct examination of friendly or neutral witnesses, but okay on cross-examination or direct examination of adverse or hostile witnesses.
Misstates the evidence; mischaracterizes the testimony	Premise of the question distorts the evidence that has been presented, or misquotes the witness's testimony.
Unintelligible; vague; ambiguous; confusing	Question is not sufficiently clear to be answered. "Unintelligible" means garbled; "vague" means not sufficiently specific; "ambiguous" means susceptible of two or more different interpretations.

OBJECTIONS TO ADMISSIBILITY OF THE ANSWER (OR PROFFERED EXHIBIT):

Hearsay	Answer to question would call for (or evidentiary item contains) a statement other than one made by the witness while testifying at trial, offered to prove the truth of the matter asserted.
Irrelevant	Answer has no probative value relating to any fact of consequence to the case.

Lack of foundation	Insufficient factual basis has been established to show that the witness has requisite knowledge (personal sensory perception or experience, expert opinion, lay opinion, knowledge of character) to give admissible testimony; or to show that exhibit is what its proponent claims.
Lack of authenticity	Insufficient factual basis to show that exhibit is what its proponent claims.
Calls for speculation, speculative	Answer to question calls for the witness to speculate or guess about matters beyond witness's factual knowledge; this is a form of "foundation" objection.
Calls for opinion; calls for conclusion	Answer would violate the rule limiting lay (nonexpert) opinion to those opinions and inferences that are based on the witness's perception of an event and are helpful to the jury in understanding the facts.
Inadmissible character evidence	Violates FRE 404.
More prejudicial/misleading/ etc. than probative, Rule 403	Probative value substantially outweighed by one or more of the Rule 403 dangers.
Cumulative	Answer would repeat earlier testimony. This is not technically improper, but comes within judge's discretion under Rule 403. This objection is often stated as "Asked and answered."
Nonresponsive	Witness has given an "evasive" answer that does not fairly meet the substance of the question.
Beyond the scope of the question	Answer has exceeded the scope of the question (i.e., the witness has "volunteered" information that was not asked for); this assumes the answer has been given, and is therefore a basis for a motion to strike.
Beyond the scope of direct/ cross-/redirect/etc. examination	Question seeks testimony that is not responsive to immediately preceding examination. Testimony is supposed to respond to matters raised in the immediately preceding examination (i.e., cross responds to direct, redirect responds to cross, recross responds to redirect, etc.).
Not the best evidence	Answer would violate the best evidence rule, which requires use of original writing, recording, or photograph to prove its contents.

G. REFLECTIONS ON NATURAL REASONING AND THE ADVERSARY SYSTEM

1. The Adversary System Reconsidered

In the United States, the adversary system remains the dominant theory of litigation. The concept that disputes are for the most part private matters controlled by private individuals before relatively passive judges does not seem under serious reconsideration on a broad scale. Perhaps it should be, however, for at least two reasons.

The first is that the adversary system is based on the assumption that each party will be effectively represented, which means among other things that the parties will have the resources necessary to fund the litigation. This assumption is often false and can lead to poor presentation of one side or the other (or both) of a dispute. Such wealth disparity can in turn lead to the dramatic effect of litigants with resources being systematically and on occasion decisively favored over their impecunious adversaries.

The second reason for reconsidering our commitment to the adversarial system is the possibility that the nature of cases being litigated is changing from the bipolar assumptions of the traditional model, which involves two private litigants disputing an essentially private matter, to a "public law model" that looks much different. Consider the following:

> The characteristic features of the public law model are very different from those of the traditional model. The party structure is sprawling and amorphous, subject to change over the course of the litigation. The traditional adversary relationship is suffused and intermixed with negotiating and mediating processes at every point. The judge is the dominant figure in organizing and guiding the case, and he draws for support not only on the parties and their counsel, but on a wide range of outsiders—masters, experts, and oversight personnel. Most important, the trial judge has increasingly become the creator and manager of complex forms of ongoing relief, which have widespread effects on persons not before the court and require the judge's continuing involvement in administration and implementation. School desegregation, employment discrimination, and prisoners' or inmates' rights cases come readily to mind as avatars of this new form of litigation. But it would be mistaken to suppose that it is confined to these areas. Antitrust, securities fraud and other aspects of the conduct of corporate business, bankruptcy and reorganizations, union governance, consumer fraud, housing discrimination, electoral reapportionment, environmental management—cases in all these fields display in varying degrees the features of public law litigation. . . .
>
> [As a consequence of this changing model of litigation] [t]he courts . . . continue to rely primarily on the litigants to produce and develop factual materials, but a number of factors make it impossible to leave the organization of the trial exclusively in their hands. With the diffusion of the party structure, fact issues are no longer sharply drawn in a confrontation between two adversaries, one asserting the affirmative and the other the negative. The litigation is often extraordinarily complex and extended in time, with a continuous and intricate interplay between factual and legal elements. It is hardly feasible and, absent a jury, unnecessary to set aside a contiguous block of time for a "trial stage" at which all significant factual issues will be presented. The scope of the fact investigation and the sheer volume of factual material that can be exhumed by the discovery process pose enormous problems of organization and assimilation. All these factors thrust the trial judge into an active role in shaping, organizing and facilitating the litigation. We may not yet have reached the investigative judge of the continental systems, but we have left the passive arbiter of the traditional model a long way behind. [Abram Chayes, The Role of the Judge in Public Law Litigation, 89 Harv. L. Rev. 1281, 1282-1283, 1284, 1297-1298, 1302 (1976).]

These two matters, wealth disparity and the changing nature of litigation, cast some doubt on the foundations of the adversarial system of litigation, although they are by no means dispositive arguments against it. As you proceed with your studies, consider on the one hand whether full-blown adversarial litigation within the rules of evidence is too complex and burdensome for simple, straightforward cases involving at least one party with relatively scarce resources, and on the other hand whether the adversarial process and strict rules of evidence are too rigid and crude to deal with complex modern litigation. Think also of what possible alternatives there might be.

Recall the connection between the adversary system and the role of limited government, mentioned at the beginning of Section B of this chapter. This conception of the role of the government in the resolution of disputes is not universally shared. In the "inquisitorial" systems of many Western European countries, disputes are not "private" matters to the extent that they are in the United States, and the adjudicative tribunal often involves itself actively in investigation, and controls the trial process much more than the litigants do. Those who favor continental systems are inclined to the view that control by a disinterested tribunal will lead to less abuse and manipulation of the evidence, thus increasing the chances that judgments consistent with the truth will emerge. For a discussion of these and related matters, see John Langbein, The German Advantage in Civil Procedure, 52 U. Chi. L. Rev. 823 (1985); Ronald J. Allen, Stefan Köck, Kurt Riechenberg & D. Toby Rosen, The German Advantage in Civil Procedure: A Plea for More Details and Fewer Generalities in Comparative Scholarship, 82 Nw. U. L. Rev. 705 (1988); Mirjan Damaska, Evidence Law Adrift (1997).

Yet another issue to consider emerges from the *Johnson* transcript. The rules of evidence are not rigidly adhered to at every turn in a trial; in many specific instances, they are either largely ignored or applied for the most part with a large dose of lenient discretion. On the other hand, at a few crucial places in the trial the rules of evidence seem to matter a great deal and lead to pointed arguments. In the *Johnson* trial, for example, this occurred where character evidence is disallowed in order to preclude inference of action in conformity therewith. See pages 11, 55, supra. Why is that? Is that a healthy or a troubling sign? How typical do you think the transcript is in this respect?

As you will also see, each year more and more cases involve expert testimony of various kinds, which means that one or both of the litigants think that the case can be tried fairly only by employing specialized knowledge that is beyond the common knowledge and experience of the layperson. As your studies progress, ask how well the legal system takes advantage of the knowledge and expertise of other disciplines. For that matter, how well does it take advantage of the knowledge of the common citizen? That question leads to the next issue.

2. Why Have Rules of Evidence?

To resolve disputes about past events, we have to make judgments about what actually happened. This means finding facts, which in turn requires evidence of those facts. The law of evidence structures the process of proof at trial, but it does so with an interesting constraint. In many instances the individuals deciding the facts will be laypersons chosen at large from the community to serve on juries. They are amateurs at legal factfinding. Jurors are not, however, amateurs at factfinding in general. Every competent member of society from an early age begins to collect and perfect methods of factfinding that facilitate navigating the environment, and most of us do so with remarkable efficiency. In large measure, the law relies on these natural reasoning processes that its factfinders (juror or judge) possess. Indeed, the law could rely on them exclusively. It could permit the parties to present whatever evidence they like, the factfinders to make whatever investigation they like, and let the natural reasoning process of the factfinders lead them to whatever decision they believe to be appropriate. This would be a system of free proof rather than one constrained by a complex law of evidence.

Obviously, the legal system has not adopted a system of free proof, or else the previous sentence would have ended your course on evidence. It instead regulates the process of proof in various ways for various reasons. Some of these ways and their underlying reasons are perfectly understandable and uncontroversial. Others are more problematic. Consider the following justifications for regulating the proof process and reflect on how persuasive they are:

(1) Efficiency. Litigants pay only a small fraction of the cost of maintaining the judicial system. Judicial resources are provided free of charge to litigants, and they constitute a large subsidy to litigation. The litigants have virtually no incentive to preserve judicial resources; indeed they have every incentive to squander them in an effort to win their cases. Economists call this problem a fundamental misalignment between private incentives to use the legal system and social good. See Steven Shavell, The Fundamental Divergence Between the Private and the Social Motive to Use the Legal System, 26 J. Legal Stud. 575 (1997). A system of free proof allowing the litigants to do more or less what they liked would lead to a substantial wasting of judicial resources. Further, a rich litigant could simply wear down a more impecunious opponent through the endless presentation of trivia. For both reasons, trials are structured by judges to keep irrelevant, redundant, and unimportant issues out of the process in order to maximize the value of the resources available to decide disputes and in order to advance the likelihood that truth will determine outcomes. See FRE 403.

Moreover, experience often allows lawmakers to identify "noisy" evidence: evidence whose probative value is generally too expensive to examine and determine. Such evidence—hearsay or a defendant's criminal record, for example,—may occasionally be probative, but in the majority of the cases factfinders would not be able to use it efficiently as a basis for decision. Setting up rules that suppress such evidence across the board thus eliminates many factfinding procedures and deliberations that are more expensive than productive. See Alex Stein, Inefficient Evidence, 66 Ala. L. Rev. 423 (2015). Such categorical exclusionary rules also eliminate errors that factfinders' improper reliance on "noisy" evidence would otherwise engender. This twin benefit offsets the social cost of the errors that factfinders commit due to their inability to use "noisy" evidence. Exclusion of "noisy" evidence thus promotes a fundamental economic objective of the legal system: It reduces the cost of errors and the cost of error-avoidance as a total sum. See Richard A. Posner, An Economic Approach to the Law of Evidence, 51 Stan. L. Rev. 1477, 1522–1530 (1999).

(2) Allocation of Errors. Allowing errors in factfinding to affect adjudicative decisions randomly may be unfair. Some adjudicative errors (e.g., conviction of an innocent defendant) are more harmful than others (e.g., acquittal of a guilty defendant). For that reason, lawmakers will do well to set up evidentiary rules that decrease the risk of error for one party (a criminal defendant) while increasing it for that party's adversary (the prosecution). But even when the stakes are symmetrical—as normally is the case in civil litigation—randomizing errors may not be a good policy because of the potential inequality in the parties' exposure to the risk of error. For example, when one party brings evidence that supports its case, but the evidence is not open to examination by the party's opponent, admitting such evidence (an out-of-court statement, for example) would create inequality in the allocation of the risk of error. The proponent of the evidence would reduce its exposure to the risk of error, while its opponent would face an increased prospect of losing the case undeservedly. Arguably, to avoid this result, lawmakers should devise evidentiary rules that equalize parties' exposure to the risk of error. See Alex Stein, Foundations of Evidence Law 118–140 (2005).

(3) Policy. Various policies extraneous to the system of litigation itself are affected by litigation. Consider two general examples. First, compelling witnesses to testify about certain kinds of communications they have had can have a destructive effect on human relationships, both professional and personal. Maintaining the privacy of these relationships are equally or more important than accurate adjudication, and thus litigation is structured to protect them through the provision of various privileges—such as attorney-client, psychotherapist-patient, or husband-wife—that exempt certain individuals from testifying in certain circumstances. See Article V of the Federal Rules of Evidence.

The second general example of extraneous policy considerations has to do with encouraging kinds of socially useful activity other those arising out of confidential communications. Suppose an accident occurs at a bridge, and the owner of the bridge does some repair to the bridge that reduces the probability of a similar accident occurring. The act of repair may indicate that the bridge was dangerous and thus be evidence of negligence on the owner's part. Admitting evidence of the act of repair at trial to prove negligence will create disincentives for future bridge owners to repair their bridges. In order to encourage the reduction of social risk, after-the-fact repairs are excluded at trial. See FRE 407. There are many similar examples. See FRE 408-410.

(4) Accuracy. Another argument for regulating the proof process is to help jurors avoid reaching erroneous results. Frederick Schauer, On the Supposed Jury-Dependence of Evidence Law, 155 U. Pa. L. Rev. 165, 199–202 (2006). One reason for the hearsay rule (Article 8 of the Federal Rules) is the belief that jurors cannot accurately appraise hearsay evidence. FRE 403 allows judges to keep "unfairly prejudicial" evidence from the jury, on the ground that admitting it risks leading jurors away from rationality. This argument, paradoxically, calls into question the very institution of jury decisionmaking. The argument is in essence that the proof process must be controlled in order to keep distracting, prejudicial, and difficult-to-appraise material away from the jury, because such material will lead the jurors to substitute emotion or caprice for rationality, thus increasing the risk of wrong results. Consider

in the next section how the trial process both accommodates and attempts to modify how the law assumes jurors will reason and behave.

(5) *Fairness.* Rules regulating admission and exclusion of evidence can also be justified for their tendency to promote fairness to the parties. One aspect of fairness relates to the system's goal of achieving factually accurate results. Rule 403, which allows the trial judge to exclude evidence that may cause "unfair prejudice" to the objecting party, is an obvious example of such a fairness-based rule. Rules restricting evidence of a party's "character" or his conduct before or after the relevant events in the case (see FRE 404) are designed, in part, to prevent juries from punishing parties for matters other than their specifically alleged wrongdoing. Another value related to fairness is that the system regards participants as fully autonomous individuals whose choices control many aspects of the proceedings, such as the responsibility to prepare and present their own case and to object to improper evidence from the opponent (see FRE 103). Finally, burdening the proponent with the obligation of presenting its own evidence with a foundation that aids the jury's decisionmaking (authenticating exhibits under FRE 901 and presenting original documents under FRE 1002) can be seen as preventing the proponent from overwhelming the opponent with unfair evidentiary burdens.

3. Natural Reasoning and the Trial Process

As we previously indicated, the trial must look somewhat strange from the point of view of the jurors. Jurors typically sit passively through disjointed presentations of evidence, although there are now some experiments being done with allowing jurors to ask questions during the presentation of evidence that suggest jury questions may promote juror understanding of the facts and issues, and alleviate doubts about the trial evidence. Steven D. Penrod & Larry Heuer, Tweaking Commonsense: Assessing Aids to Jury Decision Making, 3 Psychol. Pub. Poly. & L. 259 (1997); see also Franklin Strier, The Road to Reform: Judges on Juries and Attorneys, 30 Loy. L.A. L. Rev. 1249 (1997). Particularly because of the passivity of jurors, the judge's initial instructions to the jury and the parties' opening statements are crucial—they are the only sources of information that will create a context for the jury. Only after the close of the evidence does the judge typically give full instructions on the law, as occurred in *Johnson*. Often the instructions are not clear, although the ones in *Johnson* are for the most part fairly clear. Consider, though, the instruction on reasonable doubt, on page 71, supra:

> Reasonable doubt is defined as follows. It is not a mere possible doubt because everything relating to human affairs and depending on moral evidence is open to some possible or imaginary doubt. It is that state of the case, which after the entire comparison and consideration of all the evidence, leaves the mind of the jurors in that condition that they cannot say that they feel an abiding conviction or a moral certainty of the truth of the charge.

How helpful is that? Can it be made any clearer? This instruction is somewhat vague because the idea lying behind it is somewhat vague. In many cases, however, the instructions are vague because they are filled with incomprehensible legalese that simply leaves the jury baffled. The lack of helpfulness of many jury instructions, and the resultant lack of comprehension of them, is scandalous in a system dedicated to both lay decision makers and rationality. Again, though, can you think of any reason why such a scandal continues to persist? Jury instructions are not just the means by which jurors are controlled by trial judges. They are also one of the important means by which appellate judges control trial judges. Jury instructions embody the substantive law that the trial judge applies to the trial, and appellate courts review jury instructions nondeferentially. Moreover, in contrast to evidentiary errors, instructional errors are almost never deemed "harmless" by appellate courts. What might be the implications of that point? In any event, you should ask yourself whether this ordering of events makes sense, and whether the jury should be better informed by the trial judge at an earlier time in the process.

Professor Phoebe Ellsworth has spent considerable time studying the deliberative process of jurors. Her work confirms prior work and anecdotal experience that, notwithstanding the difficulties, juries are quite good at factfinding. Her work also confirms earlier findings that jurors are less adept at dealing with the legal issues in cases. She recently summarized her findings in a way that vividly captures the difficulty of being a juror:

> There is no reason to believe that the jurors' misunderstanding of the law is a function of their mental capacities. It seems more plausible that the system is set up to promote misunderstanding. Factors blockading the serious jury trying to perform its task include: the convoluted, technical language; the dry and abstract presentation of the law following the vivid, concrete, and often lengthy presentation of evidence; the requirements that jurors interpret the evidence before they know what the verdict choices are; the fact that juries usually do not get copies of the instructions to take with them into the jury room; the lack of training in the law for jurors as part of their jury duty; the general failure to discover and correct jurors' preconceptions about the law; the failure to inform jurors that they are allowed to ask for help with the instructions; and the fact that those who do ask for help are often disappointed by a simple repetition of the incomprehensible paragraph. [Phoebe Ellsworth, Are 12 Heads Better Than 1?, 38 Law Quadrangle Notes 56, 64 (1995).]

The jurors' task involves finding facts and applying the law to those facts. We say we want the hallmark of trials to be rational deliberation, which includes accurate factfinding and an adequate understanding of the law, yet the structure of trials is somewhat, perhaps significantly, at odds with effective learning on the part of jurors. Why might that be so? How would power shift at trials if they were structured otherwise? Is much of what you have seen designed to keep control of a trial in the hands of the lawyers? The trial judge? Is that sensible?

We have so far concentrated on the manner in which jurors learn about the litigated events. After the presentation of evidence and closing argument of counsel, juries retire to deliberate and reach a verdict. The law's reach extends to this aspect of the process as well. Because certainty is never possible to achieve at trial, jurors are instructed as to the proper decision rule to apply in the face of the inevitable uncertainty with which they will have to grapple. This comes in the form of an instruction on burdens of persuasion. In civil cases, the normal burden of persuasion is proof by a preponderance of the evidence; in criminal cases it is proof beyond reasonable doubt. Jurors are told that the relevant burden of persuasion is to be applied to "every element" of the cause of action. These matters are discussed in detail in Chapter Eleven.

Coupling the burden of persuasion to "every element" seems unproblematic on its face, but there is a problem lurking in the shadows. This coupling recommends an unnatural decisionmaking process to jurors. If followed literally, jurors would be obligated to analyze the various combinations and permutations of elements, applying the appropriate burden of persuasion as they go. There are two difficulties. First, this procedure would quickly get impossibly complicated; second, people do not typically reason about conventional, everyday affairs in this fashion. The chart below shows how complicated and unconventional the recommended decisionmaking process is. Compiled by Professors Nancy Pennington and Reed Hastie, the chart on the following page displays the jury instructions for a relatively simple homicide case involving a defense of self-defense.

Had you come across something like this chart in a book on chemical analysis or medical diagnosis, it perhaps would not have appeared strange; but as a protocol for juror decisionmaking, it appears completely out of place. The chart, and the instructions it implements, implies that the focus at trial is on the discrete issues identified as "elements"; but as we have already commented, the jurors are not fully informed of those elements until just prior to retiring to deliberate. In the *Johnson* case, for example, battery was not defined until the court's closing instructions. The focus at trial is thus not on whether some formal element is true or false; it is on competing versions of reality—in the *Johnson* case, who started the fight and why? Even the lawyers in *Johnson* more or less ignore the elements in their closing arguments, focusing again on the two competing versions of reality. To be sure, the competing versions of reality involve differing elements. And once the jury has settled on "what happened," it must consult the judge's instructions to determine who wins, which is precisely the finding that emerges from the empirical work of Nancy Pennington and Reed Hastie.

That the process of deliberation involves mediating among the conflicting versions of what happened rather than a minute parsing of the individual elements of the causes of action is supported by another consideration. Any decisionmaking methodology to which a chart like the one below could be applied would have to involve issues with relatively clear answers. Chemical analysis provides a good example.

Litmus paper turns blue or red when immersed in an acid or an alkaline solution; a solvent does or does not dissolve a substance. Trials rarely involve questions that can be answered so unequivocally. At the end of the day, the jury in the *Johnson* case will have to decide who started the fight and why, but in doing so the jurors will have to sift through a lot of ambiguous and conflicting testimony.

That the intellectual task at trial involves organizing the proffered evidence in light of competing versions of the plausible is unavoidable, given the structure of trials. Cases possess ambiguity because of the need to organize large amounts of data (evidentiary complexity), to resolve conflicting and inconsistent testimony (evidentiary tension), and to fill in intermediate premises unsupported by evidence presented at trial (evidentiary gap). The presentation of information at trial quite obviously must be incomplete in the typical case (neither Officer Huston nor Officer Van Berg could

JUROR DECISIONMAKING
Decision Alternatives and Attributes: Murder Case

Decision alternative	Attribute				Decision rule
	1. Identity	2. Mental state	3. Circumstances	4. Actions	
Not guilty	Not the right person	NA	NA	No Killing	1 or 4
Self-defense (not guilty)	Right person	(a) Fear of life (b) Fear of great bodily harm	Under immediate attack	(a) Killing (b) Exhaust escape (c) In defense (d) Reasonable retaliation	1 and (2a or 2b) and 3 and 4a and (4b and 4c and 4d)
Manslaughter	Right person	(a) Heat of sudden passion (b) Diminished capacity	(a) Great provocation (b) Threat to life not immediate	(a) Did not exhaust escape (b) Became the attacker (c) Used excessive force	1 and (2a or 2b) and (3a and 3b) and (4a and 4b and 4c)
Second degree murder	Right person	Intent to inflict injury likely to result in death	Insufficient provocation	(a), (b), (c) Like manslaughter (d) Use deadly weapon (e) Deliberate, cruel act	1 and (2 or [3 and 4d] and 4e) and (4a or 4b or 4c)
First degree murder	Right person	(a) Intent to kill (b) Purpose formed (motive)	(a) Insufficient provocation (b) Interval between plan and killing	(a), (b), (c) Like manslaughter (d) Formed plan to kill (e) Killed in accordance with plan	1 and (2a and 2b) and (3a and 3b) and (4a or 4b or 4c) and 4d and 4e

Note: NA=not applicable
Source: Nancy Pennington & Reed Hastie, Juror Decision-Making Models: The Generalization Gap, 89 Psychol. Bull. 246, 251 (1981).

say how they received their injuries) and often inconsistent information will be presented (eyewitness testimony about Officer Walker's conduct differed considerably). Witnesses testify only to what they have observed, and rarely will one witness observe everything relevant to any particular litigated issue.

Even in a case with a single witness, what is observed must be richer than what is related, if for no other reason than that memory decays with time. In addition, rhetorical skills invariably are less developed than observational skills. Consider a simple example—a case involving assault where part of the proof is testimony that the defendant made "threatening" gestures toward the plaintiff. Testimony characterizing seemingly simple gestures is often a summary of richly textured human acts that may be observed with ease but related only with difficulty, which is precisely why lay opinions such as this are often allowed. To understand such testimony, the juror must reconstruct this richly textured event. And of course in doing so, the juror may have to account for testimony to the effect that the gesture was not made in a threatening way. As case complexity increases, it is implausible that a juror merely continues to add data to the data banks rather than organizing and simplifying the data, which after all is how individuals apparently cope with the complexity of everyday life. One remembers a trip to the store yesterday rather than walking to the garage, opening the door, entering the garage, opening the car door, searching for the proper key, identifying the ignition, and so on.

There is another interesting aspect of jury decisionmaking that is highlighted by the chart. The chart suggests an orderly, deductive approach to decisionmaking: Lay out the assumptions and deduce the correct results. At some point, jurors will indeed "deduce" their verdict in such a fashion, but probably only after all the hard work is done. The hard work involves figuring out what happened. In that effort, deduction, the law's prize tool in virtually all other areas, takes a backseat to induction. Consider again the closing arguments in the *Johnson* case. Neither side attempted to lay out a formal proof of guilt or innocence; instead, they used the testimony to stitch together a story that, they hoped, would seem plausible to the jurors, given their (the jurors') general knowledge and experience.

4. The Behavior of Factfinders

The advocates at trial attempt to persuade the factfinder by advancing plausible accounts of what happened, but what seems "plausible" to a person is determined by the sum of that person's knowledge and experience rather than by the outcome of formal logical manipulations. That this is so is evident from your own experience. Reflect for a moment on how you appraise the things that you see. You look for patterns in them, searching for common threads, especially ones that tie what you are observing to what you have previously observed, although always holding yourself open to the twin possibilities that something is unique in the event under observation or that you made a mistake previously in what you came to believe. You engage in various kinds of analogical reasoning, some involving cause and effect, some filling in unobserved aspects of what you are observing by reference to what you have come to believe is commonly associated with what you presently are viewing; you rely on generalizations formed out of prior experience, and so on. These are the tools that humans use to understand, navigate, and manipulate their environment, and not surprisingly they are the tools that jurors use to resolve the disputes of historical fact before them. At the end of the day, when a consensus has emerged out of bringing the combined experience of the jurors to bear on the evidence presented at trial, the jurors look to the verdict options to determine who wins and loses. And probably on occasion when they do so and see the implications of their positions, they reconsider. To this extent there is a relationship between the largely (but not exclusively) inductive processes that drive evidence comprehension and deliberation and the virtually exclusively deductive process that drives verdict selection.

The instructions on elements, in short, merely provide the verdict options. By contrast, few instructions are given on how to reason or deliberate, because jurors, as competent members of their community, are assumed to know how to do both, an assumption that is surely correct. Judges do typically give one instruction about jury reasoning, the one given in the *Johnson* case—"use your common sense." If more elaborate instructions are necessary, the argument becomes one for deciding cases in some other way.

One last point. At the beginning of the *Johnson* transcript, the judge instructed the jury on what "evidence" is. Think about the nature of "evidence": What exactly, is it? Before reading these pages, you most likely would have thought it a dumb question— "evidence," obviously, is the testimony and exhibits at trial. Is that now so obvious? The testimony and exhibits at trial are meaningless until interpreted by a human observer—judge or juror. Moreover, the interpretation given to any piece of evidence cannot be determined in advance, for it is a function of the background and experience of the factfinder. If "evidence" is what is presented at trial, how can it be that one factfinder thinks the "evidence" proves guilt and another innocence? Does everyone in this class agree that defendant Johnson was guilty of a battery, or do some believe he should have been acquitted? The point we want you to think about, though, is the dynamic nature of trials and "evidence." There is a relational aspect to "evidence"; it (the evidence) is what some human being thinks it is, and what that person thinks it is cannot be determined in advance by a set of rules. If it could, factfinding perhaps could make the transformation from being largely inductive to largely deductive; but if it could, jurors (and judges) would become superfluous. Another way of looking at this is that historical factfinding requires judgment in addition to logic—not in contrast to logic, but in addition to it.

The necessary reliance on judgment is one of the distinguishing features of peculiarly human institutions, which the law of evidence surely is for all of its pretense to analytical rigor. These are matters we would encourage you to reflect on as you proceed throughout the course. Nor are they just matters of academic interest. You are about to turn the page to begin your study of the concept of relevancy. Right at the heart of that concept lie many of the issues we have been addressing here.

CHAPTER THREE

RELEVANCE, PROBATIVE VALUE, AND THE RULE 403 DANGERS

Relevance is the foundational principle for all modern systems of evidence law. Only *relevant* evidence helps the jury achieve rational outcomes based on the jurors' use of their reasoning capacities. The basic tenets of this principle were spelled out more than a century ago by James Bradley Thayer:

> There is a principle—not so much a rule of evidence as a presupposition involved in the very conception of a rational system of evidence . . . which forbids receiving anything irrelevant, not logically probative. How are we to know what these forbidden things are? Not by any rule of law. The law furnishes no test of relevancy. For this, it tacitly refers to logic and general experience—assuming that the principles of reasoning are known to its judges and ministers, just as a vast multitude of other things are assumed as already sufficiently known to them.
>
> There is another precept which should be laid down as preliminary, in stating the law of evidence; namely, that unless excluded by some rule or principle or law, all that is logically probative is admissible. This general admissibility, however, of what is logically probative is not, like the former principle, a necessary presupposition in a rational system of evidence; there are many exceptions to it. Yet, in order to [have] a clear conception of the law, it is important to notice this also as being a fundamental proposition. In an historical sense it has not been the fundamental thing, to which different exclusions were exceptions. What has taken place, in fact, is the shutting out by the judges of one and another thing from time to time; and so, gradually, the recognition of this exclusion under a rule. These rules of exclusion have had their exceptions; and so the law has come into the shape of a set of primary rules of exclusion; and then a set of exceptions to these rules. . . .
>
> In stating thus our two large, fundamental conceptions, we must not fall into the error of supposing that relevancy, logical connection, real or supposed, is the only test of admissibility; for so we should drop out of sight the chief part of the law of evidence. When we have said (1) that, without any exception, nothing which is not, or is not supposed to be, logically relevant is admissible; and (2) that, subject to many exceptions and qualifications, whatever is logically relevant is admissible; it is obvious that, in reality, there are tests of admissibility other than logical relevancy. Some things are rejected as being of too slight a significance, or as having too conjectural

and remote a connection; others, as being dangerous, in their effect on the jury, and likely to be misused or overestimated by that body; others, as being impolitic, or unsafe on public grounds; others, on the bare ground of precedent. It is this sort of thing, as I said before—the rejection on one or another practical ground, of what is really probative—which is the characteristic thing in the law of evidence; stamping it as the child of the jury system. [James Bradley Thayer, A Preliminary Treatise on Evidence at the Common Law 264-266 (1898).]

Thayer's analysis provides two fundamental ideas that are important to keep in mind when analyzing evidentiary issues. First, whether evidence is relevant or not will depend primarily on the "commonsense" reasoning of judges and juries (and sometimes on the reasoning of expert witnesses) and not on legal rules. This is what Thayer meant by, "[t]he law furnishes no test of relevancy," relying instead on "logic and general experience." Second, relevance is *necessary* but not *sufficient* for evidence to be admissible. In other words, many rules exclude evidence even though the evidence is, in fact, relevant. We discuss one such rule, FRE 403, in section B.

A. RELEVANCE—THE BASIC CONCEPT

The discussion of relevance under the Federal Rules of Evidence that follows is the foundation for your study of evidence law. It provides you with analytic tools to develop, articulate, and defend your own theories of why evidence is relevant in any factual dispute. This analysis is fundamental to the understanding of relevance that you must have as the proponent, opponent, or judge of the admissibility of evidence. And you will soon see that the application of all rules of evidence flows from the initial question: Why is the evidence relevant?

1. FRE 401 and 402

RULE 401. TEST FOR RELEVANT EVIDENCE

Evidence is relevant if: (a) it has any tendency to make a fact more or less probable than it would be without the evidence; and (b) the fact is of consequence in determining the action.

RULE 402. GENERAL ADMISSIBILITY OF RELEVANT EVIDENCE

Relevant evidence is admissible unless any of the following provides otherwise:

- the United States Constitution;
- a federal statute;
- these rules; or
- other rules prescribed by the Supreme Court.

Irrelevant evidence is not admissible.

2. Explanation of FRE 401 and 402

In deciding whether an item of evidence is relevant under FRE 401, a judge must consider two issues: (1) Is the item offered to prove a fact that "is of consequence" to the case? (2) Could a reasonable jury think that the item has a tendency to make that fact of consequence more (or less) probable? The common law perceived these two issues as two separate concepts—*materiality* (meaning the connection to a fact of consequence in the case) and *relevance* (meaning that the connection was logically probative). While the term "materiality" is not used in the Federal Rules, it is still common parlance among judges and lawyers and you should be familiar with it. If a proper objection is made, judges will exclude all evidence that is not relevant, under FRE 401 and 402.

a. Relevant Evidence Is Offered to Prove a Fact of Consequence

In general, a proposition of fact is "of consequence" (i.e., material) in a legal dispute if it matters to the legal resolution of that dispute. A fact matters to the legal resolution of a dispute if it is one that a jury (or a judge in a bench trial) could rationally use in determining the existence of guilt or liability. In order to determine which facts are of consequence in a particular legal dispute, one must look to the offering party's "theory of the case" (or what that party is arguing at trial) and the elements that comprise the substantive law (the crime, civil cause of action, or affirmative defense at issue). The essential elements are defined by the applicable criminal or civil law, and they are the facts that the party with the burden of proof must prove at trial. This inferential reasoning process from evidence to facts of consequence can be illustrated with a simple diagram:

Diagram 3-1

EVIDENCE ———————► FOC (EE)

The "evidence" refers to the witness testimony and exhibits presented in the courtroom. The FOC is a proposition of fact the jury can decide to believe, on the basis of drawing an inference from the evidence. The arrow represents an inference the jury can make. To be "of consequence" the inferred fact must either (1) itself be an essential element or (2) be one that a jury could rationally use in determining whether an essential element is more or less probable through one or more further inferences.

For an example of how a fact of consequence may require a further inference to connect to an essential element, consider the following:

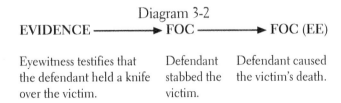

Diagram 3-2

EVIDENCE ———————► FOC ———————► FOC (EE)

| Eyewitness testifies that the defendant held a knife over the victim. | Defendant stabbed the victim. | Defendant caused the victim's death. |

The evidence is a witness's testimony that she saw the defendant holding a knife over the victim. From this testimony, the jury may infer that the defendant did in fact stab the victim. This act by the defendant is a fact of consequence because from it the jury may infer the identity of the person who caused the victim's death, which is a fact of consequence because it is an essential element in the law of homicide.

The substantive law determines the essential elements in every case. In the *Johnson* case, for example, the essential elements of the crime with which Johnson was charged were (1) the unlawful use of force or violence (2) by a person incarcerated in state prison (3) against a person not incarcerated. The prosecution presented testimony from several eyewitnesses that Johnson was kicking and struggling with the correctional officers both inside and outside his cell. This testimony was relevant to prove that Johnson used force and violence, as required by the first essential element listed above. Now consider the defense attorney's question to inmate Butler concerning the frequency with which prisoners at Pelican Bay are allowed to receive packages from home (page 48, line 1, supra). Does this information tend to prove a fact of consequence in the *Johnson* case? Can you identify any connection between it and one of the essential elements? If you cannot, then the information may be irrelevant—"immaterial," in common law parlance—and would be excluded under FRE 401 and 402.

The relevance of some evidence requires several inferences to rationally connect it to an essential element. For example, the prosecution offered testimony that Officer Huston suffered a gash on his left shin (page 16, line 44, supra). The following diagram shows how this testimony can be used to prove that Johnson used force and violence against Huston, as required by the first and third essential elements in the Johnson case:

Diagram 3-3

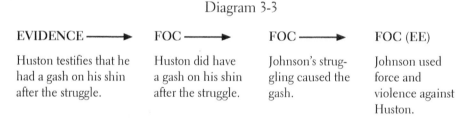

EVIDENCE ⟶	FOC ⟶	FOC ⟶	FOC (EE)
Huston testifies that he had a gash on his shin after the struggle.	Huston did have a gash on his shin after the struggle.	Johnson's struggling caused the gash.	Johnson used force and violence against Huston.

The first inference is that Huston's testimony is true—he did have the gash *after* the struggle with Johnson. From this inferred fact, the facts of consequence, including the essential element, can be identified.

Sometimes longer chains of reasoning are required. For example, inmate Butler testified that the correctional officers were wearing their gloves when they approached Johnson's cell (page 48, line 24, supra). This testimony connects to the defense theory that the guards started the fight with Johnson. The fact that a guard was wearing gloves generates the inference that the guard was prepared to have contact with an inmate, not just collect a food tray; and if the guard was prepared to have contact, then he intended to fight; and if he intended to fight, then he started the fight; and if a guard started the fight, then Johnson's use of force was self-defense and not unlawful. This chain of inferences is shown in Diagram 3-4.

Diagram 3-4

Each arrow represents an inference in the chain starting from the evidence, leading to a series of facts of consequence, including an essential element in the case. Whether the chain of reasoning is long or short, what is important to remember is that the facts of consequence in a case cannot be determined without knowing the essential elements of the substantive law that governs the dispute.

b. Relevant Evidence Must Make a Fact of Consequence More Probable or Less Probable

Once the proponent identifies the fact of consequence, the proponent must also be prepared to show how the evidence makes the fact of consequence more probable or less probable than if the evidence were not presented. The phrase "more or less probable" means that evidence is relevant if it is capable of having any rational effect at all on the jury's perception of a fact of consequence. The evidence might make that fact slightly more believable (more probable) or it might make that fact slightly less believable (less probable). In either case, it is relevant. Only when the evidence is not capable of having any rational effect in either direction is it irrelevant.

FRE 401's Minimal Standard of "Any Tendency."   FRE 401 defines relevant evidence as having "any tendency" to make the existence of a fact of consequence more or less probable. This is a minimal test of logically probable inferences from the offered item to a fact of consequence. For example, in determining the relevance of inmate Butler's testimony in the *Johnson* case that the guards wore gloves, it need only be the case that "guards who wear gloves are at least slightly more likely to have anticipated contact with inmates than if they were not wearing gloves." The judge will find evidence relevant if a reasonable jury could think that it makes a fact of consequence even slightly more or less likely than it would be were the evidence not known.

> If and only if the probability . . . is the same with and without the evidence, the evidence is irrelevant. . . . If these probabilities are different, the evidence is relevant. It seems to be recognized on all sides that the *size* of the change is of no importance in determining relevancy . . . . [T]here are no degrees of relevancy. . . . [T]he term *relevant* refers to the distinction between some probative force and no probative force . . . between some change in probability and no change. [Vaughn C. Ball, The Myth of Conditional Relevancy, 14 Ga. L. Rev. 435, 446 (1980).]

But in a specific instance, how does the proponent of evidence articulate why it makes a fact of consequence more or less probable? And if the opponent objects, how does the judge decide whether FRE 401 is satisfied? The answer to these questions requires an understanding that reasoning from evidence to a fact of consequence requires the use of generalized knowledge and experience.

Inferential Reasoning Is Based on Generalizations from Knowledge and Experience.   Inferential reasoning requires generalized knowledge and experience, as well as the various intellectual tools discussed on pages 127-32 of Chapter Two, to reason from evidence to facts of consequence. We all have a well-developed body of generalized knowledge that we use in our inferential reasoning:

> All of us . . . have accumulated vast storehouses of commonly held notions about how people and objects generally behave in our society. From this storehouse one formulates a generalization about typical behavior. The generalization, in turn, becomes the premise which enables me to link specific evidence with an element one hopes to prove. [David A. Binder & Paul Bergman, Fact Investigation 85 (1984).]

The Advisory Committee Note to FRE 402 calls these generalizations "principles evolved by experience or science, applied logically to the situation at hand."

To test whether evidence is logically probative of a specific fact of consequence, the judge examines the generalizations underlying each inference in the proponent's proposed chain of reasoning. For example, the inferential leap from "the guards wore gloves" to "the guards were prepared to fight" requires a generalization about the behavior of prison guards. Such a generalization might be articulated as follows: "Guards probably don't wear gloves to pick up food trays, but they would be likely to wear gloves when they prepare to come into contact with inmates." What do you think of this generalization? Does it support the necessary inference? Does it make the inferred fact more probable? Because such generalizations are only rough estimates of human behavior (and other kinds of occurrences), they cannot establish with certainty that an inference is true. Nevertheless, the generalizations operate logically as part of a syllogistic reasoning process: from major premise (the generalization) and minor premise (the evidence) to the conclusion (the inference to be drawn). This form of reasoning, based on generalizations from knowledge and experience, can also be diagramed:

Diagram 3-5

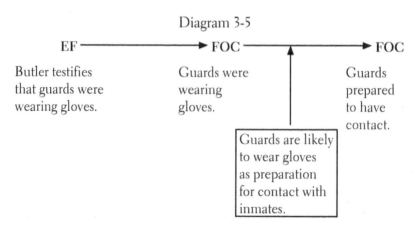

Relevance Requires Reasonable Generalizations.   Judges will admit evidence as making a fact of consequence more probable or less probable when the generalizations from common knowledge and experience are reasonable. Phrased another way, the test of relevance is "whether a reasonable person might believe the probability of the truth of the consequential fact to be different if that person knew of the proffered evidence." (2 Jack B. Weinstein & Margaret A. Berger, Weinstein's Federal Evidence §401.04[2](b) (Joseph M. McLaughlin, ed., Matthew Bender 2d ed. 2001)). The judge thus evaluates the reasonableness of the underlying generalizations from the perspective of a reasonable juror. When relevance is disputed, the offering party must be prepared to explain and justify the underlying generalization for the judge.

Generalizations Can Be the Subject of Proof.   What if the opponent objects that a generalization necessary to an item's relevance is either unknown to the jury or unreasonable, and the judge also has the same doubts? In such a case, the judge can require the proponent of the evidence to produce evidence for the generalization itself. In the *Johnson* case, for example, the judge might ask: "How would the jury know that guards wear gloves to prepare for contact with inmates?" The judge could require the defense to produce testimony about glove-wearing practices in Facility B at Pelican Bay. This evidence would then become part of the chain of reasoning:

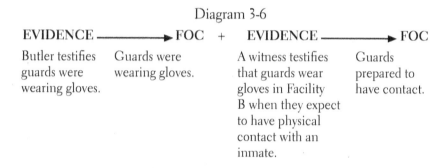

Diagram 3-6

EVIDENCE ──────────▶ FOC   +   EVIDENCE ──────────▶ FOC

| Butler testifies guards were wearing gloves. | Guards were wearing gloves. | A witness testifies that guards wear gloves in Facility B when they expect to have physical contact with an inmate. | Guards prepared to have contact. |

A proponent will have to present proof of an underlying generalization if the judge requires it. Of course, the proponent may also offer such proof simply to persuade the jury that the generalization has particularly strong probative force.

Limits on Reasonable Generalizations.   There are many types of generalized knowledge, all of which may be involved in factual adjudication:

> Generalizations range over a broad spectrum. At one end are scientific laws . . . well-founded scientific opinions . . . and widely shared conclusions based upon common experience (for instance, everyone knows that a driver must stop at a red light). In the middle are commonly held, but unproven or unprovable beliefs (for instance, fleeing the scene of a crime is evidence of a guilty conscience). At the other end are biases or prejudices that may be strongly held irrespective of available data . . . and less strongly held but still operative beliefs (for instance, men's fixed designs are probably carried out). [Terence Anderson & William Twining, Analysis of Evidence 68 (1991).]

Judges do not require objective proof of most generalizations that sound reasonable. To do so would be impractical because many aspects of common knowledge have not been validated by rigorous empirical study. Trials would grind to a halt if litigants had to offer formal proof of every generalization about human behavior and the physical world. Nevertheless, there are two limits implicit in the "reasonable juror" test: The necessary generalizations cannot be known to the judge to be false ("people can see through brick walls")[1] and they cannot be unduly speculative ("people with red hair seem to be more aggressive than people with black hair").[2] A relevance theory based on such generalizations should be rejected. Some generalizations express invidious stereotypes based on factors such as gender, race, ethnicity, religion, age, and sexual preference. Once articulated, many such generalizations probably fall within the "false" or "guesswork" categories of unacceptability, or lack any connection to the individual case. Jinro America Inc. v. Secure Investments, Inc., 2001 U.S. App. LEXIS 25987, at *37 (9th Cir. 2001) (majority held syllogism "(a) Korean businesses are generally corrupt; (b) Jinro is a Korean business; (c) therefore, Jinro is corrupt" to be impermissible under FRE 403; concurrence held that generalizations about Korean businesses were irrelevant to prove Jinro's conduct). Of course, stereotypes and biases may also surface during confidential jury deliberations if the background facts necessary to trigger them are available. Some of these problematic stereotypes have been identified and addressed in the Federal Rules. For example, FRE 610 prohibits evidence of religious beliefs or opinions on the question of credibility, and FRE 412 limits the use of evidence of a victim's sexual behavior or predisposition in cases involving allegations of sexual misconduct. It is also assumed that a diverse jury will express a range of views during deliberation and will correct for such stereotypes.

Judges Do Not Assess the Evidence Themselves. In determining whether there is a reasonable connection between evidence and a fact of consequence, judges do not assess whether they themselves believe the evidence. When the evidence is a witness's testimony, the judge does not assess whether the witness is credible. When the evidence is an exhibit, the judge does not assess whether the exhibit is genuine. Rather, for relevance determinations, the judge will assume the jury finds the witness to be credible or the exhibit is genuine and then will examine whether there is a reasonable connection to the fact of consequence. The foundational admissibility requirements for testimony and exhibits are discussed in Chapter Four.

The Policy of FRE 401 Favors Admissibility. The minimal test of relevance serves one of the most important goals of the Federal Rules of Evidence: to promote rational decisionmaking by providing the jury with as much relevant information as possible (subject to the rules that exclude otherwise relevant evidence). FRE 401

---

1. Conversations in the cockpit of an airliner just before crashing were not relevant to the mental state and psychic damages of the passengers because the passengers could not hear the conversations. Pregeant v. Pan Am. World Airways, Inc., 762 F.2d 1245, 1249 (5th Cir. 1985) (error harmless).

2. Testimony by an expert that it was "possible" but "not probable" that the defendant's Nike sneaker was the source of an inculpatory footprint was excluded as "lacking probative value" under Rule 401. United States v. Ferreira, 821 F.2d 1, 5 (1st Cir. 1987). Whether this ruling was rightly decided under FRE 401 would depend on the nature of the generalization that the expert relied on to find a "possibility."

fosters this goal by preventing the judge's own beliefs about the significance of the evidence to distort the flow of information that a reasonable jury may consider to be relevant. By contrast, suppose that a judge could reject a proponent's generalization based on the judge's own assessment of the generalization's plausibility. For example, a judge might think: "I just don't believe that guards wear gloves in anticipation of contact with inmates. I think that guards wear gloves to keep their hands clean." Excluding evidence that the guards wore gloves, based on the judge's own beliefs about the evidence and its underlying generalization, would prevent the jury from hearing this evidence, which it might reasonably consider to be relevant for determining who started the fight.

This raises the question of how certain the trial judge has to be that the evidence has the minimal relevant connection to the case. The minimal test of relevance established in FRE 401 suggests that the judge should find evidence to be relevant if the judge believes there is any probability that the relevant connection exists. Thus, even if there are alternative explanations of the glove-wearing practices of guards at Pelican Bay, if the proponent's underlying generalizations are reasonable, the evidence is relevant. For a synopsis of the philosophical, academic, and legal debates underlying "the strong federal policy favoring admissibility of, and reliance on, all helpful information . . . ," see District Judge Jack B. Weinstein's opinion in United States v. Shonubi, 895 F. Supp. 460, 492 (E.D.N.Y. 1995), 103 F.3d 1085 (2d Cir. 1997) (sentence vacated).

After a judge admits evidence under the minimal test of FRE 401, it ultimately will be up to the jury to determine the relevance and significance of the evidence. Even if a judge admits evidence over a relevance objection, the jury may nevertheless reject the evidence as irrelevant during their deliberations.

c. *Relevance Is Not Sufficiency*

The question of admissibility under FRE 401 is separate from the question of whether an item of evidence is sufficient proof of an essential element. The question of admissibility goes to logical effect, and "any tendency" under FRE 401 requires only a minimum level of logical effect. The question of sufficiency refers to the burden of production discussed in Chapter Two at pages 95-96; that is, whether a reasonable person could be persuaded by the evidence to the level demanded by the applicable burden of persuasion. Both burdens will be discussed further in Chapter Ten. Typically, a party's case will require many items of evidence to meet the burden of producing evidence sufficient to support a verdict. As the Advisory Committee Note to FRE 401 states, quoting McCormick's treatise, "A brick is not a wall." The "brick" is each item of relevant evidence; the "wall" is the totality of evidence meeting a burden of proof.

Moreover, most items of evidence will not trigger just one inference or just one underlying explanatory generalization. Evidence typically can be interpreted in several different ways, thus triggering competing and often contradictory inferences. For example, several competing explanations have probably already occurred to you as to why the guards were wearing gloves (if they were) in the *Johnson* case. These competing explanations may be made the subject of proof by the opponent, and may be argued to the jury during closing argument. It is usually for the jury, in its ultimate deliberations, to choose among them. To be admitted under FRE 401, an item of evidence is tested from the perspective of its proponent. The evidence needs only to make a fact of consequence *somewhat more or less likely than it would be were the evidence not known.*

d. Direct versus Circumstantial Evidence

The common law distinguished between two types of relevant evidence: direct and circumstantial. Direct evidence typically is defined as evidence that, if believed, establishes an essential element without any additional intervening inferences. For example, if the correctional officers had testified in the *Johnson* case that they saw Johnson kick Officers Huston and Van Berg, this testimony, if believed, would have been direct evidence that Johnson committed a battery. And the testimony of an eye-witness identifying a bank robber, if believed, would be direct evidence of the element of identity. In both examples, the fact of consequence is itself identical, or essentially identical, to the essential element, the difference being the legal terminology in which the essential element is phrased.

In most cases, however, the connection between an item of evidence and an essential element is not so immediate and may require many intervening inferences. This type of evidence is called *"circumstantial."* Suppose a witness testifies that immediately after a bank was robbed, he saw the defendant (charged with the bank robbery) running a block away from the bank. This would be viewed as circumstantial evidence of the defendant's guilt on the ground that the testimony does not directly establish the essential element of identity. Additional inferences are necessary to explain the defendant's conduct in such a way as to connect the defendant to the robbery—he was attempting to flee to avoid being caught after he had committed the crime. And because there are numerous other explanations for the defendant's running, an inference of identity does not automatically follow.

Nevertheless, direct and circumstantial evidence both require the jury to use inferential reasoning. Direct evidence establishes an essential element only if the jury believes the eyewitness, and this requires inferential reasoning about the eyewitness's ability to observe the event correctly, to remember it, and to describe it honestly and accurately. These standard issues of credibility must be resolved by the factfinder in order to evaluate any testimonial evidence, and they are the kinds of issues about which people use natural reasoning constantly in their everyday lives. Generally speaking, then, what distinguishes circumstantial from direct evidence is the length of the inferential chain.

It is important to understand, however, that the labels "direct" and "circumstantial" do not reflect the evidence's probative force. Circumstantial evidence can often be more reliable than direct evidence. A blood spot found on a murder weapon, identified as the defendant's through DNA testing, is an example of circumstantial evidence that can be very accurate, and is probably more reliable than many eyewitnesses, as will be discussed in Chapter Nine.

Virtually *all* litigated cases rely on at least some circumstantial evidence, and many essential elements (intent, for example) are typically proved only in this way. Some jurisdictions distinguish between circumstantial and direct evidence in instructing the jury, as was done in the *Johnson* case—that each fact in a chain of circumstantial evidence necessary to proof of guilt must be proved beyond a reasonable doubt (page 70, line 4, supra). This instruction cannot possibly be applied to every intermediate step in a chain of reasoning, and giving such an instruction is very confusing to the jury. The ultimate inference of guilt in a criminal case will typically depend on a number of intermediate steps, each proved by a number of individual items of evidence. Only rarely will any one such intermediate fact of consequence, of itself, be *necessary* to proof of guilt. As stated by the High Court of Australia:

[I]t may sometimes be necessary or desirable to identify those intermediate facts which constitute indispensable links in a chain of reasoning towards an inference of guilt. Not every possible intermediate conclusion of fact will be of that character. If it is appropriate to identify an intermediate fact as indispensable it may well be appropriate to tell the jury that that fact must be found beyond reasonable doubt before the ultimate inference can be drawn. But where . . . the evidence consists of strands in a cable rather than links in a chain, it will not be appropriate to give such a warning. It should not be given in any event where it would be unnecessary or confusing to do so. It will generally be sufficient to tell the jury that the guilt of the accused must be established beyond reasonable doubt and, where it is helpful to do so, to tell them that they must entertain such a doubt where any other inference consistent with innocence is reasonably open on the evidence. . . .

[T]he prosecution bears the burden of proving all the elements of the crime beyond reasonable doubt. That means that the essential ingredients of each element must be so proved. It does not mean that every fact—every piece of evidence—relied upon to prove an element by inference must itself be proved beyond reasonable doubt. . . .Indeed, the probative force of a mass of evidence may be cumulative, making it pointless to consider the degree of probability of each item of evidence separately. [51 A. Crim. R. 181, 184-185 (1990).]

e. Background Information

In most cases, judges admit some testimony that may not seem to have any obvious connection to any fact of consequence in the case. Reasonable background information about the witness who is testifying is "always admissible . . . it allows the jury to make better informed judgments about the credibility of a witness and the reliability of that witness' observations." United States v. McVeigh, 153 F.3d 1166, 1201 (10th Cir. 1998). And when witnesses describe actions or events, they are often allowed to describe them in some detail, simply to help the jury relate to and understand what it did not and cannot see for itself. Inmate Butler's explanation of how inmates receive packages from home, referred to on page 136, supra, is an example of such detail. The Latin phrase *res gestae*—meaning "things done"—is often used to justify the admission of broader context to an important incident. Parties also use many kinds of exhibits that in and of themselves do not tend to prove any fact of consequence but that are nonetheless part of, or illustrate, the story to which the jury is listening.

The Advisory Committee Note to FRE 401 explicitly approves of the admission of this kind of contextual evidence, despite its lack of immediate consequence to the case:

> Evidence which is essentially background in nature can scarcely be said to involve disputed matter, yet it is universally offered and admitted as an aid to understanding.
>
> Charts, photographs, views of real estate, murder weapons, and many other items of evidence fall in this category.

3. Applications of FRE 401 and 402

Two judicial opinions, rendered over 100 years apart, illustrate the low threshold of probative connection required by the concept of relevance.

KNAPP v. STATE[3]

168 Ind. 153, 79 N.E. 1076 (1907)

The appellant appeals from a judgment in the above-entitled cause, under which he stands convicted of murder in the first degree. Error is assigned on the overruling of a motion for new trial.

Appellant, as a witness in his own behalf, offered testimony tending to show a killing in self-defense. He afterwards testified, presumably for the purpose of showing that he had reason to fear the deceased, that before the killing he had heard that the deceased, who was the marshal of Hagerstown, had clubbed and seriously injured an old man in arresting him, and that he died a short time afterwards. On appellant being asked, on cross-examination, who told him this, he answered: "Some people around Hagerstown there. I can't say as to who it was now." The state was permitted, on rebuttal, to prove by a physician, over the objection and exception of the defense, that the old man died of senility and alcoholism, and that there were no bruises or marks on his person. Counsel for appellant contended that it was error to admit this testimony; that the question was as to whether he had, in fact, heard the story, and not as to its truth or falsity. While it is laid down in the books that there must be an open and visible connection between the fact under inquiry and the evidence by which it is sought to be established, yet the connection thus required is in the logical processes only, for to require an actual connection between the two facts would be to exclude all presumptive evidence. Within settled rules, the competency of testimony depends largely upon its tendency to persuade the judgment. As said by Wharton: "Relevancy is that which conduces to the proof of a pertinent hypothesis." 1 Wharton, Ev. §20. In Stevenson v. Stuart, 11 Pa. 307, it was said: "The competency of a collateral fact to be used as the basis of legitimate argument is not to be determined by the conclusiveness of the inferences it may afford in reference to the litigated fact. It is enough if these

3. For an interesting discussion of the *Knapp* case and the appropriate manner of analyzing the questions it raises, see Richard D. Friedman, Route Analysis of Credibility and Hearsay, 96 Yale L.J. 667, 679 (1987). —EDS.

may tend in a slight degree to elucidate the inquiry, or to assist, though remotely, to a determination probably founded in truth."

We are of opinion that the testimony referred to was competent. While appellant's counsel are correct in their assertion that the question was whether appellant had heard a story to the effect that the deceased had offered serious violence to the old man, yet it does not follow that the testimony complained of did not tend to negative the claim of appellant as to what he had heard. One of the first principles of human nature is the impulse to speak the truth. "This principle," says Dr. Reid, whom Professor Greenleaf quotes at length in his work on Evidence (volume 1 §7n), "has a powerful operation, even in the greatest of liars; for where they lie once they speak truth 100 times." Truth speaking preponderating, it follows that to show that there was no basis in fact for the statement appellant claims to have heard had a tendency to make it less probable that his testimony on this point was true. Indeed, since this court has not, in cases where self-defense is asserted as a justification for homicide, confined the evidence concerning the deceased to character evidence, we do not perceive how, without the possibility of a gross perversion of right, the state could be denied the opportunity to meet in the manner indicated the evidence of the defendant as to what he had heard, where he, cunningly perhaps, denies that he can remember who gave him the information. The fact proved by the state tended to discredit appellant, since it showed that somewhere between the fact and the testimony there was a person who was not a truth speaker, and, appellant being unable to point to his informant, it must at least be said that the testimony complained of had a tendency to render his claim as to what he had heard less probable. . . .

Judgment affirmed.

UNITED STATES v. STEVER

603 F.3d 747 (9th Cir. 2010)

[Defendant Stever appealed his conviction on one count of conspiracy to manufacture 1,000 or more marijuana plants and one count of manufacture of marijuana in violation of 21 U.S.C. §841. Stever sought to defend on the ground that the marijuana growing operation found on an isolated corner of his mother's 400-acre property was the work of one of the Mexican drug trafficking organizations (DTOs) that had recently infiltrated Eastern Oregon. Stever sought discovery from the government of materials related to the operations of DTOs in Eastern Oregon, and made proffers of proof at trial for the following purposes: (1) to rebut the inference that the owners of the property must have been involved in the marijuana operation, because Mexican DTOs have grown marijuana by trespassing on large tracts of public and private land in Eastern Oregon without the knowledge of the owners; (2) to buttress the inference that this particular marijuana operation was the work of a Mexican DTO by demonstrating that operations run by Mexican DTOs have several distinctive characteristics in common with this operation; and (3) to show that Mexican DTOs are secretive and familial and so are unlikely to have involved a local Caucasian in their operations.

The government argued that those inferences were not relevant to Stever's guilt or innocence. The district court agreed. The court refused to compel discovery and rejected Stever's proffers of proof, repeatedly insisting that evidence about who else was responsible for the marijuana operation was not relevant to assessing the likelihood that Stever was involved. On appeal, the Court of Appeals rejected both of the district court's rulings on the basis of the following analysis of relevance.]

The district court's conclusion was illogical. Evidence is relevant if it has "*any* tendency to make the existence of any fact that is of consequence to the determination of the action more probable or less probable than it would be without the evidence." Fed. R. Evid. 401 (emphasis added). The requested evidence, if it existed, tended to show that a Mexican DTO planted the marijuana. It also tended to make it more probable that Stever was not involved, as there would then be an alternative explanation for the grow that would not entail the consent, much less the participation, of any of the Stevers.

The Government makes several arguments in support of the district court's ruling. First, the Government argues that evidence must relate to a *particular* Mexican DTO to be probative of Stever's innocence. This argument fails. Evidence that makes it more likely that a Mexican DTO—any Mexican DTO—was responsible for this operation makes it less likely that Stever was.

Next, the Government argues that a showing that this grow was the work of a Mexican DTO would not tend to exonerate Stever, because Stever could have conspired with the DTO. Although such cooperation is certainly possible, Stever correctly argues that his guilt is *less likely* with Mexican DTO involvement than without it, both because without such involvement a jury would naturally assume that someone with legitimate authority over the land was at least in part responsible, and because he proffered evidence of the exclusivity of Mexican DTO operations . . . .

Finally, the Government argues that the evidence would invite the jury to engage in impermissible speculation about Mexican DTOs and their "correlat[ion] with the Stever property grow." But the district court is not free to dismiss logically relevant evidence as speculative: "[I]f the evidence [that someone else committed the crime] is in truth calculated to cause the jury to doubt, the court should not attempt to decide for the jury that this doubt is purely speculative and fantastic but should afford the accused every opportunity to create that doubt." United States v. Vallejo, 237 F.3d 1008, 1023 (9th Cir. 2001) (quoting John Henry Wigmore, Evidence in Trials at Common Law §139 (1983)) (alterations in original). The jury will still be instructed to decide whether a doubt created by the evidence is a reasonable one and, if it is not, to convict. Viewed in that light, the danger the Government invokes is only the danger that the jury will not follow the instructions given, a risk which we may not entertain in light of "the crucial assumption underlying our constitutional system of trial by jury that jurors carefully follow instructions." [Citation omitted.]

Moreover, as the Government conceded, the case against Stever was circumstantial. Prosecutors asked the jury to infer that Stever was involved in the operation based primarily on its location on his property and his various interactions with Pulido [one of his employees], who *was* linked to the operation by physical evidence. Stever sought to counter the circumstantial inferences that the Government asked the jury to draw with evidence of other, logically relevant circumstances from which obverse inferences to those sought by the Government could be drawn. The district court's conclusion that the discovery was not relevant was thus based on a misapplication of the principles of logical relevance, and the denial of Stever's motion to compel therefore an abuse of discretion.

[Judgment reversed on the ground that Stever was denied his Sixth Amendment right to make a defense, an error that was not harmless.]

NOTES AND QUESTIONS

1. Although the court in *Knapp* does not state the essential elements of the case under the substantive law, you can probably deduce those elements yourself from the *Johnson* case. What are they? How does the physician's testimony connect to a fact of consequence in the case? Can you draw a diagram of this connection? Are the tests of relevance stated in the court's opinion similar, if not identical, to FRE 401 and 402?

2. The court articulates the chain of reasoning that it relies on to establish the relevance of the physician's testimony. It requires a generalization about the truth-telling propensities of people. Is this generalization reasonable? Why does the court think so? Do you?

3. Notice the emphasis that the court gives to the defendant's inability to remember who told him about the incident involving the old man. What is the court's point? Consider this point again after reading Section B, infra on FRE 403.

4. Stever's discovery request for government reports, training materials, and other documents relating to Mexican DTOs in Eastern Oregon was made pursuant to Fed. R. Crim. P. 16(a)(1)(E)(i), which provides that the government must disclose all "documents . . . within the government's possession, custody or control . . . [that are] material to preparing the defense." The government never denied that it possessed such materials; it simply considered them irrelevant and refused to make anything available to Stever.

5. The classic articles that have forged the concept of logical relevance adopted by the Federal Rules of Evidence and described in this chapter are George F. James, Relevancy, Probability and the Law, 29 Cal. L. Rev. 689 (1941); Herman C. Trautman, Logical or Legal Relevancy—A Conflict in Theory, 5 Vand. L. Rev. 385 (1952). See also 2 Jack B. Weinstein & Margaret A. Berger, Weinstein's Federal Evidence §401 (Joseph M. McLaughlin ed., Matthew Bender 2d ed. 2001); 1A Wigmore on Evidence §37 (Peter Tillers rev. 1983).

6. The approach of the Federal Rules is typically contrasted with that of Wigmore, who argued that the law distinguished between "logical" and "legal" relevancy. 1 John Henry Wigmore, Evidence in Trials at Common Law §28, at 409-410 (3d ed. 1940): "[L]egal relevancy denotes . . . something more than a minimum of probative value." Presumably, Wigmore was attempting to distinguish between evidence that had some very slight probative value and that which had considerably more persuasive force. The concept of "legal relevancy" does not appear in the Federal Rules, but it is a term that is still used by some practicing lawyers and judges.

KEY POINTS

1. FRE 402 requires that evidence must be relevant to be admitted at trial, and that all relevant evidence is admissible unless otherwise provided.
2. FRE 401 requires that to be relevant, an evidentiary fact must connect by a process of inferential reasoning to a "fact of consequence" in the case. The essential elements of the substantive law that governs the case determine what facts are "of consequence."
3. FRE 401 requires that to be relevant, evidence must make a fact of consequence "more or less probable." The judge decides this issue under the "any tendency" standard by examining the necessary inferences and the reasonableness of the generalizations underlying them.

PROBLEMS

3.1. Consider the following items of evidence from the *Johnson* case. Are they relevant under FRE 401? State the argument for the proponent of the evidence: What fact of consequence (and essential element) is the item offered to prove? Why does the item make this fact more or less probable? Then make the opponent's argument.

  (a) The prosecution asked Officer Huston, "What type of inmates are typically housed in Facility B?" (Page 9, line 27, supra.) Why would this information be relevant?

  (b) Several correctional officers testified that the reports that they wrote following the incident did not state that they opened the food port door before the cell door was opened electronically.

  (c) The prosecution asked inmate Butler whether he was a gang member and whether defendant Johnson was a gang member. Butler answered that he himself was a Crip and that he did not know if Johnson had any gang affiliation. (Page 49, lines 33-40, supra.)

3.2. At 2:00 P.M. in the afternoon of September 15, 2010, Denise Driver stopped her school bus at its regular stop on Cedar Street. Several young school children between the ages of 8 and 12 left the bus and stood on the gravel shoulder along the side of Cedar Street. As the bus started forward, it hit one of the children, Paul Pedroso, age 10. Paul has been hospitalized since the accident.

Paul's parents have sued Driver and Driver's employer, the San Ramon School District, for negligence on Paul's behalf. They allege that Driver failed to keep a proper lookout and veered off the roadway onto the gravel shoulder where Paul was standing quietly, waiting for the bus to pass. Driver and the school district allege that Driver kept a proper lookout; that Paul was not standing quietly but was playing tag with several other children along the side of the road; and that when Paul ran out into the roadway unexpectedly, Driver had no opportunity to stop in time to avoid hitting him.

At trial in the case of Pedroso v. Driver, Denise Driver testifies in her own defense. Assume that she is a competent witness. During the direct examination of the driver, the following questions and answers occur.

1   Q: Are you still employed as a bus driver?
2   A: No, I quit after the accident.
3   Q: Why?
4   A: It is just like trying to haul a truck load of diamonds. (Voice breaks)
5   Every one of those kids were precious and I just did not have the
6   heart to go back.
7   Q: Would you like a glass of water?
8   A: No, I am okay.

During cross-examination of the driver by the plaintiffs' attorney, the following occurred:

9   Q: Isn't it true that you received a speeding ticket for driving the school bus
10   with the children in it, at 70 miles per hour in a 45 m.p.h. speed zone
11   just a month before the accident in this case occurred?
12   A: Yes.

As attorney for the defendant, what is your theory of relevance for the testimony at lines 4-6?

As attorney for the plaintiff, what is your theory of relevance for the question and answer in lines 9-12? For each item, state the connection between the evidence and the essential element.

3.3. In the case of United States v. Ray, Bernard Ray, the Chief Executive Officer of Rundown Corp., is charged with the federal crime of trading on inside information. The prosecution must prove that Ray intended to profit from the purchase or sale of securities by using "inside" information—information confidential within Rundown and not yet known to the public. Specifically, the prosecution alleges that Ray sold 100,000 shares of Rundown stock on March 16, 2015; that Ray made this sale based on his knowledge of "inside" information that Rundown was facing disastrous losses during the upcoming second quarter (April to June) of 2015; and that Ray intended to profit from this sale. In fact, Rundown Corp. did suffer disastrous financial losses between April and June of 2015, causing the company to file for bankruptcy in December of 2015.

These losses had been projected by Rundown Corp.'s outside auditing firm in early March of 2015. The chief outside auditor Arthur Andrews sent a confidential memorandum stating these loss projections to the office of June Jacobs, the Chief Financial Officer of Rundown, that was delivered to Jacobs on the morning of March 14. Later in the afternoon of March 14, chief auditor Andrews also sent an e-mail to Jacobs advising her to inform Ray about these projections. Ray claims that he was not informed about the projected losses until March 18, just before the weekly meeting of Rundown's Executive Committee. If called as a witness, Jacobs will assert her Fifth Amendment privilege to refuse to testify about these events. The government has a copy of the March 14 e-mail from

Andrews to Jacobs that it wants to enter into evidence to prove that Ray knew about the projected losses before March 16.

Is the e-mail relevant under FRE 401? Why?

3.4. In the case of State v. Blair, on September 14, 2010, Norma Waits, a 35-year-old woman, was brutally attacked in her apartment. There were no signs of forced entry. Norma's housekeeper found Norma unconscious the next morning and then called 911.

Norma was a successful and beloved singer for the local Opera Company. After an extensive investigation, police arrested Jimmy Blair, a 45-year-old prominent entertainment lawyer, and charged him with aggravated assault and battery and attempted murder. Norma does not remember the attack and cannot identify the attacker.

Jimmy and Norma had been dating since 2007. Their relationship began when they met at a fundraising gala for the Opera. Norma's friends reported that Jimmy was charming and supportive. None of them had suspected any trouble, though they did note that Norma had become more isolated in the two years preceding the attack. Norma's best friend stated that she had been unable to see much of Norma in 2010, despite repeated attempts to arrange activities. Additionally, Norma's career had begun to falter, and she took an extensive leave from the Opera, citing unspecified health problems. As the prosecution builds its case against Jimmy, many items of potentially admissible evidence are considered. For the following items, decide whether you think each item is relevant under FRE 401 and 402 and why. Identify the fact of consequence that the item might make more or less probable, and the generalizations needed to support any inferences. Is other evidence needed to determine relevance?

(a) A friend of Norma's says that a month before the attack, Norma told the friend that she planned to tell Jimmy that she was going to break up with him and leave the Bay Area soon. Norma also said that she was afraid Jimmy would be furious.

(b) A police witness would testify that on the morning after the attack, police found a suitcase in Norma's apartment half-packed with her belongings. The police also found a plane ticket for a flight to Los Angeles on that day with Norma's name on it. The ticket was torn in half.

(c) Exhibits include photographs of Norma showing severe bruising on parts of her body that would normally be covered by clothing. The photos are date stamped July 25, 2009. A police witness will testify that she found these photographs in a locked drawer in Norma's apartment, which she opened with a key found among Norma's personal effects.

3.5. During the course of a professional United States Soccer League game, a player for the Blazers, Bob Broadback, was injured by a blow struck by Tony Trapp, a player for the opposing Tomcats. The injury occurred immediately after the Blazers had scored and appeared likely to win the game. Just before the score, Broadback and Trapp had run into each other and both had fallen onto the field. As Broadback was getting up, Trapp struck a blow with his forearm to the back of Broadback's head and neck. Broadback suffered a serious neck injury.

Broadback files a personal injury lawsuit against Trapp for battery. Broadback must prove that Trapp's blow caused his injury. If Broadback also proves that Trapp struck him "with the specific intent to cause grievous injury," then Broadback can claim punitive damages. In his deposition, Trapp has testified that his contact with Broadback was a mere "slap," that "stuff like that happens all the time during games," and that Broadback must have been injured when they ran into each other on the field.

(a) At trial, Broadback offers a recorded excerpt from the televised filming of the soccer game that shows the sequence of events leading up to and including the blow by Trapp to Broadback's neck. The recording also shows an Official Referee immediately ejecting Trapp from the game. Trapp objects on grounds of relevance. What ruling and why?

(b) Broadback also offers a copy of Article V, Section A, Subsection (3) of the Official Rules Governing the Conduct of Play (Rules) of the United States Soccer League, which reads as follows:

All players are prohibited from striking another player on the head, face or neck with the hand, wrist, forearm, elbow or clasped hands.

Is this Rule relevant? To prove what?

B.   PROBATIVE VALUE AND THE RULE 403 DANGERS

FRE 403 affords the trial court authority to exclude evidence that is admittedly relevant under Rules 401 and 402, but that the judge believes might distract the jury from its role of rational decisionmaking. As you read FRE 403, you will see that the rule guides the court's discretionary power to exclude evidence. The judge is not free to choose between admission and exclusion unrestrained by fixed principles. Rather, the judge has some flexibility but is restrained by the criteria articulated. Rule 403 does not allow a trial judge "to remove relevant evidence from the jury's universe solely because he finds the evidence unpersuasive; the ultimate arbiter of the persuasiveness of the proof must be the factfinder, not the lawgiver." Blake v. Pellegrino, 329 F.3d 43, 47 (1st Cir. 2003). The judge's power to exclude under FRE 403 means that the advocates cannot present all the relevant evidence they would like to offer to the jury, and the jury will not see and hear some admittedly relevant information.

1. FRE 403

RULE 403.   EXCLUDING RELEVANT EVIDENCE FOR PREJUDICE, CONFUSION, WASTE OF TIME, OR OTHER REASONS

The court may exclude relevant evidence if its probative value is substantially outweighed by a danger of one or more of the following: unfair prejudice, confusing the issues, misleading the jury, undue delay, wasting time, or needlessly presenting cumulative evidence.

2. Explanation of FRE 403

Relevant evidence is to be excluded only if its probative value is *substantially* out-weighed by one of the rule's articulated dangers. When the opponent objects to the admission of evidence on any of the grounds stated in the rule, the judge must carefully evaluate the probative value of the offered item, estimate the Rule 403 "danger" that it poses, and then apply the terms of the balancing test that the rule sets forth. The rule itself and its Advisory Committee Note give judges little guidance in interpreting the meaning of its terms. How is the judge to measure probative value? What is the differ-ence between "confusion of the issues," "misleading the jury," and "unfair prejudice"? We will develop the meaning of these terms in some detail. We believe that careful analysis of the Rule 403 dangers can have a critical impact on the trial judge's ruling.

Consider an example of evidence raising Rule 403 dangers. James Johnson, the defendant, testified in the *Johnson* case that he observed Officer Walker attack another inmate, allegedly for no good reason: "He snatched a Hispanic guy up off the seat, took him out the kitchen, drug him by the hair out of the kitchen in the front by the sally port and jumped on the guy" (page 61, lines 7-19, supra). This testi-mony was offered to show that Johnson had good reason to fear Officer Walker when Walker came to his cell door. But the evidence presents a problem: This testimony about Officer Walker's conduct on another occasion could also cause the jury to think about Walker, not about Johnson's state of mind. The jury could think that Walker is a bad person and hold this against the government; also, the jury could think that Walker has a propensity for violence and therefore would have attacked Johnson. As we explain at page 156, infra, these are the two ways in which this evidence might be unfairly prejudicial to the government's case. Thus, Johnson's testimony might be objected to by the prosecution under the state-law equivalent of FRE 403,[4] and the judge must weigh the probative value of the evidence against these risks of unfair prejudice.

a. *Probative Value*

To decide the merits of a Rule 403 objection, the judge must first analyze the persuasive effect that the item of evidence will be likely to have on the jury's think-ing about the fact of consequence it is offered to prove. This is its *probative value*. Remember that evidence is relevant if it has "any" tendency to make the fact of con-sequence more probable or less probable; probative value measures the strength of the evidence, even if only in general terms like "highly," "somewhat," or "minimally" probative. Defendant Johnson's testimony as to Officer Walker's conduct is clearly rel-evant to show that Johnson had reason to fear Walker, but what is its probative value?

---

4. California Evidence Code §352, on which FRE 403 is based, contains essentially the same bal-ancing test:

> The court in its discretion may exclude evidence if its probative value is substantially outweighed by the probability that its admission will (a) necessitate undue consumption of time or (b) create substantial danger of undue prejudice, of confusing the issues, or of misleading the jury.

In United States v. Buchanan, 964 F. Supp. 533, 537 (D. Mass. 1997), the district court posed the issue as follows:

> In evaluating probative value I am obliged to consider first "how strong a tendency" the proffered evidence has to prove the issue of consequence in the litigation,. . . and second, the proponent's need for the evidence.

In order to examine both the strength of the evidence and the proponent's need for it, the judge will need some appreciation of the other evidence in the case.

Strength of the Underlying Inferences.   Most courts and commentators agree that the primary measure of probative value is the strength of the inferences that connect the evidence to the essential element. This strength depends on the strength of the generalizations underlying those inferences. If, as Johnson said, he saw Officer Walker beat up another inmate with no provocation, then a generalization underlying the inference that Johnson feared Walker could be articulated as follows:

Diagram 3-7

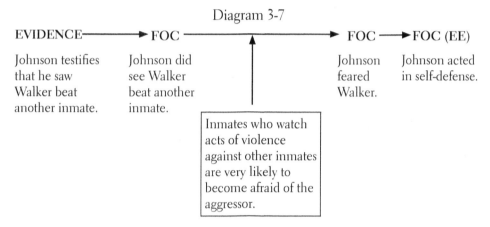

EVIDENCE⟶ FOC ⟶ FOC ⟶FOC (EE)

Johnson testifies that he saw Walker beat another inmate. | Johnson did see Walker beat another inmate. | Johnson feared Walker. | Johnson acted in self-defense.

Inmates who watch acts of violence against other inmates are very likely to become afraid of the aggressor.

The judge's rough estimate of the probability expressed in this generalization—here, the frequency with which inmates do become afraid, estimated as "very likely"—is the major component of the judge's estimate of the probative value of Johnson's testimony. There is no single "correct" way to articulate this generalization, and there is no precise or accurate way to estimate its degree of frequency. Moreover, details of the offered evidence would affect how the generalization is framed, such as was the beating extremely violent? Would it cause extreme or only mild fear in the minds of other inmates? Additional evidence can also increase or decrease the probative value of the offered item. Were such beatings frequent or unusual? Was there already "bad blood" between Johnson and Walker, or between the Hispanic inmate and Walker? Some of these facts could be the subject of further testimony from Johnson, or from additional witnesses as well. The jurors, if the evidence is admitted, will then make inferences from these facts, based on their own background knowledge and experience. You can see that the judge's estimate is just that—a rough attempt to place a value on an inference that a reasonable jury could make and that cannot be quantified with precision.

Certainty of the Starting Point.   The certainty of testimony that is the starting point of an inferential chain can also affect probative value. For example, what if Johnson testified that he "thought" it was Officer Walker who beat the other inmate but he "wasn't sure"? If witnesses admit that they are themselves uncertain about what facts they actually perceived, or if a document contains ambiguous language, judges may lower their estimate of the probative value that they attribute to the evidence for purposes of FRE 403. United States v. Rodriguez-Cabrera, 35 F. Supp. 2d 181, 184 (D.P.R. 1998) (meaning of defendant's nod so ambiguous that prejudice substantially outweighs probative value).

Judges Do Not Weigh Credibility.   Judges do not take witness credibility into account in assessing probative value. For example, should defendant Johnson be believed when he said he saw Officer Walker attack another inmate? Doubts about Johnson's credibility could reduce the probative value of the facts he testifies about. But courts *do not count the witness's credibility* when estimating probative value. 22 Charles Alan Wright & Arthur R. Miller, Federal Practice and Procedure §5214 at 265-266; United States v. Wallace, 124 Fed. Appx. 164, 167 (4th Cir. 2005) ("the credibility of a witness has *nothing to do with* whether or not his testimony is probative with respect to the fact which it seeks to prove."). The judge's role is to estimate the probative value of testimony *if believed.*

Length of the Inferential Chain.   The length of an inferential chain of reasoning does not necessarily reduce the probative value of an item of evidence. Indeed, DNA evidence, for example, requires complicated chains of reasoning and can yield a high probability. While it is true that some chains of reasoning are longer and some are shorter, the important point is that some are stronger in the sense of being more convincing, while some are weaker in the sense of being not very persuasive. At issue is the strength of the connection between the evidence and the conclusion rather than the number of steps that must be taken to get to that conclusion. This is a function primarily of the strength of the generalizations underlying each step.

Need.   The Advisory Committee Note to FRE 403 mentions two other factors that a judge may take into account in applying the rule's balancing test. First, the Note advises that judges should balance "the probative value of and *need* for the evidence against the harm likely to result from its admission" (emphasis added). Then, the Note closes with the statement that the "availability of other means of proof" may also be weighed in the decision to exclude evidence on grounds of unfair prejudice. No explanation of these terms is given, nor is the judge advised how to take these factors into account. Case law reveals that there are many ways in which judges do take need into account. The centrality of the point to be proved with the proffered evidence, the degree to which this point is disputed by the opponent, and the strength of the evidence in proving the point, can demonstrate a party's need for evidence. United States v. DeLaurentis, 83 F. Supp. 2d 455, 467-468 (D.N.J. 2000) (evidence that defendant engaged in a prior criminal scheme with government's star witness was necessary to rehabilitate that witness's credibility after defendant's attack, and was particularly probative of the witness's truthfulness).

Need for a particular item of evidence because there is no alternative means of proving a fact of consequence can also affect the FRE 403 decision. Courts have held that such need for evidence "should be weighed along with its probative value to determine whether it should be admitted under Rule 403 [but] need . . . does not make the evidence more likely to prove that which it is offered to prove." United States v. Stout, 509 F.3d 796, 800 (6th Cir. 2007). Thus, if unfair prejudice substantially outweighs the probative value of an item, the court may still exclude the item despite lack of other means of proof.

Alternatively, if there is already substantial evidence on the same point, there is less need for an additional item. Frank v. County of Hudson, 924 F. Supp. 620, 626 (D.N.J. 1996) (evidence of unrelated child sexual abuse by a defendant in a sexual harassment and discrimination case was excluded, although admissible under FRE 413-415, because four plaintiffs making similar accusations of defendant's workplace harassment "reduces the relative weight" of the proffered child abuse evidence); United States v. Bell, 516 F.3d 432, 445 (6th Cir. 2008) (quantity of illegal drugs possessed, along with drug scales, a cutting board and other drug paraphernalia, substantially reduced government's need for past drug distribution convictions to prove defendant's "intent" to distribute).

You can see that this fine-tuning of the Rule 403 factors requires that the judge be familiar with evidence that is already admitted, and that is expected to be admitted, at trial. The judge may also need to inquire about what other evidence is available to the parties. In United States v. Gonsalves, 668 F.2d 73, 75 (1st Cir. 1982), evidence of defendant's threat leveled against an eyewitness who would testify against him was admissible as showing consciousness of guilt despite the risk of unfair prejudice. The government's eyewitness identification evidence against defendant was strong, and defendant's alibi evidence was equally strong; the appellate court affirmed in part because the government had no other means to corroborate its eyewitnesses and its need was "substantial." If the judge is not able to make this contextual judgment at the time a Rule 403 objection is made, the judge can defer decision until later in the trial when more evidentiary context has been provided, using the technique of conditional admissibility that will be discussed in Chapter Four, Section E.

b. Rule 403 Dangers

The second step in resolving a Rule 403 objection is for the judge to estimate the danger that the item of evidence poses to the jury's rational decisionmaking process and to the judicial system's interest in efficient decisionmaking. FRE 403 identifies two types of dangers. One type involves major sources of risk of error in the jury's reasoning process. Evidence that is unfairly prejudicial or confusing or that will mislead the jury can be excluded. The other type involves dangers to trial efficiency. If the production of evidence will cause undue delay, is a waste of time, or is needlessly cumulative, it may be excluded. Whatever the kind of danger, the judge will attempt to make a realistic estimate of the danger posed. This will include the *nature of the danger, the likelihood that the jury will be negatively affected, and the probable degree of the harmful effect.* And if a single item of evidence raises more than one of these probative dangers, this may significantly increase the probable degree of harm.

Unfair Prejudice.   The term *unfair prejudice* refers to the danger that evidence might suggest an improper basis upon which the jury could decide the case. Evidence is *not* unfairly prejudicial simply because it is detrimental to a party's case.

> If all evidence adverse to a defendant was subject to exclusion under F.R.E. Rule 403, then no government evidence would ever be deemed admissible. The test . . . is not whether the evidence is detrimental, but whether it is so unfairly prejudicial as to substantially outweigh its probative value. [United States v. Weinstock, 153 F.3d 272, 278 (6th Cir. 1998).]

There are two principal risks of unfair prejudice within the scope of FRE 403. The first risk is that evidence about a party can trigger a response that has nothing to do with its logical connection to a fact of consequence. This response can turn the jury against that party (or in favor of that party) and improperly influence the jury's decisionmaking. The Advisory Committee Note to FRE 403 suggests that this improper reaction is "commonly, though not necessarily, an emotional one." Wigmore describes the danger as occurring when evidence would "be likely to stimulate an excessive emotion or to awaken a fixed prejudice . . . and thus dominate the mind of the tribunal and prevent a rational determination of the truth." John Henry Wigmore, Code of Evidence 355 (3d ed. 1942).

For example, recall the testimony of defendant James Johnson concerning Officer Walker's attack on another inmate, discussed on page 152, supra. Walker's attack might trigger a response of anger or disgust that prejudices the jury against Walker. There is a risk that this prejudice could influence the outcome in the *Johnson* case in an unfair way, such as the jury viewing a verdict in favor of Johnson as a punishment of Walker. If a Rule 403 objection is made, the trial judge would have to estimate this danger of unfair prejudice by identifying the nature of the danger and its likely effect. United States v. Bell, 516 F.3d 432, 445 (6th Cir. 2008) ("evidence of Bell's prior crimes painted a picture of Bell as a repeat drug offender, greatly increasing the chance that the jury would punish him not for his involvement in the offense at issue, but rather because he appeared to be a 'bad guy' "). Evidence that could generate undue sympathy for a party can also be excluded as unfairly prejudicial. Lewis v. City of Chicago Police Dept., 590 F.3d 427, 440 (7th Cir. 2009) (evidence that plaintiff suffered a broken neck when accidentally hit on the head during a forced house entry was excluded as highly inflammatory in the context of her employment claim of retaliation).

The second principal risk of unfair prejudice is if evidence admitted for a proper purpose could also be used by the jury in a manner that is prohibited by another evidence rule. For example, Officer Walker's attack on the other inmate triggers the permissible inference that defendant Johnson feared Walker. It also triggers an impermissible inference about Officer Walker's propensity to use violence against inmates in general, and thus to use violence against Johnson. This is impermissible under FRE 404(b), which prohibits the use of prior specific acts, such as Walker's attack, to prove action in conformity with character, as we will see in Chapter Five. The risk that the jury will use Johnson's testimony for this improper purpose qualifies as a danger of unfair prejudice under FRE 403. Johnson's testimony thus has a proper relevant use—to prove that he feared Walker—as well as an improper use—to prove

Walker's violent character. If the prosecution objects to Johnson's testimony, FRE 403 requires the judge to balance the testimony's permissible probative value against the danger that it will be used improperly. In Smith v. City of Oakland, 538 F. Supp. 2d 1217 (N.D. Cal. 2008), plaintiff sued two Oakland police officers for violating his constitutional rights by planting a semi-automatic rifle in his residence in order to frame him. The officers sought to cross-examine Smith about his being a candidate for "three-strikes" penalty in California if he possessed the rifle, thus giving him a powerful motive to lie. The court ruled under FRE 403:

> Mr. Smith already possessed a strong motive to lie . . . because his parole was subject to revocation for illegal possession of the gun. Moreover, any probative value to the three strikes evidence was substantially outweighed by the danger of unfair prejudice. Strikes are given for serious felonies only, and thus there was a significant risk that the jury would infer that Mr. Smith was a violent offender and improperly consider the evidence as character evidence.

When assessing unfair prejudice, courts take into account whether a jury instruction explaining the permissible and impermissible uses of evidence is likely to be effective. FRE 105. We discuss FRE 105 in more detail below.

Confusion of the Issues.   Evidence confuses the issues when it focuses the jury's attention too closely on a factual issue that is not central to the outcome of the case. Such issues are termed "collateral," which usually means that their connection to the essential elements is trivial and may be based on complicated or attenuated theories of relevance. Typically, then, proof of collateral issues will require the use of multiple witnesses or will consume considerable time in court. If the jury gets involved and interested in deciding a collateral issue, it will spend less of its attention on the important questions. It is not that these collateral issues are irrelevant; rather, they are too distracting and tend to *confuse the issues*. For example, evidence of several other incidents of violence against inmates at Pelican Bay, offered by the defense to show that defendant Johnson was justified in being fearful of prison guards, would require testimony from several witnesses, and might be hotly disputed by the prosecution. The jury might confuse the issues and focus its attention on whether those other incidents occurred, instead of on whether Johnson committed the alleged acts of battery. Halvorsen v. Baird, 146 F.3d 680 (9th Cir. 1998) (evidence from six witnesses that each had been involuntarily detained in a detoxification center when they were not drunk was not permitted to bolster plaintiff's case that he had been treated similarly; risk of confusing jury by involving it in a dispute over whether these six individuals were drunk or not).

Another risk of confusion in the *Johnson* case would be that the evidence of additional violent incidents might cause the jury to focus on an issue that is not a question that the jury is being asked to decide in the lawsuit—such as the prison's policy toward inmates at Pelican Bay. In contrast, in United States v. Crosby, 75 F.3d 1343, 1348 (9th Cir. 1996), the court held that the trial court erred in excluding as "confusing" evidence that the victim's own husband may have committed the assault for which the defendant was on trial. This evidence was not confusing, the appellate court said, because it "added no new issues to the case, as it dovetailed neatly with defendant's theory that someone else had committed the crime."

Misleading the Jury.   Courts often refer to evidence as both "confusing and mis-leading" and make no effort to distinguish between the two dangers. The danger of being *misleading,* however, usually involves a risk that an item of evidence will cause the jury to draw a *mistaken* inference. In Jones v. Ford Motor Co., 320 F. Supp. 440 (E.D. Va. 2004), plaintiff alleged that a defect in the design of the Ford cruise control system caused her automobile to accelerate suddenly, resulting in her personal injuries. To prove that Ford was on notice of the defective condition, the plaintiff offered government reports from Canada and Japan about sudden acceleration problems with cruise control systems in General Motors cars. The district court excluded these reports under Rule 403 as potentially misleading, since the cruise control systems in Ford cars were not functionally similar and the jury could mistakenly equate them to the General Motors systems. Facts taken out of context or presented in a falsely suggestive manner can also trigger this danger.

Courts are usually not persuaded by the argument that a jury will be misled into giving evidence more weight than it deserves. Juries are assumed to possess reliable generalized knowledge and experience that allows them to evaluate most aspects of human affairs that are presented at trial. Occasionally, however, the risk of over-valuation can rise to the level of "misleading" the jury. For example, videotaped reenactments of accidents or other events have been called misleading because jurors may treat them as documentations of the actual event. Many courts reject a criminal defendant's lie detector evidence on the grounds that the jury may over-value polygraph results as an indicator of truthfulness because of their scientific nature. United States v. Call, 129 F.3d 1402, 1406 (10th Cir. 1997). But a court should not exclude such testimony simply on the theory that scientific techniques by their very nature overwhelm the jury. United States v. West, 962 F.2d 1243, 1248 (7th Cir. 1992) (error to exclude psychiatrist's testimony on the ground that it would mislead the jury with confusing psychiatric terminology—"there was nothing more technical or confusing about [the doctor's] testimony here than the psychiatric testimony in most cases"); In re Paoli R.R. Yard PCB Litigation, 35 F.3d 717, 746 (3d Cir. 1994) ("[t]here must be something about the particular scientific technique such as its posture of mythic infallibility that makes it especially overwhelming").

The use of complex statistics and probabilistic evidence, such as DNA identification evidence, epidemiological studies in toxic tort cases, and employer hiring practices in discrimination cases, is also challenging for the jury. Even experts do not agree about the proper calculation and interpretation of the probability of a DNA match in "cold hit" cases, where the match is the only evidence connecting a defendant to the charged crime. David H. Kaye, Rounding Up the Usual Suspects: A Legal and Logical Analysis of DNA Trawling Cases, 87 N.C. L. Rev. 425 (2009). Even where the probability data is empirically valid, there is still a risk that the translation of statistical probability into "real numbers" that the jury can understand may mislead or confuse the jury: "The apparent precision of statistical evidence often stands in marked contrast to the uncertainties of other testimony. . . . The danger is that such evidence will overshadow equally probative but admittedly unscientific and anecdotal nonstatistical evidence." The Evolving Role of Statistical Assessments as Evidence in the

Courts 150 (Report of the Panel on Statistical Assessments as Evidence in the Courts) (Stephen E. Fienberg, ed., 1989). "The danger . . . is that statistics on the frequency with which certain blood type combinations occur in a population will be understood by the jury to be a quantification of the likelihood that the defendant, who shares that unique combination of blood characteristics, is guilty." State v. Joon Kyu Kim, 398 N.W.2d 544, 548 (Minn. 1987).

Despite the risk of over-persuasion, the probative value of, and the need for, this kind of evidence is very high. State statutes provide for the use of blood testing and probability estimates in paternity cases, and many courts have approved the admission of probability testimony about DNA testing.

Undue Delay, Waste of Time, and Needless Cumulative Evidence.   Each of these dangers illustrates a different aspect of the same underlying problem: The introduction of evidence always absorbs court time, incurs expense by the opposing parties and by the state-run judicial system, and expends the attention of the jury. The dangers of delay and waste of time are easily quantifiable. For example, if a continuance is required for production of evidence or to transport the jury to view the scene of the crime, the trial will be delayed. And if a trial judge has imposed strict time limits on the length of trials, requests for extension of time to present rebuttal evidence are decided under the FRE 403 balancing test: "As a general rule, evidence may not be excluded solely to avoid delay. . . . Under Rule 403, the court should consider the probative value of the proffered evidence and balance it against the harm of delay." General Signal Corp. v. MCI Telecommunications Corp., 66 F.3d 1500, 1509-1510 (9th Cir. 1995). Courts have held that evidence may waste the jury's time if offered to prove stipulated, collateral, or background facts. And research does show that "the longer a trial goes, the more the jury forgets and the less accurate the decision becomes." Securities and Exchange Commission v. Koenig, 557 F.3d 736, 739 (7th Cir. 2009).

The danger underlying *needless presentation of cumulative evidence* is less quantifiable. It includes the expenditure of trial time on repetitive testimony, plus the risk of losing the attention of the jury. During the *Johnson* trial, Officer Smith described for the prosecution what happened between Officer Walker and defendant Johnson when Johnson's cell door was opened. Officers Huston, Van Berg, and Walker had already testified about this occurrence. Thus, the defense might have objected, in the terms of FRE 403, that Officer Smith's testimony was a needless presentation of cumulative evidence and should be excluded. Here the judge must assess the degree to which the testimony actually is repetitive. Obrey v. Johnson, 400 F.3d 691 (9th Cir. 2005) (in an action alleging a pattern of discriminatory promotion practices, testimony from three witnesses who would have testified to their own experiences of discrimination was not cumulative or repetitive as it tended to support the pattern or practice theory). Also, there may be reasons why repetition is needed—such as the centrality of the fact of consequence being proved, the degree to which that fact is in dispute, and the probative value of the corroboration itself. It is unlikely that Officer Smith's testimony would be considered "needless" in the *Johnson* case, since Johnson's behavior was the central focus of the dispute and each side offered several witnesses to the events. *Coles v. Jenkins*, 1998 WL 964506 (W.D. Va. 1998) (court denied motion in limine to prevent defendant's use of three experts to testify regarding the dangerousness of a state highway, since each expert had a slightly different area of expertise).

c. Probative Value Substantially Outweighed by One of the FRE 403 Dangers

The final step is for the trial judge to weigh the probative value of the offered item of evidence against the danger that this item poses under FRE 403. The rule states that the evidence should be excluded only when its probative value is "substantially outweighed by" one or more of the FRE 403 dangers. The rule does not provide further explanation of how to determine when a danger *substantially outweighs* probative value. The Rule does make clear, however, by its use of the term "substantially," that the balance is tilted heavily in favor of admission of the evidence.

The Meaning of "Substantially Outweigh."   There does not appear to be a scale—a common measure—with which to compare probative value versus the degree of risk that Rule 403 dangers pose to the jury's reasoning process. If that is so, *a fortiori* there is no means of calibrating which weighs more. There is no "quantum effect on rationality" that can be assigned to an item of evidence. One way that judges might think about the balancing test is to predict an overall effect of an item of evidence on the jury: What is the likelihood that the "bad" aspect of the evidence will seriously dominate the mind of the jury, overwhelming the "good" aspect? If the likelihood seems high, admission of such evidence may lead to "bad" factfinding as the incremental "badness" of the evidence exerts itself, and exclusion under FRE 403 would be justified.

We might ask, however, why evidence should ever be admitted if its "bad" aspect appears to dominate over the "good" to even a small degree? Would not such evidence always taint the jury's factfinding? The rule's requirement that probative value be outweighed "substantially" appears to require that some risks of negative impact be tolerated. This is sensible because the judge's ability to predict such effects is so imprecise.

Another way to think about the requirement of substantiality is that it measures the judge's confidence level: Evidence should be excluded only when the judge is quite confident that the prejudicial aspects of the evidence outweigh its probative value. The requirement can be thought of, in other words, as providing a burden of proof to be applied under FRE 403 to the admission of evidence. The burden in FRE 403 favors wrongful decisions to admit evidence over wrongful decisions to exclude it. This is in keeping with the strong belief of the drafters of the Federal Rules of Evidence that the underlying principles of the rules—truth and justice—will best be furthered when more rather than less evidence is deemed admissible.

In practice, how do judges conduct the balancing test of FRE 403? One commentator suggests the following table to show how Rule 403 would properly operate:

Probative value of offered relevant evidence	Negative effect of Rule 403 listed factor	Whether trial court may exclude evidence
High	High, Mid, or Low	No
Mid	High	No (Perhaps Yes)*
	Mid or Low	No
Low	High	Yes
	Mid	No (Perhaps Yes)*
	Low	No

(Newell Blakely, Article IV: Relevancy and Its Limits, 30 U. Hous. L. Rev. 281, 317 (1993).)

The Effect of Limiting Instructions on the Balancing Process.   The balancing of probative value versus a Rule 403 danger is also affected by FRE 105, which provides as follows:

> When evidence which is admissible as to one party or for one purpose but not admissible as to another party or for another purpose is admitted, the court, upon request, shall restrict the evidence to its proper scope and instruct the jury accordingly.

The Advisory Committee Note to FRE 403 states that "[i]n reaching a decision whether to exclude on grounds of unfair prejudice, consideration should be given to the probable effectiveness or lack of effectiveness of a limiting instruction."

This means that when an item of evidence has a proper relevant use to prove a fact of consequence but also creates the risk of an improper use—an impermissible inference or an unfairly prejudicial effect—the judge may give a limiting instruction that directs the jury to consider the evidence only for its proper use. In the example from the *Johnson* case, Johnson's testimony about Officer Walker's attack on another inmate could have been accompanied by a limiting instruction—that the jury was to consider this testimony only for its effect on Johnson's state of mind, and for no other purpose. If the judge believes that the jury will probably follow such an instruction, the judge may find that the risk of unfair prejudice is lowered and will admit the item. Other instructions can be given that could reduce the confusing or misleading risks of admitted evidence. The judge's belief that the jury can and will follow limiting instructions could decrease the judge's estimation of the risk of Rule 403 dangers.

It is not clear, however, that the jury can or will follow such an instruction. Social science researchers have attempted to investigate this issue. The findings from many empirical studies are summarized in Lieberman & Arndt, Understanding the Limits of Limiting Instructions, 6 Psychol. Pub. Poly. & L. 677 (2000). Some of this research

---

* If probative value were near the bottom of the "mid" range and the negative effect extremely high, or if probative value were extremely low and the negative effect near the top of the "mid" range, Rule 403 might allow exclusion.

has concluded that the giving of an instruction may serve to emphasize the inadmissible evidence or improper inference, which may be more damaging than simply letting the matter go unnoticed. Other studies show that jurors follow limiting instructions selectively, and should be more likely to follow them when the judge offers an explanation as to why jurors should ignore certain uses of the evidence. The most common explanation for the failure of jurors to follow limiting instructions is that jurors react negatively to limits on their ability to perform "free behaviors"—especially when they are instructed to ignore uses of evidence that appear to them highly relevant. However, a recent study found that limiting instructions given *prior to* exposure to gruesome crime photos produced a pro-defense bias in survey responses. The authors hypothesize that pre-exposure instructions "function as a forewarning about the potential for bias and allow for attempts to avoid or correct bias" whereas limiting instructions given at the close of trial arrive after evidence has been encoded and perhaps judged, "when jurors are impotent to remove the influence of emotions that have infused processing." Cush & Delahunty, The Influence of Limiting Instructions on Processing and Judgments of Emotionally Evocative Evidence, 13 Psych., Psychol. & Law 110, 120 (2006). Overall, the effectiveness of limiting instructions may be hindered by the jury's lack of understanding of the policy behind a rule of exclusion and the jury's lack of comprehension of the instruction itself. See Peter Meijes Tiersma, Reforming the Language of Jury Instructions, 22 Hofstra L. Rev. 37 (1993). Lieberman & Arndt propose a number of strategies for mitigating the problem of ineffectiveness, including judicial instructions that "soft sell" the limits on the jury and emphasize issues of procedural fairness. 6 Psychol. Pub. Poly. & L. at 704-705 (2000).

As a general rule, however, courts assume that instructions do effectively exclude improper evidence from the jury's consideration. The U.S. Supreme Court has offered the following rationale:

> The rule that juries are presumed to follow their instructions is a pragmatic one, rooted less in the absolute certitude that the presumption is true than in the belief that it represents a reasonable, practical accommodation of the interests of the state and the defendant in the criminal justice process. [Richardson v. Marsh, 481 U.S. 200, 211 (1987).]

And an experienced trial judge supports the giving of limiting instructions:

> While the videos might be used by the jury improperly, a limiting instruction to the jury, here given repeatedly, specifying the purpose for which they can use the videos is sufficient to ensure that there will be no unfair prejudice to the defendant. . . .
>
>   There is always some danger that the jury will ignore the court's instructions about the limited way in which evidence should be considered. Juries in the product liability cases tried in this court have been responsible. The "runaway jury" concern is not substantiated. [Gonzalez v. Digital Equipment Corp., 8 F. Supp. 2d 194, 198 (E.D.N.Y. 1998) (Weinstein, J.).]

Judicial reliance on the use of limiting instructions to resolve FRE 403 problems will be demonstrated throughout this book. United States v. Candelaria-Silva, 162 F.3d 698 (1st Cir. 1998) (evidence of defendant's flight admitted as evidence of guilt of the crime charged; danger that jury would give it undue weight was cured by court's instruction that flight may not always reflect feelings of guilt, that many innocent people flee, and that flight alone is insufficient to sustain a conviction). In some circumstances, however, courts recognize that limiting instructions are not a "sure-fire panacea for the prejudice resulting from the needless admission of [prejudicial] evidence." United States v. Haywood, 280 F.3d 715, 724 (6th Cir. 2002). In United States v. Garcia-Rosa, 876 F.2d 209, 222 (1st Cir. 1989), the court held that the prejudicial effect of the evidence was so severe that it could not "be remedied merely through a limiting instruction . . . [and] [i]f limiting instructions could remedy all such errors, the government would easily be able to circumvent Rule . . . 403." And in Stockman v. Oakland Dental Center, 480 F.3d 791, 804 (6th Cir. 2007), the limiting instruction was not given until the jury charge, "making it all the more difficult to un-ring the bell . . . [and] opened Defendants' case to the full brunt of the injury."

Are limiting instructions the best resolution to Rule 403 problems? Some commentators urge that rather than reforming limiting instructions, they should be abolished, and that this will require trial judges to weigh probative value versus risk of unfair prejudice more carefully in making FRE 403 decisions.

3. FRE 403: Specific Problems and Applications

a. Gruesome Exhibits and Other Potentially Inflammatory Evidence

Numerous cases in federal court apply Rule 403 to the prosecution's use of photographs, videotapes, and other demonstrative evidence to portray the graphic effects of violent crime and accidents. The inflammatory nature of such exhibits calls for careful analysis of their probative value and limitations on their use.

In United States v. Yahweh, 792 F. Supp. 104 (S.D. Fla. 1992), the district judge admitted gruesome autopsy photographs from "arguably the most violent case ever tried in a federal court." The defendant objected to the use of these photographs, particularly in enlarged format, under FRE 403. To determine probative value, the judge carefully reviewed the relevance of each of the photographs and noted that the enlarged size was necessary to furnish the detail that corroborated witnesses' description of events prior to death. The judge required the medical examiners to select those photographs that illustrated their testimony and to explain the need for each photograph on the basis of content and size. In addition, the judge found that the display of the enlarged photographs enabled all jurors simultaneously to follow the witnesses' testimony. The judge also brought his own background knowledge and experience out into the open:

> For twenty years, this court has stood by the jury box to observe as witnesses testified in front of the jury box concerning exhibits being published to the jury there. In this court's view, the larger 30" × 40" pictures were the right size to illustrate and clarify the witness' testimony; in fact, even the 16" × 20" size was inadequately small by comparison. [Id. at 108.]

On the issue of unfair prejudice, the judge determined that the blown-up photos did not distort the nature of the wounds, acknowledged the grisly nature of the pictures, and ordered that the most offensive ones be reduced in size to 16" × 20" for use in jury deliberations. The photographs were not, in the judge's opinion, flagrantly or deliberately gruesome depictions of the crime. The judge also "carefully observed the jurors and their reactions to the photos. . . . [T]he jurors showed no signs of being disturbed by the exhibits." Id. at 168. Finally, the judge commented on the nature of unfair prejudice cognizable under FRE 403:

> Relevant evidence is inherently prejudicial; but it is only unfair prejudice, substantially outweighing probative value, which permits exclusion of relevant matter under Rule 403. Unless trials are to be conducted on scenarios, on unreal facts tailored and sanitized for the occasion, the application of Rule 403 must be cautious and sparing. . . . It is not designed to permit the court to "even out" the weight of evidence, to mitigate a crime. . . . [Id. at 106.]

Appellate courts are also likely to defer to the conscientious efforts of trial judges to limit the amount and impact of potentially prejudicial evidence. In a case involving the leaking of confidential government information about ongoing criminal investigations for purposes of "short-selling" in the securities market, testimony was given that some of the leaked information concerned one of the defendant's possible involvement in the attacks on September 11, 2001. That defendant objected under FRE 403. The appellate court held:

> The record thus demonstrates that, far from abusing its discretion, the district court engaged in precisely the sort of "conscientious assessment" that our precedents require . . . . It carefully weighed the probative value of the 9/11-related evidence the Government wished to offer, excluded that evidence that was more potentially prejudicial than probative (such as references to Al Qaeda), issued limiting instructions to the jury on several occasions [to the effect that the defendant was not involved in terrorism or the events of 9/11], and continued to keep tight control over the introduction of such evidence even after [a different] defendant's testimony explicitly addressed the topic of 9/11. [United States v. Royer, 549 F.3d 886, 903 (2d Cir. 2008.]

In capital punishment cases, statements from victims and victims' families about the effect of the defendant's conduct are admitted in the sentencing phase of trial, after guilt has been determined. But in the prosecution of Timothy McVeigh for the 1998 bombing of the federal building in Oklahoma City, statements from victims about the horrific injuries they and others suffered were admitted during the guilt phase of trial. The appellate court acknowledged that "[t]he description of the destruction and carnage following the explosion is the most emotionally powerful of the evidence presented during the guilt phase." United States v. McVeigh, 153 F.3d 1166, 1202-1203 (10th Cir. 1998). Proof of how the crime occurred was, however, held to be probative of the elements of the crimes charged—use of a weapon of mass destruction and a malicious intent to kill. Id. Testimony concerning long-term effects of the bombing, however, such as loss of jobs, attendance at funerals, and the lasting emotional trauma of severe injury, were found to be "not particularly relevant" to the guilt phase and to have emotional content. Any error in the admission of such testimony was, however, held to be harmless. Id. at 1203-1204.

b. Spoliation

There are many cases involving various ways in which parties, and sometimes their lawyers, attempt to destroy, alter, or suppress evidence that is adverse to their position in a lawsuit. Instances of such "spoliation" take many forms—subornation of perjury, threats to and intimidation of witnesses, solicitation of murder of a witness, and alteration or destruction of documents. Evidence of spoliation conduct is generally admissible against the spoliator—giving rise to an inference that evidence was unfavorable to the spoliator's position or to an inference of the party's general consciousness of guilt or liability. See generally Kathleen Kedigh, Spoliation: To the Careless Go the Spoils, 67 U. Mo. (K.C.) L. Rev. 597 (1999) (describing the standards of proof of spoliation and the other remedies available, including discovery sanctions, exclusion of the spoliator's evidence, and a separate tort claim against the spoliator).

For our purposes, evidence of spoliation offered at trial raises recurring questions of relevance and of unfair prejudice under Rule 403. In a civil case involving circumstantial proof that the plaintiff attempted to suborn favorable perjured testimony from a witness, the Third Circuit stated the relevance theory as follows, citing analysis from Wigmore's treatise, existing case law, and the text of FRE 401 itself:

> One who believes his own case to be weak is more likely to suborn perjury than one who thinks he has a strong case, and a party knows better than anyone else the truth about his own case. Thus, subornation of perjury by a party is strong evidence that the party's case is weak. Admittedly the conclusion is not inescapable: Parties may be mistaken about the merits or force of their own cases. But evidence need not lead inescapably towards a single conclusion to be relevant. . . . The evidence of subornation here does cast into doubt the merits of [plaintiff's] claim, even if it does not extinguish them. [McQueeney v. Wilmington Trust Co., 779 F.2d 916, 921 (3d Cir. 1985).]

Spoliation behavior is usually illegal and may involve threats of violence or worse. Thus, evidence of such behavior raises a risk of unfair prejudice, in the sense of generating an emotional response against the party as a "bad person," under Rule 403. The court in *McQueeney* reversed the trial court's decision to exclude evidence of the plaintiff's alleged attempt to suborn perjury with the following analysis of its probative value and potential for unfair prejudice:

> Intuition and the unanimity of the commentators and numerous courts that have considered it suggest not only that subornation of perjury is relevant but that it is powerful evidence indeed. . . . The court did not articulate any reasons for its finding of prejudice, and this does not appear to us to be the kind of evidence with obvious or overwhelming potential for unfair prejudice. In the absence of a showing of particularized danger of unfair prejudice, the evidence must be admitted. Were we to rule otherwise, evidence could be excluded on an unfounded fear of prejudice and we would effectively preclude all evidence of subornation of perjury. [Id. at 922-923.]

Consider whether in *McQueeney* the Third Circuit has, in effect, created a precedential ruling of law on the strong probative value and general lack of unfair prejudicial effect of spoliation evidence. We return to the topic of appellate rulings on Rule 403 questions on pages 169-71, infra.

c. Curative Admissibility

The doctrine of curative admissibility permits a party to introduce normally inadmissible evidence in order to respond to specific evidence that the opponent has introduced previously. It is related to FRE 403 in that this evidence is *needed* to respond effectively to the opponent's prior submission. The broadest statement of the curative admissibility doctrine is as follows:

> The rule of "opening the door," or "curative admissibility," gives the trial court discretion to permit a party to introduce otherwise inadmissible evidence on an issue (a) when the opposing party has introduced inadmissible evidence on the same issue, and (b) when it is needed to rebut a false impression that may have resulted from the opposing party's evidence . . . . When a defendant offers an innocent explanation he "opens the door" to questioning into the truth of his testimony, and the government is entitled to attack his credibility on cross-examination. A defendant has no right to avoid cross-examination into the truth of his direct examination, even as to matters not related to the merits of the charges against him. [United States v. Elfgeeh, 515 F.3d 100, 128 (2d Cir. 2008).]

As you can see, the doctrine permits the court to waive an opponent's evidentiary objections in order to prevent the opponent from gaining an unfair advantage.

In *Elfgeeh*, defendants were charged with operating an illegal money-transmitting business. There was evidence that some of the funds, transmitted by defendants from New York to Yemen, were being paid to groups involved in "tribal wars, blood feuds and violence" within Yemen. The trial court ruled this evidence inadmissible under FRE 403 but held that if the defendants themselves testified that they merely transmitted money to help Yemeni immigrants send money home to their family and friends, "it would open the door to allow the government to attempt to show that the [defendants] sent money instead for bellicose purposes." Id. at 128. When the defendants made three separate statements that their money transmittals were to families of their clients, the government was allowed to ask a defendant "whether he knew that the money he sent was being used to buy arms and ammunition and was allowed to submit documentary evidence obliquely referring to such use . . . in order to attack [the defendant's] credibility." Id.

Most, but not all, jurisdictions recognize some version of the curative admissibility doctrine, although there is no Federal Rule of Evidence dealing with the subject. Byrd v. Maricopa County Sheriff's Dept., 565 F.3d 1205 (9th Cir. 2009) (plaintiff's videotape initially excluded under FRE 403 later admitted under doctrine of curative admissibility after defense counsel mentioned the tape and suggested it had been edited or destroyed); Henderson v. George Washington University, 449 F.3d 127, 139 (4th Cir. 2006) (in a malpractice case, plaintiff's evidence of a report of a similar procedure on another patient excluded under FRE 403 as confusing to the jury, but admitted under the curative admissibility doctrine when the defense relied on the exclusion of the report in cross-examining the plaintiff's expert, using the court's ruling "not only to shield themselves from potentially damaging evidence, but also . . . as a sword to slice through the foundation" of plaintiff's case).

KEY POINTS

1. An objection made under FRE 403 to an item of evidence requires the trial judge to determine whether admission of the evidence creates any Rule 403 danger to the jury's decision-making process and, if so, whether this danger will substantially outweigh the probative value of the evidence.

2. Probative value refers to the strength of the evidence in proving an essential element in the case. This is determined primarily by the judge's estimate of the strength of the generalizations connecting the evidence to the disputed issue and by the proponent's need for the evidence.
3. The judge estimates the risk of harm from evidence that bears a Rule 403 danger by predicting the nature of the jury's reaction to the evidence, the degree of that reaction, and the likelihood that the harmful reaction will occur.
4. Because FRE 403's balancing test requires the danger to *substantially* outweigh the probative value, even a very significant risk of danger may not result in exclusion if there are no alternative or less dangerous means of proving the fact of consequence. The court will also use a limiting instruction to reduce the danger in order to admit the evidence.

PROBLEMS

3.6. Return to Problem 3.1, State v. Johnson, at page 148. Does the question posed to Officer Huston in (a) present any of the Rule 403 dangers? How would you rule on an FRE 403 objection?

3.7. Return to Problem 3.2, Pedroso v. Driver, at page 148. Does evidence of Driver's testimony in (a) present any of the Rule 403 dangers? How would you rule on an FRE 403 objection?

3.8. In Problem 3.2, what if the plaintiffs request that the jury be taken to the scene of the accident in order to view Cedar Street and the gravel shoulder? What arguments could be made in support of and in opposition to this request under FRE 401 and 403?

3.9. Return to Problem 3.3, United States v. Ray, at page 149. The prosecution offers the following evidence:
   (a) In October 2013, Ray sold 25,000 shares of Rundown stock one week before a major and abrupt fall in Rundown's share price.
   (b) In May 2014, Ray purchased 30,000 shares of Rundown 30 days before the company announced the profitable acquisition of a competitor, an event which caused the stock price to rise by 25 percent.
   Will the defense prevail if it objects to this evidence under FRE 403?

3.10. K and G were indicted for arson in the burning of a diner that they owned in Great Neck, New York. The report of the Fire Marshal's Office concludes that the diner fire had been intentionally set. The prosecution will prove that K and G owned two diners; that their diner in Westbury, Connecticut, operated at a profit; and that the diner in Great Neck sustained serious losses for several years. The prosecutor wants to introduce the following evidence: the fact that K and G had not paid property taxes on the Great Neck diner for several years; the fact that tax liens had been recorded against the diner; testimony from a cook at the Westbury diner that K and G asked him whether he knew anyone who would be willing to "start a fire." Are these items admissible? Are they sufficient to send the case to the jury? What if K and G testify that they were about to make a profitable sale of the Great Neck diner?

3.11. Carl Smith was arrested at Washington National Airport when the X-ray machine disclosed a suspicious metallic object in the paper bag he was carrying. This object was a loaded Beretta pistol wrapped in red cloth and a pair of pants. Smith was charged with attempting to board an aircraft with a concealed weapon. Smith claimed that the pistol was planted in his shopping bag by someone else at the airport and that he did not intend to board an airplane because he had no ticket and no luggage.

To support its claim that Smith was in knowing possession of the gun, the prosecution offered evidence of Smith's Jamaican citizenship, his possession of $450 in cash, and the presence of marijuana residue in his pants pocket. These facts, it claimed, showed that Smith met the "drug courier" profile, an informally compiled abstract of characteristics thought typical of persons carrying illicit drugs, used to argue reasonable suspicion in support of drug trafficking stops; further, it argued, drug couriers frequently carry guns for protection. Should the district court admit this evidence and permit an FBI agent to testify as an expert about the drug courier profile and its relevance to the crime charged?

3.12. Cynthia Richards allegedly slipped and fell on a Halloween costume in the "seasonal" area of a Kmart store. She claims that Kmart was negligent in failing to adequately maintain its store by not locating and picking up the costume before the accident. Kmart denies negligence, contending that its policy and practices of maintaining the store were reasonable.

During discovery, a Kmart supervisor testified that the store had no particular schedule for patrolling the store for cleanup, but that all employees were trained to pick up clutter promptly and that this policy is stated in the Handbook given to all employees. Ken Ceasar, a Kmart customer service employee on duty the night of Richards's fall, testified that he was in charge of watching the whole floor, that he had no knowledge that the costume was in the aisle, that he always walked the aisles and picked up items that were not supposed to be on the floor "as soon as he discovered them." Ceasar also stated that he had no particular memory of his own actions on the night in question.

Kmart has filed a motion in limine to exclude a videotape made secretly in the store by an investigator for Richards. The videotape was made one year after the incident, during Halloween season. It is a genuine video, and has not been altered or edited in any way. It shows merchandise on two unidentified store aisles that had fallen to the floor, and it shows Mr. Ceasar ignoring the merchandise and stepping on it, rather than promptly removing it. Prepare arguments for Kmart and for Richards on this motion in limine.

3.13. Denise McCallum is charged with armed robbery for holding up a convenience store at gunpoint. The police found a .38 caliber, "snub-nosed" revolver in a trash can a block away from the convenience store, and the store clerk told police that the robber's gun "looked just like that one." Consider arguments for and against an FRE 403 objection to the following evidence offered by the prosecutor at trial:

(a) Testimony of McCallum's roommate that two months before the robbery, she saw a snub-nosed .38 caliber revolver in McCallum's bedroom.

(b) Evidence that McCallum was unemployed for six months before the robbery.

In response to (a) above, consider arguments for and against an FRE 403 objection to the following evidence offered by the defense:

(c) Official statistics report that there are known to be at least 25,000 such handguns in the possession of individuals in the city.

4.   Appellate Review of Judicial Discretion Under FRE 403

Application of FRE 403 calls for the exercise of judicial discretion, meaning that the judge applies criteria and standards that are not mechanical but require the use of *judgment*. The trial court makes judgments that estimate the probability of inferences; that evaluate the nature, likelihood, and degree of dangers to jury decisionmaking; and that compare probative value to those dangers. On appeal, these judgments are reviewed under the abuse of discretion standard, which is a very deferential standard of appellate review. It means that appellate courts will tolerate trial court decisions that the appellate judges would not have made themselves. Reversal is justified only when the trial court "abuses" its discretion:

> Had any one of us been in a position to exercise the discretion committed to a trial judge . . . we would have no hesitancy in stating that the decision would have been otherwise; but as appellate judges we cannot find that the action of the district judge was so unreasonable and so arbitrary as to amount to a prejudicial abuse of the discretion necessary to repose in trial judges during the conduct of a trial. [Napolitano v. Compania Sud Americana De Vapores, 421 F.2d 382, 384 (2d Cir. 1970).]

There are many reasons why appellate courts defer to the trial courts' judgments under FRE 403. Here are some of them:

(1) *Complexity and Uncertainty.* The Rule 403 balancing test requires complex fact-based judgments unique to each case. Judgments about probative value and the Rule 403 dangers are at best, as we have just discussed above, rough estimates and predictions of effect on the jury's decisionmaking. The estimates that are made in one case may have little bearing in the next. The ultimate standard of "substantially outweighs" also requires balancing where there is no calibration for the weighing process, and the standard is such that precision is not called for. What is "substantial" can vary greatly among judges: "[T]he district court is engaged in a 'comparison of intangibles' and is thus 'afforded a special degree of deference.' " Estate of Moreland v. Dieter, 395 F.3d 747, 755 (7th Cir. 2005).

(2) *Competence.* The trial judge has more experience than appellate judges with making judgments of this kind. The trial judge is also closer to the evidence in the particular case, meaning that the judge has watched its presentation in the context of the entire trial and has observed its effect on the particular jury: "Only in an extreme case are appellate judges competent to second-guess the judgment of the person on the spot, the trial judge." Id.

(3) *Tolerance for Outcomes That Appear Inconsistent.* Under an abuse of discretion standard of review, appellate courts will affirm trial court outcomes that may appear to be inconsistent, even in cases that appear to be similar to the appellate court. That is what it means for the appellate court to "defer" to the trial court's judgment, even when it (or another trial court) might have decided the Rule 403 question differently. Largely because of the factors of competence, complexity, and uncertainty, appellate courts may not be able to know whether outcomes actually are inconsistent, and probably could not create sufficiently detailed precedent necessary to achieve uniform and consistent outcomes among trial courts. The contextual facts of Rule 403 decisions affect the weighing process too greatly.[5] The abuse of discretion standard of review is an acknowledgment of the limits of the knowledge of an outside reviewer.

Most appellate decisions affirm district courts' FRE 403 decisions, whether they admit or exclude the disputed evidence. The standard of review for abuse of discretion is often defined somewhat differently by the Circuit Courts of Appeal. Here is a clear statement of the applicable principles: "Under this standard, we will leave rulings about admissibility of evidence undisturbed unless we are 'left with the definite and firm conviction that the [district] court . . . committed a clear error of judgment in the conclusion it reached upon a weighing of the relevant factors or where it improperly applies the law or uses an erroneous legal standard.' " United States v. Lucas, 357 F.3d 599, 608 (6th Cir. 2004). Thus, there are some errors in applying Rule 403 that appellate courts will hold to be errors of law, such as not giving the terms of the rule their legally correct meaning, Blake v. Pellegrino, 329 F.3d 43, 45 (1st Cir. 2003) ("When . . . the admission or exclusion of evidence involves a question of law, such as the proper interpretation of a provision contained in the Federal Rules . . . , we afford de novo review"), or violating a criminal defendant's constitutional right to put on witnesses in his defense, United States v. Turning Bear, 357 F.3d 730, 734 (8th Cir. 2004) (improper exclusion of opinion testimony about a witness's credibility under Rule 403 held to violate the defendant's Fifth and Sixth Amendment rights to present witnesses in his defense).

Some balancing decisions are held to be abuses of discretion when the results are "clear errors of judgment," plainly against the logic and effect of the facts in the case. McQueeney v. Wilmington Trust Co., 779 F.2d 916 (3d Cir. 1985) (discussed at page 165, supra). And appellate courts also try to ensure that district courts will engage in the full consideration of all the Rule 403 factors. See, e.g., Securities and Exchange Commission v. Peters, 978 F.2d 1162, 1172 (10th Cir. 1992) (failure to consider adequately the possibility of a limiting instruction, contrary to suggestion in the Advisory Committee Note to FRE 403, is considered to be significant in finding abuse of discretion); United States v. McCallum, 584 F.3d 471, 477 (2d Cir. 2009)

---

5. In countering the prosecution's argument that one of its prior opinions conclusively established how a Rule 403 balancing should come out, the Ninth Circuit replied:

> [The prior opinion] doesn't help the government because it did not purport to set a minimum level for probative value under Rule 403. Nor could it, as probative value must be weighed against offsetting factors, such as delay, which differ in every case. Moreover, probative value itself can only be determined in light of the evidence and arguments of a particular case. [United States v. Crosby, 75 F.3d 1343, 1348 (9th Cir. 1996).]

(the district court gave no explanation for its conclusion under FRE 403; the appellate court held that "[w]ithout the benefit of its reasoning we are in no position to assume that the court appreciated the seriousness of the risk that introducing the convictions would undermine the fairness of the trial.").

Sometimes appellate review of FRE 403 decisions does create precedent for district courts to follow. Consider the *McQueeney* case discussed at page 165, supra. The two appellate opinions presented below will give you practice in evaluating probative value and FRE 403 dangers yourself, and in applying the rule's balancing test. You should ask yourself why the appellate court found an abuse of discretion, and whether its decision will have precedential effect.

UNITED STATES v. HITT

981 F.2d 422 (9th Cir. 1992)

KOZINSKI, Circuit Judge.

Dale Lee Hitt was convicted of possessing an unregistered machine gun in violation of 26 U.S.C. §5861(d). The government alleged he had altered a semiautomatic rifle so it would discharge more than one shot per trigger pull—the defining characteristic of a machine gun. 26 U.S.C. §5845(b). The rifle had indeed been modified in a way consistent with the government's theory, though Hitt's lawyer suggested it had been modified by its previous owner. Some internal parts usable for machine guns (but not themselves illegal) were found in a gun case in Hitt's room, but Hitt's lawyer suggested they too might have come from the rifle's previous owner.

The key question, though, was whether the rifle would in fact rapid-fire. The government and Hitt each had their own experts test-fire it: In the government's test, the rifle did fire more than one shot per trigger pull, but when Hitt's expert (witnessed by two police officers) tested it, it didn't. Hitt's expert suggested the gun may have fired automatically in the government's test because of a malfunction, perhaps because the internal parts were dirty, worn or defective. In response, the government introduced a photograph of the rifle which, it argued, showed the rifle was neither dirty, worn nor defective.

Unfortunately, the photograph showed nothing of the gun's interior. All the jury could see was the outside, and not very well at that, as the gun occupied only a small part of the 4" × 6" photograph. The rest was taken up by about a dozen other weapons—nine other guns, including three that looked like assault rifles, and several knives—all belonging to Hitt's housemate. Hitt objected to admission of the photograph under Fed. R. Evid. 403, but the district court overruled his objection.

I

A. Under Fed. R. Evid. 402, "[a]ll relevant evidence is admissible," except as otherwise provided. We let jurors see and hear even marginally relevant evidence, because we trust them to weigh the evidence appropriately. Nonetheless, when the probative value of the evidence is "substantially outweighed by the danger of unfair prejudice. . .or misleading the jury," Fed. R. Evid. 403, the evidence must be kept out.

B. The photograph's probative value was exceedingly small. The defense theory was that the gun fired as an automatic because the *internal* parts were dirty, worn or defective. The prosecution understood this too: When the prosecutor cross-examined the defendant's expert, he asked whether there was "exceptional dirt *in*" the rifle, and whether there were "worn or dirty parts *in* that machine."

But the gun's external appearance reveals nothing at all about its internal state. Firearms are designed so the internal parts suffer most of the strain from the discharge. Wear, dirt and defects that affect the internal mechanism generally have no effect on the firearm's appearance; it's not uncommon for a gun that looks clean and in working order to misfire because of dirt or defects inside. Here there was absolutely no indication that the type of wear, dirt or defect Hitt's expert was talking about could be seen by inspecting the outside of the gun.

Moreover, even if the rifle's inside condition were somehow related to its outside appearance, it's virtually impossible to tell whether the gun is clean or dirty from the photograph, in which the rifle is seen from several feet away. The photograph might well have been excludible under Rule 402 as totally irrelevant, had a Rule 402 objection been made.

C. At the same time, the photograph was fraught with the twin dangers of unfairly prejudicing the defendant and misleading the jury. It showed a dozen nasty-looking weapons, which the jury must have assumed belonged to Hitt. The photograph looked like it was taken at Hitt's residence: The guns were laid out in an obviously residential room; the jury knew Hitt was arrested at home, the photograph was talked about in the same breath as two others identified at trial as having been taken in Hitt's bedroom. Moreover, there was no one else the jury could have suspected of owning the guns. Hitt's roommate, who in fact owned all the other weapons, wasn't even mentioned during Hitt's trial. Inferring that all the weapons were Hitt's wasn't just a plausible inference; it was the only plausible inference.

Once the jury was misled into thinking all the weapons were Hitt's, they might well have concluded Hitt was the sort of person who'd illegally own a machine gun, or was so dangerous he should be locked up regardless of whether or not he committed this offense. Rightly or wrongly, many people view weapons, especially guns, with fear and distrust. Like evidence of homosexuality, see, e.g., United States v. Gillespie, 852 F.2d 475, 478 (9th Cir. 1988); Cohn v. Papke, 655 F.2d 191, 194 (9th Cir. 1981), or of past crimes, see, e.g., United States v. Bland, 908 F.2d 471, 473 (9th Cir. 1990), photographs of firearms often have a visceral impact that far exceeds their probative value. See, e.g., United States v. Green, 648 F.2d 587, 595 (9th Cir. 1981) (per curiam). The prejudice is even greater when the picture is not of one gun but of many.

But the photograph could do more than arouse irrational fears and prejudices. It could also lead the jury to draw some perfectly logical—though mistaken—inferences. Hitt's main defense was that he had the bad luck of owning a rifle that was defective or dirty, or perhaps had been modified by its previous owner. A jury that thought Hitt owned almost a dozen guns could very reasonably have viewed this argument with skepticism. The jurors could have inferred that a gun enthusiast like Hitt would be able to tell if the gun had been modified by someone else, or be able to make the modifications himself. Or they could have thought that someone that interested in guns would naturally keep them clean and in good working order. Of course, the jury shouldn't have drawn these inferences, because none of the other guns were Hitt's. Yet the inferences were entirely plausible once the jury concluded Hitt owned the whole arsenal.

D. The district judge has wide latitude in making Rule 403 decisions. But this latitude isn't unlimited. Where the evidence is of very slight (if any) probative value, it's an abuse of discretion to admit it if there's even a modest likelihood of unfair prejudice or a small risk of misleading the jury.

The evidence here was not only highly prejudicial and at most marginally probative—it was also misleading. It's bad enough for the jury to be unduly swayed by something a defendant did; it's totally unacceptable for it to be prejudiced by something he seems to have done but in fact did not. Admitting the photograph, with nothing at all to keep the jury from being misled—no limiting instruction, no redaction—violated Rule 403.

II

Having determined there was error, we must next decide whether it was harmless. There is a conflict in our circuit about the standard of review for harmless error. Some cases require that we affirm only if we can say with "fair assurance" that the error was harmless. This standard seems to have the Supreme Court's blessing. See Kotteakos v. United States, 328 U.S. 750, 764-65, 90 L. Ed. 1557, 66 S. Ct. 1239 (1946). Other Ninth Circuit cases compel affirmation if it is "more probable than not" that the error was harmless. See, e.g., United States v. Lui, 941 F.2d 844, 848 (9th Cir. 1991). . . .[6]

We needn't resolve this conflict here, though, because the error wasn't harmless under either standard. This was a close case: An expert on one side claimed the gun fired more than one shot per trigger pull; an expert on the other (corroborated by two police officers) said it didn't. The photograph may well have made the difference between acquittal and conviction. We can't say it was more probable than not that Hitt would have been convicted without the photograph. A *fortiori*, then, we can't say with "fair assurance" that he would have been convicted without it.

NOTES AND QUESTIONS

1. Judge Kozinski's opinion in *Hitt* relies on several generalizations to estimate probative value and the danger of unfair prejudice. What are they? How does Judge Kozinski know they are valid? Were they the subject of proof at trial? Is there any justification offered for them?

---

6. This isn't just wordplay: A 55% likelihood that the error was harmless qualifies as "more probable than not," but it's hardly a "fair assurance" of harmlessness. *Kotteakos* defines "fair assurance" as absence of a "grave doubt," 328 U.S. at 765, and a 45% chance that the defendant would have been acquitted but for the error certainly seems like a "grave doubt." While we obviously don't deal in such precise probabilities, "more probable than not" and "fair assurance" can, in some cases, lead to conflicting results.

2. Did the prosecution need to use the photograph in *Hitt* to rebut the suggestion that the interior of Hitt's rifle was dirty or worn? Was there alternative, less prejudicial evidence available? For example, where was the rifle itself? Who has the obligation to raise the issue of minimizing the misleading impact of the photograph?

3. Judge Kozinski also stated a general rule for conducting the balancing test under FRE 403: "Where the evidence is of very slight (if any) probative value, it's an abuse of discretion to admit it if there's even a modest likelihood of unfair prejudice or a small risk of misleading the jury." How does this language fit within the table reproduced on page 161, supra? Does it contradict the FRE 403 requirement that the danger "substantially" outweigh the probative value?

OLD CHIEF v. UNITED STATES

519 U.S. 172 (1997)

SOUTER, Justice.

Petitioner Johnny Lynn Old Chief was arrested in 1993 after a fracas involving at least one gunshot. He was charged with assault with a dangerous weapon, using a firearm in relation to a crime of violence, and with violation of 18 U.S.C. §922(g)(1), which makes it unlawful for anyone "who has been convicted in any court of a crime punishable by imprisonment for a term exceeding one year" to "possess in or affecting commerce, any firearm."[7] In the indictment, Old Chief was charged with having been convicted of an earlier assault causing serious bodily injury. Before trial, he requested that the trial court order the government not to mention any detail regarding the prior conviction except to state that defendant had been convicted of a crime punishable by imprisonment exceeding one year. This was treated as an offer to stipulate and agree that the jury could be instructed that he had been convicted of such a crime as required under §922(g)(1). Old Chief contended that Rule 403 rendered the name and nature of his prior offense unfairly prejudicial, since the jury was likely to generalize his earlier bad act into bad character, and to use his character as increasing the probability that he did the bad act with which he was now charged. The government refused to join in any stipulation and insisted on its right to prove its case its own way. The district court agreed, ruling that if the government did not want to stipulate, it did not have to. At trial, the government introduced a document regarding Old Chief's prior conviction that showed that on December 18, 1988, he did knowingly and unlawfully assault Rory Dean Fenner, said assault resulting in "serious bodily injury" for which Old Chief was sentenced to five years' imprisonment.

Justice Souter's opinion noted that the jury's potential use of this prior conviction for a propensity inference would violate FRE 404(b), and thus the admission of Old Chief's specific prior conviction raised a risk of unfair prejudice that must be analyzed under Rule 403.

---

7. "[A] crime punishable by imprisonment for a term exceeding one year" is defined to exclude "any Federal or State offenses pertaining to antitrust violations, unfair trade practices, restraints of trade, or other similar offenses relating to the regulation of business practices" and "any State offense classified . . . as a misdemeanor and punishable by a term of imprisonment of two years or less." 18 U.S.C. §921(a)(20).

As for the analytical method to be used in Rule 403 balancing, two basic possibilities present themselves. An item of evidence might be viewed as an island, with estimates of its own probative value and unfairly prejudicial risk the sole reference points in deciding whether the danger substantially outweighs the value and whether the evidence ought to be excluded. Or the question of admissibility might be seen as inviting further comparisons to take account of the full evidentiary context of the case as the court understands it when the ruling must be made. This second approach would start out like the first but be ready to go further. On objection, the court would decide whether a particular item of evidence raised a danger of unfair prejudice. If it did, the judge would go on to evaluate the degrees of probative value and unfair prejudice not only for the item in question but for any actually available substitutes as well. If an alternative were found to have substantially the same or greater probative value but a lower danger of unfair prejudice, sound judicial discretion would discount the value of the item first offered and exclude it if its discounted probative value were substantially outweighed by unfairly prejudicial risk. As we will explain later on, the judge would have to make these calculations with an appreciation of the offering party's need for evidentiary richness and narrative integrity in presenting a case, and the mere fact that two pieces of evidence might go to the same point would not, of course, necessarily mean that only one of them might come in. It would only mean that a judge applying Rule 403 could reasonably apply some discount to the probative value of an item of evidence when faced with less risky alternative proof going to the same point. Even under this second approach, as we explain below, a defendant's Rule 403 objection offering to concede a point generally cannot prevail over the Government's choice to offer evidence showing guilt and all the circumstances surrounding the offense.[8]. . .

The first understanding of the Rule is open to a very telling objection. That reading would leave the party offering evidence with the option to structure a trial in whatever way would produce the maximum unfair prejudice consistent with relevance. He could choose the available alternative carrying the greatest threat of improper influence, despite the availability of less prejudicial but equally probative evidence. The worst he would have to fear would be a ruling sustaining a Rule 403 objection, and if that occurred, he could simply fall back to offering substitute evidence. This would be a strange rule. It would be very odd for the law of evidence to recognize the danger of unfair prejudice only to confer such a degree of autonomy on the party subject to temptation, and the Rules of Evidence are not so odd.

Rather, a reading of the companions to Rule 403, and of the commentaries that went with them to Congress, makes it clear that what counts as the Rule 403 "probative value" of an item of evidence, as distinct from its Rule 401 "relevance," may be calculated by comparing evidentiary alternatives. The Committee Notes to Rule 401 explicitly say that a party's concession is pertinent to the court's discretion to exclude evidence on the point conceded.

---

8. While our discussion has been general because of the general wording of Rule 403, our holding is limited to cases involving proof of felon status. On appellate review of a Rule 403 decision, a defendant must establish abuse of discretion, a standard that is not satisfied by a mere showing of some alternative means of proof that the prosecution in its broad discretion chose not to rely upon.

. . . The Notes to Rule 403 then take up the point by stating that when a court considers "whether to exclude on grounds of unfair prejudice," the "availability of other means of proof may . . . be an appropriate factor.". . .

Old Chief's proffered admission would, in fact, have been not merely relevant but seemingly conclusive evidence of the element. The statutory language in which the prior-conviction requirement is couched shows no congressional concern with the specific name or nature of the prior offense beyond what is necessary to place it within the broad category of qualifying felonies, and Old Chief clearly meant to admit that his felony did qualify, by stipulating "that the Government has proven one of the essential elements of the offense." App. 7. As a consequence, although the name of the prior offense may have been technically relevant, it addressed no detail in the definition of the prior-conviction element that would not have been covered by the stipulation or admission. Logic, then, seems to side with Old Chief. . . .

There is, however, one more question to be considered before deciding whether Old Chief's offer was to supply evidentiary value at least equivalent to what the Government's own evidence carried. In arguing that the stipulation or admission would not have carried equivalent value, the Government invokes the familiar, standard rule that the prosecution is entitled to prove its case by evidence of its own choice, or, more exactly, that a criminal defendant may not stipulate or admit his way out of the full evidentiary force of the case as the Government chooses to present it.

This is unquestionably true as a general matter. The "fair and legitimate weight" of conventional evidence showing individual thoughts and acts amounting to a crime reflects the fact that making a case with testimony and tangible things not only satisfies the formal definition of an offense, but tells a colorful story with descriptive richness. Unlike an abstract premise, whose force depends on going precisely to a particular step in a course of reasoning, a piece of evidence may address any number of separate elements, striking hard just because it shows so much at once; the account of a shooting that establishes capacity and causation may tell just as much about the triggerman's motive and intent. Evidence thus has force beyond any linear scheme or reasoning, and as its pieces come together a narrative gains momentum, with power not only to support conclusions but to sustain the willingness of jurors to draw the inferences, whatever they may be, necessary to reach an honest verdict. This persuasive power of the concrete and particular is often essential to the capacity of jurors to satisfy the obligations that the law places on them. Jury duty is usually unsought and sometimes resisted, and it may be as difficult for one juror suddenly to face the findings that can send another human being in prison, as it is for another to hold out conscientiously for acquittal. When a juror's duty does seem hard, the evidentiary account of what a defendant has thought and done can accomplish what no set of abstract statements ever could, not just to prove a fact but to establish its human significance, and so to implicate the law's moral underpinnings and a juror's obligation to sit in judgment. Thus, the prosecution may fairly seek to place its evidence before the jurors, as much to tell a story of guiltiness as to support an inference of guilt, to convince the jurors that a guilty verdict would be morally reasonable as much as to point to the discrete elements of a defendant's legal fault.

But there is something even more to the prosecution's interest in resisting efforts to replace the evidence of its choice with admissions and stipulations, for beyond the power of conventional evidence to support allegations and give life to the moral underpinnings of law's claims, there lies the need for evidence in all its particularity to satisfy the jurors' expectations about what proper proof should be. Some such demands they bring with them to the courthouse, assuming, for example, that a charge of using a firearm to commit an offense will be proven by introducing a gun in evidence. A prosecutor who fails to produce one, or some good reason for his failure, has something to be concerned about. "If [jurors'] expectations are not satisfied, triers of fact may penalize the party who disappoints them by drawing a negative inference against that party." Saltzburg, A Special Aspect of Relevance: Countering Negative Inferences Associated with the Absence of Evidence, 66 Calif. L. Rev. 1011, 1019 (1978) (footnotes omitted). Expectations may also arise in jurors' minds simply from the experience of a trial itself. The use of witnesses to describe a train of events naturally related can raise the prospect of learning about every ingredient of that natural sequence the same way. If suddenly the prosecution presents some occurrence in the series differently, as by announcing a stipulation or admission, the effect may be like saying, "never mind what's behind the door," and jurors may well wonder what they are being kept from knowing. A party seemingly responsible for cloaking something has reason for apprehension, and the prosecution with its burden of proof may prudently demur at a defense request to interrupt the flow of evidence telling the story in the usual way. . . .

In sum, the accepted rule that the prosecution is entitled to prove its case free from any defendant's option to stipulate the evidence away rests on good sense. A syllogism is not a story, and a naked proposition in a courtroom may be no match for the robust evidence that would be used to prove it. People who hear a story interrupted by gaps of abstraction may be puzzled at the missing chapters, and jurors asked to rest a momentous decision on the story's truth can feel put upon at being asked to take responsibility knowing that more could be said than they have heard. A convincing tale can be told with economy, but when economy becomes a break in the natural sequence of narrative evidence, an assurance that the missing link is really there is never more than second best.

This recognition that the prosecution with its burden of persuasion needs evidentiary depth to tell a continuous story has, however, virtually no application when the point at issue is a defendant's legal status, dependent on some judgment rendered wholly independently of the concrete events of later criminal behavior charged against him. As in this case, the choice of evidence for such an element is usually not between eventful narrative and abstract proposition, but between propositions of slightly varying abstraction, either a record saying that conviction for some crime occurred at a certain time or a statement for admitting the same thing without naming the particular offense. The issue of substituting one statement for the other normally arises only when the record of conviction would not be admissible for any purpose beyond proving status, so that excluding it would not deprive the prosecution of evidence with multiple utility; if, indeed, there were a justification for receiving evidence of the nature of prior acts on some issue other than status (i.e., to prove "motive, opportunity, intent, preparation, plan, knowledge, identity, or absence of mistake or accident," Fed. Rule Evid. 404(b)), Rule 404(b) guarantees the opportunity to seek its admission. Nor can it be argued that the events behind the prior conviction are proper nourishment for the jurors' sense of obligation to vindicate the public interest. The issue is not whether concrete details of the prior crime should come to the jurors' attention but whether the name or general character of that crime is to be disclosed. Congress, however, has made it plain that distinctions among generic felonies do not count for this purpose; the fact of the qualifying conviction is alone what matters under the statute. . . . The most the jury needs to know is that the conviction admitted by the defendant falls within the class of crimes that Congress thought should bar a convict from possessing a gun, and this point may be made readily in a defendant's admission and underscored in the court's jury instructions. Finally, the most obvious reason that the general presumption that the prosecution may choose its evidence is so remote from application here is that proof of the defendant's status goes to an element entirely outside the natural sequence of what the defendant is charged with thinking and doing to commit the current offense. Proving status without telling exactly why that status was imposed leaves no gap in the story of a defendant's subsequent criminality, and its demonstration by stipulation or admission neither displaces a chapter from a continuous sequence of conventional evidence nor comes across as an officious substitution, to confuse or offend or provoke reproach.

Given these peculiarities of the element of felony-convict status and of admissions and the like when used to prove it, there is no cognizable difference between the evidentiary significance of an admission and of the legitimately probative component of the official record the prosecution would prefer to place in evidence. For purposes of the Rule 403 weighing of the probative against the prejudicial, the functions of the competing evidence are distinguishable only by the risk inherent in the one and wholly absent from the other. In this case, as in any other in which the prior conviction is for an offense likely to support conviction on some improper ground, the only reasonable conclusion was that the risk of unfair prejudice did substantially outweigh the discounted probative value of the record of conviction, and it was an abuse of discretion to admit the record when an admission was available. What we have said shows why this will be the general rule when proof of convict status is at issue, just as the prosecutor's choice will generally survive a Rule 403 analysis when a defendant seeks to force the substitution of an admission for evidence creating a coherent narrative of his thoughts and actions in perpetrating the offense for which he is being tried.

The judgment is reversed, and the case is remanded to the Ninth Circuit for further proceedings consistent with this opinion.

NOTES AND QUESTIONS

1. Justice Souter's discussion of the "evidentiary richness" and "narrative integrity" components of probative value reflect the theory of jury reasoning that we noted

in Chapter Two on page 131—that jurors focus at trial on competing versions of reality, not on whether a formal element of law is true or false. Considerable research indicates that juries evaluate evidence within the framework of a story, or narrative account, of the events central to the case. Jurors start to construct a story at the start of trial, and then accept or reject evidence in relation to the narratives that are available to them as the trial continues. At the end of this process, jurors will usually accept one story as the "best" account of "what happened" and match it to the verdict definitions in the instructions. This "story model" of jury decisionmaking is founded on empirical work of social scientists. A classic work is Nancy Pennington & Reid Hastie, A Cognitive Theory of Juror Decision Making: The Story Model, 13 Cardozo L. Rev. 519 (1991). Evidentiary richness and narrative integrity can be seen as contributing to the quality of an advocate's story.

Use of these factors in making and reviewing decisions under FRE 403 would not seem to be limited to §922(g)(1) cases. For example, in United States v. Vallejo, 237 F.3d 1008 (9th Cir. 2001), defendant Vallejo was charged with illegal importation of marijuana in a car he was driving from Mexico to the United States. Vallejo claimed that he did not know that the packages of marijuana were hidden inside the vehicle. The Ninth Circuit held that it was error for the district court to exclude Vallejo's evidence of the identity of the person who he claimed had hidden the drugs in the car, intending to smuggle them into the United States himself. The court made the point that the need to satisfy juror expectations added to the probative value of this evidence. The court wrote: "Vallejo . . . was not allowed to provide an answer for the jurors' question: 'If defendant did not know there were drugs in the car and did not place them there himself, who did?' " Id. at 1023.

2. Justice Souter's opinion holds that the trial court should have "discounted" the probative value of the proffered evidence of Old Chief's actual felony conviction because other evidence—the stipulation as to his status as a felon—was of equal probative force and was substantially less prejudicial. What does "discount" mean? Is this another way of stating that the prosecution did not "need" to prove the actual conviction, and that the lack of need should be dispositive in the balancing under FRE 403 under these circumstances?

3. Despite the *Old Chief* opinion, some prosecutors continue to offer evidence of the nature of a defendant's prior felony in cases filed under 18 U.S.C. §922(g)(1), and some district courts continued to admit such evidence over a defense offer to stipulate to the defendant's status as a felon. Appellate courts have found error when the prior felony would generate the risk of unfair prejudice but in many cases found the error to be harmless due to the "overwhelming evidence" of the defendant's unlawful possession of a firearm. See, e.g., United States v. Harris, 130 F.3d 829, 830 (8th Cir. 1998) ("When evidence of a defendant's guilt is overwhelming, the Old Chief violation is harmless."); Comment, The Undoing of *Old Chief*: Harmless Error and Felon-in-Possession-of-Firearms Cases, 48 Kan. L. Rev. 431, 457 (2000), suggests that the "effect-on-the-verdict" standard of harmless error replace the "weight of the evidence" standard, requiring "the judge to consider the proceedings in their entirety to determine whether the error had a substantial effect on the jury's decision."

4. Also following *Old Chief*, parties have offered a wide variety of stipulations to avoid the admission of evidence that bears the danger of unfair prejudice. In the majority of cases, trial courts have rejected such stipulations and appellate courts have refused to extend *Old Chief* beyond its holding on the issue of "status" §922(g)(1). See, e.g., United States v. Hall, 152 F.3d 381, 401 (5th Cir. 1998) (defendant's offer to stipulate to the identity of a murder victim and the cause of death did not render irrelevant photographs of victim's body in a decomposed state after defendant had buried it); United States v. Crowder, 141 F.3d 1202 (D.C. Cir. 1998) (defendant's offer to stipulate to intent element in crime of possession of drugs with intent to distribute does not render government's evidence of a similar crime inadmissible to prove intent); United States v. Hammoud, 381 F.3d 316, 342 (4th Cir. 2004) (not error to show the jury excerpts from tapes found in his home; defendant's stipulation that the tapes were produced by a terrorist organization did not relieve the government from its burden of proving that defendant *knew* that the organization engaged in terrorist activity; tapes showed speeches by organization leaders advocating violence). But see United States v. Merino-Balderrama, 146 F.3d 758 (9th Cir. 1998) (in a prosecution for possession of child pornography videos, the trial court allowed the jury to watch the videos; defendant had offered to stipulate to their pornographic content but denied ever watching them and thus denied the requisite element of *knowing* what the videos were. The appellate court held this was error because the videos were highly prejudicial, the box covers of the videos were equally probative on the issue of knowledge since they depicted child pornography, and defendant admitted he had seen the covers).

C. REFLECTIONS ON RELEVANCE, PROBATIVE VALUE, AND JUDICIAL DISCRETION

The Federal Rules of Evidence have as their central goal the factually accurate resolution of disputes that are brought to federal court. This is not to say that other values do not affect the Rules, as explicitly stated in FRE 102, or that the search for truth does not accommodate other values. It is to say, however, that the dominant policy expressed in the Rules, in the Advisory Committee Notes, in judicial interpretations, and professional and academic commentary is the pursuit of factually accurate outcomes.

This policy rests on a belief that disinterested factfinders, such as jurors, have the capacity to reconstruct prior events by using their powers of reasoning—by drawing inferences from evidence presented to them in the courtroom, based on their own generalized knowledge and experience. To the extent that the evidence presented is accurate and complete and the jury's generalizations are accurate, this reasoning process can yield accurate outcomes. The accuracy of this reasoning process is advanced in no small measure by the requirement of relevance. As we discussed at the beginning of this chapter, any evidence that jurors might rationally use in determining the existence of guilt or liability is relevant and potentially admissible (unless another rule dictates its exclusion), and irrelevant evidence—that is, evidence that has no rational bearing on the existence of guilt or liability—is inadmissible.[9]

The trial system, in short, pursues the search for truth from the perspective of a correspondence theory of knowledge. It assumes that things happen and that what happens is knowable by human beings. The system also assumes that accurate knowledge is produced through human reasoning—that persons (witnesses) can coherently communicate information about happenings to disinterested third parties (jurors) who then will draw accurate inferences based on that information. You can see that the role of witnesses and the role of the jury described on page 88, supra, are grounded in these assumptions.

These assumptions raise three issues for you to consider as you study the law of evidence: First, are relevance and probative value features of evidence that can be known and measured? Second, are juries rational? Third, how should judicial discretion in admitting or excluding evidence be regulated? We offer some brief reflections on each of these questions.

1. Can Relevance and Probative Value Be Measured?

The essence of the Federal Rules' approach to relevance is that evidence is relevant if it has the capacity to influence a disinterested person on a fact of consequence. "Influence" in this context is somewhat vague, though. We know when we have a sense of being "convinced" or "persuaded" or of being placed in "doubt" by an argument or by evidence. But must an analysis of the influence of evidence stop at such an ephemeral point? Some have argued that it must. See, e.g., Henry M. Hart, Jr. & John T. McNaughton, Evidence and Inference in the Law, 87 Daedalus 40, 44 (Fall 1958):

> The adjudicative facts of interest to the law, being historical facts, will rarely be triable by the experimental methods of the natural sciences. . . . For the most part the law must settle disputed questions of adjudicative fact by reliance upon the ambiguous implications of non-fungible "traces"—traces on human brains and on pieces of paper and traces in the form of unique arrangements of physical objects.

Perhaps Hart and McNaughton are correct that the law must be satisfied with evidence in the form of "traces on human brains." But must the implications of these traces be ambiguous? There has been great interest recently in efforts to articulate in a more rigorous fashion what it means for evidence to have persuasive force. These efforts have centered primarily on the implications of a theorem of mathematics known as Bayes's Theorem, which provides a rigorous method for combining a

---

9. The relevance requirement in the Federal Rules may be contrasted with the formal system of required proof in some continental legal systems. For example, a conviction for a serious crime could only be had upon the presentation of two eyewitnesses or a confession. Circumstantial evidence would not do. But strong circumstantial evidence constituted a "half-proof" that legitimated the use of torture in order to extract a confession. For discussions, see John Langbein, Torture and the Law of Proof: Europe and England in the Ancien Régime (1977); L. Jonathan Cohen, Freedom of Proof, in Facts in Law (William L. Twining, ed., 1983); Mirjan Damaska, The Death of Legal Torture, 87 Yale L.J. 860 (1978).

person's assessment of the probability of an event with new evidence concerning that event to arrive at a new assessment of the probability of the event.[10]

English mathematician Thomas Bayes (1702-1761) demonstrated that the following formula is derivable from the axioms of conventional probability:

O_G = odds of guilt or liability
$O_{G/E}$ = odds of guilt or liability given the new evidence (E)
$P_{E/G}$ = probability of obtaining the evidence in question if the person is guilty or liable
$P_{E/not\ G}$ = probability of obtaining the evidence in question if the individual is not guilty or liable

The formula is:

$$O_{G/E} = \frac{P_{E/G}}{P_{E/notG}} \times O_G$$

This formula expresses that the odds of guilt or liability after evidence is received are determined by the relationship between the probability of obtaining the evidence if the person is guilty or liable and the probability of obtaining the evidence if the person is not guilty or liable. In other words, to go from a prior assessment of the odds of liability to an assessment in light of the new evidence requires that the prior assessment be modified by the likelihood that the evidence would have been presented at trial if the person is liable as compared to the likelihood that it would have been presented if the person is not liable.

Do not let the discussion of probability theory obscure an important insight here. What makes evidence "relevant" is its capacity to influence the factfinder. That, in turn, is a function of the probability of receiving the evidence if the person is liable as compared to the probability of receiving the evidence if the person is not liable. Take a simple example. Suppose that in a burglary case, the prosecution wished to introduce evidence that the defendant does not like the Chicago Bears. If the defendant is guilty, the probability of receiving this evidence is a function of the proportion of burglars who are Chicago Bears fans, which we shall assume is .95 (at least in Chicago). The probability of receiving the evidence if the defendant is not guilty is a function of the proportion of nonburglars who are Chicago Bears fans, and there is no reason

<hr>

10. For what follows we are indebted to Professor Richard Lempert's work on Bayes's Theorem, which can be found in Richard Lempert, Modeling Relevance, 75 Mich. L. Rev. 1021 (1977). That work was heavily influenced by Professor John Kaplan's article, Decision Theory and the Factfinding Process, 20 Stan. L. Rev. 1065 (1968), which in turn was heavily influenced by Vaughn C. Ball, The Moment of Truth: Probability Theory and Standards of Proof, 14 Vand. L. Rev. 807 (1961). Some commentators have proposed alternatives to Bayes's Theorem, see Jonathan L. Cohen, The Probable and the Provable (1977), while others have critiqued its application to jury reasoning, among them William L. Twining & Alex Stein, Evidence and Proof, The International Library of Essays in Law and Legal Theory (1992); Ronald J. Allen, Rationality, Algorithms, and Juridical Proof: A Preliminary Analysis, 1 Intl. J. of Evidence and Proof 253 (1997); Ronald J. Allen & Michael S. Pardo, The Problematic Value of Mathematical Models of Evidence, 36 J. Legal Studies. 107 (2007); Craig R. Callen, Notes on a Grand Illusion: Some Limits on the Use of Bayesian Theory in Evidence Law, 57 Ind. L.J. 1 (1982); David Kaye, Naked Statistical Evidence, 89 Yale L.J. 601 (1980); Nancy Pennington & Reid Hastie, A Cognitive Theory of Juror Decision Making: The Story Model, 13 Cardozo L. Rev. 519 (1991).

to think that proportion would differ from the proportion of burglars who are fans of the Bears. Thus, the ratio of these probabilities (.95/.95) is 1.0, and 1.0 multiplied by the prior odds of guilt will result in no change in those odds. Therefore, this evidence is irrelevant because it has no impact on the assessment of the odds of guilt. By contrast, suppose a drop of blood found at the crime scene matches the burglar but also matches 20 percent of the population. The ratio of probabilities for this evidence (1.0/0.2) is 5. This result, when multiplied by the prior odds of guilt, makes guilt appear more likely and thus the evidence is relevant.

We do not suggest that this way of viewing relevance has any value other than perhaps explaining how some people may evaluate evidence. Even as an explanatory effort, however, it has serious limitations. The formula requires that the decisionmaker have a preliminary assessment of the odds of guilt or liability *before* the receipt of an item of evidence that is subjected to Bayesian analysis, and it is unclear what that should be in our system of trials (especially criminal trials). Davis v. State, 476 N.E.2d 127, 138 (2d Dist. Ct. App. Ind. 1985) (In applying Bayes's Theorem, expert witnesses, who testified to the probabilities of parentage derived from blood test evidence, properly employed a neutral prior probability (50/50) instead of a prior probability variable based upon circumstantial, nontest evidence of the defendants' parentage.). In addition, the probabilities associated with most evidence will virtually always defy quantification. More troublesome still, Bayes's Theorem requires that the decisionmaker evaluate each bit of evidence as it is introduced, rather than permitting the decisionmaker to hear all the evidence and deliberate on all of it at the conclusion of the trial process. At trial, by contrast, jurors are explicitly told not to form any conclusions until all the evidence is in. The reason for this is the belief that once opinions are formed, they are hard to change. Individuals will rationalize new evidence they hear to make it consistent with their preconceptions. To the extent that this is true, the party first producing evidence would have a great advantage at trial, since presumably that evidence would tend to establish that party's case. And, while it may be correct that if the likelihood ratio is 1 after the correct questions about the probabilities of obtaining evidence are asked, it is not clear that correct answers to those questions can be obtained in litigation. Care must be taken in thinking about relevance and Bayes's Theorem.

Consider evidence that a defendant (charged with bank robbery) was running from the scene of the bank robbery that took place close to a train station. Fleeing might mean that the defendant robbed the bank and was trying to escape. It also might mean that she was trying to catch a train. Assume that it could be established as an empirically valid proposition that 70 percent of the people running from the crime scene are running because of guilt. The probability of obtaining the evidence of running if the defendant is guilty is .7; the probability of obtaining the evidence if defendant is innocent is .3. So far, the prosecution would be able to show the relevance of the evidence of running. Now suppose that the defendant establishes that 70 percent of the people near a train station who are running are doing so to catch a train. Now, is the probability of obtaining the evidence of running if the defendant is innocent also .7? If so, is the likelihood ratio under Bayes's Theorem 1? The trouble with relying on this ratio in litigation is that these are not the only two explanations of people running that will occur to the jury, and these other explanations could change the ratio. Many other evidentiary facts in the case, such as how fast or slow the defendant was running, or what she was wearing, will also affect the probabilities of each explanation of what the running means. And, of course, there are very few statements about the probabilities of human behavior that can be established with such precision. In most cases, the likelihood ratio cannot be established definitively, and the judge will admit the evidence, leaving it up to the jury to interpret or explain it.

An additional limitation with a probabilistic conception is that some of the relevant evidence admitted at trial overlaps with the theories of the case or stories being offered by each side. Such "overlapping" evidence will fit with each side's explanation of what happened, even though the evidence by itself may not distinguish probabilistically between the two explanations. Consider, for example, the evidence in *Johnson* about the package sent to the defendant by his family and his failure to receive it. This evidence formed part of each side's explanation of what occurred and why, and the lawyers each made use of this evidence to argue that their version of events was more plausible.

Bayes's Theorem, in short, is an interesting way of thinking about the idea of relevance, even if it is not completely compatible with the trial process. It may also provide a useful way to think about probative value and FRE 403: Evidence is misleading whenever the jury forms a likelihood ratio that is quite different from the "true" likelihood ratio.

2. Are Juries Rational?

Regardless of whether relevance and probative value can be measured precisely, suppose you are convinced of the more fundamental points that there is a reality and that you can know it based on evidence. Are you as convinced that your fellow human beings can know it, or do you have doubts about the rationality of the human species? Even if you are a disinterested observer of events, is anyone else? How often have you seen a person's perceptions of an event determined by ideology or wishful thinking? Viewers' perceptions of the same event can differ dramatically. If that is not an uncommon occurrence, what are its implications for the social reconstruction of reality that occurs at trial based on the testimony of witnesses (whose perception may be affected by factors that are not rational)?

Moreover, how much faith do you have in disinterested third parties such as jurors drawing the appropriate inferences about what happened based on the evidence presented? How different was student opinion in your class about the credibility of witnesses in the transcript of the *Johnson* case in Chapter One? Do people use a uniform body of generalized knowledge and experience to evaluate such data? Or are you more impressed with the remarkable divergence of opinion that constantly seems to follow from the presentation of information to a group of individuals? Again, does that increase or decrease your faith in the rationality of the trial process?

Empirical research has also been done on the intellectual strategies that people use—alone and in groups—to come to conclusions about disputed facts. The landmark works in this field that may have the most compelling applications to jury decisionmaking are Michael J. Saks & Robert F. Kidd, Human Information Processing and Adjudication: Trial by Heuristics, 15 Law & Socy. Rev. 123 (1980-1981), and Amos Tversky & Daniel Kahneman, Judgment Under Uncertainty: Heuristics and Biases, 185 Science 1124 (1974). Recent work on the "narrative theory" of jury decisionmaking includes Nancy Pennington & Reid Hastie, A Cognitive Theory of Juror Decision Making: The Story Model, 13 Cardozo L. Rev. 519 (1991) and Dan Simon, A Third View of the Black Box: Cognitive Coherence in Legal Decision Making, 71 U. Chi. L. Rev. 511 (2004). The following offer good overviews of the empirical literature on juries: Vidmar & Hans, American Juries: The Verdict (2007); Shari Diamond, Beyond Fantasy and Nightmare: A Portrait of the Jury, 54 Buff. L. Rev. 717 (2006). This literature offers practitioners the opportunity to understand jurors' decisionmaking strategies, and it offers law reformers the opportunity to improve the procedures and evidentiary policies underlying our system of trial.

Questions about the validity of the assumption of jury rationality are of great importance. The outcomes of jury factfinding are always uncertain. There is no methodology and no objective point of view within the system of trials to test whether the jury has correctly decided the ultimate facts.[11] To the extent that one has doubts about jury rationality, one should have serious reservations about continuing our current system of trial. On the other hand, to the extent one has greater faith in our capacity to understand and communicate our knowledge about the world in a rational manner, then one may feel somewhat more sanguine about the model of jury reasoning. And whatever degree of skepticism you possess, you must also consider what alternatives there are to our reliance on this model.[12]

3. How to Regulate Judicial Discretion?

The exercise of judicial discretion required by FRE 403 allows the trial court considerable freedom to admit or exclude evidence. Appellate courts treat lower-court Rule 403 decisions with great deference, and appellate findings of abuse of discretion are infrequent. As you study the major rules of exclusion, you will see that these rules—the character rule, the other relevance rules, the hearsay rule, the best evidence rule, and the rules of privilege—do not grant such explicit discretion to the trial court. Rather, these exclusionary rules, and their exceptions, are so-called bright-line rules. Some of these, such as the rule prohibiting the use of extrinsic evidence to prove

---

11. The results of DNA testing may come as close to "objective certainty" as our system can provide. Numerous persons convicted of rape or murder have been freed from incarceration on the basis of subsequent DNA testing (not available at the time of trial) of body samples, such as hair and semen, found on the victim. The testing virtually excludes the defendant as the source of the samples.

12. Additional critical perspectives on the assumptions and policies that underlie the Federal Rules of Evidence can be found in Kenneth W. Graham Jr., There'll Always Be an England: The Instrumental Ideology of Evidence, 85 Mich. L. Rev. 1204, 1219-1220, 1227-1234 (1987); Rosemary C. Hunter, Gender in Evidence, Masculine Norms vs. Feminist Reforms, 19 Harv. Women's L.J. 127 (1996); Kit Kinports, Evidence Engendered, 1991 U. Ill. L. Rev. 413; Michael L. Seigel, A Pragmatic Critique of Modern Evidence Scholarship, 88 Nw. U. L. Rev. 995, 998 (1994); Frederick Schauer, On the Supposed Jury Dependence of Evidence Law, 155 U. Pa. L. Rev. 165 (2006); Todd E. Pettys, The Emotional Juror, 76 Fordham L. Rev. 1609 (2007).

specific acts that impeach a witness's truthfulness, are truly "bright line." Others control the admission/exclusion decision with doctrinal definitions and categories.

The categorical rules operate in two ways. The hearsay rule, for example, establishes categories that require judicial factfinding; the character rule establishes categories of permissible uses of specific acts that require the trial judge to identify particular noncharacter theories of relevance. Under both types of categorical rules, the trial judge's task is to determine whether the proffered item of evidence fits within a doctrinal category. This decision of whether the item "fits" usually is determinative of admission or exclusion. Thus, discretion—the estimation and balancing of probative value and dangers to jury decisionmaking—is not exercised under these categorical rules. This is not because the categorical terms are applied mechanically; they require very careful thinking by the trial judge. But it is a different kind of thinking, and it can be treated less deferentially by appellate courts if they treat the application of the categorical term as a question of law.

As you study these major exclusionary rules, you should consider the justifications for their bright-line or categorical nature as opposed to the discretionary standards of Rule 403. Think in terms of how best the exclusionary policy of the rule can be enforced; which type of rule best serves the goals of accurate outcomes, fairness to the parties, and an efficient judicial system; and which type of rule judges are most competent to decide and to review.

ASSESSMENTS

A-3.1 FRE 401-02.   Defendant is on trial for burglary. An eyewitness testifies that she saw someone wearing a Chicago Cubs baseball hat running from the crime scene on the night of the burglary. The prosecution attempts to introduce evidence that Defendant is an avid Chicago Cubs fan. Defendant objects that this evidence is irrelevant. How should the court rule on the objection, and why?

   A. Overruled. A reasonable jury could think that a fan of the Chicago Cubs is more likely to own a Cubs hat than someone who is not a fan, which would thus make it more likely that Defendant was the person seen running from the crime scene, which would make it more likely that he committed the crime.
   B. Overruled. Background information about criminal defendants is always admissible.
   C. Sustained. Just because Defendant is a fan of the Chicago Cubs, this does not mean that he owns a Cubs hat.
   D. Sustained. It is unreasonable to think that Cubs fans are more likely to commit burglary than people who are not Cubs fans.

A-3.2. FRE 401-02.   Defendant is on trial for battery. The prosecution attempts to introduce testimony from the alleged victim about injuries he suffered after being pushed by Defendant at an outdoor concert. Defendant objects that this testimony is irrelevant because injury is not an element of battery and therefore not something the prosecution must prove. In arguing for admissibility, what is the prosecution's best argument?

    A. Injuries are always relevant in criminal cases.
    B. The evidence is relevant because the injuries make it more likely that Defendant committed battery (i.e., used unlawful force or violence against the victim).
    C. The evidence is relevant because it will make the victim a more sympathetic witness.
    D. FRE 401-02 allow for the admissibility of irrelevant *res gestae* evidence.

A-3.3. FRE 403. TRUE or FALSE: When a trial judge thinks that the probative value and the potential for unfair prejudice of an item of evidence are counterbalanced, the court should exclude the evidence.

A-3.4. FRE 403. Plaintiff sued Defendant for negligence, alleging Plaintiff was injured after falling on stairs outside of Defendant's business. At trial, Plaintiff attempted to introduce testimony from a witness, a friend of Plaintiff, to testify that he fell on the same stairs six months before Plaintiff's accident. The evidence was offered to prove Defendant should have known that the stairs were potentially dangerous. The trial judge excluded the testimony after concluding that the differences between the two incidents were likely to confuse the jury, and the probative value was low because of the witness's friendship with Plaintiff. The trial court commented, "I doubt this prior incident even took place." In reviewing the trial court's ruling to exclude the evidence, how is the appellate court likely to decide the issue?

    A. There was no error because the trial court engaged in proper FRE 403 balancing.
    B. There was no error because appellate courts must review all trial court FRE 403 rulings deferentially.
    C. The trial court abused its discretion because it weighed the credibility of the witness in assessing probative value. Because of this error, the judgment must be reversed.
    D. The trial court abused its discretion because it weighed the credibility of the witness in assessing probative value. The judgment will be reversed only if the appellate court concludes the error was not harmless.

A-3.5. FRE 403. Which statement most accurately describes the U.S. Supreme Court's holding in *Old Chief?*

    A. Parties must accept any reasonable stipulations offered by the other side.
    B. The prosecution must accept all offers to stipulate by criminal defendants.
    C. When a criminal defendant's status as a felon is an essential element, the prosecution must accept an offer to stipulate on the issue.
    D. Parties can admit irrelevant evidence when it is important for the moral force of the stories they are presenting at trial.

ANSWERS

A-3.1. The best answer is **A**. Because it would be reasonable for a jury to think that fans are at least slightly more likely than nonfans to own the hat, and therefore that Defendant is at least slightly more likely to be guilty, the evidence meets the minimal test for relevance under FRE 401. B is incorrect because not all background information about criminal defendants is admissible. Such evidence might be excluded as irrelevant, under FRE 403, or under several other rules we will discuss in subsequent chapters. C is incorrect because the generalizations that underlie theories of relevance do not have to establish conclusions with certainty: The evidence has to make it only slightly more likely that he owns a Cubs hat (not establish with certainty that he owns one). D is incorrect because the theory of relevance does not depend on this generalization.

A-3.2. The best answer is **B**. Even though injury is not an essential element, evidence that an injury occurred makes it more likely that force or violence was used against the victim and thus that a battery occurred. Therefore, the evidence is relevant. A is incorrect because sometimes evidence of injury may be irrelevant (for example, a case involving the sale of illegal drugs to an undercover officer). C is incorrect because evidence that makes a witness appear sympathetic to the jury will not necessarily be relevant. Rules governing evidence relating to witness credibility will be discussed in Chapter Seven. D is incorrect because FRE 402 states that "[i]rrelevant evidence is not admissible." Courts may admit *res gestae* evidence but only when it is relevant (typically, for understanding other evidence) and otherwise admissible under the rules.

A-3.3. FALSE. FRE 403 states that evidence should be excluded only when probative value is "substantially outweighed" by one or more of the FRE 403 dangers. Therefore, when the two sides of the balancing are similar, the evidence should be admitted.

A-3.4. The best answer is **D**. Although appellate courts review FRE 403 balancing deferentially, the trial court abused its discretion by weighing the credibility of the witness. When assessing probative value for purposes of FRE 403, the trial court should assume the jury finds the witness's testimony credible and then estimate its probative value. Therefore, A and B are incorrect. Even though the trial court committed an error, the appellate court will reverse only if it concludes that the error affected the outcome (i.e., was not harmless). Therefore, C is incorrect.

A-3.5. The best answer in **C**. In *Old Chief*, the Court held that the prosecution had to accept the defendant's offer to stipulate to his status as a felon, for purposes of 19 U.S.C. §922(g)(1). In general, however, the Court explained that parties, including the prosecution, may refuse offers to stipulate when doing so would disrupt their evidentiary presentations. Therefore, A and B are incorrect. D is incorrect because *Old Chief* did not assert that parties can introduce irrelevant evidence because of narrative considerations. This aspect of the opinion concerned how to assess probative value when a party has more than one item of relevant evidence for the same fact of consequence.

CHAPTER FOUR

FOUNDATION

There is a universal principle of evidence law that no evidence is admissible until it is first shown to be what its proponent claims that it is. This principle is sometimes called "foundation." Except where expert testimony is involved (see Chapter Nine), the foundation principle requires that the party offering evidence must show that the item of evidence is rooted in (1) firsthand knowledge (2) of a specific fact that (3) is logically connected to the offering party's theory of the case. In the *Johnson* case the judge gave the jury a standard instruction that "[e]vidence consists of testimony of witnesses, writings, material objects, or anything presented to the senses and offered to prove the existence or nonexistence of a fact." Generally speaking, before an offered item of evidence of any type will be admitted, the offering party must affirmatively show its foundation, unless that foundation is readily apparent.

Practitioners, courts and commentators universally acknowledge foundation as a fundamental principal of evidence law, and use the word "foundation" to describe its various aspects. Oddly, the word foundation doesn't actually appear in any federal rule of evidence. Instead, the principle of foundation is implicit in a constellation of rules, primarily FRE 602, 901, 902, 701, and 104(b).

This chapter covers the rules that establish what foundation is required for admission of various types of evidence. Section A discusses the necessary foundation for introducing testimony from witnesses, the firsthand knowledge requirement of FRE 602. Section B presents the various foundational requirements for documents and other objects, collectively known as "exhibits." These are set out in FRE 901 and 902. Section C focuses on FRE 104, the rule distinguishing foundation questions from preliminary fact questions that trigger evidence exclusion rules. Section D concerns the cluster of rules commonly known as "the best evidence rule" (FRE 1001-1008).

A. FOUNDATION FOR WITNESSES: CREDIBILITY AND THE FIRSTHAND KNOWLEDGE REQUIREMENT

A fundamental attribute of our litigation system is that the facts of disputed cases must be established primarily through the testimony of witnesses who recount their relevant firsthand knowledge. Moreover, these witnesses are generally required to appear personally in court, where the trier of fact—the jury in a jury trial, or the judge in a bench trial—can assess their credibility while absorbing the factual information they provide. These fundamental attributes of live, firsthand testimony and factfinder control over credibility questions are reflected in FRE 601 and 602.

1. FRE 601

RULE 601.   COMPETENCY TO TESTIFY IN GENERAL

Every person is competent to be a witness unless these rules provide otherwise. But in a civil case, state law governs the witness's competency regarding a claim or defense for which state law supplies the rule of decision.

2.   Explanation of FRE 601

The first sentence of FRE 601 abolishes all categorical qualifications and disqualifications for witnesses to be allowed to testify. Common law evidence rules and numerous state statutes previously imposed rigid rules of "competency" that kept certain categories of persons off the witness stand entirely. Persons whom judges and legislators thought were categorically untrustworthy were deemed "incompetent" to testify at trial. Persons interested in the case, including parties, could not testify. Spouses were incompetent to testify for or against a spouse. Atheists were categorically held to be incompetent, as were felons, young children, the mentally ill, and, in many jurisdictions, nonwhites. It was assumed that they either possessed a motive for distorting the facts in favor of their interest, or suffered defects of character, youth, or mental capacity that created risks of untrustworthiness.

FRE 601 is extremely important as an expression of a fundamental principle of modern evidence law: that the primary authority and responsibility for determining the credibility of witnesses lies with the trier of fact. A core concern of this policy is to protect the jury's role from judicial encroachment and thereby to safeguard the parties' right to trial by jury. Judge-made categorical rules deeming witnesses incompetent to testify due to credibility concerns are no longer permitted, by implication, under FRE 601. (Likewise, FRE 603 abolishes the moral qualification inherent in the former requirement of taking an oath—swearing before God—by allowing witnesses to take a secular "affirmation" to tell the truth.) Qualities that might raise doubts about a witness's testimonial qualities can be brought out during the examination of the witness, as impeachment. You'll study impeachment of witnesses in Chapter Seven. The

Federal Rules of Evidence, and most modern state evidence codes, permit the jury to decide whether such status or interest affects a witness's credibility.

Exceptions.   The second sentence recognizes an exception for state-created categories of incompetency for state-law claims tried in federal court. FRE 605 and 606 recognize a narrow exception to the general rule of witness competence by prohibiting the presiding trial judge and members of the sitting jury from testifying in the case at issue. These prohibitions are established not because of doubts about the trustworthiness of such witnesses, but because of the procedural complications and the potentially unfair prejudicial effect such testimony would be likely to have on the (other) jurors. But apart from the judge and the jury, people who witnessed relevant events cannot be prevented from testifying solely because of their status or their interest in the case.

Testimonial Competence May Be Challenged on Individual Basis.   Although the Advisory Committee Note to FRE 601 states that "[n]o mental or moral qualifications for testifying as a witness are specified," federal case law has recognized the authority of trial judges to entertain individual challenges to the mental competency of witnesses who are "so impaired in some manner that they cannot give meaningful testimony" or who can't understand the duty to testify truthfully. See, e.g., United States v. Ramirez, 871 F.2d 582, 584 (6th Cir. 1989); see also Cal. Evid. Code §701. Child witnesses can raise troublesome issues of competence with regard to their ability to remember events and to relate them accurately and truthfully. A federal statute establishes a presumption of competency for children who are victims of crimes of abuse and who have witnessed crimes against others. 18 U.S.C. §3509(c). A competency examination may be held only if compelling reasons exist and only upon motion by the opposing party and an offer of proof of incompetency. See United States v. Allen J., 127 F.3d 1292, 1296 (10th Cir. 1997).

3.   FRE 602

RULE 602.   NEED FOR PERSONAL KNOWLEDGE

A witness may testify to a matter only if evidence is introduced sufficient to support a finding that the witness has personal knowledge of the matter. Evidence to prove personal knowledge may consist of the witness's own testimony. This rule does not apply to a witness's expert testimony under Rule 703.

4.   Explanation of FRE 602

Rule 602 sets out the personal knowledge requirement for witnesses at trial. The first sentence states the requirement and describes the evidentiary showing necessary to meet it. The second sentence tells us how that requirement can be easily satisfied. The third sentence tells us that the rule does not apply to expert witnesses.

Personal Knowledge.   Personal knowledge means firsthand knowledge acquired directly by perception through one of the five senses. Typically, this will involve perception through the senses of sight or sound, but in theory any of the five senses could be the basis for observation of a relevant occurrence. Because personal knowledge is based on perception, the witnesses who provide such testimony are often called "percipient witnesses."

Personal or firsthand knowledge is to be contrasted with speculation and hearsay. Speculation refers to a witness offering more or less plausible theories or hypotheses based on generalizing rather than direct perception. For example, a witness who comes onto the scene of a car accident at an intersection sees a red car with its front end smashed at a right angle into the rear passenger door of a blue car. At trial, the witness could testify based on firsthand knowledge of the relative positions of the two cars and the appearance of damage. This would meet the personal knowledge requirement of FRE 602. But suppose she goes on to testify, "The red car must have run a red light—otherwise I don't see how it could have hit the blue car in the side like that." That testimony would be objectionable speculation—plausible, perhaps, but not something the witness knows based on actual observation. Instead, she surmises it based on general knowledge about cars and intersections.

Hearsay is a bit more complicated. Information acquired second hand, from the statements or reports of others, is not personal knowledge and doesn't meet the requirement of FRE 602, even if it is highly reliable. Testimony offering such secondhand information will trigger the hearsay rule. The general rule excluding hearsay (FRE 802) can be seen as a close relative of the firsthand knowledge requirement. But while hearsay evidence is subject to a general rule of exclusion, there are many exceptions; as a result, a lot of what appears to be secondhand information can be admitted at trial. Does this mean that the hearsay exceptions are also exceptions to FRE 602? Not exactly. Generally speaking, a witness who testifies to the statement or report of another person must have firsthand knowledge of the statement or report, even if not of the information it contains. But you can set this problem to one side for now, until you get to your study of the hearsay rule in Chapter Eight.

Evidence Sufficient to Support a Finding.   The first phrase of FRE 602 tells us that a witness must have personal knowledge of what he testifies about. But the witness's personal knowledge is itself an evidentiary question. In other words, there must be some evidence that the witness did perceive firsthand what he's testifying about. The phrase "evidence sufficient to support a finding" sets out the evidentiary standard for that fact.

What is evidence sufficient to support a finding? (For ease of reference, we will use the abbreviation "ESSF".) It means enough evidence on which a reasonable jury could find that the fact in question is more probably than not true. It's the same standard as that used in a civil case, on a motion for summary judgment. Could a reasonable jury find this fact by a preponderance of the evidence? Putting it another way, could a reasonable jury find that it is more probably than not true that this witness has firsthand knowledge? If a reasonable jury could believe, based on the evidence, that the witness saw what he said he saw or heard what he claims to have heard, then this requirement is met.

The question of whether there is evidence sufficient to support a finding of first-hand knowledge should be treated by the judge in a similar way to questions of summary judgment. Because the finding is ultimately for the jury, ESSF must consist of admissible evidence. The judge is not supposed to decide witness credibility or resolve conflicts in the evidence. Even though it is the same as the civil summary judgment standard, the ESSF standard applies to Rule 602 in both civil and criminal cases. Deciding that there is ESSF on the question of firsthand knowledge simply submits the question to the jury. The jury *may* believe that the witness has firsthand knowledge, but doesn't have to.

A witness's own testimony asserting firsthand perception will usually suffice to establish personal knowledge for admissibility purposes. The judge cannot disregard the witness's testimony of firsthand perception based on a credibility determination or because the judge finds contradicting evidence more persuasive: Credibility and factual dispute resolution are for the jury. (There is perhaps a very limited exception for inherently incredible testimony. For example, a judge might be justified in excluding testimony of a witness who claims to have x-ray vision.) There is also a practical dimension to taking the witness's own word for it. If a second witness—"Witness 2"—were needed to establish or corroborate Witness 1's claim of personal knowledge, then Witness 2 would have to have firsthand perception of Witness 1's firsthand perception; and a third witness would have to testify to Witness 2's firsthand perception, creating an infinite regress. Thus, as a practical matter, if a witness makes a plausible claim of having firsthand knowledge, it must in most instances be assumed to be true by the judge for admissibility purposes.

Finally, it is important to note that FRE 602 does not actually call upon the jury to make an express and specific "finding" about the witness's firsthand knowledge. The rule is directed to the parties and the judge to ensure that evidence sufficient to *support* a (hypothetical) finding of the witness's firsthand knowledge has been presented. If the jury ultimately decides to believe a witness's firsthand testimony, it implicitly "finds" that the witness has firsthand knowledge. If the jury is not persuaded that the witness in fact had personal knowledge, it issues no specific finding or statement to that effect—it simply discounts that witness's testimony when weighing all the evidence during its deliberations. And if the jury believes that the witness actually had firsthand knowledge of the events, but described them incorrectly on the witness stand—due to poor memory or lying—the jury will discount the witness's testimony and the question of firsthand knowledge will be moot.

Exception for Expert Witnesses.   Expert witnesses are expressly exempted from coverage of FRE 602 and its personal knowledge requirement. As you'll see in Chapter Nine, expert witnesses are called at trial to offer information and opinions that are often not based on firsthand knowledge of the litigated events. Returning to the car accident example, an expert witness might very well be allowed to offer an opinion that the red car probably ran the red light, based on expert knowledge and analysis of the positions of the two cars after the collision, without having directly observed the collision as it occurred.

5.   FRE 602: Practical Applications

In practice, laying a foundation for firsthand knowledge under FRE 602 is very straightforward. Either the witness has personal knowledge based on firsthand sense perception of the matter in question, or she does not. If the witness did not perceive the matter firsthand, there is no set of questions and answers that can finesse the witness's inability to satisfy the personal knowledge requirement.

On the other hand, if the witness did perceive the matter firsthand, all that need be done is to have the witness explain how she came to perceive it. ESSF of personal knowledge can be established simply by having the witness explicitly or implicitly answer the question, "How do you know?" The witness's answer need only either state or imply "because I perceived it with my senses." A simple "I saw it" may be all that's needed. Even testimony from which firsthand knowledge could be inferred—such as, "I was standing right at the intersection when the accident occurred"—could be enough to establish ESSF of firsthand knowledge. The jury can decide ultimately to disbelieve that the witness "saw it," but admitting the evidence means that the jury will hear and consider it. More often than not, FRE 602 is satisfied without any special formalities. A good direct examination allows the witness to tell a coherent story, which should invariably place the witness at the scene in a position to observe relevant events. Trial lawyers who get into trouble by overlooking the FRE 602 foundation can simply lay the foundation by asking, "How do you know?" or "What did you see (hear, etc.)?"

For the sake of clear illustrations, we've been describing the personal knowledge requirement as it applies to percipient witness observation of events or occurrences, such as a car accident. Certainly, much testimony takes the form of describing such incidents, but that's not the only form. Any relevant fact that can be perceived with the senses can be the subject of percipient witness testimony. For example, if a spoken statement is relevant—"we have a deal" in a contract dispute, for instance—anyone who heard the statement could potentially testify to it as a percipient witness.

The firsthand knowledge principle of Rule 602 gives you an important insight about how to put together a case at trial or in pretrial investigation or discovery. In many cases you will know of, or at least suspect, the existence of certain facts relevant to your case through secondhand sources. In such instances, FRE 602 tells you that your task is to find a witness with firsthand knowledge of that fact—someone who perceived it with her senses. Otherwise, you may not have admissible evidence to prove the fact.

The firsthand knowledge requirement of FRE 602 also explains the basis for a general problem with trials. As discussed in Chapter Two, each party in a trial will try to present a coherent and persuasive narrative of liability or nonliability for the crime or civil claim. The coherent narrative is usually conveyed in the opening statement. But once the evidence presentation phase begins, that narrative is chopped up into bits, typically out of chronological sequence, as one witness follows another, telling a piece of the whole story. This piecemeal presentation of facts is a necessary consequence of the firsthand knowledge requirement: Each witness can tell only that part of the story about which she has personal knowledge. Typically in litigated cases, there is not one witness who knows all the facts of the case firsthand. Thus, FRE 602 explains the need for opening statements at trials. Opening statements, which are told by lawyers with secondhand knowledge of the case and are not deemed evidence, are a way to accommodate the factfinder's need to understand facts through coherent stories, while still maintaining the trial system's strong preference for evidence based on firsthand knowledge.

KEY POINTS

1. FRE 601 abolishes prior prohibitions against categories of persons from testifying as witnesses. Questions going to the credibility of a witness are for the trier of fact to determine on an individual basis.

2. FRE 602 requires that witnesses must have personal knowledge of the facts about which they testify. Personal knowledge means firsthand knowledge acquired directly by perception through one of the five senses. (Such witnesses are often called "percipient witnesses.") Personal knowledge excludes speculation, as well as information acquired second hand, through the statements of others (hearsay). Expert witnesses are exempt from this rule.

3. The party eliciting the testimony must present evidence sufficient to support a finding of the witness's personal knowledge. Evidence sufficient to support a finding ("ESSF") means enough evidence on which a reasonable jury could find that the witness more probably than not has firsthand knowledge. The jury is not asked to make a specific finding: it merely takes the matter into account in its deliberations.

4. ESSF of firsthand knowledge can be shown simply by having the witness expressly or impliedly state that she saw or heard the matter in question. It often comes out naturally through direct examination that elicits clear testimony from the witness.

5. FRE 602 tells you that your task in pretrial discovery or investigation may often be to find a witness with firsthand knowledge of a fact you want to prove, even though you may already know that fact through secondhand sources.

PROBLEMS

4.1. Reconsider the evidence offered in problem 3.13 (page 168) as well as in the *Hitt* case. Who has firsthand knowledge of the evidence to be able to testify to it, under FRE 602? Identify a witness and draft a series of direct examination (i.e., nonleading) questions to establish that witness's personal knowledge.

4.2. Review the testimony by Officers Huston and Van Berg in the *Johnson* case concerning the injuries they claimed they received in the struggle with Johnson (pages 8 and 23, supra.) Did the officers speak from personal knowledge? Would you object to any of their testimony if you were the defense? Could you lay a proper foundation under Rule 602 if you were the prosecutor?

B. FOUNDATION FOR EXHIBITS

In addition to witness testimony, parties convey facts to the jury by presenting documents and other tangible objects, known collectively as exhibits. The foundational requirements for exhibits are set forth in FRE 901 and 902.

The primary focus of this section will be on FRE 901. As noted above, the word "foundation" does not appear in FRE 901 (or any other evidence rule). Instead, the rule speaks of "authenticating" or "identifying." Moreover, FRE 901 does not mention the word "exhibits." Instead, the rule addresses the authentication and identification of "an item of evidence." This language indicates that the principles set out in FRE 901 extend beyond exhibits to other foundation questions. But for the present, our concern is with the extent to which FRE 901 governs the foundation for exhibits.

1. FRE 901

RULE 901.   AUTHENTICATING OR IDENTIFYING EVIDENCE

(a) In General. To satisfy the requirement of authenticating or identifying an item of evidence, the proponent must produce evidence sufficient to support a finding that the item is what the proponent claims it is.

(b) Examples. The following are examples only—not a complete list—of evidence that satisfies the requirement:

(1) *Testimony of a Witness with Knowledge.* Testimony that an item is what it is claimed to be.

(2) *Nonexpert Opinion About Handwriting.* A nonexpert's opinion that handwriting is genuine, based on a familiarity with it that was not acquired for the current litigation.

(3) *Comparison by an Expert Witness or the Trier of Fact.* A comparison with an authenticated specimen by an expert witness or the trier of fact.

(4) *Distinctive Characteristics and the Like.* The appearance, contents, substance, internal patterns, or other distinctive characteristics of the item, taken together with all the circumstances.

(5) *Opinion About a Voice.* An opinion identifying a person's voice—whether heard firsthand or through mechanical or electronic transmission or recording—based on hearing the voice at any time under circumstances that connect it with the alleged speaker.

(6) *Evidence About a Telephone Conversation.* For a telephone conversation, evidence that a call was made to the number assigned at the time to:

(A) a particular person, if circumstances, including self-identification, show that the person answering was the one called; or

(B) a particular business, if the call was made to a business and the call related to business reasonably transacted over the telephone.

(7) *Evidence About Public Records.* Evidence that:

(A) a document was recorded or filed in a public office as authorized by law; or

(B) a purported public record or statement is from the office where items of this kind are kept.

(8) *Evidence About Ancient Documents or Data Compilations.* For a document or data compilation, evidence that it:

(A) is in a condition that creates no suspicion about its authenticity;

(B) was in a place where, if authentic, it would likely be; and

(C) is at least 20 years old when offered.

(9) *Evidence About a Process or System.* Evidence describing a process or system and showing that it produces an accurate result.

(10) *Methods Provided by a Statute or Rule.* Any method of authentication or identification allowed by a federal statute or a rule prescribed by the Supreme Court.

2.   Explanation of FRE 901

FRE 901(a) sets out the foundational requirement that must be shown to get an exhibit admitted into evidence. A party offering evidence must present facts that (1) indicate what the proponent *claims* the exhibit to be, and (2) are "sufficient to support a finding" that the exhibit is indeed what the proponent claims. FRE 901(b) lists examples of recurring foundation issues, most (but not all) relating to exhibits, and illustrating the kinds of facts that would satisfy the foundation requirement, at least in part.

FRE 901(a), the core of the rule, is stated in somewhat abstract terms. To help you understand it, we will break it down and give examples.

What the Exhibit Is Claimed to Be.   Although the title of the rule speaks of "identifying" and "authenticating" evidence, the text of the rule uses the significant word "claims." This suggests a very particular form of identification. It is not enough, when offering an exhibit into evidence, to identify it as "a gun" or "a beer can." Exhibits are not simply random objects, but rather have specific meanings in the context of the case. Instead, the proponent of the evidence must make a claim about how the exhibit fit into the events underlying the case. "This is the gun that was used by the defendant when committing the robbery in question." "This is the can of beer that the defendant drank just a few minutes before the car accident." The "claim" about an item of evidence referred to in FRE 901 is in effect a statement showing that the exhibit is relevant, and how it is relevant.

Evidence Sufficient to Support a Finding.   As with FRE 602, the standard for establishing the foundation for an exhibit is evidence sufficient to support a finding, or ESSF. There must be ESSF that the offering party's claim about the exhibit is (more probably than not) true. This supporting evidence about the exhibit might be offered at the time the exhibit is offered into evidence, or it might come from other evidence already admitted in the case. The supporting foundation evidence must be admissible, since the test asks whether there is sufficient evidence to support a finding *by the trier of fact.* Thus, for example, a party cannot establish foundation for an exhibit by relying on inadmissible hearsay. As with any other kind of proof, the foundation evidence can be direct or circumstantial. For example, evidence that the gun being offered into evidence is the one used by the defendant in the armed robbery might consist of testimony that it had defendant's fingerprints on it and was found in a dumpster a block away from the crime scene the morning after the robbery.

How is evidence sufficient to support a finding determined? The process is the same as determining ESSF for the firsthand knowledge of a witness under FRE 602, which, again, is analogous to the civil summary judgment standard. ESSF means enough evidence of a fact that a reasonable jury could find that fact to be probably true. The judge will not assess credibility in making this determination, but assume that the witnesses supplying the foundation facts are testifying truthfully. (The jury has the prerogative to decide otherwise and disregard the testimony after it has been admitted into evidence.) Thus, in the hypothetical just discussed, if the judge thinks that a reasonable jury could find the gun to have been used by the defendant in the robbery based on testimony that the gun bore the defendant's fingerprints and was found in the nearby dumpster the next morning, then the ESSF standard has been satisfied, and sufficient foundation has been laid to admit the gun into evidence.

Like the civil summary judgment context, ESSF is in theory a burden of production—meaning that the party offering an exhibit has an affirmative obligation to make the evidentiary showing that the claim about the exhibit is probably true. The opposing party can object that an offered item of evidence lacks foundation, taking one of two different approaches to making the objection. First, the opposing party may simply argue that the foundation evidence is insufficient to support the required finding (e.g., that the gun belonged to the defendant). Second, the opposing party might offer contrary evidence. (The procedure for doing so is discussed below.) But as with summary judgment, if the offer of contrary evidence raises a factual dispute that a factfinder could reasonably resolve either way, the exhibit must be admitted and the foundation question ultimately resolved by the trier of fact. Putting this another way, once the offering party has presented ESSF that the claim about the exhibit is probably true, the exhibit should be admitted (assuming that no exclusionary rules apply to the exhibit, like hearsay). But admission of the exhibit does not bar the opposing party from presenting evidence and argument to the jury that the exhibit is *not* what the proponent claims (e.g., the gun was *not* the defendant's). Moreover, courts have consistently held that the sufficiency standard "does not erect a particularly high hurdle. . . . Indeed, the proponent of the evidence is not required to rule out all possibilities inconsistent with authenticity, or to prove beyond any doubt that the evidence is what it purports to be. Rather, a court may find proper authentication merely upon a showing that a reasonable juror could find in favor of authenticity or identification." CA, Inc. v. Simple, Inc., 2009 U.S. Dist. LEXIS 25242, at *49 (E.D.N.Y.).

3. FRE 901—Practical Applications: The Problem of Incomplete Foundations

We've seen that FRE 901's requirement to show that an item of evidence "is what the proponent claims it is" requires showing that the fact is logically connected to the offering party's theory of the case. The FRE 901 foundation rule can be restated in the following terms: A complete foundation for an item of evidence consists of all facts necessary to show the relevance of the offered evidence. This definition of foundation is theoretically correct, and useful for understanding the underlying concept of foundation. But theoretically complete foundations raise practical problems, and as a result, practitioners and judges frequently skip over them in practice. It's important to understand both the fact that this occurs, and the reason why this occurs. In this section, we'll examine those questions and, at the same time, explain the procedure for establishing exhibit foundations.

a. Basic Procedure: Offering an Exhibit Through a Foundation Witness

The first thing to know about the procedure for laying the foundation for an exhibit is this: Pretty much everything you've seen in courtroom scenes on TV and in movies about the handling of exhibits is wrong. The courtroom drama *A Few Good Men* is typical. Tom Cruise, representing two marines charged with homicide in a court martial (a tribunal that is supposed to adhere to the FRE), waves a piece of paper in the air. He says that after his clients were arrested, the barracks room of the victim, Private Santiago, was sealed off and searched. He tells us that the paper is an inventory of Santiago's closet, and then reads off a long list of clothing items—numbers of pants, shirts, boots, socks, etc.

But in real court, lawyers are not permitted, on merely their own say-so, to supply the information identifying an exhibit. There must be "evidence sufficient to support a finding" that the exhibit is what the proponent claims—whether an accurate inventory of the contents of Private Santiago's closet, or anything else. And as judges instruct juries in every trial in every jurisdiction in the United States, "statements of counsel are not evidence." (See, e.g., the transcript of the *Johnson* trial, at page 69).

What this means is that ESSF of foundation facts must be presented in the same manner as any other evidence: by witnesses with firsthand knowledge of the facts they testify to. While the FRE recognize certain exceptions (see FRE 902, discussed below), the general rule is that an exhibit must be introduced through the testimony of a percipient witness. You might think of this foundation witness as a sort of evidentiary "sponsor" for the exhibit. Thus for example, ct. kaffee would have needed to call a witness, such as a person who actually observed the contents of Santiago's closet, and wrote up the inventory. (Since that would have been tedious for moviegoers, the filmmakers dispensed with it.)

This approach to foundation is suggested in FRE 901(b)(1). Although FRE 901(b)(1) seems to suggest that "Testimony of a Witness with Knowledge. . . . that an item is what it is claimed to be" is only one of a menu of options for providing foundations, it is better to think of it as a restatement of the general rule combining FRE 602 (the firsthand knowledge requirement) and FRE 901(a), the basic foundation requirement. With a few exceptions, foundation must be provided by the testimony of a witness (or witnesses) with firsthand knowledge that the item is what the proponent claims.

Once a witness with firsthand knowledge of the relevant foundation facts has been called to the stand, establishing the foundation for the exhibit need not be all that complicated. Many trial practice handbooks provide numerous sample foundation-witness examinations. But don't be fooled into thinking that there are litanies of magic words that must always be uttered, and that these litanies differ for each different type of exhibit—as if the foundation for each exhibit were its own magic spell. Remember, all foundations are shown by ESSF that the exhibit is what the offering party wants to claim that it is. And remember too that witnesses are required by FRE 602 to testify from personal knowledge.

This means that on direct examination, most exhibit foundations can be established by asking some variation of two simple questions: (1) "What is this?" and (2) "How do you know?" The "what-is-it/how-do-you-know" approach will generate 90 percent of the foundation examinations you will ever need. Let's try applying this to the inventory of Private Santiago's closet. What is our claim about that sheet of paper? It is an inventory or list of items found in Private Santiago's closet the morning after his homicide; and it is accurate. So the direct examination would go like this:

> [Tom Cruise]:   I show you [the witness] what has been marked as Defense Exhibit 2 for identification. What is this?
>
> The Witness: It's an inventory of items found in Private Santiago's closet.
>
> Q. How do you know?
> A. Because I wrote it.
> Q. Is the inventory accurate?
> A. Yes.
> Q. How do you know?
> A. Because I carefully looked at every item in Santiago's closet and wrote it down.
> [Tom Cruise]:   Your Honor, I move exhibit 2 into evidence.

How hard is that? Note that the foundation is a kind of story about the exhibit, and one that the party offering the exhibit would want the jury to hear anyway. The foundation explains not only what the exhibit is, but vouches for its accuracy and identifies the original source of the information.

The only formalities that are not organically linked to telling the jury a persuasive story are marking the exhibit for identification and moving it into evidence. Marking the exhibit for identification is a necessary housekeeping detail. It allows the court and the parties to keep track of the exhibit through the trial, and to make clear references to it for the record on appeal. (A reference merely to "this" in a transcript is ambiguous, and it may be easier to say "Exhibit 2" than "the inventory of Santiago's closet.") Moving the exhibit into evidence signals to the judge that the offering party believes he has met his FRE 901 burden of ESSF and allows the judge to rule on it. It also signals to opposing counsel that a foundation objection, which would have been premature up to that point, should be made now if at all. If the judge admits the exhibit into evidence, it becomes part of the trial record. The jury may be allowed to examine it in the courtroom, and it will be given to the jury along with the other admitted exhibits to examine in the jury room during deliberations.

b. Partial Foundations and Connecting Up

Difficulties often arise with foundation evidence owing to the application of the firsthand knowledge requirement to foundation witnesses. As discussed in connection with FRE 602, party narratives at trial are chopped into pieces due to the personal knowledge requirement: Witnesses can tell only that part of the story they know from firsthand sense perception. This same problem can also affect foundation evidence, which after all constitutes a mini-narrative about an item of evidence. In other words, it is frequently the case that no single witness is capable of providing the entire evidentiary foundation for an exhibit through firsthand knowledge. In practice, a partial foundation will be sufficient to gain admission of an exhibit if the balance of the evidence—the additional evidence needed to meet the ESSF threshold—has been previously introduced or is promised to be introduced later in the trial.

There are two situations in which partial foundations are treated as sufficient. The first is a widely recognized situation, and is referred to by courts and practitioners as "connecting up" or "conditional admissibility." The second situation is not widely acknowledged, and does not have a name; we will refer to that situation as simply overlooking the incompleteness of the foundation.

Conditional Admissibility: "Connecting Up."   "In [some] cases it is customary to permit [the offering party] to introduce the evidence and 'connect it up' later." Huddleston v. United States, 485 U.S. 681, 690 n.7 (1988). This customary practice is called "connecting [or linking] up" or "conditional admissibility." See FRE 104(b). When an exhibit is introduced into the case through the testimony of a witness who can provide only an incomplete foundation, the judge may admit the exhibit into evidence "conditionally"—that is, on the condition that the offering party will complete the foundation through subsequently presented evidence. The offering party represents to the court—promises, in essence—to "connect up" the exhibit to the theory of the case through the anticipated further evidence.

For example, suppose the prosecution seeks to introduce into evidence a bag of cocaine allegedly sold to a government informant by the defendant. The informant can testify that he paid money to the defendant, for which he received a package of cocaine, completely wrapped in duct tape so that the contents could not be seen. But suppose he handed the package over to the police without ever having opened it; he therefore doesn't know for sure whether it contained cocaine or some other powdery substance. The police officer received a duct-taped package from an informant and was told that it was purchased from the defendant. The officer opens the package and finds a white powdery substance, from which he sends a sample to the crime lab. The officer doesn't know whether the substance is cocaine or something else, and he lacks firsthand knowledge of who sold it to the informant, not having seen the handover. Finally, the crime lab chemist knows that white powder given him by the police tested positive as cocaine, but she has no personal knowledge of how it came into the police officer's possession.

As you can see from this example, none of the three witnesses can testify to a complete foundation for the exhibit—that it is a package of cocaine sold by the defendant to the informant. Each witness can testify only to a piece. The crime lab chemist testifies that the substance is cocaine; the officer testifies that the substance was received from the informant and that the officer sent a sample to the chemist; and the informant testifies that the defendant sold him the taped package. The problem of the incomplete foundation is the same no matter the order in which the witnesses are called to testify.

Suppose the first witness to be called is the informant. He might be asked: "Do you recognize this package? What is it? How did you get it? What did you do with it after you left the scene?" The informant can testify that he gave money to the defendant and got the package in return, and that he later handed off the package to the police officer. If the prosecutor moves the package into evidence, the defense can object that the package is irrelevant, because there is no evidence that there was any cocaine in the package. Or defense counsel can object that the exhibit lacks foundation, because there is not ESSF that it was a package of cocaine. (As you can see, the two objections are essentially the same.) You can play the scenario out and make the pertinent foundation objections if the first witness is the police officer, or the chemist. (Take a moment, and try this.)

At this juncture, the court has two options. First, it can deny admission of the exhibit until the foundation is complete. The cocaine package will be admitted after the third of the three witnesses has testified, because by then there should be ESSF that the exhibit is what the prosecution claims—a package of cocaine sold by the defendant to the informant.

Second, the prosecutor can promise to the court that she will subsequently connect up the exhibit to the case through the remaining foundation evidence—here, the testimony of the other two foundation witnesses. The court can accept this promise and admit the package of cocaine after the first (or the second) of the three witnesses testifies, on the condition that the prosecutor follows through with the additional evidence. If the full foundation evidence never materializes, the court can subsequently exclude the evidence—the condition of further foundation evidence having gone unfulfilled. (In some cases, if the conditionally admitted evidence were prejudicial enough to the defendant, and the prosecutor fails to connect up, the court could declare a mistrial.) This latter option is what is meant by "conditional admissibility" of the evidence.

Reducing the "Claim" Not an Option.   It is important to note that the offering party usually can't finesse an incomplete foundation by reducing the "claim" about the exhibit. Suppose the first witness to testify is the crime lab chemist, who says, "I tested a sample of white powder provided to me by Detective Thompson. The sample, marked 'Case No. 15-241,' tested positive as cocaine." The prosecutor moves the cocaine into evidence. Defense counsel objects that the exhibit is irrelevant and lacks foundation. It won't suffice at this point for the prosecutor to say, "But your honor, I just want to prove that it was cocaine. I'm not trying to prove it had anything to do with the defendant (at least not yet)." The testimony is not ESSF that this particular sample had anything to do with the defendant. Indeed, because there is a lot of cocaine in the world, and the jury knew this fact before the trial started, as a matter of common knowledge, proof of the existence of cocaine is not by itself relevant.

So here, the prosecutor's effort to finesse a foundation problem by shrinking her purported "claim" about the exhibit necessarily fails. Her claim about the exhibit must be nothing less than that it was the cocaine sold by the defendant to the informant. The "claim" under FRE 901 is not something that can be crafted or reshaped to match the testimony of a particular witness at a particular moment in the trial. Rather, it is the claim that has to be made in order to establish the relevance of the exhibit. That claim is dictated by the offering party's theory of the case, and can't be manipulated at will to gain admissibility on an incomplete foundation.

Overlooked Incomplete Foundations.   Connecting up is a widely acknowledged and recurring situation that has a name and a procedural solution. The evidence will be admitted with an incomplete foundation, or it will be temporarily excluded until the foundation has been completed.

A second situation involving incomplete foundations is also a recurring one, but it is not widely acknowledged and does not have a name. In many instances, the foundation is not complete, but the court will fail to see the problem or will consciously ignore it. In these situations, the facts supplying a complete foundation are already in the case, or they have been implicitly promised by the very nature of the claim brought. In one sense, you could practice trial law successfully without thinking about this problem, since judges and opposing counsel are likely to overlook it. The reason we discuss it is that, by understanding it, you'll have a better grasp of foundation as a concept and avoid some of the pitfalls and confusion that judges, lawyers, and scholars sometimes fall into, by mistaking incomplete for complete foundations.

The rule drafters have contributed to this problem. FRE 901(b) purports to list examples of "evidence that satisfies the [foundation] requirement." But we can see that that's not quite true—that at least some of the examples could be incomplete foundations that do not fully satisfy the requirement of FRE 901(a). Consider the example in FRE 901(b)(5), stating that foundation can be laid for a voice (presumably on an audio recording or phone call) by "[a]n opinion identifying a person's voice—whether heard firsthand or through mechanical or electronic transmission or recording—based on hearing the voice at any time under circumstances that connect it with the alleged speaker."

Suppose that a defendant is being tried for conspiring to distribute narcotics. The prosecution offers a tape recording of the following phone conversation: Speaker 1 says "Yes?" Speaker 2 says, "It's me." Speaker 1 replies, "Let's do it." The prosecutor claims that Speaker 1 is the defendant, and that "let's do it" is a directive to Speaker 2 to buy a shipment of narcotics with Speaker 1's money. The prosecution offers a witness who is familiar with the defendant's voice through years of acquaintance, and the witness says that the voice of Speaker 1 is the defendant's. Such testimony seemingly satisfies the example in FRE 901(b)(5). It is ESSF to identify the voice on the recording as the defendant's—which is probably all that the drafters of FRE 901(b)(5) intended to convey by their example. But the evidence is hardly ESSF to show that the defendant saying "let's do it" is a green light to make a large drug buy—as opposed to, say, answering a trivia question about Cole Porter. The complete foundation must entail sufficient context so that a reasonable jury could find that "let's do it" was a directive to buy drugs, which in this example would require the testimony of other witnesses.

As noted above, incomplete foundations might sometimes be a question of linking up. But it is noteworthy that FRE 901(b) does not mention the possibility of connecting up to complete the foundation evidence; it says its examples are sufficient foundations. We think the best explanation of this is that in many cases the missing foundation evidence has already been either admitted into the case or else has been implicitly promised by the theory of the case identified in the party's opening statement. In the above example, the prosecution may already have identified Speaker 2 as the defendant's henchman who made a series of narcotics buys on behalf of the defendant based on terse, encoded commands. Perhaps this evidence came in during the course of presenting evidence on the basic narrative of defendant's alleged guilt as a narcotics dealer. At this stage in the trial, the context for "let's do it" might be sufficiently clear that neither the judge nor opposing counsel find it necessary to question the completeness of this limited foundation testimony: merely, that Speaker 1's voice is the defendant's.

Incomplete foundations are often overlooked when the complete foundation requires reference to consequential case facts that are closely linked to the essential elements of the claim. (These are facts designated "FOC(EE)" in the diagrams throughout the book.) To take another example: The defendant is charged with armed robbery, and the prosecution's theory of the case, as indicated in his opening statement, is that the weapon used by the defendant was an automatic pistol. The prosecution calls the first two witnesses, a police officer and a forensic expert, who testify respectively that an automatic pistol was found in a dumpster near the crime scene the next morning and that it had defendant's fingerprints on it. But at this point in the trial, there has been no evidence that the defendant actually committed a robbery—the prosecution plans to have the victim testify last, for tactical reasons. Technically speaking, the fact that the defendant pointed this gun at the victim is necessary to complete the prosecution's full foundational claim about the gun. But that claim closely overlaps with an essential element in the case—it is an FOC(EE). In that situation, the judge and the opposing counsel might feel that the missing foundation facts "go without saying" for purposes of admitting the gun in evidence. The prosecutor has implicitly promised, with his theory of the case, to present evidence showing that the defendant pointed a gun at the victim. Otherwise, there would be no basis for the robbery charge and the case would have to be dismissed. In such a situation, the technical incompleteness of the foundation would probably be overlooked in practice.

The important point is this: The fact that, in practice, the judge or opposing counsel might not demand more foundation does not mean that "Speaker 1 is the defendant" or "this is defendant's gun" are complete or adequate foundations in themselves.

4. FRE 901—Practical Applications: Procedural Steps

Some aspects of the procedure for admitting an exhibit into evidence under FRE 901 have been discussed, but it is worth putting them all together here in a step-by-step guide.

Step One: The Claim.   First, figure out the "claim" about the exhibit. What is the story about the exhibit that makes it relevant—that makes it fit the offering party's theory of the case? The claim need not entail every fact known about the exhibit, but rather the most pared down story of the exhibit, all those facts strictly necessary to show its relevance.

Step Two: The Witness.   Second, figure out the witnesses who have firsthand knowledge of the foundation facts you've just identified. Does one witness have all the relevant knowledge, or will you need more than one witness to lay a complete foundation? If more than one witness is required, determine whether those other facts will already have been presented before you try to introduce the evidence—in which case, your foundation will be complete—or whether, instead, those other facts will come later. In the latter instance, you'll have to say that you will "connect up" the foundation, and you'll probably ask for conditional admission of the exhibit.

Step Three: Marking the Exhibit.   Third, identify the exhibit for the record. The traditional approach is to ask the court clerk to "mark" the exhibit "for identification" with a sequential exhibit number. The clerk will literally place a sticker on the exhibit saying "Plaintiff's Exhibit no. 10" or some such. Many courts now require that exhibits be identified and marked for identification by the parties, before the trial begins. This saves time during the trial.

Step Four: Showing the Exhibit.   Now show the exhibit to the witness. For the record, narrate what you're doing. (E.g., "I'm showing you [showing the witness] what has been marked as plaintiff's Exhibit 10.")

Step Five: Laying the Foundation.   Fifth, lay the foundation through questions to the foundation witness, who, again, must have firsthand knowledge of facts relating to the exhibit. On direct examination, the foundation questions will be some variant of "What is it?" and "How do you know?" The precise questions will depend on the details of steps one and two, above.

Thus far, our examples and discussions have assumed that exhibits are always offered through friendly witnesses called by the offering party—and hence, require open-ended direct examination questions. But, in fact, any party can introduce an exhibit through any witness called by any party, as long as the witness has first-hand knowledge. You can use an adverse witness, or the other side's witness to lay a foundation. This means that, *in some instances, you will lay a foundation on cross-examination (or an adverse or hostile direct examination)*. This will permit you to ask leading questions, which makes the foundation questioning even easier. As the questioning lawyer, you simply tell the witness the foundation facts about the exhibit with the expectation of getting affirmative answers. Instead of "What is it?" and "How do you know?" you ask: "Exhibit 10 is a tape recording of a voice saying 'let's do it.'—true? And you recognize the voice as the defendant's—right? You know the defendant's voice, because you've known him for over ten years—correct?"

Step Six: Moving the Exhibit. When you, as offering party, believe the foundation is complete, you move the exhibit into evidence. "Your honor, I move plaintiff's Exhibit 10 into evidence."

Step Seven: Objection, Ruling, Counterevidence. The motion to admit the exhibit is a signal to the opposing party to make any pertinent objections to the foundation or relevance of the evidence. Since a complete foundation consists of all facts strictly necessary to make the exhibit relevant, the failure to present a complete foundation will often mean that whatever the exhibit has been shown to be is not relevant to the case. Where the offered foundation evidence fails to establish the claim about the evidence, the technically correct objection is that the exhibit lacks foundation. (E.g., the evidentiary "claim" is that the exhibit is cocaine sold by the defendant to the government informant, but the supporting evidence is limited to the lab chemist's testimony that "this is some cocaine.") Where the offering party makes a claim that is insufficient (for example, the government says, "we are simply claiming this is some cocaine"), the technically correct objection is that the exhibit is irrelevant. But in practice, there are no magic words, so long as the basic point is conveyed, and objecting on foundation or relevance grounds should suffice—the two objections are interchangeable, as a practical matter.

The contents of an exhibit normally should not be shown to the jury before the exhibit is admitted in evidence. Thus, for example, a document should not be read to the jury until its foundation has been established and the document admitted. Likewise, a video or audio recording should not be played to the jury before its admission in evidence. With certain kinds evidence, this general rule is not practical. Items of so-called real evidence, like a gun or a bag of cocaine, may have to be shown to the witness in order to lay the foundation, and the jury will see it before it is formally admitted. If the opposing counsel thinks it would be unfairly prejudicial for the jury to see the exhibit, it may be appropriate to ask the court to conduct the initial foundation inquiry outside the presence of the jury—provided, of course, that there is a good faith argument that the proper foundation cannot be laid. The rule providing for such mini-hearings outside the presence of the jury is FRE 104(c).

Objecting to foundation prematurely, before the offering party has had the chance to complete her foundation questions, should lead to the objection being overruled. That's why the step of moving the exhibit into evidence functions as a sort of cue to the opposing party to make a foundation objection. On the other hand, since contents of an exhibit normally should not be shown before the exhibit is admitted, opposing counsel has to be on the alert for premature disclosure to the jury. If the offering party tries to disclose the contents to the jury before completing the foundation, the opposing party can object to lack of foundation.

Even if the offering party provides evidence constituting a complete foundation, the opposing party can try to counter that evidence. The most direct way to do this would be to ask to cross-examine the foundation witness before the court rules on admission of the exhibit. The opposing party might also try to present affirmative counterevidence—for example, a witness who says that someone other than the defendant sold the package of cocaine to the informant. The problem here is that the ESSF standard, like the civil summary judgment standard, does not allow the court to make credibility rulings or resolve factual disputes. Thus, in the example just given, it would be for the jury to decide which witness to believe—the government informant, or the defense witness. In cases of a factual dispute, where a reasonable jury could decide the question either way, the ESSF standard has been satisfied. Only if the rebuttal evidence somehow negates the foundation evidence beyond reasonable dispute should a court rule that foundation has not been established. Assuming that the ESSF standard has been satisfied, and the evidence admitted, the jury will be allowed to hear and consider the evidence on both sides and ultimately decide for itself whether the exhibit is indeed what the proponent claims.

Streamlined Exhibit Procedures. Traditionally, the above steps are handled at trial, during the witness examination phase. However, there is a growing trend to handle some of these matters prior to trial. It has long been common for federal and state courts to require that parties exchange lists before trial of the exhibits they intend to use, at least in civil cases. Nowadays, some court rules require that the exhibits be marked for identification prior to trial, and some even specify that the parties state their objections to exhibits in writing prior to trial. The goal of such rules is to resolve as many of such objections as possible prior to empaneling the jury, thereby streamlining the trial.

KEY POINTS

1. FRE 901 is generally considered the rule governing foundation for exhibits. FRE 901(a) provides that a party offering an item of evidence (its proponent) must present evidence sufficient to support a finding (ESSF) that the item is what the offering party claims it is.
2. The "claim" about the exhibit under FRE 901(a) comprises all facts necessary to show that the offered item is relevant under the offering party's theory of the case. A complete foundation is a showing, by ESSF, of all the facts that make up the claim about the exhibit.
3. ESSF that the exhibit is what its proponent claims is evidence sufficient for a reasonable jury to make such a finding. The supporting evidence must come from witnesses with firsthand knowledge, and must itself be admissible. The judge does not determine credibility, but asks whether a reasonable jury could make the finding, assuming the witnesses are testifying truthfully.
4. If one witness can't provide a complete foundation, the offering party must either point to other facts already in the record or else should ask for conditional admission of the exhibit subject to "connecting up" the foundation—completing it with subsequent evidence.
5. In some instances, particularly where the missing facts are closely connected to the essential elements of the case and were promised in opening statement, the court is likely to overlook incompleteness of the foundation.

PROBLEMS

4.3. In the *Hitt* case, page 171 supra, how did the prosecution authenticate the photograph that included Hitt's rifle? Who do you think the foundation witness was?

4.4. Return to Problem 3.3, United States v. Ray, at page 149. For each item of evidence or alleged fact below, identify the various possibilities for laying a proper foundation under FRE 901. Note that there may be more than one approach for each item of evidence. Also, think about this from the standpoint of investigating the case: What evidence would you want to gather before trial in order to introduce the evidence at trial? Once at trial, what different witnesses could you call, and what questions would you ask?

 (a) Exhibit 1: A copy of Andrews' confidential written memo to Rundown CFO June Jacobs dated March 14, 2015.

 (b) Exhibit 2: A copy of Chief Auditor Andrews' e-mail to Jacobs, also dated March 14, 2015.

 (c) Ray's sale of 100,000 shares on March 16, 2015.

4.5. Home run king Barry Bonds testified under oath to a grand jury charged with investigating the distribution of illegal anabolic steroids by the BALCO laboratory. Bonds denied knowingly using such steroids. Bonds was then charged with ten counts of making false statements to the grand jury. Federal agents executed a search warrant on BALCO and searched its premises. The government found samples of urine that tested positive for the presence of illegal anabolic steroids. The government claims that these are samples of Bonds's urine. It contends that Bonds's urine samples were obtained by his trainer, Greg Anderson, and then taken by Anderson to BALCO employee James Valente. Valente delivered the samples to Quest Diagnostics, which sent the samples and test results back to BALCO. The test results do not identify Bonds as the source of the urine. Quest can identify the tested urine samples as coming from Valente. Valente will testify that each time Anderson gave him the urine samples, Anderson said something to the effect of "this is from Bonds." Greg Anderson refuses to testify and has been jailed for contempt of court. Have the urine samples been adequately identified as coming from Bonds?

5. FRE 901—Practical Applications: Generic Foundation Questions for Various Exhibit Types

The foundational requirements established by FRE 901 are described in the rule's title as requirements of "authentication" or "identification." These are not doctrinal terms that have a single, well-defined meaning. Instead, as we have seen, the standard of FRE 901(a) is flexible. The starting point is always to ask: Why is this exhibit relevant? What does the proponent claim it to be, based on its connection to the offering party's theory of the case? The answers to these questions are primarily case-specific and highly contextual, and will therefore vary from case to case. But there are in addition a few recurring, generic foundation issues that frequently arise in certain broad categories of exhibits. Some of these are covered by FRE 901(b)(2) through (9), which lists a set of examples of generic foundation questions. The list is nonexhaustive, and is intended to provide analogies for the authentication of exhibits of all types.

Types of Exhibits: Real versus Depictive.   It's useful to think of exhibits as falling into two broad types: things that are relevant because they were actually part of the litigated events, and things that are relevant because they describe, depict, or reconstruct the litigated events. The former are called "real" evidence. The latter category for some reason doesn't have a universally accepted name in the cases or academic literature. For ease of reference, we'll call it "depictive" evidence. It primarily consists of photographs, video and audio recordings, and so-called demonstrative evidence.

The usefulness of this division is that these two types correlate with certain recurring questions. With real evidence, it is usually necessary to show the identity and, often, the unchanged condition of the exhibit. With depictive evidence, it is usually also necessary to show the accuracy of the depiction as part of its foundation.

Written documents are sometimes viewed as a third category. While in some sense, they too could be categorized as either real or depictive, or even as a hybrid of the two, it's common for judges, practitioners, and scholars to view documents as their own category.

a. Real Evidence Foundation Issues

Real evidence refers to tangible items that played some role in the litigated event. Examples are easily thought of: the weapon used in a crime, the cocaine allegedly sold to the government informant, the allegedly defective appliance in a products liability action. The item's connection to the specific events in dispute makes it relevant, and that connection is "what the proponent claims" for purposes of satisfying FRE 901.

The foundation for real evidence typically consists of a description of the item's physical involvement in the case. We have already examined the kinds of case-specific questions that may need to be answered to establish the foundation for such items. Not just any gun, or any cocaine will do. Under FRE 901(a), the prosecution must claim that this was the gun used by the defendant in the robbery, or that this was the cocaine sold by the defendant to the government informant.

Identity.   In addition to those case-specific foundation questions, real evidence can raise recurring questions regarding identity and unchanged condition. For example, how do we know that the sample of white powder sent to the crime lab was in fact taken from the package sold by the defendant to the government informant? What if the sample really came from a supply seized in a different cocaine case? These are questions of identity of the real evidence. Identity questions often arise when an item of real evidence is generic or fungible: a gun, cocaine, or a pile of cash, for example.

Unchanged Condition.   The machine gun in the *Hitt* case was real evidence. There, the entire case turned on the question of unchanged condition. There was inevitably a lapse of time between the seizure of the gun at the time of Hitt's arrest, and the prosecution expert's test-firing of the gun to determine that it rapid fired (and so functioned as a machine gun, as opposed to a single-shot rifle). The defense argued that in the intervening time, enough dirt had accumulated in the gun's inner workings as to cause the gun to malfunction by rapid firing. Thus, the defense argued, it wasn't converted into a rapid-fire (i.e., machine) gun by Hitt. The unchanged condition of the gun thus became an element of the foundation for the gun that had to be proven by the prosecution.

Proving Identity Through an Identifiable Marking or Characteristic. Real evidence can be identified by a percipient witness who perceived the item at some relevant time during the litigated events, and who sufficiently remembers it at the time of trial. You might think of this kind of foundation testimony as "then-and-now" or "endpoint" testimony (as in the end points of a time line). This assumes, of course, that the item is sufficiently distinctive so that a person could remember it. Conceivably, the bank teller in an armed robbery might remember with some precision what the shotgun pointed at him by the robber looked like, to the extent that two years later, at the time of trial, he can plausibly identify it in court. The foundation witness testifies, in essence, "I saw it then, and I see it now in court. It is the same thing." (In-court eyewitness identifications are a form of "then-and-now" testimony applied to the person of the defendant.)

If the item is generic (a gun) or fungible (a pile of $1,000 in 20-dollar bills), the witness may not be able to remember it with particularity; conceivably, a judge could find that a claim to be able to do so is so implausible that no reasonable jury could believe it, under the ESSF standard. Such generic or fungible items might be identified in one of two ways. Perhaps the generic item had distinctive markings on it—a person's initials, or a carved design, for example. This essentially transforms the generic item into something more unique that a witness could remember and identify in court. (E.g., "The shotgun had a skull and crossbones carved on the wooden stock.")

Generic or fungible items might also be identified by a label, a number, or a tag affixed to it at the time it was discovered. Evidence collection practices of law enforcement officers require the use of evidence tags for this reason. In many cases, the evidence tag will suffice to establish the identity of a generic item. See, e.g., United States v. Abreu, 952 F.2d 1458, 1467-1468 (1st Cir. 1992) (a drug agent sufficiently identified a shotgun as the one he seized at defendant's apartment by identifying the evidence tag placed on the gun at the time of seizure and by his signature on the tag).

Proving Identity Through Chain of Custody. Chain of custody is the second typical method of identification, most often used when an exhibit is generic and has no readily identifiable characteristics. The links in the chain of custody of the item of evidence would consist of all the people who handled the evidence between the time of its discovery at the crime scene and its appearance in the courtroom. A complete chain of custody under FRE 901(b)(4) would require the testimony of *all* such people, plus testimony to show that the exhibit was stored in a secure place when it was not being handled.

Proving Unchanged Condition Through Chain of Custody.   The chain of custody can also establish that the item was not tampered with and remains in the same condition as when it was discovered. This showing may be required if the condition of the item is as important as its identity. In the examples we have been discussing, the gun found in the dumpster near the crime scene allegedly has the defendant's fingerprints on it. The substance bought from the defendant by the government informant is supposed to be cocaine. The complete chain of custody would show that these conditions existed when the items were found, when they were tested, and perhaps even when they were presented in court. If the gun is tested for fingerprints—or if a chemical test is conducted on drugs seized from a defendant—the laboratory chemist becomes part of the chain of custody. There needs to be evidence that the gun or the drug that reached the laboratory was the same gun or drug found at the crime scene or seized from the defendant, and that it has not been tampered with before or since.

A complete chain of custody can be quite burdensome to prove, as shown in Jeter v. Commonwealth, 607 S.E. 734, 737-740 (Va. App. 2005). Testimony from the detective who seized the substance from the defendant established that he immediately sealed the suspected cocaine in a "clear plastic baggie," then at the station placed it in a lock-sealed envelope, sealed the envelope with evidence tape, and marked the envelope with the date, his initials, and his identification number; gave the envelope to an authorized agent of the Division of Forensic Sciences (DFS), who gave it to a security officer at DFS, who gave the envelope to the laboratory analyst. The envelope was in the analyst's "continuous care and control" while he was performing the analytical tests on the suspected cocaine. And, after performing the analyses, the analyst resealed the envelope with evidence tape and marked the envelope with his initials, the date, and the lab number. Both the analyst and the detective identified the envelope at trial. This established every "vital link" in the chain of possession, thereby demonstrating with "reasonable certainty" that the evidence had not been altered, substituted, or contaminated.

Cases decided under FRE 901(a) make it clear that the complete chain of custody need not always be proved to satisfy the sufficiency standard. Even where gaps exist in the chain of custody of substances that require testing, courts have held that a jury *could* reasonably find that the exhibit in question was adequately identified and still in an unchanged condition. "A break in the chain of custody will not necessarily lead to the exclusion of the evidence . . . . Rather, the ultimate question is whether the authentication testimony is sufficiently complete so as to convince the court that [a reasonable jury could decline to find] that the original item had been exchanged with another or otherwise tampered with." United States v. Grant, 967 F.2d 81, 82 (2d Cir. 1992). In making this decision, courts routinely give the government the benefit of a *presumption* that evidence has been handled properly. United States v. Glawson, 322 Fed. Appx. 957 (11th Cir. 2009) (absent evidence to the contrary, the trial judge may assume that a police officer would not tamper with exhibits).

This informal but habitual presumption means that courts will typically demand that a claim of tampering must be supported by specific evidence to contest the government's proof of chain of custody. Where such evidence is offered, the court could decide to exclude the government's exhibit on the ground that it has failed to establish unchanged condition through chain of custody. Or it could admit both the disputed item of real evidence together with the defendant's evidence of changed condition. The defendant can try to persuade the jury that it has no relevance or probative value in the case. See United States v. Ladd, 885 F.2d 954, 956-957 (1st Cir. 1989) (admitting blood and urine test results from state crime lab together with defense evidence of sloppy lab practices, but excluding blood tests conducted for government by private lab). Note that the informal presumption of reliability accorded to criminal forensics labs may be subject to change, as such labs become the subject of increasingly widespread reports of negligence or fraud in handling forensic evidence.

Once an item of real evidence has been authenticated, it is still potentially subject to the judge's discretion to exclude pursuant to FRE 403. However, it is customary for judges to treat real evidence as being highly probative and thus of considerable assistance to the jury, sometimes with little analysis of what the jury would learn for purposes of deciding a fact of consequence in the case. Thus, the admission of even gruesome objects has been upheld if they played a part in the litigated events.

b. Depictive Evidence Foundation Issues

As noted above, "depictive" evidence is a term we use in this book to mean items of evidence (primarily, exhibits) that describe, depict, or reconstruct litigated events. This category does not include actual testimony from percipient witnesses recounting their firsthand knowledge of those events. Depictive evidence raises the standard foundation questions of identity and unchanged condition. Further, the relevance of an item of depictive evidence also depends on the accuracy with which it depicts an aspect of the litigated events. Accuracy therefore becomes part of the foundation for such evidence.

Recordings and Photographs. Audio, video, and photographic recordings are generally not litigated events in themselves, but are an independent record of those events. Although they may be offered together with the testimony of a witness who perceived the events, the recordings themselves are not testimony, since they are imprinted on tape or film or some other medium rather than in human memory. The recording reveals what the equipment "saw" or "heard," perhaps with less risk of human fallibility than an eyewitness. Even if there were reasonably reliable eyewitnesses, the recording in effect offers an independent version of an occurrence that could be used as substantive evidence. Such a photographic or sound recording, if properly authenticated, would be admissible as substantive proof as to what out-of-court events occurred.

The types and sources of such recordings can vary widely. Law enforcement officers produce audio recordings of intercepted phone conversations. Automatic security cameras in banks, stores, ATMs, or elsewhere create continuous audiovisual records in the hope of preserving evidence of, if not deterring, crimes. Police departments increasingly require digital cameras to be worn by their officers as "body cams," or to be mounted on police cars, in order to create independent evidentiary records. And of course, individuals with cameras may happen to capture occurrences that eventually become relevant in litigation. As individuals increasingly carry cell phones with fairly high-quality digital cameras, and as digital cameras become cheaper, easier to use, and of better recording quality, the availability of digitally recorded evidence will only increase. The impact of these technological developments may be highly significant. Consider, for example, the recent spate of police excessive force incidents captured on cell phone cameras by bystanders, compared to the extreme rarity of such footage at the time of the shocking video of the infamous Rodney King beating in 1991.

"Now-and-Then/Endpoint" Foundations for Recordings and Photographs. There are two fundamental ways to lay a foundation for recordings and still photos. As with real evidence, the foundation for a recording or photograph can be laid with "now-and-then/endpoint" testimony. This foundation is straightforward. A percipient witness who perceived the actual event at the time it occurred and remembers it now, and therefore has personal knowledge of it, can be shown the photograph or recording of the event and testify that the photograph or recording is an accurate depiction of the actual event. While technically the FRE don't require the utterance of magic words by the foundation witness, it's very common for witnesses to be asked whether the recording is a "fair," or "accurate," or "true" record or some combination of those three words. This testimony to the accuracy of the recording also suffices to establish the identity and unchanged condition of the contents without a separate or additional inquiry.

Note that it's not necessary with this type of foundation to take testimony from the photographer herself—if there even is a human photographer. Note also, that the timing for showing the photo or recording to the foundation witness is flexible. It can be done in court. Or it can have been done prior to trial, in which case the foundation witness could testify: "Two months ago, I was shown the video, and it accurately depicted the events I remember seeing." It might be necessary, in that situation, for a further foundation witness to testify that the video is now in the same condition as it has been when the other witness saw it.

"Process" Foundations for Recordings and Photographs. The second type of foundation for recordings and photographs is needed when there is no "then and now" witness available. In that situation, the fairness and accuracy of the recording or photograph will have to be inferred from testimony showing that the process of making and keeping the recording or photograph demonstrates its fairness and accuracy. Recall that a chain of custody is a process to preserve both the identity and unchanged condition of an item of real evidence. What sort of process questions would you need to answer if you wanted to show that a recording or photograph accurately recorded its content and has not been changed, due to deterioration or "doctoring"?

You could call the photographer as a foundation witness. Working behind the camera, the photographer may or may not be a useful percipient witness to events: The photographic record may have captured a lot more relevant information than the photographer was able to see or remember. Instead, she testifies about the process of taking the photograph, and we rely on the technical qualities of the equipment to infer that the recording is a "fair and accurate" depiction of the actual events. Some chain-of-custody type testimony would need to be added to establish unchanged condition, because the photographer is not acting as a "then-and-now" foundation witness.

Of course, with automated recording equipment, there is no human photographer making the recording of the relevant occurrence. In this situation, the only alternative to a then-and-now witness would be a "process" witness who can testify to the process by which the photo was taken: what sort of equipment was used, how the camera was set up to operate automatically, how the recordings were preserved, etc. Again, in this situation, the reliability of the process for producing and maintaining the recording or photograph is used as ESSF that the end product is a "fair and accurate" record of the underlying events.

The Impact of Technological Change on Foundation for Recordings and Photographs. How much evidence must be presented about the technical characteristics of the recording equipment, whether or not there was a human photographer making the recording? There is a general tendency in the cases—one that might have more to do with the human nature of judges than with the doctrinal logic of evidence law—to require more technical characteristics evidence to establish foundation for the output of novel technological processes, and less such evidence where the technology is more familiar. Compare United States v. Stephens, 202 F. Supp. 2d 1361, 1368 (N.D. Ga. 2002) (automatic recordings "may satisfy the requirements of the [FRE] . . . so long as a witness testifies to the type of equipment or camera used, its general reliability, the quality of the recorded product, the process by which it was focused, or the general reliability of the entire system") with United States v. Harris, 55 M.J. 433, 438 (CAAF 2001) ("Any doubt as to the general reliability of the video cassette recording technology has gone the way of the BETA tape"). For example, in older cases, courts adopted a much stricter attitude to ensure the accuracy of tape and film recordings, requiring proof of the equipment operator's qualifications, the working condition of the equipment, and the absence of material alterations, typically through a complete chain of custody of the recording itself from the time it was made until presentation in the courtroom. See, e.g., United States v. McMillan, 508 F.2d 101, 104 (8th Cir. 1974) (establishing seven-factor *McKeever-McMillan* test for authenticating recordings); United States v. Starks, 515 F.2d 112, 121 n.11 (3d Cir. 1975) (adopting this test). Such strict foundation requirements for now-familiar technology have eroded or been abandoned. See, e.g., United States v. Spence, 566 F. App'x 240, 242-244 (4th Cir. 2014) (rejecting *McKeever-McMillan* test in favor of simple accuracy showing); United States v. Henley, 766 F.3d 893, 912 (8th Cir. 2014) (treating *McKeever-McMillan* test as merely "helpful guidelines"). Some still-valid precedent raises the burden in criminal cases by requiring that the prosecution provide "clear and convincing evidence" that a tape recording is a "true, accurate, and authentic recording of a conversation between the parties," but the foundation requirement no longer generally requires elaborate evidence explaining the technical recording process. United States v. Emerson, 501 F.3d 804, 813-814 (7th Cir. 2007); accord United States v. Hamilton, 334 F.3d 170, 186-187 (2d Cir. 2003).

While our society, including judges, may be increasingly accepting the capacity of digital cameras to make accurate recordings and photographs, a countertrend may offset the willingness of courts to accept simple and easy foundations for such exhibits. Specifically, related technical advances may make it easier to falsify or "doctor" digital recordings and photographs. This raises a question we have already seen in the real evidence context. Who has the burden, and what is the burden, of showing unchanged condition? The general tendency of courts over the years has been to liberalize foundations and allow disputes over genuineness to go to the jury. It might be said that a minimal chain of custody to prove the continued integrity of the recording will suffice, in effect, to shift the burden to the objecting party to produce evidence raising doubts about the unchanged condition of a recording. See People v. Goldsmith, 326 P.3d 239, 248-249 (Cal. 2014) ("We decline to require a greater showing of authentication for the admissibility of digital images merely because in theory they can be manipulated."); United States v. Harris, supra, at 440 (although "technology makes alteration of photographs a *possibility*. . . . the Government need only show by direct or circumstantial evidence a *reasonable probability* that the evidence is authentic"); United States v. Stephens, 202 F. Supp. 2d at 1369 (noting that the same technical advances that make it easier to tamper with photos "have also greatly improved our ability to detect and expose such electronic tampering"). However, the case law is sufficiently variable and in flux that you would have to research this question carefully to determine the required foundation in an individual case. See Lorraine v. Markel Am. Ins. Co., 241 F.R.D. 534, 544 (D. Md. 2007) ("Obviously, there is no 'one size fits all' approach that can be taken when authenticating electronic evidence, in part because technology changes so rapidly that it is often new to many judges.").

FRE 403 and Recordings or Photographs.   Sometimes foundation questions relating to recordings will shade into FRE 403 arguments. Recordings or photographs whose accuracy is questionable can raise FRE 403 dangers of misleading the jury. And of course, photographic records that portray gruesome events such as personal injuries or autopsies of crime victims, are frequently objected to as unfairly prejudicial. The important point to remember is that FRE 403 objections are different from foundation objections, and can be made even if the ESSF standard for foundation has been met.

Demonstrative Evidence.   *Demonstrative* evidence reproduces or depicts persons, objects (such as items of real evidence that are not brought into court), or scenes that are connected to the litigated events in the case. Examples are models, diagrams, and drawings. In addition, recordings or photographs made at times different from those of the underlying events might also be classed as demonstrative. For example, a photo of an intersection made long before or after a car accident may give the jury a visual impression of the layout of the scene, or demonstrate lighting conditions at a relevant time of day. These exhibits are offered to illustrate or explain the testimony of witnesses, including experts, and to present or summarize significant portions of complex and voluminous documents.

Some demonstrative exhibits are reconstructions of litigated events or conditions, or summaries of facts, that have been created expressly for the litigation. Examples include things like a chart or tables or relevant data (for example, a one-page summary of expenditures boiled down from hundreds of checks and receipts), a map of an accident or crime scene, an organizational chart, a model of a human body with a particular type of injury, a scale model of a defectively designed car or airplane. Computer-generated animation or simulations can be used in trials to portray out-of-court events for the jury. Demonstrative exhibits are often, but need not, be fully created in advance: A witness could be asked to make a drawing from scratch, or to mark a pre-made map, to illustrate a point in his testimony.

In theory at least, such demonstrative exhibits do not have independent probative value on the substantive issues in a case. They are relevant, and permitted to be viewed by the jury, because they assist the jury in understanding testimonial, documentary, and real evidence. Such demonstrative exhibits are typically not admitted into evidence, yet they nevertheless require foundation. There must be testimony of one or more percipient witnesses to provide "then-and-now" testimony to establish ESSF that the demonstrative exhibit is a "fair and accurate" representation of the underlying events or conditions it depicts. Where the demonstrative evidence has been created by more complex technical processes, such as computer animation, some kind of process testimony will be required by someone who knows the technology and can speak to how the evidence was created. Courts also require a showing that demonstrative evidence will assist the trier of fact by increasing its understanding of the relevant events.

Some demonstrative evidence takes the form of a courtroom demonstration, which is not a tangible thing that would be marked as an exhibit. A witness might be asked to get up from the witness chair to show the jury the position of his body during a fight, perhaps with the lawyer taking part in the demonstration. A lawyer might try to demonstrate a distance in a litigated event by making reference to persons or objects in the courtroom. The proponent of the demonstration must lay a proper foundation establishing the similarity of circumstances and conditions between the out-of-court event and the in-court presentation. The conditions need not be identical, but they must be sufficiently similar to provide a fair comparison. In United States v. Gaskell, 985 F.2d 1056, 1060-1061 (11th Cir. 1993), a demonstration by an expert witness as to the amount of force needed to cause a seven-month-old infant's fatal injuries was held inadmissible. Shaking a rubber doll was not substantially similar due to stiffness of the doll's neck, differences in the weight of head, and absence of testimony concerning the number of oscillations required to produce the infant's injuries.

A Further Note About Photographs and Recordings.   We've discussed recordings and photographs as depictive evidence because they depict relevant occurrences and are not an intrinsic part of what happened that gave rise to a case. A bank robbery would be a crime whether the surveillance camera caught it on video or not. The video is evidence of "what happened," but is not itself what happened. In such circumstances, the recording or photograph is treated as depictive evidence, relevant only if it fairly and accurately depicts the relevant events.

But sometimes a photograph or recording *is* part of the chain of occurrences giving rise to a case. Suppose a robbery eyewitness identifies the defendant from a mug shot or photo array. At trial, the defendant claims mistaken identity and will want to prove that the photo identification procedure was improperly suggestive, causing the eyewitness to mistakenly select the defendant's photo. The photo or photos used in the identification procedure are thus real evidence—they played a role in the litigated events. But the manner in which they were shown to the eyewitness during the police investigation would have to be re-created in court, for the jury. That re-creation would be demonstrative evidence. The photo of the defendant may not be "fair and accurate"—indeed, the defense claims that it was misleading in some way. But a courtroom re-creation is demonstrative evidence, and must be a "fair and accurate" depiction of the manner in which the photos were shown to the witness by the police.

c.   Written Documents

Written documents tend to be treated as a separate category of evidence that is neither real nor depictive. That categorization of written documents has more to do with convention than logic. But it may stem from the fact that written documents can have elements of either or both real or depictive evidence, and that they often raise issues governed by the hearsay rule and its exceptions. The relevance of writings in a given case virtually always stems from a logical connection between their contents and the litigated events, and in many cases their language supplies sufficient context or information to make that logical connection clear. Whether that is true or not in a particular instance, a writing resembles real evidence if its creation is a relevant occurrence in itself—the signing of a written contract or the writing and publication of a libelous statement, for example. And it resembles depictive evidence if its relevance consists in its description of some relevant event, such as a diary entry recounting an instance of workplace harassment, or a time card showing that the defendant was clocked in at work when he was purportedly committing a robbery on the other side of town.

Foundation for Writings.   As with any other exhibit, the foundation for a writing will depend on how the offering party asserts it is relevant—on the claim about what the writing is. In most cases, ESSF of the authorship of the document, combined with a few case-specific context facts about the document and its contents, will provide sufficient foundation.

If the writing is an act that is relevant because of who executed it—the signature on a contract, for example—the foundation will include both facts that make the contract relevant to the case as well as ESSF that the signature was made by the relevant person. A witness who observed the defendant signing the contract could testify to that based on firsthand knowledge. See FRE 602, 901(b)(1). Alternatively, the signature could be attributed to the defendant based on the testimony of a witness familiar with the defendant's handwriting under FRE 901(b)(2), or by a comparison between the signature and a known sample of the defendant's handwriting, under FRE 901(b)(3). Authorship of a writing could even be proved by circumstantial evidence. See, e.g., United States v. Thompson, 449 F.3d 267, 274 (1st Cir. 2006) (finding ESSF that defendant authored letter that precisely fit his circumstances and conveyed facts known peculiarly to him); United States v. Gonzalez-Maldonado, 115 F.3d 9, 20 (1st Cir. 1997) (notebook found in a person's briefcase in that person's room, along with an identification card, was sufficiently authenticated as belonging to that person by such circumstantial evidence).

Depictive Writings Are Usually Hearsay.   If the writing is relevant because its contents depict relevant events, we are concerned on some level with the fairness and accuracy of the depiction. But this situation is likely to mean that the writing is hearsay—a statement made outside the trial that is relevant because the offering party claims it makes true factual assertions. In that situation, the writing will be admitted only if it fits a hearsay exception or exemption. Since many of the rules regarding hearsay exceptions or exemptions are themselves concerned with accuracy or reliability, the accuracy aspects of foundation for depictive writings will tend to be rolled into a hearsay analysis. Nevertheless, the foundation could require ESSF that the facts conveyed are accurate or reliable. Depending on the type of document, this could require, again, some showing of who authored the document. In addition, it may require a showing that the author had reason to know the facts depicted. As will be seen when we study the hearsay exceptions, this may simply be a question of showing ESSF that the author of the writing probably had firsthand knowledge of the matters stated in the writing.

Business Records.   Records of a business or other institution can be authenticated as to their source under FRE 901(b)(4) through proof of matching letterhead, comparison with matching forms, testimony about the routine practices of the institution in generating such records, and through testimony of a custodian about how the business's filing or data retrieval system operates and that the document was retrieved from a certain file or in a certain way. FRE 901(b)(7) provides for the authentication of certain types of public records or reports. Proof that they "are from the public office where items of this nature are kept" can be provided by testimony from the custodian, or by a certificate of authenticity from the public office. See FRE 902(2), discussed below.

Ancient Documents.   FRE 902(b)(8) provides that a writing that is more than 20 years old will be deemed authentic based on ESSF that it was found in a place where it would likely be if it were authentic. See Threadgill v. Armstrong World Industries, Inc., 928 F.2d 1366, 1376 (3d Cir. 1991) (admitting correspondence from the 1930s showing corporate knowledge of asbestos risks that had first been stored in a company vault, then moved to various corporate departments); and "in a condition that creates no suspicion about its authenticity." FRE902(b)(8)(A). This latter requirement refers to subsequent tampering with the document, and not its accuracy when originally created. See United States v. Demjanjuk, 367 F.3d 623, 631 (6th Cir. 2004) (suspicion about the accuracy of the original contents of Nazi document "goes to its weight and is a matter for the trier of fact"). An extremely broad "ancient documents" exception to the rule excluding hearsay, FRE 803(16), provides for the admission of a "document in existence twenty years or more the authenticity of which is established."

Electronic Writings.   Due to the enormous growth in digital document creation and storage in recent years, electronic writings (also known as "e-evidence") are
increasingly used in both civil and criminal litigation. Most common are computer-
generated data files, e-mails, chat group discussions, text messages, and web postings
of various types. The authentication of such electronic writings can be hotly contested
when authorship is in dispute.

Judicial approaches to foundation for these types of e-evidence are very much
in flux. In some instances, judges seek analogies to traditional writings, and decline
to presume technology-based accuracy problems in e-evidence. In United States v.
Safavian, the court observed:

> The possibility of alteration does not and cannot be the basis for excluding e-mails as
> unidentified or unauthenticated as a matter of course, any more than it can be the
> rationale for excluding paper documents (and copies of those documents). We live in
> an age of technology and computer use where e-mail communication now is a normal
> and frequent fact for the majority of this nation's population, and is of particular impor-
> tance in the professional world. [435 F. Supp. 2d 36, 41 (D.D.C. 2006).]

See also CA, Inc. v. Simple, Inc., 2009 U.S. Dist. LEXIS 25242, at *55-56 (E.D.N.Y.
2009) ("The mere theoretical possibility" or "bare assertions" "that the archive CD
could have been altered does not make it inadmissible"). In other cases, the tendency
to demand more exacting foundation showings for new technology is apparent. See
Devbrow v. Gallegos, 735 F.3d 584, 586-587 (7th Cir. 2013) ("While circumstantial
evidence—such as an e-mail's context, e-mail address, or previous correspondence
between the parties—may help to authenticate an e-mail, the most direct method of
authentication is a statement from the author or an individual who saw the author
compose and send the e-mail."); St. Clair v. Johnny's Oyster & Shrimp, Inc., 76 F.
Supp. 2d 773, 775 (S.D. Tex. 1999) ("Anyone can put anything on the Internet . . . the
Court holds no illusions that hackers can[not] adulterate the content on any website
from any location at any time.").

The most likely approach at present would be to require a prima facie showing of
authorship from such circumstances as e-mail headers and return addresses, ownership of accounts, access to websites, source numbers for text messages, document
metadata, and the like. Where authorship can be disputed by evidence of the likelihood of unauthorized access, shared accounts and the like, the court is likely to admit
both evidence supporting and opposing foundation and allow the jury to resolve the
factual dispute. Perhaps the primary difference between electronic and traditional
writings is the room, or need for expert testimony regarding the reliability of the processes producing the e-communications.

d. Authenticity and Genuineness of Exhibits

FRE 901 speaks of "authenticating or identifying" items of evidence. Courts and
commentators (as well as this book, in places) often use the word "authenticating"
or "authentication" essentially as synonymous with "laying the foundation" for an
exhibit. The word can be a bit misleading, to the extent that it suggests that the sole, or
even primary, concern of the foundation rules is to ensure that the exhibit is "genuine,"

meaning not a forgery. While the common law may have been exceedingly focused on preventing the use of forged or fraudulent documents, these concerns have given way to the FRE's broader emphasis on establishing relevance of evidence and on shifting credibility issues away from the judge and into the hands of the jury. (We discuss this further in the next section on FRE 104.) After all, there is little reason to believe that falsifying documents or exhibits is easier or more widespread than falsifying testimony. But such credibility issues are clearly for the jury under modern evidence rules. While "genuineness" of an exhibit (that it's not a forgery) may be an issue in specific instances, that point can be established under FRE 901 through the simple assertion of a witness purporting to have firsthand knowledge, and that witness is presumed by the court to be telling the truth for foundation purposes. The word "authenticating" may be a holdover from older doctrinal issues, or it may be a reference to the kind of showing required for real evidence, that it was the actual thing that played a role in the litigated events. The best way to define "authenticating" under current law is as synonymous with "laying the foundation for" an item of evidence.

e. Sum Up: The Flexibility of FRE 901 Foundations

We hope that the above discussions have clearly conveyed that foundation for exhibits is highly context specific, and not based on rigid rules or litanies of magic words. And the FRE's approach to exhibit foundations is intended to be sufficiently flexible to accommodate the infinite number of case-specific contexts into which exhibits must be placed.

You can see this in FRE 901(b)'s claim that its list is illustrative, and not intended to be complete. The foregoing discussions have demonstrated that the FRE 901(b) illustrations are sometimes useful in a particular situation, and sometimes not. Moreover, because the FRE 901(b) illustrations are generic, they tend to be useful only in answering generic questions about exhibits: Whose signature or voice is it? Is the exhibit accurate? The rule couldn't have been written concisely to address highly context-specific foundations, such as that "this is a package of cocaine sold by the defendant to the informant." In drafting the ultimate criterion of FRE 901(a) so broadly—that a matter is what the proponent claims it to be—the drafters of the Federal Rules have permitted flexibility in the application of the foundation requirement. Remember that the starting point of your analysis of the required foundation should always be to ask: Why is this exhibit relevant?

KEY POINTS

1. Real evidence is a tangible exhibit that played some role in the underlying litigated events. In addition to highly case-specific foundation facts linking the item of real evidence to the offering party's theory of the case, recurring generic foundation questions about real evidence usually involve the identity and unchanged condition of the item.

2. Identity of unique or recognizable objects can be established by "then-and-now" or "endpoint" testimony from a witness who saw the item during the events in question and who recognizes the item now in court. Identity of fungible or generic items can be established through a chain of custody. Where unchanged condition is an issue, a chain of custody is usually necessary, though courts do not always insist on a complete chain.

3. Depictive evidence describes, depicts, or reconstructs litigated events. It includes recordings, photographs, and demonstrative evidence. The primary generic foundation issue is that the depictive evidence fairly and accurately depicts the underlying event.

4. A witness who saw the underlying events can provide "then-and-now" testimony that the depictive evidence is "fair and accurate." In the absence of such a witness, fairness and accuracy will be an inference to be made from testimony about the accuracy of the process in which the depictive evidence was created and maintained.

5. Written documents can be real evidence, depictive evidence, or a hybrid. Generic foundation questions will tend to be about identifying the author of the document, and possibly showing his firsthand knowledge of depicted events. Writings functioning as depictive evidence are likely to be hearsay.

PROBLEMS

4.6. Jim Zeal and Stephani Goldstein were in a sailboat, the *Rastafari*, when it was stopped and boarded by the U.S. Coast Guard on the high seas, some 300 nautical miles southeast of Miami, Florida. The boarding officers searched the vessel and discovered a large quantity of a green leafy substance. Subsequently, Zeal and Goldstein were charged with conspiracy to import marijuana into the United States.

(a) At trial nine months later, the prosecution offers into evidence 11 nautical charts with navigational markings on them indicating a planned route between Kingston, Jamaica, which the government offers to show was a standard port of call for drug runners, and Miami. The prosecution asserts that the Coast Guard had seized the charts from the boat and that they are relevant to prove the conspiracy of illegal importation. To establish the authenticity of the charts, the prosecution calls Coast Guard Ensign Smythe, who testifies that he recognizes the charts as the ones he seized from the boat, and then deposited in the safe aboard the Coast Guard cutter, because of drawings of Bob Marley on each one. Is this testimony sufficient under FRE 901(b)(1)?

(b) The prosecutor also wants to establish that the leafy green substance found on board the *Rastafari* is marijuana. The prosecutor plans to show Exhibit C, a bag containing a leafy green substance, to a government chemist who testifies that, based on her in-court inspection, the substance in the bag is marijuana. But first the prosecution offers Ensign Smythe to testify that he seized a bag of a leafy green substance from the ship and placed it in the

Coast Guard safe along with the charts, and that while Exhibit C "could be" that bag, he does not know whether it is. Does this testimony satisfy FRE 901? What if FBI Agent Owens testifies that he found both the bag and the charts in the same box in the FBI evidence room and brought them to the courthouse. Would that be sufficient?

4.7. Darren is charged with possessing an unregistered sawed-off shotgun in violation of federal law. "Possession" is defined as the control of, or ability to control, the weapon. At trial, a federal agent testifies as follows: "I conducted a lawful search of the home of Rhonda Adams; I found Darren asleep in the master bedroom; I searched the master bedroom and found a black attaché case under the bed in which Darren was sleeping; I opened the case, and it contained a sawed-off shotgun." Now the prosecution wants to offer a sawed-off shotgun into evidence as Exhibit 2. The prosecutor claims that Exhibit 2 is the gun found in the black attaché case in the room where Darren was sleeping. First, the agent will identify Exhibit 2 as being a Korean-made Shinn A Sipja 12-gauge shotgun with a sawed-off barrel and cut-back stock. What additional questions would the prosecution ask the agent to satisfy FRE 901(a)? Try to use both the readily identifiable characteristic and the chain of custody methods of identifying real evidence.

4.8. In the *Johnson* case, if the prosecutor asked Officer Huston to look at a model of the food port door that was constructed before the trial, what questions would the prosecutor ask to lay the foundation to admit the model into evidence as an exhibit? Suppose that the prosecutor wants to show that two food trays cannot fit through the model food port door. Why is this relevant? What other exhibits would be needed for this demonstration? What questions would the prosecutor ask to lay the foundation for the demonstration? What other considerations should enter into the judge's decision whether to admit the model or permit the demonstration?

4.9. Return to Problem 3.5 on page 150: (a) How would Broadback's attorney lay the proper foundation for the recorded excerpt from the televised filming of the soccer game? Might defendant Trapp make any other objections? (b) Should the court permit the plaintiff, Broadback, to demonstrate to the jury the force of Trapp's blow to his neck? How might he do this?

4.10. Plaintiff Burch, an African American woman, has filed suit against her former employer, a Fifth Avenue New York department store, for discrimination against her in the terms and conditions of her employment. Plaintiff alleges that African American employees of the Fifth Avenue Store are compelled, as a condition of their employment, to either retain the hair color they were born with or color their hair only dark brown or black to conform with the color of their skin, while non-African American employees sport hair highlights and colors other than their "natural" hair color without being threatened with termination. During her testimony at trial, Burch proffers a photograph she states that she found and downloaded from Facebook that shows a white employee of the Fifth Avenue Store, Elaine, with bright red hair that is not her natural color. Is this testimony sufficient to authenticate the photograph? What additional information be would necessary to secure its admission into evidence?

6. FRE 902

RULE 902. EVIDENCE THAT IS SELF-AUTHENTICATING

The following items of evidence are self-authenticating; they require no extrinsic evidence of authenticity in order to be admitted:

(1) *Domestic Public Documents That Are Signed and Sealed.* A document that bears:

(A) a seal purporting to be that of the United States; any state, district, commonwealth, territory, or insular possession of the United States; the former Panama Canal Zone; the Trust Territory of the Pacific Islands; a political subdivision of any of these entities; or a department, agency, or officer of any entity named above; and

(B) a signature purporting to be an execution or attestation.

(2) *Domestic Public Documents That Are Not Sealed but Are Signed and Certified.* A document that bears no seal if:

(A) it bears the signature of an officer or employee of an entity named in Rule 902(1)(A); and

(B) another public officer who has a seal and official duties within that same entity certifies under seal — or its equivalent — that the signer has the official capacity and that the signature is genuine.

(3) *Foreign Public Documents.* A document that purports to be signed or attested by a person who is authorized by a foreign country's law to do so. The document must be accompanied by a final certification that certifies the genuineness of the signature and official position of the signer or attester — or of any foreign official whose certificate of genuineness relates to the signature or attestation or is in a chain of certificates of genuineness relating to the signature or attestation. The certification may be made by a secretary of a United States embassy or legation; by a consul general, vice consul, or consular agent of the United States; or by a diplomatic or consular official of the foreign country assigned or accredited to the United States. If all parties have been given a reasonable opportunity to investigate the document's authenticity and accuracy, the court may, for good cause, either:

(A) order that it be treated as presumptively authentic without final certification; or

(B) allow it to be evidenced by an attested summary with or without final certification.

(4) *Certified Copies of Public Records.* A copy of an official record — or a copy of a document that was recorded or filed in a public office as authorized by law — if the copy is certified as correct by:

(A) the custodian or another person authorized to make the certification; or

(B) a certificate that complies with Rule 902(1), (2), or (3), a federal statute, or a rule prescribed by the Supreme Court.

(5) *Official Publications.* A book, pamphlet, or other publication purporting to be issued by a public authority.

(6) *Newspapers and Periodicals.* Printed material purporting to be a newspaper or periodical.

(7) *Trade Inscriptions and the Like.* An inscription, sign, tag, or label purporting to have been affixed in the course of business and indicating origin, ownership, or control.

(8) *Acknowledged Documents.* A document accompanied by a certificate of acknowledgment that is lawfully executed by a notary public or another officer who is authorized to take acknowledgments.

(9) *Commercial Paper and Related Documents.* Commercial paper, a signature on it, and related documents, to the extent allowed by general commercial law.

(10) *Presumptions Under a Federal Statute.* A signature, document, or anything else that a federal statute declares to be presumptively or prima facie genuine or authentic.

(11) *Certified Domestic Records of a Regularly Conducted Activity.* The original or a copy of a domestic record that meets the requirements of Rule 803(6)(A)-(C), as shown by a certification of the custodian or another qualified person that complies with a federal statute or a rule prescribed by the Supreme Court. Before the trial or hearing, the proponent must give an adverse party reasonable written notice of the intent to offer the record—and must make the record and certification available for inspection—so that the party has a fair opportunity to challenge them.

(12) *Certified Foreign Records of a Regularly Conducted Activity.* In a civil case, the original or a copy of a foreign record that meets the requirements of Rule 902(11), modified as follows: the certification, rather than complying with a federal statute or Supreme Court rule, must be signed in a manner that, if falsely made, would subject the maker to a criminal penalty in the country where the certification is signed. The proponent must also meet the notice requirements of Rule 902(11).

7. Explanation of FRE 902

FRE 902 provides a list of documents that are deemed "self-authenticating." Because of their nature, appearance, or self-evident content alone, they are viewed as presenting a low risk of forgery or misidentification relative to the high degree of inconvenience and inefficiency involved in obtaining the testimony of a foundation witness. Hence, the rule dispenses with the need to produce extrinsic evidence to prove certain "authenticity" aspects of foundation: the genuineness, generic identity, and authorship of the exhibit.

What FRE 902 does not do is dispense with the case-specific aspects of foundation, an explanation of why the "self-authenticating" item is relevant to the case. Thus for example, in a drunk driving accident case, the plaintiff seeks to introduce six empty cans with the label "Duff Beer." Under FRE 902(7), the can's label by itself should be ESSF that the can contained beer, of the quantity and alcohol percentage shown on the label (and produced by the Duff Beer Co.). No witness need be offered to testify to these facts. But why are the cans relevant? Self-authentication has taken the exhibit only so far; we still need foundation witnesses to testify that the cans were found, empty but still damp and smelling strongly of beer residue, in the back seat of the defendant's car immediately following the accident. Only then might we have ESSF to support the finding that these are cans of beer consumed by the defendant shortly before the accident.

Certain kinds of public documents and public records have been produced by a formal process that triggers a generalization that the document itself, and the signatures on it, are very likely to be genuine. The formalities, such as a seal or a statement of certification as required by FRE 902(1)-(4) and (8), indicate that someone has paid attention to genuineness. Self-authentication under FRE 902(1) requires that the document bear the official seal, not a copy of it. See United States v. Hampton, 464 F.3d 687, 689 (7th Cir. 2006). For similar reasons, notarization of a signature is not sufficient under FRE 902(3); a final certification is required. Depositions, court records, public reports, notices, assessments, and payment of federal tax liens may all be self-authenticated under FRE 902(4) if accompanied by the proper certification. A public authority's printed publications, handbooks, manuals, regulations, and documents published on a website are self-authenticating under FRE 902(5) without a certification.

Various kinds of writings, just from looking at them, trigger a generalization that they are genuine because they are very difficult to forge. For example, it may more reliably be inferred that the writings defined in FRE 902(5)-(7) and (9) are from the source they appear to be from. Specht v. Google, Inc., 758 F. Supp. 2d 570 (N.D. Ill. 2010) (a news story from Forbes.com is not automatically self-authenticating as a periodical; printing a serial publication involves work and expense that make forgery unlikely while web printouts do not carry the same degree of authenticity). However, this justification for the rule has been weakened: "[M]odern technological developments [computers, scanners, publishing software, and internet access] make it easier to produce . . . a counterfeit." Wright & Gold, Federal Practice and Procedure: Evidence §7140 (2000). Pursuant to FRE 902(7), trade inscriptions and the like— "Macintosh Portable" on computers, "Product of Malaysia" inscriptions—are usually treated as establishing the authenticity of the item to which they are affixed, as well as their own genuineness. There is split authority as to whether writings such as an owner's manual, or electronic writings such as e-mail messages, that bear a company's trademark should also be considered self-authenticating.

FRE 902(11) and (12), which are referred to in the business records exception to the hearsay rule, FRE 803(6), are intended to simplify the authentication of business records and to substitute a written declaration for the production at trial of a custodian or other live witness. Courts have held that the author of the certification does not need personal knowledge of the contents of the specific business records, but must have knowledge of how the records were created and maintained. The rule does not specify whether the written declaration must include detailed information to support each factor of FRE 803(6)—that, for example, the record was made "as a regular practice"—or whether the declaration can simply recite that conclusion. Case authority is

not uniform on this point, but the majority of reported cases seem to express a preference for verbatim recitation of the required factors. Notice of a party's intent to use
Rules 902(11) and (12), together with the records themselves, must be provided to the
opponent for verification and potential challenge. If only conclusory statements are
made in written declarations, then the burden falls on the opponent to take discovery
on the underlying specific facts.

As stated in the Advisory Committee Note to FRE 902, admission of a document
pursuant to Rule 902 is not dispositive of authenticity. The opponent can offer proof
that the document is a phony or bears a forged signature. Self-authentication also
does not resolve questions as to the source or accuracy of information that is reported
in self-authenticated documents. Objections can also still be made that inadmissible
hearsay statements or expert opinions are included in, for example, newspapers or
periodicals.

KEY POINTS

1. FRE 902 provides that some exhibits can be authenticated by their appearance alone, without the testimony of a foundation witness. Authentication
   here means proving the genuineness, generic identity, and authorship of the
   exhibit. The opponent may still dispute the authenticity of these "self-authenticating" exhibits.
2. A foundation witness will still be needed to provide sufficient facts to show
   why the exhibit is relevant.

PROBLEMS

4.11. In defending a personal injury suit filed by an employee injured while operating a milling machine, the employer sought to prove the year of manufacture of
its machine. It did so by offering the serial number of its machine plus Exhibit
C, an excerpt from the "Serial Number Reference Book for Metalworking
Machinery—11th Edition," published by the "Machinery Dealers National
Association." The excerpt includes the cover, the title page, and pages 114-115;
the latter contains a list of what appear to be serial numbers for Bridgeport milling machines for each year from 1950 to 1977. The employer asserts that this
excerpt is self-authenticating under FRE 902(6) as a periodical because it is
published and updated by the Association every five years. What result?

C. PRELIMINARY FACT QUESTIONS UNDER FRE 104

FRE 104 establishes the respective roles of judge and jury in deciding fact questions
that determine the application of evidence rules. Deciding how a particular evidence

rule will apply in a specific situation always requires reference to one or more facts about the case, naturally raising the question which of the two decisionmakers at trial—judge or jury—will decide what the facts are. In a nutshell, FRE 104(a) tells us that fact questions going to application of rules of exclusion of relevant evidence are decided by the judge. FRE 104(b) tells us that fact questions going to relevance and foundation—the affirmative threshold showing that must be made by the offering party to have evidence admitted—are ultimately decided by the jury. The judge merely screens the facts to ensure that there is evidence sufficient to support a finding by the jury.

1. FRE 104

RULE 104.   PRELIMINARY QUESTIONS

(a) *In General.* The court must decide any preliminary question about whether a witness is qualified, a privilege exists, or evidence is admissible. In so deciding, the court is not bound by evidence rules, except those on privilege.

(b) *Relevance That Depends on a Fact.* When the relevance of evidence depends on whether a fact exists, proof must be introduced sufficient to support a finding that the fact does exist. The court may admit the proposed evidence on the condition that the proof be introduced later.

(c) *Conducting a Hearing So That the Jury Cannot Hear It.* The court must conduct any hearing on a preliminary question so that the jury cannot hear it if:

(1) the hearing involves the admissibility of a confession;

(2) a defendant in a criminal case is a witness and so requests; or

(3) justice so requires.

(d) *Cross-Examining a Defendant in a Criminal Case.* By testifying on a preliminary question, a defendant in a criminal case does not become subject to cross-examination on other issues in the case.

(e) *Evidence Relevant to Weight and Credibility.* This rule does not limit a party's right to introduce before the jury evidence that is relevant to the weight or credibility of other evidence.

2. Explanation of FRE 104(a)

The trial judge's decision to admit or exclude an item of evidence always requires the judge to answer one or more preliminary questions. Such preliminary matters include questions of law, questions of fact, and questions that require the exercise of discretion. Legal and discretionary questions are assigned to the judge, rather than the jury, based on fundamental understandings about our litigation system. The jury is the "trier of fact." While FRE 104(a) addresses "preliminary questions" in general, the only ones requiring a clarification with regard to a judge/jury division of responsibility are preliminary fact questions.

FRE 104(a) is written as though, in general, all of these preliminary questions are to be decided by the court: "The court must decide any preliminary question about whether ... evidence is admissible." But the breadth and nature of the exception to this general rule stated in FRE 104(b) makes clear that the concern of FRE 104(a) is with the admissibility of *relevant* evidence under the various rules that exclude relevant evidence: such as FRE 403, the hearsay rule, and, as expressly mentioned in FRE 104(a), rules concerning privilege. FRE 104(b) distinguishes and covers those fact questions that determine whether evidence is relevant, and makes the jury the ultimate decisionmaker. The judge's role under FRE 104(b) is to determine whether there is ESSF that the preliminary fact exists.

FRE 104(a) also gives the judge control over "any preliminary question about whether a witness is qualified." This phrase is understood to refer to the qualifications of expert witnesses (discussed in Chapter Nine), as well as the very narrow scope for judicial determinations of an individual witness's competence to testify. See FRE 601. It is important to understand that this language in FRE 104(a) is *not* meant to include the preliminary fact question of whether a witness has firsthand knowledge. FRE 602 makes crystal clear that that question is for the jury, subject to the judge's screening for ESSF.

Judicial Factfinding Under FRE 104(a).   The application of many evidence rules requires the judge to determine preliminary questions of fact pursuant to Rule 104(a). For example, whether a hearsay statement qualifies for one of the numerous hearsay exceptions will depend on certain facts: Was the statement made "under the stress of excitement"? FRE 803(2); or was a business record "kept in the course of a regularly conducted activity"? FRE 803(6)(B), and the like. Application of the attorney-client privilege requires determination of the preliminary fact question that the communication was made during the attorney-client relationship.

FRE 104(a) states that preliminary questions of fact to determine the applicability of such evidence exclusion rules shall be decided by the court, but it does not contain an explicit standard of proof. The Supreme Court has held that judges are to decide preliminary questions of fact under FRE 104(a) "by a preponderance of the evidence" *in both civil and criminal cases.* Bourjaily v. United States, 483 U.S. 171, 175 (1987).

> Evidence is placed before the jury when it satisfies the technical requirements of the evidentiary Rules, which embody certain legal and policy determinations. The [admissibility] inquiry ... is not whether the proponent of the evidence wins or loses his case on the merits, but whether the evidentiary Rules have been satisfied. . . . The preponderance standard ensures that before admitting evidence, the court will have found it more likely than not that [the facts that are necessary to] the technical issues and policy concerns addressed by the Federal Rules of Evidence have been afforded due consideration. [Id.]

The *Bourjaily* decision means that the party asserting an evidence exclusion rule (or an exception to that rule) has the burden to persuade the judge of all the facts necessary for the rule to apply. See United States v. Mitchell, 365 F.3d 215, 240 (3d Cir. 2004) ("Rule 104(a) places the burden of proof on the proponent of the evidence" asserting hearsay exception, under *Bourjaily*).

Under FRE 104(a), the asserting party must produce evidence that actually persuades the judge that the preliminary fact is more probably than not true. In making this decision, the judge is the factfinder: She resolves factual disputes, decides how much weight to give the evidence, and determines the credibility of witnesses. And, by the terms of Rule 104(a), the judge is not bound by the rules of evidence, except for privileges. This means that the judge may take otherwise inadmissible evidence, such as hearsay, into account. As we'll see in Chapter Eight, this also means that the judge may take the contents of the proffered item of evidence itself into account, even though it has not yet been admitted. If the judge is not persuaded on the preliminary question of fact, the judge will not apply the rule in favor of the party seeking application of the rule.

The Decision Process Under FRE 104(a).   Factfinding under FRE 104(a) is normally triggered by an objection to offered evidence, or by a pretrial motion in limine to exclude evidence. When the evidence ruling depends on preliminary facts that have already been presented earlier in the trial, the parties may simply make legal arguments. But where the evidence ruling depends on preliminary facts that have not yet been presented, or that are disputed by the parties, both sides may present evidence to the judge on the factual issue. The evidence might be presented as verbal offers of proof by the attorneys (see the discussion of FRE 103 in Chapter Two), or it might take the form of actual evidence presented by examining witnesses.

While this evidence presentation may take place in front of the jury, it is very common to hold mini-hearings outside the presence of the jury. See FRE 104(c). The reason should be apparent. The factual inquiry is to determine whether or not an item of evidence should be admitted—that is, presented to the jury. If the judge ultimately decides to exclude the evidence, it would be problematic for the jury to have heard it first. Instructions to a jury to disregard inadmissible evidence are not ideal. Moreover, FRE 104(a) expressly states that a preliminary fact showing may be based on inadmissible evidence—that is, evidence that the jury probably should not hear. There are thus good reasons to conduct FRE 104(a) factfinding outside the presence of the jury—either at the sidebar, or at a time when the jury is not present in the courtroom. FRE 104(c) expressly provides for hearings on preliminary facts to be held outside the presence of the jury, leaving the decision whether to hold such a hearing to the discretion of the judge in most instances. (Subsections 1, 2, and 3 state circumstances when the hearing *must* be held outside the presence of the jury.)

Once the judge has decided the preliminary fact question, the jury does not re-decide the preliminary question. Nor is the jury ever told what preliminary facts the judge has found. But sometimes, there is overlap between a preliminary fact determination by a judge and essential elements of a case that a jury must decide. For example, statements of co-conspirators can be admitted over a hearsay objection, if the judge finds under FRE 104(a) that a conspiracy existed. But if one of the criminal charges is the defendant's participation in the same conspiracy, this finding by the judge will not be deemed binding on (or even be told to) the jury. The jury will be fully free to decide whether or not the prosecution has proven the existence of the conspiracy at issue.

KEY POINTS

1. FRE 104(a) tells us that fact questions that determine the application of rules excluding relevant evidence are decided by the judge. FRE 104(b) tells us that fact questions that determine relevance and foundation are ultimately decided by the jury.
2. In deciding preliminary fact questions pursuant to FRE 104(a), the judge must herself be persuaded by a preponderance of the evidence that the facts warrant the application of the rule. The judge decides witness credibility, weighs the evidence, and resolves factual disputes. The judge may consider inadmissible matter. The judge may also consider the objected-to evidence itself in deciding whether the 104(a) facts have been proven.
3. The party asserting the benefit of an evidence exclusion rule, or an exception to such a rule, has the burden of production and persuasion to show that the facts warrant application of the rule.
4. After the judge decides the preliminary question under FRE 104(a), the judge either admits or excludes the item. The judge does not inform the jury about the decision on the preliminary question. If the item of evidence is admitted, the opponent may still attempt to dispute that evidence, but the jury does not redecide the preliminary question.

3. Explanation of FRE 104(b)

FRE 104(b) says:

> **Relevance That Depends on a Fact.** When the relevance of evidence depends on whether a fact exists, proof must be introduced sufficient to support a finding that the fact does exist. The court may admit the proposed evidence on the condition that the proof be introduced later.

At first glance, this rule may seem strange. Doesn't the relevance of all evidence depend on the existence of a fact or facts? Clearly, this rule is written to address a specific situation, and might have been rewritten this way: "When the relevance of an item of evidence depends on a missing fact, that item of evidence will be deemed relevant if and when the offering party introduces evidence sufficient to support a finding that the missing fact is true." Here, "missing facts" in our rewording of the rule, or "whether a fact exists" in the actual wording of the rule, refers to facts that have not yet been introduced at trial and supported with ESSF.

FRE 104(b) might thus be called "the missing fact rule." But even with this simplified name, we might still be scratching our heads over the question, "What does it mean to say that a fact is missing from the relevance of an item of evidence?" Fortunately, we've already seen and analyzed this question.

As discussed above in connection with FRE 901, the foundation for an item of evidence consists of all facts necessary to show that the evidence is relevant—that is, to show the logical connection of the offered evidence to the offering party's theory of the case. We've also seen that FRE 901 states this concept of foundation as ESSF that the item of evidence is what the offering party claims it is. We discussed FRE 901 as relating to exhibits—that is, tangible things offered in evidence—but the actual language of FRE 901 addresses any "item of evidence." Is "item of evidence" in FRE 901 properly limited to exhibits? An "item" need not be a tangible thing; dictionaries also define "item" as "a piece of information." Thus testimony about a fact or facts can constitute an item of evidence. Nothing in theory or stated in the FRE suggests that items of testimony are somehow exempt from the requirement that there be ESSF that those testimonial items are what the proponent claims. On the contrary, the theory that requires admissible evidence to be relevant implies the opposite, so that FRE 901 is probably best understood to apply beyond exhibits to testimonial "items" of evidence.

FRE 104(b) confirms that complete foundations are required for all items of evidence, including those set out entirely in testimony. In other words, FRE 104(b) tells us how to deal with incomplete foundations for evidence in general. When a fact is missing from the complete foundation, the item of evidence is not yet relevant. FRE 104(b) specifically tells us three things. First, FRE 104(b) requires that the missing fact must itself be offered in evidence such that a reasonable jury can find it to be true—ESSF of the missing fact. Second, FRE 104(b) expressly acknowledges the trial judge's authority to admit evidence conditionally on an incomplete foundation, subject to subsequent evidence completing the foundation. Third, FRE 104(b) distributes the responsibility for this factfinding between the judge and jury.

The implications of FRE 104(b) go somewhat further. As we will see, FRE 104(b) implies a broad principle of foundation that applies to all evidence. But a "problem" or objection under FRE 104(b) arises only where a necessary fact is missing from a party's offer of evidence.

Note on Conditional Relevance. FRE 104(b) is sometimes referred to as the "conditional relevance" rule. This is because the former version of the rule, before the restyling, spoke of "relevance conditioned on a fact." What we are calling the "missing fact" was formerly called the "conditional fact" or "fact condition." While it's important to know that "conditional relevance" refers to FRE 104(b), it's also important to understand that that phrase has a misleading quality. Not only does it fail to track the current language (which replaces the "fact condition" phrasing with "depends on a fact"), but it also wrongly implies that conditional relevance is a special case of relevance. In fact, FRE 104(b) is a general principle that applies to all evidence: All relevance depends on other facts. It's just that a problem only arises where one or more of those other facts are missing. Putting it differently, evidence can be relevant only when it has a complete foundation.

a. Relevance Depending on "Whether a Fact Exists": FRE 104(b) as a General Foundation Requirement

We have seen that certain facts about an offered item of evidence must be probably true if the offered item is to be relevant. The beer can is relevant only if it was a can of beer consumed by the plaintiff shortly before the accident. The package of white powder is relevant only if it contained cocaine and was sold by the defendant to the government informant. A reasonable jury must have sufficient evidence to believe that these facts about the item of evidence are probably true—that's what we mean by ESSF; otherwise, the exhibits aren't relevant. This idea is expressed in the FRE 901 language requiring the proponent of evidence to "produce evidence sufficient to support a finding that the item is what the proponent claims it is."

An example used by the Federal Rules of Evidence Advisory Committee is illustrative: "[I]f a letter purporting to be from Y is relied upon to establish an admission by him, it has no probative value unless Y wrote or authorized it." This could well have been written about FRE 901, but in fact this statement is found in the Advisory Committee Note to FRE 104(b). "No probative value," of course, means irrelevant. If the jury concludes that the letter was not written by Y, it will not hold the contents of the letter against Y as an admission. Obviously, evidence sufficient to support a finding that Y wrote the letter would be an ordinary part of the foundation for the letter; this would be one of the purposes for using the kinds of handwriting authentication listed as examples in FRE 901(b)(2) and (3). The foundational fact—that Y wrote the letter—is also the factual condition on which the letter's relevance depends. Both FRE 901(a) and 104(b) require that this factual condition be established by evidence sufficient to support such a finding. Courts and scholars have noted how, in this sense, foundation for exhibits, or FRE 901, is "a special case" of the concept of "relevance that depends on a fact" expressed in FRE 104(b).

Consider the following hypothetical example that involves an item of testimony, but not an exhibit. In a car accident case, the plaintiff's theory of the case is that the defendant caused the accident by negligently failing to maintain her car in a safe condition: specifically, that her brakes were not working properly and that she failed to get them repaired despite being on notice of the problem. To prove notice to the defendant, the plaintiff offers the testimony of a technician at Kwik Lube, a retail chain specializing in oil changes. The technician will testify that the defendant brought her car in for a routine oil change. While performing the oil change, the technician thought he noticed a possible brake problem, but believed that he lacked the equipment and expertise to confirm his suspicion.

1 Q. Did you tell the defendant about her possible brake problem?
2 A. I honestly can't remember one way or the other. I'd like to think that I did,
3   but I see lots of cars, some in better shape than others. Anyhow, I just do oil
4   changes.

At this point, the defendant objects to the whole line of testimony, arguing that it is irrelevant unless there's evidence that the technician told the defendant that he suspected her brakes were bad. The objection is sound. The "claim" about this item of testimony is that it shows that the defendant was on notice of her brake problem, and the substantive law would have required that she inquire further (by taking the car to someone who could check out the brakes). Whether the defendant was actually told about the brake problem is a missing fact from this "item" of evidence. The Kwik Lube story is not relevant without the missing fact. Using the language of FRE 104(b), we see the problem as one in which the "relevance of evidence" (here, the technician's "bad brakes" testimony) "depends on whether a fact exists" (the technician actually told the defendant about the bad brakes). This triggers the applicability of FRE 104(b), which goes on to require "proof ... sufficient to support a finding that the fact does exist." FRE 104(b); see Huddleston v. United States, 485 U.S. 681 (1988). In other words, there must be ESSF that the technician told the defendant about the brakes.

b. Conditional Admissibility

In the "bad brakes" hypothetical above, we can see that the "item" of evidence is not simply the technician's testimony. The "item" is the factual claim that someone found a brake problem that was told to the defendant. As with the earlier example of the package of cocaine that required three witnesses to complete the foundation, here the technician can't provide the complete foundation through his own testimony.

A possible solution to the problem of the admissibility of the technician's testimony is one that we have already discussed in the context of FRE 901 and exhibits: Under the doctrine of conditional admissibility, or connecting up, the plaintiff could ask that the technician's testimony be admitted conditionally, subject to the additional evidence sufficient to show that this information reached the defendant. Perhaps another witness, such as a coworker or customer, remembers hearing the technician tell the defendant, "I think your brakes may be bad." Perhaps the defendant herself remembers, and will admit to, such a conversation. There might also be circumstantial evidence of such a conversation: A witness might testify that he overheard the the Kwik Lube technician tell an unseen customer to get his or her brakes checked, at around the time the defendant was known to have been in the shop.

FRE 104(b) expressly provides that "[t]he court may admit the proposed evidence on the condition that the proof [of the missing fact] be introduced later." The device of conditional admissibility thus includes admitting an item of evidence provisionally and controlling the order of proof if necessary. FRE 104(b) questions are decided by the judge in the same manner as other foundation questions under FRE 602 and 901. The judge determines whether the offering party has presented ESSF that the missing fact is true. See Huddleston v. United States, 485 U.S. at 690 ("The court simply . . . decides whether the jury could reasonably find the [missing] fact"). If the party offering the conditionally admitted item provides this ESSF, the item will eventually be deemed admitted, and it will ultimately be up to the jurors to decide whether the item of evidence is relevant to their decision. On the other hand, if the offering party fails to provide the necessary required proof of the missing fact, the conditionally admitted item of evidence should be excluded and the jury instructed to disregard that item.[1]

---

1. There are other situations, outside the FRE 104(b) foundation context, in which evidence might be admitted "conditioned upon" the proponent offering additional proof. For example, when judges balance probative value versus a danger under FRE 403, the full probative value of the evidence, its full measure of danger, or the proponent's need for it, may not be apparent until additional evidence is taken in the case.

4. FRE 104(b) in Practice

FRE 104(b) expresses a foundation concept that applies to all evidence. Every item of evidence depends on at least some other facts in order to be relevant. Does this mean that trials become hopelessly bogged down by FRE 104(b) objections, hearings, and separate jury findings on every item of evidence? The answer is no, no, and no.

In actual practice, there are relatively few problems and objections that arise under FRE 104(b). (This is reflected in the fact that there are very few reported cases in which preliminary questions of fact are identified and formally decided under FRE 104(b), relative to other evidence issues.) Despite the ubiquity of the foundation requirement, FRE 104(b) is expressed as a rule governing missing foundation evidence. Thus, an FRE 104(b) problem arises only where there is a missing foundation fact for an offered item of evidence. Out of the hundreds of "items of evidence" (exhibits and testimonial facts) introduced in an average trial, it would be surprising to see more than a handful of missing fact problems, if any. In the remainder of this section, we will look briefly at the recurring situations in which FRE 104(b) objections arise, and how those objections are made and resolved.

Objections Under FRE 104(b).   FRE 104(b) objections arise when it appears that an offered item of evidence seems irrelevant but could potentially be made relevant with more information. There is no particular required form or phrasing to the objection. The objecting party might simply argue that the offered evidence is irrelevant, or might make a more thorough point that the evidence is irrelevant in the absence of one or more particular facts. The objecting party could cite FRE 104(b) or even FRE 401/402, the relevance rules.

There are several possible resolutions to the objection, depending on what has occurred in the trial. First, as we have seen, the offering party can ask to have the offered evidence admitted conditionally, subject to connecting up by providing ESSF of the missing fact(s).

Second, it is possible that the purportedly missing facts are already in the record. The offering party can then simply remind the judge and opposing counsel of the previously admitted evidence. In the example from *A Few Good Men*, discussed earlier in this chapter, Tom Cruise, defending two marines accused of homicide, offered evidence of the contents of the victim's closet. The evidence seemed irrelevant on the surface, until defense counsel pointed out that the prosecution's theory of the case included the assertion that the victim, Private Santiago, had been ordered to leave the base but was killed hours before his flight was scheduled to leave. The evidence that clothes remained in Private Santiago's closet suggested that he had not yet packed his bags, which could support the inference that he had not in fact been ordered to leave the base. The evidence appeared irrelevant until defense counsel pointed to an apparently missing, but previously introduced fact—Santiago had supposedly been ordered off the base—that made the evidence relevant. (Remember: Evidence can be relevant by making a fact of consequence *more* probable *or less* probable. See FRE 401.)

Third, it is possible that the judge might simply overlook the incomplete foundation, and dispense with the formality of conditional admissibility, because the missing fact is an obvious one that the offering party has promised in her theory of the case or opening statement. We discussed overlooked foundations in connection with exhibits offered under FRE 901. The same issue pertains to testimonial evidence under FRE 104(b). Suppose the first item of evidence offered by the plaintiff in a breach of contract case is the plaintiff's testimony describing an oral agreement between herself and the defendant. Technically speaking, the contract is not relevant without the "fact" that it was breached by the defendant. The complete foundation is not "this is a contract between the plaintiff and defendant," but rather "this is a contract with the plaintiff that was breached by the defendant." Yet opposing counsel and the judge are unlikely to insist that the contract testimony be "admitted conditionally" subject to ESSF that the contract was breached. Why? Because much of the plaintiff's case will be devoted to showing that the contract was breached. The plaintiff's theory of the case, probably described in her opening statement, has promised ESSF that the contract was breached. If there were not evidence sufficient to support a finding of breach, judgment as a matter of law would have to be entered against the plaintiff—perhaps even before trial, in a motion for summary judgment. To apply conditional admissibility in this context would appear to the participants as a needless formality.

Inadequate Generalizations as Missing Facts.   There is a fourth possibility for resolution of an FRE 104(b) objection. The offering party might try to argue that the evidence is relevant without the purportedly missing fact. The nature of this argument is that the missing fact can be supplied by inference. In the earlier hypothetical example, the Kwik Lube technician could not remember one way or the other whether he actually told the defendant she might have a brake problem. But plaintiff's counsel might argue that that supposedly missing fact can be inferred from his testimony. Consider the following relevance chain:

Diagram 4-1

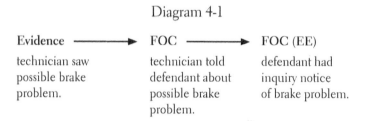

Evidence ——→	FOC ——→	FOC (EE)
technician saw possible brake problem.	technician told defendant about possible brake problem.	defendant had inquiry notice of brake problem.

Plaintiff's counsel would argue that the first inferential step can be taken by making the following generalization about the world: Oil-change technicians who see a brake problem probably notify their customers about it. As discussed in Chapter Three, a relevance chain always depends on making inferences based on applying commonsense generalizations about the world to evidence presented at trial. Here, the controversial link in the chain is between the evidence and the first FOC. What makes the inference controversial is the generalization. Is it a matter of common knowledge that oil-change technicians probably report suspected brake problems to their customers? More accurately, could a reasonable jury believe that that generalization is probably true? The relevance argument will turn on that question.

This example illustrates a recurring pattern of FRE 104(b) problems. Whenever a relevance argument arises due to an arguably inadequate generalization—one that is weak, or untrue, or not a matter of common knowledge—a judge can require that the generalization be replaced by actual evidence. The inadequate generalization becomes, in effect, a missing fact on which relevance depends, and FRE 104(b) says that such missing facts must be proven by ESSF.

There are two ways for an offering party to substitute admissible evidence for an inadequate generalization. One is to offer case-specific evidence. Evidence specifically showing that the oil-change technician's observation about the defendant's brakes was conveyed to the defendant should suffice to establish the missing fact. It thereby replaces the perhaps questionable generalization that oil-change technicians usually warn their customers.

The second way is to offer expert testimony. Sometimes the generalization will not be a matter of common knowledge, in which case the only way to prove it may be through expert testimony. This will be discussed further in Chapter Nine.

Judge and Jury Functions Under FRE 104(b). FRE 104(b) questions are decided by the judge in the same manner as other foundation questions, under FRE 602 and 901. The judge determines whether the offering party has presented ESSF that the item of evidence is what the proponent claims. The evidence may be presented in front of the jury, or might be summarized at the sidebar as an "offer of proof" under FRE 103. Judges may permit both sides to present evidence, and may even hold a hearing outside the presence of the jury pursuant to Rule 104(c). Any evidence presented (or summarized) on this question has to be admissible in order to be considered. But in screening the sufficiency of this evidence, the judge may not take witnesses' credibility into account. The sufficiency standard (ESSF) asks whether a reasonable jury could find by a preponderance of the evidence that the offering party has made out her evidentiary claim. Huddleston v. United States, 485 U.S. 681, 690 (1988). The judge does not ask whether she herself is persuaded that the evidentiary claim is probably true. Rather, "The court simply . . . decides whether the jury could reasonably find the [missing] fact." Huddleston, 485 U.S. at 690. Again, this is analogous to the civil summary judgment standard.

As implied by the foregoing discussion, the judge has four decision options: (1) admit the evidence by finding that the missing fact has been shown by ESSF; (2) admit the evidence by finding that a reasonable jury can infer the missing fact by relying on the contested generalization; (3) admit the evidence conditionally, subject to linking up later; (4) exclude the evidence as irrelevant, due to the failure to show ESSF of the missing fact.

If the evidence is admitted conditionally, and it later becomes evident that the offering party has failed to produce ESSF of the missing fact, the judge can at that time instruct the jury to disregard the evidence. In that way, the judge effectuates the admissibility condition. The judge might also, on request of the opposing party, instruct the jury that an item of evidence has been admitted only conditionally, and later advise the jury whether the condition has been fulfilled. As with other foundation questions, even if the evidence is admitted, the opposing party can still introduce evidence that the missing fact is untrue, and can argue to the jury that the item of evidence without that missing fact should be disregarded as irrelevant.

Finally, the jury is not expected to make an express, particularized finding on whether a missing fact in an FRE 104(b) situation has been proven to its satisfaction. The jury "finding" is purely hypothetical. As the Supreme Court stated in *Huddleston*, "The court simply . . . decides whether the jury *could* reasonably find the [missing] fact[.]" 485 U.S. at 690 (emphasis added). The ESSF requirement is directed to the parties and the judge to ensure that evidence sufficient to *support* a finding of the missing fact has been presented. If the jury ultimately decides to believe that the foundation for the offered evidence has been completed—because the missing fact has been proven (e.g., the technician told the defendant about her bad brakes)—then the jury will consider the entire item of evidence along with the other evidence in the case. If the jury is not persuaded that the missing fact has been proven, it simply will disregard ignores the item of evidence (e.g., the technician's unreported suspicion of a brake problem) when weighing all the evidence during its deliberations. And if the jury believes that one or more witnesses telling the story of warning the defendant about her bad brakes were lying on a significant point, the jury will discount that part of the evidence.

5. Theoretical Justifications for the FRE 104(a)/104(b) Distinction

There are important reasons for carefully maintaining the FRE 104(a)/104(b) distinction. FRE 104(a) questions are mainly those in which relevant evidence is subject to exclusion under one of the many policy-based exclusion rules in the law of evidence.[2] The facts that trigger an exclusion rule, or that qualify an offered item of evidence for an exception to an exclusion rule, can be proven by inadmissible evidence. Because 104(a) questions deal with excludable *relevant* evidence, the evidence under consideration can logically be used against the party opposing its admission even if policy reasons mandate its exclusion from evidence. To allow the jury to hear the evidence while its admissibility is being debated can prejudice the opposing party's rights if the evidence is ultimately excluded. Such a situation would leave the opposing party with the cold comfort of an instruction for the jury to disregard evidence it just heard. This is what is meant by the standard lawyers' refrain, "You can't unring a bell." While, theoretically, a judge has the training and discipline to disregard inadmissible matter that she hears, a jury is undoubtedly less able to do so.

In contrast, FRE 104(b) questions, and other foundation questions, are those in which the offered evidence is irrelevant if the preliminary facts do not pan out. In most cases, there is little or no harm done if the jury hears evidence that is ultimately deemed irrelevant. The irrelevance of the evidence means that it has no logical probative value; and because relevance is a commonsense concept, the jury can be trusted to apply logic and common sense to disregard evidence whose relevance depends on an alleged fact that turns out to be untrue. Moreover, FRE 104(b) fact conditions, as

2. The foundation for expert testimony is treated as an FRE 104(a) question, and is thus an exception to this point. See Chapter Nine.

well as FRE 901 or 602 foundations, must be based only on admissible evidence. For these reasons, the risk of unfair prejudice is much lower in FRE 104(b) situations.

The division of preliminary fact issues into FRE 104(a) questions for the judge and FRE 104(b) questions for the jury was a significant reform in federal evidence law. It was designed to liberalize the admission of evidence, to guarantee more consistently the jury's function in resolving factual disputes and credibility issues, and to reduce the ability of judges to keep strict control over the parties' presentation of their cases. Prior to the Federal Rules of Evidence, judges usually assumed the authority to decide all preliminary questions of fact themselves, pursuant to the preponderance of the evidence standard or even a higher "clear and convincing" standard of proof for some questions. The lower standard of FRE 104(b) protects, at least to some degree, the authority of the jury over factfinding, while giving more leeway to the parties and preserving the jury's function. If preliminary questions raised by FRE 602 (personal knowledge) and FRE 901 (authentication and identification) were to be decided by the judge under the preponderance standard of FRE 104(a), "the functioning of the jury as a trier of fact would be greatly restricted and in some cases virtually destroyed. These are appropriate questions for juries." Advisory Committee Notes to FRE 104. Thus, maintaining the FRE 104(a)/(b) distinction furthers the overarching goal of the Federal Rules: to promote rational decisionmaking through the liberal admission of relevant evidence.

KEY POINTS

1. FRE 104(b) fact questions are those that determine relevance and foundation. FRE 104(b) provides that when the relevance of an offered item of evidence depends on a missing fact, the offering party must also present ESSF that the missing fact is true. This is a general version of the foundation requirement applied to more specific types of evidence in FRE 602 and 901.

2. FRE 104(b) objections arise only where a fact necessary to show relevance of an offered item of evidence is missing. Where the fact is missing because it has not yet been shown by ESSF, the evidence depending on that missing fact can be admitted conditionally, subject to later proof ("connecting up") that the missing fact is probably true.

3. Both parties may present evidence on FRE 104(b) "factual condition" questions, and the judge must determine whether there is ESSF by a reasonable jury that the missing fact is true, by a preponderance of the evidence. In making this decision, the judge may consider only evidence that would be admissible to the jury. In contrast to FRE 104(a), the judge may not weigh the evidence, resolve factual disputes, or consider witness credibility. If the evidence is admitted, the opponent may still present evidence relevant to disprove the missing fact to the jury. The jury will decide the preliminary fact as part of its ultimate decisionmaking.

4. FRE 104(b) "missing fact" problems sometimes arise when the judge determines that a generalization in a chain of relevance for an offered item of evidence is doubtful.

5. The FRE 104(a)/(b) distinction preserves the jury's factfinding role by reserving to it the authority to decide all factual disputes and witness credibility issues underlying the relevance of offered evidence.

PROBLEMS

4.12. Return to Problem 4.4, United States v. Ray, at page 208. Exhibits 1 and 2 have been admitted into evidence. Exhibit 3 is a photocopy of Exhibit 1. It bears original handwritten initials "BR" on the upper left corner. Government investigators have obtained the following information from interviewing Beth Barker:

> I have been employed as Bernard Ray's executive secretary since 2005. I adhere to the following practice in handling Mr. Ray's mail, including hand delivered documents. Each work day I place incoming mail and other delivered documents in the "in" box on Mr. Ray's desk at around 10 A.M., around 1:30 P.M. and around 4:00 P.M. At 8:30 A.M. each morning, I take all of the documents in Mr. Ray's "out" box, check to make sure that Mr. Ray has initialed them, and then place them in Mr. Ray's files. Mr. Ray always reads and initials his mail and other documents and puts them in his "out" box. In response to a request from federal investigators, on September 1 of 2015 I found Exhibit 3 in Mr. Ray's files in a folder labeled "Correspondence–Andrews." I recognize the initials "BR" as Mr. Ray's handwriting.

The prosecution offers Exhibit 3 into evidence to prove that Ray read Exhibit 3 prior to his sale of stock on March 16, 2015. Is there an FRE 104(b) objection to admitting the memo? Is there an argument that the existence of the memo, without more, is sufficient to meet this objection? Would the testimony of Barker be sufficient to prove any missing facts? What should the trial court do?

4.13. Plaintiff seeks to prove that defendant Asbestos, Inc. (AI), a manufacturer of asbestos fireproofing material, knew or should have known of the dangers of asbestos before selling its product to Plaintiff, and that AI was therefore liable to Plaintiff for failure to warn. AI sold the asbestos material to Plaintiff in September of 1970. Plaintiff's only evidence that AI had knowledge of the danger of such material is an undated five-page document warning of the dangers of asbestos, found in the bottom of a file drawer belonging to an AI official, in a stack of unrelated and undated papers. The drawer was labeled "1969-1972." Should the document be admitted into evidence against AI?

4.14. Lindstrom is charged with possession and sale of two boxes of stolen smart phones. Knowledge that the smart phones were stolen is the one element of the crime that Lindstrom disputes. To prove knowledge, the prosecution offers the testimony of two witnesses, a store owner and an undercover FBI agent, in which Lindstrom had offered to sell them televisions and kitchen appliances at a suspiciously low price and without a bill of sale. It was undisputed that these other incidents occurred around the same time as the charged smart phone sale. The prosecution argues that Lindstrom's contemporaneous sale of apparently stolen TVs and appliances made it more likely that he knew the smart phones were stolen. Lindstrom claims that he did not know that the TVs and appliances had been stolen either, and he objects that the evidence of the television and kitchen appliance incidents cannot be admitted unless the trial court makes a preliminary factual finding by a preponderance of the evidence that those items had been stolen. How should the court rule?

6. Reflection on FRE 104(b): Is There a Conditional Relevance "Problem"?

A handful of commentators criticized FRE 104(b) some years ago, claiming that the rule—at that time called the "conditional relevance" rule—would undermine the efficiency of trials. "[S]topping a trial to entertain [FRE 104(b)] arguments, decide which point should be proved first, obtain a commitment to prove some other point, assess the sufficiency of proof, and even instruct the jury, would confound trials, confuse everyone, and hamstring lawyers and judges." Christopher B. Mueller & Laird C. Kirkpatrick, Evidence §1.13 (2d ed. 1999); see also Vaughn C. Ball, The Myth of Conditional Relevancy, 14 Ga. L. Rev. 435, 445-454 (1980) (worrying about requiring a separate, express jury finding on every FRE 104(b) issue). As the relative infrequency of reported FRE 104(b) cases attests, these fears have simply not born out in practice. FRE 104(b) objections arise infrequently, for the reasons discussed above. Moreover, the concern about frequent and confusing jury findings on FRE 104(b) issues was, from the start, based on a misunderstanding of the rule: As noted above, the jury finding is purely hypothetical, and the only finding actually required is the one that must be made by the judge on any disputed foundation question.

A more enduring criticism argues that the ESSF standard of FRE 104(b) appears to be a higher standard than, and inconsistent with, the "any tendency" standard stated in FRE 401. These critics argue that since *all* offered items require additional facts to link them to the case at hand, an FRE 104(b) objection can be made to any offered evidence at any time. According to these critics, the mere happenstance of basing a relevance objection on FRE 104(b) can take a relevance argument out of the permissive FRE 401/402 relevance rule, which makes clear that relevance does not depend on sufficiency. Evidence is relevant if it makes another relevant fact more probable, and does not require a showing that it makes another fact probably true (the ESSF/preponderance standard). See Ball, supra; Ronald J. Allen, The Myth of Conditional Relevancy, 25 Loyola L.A. L. Rev. 871 (1992); Dale A. Nance, Conditional Relevance Reinterpreted, 70 B.U. L. Rev. 447, 459-462 (1990); Richard Friedman, Conditional Probative Value: Neoclassicism Without Myth, 93 Mich. L. Rev. 439, 449 (1994).

The most sustained version of this argument has been made by one of the coauthors of this book. See Allen, supra, The Myth of Conditional Relevancy. Another coauthor disagrees. See David S. Schwartz, A Foundation Theory of Evidence, 100 Geo. L. Rev. 95 (2011). According to Schwartz, conditional relevance critics mix up two different things. To be sure, relevant evidence need only make another fact slightly more probable, not probably true. But in order to have that relevant quality,

D. The Best Evidence Rule   241

evidence must *itself* be based on facts that are probably true. The package of facts that make an item relevant (its foundation) must all be sustainable by ESSF. Thus, FRE 104(b)'s requirement that a missing fact must be probably true for evidence to be relevant is, he claims, consistent with FRE 401. Once the foundation is complete, the offered evidence need only have a slight tendency to make another fact more probable.

PROBLEM

4.15. Kristof is accused of first-degree homicide for the alleged premeditated killing of his uncle Max, who died in a boating incident in which Kristof was the only other person present. The prosecution's theory of the case is that Kristof was motivated by financial gain: specifically, that Max rewrote his will two months before his death to add Kristof as an heir. An earlier version of the will divided Max's estate equally between his two children, Peter and Roxana; the revised will, gave equal one-third shares to Peter, Roxana, and Kristof. In his defense, Kristof argues that Max's death was accidental. As to the will, Kristof claims he had no knowledge that he was named in it. The prosecution offers the revised will into evidence without any evidence that Kristof knew of its existence or contents. Defense counsel objects that the will is irrelevant to establish a motive without ESSF that Kristof knew about it. (No other relevance theory besides motive has been offered by the prosecution.) The prosecution argues that the mere existence of the will increases the probability that Kristof had a motive, and is therefore relevant.

How should the court rule? Consider the following subsidiary questions: Does the existence of the will make the existence of a motive probable? If not, is the prosecutor simply asking the jury to speculate about a possible motive? Does the mere possibility of a financial gain motive (through a will) increase the probability that Kristof murdered his uncle over what the probability would be without any evidence of the will? Note that, even with ESSF that Kristof knew about the will and therefore probably had a motive, the motive evidence has only slight probative value. Very few people who stand to gain from the death of another person actually kill that person; here, Peter and Roxana stood to gain to the same extent as Kristof, but they have not been charged.

D. THE BEST EVIDENCE RULE

The so-called best evidence rule requires a party to present an original or exact duplicate of any document ("writing, recording, or photograph") the party offers in evidence—at least when the original is available and the document is offered to prove its content. The theory of the rule is simple: When a writing, recording, or photograph is offered to prove the facts contained in it, the chances are good that the original will be more trustworthy than an inexact copy or a description of the original. The requirement to produce the original may be excused, and "other" or "secondary" evidence of the content may be admitted if the absence of the original is explained or justified. The best evidence "rule" is really a complex of rules in the Federal Rules, FRE 1001-1008.

The best evidence rule ("BER") is a rule for excluding relevant evidence: It excludes "other evidence" of an original document's content in any form (testimony *or* exhibits) when an original writing, recording, or photograph can and should be introduced instead. It does *not* specify a showing that must be made affirmatively to establish the relevance of an item of evidence. Thus, the BER differs from foundation rules like FRE 901, 104(b), and 602. But we include the BER in this chapter as an organizational convenience, due to its close connection to the foundation questions involved in offering exhibits into evidence.

We also note that the rule is misnamed. It does not literally require the presentation of the "best" form of evidence, as in the most reliable or persuasive, available to the party. Indeed, there may be cases where an original document is not the most reliable or persuasive evidence, and yet the only way to satisfy the rule would still be to produce the original document. More generally, there is no "best evidence principle" anywhere in the Federal Rules that requires the proponent to offer the best available evidence to prove a point: Generally speaking, a party may prove its case by any admissible evidence, regardless of whether anything "better" is available. But suggestions by some scholars to rename the rule more descriptively as "the original document rule" have not caught on.

1.   FRE 1001-1008

RULE 1001   DEFINITIONS THAT APPLY TO THIS ARTICLE

In this article:

(a) A "writing" consists of letters, words, numbers, or their equivalent set down in any form.

(b) A "recording" consists of letters, words, numbers, or their equivalent recorded in any manner.

(c) A "photograph" means a photographic image or its equivalent stored in any form.

(d) An "original" of a writing or recording means the writing or recording itself or any counterpart intended to have the same effect by the person who executed or issued it. For electronically stored information, "original" means any printout—or other output readable by sight—if it accurately reflects the information. An "original" of a photograph includes the negative or a print from it.

(e) A "duplicate" means a counterpart produced by a mechanical, photographic, chemical, electronic, or other equivalent process or technique that accurately reproduces the original.

RULE 1002.   REQUIREMENT OF THE ORIGINAL

An original writing, recording, or photograph is required in order to prove its content unless these rules or a federal statute provides otherwise.

RULE 1003.   ADMISSIBILITY OF DUPLICATES

A duplicate is admissible to the same extent as the original unless a genuine question is raised about the original's authenticity or the circumstances make it unfair to admit the duplicate.

RULE 1004.   ADMISSIBILITY OF OTHER EVIDENCE OF CONTENT

An original is not required and other evidence of the content of a writing, recording, or photograph is admissible if:

(a) all the originals are lost or destroyed, and not by the proponent acting in bad faith;

(b) an original cannot be obtained by any available judicial process;

(c) the party against whom the original would be offered had control of the original; was at that time put on notice, by pleadings or otherwise, that the original would be a subject of proof at the trial or hearing; and fails to produce it at the trial or hearing; or

(d) the writing, recording, or photograph is not closely related to a controlling issue.

RULE 1005.   COPIES OF PUBLIC RECORDS TO PROVE CONTENT

The proponent may use a copy to prove the content of an official record—or of a document that was recorded or filed in a public office as authorized by law—if these conditions are met; the record or document is otherwise admissible; and the copy is certified as correct in accordance with Rule 902(4) or is testified to be correct by a witness who has compared it with the original. If no such copy can be obtained by reasonable diligence, then the proponent may use other evidence to prove the content.

RULE 1006.   SUMMARIES TO PROVE CONTENT

The proponent may use a summary, chart, or calculation to prove the content of voluminous writings, recordings, or photographs that cannot be conveniently examined in court. The proponent must make the originals or duplicates available for examination or copying, or both, by other parties at a reasonable time or place. And the court may order the proponent to produce them in court.

RULE 1007.   TESTIMONY OR STATEMENT OF A PARTY TO PROVE CONTENT

The proponent may prove the content of a writing, recording, or photograph by the testimony, deposition, or written statement of the party against whom the evidence is offered. The proponent need not account for the original.

RULE 1008.   FUNCTIONS OF THE COURT AND JURY

Ordinarily, the court determines whether the proponent has fulfilled the factual conditions for admitting other evidence of the content of a writing, recording, or photograph under Rule 1004 or 1005. But in a jury trial, the jury determines—in accordance with Rule 104(b)—any issue about whether:

(a) an asserted writing, recording, or photograph ever existed;

(b) another one produced at the trial or hearing is the original; or

(c) other evidence of content accurately reflects the content.

2. Explanation of Best Evidence Rule

The Basic Rule.   FRE 1002 and 1003 provide the basic principle of the best evidence rule ("BER"): An original is required when a proponent seeks to prove the content of a writing, recording, or photograph. An exact duplicate (such as a photocopy) can be used instead of the original so long as there is no reason to doubt the accuracy of the duplicate. FRE 1002 says that the rule applies only to a "writing, recording, or photograph." These terms are defined in FRE 1001. For convenience, we will use the term "document" in this discussion as an occasional substitute for "writing, recording, or photograph."

Exceptions.   FRE 1004 further explains the meaning of the rule by setting out the principal exceptions. "Other evidence" of the content of the original document is admissible *if* the original document is unavailable to the offering party because it has been lost or destroyed, is being withheld by the opposing party, or can't otherwise be obtained by judicial process. But if the original was lost or destroyed by the offering party in bad faith, this exception is unavailable. Finally, the original is not required where the writing, recording, or photograph is "not closely related to a controlling issue."

What does it mean to qualify for an exception to the best evidence rule? Putting it another way, what does it mean to say that an "original [or exact duplicate] is not required" to "prove [the] content" of a writing, recording, or photograph? It means that the content of the document can be proven by "other evidence."

Other Evidence of Content.   FRE 1004's reference to "other evidence of the content" means a visual or verbal depiction or summary of a document that is not an exact duplicate. Most commonly, other evidence that is objectionable under the BER will consist of a verbal description by a witness. For example, a witness might say: "I read the contract, and it said basically that the defendant promised to pay me $50,000 for my services." "I saw the video, and it showed a police officer hitting the plaintiff with his baton." These are both examples of verbal descriptions of a document's content. They are "other evidence" of the content of the document—"other" than showing the jury the writing, recording, or photograph itself.

A verbal description is not the only prohibited means of "proving"—in essence, conveying to the factfinder—the content of a document. A party might offer a sketch that attempts to replicate a photograph. Or perhaps the lawyer's secretary listened to an original audiotape and typed up a verbatim transcript. The transcript is still "other evidence" of the content of the original tape recording. This is true even if the transcript is "better" than the tape: Perhaps the recording is of poor quality, whereas the transcript is 100 percent accurate and is more convenient than playing the tape. It is still "other evidence" of the content of the tape, and can't be admitted in evidence if the tape is available. Here, then, is an example of how the rule does not necessarily end up requiring the literal "best" evidence.

In Order to Prove Its Content. The BER, by its terms, applies when a writing, recording, or photograph is offered "in order to prove its content." In fact, a writing, recording or photograph is nearly always introduced in evidence because something contained in it is relevant to the case. If the offering party maintains that the content of the written, recorded, or photographic exhibit is relevant, then the exhibit is offered "to prove its content" within the meaning of the rule. Therefore, the BER potentially applies whenever a document is available to prove a point. The question then becomes, when such a document is available, when does the BER block "other evidence" of the content? The analysis for answering this question is probably the most difficult aspect of the BER. We address it in the next section.

3. When Is Evidence Offered to "Prove [the] Content" of a Document?

When does the Best Evidence Rule apply? The BER has no bearing when a party tries to prove a fact in the absence of any relevant documentary evidence. On the other hand, when a party seeks to introduce an original document (or exact duplicate) to prove a fact, the BER technically governs, but the party's use of the original or duplicate conforms to the rule, so there is no need to interpret or argue over the rule.

Interpretive questions and arguments about the BER thus arise only where a party seeks to prove a fact through "other evidence" when a document that could be used to prove the same point does exist (or did exist). The question then becomes whether in fact the party is trying to "prove the content" of the document. If the answer to that question is yes, then the BER does apply; and if none of the exceptions (FRE 1004, 1006, and 1007) are applicable, then the BER will prohibit the use of "other evidence." The question of whether evidence is offered to prove the content of a document is probably the most challenging concept regarding the BER. We will try to break it down in this section.

The best way to think about this question is by distinguishing broadly between two situations involving documentary evidence. In the first situation (let's call it "Type 1"), the content of a writing, recording, or photograph is a fact of independent legal significance in the case. In the second situation ("Type 2"), the goal is to prove an underlying event, one that is not itself a writing, recording, or photograph. But there may be documentary (written, recorded, or photographic) evidence depicting that event. In Type 1 situations, *the best evidence rule always applies.* In Type 2 situations, the best evidence rule applies only to the party's reliance on the document to prove the underlying event; but it does not bar evidence that avoids reliance on the document, to prove the underlying event.

Type 1: Document Content Has Independent Legal Significance. In some instances, the content of a writing, recording, or photograph has independent legal significance. A common example is a written contract. The content of such a writing is a relevant occurrence in itself, and has independent legal significance: It is the manifestation of the exchange of promises creating legally enforceable obligations. The terms of other legal instruments, such as wills, are likewise legally significant occurrences. A document might also constitute a crime or tort. For instance, a libel is a printed and published statement that is false and damaging to the plaintiff's reputation. This, too, is in itself a relevant occurrence manifested in the written document. If notice or knowledge is an issue in the case, the content of the document giving that notice or knowledge is likewise a relevant event.

Putting it another way, in each of the above examples the writing, recording, or photograph is the source of the relevant fact. Where this is the case, the content of the document must necessarily be proven somehow in order to get the relevant fact into the record. The best evidence rule always applies in this situation.

Documents whose contents have independent legal significance have two other characteristics that might help you identify them as belonging to this category. First, in all of these examples, the writings and recordings are "nonhearsay" statements that are relevant as legally operative facts or for their effect on the listener (or viewer), as will be discussed in Chapter Eight, infra. Their relevance is not that they contain truthful assertions of fact, but rather that they manifest intentions or opinions or that they had a certain effect on persons who saw or read them. Second, such documents are "real" rather than "depictive" evidence, as discussed above in connection with FRE 901. They played a role in the litigated events, rather than simply recording or depicting relevant events.

Type 2: Document Could Be Used to Prove an Underlying Event.   Writings, recordings, and photographs can also be relevant as evidence because they provide a record of what happened. But when the proponent uses a percipient witness to prove that an event happened, there is no requirement that the proponent produce a recorded version of that event instead.

In such instances, the underlying event occurs outside of the writing, recording, or photograph, but is captured or described in the document. In this situation, the writing, recording, or photograph is depictive (as opposed to real) evidence. The best evidence rule applies only to evidence that relies on the writing, recording, or photograph to prove the underlying event. Other evidence offered to prove the underlying event without relying on the medium of the writing, recording, or photograph is not affected by the BER. Even though a writing, recording, or photograph exists depicting the same underlying event, that does not bar "other evidence" of that underlying event, in the form of testimony, visual reconstructions, or the like—so long as that other evidence is not derived from viewing the writing, recording, or photograph. The witness's testimony is being used to prove the *event*, not the *content of a record*. "The fact that a video recording may at times be in fact the 'best' evidence of what occurred does not render first-hand testimony of the event incompetent." Jackim v. Sam's E., Inc., 378 Fed. Appx. 556, 565-566 (6th Cir. 2010).

A "Type 2" Example.   An example can make this point clearly. Suppose in a police excessive force case, a police officer was seen by several eyewitnesses hitting an unresisting suspect with a baton. In addition to the eyewitnesses, a passerby captures the incident on a video taken with his cell phone. The plaintiff offers testimony from one of the eyewitnesses describing the entire incident. The plaintiff then offers the testimony of the passerby to corroborate the eyewitness. On direct examination, the passerby admits "I did not actually see the incident, because I was looking into my cell phone to aim the camera at the officer and the plaintiff. There was glare from bright sunlight, so I couldn't see the image while it was recording. However, I later watched my video, and saw the whole thing on the video. Here's what happened. . . ."

How does the best evidence rule apply to these two witnesses' testimony? The first witness is simply presenting relevant eyewitness testimony based on firsthand knowledge, in accord with FRE 602. This testimony is not objectionable. Even though there happens to be a video of the incident, the BER does not apply to the eyewitness's testimony, because the eyewitness is not proving the contents of the video: He is proving what he saw, directly. This analysis would not change even if the video were introduced in evidence—the witness is still testifying to what he saw. Nor would the analysis change even if the eyewitness also served as a foundation witness to introduce the video—by offering "then and now" testimony to say that the video is a fair and accurate depiction of what he saw. In that case, the eyewitness has still provided a firsthand account of what he saw, plus foundation testimony for introducing the original (or a duplicate) of the video. Since the original video is offered, it conforms to the best evidence rule. What the eyewitness is *not* doing is trying to describe the content of the video in lieu of his own firsthand perception. Testifying that the video is a fair and accurate depiction of what happened is not what the BER means by the phrase "other evidence of content."

However, the passerby's testimony *does* trigger, and violate, the BER. The passerby is not describing the excessive force incident as he saw it firsthand, but rather describing *what the video shows*. Although the plaintiff's ultimate objective in presenting the passerby's testimony is to prove the underlying excessive force incident, here—unlike with the eyewitness testimony—the passerby's testimony does so only by proving what was on the video. The passerby's testimony relies on the video, not on firsthand knowledge of the underlying event. The passerby's description of what he saw on the video is what the BER means by "other evidence" of a recording. But the BER prohibits the use of "other evidence" of a recording if the recording is available. Rather than having the passerby testify to what he saw on the video, the plaintiff would have to offer the video itself into evidence.

"Type 2" Situations: Document and Other Evidence Both Permitted.   As this last comment should make clear, when there are both one or more eyewitnesses to an underlying event *and* a document recording that event, both can be offered in evidence. The only restriction is that a witness will not be allowed to summarize or describe the content of the document.

4. Best Evidence Rule: Definitions and Exceptions

a. Definitions

Writings, Recordings, or Photographs.   The definition of writings, recordings and photographs in FRE 1001 is broad, and probably intended to convey common understandings of these things. Where the applicability of the definition is debatable, it may be useful to refer to the pre-restyling version of the rule. For example, is a video a "recording" or "photograph" (or a combination of the two)? The former rule explicitly defined "photograph" to include "still photographs, X-ray films, videotapes and motion pictures." Remember that the re-styling was not intended to change the substance of any rule. The main difference in language is a switch from an effort to list various technologies to a broad definition intended to encompass technological changes in the production of writings, recordings, or photographs.

Originals and Duplicates. An "original" of a document includes the intuitive sense of the word "original" with certain additions: An accurate printout of an electronic document or photographic print from a negative (or the negative itself), are originals. "Counterparts" intended to function as originals are both (or all) deemed original. For example, a frequently followed contracting formality is to print two identical contracts with signature lines; each party signs both copies, so that each party may have a contract bearing original (rather than photocopied) signatures. Both are deemed originals by FRE 1001(d).

A duplicate is an accurate copy reproduced from the original by an automated technological process, like photocopying. FRE 1001(e). (Gone are the days when legal secretaries, like Melville's "Bartleby, the Scrivener," copied out legal documents by hand. A handwritten copy would be deemed "other evidence" under the modern BER.) Under FRE 1003, a duplicate can be used instead of the original, unless there is an actual reason to question its accuracy or it would somehow be unfair to use it in place of the original. A duplicate need not take the same technological form as the original, so long as the contents are accurately reproduced: For example, a digitally enhanced recording, or a CD version of an audio recording originally made on tape, qualifies as a duplicate. (A court might require some foundation-type testimony to establish the accuracy of the copy.)

Inscriptions on Objects Are Not Writings. Inscriptions on objects are usually not treated as "writings" under FRE 1002, and the best evidence rule does not apply. Courts have discretion to treat such objects as a writing depending on the need for the exact inscription, the simplicity or complexity of the inscription, and the ease or difficulty of production. Presumably, this principle would apply to street signs giving the names of streets or traffic instructions. A witness could testify to having seen a stop sign, or to knowing his location by having seen a sign identifying the street name, without producing the original signs in court.

b. Exceptions

Other evidence of the content of a writing, recording, or photograph is permitted in situations described in FRE 1004, 1006, and 1007.

FRE 1004: Originals Unavailable. The most prevalent exception to the BER occurs when the original document is not available to the offering party. FRE 1004(a) states that other evidence is admissible to prove the content of original documents that have been "lost or destroyed, unless the proponent lost or destroyed them in bad faith." Loss or destruction of the original, pursuant to FRE 1004(a), may be proved by testimony from a person with knowledge, or by circumstantial evidence that the proponent has made a reasonable, diligent, and unsuccessful search for the original. The proponent need not explain with absolute certainty what happened to the original, but has the burden to prove that its loss or destruction was not in bad faith. See, e.g., Knit With v. Knitting Fever, Inc., 742 F. Supp. 2d 568, 586 (E.D. Pa. 2010); Seiler v. Lucasfilm, 613 F. Supp. 1253, 1260 (N.D. Cal. 1984) aff'd, 808 F.2d 1316 (9th Cir. 1986). Negligent destruction of documents has been held insufficient to establish bad faith. Likewise, destruction of documents as part of a routine purge, pursuant to a document retention policy or practice, is generally not deemed bad faith. See Cross v. United States, 149 F.3d 1190 (10th Cir. 1998) (negligent destruction); United States v. Balzano, 687 F.2d 6 (1st Cir. 1982) (routine purging).

Under FRE 1004(b), if the originals are not lost but are in the possession of others, the court may require the proponent to show that they cannot be obtained by the proponent's reasonable, diligent, and unsuccessful use of judicial process or other inquiry (such as pretrial discovery or investigation). If the original is in the possession of the opposing party, then, pursuant to the requirements of FRE 1004(c), secondary evidence of its content may be offered if the opponent was on notice that the original would be the subject of proof but failed to produce it at trial.

FRE 1004 permits the proponent to use any "other evidence" of the content of the original. No preference is given to any particular type of secondary evidence once the original is not available. A common form of secondary evidence is the oral testimony of a witness who once perceived the original and claims to remember it. All types of copies are also equally acceptable, such as a transcripts of an audiotape. Official records are an exception to this principle of equal acceptability. FRE 1005 establishes a priority for proof of such official records: A certified copy or a copy that a witness can testify is correct is preferred over other types of secondary evidence. Only if such copies cannot be obtained with "reasonable diligence" may other evidence of contents be given.

FRE 1006: Voluminous Originals.   FRE 1006 permits the proponent of voluminous writings, recordings, and photographs to present the contents of these items in the form of a summary, chart, or calculation. The FRE 1006 summary is treated as evidence *in place of* the voluminous underlying documents. The underlying voluminous materials need not *actually be* admitted at trial. In this sense, an FRE 1006 summary or chart is not the same as a visual aid that is used simply to summarize or illustrate other evidence—exhibits or testimony—that has already been, or will be, admitted at trial. In contrast to FRE 1006 summaries, mere demonstrative aids are not deemed evidence, and many courts don't allow them to be taken into the jury room during deliberations.

Even though the voluminous materials don't have to be admitted in evidence, FRE 1006 requires a showing that they would have been admissible, including the laying of a proper foundation. The proponent is also obligated to produce the originals in time to permit the opponent to examine and copy them, obviously to check the summary for any errors or inconsistencies, and for purposes of cross-examination. Courts are strict in enforcing this requirement. United States v. Modena, 302 F.3d 626, 633 (6th Cir. 2002) (willingness to provide underlying documents, if requested prior to trial, is inadequate; opponent has absolute right to production of underlying material, and party seeking to use summary must state when and where material may be reviewed even absent a discovery request).

FRE 1007: Opposing Party Description of Content.   If the opposing party in the litigation has described the content of a writing, recording, or photograph, FRE 1007 permits the use of this description against that party to prove that content, without accounting for the absence of the original. Clearly, the opposing party's verbal description is "other evidence" of content. But this exception, in addition to its potential convenience, is justified by the general principle that it is not unfair to use a party's own words against him. The only restriction on this form of other evidence is that it must have been committed to writing: It must be testimony at a hearing or deposition, a written response to a discovery request, or a written statement.

5. Best Evidence Rule: Practical Applications

Objecting to "Other Evidence" Under the BER.   If a party offers testimony verbally describing the content of a document, or some other form of depiction or reproduction of an original document that is not an accurate duplicate, the opposing party should object that the offer is "not the best evidence." The offering party's response depends on whether, in fact, she is offering "other evidence." If the answer to this question is yes, then the offering party needs to establish an exception to the BER under FRE 1004, 1006, or 1007. But if the answer is no—if the offered evidence is *not* offered to prove the content of a writing, recording, or photograph, the BER doesn't apply to bar the evidence.

We have seen that testimony about an underlying event that happens to have been captured on video or otherwise described in a document can be proven with testimony and other evidence, so long as the evidence recounts the underlying event itself rather than recounting a document's description of the underlying event. In addition, it may be the case that evidence relates to a document, but is not offered to prove its content.

Facts About the Document Are Not "Other Evidence of Content."   It is extremely important (though at times difficult) to distinguish between a description of the content of the document and facts about the document—its surrounding circumstances or "envelope information." For example, foundation testimony about an exhibit—identifying its author, explaining the circumstances of its creation, or describing it as a "fair and accurate" depiction of some underlying event—is not what the BER means by "other evidence of content." Rather, that is simply laying the foundation for admitting an original (or duplicate) writing, recording, or photograph so that the document can prove its own content, in conformity with the

BER. In addition, testimony that a document exists, or testimony describing the circumstances of its creation, is not what the BER means by evidence of content. This is more in the nature of "envelope information" about the document, rather than some sort of recapitulation of its content. Finally, in many cases it may be relevant to know what a particular person understood a document to mean, or how he reacted or responded to it.

In the foregoing examples, a witness can testify "about" a document without really attempting to prove what its contents are. This testimony is permissible under the BER, whether or not the document is introduced in evidence.

A commonly heard objection is that "the document speaks for itself." This is an imprecise, and potentially incorrect attempt to get at a BER objection. It is true that a document "speaks for itself," insofar as an original or accurate duplicate must be used to prove the document's content under the BER (in the absence of an exception, anyway). But the document doesn't necessarily speak for itself in the other important senses just described: A document may or may not contain information about its own creation or information sources. And a document generally does not contain information about how its readers or viewers perceived or understood it. If those latter facts are relevant, then testimony about the document is admissible, and a BER or "the document speaks for itself" objection should be overruled.

6. Explanation of FRE 1008

FRE 1008 makes a specific allocation of factfinding between judge and jury in the application of the best evidence rule's various provisions. The judge's general authority to make the preliminary fact determinations necessary to apply exclusionary rules of evidence is established in FRE 104(a). What rule FRE 1008 does is to distinguish between FRE 104(a)- and 104(b)-type questions in the application of the BER.

FRE 1008 explains that preliminary facts necessary to the application of FRE 1001–1007 are 104(a) questions for the judge to decide. But FRE 1008(a), (b), and (c) go on to identify three specific factual questions that are for the trier of fact to determine "in accordance with Rule 104(b)." This means that the judge should not decide the question by a preponderance of the evidence, but should determine only whether there is evidence sufficient to support a jury finding on the matter. The Advisory Committee Note to Rule 1008 explains that these are questions that "go beyond the mere administration of the rule preferring the original and into the merits of the controversy."

FRE 1008(a), (b), and (c) in essence involve disputed relevance and foundation questions about a writing, recording, or photograph offered into evidence. Recall that FRE 901 requires ESSF that the item in question is what its proponent claims. And FRE 104(b) requires ESSF of the probable truth of an underlying fact on which relevance depends. FRE 1008(a), (b), and (c) are each examples of a contention that the item in question is not what the proponent claims. If an offered document is not a genuine original because no original ever existed, or because there is a different original, then the offered document is not relevant to prove the fact in question. Likewise, if other evidence of the content of a document (e.g., testimony purporting to describe or summarize it) is false or inaccurate, the testimony will not be relevant to prove the contents. To maintain consistency with FRE 901 and 104(b), these issues are treated as foundation issues that must be decided by the trier of fact. The judge screens for ESSF rather than reaching her own factual conclusion under FRE 104(a).

KEY POINTS

1. The best evidence rule prohibits a party from proving the content of a writing, recording, or photograph by verbal descriptions or inexact reproductions. Instead, the original document or an exact copy must be used. FRE 1001–1003.
2. "Other evidence" of the content of a document—typically, verbal descriptions or inexact reproductions—may be used to prove the content of the original, if the original was justifiably unavailable. The proponent of the other evidence has the burden to prove the facts justifying the unavailability of the original, under FRE 104(a). The proponent of the other evidence must show that any loss or destruction of the original was not due to his own bad faith.
3. The BER applies to all instances where the original writing, recording, or photograph would be real evidence, if offered. But where the writing, recording, or photograph is relevant only to prove the underlying events it depicts, then the BER applies only to evidence attempting to summarize or inexactly reproduce the writing, recording, or photograph. The BER imposes no restriction on other evidence proving the underlying event without the writing, recording, or photograph, such as direct eyewitness testimony.
4. FRE 1006 permits the use of summaries of voluminous writings, recordings, and photographs without the admission of the originals into evidence. The originals or duplicates must, however, be available to the opponent. A summary admitted under Rule 1006 is itself substantive evidence.
5. FRE 1008 provides that most preliminary questions of fact under the best evidence rules are for the judge to decide pursuant to FRE 104(a). The only FRE 104(b) questions for the jury are disputes as to the true content or existence of the original.

PROBLEMS

4.16. Return to Problem 4.4, United States v. Ray, at page 208. Does FRE 1002 apply to the government's offer of Exhibits 1 and 2? Why? Do Exhibits 1 and 2 satisfy FRE 1002? Could the government prove Ray's stock sale on March 16, 2015, by calling Ray's stockbroker as a witness and asking her whether she sold Ray's 100,000 shares of Rundown stock at his direction on March 16th? Would this violate FRE 1002?

4.17. Workman, a dentist, was indicted for his participation in a scheme to conceal his income and assets from the Internal Revenue Service. In 2011, before the indictment was issued, Workman was interviewed by Donna Jackson, a lawyer representing Workman's wife in their divorce proceedings. The conversation, in which Workman made statements about concealing assets, was tape recorded. Jackson also took notes. Jackson's secretary, who was not present at the interview, typed a transcription of the conversation based on the tape recording. Assume that the tape, the notes, the transcript, Jackson, and her secretary are still available. What are the several ways in which the prosecution could present the content of the 2011 conversation at Workman's trial? Would any of the best evidence rules apply?

  The prosecution now learns that Jackson erased the tape in the ordinary course of business, lost her notes, and does not remember the contents of the conversation. Can the transcript be admitted into evidence?

4.18. In a wrongful death case alleging that the defendant driver was intoxicated when his car crossed a median strip in a divided highway, causing a head-on collision with the plaintiff's intestate, the plaintiff offers testimony from the state police officer who was first on the scene of the accident. The officer would testify that when he approached the defendant's car and saw several empty bottles of Budweiser beer on the front seat. Must the plaintiff produce the original labels and bottles?

4.19. Return to Problem 4.6 at page 221. To prove that Jim Zeal and Stephani Goldstein were conspiring to import marijuana from outside of the United States, the prosecution offers the testimony of Ensign Chandler who also boarded the *Rastafari*. Chandler will testify that he discovered a global positioning system (GPS) in the boat; that a GPS device uses global positioning satellites to track and record the location of any device and therefore the location of an object, such as the boat, to which the device is attached; and that the backtrack feature on the GPS graphed the *Rastafari*'s journey from Kingston, Jamaica, to the point at which it was seized by the Coast Guard. Chandler will have to admit that he did not seize the GPS or obtain any record of the data he observed as a display on its screen. The defendants object on the grounds that Chandler's testimony violates the best evidence rule. What result?

4.20. Flanagan sues Zeppelin Electric Products, Inc., alleging that an oral agreement was made whereby Flanagan would remove gravel from Zeppelin's lot for consideration of $65 per hour. Flanagan and his crew toiled away until the gravel was completely removed. Zeppelin refused to pay Flanagan's bill, disputing the actual number of hours worked. At trial Flanagan offers into evidence a summary of data that he says he transcribed each week from tally sheets recorded at the worksite, indicating the number of hours worked by each employee. He claims that the tally sheets were discarded or lost. Defense counsel objects on the ground that the summary violates the best evidence rule and claims that the so-called tally sheets probably never existed. What result under FRE 1004, 1006, and 1008? What fact questions would the judge instruct the jury to decide?

7. The Best Evidence Rule: Policies and Problems

The following opinion of the Ninth Circuit Court of Appeals concerns a party's attempt to offer secondary evidence of detailed drawings when that party's good-faith loss of the originals had not been proved. The opinion discusses the policies that justify requiring production of originals in general, as well as when nonproduction is not excused.

SEILER v. LUCASFILM, LTD.

808 F.2d 1316 (9th Cir. 1986)

FARRIS, Circuit Judge.

Lee Seiler, a graphic artist and creator of science fiction creatures, alleged copyright infringement by George Lucas and others who created and produced the science fiction movie *The Empire Strikes Back*. Seiler claimed that creatures known as "Imperial Walkers" which appeared in *The Empire Strikes Back* infringed Seiler's copyright on his own creatures called "Garthian Striders." *The Empire Strikes Back* appeared in 1980; Seiler did not obtain his copyright until 1981. . . .

FACTS

Seiler contends that he created and published in 1976 and 1977 [drawings of] science fiction creatures called Garthian Striders. In 1980, George Lucas released *The Empire Strikes Back*, a motion picture that contains a battle sequence depicting giant machines called Imperial Walkers. In 1981 Seiler obtained a copyright on his Striders, depositing with the Copyright Office "reconstructions" of the originals as they had appeared in 1976 and 1977.

Seiler contends that Lucas's Walkers were copied from Seiler's Striders which were allegedly published in 1976 and 1977. Lucas responds that Seiler did not obtain his copyright until one year after the release of *The Empire Strikes Back* and that Seiler can produce no documents that antedate *The Empire Strikes Back*.

Because Seiler proposed to exhibit his Striders in a blow-up comparison to Lucas's Walkers at opening statement, the district judge held an evidentiary hearing on the admissibility of the "reconstructions" of Seiler's Striders. Applying the "best evidence rule," Fed. R. Evid. 1001–1008, the district court found at the end of a seven-day hearing that Seiler lost or destroyed the originals in bad faith under Rule 1004(1) and that consequently no secondary evidence, such as the post–*Empire Strikes Back* reconstructions, was admissible. In its opinion the court found specifically that Seiler testified falsely, purposefully destroyed or withheld in bad faith the originals, and fabricated and misrepresented the nature of his reconstructions. The district court granted summary judgment to Lucas after the evidentiary hearing.

On appeal, Seiler contends (1) that the best evidence rule does not apply to his works, [and] (2) that if the best evidence rule does apply, Rule 1008 requires a jury determination of the existence and authenticity of his originals. . . .

DISCUSSION

1. Application of the Best Evidence Rule

. . . We hold that Seiler's drawings were "writings" within the meaning of Rule 1001(1); they consist not of "letters, words, or numbers" but of "their equivalent." To hold otherwise would frustrate the policies underlying the rule and introduce undesirable inconsistencies into the application of the rule. . . .

In the days before liberal rules of discovery and modern techniques of electronic copying, the rule guarded against incomplete or fraudulent proof. By requiring the possessor of the original to produce it, the rule prevented the introduction of altered copies and the withholding of originals. The purpose of the rule was thus long thought to be one of fraud prevention, but Wigmore pointed out that the rule operated even in cases where fraud was not at issue, such as where secondary evidence is not admitted even though its proponent acts in utmost good faith. Wigmore also noted that if prevention of fraud were the foundation of the rule, it should apply to objects as well as writings, which it does not. . . .

The modern justification for the rule has expanded from prevention of fraud to a recognition that writings occupy a central position in the law. When the contents of a writing are at issue, oral testimony as to the terms of the writing is subject to a greater risk of error than oral testimony as to events or other situations. The human memory is not often capable of reciting the precise terms of a writing, and when the terms are in dispute only the writing itself, or a true copy, provides reliable evidence. To summarize . . . the importance of the precise terms of writings in the world of legal relations, the fallibility of the human memory as reliable evidence of the terms, and the hazards of inaccurate or incomplete duplication are the concerns addressed by the best evidence rule. . . .

. . . The contents of Seiler's work are at issue. There can be no proof of "substantial similarity" and thus of copyright infringement unless Seiler's works are juxtaposed with Lucas's and their contents compared. Since the contents are material and must be proved, Seiler must either produce the original or show that it is unavailable through no fault of his own. Rule 1004(1). This he could not do.

The facts of this case implicate the very concerns that justify the best evidence rule. Seiler alleges infringement by *The Empire Strikes Back*, but he can produce no documentary evidence of any originals existing before the release of the movie. His secondary evidence does not consist of true copies or exact duplicates but of "reconstructions" made after *The Empire Strikes Back*. In short, Seiler claims that the movie infringed his originals, yet he has no proof of those originals.

The dangers of fraud in this situation are clear. The rule would ensure that proof of the infringement claim consists of the works alleged to be infringed. Otherwise, "reconstructions" which might have no resemblance to the purported original would suffice as proof for infringement of the original. Furthermore, application of the rule here defers to the rule's special concern for the contents of writings. Seiler's claim depends on the content of the originals, and the rule would exclude reconstituted proof of the originals' content. Under the circumstances here, no "reconstruction" can substitute for the original.

Seiler argues that the best evidence rule does not apply to his work, in that it is artwork rather than "writings, recordings, or photographs." He contends that the rule both historically and currently embraces only words or numbers. Neither party has cited us to cases which discuss the applicability of the rule to drawings.

To recognize Seiler's works as writings does not, as Seiler argues, run counter to the rule's preoccupation with the centrality of the written word in the world of legal relations. Just as a contract objectively manifests the subjective intent of the makers, so Seiler's drawings are objective manifestations of the creative mind. The copyright laws give legal protection to the objective manifestations of an artist's ideas, just as the law of contract protects through its multifarious principles the meeting of minds evidenced in the contract. Comparing Seiler's drawings with Lucas's drawings is no different in principle than evaluating a contract and the intent behind it. Seiler's "reconstructions" are "writings" that affect legal relations; their copyrightability attests to that.

A creative literary work, which is artwork, and a photograph whose contents are sought to be proved, as in copyright, defamation, or invasion of privacy, are both covered by the best evidence rule. We would be inconsistent to apply the rule to artwork which is literary or photographic but not to artwork of other forms. Furthermore, blueprints, engineering drawings, architectural designs may all lack words or numbers yet still be capable of copyright and susceptible to fraudulent alteration. In short, Seiler's argument would have us restrict the definitions of Rule 1001(1) to "words" and "numbers" but ignore "or their equivalent." We will not do so in the circumstances of this case.

Our holding is also supported by the policy served by the best evidence rule in protecting against faulty memory. Seiler's reconstructions were made four to seven years after the alleged originals; his memory as to specifications and dimensions may have dimmed significantly. Furthermore, reconstructions made after the release of *The Empire Strikes Back* may be tainted, even if unintentionally, by exposure to the movie. Our holding guards against these problems.

NOTES AND QUESTIONS

1. The key to the *Seiler* court's decision to apply the BER to Seiler's lost original drawings was that they were "equivalent" to "letters, words or numbers." Are you convinced? If this interpretation is a stretch, is it justified by its arguable furtherance of the policy of the BER? Suppose that Seiler's 1976 and 1977 original Garthian Striders had been models, instead of drawings, and that he had obtained a copyright based on a reconstruction of those models in 1981. Would the result be different? Do the policies of the best evidence rule apply equally to models?

2. The district judge had decided under FRE 1004(a) that Seiler had destroyed all originals of his drawings in bad faith, obviously taking Seiler's credibility into account—as he was allowed to do under FRE 104(a). This ruling meant that Seiler's nonproduction of his original drawings was not excused, and therefore no secondary evidence of their contents (his reconstructions) could be admitted. Seiler argued on appeal that the judge was required to give to the jury the question under FRE 1008(c) whether "other evidence of contents" (his reconstructions) correctly reflected the contents of his original drawings, and thus had to admit his reconstructions. The appellate court held, however, that the Rule 1008(c) did not come into play unless the district court had decided the Rule 1004(a) issue in Seiler's favor. If the district judge had decided that Seiler's loss of his original drawings was in good faith, the judge would not then be permitted to refuse admission to Seiler's reproductions because the court did not believe that the reconstructions genuinely reflected Seiler's originals. It would be for the jury to resolve this issue under FRE 1008(c). It seems logical to view the FRE 1004(a) question as logically prior to the 1008(c) question.

How would the issues have been analyzed if Lucasfilms had contended that the original, pre-*Star Wars* Garthian Striders had never existed?

ASSESSMENTS

A-4.1. FRE 602.   The plaintiff in an automobile accident case testifies that, almost immediately after impact with the other car, he lost consciousness; that when he came to, he had an intense pain in his right knee; and that he had suffered a fractured tibial plateau (where the tibia bone ends at the knee). The defendant objects that the testimony is inadmissible. The objection should be:

   A. Overruled, because the plaintiff is describing physical occurrences to his own body, of which he has personal knowledge through sensory perception.
   B. Overruled as to the loss and regaining of consciousness and knee pain, but sustained as to the facture.
   C. Sustained, because the loss of consciousness makes it implausible that he can remember details immediately before and after.
   D. Sustained, if the judge believes the witness's claim of memory is unlikely, given the trauma and loss of consciousness.

A-4.2. FRE 901.   Plaintiff Jason Jones is suing his former employer, Acme Corp., for employment discrimination. Jones contends that Acme fired him because of his disability in violation of the Americans with Disabilities Act. Acme contends that it fired Jones legitimately, for falsely stating on his employment application that he had never been convicted of a felony. Jones testifies first in the plaintiff's case in chief. On cross-examination of Jones, defense counsel introduces "Defendant's Exhibit 1." Jones admits on cross-examination that he recognizes Exhibit 1 as an Acme employment application, and that he filled out and signed it. Next to the question "Have you ever been convicted of a felony?", are two check boxes, one on top of the other, labeled "no" and "yes." Jones testifies that he checked the top box, "no," thinking it was the "yes" box, because he believed that "yes" boxes always come before "no" boxes on forms. He further testifies that he would have readily admitted his prior felony conviction had anyone ever asked him. Defense counsel moves Exhibit 1 into evidence. The exhibit should be:

A. Admitted, because defense counsel has offered ESSF that the exhibit is what the proponent claims.

B. Admitted conditionally, pending ESSF from official records that Jones had a felony conviction.

C. Admitted conditionally, pending affirmative testimony from a defense witness with firsthand knowledge that Jones knowingly checked the "no" box.

D. Excluded, because at this stage in the trial, there is not ESSF that Jones intentionally checked the "no" box.

A-4.3. FRE 104(b). Steven Cross is charged with possession with intent to sell cocaine, and conspiracy to sell cocaine. Government informant Tony Genovese will testify that Cross drove to a motel parking lot, where Genovese was waiting for him. Genovese said, "Let's open the trunk." When the automatic trunk latch didn't work, Cross got out and the two men went to the back of the car. Cross opened the trunk with the car key, revealing ten 16-oz. packages of Gold Label brand granulated sugar. Cross was arrested in the parking lot by waiting FBI agents. It is undisputed that the packages contained cocaine. But Cross testifies that he thought he was merely dropping off the car for his friend Barry Styles, whom he claims told Cross he was loaning the car to Genovese. As evidence tending to show Cross's guilty knowledge, Genovese testifies that Cross "did not look surprised" to see the packages of sugar in the trunk. The defendant's best argument for excluding Genovese's "did not look surprised" testimony is:

A. The packages are not self-authenticating under FRE 902, because they were obviously tampered with, even though the "Gold Label" trade inscription appears genuine.

B. The testimony is irrelevant absent ESSF that Cross put cocaine in the packages.

C. The testimony is irrelevant absent ESSF that Cross knew they contained cocaine.

D. Genovese's testimony is self-serving and therefore not credible.

A-4.4. Best Evidence Rule. In an employment discrimination case, the defendant Store Mart asserts that it fired the plaintiff Victor Diaz a year into the Diaz's employment because of an alleged discovery that Diaz had lied on his job application form by falsely stating that he had an Associate of Arts degree from community college. It is undisputed that he had no such degree, but Diaz asserts that he never claimed he did on his employment application. Donald Clay, the Store Mart manager who hired Diaz, will testify as follows (in the absence of an objection): "I have made a diligent search through the files and have been unable to find Diaz's application form. However, I distinctly remember reviewing Diaz's employment application at the time we hired him. He wrote in the 'education' section of the application form that he had an Associate of Arts Degree from Northern Virginia Community College." Does the plaintiff have a basis to object to this testimony under the best evidence rule?

A. Yes, because the testimony seeks to prove the content of a writing.

B. Yes, because Clay's purported memory is self-serving and the original document would be more probative evidence of whether Diaz lied on his application, since it does not raise the same credibility issues.

   C. No, because the purported lie is an underlying event that can be proven through any firsthand witness even though it also happened to take written form.

   D. No, because the original document is the blank application form, and Diaz's answers on the form do not qualify as a writing, recording or photograph.

ANSWERS

A-4.1. FRE 602. The best answer is B. The witness has direct firsthand perception of his own loss and regaining of consciousness, and feeling of pain. The particular cause of the pain—a knee fracture—is not observable through the senses, however, and instead requires some sort of expert medical diagnosis or opinion. Therefore, A is wrong: in contrast to observable symptoms, internal physical processes are not within a person's firsthand knowledge, even those within one's own body. D is plainly wrong, because ESSF of personal knowledge asks whether a reasonable jury could believe the witness, not whether the judge does. For related reasons, C is not a good answer: although a judge can screen out "implausible" testimony (i.e., that a jury couldn't reasonably believe), the idea that a person remembers events shortly before losing and after regaining consciousness does not rise to the level of implausibility of, say, a claim of super-human perception.

A-4.2. FRE 901. The best answer is A. The claim about the exhibit is that Jones knowingly put a false answer on the form. The answer is concededly false, and the question on the form is sufficiently straightforward that a reasonable jury could infer that Jones understood what he was doing; mental states like knowledge and intent must usually be inferred from such circumstantial evidence. Therefore, C and D are wrong. There is no requirement that the final inference in a relevance chain (Jones's knowledge or intent) be proven by direct firsthand knowledge; only that the evidence starting the chain be within the witness's firsthand knowledge. Nor is there a requirement that an exhibit be offered with evidence supplied by witnesses called by the party; foundations can be laid on cross-examination. Moreover, while Jones has raised a factual dispute about his intent, that is a jury question; the judge can't resolve factual disputes in ruling on foundation matters. B is not the best answer, because Jones has firsthand knowledge of his own felony conviction; therefore, "official" corroboration is not required.

A-4.3. FRE 104(b). The best answer is C. The testimony implies that Cross knew there was cocaine in the trunk because he was "unsurprised" when he saw it. Therefore, there should be ESSF that Cross knew what he was looking at when he was unsurprised. Arguably, there already is ESSF, insofar as a jury could infer guilty knowledge from Cross's unsurprised expression. But that doesn't make any of the other answers better than C. A is nonsensical, since the government is not offering the packages to show that they contained sugar. B is not the best answer, since the government does not necessarily contend (or need to contend) that Cross packed the cocaine himself—only that he knowingly delivered it. D is wrong because the objection is based on a missing fact under FRE 104(b): the judge does not determine witness credibility in ruling on admissibility.

A-4.4. Best Evidence Rule.   The best answer is A, for the reason stated. B is wrong; even though it may reflect part of the BER's underlying policy, the rule itself does not depend on which evidence is more probative, but on whether the offering party seeks to prove the content of a writing. C is wrong because the lie is a writing with no independent evidentiary existence apart from the written job application. Nothing in the fact pattern suggests that he also lied orally, and in any event the accusation is that he lied *on his* application form. D is wrong because the relevant writing necessarily includes Diaz's allegedly false answer; nothing in the BER's definitions excludes writing added to a document after the document was first created.

CHAPTER FIVE

THE CHARACTER, PROPENSITY, AND SPECIFIC ACTS RULES

The law of evidence would be very simple if it were the case that "all relevant evidence is admissible," but FRE 402 goes on to say "*except* as otherwise provided . . . by these rules." The exceptions and qualifications to the general rule admitting relevant evidence are the focus of many of the Federal Rules of Evidence. FRE 403, as you have seen, allows the trial judge to exclude relevant evidence on a discretionary, case-by-case basis. In contrast, FRE 404-415 establish certain categorical exclusions of otherwise relevant evidence. In this chapter, we will focus on the most important of these rules: the exclusion of otherwise relevant character evidence and evidence of specific acts. FRE 404-406 and 412-415.

As we begin our examination of these rules, you should keep in mind that the exclusionary provisions may not be a complete bar to the admissibility of a particular piece of evidence. Rather, they prohibit the proponent from offering the evidence only in a particular context or for a particular purpose. For example, FRE 404(b) limits the use of specific acts to prove character but authorizes their use for other purposes, such as to prove motive or intent. Thus, in order to apply the rules properly, you must ask the question that should always be your first question: What is the proponent of the evidence trying to prove? In other words, what is the proponent's theory of relevance? Only after you answer this question will you be able to apply the rules.

A. THE RELEVANCE OF CHARACTER EVIDENCE TO PROVE CONDUCT ON A PARTICULAR OCCASION

Imagine a simple tort case in which a pedestrian is hit by a car and injured. The plaintiff pedestrian claims that he was walking in a clearly marked crosswalk when the defendant driver negligently drove his SUV into him. The defendant claims that the plaintiff was contributorily negligent because he darted out into the middle of the street and was not in the crosswalk. What sort of evidence would the attorneys want to put before the jury to corroborate the testimony of their clients?

Suppose counsel for the plaintiff has the following evidence.

(1) Witness 1, who has seen the defendant drive on many occasions, to testify that the defendant is a careless driver who often fails to stop for pedestrians in crosswalks;

(2) Witness 2, a public records custodian, together with Exhibits A through E, public records establishing that the defendant has had several car accidents and traffic infractions in the past;

(3) Witness 3, a shopkeeper whose storefront overlooks the crosswalk, to testify that he sees the plaintiff cross the street nearly every day, and that he invariably uses the crosswalk.

And the defendant offers:

(4) Witness 4, a friend of the defendant, to testify that the defendant has remade himself into a very safe driver in the past two years.

All of this evidence meets the basic test of relevance under FRE 401, tending to make a fact of consequence (was the driver negligent? was the pedestrian contributorily negligent?) more likely or less likely. While this evidence may not be compelling by itself, you can see that a rational jury could find it useful to consider. As a matter of common sense, it is easy to see how each item of evidence is logically connected to the issues that the parties have to prove in the case. Yet, for reasons that will be explained in this chapter, only the testimony of Witness 3 is likely to be admitted; the rest should be excluded as improper character evidence under FRE 404.

A few definitions will be helpful in analyzing the material presented in this chapter.

1. *Propensity* means a tendency of a person or thing to behave in a certain way. A common thread in this chapter is the "propensity inference"—an argument that evidence about propensity is relevant to show how a person or thing behaved or operated on a specific occasion that is the subject of the litigation. All four of the examples of evidence in the Pedestrian v. Driver hypothetical are of this nature.

2. *Character* (FRE 404) is a type of propensity, probably the most common and familiar. The Federal Rules, however, do not define the terms *character* or *character trait*. This absence of a definition can occasionally raise difficulties. For a working definition, "character" in evidence law refers to the general traits, qualities, or characteristics that make up an individual's personality or behavioral tendencies. Evidence that the defendant is a "negligent" or "careless" driver is character evidence. Evidence of a person's character is relevant—but, as we shall see, generally inadmissible—to show that he committed a particular act consistent with his character on a specific occasion that is the subject of the litigation. Importantly, the character inferences that the rules generally prohibit are propensity inferences, but *not all propensity inference are character inferences*. Evidence can be relevant because of a propensity inference even though it does not depend on an individual's character or character trait.

3. *Specific Acts*, also known as "crimes, wrongs, or other acts" (FRE 404(b)) are instances of a person's conduct that are not the subject of the case being litigated.

That is, they are not the conduct giving rise to alleged civil or criminal liability in the litigation before the court—they are most often specific acts that took place in the past (before the litigated events occurred) but they may also have taken place after the litigated events occurred. Although they are not part of the litigated events, such specific acts may nevertheless be *relevant* to the current case. In the Pedestrian v. Driver hypothetical, the driver's past accidents and traffic infractions are examples of past specific acts. The driver's previous accidents and infractions (other than hitting Plaintiff Pedestrian) are relevant to the case because they give rise to an inference that Driver may have driven negligently on the occasion in question when he collided with Plaintiff Pedestrian. Similarly, the many specific times Pedestrian walked in the crosswalk prior to the accident are not themselves the subject of the litigation. What matters is whether Pedestrian walked inside the crosswalk when he was hit by Driver. But the prior instances may give rise to an inference that he stayed inside the crosswalk on the occasion in question.

4. *Habit* (FRE 406) refers to a type of propensity evidence that the law of evidence distinguishes from character. While character evidence is generally excluded, evidence of habit is admissible. Generally speaking, propensities toward conduct that is more consistent, routine, and repetitive tend to be categorized as "habit," while conduct that is less so tends to be called "character." "Habits" also tend to be somewhat more morally neutral while behavior that is more morally loaded tends to be categorized as "character." The testimony of Witness 3 in the above hypothetical, that Pedestrian invariably walks within the lines of the crosswalk, would probably be admitted as habit evidence.

In preparing a case for trial, it is natural for litigants to search out evidence of character and evidence of relevant specific acts beyond the litigated events. In terms of sheer volume, most evidence introduced in trials (civil or criminal) is circumstantial evidence, and evidence of character and past specific acts is a very commonplace, easily found, and intuitive form of circumstantial evidence. The personalities of all of us are often conceived of as a set of "character traits," and our lives are a constant stream of actions. Who we are and what we do are closely intertwined. In a typical litigated case, where it is disputed whether a (civil or criminal) defendant acted in a certain way, what could be more natural than to look at the kind of person the defendant is, and what he has done before, in order to determine whether he committed the acts alleged in the litigation? If a person is charged with fraud, it would be useful to know whether he is "honest." If he is alleged to have committed an assault, it seems relevant to know whether he is "violent." The "character" inference is a commonsense form of reasoning which holds that a person with a dishonest character is more likely than an honest person to have committed the fraud in question; or that a violent person is more likely than a nonviolent one to initiate a physical assault. (See Diagram 5-1, infra.) Thus, use of character evidence is tempting for litigants.

It is crucial to see how specific acts fit into the character inference. How do we know what someone's character is? How do we know whether a person is "careless" or "dishonest" or "violent"? And how would we prove that in court, in the absence of a rule restricting such proof? Perhaps the most intuitive answer is to look at the person's conduct. Character traits are ultimately generalizations based on specific instances of conduct. Thus, specific acts are the intuitively obvious source of character evidence and in practice are often relevant to prove character, which in turn is relevant as circumstantial evidence of how a person may have acted on a particular (disputed) occasion. This chain of reasoning is illustrated in Diagram 5-2, infra. As commonsense and intuitive as this chain of reasoning may be, it is precisely what the Federal Rules *prohibit*. As we will see, while evidence of character may *sometimes* be used to prove or disprove conduct on a specific occasion, FRE 404(b) does not allow specific acts to prove *character* in order to prove, in turn, conduct on a particular occasion.

B. GENERAL PROHIBITION ON USE OF CHARACTER AND "CRIME, WRONG, OR OTHER ACT" EVIDENCE

1. FRE 404

RULE 404.   CHARACTER EVIDENCE; CRIMES OR OTHER ACTS

(a) Character Evidence.

(1) *Prohibited Uses*. Evidence of a person's character or character trait is not admissible to prove that on a particular occasion the person acted in accordance with the character or trait.

(2) *Exceptions for a Defendant or Victim in a Criminal Case*. The following exceptions apply in a criminal case:

(A) a defendant may offer evidence of the defendant's pertinent trait, and if the evidence is admitted, the prosecutor may offer evidence to rebut it;

(B) subject to the limitations in Rule 412, a defendant may offer evidence of an alleged victim's pertinent trait, and if the evidence is admitted, the prosecutor may:

(i) offer evidence to rebut it; and

. (ii) offer evidence of the defendant's same trait; and

(C) in a homicide case, the prosecutor may offer evidence of the alleged victim's trait of peacefulness to rebut evidence that the victim was the first aggressor.

(3) *Exceptions for a Witness*. Evidence of a witness's character may be admitted under Rules 607, 608, and 609.

(b) Crimes, Wrongs, or Other Acts.

(1) *Prohibited Uses*. Evidence of a crime, wrong, or other act is not admissible to prove a person's character in order to show that on a particular occasion the person acted in accordance with the character.

(2) *Permitted Uses; Notice in a Criminal Case*. This evidence may be admissible for another purpose, such as proving motive, opportunity, intent, preparation, plan, knowledge, identity, absence of mistake, or lack of accident. On request by a defendant in a criminal case, the prosecutor must:

   (A) provide reasonable notice of the general nature of any such evidence that the prosecutor intends to offer at trial; and

   (B) do so before trial—or during trial if the court, for good cause, excuses lack of pretrial notice.

2. Explanation of FRE 404(a) and (b)

Our initial focus is on two parts of FRE 404:
  (a) Character Evidence.
   (1) *Prohibited Uses*. Evidence of a person's character or character trait is not admissible to prove that on a particular occasion the person acted in accordance with the character or trait . . . .
  (b) Crimes, Wrongs, or Other Acts.
   (1) *Prohibited Uses*. Evidence of a crime, wrong, or other act is not admissible to prove a person's character in order to show that on a particular occasion the person acted in accordance with the character.

The text of FRE 404(a) begins by prohibiting the use of evidence of a person's character to prove action in accordance with that character trait on a particular occasion. This general prohibition provides the backdrop against which the more specific and detailed rules admitting and excluding various forms of character evidence must be understood. The basic prohibitions of FRE 404(a) and 404(b) (putting aside, for the moment, the qualifications and exceptions stated in the rule) are broad and straightforward. Under FRE 404(a), evidence of character is not permitted to show action on a particular occasion. This bars the basic inference shown in Diagram 5-1:

Diagram 5-1

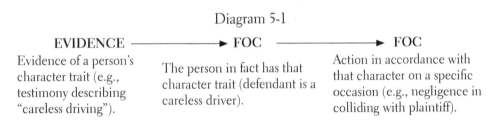

EVIDENCE	FOC	FOC
Evidence of a person's character trait (e.g., testimony describing "careless driving").	The person in fact has that character trait (defendant is a careless driver).	Action in accordance with that character on a specific occasion (e.g., negligence in colliding with plaintiff).

FRE 404(b) elaborates on this principle by making clear that crimes, wrongs, and other specific acts cannot be admitted to prove that a person had a certain character trait and in order "to show" the person acted in accordance with the character trait on a particular occasion. (Note: to "show" in FRE 404(b) simply means to "prove.") This inference, too, relies on the prohibited character inference. As a matter of logic, evidence of past conduct similar to the acts that allegedly give rise to liability—for instance, evidence of past driving infractions and accidents to show that it is more likely that the driver was negligent in the incident in question—is usually relevant precisely because we make the character inference. Driver's past driving conduct shows him to be a certain type of driver, the kind who is more likely to do that type of thing—negligent driving—on further occasions. FRE 404(b) thus prohibits the chain of inferences shown in Diagram 5-2:

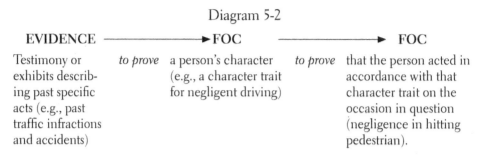

FRE 404(b)'s prohibition of a particular mode of proving character to prove action in accordance with that character trait may seem unnecessary given the general prohibition in FRE 404(a). But there are two good reasons for spelling it out. First, there are limited exceptions set out in FRE 404(a)(2) in which character evidence may be offered to prove conduct on a specific occasion. FRE 404(b) makes clear that even when these exceptions apply, the means of proving character cannot include specific acts.

Second, as suggested above, past specific acts are a common and intuitively obvious form of evidence that litigants are naturally inclined to look for. Absent the express prohibition in FRE 404(b), it might not be sufficiently clear to courts and litigants that specific acts evidence is in many instances relevant only because it proves character in order to prove actions in accordance with character, i.e., that the relevance of this evidence depends on the prohibited character inference. FRE 404(b) stands as a reminder that specific acts evidence is objectionable on this ground.

a. The Rationale for Restricting Evidence of a Person's Character

There are good reasons for restricting the use of character evidence to prove a person acted in accordance on a particular occasion:

Weakness of the Propensity Inference.   First, the probative value of character evidence to show action in accordance with character will seldom, if ever, be very great. A person who is generally honest will at least occasionally be less than fully honest; a person whom we may fairly describe as having a violent character will on many occasions react to adverse situations in a peaceful manner. Moreover, on the occasion giving rise to the litigation, there may have been particular stresses on the individual or some other unusual circumstances that increased the likelihood of acting "out of character."

In the *Johnson* case, for example, evidence of Walker's reputation for violence is relevant to show that he was violent at the time of the alleged jail cell altercation. Yet the evidence does not suggest that Walker was violent in a majority of his encounters with inmates. If that were the case, it is unlikely that he would have retained his job.

Rather, the defendant's evidence suggests only that Walker happened to be violent somewhat more often than the other correctional officers. Alternatively, consider the prosecution's evidence about Walker's *good* character. Walker may have been a generally peaceful person, but the stress of the incident with Johnson could have caused Walker to act "out of character." Even if one fully credits the defense evidence and discounts the prosecution evidence (or vice versa), the evidence tells the fact finder very little about the likelihood that Walker behaved violently at the one specific time that is the focus of the litigation. In short, the inference in Diagram 5-1 from a general character trait like violence, peacefulness, honesty, or dishonesty to action in accordance with that character trait on a particular occasion is likely to be quite weak.

Low Probative Value of the Evidence to Prove Character.   Furthermore, the inference from the evidence offered (e.g., the testimony about Walker's reputation for violence) to what a person's character actually is may itself be weak. As will be seen below, when character evidence is permitted, it must take the form of the witness's opinion about a person's character or that person's "reputation" in the community. Such evidence often comes across as too vague and general to be convincing. How convinced were you by the inmates' testimony about Walker's reputation for violence in the *Johnson* case?

Evidence of past specific acts—for instance, specific instances in which Walker beat an inmate, if such evidence existed—may be much more powerful than general opinions, but even that evidence may not be very probative of a person's character. While a person's character is undoubtedly reflected in his conduct, how much conduct do we need to observe before we can make reliable "character" judgments? Would two instances of Walker assaulting inmates suffice to prove that he had a "character" to be violent toward inmates? What if those incidents were "out of character" for him?

Diversion from Main Issues.   If the character evidence is disputed, there is a risk of digressing into a "minitrial" on character and diverting the factfinder's attention from the main issues in the case. In *Johnson*, for example, there was conflicting testimony about Walker's reputation for violence or nonviolence. Moreover, the risk of confusion of issues would be heightened if character were to be proven by past specific acts. If, for instance, the defense in *Johnson* wanted to introduce evidence that Walker had previously assaulted two inmates, we can easily see the potential for minitrials on those incidents. Were those prior assaults similar in relevant respects to Johnson's situation? Did Walker provoke the assault or simply defend himself? How many facts are disputed about the prior assaults, and how many witnesses are there to those events?

"Bad Person" Prejudice.   Character evidence may also be unfairly prejudicial, particularly if it is evidence of the character of a party to the lawsuit. Inherent in the concept of character—or at least in the attributes that most people and most courts think of as character—is a moral quality or sense of rightness or wrongness. Consider, for example, the meaning of the words we use to describe what we refer to as character traits, e.g., *honesty, dishonesty, peacefulness,* and *violence.* Evidence that a litigant possesses one of these traits may arouse an emotional response and dispose the jury to decide in favor of that person if it is a positive character trait or against the person if it is a negative one.

This danger is intensified when a negative character inference might be drawn from past specific acts. Consider, for example, a murder case in which the prosecutor offers evidence that the defendant has committed an unrelated murder on a prior occasion. One way that this evidence is relevant is to show that the defendant has a generally violent character—and more specifically, a character trait to commit murder—and thus may have committed the murder on the occasion in question. At the same time, the prejudicial impact of the evidence may be substantial. The jury is likely to have little sympathy for a one-time murderer even if it has a reasonable doubt about the defendant's guilt on the current charge. The jurors may also make unfounded assumptions about the likelihood that someone who has committed murder in the past will do so again. The risk is probably especially great that a jury, on hearing about a criminal defendant's bad character, may be willing to ignore a reasonable doubt and convict a person who may not (in the jurors' view) have been sufficiently punished in the past and who may commit crimes in the future. But as Justice Cardozo famously said, "the law has set its face against the endeavor to fasten guilt upon [a criminal defendant] by proof of character or experience predisposing to an act of crime." People v. Zackowitz, 254 N.Y. 192, 172 N.E. 466 (1930).

As you can see from the foregoing points, character evidence raises classic FRE 403 issues, in which probative value must be weighed against FRE 403 dangers of consumption of time, confusion of issues, and unfair prejudice. FRE 404 can be understood as reflecting a judgment that the FRE 403 dangers inherent in character evidence will so often substantially outweigh the probative value that it makes sense to exclude it as a general rule rather than to permit case-by-case decisions on whether to admit it. And while character evidence admissible under the FRE 404(a) exceptions can be proven by opinion or reputation testimony, it cannot be proven by specific acts. Although specific acts may be slightly more probative of character than vague, general reputation or opinion evidence, the FRE 403-type dangers of minitrials and unfair prejudice are probably much greater.

b. Exceptions to the FRE 404(b) Prohibition Against the Use of Specific Acts

Despite the unqualified nature of the prohibition against specific acts evidence in FRE 404(b), there are limited instances in which it is permissible to use evidence of a person's specific acts to prove that person's character to prove action in accordance with character. FRE 608(b) and 609, which we will consider in Chapter Seven, explicitly authorize the use of specific acts for this purpose. The revised Federal Rules dealing with the admissibility of sexual misconduct evidence, FRE 413-415, also contemplate the use of specific acts to prove character to show action in accordance with character.

KEY POINTS

1. Evidence of a person's character is relevant to prove the person's action in accordance with character on a particular occasion.
2. The Federal Rules, however, prohibit the use of character evidence to prove action in accordance with character except in the situations set forth in FRE 404(a) (discussed in Section G, infra).
3. The Federal Rules do not define "character" or "character trait." Typically, "character" refers to the general traits, qualities, or characteristics of a person that makeup that person's personality or behavioral tendencies. Character traits tend to be reflected in occasional, rather than routine, conduct and tend to have moral overtones (e.g., honesty or dishonesty) and, therefore, inherent prejudice.
4. Crimes, wrongs, or other acts that are not part of the events being litigated are often relevant to prove character in order to prove action in accordance with that character trait on a particular occasion. However, they are excluded from evidence for this purpose by FRE 404(b).

PROBLEMS

5.1. Return to Problem 3.3, United States v. Ray, at page 149. The prosecution offers evidence that (a) in October 2013, Ray sold 25,000 shares of Rundown stock one week before a major and abrupt fall in Rundown's share price; and (b) in May 2014, Ray purchased 30,000 shares of Rundown 30 days before the company announced the profitable acquisition of a competitor, an event that caused the stock price to rise by 25 percent. For what purposes is this evidence relevant? Is it objectionable?

5.2. Return to Problem 3.4, State v. Blair, at page 150. The prosecution offers the following evidence. For what purposes is this evidence relevant? Is it objectionable?
  (a) That in 2008, Blair pleaded guilty to a charge of simple assault after making an unprovoked attack with his fists on a man in a bar.
  (b) Testimony from Blair's then-girlfriend that on two occasions in 2005 she called 911 because Blair had beaten her. She received medical treatment on both occasions, though she did not press charges against Blair.
  (c) That Blair was arrested for battering Norma in September 2008. Norma received medical treatment for her injuries, but no charges were filed against Blair.

5.3. Return to the case of United States v. Hitt, at page 171. Recall that the prosecution offered a photograph of the defendant's rifle surrounded by several guns that were not his. Suppose that the guns did in fact belong to Hitt. With that assumption, what arguments could be made for the relevance of the photograph? Can any objection be made under FRE 404(b)? Can you think of any additional arguments in support of an FRE 403 objection?

5.4. Return to Problem 3.2, Pedroso v. Driver, at page 148. The defendant offers the following evidence. For what purposes is this evidence relevant? Is it objectionable?

(a) Testimony of the transportation supervisor for the entire school district that defendant Driver "is the best and most safety conscious driver in the district."

(b) Testimony from the same witness that Driver "had a spotless driving record prior to this incident."

The plaintiff offers the following evidence. For what purpose is this evidence relevant? Is it objectionable?

(c) Testimony from Driver's neighbor that Driver had been depressed for weeks prior to the incident and that "half a dozen" empty liquor bottles could be seen in Driver's trash each week.

(d) Driver's admission that she had been speeding while driving her bus route prior to the incident.

5.5. Joseph Zachary has been convicted of first degree murder for the premeditated killing of Marty Coppola. According to the evidence presented to the jury, Zachary got into a heated argument with Coppola at a bar. He went back to his apartment where he retrieved a 9 mm pistol, returned to the bar and shot Coppola. To prove premeditation, the prosecution argued that Zachary returned to the bar intending to kill Coppola. The defense argued for first degree manslaughter based on (1) Zachary's testimony that he did not intend to use the gun on Coppola and (2) corroborated testimony that Zachary pulled the gun only after Coppola tried to punch him in the face. The prosecution, over defense counsel's objection, introduced evidence that Zachary also owned a .38 caliber magnum revolver and a .45 caliber pistol in addition to the murder weapon. No evidence was offered about how or why Zachary chose the 9 mm pistol. In admitting the evidence of the other guns, the trial judge agreed with the prosecutor's argument that the evidence "shows the defendant had a murderous propensity."

Assuming that all arguments have been properly preserved for appeal, what arguments should the defense make to the appellate court that the evidence concerning the other guns should have been excluded from the trial? How should the prosecutor respond?

C. THE ADMISSIBILITY OF SPECIFIC ACTS THAT ARE DEEMED RELEVANT WITHOUT A CHARACTER INFERENCE

Rule 404(a)(1) prohibits a certain kind of propensity inference—specifically, a "character" inference, one that asks the jury to infer that a person acted a certain way on the occasion in question because it was his "character" to act that way. FRE 404(b)(1) emphasizes this prohibition with respect to evidence of specific acts. But nothing in these rules prohibits the use of specific acts that are relevant for some purpose other than to prove character to prove, in turn, conduct on a particular occasion. In other words, specific acts that are relevant without making the full character inference illustrated in Diagram 5-2, supra, are not excluded by FRE 404(b)(1).

Because past specific acts are an important and common type of evidence, the drafters of the rules did not leave this point about their admissibility for noncharacter purposes to implication, but chose instead to spell it out in FRE 404(b)(2).

1. Explanation of FRE 404(b)(2)

FRE 404(b)(2) provides:

> (2) *Permitted Uses; Notice in a Criminal Case.* This evidence [of a crime, wrong or other act] may be admissible for another purpose, such as proving motive, opportunity, intent, preparation, plan, knowledge, identity, absence of mistake, or lack of accident. On request by a defendant in a criminal case, the prosecutor must:
>
> > (A) provide reasonable notice of the general nature of any such evidence that the prosecutor intends to offer at trial; and
> >
> > (B) do so before trial—or during trial if the court, for good cause, excuses lack of pretrial notice.

Specific acts may be admissible pursuant to FRE 404(b)(2) to prove a fact of consequence without proving "character" or a "character trait." In order to admit evidence pursuant to FRE 404(b)(2), the proponent must satisfy three requirements. First, the proponent must articulate some noncharacter purpose for which the specific acts evidence is relevant. Second, the proponent must introduce evidence that the person who allegedly committed the act in fact did commit the act. Third, the proponent must be prepared to respond to a likely FRE 403 objection to the evidence.

Assume, for example, a case in which the defendant is charged with shooting a police officer, and the prosecution wants to introduce evidence that the defendant robbed a bank shortly before the shooting. The prosecution would first have to articulate a noncharacter purpose for introducing evidence of the defendant's involvement in the bank robbery. In this case, the prosecution would maintain that the bank robbery evidence is offered, not to show that the defendant more likely shot the police officer in accordance with a general character for dishonesty or lawlessness, but rather to establish a motive for the shooting: Because the defendant had recently robbed a bank, the defendant had a particular fear of capture and, therefore, a motive for shooting the police officer. Second, the prosecution would have to have evidence— perhaps, for example, a videotape of the robbery or eyewitness testimony—sufficient to support a finding that the defendant was indeed the bank robber. (Note: This is a finding under 104(b). See Chapter Four, Section E.) Finally, the prosecution would have to be prepared to respond to an objection that the probative value of the bank robbery evidence (to prove that the defendant had a motive for the shooting and, therefore, that the defendant did shoot the officer) is substantially outweighed by the FRE 403 dangers.

If the proponent of the evidence is the prosecutor, there is a fourth requirement— that the prosecution respond to a criminal defendant's demand for notice. According to the Advisory Committee Note on this notice requirement, its purpose is "to reduce surprise and promote early resolution on the issue of admissibility." The rule states no absolute time limits and no particular form that the request and response must take.

a. *Types of 404(b)(2) Evidence*

The eight examples listed in FRE 404(b)(2)—motive, opportunity, intent, preparation, plan, knowledge, identity, or absence of mistake or accident—can be grouped into three broad and overlapping categories. However, the phrase "such as" in FRE 404(b)(2) expressly makes clear that the list is not exhaustive. To secure admission pursuant to FRE 404(b)(2), it is not necessary to identify one of the listed purposes. It is sufficient for the proponent of specific acts evidence to convince the court that the evidence is outside the scope of FRE 404(b)(1)—i.e., it is offered for some purpose other than proving a person's character to prove conduct in accordance with character on a particular occasion.

Evidence of Motive, Opportunity, Preparation, or Plan.   Sometimes the events giving rise to civil or criminal liability are an inextricable part of a larger story involving other actions by a party. These other actions are in turn relevant to an essential element, tending to prove who did the act or what the act was. The prosecution in a homicide case might want to present evidence that the defendant stole a gun in a burglary a week before the homicide to explain how he came into possession of the gun used in the crime—an example of *opportunity* or *preparation*. In the same homicide case, the prosecution might offer evidence that the defendant was involved with the victim in a drug deal that went bad, in order to establish the defendant's *motive* to kill the victim. Or, under a different set of facts, a homicide might be part of a broader *plan* or scheme to further a drug-dealing conspiracy—if the victim were a potential witness against the conspirators, or a competing drug dealer—in which case the prosecution might offer specific acts evidence in the form of evidence of the (uncharged) drug dealing conspiracy.

"Motive," "opportunity," "preparation," and "plan," are all terms that capture the idea of essential aspects of the story of the case, such that the story can only be fully understood if the other actions are presented to the jury. As we saw in the *Old Chief* case, litigants have an acknowledged strong interest in presenting evidence that tells the jury a story that is coherent and has "narrative integrity"—that doesn't leave the jury wondering "how" and "why." In addition, these kinds of facts are relevant in other ways, typically as circumstantial evidence tending to show *identity*—who committed the crime or conduct that is the subject of the litigation—or the fact that the crime or conduct occurred, where those facts are in dispute.

It could be said that the examples given above are not properly considered past specific acts at all, in the sense we that have been using the term. Why not? Because, at least in some cases, they arguably are indeed part of a single, cohesive chain of events giving rise to liability. Even if this is so, they nevertheless are frequently lumped into the 404(b)(2) category to the extent that they theoretically could have been the subject of additional civil claims or criminal charges.

Evidence Showing Relevant States of Mind. States of mind are at issue in many litigated cases: Mental states may be an element of the criminal charge or the civil claim, and the defendant can put his state of mind at issue by asserting mistake, accident, or lack of knowledge. In such cases, past specific acts can be admissible for the noncharacter purpose of proving *knowledge, intent* or *absence of mistake or accident.* The same evidence that showed "preparation" or "motive" in the homicide example above, may also be relevant to show an intent to kill or the kind of premeditation that must typically be shown in a murder case. Past specific acts might also show the requisite knowledge. For instance, in a prosecution for conspiracy to distribute narcotics, the prosecution might offer a prior conviction for dealing cocaine to show the defendant's knowledge that the substance he transported was in fact cocaine.

This last example also illustrates what is meant by *absence of mistake or accident.* Past specific acts may be relevant to rebut a defendant's assertion that he is not liable or guilty because he was mistaken about crucial facts or that the conduct was unintentional. In the cocaine dealing example, if the defendant claims he did not know the white powder was cocaine, his past conviction for dealing powder cocaine would be relevant to undermine that claim. Past specific acts are also occasionally offered to rebut a claim of accident. For instance, in a case where an alleged arsonist charged with burning down his business to collect insurance proceeds claims that the fire was an accident, the prosecution might introduce evidence of prior purported accidents in which the same defendant lost other businesses in fires and collected insurance proceeds. The theory is that such accidents are unlikely to recur with the same person so frequently, implying that intentional conduct must be involved.

Evidence Showing Identity. In cases where the defense theory is that the wrongful conduct was perpetrated by some other known or unknown person, specific acts can be relevant as circumstantial evidence that the defendant is indeed the perpetrator. To be sure, "other conduct" offered for any of the other noncharacter purposes above is ultimately relevant to "identify" the defendant as the culprit. *Identity* is probably listed separately as a way of including the "modus operandi" theory: Where other conduct is so distinctive and nearly identical in its attributes or methods to the litigated conduct as to suggest by itself that the same perpetrator did the past and present acts, it can be admitted as showing identity.

b. Preliminary Factfinding with Respect to Whether the Person in Question Committed the Act

The probative value of specific acts evidence for any of the noncharacter purposes covered by FRE 404(b) depends in part on the strength of the proof that the person committed the act and, if culpability is important to the relevance of the evidence, that the person did so culpably. What standard should the trial judge use in determining whether to admit the specific acts evidence? In Huddleston v. United States, 485 U.S. 681 (1988), the Supreme Court resolved a conflict in the federal circuits by holding that the question of the person's culpable involvement was one of conditional relevance governed by FRE 104(b). Thus, under the Federal Rules, the proponent of the evidence can satisfy the preliminary fact requirement by introducing "evidence sufficient to support a finding" by a preponderance of the evidence that the person was culpably involved in the act. This standard of proof is relatively low, as we discussed at pages 192-93, supra. Despite *Huddleston*, some state courts apply a higher standard in assessing a person's involvement in prior acts.

c. Probative Value and Prejudice Generally

Finding a relevant "noncharacter" purpose for specific acts evidence under FRE 404(b)(2) and satisfying the preliminary fact standard does not mean that the evidence is automatically admissible. The term "may" in FRE 404(b) makes it clear that admissibility is subject to compliance with the other rules of evidence, the most important of which in the context of specific acts evidence is FRE 403. FRE 404(b)(2) evidence nearly always raises a potential FRE 403 objection. This is because in virtually every (perhaps every) instance in which evidence offered for one of the FRE 404(b)(2) purposes, there will still be the risk that the jury will consider the conduct for the impermissible purpose of proving character to prove conduct in accordance with character on a specific occasion. Thus, for example, if the prosecutor in a homicide case offers evidence of the defendant's burglary-theft of a gun to show preparation and opportunity, the jury may nevertheless use the evidence to determine that the defendant has a character to commit crimes and is therefore more likely to have committed the homicide—or is just a bad person who should be punished on that basis. In other words, FRE 404(b)(2) evidence is likely to be relevant for two purposes—one admissible, the other not. Thus, a classic FRE 403 objection is presented, based on the argument that the prejudice flowing from the impermissible purpose substantially outweighs the probative value of the permissible purpose.

Factors for the court to consider in making the FRE 403 balancing decision include

(1) how probative the noncharacter purpose is of some contested issue in the case;

(2) how probative the specific act is to prove the noncharacter purpose (e.g., whether there is a sufficiently close temporal proximity between the specific act and the crime charged; whether there is a "substantial similarity" between the past act and the crime charged, see United States v. Haywood, 280 F.3d 715 (6th Cir. 2002));

(3) how probative the evidence is to establish that the act occurred (e.g., whether there is a dispute about the nature of the act or the defendant's involvement in it);

(4) how much of a risk of unfair prejudice would result from introduction of the evidence (e.g., how heinous is the specific act); and

(5) how effective a limiting instruction is likely to be in reducing the risk of unfair prejudice.

In sum, when the prosecution offers specific acts evidence against a criminal defendant, there inevitably will be the risk of "bad person" prejudice: Jurors may be willing to ignore a reasonable doubt because they regard the defendant as a bad person who perhaps has not been sufficiently punished for prior misdeeds and who may commit similar bad acts in the future. In addition, there is a risk that the jury may use the act in an improper character-propensity sense as evidence that the defendant committed the crime charged. Keep in mind, though, that FRE 403 is a rule favoring admissibility (probative value must be "substantially outweighed" by the countervailing factors) and that courts often admit potentially prejudicial 404(b)(2) evidence.

KEY POINTS

1. FRE 404(b)(1) prohibits the use of specific acts *only* to prove character to prove action in accordance with character.
2. Admissibility of specific acts for noncharacter purposes requires the proponent to do three things: (a) convince the judge that there is a legitimate noncharacter purpose for the evidence; (b) satisfy the preliminary fact standard for the specific act; and (c) respond to an FRE 403 objection.
3. The list of purposes in FRE 404(b)(2) for which specific acts evidence may be admissible is not exhaustive. Specific acts evidence may be admissible for *any* noncharacter purpose.
4. Under the Federal Rules, the question of whether a person was culpably involved in the specific acts is an FRE 104(b) preliminary fact question. The proponent can satisfy the standard by offering evidence sufficient to support a finding by a preponderance of the evidence that the person was culpably involved in the act.
5. FRE 403 may sometimes require exclusion of specific acts evidence offered for noncharacter purposes.

PROBLEMS

5.6. Consider whether the specific acts evidence should be admissible in the following cases:
  (a) Jill's home was burglarized, and there was no evidence of a forced entry. In the case against the defendant, the prosecution offers evidence that a week before the burglary, the defendant stole Jill's purse containing her key ring.
  (b) The defendant is charged with growing marijuana. She claims that her friends are responsible and that she thought the plants were weeds. The prosecution offers eyewitness testimony from a neighbor that he had seen the defendant harvest marijuana on her property the year previously.
  (c) The defendant is charged with killing X, who was about to testify as an eyewitness in a major drug conspiracy trial. The prosecution offers evidence of the defendant's participation in the conspiracy.
5.7. Jerry Kozinski is being tried for burglary of an office building. A "Z" was found spray-painted on the front door of the burglarized building the same morning

the burglary was discovered. The prosecution offers the following evidence. Is it admissible?

(a) Evidence that Kozinski had pleaded guilty to a residential burglary two years ago in which a "Z" was found spray-painted on the front door of the burglarized house.

(b) Records from Blockbuster Video showing that Kozinski had rented "The Mark of Zorro" (in which the protagonist leaves behind a letter "Z" at the scenes of his exploits) eight times in the past three years.

5.8. Return to Problem 5.4, Pedroso v. Driver, at page 148. Reconsider each of the offered items of evidence in light of FRE 404(b)(2). Is the admissibility of any of this evidence affected in light of the additional rule?

5.9. Return to Problem 3.3, United States v. Ray, at page 149. The prosecution offers evidence that (a) in October 2013, Ray sold 25,000 shares of Rundown stock one week before a major and abrupt fall in Rundown's share price; and (b) in May 2014, Ray purchased 30,000 shares of Rundown 30 days before the company announced the profitable acquisition of a competitor, an event which caused the stock price to rise by 25 percent. Assume that the defense counsel's earlier FRE 403 objection to this evidence (see Problem 3.9, at page 167) has been overruled. Can the defense object to this evidence under FRE 404? Does that objection suggest any additional arguments for an FRE 403 objection? How should the prosecutor respond?

5.10. Return to Problem 3.4, State v. Blair, at page 150. The prosecution offers the following evidence. What arguments can be made for and against admission?

(a) That in 2008, Blair pleaded guilty to a charge of simple assault after making an unprovoked attack with his fists on a man in a bar.

(b) Testimony from Blair's ex-girlfriend that he had beaten her on two occasions in 2005. She received medical treatment on both occasions, though she did not press charges against Blair.

(c) That Blair was arrested for battering Norma in September 2008. Norma received medical treatment for her injuries, but no charges were filed against Blair.

5.11. Return to Problem 3.5 on page 150. A retired player on the Tomcats team who has played with Trapp for the past ten years would testify that Trapp often has extreme outbursts of rage when the Tomcats are losing. He also would testify that when that happens, he has seen Trapp hit players from the opposing team on several occasions.

5.12. Greg Simpson is charged with armed robbery and burglary. According to the testimony of Fred Able, a knife-wielding man wearing jeans, a T-shirt, and a ski mask broke into his home by coming through an unlocked window. The intruder, who had a slight limp and appeared to be over six feet tall, demanded Able's money and threatened to kill him if he called the police. The prosecution offers the testimony of Pam Wellington that one week before the incident at Able's house, a man who she identifies as Simpson came to her door, said his car had broken down, and asked to use the telephone. He was wearing jeans and a T-shirt. Before Wellington could respond, Simpson pushed his way into the house, pulled out a knife and demanded Wellington's money and jewelry. As Wellington began to comply, her dog attacked Simpson and bit him in the leg. Simpson fled through the front door. Simpson is six feet tall. Both crimes occurred at approximately 11:00 A.M. in the same neighborhood. Simpson objects to Wellington's testimony on the grounds that the evidence (a) is impermissible character evidence, (b) should be excluded because of FRE 403, and (c) should be excluded because he was acquitted of burglary and attempted robbery in the Wellington incident. How should the court rule?

5.13. Garvin is charged with illegal possession of a firearm, which was discovered in a Cadillac parked outside Garvin's house. Garvin frequently used the Cadillac, which belonged to his aunt. The prosecution wishes to introduce evidence that Garvin had previously been arrested for robbery, that the police were at his house to execute a warrant to search for proceeds of robbery, that they discovered the key to the Cadillac during the search, and that Garvin's aunt then identified herself as the owner of the Cadillac and consented to its search. How much of this evidence should be admissible? For what purpose?

2. Difficulties Distinguishing FRE 404(b)(2) Evidence From Prohibited Character Evidence

Our description of three categories of specific acts evidence admissible under FRE 404(b)(2)—essential parts of a larger story (motive, opportunity, preparation, plan), states of mind (knowledge, intent, absence of mistake, lack of accident), and identity (including modus operandi)—was not intended to suggest that any past specific act that can be shoehorned into one of these descriptors should be deemed admissible. On the contrary, we believe that lax application of the 404(b)(2) categories poses a real risk of undermining the policies behind the 404(b)(1) prohibition of specific acts to prove character to prove conduct on a particular occasion. In this section we discuss five areas in which applications of FRE 404(b)(2) may be in tension with the FRE 404(b)(1) ban on character evidence.

a. The Problem of "Res Gestae"

While evidence of past acts to show "motive" or "opportunity" might supply elements that fill out the story of the case, they are also independently relevant: for example, a person with a motive is more likely to have done the act in question than someone with no motive. However, parties sometimes argue for admission of evidence that is not technically relevant on the ground that it purportedly involves the "same transaction" as the conduct at issue in the case, or helps to "complete the story" of the case. Such evidence is often called *res gestae*, a Latinism that may give the argument to admit such evidence more weight than it deserves. For example, it is all too easy for a prosecutor to argue that prior criminal acts of a defendant are part of the "larger narrative" the prosecution wants to tell. Consider People v. Zackowitz, 254. N.Y. 192, 172 N.E. 466 (1930), which forms the basis of Problem 5.5 at page 270, supra. The prosecution did in fact argue that the past acts evidence was relevant background narrative (using the term *res gestae*). But why was that particular part of the narrative at all helpful, let alone necessary to understanding the "story" of the crime? Judge Cardozo, writing for the court, plainly believed it was not.

Courts have taken different views on how carefully to limit marginally relevant or irrelevant past acts evidence that is offered only to "complete the story." Compare United States v. Bowie, 232 F.3d 923, 929 (D.C. Cir. 2000) ("there is no general 'complete the story' or 'explain the circumstances' exception to Rule 404(b) in this Circuit") with United States v. Brooks, 670 F.2d 625, 628-629 (5th Cir. 1982) (admitting evidence that marijuana was found in defendant's car as "arising out of the same transaction or series of transactions as the charged offense" of possession of cocaine with intent to distribute). In our view, courts should not admit such evidence unless it is necessary to a coherent and intelligible description of the conduct giving rise to civil or criminal liability.

b. The Problem of Specific Acts Evidence to Prove Intent or Knowledge

FRE 404(b) identifies "intent" and "knowledge" as two of the permissible non-character uses of specific acts evidence. "Intent" and "knowledge" are two mental states that permeate our laws. Acts that may be deemed nonculpable when done with an "innocent" state of mind might give rise to civil or criminal liability with a "guilty" state of mind. The presence of "knowledge" or "intent" may convert an accident or innocent mistake into a crime or tort. (Consider Holmes's famous quip, "even a dog knows the difference between being tripped over and being kicked.")

Some courts have formulated the admissibility of past specific acts evidence to prove such states of mind this way: "Where a defendant claims that his conduct has an innocent explanation, prior act evidence is generally admissible to prove that the defendant acted with the state of mind necessary to commit the offense charged." United States v. Zackson, 12 F.3d 1178, 1182 (2d Cir. 1993). In *Zackson*, for example, the prosecution introduced evidence that the defendant had previously participated in a marijuana-selling conspiracy to rebut his contention that he did not willingly participate in a cocaine-dealing conspiracy.

Does the prior marijuana selling prove intent without relying on a character inference? The relevance of the prior marijuana conspiracy is to prove that the defendant has a propensity to engage intentionally in drug-selling activities, offered to show that he so intended on the occasion of the charged cocaine conspiracy. If the defendant's propensity to sell drugs illegally implicates a character trait, then this use of past specific acts requires the very type of character inference prohibited by FRE 404(b)(1).

Finally, consider how "knowledge" and "intent" are different? They may be distinguished this way: "knowledge" is an understanding of the nature of the elements of an act, while "intent" is the conscious purpose to do that act. But in application, such a distinction may be overly subtle or even a moot point. Many legal rules lump "intent" and "knowledge" together. The federal Controlled Substances Act, for instance, defines numerous drug crimes in terms of acts that are done "knowingly *or* intentionally." 21 U.S.C. §§841, 846 (emphasis added). Nevertheless there may be instances in the context of past specific acts evidence where this distinction could matter. Perhaps knowledge may be something that, once acquired, is usually retained indefinitely, so that proving that someone knew something in the past proves that he knew it on a subsequent occasion without a character inference. In contrast, intentions are subject to change and vary with circumstances. There is no reason to infer that someone who intentionally kicked a dog a year ago also intended to kick a different dog yesterday rather than, as claimed, accidentally tripped over it—unless one infers a propensity (and related character trait) for kicking dogs.

c. The Problem of Specific Acts Evidence to Prove Mental States That Are Not Disputed

The danger of allowing specific acts to prove character to prove mental states is particularly troubling in the following scenario. Suppose the defendant is charged with the sale of heroin. Prosecution witnesses will include the alleged purchaser and individuals who can identify the substance as contraband and establish a chain of custody. The defense will be that the police arrested the wrong person and that the defendant had nothing to do with the heroin transaction to which the prosecution's evidence relates. The prosecution offers evidence that the defendant knowingly sold heroin two years ago on the ground that this prior sale is evidence of the defendant's knowledge, which is one of the elements of the offense. The defendant objects: "knowledge of what"? The prosecution responds: "knowledge of what heroin is and knowledge of what a heroin sale is." The defendant then objects that the evidence should be excluded according to FRE 403. In support of the objection, the defendant offers (a) to stipulate that whoever sold the heroin did so with the requisite knowledge and (b) to accept a jury instruction explaining the stipulation to the jury.

The Argument for Exclusion.   As we discussed in Chapter Three, the need for evidence is one of the factors to applying FRE 403. Even without the stipulation and jury instruction, there may be little need for the prior act evidence in the heroin sale case as long as the defendant does nothing to suggest lack of knowledge. It seems likely that the jury would infer knowledge from the facts of possession and sale and from the failure to deny knowledge. Thus, even if one believes there is a strong inferential link between the prior knowing sale and present knowledge, the evidence, in context, appears to have low probative value. (Do you think the prosecutors would consider dropping the drug sale case if they did not have evidence of previous drug selling?) The stipulation and jury instruction further decrease the need for the evidence.

Against this low probative value, one must assess the FRE 403 risk of unfair prejudice. If the evidence were admitted, there is the risk that the jury would consider it in two improper ways: first, the jury might infer that because the defendant sold heroin once before, the defendant is the kind of person who has a character trait for selling heroin and, therefore, probably sold it on this occasion. This particular chain of inferences, however, is clearly prohibited by FRE 404(b)(1). Second, there is the risk of "bad person" prejudice: the jurors may be willing to forgo a reasonable doubt in order to convict and remove from the streets someone who is involved with drugs. The lack of need for the evidence coupled with the possibility of misuse of the evidence by the jurors creates a strong argument to exclude the prior heroin sale evidence on FRE 403 grounds.

Early leading cases on this issue held that the past specific act evidence should be excluded where the defendant offered to stipulate. See United States v. Colon, 880 F.2d 650, 660 (2d Cir. 1989); United States v. Jenkins, 7 F.3d 803, 806-807 (8th Cir. 1993); United States v. Crowder, 87 F.3d 1405, 1410 (D.C. Cir. 1996), *vacated and remanded*, 519 U.S. 1087 (1997), *reversed on remand*, 141 F.3d 1202 (D.C. Cir. 1998) (en banc).

The Impact of *Old Chief*.   Recall that in Old Chief v. United States, page 174, supra, the Supreme Court acknowledged that the FRE 403 balancing process must include the "assessment of evidentiary alternatives." The Court then held that the defendant's stipulation precluded the prosecution from introducing evidence of the defendant's prior conviction when the conviction was relevant only to show the defendant's legal status as a former felon. At the same time, the Court observed that the probative value of evidence includes its "descriptive richness," its contribution to the "narrative integrity" of a party's case, and its ability to convince a jury of what is "morally reasonable." With respect to FRE 404(b) issues, the Court stated in dictum:

> The issue of substituting one statement [i.e., the stipulation] for the other [i.e., the evidentiary proof] normally arises only when the record of conviction would not be admissible for any purpose beyond proving status, so that excluding it would not deprive the prosecution of evidence with multiple utility; if, indeed, there were a justification for receiving evidence of the nature of prior acts on some issue other than status (i.e., to prove "motive, opportunity, intent, preparation, plan, knowledge, identity, or absence of mistake or accident," Fed. Rule Evid. 404(b)), Rule 404(b) guarantees *the opportunity to seek* admission. [519 U.S. at 190 (emphasis added).]

What impact should *Old Chief* have on our sale-of-heroin hypothetical? Superficially, *Old Chief* seems to state two general rules about when prosecutors are free to decline defense stipulations that would eliminate prosecution evidence: a general rule that prosecutors may decline such stipulations, and a narrow exception in the circumstances of a defendant's "status." Yet the central focus of *Old Chief* is less about "stipulations" than about the FRE 403 balancing process. In the above drug-dealing hypothetical, there seems to be no greater need to prove intent than to prove a defendant's status as a felon because it is not disputed; intent is reduced to something of a technicality and is not part of the narrative of the prosecution's case. It seems clear to us that under the FRE 403 balancing process, the past acts of drug dealing to prove (undisputed) intent should usually be excluded.

In fact, some courts have taken the opposite view, holding that *Old Chief* generally supports the admissibility of such evidence. United States v. Bilderbeck, 163 F.3d 971, 977-978 (6th Cir. 1999); United States v. Williams, 238 F.3d 871, 876 (7th Cir. 2001). At least two courts of appeals have held that *Old Chief* overrules or at least greatly restricts prior circuit precedent allowing defendants to rely on stipulations to avoid the prejudicial impact of prior crimes offered to show intent or knowledge. United States v. Hill, 249 F.3d 707 (8th Cir. 2001); United States v. Crowder, 141 F.3d 1202

(D.C. Cir. 1998) (en banc). We view these cases as mistakenly decided, to the extent that they seem to construe *Old Chief* as a restriction on the need for a careful FRE 403 balancing.

d. Past "Accidents" or "Coincidences" and the Anticoincidence Theory

What does FRE 404(b) have to say in cases where the defendant disputes intent—by claiming mistake or accident—and the prosecution (or plaintiff) wants to offer evidence of prior similar purported "accidents"? Another application of FRE 404(b)(2) that carries the potential for misuse are *anticoincidence theories of relevance*, also known as "the doctrine of chances." Used to refute a defense of "mistake or accident," an anticoincidence theory is based on the generalization that if the specific acts are sufficiently numerous and similar to the crime charged, "coincidence" or "randomness" is unlikely to explain their occurrence. Instead, it is more likely that there is some unifying causal explanation—for example, a single person's intentional, repetitive action—for the occurrence of such numerous and similar events. As one court colorfully put it, "The man who wins the lottery once is envied; the one who wins it twice is investigated." United States v. York, 933 F.2d 1343, 1350 (7th Cir. 1991); see United States v. Beechum, 555 F.2d 487, 495 (5th Cir. 1977), *vacated on other grounds*, 582 F.2d 898 (5th Cir. 1978) (en banc) ("doctrine of chances is the idea that '[t]he prior commission of similar acts reduces the possibility that a conceded act of disputed intent was performed with innocent intent'"); Paul F. Rothstein, The Doctrine of Chances, Brides of the Bath, and a Reply to Sean Sullivan, 14 Law, Probability & Risk 51 (2015).

Consider the following hypothetical: Adam White is charged with aggravated battery on his three-year-old son, Jeremy, who suffered a facial bruise and a broken left arm. White claims that the injuries occurred when Jeremy accidentally fell down a flight of stairs. The prosecution offers to prove that on three prior occasions when Jeremy was in the custody of his father he suffered broken bones, and that on two occasions White brought Jeremy's younger sister, Ruth, to the hospital emergency room with severe head injuries.

Defense counsel objects that the past specific acts are offered to prove that White has a character trait for physically abusing his children and is therefore barred under FRE 404(b)(1). The prosecutor responds that the evidence is offered for the noncharacter purpose of proving "absence of mistake or accident" pursuant to FRE 404(b)(2). Defense counsel then objects that there is not evidence sufficient to support a finding, as required under *Huddleston* and FRE 104(b), that any of the prior incidents are (as the prosecution claims) intentional batteries by White rather than accidents or batteries committed by someone else.

Viewing each incident in isolation, the defense argument seems to have merit: there is not evidence sufficient to support a finding of the defendant's culpable involvement with respect to any single incident. But how likely is it that mere coincidental occurrence of similar "accidents" can explain all of the injuries? Instead, it may be rational to infer that intentional acts account for at least some of the injuries. Moreover, the defendant is the only identifiable person present at the time the

incidents occurred. Thus, it seems reasonable to believe—perhaps even highly probable—that the defendant was culpably involved in one or more of the incidents, even
though we do not know which one(s). Is the evidence sufficient to support a finding by
a reasonable trier of fact under FRE 104(b) that the defendant was probably culpably
involved in one or more of the past incidents as well as the present one? However that
question is answered, it seems appropriate in this type of situation to focus attention
for preliminary factfinding on the acts in the aggregate rather than on each individual
incident viewed separately.

Finally, defense counsel could object under FRE 403 that, even if there is evidence sufficient to support a finding that the *prior* acts were intentionally committed
by White, that is insufficiently probative that the *current* incident was nonaccidental
to overcome the FRE 403 dangers of undue prejudice and confusion of issues.

As you can see, the doctrine of chances allows past specific acts to prove intent
where there may not be evidence sufficient to support a finding that any single past
specific act was itself intentional. To be relevant, "anticoincidence" evidence has to
support the inferences both that at least some of the past "accidents" were not in fact
accidents and that the number of past nonaccidents suffices to refute the defense of
accident on the occasion giving rise to the current claim or charge.

This reasoning process poses a danger of creating a significant "doctrine of chances"
loophole in FRE 404(b)(1)'s specific acts prohibition. As Professor Imwinkelried has
pointed out, one can always conceptualize the inference from specific act to character
to action in accordance with character in terms of the doctrine of chances. Edward
J. Imwinkelried, The Use of Evidence of an Accused's Uncharged Misconduct to
Prove Mens Rea: The Doctrines That Threaten to Engulf the Character Evidence
Prohibition, 130 Mil. L. Rev. 41, 54-75 (1990). For example, evidence of a murder
defendant's prior violent acts—which would be objectionable as evidence of the
defendant's violent character to show action in accordance with that character—can
be portrayed as "doctrine of chances" evidence. The prosecutor could focus on the
objective improbability that the prior acts and the act in question would have occurred
randomly and suggest that, therefore, the defendant must be culpably responsible for
them as well as the act that is the subject of the current prosecution.

Moreover, how do we know when we have enough past purported "accidents" to
refute the current claim of accident or coincidence? Prosecutors have often argued—
sometimes successfully—that one prior incident is enough. Compare United States v.
York, 933 F.2d 1343, 1350 (7th Cir. 1991) (upholding admission of evidence of prior
unsolved murder of defendant's wife to rebut claim that death of defendant's business partner was accidental) with Wynn v. State, 718 A.2d 588 (Md. 1998) (reversing
admission of prior incident of allegedly knowing possession of stolen goods offered to
rebut defense that current possession of stolen goods was not knowing). But if one or
two or even a few prior incidents are deemed enough to satisfy the anticoincidence
theory—at least for occurrences more commonplace than winning the lottery—much
of FRE 404(b)(1)'s prohibition could be eroded, at least in cases where a party claims
mistake or accident.

On closer examination, the doctrine of chances looks a lot like a version of the
character inference prohibited by FRE 404(b)(1). If it is justified, it is in cases where

the statistical inference is strong enough to make the evidence more probative than garden-variety evidence of past specific acts. The question is: "How frequently does a typical, innocent person suffer this type of loss?. . .Once the inquiry focuses on relative frequency, it is evident that sometimes even just one uncharged incident will be admissible to trigger the doctrine of chances." Imwinkelreid, supra, at 282; see also Westfield Ins. Co. v. Harris, 134 F.3d 608, 615 (4th Cir. 1998) (evidence that defendant made at least seven prior fire insurance claims probative of whether fire in question was deliberately set or an accident).

A final concern is this: are unaided intuitions of jurors sufficient to make what is arguably a complex statistical inference? You have undoubtedly encountered instances in which statisticians have estimated the likelihood that a certain eventuality "could have occurred by chance." Indeed, in criminal cases, forensic evidence is often expressed in terms of statistical probabilities. An argument could be made that, in many—if not all—cases, courts should require expert statistical evidence to establish how many incidents are sufficient to trigger the doctrine of chances.

e. Modus Operandi and the Character Inference

A "modus operandi" is a pattern of behavior sufficiently distinctive or idiosyncratic to support the inference that the same person who committed the prior act must also have committed the one in question in the current case. It is thus relevant where the defendant denies committing the act in the case before the court. Because a high degree of distinctiveness and similarity is required to establish modus operandi, the doctrine will necessarily apply only in limited circumstances. See United States v. Thomas, 321 F.3d 627, 635 (7th Cir. 2003).

Courts have traditionally accepted past specific acts evidence under a "modus operandi" theory for the noncharacter purpose of proving "identity." Yet, modus operandi evidence to prove identity may be difficult to distinguish from prohibited character evidence. With each, the proponent asks the fact finder to infer that the defendant has a propensity to act in a certain distinctive way, as shown by past instances, and therefore acted in that way on the occasion in question. The only justification to treat modus operandi evidence differently from prohibited character evidence is that, because of the high standard of uniqueness and similarity of the behavior, it is more probative than generic character traits.

KEY POINTS

1. FRE 404(b)(2) permits use of past specific acts to prove "intent" even though the relevance of such evidence may depend on making the same sort of character inference usually prohibited by FRE 404(b)(1).

2. Where "intent" or "knowledge" is an element of the criminal charge or civil claim but is not disputed by the defendant, the use of past specific acts to prove intent should arguably be excluded under FRE 403. However, some courts have held that *Old Chief* supports admission of such evidence.

3. The "doctrine of chances" allows admission of prior incidents as to which the defendant denies culpable involvement in order to rebut a defense of "mistake or accident" under an "anticoincidence" theory of relevance—the argument that it is extremely unlikely that the past and current incidents could have occurred randomly without the defendant's intentional involvement.

D. AN APPLICATION OF FRE 404(B) AND FRE 403

UNITED STATES v. VAROUDAKIS

233 F.3d 113 (1st Cir. 2000)

LIPEZ, Circuit Judge. . . . The government alleged that defendant George Varoudakis, charged with arson and conspiracy to commit arson in violation of 18 U.S.C. §844(i) and 18 U.S.C. §371, hired an acquaintance to burn down his failing restaurant, Destinations, in order to collect insurance proceeds. Following his conviction, Varoudakis argues on appeal that the district court abused its discretion by admitting evidence of a prior bad act, namely, testimony by Varoudakis's long-time girlfriend and co-conspirator in the Destinations arson, Cheryl Britt, that she saw Varoudakis set fire to his leased car sixteen months before the Destinations fire. We agree with Varoudakis that the evidence should have been excluded under Rule 403, and that the error was not harmless. Accordingly, we vacate the judgment.

I.

In 1991, George Varoudakis opened a restaurant and night club called Destinations at One Congress Street in Boston. The establishment's general manager was Cheryl Britt, Varoudakis's girlfriend since the mid-1980s. Initially, Destinations succeeded financially, but business declined about a year after it opened. Varoudakis paid his suppliers cash on delivery and owed his workers back wages. His landlord claimed $600,000 in back rent and damages, and began eviction proceedings in December 1994.

In late 1994, after several years of carrying insurance that was inadequate under the terms of his lease, Varoudakis increased the contents insurance coverage for Destinations to $500,000 and bought business interruption insurance for $100,000.

Cheryl Britt testified that Varoudakis told her he increased the insurance so he could burn the restaurant and collect the insurance proceeds.

Britt testified that several weeks before the April 1995 fire, Varoudakis told her to stop paying Destinations's bills. As a result, Britt did not pay the February 1995 insurance bill. On March 27, 1995, the insurance policy was cancelled. At trial, Varoudakis relied on the cancellation to contest the government's theory that he burned Destinations to collect insurance. Britt, however, testified that Varoudakis did not know the insurance was cancelled.

Also sometime in March, Varoudakis began moving sound and lighting equipment from Destinations to a property he owned in Everett. Several employees worked long hours loading the equipment into trucks on the days and nights leading up to the fire. According to Britt and others, the removal included a drop-safe, tables, kitchen equipment, liquor, and paperwork. More than $100,000 worth of equipment was removed.

Britt and her sister, Diane Casey, testified that at the end of March 1995, Varoudakis hired Casey's boyfriend, Nick Adams, to torch Destinations. Britt said that Varoudakis told her to pay Adams $2,000 when the job was completed.

Destinations burned on April 4, 1995. Investigators determined that arson caused the fire. Varoudakis did not dispute this finding at trial.

Cheryl Britt initially denied to investigators that Varoudakis had hired Adams to set the fire. After she learned that Varoudakis had accused Casey and Adams, and after investigators told her she could be indicted, she implicated Varoudakis. In the course of these discussions with investigators in October 1995, Britt was promised immunity. However, she lied about her involvement in the fire and her relationship with Varoudakis to investigators and in two grand jury appearances. The government did not revoke her immunity. At Varoudakis's trial, Britt was one of the government's main witnesses.

[A]fter a thirteen-day trial, a jury convicted Varoudakis of both arson and conspiracy to commit arson. . . .

II.

At trial, the court allowed Cheryl Britt to testify that in December 1993 she saw Varoudakis set fire to a Cadillac he had leased. Britt said that Varoudakis parked the car on a piece of property he owned in Everett and that he left in another car to buy gasoline, with her as a passenger. When he returned, he threw newspapers into the back of the Cadillac, poured gasoline over them, and ignited the newspapers. Britt said Varoudakis told her that he torched the car because the lease had expired and he owed excess mileage charges, and that he expected insurance to cover the loss. On cross-examination of Britt, Varoudakis offered the car lease agreement to impeach Britt's testimony that the lease had expired. The agreement showed that the lease had 23 months remaining. Following Britt's testimony, Officer Richard Gamby of the Everett Police Department testified that he investigated the burning of a Cadillac in December 1993 that matched Britt's description.

Varoudakis argues that the car fire evidence should not have been admitted under Rule 404(b) because its sole purpose was to demonstrate criminal propensity, or that the evidence should not have been admitted under Rule 403 because its probative value was substantially outweighed by its unfairly prejudicial effect. The government responds that the car fire evidence was properly admitted, or, if not, that its admission was harmless error.

We review the district court's determination that the prior bad act evidence was admissible under 404(b) and 403 for an abuse of discretion.

A. STANDARD FOR ADMISSION UNDER FEDERAL RULE OF EVIDENCE 404(B)

Rule 404(b) provides that evidence of a defendant's prior bad acts may not be admitted to prove his criminal character or propensity to commit crimes of the sort for which he is on trial. To admit evidence of prior bad acts, a trial court must find that the evidence passes two tests. First, the evidence must have "special relevance" to an issue in the case such as intent or knowledge, and must not include "bad character or propensity as a necessary link in the inferential chain." Second, under Rule 403, evidence that is specially relevant may still be excluded if its probative value is substantially outweighed by the danger of unfair prejudice.

As the text of Rule 404(b) indicates, prior bad act evidence may be specially relevant if, for example, it goes to the defendant's intent, knowledge, plan, absence of mistake, or identity. Additionally, prior bad acts may be admitted in conspiracy cases under 404(b) if they "explain the background, formation, and development of the illegal relationship." We have focused on two factors to determine the probative value of prior bad act evidence: "the remoteness in time of the other act and the degree of resemblance to the crime charged."

B. APPLYING RULE 404(B)

1. The Court's Ruling

Immediately before the opening statements of counsel, in response to a motion in limine filed by the defendant to exclude the car fire evidence, the court ruled that Britt's testimony about the car fire would be admissible to show Varoudakis's "plan, knowledge, and intent" in relation to whether he "knowingly participated in a common scheme to defraud." In support of this rationale, the court cited the government's allegations that Varoudakis committed both the car fire and the Destinations arson "for a financial motive" and with "one of the same conspirators [Britt]."

The court cited United States v. Gonzalez-Sanchez, 825 F.2d 572 (1st Cir.), cert. denied, 484 U.S. 989 (1987), as authority for its ruling. In Gonzalez-Sanchez, the defendants, who were gang members, were convicted of an October 1981 arson. The trial court admitted prior bad act evidence primarily concerning two other recent fires. Like the arson charged, both fires had also destroyed businesses owned by the defendants and insured by the same insurance company. These fires occurred just two months and six months before the October 1981 fire. In upholding the court's decision to admit the evidence, we said: "The issue at trial was not just whether [defendant] Latorre committed arson. The broader issue was whether Latorre knowingly participated in a common scheme to defraud." Id. at 581.

There are important differences between the facts supporting a common scheme rationale in Gonzalez-Sanchez and this case. Unlike the recurring fires in Gonzalez-Sanchez—three arsons of business properties in six months—Britt's testimony does not suggest a plan connecting the car fire to the Destinations fire. In United States v. Lynn, 856 F.2d 430 (1st Cir. 1988), we held that evidence of a prior conviction for marijuana was not admissible to show a common plan or scheme connected to the defendant's instant prosecution for marijuana distribution because there was no evidence that the previous offense "leads in a progression" to the second. Id. at 435. Similarly here, no evidence suggests that "a continuing or connected scheme" linked the car fire and the Destinations fire. Id.

Finally, the court said that the car fire was specially relevant to Varoudakis's motive to commit the Destinations fire because, in both instances, he allegedly committed arson to alleviate a financial burden by collecting insurance proceeds. Unlike knowledge and intent, motive is not an element of the crime that the government must prove. For that reason, proof of motive must be offered to show some other element, for example, that the crime was committed, the identity of the accused, or the accused's requisite mental state.

When prior bad act evidence is offered to prove a motive for the crime, "courts must be on guard to prevent the motive label from being used to smuggle forbidden evidence of propensity to the jury." That is the problem here. As proof of motive, the car fire testimony is offered as circumstantial evidence that Varoudakis committed the Destinations fire. It involves an inference of propensity as "a necessary link in the inferential chain." *Frankhauser*, 80 F.3d at 648. Put most simply, the government argues that Varoudakis's commission of the car fire arson in response to financial stress makes it more likely that he committed the restaurant arson in response to financial stress. Contrast this forbidden inference with the permissible inference to be drawn in a case in which the prior bad act—say, a botched robbery by the defendant that was frustrated by the ineptitude of his cohort—provided the motive for the defendant's subsequent assault on his cohort. There the prior bad act would provide circumstantial evidence of the commission of the assault without the involvement of any propensity inference.

In a case that also involved arson of a restaurant owned by the defendant, the Eleventh Circuit excluded evidence that the defendant, in a separate incident, threatened to "burn out" a tenant after she did not pay a full month's rent. See United States v. Utter, 97 F.3d 509, 514 (11th Cir. 1996). As in this case, the government argued that the tenant's testimony would show "how the defendant reacts to financial stress." Id. The court rejected this rationale, stating: "This is the type of character and propensity evidence prohibited by Rule 404(b)." Id. See also *Lynn*, 856 F.2d at 436. For the same reason, we find error in the district court's financial motive rationale.

2. The Britt-Varoudakis Relationship

There is, however, a proper rationale for admitting the car fire evidence under 404(b) that differs subtly, but importantly, from the district court's rationale that Britt was a co-conspirator in both fires. The government urges on appeal that the car fire evidence was properly admitted because it demonstrates the background and formation of the conspiratorial relationship between Varoudakis and Britt during the planning for and commission of the Destinations fire.

In United States v. Escobar-De Jesus, 187 F.3d 148, 169 (1st Cir. 1999), we said that prior bad act evidence is admissible "to help the jury understand the basis for the co-conspirators' relationship of mutual trust."

Cheryl Britt's relationship with George Varoudakis was similarly material to the conspiracy case against him. Britt testified to the key facts that Varoudakis hired Nick

Adams to torch Destinations and that he believed he still had insurance when the arson took place. Britt's testimony also refuted Varoudakis's alibi, and his claim that he removed the sound system and other equipment for a legitimate purpose.

Britt knew these things because Varoudakis trusted her. Her testimony that he allowed her to watch him torch his Cadillac demonstrated that trust. It also demonstrated Varoudakis's willingness to involve her in some way in his illegal acts. Like the prior bad act evidence admitted in *Escobar-De Jesus*, Britt's car fire testimony helped explain the nature of their relationship.

The defense argues that the prior bad act evidence should not be admissible to show the background and formation of Britt's relationship with Varoudakis because Varoudakis did not dispute that he and Britt were long-time intimates. At first blush, this argument seems plausible. However, we have held that evidence of prior bad acts may be probative even when it is relevant to an issue that the defendant does not contest. . . . [T]he fact that the defendant does not contest the issue for which the prior bad act evidence is offered does not, "by itself, remove those issues from the case."

We conclude, therefore, that the car fire evidence is specially relevant under Rule 404(b) to Varoudakis's relationship with Britt because it shows that he trusted her so much that he was willing to commit a crime in her presence. . . .

C. RULE 403

Prior bad act evidence that surmounts the bar of Rule 404(b) may still be inadmissible under Rule 403. This rule requires the trial court to exclude the evidence if its probative value is substantially outweighed by "the danger of unfair prejudice." Fed. R. Evid. 403. Otherwise relevant evidence may also be excluded if its probative value is substantially outweighed by "confusion of the issues, or misleading [of] the jury, or by considerations of undue delay, waste of time, or needless presentation of cumulative evidence."

The district court's determination on this issue merits great deference on appeal. Nonetheless, we find that in this case the district court erred in finding that the car fire evidence was admissible under Rule 403.

Under Rule 403's weighing test, "it is only unfair prejudice which must be avoided." We stress "unfair" because "by design, all evidence is meant to be prejudicial." Id. Usually, courts use the term "unfair prejudice" for evidence that invites the jury to render a verdict on an improper emotional basis. For example, we have upheld the exclusion of prior bad act evidence in part because it was "undeniably explosive," *Gilbert*, 229 F.3d at 26. We are also cautious when the prior act is a "shocking or heinous crime likely to inflame the jury."

As the district court noted, the car fire evidence is not particularly shocking. There is little danger that it swayed the jury toward a conviction on an emotional basis. But Rule 403 also protects defendants from unfair prejudice resulting from criminal propensity evidence. As the Supreme Court has stated, improper grounds under Rule 403 "certainly include . . . generalizing a defendant's earlier bad act into bad character and taking that as raising the odds that he did the later bad act now charged." Old Chief v. United States, 519 U.S. 172, 180 (1997).

To be sure, all prior bad act evidence involves some potential for an improper propensity inference. That is why, under Rule 404(b), the possibility that a jury may infer something negative about a defendant's character or propensity to commit crime does not make the evidence inadmissible unless *no* permissible inference may also be drawn. Under Rule 403, however, that risk of an improper criminal propensity inference should be considered in light of the totality of the circumstances, including the government's need for the evidence given other available testimony, to prove the issue identified pursuant to the 404(b) special relevance analysis. See *Old Chief*, 519 U.S. at 184 ("what counts as the Rule 403 'probative value' of an item of evidence, as distinct from its Rule 401 'relevance,' may be calculated by comparing evidentiary alternatives").

Here is the crux of our analysis. "The prejudice to an opponent can be said to be 'unfair' when the proponent of the evidence could prove the fact by other, non-prejudicial evidence." Wright & Graham, supra, §5214. Doubts about the probative value of prior bad acts evidence are thus "compounded" when prosecutors have other evidence available, "rendering negligible their need to show intent by the prior bad acts."

There is clearly a tension between Rules 404(b) and 403. The more similar the prior bad act evidence is to the charged crime, the more likely it is to be deemed relevant under 404(b). Yet the more the prior bad act resembles the crime, the more likely it is that the jury will infer that a defendant who committed the prior bad act would be likely to commit the crime charged. This is precisely the kind of inference that Rule 403 guards against.

D.   APPLYING RULE 403

The government primarily used the car fire evidence to cast Varoudakis as an arsonist. In its opening statement, the government said the following: "Now, the Defendant knew very well how to plan an arson because this wasn't the first arson he had planned." Although Rule 404(b) permits the admission of prior bad acts evidence as proof of plan, we have already concluded that no common plan or scheme linked the car fire and the Destinations fire. In reality, this opening statement underscored Varoudakis's criminal propensity to burn Destinations because of the car fire. In questioning Britt about the car fire, the government did not stress the development of her relationship with Varoudakis, a proper rationale for admission under 404(b). Instead, Britt's testimony focused on the facts of the car fire and Varoudakis's statement to her that he burned the car to collect insurance coverage.

Moreover, as in *Gilbert*, the probative value of the car fire evidence was minimal. The government did not need the car fire to demonstrate the close nature of Varoudakis's relationship with Britt. Britt testified that she and Varoudakis began a romantic relationship in about 1985, and that they lived together for six years, beginning in about 1989, in an apartment that Varoudakis helped Britt purchase. Britt said Varoudakis bought her jewelry and furniture and took her on expensive vacations.

The government also did not need the car fire evidence to prove Varoudakis's knowledge or intent relating to the Destinations arson. Varoudakis denied setting the fire at all, rather than arguing that he burned Destinations unknowingly or unintentionally. There was no evidence suggesting that Varoudakis was an innocent "tool" of others in the arson conspiracy like the defendant in *Gonzalez-Sanchez*, 825 F.2d at 581. The absence of a dispute on these issues weighs against admitting the evidence under 403. See *Gilbert*, 229 F.3d at 24 (citing as a factor weighing in favor of exclusion that "four of the five issues adduced by the government in support of admitting the [prior bad act] evidence do not appear to be much in dispute in this case.").

Britt's testimony revealed that the government did not need the car fire evidence to establish Britt's close relationship with Varoudakis, the only legitimate purpose of the evidence under 404(b). The absence of any other special relevance under 404(b), including those cited by the court and the government, was also discernible at this juncture. The propensity danger of the evidence was unmistakable. Thus the probative value of the car fire evidence was substantially outweighed by the danger of unfair prejudice at the time the district court admitted it. That ruling was erroneous.

We add two further observations. First, given the nature of appellate review, with its restrictions to the cold record, we rarely reverse a district court's judgment about the admissibility of prior bad act evidence pursuant to the weighing analysis of Rule 403. Indeed, as we have said repeatedly, "only in exceptional circumstances will we reverse the exercise of a district court's informed discretion vis-à-vis the relative weighing of probative value and unfairly prejudicial effect." We reiterate our commitment to that principle. Here, however, we have the exceptional case that requires us to intervene.

Second, although we do not reach the conclusion that we must intervene on the basis of hindsight, we do reach it with advantages unavailable to the district court. By contrast, the prosecution does have these advantages of context and time. Before trial, the prosecution generally knows the totality of its case and how the prior bad act evidence fits into it. The prosecution also has the time to analyze rigorously whether the exceptions to Rule 404(b),[1] and the limitations of Rule 403, apply to the facts. The failure to engage in that analysis leads to the needless complications we find in this case and others. . . . United States v. Simon, 842 F.2d 552, 556 (1st Cir. 1988) (Torruella, J., concurring) ("Almost any excuse or far-fetched theory is made to fit within [Rule 404(b)'s] truly exceptional language.").

In oft-quoted language, Justice Jackson explained why our rules of evidence are so wary of propensity evidence:

> The State may not show defendant's prior trouble with the law, specific criminal acts, or ill name among his neighbors, even though such facts might logically be persuasive that he is by propensity a probable perpetrator of the crime. The inquiry is not rejected because character is irrelevant; on the contrary, it is said to weigh too much with the jury and to so overpersuade them as to prejudge one with a bad general record and deny him a fair opportunity to defend against a particular charge. [Michelson v. United States, 335 U.S. 469, 475-76 (1948) (footnotes omitted) (quoted approvingly in Old Chief, 519 U.S. at 181)].

---

1. Because of its many exceptions to the general statement that prior bad act evidence should not be admitted, Rule 404(b) is sometimes understood as one of inclusion, and sometimes as one of exclusion. Whatever the proper formulation, the exceptions must not . . . the rule.

Despite the fairness implications of the prosecution's use of prior bad act evidence, the prosecution too often pushes the limits of admissibility of this evidence, knowing its propensity power and gambling that the time constraints on the trial court, the court's broad discretion, the elasticity of Rule 404(b), and the harmless error rule of the appellate court, will save it from the consequences of overreaching. That is not always a good gamble.

[The judgment was vacated after the court further found that the error at trial was not harmless.]

NOTES AND QUESTIONS

1. *Varoudakis* replicates the three-step analytical process described in subsection C.1 for offering specific acts as evidence. The prosecution articulated a noncharacter purpose (several in fact) for which the evidence of the car-arson was relevant. The parties litigated a factual dispute over whether in fact the car fire was an arson to recover insurance proceeds. And finally, an FRE 403 objection was considered, since the danger of unfair prejudice due to the jury's drawing the impermissible character inference is present, despite the apparent existence of valid noncharacter purposes.

2. See if you can answer the following questions about FRE 404 and the *Varoudakis* case:

(a) The defendant disputed the prosecution's claim that the car fire was in fact an arson to recover insurance proceeds. Conflicting evidence on that point was presented to the jury. If the question of whether the past specific act occurred at all (or occurred in the relevant way asserted by the offering party) is disputed, why would the jury be permitted to hear that evidence? Under what rule?

(b) Apparently, the prosecution offered other instances of past specific acts of defendant Varoudakis that were not objected to (or at least not discussed by the court as raising difficulties). These included his decision to stop paying the restaurant's bills and his landlord's claim of $600,000 in unpaid rent and unspecified "damages." Suppose the defense had objected to this evidence as inadmissible under FRE 404(a) and (b)(1) because it was offered to show his generally bad character as a deadbeat and an irresponsible tenant. How should the court have ruled on such an objection?

(c) Why wasn't the alleged car-arson admissible to show Varoudakis's "knowledge, plan, intent or motive" as argued by the prosecution? Did the court of appeals get that issue right?

(d) Nevertheless, the appellate court held that the car-arson evidence overcame an FRE 404(b)(2) objection. On what theory? Does that theory fall within any of the categories in 404(b)(2)? If not, does that mean the court made a mistake?

(e) What ultimately is the basis for excluding the evidence?

(f) The court seemed concerned about what the prosecution said about the car-arson evidence in its opening statement and closing argument. How did that factor into the court's analysis? A standard principle of trials is that "statements and arguments of counsel are not evidence." Shouldn't a reviewing court look only at the evidentiary record, and not at counsel's statements and arguments, in determining the FRE 403 and 404 issues raised in this case?

3. It is unusual for courts to be openly critical of attorneys, as the *Varoudakis* court was in the last few paragraphs of the opinion. What was the court getting at?

4. Courts and commentators frequently refer to the prohibition against use of specific acts evidence in FRE 404(b)(1) as a prohibition against the use of "propensity evidence" or a prohibition against making "propensity inferences" or using specific acts for "propensity purposes." Almost all of the permissible uses of specific acts evidence, however, also require the factfinder to make propensity inferences. Thus, despite the common association of the term *propensity* with FRE 404(b)(1), the concept of "propensity" is not helpful in determining what FRE 404(b) prohibits and what it permits.

PROBLEMS

5.14. Felix Unger is charged with arson for allegedly intentionally setting fire to a business he owns, the Odd Cuppa Joe Diner, in order to collect on insurance proceeds. Unger contends that the fire, which destroyed the diner, was an accident. The prosecution offers the following evidence. Is it admissible?

(a) Evidence that two other businesses owned by Unger burned down, one 20 years ago and one 10 years ago, and that he claimed the fires were accidental. In each instance, he collected insurance proceeds.

(b) Evidence that Unger pleaded guilty to arson in connection with the fire 10 years ago.

5.15. Return to Problem 5.5 at page 270. Assume that the trial court admitted evidence of the other guns, not to show Zachary's "murderous prosperity," but to "complete the story of the crime." Based on all that you have read, how should Zachary's appeal be argued by the defense and prosecution? How should the appeal be decided?

5.16. (a) In her trial for possession of one kilogram of cocaine with intent to sell, Ann has pleaded not guilty. The prosecution offers the testimony by a police officer that three weeks prior to the charged crime, Ann sold cocaine to Brenda. The defense objects, and the following colloquy takes place at the side bar:

1 *Defense:*   It's improper character evidence, Your Honor.
2 *Prosecutor:*   No, it's admissible on the issue of intent.
3 *Defense:*   We haven't put intent in issue here, Your Honor, so at best the testi-
4   mony is premature. And there wasn't even a conviction, so it can't get in.

What should be the ruling of the trial court on these arguments, and why?

(b) During the defense case-in-chief, Ann testifies that she didn't know that the one kilogram of material found in the trunk of her car was cocaine. On cross-examination, the prosecutor asks, "Isn't it true, Ann, that you were involved in drugs 11 years ago, which led to a conviction for selling heroin?" Ann's truthful answer would be "Yes." The defense again invokes the rule against character evidence, but the prosecutor claims, "It goes to knowledge, intent, and plan, Your Honor." What should be the ruling of the trial court on this argument, and why?

E. HABIT AND ROUTINE PRACTICE

Although the Federal Rules severely limit the circumstances in which a party may introduce character evidence to show action in accordance with character, the Federal Rules permit the use of evidence of a person's habit to show action in accordance with that habit on a particular occasion. Similarly, they permit evidence of business custom or the routine practice of an organization to show action in accordance with that custom or practice.

1. FRE 406

RULE 406.   HABIT; ROUTINE PRACTICE

Evidence of a person's habit or an organization's routine practice may be admitted to prove that on a particular occasion the person or organization acted in accordance with the habit or routine practice. The court may admit this evidence regardless of whether it is corroborated or whether there was an eyewitness.

2. Explanation of FRE 406

Most of the Federal Rules address the issue of exclusion or admissibility; FRE 406, which announces that a certain category of evidence is admissible, seems technically unnecessary: FRE 402 makes all relevant evidence admissible unless it is subject to an exclusionary rule, and nothing in the Federal Rules excludes evidence of "habit" (as distinct from "character").[2] Nonetheless, FRE 406 serves two important functions.

First, FRE 406 places no special restrictions on admitting habit evidence. Although most jurisdictions today do not limit the use of habit and routine practice evidence, many older cases—including some federal cases—required eyewitnesses or other corroboration to admit the evidence. FRE 406 makes clear that these former restrictions no longer apply.

---

2. Prior to the restyling, FRE 406 provided that evidence of habit or organizational routine is "*relevant* to prove that the conduct of the person or organization on a particular occasion was in conformity with the habit or routine practice." FRE 406 (2010) (emphasis added). The relevance of such evidence is even more obvious than its admissibility. Clearly, FRE 406 was always intended to distinguish this type of "propensity" evidence from character evidence barred by FRE 404, and the replacement of the word "relevant" with "may be admitted" in the restyled rule should not change the rule in substance.

Second, FRE 406 provides a useful clarification that habit evidence is not subject to the strictures of the character provisions even though habit evidence closely resembles character evidence in its form and logic. Like traits of "character," "habits" are tendencies or propensities of persons to behave in certain predictable ways. Like character evidence, the relevance of habit evidence depends on a "propensity inference"—the inference that a person is more likely to have acted in a certain way on a particular occasion if it was his propensity (character or habit) to act in such a way.

Organizations may also have behavioral propensities. FRE 406 implies that inadmissible character traits are understood by evidence law to be traits of individual persons, rather than collective groups of persons.

a. The Importance of Habit and Routine Practice Evidence

Habit or routine practice evidence can be very useful circumstantial proof of action on a particular occasion. For example, to show that Alex was in the crosswalk of an intersection when he was hit by the defendant's car, Alex may introduce evidence of his habit for using the crosswalk at that intersection. To establish this habit Helen may testify, "I have seen Alex cross the street at this intersection hundreds of times, and every time he has used the crosswalk."

Moreover, evidence of routine practice of an organization may sometimes be the only way to prove action on a particular occasion. Consider, for example, how an insurance company could prove that it had sent out a cancellation notice. It seems unlikely that any employee would have a specific memory of mailing the notice in question. The insurance company, however, will probably be able to rely on its routine practice to prove that the notice was sent: The company could introduce a copy of the cancellation notice along with the following testimony of one of the company employees: "This copy came from our filing cabinet. It is the routine practice of the company to put such copies in the file only when originals are prepared, signed, and placed in the outgoing mail box. Every day at 3:00 P.M., a designated employee takes mail from our outgoing mailbox and deposits it with the U.S. mail." The sorts of organizations to which FRE 406 applies must be cohesive enterprises rather than loose associations. See United States v. Rangel-Arreola, 991 F.2d 1519, 1523 (10th Cir. 1993).

b. Methods of Proving Habit and Routine Practice

FRE 406 does not deal with the types of evidence that a proponent may use to prove habit or routine practice in order to prove conduct on a particular occasion, but that would be unnecessary. The FRE 404(b) prohibition on specific acts evidence to prove "character" does not apply to the use of specific acts to prove "habit," which by definition is distinct from character. Typically, proponents use evidence of the type described in the foregoing illustrations: The habit witness is likely either to mention a number of specific acts or to offer a summary or "opinion" based on a large number of observations that are not individually described. If the court characterizes the summary as opinion testimony rather than specific act testimony, that characterization should cause no problem as long as the opinion meets the helpfulness and firsthand knowledge requirements of FRE 701, the lay opinion rule. A routine practice witness may describe specific instances or, as in the illustration, describe generally what the practice is.

Although reputation evidence is one of the traditional methods of proving a character trait, a proponent should not be able to use reputation evidence to prove habit or routine practice. Reputation evidence offered for this purpose would be hearsay, and while there is a hearsay exception for reputation evidence offered to prove character, FRE 803(21), there is no exception for reputation evidence offered to prove habit or routine practice.

c. The Distinction Between Habit and Character

Federal Rules 404-406 restrict the use of character evidence but not habit evidence to show conduct on a particular occasion, and as suggested above, habit evidence closely resembles character evidence and relies on the same kind of "propensity" inference in order to be relevant. Thus, the classification of a person's propensity as "habit" rather than "character" is frequently dispositive of its admissibility.

The Federal Rules define neither "character" nor "habit." However, both common usage and the case law suggest that the term *habit* refers to a propensity that is much more specific and routine than a character trait. For example, getting up every morning at 6:00 A.M. is an activity that as a matter of common usage we would refer to as a habit, whereas being violent (which typically is not something that occurs in a regularized, routine manner) is something we would call a character trait. Similarly, as we suggested, a court would probably regard testimony about Alex's crossing the same intersection in the crosswalk as habit evidence. Charmley v. Lewis, 302 Or. 324, 729 P.2d 567 (1986). Courts, however, would consider testimony that Alex acted carefully and cautiously *in general* as evidence of a character trait. Should evidence that a person "regularly stayed within crosswalks when crossing the street" be regarded as character evidence or habit evidence? Cf. Kovacs v. Chesapeake & Ohio Ry., 134 Mich. App. 514, 351 N.W.2d 581 (1984) (testimony that person approached railroad crossings in prudent, careful manner admissible as evidence of habit).

Although courts rely almost exclusively on the extent to which activity is specific and routine in deciding whether to call it habit evidence, there is another factor that tends to distinguish habit from character. As the preceding crosswalk and 6:00 A.M. rising examples suggest, activity that we think of as constituting a habit tends to be morally neutral, at least compared to character traits, which have a more salient moral connotation: being violent is bad; being careful is good.

The same factors that distinguish habit from character—regularity, specificity, and moral neutrality—inhere in what the common law referred to as business custom and what FRE 406 refers to as "routine practice of an organization." Indeed, according to the Advisory Committee Note to FRE 406, this phrase refers to "behavior on the part of a group" that is "equivalent" to the behavior of an individual that we characterize as habit.

d. The Rationale for Permitting Habit and Routine Practice Evidence

The factors that tend to distinguish habit and routine practice from character—the relatively more routine and specific nature of the activity and the absence of moral connotation—suggest the rationales for permitting evidence of the former and severely restricting evidence of the latter. First, because of the regularized, specific nature of habit and routine practice evidence, it is likely to be much more probative of action on a particular occasion than is character evidence. In other words, the generalization that people have a propensity to act in accordance with their habits is likely to be true more of the time than the generalization that people act in accordance with their character traits. Second, to the extent that habit or routine practice evidence is morally neutral, it does not have the potential for prejudice that inheres in character evidence. Gamerdinger v. Schaefer, 603 N.W.2d 590, 594 (Iowa 1999). In addition, given the difficulty of recalling a specific instance of routine, repetitive behavior, habit, or routine practice may be the only evidence available for an individual, or particularly an organization to prove a particular instance of conduct.

e. Strategies for Distinguishing Between Habit and Character

Legal authority distinguishing habit from character is less clear than one would like. The Advisory Committee Note to FRE 406 is vague, if not inconsistent, on this point. The Note begins by quoting McCormick's Handbook on the Law of Evidence that habit is "more specific" than character and is defined as a "person's regular practice of meeting a particular kind of situation with a specific type of conduct, such as the habit of going down a particular stairway two stairs at a time, . . . or of alighting from railway cars while they are moving." But the Note follows this only slightly helpful definition by citing language from a case suggesting that habit means activities of "invariable regularity that are perhaps not 'volitional.' " Advisory Committee Note to FRE 406 (quoting Levin v. United States, 338 F.2d 265 (D.C. Cir. 1964)).

While the *Levin* definition seems unduly narrow, the McCormick passage does not tell us much about any qualitative difference between character and habit; nor does it provide us with much of a basis for labeling activity that falls between the fairly extreme examples of generality and specificity. For example, what about evidence that a person (a) is a careful driver, (b) always or usually stops at stop signs, (c) always or usually stops at a particular stop sign? The case law indicates that the first and probably the second pieces of evidence would be character evidence and that the last piece of evidence would be habit evidence. Jones v. Southern Pacific Railroad Co., 962 F.2d 447, 448 (5th Cir. 1992) (nine various safety violations over 29-year period not evidence of habit); Weil v. Seltzer, 873 F.2d 1453 (D.C. Cir. 1989) (passing off steroids as antihistamines not habit; habit is something that occurs with "invariable regularity"); Simplex Inc. v. Diversified Energy Systems, Inc., 847 F.2d 1290 (7th Cir. 1988) (supplier's conduct in making late deliveries on other contracts not a habit); Charmley v. Lewis, 302 Or. 324, 729 P.2d 567 (1986) (frequently crossing same intersection within unmarked crosswalk is habit evidence). These results, however, are by no means obvious from McCormick's description. For an excellent discussion of the difficulties in distinguishing between character and habit, see 1A John Henry Wigmore, Evidence in Trials at Common Law 1624-1630 (Peter Tillers rev. 1983).

Given the difficulty in articulating *a priori* criteria for distinguishing between habit and character, the advocate who wishes to convince a judge that evidence should fall into one category or the other should follow a twofold strategy. First, of course, it will be important to look at the existing case law and to draw analogies to and distinctions from situations in which courts have designated evidence as habit or character. Second, one should try to relate the desired classification to the evidentiary justifications for having different rules for habit evidence and character evidence in the first place. For example, if the specificity of the conduct, the consistency of the behavior, and its contextual similarity to the conduct at issue suggest relatively high probative value, argue that these specific factors warrant placing the evidence in the habit category. Similarly, to the extent that there is a risk of unfair prejudice, argue that risk of prejudice is one of the hallmarks of character evidence and that the evidence in question therefore should fall in the character category. Focusing on probative value and prejudice has the benefit of promoting rational evidentiary decisionmaking, though to be sure, this focus will not always provide easy answers to the question whether one is dealing with habit or character. The reality seems to be that the distinction between habit and character is a difference of degree rather than a clear categorical distinction.

f. Judicial Factfinding on the Question of Habit

The immediately preceding discussion has dealt with whether a particular activity is a habit or a character trait. A closely related but distinct issue, which can arise both with proffered habit evidence and with proffered routine practice evidence, is whether the evidence establishes the existence of the habit or routine practice in the particular case. Reconsider, for example, the illustration in which Helen offered to testify about Alex's habit of using the crosswalk at a particular intersection. The first question that one must ask is whether the activity is the type that can qualify as a habit rather than a character trait. In other words, is crossing a particular intersection in the crosswalk, if sufficiently regularized, a habit as opposed to a character trait? Assuming that the answer is affirmative, one must then consider whether the witness's testimony can establish that Alex's activity is sufficiently regularized to be his habit. If Helen had seen Alex cross the intersection many times, always using the crosswalk, the answer to this second question would also be affirmative. On the other hand, if Helen offered to testify (1) that Alex used the crosswalk only 60 percent of the time or (2) that she had seen Alex cross at the intersection only three times, a court would exclude the evidence on the ground that it does not show Alex's habit. In the first alternative, Alex's activity is not sufficiently regularized or routine; in the second alternative, Helen's knowledge of Alex's activity is insufficient to determine whether the activity is regularized and routine. Consider what the result should be if Helen offered to testify that on all of the hundreds of times she had seen Alex use the crosswalk she was crossing the street with him. Should this evidence be admissible to prove Alex's habit to show that he was using the crosswalk on the occasion in question, when he was alone?

In situations in which it is arguably a close question (1) whether the type of activity could fit within the habit or routine practice category or (2) whether in the particular case the evidence is sufficient to establish the habit or routine practice, courts tend to exercise fairly tight control over the admissibility of the evidence. Courts rarely articulate the precise bases for their conclusions, however. Consider, for example, a situation in which a court has excluded proffered habit evidence on the ground that the witness has not observed the activity enough times to establish whether the habit in fact exists. The court may have decided by a preponderance of the evidence pursuant to FRE 104(a) that the evidence did not establish a habit. Alternatively, the court, applying FRE 403, may have concluded that the relatively low probative value of the evidence (in light of the few instances to which the witness could testify) did not warrant taking the time to litigate the matter. It may not be clear which of these theories the court relied on. Indeed, the court may not specifically have considered these two theoretically distinct justifications for its exclusionary decision.

g. An Application of the Character/Habit Distinction: Drinking "Habits"

The occasional difficulties in distinguishing character from habit are well illustrated by the special, but frequently recurring, situation of evidence of a person's alcohol consumption practices offered as circumstantial evidence of intoxication on a specific occasion. Consider a case in which the defendant is charged with vehicular homicide following a hit-and-run accident on a Friday evening and the prosecution wants to establish that the defendant was drunk at the time of the accident. Assume that the prosecutor is prepared to introduce eyewitness testimony about the defendant's propensity to drink and drive. Regardless of whether one regards a drinking problem as an illness, presenting such evidence to the jury is likely to be prejudicial in the sense that jurors may tend to ignore a reasonable doubt because of their lack of sympathy for a person who drinks and drives. Thus, in this respect, for evidentiary purposes a tendency to drink too much—or at least a tendency to drink too much and then drive—is like a character trait. On the other hand, if the evidence of drinking were quite specific—for example, drinking six or seven shots of whiskey between 5:00 P.M. and 6:00 P.M. every Friday after work for the last 50 Fridays—the activity is as regular and routine as much of the evidence that gets the label *habit*.

Ultimately, admissibility of the prosecution's evidence in our vehicular homicide prosecution will turn on comparing the precise nature of the evidence with the existing case law. As the Advisory Committee's Note to FRE 406 points out, "evidence of intemperate 'habits' is generally excluded when offered as proof of drunkenness in accident cases." A number of courts, however, admit evidence of a person's drinking propensities that tend to be specific and routine. Loughan v. Firestone Tire & Rubber Co., 749 F.2d 1519, 1522-1523 (11th Cir. 1985) ("uniform pattern of behavior" over six years that included drinking on job, usually drinking in early morning hours, and carrying beer cooler in truck); State v. Kately, 270 N.J. Super. 356, 637 A.2d 214 (1993) (admitting testimony that defendant had been drinking in field across from defendant's home every night each week for about a year, that defendant would consume from one to two six-packs of beer, and that defendant was drunk four or five nights a week).

h. Evidence of Custom or Routine Practice of an Organization

Do organizations have character traits? An argument can be made that, as far as the law of evidence is concerned, they do not: The character evidence prohibitions set out in FRE 404 apply to evidence of the character of "a person." While corporations and other organizations may be treated as a "person" for certain legal issues, FRE 406 distinguishes between the conduct of "a person" and that of "an organization." Reading FRE 404 and 406 together, and giving the same terms the same meaning, thus suggests that "a person" in FRE 404 does not include organizations.

If a court assumes that organizations do not have character traits, then there is no risk of slipping across the "line" that theoretically distinguishes habit from character, and these courts may not look to precisely the same criteria for proving the custom or practice of an organization as they do for proving the habit of an individual. While courts may insist upon a showing that an organizational practice is routine and repetitive, they might not insist that the conduct be morally neutral or even so commonly repeated as to happen on a daily basis. See Vining ex rel. Vining v. Enterprise Financial Group, 148 F.3d 1206 (10th Cir. 1998) (applying FRE 406 to admit routine practice evidence of abusive pattern of insurance policy rescissions); United States ex rel. Koch v. Koch Industries, 1999 U.S. Dist. LEXIS 16632 (N.D. Okla. Sept. 28, 1999) (applying FRE 406 to admit routine practice evidence of company-wide, management-directed scheme to mismeasure the volume of oil it produced on virtually all leases).

As with habit, an objection can be made to evidence of the custom or routine practice of an organization on the ground that the proffered specific acts of the organization are insufficient to establish the custom or practice, or that the witness offering an opinion of the organizational practice lacks sufficient firsthand knowledge of the claimed practice. In addition, the opponent can object to organizational practice evidence under FRE 403 by arguing that, for example, past bad acts of the organization have low probative value for proving a routine practice, but high prejudicial effect. However, in one important respect, the objections to organizational practice evidence may differ from the objections that can be made to individual habit evidence. The opponent can object to evidence offered to show the habit of a person by arguing that the propensity is in fact not a habit, but rather a character trait. In contrast, there may be no "character" objection to evidence of organizational practice. Note, however, that even where past specific acts of an organization may be deemed insufficiently routine to fit within FRE 406, the evidence may still be deemed admissible as "similar happenings," discussed in Section F, infra.

The kinds of organizations contemplated in FRE 406 are made up of human beings, and in many cases, the custom or practice of the organization will necessarily be shown by evidence of specific acts of individuals who work for or otherwise constitute the organization. Likewise, when FRE 406 speaks of using "routine practice" to prove the "conduct of . . . [an] organization on a particular occasion," the rule glosses over the reality that organizations act through their individual agents or employees. This reality should occasionally raise the red flag of an objectionable character inference if the proponent of the evidence is trying to use purported organizational practice to prove the conduct of an individual.

In a comparatively straightforward case of routine organizational practice, consider again the problem of an insurance company proving it sent out a cancellation notice based on an inference from its routine practice of mailing such notices. The inference from the routine practice is that the notice "was sent by the company." Clearly, some unidentified person or persons did the sending, but the law of evidence seems to gloss over this on the theory that the identity of the employee(s) who did the sending is not so important, and the conduct is legally attributable to the organization anyway.

A somewhat more problematic example might arise where the routine practice of the organization involves misconduct. Numerous instances of police brutality or employment discrimination might be offered to show a "pattern and practice" of such misconduct as circumstantial evidence that the plaintiff suffered such a wrong on a particular occasion. If the numbers are sufficient to establish the "routine practice" of the organization, it should be permissible for the jury to infer conduct on a particular occasion so long as the proponent seeks to prove the organization's conduct, as opposed to the conduct of a particular person. It is unclear whether such evidence is more appropriately admitted as "routine practice" under FRE 406, see *Vining*, supra, or instead as evidence of "similar happenings" governed by FRE 401-403. See Sprint/United Management Co. v. Mendelsohn, 552 U.S. 379 (2008) (analyzing alleged company-wide pattern of discriminatory acts under FRE 403). The distinction is probably academic, however.

KEY POINTS

1. FRE 406 places no specific limitations on the use of habit or routine practice evidence to show action on a particular occasion.
2. The admissibility of habit or routine practice evidence is likely to turn on the resolution of two closely related but distinct questions: Is the activity in question a habit (or routine practice), or is it a character trait? Is the evidence in the particular case sufficient to establish the existence of the habit or routine practice?

PROBLEMS

5.17. Return to Problem 3.2 at page 148, supra. Leaving aside any problem of hearsay, is Driver's Exhibit A admissible to show her habit of good driving?

5.18. Consider the following two offers of evidence:

(a) Defendant Lefty Frizzell is charged with shoplifting some tools from Deuce Hardware. At trial, he testifies that he bought the items but was not given a sales receipt. In rebuttal, the prosecution offers testimony of the store manager that it was the standard practice of the cashiers to give sales receipts for every purchase. Is the testimony admissible over the defense's objection that this is inadmissible character evidence?

(b) Defendant Harry Lately is being sued for negligence for speeding through a yellow light and colliding with the plaintiff's car on Lately's way to work. The plaintiff offers the testimony of Lately's supervisor that Lately was "frequently late to work and always seemed to be in a rush." Is the testimony admissible over the defense's objection that this is inadmissible character evidence?

5.19. Return to Problem 3.3, United States v. Ray, at page 149. The prosecution offers Beth Barker as a witness. On direct examination, Barker is prepared to testify:

> I have been employed as Bernard Ray's executive secretary since 2008. I followed the following practice in handling Mr. Ray's mail, including hand-delivered documents and intra-office memos. I would place incoming mail and other delivered documents in the "in" box on Mr. Ray's desk three times each day, at around 10 A.M., around 1:30 P.M. and around 4:00 P.M. At 8:30 A.M. each morning, I take all of the documents in Mr. Ray's "out" box, check to make sure that Mr. Ray has initialed them, and then place them in Mr. Ray's files. Mr. Ray always reads and initials his mail and other documents and puts them in his "out" box. In response to a request from federal investigators, on September 1, 2016, I found Exhibit 3 in Mr. Ray's files. Exhibit 3 is a March 14, 2015 memo from auditor Arthur Andrews to Rundown CFO June Jacobs. It has Mr. Ray's initials in the top left corner.

Any objections? What additional questions might the prosecution have to ask in order to secure admission of this testimony?

5.20. You are preparing to prosecute Petro R. for aggravated manslaughter involving a fatal hit-and-run accident. There is no dispute that Mr. R. was driving his car on a Sunday evening and that he hit another car that was waiting to make a turn, killing the driver. Your theory of the case is that Mr. R. was drunk at the time of the accident and that his intoxication supports the aggravated manslaughter charge, which requires "extreme indifference to human life." Mr. R. was never tested for drunkenness because he had left the scene.

You have a witness, Bernie Zurella, the bartender, who is prepared to testify as follows:

> For the past five years Mr. R. has come into the bar virtually every weekend; usually both Saturday and Sunday nights. He always stays about an hour, drinks vodka steadily, becomes loud and noisy, and leaves. I really cannot remember whether he was actually at the club on the night of the accident.

Will you be able to use this testimony?

5.21. The plaintiff has sued the defendant manufacturer for injuries sustained when a can of refrigerant exploded. The plaintiff claims that the explosion was caused by a defect in the product, and the manufacturer claims that the explosion resulted from the plaintiff's use of a heating coil to heat the refrigerant before pouring it, contrary to the instructions on the can. Should the court admit the manufacturer's evidence that it was the plaintiff's habit to use an immersion heating coil to heat cans of refrigerant? What additional information, if any, would you want to know to decide the admissibility issue?

F. SIMILAR HAPPENINGS

In thinking about "specific acts" or occurrences other than those giving rise to the civil claim or criminal charge, there remains one further category. This category is typically referred to as "similar happenings," and it entails prior conduct by persons or occurrences involving inanimate objects that are offered for some purpose other than to prove character, habit, or routine practice. Evidence of similar happenings (or nonhappenings) falls into three broad categories:

> (1) **Organizational propensity offered to prove conduct on a specific occasion.** Past similar conduct of, or occurrences within, an organization, offered to show that the organization has a "propensity" toward certain acts or occurrences to prove the organization's conduct (strictly speaking, the conduct of one or more agents or employees of the organization) on a specific occasion. Organizational "propensity" is some factor attributable to the organization, rather than to chance (typically a formal or informal policy), that would tend to cause the acts or occurrences. (Some of this type of evidence may fall within FRE 406.)

Examples include evidence of numerous instances of race discrimination against others to show a company-wide practice offered as circumstantial proof that the company discriminated against the plaintiff; evidence of other contracts between the plaintiff and the defendant offered to prove the terms of the current contract between the plaintiff and the defendant; evidence of prior safety violations of a company to raise an inference of negligent behavior on the occasion giving rise to the plaintiff's injury; past fraudulent transactions by a company to show fraud against the plaintiff on a particular occasion.

> (2) **Organizational liability based on policy, practice or notice.** Past similar conduct of, or occurrences within, an organization, offered to establish an element of liability, such as "notice" or "pattern or practice" liability, or to establish a standard of care.

Examples include prior safety violations of a company to show that the company "knew or should have known" about potentially tortious conditions; repeated acts of police misconduct to show an institutional "policy, pattern or practice," the latter being an element of municipal liability for torts of employees; evidence of a routine custom of vehicle safety inspections to show a standard of care that was breached in a case where no safety inspection was made prior to the accident in question.

> (3) **Characteristics of objects.** Past similar behavior or operation of, or occurrences involving, an inanimate object.

Examples include evidence that an instrumentality has caused other similar injuries in the past (e.g., that people have injured themselves falling on the same set of stairs, or that an allegedly defective product or machine has malfunctioned in the past); or evidence that similar objects have had other characteristics similar to an object at issue in the case (such as evidence that similar real properties have a value comparable to the value claimed in a property dispute).

1. No Specific Federal Rule for Similar Happenings

There is no specific Federal Rule dealing with similar happenings. Indeed, you might wonder why it is even considered a particular category of evidence at all.

Yet courts and commentators do, in fact, usually treat evidence of similar happenings or nonhappenings as a distinct category of evidence, see, e.g., 1 McCormick on Evidence §196-200 at 691-710 (John W. Strong, ed., 5th ed. 1999), for two reasons. First, similar happenings evidence bears close resemblance to the kinds of "specific acts" evidence that is strictly regulated by the character provisions. Second, the reasoning process that makes "similar happenings" evidence relevant often relies on a propensity inference similar to that involved in character evidence. Thus, the same kinds of recurring FRE 403 dangers that undoubtedly underlie FRE 404 may arguably exist for similar happenings. Perhaps for this reason, many older cases reflect a fairly strict judicial control—as a matter of case law applying FRE 403 and its common law analogues—over similar happenings evidence. Modern cases have liberalized admission of similar happenings evidence and tend to treat it as a classic instance of FRE 403.

2. Similar Happenings, Character, and Habit Evidence Compared

If you take another look at the examples of the three categories of similar happenings evidence, you can see some obvious points of comparison with the kinds of "propensity" evidence we have studied so far in this chapter. Category (1) resembles character evidence prohibited by FRE 404(b)(1), in that past similar happenings are being offered to show organizational propensity to prove the conduct of the organization on a specific occasion. The reason FRE 404(b)(1) does not apply is that the propensity in question is not that of a person, but a thing. Even though most organizations consist of groups of people, so long as the propensity is being attributed to an organization, courts will usually not consider it to be "character" evidence. Similarly, category (3) evidence is offered to show the propensity of a thing (like a machine or a piece of property). This too falls outside the scope of FRE 404 since character (as that term is understood by most courts) is an attribute of individual people, not inanimate objects.

Category (1) of similar happenings evidence will sometimes overlap with routine practice evidence under FRE 406, which allows proof of the routine practice of an organization in order to prove conduct on a specific occasion. But there will also be instances in which a court will find evidence of organizational behavior to be insufficiently routine or morally neutral to qualify as FRE 406 evidence. For instance, a company may often defraud customers, but perhaps not so often as to make it a "routine." Again, such evidence is analogous to evidence of an organization's "character," but the law of evidence recognizes character traits only of individual persons. Therefore, specific acts to prove the (quasi) "character" of an organization to prove the organization's conduct on a specific occasion comes within the "similar happenings" rather than the "character" rubric. Ultimately, it is somewhat academic whether such evidence is deemed to fall within FRE 406 or the "similar happenings" category: either way, the admission or exclusion is likely to depend on an application of FRE 403. See Sprint/United Management Co. v. Mendelsohn, 552 U.S. 379 (2008) (rejecting per se rule against admitting evidence of discriminatory acts by supervisors other than the alleged perpetrator in the particular case, and analyzing such evidence under FRE 403).

Where the proponent offers evidence of an "institutional propensity," the opponent of the evidence should be alert to the possibility that the evidence is really a disguised effort to prove the character of an individual. The use of past specific acts to show organizational propensity makes sense if the acts tend to show a causal mechanism by which some factor intrinsic to the organization—a formal or informal policy, for example—supports the inference that the individual acts or occurrences are not based on random factors. (The relevance of such similar acts evidence may be, in effect, a kind of "doctrine of chances" theory raising similar dangers of misuse.)

If, however, the purported "similar happenings" are really the actions of a person offered to show how that person behaved on a particular occasion, the admissibility of the proffered evidence will involve the character provisions. Consider a product liability case in which the plaintiff sustained injuries after a can of refrigerant exploded. The defendant claims the can exploded because, contrary to the instructions on the can, the plaintiff used an immersion heating coil to heat the refrigerant. To substantiate this claim, the defendant offers evidence that on other occasions the plaintiff used a heating coil to heat cans of refrigerant. If the court regards the evidence as showing the plaintiff's character trait for carelessness, it is inadmissible under FRE 404. On the other hand, (1) if the court finds that the evidence falls within some noncharacter FRE 404(b) purpose or (2) if the court regards the evidence as sufficient to establish a habit, the evidence is potentially admissible. Either way, however, what on the surface appears to have been a past similar happening involving the can of refrigerant turns out to be a question of individual human behavior.

3. The Admissibility of Similar Happenings Evidence Depends on FRE 403

Don't be too caught up in the notion of "similarity" with similar happenings evidence. Assuming the proponent of similar happenings evidence offers witnesses with firsthand knowledge of these events, the only rules that a judge will probably have to consider are FRE 401-403. Since no rule makes similarity a special condition of admissibility, it is not an FRE 104 preliminary fact for the judge to consider. Rather, the judge's task is to determine only whether the evidence is relevant and if so whether the probative value is substantially outweighed by the countervailing FRE 403 factors. As with any evidence, the probative value of similar happenings evidence depends on the purpose for which the evidence is offered. The probative value may or may not depend heavily on similarity of the proffered happenings. For example, in a civil rights suit alleging municipal liability based on a "pattern and practice" of excessive force by police, it may be that the only relevant "similarity" of the incidents is that they were all committed by members of the defendant's police force. On the other hand, in a product liability case, courts may require a showing of similarity of past injury incidents to establish that the other users all used the product as directed and thereby eliminate possible causes of injury other than product defect. *Similarity* in this category of evidence really refers to the presence or absence of extraneous factors that will make the past happenings more or less probative for the case at hand. This probative value is balanced against the FRE 403 dangers: waste of time, confusion of issues, and unfair prejudice caused by risk of improper inferences.

4. Applications of FRE 403 to Similar Happenings Evidence in Practice

Since the FRE 403 balancing test favors admissibility, one's initial instinct may be that courts should be liberal in admitting similar happenings evidence when the only barrier to admissibility is FRE 403. The case law is consistent with this instinct when similar happenings evidence is offered to show *notice* of a possible defect (e.g., prior fuel tank explosions offered to show defendant had notice of dangerous placement of fuel tank). Four Corners Helicopters, Inc. v. Turbomeca, 979 F.2d 1434 (10th Cir. 1992). When the issue is notice, the probative value of the evidence depends primarily on whether the defendant was or should have been aware of the other incidents and not on how similar they are to the incident that gave rise to the litigation. But see First Security Bank v. Union Pac. R. Co., 152 F.3d 877 (8th Cir. 1998) (substantial similarity required even when evidence offered to show notice).

By contrast, when the probative value of the evidence depends on the degree of similarity among the happenings, courts are likely to require a high degree of similarity as a condition of admissibility. Most federal courts speak of a requirement of "substantial similarity." First Security Bank v. Union Pac. R. Co., supra; Wheeler v. John Deere Co., 862 F.2d 1404, 1407 (10th Cir. 1988). For example, if the plaintiff offers incidents of uncontrollable skidding by cars with Acme tires to prove Acme tires caused the plaintiff's car to skid uncontrollably, the evidence is not likely to be admissible unless the plaintiff can introduce evidence of similarity in the type of road, weather conditions, and other factors that tend to eliminate alternative causal explanations for the skidding incidents. Brooks v. Chrysler Corp., 786 F.2d 1191 (D.C. Cir. 1986) (excluding other automobile accidents because of insufficient showing of substantial similarity). Perhaps one can justify this careful screening by courts on the ground that the probative value of similar incidents standing alone is sufficiently low that it is substantially outweighed by the FRE 403 efficiency and confusion factors.

In making the FRE 403 determination, one should look not merely at the time that it will take initially to introduce the evidence but also at the total time that it will take to deal with the evidence. Once the proponent introduces the evidence, the other party is likely to feel compelled to respond with evidence suggesting that the events did not occur at all or that there are not relevant similarities among the events—a process that may be quite time consuming. Thus, unless the proponent is prepared to demonstrate at the outset that the evidence has more than minimal probative value, an FRE 403 decision to exclude similar happenings evidence may often be warranted.

5. Similar Happenings Offered to Show an Institutional Policy or Practice

One of the most important uses of similar happenings is to show an institutional policy or practice. For example, in a prisoners' class action challenging the practices of violence at Pelican Bay Prison, the setting that gave rise to the *Johnson* case in Chapter One, the plaintiffs relied on testimony and records describing numerous incidents of excessive force against inmates to establish their claim that state prison officials were aware of the problem at Pelican Bay and, in fact, "implicitly sanctioned the misuse of force and acted with knowing willingness that harm occur." Madrid v. Gomez, 889 F. Supp. 1146, 1199-1200 (N.D. Cal. 1995). See also Austin v. Hopper, 15 F. Supp. 2d 1210 (M.D. Ala. 1998). In that lawsuit, the institutional practice was itself the focal point of the suit: liability followed directly from the establishment by the plaintiffs of the institutional practice, without having to draw further inferences about conduct on a specific occasion.

In civil rights cases brought by individuals against a municipal police force for police brutality, evidence of other incidents of excessive force is legally necessary in order for plaintiffs to win a judgment against a city, county, or other "municipality": "[A] plaintiff must prove a specific pattern of conduct or series of incidents violative of constitutional rights in order to sustain the existence of a municipal policy or custom." Sherrod v. Berry, 827 F.2d 195, 206 (7th Cir. 1987); see Monell v. New York City Dept. of Social Servs., 436 U.S. 658 (1978).

6. Evidence of Similar Nonhappenings

"Similar happenings" evidence is also understood to include evidence of nonhappenings offered to prove lack of notice or that an event did not occur or did not occur in the manner or for the reason alleged (e.g., evidence of the absence of people falling down a staircase to rebut the plaintiff's claim that the staircase was dangerous). See Landis v. Jarden Corp., 5 F. Supp. 3d 808, 818 (N.D. W.Va. 2014) ("In general, courts have recognized that the absence of prior accidents involving a product may be admissible in a product liability case to show (1) absence of defect, (2) the lack of a causal relationship between plaintiff's injury and the defect alleged, (3) the nonexistence of an unduly dangerous situation, and (4) lack of notice."). In this type of case a court is likely to require evidence that the conditions were similar during the time of the nonhappenings. In addition, the court is likely to require a significant number of nonhappenings. Whereas evidence that two or three people fell down a staircase may be quite probative to show that the staircase was dangerous, evidence that two or three people managed to use the staircase without falling is not very probative of the proposition that the staircase is safe. Those two or three people may fortuitously have avoided the dangerous spot. Evidence that several hundred people used the staircase without falling under conditions similar to the conditions that existed when the plaintiff fell, however, is quite probative of the proposition that the staircase was not dangerous at the time of the plaintiff's fall.

KEY POINTS

1. Evidence of similar happenings or nonhappenings is offered to show such matters as (a) the behavioral propensity of an organization or an object, (analogous to the "character" of a person) to show the behavior of the organization (or its agents or employees) on a specific occasion, (b) the institutional policy of an organization where that is a fact of consequence or essential element, or (c) the behavior or characteristics of an inanimate object.
2. There is no specific Federal Rule governing the use of similar happenings. Admissibility depends on an application of FRE 401-403.
3. Because similar happenings evidence involves either no propensity inference at all, or else a propensity inference about organizations or things rather than individual persons, it is not considered to be evidence of "character" and is therefore not governed by FRE 404.
4. Except when similar happenings evidence is offered to show notice, courts tend to require a showing of similarity as a condition of admissibility.

PROBLEMS

5.22. Henry purchased Acme Household Cleanser and used it for the first time to clean his kitchen. He suffered severe burns where the cleanser came into contact with his skin. Henry sues Acme Corp., the manufacturer, for strict product liability, alleging $50,000 in damages. Henry offers testimony that during the five years before the incident seven people were severely burned by Acme Household Cleanser and that four of these instances were reported to Acme. Should any of this evidence be admissible?

5.23. Paul Preston has sued National Motor Corporation (NMC) for personal injuries arising out of an auto accident in which his "Bounder" sports utility vehicle rolled over while making a tight turn on a highway entrance ramp. Preston claims that a design defect in the Bounder makes it prone to rollover accidents. Preston offers evidence showing 50 incidents of rollovers by Bounders on entrance or exit ramps while traveling at or below the speed limit. On what basis could the defense object? Should the evidence be admitted?

5.24. The plaintiff William Lane has brought a damages action against the Los Angeles Police Department for violating his civil rights by using a potentially lethal "chokehold" in making arrests under circumstances where deadly force is not warranted. Lane offers evidence of 20 incidents in which the chokehold was applied to persons other than himself. Lawyers for the LAPD argue that the evidence is inadmissible character evidence to prove that Lane was choked on a specific occasion and that the other incidents are too dissimilar from one another to be probative and too sporadic to constitute a routine practice under FRE 406. Lane argues that the evidence is offered to prove that the LAPD had a "custom, policy, pattern or practice" of unwarranted use of the chokehold. Should the evidence be admitted?

5.25. Fred Johnson is suing Farming Partners for breach of an oral contract for the sale of tomatoes grown by Johnson. Johnson claims that the contract was for the sale of tomatoes outright at a quoted price. Farming Partners claims that the agreement was for it to take the tomatoes on consignment. To establish Farming Partners' routine business practice, Johnson offers the testimony of two other tomato farmers that they entered into oral contracts with Farming Partners for the sale of tomatoes, that the contracts were for outright sales, and that Farming Partners breached the contracts by maintaining the position that they had accepted the tomatoes only on a consignment basis. Is this evidence admissible?

5.26. Ed Naples has brought an action against Acme Lawn Tool Company for breach of an oral employment contract. Acme fired Naples six months after he had been hired as Vice President for Sales. Naples claims the contract was for a fixed term of one year; Acme claims that it was an "at will" contract. Acme offers the testimony of several members of the Acme Board of Directors that all officers of the company are employed on an at-will basis. Should this evidence be admitted? What, if any, additional information would be helpful to your decision?

5.27. Pamela King has sued the Whoopie Amusement Park for personal injuries she sustained riding on Whoopie's roller coaster. According to Pamela's testimony, "A tree limb hit me in the face when I was riding on the roller coaster." The force of the blow broke her glasses and pieces of the lens were lodged in her eye. As part of its defense Whoopie offers the testimony of the amusement park manager (a) that during the entire summer up to the time of the plaintiff's injury nobody had complained about low-hanging branches along the path of the roller coaster and (b) that on the day the plaintiff was injured over 1,000 other persons rode the roller coaster without incident. For what purposes is the defendant's evidence relevant? Should it be admitted?

5.28. Return to Problem 3.2 at page 148. Should Driver be permitted to testify on direct examination that she has never had a driving accident?

G. EXCEPTIONS TO THE PROHIBITION ON USE OF CHARACTER TO PROVE CONDUCT ON A PARTICULAR OCCASION

1. Explanation of FRE 404(a)(2), (3)

There are four exceptions to FRE 404(a)'s prohibition on character evidence to prove conduct on a specific occasion. These are set out in FRE 404(a)(2) and (3). FRE 404(a) provides:

(a) *Character Evidence.*

(1) *Prohibited Uses.* Evidence of a person's character or character trait is not admissible to prove that on a particular occasion the person acted in accordance with the character or trait.

(2) *Exceptions for a Defendant or Victim in a Criminal Case.* The following exceptions apply in a criminal case:

(A) a defendant may offer evidence of the defendant's pertinent trait, and if the evidence is admitted, the prosecutor may offer evidence to rebut it;

(B) subject to the limitations in Rule 412, a defendant may offer evidence of an alleged victim's pertinent trait, and if the evidence is admitted, the prosecutor may:

(i) offer evidence to rebut it; and

(ii) offer evidence of the defendant's same trait; and

(C) in a homicide case, the prosecutor may offer evidence of the alleged victim's trait of peacefulness to rebut evidence that the victim was the first aggressor.

(3) *Exceptions for a Witness.* Evidence of a witness's character may be admitted under Rules 607, 608, and 609.

a. FRE 404(a)(2)(A) and (B): A Criminal Defendant's Right to Open the Door to Character Evidence

A criminal defendant is free to introduce evidence of the defendant's own "pertinent trait" of character (FRE 404(a)(2)(A)) or of the victim's character (FRE 404(a)(2)(B)). This is often called "opening the door" to the character issue. For example, in the *Johnson* case the defendant could have introduced evidence of his own peaceful character for the purpose of showing action in accordance with that character trait at the time of the altercation with the prison guards (i.e., for the purpose of showing that he was behaving peacefully and was not the aggressor). FRE 404(a)(2)(A). Similarly, Johnson could have introduced evidence that one or more of the prison guards who were victims had a violent character in order to suggest that they were the aggressors in the incident. FRE 404(a)(2)(B). In fact, Johnson did introduce evidence of prison guard Walker's character for violence (see, e.g., pages 54, 59-61. As we discuss in subsection g, infra, however, it is not clear that Johnson introduced the evidence to suggest that Walker was the first aggressor.

b. FRE 404(a)(2)(A) and (B): The Prosecution's Right to Respond to a Defendant's Character Evidence

When a defendant elects to open the character evidence door, the prosecution in its rebuttal case may introduce character evidence to rebut the defendant's evidence. For example, if an assault defendant introduces evidence of the defendant's own good character for peacefulness, the prosecution can respond with evidence that the defendant has a character trait for violence in order to show that the defendant was the aggressor. FRE 404(a)(2)(A). Similarly, if an assault defendant introduces evidence of the victim's character for violence in order to suggest that the victim was the aggressor, the prosecution may respond with evidence of the victim's character for peacefulness. FRE 404(a)(2)(B)(i). In the *Johnson* case, some of the prosecution's rebuttal focused on Officer Walker's good character (page 67, supra). One thing the prosecution may have been attempting to do was to prove Walker's good character so that the jury could infer that Walker did not act improperly at the time of the altercation with Johnson.

Note that when defendants open the door to a victim's bad character, they also open the door to their own bad character. FRE 404(a)(2). Thus, in the preceding hypothetical where the assault defendant introduced evidence of the victim's character for violence, the prosecutor could respond not only with evidence of the victim's character for peacefulness, FRE 404(a)(2)(B)(i), but also with evidence of the defendant's character for violence, (B)(ii).

Whenever the prosecution is rebutting the defendant's character evidence, the prosecution's evidence must be about the same character trait addressed by the defendant's evidence. This limitation is implicit in the term *rebut*, and FRE 404(a)(2)(B)(ii) makes the limitation explicit when the prosecution responds to evidence of the victim's bad character with evidence of the defendant's "same" bad character. Thus, in the foregoing hypotheticals, the prosecutor could not respond to the defendant's evidence about the victim's violence or the defendant's peacefulness with evidence of the victim's honesty or the defendant's dishonesty. This prosecution evidence would not *rebut* the defendant's evidence because a person can be both violent and honest or peaceful and dishonest.

c. FRE 404(a)(2)(C): The Prosecution's Right to Use Character Evidence to Respond to Defense Attacks on a Homicide Victim's Conduct

FRE 404(a)(2)(C) also provides that the prosecution may introduce evidence of a homicide victim's character for peacefulness, if the defendant has suggested that the victim was the first aggressor. Assume, for example, that Johnson had killed Officer Walker and was being prosecuted for homicide. Assume further that Johnson or other defense witnesses testified that Walker was the first aggressor and that Johnson had acted in self-defense. This defense testimony is not character evidence. The defendant is not trying to show Walker's general character for violence. Rather, the defendant is offering evidence of specific actions of Walker that constitute an element of the self-defense claim. The prosecutor, however, can respond to this testimony with evidence of Walker's good character for peacefulness. This character evidence is admissible because Johnson introduced evidence that Walker had been the first aggressor; it is not dependent upon Johnson's opening the door to his own or Walker's character. However, since *Johnson* was not actually a homicide case, the prosecution could not open the door to Walker's peaceful character to show action in accordance with character.

Even if *Johnson* had been a homicide case, the prosecution could not have opened the door to defendant Johnson's character for violence. The prosecution can never introduce evidence of the defendant's character unless the defendant has first introduced character evidence. The possibility that the prosecution might improperly open the door to Johnson's character was the focus of a sidebar early on in the *Johnson* case. When the prosecution sought, over objection, to inquire into the nature of the facility where the defendant was housed, the court indicated that the prosecution witnesses could describe Facility B but could not directly state that the inmates in that facility tended to be violent (pages 9-10, supra). If the jurors heard such testimony about the inmates, they might infer that Johnson, one of the inmates, was a violent person and therefore probably had acted violently at the time of the alleged attack on the guards.

d. The FRE 404(a)(2) Requirement of Pertinence

According to FRE 404(a)(2)(A) and (B) the defendant's and the prosecution's character evidence must tend to establish a "pertinent" character trait. For example, in the *Johnson* case it would have been permissible for the defendant to introduce evidence of his own character for peacefulness or evidence of a prison guard victim's character for violence to show that the guard, not Johnson, was the aggressor. Similarly, it would be permissible for a defendant charged with perjury to introduce evidence of the defendant's character for honesty to show that the defendant did not intentionally lie on the particular occasion in question. In the *Johnson* case, however, it would not have been permissible for the defendant to introduce evidence of a prison guard's character for dishonesty to show that the guard was the aggressor; and it would not be permissible to introduce evidence of a perjury defendant's character for peacefulness to show that the defendant did not commit the perjury.

e. The Rationales for the FRE 404(a)(2) Exceptions

As we have seen, there are substantial concerns justifying the FRE 404(a)(1) prohibition against the use of character evidence to show a person's action in accordance with character. One might ask why, then, there are any exceptions to the FRE 404(a) (1) general rule of exclusion. First, as we suggested in subsection B.3.a, above, the problem of unfair prejudice is likely to be greatest with respect to evidence of a criminal defendant's bad character. This type of evidence, however, will never be admissible unless the defendant chooses to open the door to the character evidence inquiry. Second, despite the low probative value of character evidence to show action on a particular occasion and despite the risk of unfair prejudice to the prosecution (e.g., the jury may be willing to acquit a guilty defendant who assaulted a person with a bad character), a criminal defendant should not have to face the consequences of conviction without having had every opportunity to establish a reasonable doubt. Proof of the defendant's good character or the victim's bad character may establish such a doubt.

Third, any risk of unfair prejudice to the defendant from evidence of a victim's good character seems relatively remote. The concern here is that jurors, on hearing of the victim's good character, would be willing to convict a defendant about whose guilt they had a reasonable doubt but who they believe nonetheless may have committed a crime against a good person. Moreover, the defendant has the right to keep the victim-character evidence door closed except in homicide cases where the defendant claims that the victim was the first aggressor. In these relatively rare instances, the defendant and the victim may have been the only persons present at the time of the killing. The unavailability of the victim to contradict the defendant's evidence arguably justifies allowing the prosecution to resort to character evidence to establish its case.

f. FRE 404(a)(3): The Character of Witnesses

FRE 404(a)(3) is a cross-reference to the rules that permit the impeachment and rehabilitation of witnesses with evidence of their character for truthfulness. FRE 404(a)(3) allows impeachment and rehabilitation of witnesses based on their character for truthfulness pursuant to FRE 607-609, which applies to both criminal and civil actions. Otherwise, there are no exceptions in civil cases to 404(a) (1)'s prohibition on character evidence to prove action on a particular occasion. The relevance of any witness's testimony depends upon the assumption that the witness is testifying truthfully. Thus, parties are permitted to introduce evidence that either undermines or supports a witness's truthfulness. One way to do this is to show the witness's character for truthfulness. From evidence that a witness has a bad (or good) character for truthfulness, one can infer that the witness is acting in accordance with that character trait by being untruthful (or truthful) on the witness stand. We will consider the rules that govern evidence of a witness's character for truthfulness in Chapter Seven.

g. An Application of the Character Rules: People v. Johnson

The evidence of Walker's character in the *Johnson* case is relevant for two distinct purposes. Diagrams 5-3 and 5-4 illustrate these two purposes.

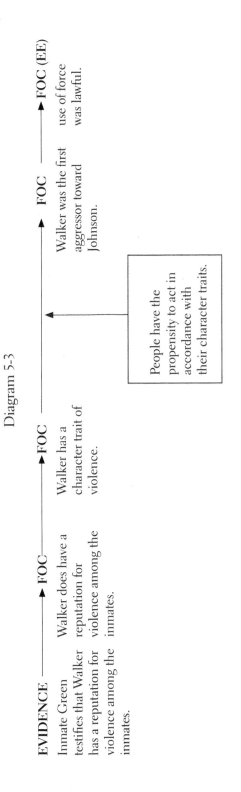

Diagram 5-3

Diagram 5-4

EVIDENCE ⟶ FOC

Inmate Green testifies
that Walker has a
reputation for violence
among the inmates

Walker does have a
reputation for violence
among the inmates

FOC ⟶

+

FOC ⟶

Johnson knew of
Walker's reputation
for violence

FOC ⟶

Johnson feared Walker's
use of force against him

FOC (EE)

Johnson's use of force
was reasonable

As Diagram 5-3 indicates, reputation evidence of Walker's character is relevant to show that Walker acted in accordance with that character on March 28, 1992 (i.e., to show that he may have been the aggressor against Johnson). The evidence, however, may not be admissible for this purpose under FRE 404(a)(2), which permits the defendant to open the door to a pertinent character trait of "the victim of the crime." Although Walker was one of the correctional officers present at the scene, the defendant was charged with battery against only Officers Huston and Van Berg (pages 2-3, supra). Thus, in a formal sense, Walker was not the victim of any crime. What arguments can you make that the evidence of Walker's character should nonetheless be admissible to prove that Walker was the first aggressor?

Diagram 5-4 illustrates an alternative theory of relevance. Because the reputation evidence of Walker's violent character was introduced in conjunction with evidence that the defendant knew of the reputation, the evidence is relevant to a claim of self-defense. One element of self-defense is that any aggressive action by a defendant must be the result of a reasonable fear of bodily harm. Johnson's awareness of Walker's reputation for violence suggests the reasonableness of Johnson's actions. Similarly, the prosecution testimony that Walker was not known among the inmates as a violent person is evidence from which one may infer that Johnson had no reason to fear Walker.

This second theory of relevance does not involve using character evidence to show action in accordance with character. Therefore, it is not within the scope of FRE 404; rather, admissibility of the evidence for this purpose depends solely on the application of the basic relevance concepts embodied in FRE 401-403. The fact of consequence is what Johnson was thinking when Johnson acted, not whether Walker acted in accordance with Walker's character. Indeed, for the purpose of showing what Johnson was thinking, it does not matter whether Walker really was a violent or peaceful person. What is important is whether the defendant had a reasonable (even if incorrect) belief that Walker was violent.

We suggest that you reread pages 45-46, 59-60, 62-63, and 79-81, supra, in Chapter One. Did the judge and the attorneys adequately distinguish these two theories of relevance?

KEY POINTS

1. The Federal Rules allow character evidence to prove action in accordance with character in the situations set forth in FRE 404(a)(2):
   (a) a criminal defendant may open the door to a pertinent trait of the defendant's own good character, in which case the prosecution may then offer evidence to rebut that same character trait;
   (b) a criminal defendant may open the door to a pertinent trait of the victim's bad character, in which case the prosecution may then offer evidence to rebut that same character trait of the victim and to prove the same pertinent trait of the defendant's bad character;
   (c) in a homicide case the prosecution may open the door to the victim's character for peacefulness in order to rebut the defendant's claim that the victim was the first aggressor.

2. Any party may introduce character evidence for impeachment and rehabilitation purposes to the extent allowed by FRE 607-609.
3. When the use of character evidence is permissible, the character evidence must relate to a pertinent character trait.
4. Except in the context of impeaching and rehabilitating witnesses, FRE 404 prohibits the use of character to prove action in accordance with character in civil cases.

2. Explanation of 405(a): How Character Is Proven When the FRE 404(a)(2) and (3) Exceptions Apply

When character evidence is admissible under one of the FRE 404(a)(2) or (3) exceptions, in what form can the evidence be offered? Rules 404(b)(1) and 405(a) govern this question. FRE 404(b)(1) provides:

> Evidence of a crime, wrong, or other act is not admissible to prove a person's character in order to show that on a particular occasion the person acted in accordance with the character. . . .

RULE 405. METHODS OF PROVING CHARACTER

(a) *By Reputation or Opinion.* When evidence of a person's character or character trait is admissible, it may be proved by testimony about the person's reputation or by testimony in the form of an opinion. On cross-examination of the character witness, the court may allow an inquiry into relevant specific instances of the person's conduct.

There are three possible ways one might try to prove character in the absence of the above rules. First, a witness might offer specific instances of conduct of the person whose character is in question. One's character, after all, is known to others by how one behaves. Second, a witness could offer to testify that in the witness's opinion the person in question has the particular character trait. Finally, a witness could offer to testify that the person has a reputation in the community for having the kind of character trait that is relevant to the litigation. An individual's reputation is what people say about the individual, and when reputation evidence is offered to prove character, it is the truth of the reputation that is important. Thus, reputation evidence is hearsay—evidence of what people out of court say about the individual offered to prove the truth of what they say. FRE 803(21) provides an exception to the hearsay rule for evidence of reputation offered to show an individual's character.

FRE 404(b)'s prohibition on the use of specific acts to prove a person's character for the purpose of showing action in accordance with that character trait expressly applies to the FRE 404(a) exceptions. Therefore, even when character evidence is admissible under FRE 404(a)(2), it may not be proven by past specific acts. For example, during the prosecution's rebuttal in the *Johnson* case, the trial judge made it clear that Lieutenant Stokes could not testify about specific acts for the purpose of proving Walker's good character (page 65, supra).

FRE 405(a) provides that reputation evidence and opinion evidence are permissible means of proving character *whenever* a party offers admissible character evidence to show action in accordance with that character. Assume, for example, that in the *Johnson* case, Walker was properly considered a victim (which technically he was not, because no charge was based on the alleged assault on him). Assume further that the defense and the prosecution were interested in proving Walker's character for violence or peacefulness for the purpose of showing whether he was the first aggressor. See Diagram 5-3 at page 313, supra. The following evidence could be used for this purpose: Inmate Green, a defense witness, testified on direct examination that Walker had a reputation for being a "bad cop" (page 54, supra); on redirect examination Green testified that Walker was known among the inmates—that is, had a reputation among the inmates—for violence; and during the prosecution's rebuttal case, Lieutenant Stokes testified Walker had the reputation as a good correctional officer (page 67, supra). Pursuant to FRE 405(a) it also would have been permissible for these witnesses to offer their opinions about Walker's violence or peacefulness.

For ease of reference, we will refer to witnesses who give reputation or opinion testimony about a person's character pursuant to FRE 405(a) as "character witnesses." The last sentence of FRE 405(a) permits the opposing party to ask character witnesses questions about specific acts on cross-examination. We discuss this part of the rule in subsection 5, infra.

a. The Prohibition Against Using Specific Acts to Prove Character

The FRE 404(b)(1) prohibition against the use of specific acts to prove character to show action in accordance with character may seem counterintuitive. The people that we know—or that we think we know—the best are likely to be people that we know by their deeds. Thus, it would seem that specific acts evidence would often be the most probative form of character evidence. Nonetheless, as discussed above, there are substantial FRE 403-type countervailing concerns that justify excluding specific acts to prove character to show action in accordance with character. These include: bad person prejudice stemming from evidence of prior *bad* acts; confusion of issues and undue consumption of time if there are factual disputes surrounding the alleged prior conduct; and the relatively low probative value of the character inference generally.

There are limited instances in which it is permissible to use evidence of a person's specific acts to prove that person's character to show action in accordance with character. FRE 608(b) and 609 contemplate use of specific acts to prove the character of a witness for truthfulness or untruthfulness, and FRE 413-415 contemplate the use of specific acts to prove character to show action in accordance with character in certain cases of sexual misconduct.

b. The Probative Value of Opinion and Reputation Evidence to Prove Character

The probative value of opinion or reputation evidence to prove a person's character will depend in part on how long, how well, and in what contexts the witness has known (opinion) or has known about (reputation) the person whose character the evidence is offered to prove. The common law (which did not permit opinion evidence at all in most jurisdictions) required that a reputation witness testify to the person's reputation in the community. In theory, this focus on the community as a whole was designed to ensure that evidence be fairly reflective of the views about the person in question. As a practical matter today, however, there will not be many instances in which an individual has a reputation throughout the entire community in which the person lives. Indeed, in our complex, urbanized society, it is not clear what the entire community would be. Courts wisely recognize this fact and permit reputation testimony to be based on what a witness has heard in some relevant community — perhaps the neighborhood where the person lives or the place where the person works. Consider, for example, the *Johnson* case, where defense counsel objected on relevance grounds to evidence of Walker's good reputation among the prison staff. According to the defense, the evidence should have been limited to Walker's reputation among the inmates, but the judge disagreed:

> I am going to overrule the objection because although the inmates and the staff are not precisely the same, they are a part of the community within the prison and are in communication with one another on a constant basis. So reputation is something that is back and forth and it is the kind of thing that would be known. [Page 65, supra.]

Even if there is no difficulty in defining the relevant community, there may be a question whether the witness knows or knows about the individual well enough to testify in the form of opinion or reputation. The Federal Rules do not deal specifically with the foundation requirement for character witnesses. FRE 403, however, provides latitude for trial judges to exclude testimony that is marginally probative because the witness does not have much of a basis for knowing or knowing about the person in question. United States v. Watson, 669 F.2d 1274 (11th Cir. 1982) (not error to exclude testimony of character witness who knew individual for brief period of time, which did not coincide with relevant events at trial).

Character witnesses are likely to be friendly, cooperative witnesses on direct examination. Thus, if the witness in fact has a sufficient basis for offering character evidence, there should seldom be any difficulty in eliciting the appropriate foundational information and in getting responses in the form of reputation or opinion testimony to questions about pertinent character traits. Michelson v. United States, 335 U.S. 469, 471 (1948), where a bribery defendant opened the door to his own character, provides a good, albeit somewhat sparse, example of a direct examination of a character witness:

Q: Do you know the defendant Michelson?
A: Yes.
Q: How long do you know Mr. Michelson?
A: About 30 years.
Q: Do you know other people that know him?
A: Yes.
Q: Have you had occasion to discuss his reputation for honesty and truthfulness and for being a law-abiding citizen?

A: It is very good.
Q: Have you talked to others?
A: Yes.
Q: And what is his reputation?
A: Very good.

For an elaboration of the common law foundation requirements for reputation and opinion testimony, see Mason Ladd, Techniques and Theory of Character Testimony, 24 Iowa L. Rev. 498 (1939).

c. Reputation Evidence versus Opinion Evidence

Opinions are generalizations from more specific facts, and an opinion about a person's character will naturally be a generalization based on the witness's perception of that person's behavior. In situations other than character testimony, when a witness testifies in the form of opinion, it is permissible—indeed, desirable—to inquire into the underlying basis for the opinion on both direct and cross-examination. Because of this standard practice, the use of opinion evidence to prove character creates the possibility that the opinion witness could testify about various specific acts that provide the basis for the opinion. The common law's reluctance to permit litigation over specific acts is precisely the reason that the majority common law rule prohibited opinion testimony, along with specific acts testimony, to prove character to show action in accordance with character.

Nonetheless, witnesses who are called to testify about an individual's character are likely to have rather strong personal feelings about the individual who is the subject of their testimony. If they testify in terms of reputation, the real gist of what they are thinking and of what motivates their testimony may well be their *opinion* about the defendant's character. Recognizing this possibility, the drafters of the Federal Rules took the position that these character witnesses should be permitted to offer their opinions directly. Thus, FRE 405(a) permits both reputation and opinion testimony in all instances in which character evidence is admissible. At the same time, however, the Advisory Committee Note to FRE 405 makes it clear that the use of opinion testimony to prove character to show action in accordance with character should "be confined to the nature and extent of observation and acquaintance upon which the opinion is based." Opinion testimony should not be allowed to evolve into testimony about specific acts on which the opinion may be based.

KEY POINTS

1. FRE 404(b) prohibits the use of specific acts to prove a defendant's character for the purpose of showing action in accordance with character, except in the limited situations governed by FRE 413-415, FRE 608(b), and FRE 609, which we will consider later.
2. FRE 405(a) permits the proponent to offer both reputation and opinion testimony in the limited situations in which FRE 404(a) allows the use of character evidence to prove action in accordance with character.

3. If a character witness offers opinion testimony, it is not permissible to explore on direct examination the specific acts that may be the basis for the witness's opinion.

PROBLEMS

5.29. In the *Johnson* case, assume that one of the charges was assaulting Officer Walker. For what purposes, if any, should the following evidence be admissible?

   (a) Officer Huston's testimony for the prosecution that on several previous occasions Johnson had assaulted other prisoners and prison guards;

   (b) Inmate Green's testimony for the defense that Officer Walker has a reputation for violence;

   (c) Officer Walker's testimony for the prosecution in rebuttal that Johnson has a reputation for violence.

5.30. Mayer is charged with assault with a deadly weapon and claims self-defense. In his defense, Mayer offers testimony that (a) two weeks before the alleged assault the victim had threatened him with a knife, (b) the victim had a reputation for carrying weapons, and (c) on the morning of the trial the victim threatened to kill Mayer's sister. For what purposes is this evidence relevant? Is it admissible?

5.31. Clarence Hill is being prosecuted for the attempted murder of Ted Ellsworth in a jurisdiction that views mere words as potentially adequate provocation, which would be a defense to the attempted murder charge.

   Clarence and several eyewitnesses testify as follows: They and Ted Ellsworth were all in a local tavern, and Hill and Ellsworth were at opposite ends of the bar. Ellsworth taunted Hill with racial slurs and derogatory references to Hill's wife. Hill became enraged and shot Ellsworth.

   The prosecutor is convinced that these witnesses are lying and wants to introduce the testimony of Ruth Watson that Ellsworth has a reputation in the community for peacefulness, compassion, and absence of racial prejudice. Ellsworth is not available to testify. Is Ruth Watson's testimony admissible?

5.32. On the night of October 7, Elton Haywood called the police to report a prowler in his backyard and then went outside with a shotgun to search for the prowler. When the police arrived, they mistook Haywood for the prowler, and despite—or perhaps because of—Haywood's loud, persistent protestations, they handcuffed him. Eventually the police took Haywood to the Dry-U-Out Detoxification Facility, where he spent the night locked in a cell with a urine-soaked floor. Haywood has filed a civil rights and false imprisonment suit against the facility and several of its employees. Although Haywood has had a drinking problem in the past, he claims that he had had nothing to drink on the night of the incident and that he was wrongfully detained. The defendants offer expert opinion testimony that Haywood is an alcoholic and that a common characteristic of alcoholics is to deny that they have been drinking when they plainly have. Is the evidence admissible?

3. The Cross-examination of Character Witnesses

Although a character witness cannot testify about specific acts on direct examination, the cross-examiner is allowed to question the character witness about specific acts relevant to character, pursuant to the last sentence of FRE 405(a). Assume, for example, that John Smith is charged with murder and that as part of the defense Mary Martin testifies, pursuant to FRE 404(a)(1), that John has a good reputation in the community for peacefulness. The prosecutor, when cross-examining Mary, can ask about various violent acts that John supposedly committed.

a. The Relevance of the Specific Acts Inquiries

The permissible relevant purpose for asking specific acts questions in the preceding example is *not* to prove John's character for violence. Indeed, FRE 404(b) prohibits questions about specific acts to prove John's character. Rather, the permissible relevant purpose of the prosecutor's questions is to test Mary's credibility as a reputation witness: If she denies having heard of the acts of violence, one can infer that she does not have a very good sense of what John's reputation is; and if she has heard of the acts, one may doubt the truth of her testimony (or question her conception of what a reputation for peacefulness means). United States v. Adair, 951 F.2d 316, 319 (11th Cir. 1992); United States v. Alvarez, 860 F.2d 801, 826-827 (7th Cir. 1988).

Because the specific act questions are admissible only to impeach the character witness and not to prove the character of the person who is the subject of the testimony, the party calling the character witness is entitled to a limiting instruction pursuant to FRE 105. For example, in our John and Mary hypothetical, the judge might say, "Ladies and gentlemen of the jury, I instruct you that the questions the prosecutor asked Ms. Martin about various acts of violence allegedly engaged in by Mr. Smith were asked for the sole purpose of assessing Ms. Martin's knowledge of Mr. Smith's reputation. You must not consider them as evidence of Mr. Smith's character."

b. The Prejudicial Impact of Specific Acts Questions

To the extent that jurors are unwilling or unable to follow a limiting instruction regarding specific acts questions posed pursuant to FRE 405(a), there is a two-fold risk of prejudice. In the preceding hypothetical, for example, the jurors may infer from the questions to Mary about John's violent acts that John is a violent person and may have acted in accordance with that violent character trait by murdering the victim of the charged crime, as the prosecution has alleged. This use of the evidence would violate FRE 404(b), thereby raising the FRE 403 danger of unfair prejudice in the sense that the jury may use the evidence in a logically relevant but legally impermissible manner. In addition, the jurors may be willing to ignore a reasonable doubt if they regard John as a bad, dangerous person. This possibility raises the FRE 403 danger of unfair prejudice in the sense that the jurors may base their decision on an emotional and legally improper ground.

The most prejudicial specific acts questions, as the preceding hypothetical demonstrates, are those that relate directly to the character trait about which the character witness testified. These questions, however, are also likely to be the most probative for the legitimate purpose of testing a character witness's knowledge of the defendant's character for peacefulness. Since FRE 405(a) specifically authorizes these questions, and since high prejudice is likely always to be a concomitant of high probative value with FRE 405(a) specific acts questions, courts regularly permit the cross-examiner to ask character witnesses questions that are in fact extremely prejudicial.

c.   The Relationship Between the Character Trait and the Specific Acts Inquiries

Specific act inquiries made pursuant to FRE 405(a) must be "relevant" to the character trait about which the character witness testified on direct examination. One aspect of this relevance requirement is that the specific acts must relate to the character trait in question. For example, in our hypothetical involving Mary's testimony about John's reputation for peacefulness, it would be appropriate to ask Mary about John's specific acts of violence but not about acts of dishonesty. United States v. Westerbrook, 896 F.2d 330, 335 (8th Cir. 1990) (character witness testified as to defendant's honesty; it is improper to ask character witness about defendant's conviction for possessing controlled substance).

One might argue that, in a minimal FRE 401 sense, any bad act is relevant to a bad character trait, and any good act is relevant to a good character trait. Moreover, since the purpose of the inquiry is to test the character witness's knowledge of the principal witness's character, the key to relevance arguably should be the likely notoriety of the act rather than its relationship to the character trait about which the witness testified. Nonetheless, courts are likely to require that FRE 405(a) specific acts questions to character witnesses relate to the character trait about which the witness has testified—a result that one can probably justify under FRE 403, if not FRE 401.

d.   The Character Witness's Likely Knowledge of the Specific Act

A second restriction on the use of specific acts evidence to impeach a character witness is also a matter of relevance—or at least probative value for the purpose of FRE 403 balancing.

The questions should be limited to acts about which the witness is likely to have known or to have heard. United States v. Alvarez, 860 F.2d 801, 827 (7th Cir. 1989). For example, if Mary on direct examination testified that she had known John well for five years and was familiar with his reputation during that time, it may not be reasonable to expect that she would have heard about an isolated act of violence that occurred 15 years ago. Even if she had heard about the act, it may not be reasonable to expect a single 15-year-old act of violence to affect her view of John's reputation for peacefulness during the past five years. But see Alvarez, supra (trial court did not abuse its discretion by permitting inquiry about specific act occurring ten years before character witness giving reputation testimony knew the defendant). Cf. Michelson v.

United States, 335 U.S. 469 (1948) (where two character witnesses testified to know-ing defendant 30 years and a third character witness testified to knowing defendant half that long, not error to allow questions about matters that occurred 20 and 27 years ago).

Assessing whether a character witness is likely to have heard of any particular act will involve consideration of several factors. For example, in our Mary and John hypo-thetical, how well and how long has Mary known or known about John? Is John's act likely to have been the subject of discussion because of the nature of the act? Is John the kind of person whose activities are likely to be known to people situated similarly to Mary? Questions that are only marginally probative for legitimate impeachment purposes may be excluded because of their low probative value and high degree of unfair prejudice.

e.   The Cross-examiner's Reasonable Belief That the Act Occurred

A third limitation on the use of specific acts questions (not specifically mentioned in FRE 405(a)) relates to the cross-examiner's belief that the specific acts occurred. If the prosecutor had no knowledge about whether John, in our hypothetical, had committed any violent acts, it should be permissible to ask Mary in a nonsuggestive manner, "Do you know of any violent acts that John has committed?" However, any but the most general inquiry about specific acts is likely to suggest to the jury that the cross-examiner believes that the act occurred. When such an implication inheres in the question, the cross-examiner must have a reasonable basis for believing that the act occurred. United States v. Adair, 951 F.2d 316, 319 (11th Cir. 1992); United States v Alvarez, supra.

Some courts have suggested that the better practice is to require the cross-exam-iner to demonstrate the factual basis to the judge, outside the presence of the jury, before asking the questions. United States v. Reese, 568 F.2d 1246 (6th Cir. 1977). In *Alvarez*, supra, the court followed this practice, and the prosecutor responded with an affidavit from an FBI officer stating that defendant had confessed to the act in question.

In discussing this limitation on the cross-examination of character witnesses, the Supreme Court in Michelson v. United States, supra, noted that as a matter of logical relevance the requirement should be that the cross-examiner of the reputation witness have a reasonable belief that there were *rumors about the act*, regardless of whether it in fact occurred. Nonetheless, the Court approved the existing rule requiring the cross-examiner to demonstrate to the judge the reasonable basis for believing that the *act in fact occurred*:

> But before this relevant and proper inquiry [here, a question to the defendant's char-acter witness about the defendant's arrest] can be made, counsel must demonstrate privately to the court an irrelevant and possibly unprovable fact—the reality of the arrest. From this permissible inquiry about reports of arrest, the jury is pretty certain to infer that defendant had in fact been arrested and to draw its own conclusions as to character from that fact. The [requirement of a reasonable basis] thus limits legally relevant inquiries to those based on legally irrelevant facts in order that the legally

irrelevant conclusion which the jury probably will draw from the relevant questions will not be based on unsupported or untrue innuendo. It illustrates Judge Hand's suggestion that the system may work best when explained least. Yet, despite its theoretical paradoxes and deficiencies, we approve the procedure as calculated in practice to hold the inquiry within decent bounds. [335 U.S. at 481 n.18.]

Although the cross-examiner needs a reasonable belief for believing the act occurred, the cross-examiner may not introduce evidence at trial for the purpose of proving that the acts occurred, even if the character witness denies them. See, e.g., United States v. Benedetto, 571 F.2d 1246, 1250 (2d Cir. 1978); see also United States v. Pruitt, 43 M.J. 864, 868 (U.S. A.F. Ct. Crim. App. 1996) ("it is a strange cross-examination, because the cross-examiner is not allowed to prove the existence of the acts about which he asks" quoting Saltzburg et al., Military Rules of Evidence Manual (3d ed. 1991)).

f. Acts, Arrests, and Convictions

Like *Michelson*, decisions under the Federal Rules permit prosecutors to ask defense character witnesses not only about defendants' prior *acts* but also about their prior *arrests*. United States v. Wellons, 32 F.3d 117 (4th Cir. 1994); United States v. Jordan, 722 F.2d 353, 358 (7th Cir. 1983). An arrest, however, is "conduct" by the police, not the defendant.

As a matter of logical relevance, asking about the arrest rather than the conduct leading to it is not inappropriate. The purpose of the question is to test what the character witness knows or has heard about the defendant, and in some instances there may have been as much or more publicity about the arrest than the underlying acts. On the other hand, if there is reason to believe that the defendant did not engage in the conduct leading to the arrest, the question may be particularly prejudicial. There is always the risk that the jury may use a specific act question improperly to infer that the defendant has a bad character. If the defendant has engaged in the conduct suggested by the question, the jury at least gets an accurate assessment of the kind of person the defendant is. Evidence of the defendant's arrests creates not only this risk but also the risk that the jury will regard the arrest, perhaps incorrectly, as evidence that the defendant actually engaged in the illegal activity. Nonetheless, inquiry about arrests may be appropriate. United States v. Grady, 665 F.2d 831, 834-835 (8th Cir. 1981) (permitting inquiry about arrests on charges that were later dismissed).

Sometimes specific act questions to a defendant's character witness refer to the defendant's prior convictions. United States v. Collins, 779 F.2d 1520 (11th Cir. 1986). Like an arrest, a defendant's prior conviction is logically relevant—without regard to the truth of the underlying facts—to test the character witness's awareness of the defendant's background or reputation. Permitting questions about convictions, however, may be even more prejudicial than permitting questions about arrests. While there may be little likelihood that the defendant did not commit the acts leading to a conviction, the very certainty of those facts, as validated by the conviction, may make it especially difficult for the jury to disregard the improper inference that the defendant is a bad person.

g.   The Form of the Questions on Cross-examination

The common law, which in most jurisdictions permitted a criminal defendant to use only reputation evidence when opening the door to character, was quite exacting about the proper form of specific acts questions on cross-examination. Since the direct examination testimony was limited to what the witness had *heard* people say about the defendant, asking on cross-examination whether the witness *knew* about some bad act was objectionable. The proper form for the specific acts questions on cross-examination was, "Have you heard . . . ?" not "Did you know . . . ?" By contrast, if the jurisdiction happened to permit opinion testimony on direct examination, a witness offering an opinion about the defendant's character presumably would be basing that opinion in whole or in part on personal knowledge. Thus, it would be proper to ask on cross-examination whether the opinion witness knew about specific acts.

If there were ever sound reasons for insisting on the proper form of cross-examination questions about specific acts, those reasons have been seriously eroded by the allowance of opinion as well as reputation testimony on direct examination. The Advisory Committee Note to FRE 405 asserts that the distinctions in the form of the cross-examination questions "are of slight if any practical significance" and that the second sentence of FRE 405(a) "eliminates them as a factor in formulating questions." United States v. Scholl, 166 F.3d 964, 974 (9th Cir. 1999) (no merit to argument that "Did you know . . . ?" rather than "Have you heard . . . ?" was improper in cross-examining character witness).

4. Limitations on the Use of Character Evidence in Practice

a.   The Inherent Weakness of Good Character Evidence

The most common use of character evidence to show action in accordance with character pursuant to FRE 404(a)(2) is a criminal defendant's opening the door with evidence of the defendant's own *good* character. Nonetheless, for reasons that are probably apparent, the occasions on which criminal defendants elect to open the door to the character evidence inquiry are relatively rare. In most cases, reputation and opinion evidence about a defendant's good character is not likely to be highly persuasive. The ban on using specific acts to prove character means that the opinion or reputation witness cannot provide persuasive or illustrative examples to support the opinion or reputation testimony. As a result, that testimony will necessarily take the form of (often bland) generalities. In sharp contrast, the cross-examiner of such character witnesses can go into specific bad acts under FRE 405(b). Depending on what the prior bad acts look like, they are potentially very persuasive and effective in undermining the positive character testimony.

Consider, then, who is likely to benefit from a rule that permits criminal defendants to open the door to character evidence. Or to put the issue somewhat differently, consider what kinds of people you would like to be able to call as character witnesses if you were a criminal defendant. To the extent that criminal defendants may benefit from the use of character evidence, is the benefit likely to be derived from the content of the character testimony or from the character (and/or reputation) of the character witnesses? If the character of the character witnesses is likely to make the biggest difference, is it desirable to have a rule that, in effect, benefits people primarily because of whom they know?

b. The Potential Unfairness of FRE 405

We have already noted that courts may exclude on FRE 401-403 grounds questions about acts that do not relate to the character trait in issue and that are sufficiently remote from the time frame about which the character witness testified. As we pointed out above, however, FRE 403 is not often applied to exclude Rule 405 specific acts questions. As a result, FRE 405 appears to give a significant unfair advantage to the cross-examiner. For example, in our preceding murder hypothetical, the defendant, John, is limited to the use of relatively bland reputation or opinion evidence of his peaceful character. The prosecutor, by contrast, can ask Mary, the character witness, about all sorts of violent acts in which

John may have engaged. Granted, in theory the purpose of the prosecutor's questions is not to prove the defendant's character but only to impeach the credibility of the character witnesses. And granted, the defendant is entitled to a limiting instruction from the judge. How likely is it, though, that the jury will be able to confine its consideration of the violent acts to the theoretically legitimate impeachment purpose?

Is it sufficient to answer that the process is not unfair because the defendant has the choice initially to decide whether to open the door to character evidence? If you are defense counsel and if you feel compelled to call character witnesses, what can you do to blunt the effect of the prosecutor's cross-examination of your character witnesses?

KEY POINTS

1. Whenever a character witness testifies in the form of reputation or opinion about a person's character, FRE 405(a) permits the opposing party to ask the witness on cross-examination about specific acts committed by the person who is the subject of the character testimony. Courts also permit questions about the person's arrests or convictions.
2. The specific acts (or arrests or convictions) must relate to the character trait about which the witness has testified.
3. The purpose of the specific acts question is to impeach the testimony of the character witness, not to show the character of the person about whom the witness has testified.

PROBLEMS

5.33. Dick Davis is charged with the murder of Ralph Green and claims self-defense. After the prosecution has presented its case, Davis offers the following evidence:

> (a) Witness$_1$ to testify that he and Davis are Elks, that he knows Davis well from weekly meetings, and that Davis has an excellent reputation for honesty among the Elks.
>
> (b) Witness$_2$ to testify that Ralph Green has a reputation in the community for violence.
>
> (c) Witness$_3$ to testify that two years ago Ralph Green was convicted of aggravated assault, a felony.
>
> (d) Witness$_4$ to testify that she told the defendant of three different times that she had seen the victim make unprovoked attacks on other people.
>
> In rebuttal, the prosecution offers the following evidence:
>
> (e) Witness$_5$ to testify that Ralph Green has a reputation in the community for peacefulness.
>
> (f) Witness$_6$ to testify that Davis has a reputation in the community for violence.
>
> Which evidence is objectionable?

5.34. Return to Problem 3.3, United States v. Ray, at page 149. Is the following evidence admissible? Might the answer change depending on the order in which the evidence is offered?

> (a) For the prosecution: Testimony from a partner in the brokerage firm that handled Bernard Ray's stock transactions: "Bernard Ray is an unusually shrewd and well-informed investor. He personally directs each and every trade of shares in his account."
>
> (b) For the defense: Testimony from June Jacobs, Rundown's CFO: "Bernard Ray, although a great salesman and inspirational leader to the company, is extremely unsophisticated about finance and securities markets. He delegated all financial matters to others in both the running of the company and in decisionmaking regarding his personal investments."
>
> (c) For the defense: Five instances since the year 2013 in which major trades of securities (other than Rundown stock) were made at the discretion of one of Bernard Ray's brokers.
>
> (d) For the prosecution: Evidence that Ray has a PhD in economics.

H. EVIDENCE OF A PERSON'S CHARACTER WHEN CHARACTER IS AN ESSENTIAL ELEMENT OF A CLAIM OR DEFENSE

Consider an action in which Martha sues George for libel because George has circulated a leaflet claiming that Martha was dishonest. An element of Martha's claim is that the allegedly libelous statement is false. Since the statement that Martha is dishonest is a statement about her character, Martha's actual character for dishonesty is an essential element of her claim.

Nothing in FRE 404 or in any other Federal Rule specifically prohibits or restricts the use of character evidence when character *is an essential element of a claim or a defense*. FRE 405, however, addresses the type of character evidence that one can use in this type of situation.

1. Explanation of FRE 405(b)

RULE 405.   METHODS OF PROVING CHARACTER

(b) By Specific Instances of Conduct. When a person's character or character trait is an essential element of a charge, claim, or defense, the character or trait may also be proved by relevant specific instances of the person's conduct.

Occasionally, the substantive law makes a person's character an essential element of a claim or a defense, as the element of falsity (or in some jurisdictions, the defense of truth) does in a defamation action when an allegedly defamatory statement is a statement about a person's character. For example, the fitness or character of a person is a factor to consider in deciding whether to award child custody to that person. A claim that a hospital was negligent in hiring a careless physician makes the physician's carelessness—that is, character for lack of care—an element that the plaintiff must establish in order to recover. Similarly, a negligent entrustment claim that the defendant was negligent in permitting a careless, unqualified employee to drive the plaintiff's vehicle makes the employee's character for lack of care an element that the plaintiff must prove in order to prevail. In wrongful death cases, the plaintiff's damages may depend in part on the character of the decedent, thereby making the decedent's character an essential element of proof.

FRE 405(b), in conjunction with FRE 405(a), makes it clear that all three forms of character evidence—reputation, opinion, and specific acts—are potentially admissible when character is an essential element of a claim or defense. For example, in our libel hypothetical in which George wants to establish the truth of the statement that Martha is a dishonest person, George could call witnesses to testify (1) that Martha had a reputation for dishonesty in the community, (2) that in the witnesses' opinion Martha was dishonest, and (3) that Martha had engaged in specifically described dishonest acts.

The only limitation on the use of any of these types of evidence to prove character when character is an essential element of a claim or defense is FRE 403. In particular with respect to specific acts, courts should balance the probative value of the acts in proving the character trait at issue against (1) the risk that the evidence may engender an emotional response from the jury, and (2) the time and effort it would take to litigate the details of what the person may or may not have done.

It is important to understand that FRE 405(b) is not an exception to FRE 404(b)(1)., which prohibits using character evidence *only* to prove conduct on a particular occasion. When character is an essential element, however, it is not being offered to prove that someone acted a certain way on a particular occasion. Proof of character under 405(b) is an end in itself—it is proof of the essential element or fact of consequence—rather than circumstantial proof of some further conduct. Looked at another way, the use of character in FRE 405(b) does not fall within the chain of inferences described in Diagrams 5-1 and 5-2 at pages 265-66, supra, and does not fall within 404(b)(1)'s prohibition at all. So even if 405(b) did not expressly mention that specific acts are permitted—indeed, even if it had not been written at all—it would still be the case that character as an essential element would be subject to proof by any relevant means. FRE 405(b) is thus another "reminder" to courts (like FRE 404(b)(2) and FRE 406) not to apply the character prohibitions beyond their confined boundaries.

2. An Application: Reputation versus Character in Defamation Cases

In our discussion of FRE 404(a), we noted that evidence of a person's reputation is one way to prove a person's character. It is important to keep in mind, particularly in the context of defamation actions, the difference between "character" and "reputation." *Character* is an integral part of a person. *Reputation*, by contrast, is what people say about a person. In defamation actions, a plaintiff's reputation—regardless of whether it happens to coincide with the plaintiff's actual character—is always relevant, because the substantive law makes injury to reputation the basis for assessing damages. Consider, for example, the previous hypothetical in which George circulated a pamphlet stating that Martha was dishonest. Her damages, if she prevails on the substantive claim, will be based on how much George's statement damaged her reputation, not on what kind of a person she is or was. Character becomes an essential element in a defamation action, as we illustrated previously with the George and Martha example, only if (1) the defendant claims that the allegedly defamatory statement is true and (2) the statement is one about the plaintiff's character.

KEY POINTS

When character is an essential element of a claim or a defense, FRE 405(b) permits proof of character with evidence of specific acts. In addition, it is permissible to prove character with reputation or opinion evidence pursuant to FRE 405(a).

PROBLEMS

5.35. Paul Vincent has sued Office Barn for injuries he sustained from being physically abused by store security guard Arnold Stallone, who mistakenly believed Vincent had been shoplifting. The claim is negligent supervision and/or hiring, and the plaintiff must prove (1) that Stallone had a propensity for violence and (2) that Office Barn knew or should have known of the propensity and was therefore negligent in hiring him as a security guard and in failing to supervise him adequately. Vincent offers the following testimony. Is it admissible?

   (a) Witness$_1$ to testify that he has known Stallone for ten years, and in his opinion, Stallone is a violent person.

   (b) Witness$_2$ to testify that Stallone beat him up with no provocation in a bar one year before Stallone began working at Office Barn.

   (c) Witness$_3$ to testify that Stallone had been arrested four times, and convicted twice, for assault prior to working for Office Barn.

Office Barn offers the following testimony. Is it admissible?

    (d) Witness$_4$ to testify that she has lived in the same neighborhood as Stallone for five years and that he has a reputation as a peaceful person.

5.36. Return to Problem 3.2 at page 148. Is the evidence of Driver's speeding ticket likely to be admissible? For what purpose(s)?

5.37. Paul Plant, a candidate for public office, has sued Diane Daniels for defamation for circulating a pamphlet stating that Paul is a violent person with a bad temper and that on May 23 Paul stole a pistol from a local sporting goods store. Paul testifies that both statements are untrue.

    (a) Paul calls Edgar James, who offers to testify that since the publication of the pamphlet Paul has had a reputation in the community for violence and for dishonesty.

    (b) Diane calls Zelda Young, who offers to testify that she observed Paul engaged in a fistfight at a local tavern last year.

    (c) Diane calls Florence Newman, who offers to testify that before the alleged defamation Paul had a reputation in the community for being violent and for being dishonest.

    (d) Diane calls Winston Hampton, who offers to testify that on two occasions last year when he was with Paul, Paul stole merchandise from a local department store.

    Assuming that proper objections are made, which pieces of evidence should be admissible?

5.38. The defendant is charged with the sale of heroin. He claims that he was entrapped by the entreaties of the purchaser, a supposed friend who was in fact an undercover narcotics officer. According to the substantive law, the defense of entrapment is not available if the defendant was predisposed to commit the crime. To show predisposition the prosecution offers evidence (a) that the defendant has the reputation in the community as a drug dealer and (b) that on five specific occasions the defendant has sold drugs to schoolchildren. Should the defendant's objections to these pieces of evidence be sustained?

I. EVIDENCE OF SEXUAL ASSAULT AND CHILD MOLESTATION

As part of the Violent Crime Control and Enforcement Act of 1994, Congress enacted three rules, FRE 413-415, that relate to the admissibility of sexual misconduct evidence in cases involving charges of sexual assault and child molestation. The obvious purpose of the rules is to make sexual misconduct evidence more freely admissible. In our discussion of these rules, the terms *sexual assault* and *sexual misconduct* include both sexual assault and child molestation.

Evidence commentators have been particularly critical of FRE 413-415, which were enacted directly by Congress and not subject to the typical rule-making process. Charles Alan Wright & Kenneth W. Graham Jr., Federal Practice and Procedure §5411-5417B (Supp. 2001); Edward J. Imwinkelried, A Small Contribution to the

Debate over the Proposed Legislation Abolishing the Character Evidence Prohibition in Sex Offense Prosecutions, 44 Syracuse L. Rev. 1125 (1993); Perspectives on the Proposed Federal Rules of Evidence 413-415, 22 Ford. Urban L.J. 265 (1995).

Because most criminal sexual assault cases arise in state courts, a significant potential impact of FRE 413-415 is as a model for state evidence codes. The idea here was also to give states a "safe harbor": a dependable indication as to when prosecutors can constitutionally use prior sexual misconduct evidence to prove guilt. Presumptively, FRE 413-415 comport with Due Process. As stated by a chief sponsor of FRE 413-414, Senator Robert Dole, "it's possible – perhaps even likely – that the States may follow suit and amend their own rules of evidence [accordingly]."140 Cong. Rec. S10,276 (daily ed. Aug. 2, 1994). See also Alex Stein, Constitutional Evidence Law, 61 Vand. L. Rev. 65, 112-13 (2008). Approximately three-quarters of the states have evidence rules based on the Federal Rules. States, however, have not rushed to adopt these new rules. But see Ariz. R. Evid. 404(c); Cal. Evid. Code §1108 (West 1995); Mo. Ann. Stat. §566.025 (Vernon Supp. 2001).

1. FRE 413-415

RULE 413. SIMILAR CRIMES IN SEXUAL-ASSAULT CASES

(a) *Permitted Uses.* In a criminal case in which a defendant is accused of a sexual assault, the court may admit evidence that the defendant committed any other sexual assault. The evidence may be considered on any matter to which it is relevant.

(b) *Disclosure to the Defendant.* If the prosecutor intends to offer this evidence, the prosecutor must disclose it to the defendant, including witnesses' statements or a summary of the expected testimony. The prosecutor must do so at least 15 days before trial or at a later time that the court allows for good cause.

(c) *Effect on Other Rules.* This rule does not limit the admission or consideration of evidence under any other rule.

(d) *Definition of "Sexual Assault."* In this rule and Rule 415, "sexual assault" means a crime under federal law or under state law (as "state" is defined in 18 U.S.C. § 513) involving: (1) any conduct prohibited by 18 U.S.C. chapter 109A; (2) contact, without consent, between any part of the defendant's body—or an object—and another person's genitals or anus; (3) contact, without consent, between the defendant's genitals or anus and any part of another person's body; (4) deriving sexual pleasure or gratification from inflicting death, bodily injury, or physical pain on another person; or (5) an attempt or conspiracy to engage in conduct described in subparagraphs (1)-(4).

RULE 414. SIMILAR CRIMES IN CHILD MOLESTATION CASES

[This rule is similar in structure and content to FRE 413, but it applies to offenses of child molestation rather than sexual assault. Section (d) defines "child" as "a person below the age of fourteen" and removes the "without consent" phrase that occurs in subdivisions (2) and (3) of FRE 413.]

RULE 415. SIMILAR ACTS IN CIVIL CASES CONCERNING SEXUAL ASSAULT OR CHILD MOLESTATION

[This rule makes FRE 413 and FRE 414, including the notice requirement, applicable to civil cases in which a claim is based on a party's alleged sexual assault or child molestation.]

2. Explanation of FRE 413-415

a. The Relationship Between FRE 413-415 and Other Rules of Evidence

FRE 413-415 and FRE 404.   The purpose of FRE 413-415 is to liberalize the admissibility of character evidence in sexual assault and child molestation cases by removing the two primary objections that would otherwise be available under FRE 404. First, the prosecution is permitted to open the door to use of propensity evidence in such cases, a right otherwise reserved to criminal defendants under FRE 404(a). Second, the prosecution may offer past specific acts of sexual assault or child molestation as evidence that the defendant committed the current offense, notwithstanding the FRE 404(b) ban on past specific acts to prove character to show action in accordance on a particular occasion. United States v. Enjady, 134 F.3d 1427, 1431 (10th Cir. 1998) (Congress intended "to lower the obstacles to admissibility of propensity evidence in a defined class of cases"). This liberalization of the preexisting rules is consistent with the language of FRE 413-415: sexual assault evidence "may be considered on any matter to which it is relevant." In addition, this understanding of FRE 413-415 is suggested by their legislative history (David J. Karp, Evidence of Propensity and Probability in Sex Offense Cases and Other Cases, 70 Chi.-Kent L. Rev. 15, 15 n.* (1995); Dale A. Nance, Forward: Do We Really Want to Know the Defendant?, 70 Chi.-Kent L. Rev., 3, 8 (1994)) and by the Justice Department, which lobbied for the enactment of the rules (Karp, supra at 19).

Consider, for example, a case in which the defendant is charged with attempted rape and the prosecution offers to prove that on two occasions within the past five years the defendant had sexually assaulted two women. Assume that the two women were unrelated to the victim of the attempted rape and that there were no unusual similar features among the three incidents. Are the two prior incidents relevant to identify the defendant as the perpetrator of the crime charged? Perhaps, but only because the evidence shows a general tendency to engage in sexual assaults. That sounds like a description of propensity evidence. If so, then the evidence, before the adoption of FRE 413, would have been inadmissible pursuant to both FRE 404(a) and FRE 404(b)(1). FRE 413 removes the FRE 404 impediments to the admissibility of relevant sexual assault evidence.

FRE 413-415 and FRE 403.   When FRE 413-415 were first enacted, there was some concern that these rules made no explicit reference to existing exclusionary rules and no indication of the extent to which judges may have discretion to exclude sexual misconduct evidence under FRE 403.[3] However, every appellate case dealing with this issue has concluded that sexual misconduct evidence is subject to FRE 403 balancing. United States v. Guardia, 135 F.2d 1326 (10th Cir. 1998). In fact, some federal court decisions have suggested that if FRE 403 were not available to exclude prejudicial evidence of sexual misconduct, admitting such evidence would violate a defendant's due process right to a fair trial. United States v. Castillo, 140 F.3d 874 (10th Cir. 1998) (FRE 414); United States v. Enjady, 134 F.3d 1427 (10th Cir. 1998) (FRE 413); United States v. Mound, 149 F.3d 799, 801 (8th Cir. 1998) (holding that FRE 413 does not violate due process and that neither FRE 413 nor FRE 414 violates equal protection because trial judges' discretion under FRE 403 to exclude excessively prejudicial evidence adequately protects defendants against prejudice); see also Aviva Orenstein, Deviance, Due Process, and the False Promise of Federal Rule of Evidence 403, 90 Cornell L. Rev. 1487, 1517 (2005) ("it would be foolish for those who are concerned about the reach of FRE 413 and 414 to count on a successful due process challenge"). Thus, in the attempted rape hypothetical, the defendant could argue that the prior sexual assaults should be excluded on FRE 403 grounds.

FRE 413-415 and Other Rules of Evidence. Can the FRE 413-415 language that prior sexual assault evidence is admissible be construed as an exception to other exclusionary rules of evidence, such as the hearsay rule? The argument strikes us as unsound. "Congressional proponents of the legislation creating Rule 413 intended that 'the general standards of the rules of evidence will continue to apply, including the restriction on hearsay evidence and the court's authority under rule 403 to exclude evidence whose probative value is substantially outweighed by its prejudicial effect.'" 2 Weinstein's Federal Evidence 413-411 (2d ed. 2005). In light of the uniform view that FRE 403 can be invoked to exclude sexual assault evidence, it seems likely that courts will conclude that other established rules—for example, the hearsay rule—are also applicable to evidence offered pursuant to FRE 413-415. Thus, in the attempted rape hypothetical, it is unlikely that a court would permit the prior sexual assaults to be proven by out-of-court hearsay statements that would not otherwise be admissible. In cases involving the defendant who was convicted for his prior act of sexual misconduct, the prosecution would be able to introduce it into evidence under the hearsay exception for judgments of conviction, FRE 803(22). When the prosecution relies on uncharged sexual misconduct, it must prove it to the jury by admissible evidence.

b. FRE 413-415 and Preliminary Factfinding

As is the case with specific-act evidence admissible pursuant to FRE 404(b)(2), there is no requirement that the sexual assault resulted in a conviction or even a criminal charge. If there is a question about the nature of the defendant's involvement in an alleged sexual assault, a court should resolve this issue in the same manner that it

---

3. *May admit evidence* indicates that admissibility is subject to other exclusionary provisions, including a court's power to exclude probative evidence pursuant to FRE 403. Note that in the one instance where the drafters of the Federal Rules clearly intended for admissibility to be mandatory, the rule states that the evidence *"must be admitted."* See FRE 609(a)(2), discussed in Chapter Seven.

resolves the issue when there is a question about a defendant's culpable involvement in other types of specific acts. Under the Federal Rules, as a result of the Supreme Court's decision in *Huddleston*, discussed at page 236, supra, there must be "evidence sufficient to support a finding" (FRE 104(b)) that the defendant was culpably involved in the act. United States v. Mann, 193 F.3d 1172 (10th Cir. 1999). For example, in the preceding rape hypothetical, assume that the defendant offers the testimony of a friend who provides the defendant with an alibi for the times of the noncharged sexual assaults; assume further that the prosecution's proof of those specific acts consists of the alleged victims' testimony and that there is a history of personal animosity between the alleged victims and the defendant. Even though the judge may disbelieve the alleged victims, there is sufficient "evidence to support a finding" under FRE 104(b) that the assaults occurred, because the judge is not permitted to take credibility into account. Importantly, prior to admitting evidence of uncharged sexual misconduct under FRE 413-414, the judge must also "make a preliminary finding that a jury could reasonably find by a preponderance of the evidence that the 'other act' occurred." In United States v. Enjady, 134 F.3d 1427, 1433 (10th Cir.1998).

The prosecution also can rely on prior sexual-misconduct evidence even when the defendant was acquitted of the underlying misconduct. Because acquittals can rest on a reasonable doubt and thus do not constitute an affirmative finding of innocence, the prosecution cannot be barred from adducing such evidence, subject to the trial judge's discretion to exclude it pursuant to FRE 403. See Dowling v. United States, 493 U.S. 342, 347-53 (1990) (holding that admission of inculpatory similar-act evidence pursuant to FRE 404(b)(2) does not violate the defendant's right to due process and protection against double jeopardy even when the evidence relates to accusations of which he was acquitted). Note, however, that *Dowling* relates to similar-act evidence that falls under FRE 404(b)(2) and thus arguably does not extend to general propensity evidence made admissible by FRE 413 and 414. *Cf.* Hess v. State, 20 P.3d 1121, 1129 (Alaska 2001) (holding that although the prosecutor could rely on the defendant's prior sexual assault despite the acquittal, "it was error not to inform the jury of [the] acquittal").

That the defendant was acquitted of the prior sexual misconduct would often prevent the evidence from passing the *Enjady* multifactor test, which requires the trial judge to consider "(1) how clearly the prior act has been proved; (2) how probative the evidence is of the material fact it is admitted to prove; (3) how seriously disputed the material fact is; and (4) whether the government can avail itself of any less prejudicial evidence." Id. at 1433. See also United States v. Benally, 500 F.3d 1085, 1090 (10th Cir. 2007) (approving district court's application of the multifactor test to uncharged sexual misconduct); United States v. Pascal, 2015 WL 2384347, (10th Cir. 2015).

c. The Broad Definition of "Offense of Sexual Assault"

The definition of what constitutes an "offense of sexual assault" is potentially very broad. Any acts having the characteristics described in §§(d)(2) through (d)(5) are apparently included as long as some state has enacted a criminal statute that prohibits that conduct. Assume, for example, in our rape hypothetical that the prosecution seeks to introduce evidence that the defendant has engaged in consensual sexual activity that involves pain or injury. If any state happens to encompass that sexual activity within its criminal law, the prosecution's evidence arguably falls within the scope of the rule as admissible even if the activity is not a federal crime or a crime in the state where the defendant is being prosecuted.

d. The Meaning of "Without Consent" in FRE 413(d)(2) and (3)

Nothing in FRE 413 indicates whether the term *consent* in section (d) means legal or actual consent. Consider a situation in which a defendant is charged with the rape and the victim is an adult. Prior sexual contact with other adults against their will (i.e., without *actual* consent) is without question a type of sexual assault that falls within the scope of FRE 413. What about prior sexual contact with a minor that was with the minor's actual consent but not legal consent because of the minor's age? Should this type of evidence be admissible? Should it matter whether the defendant was aware of the minor's age?

3. Elaboration of FRE 413-415

a. The Application of FRE 403 to Previously Inadmissible Character Evidence

The clear intent of FRE 413-415 is to make previously inadmissible evidence admissible. How, if at all, is a judge to take into account this mandate for more liberal admissibility in making the FRE 403 determination with respect to a particular piece of evidence?

Perhaps not surprisingly, the cases take a variety of approaches to this issue. At one extreme is Frank v. County of Hudson, 924 F. Supp. 620 (D.N.J. 1996), where the court stated, "Child sexual abuse deservedly carries a unique stigma in our society; such highly prejudicial evidence should therefore carry a very high degree of probative value if it is to be admitted." Id. at 626-627. The analysis in *Frank* suggests that FRE 403 is likely to require exclusion of sexual misconduct evidence not falling within one of the traditional noncharacter purposes for admitting specific acts evidence. That may or may not be desirable as a matter of policy. As a matter of law, it is wrong because it makes FRE 413-415 a nullity.

At the other extreme, some courts have been willing to admit evidence of very old, seemingly isolated, and sometimes dissimilar instances of sexual misconduct. For example, in United States v. Meacham, 115 F.3d 1488 (10th Cir. 1997), where the defendant was charged with transporting a minor in interstate commerce with the intent that she engage in sexual activity, the court held that it was proper to admit two similar incidents of child molestation that occurred over 30 years earlier. There was no evidence of more recent incidents with third persons to indicate a continuing pattern of conduct. See also United States v. Gabe, 237 F.3d 954 (8th Cir. 2001) (20-year-old incident of child molestation admissible); United States v. Eagle, 137 F.3d 1011 (8th Cir. 1998) (upholding admission of evidence of prior statutory rape of defendant's current common law wife in prosecution for child molestation); United States v. Larson,

112 F.3d 600 (2d Cir. 1997) (16- to 20-year-old similar incidents of child molestation admissible; 21- to 23-year-old similar incidents excluded). For two cases in which the court of appeals first held that the admission of specific acts evidence pursuant to FRE 404(b) was prejudicial error and then later held that the same evidence was properly admissible pursuant to FRE 414, see United States v. Sumner, 204 F.3d 1182 (8th Cir. 2000), and United States v. LeCompte, 131 F.3d 767 (8th Cir. 1997).

Despite—or perhaps because of—the variety of approaches to FRE 403, the results in particular cases may sometimes have more to do with the nature of the case than with what the court articulates about the relationship between FRE 403 and FRE 413-415. Although in the past courts have been divided on the admissibility of sexual assault evidence in child molestation cases, David P. Bryden and Roger C. Park, "Other Crimes" Evidence in Sex Offense Cases, 78 Minn. L. Rev. 529, 531 n.12 (1992), the trend seems to be strongly in favor of admitting such evidence under FRE 414. United States v. Gabe and United States v. LeCompte, supra; Christina E. Wells & Erin Elliott Motley, Reinforcing the Myth of the Crazed Rapist: A Feminist Critique of Recent Rape Legislation, 81 B.U. L. Rev. 127, 177-178 (2001). In rape cases, on the other hand, courts traditionally appear to have been less willing to admit prior sexual assault evidence in acquaintance rape cases than in stranger rape cases, see Bryden & Park, supra at 531 n.11, and this tendency may be continuing. Both in acquaintance rape cases (FRE 413) and in sexual harassment actions involving acquaintances (FRE 415), courts have seemed particularly sensitive to unfair prejudice concerns and have not been reluctant to exclude sexual misconduct evidence. United States v. Acevedo, 117 F.3d 1429 (table of unpublished decisions), No. 96-2149, 1997 U.S. App. LEXIS 17578 (10th Cir. July 14, 1997); Cleveland v. KFC Natl. Mgmt. Co., 948 F. Supp. 62 (N.D. Ga. 1996). For a discussion of these and other similar cases, see Wells & Motley, supra; Jane Harris Aiken, Sexual Character Evidence in Civil Actions: Refining the Propensity Rule, 1997 Wis. L. Rev. 1221.

The apparent willingness to exclude sexual assault evidence in cases involving alleged sexual misconduct by an acquaintance may be undermining one of the objectives of FRE 413 and FRE 415. Bryden & Park, supra at 576-582, note that in acquaintance rape cases in which defendants claim consent, there may be a relatively greater need for sexual assault evidence. There is not as likely to be physical evidence to establish that a rape occurred. Thus, the defendant's prior sexual misconduct may be particularly important in resolving the inevitable credibility conflict between the defendant and alleged victim. Karen Andrews, The Admissibility of Other-Crimes Evidence in Acquaintance-Rape Prosecutions, 17 S. Ill. U. L.J. 341 (1993); Sara Beale, Prior Similar Acts in Prosecutions for Rape and Child Sex Abuse, 4 Crim. L.F. 307 (1993).

b. The Underlying Rationale for Rules 413-415

Regardless of how much or how little FRE 413-415 in practice have liberalized the use of sexual misconduct evidence, their underlying premises must be (1) that sexual misconduct evidence has relatively high probative value to show action on a particular occasion and (2) that the probative value of this type of evidence is not likely to be outweighed by its prejudicial impact. Both of these propositions may be true, but neither is free from doubt. Because of the controversy surrounding FRE 413-415, we include references here to some of the legal and social science literature that has examined these two basic propositions.

Unfair Prejudice.   The prejudicial impact of any specific acts evidence—that is, the extent to which it may make the jury willing to ignore a reasonable doubt and convict a bad, perhaps dangerous person—is a function of how bad or dangerous the specific acts are in the minds of the factfinder. We suspect many of you and many jurors share the view that child molestation and sexual assault are among the most serious and heinous crimes. To the extent that this assessment is correct, the only justification for creating an exception to the prohibition against the prosecution's opening the door to proof of the defendant's character and doing so even with specific acts evidence is the relatively high probative value of such evidence.

Probative Value and Recidivism.   The already liberal admissibility of sexual misconduct evidence in some jurisdictions suggests that at least some courts regard sexual assault evidence as more probative than other types of character evidence. Moreover, some—perhaps many—of you may believe intuitively that prior sexual misconduct evidence is particularly probative propensity evidence. The important empirical question is whether this intuition is in fact true with respect to sexual misconduct against third persons. Repeated abuse of the same person—particularly a spouse or son or daughter—may be quite common. Evidence of repeated sexual violence against the same person, however, is likely to be considered noncharacter evidence and, therefore, potentially admissible in any event pursuant to FRE 404(b)(2).

Studies of recidivism indicate that the recidivism rate for sexual offenders is not consistently higher than for other serious crime offenders. Roger Park, however, has argued that the important recidivism factor should be how often sex offenders commit other sex crimes in comparison to how often other offenders commit crimes similar to the ones of which they were convicted. Roger C. Park, Character at the Crossroads, 49 Hast. L.J. 717, 756-754 (1998). By this standard, the propensity of rapists to be recidivists is relatively high. Id. at 762. Moreover, sex crimes are known to be underreported, and recidivism statistics rely on arrest and conviction rates. A. Nicholas Groth, Robert E. Longo & J. Bradley McFadin, Undetected Recidivism among Rapists and Child Molesters, 28 Crime & Delinquency 450 (1982). Forty-five percent of all rapes in the United States are never reported, and studies show that only 5 to 10 percent of acquaintance rape cases are reported. Karen Andrews, The Admissibility of Other-Crimes Evidence in Acquaintance-Rape Prosecutions, 17 S. Ill. U. L.J. 341, 342-343 (1993). Moreover, there is evidence that police do not pursue an arrest if they do not believe the victim. Gary D. LaFree, Rape and Criminal Justice: The Social Construction of Sexual Assault 59-60, 66-69, 207-226 (1989); Julie Horney & Cassia Spohn, Rape Law Reform and Instrumental Change in Six Urban Jurisdictions, 25 Law & Soc'y Rev. 117 (1991). Cf. Tamara Rice Lave & Aviva Orenstein, Empirical Fallacies of Evidence Law: A Critical Look at the Admission of Prior Sex Crimes, 81 U. Cin. L. Rev. 795 (2013) (criticizing psychological and empirical justifications for

FRE 413-415 for failing to account for important nuances in interpreting recidivism in and under-reporting of sex crimes).

A Contextual Assessment of Probative Value.   Consider the likely impact of one's political and social values in assessing the probative value of sexual assault evidence. If one regards sexual assaults as largely analogous to all other violent crimes, then there is no reason for character evidence rules to differ across those crimes. The generally low probative value of character evidence to show action in accordance with character and the potential for unfair prejudice to criminal defendants would militate against using the action-in-accordance with character inference in all cases.

On the other hand, if one considers sexual assaults as one manifestation of a male-dominated social structure that tends to discriminate against and oppress women — especially women of color and poor women — in a variety of ways, it is reasonable to expect that prosecutors, judges, and factfinders may approach sexual assault cases with some of the biases that inhere in that societal oppression. Special rules of admissibility to compensate for those biases may be appropriate. Bryden and Park, supra at 583.

Legal literature suggests that this type of discriminatory bias does exist. Empirical research based on Uniform Crime Reports and real and mock jury trials reveals that men are more likely to rape women of color and poor women, but are less likely to be convicted when they do so. If the perpetrators are convicted, they serve less jail time when these women are their victims. One explanation is that judges and juries are more likely to see these women as sexually available and therefore not capable of being assaulted. Gary D. LaFree, Rape and Criminal Justice: The Social Construction of Sexual Assault 219-220 (1989); G. Chezia Carraway, Violence Against Women of Color, 43 Stan. L. Rev. 1301 (1991); Kimberle Crenshaw, Mapping the Margins: Intersectionality, Identity Politics, and Violence Against Women of Color, 43 Stan. L. Rev. 1241 (1991); Dorothy E. Roberts, Rape, Violence, and Women's Autonomy, 69 Chi.-Kent L. Rev. 359 (1993). In addition, traditional and still currently powerful stereotypes blame the woman for acquaintance rape or even deny that the activity is rape when the woman is seen as contributing to her predicament. Lois Pineau, Date Rape: A Feminist Analysis, 8 Law and Philosophy 217 (1989). See also Andrews, supra; David P. Bryden & Sonja Lengnick, Rape in the Criminal Justice System, 87 J. Crim. L. & Criminology 1194 (1997); Karen M. Kramer, Note, Rule by Myth: The Social and Legal Dynamics Governing Alcohol-Related Acquaintance Rapes, 47 Stan. L. Rev. 115 (1994). These attitudes make jurors willing to discount, if not disbelieve, victims' stories, and since there often will be no evidence of physical injury in an acquaintance rape situation, the victim's credibility will usually be critical to a successful prosecution. To the extent that jurors share these stereotypical attitudes, the likelihood of a conviction is small; and if juries are unlikely to convict, prosecutors are unlikely to bring cases. Admitting evidence of a defendant's prior sexual assaults may challenge the jurors' stereotypes and in turn make prosecutors more willing to pursue acquaintance rape cases. Allowing evidence of a defendant's prior sexual assault record also may increase convictions in cases where poor women and women of color are the victims.

Perhaps this bias and stereotyping explains the pre-FRE 413-415 state of the law. As we noted there, many courts have tended to be relatively liberal in admitting evidence of a defendant's prior sexual conduct in child molestation cases and in cases involving sexual assaults by strangers. This same liberal view of admissibility, however, has not extended to cases involving sexual assault by an acquaintance. We can think of no basis for believing that a sexual assault defendant's prior sexual conduct is likely to be less probative in acquaintance assault situations than in stranger assault situations.

Some scholars have argued that FRE 413-415 merely reenforce societal stereotypes of rapists as vicious predators and revive the idea that women who make accusations of rape need to have a corroborating witness (in these cases, women who have been prior victims). Aviva Orenstein, No Bad Men!: A Feminist Analysis of Character Evidence in Rape Trials, 49 Hastings L.J. 663 (1998); Wells and Motley, supra. See also Katharine K. Baker, Once a Rapist? Motivational Evidence and Relevancy in Rape Law, 110 Harv. L. Rev. 563 (1997) (criticizing FRE 413 for creating a dangerous sex-offender stereotype that increases the risk of wrongful conviction for certain underprivileged defendants, while allowing date-rapists who don't fit the stereotype to escape conviction). Do these analyses change your views about the desirability of FRE 413-415?

c. The Significance of FRE 413-415 to Federal Litigation

The controversy surrounding the adoption of FRE 413-415 focused almost exclusively on the role of FRE 413 and FRE 414 in criminal prosecutions. As we noted at the outset of Section E, however, sexual assault and child molestation are predominantly state crimes. Thus, although most of the limited number of FRE 413-415 cases to date are criminal cases, there will probably be relatively few opportunities for federal courts to apply FRE 413 and FRE 414. By contrast, FRE 415—the civil case counterpart to FRE 413 and FRE 414—may become the primary vehicle for giving content to the federal sexual misconduct rules. 23 Wright and Graham, supra at §5411B (Supp. 2001). For example, plaintiffs with sexual harassment claims (including federal civil rights suits) based on unlawful sexual touching may seek to introduce evidence of the defendants' prior sexual misconduct pursuant to FRE 415. Cleveland v. KFC Natl. Mgmt. Co., 948 F. Supp. 62 (N.D. Ga. 1996); Jane Harris Aiken, Sexual Character Evidence in Civil Actions, 1997 Wis. L. Rev. 1221.

KEY POINTS

1. FRE 413-415 permit the use of specific acts to establish a person's character or propensity for engaging in sexual assault and prove action on a particular occasion.
2. Evidence potentially admissible under FRE 413-415 may be excluded pursuant to FRE 403.

PROBLEMS

5.39. Defendant has been charged with "intentionally having sexual contact with a minor with the intent to become sexually aroused or gratified." During its case in chief, the prosecution introduced evidence that the defendant lured a three-year-old girl into his home, fondled her, and gave her a piece of candy. Defendant testified in his own behalf and denied the incident. On rebuttal, the prosecution offers the testimony of a 12-year-old girl that, a week before the alleged incident with the three-year-old girl, the defendant offered the witness $20 if she would come into his home and expose herself. Should the evidence be admitted?

5.40. Alex Abrams is charged with attempted sexual assault and battery. Brenda Bailey, the alleged victim, testifies that she was at a bar where she met a man whom she identifies as the defendant Abrams; that he followed her to her car as she left the bar after midnight; that he grabbed her from behind, pinned her to the ground, and attempted to assault her sexually; and that her screams brought other patrons from the bar and her assailant ran away. Abrams testifies that Bailey has misidentified him; that it was a dark night; and that he had been at the bar earlier but left before midnight and was at home when the alleged attack occurred.

The prosecution seeks to admit the following evidence: testimony from two women that seven years ago and five years ago, respectively, they were sexually assaulted by Abrams after he followed them out of a bar. Should this evidence be admitted prior to the adoption of FRE 413-415? After their adoption?

Would the result be different if the sexual assaults were more recent? If they had occurred during the daytime at the women's homes?

5.41. Carl Corbin is charged with rape. Doris Davis, the alleged victim, testifies that she met Corbin in a bar; that they talked for a while and she agreed to accompany him to another bar for drinks and dancing; that after spending a few hours at this second bar she accepted his offer of a ride back to her car; that along the way he stopped at a park and said he wanted to have sex with her; that she said no and told him she was afraid she would get pregnant; and that he forcibly raped her. Corbin testifies that Davis consented to have sexual relations with him after a fun evening.

The prosecution seeks to admit the following evidence: testimony from a woman that she had dated Corbin for a brief period of time three years ago; that he wanted to have sexual relations with her; that she told him no but he then forced her to have sex; and that she never reported the incident to anyone. Should this evidence be admitted prior to the adoption of FRE 413-415? After their adoption?

Would the result be different if the woman would testify that she met Corbin in a bar; that after a few drinks and dancing he offered to drive her home; that he stopped at the same park where he had stopped with Davis; and that he forced her have sex after she said no?

5.42. Agatha Lewis has brought an action for damages against Brian Bellows, who, she alleges, transmitted AIDS to her. Agatha establishes with blood test evidence that she did not have the AIDS virus 18 months ago, that she now has the virus, and that Brian has the virus. Agatha testifies that she is not an intravenous drug user, that she has not had a blood transfusion, and that the only person with whom she has had intimate sexual contact subsequent to the negative AIDS test was Brian. She further testifies that she met Brian at a party; that they went to his apartment after the party and had sexual intercourse; that she had sexual intercourse with him two or three additional times in the next two weeks; and that she had no further contact with him. In his defense, Brian admits that he met Agatha at a party. He claims that he gave her a ride to her apartment after the party and that he did not on that night or on any other occasion have sexual intercourse with Agatha. In rebuttal, Agatha offers the testimony of three women that during the past year they met Brian at parties and had brief sexual affairs with him. Should this evidence be admitted prior to the adoption of FRE 415? After its adoption?

5.43. Steve Sanders, a 21-year-old college junior, is charged with the rape of Betty Brown, a classmate. According to the prosecution, the rape occurred during their first (and only) date. Sanders admits having had intercourse but claims that Brown consented. The prosecution offers the following pieces of evidence:

(a) the testimony of Ann Williams, a 16-year-old high school student, that she recently had consensual sexual intercourse with Sanders;

(b) the testimony of Ellie Wilson, another student, that on her first date with Sanders he was extremely aggressive and ripped some of her clothing before she could stop him;

(c) a wallet belonging to Mary Miller that was seized from Sanders's room and Mary Miller's testimony that one month ago a masked man raped her in the laundry room of the dormitory and stole her wallet (Sanders claims that he found the wallet on a street corner the night before it was seized from his room, and that he was studying in the library at the time of the rape).

How should the court rule prior to the adoption of FRE 413-415? After their adoption?

J. EVIDENCE OF AN ALLEGED VICTIM'S PAST SEXUAL BEHAVIOR OR DISPOSITION IN SEX OFFENSE CASES

Until fairly recently, many courts were quite liberal in permitting rape and other sex crime defendants to introduce evidence of the alleged victim's sexual history when the defendant claimed that the victim had consented. The most common form of prior sexual history evidence was reputation testimony, but a number of jurisdictions also permitted specific acts evidence. Starting in the 1970s, states began to enact "rape shield" legislation to curb the admissibility of some of this evidence. FRE 412, subsequently amended in 1994, was also the product of specific legislative action. Congress added FRE 412 to the Federal Rules in 1978. For a discussion of the background and legislative history of Rule 412, see 23 Charles Alan Wright & Kenneth W. Graham Jr., Federal Practice and Procedure §5381 at 483-491 (1980), §5381.1 at 190-199 (Supp. 2001).

1. FRE 412

RULE 412. SEX-OFFENSE CASES: THE VICTIM'S SEXUAL BEHAVIOR OR PREDISPOSITION

(a) *Prohibited Uses.* The following evidence is not admissible in a civil or criminal proceeding involving alleged sexual misconduct: (1) evidence offered to prove that a victim engaged in other sexual behavior; or (2) evidence offered to prove a victim's sexual predisposition.

(b) *Exceptions.*

(1) *Criminal Cases.* The court may admit the following evidence in a criminal case:

(A) evidence of specific instances of a victim's sexual behavior, if offered to prove that someone other than the defendant was the source of semen, injury, or other physical evidence;

(B) evidence of specific instances of a victim's sexual behavior with respect to the person accused of the sexual misconduct, if offered by the defendant to prove consent or if offered by the prosecutor; and

(C) evidence whose exclusion would violate the defendant's constitutional rights.

(2) *Civil Cases.* In a civil case, the court may admit evidence offered to prove a victim's sexual behavior or sexual predisposition if its probative value substantially outweighs the danger of harm to any victim and of unfair prejudice to any party. The court may admit evidence of a victim's reputation only if the victim has placed it in controversy.

(c) *Procedure to Determine Admissibility.*

(1) *Motion.* If a party intends to offer evidence under Rule 412(b), the party must:

(A) file a motion that specifically describes the evidence and states the purpose for which it is to be offered;

(B) do so at least 14 days before trial unless the court, for good cause, sets a different time;

(C) serve the motion on all parties; and

(D) notify the victim or, when appropriate, the victim's guardian or representative.

(2) *Hearing.* Before admitting evidence under this rule, the court must conduct an in camera hearing and give the victim and parties a right to attend and be heard. Unless the court orders otherwise, the motion, related materials, and the record of the hearing must be and remain sealed.

(d) *Definition of "Victim."* In this rule, "victim" includes an alleged victim.

2. Explanation of FRE 412

FRE 412 has a twofold rationale. First, the combination of relatively low probative value and significant countervailing FRE 403 concerns warrants a flat rule of exclusion rather than individual case-by-case balancing to determine admissibility. Second, independent of FRE 403 concerns, substantive policy considerations justify the exclusion of relevant evidence. Thus, FRE 412 excludes some evidence of an alleged sexual assault victim's sexual conduct in order to protect the alleged victim from harassment and embarrassment and to avoid deterring such a person from coming forward to complain and testify about the sexual assault.

a. Relevancy of an Alleged Victim's Sexual Behavior or Disposition

Some people adamantly maintain that evidence of a sexual assault victim's prior sexual history is irrelevant to the issue of consent. FRE 412 (b)(1)(B), however, explicitly permits evidence of sexual behavior between the defendant and the alleged victim to prove the victim's consent. Moreover, there is no explicit limitation on the use of prior sexual conduct to prove consent in civil cases. Is such conduct relevant under the minimal threshold of FRE 401? Consider an alleged victim whose only prior consensual intercourse was in the context of a marriage relationship. What generalizations can you frame that say something about the likelihood that such a victim consented or did not consent to sexual intercourse with a stranger? With an acquaintance? If the defendant's defense of consent is based on evidence that is arguably ambiguous as to whether the victim consented, is evidence of the alleged victim's prior consensual sexual conduct with third persons probative of consent? Again, can you think of a generalization that permits one to make the inference from the evidentiary fact (prior sexual conduct) to the fact of consequence (consent)? We suggest that in both examples the relevance of the evidence depends on whether one can frame a valid generalization about the alleged victim's sexual conduct.

b. The Underlying Propensity Theory

The concept of relevance with which we have been dealing explicitly and implicitly throughout the course rests on the premise that individuals have propensities to behave in particular ways and that we can arrive at reasonable conclusions about historical facts by taking these propensities into account. For example, at the most basic level, when a person says that event X occurred, we regard the person's statement as relevant, at least in a minimal FRE 401 sense, to establish that X occurred because we assume, on the basis of our common experience, that individuals generally have a propensity to tell the truth. Similarly, a premise underlying the character evidence rules is that individuals have propensities to behave in characteristic ways and that if we know something about the individuals' conduct on some occasions, we can make reasonable—although sometimes weak—inferences about their conduct on other occasions. Given this pervasive reliance on the premise that we can infer something about an individual's conduct on some occasions if we know how the individual behaved on other occasions, and given the very low FRE 401 threshold requirement for "relevance," courts have not been willing to reject all evidence of an alleged victim's prior sexual behavior as irrelevant to the issue of consent.

Indeed, before rape shield legislation such as FRE 412, the rape defendant's right to introduce reputation evidence about the victim's prior sexual conduct was regarded as an application of the general principle, codified in FRE 404(a)(2), that a defendant can introduce reputation (and under FRE 405(a), opinion) testimony to prove the victim's character trait to show action in conformity with that trait. In other words, just as a homicide defendant claiming self-defense could introduce evidence of the victim's reputation for violence to suggest that the victim was the first aggressor, it was regarded as appropriate for a rape defendant claiming consent to introduce evidence of the victim's reputation for promiscuity or lack of chastity to suggest that the victim consented to the intercourse.

The theoretical justification for introducing evidence of specific instances of the victim's consensual sexual intercourse was more varied. Some courts claimed that the evidence was admissible to show the victim's "intent." Other courts admitted the evidence to "impeach" the credibility of the rape victim without bothering to explain what relationship existed between consensual sexual intercourse and truth-telling. Still other courts frankly admitted that the specific-act evidence was being used in a propensity sense or that it was being used to show character. These latter courts took the position that there was an exception to the propensity-character rule for evidence of prior sexual conduct, an exception that one might analogize to the use of a criminal defendant's prior sexual misconduct in sexual assault prosecutions.

c. The Scope of FRE 412

FRE 412 excludes most evidence of an alleged victim's prior sexual behavior and sexual predisposition, even when it is relevant under the above-described propensity theory. We will deal with the reasons for this rejection of past practice in the next section. Here we want to focus on the actual application of FRE 412.

The Meaning of "Other Sexual Behavior" and "Sexual Predisposition." The exclusionary provisions in FRE 412(a) come into play only with respect to evidence of "other sexual behavior" and "sexual predisposition." The rule does not define either of these phrases, but the Advisory Committee's Note provides some examples. *Sexual behavior* "connotes all activities that involve actual physical conduct . . . or that imply sexual intercourse or conduct"—for example, "use of contraceptives," "birth of an illegitimate child," or "venereal disease." It also includes "activities of the mind, such as fantasies or dreams." *Sexual predisposition* includes "evidence that does not directly refer to sexual activities or thoughts but that the proponent believes may have a sexual connotation for the factfinder"—for example, evidence "relating to the alleged victim's mode of dress, speech, or lifestyle. FRE 412(a) applies to all general sexual propensities of the alleged victim, and operates similarly to FRE 404(a)(1), which provides that "Evidence of a person's character or character trait is not admissible to prove that on a particular occasion the person acted in accordance with the character or trait."

The Applicability of FRE 412 When the Issue Is the Victim's Behavior on a Particular Occasion. If a defendant offers evidence for the purpose of showing the alleged victim's sexual conduct on a particular occasion, the theory of relevance presumably will be that the evidence shows something about the sexual predisposition (i.e., propensity) of the individual and that from this predisposition one can infer how the victim behaved on a particular occasion. Thus, all evidence (whether in the form of reputation, opinion, or specific act) offered to show conduct on a particular occasion would be evidence of "sexual predisposition." If evidence of dressing in a provocative manner, telling lewd jokes, or soliciting sex were offered for this purpose, it would not be necessary to determine whether the evidence constituted "other sexual behavior." Such evidence, however, to the extent it purports to show the alleged victim's sexual conduct on a particular occasion, either falls into the excluded "sexual predisposition" category or is altogether irrelevant. Such evidence, when offered by a criminal defendant, ostensibly falls within the terms of FRE 404(a)(2)—opening the door to a "pertinent" character trait of the victim. However, FRE 404(a)(2)(B) makes clear that character evidence relating to the victim's sexual predisposition is governed by the stringent "rape shield" limitations of FRE 412.

The Applicability of FRE 412 in Other Contexts. The definitions of "other sexual behavior" and "sexual predisposition" become important when evidence of an alleged victim's prior activity is offered for some purpose other than to show sexual conduct on a particular occasion. Assume, for example, that a defendant is charged with rape and claims that the alleged victim has falsely accused him. To suggest a motive for the false accusation the defendant offers to testify that he had threatened to reveal to the alleged victim's spouse that she had a secret job as a nude dancer and had solicited sex from him.

Do these activities constitute "sexual behavior"? Perhaps the answer is yes with respect to soliciting sex, for the Advisory Committee's Note indicates that sexual behavior includes "activities of the mind, such as fantasies or dreams." Nude dancing, on the other hand, seems to fall more readily into the Advisory Committee's description of "sexual predisposition"—activity that "may have a sexual connotation for the factfinder . . . [such as] mode of dress . . . or lifestyle." It is not clear, however, that evidence is governed by FRE 412 merely because it may suggest a sexual predisposition to the factfinder. If the activity in question is not "sexual behavior," it falls within the scope of FRE 412 only if it is "offered to prove any alleged victim's sexual predisposition." Does the language "To prove . . . sexual predisposition" apply only to evidence offered to show action in accordance with that predisposition, or does it apply to evidence that may suggest to the factfinder a sexual predisposition but that is offered for some other purpose? In our hypothetical, the defendant would argue that the evidence of nude dancing (and soliciting sex, if that activity is not "sexual behavior") is being offered to prove the alleged victim's motive for lying, not her sexual predisposition.

If nude dancing and soliciting sex fall within the FRE 412(a) general exclusionary rule for "other sexual behavior" or "sexual predisposition," then the evidence would be inadmissible unless it falls within one of the FRE 412(b) exceptions (the defendant would argue that the court must admit the evidence pursuant to FRE 412(b)(C) because the Constitution's Due Process and Compulsory Process Clauses entitle him to use it in his defense). If these activities do not fall within either of the prohibited categories of evidence, the only limits on the admissibility of the evidence are FRE 401-403.

Hostile Work Environment Cases. There is at least one line of cases holding that FRE 412 applies to evidence suggesting a sexual predisposition even when the evidence is offered to prove something other than the alleged victim's action in accordance with the predisposition. In sex discrimination suits based on a hostile work environment, defendants frequently contend that the plaintiffs welcomed or created the environment that they claim to be discriminatory. To establish this defense, defendants offered evidence showing that the plaintiffs have behaved provocatively, used vulgar, sex-charged language, and engaged in other behavior that is similar to the activity about which they are complaining. Courts have held that FRE 412 applies to this evidence. Socks-Brunot v. Hirschvogel Inc., 184 F.R.D. 113 (S.D. Ohio 1999); Sheffield v. Hilltop Sand & Gravel Co., 895 F. Supp. 105, 108-109 (E.D. Va. 1995). According to *Socks-Brunot*:

> Evidence tending to prove both prior sexual conduct of the plaintiff and workplace conversations of the plaintiff is covered by Rule 412. Generally, evidence admissible for one purpose but inadmissible for another may be heard by a jury, pursuant to Federal Rule of Evidence 105. The general rule is inapplicable with regard to evidence covered by Rule 412. [184 F.R.D. at 119.]

But cf. Morales-Evans v. Administrative Office of the Courts, 102 F. Supp. 2d 577, 581 n.7 (D.N.J. 2000) (evidence of prior sexual relationship with supervisor considered only "to provide context" for supervisor's allegedly inappropriate remark; "not . . . considered as evidence of sexual predisposition or behavior . . .; therefore this consideration does not run afoul of Rule 412.").

The Admissibility of "Other Sexual Behavior" and "Sexual Predisposition" Evidence in Civil Cases. In hostile work environment and other civil cases, the balancing test in FRE 412(b)(2) governs admissibility of evidence of an alleged victim's sexual behavior and predisposition. This test differs from the FRE 403 balancing test in two respects. First, it is a reverse FRE 403 test. In contrast to FRE 403, which favors admissibility, FRE 412(b)(2), by requiring that the probative value must substantially outweigh countervailing factors, favors exclusion. Wolak v. Spucci, 217 F.3d 157, 163 (2d Cir. 2000).

Second, as per the Advisory Committee Note to FRE 403, one should interpret "unfair prejudice" in FRE 403 as referring to the evidence's "undue tendency to suggest decision on an improper basis, commonly, though not necessarily, an emotional one." By contrast, FRE 412(b)(2) specifically refers to prejudice against a party *and* harm to the alleged victim. Consider, for example, an alleged rape victim's civil suit against a defendant who claims that the plaintiff consented to the intercourse. If the defendant offers evidence of prior consensual intercourse with the plaintiff, the court must weigh the probative value of this evidence against both the risk that the evidence may make the jury improperly discount the plaintiff's credibility as a witness (FRE 403-type prejudice) and the harm to the victim (such as embarrassment and invasion of privacy) from the presentation of evidence about the victim's prior sexual activity. The court must also consider the risk that the jury might discount the plaintiff's moral worth as a person and effectively modify the burden of proof by making itself more willing than it should be to err against her interest in the face of uncertainty.

The Admissibility of "Other Sexual Behavior" and "Sexual Predisposition" Evidence in Criminal Cases.   For criminal cases, FRE 412(b)(1) delineates only three exceptions to the general rule of exclusion. The first two exceptions are quite narrow. Both refer to case-specific evidence of (a) the victim's sexual behavior with third persons to suggest that they may be the source of semen or injury and (b) the victim's sexual behavior with the defendant to suggest consent. As a result, these exceptions may not encompass all of the situations in which, in fairness, a court should permit a criminal defendant to introduce evidence of an alleged victim's sexual behavior or predisposition. The rule acknowledges this possibility by providing in the third exception for admission in those cases in which "exclusion . . . would violate the constitutional rights of the defendant." This language is a reference (1) to the due process and compulsory process doctrines that embody criminal defendants' constitutional right to present a defense and (2) to the Sixth Amendment Confrontation Clause right to confront and cross-examine witnesses. While these rights do not allow criminal defendants to present evidence and cross-examine witnesses in complete disregard of the rules of evidence, the Supreme Court has held on numerous occasions that rules of evidence can restrict these rights only for compelling reasons. See Alex Stein, Inefficient Evidence, 66 Ala. L. Rev. 423, 460-69 (2014). There was, of course, no need to expressly state this third exception in the rule. The Constitution is the supreme law of the land. When the defendant has a constitutional right to introduce the evidence, this right trumps any exclusionary rule.

The "constitutionally required" exception to the Kentucky version of FRE 412(a) was at work in the Supreme Court's decision Olden v. Kentucky, 488 U.S. 227 (1988). The defendant responded to the complainant's kidnapping and rape accusations by introducing evidence that he and the complainant had consensual sex, after which he and his friend drove the complainant—at her request—to the house belonging to a person named Russell, with whom she had an extramarital relationship. This evidence was supposed to impeach the complainant's testimony by showing that she feared jeopardizing her relationship with Russell and thus had a motive to fabricate the rape story. On both trial and appellate levels, Kentucky courts held that the state's "rape shield" statute does not permit the defendant to use this evidence, but the Supreme Court disagreed. The Court ruled that the suppression of the defendant's exculpatory evidence violated his Sixth Amendment right "to be confronted with the witnesses against him." Id. at 231. Importantly, the defendant's evidence implicated, but did not rely on, the alleged victim's general promiscuity. Rather, it relied on her case-specific motive to lie. This characteristic puts the defendant's evidence on a par with evidence admissible under the first two exceptions to the "rape shield," FRE 412(b)(1)(A)&(B).

When the defendant's evidence falls within one of those exceptions, it is not automatically admissible. Rather, the evidence must be "otherwise admissible under these rules." Consider, for example, a rape case in which the defendant claims that the alleged victim consented to the sexual intercourse. To prove consent, the defendant offers to testify that on one occasion three years ago he had consensual sex with the victim. This evidence falls within the FRE 412(b)(1)(B) exception, but the court retains discretion to exclude the evidence on FRE 403 grounds.

The Notice Requirement.   The notice and hearing requirement in FRE 412(c) is more demanding than any other notice requirement in the Federal Rules. Cf. FRE 404(b), FRE 413-415. Any notice requirement makes the decisionmaking process more rigorous because it gives the parties time to prepare their arguments. A stringent notice requirement may have the additional impact of deterring litigants from pressing weak claims.

3. Elaboration of FRE 412

a. The Rationale for a Rule Excluding Evidence of Prior Sexual Behavior and Sexual Predisposition

There are substantial reasons to be concerned about the liberal admissibility of an alleged sexual assault victim's sexual history. The ability to introduce evidence of the victim's sexual history gives the defendant the opportunity to try to make the victim and the victim's character the focal point of the litigation. The prospect of a degrading and humiliating examination by defense counsel may discourage many victims from cooperating with prosecutors, or even reporting sexual assaults in the first place. One cannot, however, attribute the humiliation and degradation of rape victims solely—or perhaps even primarily—to liberal rules of admissibility for prior sexual conduct. Disbelief of, disrespect for, and insensitivity toward rape victims have existed throughout the criminal justice system. Susan Brownmiller, Against Our Will: Men, Women and Rape 408-420 (1976); Colleen A. Ward, Attitudes Toward Rape: Feminist and Social Psychological Perspectives (1995); Morrison Torrey, When Will We Be Believed? Rape Myths and the Idea of a Fair Trial in Rape Prosecutions, 24 U.C. Davis L. Rev. 1013 (1991).

In cases that are tried, there may be disputes about whether the victim in fact engaged in any of the conduct that the defendant wishes to attribute to the victim. In addition, the jury might overestimate the probative value of the prior sexual history evidence on the question of consent or be prejudiced against the victim because of the sexual conduct. There is evidence that juries may too readily acquit defendants because they disbelieve a female victim or believe that "she got what she deserved." Harry Kalven & Hans Zeisel, The American Jury 249-54 (1966); David P. Bryden & Sonja Lengnick, Rape in the Criminal Justice System, 87 J. Crim. L. and Criminology 1194 (1997); Aviva Orenstein, No Bad Men!: A Feminist Analysis of Character Evidence in Rape Trials, 49 Hastings L.J. 663 (1998); Beverly J. Ross, Does Diversity in Legal Scholarship Make a Difference?: A Look at the Laws of Rape, 100 Dick. L. Rev. 795 (1966); Torrey, supra. Because of widespread racism, class biases and sexual stereotypes, this phenomenon is particularly likely to occur when the victim is a woman of color or poor, or when she was acquainted with the man who raped her. Gary D. LaFree, Rape and Criminal Justice: The Social Construction of Sexual Assault 219-220; G. Chezia Carraway, Violence Against Women of Color, 43 Stan. L. Rev. 1301 (1991); Kimberle Crenshaw, Mapping the Margins: Intersectionality, Identity Politics, and Violence Against Women of Color, 43 Stan. L. Rev. 1241 (1993); Lois Pineau, Date Rape: A Feminist Analysis, 8 Law & Philosophy 217 (1989);

Dorothy E. Roberts, Rape, Violence, and Women's Autonomy, 69 Chi.-Kent L. Rev. 359 (1993).

Finally, there is the problem that prior sexual history will frequently be of no more than marginal relevance to the question of whether the victim consented on the occasion in question. Indeed, as we noted earlier, one of the principal reasons that the rules of evidence severely restrict the use of character to show action in conformity is that the strength of the inference from character to action on a particular occasion is almost invariably weak. We can think of no reason to believe that the inference from prior consensual intercourse—especially when the activity is with third persons—to consensual sex with the defendant is valid.

In theory, FRE 403 and its common law counterparts might have been adequate devices for taking into account these concerns that warrant caution in the use of evidence of a rape victim's prior sexual conduct. However, the policy of protecting a rape victim from humiliation is not, strictly speaking, the sort of concern that readily fits among the FRE 403 dangers. Moreover, in practice, many individuals perceived—correctly, we believe—that courts were often too willing to admit marginally probative, highly prejudicial evidence of the victim's prior sexual activity in rape and other sexual assault prosecutions. The response to this perception has been the adoption of "rape shield" rules or statutes such as FRE 412 that specifically address and limit the situations in which evidence of a victim's prior sexual conduct may be admitted. Rape victims need an assurance against bias and mistreatment by the justice system, and FRE 412 aims at satisfying that need as well.

Because "rape shield" provisions are now common, it is difficult to assess how liberal judges would have been in admitting evidence of victims' past sexual behavior and sexual predisposition in the absence of such rules. Some might argue that recent increased public awareness and concern with sexual assault crimes (exemplified by the enactment of FRE 413-415) make "rape shield" provisions less necessary today than when they were first enacted. Others firmly believe, as we suggested earlier, that social attitudes that stereotype women as sexual objects and as provoking sexual contact will somehow find their way into the jury box. From this perspective, "rape shield" provisions continue to be vitally important both as devices for contributing to accurate factfinding and as affirmations of the autonomy of women.

b. Two Approaches to the Exclusion of Other Sexual Behavior and Sexual Predisposition Evidence

FRE 412 presents an interesting example of two quite different approaches to the problem of regulating the admissibility of sexual behavior and sexual predisposition evidence. In civil cases, where there is no established doctrine of constitutionally required evidence, Congress chose to rely exclusively on a balancing test that favors exclusion. By contrast, in criminal cases, where the constitutionally required evidence doctrine provides what is in effect a safety valve for an overly strict exclusionary rule, Congress created only two specific, very narrow, exceptions to a general rule of exclusion.

Do you think it is desirable to have an evidentiary rule that tends to force courts to resolve issues of admissibility in terms of constitutional law? In any event, are the criteria for determining whether evidence is constitutionally required likely to be applied consistently from case to case?

Particularly in light of your analysis and discussion of the following problems, consider whether it would be preferable to have a general balancing test for both criminal and civil cases. If your answer is no, are there any additional exceptions that you would add to FRE 412(b)(2)?

c. Rape Shield Rules and the Defendant's Right to Testify

When a criminal defendant seeks to testify about a rape victim's prior sexual conduct, there may be a conflict between the jurisdiction's rape shield rule and the constitutional right to testify, a right closely related to the due process and confrontation clause rights that we have been discussing. The Seventh Circuit dealt with such a situation in Stephens v. Miller, 13 F.3d 998 (7th Cir. 1994) (en banc), a case involving suppression of the defendant's testimony about the remark he made to the alleged victim during what he described as consensual sex. This remark referred to the way the victim allegedly had sex with another man, and its suppression generated seven opinions that included concurrences and dissent. We urge you to read *Stephens* and to consider (1) whether the court resolved the constitutional issue properly and (2) what implications *Stephens* may have for the questions we raised at the end of subsection b, supra.

d. FRE 412 and Discovery in Civil Cases

The prohibition in FRE 412 raises recurring questions in certain civil cases, particularly sexual harassment cases, about the scope of pretrial discovery into, for example, the sexual behavior or predisposition of a plaintiff alleging sexual harassment. It is a black-letter principle of civil procedure that the scope of discovery is broader than the scope of evidentiary admissibility at trial. The Federal Rules of Civil Procedure require parties to respond fully to discovery requests that are "reasonably calculated to lead to the discovery of admissible evidence." Fed. R. Civ. P. 26. The prospect of compelled disclosure of private or embarrassing information in discovery raises many of the same problems: deterring plaintiffs from filing meritorious claims and witnesses from coming forward. These problems are addressed by FRE 412, but FRE 412 deals expressly only with admission of evidence at trial, not disclosure in pretrial discovery. For a compelling instance of invasive discovery into female plaintiffs' sexual histories in a sexual harassment case, see Jenson v. Eveleth Taconite Co., 130 F.3d 1287 (8th Cir. 1997); Clara Bingham & Laura Leedy Gansler, Class Action: The Story of Lois Jenson and the Landmark Case That Changed Sexual Harassment Law (2002).

Courts have held, in the context of objections to discovery requests or motions for protective orders, that discovery requests into a plaintiff's sexual behavior are governed by Fed. R. Civ. P. 26(c). However, because that provision expressly incorporates the ultimate admissibility of evidence as a benchmark, it is clear that FRE 412 should be taken into account in deciding discovery motions on these issues. See Sanchez v. Zabihi, 166 F.R.D. 500, 510-502 (D.N.M. 1996). Indeed, the Advisory Committee

Note to proposed FRE 412 states that "in order not to undermine the rationale of Rule 412, however, courts should enter appropriate orders pursuant to Fed. R. Civ. P. 26(c) to protect the victim against unwarranted inquiries and to ensure confidentiality. Courts should presumptively issue protective orders barring discovery unless the party seeking discovery makes a showing that the evidence sought to be discovered would be relevant[.]" Arguably, the party seeking discovery should also show that the evidence would not be barred by FRE 412, which means that FRE 412 would have the same effect on discovery as privileges.

KEY POINTS

1. FRE 412 severely limits the extent to which a party can introduce evidence of an alleged victim's sexual predisposition or sexual behavior in both criminal and civil cases.
2. FRE 412(a) and (b)(1) prohibit a criminal defendant from introducing such evidence unless it is (1) specific instances of sexual behavior with a third person offered to show the source of semen, injury, or other physical evidence; (2) specific instances of sexual behavior with the defendant offered to show consent; or (3) constitutionally required evidence.
3. In civil cases, evidence of an alleged victim's sexual predisposition or behavior is admissible only if it satisfies the FRE 412(b)(2) reverse FRE 403 balancing test that takes into account both prejudice to a party and harm to the alleged victim.

PROBLEMS

5.44. Return to Problem 5.41 at page 326. To prove that Davis in fact consented to sexual intercourse, the defense seeks to admit the following evidence:
  (a) testimony from Corbin that he and Davis had consensual sexual relations on several prior occasions;
  (b) testimony from three men that they had met Davis at bars and had consensual sex with her;
  (c) testimony that Davis has a reputation in the community for promiscuity;
  (d) testimony from Sue Smith, a friend of Corbin, that at the first bar on the night in question Davis told Smith that she was attracted to Corbin and would like to have sexual relations with him.
Should this evidence be admitted prior to the adoption of FRE 412? Should it be admitted under FRE 412, assuming the defense has complied with the procedural requirements of FRE 412(c)?

5.45. In Problem 5.41, assume that Corbin claims that he did not have the requisite mental state for rape because he reasonably (although perhaps mistakenly) believed that Davis had consented to sexual intercourse. Should any of the evidence be admissible to support his claim prior to the adoption of FRE 412? After its adoption?

5.46. The defendant, a successful banker with no known history of sexual misconduct, is accused of sexually assaulting the teenage daughter of his next door neighbor. He claims that she is falsely accusing him because he threatened to reveal to her parents that she and the defendant's son were having a sexual affair. FRE 412 is applicable. Should the court sustain the prosecution's objection to the defendant's evidence about the alleged victim's sexual affair?

5.47. Dawkins, age 23, has been charged with forcibly raping M.M., a 15-year-old girl. Dawkins claims that he believed M.M. was 18 and that she consented. M.M. will testify about the rape. The medical evidence is inconclusive on the question of whether there had been forcible rape. The prosecution wants to offer evidence that two years ago Dawkins forcibly raped his 12-year-old niece and claimed that she had consented. Dawkins wants to offer evidence that last year M.M. charged Craig Wilson with rape. Assume, alternately, (a) that Wilson is unavailable to testify, (b) that, if permitted, Wilson will testify and deny the rape, and (c) that, if permitted, Wilson and other witnesses will present compelling evidence that the rape charge against Wilson was false. FRE 412-414 are applicable. How should the court rule?

5.48. Frances Meyer, a police officer, has brought sex discrimination hostile work environment action against the police chief, the mayor, and the town of Pleasantville. Her claim includes allegations that pornographic magazines and wall posters were continually on display at the police station despite her objections; that the police chief would regularly relate in her presence the plots of pornographic movies; that he pinched her buttocks; that he continually told her she was "really missing something" by not having sex with him; and that he used lewd language in her presence. The defense is based on the theory that Meyer welcomed or encouraged this type of behavior. For this purpose, the defense offers evidence that Meyer herself told lewd jokes at the police station; that she regularly watched pornographic movies at home; that she was having a very public affair with a married man; that she would talk at the police station about her sexual fantasies; and that on several occasions she had gone to a strip club. FRE 412 is applicable. Should some or all of the defense evidence be admissible?

5.49. Bryan, a 25-year-old superstar basketball player, is charged with felony sexual assault on a 19-year-old woman, Mary, who worked at the front desk in a resort hotel where Bryan was staying. Bryan admits having sex with Mary in his hotel room but asserts it was consensual. Mary asserts that Bryan forced her to have sexual relations and that she said "no" several times. There are no other witnesses to these events.

Mary received a medical examination approximately 15 hours after the encounter with Bryan. The exam revealed some internal injuries that the prosecution claims are consistent with the use of force during sexual relations, although the report of a prosecution expert states that the injuries could also be consistent with consensual sex. Bryan's T-shirt was found to have a small stain of Mary's blood on it. Are the following items of evidence admissible?

(1) In its case in chief, the prosecution offers the testimony of three women as follows: Witness₁ says that ten years ago, she and Bryan were "making out" when he tore her blouse off and fondled her; Witness₂ says that in college she and Bryan were dating and having consensual sex but that several times he was very aggressive and intimidated her into having sexual relations when she didn't want to; Witness₃ says that she met Bryan in a hotel a year ago, flirted with him, and then went to his hotel room where he forced her to have sex.

(2) The defense will ask several witnesses about Mary's sexual activities in the three days before her hospital examination. Their answers will reveal several sexual encounters, possibly including one (based on DNA evidence) after the events with Bryan and before Mary's hospital exam.

(3) For the defense, hospital records showing that Mary was treated for an intentional overdose of a prescribed antidepressant medication one month before the encounter with Bryan, which the defense claims was an "attention-seeking" suicide attempt. (The court would first have to hold that Mary waived her right to keep her medical records private.)

5.50. In the British case, R. v. Funderburk, [1990] 2 All E.R. 482, the defendant responded to statutory rape charges accusing him of having sex with a 13-year-old girl by introducing evidence of the girl's prior sexual encounters with other men. He claimed that he needed this evidence to make the jury properly understand the girl's ability to give a graphic description of the alleged intercourse, as well as to show that the girl had fantasized or transposed her experience of other liaisons to him. The court decided that the British "rape shield" statute (the Sexual Offenses (Amendment) Act of 1976) does not block this evidence. How should a federal court rule on that evidence under FRE 412?

ASSESSMENTS

A-5.1 FRE 404. Defendant is on trial for burglary. At trial, the prosecution attempts to introduce evidence that when the police arrested Defendant at his home, the police also seized a firearm, which had previously been reported as stolen six months prior to the burglary. The prosecution contends that evidence of the stolen firearm makes it more likely Defendant committed the subsequent burglary. Defendant objects that the evidence is inadmissible character evidence. How should the court rule, and why?

A. Sustained. The prosecution's theory of relevance depends on an impermissible character inference.

B. Sustained. Evidence of other crimes is not admissible in criminal cases.

C. Overruled. The evidence is not offered to prove Defendant's character.

D. Overruled. Either party can introduce character evidence in criminal cases.

A-5.2 FRE 404. Plaintiff sues Defendant for negligence, alleging that Defendant, a car mechanic, was negligent in installing a tire in Plaintiff's car. According to Plaintiff, the tire blew out shortly after installation, causing an accident and injuries to Plaintiff. Defendant contends that Plaintiff's negligent driving caused the accident. Defendant attempts to introduce evidence that Plaintiff was involved in another car accident two months after the one at issue in the case, for which Plaintiff received a ticket. Defendant also contends Plaintiffs injuries are the result of this second accident, not the first one. Plaintiff objects that any evidence regarding the second accident is inadmissible under FRE 404 and FRE 403. Which statement most accurately reflects how the court should rule on the objection?

A. The evidence is inadmissible because Defendant's theory of relevance is not listed in FRE 404(b)(2).

B. The evidence is inadmissible under FRE 404(b)(2) because the evidence involves an act that did not occur prior to the events being litigated.

C. The evidence is inadmissible because this is a civil case.

D. The evidence is relevant for both a permissible purpose under 404(b)(2) and for an impermissible character purpose. Admissibility will depend on an application of FRE 403.

A-5.3 FRE 406. In a products liability suit against a drug manufacturer, Defendant claims that it is not liable because its sales representative fully informed the treating doctor of the dangers associated with the drug. Defendant offers the testimony of the sales representative that he always discusses the dangers of the drug in question with physicians; that the discussions include information about a particular study detailing the dangers; and that the presentations to physicians would "go virtually the same way every time." Moreover, he estimates that he has made approximately 20 or 25 such presentations. Plaintiff objects that this is inadmissible character evidence. How is the court likely to rule, and why?

A. The evidence is admissible as habit evidence.

B. The evidence is admissible as character evidence.

C. The evidence is inadmissible character evidence.

D. The evidence is inadmissible under FRE 403.

A-5.4. FRE 404-05. Defendant has been charged with committing perjury before a federal grand jury. As part of its case-in-chief at trial, the prosecutor offers the following evidence:

(1) Witness$_1$'s testimony that he knows of at least five occasions on which Defendant has lied.

(2) Witness$_2$'s testimony that Defendant has a reputation in the community for dishonesty.

How should the court rule on these two items of evidence?

A. Both are admissible.

B. (1) is admissible but (2) is inadmissible.

C. (2) is admissible but (1) is inadmissible.

D. Both are inadmissible.

A-5.5. FRE 413-14. New State legislates a rule that mandates admission of the defendant's prior sexual misconduct as evidence of guilt in any trial involving accusations of rape, sexual assault, or child molestation, while giving courts no discretion to exclude such evidence due to its prejudicial effect on or confusion of the jury. This rule likely violates constitutional due process. TRUE or FALSE?

ANSWERS

A-5.1. The best answer is **A**. The evidence makes it more likely Defendant committed the burglary by relying on an implicit character inference. There is no evidence the firearm was even used in the burglary. The theory of relevance depends on an inference about Defendant's general propensity for crime. Therefore, C is incorrect (assuming the above theory of relevance). B is incorrect because evidence of other crimes is sometime admissible in criminal cases (so long as it doesn't violate the character rules). D is incorrect because none of the exceptions that would allow the prosecution to introduce character evidence (for example, those involving homicide, sexual assault, or witnesses) apply in this case.

A-5.2. The best answer is **D**. There is a non-character theory of relevance for this evidence (i.e., the cause of Plaintiff's injury) and a character theory of relevance (i.e., the second accident makes it more likely Plaintiff is a negligent driver and drove negligently on the occasion at issue). Therefore, admissibility of the evidence, and how many details to admit, will depend on an application of FRE 403. A is incorrect because FRE 404(b)(2) does not require that the theory of relevance fit one of the enumerated categories—any non-character theory will do. B is incorrect because FRE 404(b)(2) does not require that the "other acts" must have occurred prior to the litigate events; relevant acts occurring after the litigated events are also potentially admissible. C is incorrect because FRE 404(b)(2) evidence is permitted in civil cases as well as in criminal cases.

A-5.3. The best answer is **A**. The evidence is specific enough and involves a sufficient number of incidents to qualify as habit (as opposed to character) evidence. Therefore, B and C are incorrect. (If the evidence were character evidence, it would be inadmissible to prove the representative's conduct on the particular occasion.) D is unlikely because the probative value of this evidence appears to be high and there do not appear to be any countervailing FRE 403 dangers.

A-5.4. The best answer is **D**. Because Defendant has not "opened the door" by introducing character evidence, the prosecution may not introduce evidence about Defendant's character for truthfulness. Therefore, A, B, and C are incorrect. If an exception to the general ban character evidence applied, then the prosecution would be limited to reputation or opinion evidence on direct (in which case, (2) but not (1) would be admissible).

A-5.5. TRUE. The trial court's discretion to exclude overwhelmingly prejudicial past-crime evidence is what makes FRE 413-414 and their state equivalents constitutional, as emphasized by several circuit court decisions (cited above).

CHAPTER SIX

THE OTHER RELEVANCE RULES

In Chapter Five we noted that the Federal Rules—like the common law—have a variety of rules, sometimes referred to as "relevance rules," which exclude relevant evidence. In Chapter Five we discussed the relevance rules regulating character evidence. Our focus in this chapter will be on relevance rules that make evidence inadmissible to prove fault or liability, but that permit such evidence for other purposes. FRE 407-409, 411. What unites these rules is that they exclude relevant evidence, in part, to encourage various types of out-of-court conduct, deemed socially desirable, and to serve policy goals external to the goal of accurate factfinding at trial. We conclude the chapter with a discussion of FRE 410, which makes inadmissible certain evidence relating to guilty pleas.

A. INADMISSIBLE TO PROVE "NEGLIGENCE," "CULPABLE CONDUCT," OR "LIABILITY"

The Federal Rules preclude evidence of subsequent remedial measures (FRE 407), compromises and offers of compromise (FRE 408), payment of medical and other similar expenses (FRE 409), and liability insurance (FRE 411) to prove fault or liability. These rules do not exclude evidence altogether. Rather, they prohibit the proponent from offering the evidence to prove liability or fault. For example, FRE 408, which prohibits offer-of-compromise evidence for this purpose, acknowledges that offers of compromise may be admissible for other purposes, such as showing the bias of a witness. Thus, as with the character evidence rules we examined in Chapter Five—and as you will see with the impeachment and hearsay rules we examine in Chapters Seven and Eight—your analysis of admissibility must always begin with the question of relevance: *What* is the proponent of the evidence trying to prove; *what* is the proponent's theory of relevance? Only after you answer these questions will you be able to apply FRE 407, 408, 409, or 411.

If the answer to the relevance inquiry is that there is both a permissible and an impermissible purpose for which the proponent may wish to offer the evidence, admissibility of the evidence will depend on the application of FRE 403: Is the probative value of the evidence for the permissible purpose substantially outweighed by the risk that the jury may consider the evidence for the impermissible purpose? If the answer is no (i.e., if the answer is that the evidence is admissible), the party against whom the evidence is admitted will be entitled to a limiting instruction pursuant to FRE 105.

1. FRE 407

FRE 407.   SUBSEQUENT REMEDIAL MEASURES

When measures are taken that would have made an earlier injury or harm less likely to occur, evidence of the subsequent measures is not admissible to prove:

- negligence;
- culpable conduct;
- a defect in a product or its design; or
- a need for a warning or instruction.

But the court may admit this evidence for another purpose, such as impeachment or—if disputed—proving ownership, control, or the feasibility of precautionary measures.

2. Explanation of FRE 407

a. The Exclusionary Mandate

The Inference of Negligence or Culpable Conduct.   When a person alters a condition or object that caused an injury and the change could make future injury less likely, one possible inference to draw from the remedial action is that the person who made the alteration believed that the object or condition before the alteration posed an unreasonable risk of injury. If we know that the person (or organization) responsible for the object or condition had this belief, it is more likely that the object or condition did create an unreasonable risk of injury than if we knew nothing about the person's belief. Indeed, pursuant to this theory of relevance, when a party to an action takes subsequent remedial action, it is equivalent to a recognition or implicit acknowledgment of fault. Diagram 6-1 illustrates this reasoning.

There is, however, an alternative explanation. The person (or organization) may have carried out the remedial measure to improve safety conditions that were not inadequate. That scenario involves no acknowledgment of fault whatsoever. To paraphrase Baron Bramwell's saying in Hart v. Lancashire & Yorkshire Ry. Co., 21 L.T.R. N.S. 261, 263 (1869), "because the world gets wiser as it gets older," it doesn't

Diagram 6-1

EVIDENCE →FOC→	FOC →	FOC →	FOC (EE) →
Eyewitness testifies that, after an accident in which a toy rifle discharged, the manufacturer designed a safety catch for the toy.	Manufacturer did design a safety catch for a toy rifle after an accident.		
	Manufacturer believed that the toy rifle created an unreasonable risk of injury without the safety catch.	The toy rifle did create an unreasonable risk of injury without the safety catch.	TThe manufacturer was negligent in producing the toy rifle without the safety catch (alternatively, the toy rifle was a defective product prior to the safety catch's installation).

mean that "it was foolish before." Subsequent remedial measures evidence is therefore inherently ambiguous. More often than not, its contribution to factfinding would be minimal. At the same time, allowing tort plaintiffs to use such evidence as proof of the defendant's acknowledgment of fault would discourage individuals and firms from implementing subsequent remedial measures. This twin vice of evidentiary ambiguity and the potential chilling of socially desirable conduct justifies the exclusionary mandate of FRE 407. Flaminio v. Honda Motor Company, Ltd., 733 F.2d 463 (7th Cir. 1984). In addition to negligence and culpable conduct, FRE 407's exclusionary mandate extends to subsequent remedial measures offered to prove product defects and the need for a warning or instruction.

Activities That May Be Subsequent Remedial Measures. A subsequent remedial measure includes any action that a person takes after a damaging event that reduces the likelihood of the event's reoccurrence. It may include, for example, an employer's change in its promotion policy, Hamilton v. New York, 627 F.3d 50, 53 (2d Cir. 2010) (evidence employer changed promotion policy to involve more individuals to "help prevent unsuccessful candidates from feeling as if they were unfairly passed over" excluded as a subsequent remedial measure in employment-discrimination case); sending a memorandum to employees urging them to observe safety regulations, First Security Bank v. Union Pac. R. Co., 152 F.3d 877 (8th Cir. 1998) (admonishing employees about location of rail cars in relation to crossing); altering the design of a product, Flaminio v. Honda Motor Co. 733 F.2d 463 (7th Cir. 1984) (motorcycle design); repairing or altering the condition of property, Knight v. Otis Elevator Co., 596 F.2d 84 (3d Cir. 1979) (placing "guards" around elevator buttons); disciplining or firing an individual whose alleged negligence was responsible for an accident, Specht v. Jensen, 863 F.2d 700 (10th Cir. 1988) (disciplining police officers for violation of Fourth Amendment); Hull v. Chevron U.S.A., Inc. 812 F.2d 584 (10th Cir. 1987) (firing forklift operator following accident); sending a recall notice, Chase v. General Motors Corp., 856 F.2d 17 (4th Cir. 1988) (recall of cars manufactured before design change); changing rules or regulations, Ford v. Schmidt, 577 F.2d 408 (7th Cir. 1978) (change in prison regulations); or posting warning signs, In re Joint Asbestos Litigation, 995 F.2d 343 (2d Cir. 1993) (posting warning sign on asbestos product); Tuer v. McDonald, 684 A.2d 478 (Md. 1996), decided under a Maryland rule identical to FRE 407 (changing medical protocols for treating patients with anticoagulants).

There Is No Intent or Motive Requirement. FRE 407 applies to measures that would have made earlier injuries less likely had the measures been implemented before the injuries. The inferences prohibited by FRE 407—from subsequent action to negligence, culpable conduct, defect, or the need for a warning—depend on beliefs by those engaging in subsequent actions that prior conditions were unreasonably dangerous. In other words, without these beliefs, the evidence is irrelevant for proving the prohibited purposes. David P. Leonard, The New Wigmore §2.2 (2002) ("Relevancy is assumed on the basis that the evidence constitutes a recognition of fault by the party whose conduct is in question."). In applying FRE 407's exclusionary mandate, however, there is no additional requirement that the subsequent actions were done with the proven intent or motive to prevent future injuries or to make conditions safer. See Chlopek v. Federal Ins. Co., 499 F.3d 692, 700 (7th Cir. 2007) (rejecting argument that a change in a warning was not "remedial" because it was not prompted by safety concerns: "motive for making the change is irrelevant.").

The Effectiveness of the Remedial Action. Courts rarely focus on how effective a remedial measure would have been in making earlier injury or harm less likely. For example, courts readily accept that firing an employee can be a subsequent remedial measure within the meaning of FRE 407 without examining whether the action is likely to reduce the chance of future accidents. There is, however, precedent for the proposition that FRE 407 does not apply to investigations that are not "remedial" but only "initial steps toward ascertaining whether any remedial measures are called for." Fasanaro v. Mooney Aircraft Corp., 687 F. Supp. 482, 487 (N.D. Cal. 1988); Fox v. Kramer, 994 P.2d 343 (Cal. 2000) (accepting the prevalent view that doctors' peer review and other investigative procedures are not "subsequent remedial measures"). Compare Rocky Mountain Helicopters, Inc. v. Bell Helicopters, 805 F.2d 907, 918 (10th Cir. 1986) (investigative reports not subsequent remedial measures) with Maddox v. Los Angeles, 792 F.2d 1408, 1417 (9th Cir. 1986) ("investigation and measures taken were remedial measures").

The Timing of the Remedial Action. For evidence of a remedial measure to be inadmissible under FRE 407, it must occur after "an earlier injury or harm." The purpose of this language, according to the Advisory Committee Note, is to make it clear that "the rule applies only to changes made after the occurrence that produced the damages giving rise to the action." Thus, if the defendant changed a product design after the plaintiff was injured, FRE 407 would apply to prevent the plaintiff from introducing evidence of the design change to show defect. On the other hand, if the defendant took the remedial action subsequent to the injuries of several other people but prior to the plaintiff's injury, FRE 407 would not preclude admissibility of the design change. Trull v. Volkswagon, Inc., 187 F.3d 88 (1st Cir. 1999). In appropriate cases, however, the court may still exclude such evidence pursuant to FRE 403.

Remedial Actions Mandated by the Law and Government Agencies. Compliance with a statute, regulation, or a government agency's requirement is not a "remedial" measure. Such compliance is primarily motivated by the person's or the firm's desire to avoid penalty rather than to fix a safety problem. Furthermore, penalties for noncompliance sufficiently incentivize individuals and firms to take the mandated actions. This "stick" renders the FRE 407 "carrot" redundant and, consequently, inapplicable. See O'Dell v. Hercules, Inc., 904 F.2d 1194, 1204 (8th Cir. 1990) ("An exception to Rule 407 is recognized for evidence of remedial action mandated by superior governmental authority or undertaken by a third party because the policy goal of encouraging remediation would not necessarily be furthered by exclusion of such evidence."). Compliance evidence, however, would normally be irrelevant as proof of negligence, fault, or a product defect.

b. Permissible Uses of Subsequent-Remedial-Measure Evidence

FRE 407 makes it clear that subsequent-remedial-measure evidence may be admissible for other purposes. As with FRE 404(b), the list of permissible purposes in FRE 407 is not exclusive. Subject to FRE 403 and other exclusionary rules, subsequent-remedial-measure evidence may be admissible for *any* purpose other than to show negligence, culpable conduct, defect, or the need for a warning or instruction.

The purposes listed in the second sentence of FRE 407 are the permissible purposes for which subsequent-remedial-measure evidence is most likely to be relevant. For example, the fact that the defendant repaired a staircase suggests that the defendant was the owner of the building containing the staircase or that the defendant, rather than somebody else, had control over the staircase and was responsible for keeping it in good order. Cf. Lee v. E.I. Dupont, 249 F.3d 362 (5th Cir. 2001) (subsequent design change to scaffold admissible against defendant to show that defendant rather than plaintiff's employer was responsible for maintaining the scaffold). If a defendant testifies that the staircase was in good condition at the time of the accident, the fact that the defendant had repaired or authorized the repair of the staircase is relevant to impeach the defendant's credibility: Making or authorizing the repair seems inconsistent with the witness's testimony that the staircase was safe at the time of the accident. Cf. Anderson v. Malloy, 700 F.2d 1208 (8th Cir. 1983) (in rape victim's negligence action against motel operator, defendant testified that safety chains and peep holes on doors would only provide false sense of security and that everything necessary for security had been done; plaintiff permitted to show subsequent installation of safety chains and peep holes both to show feasibility and to impeach defendant).

Finally, as we suggested previously, taking subsequent remedial action may rebut a defendant's claim that it was not feasible to maintain the staircase in a safer condition. Cf. Dixon v. International Harvester Co., 754 F.2d 573 (10th Cir. 1985) (defendant claimed additional protective metal on logging vehicle not feasible because it would impair vision; evidence of subsequent installation of protective metal on similar vehicles held admissible). Importantly, however, when a defendant testifies that he acted according to the then-applicable safety standards, his denial of the negligence allegations cannot be interpreted as disputing the feasibility of the safety improvements that he subsequently implemented. For the FRE 407 exception to apply, the defendant must argue that those improvements were not feasible at the time of the accident. Tuer v. McDonald, 684 A.2d 478 (Md. 1996).

c. The "If Disputed" Requirement

Even if the "if disputed" phrase did not appear in FRE 407, FRE 403 should be a basis for excluding evidence of a subsequent remedial measure offered to prove an issue that is not disputed. By the terms of the rule, the "if disputed" phrase does not apply to evidence offered for impeachment. There is no need for it to do so. Impeachment evidence is evidence offered to undermine the credibility of a witness, and every witness's credibility is regarded as a matter that can be disputed. See FRE 611(b). Prior to the 2011 restyling amendments to the FRE, the "if disputed" requirement was phrased as "if controverted," and therefore prior judicial opinions applying FRE 407 will use the "if controverted" language.

d. The Relationship Between FRE 407 and FRE 403

When a party offers subsequent-remedial-measure evidence for a legitimate, disputed purpose, the question of admissibility in theory should turn on the applicability of FRE 403: Is the probative value of the evidence for the legitimate purpose (e.g., feasibility) substantially outweighed by the possibility that the jurors may use the evidence for the impermissible purpose of inferring negligence or other culpable conduct? In fact, if subsequent-remedial-measure evidence is relevant to prove some contested issue other than negligence, culpable conduct, defect, or need for a warning, the result almost invariably is that the evidence is admissible. Christopher B. Mueller and Laird C. Kirkpatrick, Federal Evidence §130 (2d ed. 1994). If so, the party against whom the evidence is admitted is entitled to a limiting instruction pursuant to FRE 105.

Courts, however, do sometimes rely on FRE 403 to exclude evidence that does not fit within FRE 407's language but that may raise similar policy concerns. See, e.g., Bogosian v. Mercedes Benz, Inc., 104 F.3d 472 (1st Cir 1997) (excluding evidence of modifications made to a product after purchase by plaintiff, but before injury, because jurors may overestimate probative value).

3. Elaboration of FRE 407

a. The Rationales for FRE 407

There are four rationales for FRE 407. Some of them also apply to other rules — FRE 408 (offers of compromise), 409 (medical expenses), and 411 (liability insurance) — that exclude evidence to prove negligence, liability, or culpable conduct. We discuss these other rules later in this chapter.

Low Probative Value.   First, as we already mentioned, the evidence may have relatively low probative value because of its ambiguity. Although a defendant may have engaged in subsequent measures to remedy prior negligence, culpability, defect, or the need for a warning, the defendant may have engaged in the same conduct for a variety of other reasons. For example, a defendant may take subsequent remedial action to make a product safer out of an abundance of caution even though there was no negligence or design defect at the time of an injury. (Indeed, the injury or harm at issue may have revealed information for making conditions safer, which the defendant could not have reasonably foreseen beforehand.) The defendant may also undertake subsequent changes for reasons unrelated to improving safety. Similarly, a party may offer to settle a claim (FRE 408) in order to avoid litigation costs, not because the party is at fault.

Countervailing FRE 403 Factors. Second, countervailing FRE 403 considerations may warrant exclusion. These considerations include a concern that admission of the evidence to prove negligence or fault may tend to mislead the jury. Jurors may reasonably expect that the evidence they hear has a bearing on what they are supposed to decide. Thus, if they hear evidence that in fact has low probative value, they may be misled into thinking that the evidence is more probative than it really is. Moreover, jurors may overestimate the probative value of the evidence because of "hindsight bias." Jurors who learn that a defendant responded to an accident or injury by making changes may overestimate how likely the defendant should reasonably have foreseen the accident or injury ahead of time. See Dan M. Kahan, The Economics—Conventional, Behavioral, and Political—of "Subsequent Remedial Measures" Evidence, 110 Colum. L. Rev. 1616 (2010).

Although jurors may overestimate the probative value of evidence of subsequent remedial measures (and this overvaluation may contribute to erroneous decisions), keep in mind that depriving jurors of relevant and probative remedial evidence may also contribute to erroneous decisions.

Not Discouraging Desirable Conduct. Third, the rules excluding evidence to prove liability or fault traditionally have been justified on the ground that we do not want to discourage individuals from engaging in socially desirable conduct such as making conditions and products safer. In this respect, these rules are similar to some rules of privilege. We exclude evidence of confidential communications between lawyers and clients in part because we do not want to discourage clients from being candid when they consult lawyers for legal advice. Similarly, we exclude evidence of subsequent remedial measures, offers of compromise (FRE 408), payment of medical expenses (FRE 409), and maintaining liability insurance (FRE 411) to prove fault, in part because we do not want to discourage individuals from engaging in these types of socially desirable conduct.

Consider whether this justification provides a sufficient basis for excluding relevant evidence. To what extent do you think individuals take into account—or even know—the rules of evidence in making decisions about subsequent remedial measures, offers of compromise, or payments of medical expenses? Would you distinguish in this context between individuals and firms? (The answers may depend to a substantial extent on whether the individual has sought the advice of counsel before engaging in the activity.)

Not Punishing Desirable Conduct. A fourth rationale for these rules is that—regardless of low probative value, misleading the jury, or deterring socially desirable conduct—we do not want to punish or disadvantage individuals for doing good things. This rationale is most frequently associated with the exclusionary rule for payment of medical expenses, sometimes referred to as the "good Samaritan" rule. We suggest, however, that the rationale is equally applicable to—and perhaps more compelling than the deterrence rationale for—the limitations on the use of remedial measures, offers to compromise, and insurance.

b. Subsequent Remedial Measures by Third Persons

Courts frequently admit evidence of remedial measures taken by persons other than the party against whom the evidence is offered. See Diehl v. Blaw-Knox, 360 F.3d 426, 430 (3d Cir. 2004) (following plaintiff's injury, employer modified piece of road-widening equipment that injured plaintiff; evidence of modification admissible against manufacturer of equipment); Mehojah v. Drummond, 56 F.3d 1213 (10th Cir. 1995) (suit against ranch by couple whose automobile struck cattle on highway; FRE 407 not applicable to subsequent installation of fence by owner of land leased to ranch); Pau v. Yosemite Park & Curry Co., 928 F.2d 880 (9th Cir. 1991) (suit against bike rental company following fatal accident on National Park trail; evidence that Park Service posted sign prohibiting bikes following the accident not precluded by FRE 407); but see In re Air Crash Disaster, 86 F.3d 498 (6th Cir. 1996).

KEY POINTS

1. FRE 407 makes evidence of subsequent remedial measures inadmissible to prove negligence, culpable conduct, defect in a product, or need for a warning or instruction.
2. FRE 407's exclusionary mandate applies only to remedial action taken after the event that is the subject of the litigation.
3. Subject to FRE 403, subsequent-remedial-measure evidence may be admissible for other purposes, the most likely of which are those listed in FRE 407: to show ownership, control, feasibility, or to impeach the credibility of a witness. The evidence should be admissible for these other purposes only if they are disputed issues in the case.

PROBLEMS

6.1. Return to Problem 3.2 at page 148. Assume that six months ago the San Ramon School District adopted a policy requiring all of its bus drivers to take a special driver education course each year. Will the plaintiff be able to admit evidence of this policy adoption?

6.2. Return to Problem 3.12 at page 168. The plaintiff, Cynthia Richards, offers evidence that shortly after the accident the Kmart supervisor who testified during discovery required store employees to walk the aisles every 15 minutes to look for clutter on the floor. Can you articulate a theory of relevance for this evidence? For the theory of relevance you have identified, should the evidence be excluded under FRE 407?

Would your answers change if the supervisor testifies at trial: "At the time of Ms. Richards's accident our store was very safe; no policy of patrolling the store was necessary because our employees always picked up clutter in the aisles immediately"? Again try to articulate a theory of relevance for this evidence and explain whether it should be excluded under FRE 407.

6.3. Lisa Evans is suing the Jones Manufacturing Co. for the wrongful death of her husband, Edward. Edward suffered injuries that resulted in his death when a coworker turned on an industrial baling machine, manufactured by the defendant, when Edward was inside the hopper attempting to clear a jam. Lisa wishes to introduce evidence that after Edward's death

(a) Jones Manufacturing Co. fired the individual responsible for designing safety features on the baler; and

(b) Edward's employer, Loman Industries, modified the baler by installing an access door to the hopper and by making the baler inoperable when the access doors were open.

Jones objects that both items of evidence should be excluded under FRE 407. Should Jones's objections be sustained?

6.4. Eugene Wright is suing the Loop Ladder Co. for personal injuries that he received when a ladder on which he had been standing fell to the ground with him on it. Eugene claims that a plastic tip on the ladder was too weak and that it broke, causing the ladder to fall. The defendant claims that the plastic tip broke from the impact of the fall or at some later time. An expert witness testifies for the defendant that the tip was adequate for its purpose. Plaintiff offers evidence that shortly after his accident, the Loop Ladder Company substituted a strengthened plastic cap on all of its ladders. Should this evidence be excluded under FRE 407? Would it make any difference in your analysis if the expert were a Loop employee who had authorized the change in the plastic tip?

6.5. Return to Problem 5.22 at page 307. Consider the admissibility of the following evidence against Acme:

(a) testimony that following the incident involving Henry, Acme hired outside consultants to prepare a report on the safety of its cleanser;

(b) the consultants' post-accident report analyzing the toxicity of the cleanser;

(c) testimony that following the report Acme reduced the toxicity of its cleanser formula.

Would any of your answers change if an Acme executive had testified, "There is nothing safer than Acme Cleanser"?

3. FRE 408

RULE 408. COMPROMISE OFFERS AND NEGOTIATIONS

(a) Prohibited Uses. Evidence of the following is not admissible—on behalf of any party—either to prove or disprove the validity or amount of a disputed claim or to impeach by a prior inconsistent statement or a contradiction:

(1) furnishing, promising, or offering—or accepting, promising to accept, or offering to accept—a valuable consideration in compromising or attempting to compromise the claim; and

(2) conduct or a statement made during compromise negotiations about the claim—except when offered in a criminal case and when the

negotiations related to a claim by a public office in the exercise of its regulatory, investigative, or enforcement authority.

(b) *Exceptions.* The court may admit this evidence for another purpose, such as proving a witness's bias or prejudice, negating a contention of undue delay, or proving an effort to obstruct a criminal investigation or prosecution.

4. Explanation of FRE 408

a. *The Exclusionary Mandate; Permissible Uses; FRE 403*

One plausible inference to draw from offers of compromise is that the offerors—like people who take subsequent remedial action—believe they were at fault in the incident giving rise to a claim against them. If they have this belief, one can then make the further inference that they were in fact at fault. In short, one way in which compromising or offering to compromise a claim is relevant is as a tacit recognition of fault or liability.

As is the case with subsequent-remedial-measure evidence, there are other possible explanations for wanting to compromise a claim. For example, some individuals who adamantly believe they are not at fault may be willing to settle a claim because their potential litigation costs are too high or because their involvement in the litigation may hurt their business or reputation.

The FRE 408 exclusionary mandate and its exceptions are the equivalent of the two sentences in FRE 407. To encourage settlements, FRE 408 excludes evidence of compromises and of offers to compromise on the questions of liability for or the amount of claims. At the same time, the rule makes it clear that such evidence may be admissible for other purposes. The list of other purposes, which is not exclusive, includes the purposes for which offers of compromise are most likely to be relevant. For example, to show the bias of a witness who testifies for the plaintiff, the defendant may want to establish that the witness had previously settled a similar claim with the defendant for less than the witness had wanted, see Croskey v. BMW of North America, Inc., 532 F.3d 511, 519 (6th Cir. 2008), or that the witness's claim against the plaintiff includes a provision for the plaintiff to pay to the witness a portion of any judgment obtained against the defendant, see Brocklesby v. United States, 767 F.2d 1288 (9th Cir. 1985). More contestably, a municipality's settlement of a police brutality action may be admissible to show that the municipality knew of and condoned the officer's conduct. Spell v. McDaniel, 824 F.2d 1380 (4th Cir. 1987). Proof of negotiations and offers to compromise may indicate that a party was acting in good faith to resolve a claim and thus rebut a charge of undue delay, Californian & Hawaiian Sugar Co. v. Kansas City Terminal Warehouse Co., 602 F. Supp. 183 (W.D. Mo. 1985), or was acting in bad faith, Athey v. Farmers Ins. Exch., 234 F.3d 357 (8th Cir. 2000) (compromise negotiations admissible to show bad faith in negotiating); Bankcard Am., Inc. v. Universal Bancard Sys., Inc., 203 F.3d 477, 484 (7th Cir. 2000) ("It would be an abuse of Rule 408 to allow one party during compromise negotiations to lead his opponent to believe he will not enforce applicable time limitations and then object when the opponent attempts to prove the waiver of time limitations").

Offers of compromise during an income tax audit may be admissible to show the taxpayer's knowledge and to rebut a claim of good faith in a tax evasion prosecution. United States v. Hauert, 40 F.3d 197 (7th Cir. 1994). Compromise evidence may also be admissible to prove "absence of mistake" or that an event was not an "isolated incident." See Orr v. Albuquerque, 531 F.3d 1210, 1219 (10th Cir. 2008) (compromise evidence admissible to prove that "Ms. Vigil's treatment of Officers Orr and Paiz was not a random accident, as defendants claim, but part of a larger and deliberate pattern of treating pregnant women differently from other employees.").

FRE 408 also prohibits using compromise evidence to impeach a witness "by a prior inconsistent statement or a contradiction." Such uses of compromise evidence, according to the Advisory Committee, "would tend to swallow the exclusionary rule and would impair the public policy of promoting settlements."

Unlike FRE 407, FRE 408(b) does not contain "if disputed" language in specifying permissible uses. Nonetheless, in order to have sufficient probative value to overcome an FRE 403 objection, the purpose for which the evidence is offered should be a disputed issue in the case.

b. Conduct or Statements Made During Negotiations

FRE 408 excludes not only compromises and offers of compromise but also — at least in civil actions — conduct or statements made during compromise negotiations. (We discuss FRE 408 and criminal prosecutions in subsection d.) This is a significant departure from the common law rule, which excluded only statements of offer and acceptance. Consider, for example, a situation in which Amy and John are involved in an automobile accident. Amy threatens to sue, asserting that John was at fault and must pay for the damage to Amy's car. In response, John says:

(1) "Let's settle this matter ourselves so we don't have to pay fat fees to lawyers. I'll give you $500 and we'll call everything even."

Alternatively, he says:

(2) "There's no need to deal with lawyers, who'll demand a fat fee. This was my fault. I'll give you $500 and we'll call everything even."

Assume that Amy rejects the settlement offer and sues John. Both the common law and FRE 408 would preclude use of the offers of compromise against John to prove liability. The common law, but not FRE 408, would permit Amy to use John's acknowledgment of fault in the second statement to prove liability.

c. The "Disputed Claim" Requirement

Offers of compromise and statements of fault are inadmissible pursuant to FRE 408 only if made during compromise negotiations over a disputed claim. If there is no disputed claim or if the statement of fault occurs outside the context of compromise negotiations, the statement of fault will be admissible. For example, in the preceding hypothetical if John made the offer and statement of fault before Amy made any claim, the statement would be admissible. Big O Tire Dealers, Inc. v. Goodyear Tire & Rubber Co., 561 F.2d 1365, 1372-1373 (10th Cir. 1977) (statements admissible as "business communications"; "discussions had not crystallized to the point of threatened litigation"). If John conceded full liability and was not attempting to reach a compromise, his statements also would be admissible. Perzinski v. Chevron Chem. Co., 503 F.2d 654 (7th Cir. 1974) (salesperson's statement that company would "take care of" plaintiff admissible).

In applying FRE 408, the trial judge must usually decide some preliminary questions of fact. What type of information is likely to be important to the preliminary question whether there is a disputed claim and a legitimate attempt to compromise that claim? Reconsider whether John's initial two statements, which we characterized as having been made after Amy threatened to sue, would be admissible under the following circumstances:

(a) There had been no threat to sue.
(b) The threat had been a spontaneous outburst at the time of the accident.
(c) The possible suit had been mentioned in the context of a polite but restrained conversation between Amy and John about various options available to them.
(d) The value of Amy's claim did not exceed $500. (Does it matter whether John or a reasonable person would probably have been aware of this fact?)

To what extent are the foregoing factors relevant to the judge's decision whether Amy and John were engaged in compromise negotiations over a disputed claim?

The answer to the foregoing question, of course, depends in part on how courts interpret "a disputed claim," and the courts of appeals provide varying answers. For example, compare Blu-J, Inc. v. Kemper C.P.A. Group, 916 F.2d 637, 642 (11th Cir. 1990) (FRE 408 exclusionary rule applies to "statements or conduct . . . intended to be part of the negotiations toward compromise") with Big O Tire Dealers v. Goodyear Tire & Rubber Co., supra at 1373 (FRE 408 exclusionary rule applies only after discussions "crystalize to the point of threatening litigation").

d. The Applicability of FRE 408 to Criminal Cases

If a person admits some wrongdoing in the course of negotiations to settle a civil claim, may the prosecution use the statement against the wrongdoer in a subsequent criminal prosecution? FRE 408 prohibits the use of compromises and offers and acceptances in criminal prosecutions, but it creates a limited exception to the general prohibition against the use of *conduct or a statement made during compromise negotiations*. The exception—that is, the right to use in criminal prosecutions conduct and statements made during civil compromise negotiations—exists when "negotiations related to a claim by a public office in the exercise of its regulatory, investigative, or enforcement authority." To illustrate a factual scenario that fits the scope of this exception, the Advisory Committee cited United States v. Prewitt, 34 F.3d 436, 439 (7th Cir. 1994). *Prewitt* was a mail fraud prosecution in which the court upheld the admissibility of statements of fault made during the compromise of a civil securities enforcement action. According to the Advisory Committee, "Where an individual makes a statement in the presence of government agents, its subsequent admission in a criminal case should not be unexpected."

e. A Party's Own Offer of Compromise

In Pierce v. F.R. Tripler & Co., 955 F.2d 820, 828 (2d Cir. 1992), the court held that FRE 408 applies to a party's effort to introduce its own offer of compromise. *Pierce* was an age discrimination suit in which the defendant, to show mitigation of damages, sought to introduce its offer of a job to the plaintiff. Although the purpose of the offer was to contest the amount of a claim, the defendant had argued that the policies underlying FRE 408 were inapplicable when a party sought to introduce evidence of its own offer of compromise. The "on behalf of any party" language in FRE 408 was intended to codify the result in *Pierce*. The Advisory Committee offered two reasons for the amendment. First, the offeror's revealing its own offer could "reveal the fact that the adversary entered into settlement negotiations," which would undermine the policy of FRE 408. Second, "proof of statements and offers made in settlement would often have to be made through the testimony of attorneys, leading to the risks and costs of disqualification." There is yet another, possibly more compelling, reason for suppressing "own settlement offer" evidence under FRE 408 or 403. Making such evidence admissible would motivate parties to make unattractive settlement offers strategically in order to use them as evidence in a subsequent litigation. This strategic behavior would impede settlements while unnecessarily increasing the cost of settlement negotiations for all parties involved. See generally Gideon Parchomovsky & Alex Stein, The Distortionary Effect of Evidence on Primary Behavior, 124 Harv. L. Rev. 518 (2010).

f. Compromises and Offers of Compromises by Third Persons

Consider a case in which the plaintiff sues the defendant, a restaurant, for food poisoning. The plaintiff claims that the restaurant was responsible for mishandling the food. The defendant seeks to introduce evidence that it had made a claim against its food supplier for $300,000, and that the supplier had settled the claim for $250,000. The defendant argues that the settlement evidence is an admission by the supplier that the supplier provided the restaurant with adulterated food, and that the adulteration—not the defendant's alleged mishandling of the food—was responsible for the food poisoning. Assume that the court must decide this case under the negligence rule, rather than the doctrine of strict liability for defective products.

Just as we suggested that evidence of a third person's subsequent remedial measure does not implicate the policies underlying FRE 407 (see page 365, supra), evidence of a third person's offer of compromise does not implicate the policies underlying FRE 408. The negotiations and settlement have nothing to do with the party against whom the evidence is offered, and it will be adequate protection for the third person to exclude the evidence if and when the third person becomes a party. Courts, however, have taken different approaches for compromise evidence involving distinct claims and third parties. Compare Towerridge, Inc. v. T.A.O., Inc., 11 F.3d 758, 770 (10th

Cir. 1997) ("Rule 408 does not require the exclusion of evidence regarding the settlement of a claim different from the one litigated") with C&E Serv., Inc. v. Ashland, Inc., 539 F. Supp. 2d 316, 320 (D.D.C. 2008) ("The very policy of Rule 408 would be defeated if it did not operate to preclude the admissibility of settlement negotiations in a case involving another party or another claim.").

5. FRE 409

RULE 409.   OFFERS TO PAY MEDICAL AND SIMILAR EXPENSES

Evidence of furnishing, promising to pay, or offering to pay medical, hospital, or similar expenses resulting from an injury is not admissible to prove liability for the injury.

6. Explanation of FRE 409

a. The Exclusionary Mandate

Just as evidence of a subsequent repair or an offer to compromise may be relevant as a recognition of fault, paying or offering to pay another person's medical expenses may be relevant for similar reasons: The payments may imply that those paying believe they are legally responsible for the injuries.

For reasons similar to Rules 407 and 408, FRE 409 excludes such evidence to prove liability. For example, if a driver hits a pedestrian and offers to pay the pedestrian's medical expenses, neither the offer nor the payment is admissible to prove the driver's liability. Similarly, if an insurance company pays a person's medical expenses before any trial or settlement, evidence of the payment is not subsequently admissible to prove the insurance company's liability. See Galarnyk v. Hostmart Mgmt., 55 Fed. Appx. 763 (7th Cir. 2003) (plaintiff "fell in the bathroom of [a motel], converting gravitational energy to kinetic energy with such effectiveness that he punched a hole in the wall"; offers by defendant and defendant's insurance carrier to pay medical expenses not admissible to show liability).

b. The Admissibility of Statements Made in Conjunction with Medical and Similar Payments

In one significant respect FRE 409 differs from FRE 408: Statements made in conjunction with the payments—including statements of fault—are *not* excluded. According to the Advisory Committee:

> This difference in treatment arises from fundamental differences in nature. Communication is essential if compromises are to be effected, and consequently broad protection of statements is needed. This is not so in cases of payments [governed by FRE 409], where factual statements may be expected to be incidental in nature.

c. FRE 409 Permits Evidence of Payment for Purposes Other Than to Show Liability

Although FRE 409 does not include an illustrative list of possible permissible uses for evidence of medical and similar payments, this evidence—like FRE 407, 408, and 411—may be admissible for any relevant purpose other than to prove liability. See, e.g., Savoie v. Otto Candies, Inc., 692 F.2d 363 (5th Cir. 1982) (maintenance payments to prove status as seaman).

d. What Constitutes a "Similar" Expense?

FRE 409 is rarely invoked, perhaps because there are not enough good Samaritans among us. If there were, an issue that would undoubtedly arise in applying FRE 409 is what constitutes "similar expenses." For example, should evidence of paying to have an automobile repaired or paying subsistence income while an individual is recuperating from injury be excluded? See Great Coastal Express, Inc. v. Atlanta Mut. Cos., 790 So. 2d 966 (Ala. Civ. App. 2000) (state equivalent of FRE 409 not a bar to evidence that defendant paid for some of clean up following fuel leak; evidence admissible to infer defendant's negligence).

7. FRE 411

RULE 411.   LIABILITY INSURANCE

Evidence that a person was or was not insured against liability is not admissible to prove whether the person acted negligently or otherwise wrongfully. But the court may admit this evidence for another purpose, such as proving a witness's bias or prejudice or proving agency, ownership, or control.

8. Explanation of FRE 411

a. The Exclusionary Mandate

This rule is similar in purpose, structure, and application to FRE 407-409. With respect to liability insurance, however, the probative value of the forbidden inference is particularly weak. This inference holds that people with liability insurance are likely to be less careful than people without insurance, who must pay their own money for the injuries they cause. Apart from being empirically unfounded, this inference pays no regard to the "moral hazard" exceptions to insurance and to the premium increases charged to people responsible for accidents.

The exclusionary mandate of FRE 411 is often rationalized by the need to prevent jurors from basing their verdict on "deep pocket" considerations. Arguably, if evidence of liability insurance were admissible on the question of fault, there would be a substantial risk of unfair prejudice. Jurors might be inclined to impose damages because of insurance or to forgo or minimize damages out of sympathy for the uninsured. On the other hand, given the pervasiveness of liability insurance, if an uninsured party is not able to present evidence of absence of insurance, there is a risk that the jury may assume that the party is insured and impose damages on the basis of this incorrect assumption. Moreover, empirical studies of jurors indicate that, despite instructions to the contrary, jurors frequently discuss and make assumptions about insurance. See, e.g., Shari Seidman Diamond & Neil Vidmar, Jury Ruminations on Forbidden Topics, 87 Va. L. Rev. 1857, 1876 (2001) (in a study of 40 tort cases, jurors discussed insurance in 85% of the cases). Granted that jurors rely on their beliefs about insurance in their deliberations (even when they are instructed not to), why not set up a rule that provides the jury with accurate information about insurance? Would such a rule improve the existing legal regime?

b. The Permissible Uses of Evidence of Liability Insurance

Like FRE 407-409, FRE 411 excludes evidence of liability insurance only to prove negligence or wrongful conduct. The second sentence of FRE 411 lists the most common permissible uses of evidence of liability insurance. Like the lists of permissible purposes in FRE 407 and FRE 408, the FRE 411 list is not exhaustive. When there is a permissible purpose, the admissibility of the evidence should depend on the application of FRE 403, and FRE 403 should require at a minimum that the issue for which the evidence is offered is disputed.

Liability insurance offered for some legitimate, disputed purpose is usually admitted. Morton v. Zidell Explorations, Inc., 695 F.2d 347 (9th Cir. 1982) (proof of purchasing insurance to rebut claim that contract not in effect); Hunziker v. Scheidemantle, 543 F.2d 489 (3d Cir. 1976) (proof of insurance covering alleged agent to prove agency); Newell v. Harold Shaffer Leasing Co., 489 F.2d 103 (5th Cir. 1974) (maintaining insurance introduced to show ownership or control). If, as is frequently the case, an insurance investigator testifies about the results of an investigation, evidence that the investigator represents a company that insures one of the parties will probably be admissible both as part of the general background information about the witness and as an indication of the possible bias of the witness. Conde v. Starlight I, Inc., 103 F.3d 210 (1st Cir. 1997); see also Cook v. Rockwell Intl. Corp., 580 F. Supp. 2d 1071, 1155 (D. Colo. 2006) (evidence of indemnification obligations to defendants admissible to prove bias or prejudice of witnesses affiliated with indemnitor).

KEY POINTS

1. Under FRE 408, 409, and 411, evidence of compromises, offers of compromise, payment or offers to pay medical and similar expenses, and liability insurance is not admissible to prove liability.
2. Subject to FRE 403, such evidence may be admissible for other purposes. The permissible purposes listed in FRE 408 and FRE 411, like the permissible purposes listed in FRE 407, are the most common purposes for which evidence governed by those rules is likely to be admissible, but the lists are not exclusive.
3. When evidence is offered for a theoretically legitimate permissible purpose, FRE 401-402 or 403 would require exclusion if the issue is not a disputed one.

PROBLEMS

6.6. Return to Problem 3.2 at page 148.

    (a) Paul's mother offers to testify that shortly after the accident she received a note from Driver with $200. The note, which the plaintiff would like to introduce into evidence, says: "I'm so sorry about Paul's accident. I'm not a rich person but I hope this will help with some of the expenses."

    (b) Plaintiff wishes to introduce evidence that, after the lawsuit was filed, the school district offered to settle the suit for $25,000.

    (c) In cross-examining the school district's accident reconstruction expert, plaintiff wishes to show that the witness has a professional relationship with the School District's liability insurance carrier.

    Should any of this evidence be admitted?

6.7. While sitting in Evidence class, Dave was preoccupied with his plans for the semester break. His hot coffee spilled on Paula, who was sitting next to him. Paula suffered a serious burn in the area where the coffee spilled. She sued Dave for negligence and Espresso-to-Go, where Dave purchased the coffee, for a defectively designed take-out cup, alleging $50,000 in damages. Paula offers to testify as follows on direct examination:

    Q: Paula, what happened immediately after the spill?
    A: Dave said he would pay for my ruined clothes.
    Q: Did you ever talk to Dave about the case again?
    A: Yes. After I filed this suit, Dave saw me in the hall one day and said he was sorry I had been hurt because he had been so clumsy and that he'd like to talk more, but he was late for class. Then the next day he said he didn't think my case was worth $50,000, but that he'd like to pay all my bills and give me money for a "bar trip" after graduation.

    What objections should defense counsel make to this testimony?

6.8. Assume that Paula settles with Dave and proceeds to trial against Espresso-to-Go.

    (a) Paula calls Dave to testify about the incident and to describe the severity of her burns. Are the following questions by defense counsel on cross-examination objectionable: "Isn't it true that you were sued by Paula for your own negligence? And isn't it true that you and Paula reached a compromise of that claim for a mere $500? And isn't it true that Paula really dropped the suit against you in exchange for your testimony here today?"

    (b) Can Paula introduce evidence of Espresso-to-Go's substantial liability insurance policy? Would your answer change if, at trial, the owner of Espresso-to-Go had mentioned during testimony (1) that its products were so low risk that the company did not carry much insurance or (2) that he could not afford to lose the lawsuit because he needed everything to care for his ailing mother?

6.9. Paul Preston has sued Daniel Dripps for damages for assault and battery after Dripps attacked Preston at their daughters' hockey game. In a mediation session to discuss settlement, Preston's lawyer says that Preston would settle for payment of his medical expenses plus $5,000 if Dripps would admit he was wrong and apologize. Dripps says, "Well, I am sorry—I was in the wrong." He counter-offers to offer an apology and pay the medical expenses and no more. Preston says he doubts Dripps's sincerity about the apology. To demonstrate Dripps's sincerity, Dripps's attorney shows Preston's attorney an entry from Dripps's diary the day of the fight saying that he was at fault and was sorry. Negotiations break down over the $5,000. The day after the mediation, Preston's counsel sends out a document request demanding production of the diary, which the plaintiff had not known about prior to the mediation. Eventually, the case goes to trial. Is the following evidence offered by Preston admissible?

(1) Dripps's statement at the mediation that he was sorry and is in the wrong;

(2) Dripps's willingness to cover Preston's medical expenses;

(3) The entry from Dripps's diary admitting fault; and

(4) Evidence that Dripps's homeowners' insurance company denied coverage for the alleged assault and battery on the ground that the policy did not cover intentional wrongful acts. (Preston argues that it shows that the insurance company found Dripps to have acted wrongfully and intentionally.)

Would any of your answers be different if this were a criminal prosecution of Dripps for battery?

6.10. Pam Palmer has sued Dick Davis for injuries she received in an automobile accident involving her car and the cars of Davis and Walter Williams. According to the plaintiff's complaint she was headed west on a two-lane road when Davis, who was heading east, crossed the road into her lane of traffic and hit her. Davis claims that he had been taking necessary evasive action in an unsuccessful effort to avoid hitting another car that had suddenly pulled in front of him from a side street. The driver of the third car was Walter Williams.

Williams has testified for the plaintiff that Davis was responsible for the accident. According to Williams, he had been traveling east at a normal rate of speed when Davis, who was speeding, suddenly approached from the rear. In an unsuccessful effort to avoid hitting Williams, Davis veered to the left, clipping the rear end of Williams's car and hitting the plaintiff's car as well.

Davis offers to show that he had filed suit against Williams for damage to his automobile and that Williams had paid Davis $500 to settle the suit, in which Davis had asked for $2,000. Should this evidence be admitted over plaintiff's objection?

6.11. Roland Nast has filed an age discrimination suit against the Jones Hardware Co. for failing to promote him to a manager position and giving the job instead to a much younger employee.

(a) Although Nast had a reputation for being a bit hotheaded and argumentative, Jim Jones, president of Jones Hardware, maintained during settlement negotiations that Nast's attitude and personality had nothing to do with his not getting the manager job. Instead, according to Jones, the problem was Nast's tardiness record. At trial, however, Jones testified that Nast's attitude and personality were primary factors in the decision not to promote him to a manager position. Can Nast introduce Jones's settlement negotiation statements?

(b) To rebut the claim of discrimination, Jones Hardware offers evidence that after Nast filed his complaint Jones Hardware offered Nast a position at a different branch store. This newly offered position had the same salary as the manager salary. Should the evidence be admitted?

B. REFLECTION ON RULES 407-409, 411

Consider whether it makes sense for the Federal Rules to retain the exclusionary mandates set forth in FRE 407-409 and FRE 411. Commentators have pointed out, particularly with respect to FRE 407, that it is common for proponents to be able to articulate some alternative, permissible reason for admitting the evidence. See, e.g., David. P. Leonard, Selected Rules of Limited Admissibility, The New Wigmore §2.8 (2002). To the extent that one can readily find some alternative permissible theory for the use of evidence that is subject to these rules, one can with good reason question the desirability of the rules in their present form: If courts tend to resolve the FRE 403 balance between the permissible and impermissible use in favor of admissibility (which is usually the case), and if one doubts the efficacy of limiting instructions, the rules in fact would seem not to be serving their designed purposes very well. Alternatively, if the FRE 403 balance were usually to come out in favor of exclusion, the rules would be stated in a deceptively (and thus perhaps undesirably) narrow manner: Despite the limited nature of the express exclusionary mandates, FRE 403 concerns could make the mandates quite broad.

Regardless of whether most decisions involving FRE 407-409 and FRE 411 result in admission or exclusion of the evidence, it may be that judges are simply applying the FRE 403 balancing test wisely on a case-by-case basis. Or perhaps the inherent difficulty of balancing and the breadth of judicial discretion lead to arbitrary and inconsistent results from case to case. Unfortunately, we do not have enough reliable information to assess the need for these rules. Consider, for example, FRE 407's limitation on evidence of subsequent remedial measures. The rule depends on assumptions regarding how the presence or absence of the rule affects or would affect behavior—i.e., that the rule encourages people to make conditions safer and that its absence would discourage such behavior—but we do not have reliable information about whether the rule actually produces or would produce these effects. (For further discussion of the empirical assumptions underlying FRE 407 and the limited information available regarding these assumptions, see Kahan, supra.)

Perhaps answers will emerge as we gain more experience and sophistication in studying the operation of the rules of evidence in practice. In the meantime, however, these potential problems should not be ignored. The task of the rule drafters should be to devise the best possible rules in light of the best available information (based on rational choice, logic, empiricism, and intuition) as to how various alternative formulations of the rules are likely to work in practice.

C. WITHDRAWN GUILTY PLEAS, PLEAS OF NO CONTEST, AND STATEMENTS MADE DURING PLEA DISCUSSIONS

1. FRE 410

RULE 410.   PLEAS, PLEA DISCUSSIONS, AND RELATED STATEMENTS

(a) *Prohibited Uses.* In a civil or criminal case, evidence of the following is not admissible against the defendant who made the plea or participated in the plea discussions:

(1) a guilty plea that was later withdrawn;

(2) a nolo contendere plea;

(3) a statement made during a proceeding on either of those pleas under Federal Rule of Criminal Procedure 11 or a comparable state procedure; or

(4) a statement made during plea discussions with an attorney for the prosecuting authority if the discussions did not result in a guilty plea or they resulted in a later-withdrawn guilty plea.

(b) *Exceptions.* The court may admit a statement described in Rule 410(a) (3) or (4):

(1) in any proceeding in which another statement made during the same plea or plea discussions has been introduced, if in fairness the statements ought to be considered together; or

(2) in a criminal proceeding for perjury or false statement, if the defendant made the statement under oath, on the record, and with counsel present.

2. Explanation of FRE 410

a. Withdrawn Guilty Pleas

Once a defendant has pleaded guilty, the defendant may withdraw the plea only with the permission of the court. The standards for permitting withdrawal of a plea typically are not articulated with any degree of specificity, but there must be "cause" or some good reason to permit the withdrawal. A court is likely to permit withdrawal of a plea if there is reason to believe that the plea is inaccurate because the defendant is innocent or if it appears that the defendant's rights were violated in the process of procuring the plea. To the extent that the concern is with the violation of the defendant's rights, exclusion may be necessary in order to make the remedy for the violation meaningful. If the prosecutor could respond to a withdrawn plea by using that plea against the defendant in a subsequent proceeding, the value of withdrawal as a remedy would often be substantially undermined. To the extent that the concern is with the reliability of a plea, the fact that a judge has already determined that the plea is unreliable casts doubt on the plea's probative value.

b. Pleas of No Contest

Only some jurisdictions permit pleas of no contest, and where they are permitted the court usually must approve the pleas. Pleas of no contest are by their nature compromises. They constitute acquiescence to a criminal conviction without an admission of guilt or a determination of guilt after an adjudicatory trial. Their compromise nature makes uncertain their probative value to prove that the person committed the acts charged. Moreover, use of no-contest pleas for this purpose may undermine the initial value of the plea as a device to encourage settlement. Olsen v. Correiro, 189 F.3d 52 (1st Cir. 1999).

c. Statements Made in Conjunction with the Process of Making and Negotiating Pleas

Federal Rule of Criminal Procedure 11, to which FRE 410(a)(3) refers, governs plea bargaining and the judicial acceptance or rejection of guilty pleas. By specifically excluding (a) statements made in Rule 11 plea bargaining proceedings and (b) statements made in the course of plea bargaining with prosecutors, FRE 410(a)(3) and (4) operate in the criminal negotiating process as the counterpart to FRE 408's prohibition against using evidence of attempts to settle or compromise civil claims.

As a matter of general principle, and perhaps even as a matter of practical reality, one may question the soundness of such a rule. An offer to plead guilty, at least if the plea is to a relatively serious charge, may have more probative value than the offer to settle—even for a substantial amount of money—a civil claim. Moreover, offers to plead guilty that FRE 410 excludes usually occur in the context of plea negotiations, and there are several reasons why settling or compromising criminal charges may be regarded as undesirable and, therefore, something to be deterred. First, the possibility of pleading guilty to a charge that is substantially less severe than the crime initially charged may have the undesirable effect of pressuring an innocent individual to plead guilty in order to avoid the risk of possible conviction on the more serious charge. Second, the possibility of a plea to a lesser charge may have the arguably undesirable effect of undermining a legislatively dictated mandatory sentence for the crime initially charged or of limiting the range of the judge's sentencing discretion. Finally, a consequence of encouraging or even condoning plea bargaining is the possibility of unfairness or at least the appearance of unfairness from what are or seem to be inconsistent and arbitrary plea bargaining decisions from case to case by prosecutors. This, in turn, may lead to cynicism about or disrespect for the criminal law and perhaps undermine the force of criminal prohibitions and penalties as general deterrents.

Despite these concerns, the Supreme Court has acknowledged that plea bargaining is an acceptable method for disposing of criminal cases, Santobello v. New York, 404 U.S. 257 (1971), and the reality is that plea bargaining is pervasive in the criminal justice system. Depending on the jurisdiction, anywhere from 70 percent to 95 percent of all criminal charges are disposed of by guilty pleas, and many of these pleas are the result of plea negotiations. Moreover, the criminal justice system does not have the resources to process the current and ever increasing volume of cases without heavy reliance on guilty pleas. Thus, as a practical matter, plea bargaining is a fact of life. In light of this reality, it may be at least as important to encourage guilty pleas as it is to encourage settlement of civil cases. Just as excluding statements made in conjunction with offers to settle a civil suit may facilitate the negotiating process, excluding statements made during plea negotiations may motivate criminal defendants to enter into a plea bargain and plead guilty.

d. The Scope of FRE 410(a)(4)

There are two important limitations on the scope of the rule excluding statements covered by FRE 410(a)(4). First, the statements must be made "in the course of plea discussions." For example, if a defendant is merely seeking leniency in the charging decision without suggesting any possibility of pleading guilty, a court may conclude that the conversation is not a plea discussion. Similarly, seeking dismissal of charges against third persons may be outside the scope of plea negotiations, United States v. Doe, 655 F.2d 920 (9th Cir. 1980), as are statements made following the completion of plea negotiations, United States v. Perry, 643 F.2d 38 (2d Cir. 1981). Second, the defendant's statements must be made "to an attorney for the prosecuting authority."

For example, statements to police officers, who have no formal authority to plea bargain in any event, do not fall within the FRE 410(a)(4) exclusion. United States v. Stern, 313 F. Supp. 2d 155, 167-168 (S.D.N.Y. 2003); United States v. Brumley, 217 F.3d 905 (7th Cir. 1997). Statements made to police officers as part of the plea negotiation, however, may be covered by the rule if the police are acting as agents of the prosecutor. United States v. Millard, 139 F.3d 1200 (8th Cir. 1998).

Even if the statements are made to a prosecuting attorney, they may not be protected. There is a split of authority on the question of whether proffer sessions that explore possible cooperation with the government but that do not include discussions of a guilty plea fall within the FRE 410 exclusionary mandate. Compare United States v. Morgan, 91 F.3d 1193, 1195-1196 (8th Cir. 1996) (statements not protected) with United States v. Frank, 173 F.R.D. 59, 69 (W.D.N.Y. 1997) (statements protected). See United States v. Stein, 2005 U.S. Dist. LEXIS 11141 (E.D. Pa.) (collecting cases).

Importantly, a defendant's statement will receive the FRE 410 protection only when he (or his attorney speaking as an agent) has a subjective belief that plea negotiations with a prosecuting authority are taking place and that belief is objectively reasonable. United States v. Olsen, 450 F.3d 635 (7th Cir. 2006); United States v. Sayakhom, 186 F.3d 928 (9th Cir. 1999); United States v. Bridges, 46 F. Supp. 2d 462 (E.D. Va. 1999) (collecting cases).

e. The FRE 410(b) Exceptions

The two enumerated exceptions in FRE 410(b) will rarely be of consequence. The first exception merely acknowledges the rule of completeness encompassed in FRE 106. For example, if a defendant introduces part of a statement made in conjunction with plea negotiations, the prosecution can introduce other statements that provide a context or explanation for the statement introduced by the defendant. The second exception in effect permits the prosecution to bring perjury charges against a defendant who lies under oath during plea negotiations. Perjury prosecutions are relatively rare, however; and in any event, plea negotiations are seldom carried out under oath.

f. Waiver of FRE 410's Exclusionary Mandate

In United States v. Mezzanatto, 513 U.S. 196 (1995), the Supreme Court held that a defendant may waive the FRE 410(a)(4) exclusionary mandate with regard to the impeachment use of statements made in the process of plea negotiations as part of an agreement with the prosecutor in which the defendant obligated himself to reveal the truth. In *Mezzanatto*, the prosecutor, at the outset of plea discussions with the defendant and his counsel required the defendant to undertake to tell the truth and insisted on the right to be able to use the defendant's statements against him for impeachment purposes in the event of a trial. Mezzanatto agreed to this waiver, and during the plea discussions he made some incriminating statements. The prosecutor, however, terminated the plea negotiations for reasons that included false statements that Mezzanatto had made. The case proceeded to trial. Mezzanatto testified, and over his objection the prosecution introduced into evidence some of Mezzanatto's plea bargain statements to impeach his testimony. In his opinion for the Court, Justice Thomas rejected the defendant's claims that waiver was inconsistent with the purpose of FRE 410 and that the possibility of waiver provided potential for prosecutorial over-reaching. Moreover, Justice Thomas suggested that the waiver would be valid even if it were not limited to the impeachment use of the statements. Only Chief Justice Rehnquist and Justice Scalia expressed agreement with this dictum.

Nonetheless, several federal circuits have extended *Mezzanatto* by upholding waivers that allow prosecutors to use FRE 410 evidence substantively to rebut any contrary evidence offered by the defendant, United States v. Hardwick, 544 F.3d 565 (3d Cir. 2008); United States v. Velez, 354 F.3d 190, 196 (2d Cir. 2004); United States v. Rebbe, 314 F.3d 402 (9th Cir. 2002); United States v. Krilich, 159 F.3d 1020 (7th Cir. 1998); or even substantively in their cases-in-chief: United States v. Mitchell, 633 F.3d 997 (10th Cir. 2011); United States v. Sylvester, 583 F.3d 285 (5th Cir. 2009); United States v. Young, 223 F.3d 905 (8th Cir. 2000); United States v. Burch, 156 F.3d 1315 (D.C. Cir. 1998). Importantly, a defendant's *Mezzanatto* waiver is held to be effective only when it is drafted in unambiguous terms: United States v. Escobedo, 757 F.3d 229 (5th Cir. 2014).

Consider the effects of the *Mezzanatto* decision. It seems likely that at least some defendants will be unwilling to enter into plea negotiations if prosecutors demand waivers. Of course, prosecutors could choose to forgo the demand in some or all of those cases. If a demand for waiver becomes the standard prosecutorial policy, however, there may well be a net decrease in the number of defendants willing to enter into plea negotiations. On the other hand, the *Mezzanatto* waiver allows defendants to credibly commit themselves to telling the truth in plea bargain discussions. If the waiver were ineffectual, the defendants would have suffered no penalties for lying. Their promise to tell the truth would consequently be "cheap talk" that prosecutors cannot rationally trust. Facing this predicament, prosecutors would tend to steer away from plea bargains that could benefit both sides. The *Mezzanatto* waiver thus produces a socially beneficial sorting effect: It facilitates plea bargains between prosecutors seeking to obtain truthful statements from defendants and defendants willing to commit themselves to providing those true statements. See Eric B. Rasmusen, *Mezzanatto* and the Economics of Self Incrimination, 19 Cardozo L. Rev. 1541 (1998).

KEY POINTS

1. FRE 410(a)(1) and (2) provide that a defendant's withdrawn guilty pleas and pleas of nolo contendere are not admissible against the defendant.
2. FRE 410(a)(3) provides that a defendant's statements made during a judicial plea-acceptance proceeding are not admissible against the defendant if the guilty plea was withdrawn or was a plea of no contest.
3. FRE 410(a)(4) provides that a defendant's statements made during plea discussions are not admissible against the defendant. According to the language of FRE 410(a)(4), statements qualify for exclusion only if they are made (a) to a prosecuting attorney, (b) during plea discussions, and (c) the discussion failed to result in a guilty plea or it resulted in a plea that was later withdrawn.
4. In determining whether the "plea discussions" and "attorney for the prosecuting authority" requirements are satisfied, courts consider the matter from the defendant's perspective. The defendant's statement will be excluded only if he had a subjective belief that he was engaging in plea discussions with a prosecuting attorney and if that belief was objectively reasonable.
5. Defendants may waive the right not to have plea bargaining statements used against them, at least for impeachment purposes (the "*Mezzanatto* agreement").

PROBLEMS

6.12. Attorney Yvonne Gruber heard a rumor that her client, Dawn Carson, was about to be indicted for income tax evasion. On behalf of Carson, Gruber spoke with an assistant U.S. Attorney about the possibility of a plea bargain. In response to a question, Gruber acknowledged that her client would be willing to plead guilty to a relatively minor charge. There were no further discussions, and Carson was eventually indicted for income tax evasion. Can the prosecution use Gruber's statement about Carson's willingness to plead guilty? Would your answer be different if Gruber had contacted the IRS and had the conversation with an IRS agent?

6.13. In the course of plea negotiations with an assistant U.S. Attorney, Tom Mason, after acknowledging that he sold heroin on three specific occasions, entered into a cooperation agreement. According to the agreement, Mason would not be prosecuted if he helped the police develop evidence against his supplier. Mason reneged on the agreement and is now being prosecuted for sale of heroin. During its case in chief the prosecution offers Mason's statement about selling heroin. Should Mason's objection be sustained? Does you answer depend upon whether the cooperation agreement contained a waiver of Mason's FRE 410 rights?

6.14. Return to Problem 3.2 at page 148. Assume that Driver was charged with reckless driving, a misdemeanor, as a result of the accident with Paul. Driver is grief stricken and has no interest in fighting the charge. Moreover, she is worried that if she seriously contests the ticket and is found guilty, the penalty may be stiffer than if she pleads guilty. If Driver pleads guilty, however, the plea can be used against her in a civil suit. The jurisdiction does not permit nolo pleas. What advice can you give her?

ASSESSMENTS

A-6.1. FRE 410. A criminal defendant made a plea bargain agreement with the prosecution in which he acknowledged his participation in a criminal enterprise and named his accomplices. The agreement entitles the prosecution to rescind it and use the defendant's confession as evidence against him if it turns out that the defendant lied about any of the accomplices.

A. This agreement is void because it violates the Fifth Amendment (but not FRE 410).
B. This agreement is void because it violates FRE 410 (but not the Fifth Amendment).
C. Under the prevalent view, this agreement is valid, but the prosecution can use the defendant's self-incriminating statement for impeachment purposes only.
D. Under the prevalent view, this agreement is valid and the prosecution can use the defendant's self-incriminating statement for any purpose to which it is relevant.

A-6.2. FRE 407. Hospital patient P fell on the floor and broke her hip when she tried to step down from an MRI machine. Following this event, the hospital appointed a committee of safety experts that recommended requiring MRI technicians to help patients step down. P's tort suit against the hospital goes to trial in a federal court. P subpoenas one of the safety committee members to testify about the committee's findings and recommendation. The hospital objects.

A. The court must sustain this objection.
B. The court must overrule this objection.
C. Pursuant to FRE 403, the court ought to use its discretion and sustain the hospital's objection.
D. More information is needed to properly deal with this objection.

A-6.3. FRE 407.   To prove that the elevator in D's store was unsafe on the day of the accident, P testifies that D had it fixed the day after the accident. P's testimony is clearly inadmissible. TRUE or FALSE?

A-6.4. FRE 408-09. P sues D in tort. To prove that she tried to mitigate her damage, P testifies that she offered D to settle the case by agreeing to pay her medical expenses.

- **A.** P's testimony should be excluded pursuant to FRE 409.
- **B.** P's testimony should be excluded pursuant to FRE 408.
- **C.** P's testimony should be excluded pursuant to FRE 403.
- **D.** P's testimony is admissible.

A. 6.5. FRE 411.   Car accident victim V sues O for negligently entrusting his vehicle to unlicensed driver D, who caused the accident. O claims that he did not own the vehicle. To support this claim, O produces a car-sale agreement naming D as the purchaser of the vehicle. For her part, V offers into evidence a liability insurance policy purchased by O. The policy names O as the owner of the vehicle and covers his liability for accidents up to $2,000,000.

The proffered insurance policy is:

- **A.** Clearly admissible.
- **B.** Clearly inadmissible.
- **C.** Facially admissible, but most courts exclude such evidence to avoid prejudicing the jury, pursuant to FRE 403.
- **D.** Potentially admissible, but more information is needed to answer this question.

ANSWERS

A-6.1. The best answer is **D**, as per United States v. Mezzanatto, 513 U.S. 196 (1995), discussed earlier on page 380-381.

A-6.2. The best answer is **D**. Under FRE 407, remedial measures do not include internal investigations and recommendations when these are merely initial steps toward ascertaining what, if any, remedial measures are called for. However, expert recommendations that the organization will likely implement are remedial measures that fall under the FRE 407 exclusionary mandate. See supra page 361. The court therefore needs to ascertain the likelihood of the hospital's acting upon the committee's recommendations.

A-6.3. TRUE.   This is a straightforward application of the FRE 407 ban on subsequent remedial measures evidence, however probative of negligence it might be.

A-6.4. The best answer is **D**. P's testimony is admissible because it falls under the "another purpose" exception to the FRE 408's ban on settlement negotiation evidence. P's testimony purports to show that she attempted to mitigate her injury and not that D implicitly acknowledged its liability by agreeing to negotiate a settlement. Hence, B is false. A is false as well because FRE 409 only excludes a defendant's offer—as opposed to a plaintiff's request—to pay the injured party's medical expenses. P's testimony also does not purport to prove "liability for the injury." Rather, it negates the "avoidable consequence" exception to the defendant's potential liability, which *P* must establish independently. C is false, too, because *P*'s testimony is probative and has no prejudicial effect since it attributes no acknowledgment of fault to *D*.

A-6.5. The best answer is **A**. The proffered insurance policy falls under the "another purpose" provision of FRE 411 that explicitly lists "ownership" as an admissible purpose.

CHAPTER SEVEN

THE IMPEACHMENT
AND REHABILITATION
OF WITNESSES

Many trials turn on the question of credibility. The rules of evidence considered in this chapter establish the framework within which the parties may present evidence of witnesses' credibility to the jury. Many of the issues and techniques discussed in this chapter will also apply to impeaching and rehabilitating the credibility of hearsay declarants (i.e., those who make statements out of court that are admitted as evidence at trial). See FRE 806. We discuss the impeachment of hearsay declarants in Chapter Eight.

A. BASIC CONCEPTS

1. Impeachment: The Inferential Process

a. The Testimonial Inferences

The strength and accuracy of any witness's testimony depends upon certain testimonial abilities: A witness must be able to observe events, to remember them, and to relate them honestly and accurately. The jury must make inferences about these abilities—the ability to narrate accurately, to be honest, to perceive, and to remember—in order to credit the truth of what a witness says. For example, when a witness testifies, "The defendant's car ran the red light," the jury, in crediting this testimony, must infer that (1) the witness is communicating that the defendant was driving a car that did not stop at a red light; (2) the witness believes this assertion; (3) the witness's belief is based on the witness's accurate perception of what happened; and (4) the witness accurately remembers what happened.

Diagram 7-1 illustrates these inferences. If any of the inferences in the diagram is false, the evidence is not relevant to prove that the defendant did not stop at the red

Diagram 7-1

EVIDENCE ──▶FOC ──▶FOC ──▶FOC ──▶FOC ──▶FOC

W says, "Defendant's car ran the red light".

W means, "Defendant did not stop the car at the red light." (narration)

W honestly believes that the defendant did not stop the car at the red light. (sincerity)

W perceived the event accurately (perception).

W remembers the event accurately (memory).

Defendant did not stop the car at the red light.

light. To help ensure that they are not false, the law requires witnesses to testify from firsthand knowledge (FRE 602) and to affirm that they will testify truthfully (FRE 603). For several reasons, however, the law does not generally require the proponent of evidence to make any other special showing regarding the accuracy of these inferences as a condition of admissibility. First, although there are obvious exceptions, our common experience tells us that people tend to be honest and accurate in most situations. (Consider the chaos in which we would live if the foregoing statement were not generally true.) Second, typically witnesses will testify to general background information about their residences and occupations, which will provide some minimal personal information for the jury to consider in assessing the strength of the inferences. Third, in the Anglo-American legal system, the task of assessing the accuracy of these inferences traditionally has been one for the jury rather than the judge. Finally, opposing counsel will have the opportunity to try to raise doubts about the strength of these inferences.

b. Types of Impeachment Evidence

Impeachment is the process of trying to raise doubts about the inferences illustrated in Diagram 7-1. It is, in other words, an attempt to show that a witness may have inadvertently narrated the events incorrectly, lied, misperceived the events about which the witness testified, or forgotten some or all of what happened. To the extent that the jury believes the impeaching evidence, the jury should conclude that what the witness said is less likely to be accurate than if there had been no impeaching evidence.

If the witness has offered an opinion or conclusion about some matter, there is a further impeachment concern. Consider, for example, a witness's testimony that the defendant was drunk. Even if the witness is sincere, is using the term *drunk* in a commonly understood sense, correctly perceived the events, and recalls them accurately, the witness may have misevaluated the defendant's symptoms and used erroneous generalizations for either of two reasons. First, the witness may not be a very good judge of drunkenness. For example, the witness may have associated loud, boisterous talk with drunkenness without realizing that the defendant always speaks in a loud, boisterous manner. Second, the defendant's symptoms, although indicative of drunkenness, may in fact have had some other source. The impeaching party may suggest both of these possibilities to the jury, and the jury may then tend to disregard the witness's opinion.

There are a variety of ways to impeach a witness:

(1) Evidence that a witness has a character trait for untruthfulness suggests that the witness may be untruthful on the witness stand.
(2) Showing that the witness has a bias or interest in the case suggests a motive for being untruthful.
(3) Attacks on other testimonial qualities such as the witness's narrative or perceptive abilities may also undermine a witness's credibility. Such attacks may focus on general abilities (e.g., color blindness) or on the specific exercise of those abilities on the occasion relevant to the case (e.g., witness not wearing glasses at time event observed).

(4) Proof of a witness's inconsistent statements suggests that the jury should be skeptical about the accuracy of the witness's testimony.

(5) Testimony from other sources that contradicts the witness may reduce the witness's believability.

c. Impeachment Evidence versus Substantive Evidence

Evidence offered to impeach the credibility of a witness—like all other evidence that is admitted—must be relevant to prove or disprove some fact that is of consequence to the litigation. If it were not, the impeachment evidence would be inadmissible pursuant to FRE 402. The difference between evidence offered for "impeachment" purposes and evidence offered for "substantive" purposes is in the relevance theory that leads to a fact of consequence.

The evidentiary facts discussed in this chapter relate to essential elements of a case because they may influence the jury's evaluation of witnesses. Sometimes evidence that impeaches the credibility of witnesses will also be relevant and admissible as substantive evidence of an essential element. When this is the case, there is no need to consider whether the evidence is admissible to impeach a witness because the evidence will already be admitted for its substantive purpose (i.e., as evidence that makes a fact of consequence more or less probable independent of its effect on the credibility of a witness). In other words, evidence must be analyzed for its impeachment purpose only when it is inadmissible for a substantive purpose, which will often be the case. Here are three examples to illustrate these points:

(1) In the case of a bank robbery, the teller who handed money over to the robber may testify that the defendant was not the robber. Other witnesses, customers in the bank, may identify the defendant as the robber. A police officer may establish that the teller is the sister of the defendant. The testimony of the customers contradicts—and therefore implicitly impeaches—the credibility of the teller (and vice versa), but each witness's testimony is also independently admissible on the substantive question of the robber's identity. The testimony of the police officer is not independently admissible for a substantive purpose; its only relevance is to impeach the credibility of the teller by showing bias.

(2) In the running-the-red-light hypothetical, the defendant wishes to impeach the plaintiff's witness with the witness's prior inconsistent statement, not made under oath, that the light was green when the defendant entered the intersection. Because of the hearsay rule, the prior statement is inadmissible as substantive evidence that the light was green. FRE 801(d)(1)(A). The defendant, however, may use the prior inconsistent statement, without regard to its truth, to infer that the witness's direct examination testimony is not accurate. Knowing that the witness has made inconsistent statements about the same subject, regardless of which statement is true, casts some doubt on the witness's credibility. On one of the two occasions the witness may have been lying; at the very least, the inconsistency shows that the witness is not particularly careful about narrating the events of the accident.

(3) Della Dean is charged with perjury and testifies in her own defense. To impeach the truthfulness of Della's testimony, the prosecution offers evidence that Della was convicted of perjury two years ago. It would be impermissible under FRE 404 to introduce evidence of past perjury to prove that Della committed perjury on the occasion charged in the current indictment. Because Della has testified as a witness, however, it will be permissible to introduce her prior conviction in order to impeach her character for truthfulness. FRE 609(a). The inferential process is as follows: Because Della has committed perjury, she is a generally untruthful person, who may be lying on the witness stand.

Evidence admitted for the purpose of impeaching the credibility of a witness will sometimes not be admissible for a substantive purpose—either because it would be irrelevant, as in the first hypothetical, or because some exclusionary rule (e.g., the hearsay rule or FRE 404(b)) would prohibit its substantive use, as in the latter two hypotheticals. When evidence is not admissible for a substantive purpose, you must also evaluate whether it may be admitted for an impeachment purpose.

When evidence is admissible only to impeach the credibility of a witness, the limited admissibility has three significant consequences. First, the proponent of the evidence cannot rely on that evidence as substantive evidence to satisfy a burden of production in response to a motion for summary judgment or judgment as a matter of law. Second, the proponent cannot rely on the evidence as substantive proof of disputed facts during closing argument. Third, whenever the evidence is relevant but inadmissible for a substantive purpose, the party against whom the evidence is offered can make an FRE 403 objection and, if the evidence is admitted, is entitled to a limiting instruction. Consider, for example, the hypothetical in which the defendant introduced evidence that a plaintiff's witness had made an inconsistent statement about whether the defendant ran the red light:

- The defendant could not rely on the substance of the inconsistent statement to support the production burden on the question of contributory negligence.
- If the case went to the jury, the defendant could argue that the inconsistency suggested the witness was mistaken or lying about the color of the light, but the defendant could not argue that the statement was a truthful assertion that the light was green for the defendant.
- The plaintiff would be entitled to an instruction that the jury could use the statement only to assess the witness's credibility, not as substantive evidence of the color of the light.

Do you think jurors are likely to be able to understand or follow a limiting instruction? If not, would it be desirable either (1) to exclude the evidence altogether on FRE 403 grounds or (2) to forgo the limiting instruction?

2. "Extrinsic Evidence" and Impeachment

One can impeach a witness (1) by examining (usually cross-examining) the witness and (2) by introducing extrinsic evidence. *Extrinsic evidence* means any evidence other than that developed through direct or cross-examination of the witness. It may be an exhibit, such as a record of a prior conviction, or the testimony of another witness that impeaches the first witness by showing, for example, bias or an inconsistent statement that the first witness denied making.

As we discuss various impeachment techniques, we will consider the extent to which the impeachment rules permit extrinsic evidence.

3. "Rehabilitating" versus "Bolstering" Evidence

When a witness has been impeached, the nonimpeaching party may respond with evidence that attempts to counter or undue the impeachment evidence. For example, if one side impeaches a witness with evidence that the witness has an untruthful character, the opposing party may respond with evidence purporting to prove that the witness is a truthful person. Evidence that rebuts impeachment evidence is known as "rehabilitation" evidence. The relevance of such evidence is the opposite of impeachment evidence — rehabilitation evidence is relevant because it makes it less likely that the witness's testimony has the testimonial problems that were the subject of impeaching evidence. Just as impeachment may relate to any of the four testimonial problems (narration, sincerity, perception, or memory), rehabilitation evidence may likewise be relevant for any of these issues.

Parties may also attempt to introduce evidence that purports to make a witness's testimony more believable when the witness has not been impeached. Such evidence is known as "bolstering" the credibility of a witness and is generally disfavored. A general common law rule prohibited bolstering evidence. See, e.g., United States v. Bolick, 917 F.2d 135, 137-140 (4th Cir. 1990) (referring to a general ban on preimpeachment bolstering: "We are among the courts to adhere to that time-honored principle."); United States v. Wells, 623 F.3d 332, 345 (6th Cir. 2010) ("By prematurely calling attention to prior consistent statements in the opening statement, a prosecutor creates the chance of mistrial and an issue for appeal."). The Federal Rules contain provisions that prohibit bolstering with character evidence, FRE 608(a), and with prior consistent statements, FRE 801(d)(1)(B). Other types of bolstering evidence are governed by FRE 403.

B. IMPEACHMENT AND REHABILITATION WITH CHARACTER EVIDENCE

In Chapter Five we considered evidentiary restrictions on the substantive use of character evidence. We noted that one of the FRE 404(a) exceptions to the general prohibition against using character evidence to show action in conformity with character was the use of character evidence for impeachment and rehabilitation. FRE 404(a)(3). It is to this subject that we now turn. We are concerned here with using evidence of a witness's character for truthfulness to infer action in conformity with that character trait on a particular occasion (i.e., to infer that the witness is either lying or telling the truth on the witness stand). FRE 608 refers to a witness's "character for truthfulness or untruthfulness." Unless the context suggests a contrary meaning, our use of the term *truthfulness* includes both truthfulness and untruthfulness.

The rules governing impeachment and rehabilitation with character evidence, as well as the rules governing other forms of impeachment and rehabilitation evidence, apply to *all* witnesses and to *all* kinds of cases. With some minor exceptions that we will discuss in due course, it makes no difference whether the witness happens to be a party. A party may use character evidence to impeach a witness in civil as well as criminal trials, and criminal defendants do not have the option to keep the door closed to inquiries about any witness's character for truthfulness.

Because the rules governing the use of character evidence for impeachment purposes (FRE 404(a)(3), 608, and 609) are different from the rules governing character evidence for substantive purposes (FRE 404(a)(1) and (2), 404(b), and 405) and because both sets of rules are intricate, the general subject of character evidence may seem confusing. The best way to eliminate the confusion is to focus initially on what should always be the first question: How is the evidence relevant? Once you answer this question, it should be relatively easy to apply the proper rules.

1. FRE 608

RULE 608. A WITNESS'S CHARACTER FOR TRUTHFULNESS OR UNTRUTHFULNESS

(a) Reputation or Opinion Evidence. A witness's credibility may be attacked or supported by testimony about the witness's reputation for having a character for truthfulness or untruthfulness, or by testimony in the form of an opinion about that character. But evidence of truthful character is admissible only after the witness's character for truthfulness has been attacked.

(b) Specific Instances of Conduct. Except for a criminal conviction under Rule 609, extrinsic evidence is not admissible to prove specific instances of a witness's conduct in order to attack or support the witness's character for truthfulness. But the court may, on cross-examination, allow them to be inquired into if they are probative of the character for truthfulness or untruthfulness of:

(1) the witness; or

(2) another witness whose character the witness being cross-examined has testified about.

By testifying on another matter, a witness does not waive any privilege against self-incrimination for testimony that relates only to the witness's character for truthfulness.

2. Explanation of FRE 608(a)

a. *Reputation and Opinion Evidence to Prove Character for Untruthfulness*

One method to impeach a witness is with reputation or opinion evidence offered to prove the witness's character for untruthfulness in order to suggest that the witness is lying on the witness stand. For example, in the *Johnson* case the defendant could have called witnesses to testify that Officer Huston (or any other prosecution witness) had a reputation for being untruthful. FRE 608(a) permits both reputation and opinion evidence of character for untruthfulness. The process of eliciting reputation or opinion testimony from a character witness pursuant to FRE 608(a) is identical to the process described in Chapter Five, where we dealt with the use of reputation and opinion evidence for substantive purposes. For a review of the foundation requirement and a discussion of why opinion witnesses should not be permitted to set forth the factual bases for their opinions, see pages 316-19, supra. FRE 608(a) limits the use of reputation or opinion evidence to "character for truthfulness or untruthfulness." This limitation repudiates the position of a few jurisdictions, which have permitted parties to impeach witnesses with evidence of general bad character or bad moral character. According to the Advisory Committee Note:

> In accordance with the bulk of judicial authority, the inquiry is strictly limited to character for veracity, rather than allowing evidence as to character generally. The result is to sharpen relevancy, to reduce surprise, waste of time, and confusion, and to make the lot of the witness somewhat less unattractive.

After a witness's character for truthfulness has been attacked, the opposing party may then rehabilitate the witness by introducing evidence regarding the witness's good character for truthfulness. Just as the impeaching evidence is offered to suggest the witness is lying on the witness stand, the rehabilitation evidence is offered to suggest the witness is being sincere on the witness stand.

b. The FRE 608(a) Limitation on Evidence of Good Character for Truthfulness

According to FRE 608(a) reputation or opinion testimony regarding a witness's good character for truthfulness is not admissible until the witness's character has been "attacked." It is not entirely clear, though, what kind of impeachment constitutes an attack on character for truthfulness. Courts traditionally have regarded impeachment by showing prior convictions, FRE 609, or bad acts that did not result in convictions, FRE 608(b), as an attack on a witness's character. Thus, rehabilitation with reputation or opinion evidence would be appropriate. For example, since the prosecution in the *Johnson* case impeached the credibility of both inmate Michael Green and the defendant with evidence of prior convictions (page 55, lines 20, 34; page 61, line 30, supra), it would have been permissible for the defendant to call witnesses who would offer their opinions that Green and Johnson were truthful individuals. On the other hand, courts have declared that some prior acts are not relevant to attack a witness's character for truthfulness. See United States v. Holden, 557 F.3d 698, 702 (6th Cir. 2009) ("As a general matter, prior drug use is not relevant to a witness's character for truthfulness.").

Although proof of bias may suggest that a witness is not testifying truthfully, courts generally regard proof of a witness's bias as not being an attack on the witness's *character* for truthfulness. United States v. Figueroa, 548 F.3d 222 (5th Cir. 2008) (cross-examining witness about swastika tattoos relevant to bias toward defendant not character for untruthfulness). For example, in the *Johnson* case, if the prosecution could have established that Johnson and his cellmate belonged to the same gang (page 49, line 32, supra), this evidence would show the cellmate's possible bias but not the cellmate's bad character for truthfulness. Similarly, proof in a civil case that a witness for the plaintiff had recently gone through an acrimonious, contested divorce with the defendant suggests that the witness may be biased against the defendant but not that the witness is a generally untruthful person. Thus, FRE 608(a) would not permit Johnson or the defendant in the civil action to rehabilitate the impeached witness by offering opinion or reputation evidence of that witness's good character for truthfulness. Depending on the circumstances of the case, however, some evidence of bias may also constitute an attack on the witness's character, thus permitting FRE 608(a) rehabilitation evidence. See, e.g., United States v. Medical Therapy Sciences, Inc., 583 F.2d 36, 41 (2d Cir. 1978) (evidence of corrupt conduct by a witness that indicates bias, such as embezzling money, may also constitute an attack on witness's character for truthfulness). The key inquiry is whether the evidence of bias also suggests that the witness has a character for untruthfulness.

Sometimes there will be disagreement about how to categorize the impeaching evidence. For example, recall in the *Johnson* case that defense counsel on cross-examination of Officer Huston suggested Huston's alleged injury in the altercation with Johnson was fabricated because of the workers' compensation rules (page 21, line 4, supra). This inquiry suggests a particular bias or motive to lie. Does it also impugn Huston's character for truthfulness, so that the prosecution could have responded with FRE 608(a) character witnesses to testify about Huston's reputation for truthfulness? See if you can articulate a difference between character and bias that justifies different treatment under FRE 608(a).

KEY POINTS

1. FRE 608(a) permits a party to impeach the credibility of a witness by offering extrinsic evidence in the form of opinion or reputation testimony about the witness's character for untruthfulness. The evidence must focus on untruthfulness, not general moral character.

2. FRE 608(a) permits reputation or opinion evidence offered to prove a witness's good character for truthfulness only after the opposing party has attacked the witness's character for truthfulness.

PROBLEMS

7.1. Darby is being prosecuted for the armed robbery of a liquor store proprietor. During the presentation of the prosecution's case the proprietor made a positive identification of Darby as the robber. As part of the defense, Darby calls Sue Williams to testify that the proprietor has a reputation in the community for lying. Is the evidence admissible?

7.2. In the same case, another defense witness offers to testify that the proprietor has a reputation in the community for not remembering faces and for misidentifying people. Is the evidence admissible? Would your answer be different if the witness offered to testify that on the basis of her experience with the proprietor she is of the view that the proprietor has difficulty remembering faces and often misidentifies people?

7.3. Harper was arrested for sale of cocaine and accepted the government's offer to cooperate in obtaining evidence against his supplier. Harper identified Ellsworth as the supplier, and Ellsworth was eventually charged with sale of cocaine. At Ellsworth's trial, Agent Fowler, who was in charged of the investigation, testified that Harper had delivered what was in fact cocaine to him, and Harper testified that he had obtained the cocaine from Ellsworth. During the cross-examination of Harper, defense counsel elicited information about Harper's cooperation with the police. During the cross-examination of Agent Fowler, defense counsel elicited that Harper had three independent sources for cocaine. On redirect of Agent Fowler, the prosecutor asks:

    (a) Do you believe Mr. Harper received the cocaine involved in this case from a source other than the defendant, Ellsworth?

    (b) In your opinion is Mr. Harper's testimony in this case truthful?

    (c) In your opinion is Mr. Harper a truthful person?

    How should the court rule on Ellsworth's objections to these questions? Would any of your answers be different if defense counsel had referred to Harper as a liar in the opening statement? If defense counsel had elicited from Harper on cross-examination that two years ago he was convicted of embezzlement?

7.4. Dan Dickson is charged with perjury and testifies in his own behalf. The prosecutor's cross-examination fails to shake Dickson's story or cast doubt on his credibility. Dickson then offers the testimony of Willa Wilson that Dickson has a good reputation in the community for truthfulness. Is Wilson's testimony admissible?

3. Explanation of FRE 608(b)

FRE 608(b) provides:

> (b) *Specific Instances of Conduct.* Except for a criminal conviction under Rule 609, extrinsic evidence is not admissible to prove specific instances of a witness's conduct in order to attack or support the witness's character for truthfulness. But the court may, on cross-examination, allow them to be inquired into if they are probative of the character for truthfulness or untruthfulness of:
>
> > (1) the witness; or
> >
> > (2) another witness whose character the witness being cross-examined has testified about.
>
> By testifying on another matter, a witness does not waive any privilege against self-incrimination for testimony that relates only to the witness's character for truthfulness.

a. The Prohibition Against the Use of Extrinsic Evidence

FRE 608(b) prohibits the use of extrinsic evidence of a witness's specific acts to *support or attack* the witness's character for truthfulness. FRE 608(b) and a majority of states, however, do permit inquiry into (1) a witness's own acts during the examination of that witness, and (2) the acts of "another witness whose character the witness being cross-examined has testified about." The prohibition against the use of extrinsic evidence means that the examiner is bound by the answer of the witness; the impeaching party cannot introduce extrinsic evidence to contradict the witness. For example, in the *Johnson* case, defense counsel could have asked Officer Huston if he lied on his job application form. If Huston denied lying, however, defense counsel could not prove the lie by introducing the job application form, which would be extrinsic evidence, and then proving with other extrinsic evidence that the information contained on the form was false. Similarly, if another witness had testified that Huston had a good reputation for truthfulness, then that witness could be asked on cross-examination whether he knew Huston had lied on the job application form. However, defense counsel could not prove the lie with extrinsic evidence.

Not permitting the examiner to challenge the witness's answer with extrinsic evidence of bad character for truthfulness may sometimes appear unfair. For example, in our hypothetical in which Officer Huston denies that he lied on his job application form, assume that defense counsel is prepared to authenticate the job application form and to call ten witnesses who will testify that the facts stated in the application are false. What could be better impeaching evidence than this extrinsic proof that the witness had lied not only on the job application form but also on the witness stand?

There may be no more relevant or more effective impeachment. But fairness dictates that if the impeaching party is allowed to introduce the extrinsic evidence, the party whose witness was impeached should have an opportunity to counter that evidence. It may be, for example, that the job application form is a forgery, that the statements on the job application are reasonably subject to more than one interpretation, or that the witnesses who would testify that Officer Huston lied on the application are themselves dishonest. And if that opportunity exists, a substantial amount of time and energy could be devoted to litigating the truth or falsity of facts whose only value is to impeach the credibility of a witness. Moreover, there would be the potential for this type of minitrial with every witness. Thus, while it may be true that catching the witness in a lie on the stand would be extremely effective impeachment, FRE 608(b), out of concern with the time and distraction that could result from litigating collateral matters, prohibits the impeaching party from introducing extrinsic evidence to prove the lie.

b. The Limited Scope of Permissible Inquiry

FRE 608(b) is consistent with FRE 608(a) in that the specific acts must relate to character for truthfulness. See, e.g., United States v. Holden, supra (witness's prior marijuana use is not relevant impeachment evidence under 608(b)). This rule is considerably narrower than the rules in some state jurisdictions, which permit inquiry into acts relevant to prove a generally bad moral character.

c. No Fifth Amendment Waiver

Because of the centrality of cross-examination to our adversary system, the giving of testimony by a witness is regarded as a waiver or forfeiture of the witness's Fifth Amendment right against self-incrimination, at least with respect to the subject matter of the witness's direct examination testimony. The last sentence of FRE 608(b) makes it clear that testifying is not a waiver of the privilege with respect to questions that are permissible only to undermine the witness's credibility. Consider, for example, our hypothetical question about whether Officer Huston had lied on his job application form. If making false statements on the form were a crime, Officer Huston could rely on the Fifth Amendment to refuse to answer.

d. The Scope of 608(b)(1): Questioning Witnesses About Their Own Specific Acts

The Meaning of Untruthfulness.   Although the Advisory Committee Note to FRE 608(b) makes it clear that the terms *truthfulness* and *untruthfulness* are intended to limit the types of specific acts about which one may inquire, there is not uniform agreement about the scope of the limitation. At the extremes, courts tend to find that perjury or other instances of making false statements suggest untruthfulness, United States v. Velarde, 485 F.3d 553 (10th Cir. 2007) (prior false accusations by witness); United States v. Jensen, 41 F.3d 946 (5th Cir. 1994) (submission of false tax return and false loan documents to obtain loan); see also United States v. Torres, 569 F.3d 1277 (10th Cir. 2009) (prosecution witness's prior breach of agreement with DEA relevant under FRE 608(b)), and that acts of violence (e.g., murder, destruction of property) or drug crimes do not suggest untruthfulness, United States v. Geston, 299 F.3d 1130, 1137 (9th Cir. 2002) (violent conduct while under influence of alcohol not probative of untruthfulness); United States v. Wilson, 344 F.2d 1208 (10th Cir. 2001) (drug crimes not probative of truth or untruth). There is, however, a gray area where courts sometimes reach seemingly inconsistent results. Compare, e.g., United States v. Wilson, 985 F.2d 348, 352 (7th Cir. 1993) (bribery probative of untruthfulness) with United States v. Rosa, 891 F.2d 1063, 1069 (3d Cir. 1989) (bribery "not the kind of conduct which bears on truthfulness or untruthfulness").

Questions about Arrests, Charges, and Administrative or Judicial Findings. Sometimes an impeaching party will have evidence that a witness was arrested or charged with some offense relating to untruthfulness or that an administrative or judicial body has found that a witness behaved in a manner indicating untruthfulness. For example, the witness may have been arrested for or charged with falsifying loan documents; the witness may have been disbarred for deceitful conduct; or a judge in an earlier proceeding may have implicitly or explicitly found that the witness had lied. In these situations FRE 608(b) permits the impeaching party to ask about the underlying conduct—whether the witness in fact falsified documents, engaged in deceitful conduct, or lied in an earlier proceeding. But what about asking whether the witness was *arrested* or *charged* with falsifying documents, whether the witness was *disbarred* for the deceitful conduct, or whether a *judge found* that the witness had lied?

A witness's arrest or a factual finding about the witness is not a specific instance of the *witness's* conduct. Rather, as we pointed out in Chapter Five at page 324, an arrest or a finding is activity engaged in by the arresting officer or the fact finder. Moreover, as we point out in Chapter Eight at pages 468, this type of evidence is hearsay. The witness is not being asked directly whether the witness engaged in the conduct. Instead, the witness is being asked whether somebody else—the arresting officer (or person who authorized the arrest) or the factfinder—said that the witness engaged in the conduct. And, of course, that statement of the police officer or the factfinder is relevant to impeach the witness only if one believes the truth of what the officer or fact finder said. For this reason, some courts have limited FRE 608(b) questioning to the witness's conduct in these instances. See, e.g., United States v. Holt, 486 F.3d 997 (7th Cir. 2007) (not abuse of discretion for trial court to allow cross-examination of police officer about his conduct but to exclude questioning about whether the officer was suspended for the conduct); United States v. Davis, 183 F.3d 231, 257 n.12 (3d Cir. 1999) ("the government cannot make reference to [the defendant's] . . . suspension or that Internal Affairs found he lied . . . . The government needs to limit its cross-examination to the facts underlying those events."). Other courts, however, have permitted these questions. See, e.g., United States v. Whitmore, 359 F.3d 609 (D.C. Cir. 2004) (judge's finding that witness had lied); United States v. Scott, 74 F.3d 175,177 (9th Cir. 1996) (question about prior arrest).

e. Questions About Specific Acts and FRE 403

FRE 608(b) states that courts "may" allow questions about specific acts when they are probative of character for truthfulness. Even when specific acts are probative of character for truthfulness, courts may exercise their discretion and exclude such questions because of FRE 403 concerns. First, in some instances the witness's conduct, even if relevant for untruthfulness, may have low probative value. Compare Ad-Vantage Telephone Directory Consultants, Inc. v. GTE Directories Corp, 37 F.3d 1460 (11th Cir. 1994) (accountant's 1969 sanction for ethical violation inadmissible on FRE 403 grounds because of remoteness in time) with United States v. Munoz, 233 F.3d 1117, 1135 (9th Cir. 2000) (14- to 16-year-old incident not too remote). Second, if the witness acknowledges an act of untruthfulness, there is a risk of unfair prejudice. See United States v. Bunchan, 580 F.3d 66 (1st Cir. 2009) ("The district court's determination that the nature of sexual assault charges was not sufficiently probative of [the witness's] character for truthfulness to outweigh the serious danger of prejudicing the jury against him was well within its discretion."). This risk is particularly great if the witness happens to be a party: The jury may be willing to decide against the party because the jury regards the witness as a bad person. United States v. DeGeratto, 876 F.2d 576, 582-583 (7th Cir. 1989) (emphasizing prejudicial nature of cross-examination about defendant's involvement in prostitution without discussing how such evidence was probative of truthfulness). Third, if there are numerous inquiries about the specific acts of truthfulness, there are likely to be concerns with time-consumption and confusion of the issues. Fourth, even if the witness honestly denies having committed a dishonest act, there is a risk that the jury may be more swayed by the suggestiveness of the question than by the answer. United States v. Dring, 930 F.2d 687, 692 (9th Cir. 1991) (quoting McCormick on Evidence for proposition that a " 'slashing cross-examination may carry strong accusations of misconduct and bad character, which the witness's denial will not remove from the jury's mind' "). Finally, if the witness is a party and if the question relates to conduct similar to the conduct that is the subject of the litigation, there is a risk that the jury will consider the evidence, contrary to the dictate of FRE 404(b), as evidence that the defendant engaged in the conduct that is the subject of the litigation. United States v. Pintar, 630 F.2d 1270, 1285-1286 (8th Cir. 1980) (prosecution unduly emphasized illegal kickbacks that were not part of the charge and not admissible pursuant to FRE 404(b) in cross-examination of defendant).

Despite the FRE 403 grounds for objecting to FRE 608(b) questions, courts typically are quite liberal in permitting inquiry about specific acts to prove character for impeachment purposes. According to the Advisory Committee, "Effective cross-examination demands that some allowance be made for going into matters of this kind." See also David P. Leonard, Appellate Review of Evidentiary Rulings, 70 N.C. L. Rev. 1155 (1992), a particularly thoughtful analysis of the role of appellate courts in reviewing trial judges' FRE 608(b) decisions.

f. Good-Faith Requirement; Practical Considerations

Because of the suggestiveness that is likely to inhere in a question about a specific act relating to truthfulness, courts have held that the examiner must have a good-faith basis for believing that the act occurred. United States v. DeGeratto, 876 F.3d 576, 584 (7th Cir. 1989). Such a requirement is probably satisfied, for example, by knowledge that the witness had been arrested for the activity that is the subject of the question or by hearsay information obtained during the investigation of the case. See United States v. Whitmore, 359 F.3d 609 (D.C. Cir. 2004) (record from state Motor Vehicle Administration provided reasonable basis to ask witness about suspended driver's license, even though record was hearsay).

A litigant who suspects that the opponent may ask a question without a factual basis for the inquiry should request a hearing on that issue outside the presence of the jury. Similarly, if a litigant suspects that the opponent may ask about some act falling outside the truthfulness limitation in FRE 608(b), the litigant should consider filing a motion in limine seeking a ruling on the issue. Unless the litigant knows that the opponent is aware of the potential impeaching evidence, however, filing such a motion may have the undesirable effect of alerting the opponent to the evidence.

An additional practical consideration in criminal cases concerns the constitutional obligation of prosecutors under Brady v. Maryland, 373 U.S. 83 (1963), to turn over evidence favorable to the defense. This obligation extends to evidence that the defense may use to impeach government witnesses under FRE 608(b). United States v. Torres, 569 F.3d 1277 (10th Cir. 2009) (abuse of discretion by trial court in failing to find *Brady* violation when prosecutor failed to disclose government witness, a confidential informant, had previously breached an agreement with the government and had been involved in unrelated criminal conduct); see also United States v. Price, 566 F.3d 900 (9th Cir. 2009); United States v. Johnson, 519 F.3d 478 (D.C. Cir. 2008); United States v. Velarde, 485 F.3d 553 (10th Cir. 2007).

g. Specific Acts Showing Good Character for Truthfulness

Most FRE 608(b) questions involve attempts to impeach witnesses with their untruthful acts; however, the rule also permits questions about truthful acts. For example, a witness who has been impeached with character evidence may be asked about specific truthful acts as a means of rehabilitating the witness's character. FRE 608(b) prohibits extrinsic evidence for specific acts relating to truthfulness as well as untruthfulness. See United States v. Melia, 691 F.2d 672, 674-675 (4th Cir. 1982) (improper to rehabilitate witness with extrinsic evidence that witness helped to solve various crimes). Technically, FRE 608(b), unlike FRE 608(a), does not contain a provision that permits questions about truthful acts only after the witness has been impeached with character evidence. Nevertheless, this kind of bolstering evidence is unlikely to be allowed (because of either FRE 403 or FRE 608(a)'s prohibition on preimpeachment character evidence). The reported cases and academic commentary devote little attention to FRE 608(b) truthful acts. This category of evidence does not appear to generate problems for courts. The evidence is obviously self-serving and, therefore, seldom worth introducing or challenging.

h. "Cross-Examination"

FRE 608(b) states that the court may allow specific instances to be inquired into on "cross-examination." Although FRE 608(b) questions about untruthful acts arise most often during cross-examination (as an attempt to impeach a witness called by the opposing party), there are other instances in which FRE 608(b) questions will be allowed. Therefore, the term "cross-examination" should not be interpreted to limit the scope of the rule. For example, FRE 607 permits parties to impeach the credibility of their own witnesses. Therefore, a party who calls a witness, and attempts to impeach that witness, may ask 608(b) questions on direct examination. Moreover, if one party asks 608(b) questions relating to *untruthfulness* on cross-examination, then the opposing party may attempt to rehabilitate the witness by inquiring into specific acts relating to *truthfulness* on redirect examination, or vice versa. See, e.g., United States v. Powell, 124 F.3d 655, 661 n.4 (5th Cir. 1997) (when defendant raised issue of his own truthful character during cross-examination of a witness, it was permissible for the prosecution to ask about specific acts of the defendant during redirect).

i. The Scope of FRE 608(b)(2): Questioning Character Witnesses Regarding Specific Acts of the Witnesses They Testify About

FRE 608(b)(2) addresses an issue we have considered previously in Chapter Five: the cross-examination of reputation or opinion witnesses to test their knowledge of the reputation or the basis for the opinion about which they testify.

Once a character witness has given reputation or opinion testimony pursuant to FRE 608(a), the opposing party—in addition to impeaching the character witness with questions about the character witness's own acts of untruthfulness (FRE 608(b)(1))—may impeach the character witness in the same manner in which a party may impeach character witnesses who give reputation or opinion testimony pursuant to FRE 404(a)(2): The impeaching party may ask the character witness if the character witness is aware of relevant specific acts committed by the person whose character was the subject of the witness's testimony. For example, if, as we hypothesized earlier about the *Johnson* case, the defense had called witnesses to testify that in their opinion Johnson was a truthful person, it would have been appropriate to ask these witnesses on cross-examination both about their own acts of untruthfulness (FRE 608(b)(1)) and about their knowledge of acts of dishonesty in which Johnson had engaged (FRE 608(b)(2)). It would not have been appropriate, however, to ask them if they knew about Johnson's previous violent acts. As FRE 608(b) makes clear, the specific acts must relate to the character trait about which the FRE 608(a) character witness testified—truthfulness—and acts of violence are not probative of truthfulness.

This FRE 608(b)(2) impeachment process is identical to the process for impeaching character witnesses that we described in Chapter Five. In effect, FRE 608(b)(2) is a specific, somewhat awkwardly worded application to FRE 608(a) character witnesses of the general principle set forth in the second sentence of FRE 405(a): "On cross-examination [of a character witness who offers reputation or opinion testimony], the court may allow an inquiry into relevant specific instances of the person's conduct." As is the case in the context of relying on FRE 405(a) to impeach FRE 404(a) character witnesses, (1) the cross-examiner must have a good-faith basis for asking the questions, United States v. Reese, 568 F.2d 1246, 1249 (6th Cir. 1977), and (2) the legitimate purpose of the inquiry is to impeach the credibility of the character witness, *not* to prove the character of the principal witness, about whom the question is asked. Indeed, using the character witness's testimony about the principal witness's specific act to prove the principal witness's truthfulness would violate the FRE 608(b) prohibition against using extrinsic evidence to prove the principal witness's character.

KEY POINTS

1. FRE 608(b)(1) permits the impeachment and rehabilitation of witnesses with questions about the witnesses' own specific acts that show character for truthfulness. The examiner is bound by the witness's answer to such questions and may not introduce extrinsic evidence to challenge the answer.
2. FRE 608(b)(1) specific-acts questions must relate to character for truthfulness, and they are subject to exclusion on FRE 403 grounds.
3. When an FRE 608(a) character witness offers opinion or reputation testimony about another witness's character for truthfulness, FRE 608(b)(2) permits the opposing party to ask the character witness about specific acts probative of truthfulness that the other witness may have committed. The purpose of the questions is to test the basis for the character witness's reputation or opinion testimony.

PROBLEMS

7.5. Defendant is on trial for a burglary, which took place at 10:00 P.M. in a house at 1251 Hazel Street. Defendant has bright red hair. The defense calls Jones to testify, and Jones testifies as follows: "On the night of the burglary, I was walking out of the Century Pub around 10:00 P.M. The Pub is across the street from 1251 Hazel Street. I saw a man with black hair running out of the house at 1251 Hazel Street."

In order to impeach Jones, may the prosecution:

(a) call another witness, Smith, to testify that Jones has a bad reputation for truthfulness in their neighborhood? (;)

(b) ask Jones whether he lied on a job application a year ago when he denied ever having been convicted of a crime? Suppose the prosecution has a copy of both the job application and a record of Jones's conviction for armed robbery four years ago. If Jones denies lying on the job application, may the prosecution respond by admitting an authenticated copy of the job application? An authenticated record of the conviction?

7.6. Sam Browning is charged with murder. He plans to testify in his own behalf and to call Walt Williams to testify that Browning has a good reputation for peacefulness. The prosecutor has a good-faith basis for believing that three years ago Browning was involved in a bribery scheme; that he beat his wife (although no charges have ever been filed); and that last year Williams filed a false income tax return.

(a) Can the prosecutor ask Browning about the bribery incident? The beating?

(b) Can the prosecutor ask Williams if he has heard that Browning was involved in a bribery scheme three years ago? That Browning beat his wife three years ago?

(c) Can the prosecutor ask Williams if he intentionally filed a false income tax return last year?

7.7. Ed Duke is being prosecuted for murdering Harry Howe, owner of Harry's Hash House. Harry was found dead on the floor of his Hash House and the till was open and empty. At trial Fred Finley testifies for the prosecution that the day before the murder Ed Duke said he was going to get Harry.

(a) On cross-examination of Finley, defense counsel asks Finley whether he has ever been arrested for possession of marijuana.

(b) Alex Adams offers to testify that several years ago he was an altar boy at the local church, that Finley was a chorister, and that several times Alex saw Finley steal church property such as cups and other religious objects.

(c) Jane Jackson, a neighbor of Finley's parents, offers to testify that she has known Finley for Finley's entire life and that in her opinion he is untruthful.

(d) In rebuttal, the prosecution calls Mark Mayer, who offers to testify that he lives in the same neighborhood as Fred Finley and that he knows Finley's reputation in the neighborhood for truth and veracity is good.

(e) On cross-examination of Mayer, defense counsel asks if Mayer has heard that Finley was convicted of perjury two years ago.

Should objections to any of this evidence be sustained?

7.8. Williams is charged with being a convicted felon in possession of a firearm. The only evidence of his possession was the testimony of Detective David Martin. Martin testified that while giving chase, he saw Williams throw a black object. After arresting Williams, Martin returned to the area and found a gun that showed signs of being thrown against a wall. Williams claims that he had no gun and that it was planted by Martin.

Can Williams cross-examine Martin about (a) a Superior Court judge's finding that Martin lied on the stand during a trial, (b) Martin's driver's license being suspended for driving while intoxicated and the fact that Martin never reported the information to his superiors, and (c) Martin's failure to comply with a court order to pay child support?

Consider whether the court should permit Williams to call the following witnesses:

(a) Johnny Caravella to testify about a news story he wrote five years ago that identified Detective Martin as the subject of many police harassment complaints in the neighborhood. The sources for the story were unnamed people who lived in Martin's neighborhood.

(b) Defense attorney Alice Weaver to testify that Martin has a reputation in the "court community" for being untruthful. Weaver's testimony is based on the opinions of three other defense lawyers she knows and her own experience with cases in which Martin has been a witness.

(c) Chris Brown, an acquaintance of Martin, to testify that Martin wrongfully arrested him for drug possession, that a friend's belongings went missing when Martin arrested the friend, and that in his (Brown's) opinion Martin is very dishonest. Until six years ago Brown lived in Martin's neighborhood and saw Martin almost daily. Brown continues to see Martin regularly when he returns to the neighborhood to visit his mother.

4. FRE 609

RULE 609. IMPEACHMENT BY EVIDENCE OF A CRIMINAL CONVICTION

(a) In General. The following rules apply to attacking a witness's character for truthfulness by evidence of a criminal conviction:

(1) for a crime that, in the convicting jurisdiction, was punishable by death or by imprisonment for more than one year, the evidence:

(A) must be admitted, subject to Rule 403, in a civil case or in a criminal case in which the witness is not a defendant; and

(B) must be admitted in a criminal case in which the witness is a defendant, if the probative value of the evidence outweighs its prejudicial effect to that defendant; and

(2) for any crime regardless of the punishment, the evidence must be admitted if the court can readily determine that establishing the elements

of the crime required proving—or the witness's admitting—a dishonest act or false statement.

(b) Limit on Using the Evidence After Ten Years. This subdivision (b) applies if more than ten years have passed since the witness's conviction or release from confinement for it, whichever is later. Evidence of the conviction is admissible only if:

(1) its probative value, supported by specific facts and circumstances, substantially outweighs its prejudicial effect; and

(2) the proponent gives an adverse party reasonable written notice of the intent to use it so that the party has a fair opportunity to contest its use.

[Section (c) restricts the use of convictions that have been the subject of pardon or annulment; section (d) restricts the use of juvenile adjudications; and section (e) provides that the pendency of an appeal does not make evidence of a conviction inadmissible.]

5. Explanation of FRE 609(a) and (b)

FRE 609(a) permits impeachment with two types of convictions: (1) convictions for serious crimes (i.e., those punishable by imprisonment for more than one year, which is the federal definition of a felony), and (2) convictions, regardless of potential punishment, for crimes involving a dishonest act or false statement. The theory of relevance underlying the use of both types of prior convictions is similar to the theory of relevance underlying inquiries about specific instances of conduct pursuant to FRE 608(b)(1): The witness's specific acts that are the basis for the conviction show a general character trait or disposition for untruthfulness from which one can infer that the witness may not be telling the truth on the witness stand. The limitations of FRE 609 do not apply when prior convictions are offered for a relevant purpose other than to prove the witness's character for truthfulness, such as to show contradiction or bias. United States v. Gilmore, 553 F.3d 266, 272 (3d Cir. 2009) (defendant's prior drug convictions admissible to contradict his testimony that he never sold drugs); United States v. Allen, 540 F.3d 821, 824 (8th Cir. 2008) (witness's prior conviction for misdemeanor domestic battery admissible to show witness was prohibited from possessing a firearm and, therefore, had a self-interested motive in denying knowledge or possession of a firearm in a car in which he and defendant were arrested).

An essential feature of FRE 609 is that, unlike FRE 608(b), it contains no prohibition against the use of extrinsic evidence. Thus, if a witness denies a conviction, it is permissible to establish the conviction with extrinsic evidence—for example, with a record of the conviction.

a. The Two FRE 609(a)(1) Balancing Tests

If a conviction falls within FRE 609(a)(1)—that is, if it is a felony that is *not* a crime involving a dishonest act or false statement (e.g., if it is murder)—its admissibility to impeach a witness is subject to a balancing test. The balancing test for all witnesses *except* criminal defendants is FRE 403. For criminal defendants who are witnesses, FRE 609(a)(1) mandates a reverse-FRE 403 test: The probative value must outweigh the prejudice to the defendant. Whereas FRE 403, by requiring that the probative value must be substantially outweighed by the countervailing factors, favors admissibility, and in effect puts the burden on the party arguing for exclusion to justify that result, the reverse FRE 403 test in FRE 609 favors exclusion and in effect puts the burden on the prosecution to justify admissibility.

Consider, for example, a situation in which a witness has been released from imprisonment for murder six years ago. In deciding whether to admit evidence of the murder conviction to impeach the witness, the judge must first assess the probative value of the conviction. Then the judge must assess the prejudicial impact of the evidence and apply the appropriate balancing test. All of the issues that you studied in Chapter Three concerning the application of FRE 403 apply to the trial judge's decision.

Probative Value.   The evidentiary fact that the conviction is offered to prove is the truthfulness of the witness at the time of the witness's testimony. Thus, the probative value assessment should include consideration of (1) the age of the conviction, (2) how probative murder is to show bad moral character or general disposition for law-breaking, which in turn shows a disposition for untruthfulness, and (3) the witness's intervening behavior. Six years may seem like a long time, and murder may not seem very probative of untruthfulness. On the other hand, six years is only slightly more than half of the time period prescribed in FRE 609(b), and in the absence of mitigating circumstances relating to the murder, it may be reasonable to infer that a person who is willing to commit such a serious crime has little regard for the law, including the requirement to testify truthfully. Moreover, a crime that in isolation may not seem very probative of truthfulness may be more probative if it is part of a continuing pattern of untruthfulness. Thus, conduct reflecting on truthfulness during the time between release from imprisonment and giving testimony should be an important part of the probative value determination. United States v. Gilbert, 668 F.2d 94, 97 (2d Cir. 1981) (conviction admissible; age of conviction and subsequent history did not suggest abandonment of earlier ways).

Unfair Prejudice.   Against the probative value assessment the judge must balance the potential for unfair prejudice. Here there are two primary concerns: First, to what extent will the jury consider the witness to be a bad person and, therefore, be disposed against the witness? For example, if the witness is the defendant, there is a risk that jury may ignore the reasonable doubt standard because it regards the defendant as a bad or dangerous person. Even if the witness is not a party, there is a risk that prejudice against the witness may spill over and affect the jury's attitude about the party who called the witness.

Second, to what extent is there a risk that the jury may use the conviction not only in its proper propensity sense to prove that the witness may be untruthful on the witness stand but also in an improper propensity sense? For example, if the witness is a defendant charged with a crime of violence, there is a risk that the jury, in violation of the prohibition in the first sentence of FRE 404(b), may use the murder conviction as evidence of the defendant's character for violence, for the purpose of inferring that the defendant behaved violently in committing the crime charged. This risk is particularly high when the witness is the defendant and the prior crime is similar in nature to the one at issue in the current trial.

The Reverse FRE 403 Balancing Test for Criminal Defendants. The probative value of the murder conviction to prove untruthfulness remains the same regardless of whether the witness is a party to the action. The prejudice, however, is likely to be greatest when the witness is a criminal defendant. Even if the jury regards a nonparty witness as a bad person, it seems less likely that the jury would respond by thinking ill of and, as a result, punishing the party who called the witness. And the risk that a jury may utilize a prior conviction in an improper propensity sense exists only if some conduct of the witness is the subject of the current litigation. That, of course, will always be the case with criminal defendants who testify on their own behalf.

Because the risk of prejudice to criminal defendants is particularly high and because the probative value versus prejudice balancing process is inherently imprecise, FRE 609(a)(1) employs a reverse FRE 403 balancing test for witnesses who are criminal defendants. As a result, it is somewhat more likely, at least in theory, that the murder conviction— and other FRE 609(a)(1) convictions—will be admissible against witnesses who are not criminal defendants than against criminal defendants. See United States v. Caldwell, 760 F.3d 267, 285-289 (3d Cir. 2014) (excluding the defendant's prior convictions under reverse 403 balancing test after considering: (1) the nature of the crime, (2) the date of conviction, (3) the importance of the defendant's testimony, and (4) the importance of the defendant's credibility).

The FRE 403 Balancing Test for Other Witnesses. FRE 609(a) does not give civil parties who are witnesses the benefit of the reverse FRE 403 balancing test. Rather, FRE 609(a) treats them in the same manner as it treats nonparty witnesses. Their prior convictions will be admissible unless the probative impeachment value of the convictions is substantially outweighed by the FRE 403 countervailing factors.

The subject matter of civil litigation often does not involve the same type of morally culpable conduct that is typically the subject of criminal prosecutions. As a result, the risk of prejudice from using prior convictions for impermissible propensity purposes may be less in civil cases generally than in criminal prosecutions. Moreover, civil litigants as a class are not as likely to have prior convictions as are criminal defendants. On the other hand, some civil claims—for example, fraud or sexual assault—involve allegations of criminal conduct; and as we suggested in subsection iii, supra, the risk of bad person prejudice is likely to be greater with party witnesses than with nonparty witnesses. Do you think civil party witnesses should receive the same reverse balancing test that criminal defendants receive?

The Factual Circumstances of the Crime. When courts balance the probative value of a conviction against its unfair prejudice and other countervailing factors, they frequently discuss the issue in only general terms—such as the type, the punishment, the date, and the number of convictions—because this is the information that will be presented to the jury. United States v. Howell, 285 F.3d 1263 (10th Cir. 2002). We discuss the factual details that may be presented below in subsection 6(d). Courts also inquire into the facts underlying a conviction when determining whether a conviction involves a "dishonest act or false statement" for purposes of FRE 609(a)(2). We discuss this issue below in subsection 5(b).

b. The Automatic Admissibility of FRE 609(a)(2) "Dishonest Act or False Statement" Convictions

The Rule.   "Dishonest act or false statement" convictions, as the language of FRE 609(a)(2) makes clear, are automatically admissible without regard to balancing and without regard to the seriousness of the crime. In short, if the conviction is for a crime involving a dishonest act or false statement, it is unnecessary to consider what the potential penalty for the crime is or any potential prejudicial impact of the conviction. As long as the conviction falls within the time limitation set forth in FRE 609(b), a court has no discretion to exclude it. For example, if a witness had been convicted of a misdemeanor offense of making a false statement on some type of application form, the impeaching party could admit the conviction to impeach the witness even if the conviction were nine years old and thus arguably not very probative of the witness's truth-telling on the witness stand now, nine years later. Even if the witness were a criminal defendant charged with the identical crime the evidence would be admissible.

The Meaning of "Dishonest Act or False Statement."   Because of the automatic admissibility for crimes involving dishonest acts or false statements, the contours of this category of crimes are extremely important. To the extent that one equates "dishonest act" with "illegal," all crimes are crimes involving a dishonest act. Clearly, however, the term *dishonest* in FRE 609(a)(2) should not be interpreted that broadly, for limitations in FRE 609(a)(1) would then be meaningless.

Prior to the 2011 restyling amendments, FRE 609(a)(2) referred to crimes involving "dishonesty or false statement," and the Advisory Committee Note to FRE 609 equates "dishonesty or false statement" with the common law classification *crimen falsi*. The Senate Judiciary Committee Report and the Conference Report on the Federal Rules contain the following identical elaboration:

> [It means] crimes such as perjury or subornation of perjury, false statement, criminal fraud, embezzlement or false pretenses, or any other offense, in the nature of *crimen falsi* the commission of which involves some element of untruthfulness, deceit or falsification bearing on the accused's propensity to testify truthfully.

Federal courts have interpreted "dishonesty or false statement" relatively narrowly. United States v. Osazuwa, 564 F.3d 1169, 1175 (9th Cir. 2009) ("It is undisputed that bank fraud is an act of dishonesty"); United States v. Harper, 527 F.3d 396, 408 (5th Cir. 2008) ("theft by check convictions fall under Rule 609(a)(2)"); United States v. Morrow, 977 F.2d 222 (6th Cir. 1992) (counterfeiting is crime of "dishonesty or false statement"); Wagner v. Firestone Tire & Rubber Co., 890 F.2d 652 (3d Cir. 1989) (forgery is crime of "dishonesty or false statement"); Walker v. Horn, 385 F.3d 321, 334 (3d Cir. 2004) (robbery is not crime of dishonesty or false statement); United States v. Mejia-Alarcon, 995 F.2d 982 (10th Cir. 1993) (conviction for unauthorized use of food stamps not within FRE 609(a)(2)); United States v. Karmer, 923 F.2d 1557 (11th Cir. 1991) (misdemeanor theft not usually within FRE 609(a)(2)). There are gray areas, however, and the case law is not entirely consistent. Compare, e.g., United States v. Wilson, 985 F.2d 348 (7th Cir. 1993) (failure to file income tax return is crime of "dishonesty or false statement") with Cree v. Hatcher, 969 F.2d 34 (3d Cir. 1993), (failure to file income tax return not within FRE 609(a)(2)). See generally Stuart P. Green, Deceit and Classification of Crimes: Federal Rule of Evidence 609(a)(2) and the Origins of Crimen Falsi, 90 J. Crim. L. & Criminology 1087 (2000).

The Significance of the Underlying Details of the Crime. FRE 609(a)(2) provides that a conviction falls within its scope when "the court can readily determine that establishing the elements of the crime required proving—or the witness's admitting—a dishonest act or false statement." In the absence of the witness's admission, the Advisory Committee provides examples of what may satisfy the "readily apparent" requirement:

> Where the deceitful nature of the crime is not apparent from the statute and the face of the judgment—as, for example, where the conviction simply records a finding of guilt for a statutory offense that does not reference deceit expressly—a proponent may offer information such as *an indictment, a statement of admitted facts, or jury instructions to show that the factfinder had to find, or the defendant had to admit, an act of dishonesty or false statement in order for the witness to have been convicted.* (Emphasis added.)

In United States v. Jefferson, 623 F.3d 227, 234-235 (5th Cir. 2010), for example, the court concluded that a prior conviction for obstruction of justice involved a dishonest act or false statement, and thus qualified under FRE 609(a)(2), because the indictment in that case alleged that the witness attempted to persuade another to lie to federal law enforcement authorities. See also United States v. Collier, 527 F.3d 695, 699 (8th Cir. 2008) (conviction for credit card fraud within 609(a)(2) because offense included "intent to defraud" as a statutory element).

c. The FRE 609(b) Reverse Balancing Test

All prior convictions falling within the scope of FRE 609(a)—including dishonest act and false statement convictions—are subject to a reverse FRE 403 balancing test in FRE 609(b) if they fall outside the ten-year time period specified in that subsection. The ten-year time period runs from the date of conviction or release from imprisonment, whichever is later. See United States v. Rogers, 542 F.3d 197, 201 (7th Cir. 2008) ("confinement" for purposes of FRE 609(b) "does not include periods of probation or parole"—"The clock starts at the witness's release from any physical confinement."). Thus, for example, a 12-year-old perjury conviction for which the witness served a three-year sentence would be automatically admissible despite the age of the conviction. If the witness had been imprisoned for only one year, however, FRE

609(b) would apply, and the conviction would be admissible only if its probative value substantially outweighed its prejudice—a test that, by virtue of the term *substantially*, is even more stringent than the reverse FRE 403 test in FRE 609(a).

Indeed, although courts have not developed specific standards to distinguish FRE 609(b) balancing from FRE 609(a) balancing, they have indicated that FRE 609(b) convictions should rarely be admissible. United States v. Bensimon, 172 F.3d 1121, 1126-1127 (9th Cir. 1999).

6. FRE 609(a) Impeachment: Policy and Practical Considerations

a. The Rationale for FRE 609(a)(1)

FRE 609(a)(1)—like the rules in most states—permits a trial judge to balance probative value and prejudice in deciding whether to admit evidence of felonies, regardless of whether the underlying conduct could reasonably be described as having a bearing on the witness's character for truthfulness. The rule is thus far broader than FRE 608(b).

The common law origin of impeachment with prior convictions probably accounts in part for its breadth and its uniform acceptance:

> At common law a person's conviction of treason, any felony, or a misdemeanor involving dishonesty (*crimen falsi*), or the obstruction of justice, rendered the convict completely incompetent as a witness. These were said to be "infamous" crimes. Thanks to statutes or rules virtually universal in the common law world, this primitive absolutism has been abandoned. The disqualification for conviction of crime has been repealed, and by specific provision or by decision it has been reduced to a mere ground for impeaching credibility. [1 McCormick on Evidence §42, at 184-85 (Kenneth S. Broun ed., 6th ed., 2006).]

In addition, the rule is justified by the belief that prior convictions, even if they are based on activity that does not relate very directly to truthfulness, may be especially relevant to the question of the witness's general credibility. Neither courts nor commentators, however, attempt to justify the assumption that convictions for acts only remotely related to truthfulness (e.g., aggravated assaults) may be especially probative of truthfulness on the witness stand. But see Campbell v. Greer, 831 F.2d 700 (7th Cir. 1987) ("The proposition that felons perjure themselves more often than other, similarly situated witnesses . . . is one of many important empirical assertions about law that have never been tested, and may be false."); Schmude v. Tricam Indus., Inc., 556 F.3d 624, 628 (7th Cir. 2009) (asserting that the assumption that convicted felons are more likely to lie on the witness stand is "underinclusive, since many people who have committed a felony have not been caught.").

Consider to what extent the following explanation justifies FRE 609: A person of generally bad moral character is more likely to lie than a person of generally good moral character. Indeed, compelling proof of bad moral character may be particularly probative of untruthfulness. All of us, however, from time to time engage in "bad" acts that tend to suggest bad moral character; and since few, if any, of us are likely to consider ourselves to be of bad moral character, it must follow that a single bad act—or even a series of bad acts—is not necessarily very probative of general moral character. Thus, in the absence of a conviction, most jurisdictions prohibit inquiry into these acts unless they are likely to have more than very marginal value to the question whether the witness is lying—that is, unless they relate fairly directly to that issue by suggesting a character trait of untruthfulness as opposed to general bad moral character. On the other hand, because the criminal law traditionally has tended to proscribe only the most reprehensible activities, convictions (especially when they are for serious crimes) are likely to be particularly probative of bad moral character and, therefore, untruthfulness. Of course, this justification for FRE 609 is weakened by the modern trend to also criminalize conduct that many do not consider to be morally reprehensible.

b. Prior Convictions and Prejudice

Most prior convictions admissible under FRE 609(a) are likely to be more prejudicial than most nonconviction bad act evidence admissible under FRE 608(b). This is so because the substantive law tends to criminalize the most reprehensible behavior; because police and prosecutors tend to focus their limited resources on the most serious offenders; and because the fact of conviction represents the community's judgment of moral condemnation. As a result, there is a relatively high risk that juries may be predisposed against witnesses who are shown to have prior convictions. Whenever the witness is a party or somebody closely associated with the party, jurors' attitudes about the witness may improperly affect their decision.

In assessing probative value and prejudice, it is important to keep in mind the significance of the similarity between the prior conviction evidence and the current criminal charge. When the witness is a criminal defendant (or some other person whose alleged actions are the basis for the current litigation), similarity between the current criminal allegations and the facts underlying the impeachment evidence enhances the *prejudice*, not the probative value, of the prior conviction. The only permissible inference to draw from the conviction is that the witness is an untruthful person and therefore may be lying on the witness stand.

c. Extrinsic Evidence

Convictions are the result of a plea or a factfinder's beyond-a-reasonable-doubt finding of guilt. They provide highly probative evidence that the underlying bad acts occurred, and the fact of a conviction can be easily established with a public record. Thus, the concern with time-consuming litigation about collateral matters that arguably justifies the FRE 608(b) prohibition against extrinsic evidence, see page 395, supra, does not apply to convictions offered pursuant to FRE 609, which may be proven with extrinsic evidence. In practice, however, there is seldom any need for such extrinsic evidence. Because a party can so easily establish a conviction, it is unlikely that a witness will deny the conviction in the first place. Indeed, as we discuss at page 412, infra, if a prior conviction will be admissible to impeach a witness, the party calling the witness may have the witness acknowledge the conviction on direct examination.

d. The Factual Details of the Conviction

Just as courts have an interest in avoiding lengthy inquiry into alleged bad acts that have not resulted in convictions, courts also have an interest in not spending a great deal of time exploring the facts underlying a witness's conviction. Moreover, eliciting the factual details underlying a conviction is likely to increase its prejudicial impact. Thus, courts typically will permit the impeaching party to mention the name of the crime, when and where it occurred, what sentence was imposed, and nothing more. United States v. Lopez-Medina, 596 F.3d 716, 738 (10th Cir. 2010) ("Ordinarily it is improper for the prosecution to examine into the details of the crime . . . . The cross-examination should be confined to the essential facts of conviction, nature of crime, and the punishment."); United States v. Osazuwa, supra ("Absent exceptional circumstances, evidence of a prior conviction for impeachment purposes may not include collateral details and circumstances attendant upon the conviction."); United States v. Commanche, 577 F.3d 1261 (10th Cir. 2009) (abuse of discretion for trial court to allow detail that defendant's prior two felony convictions involved sharp objects when defendant was on trial for allegedly stabbing two men); United States v. Pandozzi, 887 F.2d 1526, 1534-1535 (1st Cir. 1989) (impeachment with sexual assault conviction; proper to elicit that crime was sexual assault and to prohibit reference to fact that victim was a child). The details of a conviction that may be admitted will depend on an application FRE 403. See United States v. Lopez-Medina, supra ("A district court must conduct a Rule 403 balancing test before determining [whether to admit or exclude evidence] other than the fact and date of such convictions."). Further details regarding a crime may be admissible if, for example, the witness tries to explain away or minimize the seriousness of the crime. United States v. Amachia, 825 F.2d 177 (8th Cir. 1987); see also United States v. Commanche, supra (witness does not "open the door" to details about the conviction merely by answering questions about it).

e. The Relationship Between FRE 609(a) and FRE 608(b)

To what extent may parties rely on FRE 608(b) to admit additional details or specific acts related to criminal convictions that may be admitted under FRE 609? Recognizing the potential for FRE 608(b) to undermine limitations on the details of criminal conduct that may be presented under FRE 609, several federal appellate courts have clarified recently that FRE 608(b) may not be used to admit specific acts related to criminal convictions. FRE 608(b) applies only to specific acts that did not result in a criminal conviction; FRE 609 governs impeachment with criminal convictions and any underlying conduct. United States v. Osazuwa, 564 F.3d 1169 (9th Cir. 2009) ("Echoing the observations of the Fifth, Eighth, and Tenth Circuits, we hold that Rule 608(b) permits impeachment only by specific acts that have not resulted in a criminal conviction. Evidence relating to impeachment by way of criminal conviction is treated exclusively under Rule 609"); United States v. Lightfoot, 483 F.3d 876 (8th Cir. 2007); United States v. Parker, 133 F.3d 322 (5th Cir. 1998); Mason v. Texaco, Inc., 948 F.2d 1546 (10th Cir. 1991).

f. Hearsay

Regardless of whether the prior conviction is elicited from the witness or proved extrinsically with the record of conviction, the evidence is hearsay. The theory underlying FRE 609 is that the witness committed the acts that constitute the elements of the crime for which the witness was convicted and that proof of these acts suggests something important about the witness's credibility. In other words, the conviction is a manifestation of the jury's or the judge's assertion in an earlier proceeding that the witness committed the acts essential for the conviction, and it is the truth of this assertion that is critical to the relevance of the evidence. To the extent one doubts the reliability of this assertion, one should also doubt the probative value of the evidence for its impeaching purpose. For a recent argument that problems regarding the reliability of convictions and guilty pleas fall disproportionately on racial minorities, and that FRE 609 exacerbates these problems by generating evidence for further convictions, see Montré D. Carodine, "The Mis-Characterization of the Negro": A Race Critique of the Prior Conviction Impeachment Rule, 84 Ind. L.J. 521, 526 (2009) ("Rules such as Rule 609 keep Blacks ensnared in the criminal justice system, perpetuating the criminalization of a staggering percentage of the Black population.").

The Federal Rules, as well as a number of other jurisdictions, have a judgments exception to the hearsay rule. Typically, however, the judgments exception is narrower than the rule authorizing impeachment with prior convictions. For example, FRE 803(22) extends the judgments exception only to convictions for crimes punishable by imprisonment for more than one year, whereas FRE 609(a)(2) authorizes the use of "dishonest act or false statement" convictions regardless of the potential penalty. If courts have even noticed this conflict between FRE 609(a) and FRE 803(22), they have not been bothered by it. Courts considering the admissibility of misdemeanor convictions for impeachment under FRE 609(a)(2) have relied on that rule, which deals specifically with that issue, and have ignored the limitations in the more general FRE 803(22).

g. Practical Considerations

Frequently parties will file motions in limine seeking an advance ruling on whether prior convictions will be admissible against them. In deciding whether or not to testify in their criminal trials, defendants will want to know ahead of time whether their prior convictions will be admissible to impeach them. The admissibility determination may affect a defendant's trial strategy in two important ways. First, defendants who learn their prior convictions will be admissible for impeachment purposes may choose not to testify in order to prevent the jury from learning about the convictions. There is some empirical evidence suggesting that the admission of a criminal defendant's prior convictions contributes to the likelihood of a guilty verdict. Harry Kalven Jr. & Hans Zeisel, The American Jury 159-160 (1966); Anthony N. Doob & Hershi M. Kirshenbaum, Some Empirical Evidence on the Effect of Sec. 12 of the Canada Evidence Act Upon the Accused, 15 Crim. L.Q. 88, 91-95 (1972-1973). However, other evidence suggests that the prejudicial impact of prior convictions may not be as strong as is commonly asserted or assumed. See Ronald J. Allen &

Larry Laudan, The Devastating Impact of Prior Crimes Evidence and Other Myths of the Criminal Justice Process, 101 J. Crim. L. & Criminology 493 (2011) (discussing a study of over 350 state court criminal trials in which the acquittal rates for defendants with prior convictions was similar for defendants who had their convictions admitted at trial and for those who did not have their convictions admitted: 20.3% versus 23.9%).

Second, when a defendant chooses to testify and the defendant's prior convictions will be admissible, it will often be tactically important for the defendant to mention admissible prior convictions on direct examination. If the jury learns of the convictions for the first time on cross-examination, there is the risk that the jury will be prejudiced against the defendant for not "coming clean" on direct examination. The direct examiner, however, obviously has no interest in calling to the jury's attention convictions that would not otherwise be admissible.

In the *Johnson* case, defense counsel brought out on direct examination the prior convictions of the defendant, his cellmate, Butler, and inmate Green. Unfortunately, however, the direct examination was not complete with respect to Green's prior convictions. Thus, the prosecution was still able to benefit from the implication that the witness was not fully forthcoming on direct examination (page 55, lines 20-39, supra).

Judges will frequently rule on motions in limine regarding the admissibility of convictions before a defendant has to decide whether to testify. There is apparently no obligation to make such a ruling, however. In Luce v. United States, 469 U.S. 38 (1984), the Supreme Court held that a defendant who chose not to testify after the trial judge refused to rule on his motion in limine could not seek reversal on the ground that the convictions should not have been admissible. To preserve that claim, the Court held, the defendant must testify.

The *Luce* Court relied primarily on two factors. First, there was a concern that with a contrary holding defendants who had no genuine interest in testifying might file motions in limine in the hope of creating reversible error in the event that the court ruled the convictions to be admissible. Second, Luce made his motion before trial and did not accompany it with any indication of how he planned to impeach prosecution witnesses or what the testimony of defense witnesses (including himself) would be. In this context, the Supreme Court quite reasonably took the position that the trial judge may not have had enough information to engage in the balancing process required by FRE 609.

Consider what should happen if the defendant receives an unfavorable ruling on a motion in limine before testifying. Can the defendant acknowledge the conviction on direct examination in order to remove any inference of hiding unfavorable information and at the same time preserve the admissibility issue for appeal? Despite the fact that this situation does not implicate the two concerns that were central to *Luce*, the Supreme Court in Ohler v. United States, 529 U.S. 753 (2000), held 5 to 4 that a defendant who acknowledges prior convictions on direct examination after a ruling that they will be admissible pursuant to FRE 609 cannot claim on appeal that the admissibility decision was erroneous. See also United States v. McConnel, 464 F.3d 1152, 1162 (10th Cir. 2006) (extending *Ohler*'s waiver rule to impeachment evidence under FRE 608(b)). For a case refusing to follow *Ohler* and reaching the opposite result, see State v. Daly, 623 N.W.2d 799 (Iowa 2001). Which decision do you think is better — *Ohler* or *Daly*?

Even after *Ohler* and *Luce*, a defendant who contemplates the possibility of testifying should probably pursue a motion in limine to exclude prior convictions. If the judge rules on the motion, the defendant at least will have a better sense of the consequences of testifying.

For defense counsel who pursue such motions, there are several important considerations. First, and most important, while there may be legitimate tactical reasons for withholding some information from the court and the prosecution, a defense counsel who is serious about wanting a ruling on the motion should provide the trial court with as much information as possible to make the decision. For example, the defense should indicate what the impeachment of prosecution witnesses is likely to entail, what the defense testimony will probably be, and why the defendant's testimony is important for a fair trial. Providing the judge with this information removes one of the principal concerns expressed by *Luce*.

Second, if the court does not grant the motion before trial, defense counsel should renew the motion at the close of the prosecution case and, if necessary, again immediately before the defendant will have to decide whether to take the stand. At each renewal of the motion defense counsel should refine the argument for exclusion of the convictions in light of the evidence that has been presented and the anticipated evidence. At some point along the way it is likely that the court will have sufficient information to make a reasoned FRE 609 ruling. And if the judge has all of the relevant information, there is no reason why the judge should not rule on the motion. Indeed, in this type of situation the defendant might argue that — particularly in light of the *Luce* and *Ohler* — it is an abuse of discretion and an unreasonable burden on the defendant's right to testify for the judge to refuse to make the ruling.

Third, if the trial judge is reluctant to make a definitive FRE 609 balancing decision without knowing what the evidence in the case actually is, defense counsel should seek a conditional ruling: For example, as long as the evidence presented by the defendant is limited to the representations accompanying this motion, the defendant's prior convictions are not admissible.

KEY POINTS

1. FRE 609(a)(2) provides that convictions involving dishonest acts or false statements falling within the ten-year time limit described in FRE 609(b) are automatically admissible to impeach all witnesses (including criminal defendants) without regard to penalty or balancing.
2. FRE 609(a)(1) provides that other convictions falling within the ten-year time limit are admissible only if they are punishable by more than a year's imprisonment and if they satisfy the appropriate balancing test.
3. The balancing test for all witnesses except criminal defendants is FRE 403 (admissible unless probative value substantially outweighed by countervailing

factors); the balancing test for criminal defendants who are witnesses is a reverse FRE 403 test (probative value must outweigh the prejudicial impact on defendant).

4. The ten-year time limitation in FRE 609(b) runs from the date of conviction or the date of release from imprisonment, whichever is more recent.

5. In federal courts, a defendant who acknowledges prior convictions on direct examination following an in limine ruling that the convictions will be admissible cannot challenge the in limine ruling on appeal.

PROBLEMS

7.9. Return to Problem 7.5 at page 401. During cross-examination, may the prosecution ask Jones whether he has ever been convicted of armed robbery? If Jones answers, "No," may the prosecution respond by admitting an authenticated record of Jones's conviction from four years ago?

7.10. Return to Problem 3.5 at page 150. Suppose Trapp testifies consistently with his deposition. Broadback's attorney has an authenticated record of Trapp's felony conviction for illegally possessing methamphetamine. The attorney also has an authenticated copy of a recent application for a life insurance policy in which Trapp denied ever using illegal drugs. During cross-examination, may Broadback's attorney:

(a) Ask Trapp whether he was convicted for possessing methamphetamine? If Trapp denies the conviction, may Broadback's attorney introduce the record of conviction?

(b) Ask Trapp whether he lied on his life insurance application? If he denies doing so, may the attorney introduce the application and the record of conviction?

7.11. Ellen Jamison is being prosecuted for perjury, and she testifies in her own defense. Eight years ago Ellen was convicted of perjury, and last year she was convicted of felonious assault against her husband. Can the prosecutor introduce evidence of these convictions?

7.12. In the *Johnson* trial, which occurred in 1992, the following convictions were used to impeach the credibility of defense witnesses:

(a) robbery and battery (years not specified) by George Butler, the defendant's cellmate;

(b) first degree murder, assault with a deadly weapon, and first degree burglary (years not specified) by Michael Green, another inmate;

(c) rape (paroled in 1984) and first degree burglary (1985) by the defendant, Johnson.

Which of these convictions would be most likely and least likely to be admitted pursuant to FRE 609?

7.13. Tom Jackson has filed a federal civil rights against Larry Oster, a prison guard, for injuries sustained in what Jackson claims was an unprovoked assault. Jackson is currently in prison for life with no possibility of parole as a result of his conviction eight years ago for aiding and abetting his brother in the murder of a police officer. Jackson has filed a motion in limine asking the court to exclude any reference to the conviction. Oster has filed a motion in limine asking the court to rule that for impeachment purposes the defendant can introduce evidence that the conviction was for murdering a police officer and that Jackson is serving a life sentence without possibility of parole. How should the court rule?

7.14. Houghton has been charged with bank robbery, using a firearm during the robbery, and possession of a firearm after having been convicted of a felony. Houghton was convicted of murder 15 years ago and paroled three years ago. He is willing to stipulate that he has been "convicted of a felony," and he plans to testify that he was not the robber. In a motion in limine he asks the court to exclude any evidence of or reference to the prior conviction except for the stipulation. How should the court rule?

7.15. Dawn Drabble is charged with robbery. In cross-examining a prosecution witness, Dawn wishes to show that the witness was convicted of felonious assault eight years ago. Later, Dawn testifies in her own defense, and the prosecution offers to show that she was convicted of felonious assault eight years ago. Are the convictions admissible?

7.16. Jane and Ed Farley are charged with embezzlement, and they both plan to testify. Dan Evans will testify for them as a character witness. Jane Farley was convicted of filing a false income tax return 15 years ago, and Ed Farley was convicted of felonious theft five years ago. Dan Evans was convicted of misdemeanor battery two years ago. Pursuant to FRE 608(b) the prosecutor plans to ask the following questions on cross-examination:

(a) To Jane Farley: Isn't it true that you filed a false income tax return 15 years ago?

(b) To Ed Farley: Isn't it true that five years ago you made false representations to induce individuals to invest in a get-rich-quick scheme? (As the prosecutor knows, this was the underlying basis for theft charge.)

(c) To Dan Evans: Isn't it true that two years ago you pretended to be a friend to Joe Newhouse and lured him to a deserted building where you knew he would be beaten? (As the prosecutor knows, this was the basis for the battery charge; Evans was convicted as an aider and abettor.)

Are any of these questions objectionable?

C. IMPEACHMENT AND REHABILITATION WITH A WITNESS'S PRIOR STATEMENTS

A witness's prior statement—that is, a statement made at another time and place prior to the witness's current testimony—falls within the core definition of hearsay, and thus may be inadmissible, if the statement is offered to prove its truth. FRE 801(a)-(c); FRE 802. Sometimes a witness's prior statement will be admissible for its truth because it falls within an exception to the hearsay rule or an explicit exemption from the definition of hearsay. FRE 801(d), 803-804, 807. If a witness's prior statement is admissible for its truth, there is no need to consider whether it may *also* be admissible for the nonhearsay purpose of impeaching or rehabilitating the witness. We discuss hearsay in Chapter Eight. Our focus here is on the nonhearsay use of prior inconsistent and consistent statements that are not independently admissible for their truth.

When a witness's prior inconsistent statements are offered to impeach the witness, the relevance of this evidence derives not from its truth but from its inconsistency with the witness's trial testimony. Proof of an inconsistency, regardless of which statement is true, suggests that the witness may have lied in making one of the statements or that the witness for some other reason — for example, faulty memory or lack of interest in the subject matter — has on one occasion not reported accurately what happened. Such proof allows the impeaching party to argue to the jury that the witness is not reliable. The admissibility of a prior inconsistent statement for an impeaching purpose is governed by FRE 401-403, that is, whether it is relevant for an impeaching purpose, its probative value for this purpose, and whether its probative value is substantially outweighed by FRE 403 concerns. In addition, FRE 613 establishes the process for admitting prior inconsistent statements that are relevant and admissible under FRE 403.

A witness's prior consistent statements may also be relevant for rehabilitating a witness's testimony. The theory of relevance is similar to that for prior inconsistent statements. Proof that a witness has made statements consistent with the witness's current testimony suggests that the witness is careful and thoughtful in speaking about the matter to which the statements relate. Thus, except to the extent that there is reason to believe the witness is deliberately telling consistent lies, knowing about the consistency gives us more reason to credit and rely on the witness's testimony.

1. FRE 613

RULE 613.   WITNESS'S PRIOR STATEMENT

(a) *Showing or Disclosing the Statement During Examination.* When examining a witness about the witness's prior statement, a party need not show it or disclose its contents to the witness. But the party must, on request, show it or disclose its content to an adverse party's attorney.

(b) *Extrinsic Evidence of a Prior Inconsistent Statement.* Extrinsic evidence of a witness's prior inconsistent statement is admissible only if the witness is given an opportunity to explain or deny the statement and an adverse party is given an opportunity to examine the witness about it, or if justice so requires. This subdivision (b) does not apply to an opposing party's statement under Rule 801(d)(2).

2. Explanation of FRE 613

FRE 613 establishes the process by which an examiner may introduce evidence of a witness's prior inconsistent statement for the purpose of impeaching the witness's credibility. Typically, the examiner will confront the witness with a prior inconsistent statement during cross-examination.

a. FRE 613(a)

FRE 613(a) makes it clear that the examiner need not disclose the contents of a prior inconsistent statement to the witness before asking whether the witness made the statement. This provision formally abolishes the rule derived from the Queen Caroline's Case, 2 Br. & B. 284, 129 Eng. Rep. 976 (1820), which required, at least with respect to written statements, that the witness be shown the statement prior to any questioning about the statement. The rationale for the rule of the *Queen's Case* stems from a concern that the witness may honestly have forgotten what is or appears to be an inconsistent statement. If such a witness were not shown the statement prior to questioning, a clever cross-examiner might be able to get the witness to deny having made the statement, thereby giving the false impression that the witness was a liar. On the other hand, showing the statement to the witness before questioning gives the dishonest witness the opportunity to concoct a false story that minimizes the impact of the inconsistency. For this reason many commentators have criticized the *Queen's Case* rule, which the Advisory Committee Note to FRE 613(a) characterizes as a "useless impediment to cross-examination."

FRE 613(a) provides that opposing counsel has the right, upon request, to learn of the statement. According to the Advisory Committee Note, this provision "is designed to protect against unwarranted insinuations that a statement has been made when the fact is to the contrary." Assume, for example, that defense counsel had reason to believe that one of plaintiff's eyewitnesses to an automobile accident had made a statement inconsistent with the witness's trial testimony about who was at fault. Counsel could interrogate the witness about whether the witness had ever made such a statement without first revealing its contents to the witness. Upon request, however, defense counsel would have to reveal the inconsistent statement to plaintiff's counsel.

b. FRE 613(b)

FRE 613(b) also acknowledges that extrinsic evidence of inconsistent statements may be admissible, but it provides that in most instances there is a twofold condition for the admissibility of extrinsic evidence. The witness must have an opportunity to explain the statement, and the opposing party must have an opportunity to explore the inconsistency with the witness. To fulfill these requirements the party offering the prior inconsistent statement must generally do so when the witness is still testifying or must make sure that the witness is available for recall. United States v. Moore, 149 F.3d 773, 781-782 (8th Cir. 1998).

Requiring that the witness have the opportunity to explain the statement gives the factfinder a reasonable basis for evaluating the alleged inconsistency. For example, the witness may have a plausible explanation for why an apparently inconsistent statement is not in fact inconsistent, or the witness may deny having made the statement, in which case the factfinder will have to assess the relative weight of the extrinsic evidence and the witness's denial.

The "if justice so requires" exception exists because there may be situations in which it is not possible to give the witness an opportunity to explain the apparent inconsistency. Consider, for example, a situation in which the impeaching party becomes aware of the prior inconsistent statement only after the witness has been dismissed and is no longer available. In such a case it may further the search for truth to permit extrinsic evidence of the inconsistent statement without any opportunity for the witness's explanation rather than to exclude the impeaching evidence altogether.

The final sentence of FRE 613(b) provides another exception to the usual requirement that the witness have an opportunity to explain or deny the statement: The requirement is inapplicable to inconsistent statements by a party falling within FRE 801(d)(2). That rule provides that a party's prior statements may be admissible for their truth regardless of whether the party testifies. Thus, there is no need to restrict admissibility under FRE 613 when the party happens to be a witness.

c. FRE 613(b)'s Departure from the Common Law

The common law imposed a rigorous foundation requirement as a condition for introducing extrinsic evidence of an inconsistent statement. The impeaching party could not introduce extrinsic evidence of a witness's statement without first indicating the precise time and place of the statement and the person to whom it was made and then asking the witness whether the witness had made the statement. The drafters of the Federal Rules made clear their intent to have a more flexible foundation requirement. According to the Advisory Committee Note to FRE 613(b):

> The traditional insistence that the attention of the witness be directed to the statement on cross-examination is relaxed in favor of simply providing the witness an opportunity to explain and the opposite party an opportunity to examine on the statement, with no specification of any particular time or sequence.

As a result of this liberalization of the common law foundation requirement, it is possible that an impeaching party may introduce extrinsic evidence of an inconsistent statement without ever having mentioned the statement to the witness. Consider, for example, a situation in which the witness suggests on direct examination that the defendant was speeding. Now suppose that the opposing counsel has information that the witness had said the defendant was not speeding. Under FRE 613, opposing counsel on cross-examination may do nothing more than get the witness to reconfirm the direct examination testimony. Then, later in the trial during the presentation of the defense case, counsel may attempt to introduce extrinsic evidence of the inconsistent statement. As long as the witness has not been dismissed and is subject to recall (or perhaps as long as witness is available and can be called anew by the opposing party), extrinsic evidence of the statement may be admissible.

d. Extrinsic Evidence in Practice: Practical Considerations

Some trial judges have prohibited litigants from introducing extrinsic evidence of prior inconsistent statements that they made no effort to explore with the witness on cross-examination, and appellate courts have upheld these decisions on the ground that the trial judges were appropriately exercising discretion to control manner and order of proof. FRE 611(a). United States v. Sutton, 41 F.3d 1257, 1260 (8th Cir. 1994). As a result, the impeaching party in these cases lost the opportunity to show the inconsistent statement. To avoid this situation, unless counsel feels that there is a compelling tactical reason not to do so, the safe course of action is to lay the traditional common law foundation and to confront the witness with the inconsistent statement on cross-examination. (Indeed, many cross-examiners regularly use the elements of that foundation as part of their impeachment technique.) If the impeaching party lays the common law foundation and the witness denies making the inconsistent statement, the door should be open to proof of the statement with extrinsic evidence. If the party admits the statement, it is less clear whether extrinsic evidence of the statement will be admissible. Some courts take the position that the witness's acknowledgment of the statement removes any need for the extrinsic evidence, while other courts permit extrinsic evidence. The appropriate course of action, in our view, is not to have a flat rule of inadmissibility or admissibility but rather to view the issue as one governed by FRE 401-403.

e. Probative Value and FRE 403 Concerns

Since everyone occasionally makes inconsistent statements, proof of an apparently trivial inconsistency does little, if anything, to impeach a witness's credibility. If the inconsistency relates to the subject matter of the lawsuit, however, it provides a reason to be wary generally of the witness's testimony. The inconsistency, regardless of which statement is true, suggests either that the witness is willing intentionally to lie about the subject matter of the litigation or at least that the witness has been careless and inaccurate in reporting information important to the resolution of the litigation.

The Risk of Improper "Substantive" Use. When an inconsistent statement relates to an issue in the lawsuit, there is, of course, the possibility that the jury will consider the statement not merely for its impeachment value but also for its truth. The risk of improper use is a danger of unfair prejudice within the scope of FRE 403. This risk of unfair prejudice, however, will seldom, if ever, be a basis for exclusion of the evidence. Inconsistent statements about the issues in the lawsuit are likely to be more probative for impeachment purposes than inconsistent statements about unrelated matters. Thus, the most prejudicial inconsistent statements are also the most probative for their impeachment value. As you know, the FRE 403 balancing test favors admissibility. Thus, the FRE 403 unfair prejudice argument is not likely to succeed unless the objecting party can show some way in which the statement at issue is likely to be uniquely prejudicial in comparison to other inconsistent statements. For a rare example of a case holding that prior inconsistent statements should have been excluded because their impeachment value was outweighed by the risk that the jury would use the statements for their truth, see United States v. Logan, 121 F.3d 1172 (8th Cir. 1997). Cf. United States v. Young, 248 F.3d 260, 268 (4th Cir. 2001) (probative value of witness's ambiguous responses to questions (e.g., "uhm-hmm") outweighed by risk that jury would consider truth of matters asserted in questions).

Loss of Memory and Inconsistency.   There is at least one type of situation in which an FRE 403 unfair prejudice argument should have a reasonable chance of succeeding. If a witness who testifies to a lack of memory about an event has made a prior statement about the event, some courts view the claimed current loss of memory and the prior statement as inconsistent with each other. When it is reasonable to regard the loss of memory as feigned and, therefore, tantamount to a denial of the earlier statement, the characterization of the statements as inconsistent is reasonable. To the extent that the claimed loss of current memory seems plausible, however, there is no inconsistency between the witness's testimony and the prior statement. United States v. DeSimone, 488 F.3d 561, 572 (1st Cir. 2007) (not abuse of discretion to find no inconsistency between prior statement and trial testimony because it was "not implausible" that the witness did not recall a conversation that took place five years before trial). Thus, the prior statement has relatively low probative value for its legitimate impeachment use, but there is no reduction in the likelihood that the jury will consider the prior statement for its truth.

Inconsistent Statements About Collateral Matters.   Sometimes a witness's alleged inconsistent statement will be about a "collateral" matter—a matter that is wholly unrelated to the issues in the case. If an inconsistent statement is about a collateral matter, its probative value may be so low that on at least some occasions the FRE 403 efficiency concerns should require its exclusion. Consider, for example, a situation in which George sees an automobile accident as he is leaving a movie theater. A month later, in an interview with an insurance investigator, George states that he had been going to the theater every night the week of the accident because there was a Bogart festival. He further relates that he had seen *Casablanca* on the night of the accident. (Which Bogart movie George saw may be technically irrelevant to the issues in the case, but it is not unusual for a witness to include such details as part of a narrative of events.) At the trial George's testimony is consistent with his earlier statement in every respect except that he says he had seen *Key Largo* on the night of the accident. Assume that there is no dispute about what night the accident occurred and that it was the night that *Key Largo* was shown. Assume further that everyone concedes that there was not an accident on the night *Casablanca* was shown. Despite the facts that the inconsistency is collateral to the issues in the case and that it seems plausible that a person might have conflicting memories about which of two Bogart movies was showing on a particular night during the Bogart festival, one might want to permit the impeaching party to examine George about the inconsistency. The very low probative value of the evidence, however, may not warrant the consumption of time required to call an additional witness to offer extrinsic evidence of the inconsistency. Indeed, this is the result mandated by a common law rule that prohibited extrinsic evidence of an inconsistent statement about a collateral matter. Moreover, some federal courts have specifically adopted this rule. United States v. Grooms, 978 F.2d 425 (8th Cir. 1992); United States v. Tarantino, 846 F.2d 1384, 1409-1410 (D.C. Cir. 1998) (reciting the FRE 403 discretionary balancing test as authority).

Despite the cases approving the "collateralness" doctrine, the admissibility of extrinsic evidence of inconsistent statements under the Federal Rules should turn on an application of FRE 403 to the details of the case.

3. Prior Consistent Statements

A witness's prior *consistent* statements may be relevant to rehabilitate a witness's credibility by demonstrating that the witness has spoken consistently about a matter. The prior statements may also be relevant for their truth, in which case they implicate hearsay concerns. FRE 801(d)(1)(B), however, exempts from the definition of hearsay a witness's prior consistent statements. This means that consistent statements admitted for rehabilitation purposes may also be considered for their truth.

FRE 801(d)(1)(B) exempts two categories of prior consistent statements. The first category (FRE 801(d)(1)(B)(i)) applies to a statement offered "to rebut an express or implied charge that the [witness] recently fabricated it or acted from a recent improper influence motive in so testifying." As we discuss in Chapter Eight at pages 494-95, infra, the Supreme Court in Tome v. United States has interpreted this category narrowly: Only prior consistent statements made prior to the time that a motive to fabricate or an improper influence arose fall within the scope of this category. The second category (FRE 801(d)(1)(B)(ii)), created by a recent amendment to the Federal Rules, exempts prior consistent statements offered "to rehabilitate the [witness's] credibility as a witness when attacked on another ground." We discuss the hearsay exemptions in detail in Chapter Eight.

If a prior consistent statement is admissible, there is no specific limitation on proof of the statement by extrinsic evidence. Typically, however, a party will be eliciting the statement from the witness who made it, and the witness is likely to be friendly to the examiner. Thus, there will seldom be any need for extrinsic evidence.

KEY POINTS

1. Prior inconsistent statements may be admissible for the nonhearsay purpose of impeaching the credibility of a witness.

2. FRE 613(b) provides that normally a party may not introduce extrinsic evidence of a prior inconsistent statement unless the witness has an opportunity to explain or deny the statement and opposing counsel has an opportunity to question the witness about the statement.

3. Although FRE 613(b) liberalizes the common law foundation requirement for extrinsic evidence of inconsistent statements, some federal courts prohibit extrinsic evidence if the impeaching party does not call the statement to the witness's attention.

4. Prior consistent statements offered to rebut an express or implied charge of recent fabrication or improper influence are admissible for their truth pursuant

to FRE 801(d)(1)(B)(i) as long as the statements were made before the motive to fabricate arose.

5. Prior consistent statements offered to rehabilitate a witness whose credibility has been attacked on another ground are admissible for their truth pursuant to FRE 801(d)(1)(B)(ii).

PROBLEMS

7.17. Return to Problem 7.5 at page 401. May the prosecution introduce testimony from a police officer who investigated the burglary that, when he first spoke with Jones the night of burglary, Jones said that he saw someone running from the house at 1251 Hazel Street but that it was dark and he could not see who it was?

7.18. Return to Problem 3.2 at page 148. Assume that Jake O'Leary, an eyewitness, testifies for the defense that Driver did not veer off the roadway onto the gravel shoulder. Plaintiffs' counsel has a written statement from Pam Peters, Jake's former girlfriend, that the evening after the accident Jake said, "That bus driver should have been more careful." Can plaintiffs' attorney ask O'Leary about the statement on cross-examination? If the question is permitted and Jake denies having made the statement, can plaintiff's attorney call Pam to testify that Jake made the statement?

7.19. Danny Dickson has been charged with murdering a fellow prison inmate. Three inmates testified for the prosecution that Danny committed the murder, and none of them was cross-examined. Later in the trial Danny offered the testimony of two other inmates to the effect that the prosecution witnesses had told them that Danny had not committed the murder. The prosecution objects to this evidence. What result?

7.20. Return again to Problem 3.2 at page 148. Plaintiffs' counsel has located Wanda White, another school bus driver, who had dinner with Driver shortly after the accident. According to White, Driver said that she was going to quit her job because she hated "having to deal with those little brats every day." Can plaintiff's attorney call White to testify to this statement? Does your answer depend upon (a) whether Driver testifies as set forth at page 149, line 4? (b) whether plaintiff's counsel first asks Driver about the statement on cross-examination?

7.21. Review the direct and cross-examination of Officer Huston in the *Johnson* case (page 8, line 27, supra). What was the relevance of defense counsel's questions on cross-examination about whether the incident report prepared by Officer Huston made any reference to an open food port? Would that inquiry be appropriate under the Federal Rules? Would it be appropriate under the Federal Rules to introduce the incident report to show that it contained nothing about the food port?

7.22. Return to Problem 3.2 at page 148. Assume the following occurred on direct examination of Driver after the direct examination set forth at page 149:

1   Q: Did you drive the bus onto the gravel shoulder?
2   A: No.
3   Q: In the days following the accident did you discuss it with anyone?
4   A: Yes, with my friend Wanda.
5   Q: And what did you talk about.
6   A: I told her that I'd been very careful, that I hadn't driven the bus onto the
7   gravel shoulder, and that I felt so sad for those dear little children that I
8   thought I was going to have to quit my job.

Is any of this evidence objectionable? Would your answer be different if this were redirect and if evidence of the "little brats" statement (see Problem 7.20 at page 422) had been elicited on cross-examination? In answering this last question, does it matter whether the discussion with Wanda referred to in Problem 7.20 and the discussion with Wanda referred to here were (a) part of the same conversation or (b) conversations occurring on different days?

7.23. Pam Peters has brought an action for personal injuries against the Ace Department Store for injuries that she claims to have sustained when she fell on some ice in the parking lot on January 23. Peters first consulted an attorney in March, and the suit was filed in April. The trial is taking place the following December. On direct examination Peters testified about the accident, the severe bruises that she suffered, and the continuing backaches and headaches that she has had continually from the day of the injury. During cross-examination defense counsel elicited the fact that Peters did not mention the fall or her alleged injuries when she visited her doctor for a routine checkup on March 1. Later in the trial the defendant offered the testimony of two women who have monthly bridge games with Peters to the effect that Peters said nothing about the fall or any injuries at their bridge games on January 30 and on February 28. Plaintiff objects to the admissibility of this evidence.

In rebuttal, the plaintiff offers the testimony of Ed Peters, Pam Peters's husband, that she told him about the accident on January 23 and that she has frequently mentioned headaches and backaches — at least two or three times a week ever since January 23. The defendant has objected to Ed Peters's testimony.

Should either plaintiff's or the defendant's objection be sustained?

7.24. Return to Problem 3.3 at page 149. On direct examination, Beth Barker testifies for the prosecution that she definitely remembers placing the March 14, 2015, auditor's memo in Ray's "in box" on the afternoon of March 14 and removing it the next day from his "out box," and that Ray's initials were on the memo.

(a) Consider the following cross-examination of Ms. Barker:

9   Q: Ms. Barker, on July 10, 2016, you made a statement in my office that was
10   recorded by my assistant, did you not?
11   A: Yes.
12   Q: And at that session in my office I asked you some questions about a
13   March 14, 2015, auditor's memo, did I not?
14   A: Yes.

1   *Q*: Isn't it true that I asked you the following questions and you gave the fol-
2   lowing answers: [reading from the transcript prepared by the assistant]
3   *Q*: Ms. Barker, of all the memos you deal with, do you specifically recall the
4   March 14 memorandum from Rundown's auditors?
5   *A*: No, I can't say that I recall that specific memo.

Should the prosecutor's objection to defense counsel's reading from the transcript be sustained?

(b) Defense counsel next offers into evidence Exhibit B, an authenticated written statement of Beth Barker dated December 19, 2015, which states (in pertinent part):

> I, Beth Barker, declare
> I have removed hundreds of documents from Bernard Ray's "in box" in the years I worked as his secretary.
> I do not have a specific recollection of the March 14, 2015, auditor's memo.
> I declare under penalty of perjury that the foregoing is true and correct to the best of my knowledge.
>
> [signed] Beth Barker

Should the prosecutor's objection to the admission of Exhibit B be sustained?

(c) On cross-examination, defense counsel asks Barker the following:

6   *Q*: Ms. Barker, on August 12, 2016, were you arrested for embezzling $250
7   from a petty cash fund while you were employed at Rundown?
8   *A*: Yes.
9   *Q*: And when did the alleged embezzlement occur?
10   *A*: I don't remember?
11   *Q*: Was it before August 1st?
12   *A*: I don't remember.
13   *Q*: Ms. Barker, isn't it a fact that you made up this story about seeing the
14   signed memo in Bernard Ray's mail box in order to get a deal with the
15   prosecutor on your embezzlement charge?
16   *A*: No, that's not true.
17   *Defense Counsel*:   I have no further questions.

On redirect, the prosecutor offers into evidence an authenticated written statement of Beth Barker dated June, 30, 2016, stating that "I recall removing the March 14, 2015, auditor's memo from Mr. Ray's "out box" on March 15, 2015. It had Mr. Ray's initials on it, and I filed it." There is a dispute as to whether the alleged embezzlement occurred before or after June 30.

Should the June 30 statement be admitted over defense counsel's objection?

D. OTHER IMPEACHMENT TECHNIQUES

Recall that at the outset of the impeachment discussion we described impeachment as the process of attempting to raise doubts about the testimonial abilities of witnesses—that is, to show that the witness is lying, careless with words, imperceptive, or forgetful. The Federal Rules specifically address only two permissible methods for raising these doubts: attacking a witness's character and showing a witness's prior inconsistent statement. The process of impeachment, however, is not so limited. The common law permitted the impeachment of witnesses with evidence of unorthodox religious beliefs, bias, mental or sensory incapacity, and contradiction.

FRE 610 prohibits relying on the content of a witness's religious beliefs to assess credibility: "Evidence of a witness's religious beliefs or opinions is not admissible to attack or support the witness's credibility." For impeachment techniques that the Federal Rules do not specifically address, FRE 401-403 determine the admissibility of evidence.

1. Bias

a. Relevance

Courts and commentators frequently attach the label "bias" to what Wigmore identified as three methods of showing a witness's "emotional incapacity." According to Wigmore:

> Three different *kinds of emotion* constituting untrustworthy partiality may be broadly distinguished—bias, interest, and corruption: *Bias*, in common acceptance, covers all varieties of hostility or prejudice against the opponent *personally* or of favor to the proponent personally. [E.g., intimate family relationship with one of the parties.] *Interest* signifies the specific inclination which is apt to be produced by the relation between the witness and the *cause at issue* in the litigation. [E.g., the expectation of favorable treatment from the prosecutor or sentencing judge in return for the testimony.] *Corruption* is here to be understood as the *conscious false intent* which is inferable from giving or taking a bribe or from expressions of a general unscrupulousness for the case at hand. [E.g., an attempt to bribe another witness or the receipt of money for *testimony*.] The kinds of evidence available are two:
>
> [1] the *circumstances of the witness' situation*, making it "a priori" probable that he has some partiality of emotion for one party's cause;
> [2] the *conduct of the witness* himself, indicating the presence of such partiality, the inference here being from the expression of the feeling to the feeling itself.
>
> [3A John Henry Wigmore, Evidence §947, at 782 (James Chadbourn rev. 1970) (emphasis original).]

Proof of any of these types of bias can be particularly effective in discrediting a witness because it is highly probative of insincerity. Compare, for example, the likely impact of a prior inconsistent statement or an FRE 608(b) bad act with proof of a witness's close relationship with or expected favorable treatment from one of the parties. All of us make inconsistent statements at least occasionally, and having a bad character for truthfulness may mean nothing more than that the person is untruthful a bit more often than most people. Neither of these forms of impeachment suggests any particular reason to believe that the witness is being untruthful on the particular occasion of the witness's current testimony. By contrast, the types of bias described by Wigmore suggest a specific, concrete motive for fabricating testimony or at least being less than fully candid.

b. Extrinsic Evidence

In United States v. Abel, 469 U.S. 45 (1984), the Supreme Court upheld the proof of bias with extrinsic evidence under the Federal Rules. The evidence in *Abel* consisted of testimony from a prosecution witness that a defense witness and the defendant were both members of the same secret prison gang that required its members to commit perjury, theft, and murder on each member's behalf. Which type of bias, under Wigmore's analysis, does this suggest? Remember that the prosecution in the *Johnson* case tried to prove that defendant Johnson and his cell mate, Butler, belonged to the same gang outside of prison.

c. Possible FRE 403 Limitations on Extrinsic Evidence of Bias

Despite *Abel*, the right to introduce extrinsic evidence of bias is not automatic under the Federal Rules. Typically, evidence of bias is highly probative, but if the witness fully admits the bias or if the evidence in fact suggests little about the witness's possible bias, a court should probably sustain an FRE 403 objection to extrinsic evidence. United States v. Adams, 799 F.2d 665, 671 (11th Cir. 1986) (extrinsic evidence of bias excluded because bias adequately shown through cross-examination). Evidence of bias may also raise the FRE 403 issue of unfair prejudice. Consider, for example, United States v. Abel, supra:

> Respondent argues that even if the evidence of membership in the prison gang were relevant to show [witness Mills's] bias, the District Court erred in permitting a full description of the gang and its odious tenets . . . .
>
> Respondent specifically contends that the District Court should not have permitted Ehle's precise description of the gang as a lying and murderous group. Respondent suggests that the District Court should have cut off the testimony after the prosecutor had elicited that Mills knew respondent and both may have belonged to an organization together. This argument ignores the fact that the type of organization in which a witness and a party share membership may be relevant to show bias . . . . The attributes of the Aryan Brotherhood—a secret prison sect sworn to perjury and self-protection— bore directly not only on the fact of bias but also on the source and strength of Mills' bias. The tenets of this group showed that Mills had a powerful motive to slant his testimony towards respondent, or even commit perjury outright.
>
> A district court is accorded a wide discretion in determining the admissibility of evidence under the Federal Rules. Assessing the probative value of common membership in any particular group, and weighing any factors counseling against admissibility is a matter first for the district court's sound judgment under Rules 401 and 403 . . . . [469 U.S. at 53-54.]

Some courts also consider whether the witness was given an opportunity to explain or deny the evidence of bias in determining whether extrinsic evidence ought to be admitted. United States v. Betts, 16 F.3d 748, 764 (7th Cir. 1994).

d. Bias versus Character

A troublesome issue that sometimes arises—particularly with the type of evidence that Wigmore refers to as "corruption"—is whether the evidence should fit within the "bias" category or the "character" category. For example, is proof that the witness attempted to bribe another witness evidence of corruption-bias, or is it evidence of character, or both? Is the evidence of gang membership in *Abel* character evidence or evidence of bias or both? The issue is important because extrinsic evidence of the witness's conduct is admissible to prove bias but not to prove character under FRE 608(b).

The issue is difficult to resolve in part because the term *character* is not defined. Similarly, the contours of *corruption*, which the Advisory Committee's Note to FRE 608 equates with "character" and distinguishes from "bias" and "interest," are not clear. Moreover, it is not clear to what extent one should regard the concepts of character and bias as mutually exclusive or as potentially overlapping. In *Abel* the Court noted that the evidence of gang membership may show a bad character for truthfulness as well as bias. The Court suggested but did not decide that the FRE 608(b) prohibition against extrinsic evidence to prove character should not apply when the evidence is relevant and otherwise admissible to show bias.

To the extent that it is reasonable to infer from the corrupt act that the witness has some particular concern about or interest in the outcome of the present litigation, the evidence has relatively high probative value on the question of whether the witness's testimony is tainted because of this interest. Thus, it seems appropriate to attach the bias label to the evidence in order to permit exploration of the matter with extrinsic evidence. On the other hand, if the *only* reasonable inference to draw from the corrupt act is that the individual has a general lack of integrity or disregard for the truth, the probative value of the evidence to suggest untruthfulness on one specific occasion on the witness stand is relatively low. This evidence should receive the "character" label in order to prevent the possibility of time-consuming and distracting exploration of the matter with extrinsic evidence. In short, as Wigmore observed, "The only distinction that is here legitimate is between conduct indicating a corrupt moral character in general and conduct indicating a specific corrupt intention for the case at hand." 3A John Henry Wigmore, Evidence §963, at 808-810 (James Chadbourn rev. 1970).

KEY POINTS

1. Showing a witness's bias is relevant to impeach the witness's credibility, because the bias suggests a particular reason or motive for the witness to lie or at least be less than completely candid.
2. FRE 401-403 govern questioning regarding bias and the admissibility extrinsic evidence.

PROBLEMS

7.25. Return to Problem 3.2 at page 148. Assume that plaintiff called Nancy Patterson, an accident reconstruction expert, who testified that in her opinion the bus veered on the roadway and was on the gravel shoulder when it hit Paul. Defense counsel has learned that Patterson is receiving a $5,000 fee, that she has testified ten times on behalf of plaintiffs and only once on behalf of defendants, and that her husband's sister is married to Paul's uncle. Plaintiff's counsel has filed a motion in limine requesting that the court not permit any mention of these matters on the grounds that they are irrelevant and prejudicial. The motion is accompanied by affidavits from Patterson and other accident reconstruction experts stating that a $5,000 fee is in the low to normal range for the work that she has done and an affidavit from Patterson stating that she has not seen or heard from her husband's sister in over five years.

How should the court rule on the motion?

If the court denies the motion, can plaintiffs' counsel call other experts to testify that the fee is in the low to normal range?

7.26. Joan Dominick is being prosecuted for selling and conspiring to sell controlled substances. According to the prosecution's case, the conspiracy has lasted for a number of years and has involved three closely knit families. Joan acknowledges that some members of her family were involved in the conspiracy, and she admits being acquainted with the other alleged co-conspirators. However, she claims that she was not involved in any illegal activity. The principal witness against Joan is Sean Matthews, an acknowledged member of the conspiracy, who has pleaded guilty and entered into a cooperation agreement with the government. According to Sean, Joan supplied him with large quantities of drugs on a number of occasions. On cross-examination, Joan wants to inquire about (a) the extent of Sean's involvement in the conspiracy, (b) his plea, and his cooperation agreement, (c) an occasion five years ago when she rejected his sexual advances and he became angry, and (d) a ten-year-old drug scam in which Sean lost $30,000 and claimed (incorrectly, according to Joan) that Joan was responsible for defrauding him. How much of this inquiry should the court permit?

7.27. Stella Starlet is a rising movie star, rock singer, and television personality. She has sued Frances Fisher, her former manager and agent, for fraud and breach of contract. Stella's services were in great demand, and according to the complaint Fisher would negotiate contracts only with individuals willing to pay a substantial sum, above the negotiated contract amount, in cash directly to Frances. One of Stella's key witnesses is Ken Olsen, a former employee of Fisher. Olsen testified in detail about Fisher's demanding and receiving sums to book Stella that were never accounted for. The following cross-examination of Olsen took place without objection:

```
1    Q:  Do you know Stella Starlet personally?
2    A:  Yes.
3    Q:  You're quite fond of her, aren't you?
4    A:  Well, I like her and respect her.
```

Q: You feel indebted to her, don't you?
A: Indebted? No.
Q: Isn't it true that in the two months prior to this trial she has taken you to dinner at expensive restaurants on at least seven occasions?
A: No, she has never done that.
Q: And isn't it true that last month she bought you diamond cuff links and a new set of expensive golf clubs?
A: No.
Q: Two weeks ago when you were having lunch with your friend Tom Thompson at the River Edge Cafe, didn't you tell Thompson that Stella had taken you to dinner seven times in the last two months and that she had bought you diamond cuff links and new golf clubs?
A: No.

As part of its defense, the defendant calls Tom Thompson to testify that two weeks ago at the River Edge Cafe, Ken Olsen was bragging that he had had dinner with Stella Starlet on seven occasions in the last two months and that she recently bought him diamond cuff links and new golf clubs. Should this evidence be admitted over plaintiff's objection?

2. Mental or Sensory Incapacity

a. Relevance

Any sensory or mental deficiency that inhibits a witness's ability to perceive events accurately at the time they occur or to remember and to narrate accurately what happened at the time of trial is relevant to cast doubt on the witness's credibility. Thus, for example, it is relevant to prove that a witness suffers from faulty memory; some form of mental illness that contributes to a witness's inability to distinguish fact from fantasy; intoxication at the time of the event to which the testimony relates or while on the witness stand; or color blindness if accuracy with respect to color is important. Indeed, any fact relating to the witness's general testimonial capacities for narration, perception, and memory or about the exercise of these capacities on the occasion in question is relevant to impeach the witness. Subject to a court's discretion to control the mode of cross-examination (FRE 611(a)) and to FRE 403, it is permissible to inquire about these matters during the examination of the witness whose sensory or mental condition is at issue. United States v. Robinson, 583 F.3d 1265 (10th Cir. 2009) (reversible error to exclude evidence about prosecution witness's mental health, prescription medication use, and auditory hallucinations); United States v. Pryce, 938 F.2d 1343, 1345 (D.C. Cir. 1991) (prejudicial error to limit questions about witness's hallucinations to the time frame of the events about which witness testified); United States v. DiPaola, 804 F.2d 225, 229-230 (2d Cir. 1986) (permissible to exclude questions about witness's drinking problem in the absence of any showing that witness was under the influence at the time of the events or when giving testimony); Roberts v. Hollocher, 664 F.2d 200, 203 (8th Cir. 1981) (questions about Roberts's drug use permissible because they were "relevant to Roberts' physical state at the time of the alleged incidents and to his ability to accurately recall those incidents").

b. Extrinsic Evidence

In addition to making inquiry on cross-examination, parties may introduce extrinsic evidence of a witness's mental or sensory incapacity. Courts traditionally have regarded such evidence as showing something different from a moral incapacity or character trait. Thus, the restrictions on the proof of character are not applicable. As a result, for example, courts have permitted extrinsic evidence of such matters as strange, seemingly irrational acts of a witness, expert testimony from a psychiatrist about a witness's mental capacity, and courtroom experiments to demonstrate a witness's poor memory or eyesight.

It is appropriate to decide on a case-by-case basis how extensive a cross-examination to permit and how much, if any, extrinsic evidence to introduce about a witness's sensory or mental incapacity. The Federal Rules take this approach. In the absence of any exclusionary rule, admissibility decisions should turn on the application of FRE 401-403 and, if expert testimony is offered, FRE 702-706.

c. Mental Incapacity as a Bar to Testimony

In considering an individual's mental incapacity it is important not to confuse mental incapacity as a subject matter for impeachment with mental incapacity as a complete bar to testimony. Early in the development of the common law, courts barred individuals regarded as mentally deranged or defective from testifying. As we discussed in Chapter Four, FRE 601 now presumes that every person is competent to be a witness, including a person with mental illness. If an individual's mental condition prevents the individual from understanding the oath or the obligation to testify truthfully, however, that would be a legitimate reason for refusing to let the individual testify.

KEY POINTS

1. Courts regard a witness's sensory or mental incapacity as something different from a character trait. Thus, impeachment on these grounds is not limited by FRE 404 or FRE 608.
2. FRE 401-403 and, if expert testimony is involved, FRE 702-706 govern proof of a witness's sensory or mental incapacity.

PROBLEMS

7.28. Al Drummond has been charged with possession and sale of cocaine. The key government witness is Jimmy Jones, an informant and, according to the government, a former co-conspirator in drug trafficking with Drummond. Jones had already pleaded guilty and been sentenced for his involvement in the drug incident for which Drummond is on trial. On cross-examination of Jones, defense counsel (with a factual basis for each question) asks:

(a) "Isn't it true that you are a heroin addict?"
(b) "Isn't it true that you are under the influence of heroin right now on the witness stand?"
(c) "Isn't it true that last week you sold two ounces of heroin to James Edwards?"

Are any of these questions objectionable? If objections are not made or are overruled, can the defendant later introduce extrinsic evidence to prove that Jones is an addict? Was under the influence of heroin on the witness stand? Sold heroin last week to James Edwards?

The defense calls as a witness Dr. Helen James, who is qualified as an expert on mental disorders. She offers to testify that she recently diagnosed Jimmy Jones as suffering from AKSS syndrome, a severe mental disorder. Should plaintiff's objection to this evidence be sustained?

7.29. Return to Problem 5.32 at page 320. If the court rules that the evidence is not admissible substantively, may the defendant nonetheless introduce the expert testimony to impeach Haywood's credibility?

3. Contradiction

a. Relevance

The last traditional method of impeaching a witness's credibility is by means of contradiction—that is, introducing evidence that contradicts something the witness has said. For example, if the witness said that she was wearing a yellow dress when she saw the automobile accident, it would contradict her testimony to establish that she was wearing a blue dress on that occasion; and if one can establish that a witness is incorrect about one thing, it is arguably appropriate to infer that the witness may be wrong about other things, including perhaps the substantively important aspects of the witness's testimony.

As Wigmore observed:

The peculiar feature of [the] probative fact of error on a particular point [i.e., contradiction] is its *deficiency with respect to definiteness* and its *wide range with respect to possible significance.* Looking back over the various [impeachment devices] already considered, it will be seen that the evidence in those classes of cases was aimed clearly and specifically at a particular defect; it showed either that or nothing. Former perjury would indicate probably a deficient sense of moral duty to speak truth; relationship to the party, a probable inclination to distort the facts, consciously or unconsciously . . . .

[Evidence of contradiction] is not offered as definitely showing any specific defect of any of these kinds, and yet it may justify an inference of the existence of any one or more of them. We know simply that an erroneous statement has been made on one point, and we infer that the witness is capable of making an erroneous statement on other points. We are not asked, and we do not attempt to specify, the particular defect which was the source of the proved error and which might therefore be the source of another error. The source might be a mental defect as to powers of observation or recollection; it might be a lack of veracity character; it might be bias or corruption . . . . The inference is only that since, for this proved error, there was *some unspecified defect* which became a source of error, the same defect may equally exist as the source of some other error, otherwise not apparent. [3A John Henry Wigmore, Evidence §1000, at 957-958 (James Chadbourn rev. 1970) (emphasis original).]

All of us, of course, from time to time make erroneous statements that can be contradicted. Thus, at least in the absence of showing many contradictions by the same witness, see id. §1000, at 958, proof of contradictions about matters unrelated to the issues being litigated—for example, that the witness in the preceding example was wearing a blue dress instead of a yellow dress—are often of only marginal probative value to impeach the witness's credibility.

b. Extrinsic Evidence

FRE 401-403 govern the admissibility of evidence of contradiction, and as is the case with evidence of sensory or mental defects, courts applying FRE 403 may permit cross-examination but exclude extrinsic evidence to prove the contradiction if the contradiction appears to have little probative value to impeach the witness. For example, in our blue dress hypothetical, a court may permit some cross-examination about the color of the witness's dress, but if the witness does not admit being wrong about the color of her dress, the court may not permit the impeaching party to establish the contradiction with extrinsic evidence by calling other witnesses to testify that the dress was in fact blue. The color of the witness's dress is not relevant to any issue in the case; and although it is not uncommon for witnesses to include irrelevant details in their testimony, contradicting such matters is typically not very probative of how reliable the witness's testimony is on relevant, disputed facts. Thus, under FRE 403, it will seldom if ever be worth the time and risk of confusing the jury to prove these contradictions with extrinsic evidence. As we observed earlier, all of us occasionally make statements that are subject to contradiction, and as the Wigmore excerpt points out it is seldom clear precisely what testimonial deficiency a contradiction shows.

c. The Impeachment of Experts with Statements in Treatises

Parties may attempt to impeach an expert witness with statements made by other experts. FRE 803(18) contains a relatively broad hearsay exception for learned treatises. The Advisory Committee acknowledged that, in part, the rationale for this hearsay exception is that it "avoids the unreality of admitting evidence for the purpose of impeachment only, with an instruction to the jury not to consider it otherwise." The hearsay exception, however, does more than merely eliminate the need for a limiting instruction. FRE 803(18) does not require that any particular expert rely on or acknowledge the treatise as authoritative, nor does it require that the statements in the treatise be inconsistent with any expert's testimony. Thus, as other portions of the Advisory Committee Note make clear, the purpose of the exception is to permit affirmative use of statements in learned treatises apart from whatever impeachment value they may have.

d. The "No Extrinsic Evidence to Impeach on a Collateral Matter" Doctrine

At common law the admissibility of extrinsic evidence to contradict a witness was governed by the general principle that one may not introduce extrinsic evidence to impeach on a collateral matter. This is the same principle that we mentioned earlier in discussing extrinsic evidence of prior inconsistent statements, at pages 420-21, supra. For example, in the blue dress hypothetical, the collateralness doctrine would require exclusion of extrinsic evidence contradicting the witness's testimony that she had been wearing a yellow dress and also extrinsic evidence of a prior inconsistent statement in which she stated that she had been wearing a blue dress at the time of the accident. The color of the dress is collateral in that it has no bearing on an issue in the case.

We offer an examination of the collateralness doctrine here for two reasons. First, although the Federal Rules do not mention the collateralness doctrine, some federal courts have adopted and apply it both in the contradiction context, United States v. Catalan-Roman, 585 F.3d 453, 469 (1st Cir. 2009), and in the inconsistent statement context, United States v. Grooms, 978 F.2d 425 (8th Cir. 1992). Second, mastering the collateralness doctrine requires focusing on the inferential process involved in the use of evidence that contracts a witness, and this focus is critical to a reasoned, persuasive argument about admissibility in FRE 403 terms.

What Is Not Collateral Generally. Whether extrinsic evidence is collateral and therefore inadmissible pursuant to the collateralness doctrine is not always intuitively obvious. Three types of facts are *not* collateral:

(1) facts relevant to the substantive issues in the case;
(2) facts relevant, apart from the contradiction, to impeach the credibility of a witness, if extrinsic evidence is generally admissible for the noncontradiction impeachment purpose; and
(3) facts recited by the witness that, if untrue, logically undermine the witness's story.

See 1 McCormick on Evidence §49, at 232-238 (Kenneth S. Broun ed., 6th ed., 2006).

Evidence That Is Directly Relevant to the Issues in Litigation. Evidence that is directly relevant to substantive issues can be introduced for its substantive value apart from any impeachment value that it may have. In effect, the impeachment value of the evidence is secondary. As we stated earlier, if evidence is independently admissible, there is no need to consider whether it is also admissible for impeachment purposes.

Evidence That Impeaches a Witness Apart from Contradiction. The collateralness doctrine should not prohibit the use of extrinsic evidence that both contradicts the witness and also impeaches credibility in some other way, as long as it is clear that extrinsic evidence would be admissible for that independent impeachment purpose (e.g., to prove bias or a prior conviction). On the other hand, if a specific impeachment rule prohibits extrinsic evidence as FRE 608(b) does, it would undermine that prohibition to admit extrinsic evidence on the theory that the evidence contradicts the witness. Consider for example, the impact of a contrary rule with respect to FRE 608(b). In every case in which the witness denied committing a bad act, the proponent of the extrinsic evidence could argue that extrinsic evidence of the bad act was being offered not to prove character for untruthfulness but to show a contradiction. If that argument were accepted, the prohibition against extrinsic evidence in FRE 608(b) would become meaningless.

Evidence That Logically Undermines a Witness's Story.   Contradictions that logically undermine the witness's story are also considered noncollateral. To illustrate this third category, consider a personal injury action in which Sadie testifies for the plaintiff and explains that she happened to see the accident as she was walking home from the grocery store where she had gone to purchase milk for her children. Proof that Sadie bought beer instead of milk would contradict her story, but such proof would not logically undermine her testimony. What she bought is collateral. Thus, on cross-examination counsel could question Sadie about what she bought, but the counsel would have to accept her answers; extrinsic evidence would be inadmissible. On the other hand, evidence that Sadie had not been in the area of the grocery store at all suggests that she may not have seen the critical events to which she testified. Just as there would be no general prohibition against extrinsic evidence that Sadie was almost blind, there should be no prohibition against the use of extrinsic evidence suggesting that Sadie might not physically have been in a position to observe what she claimed to have seen. In short, proof that Sadie had not been near the grocery store on the day of the accident tends logically to undermine her story about the accident. Thus, it should not be regarded as collateral, and extrinsic evidence of her absence from the store should be admissible.

A Test for "Collateralness."   There is a commonly stated test for collateralness that, if properly understood and applied, is consistent with all we have said so far: Could the fact have been proven with extrinsic evidence for any purpose except to show a (mere) contradiction? If the answer is yes, if, in other words, there is some relevant, permissible use for extrinsic evidence above and beyond its value as showing a mere contradiction, it is not collateral. On the other hand, if the only permissible purpose for offering the evidence is to prove a contradiction, the extrinsic evidence is collateral. Thus, for example, in our preceding illustrations it would not be collateral to prove by extrinsic evidence (a) a prior conviction that the witness denied, (b) facts constituting bias that the witness denied, (c) substantively relevant events that the witness denied, or (d) Sadie's absence from the grocery store. It would be collateral to prove (a) that the witness was wearing a blue dress instead of a yellow dress, (b) that the witness falsely denied committing a dishonest act, or (c) that Sadie bought beer.

KEY POINTS

1. Proving a contradiction is relevant to cast doubt on the credibility of a witness. FRE 401 and 403 govern the admissibility of evidence for this purpose.
2. Rather than invoking FRE 401-403, some federal courts rely on the common law prohibition against the use of extrinsic evidence to impeach on a collateral matter to exclude extrinsic evidence that contradicts a witness on a collateral matter. Extrinsic evidence is collateral if the fact that the evidence establishes cannot be proven with extrinsic evidence for any purpose other than to show the contradiction.
3. In most cases proper application of FRE 403 would probably lead to the same result as the common law prohibition against extrinsic evidence to contradict on a collateral matter.

PROBLEMS

7.30. Return to Problem 7.5 at page 401. For the following evidence, may the prosecution (1) question Jones about it during cross-examination, and (2) introduce extrinsic evidence if he denies it:
  (a) that Jones had ten beers at the Pub;
  (b) that the woman he was speaking with at the Pub was wearing a red dress;
  (c) that Jones left the Pub at 11:00 P.M.?
7.31. Return to Problem 3.2 at page 148. Assume that Eddie Keller, a 13-year-old who had been on the bus with Paul, testifies for the plaintiff that Driver veered onto the gravel shoulder and hit Paul. Plaintiff's counsel then asks Eddie what happened next and he replies, "I don't know. I was scared. I went straight home and stayed in my room until supper." Defense counsel has learned from Jim Tobin, one of Eddie's classmates, that Eddie did not go straight home. Instead, he went to the local playground where he found Jim and beat him up in order to settle an argument that had developed earlier in the day. Can defense counsel ask Eddie about the incident with Jim? If there is no objection and Eddie denies the incident, can defense counsel call Jim to testify that Eddie beat him up?
7.32. See Problem 7.31. After beating up Jim, Eddie went to the corner drug store, where he was caught trying to steal comic books and candy. Can defense counsel ask Eddie about this incident? If there is no objection and Eddie denies the attempted theft, can defense counsel call Mark Manning, the druggist, to testify about what happened?
7.33. Defendant is charged with a liquor store robbery that occurred Sunday shortly after noon. To establish an alibi, Witness₁ testifies for Defendant as follows: "On Sunday morning at 12:15 P.M., as I was walking out of church, I observed Defendant across the street." (Other testimony establishes that the church and the liquor store are at opposite ends of the city.) Witness₂ offers to testify for the prosecution that on Sunday morning at about 12:15 P.M. he saw Witness₁ walking out

of an all-night bar. Defendant objects to this evidence on the ground that its admission would violate (a) FRE 608(b)'s prohibition against extrinsic evidence of specific instances of conduct, (b) the general prohibition against the use of extrinsic evidence to impeach on a collateral matter, and (c) FRE 403. How should the court rule?

7.34. Daniels is charged with selling cocaine to an undercover police officer. Daniels testified on direct examination that he did not sell the drugs. He further testified that at the time of the alleged sale he had been playing dice with several other people, one of whom periodically left the game and returned with cash. Daniels suggested that the companion was the seller and that the undercover officer identified the wrong person. On cross-examination, the prosecutor asked if Daniels had actually seen the companion sell the cocaine. Daniels responded negatively. The prosecutor then asked Daniels if he was familiar with cocaine, and Daniels responded that he had never seen cocaine.

The prosecutor knows that Daniels tested positively for cocaine use three times in the last two years. Can the prosecutor inquire about these matters on cross-examination or introduce extrinsic evidence of the tests?

E. REFLECTION ON THE IMPEACHMENT PROCESS

In our initial discussion of the difference in the inferential process between using evidence for impeachment purposes and using evidence for substantive purposes, we used two examples of situations in which evidence is relevant for both substantive and impeachment purposes but potentially admissible only for the latter purpose. See pages 388-89, supra. One involved a witness's inconsistent statement not under oath about the color of a traffic light at the time of an automobile accident. On direct examination the witness testified that the light was red. The inconsistent statement was that the light was green. The other example involved a prior conviction for perjury by a defendant-witness who was charged with perjury. In both examples the permissible impeachment use of the evidence involves an inferential chain of reasoning that arrives at an essential element in the case by a route that is more circuitous than the chain of reasoning required to make the evidence relevant for its prohibited substantive purpose: This circuitous route requires the factfinder to make an inference that what the witness says is not reliable.

The Inconsistent Statement Case. Because of the hearsay rule the witness's inconsistent statement is not admissible as a direct assertion that can be relied on to prove that the light was green. The statement is admissible, however, because its inconsistency suggests fabrication or lack of care in making the statement that the light was red. Thus, the witness may have been unreliable in claiming that light was red. And, if it was not red, it must have been some other color—green, or perhaps yellow.

The Perjury Case. Because of FRE 404(b) the witness-defendant's prior perjury conviction is not admissible as evidence of the defendant's character for untruthfulness to prove directly that the defendant lied at the time of the alleged perjury. The conviction is admissible, however, to suggest that the defendant is an untruthful person who may be lying on the witness stand. Thus, the defendant may have been unreliable in denying the alleged perjury. This leaves as the alternative the proposition that the defendant committed the perjury as charged.

What justifies permitting the jury to take the circuitous route but not the direct route to the same conclusion? Even if there is a reasonable answer to the preceding question, do you believe that trial judges are capable of instructing juries on the distinction and that jurors are capable of comprehending and acting on the instruction?

If the distinction between the impeachment use and the substantive use of a prior inconsistent statement or a prior perjury conviction is not one that judges and juries are likely to be able to appreciate and understand, there is a fundamental problem with our current approach to "impeachment" evidence. Moreover, it is a problem that, at least in practice, is not adequately addressed by the balancing process of FRE 403: In the overwhelming number of cases in which there is more than very marginal impeachment value to evidence that is inadmissible substantively, it will be admitted with limiting instructions. For example, in the perjury hypothetical, the defendant is entitled to an instruction that the prior perjury conviction is admissible only to impeach the credibility of the defendant as a witness and that it is not proper to infer that because the defendant committed perjury once before it is more likely that the defendant committed perjury on the occasion in question. If we are serious about the "substantive" prohibitions, we should not be so ready to admit for impeachment purposes evidence that in theory is inadmissible for substantive purposes; or if we want to admit evidence for impeachment purposes that theoretically is not admissible substantively, we need to rethink the desirability of the substantive prohibitions.

One possibility would be to retain the current distinctions between impeachment and substantive uses of evidence only for the purpose of deciding whether or at what point evidence will be admissible. In other words, specific acts would still be inadmissible as part of a prosecutor's case-in-chief to prove character to show action in accordance with character, and unsworn prior inconsistent statements would initially be inadmissible for their truth. However, if this type of evidence gains enough added relevance from its impeachment value that it should be admissible for that purpose, it should be admissible for whatever probative value it has for any matter of consequence in the litigation. The primary benefit of this proposal is that it would eliminate often confusing and difficult-to-follow limiting instructions.

ASSESSMENTS

A-7.1 FRE 608.   Defendant is on trial for murder. Defendant claims self-defense and testifies that the alleged victim followed him home and attacked him in his driveway. At trial, Neighbor gave testimony corroborating the self-defense theory. During cross-examination, the prosecution asks Neighbor whether Neighbor violated her law school's honor code two years ago. The defense objects. How should the court rule, and why?

A. The question is permissible, but only if the prosecutor persuades the judge that there is a reasonable basis for believing that the violation occurred.
B. The question is permissible because the defendant first introduced character evidence.
C. The question is impermissible because it does not call for opinion or reputation testimony.
D. The question is impermissible because Neighbor's character is irrelevant.

A-7.2 FRE 609. Defendant is on trial for aggravated assault. At trial, Defendant testifies that he acted in self-defense. The prosecution seeks to introduce evidence that Defendant pleaded guilty five years ago to making a false statement to a federal agent. Defendant pleaded guilty as part of a plea agreement, after he was arrested for participating in an illegal drug conspiracy. The false statement concerned his denial of any involvement in the conspiracy when first questioned by federal drug agents. The defense objects. How should the court rule, and why?

A. Admissible under FRE 609 regardless of any FRE 403 dangers.
B. Admissible under FRE 609 because the probative value substantially outweighs any FRE 403 dangers.
C. Inadmissible because the defendant has not introduced any character evidence.
D. Inadmissible under FRE 609 because the potential for unfair prejudice substantially outweighs the probative value of the evidence.

A-7.3. FRE 609. TRUE or FALSE: When considering the admissibility of a testifying criminal defendant's prior conviction for impeachment purposes under FRE 609(a)(1), if a court thinks that its probative value and its potential for unfair prejudice to the defendant are counterbalanced, the court should exclude the evidence.

A-7.4. FRE 613. Ed Macy is charged with felonious assault. He claims not to have been the assailant and will present an alibi defense. During his incarceration prior to trial, Macy's cellmate told him that Wally Wilder had confessed to committing the assault. At trial, Macy calls Wilder as a defense witness, and Wilder denies any involvement in the assault. Can Macy (1) ask Wilder about Wilder's alleged confession to the cellmate, and (2) call the cellmate to testify about Wilder's alleged confession if Wilder denies confessing?

A. Both items of evidence are admissible under FRE 613.
B. (1) is admissible but (2) is not.
C. (2) is admissible but (1) is not.
D. Both items are inadmissible under FRE 613.

A-7.5 Other Impeachment Techniques. Extrinsic evidence to prove a witness's bias is admissible:

A. Whenever it is relevant.
B. Never.
C. Only if it satisfies FRE 403 balancing.
D. Only if the witness is first given an opportunity to explain.

ANSWERS

A-7.1. The correct answer is **A**. Under FRE 608(b), witnesses can be asked about their own specific acts that relate to untruthfulness. Here, violating the honor code is relevant for Neighbor's character for untruthfulness; however, the prosecution must have a good faith or reasonable basis for believing that the act occurred. B is incorrect because the prosecution can ask this question regardless of whether the defendant first introduces character evidence. C is incorrect because FRE 608(b) permits questions about specific acts. D is incorrect because a witness's character for truthfulness is relevant.

A-7.2. The correct answer is **A**. Because the defendant testified, the evidence is admissible under FRE 609(a)(2). The crime involved a false statement and thus is admissible without the need for FRE 403 balancing or "reverse 403" balancing for criminal defendants. Therefore, B and D are incorrect. C is incorrect because the evidence is admissible regardless of whether the defendant introduces character evidence.

A-7.3. TRUE. When the witness is a criminal defendant, "reverse 403" balancing applies. FRE 609(a)(1)(B). According to the rule, the evidence must be admitted only when probative value outweighs prejudicial effect to the defendant. Therefore, when the two are counterbalanced the evidence should be excluded.

A-7.4. The best answer is **A**. Both are permissible under FRE 613. Even though Wilder is a defense witness, parties can impeach their own witnesses. FRE 607. External evidence is also admissible, subject to FRE 403. If Wilder denies making the confession, the probative value of the external evidence should be sufficiently high to survive an FRE 403 objection.

A-7.5. The best answer is **C**. FRE 403 governs the admissibility of evidence of bias—both the questioning of witnesses and external evidence. A is incorrect because some relevant bias evidence should be excluded by FRE 403, and B is incorrect because some relevant bias evidence should be admissible under FRE 403. D is incorrect because there is no requirement that witnesses must first be given an opportunity to explain any bias evidence.

CHAPTER EIGHT

THE HEARSAY RULE

The general rule excluding hearsay is one of the hallmarks of the Anglo-American law of evidence. It establishes as a general proposition that when statements are made by people outside of court, those statements are not admissible when offered to prove the truth of the matters asserted therein. But recall the excerpt from Thayer's Treatise quoted in Chapter Three: "[T]he law has come into the shape of a set of primary rules of exclusion; and then a set of exceptions to these rules. . . ." James Bradley Thayer, A Preliminary Treatise on Evidence at Common Law 26 (1898). The hearsay rule illustrates this principle. FRE 802 is the primary rule of exclusion. It is, however, subject to 8 exceptions and 29 exemptions pursuant to which many kinds of hearsay statements are admitted.

We will examine the exemptions in Section C and the exceptions in Sections D, E, and F of this chapter. Initially, however, it is important to understand what hearsay is, how it is defined, and what justifies its exclusion from the factfinding process of trial. Remember that the classification of evidence as hearsay or not hearsay is not necessarily determinative of admissibility. Evidence of an out-of-court statement that is not hearsay may be inadmissible for some other reason (e.g., privilege), and evidence that is hearsay may be admissible under one of the exemptions or exceptions. Your desire ultimately to admit or exclude a particular out-of-court statement should not influence your initial analysis of whether that statement falls within the definition of the exclusionary rule.

A. THE GENERAL RULE OF EXCLUSION AND THE DEFINITION OF HEARSAY

Exclusion of hearsay requires a test that judges apply to individual items of evidence. Under FRE 801(c), hearsay is a statement offered "to prove the truth of the matter asserted." This brief definition of hearsay is deceptively simple. Its application will require an understanding of the reasons for the hearsay prohibition—reasons that are captured only imperfectly in any brief doctrinal definition.

1. FRE 801 and 802

RULE 801. DEFINITIONS THAT APPLY TO THIS ARTICLE; EXCLUSIONS FROM HEARSAY

(a) *Statement.* "Statement" means a person's oral assertion, written assertion, or nonverbal conduct, if the person intended it as an assertion.

(b) *Declarant.* "Declarant" means the person who made the statement.

(c) *Hearsay.* "Hearsay" means a statement that:

(1) the declarant does not make while testifying at the current trial or hearing; and

(2) a party offers in evidence to prove the truth of the matter asserted in the statement.

(d) *Statements That Are Not Hearsay.* A statement that meets the following conditions is not hearsay:

(1) A *Declarant-Witness's Prior Statement.* The declarant testifies and is subject to cross-examination about a prior statement, and the statement:

(A) is inconsistent with the declarant's testimony and was given under penalty of perjury at a trial, hearing, or other proceeding or in a deposition;

(B) is consistent with the declarant's testimony and is offered:

(i) to rebut an express or implied charge that the declarant recently fabricated it or acted from a recent improper influence or motive in so testifying; or

(ii) to rehabilitate the declarant's credibility as a witness when attacked on another ground; or

(C) identifies a person as someone the declarant perceived earlier.

(2) *An Opposing Party's Statement.* The statement is offered against an opposing party and:

(A) was made by the party in an individual or representative capacity;

(B) is one the party manifested that it adopted or believed to be true;

(C) was made by a person whom the party authorized to make a statement on the subject;

(D) was made by the party's agent or employee on a matter within the scope of that relationship and while it existed; or

(E) was made by the party's coconspirator during and in furtherance of the conspiracy.

The statement must be considered but does not by itself establish the declarant's authority under (C); the existence or scope of the relationship under (D); or the existence of the conspiracy or participation in it under (E).

RULE 802. THE RULE AGAINST HEARSAY

Hearsay is not admissible unless any of the following provides otherwise:

- a federal statute;
- these rules; or
- other rules prescribed by the Supreme Court.

Our initial discussion focuses on FRE 801(a)-(c) and 802. We discuss FRE 801(d) in Section C.

2. Explanation of FRE 801 and 802

To appreciate the significance of the general rule of exclusion, consider that a friend of yours, Sally, tells you that she saw a gray SUV run through a red light and hit a pedestrian. Would you believe Sally? Would you rely on her information? If you know that Sally is a trustworthy person, and that she usually is a careful observer of things and has a good memory, you would probably have little reason to doubt what she says. You would view Sally as a reliable source of information about the accident. We learn many useful things about people, events and conditions from what others tell us.

Sally's knowledge about the accident would be particularly useful in a lawsuit brought by the pedestrian against the driver of the SUV. Sally herself could be called to testify as a *witness*. In response to a question about what she saw, she would testify: "On June 1, I observed the gray SUV run a red light and hit a pedestrian." But now assume that Sally made this same statement to her friend George after the accident. Subsequently, George is called as a witness to testify that "On June 2, Sally told me that on June 1 she had seen a gray SUV run a red light and hit a pedestrian." Sally's own testimony would be welcome in any courtroom in America. But George's testimony would be excluded by the hearsay rule. Why? Apply the terms of FRE 801(a)-(c): George's testimony describes (1) a *statement* (an "oral assertion"); (2) the statement is made by a *declarant* (Sally is "the person who made the statement"); (3) the statement was *not* made by Sally *while testifying at the current trial or hearing*; and (4) the statement is being offered by the pedestrian *to prove the truth of the matter asserted by the declarant* (that the gray SUV ran the red light). Thus, Sally's statement is *hearsay* and George's testimony about that statement would consequently be inadmissible under FRE 802.

Notice that the term *hearsay* applies to Sally's statement because when she made it she was an out-of-court declarant; the hearsay rule operates to exclude evidence of that statement no matter how it is presented in court—through testimony such as George's, through a letter Sally wrote to George, through her diary, through a tape-recording of Sally speaking to George, or even if Sally testified about her own out-of-court statement. And, by the way, there is no traditionally recognized hearsay exception that could make Sally's out-of-court statement admissible.

a. The Relevancy of Sally's Testimony Depends on Generalizations About Sally's Testimonial Qualities

Why should Sally's statement of belief about the gray SUV be admitted if Sally says it in court as a witness, but be excluded if George reports her statement to the jury? The answer to this question, which involves an explication of hearsay policy, begins with relevancy. Under FRE 401, Sally's testimony as a witness is offered to prove that it is more likely that the SUV did run the red light and hit a pedestrian. We know from our study of impeachment in Chapter Seven that inferences about Sally's narration, sincerity, perception, and memory are necessary to connect her statements to the fact of consequence. These inferences about Sally's four testimonial qualities, and the generalizations that underlie them, are shown in Diagram 8-1. The final inference—from the accuracy of Sally's belief to the conclusion about the event itself—is an inference that does not rest on a generalization about one of Sally's testimonial qualities. Rather, it expresses the assumption underlying the model of rational factfinding that people's beliefs about the world can and do generally correspond to reality.

It is possible that, contrary to the generalizations articulated in Diagram 8-1, Sally did not speak accurately and honestly, or did not perceive accurately or remember accurately the event involving the SUV. If this is so, then relying on her belief about this event generates risks of error. We refer to these four risks as *testimonial dangers*, or as *hearsay dangers* when an out-of-court statement is being considered.

Diagram 8-1

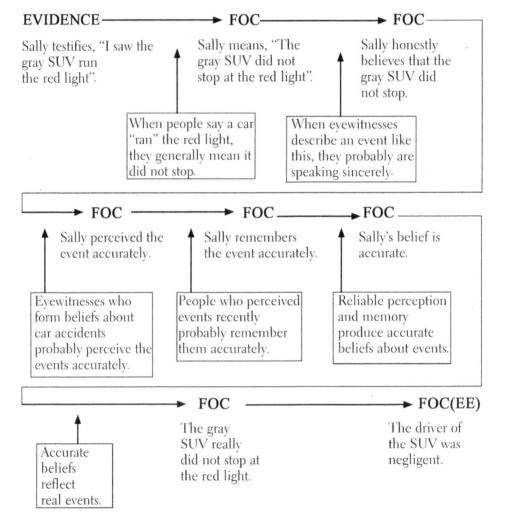

A narration danger is present when a person uses a wrong or ambiguous word or expression, by failing to articulate in sufficient detail, or by otherwise conveying a misleading version of what s/he intended to say. For example, Sally may mistakenly call the SUV's color gray, despite intending to report its color as green. To illustrate ambiguity, consider a person who says, "Jon had a great catch" and try to determine whether s/he is referring to fishing or baseball. The answer may be clear from the context within which the statement is made, but ambiguity problems arise when the hearer or reader might misinterpret what the speaker is thinking and communicating. Thus, even when Sally is sincere and has an impeccable memory of the event after properly perceiving it, the narration danger means that an inference from her words to what she means to say—FOC-1 in the Diagram 8-1—may be incorrect.

If Sally is trying to deceive the listener (a *sincerity* danger), her words will misrepresent what she really perceived and remembers. If Sally is lying, then the inference from Sally's words to her belief about the SUV that we (or the jury) as listeners attribute to Sally—FOC-2 in the Diagram—will not correspond to what she actually knows about the accident.

Inferences about Sally's perception and memory affect the congruity between what Sally honestly believes she saw and what actually happened. To prove that the SUV did fail to stop at the red light, Sally's belief about what happened must be accurate—Sally must have observed and understood the incident properly. The prospect of her not observing and understanding the event properly is called the *perception* danger. Perception, as used here, includes impressions received from any of the person's senses. The identification of an odor or the hearing of another person's speech might present perception issues. A memory problem arises when Sally forgets some or all of the details of the event she perceived; for example, that the gray car was a truck rather than an SUV (a *memory* danger). If there are perception or memory problems with Sally's statement, then the inferences of perception (FOC-3) or memory (FOC-4) will be incorrect and the ultimate inference that Sally's belief accurately reflects what the SUV did (the FOC(EE)) will also be incorrect.

To summarize: We cannot know with absolute certainty whether Sally is lying or using the wrong or ambiguous words, or whether she misperceived or has forgotten what happened. Each of these risks—faulty narration, insincerity, faulty memory, and misperception—affects the trustworthiness of Sally's testimony. We assume, on the basis of our common experience, that people generally tend to be truthful and accurate in their statements. Sally's statement that the gray SUV ran the red light is relevant to the trial and we leave it to the jury to evaluate her testimonial qualities.

b. The Relevancy of Sally's Hearsay Statement Also Depends on Generalizations About Sally's Testimonial Qualities

The very same inferences about Sally's testimonial qualities are necessary if Sally's statement is presented to the jury as hearsay. This can be illustrated with the example of George testifying about Sally's out-of-court statement to the jury. The inferential chain of reasoning shown in Diagram 8-2, an abbreviated version of Diagram 8-1, would be necessary to the relevancy of George's testimony.

Diagram 8-2

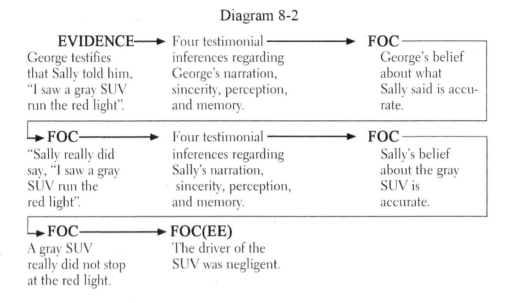

EVIDENCE →	Four testimonial →	FOC
George testifies that Sally told him, "I saw a gray SUV run the red light".	inferences regarding George's narration, sincerity, perception, and memory.	George's belief about what Sally said is accurate.
↳ FOC →	Four testimonial →	FOC
"Sally really did say, "I saw a gray SUV run the red light".	inferences regarding Sally's narration, sincerity, perception, and memory.	Sally's belief about the gray SUV is accurate.
↳ FOC →	FOC(EE)	
A gray SUV really did not stop at the red light.	The driver of the SUV was negligent.	

As you can see, inferences about Sally's testimonial qualities are the same in form and in basic content as they were in Diagram 8-1. Essentially, then, the content of the jury's inferential reasoning process about the probative value of what Sally says about the SUV is the same whether she testifies or not. Moreover, the same potential risks of error, associated with Sally's faulty narration, insincerity, faulty memory, and misperception, are present here as well.

The relevance of hearsay has also been illustrated with a "testimonial triangle,"[1] which collapses the four inferences into two legs of a triangle:

Diagram 8-3

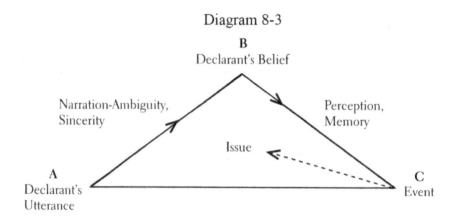

B
Declarant's Belief

Narration-Ambiguity, Sincerity

Perception, Memory

Issue

A
Declarant's
Utterance

C
Event

---

1. The testimonial triangle concept was first popularized for the academic legal community by Professor Laurence Tribe in his article Triangulating Hearsay, 87 Harv. L. Rev. 957 (1974), and in Richard O. Lempert and Stephen A. Saltzburg, A Modern Approach to Evidence (1977). For a much earlier version of the triangle, see Charles Kay Ogden & Ivor Armstrong Richards, The Meaning of Meaning 10-12 (1927).

The triangle starts with the declarant's words—spoken or written outside of court—which are usually presented to the jury through testimony or an exhibit. The left leg of the triangle from A to B represents the inference from the declarant's words to the declarant's state of mind of "belief," an inference that requires reliance on the declarant's sincerity and narrative ability. The right leg from B to C represents the inference from the declarant's state of mind of belief to the existence of an event that caused that belief. This inference requires reliance on the declarant's perception and memory (and, again, on our general assumption that accurate beliefs correspond to real events). Thus, the relevance of Sally's statement requires both legs of the testimonial triangle, and requires that we make the inferences about all four of Sally's testimonial qualities. Once again, this is the same structure of inferential reasoning that the jury would make if Sally were presented to testify as a witness. If so, why then does the hearsay rule differentiate so sharply between Sally's admissible statement as a witness and her inadmissible statement as a hearsay declarant?

c. Hearsay Policy Differentiates Between Witnesses and Hearsay Declarants

The most common answer to this question focuses on three factors that differentiate witnesses (like Sally speaking in court) from hearsay declarants (like Sally speaking out of court). First, the witness in the courtroom is always under oath, thereby reducing the likelihood of insincerity, whereas a declarant's out-of-court statement may or may not be made under oath. Moreover, the solemnity and formality of the court proceedings may cause the witness to be particularly careful about properly narrating the event.

Second, the jury is able to observe the demeanor of the in-court witness. Observing how the witness responds and reacts to questions, particularly on cross-examination, may give the jurors a somewhat better sense of the witness's sincerity, narrative ability, perception, and memory than they would get from having the content of the statement related to them by some third person. While demeanor evidence is often criticized as an ineffective indicator of outright insincerity, its use in evaluating other aspects of witness and party behavior has been noted. The opportunity for the trier of fact to assess the credibility of witnesses in person is a principal reason for the deference that appellate courts afford to factual findings at the trial level. See, e.g., Olin Guy Wellborn III, Demeanor, 76 Cornell L. Rev. 1075, 1077 (1991).

Third, and most important, the in-court witness is subject to cross-examination, which the opponent may use to elicit facts from the witness that are relevant to all four of the witness's testimonial qualities. We have seen in Chapter Seven how the topics of impeachment can all be addressed through cross-examination of a witness. The witness's answers, and the behavior of the witness in responding to questions, may clarify ambiguity, reveal mistakes in narration, reveal weaknesses in perception or memory, and provide information about the witness's character for truthfulness, the witness's bias, or the witness's motive to misrepresent the facts of the case. In addition, fear of cross-examination may motivate witnesses to be truthful and accurate in their testimony.

Without cross-examination, it is feared, hearsay statements may bear more testimonial dangers that are not exposed to the jury and hence may be *less reliable* than in-court testimony. Some witnesses, of course, may beat the system and lie quite persuasively. But to recognize that possibility is to recognize only that our adjudicatory system is not perfect. It is a truism, and many trial lawyers believe, that in the context of our adversary system, cross-examination is "beyond any doubt the greatest legal engine ever invented for the discovery of truth." 5 John Henry Wigmore, Evidence in Trials at Common Law 32 (James Chadbourn ed. 1974).

The problem with hearsay is succinctly stated by the District of Columbia Circuit:

> The problem with hearsay is that it deprives the defendant of the opportunity to cross-examine the person who uttered the statement at issue. Here, the government presented allegations of prior drug dealing, and the defendant was unable to cross-examine the person who made them. At the time of the testimony, that person—the less-than-reputable convict, Thomas Rose—was sitting in a federal correctional institution. Meanwhile in court, telling Rose's story, was the clean-cut FBI agent, Neil Darnell. Thus, Evans had no opportunity to "test the recollection and sift the conscience" of his accuser . . . Cross-examination may be the "greatest legal engine ever invented for the discovery of truth," . . . but it is not of much use if there is no one to whom it can be applied. [United States v. Evans, 216 F.3d 80, 84 (D.C. Cir. 2000).]

However, even though cross-examination of a hearsay declarant is usually not possible, it is not the only way to expose potential hearsay dangers. A hearsay declarant's inconsistent statements, bias against one of the parties, or untruthful character may be shown through the testimony of other witnesses or exhibits. FRE 806 explicitly permits impeachment of hearsay declarants: "When a hearsay statement . . . has been admitted in evidence, the declarant's credibility may be attacked . . . by any evidence that would be admissible for those purposes if the declarant had testified as witness." Furthermore, cross-examination may not always contribute to accurate factfinding. Cross-examination leads to the exposure of a witness's deliberate falsehood much less frequently in real life than in courtroom dramas. It may yield only the jury's intuitive sense about a witness's general credibility. But some witnesses may appear to be less than reliable, when in fact they are only shy or nervous or scared. Stereotypes can also affect the jury's perception of who is, or is not, a reliable witness.

Nevertheless, it is certainly more difficult and burdensome for the opponent to obtain and present impeaching facts about hearsay declarants. Cross-examination of a live witness does operate as an efficient means of providing relevant information about a witness's testimonial qualities to the jury. And the *Evans* case above also shows that a proponent could use hearsay as a strategic choice to keep a less-than-convincing declarant off the witness stand. For all these reasons, the opponent's lack of ability to cross-examine a hearsay declarant is the primary reason for excluding hearsay evidence.

Hearsay policy may be summarized as follows: A witness's oath, demeanor, and cross-examination are thought to reduce testimonial dangers and to make in-court testimony *more reliable*. Cross-examination also increases the likelihood that testimonial dangers—sincerity, narration-ambiguity, perception, or memory problems—will be exposed and evaluated by the jury. And it generates information that helps the jury decide whether to rely on a witness's statement. Therefore, because of these differences between a witness's in-court testimony and declarant's out-of-court statement, hearsay is viewed as less reliable and more difficult for the jury to evaluate. It is excluded in the interest of increasing the accuracy of jury decisionmaking. And we remind you that whenever the relevance of an out-of-court statement requires inferences about all four testimonial qualities of the declarant, or the complete trip around the triangle, then hearsay policy is implicated.

It is not an argument for excluding hearsay that the witness who reports a hearsay statement to the jury while on the stand (like George) may be lying, or be mistaken, about what the hearsay declarant (like Sally) said. All testimony bears risks of misperception, faulty memory, and fabrication. A witness who reports hearsay is no different. We rely on oath, the formalities of the courtroom, demeanor, and cross-examination to help the jury evaluate the testimonial qualities of all witnesses (including George).

Hearsay policy could operate as a rule of preference. If a hearsay declarant like Sally is *available* to testify as a witness, it may be preferable to have her testify at the trial. But what if the hearsay declarant is not available to testify? Sally may be ill or out of the country. If we still want to exclude her hearsay statement, we are not talking about a rule of preference but about whether the jury will hear Sally's information at all. If Sally is unavailable, how critical is it to provide the opportunity for the opponent to cross-examine her? Should we exclude relevant evidence for the sake of whatever benefit cross-examination might have brought? See, e.g., Justin Sevier, Testing Tribe's Triangle: Juries, Hearsay, and Psychological Distance, 103 Geo. L.J. 879, 923-924 (2015) (demonstrating experimentally that "jurors attend to the infirmities that lurk beneath the evidence provided by out-of-court hearsay declarants" and properly discount the credibility of such evidence). It is still much too soon for you to be formulating any definitive judgments about these issues. But you should keep them in mind as you continue to study the definition of hearsay.

KEY POINTS

1. Hearsay is a person's statement (a) that is made at a time other than while the person is testifying at the hearing in which the statement is offered and (b) that is offered to prove the truth of the matter asserted in the statement.
2. A hearsay statement may be oral or it may be written.
3. Hearsay policy is to exclude hearsay because there is no oath, no observation of demeanor, and no opportunity to cross-examine the hearsay declarant to determine if there are sincerity, narration-ambiguity, perception, or memory problems (the hearsay dangers).
4. If an out-of-court statement is offered to prove the sincere belief of the declarant in the matter asserted, and then to prove the accuracy of that belief about an event, then all four testimonial qualities of the declarant are involved in the relevancy of the statement and hearsay policy is implicated.

PROBLEMS

8.1. Return to Problem 3.2, Pedroso v. Driver, at page 148. If the defendant denies (on line 00) that she received a speeding ticket, the plaintiffs will offer the ticket itself into evidence. How can the ticket be authenticated? Defendants will object that it is hearsay. Is it?

8.2. Return to Problem 3.3, United States v. Ray, at page 149. June Jacobs' assistant would testify for the prosecution that on the afternoon of March 14, 2015, Jacobs told the assistant that she had just gotten some bad news and that she was going to Ray's office to tell him. Would this testimony be hearsay? What if Jacobs sent a text message to the outside auditor Andrews: "Just told CEO about loss projections." Hearsay? What if Jacobs testified under oath to a grand jury that on March 14, 2015 she told Ray about the loss projections?

8.3. Return to Problem 3.4, State v. Blair, at page 150. The prosecutor seeks to admit the following out-of-court statements by Norma. Who would testify to present this evidence? Are the statements hearsay? Do you think they should be excluded?

    (a) A friend of Norma's says that a month before the attack, Norma told the friend, "Last week I told Jimmy that I was going to break up with him and leave the Bay Area soon. Jimmy was furious."

    (b) In 2008, Norma's mother visited her apartment. Norma was upset and crying. Norma said to her mother that Jimmy had lost his temper and hit her earlier that day, and that when she tried to leave her apartment, he threw a vase at her. The mother saw the shattered vase on the floor.

    (c) Inside the locked drawer in which police found photographs of Norma showing severe bruising and date-stamped July 25, 2009, a handwritten diary was also found. On the page dated July 21, 2009, it stated: "Jimmy beat me after an argument."

3. Elaboration of FRE 801 and 802: Implications of the General Rule of Exclusion

a. Identifying What a Hearsay Statement Is Offered to Prove

The truth-of-the-matter-asserted test of FRE 801(c) requires the identification of the "matter" that an out-of-court statement is offered to prove. Looking at the testimonial triangle in Diagram 8-3 on page 446, supra, the event at point C—that the SUV failed to stop at the red light—is the fact of consequence that, for purposes of FRE 801(c), the declarant's utterance is offered to prove. This fact must then be connected to an essential element in a lawsuit. The line running from point C to "Issue" represents any further inferences that may be necessary to reach the essential element in the case. In this hypothetical, the only remaining inferential task after reaching point C is to decide whether failing to stop at the red light violated the requisite standard of care and therefore satisfies the essential element of negligence.

In many cases, however, after reaching point C, several additional inferences will be necessary for the utterance to be relevant to an essential element in the case. For example, George might testify that Sally said to him, "I had the green light and was just about to cross Main Street when I saw the gray SUV coming toward me down Main Street. It passed in front of me and hit a pedestrian who was also crossing Main Street with the green light." For this evidence to be relevant, the complete trip around the testimonial triangle is necessary to prove that Sally's statements—that she and the pedestrian had the green light—are true. Then, further inferences can be made: first, that if Sally and the pedestrian did have the green light, the red light must have been showing for oncoming traffic on Main Street; second, that the SUV therefore had the red light; third, that the SUV therefore failed to stop at this red light as illustrated in Diagram 8-4.

Diagram 8-4

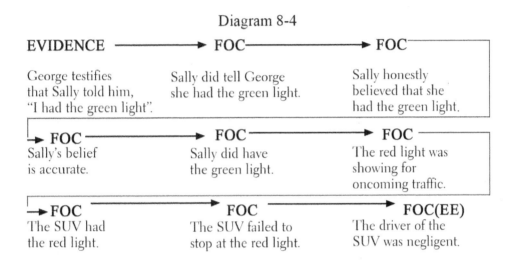

Are Sally's out-of-court statements to George hearsay? Clearly, they are *statements* made by a *declarant not while testifying at the trial.* Applying FRE 801(c), are they *offered to prove the truth of the matter asserted*? You might answer "no," because it seems that her statements are offered to prove that the driver of the SUV failed to stop at the red light and Sally's statement did not assert this. But this is not a correct analysis. The truth-of-the-matter-asserted test should be applied to the last inference that depends on Sally's testimonial qualities. This is FOC-1—that Sally did have the green light. Sally's statement *is* being offered to prove the truth of this assertion. Only if FOC-1 is true can the conclusion about the driver being negligent be drawn. The truth of FOC-1 rests on generalizations about all four of Sally's testimonial qualities; thus hearsay policy is implicated. The further inferences that connect Sally's statements to the essential element in the case *do not relate to her beliefs and do not require any further reliance on her narrative ability, sincerity, perception, or memory.* Thus, they do not implicate hearsay policy. Do not be misled into applying FRE 801(c) to the final conclusions—that the light for the SUV was red, that the SUV failed to stop at the red light, or that the SUV driver was negligent. Sally's statements are hearsay.

They are offered to prove the truth of the matters "asserted in the statement," as FRE 801(c) defines hearsay.

This same analysis must be made each time you apply the truth-of-the-matter-asserted test of FRE 801(c). If an inference that the matters contained in the declarant's assertions are true is required for relevance, then the assertions are "offered to prove" those matters, even if those matters are just a necessary step in the chain of reasoning that continues to some further conclusion.

b. Testimony by Witnesses About Their Own Out-of-Court Statements May Still Be Hearsay

FRE 801(b) defines a "declarant" as a person who made a statement. This term generally is used to refer to people when they made statements *outside of court*, and we have used it that way in the preceding sections. When people make statements to the jury in court, under oath, and subject to cross-examination, they are, obviously, functioning as witnesses. When witnesses testify in court about statements that they themselves made *not while testifying in the current trial or hearing*, those statements are defined as hearsay by FRE 801(c). For example, in the case of the gray SUV, suppose that Sally testifies as a witness that "right after the accident, I remember telling George that the gray SUV ran the red light." Sally is testifying about her own hearsay statement. In this circumstance the hearsay declarant (Sally) is in fact in the courtroom and can be cross-examined. Some commentators have therefore argued that if witnesses report their own out-of-court statements, their evidence should not be regarded as hearsay. See, e.g., Edmund M. Morgan, Hearsay Dangers and the Application of the Hearsay Concept, 62 Harv. L. Rev. 177, 192-193 (1957). Others disagree, contending that cross-examination is less valuable when it is conducted long after the statement was made. And, if a witness's prior statements were not hearsay, witnesses could refer to and rely on their own prior *prepared* statements in their testimony. This is undesirable since the witness was not subject to cross-examination or to the scrutiny of the jury when preparing those statements. The various positions in the debate over the hearsay status of prior statements of witnesses are described in the Advisory Committee Note to FRE 801(d)(1). Under FRE 801(c), prior statements of witnesses are defined as hearsay unless specifically exempted. See FRE 801(d)(1), which we will examine in Section C infra.

c. Hearsay, Lay Opinions, and the Firsthand Knowledge Rule

You have previously encountered the lay opinion rule (FRE 701) and the firsthand knowledge rule (FRE 602) in Chapter Four. Here we address briefly the relationship between those rules and the hearsay rule.

Consider a situation in which Ellen, a bystander, is prepared to testify in the suit between the pedestrian and the driver of the gray SUV. Ellen might testify that "The gray SUV ignored the red light and hit the pedestrian in the crosswalk." There are three possible bases for Ellen's belief: First, she may have observed the entire incident; second, Sally may have told her what happened; or third, on the basis of her observation of the position of the car and the pedestrian after the accident, she could have concluded that the defendant's SUV must have run the red light. If the second variation were true, Ellen would in effect be relating a hearsay statement. She has no firsthand knowledge of the event herself. In the third variation, Ellen's testimony that the defendant ignored the red light would be a lay opinion, based on her firsthand knowledge of the position of the car and the person who was hit. If she testified about the facts she did observe, instead of just stating her conclusion, the jury might be just as capable as she is to draw the appropriate inference.

If the opponent is unsure about the basis for Ellen's testimony, the initial objection can always be "lack of firsthand knowledge." The objecting attorney should immediately ask the judge to permit inquiry, outside the presence of the jury, into the basis for Ellen's testimony. The opponent should ask, "How do you know that the defendant ignored a red light?" If this inquiry reveals that Ellen is in fact relating hearsay ("Sally told me what happened"), the objecting attorney can then change the objection to hearsay. If the inquiry reveals that Ellen is expressing an opinion that is not based on her observation of the accident itself, then the objection would be lack of firsthand knowledge or a lay opinion objection. What is important, as a practical matter, is for the attorney to make some objection that will get the judge's attention and permit inquiry, preferably without the jury listening, into the basis for the witness's knowledge. Once the basis of knowledge is established, it should be relatively easy for the parties to address the question of why the evidence should or should not be admissible.

d. Multiple Hearsay

On some occasions evidence will contain multiple hearsay. Consider, for example, the pedestrian's attempt to prove that the gray SUV went through a red light by offering a properly authenticated police report that states "George reports that 'Sally told me that the gray SUV ran the red light.'" Here we have multiple hearsay. We care about the sincerity, narration, perception, and memory of the police officer who wrote the report, as well as both Sally and George, and none of them is on the witness stand subject to cross-examination when making their statements.

If the plaintiff called George as a witness to testify from memory about what Sally said, we would have single hearsay. If the plaintiff called the police officer as a witness to testify about what George said, we would still have double hearsay. Sally is still a declarant because her statement continues to be offered for its truth. In addition, George is a declarant as well. In multiple hearsay situations, the evidence will be inadmissible unless there is a hearsay exception or exemption for each layer of hearsay. FRE 805 provides that "[h]earsay within hearsay is not excluded by the rule against hearsay if each part of the combined statements conforms with an exception to the rule."

KEY POINTS

1. If a statement made outside of court is offered to prove the truth of what it asserts, it is defined as hearsay even though the declarant is the witness who is testifying about the statement.

2. A hearsay objection is appropriate after determining that a witness does not have firsthand knowledge of the events testified to, but is relying on what others have said.

3. Some hearsay statements include additional hearsay within them. In such cases of multiple hearsay, each hearsay component must be admissible through an exception or exemption.

PROBLEMS

8.4. Return to Problem 3.5, Broadback v. Trapp, on page 150. During his own testimony, plaintiff Broadback testifies as follows:

(a) "I told the ambulance driver that I felt tremendous pain after my collision with Trapp."

The ambulance driver then testifies that one of Broadback's teammates spoke to her on the way to the hospital:

(b) "The teammate told me that 'Trapp has always had it in for Broadback.'"

(c) "The teammate also said that he heard Trapp say 'I did this on purpose.'"

Are any of these statements objectionable as hearsay?

8.5. John and Mary Smith had a son, Brent, who was born on August 20, 1976. John and Mary were killed in a plane crash, and their son, if he survived them, was entitled to inherit their entire estates. In a probate proceeding in December 2000, an individual offers to testify as follows to establish his right to inherit the assets of John and Mary Smith: "My name is Brent Smith. I was born on August 20, 1976. I am 24 years old. I am the son of John and Mary Smith." Is any of this testimony objectionable as hearsay?

4. Explanation of FRE 801(c): Nonhearsay Statements with No Hearsay Dangers

Not all out-of-court statements are hearsay. A critical aspect of the definition of hearsay is that, under the proponent's relevance theory, the statements are offered to prove the *truth* of the matters they assert. Many out-of-court statements are not offered for this relevance theory; they are offered for a *nonhearsay* use.

a. Nonhearsay Uses

In our hypothetical concerning the gray SUV and the pedestrian, consider the following testimony of Sally about an event she witnessed: "In the morning, just before the accident, when I was getting gasoline at the service station, I heard Mike, a mechanic, say to the defendant who was driving a gray SUV, 'Your brakes are in bad shape. It would be dangerous for you to drive that SUV.'" Is Mike's statement hearsay? It is a statement made by a declarant who is not testifying at trial, but is it offered for the relevance theory of proving the truth of the matter Mike is asserting? The proponent of Sally's testimony, the plaintiff, might well argue as follows:

> Your Honor, we are not offering this evidence to prove the truth of the matter asserted by the mechanic—that the brakes were in fact bad. Rather, we are offering the evidence to prove only that the mechanic spoke those words. This is relevant to show that the defendant had notice of the dangerous condition of his brakes before he got into his car and drove through the red light. One of the things that we must prove in order to prove one of our claims of negligence is that the defendant either knew or should have known about the dangerous condition of his brakes. This out-of-court statement is relevant to show that the defendant heard it, that he had knowledge that his brakes were bad, and that he should have had his brakes repaired.

This theory of nonhearsay relevance is known as "effect on the listener." Under this theory, evidence of Mike's statement is not hearsay. Sally's testimony tends to prove that Mike's statement was made, and Mike's statement is relevant for what is called the "nonhearsay" use of "notice." It tends to prove that the driver heard these words and knew his brakes were bad, a fact of consequence in the case. In terms of FRE 801(c), the proponent is not offering Mike's statement to prove that the matters asserted are true. In terms of the inferential process in Diagram 8-1, the proponent is not offering Mike's statement to prove that Mike's beliefs about the condition of the brakes are accurate in order to prove that the brakes were bad. Indeed, it is not being offered to prove anything about the Mike's belief. This can be illustrated with the testimonial triangle, below.

The line from the declarant's utterance at point A to the Issue represents the inference required to use Mike's statement to prove the fact of consequence—that the driver of the SUV had notice that his brakes were bad. The relevance of the evidence does *not* depend on making the inference from A to B or from B to C. Relevancy does not depend on what belief was in Mike's mind, or on whether that belief was accurate and corresponded to some event in the real world. Stated another way, relevance does not depend on Mike's memory, perception, sincerity, or narration. Therefore, hearsay policy is not implicated. There is no need to be concerned about the lack of oath, demeanor, and cross-examination of Mike.

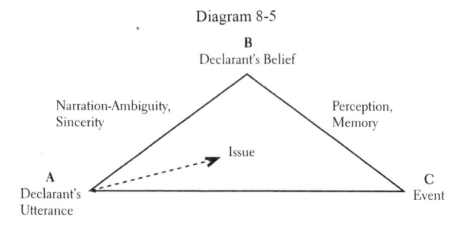

Diagram 8-5

Effect on the Listener.   As we noted, the proponent of Mike's statement is offering it for the relevant nonhearsay use of showing its *effect on the listener*. Arguably, given the warning, the driver of the SUV had notice and therefore had the opportunity to respond. How the warning affected him—his conduct in responding to it—is relevant to whether he breached a requisite duty of care, which is an essential element of a negligence case. Under this theory of relevance, Mike's testimonial qualities become virtually insignificant, as shown in Diagram 8-6.

Diagram 8-6

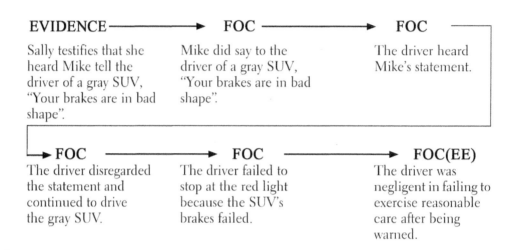

Of course, we do care about whether Mike spoke any words at all (is Sally lying?), whether Sally heard the words correctly, and whether, at the time she testifies, Sally remembers accurately what was said. But Sally is a witness, making her statement in court, under oath, and can be cross-examined on all these points. The proponent's theory of relevance—that the driver was *unreasonable* in disregarding Mike's warning—depends on Mike's *apparent* sincerity, not on Mike's *actual* sincerity. It also requires that the driver hear Mike's statement—thus, that Mike's words were spoken loudly enough for the driver to hear. Anybody who heard the warning—Sally, Mike himself, a bystander—can testify about the loudness of the warning and the apparent sincerity with which it was given. In his own defense, the driver of the SUV may claim that it was reasonable for him to disregard what the mechanic said because Mike was always joking about brakes. But that is a defense, and does not alter the nonhearsay status of Sally's testimony for the plaintiff as to what she heard Mike say.

Out-of-court statements offered to prove their *effect on the listener* are relevant in many different kinds of cases. The classic English hearsay law decision, Subramaniam v. Public Prosecutor [1956] 1 W.L.R. 965, provides a vivid illustration. Subramaniam was accused of aiding and abetting terrorists and pled not guilty by reason of duress. He took the stand to testify about his out-of-court conversations with terrorists that included the terrorists' threat to kill him if he did not help them. The trial court excluded this part of Subramaniam's testimony as hearsay, but the Privy Council (the British Commonwealth's highest court) disagreed. It held that Subramaniam did not purport to prove that the terrorists' statements were true. Rather, he wanted to prove that those statements made him fear for his life and do what the terrorists wanted him to do because of that fear. These facts made the defense of duress available to him. The same is true about different rules of substantive law that make liability depend on the reasonableness of a listener's response to *warnings, notices, and instructions.* For example, in a civil rights action for an unwarranted shooting by police officers, brought against the officers and their supervisors, prior complaints charging abuse by one of the officers were not hearsay because they were offered to show the failure of the supervisors to respond to those prior complaints. Gutierrez-Rodriguez v. Cartagena, 882 F.2d 553, 575 (1st Cir. 1989). The effect of a statement can also be to create a specific state of mind, such as *knowledge, good faith, provocation, or reasonable apprehension of bodily harm.* This state of mind may be an essential element in a civil or a criminal case. For example, whether a police officer acted with "probable cause" in making an arrest may be determined by what the officer was told the arrested person was doing. Reports of "homosexual violence" among prison inmates to prison officials are relevant to prove the officials' "deliberate indifference"—the state of mind required in a civil rights suit. Roland v. Johnson, 933 F.2d 1009 (6th Cir. 1991). In a case involving the issue of bad-faith denial of insurance coverage, appraisal reports were not offered to show the amount of loss actually suffered, but instead to show what information the insurance company had when it denied the claim. Talmage v. Harris, 486 F.3d 968, 975 (7th Cir. 2007). Finally, statements made to a listener can provide *motive* for conduct, and thus are relevant to explain the listener's subsequent behavior.

Legally Operative Facts. Another relevant nonhearsay use for an out-of-court statement is when the statement is itself a *legally operative fact.* For example, suppose Paul says to Sarah outside of court, "I offer to sell you my five-year old horse for $500." To prove the age of the horse, Paul's statement to Sarah is hearsay. However, in an action to establish that there was an offer for the sale of the horse, Sarah—or Paul or anyone else who heard the words—could testify to what Paul said. Under the substantive law of contracts, the words are themselves the event to be proved—the offer. McNaboe v. NVF Co., 2000 U.S. Dist. LEXIS 4418, at *39 (D. Del. 2000) ("The words the offerors . . . uttered in making the offer are admissible as nonhearsay as they are utterances to which the law attaches duties and liabilities."). Anyone who heard Paul's statement can testify that it was made, just as any eyewitness to an automobile accident could testify to the event that the gray SUV ran a red light. In the words of the Seventh Circuit:

> [This kind of utterance echoes] the linguist's distinction between performative and illocutionary utterances. The latter narrate, describe, or otherwise convey information, and so are judged by their truth value (information is useful only if true—indeed it is *information* only if it is true); the former—illustrated by a promise, offer, or demand— commit the speaker to a course of action. Performative utterances are not within the scope of the hearsay rule, because they do not make any truth claims. [United States v. Montana, 199 F.3d 947, 949 (7th Cir. 1999).]

Such utterances do not make truth claims because none of the inferences required for relevance depend on Paul's testimonial qualities. No memory or perception danger exists because Paul is not relating some fact that he has observed. Moreover, under the prevalent objective theory of contract formation, there is no sincerity or narration-ambiguity danger here, for we do not have to make any inference that Paul is sincere. The proponent's theory of relevance is that Paul said the words in an *apparent* manner such that the offeree might reasonably be expected to take it seriously; this would be a valid and binding offer. And whether the words were spoken in an *apparently* serious manner is something about which anyone who heard the words can testify and be fully cross-examined. Paul's subjective intent or understanding may be relevant to the issue of mutual mistake, which Paul may raise as a defense. But mistake only becomes an issue once there has been an offer and an acceptance. Thus, to prove the offer, Paul's statement is nonhearsay. Its relevance can be shown on the testimonial triangle as the line from A to the Issue: From the fact that Paul spoke the words, we infer an essential element in a contract case.

Many different kinds of statements are *legally operative facts* because principles of substantive law give them independent legal significance. For example, in litigation over whether a group insurance policy is excluded from ERISA coverage, the policy itself is admissible as nonhearsay, "excluded from the definition of hearsay . . . because it is a legally operative document that defines the rights and liabilities of the parties." Stuart v. Unum Life Ins. Co., 217 F.3d 1145, 1153 (9th Cir. 2000). Some statements are acts done with words that, under the substantive law, give rise to civil obligations or consequences—e.g., acknowledging debts, agreeing to marry a person in an official ceremony, and uttering words of defamation or slander. And some words are criminal acts—perjury, extortionate threats, offers to sell drugs, statements forming a conspiracy. For example, a statement soliciting a bribe was held to be a legally operative fact, "important for the mere fact that the words were said and not for the truth of the matter." Transportes Aereos Pegaso v. Bell Helicopter Textron, Inc., 623 F. Supp. 2d 518, 530 (D. Del. 2009). Sometimes verbal statements have immediate legal significance when they also accompany nonverbal acts. If information about the context within which such statements were made is necessary, it can be supplied by anyone who was there. Cross-examination of the declarant is not necessary to supply it.

Credibility-related Statements.   An out-of-court statement is often instrumental for discrediting a testifying witness's testimony. For example, when a declarant's statement is offered to show that it contradicts his in-court testimony, it becomes relevant and admissible as nonhearsay. The theory of relevance is not that the prior statement is necessarily true, but that the equivocation reflected in the inconsistent statements—whichever one, if any, is true—suggests that the witness is not credible.

Identifying Nonhearsay Uses.   A proponent's boilerplate response to a hearsay objection in court is, "Not offered for its truth, Your Honor." That response will not satisfy a thoughtful judge or a well-trained opponent. The proponent should be able to articulate the nonhearsay theory of relevance; for example, that the statement is offered to prove an effect on the listener (regardless of its truth) and that this effect on the listener is a fact of consequence in the case. The proponent should also be able to explain *why* exclusion of the statement is not appropriate; that is, why hearsay policy is *not* implicated. The critical point is that the evidence is relevant without reliance on the declarant's testimonial qualities that purport to establish the statement's truth.

Some texts and study aids provide a laundry list of nonhearsay uses for out-of-court statements. Such lists typically include the three nonhearsay uses already identified—statements relevant for their effect on the listener; statements that are legally operative facts; and credibility-related statements, discussed in Chapter Seven at pages 415-416, supra. The lists also include statements offered as *circumstantial evidence of the declarant's state of mind*. A leading treatise, Christopher B. Mueller & Laird C. Kirkpatrick, Evidence §8.20-21 at 829-834 (2d ed. 1999), also includes words that operate as identifying characteristics of an object (a license plate, a trade insignia) and words that have a performative aspect that dominates the assertive aspect (the ability to speak French, or to speak at all). These written or spoken words generate logical factual inferences that have nothing to do with their "truth" value; thus they might be called *"logically operative facts."* While these lists may help you to identify some common nonhearsay uses for out-of-court statements, the key to understanding nonhearsay is to focus on the inferences necessary to the relevance of the out-of-court statement. The list is no substitute for the analysis that underlies it.

b. Statements Relevant for Both Nonhearsay and Hearsay Uses

Sally's testimony about what Mike the mechanic said to the driver of the gray SUV could also be relevant to prove that the brakes on the Honda were in fact bad. If offered for this purpose, the evidence is clearly hearsay. Relevance would depend on the mechanic's sincerity, narration, perception, and memory. It would be excluded if no hearsay exception applies.

When a particular piece of evidence is admissible for one purpose (to prove notice) but inadmissible for another (to prove the brakes were bad), the question of admissibility is one of discretionary balancing for the trial judge under FRE 403. The risk of unfair prejudice is that the jury, even after being given limiting instructions, will use the evidence for its improper hearsay purpose (here, to prove bad brakes). Is the probative value of the evidence for the admissible purpose (here, notice) substantially outweighed by the danger of unfair prejudice? We have seen in the discussion of FRE 403 in Chapter Three that need for the evidence can alter the balancing when there are alternative means to prove notice. If there are not, the need for evidence of Mike's warning will be very high. And in many cases, other evidence to prove the truth that the SUV's brakes were bad will already have been admitted. This diminishes the risk of unfair prejudice. The Rule 403 decision is made within these contextual facts of the specific case.

KEY POINT

When an out-of-court statement is offered to prove its effect on the listener, some legally operative fact, some factor pertaining to the declarant's credibility as a witness, or some other matter where relevance does not depend on inferences about the accuracy of the declarant's belief about an event, the statement is not hearsay. It is not offered for the truth of the matter it asserts.

PROBLEMS

As you examine the following problems, consider why the out-of-court statements are relevant and whether they are hearsay or nonhearsay. We have discussed three ways of articulating the hearsay test, and you should try to apply each one. Ignore the possibility that the statement may fall within a hearsay exception and focus solely on the question of whether the evidence is hearsay.

8.6. The Federal Election Commission (FEC) has brought an enforcement action against the Christian Coalition for violating federal campaign finance laws during congressional elections in 2000, 2002, and 2004. Federal law prohibits corporations and labor unions from using their general treasury funds to make direct contributions to candidates; but they can make expenditures related to federal elections so long as these expenditures are for communications that do not expressly advocate the election or defeat of a clearly identified candidate. The Christian Coalition is a corporation and in 2002 it paid for its Executive Director to speak at a conference in Montana. In this videotaped speech, the Executive Director said that Montana's Democratic Congressman Pat Williams "is one of your top targets in the entire nation," and, "We're going to see Pat Williams sent bags-packing back to Montana in November of this year." The FEC asserts that this violates federal law. The Christian Coalition objects that the videotape of the speech is hearsay. What result?

8.7. Lucy Rawlins is suing Lagoon Resort in the State of Hawaii for injuries she allegedly suffered during a scuba diving trip organized by the Resort. Resort's defense is that Rawlins signed a valid form that releases it from liability for the claim Rawlins has alleged against it. The general manager of Lagoon Resort testifies that he is responsible for explaining the release to guests, obtaining signatures, and filing and storing these records. He claims that Exhibit A is the Liability Release Form signed by Rawlins. Rawlins does not contest that she signed Exhibit A but objects that it is hearsay. What result?

8.8. In a libel suit, Plaintiff alleges that the defendant sent a signed, typewritten letter to Plaintiff's employer stating that plaintiff was a liar and thief. Plaintiff offers an authenticated photocopy of the letter into evidence. Defendant objects that the letter is hearsay. What result? Defendant then calls a coworker of Plaintiff who will testify that Plaintiff lied on the job and stole from the company. Plaintiff objects that this testimony is hearsay. What result? Coworker also testifies that "For years Plaintiff has had a reputation in the company for lying and stealing on the job." Is this testimony hearsay? Is it inadmissible character evidence?

8.9. Return to Problem 3.3, United States v. Ray, at page 149. To prove that Ray was responsible for the sale of his 100,000 shares of Rundown stock, the prosecution offers Ray's e-mail to his broker directing the broker to make the sale. Hearsay? To prove that Ray gave this order on March 16, 2015, the prosecution points to the typed date of "March 16, 2015" in the e-mail. Hearsay?

8.10. In a prosecution of Joe Jamal for bank robbery, FBI Agent Guerrero testifies that a confidential FBI informant identified Jamal as a suspect. Defense counsel objects that the testimony is hearsay, offered to prove the truth of the matter asserted. The government claims that the testimony is offered to explain the Agent's investigatory procedures and to show why he developed a photo identification display for witnesses that included Jamal's photograph. What ruling?

8.11. In a racketeering prosecution pursuant to the RICO statutes, a witness for the prosecution appears visibly nervous, speaks haltingly, and changes his testimony several times, but finally does identify one of the defendants as the person who paid him to deposit cash in phony bank accounts, a violation of RICO. At the close of the witness's testimony, the prosecutor asks whether the defendants have threatened him. The witness responds that two of the defendants called him at his home a week before the trial and made threats on his life if he testified. Hearsay?

8.12. Joseph Blackstone, a professor of economics at a leading business school, is charged with insider trading in violation of 18 U.S.C. §78. Blackstone was a director of NF, a small natural foods company that was purchased by the Kellogg Company in February of 2011. Just prior to the purchase, several of Blackstone's family and friends purchased large amounts of stock in NF and made a significant profit when Kellogg purchased the company. Blackstone is charged with tipping all of these individuals with inside information about the impending Kellogg purchase. Blackstone denies communicating any tips about the purchase and states that all of the individuals could have learned of the purchase through "leaks" in the industry and in the press. At trial, Blackstone offers the following testimony of Voss, one of his friends: "In January of 2011, I heard that a Yahoo message board contained a rumor about the Kellogg purchase." Should the court exclude this testimony as hearsay?

8.13. Sondra Evers is suing Jones's Deli for personal injuries sustained when she slipped and fell on a pool of spilled ketchup near the food takeout counter. Sondra claims that the ketchup had been on the floor long enough for Jones's employees to have known about it. Sondra calls Bertha Barlow, who offers to testify as follows: "About half an hour before Ms. Evers had her accident, I was walking past the takeout counter when I overheard someone exclaim loudly, 'There's ketchup on the floor!'" Should this testimony be excluded as hearsay? What if Bertha also testifies that she saw a Jones's Deli clerk near the takeout counter when she heard the statement?

8.14. Return to Problem 3.2, Pedroso v. Driver, at page 148. Max testifies for defendants that he always rode the same school bus with Paul Pedroso and Paul's friend Tom, and that Paul and Tom used to play tag after getting off the bus together. Max testifies that on the day of the accident, he heard Tom say "Paul, you're *it*" as the two boys left the bus. Plaintiffs object to this testimony as hearsay. What result?

8.15. Brian Andronico is charged with conspiracy to distribute counterfeit currency. An undercover agent, Pamela Mertz, testified that she made purchases of counterfeit money from a man driving a car with the license plate "ICE 2000." The prosecution can prove that the license plate "ICE 2000" is registered to Andronico. The defendant objects on grounds of authentication, best evidence, and hearsay. Should Mertz's testimony be admitted?

8.16. To prove consciousness as a basis for pain and suffering after an accident, plaintiff offers a witness to testify as follows: "Within 30 seconds of the accident I was at the plaintiff's side. She was lying on the ground, and I shouted to a passerby, 'Get help; she's unconscious.' At that moment the plaintiff said, 'I'm not unconscious.'" Is the evidence hearsay?

5. Explanation of FRE 801(a)(2): Nonverbal Conduct

a. The Relevancy of Nonverbal Conduct to Prove Belief

Thus far, all of our examples of hearsay have involved oral or written utterances, but in some instances hearsay is completely nonverbal. Consider, for example, the following testimony offered by a police officer in a battery prosecution: "When I arrived at the bar that was the scene of the fight, I asked who threw the first punch. One of the women who was present pointed at Jim Harris, the defendant, who was wearing a red shirt." This testimony is relevant to prove the woman's belief, as shown by her nonverbal conduct, that Harris threw the first punch. Consider Diagram 8-7 on page 463.

This theory of relevance depends on inferences about the testimonial qualities of the police officer, who is a witness, and of the woman. The inference from the woman's conduct (IF_1) to her belief (IF_3) (from A to B on the testimonial triangle) and the inference from her belief to the occurrence of the event at issue (FOC) (from B to C on the testimonial triangle) show that all of the hearsay dangers are present. The woman may have been falsely representing her belief to get Jim Harris in trouble (a sincerity risk); the arm movement may have been an involuntary tic that was not based on any belief about Jim (an ambiguity risk); the woman may not have seen clearly who threw the first punch (a perception risk); and she may have forgotten who threw the first punch by the time the officer asked (a memory risk). Indeed, in terms of the inferential process involved in using this evidence to prove that Harris threw the first punch, there is no pertinent difference between the intentional pointing and a verbal response that identifies Harris (e.g., "It was Jim Harris" or "It was the man in the red shirt").

Remember that often conduct is just conduct, offered to prove that an act was done, without regard to the actor's belief. In a medical malpractice case, the defendant physician testified that while treating his patient's snake bite, he placed a telephone call to a toxicology specialist. Since the content of that call was not disclosed, this testimony revealed only the doctor's intent to place the call and was not hearsay. Field v. Anderson, 2006 WL 3043431 (W.D. Ky.).

Diagram 8-7

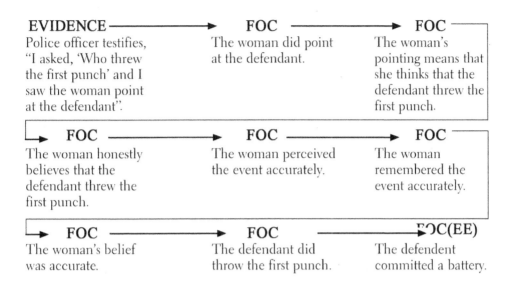

b. Application of FRE 801(a)

FRE 801(a) defines a "statement" as "a person's oral assertion, written assertion, or *nonverbal conduct, if the person intended it as an assertion.*" (Emphasis added.) Applying this definition to our hypothetical raises a preliminary question of fact: Did the woman intend her nonverbal conduct (pointing) to be an assertion of her belief that Jim threw the first punch? What facts would you contend are relevant to the question of her intent? If the woman did so intend, her act of pointing, commonly called *assertive conduct*, will be found to be a "statement" and will be excluded as hearsay. If she did not so intend, her act is commonly called *nonassertive conduct*, and it may be admitted because it is not a "statement" and therefore not hearsay.

Assertive Conduct. Sometimes conduct is intentionally used by the actor as a substitute for words. That is, the actor wants to communicate a belief and uses conduct to do so. By raising your hand in class, for example, you communicate "I want to speak." Or by shaking your head from side to side when asked a question, you communicate that your answer is "no." Both of these actions would usually be *intended by the actor to be assertions* of what the actor is thinking. If they are so intended, then in the words of the Advisory Committee Note, such conduct "is clearly the equivalent of words, assertive in nature, and [is] to be regarded as a statement." The act of pointing, mentioned in the Note, would typically be found to be assertive conduct, intended by the actor as the equivalent of words, and thus would be hearsay.

Nonassertive Conduct. Sometimes conduct is not intended by the actor as an assertion. In our hypothetical about the fight in the bar, what if the woman did not point at Jim Harris but instead carefully maneuvered Jim to the back door of the bar and gave him a push out the door? If the police officer saw her do this and arrested

Jim Harris, would the officer's testimony as to what the woman did be relevant in the battery prosecution? Would it be hearsay? It can be inferred from her conduct that the woman believed Jim started the fight, that her belief was accurate, and that Jim did in fact start the fight. Thus, her conduct is relevant. But unlike the act of pointing, the act of carefully pushing Jim out of the back door may not be intended by the woman to assert her belief in Jim's guilt. She may be trying to protect Jim, and the last thing she wants is for the police officer to arrest him. If she does not intend to communicate her belief, then her conduct is nonassertive and, under the definition of FRE 801(a), would not be a "statement" and hearsay. Notice that the woman's conduct communicates her underlying belief or intent to people who observe it, and that the key question here is whether she intended to make that communication. If she did, the conduct would be hearsay (deeds substituting for words). If she had no such communicative intent, the conduct would not be hearsay ("deeds speak louder than words").

However, you can still see that the relevance of the woman's conduct, even if it is nonassertive, depends on inferences about all of her testimonial qualities. If any of these inferences is false, the woman's conduct is not relevant to prove Jim started the fight. For example, the woman may actually think Jim did not start the fight but wants the police to think he did (a sincerity risk); or she may want him to leave the bar for other reasons, such as that he has illegal drugs in his possession (an ambiguity risk). There are also potential perception and memory dangers: The woman may have confused Jim with another man wearing a red shirt who actually threw the first punch, or she may have forgotten what she actually saw. These are the same risks we have previously identified with regard to the woman pointing at Jim; and if the woman shouted "Jim Harris" in response to the officer's question, the same risks would be present. The intended and the unintended communication scenarios still differ from each other: In the intended-communication scenario, factfinders must rely on the woman as a truth teller, whereas in the unintended-communication scenario, they do not have to do so. Instead, they can use their general knowledge of the world to infer what people normally want to accomplish when they do what the woman did under similar circumstances. Arguably, this substitution would reduce the hearsay risks (without eliminating them completely). We analyze this argument in Section 6 below.

FRE 801(a)'s Intent Test. FRE 801(a) creates a doctrinal test for determining whether any particular item of nonverbal conduct evidence is or is not hearsay. Nonverbal conduct intended as an assertion, is hearsay; nonverbal conduct not intended as an assertion is not hearsay. This test thus involves a preliminary question of fact: Was the actor's nonverbal conduct intended as an assertion? This preliminary question will be decided on the basis of the *nature of the conduct* and the *circumstances surrounding it* as presented by both parties. There will be some close cases, and there may be situations in which conduct that is normally nonassertive is in fact intended to be assertive. For example, if the woman pushing Jim Harris out the back door made a lot of noise and called attention to her conduct, these contextual facts could generate the inference that she was intending to communicate her belief in Jim's guilt to the police officer.

FRE 104 governs the preliminary factfinding that is necessary to the judge's application of FRE 801(a)'s intent test. Should the question of "intent" be governed by FRE 104(a) or (b)? As you know from Chapter Four, preliminary questions of fact are for the judge under FRE 104(a), unless they establish the relevance of the offered evidence. In the hypotheticals that we have just discussed, the woman's intent to use her conduct to assert Jim's guilt is not necessary to the relevance of that conduct. The relevance of her conduct does depend on *her belief* about who started the fight; but that she *intends to assert that belief* is not an inference that is necessary to relevance. Instead, it is a test imposed by hearsay policy. Thus, under FRE 104(a), the judge must be persuaded by a preponderance of the evidence on the question of intent. This rule reflects the general policy of FRE 402, which deems all relevant evidence presumptively admissible: if the evidence is relevant, the burden always shifts to the opponent to show the judge that a rule of exclusion applies. Furthermore, as explained by the Advisory Committee Note to FRE 801, "the rule is so worded as to place the burden upon the party claiming that the intention existed; ambiguous and doubtful cases will be resolved against him and in favor of admissibility." To what language in FRE 801 do you think the Advisory Committee is referring?

6. Elaboration of FRE 801(a): Justification for the Distinction Between Assertive and Nonassertive Conduct

Since the relevance of both the woman pointing and the woman pushing Jim out the back door depends on the accuracy of her belief and requires a complete trip around the testimonial triangle, both kinds of conduct implicate hearsay policy. Yet only the assertive conduct of the woman pointing is defined as hearsay; the nonassertive conduct of pushing Jim is not hearsay under FRE 801(a)'s definition. Why?

a. *Absence of Hearsay Danger*

The Advisory Committee's Note to FRE 801(a) suggests that nonassertive conduct should not be defined as hearsay because of the probable absence of any sincerity danger. If an actor has a belief about a disputed fact—that Jim Harris threw the first punch—but is not intending to assert or to communicate that belief, then the actor cannot be "lying" about it. It is the view of the Advisory Committee that a person can be insincere—can tell a lie—only if the person is intending to communicate a particular fact that would be the subject of the lie. Without the intent to assert that fact, there is no opportunity to fabricate it. Is this a common sense generalization? Do you agree with it? Is the absence of sincerity risk a sufficient reason to admit the woman's pushing Jim as not hearsay?

Surprisingly and unaccountably, the Advisory Committee Note to FRE 801(a) asserts that the testimonial qualities other than sincerity also do not present a high risk: "Admittedly [nonassertive conduct] is untested with respect to the perception, memory, and narration (or their equivalents) of the actor, but the *Advisory Committee is of the view that these dangers are minimal in the absence of an intent to assert . . .*"

(emphasis added). On what empirical data does the Advisory Committee base this conclusion? There seems to be nothing inherent in nonassertive conduct that tends to reduce or eliminate the other hearsay dangers. Can you think of anything about the woman's conduct in pushing Jim out the back door that reduces the danger of ambiguity (she was worried about illegal drugs) or perception (she confused Jim with another man in a red shirt)? The Note indicates that the actor's motivation to be accurate and the need to rely on the actor's own conduct can reduce the degree of perception and memory dangers. But these factors are not automatically present in every case. As a result, the woman's conduct in pushing Jim could be admitted as not hearsay without any reduction in the perception or memory danger involved.

Thus, you should ask yourself whether the probable absence of just one hearsay danger (sincerity) is sufficient justification for removing nonassertive conduct from the definition of hearsay altogether. When we study the hearsay exceptions, we will see that the probable absence of one or more of the hearsay dangers is a principal justification for many of them.

b. Necessity

In general, excluding relevant evidence because of some hearsay dangers may be too great a price to pay when it is very burdensome or perhaps even impossible to obtain other, "better" evidence on the same point. Thus, "necessity" is a reason for many of the exceptions to the hearsay rule. The concern about nonassertive conduct is that it is so pervasive and so often relied on as a matter of course in our everyday lives that we would be giving up too much relevant evidence by classifying such conduct as hearsay. For example, if we look out the window and see people wearing heavy overcoats, we assume it is cold outside; if a northbound vehicle proceeds through an intersection with a traffic light, we assume the driver thinks that the light is green for that vehicle; if we see people on the street begin to put up their umbrellas, we assume they believe it has begun to rain; if a shopkeeper repairs a loose board in the threshold to a shop after someone has tripped on it, we assume the shopkeeper thinks the loose board was dangerous. In these situations, the individual actors have beliefs about events or conditions that motivate their conduct; but they are probably not *intending to assert* the belief that it is cold, that the light is green, that it is raining, or that the loose board is dangerous.[2] Consequently, their conduct would not be defined as hearsay under FRE 801(a).

Another variation of the necessity argument for treating nonassertive conduct as not hearsay is that attorneys are not immediately sensitive to the hearsay characteristics of such evidence. If a rule treating nonassertive conduct as hearsay would be only sporadically applied, the rule arguably ought not to exist at all.

---

2. In Chapter Six, page 358, supra, we noted that subsequent remedial measures might be relevant to prove the belief of the actor that the situation remedied was dangerous. Now you can see why such conduct is unlikely to be classified as hearsay — it is unlikely that such actors are intending by their conduct to assert "dangerousness." But do not forget that the relevance of remedial measures to prove liability or fault still requires a complete trip around the testimonial triangle.

c. Should Nonassertive Conduct Be Excluded from the Definition of Hearsay?

Whether the foregoing reasons are sufficient to exclude nonassertive conduct from the hearsay prohibition has long been the subject of academic debate.

The Difficulty of Applying the Intent Test.   One concern relates to the task of classifying conduct as assertive or nonassertive. The judicial task of determining under FRE 801(a) whether conduct is intended as an assertion is not easy, and inevitably entails the risk that the wrong decision will be made, either because the actor has cleverly disguised an assertion (e.g., the woman is trying to communicate that Jim is guilty by pushing him out the door when she knows he is not), because sufficient evidence of intent is not available, or because the court misapplies the concept of intent to assert. Even if judges reach the correct result most of the time, too much time and effort are spent on arguing and deciding the question of intent.

The Danger of Ambiguity.   A second, and perhaps more substantial, concern is that significant hearsay dangers are still attached to such conduct. The lack of intent to assert inevitably increases the ambiguity danger. Conduct can be the product of many different beliefs, and the factfinder may attribute a belief to the actor that the actor does not in fact hold. We have seen that the woman may have other reasons for pushing Jim out the back door. Similarly, a driver going through the intersection is unlikely to be intending to assert that the light is green but it may also be wrong to infer that the driver believes that the light is green. The driver may know that the light is red but because of some emergency the driver feels compelled to ignore the red light. A substantial ambiguity problem means the conduct has low probative value to prove the specific belief for which it is offered. At some point the conduct may be so ambiguous, and the probative value so low, that a court could rely on FRE 403 to exclude the evidence. Moreover, the driver of the car may be color-blind, or distracted, and may not have perceived the color of the stop light. As noted previously, there is nothing about all nonassertive conduct that tends to minimize perception or memory problems.

Is the Admission of Nonassertive Conduct Good Policy?   Remember that the principal impact of the rule excluding hearsay is to require the presentation of witnesses, subject to oath, demeanor, and cross-examination. If the woman's pointing is assertive conduct, the proponent *must produce that woman as a witness* (unless her conduct falls within a hearsay exception or exemption). If her conduct is nonassertive, she *need not be called as a witness.* However, cross-examination of the woman might uncover some risk of her insincerity. And, it might provide specific information about her belief that would obviously reduce the ambiguity risk. Furthermore, it is generally thought that cross-examination is most effective in exposing perception and memory problems, neither of which is minimized by the fact that out-of-court conduct is nonassertive. These factors might call for defining nonassertive conduct as hearsay, which would require the proponent to bring the actor to court to testify and to be cross-examined. There is a middle ground between defining all nonassertive conduct as hearsay, thus excluding it wholesale, and FRE 801(a)'s position of allowing it to be admitted wholesale. It would be possible to define hearsay as including all conduct relevant to prove belief; then to create a hearsay exception for nonassertive conduct; and to condition the applicability of that exception on the unavailability of the actor. Alternatively, the exception for nonassertive conduct could depend on a case-by-case showing of the kind of motivation or reliance by the actor that minimizes perception and memory dangers. Do you think such alternatives would be preferable to the Federal Rules' approach? Consider a rule that allows jurors to draw adverse inferences against a party who fails to call an available and potentially important witness. United States v. Pierce, 785 F.3d 832, 843-844 (2d Cir. 2015) (confirming appropriateness of "adverse inference against a party that fails to call a witness whose production . . . is peculiarly within [that party's] power." (citing United States v. Gaskin, 364 F.3d 438, 463 (2d Cir. 2004)). Does this rule change anything in your analysis?

d. Disguised Assertions

Sometimes evidence that appears to be nonassertive conduct is in fact relevant only because of underlying assertive behavior of particular persons. The easiest example is when a judgment of conviction for a crime is used to prove that the defendant did do the illegal act. The conviction is relevant because it is evidence that 12 jurors voted, or one judge decided, that the defendant did do the act. Such conduct clearly is *intended to assert the belief in guilt*. Because the jury's vote may not appear on the face of the judgment of conviction itself, it is what we call a *disguised* assertion. Convictions are uniformly classified as hearsay (and are generally admissible pursuant to FRE 803(22)). Once again, locating the hidden declarant (the jury) who is making a disguised assertion (the verdict of guilt) depends on your identification of the inference of belief that is necessary for the relevance of the offered item of evidence.

Now consider evidence that Greta was arrested (not convicted) for robbery. Is the arrest hearsay, if used to prove that Greta actually committed the illegal act? The answer depends on whether the arrest is assertive or nonassertive conduct of the hidden declarants, the officers who arrested Greta. There are several ways to analyze this problem. The officers may have been making the arrest because they observed Greta in the act and thus they believed that she did commit the robbery. If so, we think it is appropriate to regard their conduct in arresting her as their intended assertion of that belief. Alternatively, the officers may have been executing a warrant or acting in response to a victim's accusation. They have no firsthand knowledge of Greta's behavior and may not be intending to assert their own belief about her criminal activity. But the officers are making the arrest only because another hidden declarant—the individual who made an accusation or the officer who signed the affidavit for the warrant—did make an intended assertion of belief that Greta robbed the bank. The apparently nonassertive arrest is occurring only because of, and is relevant only because of, this disguised assertion of belief in Greta's guilt, the fact that the evidence is being offered to prove. The evidence, therefore, should be regarded as hearsay.

Consider also testimony that John's driver's license was revoked, which is offered to prove that John engaged in unsafe driving. It may well be that the hidden declarant, the person who generated the paperwork that officially revoked John's license, was acting in a bureaucratic manner and was not intending to assert anything about how John drove. Nonetheless, the revocation is occurring only because somebody—presumably the judge who found John guilty of a traffic offense—asserted that John had engaged in some illegal driving activity.

Our characterization of the arrest and revocation evidence as assertive is either a minority position or a refinement that most discussions of nonassertive activity do not bother to make. McCormick classifies the revocation evidence as nonassertive. See Charles T. McCormick, The Borderland of Hearsay, 39 Yale L.J. 489, 491 (1930). See also Ted Finman, Implied Assertions as Hearsay: Some Criticisms of the Uniform Rules of Evidence, 14 Stan. L. Rev. 682, 683 n.4 (1962) (citing conduct that leads to the institutionalization of a patient as nonassertive). Morgan, on the other hand, characterizes the institutionalization evidence and the revocation evidence as assertive. Edmund M. Morgan, Hearsay Dangers and the Application of the Hearsay Concept, 62 Harv. L. Rev. 177, 190 (1948). What do you think?

KEY POINTS

1. Evidence of nonverbal conduct is sometimes offered to prove the accuracy of the beliefs of the actor about events. If the actor is intending to communicate that belief through conduct, then the evidence is defined as hearsay. The actor's testimonial qualities of sincerity, perception, and memory are involved in the relevancy of the conduct.

2. If the actor is not intending to communicate belief, then the evidence is defined as not hearsay and is admitted to prove the truth of that belief, even though the actor's testimonial qualities of perception and memory are still involved.

3. The question of the actor's intent is a preliminary question of fact for the judge to decide pursuant to FRE 104(a). The burden to persuade the judge on the question of intent is on the opponent who is objecting to the admission of the actor's conduct as hearsay.

PROBLEMS

8.17. Ed Stephens is being prosecuted for bank robbery. Eyewitnesses claim that the robber wore a loud Hawaiian shirt. The prosecution offers the following testimony of Officer Emily James:

> The day after the robbery, I was following leads on various possible suspects. I went to the Stephens's home, and found only Mrs. Stephens there. I asked her if she would give me the shirt that her husband wore the previous day. She handed me a Hawaiian shirt, which is marked as Exhibit A. I also watched her as she entered the bedroom and I saw her conceal a leather bag under the bed. After she gave me the shirt, I conducted a search for the leather bag and found that it was full of money, which is marked as Exhibit B.

Defense counsel has objected to this entire testimony, and to Exhibits A and B on grounds of hearsay. What result?

8.18. Ralph Benson and Jerry Jackson owned a small yacht that they kept docked on Leech Lake, Minnesota. On the morning of June 15, Ralph, his wife, and two children set off across the lake in the yacht. A storm suddenly arose on the lake, and nobody has seen the Benson family or the yacht since that morning. Jackson sued the company that insured the yacht against damage or loss due to bad weather. The insurance company relies on a clause in the policy that permits recovery only if the yacht was navigable at the time of the loss. To prove that the yacht was navigable, Jerry Jackson offers to testify, "On the morning of June 15, I observed Ralph Benson carefully look around the yacht, place his wife and children on board, and set off across the lake." Counsel for the insurance company objects to this testimony on the ground that it is hearsay.

8.19. Return to Problem 8.13 at page 461, supra, Sondra Evers's case against Jones's Deli.

    (a) Plaintiff Evers offers a videotape prepared at the request of her attorney showing her activities at her home, as relevant to prove the serious effect of the fall on her physical condition.

    (b) For the defendant, Karen Larson would testify: I am the manager of Jones's Deli and I was at the store from 8:00 A.M. until 5:30 P.M. on the day Ms. Evers fell. On that day I received no complaints about any spilled ketchup on the floor. Is this testimony relevant? What additional facts might the proponent need to present? Should the testimony be excluded on grounds of hearsay?

8.20. Ben Jacobsen, a 50-year-old former railroad firefighter, is charged with homicide for fatally shooting a man who had been sleeping in a box car in an infrequently used area of the switching yard. The crime occurred at approximately 11:00 A.M. on Tuesday, July 23. Jacobsen claims that he is not guilty and suggests that two teenage boys committed the crime. He calls to the stand Harry Winters, a railroad employee, who offers to testify as follows: "Shortly after 11:00 A.M. on Tuesday, July 23, I observed two teenage boys near the box car. They were running away from it." Is this evidence hearsay?

8.21. Plaintiff is suing a police officer for false arrest. The officer arrested Plaintiff for driving while under the influence of intoxicating liquor. At trial, Plaintiff submits properly authenticated proof that she had been acquitted by a jury of the charge in question. Hearsay?

8.22. Return to Problem 8.10 at page 461, supra. What if Agent Guerrero had not testified as to the specific contents of the confidential informant's statement but did testify that "in the course of my investigation leading to defendant Jamal's arrest, I had contact with a confidential informant." Hearsay?

8.23. To prove that Darcey had been using drugs, testimony of one of Darcey's friends is offered: "Last December 31, I visited Darcey at the State Drug Rehabilitation Center, where he is a patient." Hearsay?

8.24. In the prosecution of Donna Draper for conspiracy to import heroin, an illegal substance, the prosecution offered the testimony of Sergeant Edward Conley concerning a nine-year-old German shepherd named Bosco. Sergeant Conley testified that Bosco was trained to detect narcotics by smell. Sergeant Conley further testified that he took Bosco to a room in a bank in which a bag containing $9,000 was located, and, when he instructed Bosco to search for drugs, the dog "showed a strong, positive aggressive alert, shaking the bag, ripping it apart, grabbing the money in his mouth, and ripping the money." Other evidence establishes that the currency to which Bosco reacted had been brought to the bank by Draper in order to purchase cashier's checks. Should this evidence be excluded on the ground that it is hearsay? On any other ground?

8.25. Return to Problem 4.19 at page 253. Is Ensign Chandler's testimony about the display on the GPS screen hearsay?

8.26. In the prosecution of Clive Bailey for conspiracy to possess marijuana with the intent to distribute, the prosecution offered the testimony of the arresting officer. The officer testified that a Ms. Washington had been caught collecting a shipment of a barrel of marijuana. Washington agreed to cooperate with the government by having agents accompany her to deliver the barrel to the intended recipient. She then drove her van to her residence, with two task force agents hiding in the back, and placed a phone call, punching in a code. Fifteen minutes later, Clive came up to the van, opened the back of the van, and fled upon seeing the agents, but was apprehended. The agents recovered his pager, which reflected receipt of the call from Ms. Washington's telephone and the code she had entered. Is any of this testimony hearsay?

7. Utterances Relevant for the Truth of the Declarant's Unstated Beliefs

Verbal conduct, that is, oral or written words of a declarant, often expresses the belief of a declarant explicitly. But sometimes, the beliefs of the declarant that generate verbal conduct are not stated explicitly but can be inferred from the words that are spoken or written. Is verbal conduct hearsay when offered to prove the truth of the unstated (inferred) beliefs? To answer this question we must first address the relevancy of such utterances.

a. The Relevancy of Unstated Beliefs

Here are some examples of utterances that can be relevant only if they are offered to prove beliefs that the declarant holds but does not state explicitly (see also supra, page 463-467). In our hypothetical case brought by the pedestrian against the driver of the gray SUV, suppose that Sally says to George "That SUV driver must be drunk" just after the pedestrian is struck. And suppose that the pedestrian is *not* trying to prove that the driver was drunk. The relevance of Sally's statement would depend on the inference that Sally has an unstated belief that the driver of the gray SUV was driving in a careless or wrongful manner when his car hit the pedestrian. The pedestrian would offer Sally's statement to prove that this *unstated belief is true.* The fact of consequence is that the driver was driving carelessly or wrongfully. Under this theory, the relevance of the statement depends on all of Sally's testimonial qualities, thus requiring a complete trip around the testimonial triangle, as Diagram 8-8 illustrates:

Diagram 8-8

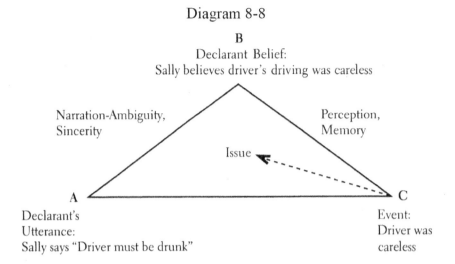

B
Declarant Belief:
Sally believes driver's driving was careless

Narration-Ambiguity,
Sincerity

Perception,
Memory

Issue

A

C

Declarant's
Utterance:
Sally says "Driver must be drunk"

Event:
Driver was
careless

Further inferences to reach the issue in the pedestrian's case will involve deciding what kind of wrongful driving Sally perceived. Other facts about the incident will show that Sally was probably referring to the driver's failure to stop at the red light.

In the hypothetical about Jim Harris's prosecution for battery, suppose that the woman said to Jim "get out of here quick" just after the police officer asked who had thrown the first punch. Or, a man said, "Jim Harris ought to confess." These statements might be relevant to the prosecution's case, but not to prove that Jim ought to get out or confess. The relevance of the statements would depend on an inference that the woman and the man held the belief that Jim had thrown the first punch. Again, this belief is unstated, but the prosecution would be offering the two statements to prove that this unstated belief is true. And again, this theory of relevance requires reliance on all of the testimonial qualities of the woman and man.

It may occur to you to ask why the pedestrian would want to use Sally's out-of-court statement when questioning Sally at trial would reveal with more certainty what she believed about the accident. The same is true for the woman and man in the bar. Why not call them as witnesses and ask them whether they saw Jim throw the first punch? The answer is that sometimes declarants cannot be called as witnesses—they are unavailable, unwilling, or forgetful. Their out-of-court statements are the best source of their knowledge and beliefs, even if those beliefs are unstated.

One final example will help to make this point. In State v. Dullard, 668 N.W.2d 585 (Iowa 2003), Brent Dullard was convicted of possession of the precursor materials with intent to manufacture methamphetamine, a controlled substance. On a tip, police had conducted a legal search of the house and garage that Dullard shared with his mother. In the garage, police found materials that are potential precursors of methamphetamine (ephedrine and ether) plus items commonly used in the manufacture of methamphetamine. Under Iowa law, Dullard and his mother had joint possession of the garage where all of the substances were found. Thus, the prosecution had to prove Dullard's "actual knowledge or circumstances from which a jury could infer knowledge" in order to establish his possession of the precursors. This led the prosecution to offer into evidence a small spiral notebook found in a wooden desk in the garage that contained a handwritten note from an unknown person. The note read:

> B-
> I had to go inside and pee + calm my nerves somewhat down. When I came out to go get Brian I looked over to the street North of here + there sat a black + white w/ the dude out of his car facing our own direction—no one else was with him.

The prosecution contended that the note was intended for Dullard ("B") and that it was relevant to show the writer's belief that Dullard needed to be told about the policeman because he was involved in, and had actual knowledge of, the drug activity in the garage. This relevant belief was unstated; and, the unknown writer was not available as a witness.

You can see that, just as with the hypothetical statements of Sally and about Jim Harris discussed above, inferences about all of the unknown writer's testimonial qualities are necessary to the relevancy of the note. Perhaps the author knew that Brent Dullard was ignorant of the contents of his garage and wanted to misrepresent his involvement (a sincerity risk); perhaps the author mistakenly wrote "B" and intended the note for "E" (a narration risk); perhaps the author had misperceived or forgotten about Brent's actual conduct and was mistaken about Brent's involvement (perception and memory risks). Even if all of these risks, or some of them, seem small to you, their existence implicates hearsay policy. If you were the attorney for Dullard, you would certainly want the opportunity to cross-examine the author of the note.

b. Application of FRE 801(a) and (c)

Courts and commentators have struggled for two centuries with the problem of how the rule against hearsay should classify the kinds of utterances that we have been discussing. The Iowa Supreme Court posed the question of whether this implied, unstated belief—which it also called an "implied assertion" using the terminology of the common law—is a hearsay statement under the definition contained in the Iowa rule of evidence identical to FRE 801(a) and (c).

The Literal Approach. FRE 801(a) defines a "statement" as "a person's oral assertion, [or] written assertion." FRE 801(c) defines hearsay as a "statement [of a declarant] that a party offers in evidence to prove the truth of the matter asserted in the statement." Taking these terms literally, the declarant's written assertions in the note in *Dullard* were not offered to prove the truth of the matters or propositions that they assert. Instead, the Court wrote, "the handwritten note is offered solely to show the declarant's belief, implied from the words and the message conveyed" that Dullard, the alleged recipient, had knowledge and thus possession of the drug lab materials. 668 N.W.2d at 591.

Under a literal approach to FRE 801(a) and (c), since that relevant belief was not stated as an assertion in the note, the note could not be a statement that was offered to prove the truth of the matter it asserted. The same result would be reached if these definitions were applied to Sally's statement that the "driver must be drunk" and to the statements that Jim Harris should "get out quick" or "ought to confess" in the hypotheticals we have just discussed. These utterances would not be hearsay because they are not offered to prove the truth of the matters they explicitly and literally assert.

The Common Law Approach.   At common law, courts used the phrase *implied assertions* to identify those utterances that were relevant not for the stated beliefs but for the implied unstated beliefs of the declarant. The Iowa Supreme Court in *Dullard* treated the note as containing an "implied assertion" of the author's belief that Dullard had knowledge and possession of the drug lab materials. The court described the common law approach:

> The starting point for the common law approach to implied assertions inevitably begins with the celebrated and durable case of Wright v. Tatham, 112 Eng. Rep. 488 (Ex. Ch. 1837). The case involved an action to set aside a will based on the incompetency of the testator . . . . At trial, the proponents of the will offered several letters written to the testator by various individuals concerning a variety of business and social subjects . . . . The purpose of the letters was to show the absent declarants must have believed the testator was able to engage in intelligent discourse on the various topics discussed in the letters . . . . This belief, therefore, constituted evidence of the testator's competency. [668 N.W. 2d at 591.]

The opinion in *Wright* became the general rule at common law. The court analogized the written letters to nonverbal conduct, the relevance of which depends on the belief of the actor. It held that "assertions that are relevant only as implying a statement or opinion of the absent declarant on the matter at issue constitute hearsay in the same way the actual statement or opinion of the absent declarant would be inadmissible hearsay."

If the goal of a definition of hearsay is to identify those out-of-court utterances that require evaluation of *all* of the declarant's testimonial qualities—where the trip around the complete testimonial triangle is required—then the holding in *Wright* makes sense. All of the examples of utterances relevant to prove unstated beliefs that we have discussed so far (which the common law would call implied assertions) require inferences about *all* of the declarants' testimonial qualities. Under hearsay policy, this justifies requiring oath, demeanor, and cross-examination. Professor Roger Park labeled this common law risk analysis a "declarant-oriented" test for hearsay; a test that "focuses on whether the use of the utterance will require reliance on the credibility of the out-of-court declarant." Roger C. Park, McCormick on Evidence and the Concept of Hearsay: A Critical Analysis Followed by Suggestions to Law Teachers, 65 Minn. L. Rev. 423, 424 (1981).

FRE 801(a)-(c) Rejects the Common Law Approach.   The Advisory Committee Note to FRE 801(a) states that certain utterances are removed from the definition of hearsay, even though their relevance depends on the testimonial qualities of the declarant. This rejection of the "declarant-oriented" common law approach is briefly stated and sparingly justified as follows:

> [S]ituations giving rise to [nonassertive] . . . conduct are such as virtually to eliminate
> questions of sincerity. Similar considerations govern nonassertive verbal conduct and
> verbal conduct which is assertive but offered as a basis for inferring something other
> than the matter asserted, also excluded from the definition of hearsay by the language
> of subdivision (c).

The Note relies on an analogy between nonassertive *conduct*, defined as not hearsay
by FRE 801(a), and two kinds of *verbal utterances*. The first sentence states that evidence of an actor's nonassertive conduct involves no sincerity danger. Why? Because
the actor has no intent to use his conduct to communicate his belief. Think back
to the earlier examples of nonassertive conduct admitted as not hearsay under FRE
801(a). Without the intent to communicate, there is no opportunity for the actor to
lie, that is, to decide to communicate false information through conduct. In the next
sentence, the Note implies that the risk of insincerity is also nonexistent for *all* "nonassertive verbal conduct and verbal conduct which is assertive but offered as a basis for
inferring something other than the matter asserted" and that therefore such utterances
should also be defined as not hearsay.

  "Nonassertive verbal conduct" may refer to hortatory declarations, instructions,
and commands. The exclamation "Jim, get out quick" would be an example of this
type of utterance. Assertive verbal conduct "offered as the basis for inferring something other than the matter asserted" may refer to assertions like the note in *Dullard*—
utterances relevant for unstated beliefs that still bear hearsay dangers. The Note does
not explain or give examples of either kind of statement, however, so its meaning
is somewhat ambiguous. Furthermore, "nonassertive verbal conduct" is an oxymo-
ron, for virtually all conscious utterances are efforts to assert something. Nonetheless,
when utterances are offered as relevant to prove the declarant's unstated beliefs, the
Advisory Committee appears to reject the common law approach to the definition of
hearsay.

8. Elaboration of FRE 801: Courts Reject the Literal Approach and Apply an "Intent" Test

Many federal courts faced with a choice between the literal approach of FRE
801(c) and the common law approach to statements relevant for unstated beliefs
have rejected both. Instead, they have sought to identify those statements that bear
the highest risk of insincerity and to exclude only those statements as hearsay. This
approach rests on the understanding that words may be spoken or written with the
intent to communicate something different from, or in addition to, what the words
themselves formally articulate. People use language in many different ways to communicate. If the man stating "Jim Harris ought to confess" is intending to communicate his unstated belief that Jim threw the first punch by using this form of speech,
it follows that he could choose to "lie" by communicating false information about
Jim. When a speaker intends to communicate an unstated belief, there is enhanced
danger of insincerity.

a. The Judicially Created Intent Test

The test used by courts to identify those statements with the greatest sincerity danger has been articulated in different ways. Some courts have read "matter asserted" broadly enough to include matters that are *intentionally implied*, as well as explicitly stated—hence the label "implied assertions" for this type of hearsay. In Park v. Huff, 493 F.2d 923, 927 (5th Cir.), *rev'd on other grounds*, 506 F.2d 849 (5th Cir. 1974) (en banc), the court said that a declarant's statements implying that the defendant was financing a murder conspiracy are hearsay when there is a "possibility that the declarant intended to leave a particular impression." The court in United States v. Zenni, 492 F. Supp. 464, 468-469 and n.21 (E.D. Ky. 1980) acknowledged that FRE 801(a) "does not seem to require a preliminary determination by the trial court whether verbal conduct is intended as an assertion" but the court held that such a determination of intent would be required to include some "implied assertions" within the definition. *Zenni* involved callers placing bets with the defendant, which led to criminal charges alleging that the defendant carried out unlawful bookmaking. The callers only wanted to place their bets: Neither of them intended to communicate that Zenni was a bookmaker. For that reason, the court categorized those calls as nonhearsay. Compare this decision with the English case, R. v. Kearley, 2 App. Cas. 228 (H.L. 1992), decided under the old authority of Wright v. Tatham. *Kearley* held that statements made by individuals who called the defendant's residence to ask for drugs were hearsay. Which of the two decisions best fits FRE 801(a)-(c): *Zenni* or *Kearley*? Which of them stands on firmer policy grounds than the other?

The intent test has been largely a judicial creation. Prior to the restyling of the Federal Rules, FRE 801(a)(1), defined verbal assertions as "statements" and did not contain an intent test, in contrast to the definition of nonverbal conduct as "statements" in FRE 801(a)(2), which did.[3] In creating this test, courts relied on the somewhat backhanded language of the Advisory Committee Note to FRE 801(a) that does emphasize that an intent to assert is critical to identifying hearsay: "The key to the definition is that nothing is an assertion unless intended to be one." Conversely, it would seem that if there is intent to assert, there is hearsay. Many evidence commentators agree:

> A number of scholars have advocated using the declarant's intent, or some objective manifestation of it, in determining what the declarant's statement asserts. Some version of an intent test seems necessary to keep the assertion definition [the literal truth-of-the-matter-asserted test] from being wholly arbitrary. [Roger C. Park, "I Didn't Tell Them Anything About You": Implied Assertions as Hearsay Under the Federal Rules of Evidence, 74 Minn. L. Rev. 783, 800 (1990).]

---

3. But see the text of the restyled FRE 801(a): "Statement" means a person's oral assertion, written assertion, or nonverbal conduct, if the person intended it as an assertion. Could it be argued that the "it" in the final clause refers to oral and written assertions, as well as conduct, and thus the Rule itself applies the intent test to verbal statements of unstated belief as well? Probably not, as this would be a substantive change in the Rule.

b. The Difficulties of Applying an Intent Test

An intent test might be stated as follows: *When an out-of-court utterance is relevant to prove the truth of a belief that is different from or more than the truth of the declarant's literal utterance, the evidence is hearsay if the declarant is intending to communicate the truth of the unstated belief that is critical to the relevance of the evidence.*

One problem with such a test is that it is not clear what the meaning of "intent" is. When people speak, they have many beliefs in mind all at the same time. How central to the declarant's consciousness or thinking does a matter have to be for it to qualify as an "intended" communication? Consider Jill's statement to a friend of hers to whom she has been complaining about one of her coworkers, Mary. Jill says: "Well, at least I never stole from the company!" It seems clear from the context of the conversation that Jill has the specific intent to communicate to her friend the specific unstated proposition that Mary *did* steal from her employer. Jill has chosen a somewhat unusual way of expressing that proposition, but this does not diminish any of the hearsay dangers, including the danger of insincerity. Since she is intending to make an implicit communication, Jill has the opportunity to imply deliberately and falsely that Mary steals. The same analysis would seem to apply to the man's statement "Jim Harris ought to confess" in our hypothetical about who started the fight in the bar.

But while Jill's intent, and the man's intent, may be reasonably clear, in many cases it may be quite difficult to determine whether specific intent exists to communicate an unstated proposition. Consider the following:

> During the search of [codefendant] Mayfield's apartment, the telephone rang, and a police officer answered it. An unidentified female voice asked to speak with "Keith." The officer replied that Keith was busy. The caller then asked if Keith "still had any stuff." The officer asked the caller what she meant, and the caller responded "a fifty." The officer said "yeah." [United States v. Long, 905 F.2d 1572, 1579 (D.C. Cir. 1990).]

The defendant, Keith Long, was charged with possession of cocaine with intent to distribute. The caller's questions were clearly based on her belief that Keith was a drug-seller and had sold her drugs in the past. But what was the declarant intending to communicate? It may be that the declarant was simply intending to express her desire for drugs and not trying to assert the proposition "Keith is a drug-seller." Nonetheless, the declarant, at some level of consciousness, is basing her conduct on her knowledge that Keith has sold to her in the past and that her questions will communicate this fact. The declarant's out-of-court utterance was admitted at trial and Long was convicted. On appeal, Long argued that "the questions plainly revealed assumptions that are the functional equivalent of direct assertions . . . . [T]he caller, through her questions, in effect asserted that 'Keith ha[d] crack and s[old] it out of Mayfield's apartment.'" Id. The appellate court disagreed that "intent" was involved:

> With our inquiry focused on the *intent* of the caller, we have little trouble disposing of Long's theory about implied assertions. Long has not provided any evidence to suggest that the caller, through her questions, intended to assert that he was involved in drug dealing. The caller may indeed have conveyed messages about Long through her questions, but any such messages were merely incidental and not intentional. [Id. at 1580.]

Do you agree with the court's conclusion? Is the caller's statement more like Jill's "at least I never stole from the company" or like the statement of the note writer in *Dullard*?

To make an accurate decision about a speaker's intent, the jury will require sufficient factual information. Out-of-court utterances are typically described to the jury by someone who overheard them. Testimony from this witness about the immediate context in which the utterance was made may be the only information available to the jury. If the utterance was written, the document, and the witness authenticating it, may provide even less information pertinent to intent. 3 Stephen A. Saltzburg, Michael M. Martin & Daniel J. Capra, Federal Rules of Evidence Manual 1473 (7th ed. 1998), suggests that factual difficulties in applying an "actual intent" test can be adequately handled by an objective, rather than subjective, test of intent: "The question should be whether a reasonable person making a statement such as the declarant made would have intended to communicate the implied assertion that the proponent is offering for its truth."

Finally, which party should bear the burden of persuading the judge as to whether the declarant has or does not have the requisite intent? The traditional legal device for dealing with uncertainty about factual issues is allocating the burden of proof. By assigning the burden of proving intent, or lack thereof, the risk of erroneous decisions can be assigned to one party instead of the other to further evidentiary policy. Most proposed intent tests do place the burden to prove intent on the opponent of the evidence in accordance with the inclusionary presumption of FRE 402: "As with conduct, the burden should be placed on the non-offering party to show that the declarant had the intent to communicate the implied assertion." 3 Stephen A. Saltzburg, Michael M. Martin, & Daniel J. Capra, Federal Rules of Evidence Manual at 1473.

c. Some Courts Still Adhere to the Common Law Approach

The Iowa Supreme Court in *Dullard* rejected both the literal approach and an intent test, and adopted the common law's "declarant-oriented" approach to the definition of hearsay. The court held that the note written by the unknown declarant was hearsay, even if its author did not intend to assert that Brent Dullard had knowledge of and possession of the substances in his garage.

> The distinction drawn between intended and unintended conduct or speech only implicates the danger of sincerity . . . other 'hearsay dangers remain viable, giving rise to the need for cross-examination. Moreover, even the danger of insincerity may . . . be present . . . where the reliability of the direct assertion . . . is insincere . . . . Implied assertions can be no more reliable than the predicate expressed assertion. [668 N.W.2d at 594-595.]

Two years after *Dullard*, the Maryland Court of Appeals made a thorough analysis of the common law approach and the federal intent test, as well as much of the scholarly literature. It broadened the meaning of "matter asserted" and held that

> where the probative value of words, as offered, depends on the declarant *having communicated a factual proposition*, the words constitute an "assertion" of that proposition. The declarant's intent . . . is irrelevant. If the words are . . . offered in court to prove

the truth of the [communicated] proposition—*i.e.* of the "matter asserted"—they are hearsay under our rules. [Stoddard v. State, 887 A.2d 564, 577 (Md. 2005) (emphasis added).]

Some federal circuit courts also seem to have applied the common law approach by excluding statements that are relevant only for the declarant's unstated belief without making any finding that the declarant intended to assert that belief. See Weinstein and Berger, Weinstein's Federal Evidence §801.10[2][c], at 801-10 to 801-12 nn.13, 15 (McLaughlin ed., 2d ed. 2003); Callen, Hearsay and Informal Reasoning, 47 Vand. L. Rev. 43, 47-48 n.18 (1994). Nevertheless, it is fair to say that the prevailing judicial practice is to admit as not hearsay statements relevant for unstated beliefs when the declarant did not intend to assert those beliefs, and to apply an intent test to exclude those statements that appear to bear significant sincerity danger due to opportunity to fabricate.

KEY POINTS

1. The Advisory Committee Note to FRE 801 construes FRE 801(a) and (c) as excluding oral and written utterances that are offered to prove a declarant's unstated beliefs from the definition of hearsay. Such utterances are not offered to prove the truth of the literal matters they assert.
2. The relevancy of these utterances still depends on the declarants' testimonial qualities. However, when the declarant is not intending to communicate the unstated belief, the sincerity danger may be minimal, and the utterance is analogous to nonassertive conduct.
3. In the majority of jurisdictions, if a court finds that the declarant specifically intends to communicate an unstated belief, it will usually exclude the utterance as hearsay.
4. Intent to communicate may be difficult to prove either because of factual uncertainty or because of ambiguity in the meaning of intent.

NOTES AND QUESTIONS

1. Ever since Wright v. Tatham, there has been a continued practical and academic debate about whether these utterances—also called "implied assertions"—should be classified as hearsay or as not hearsay, and about the most effective doctrinal test for accomplishing this. An informative contribution to this debate is the Symposium on Hearsay and Implied Assertions: How Would (or Should) the Supreme Court Decide the *Kearley* Case?, 16 Miss. C. L. Rev. 1 (1995). Other articles include Michael S. Pardo, Testimony, 82 Tul. L. Rev. 119 (2007); Michael H. Graham, Handbook of Federal Evidence Section 801.7, at 73-77 (5th ed. 2001); Craig R. Callen, Hearsay and Informal Reasoning, 47 Vand. L. Rev. 43 (1994); Paul S. Milich, Re-examining Hearsay Under the Federal Rules: Some Method for the Madness, 39 Kan. L.

Rev. 893 (1991); Roger C. Park, I Didn't Tell Them Anything About You: Implied Assertions as Hearsay Under the Federal Rules of Evidence, 74 Minn. L. Rev. 783 (1990). As noted earlier, in 1992, the English House of Lords reaffirmed the common law approach to implied assertions set forth in Wright v. Tatham. Regina v. Kearley, 2 App. Cas. 228 (1992). However, some ten years later, section 115 of the Criminal Justice Act of 2003 rejected this approach. The key text is that the definition of hearsay includes only those statements where "the purpose of, or one of the purposes, of the person making the statement appears to the court to have been (a) to cause another person to believe the matter, or (b) to cause another person to act . . . on the basis that the matter is as stated." Would the note in *Dullard* be hearsay under this test?

PROBLEMS

8.27. Return to Problem 8.13 at page 461, supra. To prove that there was ketchup on the floor where she fell, Sondra Evers presents Joel as a witness who will testify that shortly before Sondra's fall he heard another customer say, "Watch out for that ketchup!" Joel was standing in an aisle and did not see what the customer was looking at. Is it hearsay?

8.28. Return to Problem 3.4, State v. Blair, at page 150 supra. In Norma's private diary, on a page dated the day before the attack on her, Norma has written:

> Jimmy has really hurt me this time. He is getting more violent when I tell him I want to leave. I don't want anyone to read this and I am going to burn this diary when I leave for L.A.

Hearsay?

8.29. Victim was alone with Fred and Stanley when he was shot. To prove Fred shot the victim, the prosecution offers the following:
   (a) The victim's statement immediately thereafter: "Help me, Stanley, I've got a bullet in me."
   (b) The victim's statement at the hospital: "Whatever you do, don't let Fred in here. He wants to hurt me."

8.30. Fred and John have just been arrested by the police for a robbery. Fred says to John: "Don't worry, I didn't tell them anything about you." Hearsay if offered to prove John participated in the robbery?

8.31. Roger was arrested in the parking lot of a shopping center after selling two golf ball-sized packages of heroin to an undercover police agent. Roger told police that Frank was acting as his look-out during the transaction and was circling the parking lot in a blue van. The police questioned Frank, who insisted he knew nothing about a drug deal and denied that he had been circling the parking lot. Frank is now on trial for conspiracy to distribute heroin. Evidence is presented that while the police were talking to Frank, his cell phone rang repeatedly. An officer answered the cell phone ten times and each time the caller "was someone requesting heroin." There is no evidence as to what the anonymous callers actually said to the officer. The court held that the calls were not hearsay:

> Even if the calls included assertions, the government offers them, not for their truth, but for the fact they were made. The fact that Frank received ten successive solicitations for heroin is probative circumstantial evidence of his involvement in a conspiracy to distribute heroin. The defense argues that the calls contain implicit factual assertions about the callers' belief that the defendant could supply the desired heroin. But the government did not offer the calls to prove the truth of these implicit assertions. Even if the callers had no real desire for the drug, and no faith that Frank could deliver it, the fact that he received ten of these calls is still evidence of his participation in a heroin distribution conspiracy.

What do you think of the court's reasoning? Why would anyone make such a call if he had no desire for the drug or belief that Frank could supply it? Could the reasoning be the same if Frank had received only one call? What result if the court had applied the "intent" test?

9. Reflection on the Definition of Hearsay: Should FRE 801 Be Revised?

The goal of a definition of hearsay is at least twofold. It should advance hearsay policy by identifying evidence that should be subject to the hearsay prohibition of FRE 802. It should also provide rules that are as clear and as simple as possible for judges to apply quickly in the charged atmosphere of an ongoing trial. Thus, it may be undesirable to burden the definition of hearsay with an intent test, both in terms of time and factfinding competence. If so, must intent be ignored and the identification of hearsay remain focused solely on the literal content of the words uttered to see whether the evidence was offered to prove the truth of those words?

An alternative is, of course, the "declarant-oriented" approach to defining hearsay adopted in *Dullard*. This approach would define all of these problematic utterances as hearsay without the necessity of any "intent" test at all. The result would be wholesale exclusion of utterances whenever relevance depends on the complete trip around the testimonial triangle.

There are other options for the definition. In Tex. R. Crim. Evid. 801(c) and Tex. R. Civ. Evid. 801(c), Texas has adopted a definition of "matter asserted" that focuses on the use of utterances to prove the beliefs of the declarant. "Matter asserted" includes "any matter explicitly asserted, and any matter implied by a statement, if the probative value of the statement as offered flows from declarant's belief in the matter." Professor Michael Graham proposes a similar definition that focuses on the presence of a necessary inference of sincerity:

> "Hearsay" is a statement offered in evidence, other than one made by the declarant while testifying at the trial or hearing, to the extent relevance depends upon (1) the truth of the matter asserted or (2) the declarant's belief in the truth or falsity of the

matter asserted. [Michael Graham, Stickperson Hearsay: A Simplified Approach to Understanding the Rule Against Hearsay, 1982 U. Ill. L. Rev. 887, 921 (1982).]

In practice, judges probably apply the truth-of-the-matter-asserted language of FRE 801(c) in a literalistic fashion, until they are confronted with an out-of-court utterance where the declarant's specific intent to communicate an unstated belief is clear. Then they craft some kind of intent test to exclude it. Is such muddling through acceptable? Professor Roger Park contends that judges are doing fine with the current rule:

> A review of the published caselaw does not reveal any obvious signs of injustice . . . . The cases generally involve utterances classed as [not hearsay] that raise no real insincerity dangers affecting the purpose for which they are being used . . . . [F]ederal courts are reaching fair results in resolving implied assertion problems under the existing assertion definition. [Park, 74 Minn. L. Rev. at 836-838.]

It would be possible to abandon the categorical thinking that underlies the truth-of-the-matter asserted test, the intent test, and the declarant-oriented test. The definition could focus on the more functional question whether the utterance is one that, from its content or context, appears to raise few sincerity risks. Professor Paul Milich suggests a specific test that would require judicial appraisal of the risk of insincerity:

> If it appears from the circumstances and the language used that the declarant probably would not have used that particular locution to lie about the fact in question, then the reduced risk of insincerity frees the evidence from the definition of assertion and the federal definition of hearsay. [Paul S. Milich, Re-examining Hearsay Under the Federal Rules: Some Method for the Madness, 39 Kan. L. Rev. 893, 909 (1991).]

A shift in the definition toward an explicit appraisal of sincerity risk on a case-by-case basis affords the trial judge more discretion in applying the basic hearsay rule of exclusion. Lack of sincerity danger would be a stand-in for greater probative value, and out-of-court utterances would escape the definition because trial judges evaluate them as more probative. If appellate courts defer to this evaluation, then there could be less appellate review than is currently afforded under any of the more categorical "truth of the matter asserted," "intent" and "declarant-oriented" definitions. See also Alex Stein, Foundations of Evidence Law 193-196 (2005) (arguing that the statement-oriented definition of hearsay is too narrow, while the declarant-oriented definition is overinclusive, and suggesting adoption of a broad standard authorizing courts to admit any hearsay statement, express or implied, when the witness testifying about that statement provides factfinders with testable information about the statement's credibility and background conditions).

We have discussed here only a fraction of the academic ink that has been spilled on the question of the definition of hearsay. As we stated at the beginning of this chapter, a brief doctrinal definition can only imperfectly capture all of the reasons for the hearsay prohibition. Any test of hearsay that focuses solely on identifying sincerity danger reflects a choice to ignore perception and memory dangers. This reflects a compromise with other values at stake in our system of trial, including the efficiency of trials, confidence in jury factfinding, the role of the trial judge and the nature of appellate review. Different definitions reflect a difference in thinking about where the compromise should be drawn. After you have studied the exemptions and exceptions to the general rule of exclusion, we will again examine some of the current and diverse thinking on the meaning, function, and future of the entire hearsay rule.

B. A GENERAL APPROACH TO THE ADMISSION OF HEARSAY UNDER THE EXEMPTIONS AND EXCEPTIONS

Many out-of-court statements, although they are hearsay, are admitted into evidence to prove the truth of the matters they assert. FRE 801(d) *exempts* eight types of out-of-court statements from the definition of hearsay, and FRE 803, 804, and 807 create 29 explicit *exceptions* to FRE 802's rule of exclusion. In terms of the process by which judges admit these various statements, there is no difference between an FRE 801(d) hearsay exemption and an FRE 803, FRE 804, or FRE 807 hearsay exception. Exemptions and exceptions are the same. As we explain below, the United States Supreme Court also treats them as indistinguishable for purposes of the Sixth Amendment Confrontation doctrine. We discuss exemptions and exceptions separately in the sections of this chapter only as a matter of organizational convenience.

1. Justification for the Exemptions and Exceptions

There are differences, however, in the justifications for admitting all these different types of hearsay statements. The drafters of the Federal Rules created the new status of *exemption* under FRE 801(d) to admit hearsay statements whose principal rationale for admission is the possibility for cross-examining the declarant. Most hearsay *exceptions* admitted under FRE 803, 804, and 807 are justified by the presence of circumstances that tend to minimize one or more of the hearsay dangers, making these statements perhaps more "trustworthy"—and certainly more amenable to in-court adversarial scrutiny—than other hearsay. Thus, there would be, in theory, less reason for concern about the absence of cross-examination.

We analyze these justifications in more detail in each of the following sections in this chapter, and you should ask yourself how persuasive you think they are. After you have spent considerable time and effort on identifying hearsay and on understanding how and why hearsay policy operates to exclude it, it may come as something of a shock to see how freely a lot of hearsay is admitted through the exemptions and exceptions.

2. The Categorical Approach

FRE 801(d), FRE 803, and FRE 804 all apply a categorical approach to the admission of hearsay. FRE 807 applies a noncategorical "trustworthiness" approach, which will be discussed separately in Section F. By "categorical approach" we mean that the rules establish specific categories of out-of-court statements that can be admitted for their truth. These categories are sometimes defined by who the declarant is, sometimes by the content of the statement, and sometimes by the circumstances in which the statement was made. You should read through these rules now to get a general sense of what these categories are like.

3. The Process of Admission

The process of admission under FRE 801(d), FRE 803, and FRE 804 goes something like this: A proponent typically offers to prove a declarant's out-of-court statement through the testimony of a witness who overheard it or through an exhibit that contains it, such as a document in which the statement is written or a tape or some other recording of it. The opponent typically objects on grounds of hearsay. In order to rule on this objection, the judge must decide whether the statement is hearsay under FRE 801(a)-(c). If it is, then the burden is on the proponent of the statement to produce foundational evidence—typically evidence of who the declarant is, or what the content of the statement is, or the out-of-court circumstances in which the hearsay statement was made—that satisfies the categorical terms of a specific exemption or exception. The doctrinal terms of the exemption or exception tell you what foundational evidence needs to be produced. The judge then decides whether the proffered statement fits within the specific categorical exemption or exception.

4. The Foundational Requirements

We call this foundational evidence *foundation facts*. See Eleanor Swift, A Foundation Fact Approach to Hearsay, 75 Calif. L. Rev. 1339 (1987). You saw in Chapter Four that the proponent of an exhibit must produce foundation facts that satisfy the standard for authentication and identification set by FRE 901(a). In the same way, under FRE 801(d), FRE 803, and FRE 804, the proponent must produce foundation facts that satisfy the standards set by the categorical subsections of those rules. Typically, this will mean that the proponent must produce a witness who can testify about these foundation facts. We call this witness a *foundation witness*.

Take as one example a witness, Joe, who testifies in court and identifies Sam, the defendant, as the perpetrator of a crime or tort. At a lineup held at a police station just a few days after the crime or accident, Joe made a statement that the perpetrator was Peter, not Sam. Sam, the defendant, would obviously want to offer this prior statement into evidence to prove that he was *not* the perpetrator. Can Joe's prior statement be admitted for the truth of the matter it asserts? Yes, if it fits within a categorical exemption or exception. By reading FRE 801(d)(1)(A), you will see that the foundational requirements for it are as follows:

- the statement was made by a declarant who is now testifying in court as a witness;
- the declarant is subject to cross-examination about the statement;
- the contents of the statement are inconsistent with testimony given at trial;

- the statement was made under penalty of perjury; and
- the statement was made at a trial, hearing, other proceeding, or in a deposition.

Focusing for now just on the fourth requirement, the proponent will have to produce foundational evidence as to whether the statement was made under penalty of perjury. A foundation witness who can present foundation facts that Joe made his statement subject to a formal oath or attestation might be Joe himself; it might be the police officer at the lineup; or, it could be anyone else who observed Joe and who could describe the oath or attestation. After hearing this foundational testimony, the judge will decide whether the categorical requirement has been satisfied. This is a preliminary question that is necessary to the application of an evidence rule. FRE 104 governs such questions, as you know. Applying the policies underlying Rule 104 you should be able to determine whether the judge applies Rule 104(a) or (b). As a general principle, FRE 104(a) applies unless the facts listed above as foundational requirements are necessary to the out-of-court statement's relevancy. Are they? You can see that they are not. Joe's prior statement would be relevant to prove that Sam was *not* the perpetrator whether or not it was under penalty of perjury. This requirement is, instead, a matter of hearsay policy. Thus, the judge would have to be persuaded by a preponderance of the evidence, pursuant to FRE 104(a), that the foundational requirement was satisfied. This is the proponent's burden, and it is the key to the admission of hearsay. We will have more to say about this judicial decisionmaking process as we discuss Rules 801(d), 803, and 804 in greater detail.

5. Multiple Exemptions and Exceptions May Apply

As you study the hearsay exemptions and exceptions, keep in mind that an out-of-court statement may sometimes be admissible pursuant to more than one of them. For example, the deposition testimony given by a party who is now testifying as a witness could be admissible against the party as an admission under FRE 801(d)(2)(A) or as a prior inconsistent statement under oath under FRE 801 (d)(1)(A); a statement may be both a present sense impression under FRE 803(1) and an excited utterance under FRE 803(2); a document may qualify for admission as a public record under FRE 803(8) and as a business record under FRE 803(6). When this is the case, it is sufficient to overcome a hearsay objection to show that the evidence falls within one exemption or exception. Similarly, except in one context that we will consider later, the fact that evidence does *not* quite fit within a particular exemption or exception does not prevent its admission under a different one.

6. FRE 805

It's fairly common for one statement to contain another. Consider a police report of an assault with a deadly weapon quoting a physician who treated the victim: "The victim told me that he was stabbed three times." Alternatively, a friend might tell you: "You'll never believe what Professor X just said," and then summarize what Professor

X said. The police report and your friend's summary of Professor X are both statements that contain statements. If both the outer statement-containing statement and the inner (contained) statement are offered for their truth, this raises a problem of "hearsay within hearsay," sometimes also referred to as "double hearsay" or "multiple hearsay." FRE 805 addresses this issue.

FRE 805: HEARSAY WITHIN HEARSAY

Hearsay within hearsay is not excluded by the rule against hearsay if each part of the combined statements conforms with an exception to the rule.

This means that whenever multiple layers of hearsay are present, each hearsay statement must fall within either an FRE 801(d) exemption or an FRE 803, 804, or 807 exception. Every individual hearsay statement must be identified as admissible by its own exception or exemption.

The burden is on the proponent of multiple hearsay to satisfy the factual requirements of all of the exemptions and exceptions being used. Any combination of exceptions and exemptions is permitted.

Calling these examples "multiple hearsay" presupposes that each level of statement is offered for its truth. That might not always be the case. One or more levels might be offered for a nonhearsay purpose of the type discussed earlier in the chapter. In this sense, it might be more accurate to define the problem as that of "statements within statements." To cross the admissibility barrier, each statement must either fall within a hearsay exception or exemption *or* serve a nonhearsay purpose. Consider Back v. Nestle USA, Inc., 694 F.3d 571, 577-578 (6th Cir. 2012). This age discrimination suit was supported by an affidavit from the plaintiff's coworker. According to that affidavit, the defendant's human resources director repeated a statement by someone in higher management about a plan to terminate the oldest employees. The Sixth Circuit decided that the director's statement was admissible pursuant to FRE 801(d)(2)(D). The higher management's statement, the Court explained, could also be admitted under FRE 801(d)(2)(D) if the plaintiff could prove by independent evidence that the declarant spoke within the scope of his employment. Because the plaintiff offered no such evidence, his coworker's affidavit failed to satisfy FRE 805.

7. The Confrontation Clause

There is one more introductory point to be made. In criminal prosecutions, defendants have a right "to be confronted with the Witnesses against them," which is protected by the Sixth Amendment to the U.S. Constitution. This right has been construed by the Supreme Court to mean that so-called "testimonial" hearsay statements generally may not be used by the prosecution in criminal trials. Crawford v. Washington, 541 U.S. 36 (2004). We will discuss the meaning given to the term *testimonial* and the complexities of applying the testimonial standard in Section G of this chapter. *Crawford* and its progeny affect some, but not all, of the hearsay exceptions, and there are also exceptions to its prohibition, including that the declarant is testifying as a witness at the trial. We raise the confrontation issue now because some inculpatory hearsay statements that you will find to be admissible under a hearsay exemption or exception must still undergo scrutiny under *Crawford* as well. We raise the *Crawford* issue explicitly at a few points in Sections C, D, E, and F.

C. HEARSAY EXEMPTIONS

FRE 801(d) exempts certain types of out-of-court statements from the definition of hearsay. These statements are admissible to prove the truth of the matters they assert, assuming that they are otherwise unobjectionable. FRE 801(d)(1) exempts certain kinds of statements previously made out of court by a testifying witness. FRE 801(d)(2) exempts out-of-court statements made by a party or by persons affiliated with a party, so long as the statements are offered *against* that party. Reading the Advisory Committee Notes to FRE 801(d) will give you some idea of the controversy surrounding the hearsay status of these two broad categories of out-of-court statements.

1. FRE 801(d)(1) and (2)

RULE 801.   DEFINITIONS

(d) *Statements That Are Not Hearsay.* A statement that meets the following conditions is not hearsay:

(1) A *Declarant-Witness's Prior Statement.* The declarant testifies and is subject to cross-examination about a prior statement, and the statement:

(A) is inconsistent with the declarant's testimony and was given under penalty of perjury at a trial, hearing, or other proceeding or in a deposition;

(B) is consistent with the declarant's testimony and is offered to rebut an express or implied charge that the declarant recently fabricated it or acted from a recent improper influence or motive in so testifying; or

(C) identifies a person as someone the declarant perceived earlier.

(2) An *Opposing Party's Statement.* The statement is offered against an opposing party and:

(A) was made by the party in an individual or representative capacity;

(B) is one the party manifested that it adopted or believed to be true;

(C) was made by a person whom the party authorized to make a statement on the subject;

(D) was made by the party's agent or employee on a matter within the scope of that relationship and while it existed; or

(E) was made by the party's co-conspirator during and in furtherance of the conspiracy.

The statement must be considered but does not by itself establish the declarant's authority under (C); the existence or scope of the relationship under (D); or the existence of the conspiracy or participation in it under (E).

2. Explanation of FRE 801(d)(1): The Testifying Declarant Must Be "Subject to Cross-examination About a Prior Statement"

FRE 801(d)(1) admits statements made outside of court by a hearsay declarant who is testifying as a witness at trial. With the declarant-witness in court, subject to cross-examination, you might think that *all* of that witness's out-of-court statements should be admitted as exempt from the hearsay rule of exclusion. This is not the case, however, as the rule admits only three categories of prior statements. There are two basic requirements that apply to all three categories:

- the out-of-court declarant is testifying at trial; and
- the declarant is subject to cross-examination about the prior statement.

Consider the example presented on page 484, supra: Joe is an eyewitness to a crime or accident and he testifies in a criminal or civil case brought against Sam, the alleged wrongdoer. At trial, Joe identifies Sam as the wrongdoer. Suppose that Joe had been brought to a police lineup that included Sam just a few days after the incident. After viewing the lineup Joe identified Peter, not Sam, as the perpetrator. Sam would like to offer evidence of this prior statement in his own defense. Would it be admissible under FRE 801(d)(1)(A), or (B), or (C)?

a. Preliminary Factfinding

The Declarant Is Testifying at Trial.   The first foundational requirement is that the person testifying—Joe—be identified as the same person—Joe—who made the proffered out-of-court statement. United States v. Byrd, 210 Fed. App'x 101 (2d Cir. 2006) (defendant's offer of his probation officer's testimony about statements made by defendant himself was inadmissible because defendant did not testify). The proponent of Joe's hearsay statement can fulfill this requirement through Joe's own acknowledgment that he made the out-of-court statement, or through the testimony of another witness who can say that the witness Joe was the out-of-court speaker.

Examination Concerning the Statement.   Then the judge must determine that Joe is *subject to cross-examination about the prior statement*. The opponent's opportunity to cross-examine the declarant-witness is, as we have said, the principal justification for admitting Rule 801(d)(1) statements. Although the rule speaks in terms of *cross-examination* only, it has been construed to mean redirect examination as well. Thus, either party may introduce a prior statement of a witness, either on direct or cross-examination, and the opposing party must then have the opportunity to examine the witness about the statement. Prior statements can also be admitted after the witness has testified. The declarant-witness must still be available in court or subject to recall by the opposing party to satisfy the requirement of cross-examination *about* the statement, if the witness was not asked about it during the original examination by the opponent.[4]

Remember that the declarant-witness's prior hearsay statement is now being offered for its truth. Thus, the opponent of the statement will want to examine the declarant-witness *about* the hearsay statement in order to expose reasons why it should not be relied on by the jury. If the declarant-witness remembers both making the prior statement and the events that are the subject of the statement, the cross-examiner can elicit information pertinent to evaluating the declarant-witness's testimonial qualities at the time the statement was made. If the declarant-witness denies the truth of the prior statement, or attempts to explain it, the jury will decide what weight to give it. If the witness adopts as true the contents of a prior inconsistent statement, there is then no hearsay problem because the adopted inconsistency corrects and becomes a part of the witness's in-court testimony. United States v. Lopez-Lopez, 282 F.3d 1, 17 (1st Cir. 2000) (witness adopted prior statement that he had observed defendant for "only two or three seconds" as opposed to his trial testimony of "four or five" seconds; "adoption bypasses . . . the entire hearsay problem"). But "adoption" of a prior *consistent* statement does not eliminate the hearsay problem.

Denial of, or Inability to Remember, the Prior Statement. What if the witness denies making or cannot remember making the prior statement? If the prior statement is an authenticated writing or recording, there may be little doubt that it was made. If the prior statement was not recorded, then it will be the subject of testimony from someone who was present at the time—the police officer, for example, who was with Joe at the police lineup when Joe identified Peter and not Sam. At trial, if Joe denies that he made the prior inconsistent identification, he will still be considered to be a witness *subject to cross-examination about the statement.* But how would you cross-examine him? There is likely to be nothing more than a swearing contest between two witnesses, such as Joe and the police officer, about whether the statement was made.

Inability to Remember the Underlying Events. It may also happen that the witness cannot remember the underlying event that is the subject of the statement. If this seems far-fetched to you, consider United States v. Owens, 484 U.S. 554 (1988), in which a battery victim's prior statement identifying defendant Owens as his assailant was admitted under FRE 801(d)(1)(C). At trial, the victim had no memory of seeing the assailant. He could remember the attack and making the prior identification of Owens at the hospital, but he could not recall how he knew it was Owens who attacked him. How would you cross-examine this victim about his perception or memory of the assailant? Should the victim be considered to be a witness *subject to cross-examination about the statement,* in fulfillment of FRE 801(d)(1)?

---

4. Note that this protection of the right of the opponent to examine the witness concerning the prior statement under FRE 801(d) is equivalent to the protection afforded under FRE 613(b) when a witness's prior inconsistent statement is offered only for impeachment, as discussed in Chapter Seven, page 417.

In *Owens*, the Supreme Court rejected both a confrontation clause and a Rule 801(d)(1) challenge to the admission of the prior statement of identification. With respect to the adequacy of cross-examination under FRE 801(d)(1) the Court said:

> Ordinarily a witness is regarded as "subject to cross-examination" when he is placed on the stand, under oath, and responds willingly to questions. Just as with the constitutional prohibition, limitations on the scope of examination by the trial court or assertions of privilege by the witness may undermine the process to such a degree that meaningful cross-examination within the intent of the rule no longer exists. But that effect is not produced by the witness's assertion of memory loss—which . . . is often the very result sought to be produced by cross-examination, and can be effective in destroying the force of the prior statement. Rule 801(d)(1)(C), which specifies that cross-examination need only "concer[n] the statement," does not on its face require more. [Id. at 561-562.]

Owens thus imposes a minimal requirement of what it means to cross-examine a witness "concerning" a prior statement, which was the applicable term prior to the restyling of the rule. There is no reason to think that the new text—"about" the statement—changes its meaning. Under *Owens*, it does not matter that the witness denies making, or cannot remember, either the prior statement or the underlying event, or perhaps even both. United States v. Harty, 476 F. Supp. 2d 17, 25 (D. Mass. 2007) (witness's hearsay identification of defendant's photograph admissible under FRE 801(d)(1)(C) despite the witness's inability to remember the alleged crime, to recognize the photo currently, and to remember why he had picked out defendant's photo originally).

Lower courts following *Owens* have applied this minimalist position to statements governed by FRE 801(d)(1)(A). In United States v. Milton, 8 F.3d 39 (D.C. Cir. 1993), the court held that a witness who claimed to have forgotten both the underlying events and the making of the prior inconsistent statement was nevertheless subject to cross-examination concerning it:

> When a witness has forgotten the basis for and the giving of testimony under oath in an earlier proceeding and that testimony is then introduced into evidence, defense questioning, though impaired, is not futile for the reasons given in Owens. It is still possible to bring out on cross-examination the "witness' bias, his lack of care and attentiveness . . . and even (what is often a prime objective of cross-examination) the very fact that he has a bad memory." And that is precisely what took place in this case. Defense counsel elicited testimony from Jones that tended to discredit her grand jury testimony. She admitted that when she appeared before the grand jury she was addicted to drugs, was suffering from withdrawal and was on the verge of a nervous breakdown. [Id. at 46-47.]

In United States v. Keeter, 130 F.3d 297 (7th Cir. 1997), the defendant claimed that the witness was feigning a loss of memory of both the litigated event and the prior statement, and thus could not be cross-examined. The Seventh Circuit, relying on *Owens*, held that the "Supreme Court's point was that the confrontation clause (and the rule) are satisfied when the witness must look the accused in the eye in court; shortcomings in the declarant's memory may be made known to the jury." Id. at 302.

Personal Knowledge Is Required. The Ninth Circuit opinion in *Owens*, 789 F.2d 750 (9th Cir. 1986), also discussed the requirement of personal knowledge. Courts and commentators are agreed that the requirement applies to statements admitted under FRE 801(d)(1). Thus, in *Owens*, where the witness-declarant could not remember seeing his assailant at the time of the attack, the defendant Owens argued that personal knowledge had not been shown. The appellate court concluded that it could not say whether the district court had actually decided the personal knowledge issue. Most courts have applied FRE 104(a) to the personal knowledge requirement for hearsay declarants. This requires a higher threshold of proof to be met by proponents, and requires a decision by the judge under the preponderance of the evidence standard. In cases of failed memory, such a decision may be difficult to make.

b. Other Justifications for the FRE 801(d)(1) Exemptions

In addition to the witness-declarant being subject to some form of cross-examination, the foundational requirements of prior statements admitted under subsections (A), (B) and (C) may make those statements more reliable than other hearsay.

3. Explanation of FRE 801(d)(1)(A): Prior Inconsistent Statements

a. Preliminary Factfinding

The foundational requirements for FRE 801(d)(1)(A) are:

- the contents of the statement are inconsistent with testimony given at trial;
- the statement was given under the penalty of perjury; and
- the statement was made at a trial, hearing, other proceeding, or in a deposition.

Inconsistency. In the example of Joe's prior identification of Peter, the foundational requirement of its inconsistency with his in-court identification of Sam is determined by comparing the contents of the two statements. Generally, the inconsistency will appear from the contents alone, particularly when the statements are diametrically opposed such that the truth of one implies the falsity of the other. But inconsistency is not limited to such opposition; "any substantive divergence between two statements" will permit use of the prior statement. United States v. Jasin, 215 F. Supp. 2d 552, 591 (E.D. Pa. 2002) (citing Weinsten's Federal Evidence §801.21(2)(b)). Sometimes there may be doubt about the fact of inconsistency, particularly if the allegedly inconsistent statement is ambiguous. The judge should make an FRE 104(a) determination of inconsistency—under the higher standard of preponderance of the evidence. The relevancy of the prior statement is to prove the truth of its own content; relevancy is not dependent on whether the statement is actually inconsistent with the witness's trial testimony.

Inconsistency Due to Evasion.   Some courts have found inconsistency when a witness claims a loss of memory of relevant events while testifying at trial, but had previously testified in detail about them before a grand jury. "We have previously concluded that a witness's 'feigned' memory loss can be considered inconsistent under the Rule, for 'the unwilling witness often takes refuge in a failure to remember.'" United States v. Cisneros-Gutierrez, 517 F.3d 751, 757 (5th Cir. 2008). Inconsistency may be found in evasive answers, silence, or changes in position. United States v. Iglesias, 535 F.3d 150, 159 (3d Cir. 2008) (prior testimony from a suppression hearing admitted when, just two days later, witness's testimony "included one word admissions, evasive and rambling responses, and equivocations").

Under Penalty of Perjury and at a Trial, Hearing, or Other Proceeding.   The circumstances in which the inconsistent statement was made are also part of the FRE 801(d)(1)(A) foundation. The proponent must show that the statement was made under penalty of perjury and that the statement was made in a trial, hearing, deposition, or other proceeding. These foundation facts are relatively easy to prove, although you can see that Joe's prior inconsistent statement, made at the lineup, would not satisfy the requirement of being made at a hearing. But is a lineup an *"other proceeding"* that would satisfy the rule's requirement? Typically, statements made in the course of interviews and lineups are held not to be within the meaning of "other proceedings." They are not made under penalty of perjury, and the formality of trials, hearings, and depositions is thought to be conducive to reliability and truthfulness; the informality of most other interrogations is not. In United States v. Perez, 870 F.2d 1222 (7th Cir. 1989), the transcript of defense counsel's pretrial interview with an adverse government witness was held not admissible under FRE 801(d)(1)(A). The statement was under oath and recorded by a court reporter. But it did not meet the requirements of a deposition under the Federal Rules of Criminal Procedure. The government was not present and the court did not authorize the interview (note that such a statement might still be admitted pursuant to a criminal defendant's entitlement to compulsory process under the Sixth Amendment: see page 611 below). Some interrogations by immigration officers have been held to be "other proceedings." United States v. Castro-Ayon, 537 F.2d 1055, 1058 (9th Cir. 1976) (interrogation bore "many similarities to a grand jury proceeding; both are investigatory, ex parte, inquisitive, sworn, basically prosecutorial . . . recorded, and held in circumstance of some legal formality").

b. Justification for the FRE 801(d)(1)(A) Limitations

The Advisory Committee originally proposed that *all* prior inconsistent statements could be used for their truth, as is true in California under Evidence Code §1235. Because such statements are closer in time to the events they relate to, and the declarant-witness is testifying before the jury, hearsay dangers are attenuated. The House of Representatives, however, decided that admissibility should be limited to statements made under oath and *subject to cross-examination at the time they were made.* The final version of FRE 801(d)(1)(A) represents a compromise between these two positions: A witness's inconsistent statement may be used for its truth only if made at a trial, hearing, other proceeding, or in a deposition, but without the requirement of cross-examination. The compromise permits admission of statements made to grand juries under FRE 801(d)(1)(A), used most commonly when government witnesses change their stories at trial or claim not to remember the facts about the defendant's culpability to which they testified previously.

Most hearings or other proceedings are likely to be transcribed, so the fact that the prior statement was made at all will be easier to prove. Both sides to the debate over FRE 801(d)(1)(A), reported in the Advisory Committee Note, also used arguments about the reliability of prior inconsistent statements. The potential penalty of perjury, and the requirement of being made at a hearing, were intended to increase the trustworthiness of the statement. As we have said before, admitting hearsay for such reasons of increased trustworthiness is typical under the hearsay exceptions.

c. Prior Inconsistent Statements Not Within FRE 801(d)(1)(A)

At common law, any prior inconsistent statement could be admitted, but only as nonhearsay to impeach the testifying witness, not for its truth. Today, an allegedly inconsistent statement that does not fit within FRE 801(d)(1)(A) may still be admitted just to show that the witness has said inconsistent things and should not be relied on. Any such statement qualifies as relevant and consequently admissible pursuant to FRE 401 and 402. The use of prior inconsistent statements for this impeachment purpose was discussed in Chapter Seven. Notice that when a prior inconsistent statement is admissible to prove its truth under FRE 801(d)(1)(A), its proponent must still give the declarant an opportunity to explain the discrepancies between the statement and her testimony, as required for all prior inconsistent statements by FRE 613(b). Failure to give the witness that opportunity and to allow "an adverse party . . . to examine the witness about it" would prevent the statement's proponent from introducing it, unless "justice so requires." As provided by FRE 613(b), this limitation does not apply only to party admission evidence that falls under FRE 801(d)(2).

4. Explanation of FRE 801(d)(1)(B): Prior Consistent Statements

a. Preliminary Factfinding

In our previous example, Joe might have told the police the license plate number of the car involved in the crime or tort and then testified to this same number at trial. The statement to the police could be admissible for its truth as a prior consistent statement if the requirements of FRE(d)(1)(B) are satisfied. According to these requirements, the statement must be consistent with the declarant's testimony and be offered:

(1) to rebut an express or implied charge that the declarant recently fabricated it or acted from a recent improper influence or motive in so testifying; or

(2) to rehabilitate the declarant's credibility as a witness when attacked on another ground.

The consistency of Joe's two statements would be apparent. If there are doubts about consistency, the preliminary question would be decided similarly to the question of inconsistency, discussed above.

An Express or Implied Charge of Recent Fabrication or Improper Influence or Motive. It seems obvious that parties would find it advantageous to present their witnesses' prior consistent statements to the jury for their truth. But FRE 801(d)(1)(B) applies only if the credibility of the testifying witness has been attacked. Proof of such attack will be apparent to the judge from the opponent's cross-examination of the witness or from the admission of other impeaching evidence. Prior consistent statements should not be admitted for their truth until such an attack has actually occurred. The kinds of impeachment techniques that qualify as charges of *recent fabrication or improper influence or motive* are analyzed in Chapter Seven. A common example of a motive to fabricate arises in criminal cases where confederates of the defendant negotiate a plea bargain and then testify against the defendant. The defense will seek to impeach such witnesses with the suggestion that they have received favorable treatment from the government in exchange for testimony inculpating the defendant. United States v. Washington, 462 F.3d 1124, 1135 (9th Cir. 2006) (defense counsel accused witnesses of colluding with each other, because of their plea agreements, "to make up stories implicating [defendant] in the bank robbery").

To "Rebut" the Charge. In Tome v. United States, 513 U.S. 150 (1995), decided prior to the introduction of subsection B(ii), the question was raised whether the consistent statement could *rebut* the charge of improper influence or motive, as required by Rule 801(d)(1)(B), only if it was made *prior* to the date at which the improper influence or motive allegedly arose. In *Tome*, a child witness testified in court about acts of sexual assault by her father. After cross-examination, several of her prior statements making the same accusations were then admitted under FRE 801(d)(1)(B) to rebut the implicit charge that the child's in-court testimony was fabricated and was motivated by a desire to live with her mother. The child's out-of-court accusations had been made, however, *after* the child's motive to fabricate arose; that is, *after* primary custody had been awarded to the father. The Supreme Court majority held that the prior accusations did not, therefore, fall within the meaning of *rebut* under subsection (B). The majority reasoned first that the term meant rebutting a specific charge, not just bolstering credibility:

> [T]he question is whether A.T.'s out-of-court statements rebutted the alleged link between her desire to be with her mother and her testimony, not whether they suggested that A.T.'s in-court testimony was true. The Rule speaks of a party rebutting an alleged motive, not bolstering the veracity of the story told. [Id. at 157-158.]

The majority noted that this same common law meaning of "to rebut" had been adopted by the Advisory Committee in its Note to FRE 801(d)(1)(B), limiting the scope of subsection (B)(i) to statements made *before* the motive to fabricate arose. Only pre-motive statements could *rebut* an improper motive because their consistency would show that the in-court testimony was not tainted by that motive. Four dissenting Justices read the term *rebut* as raising a relevance issue rather than a rigid pre-motive timing requirement. In their view, not only pre-motive but some post-motive consistent statements might be relevant to rebut a charge of recent fabrication or improper influence or motive, and should be admitted under the rule.

Cases decided since *Tome* raise the question as to when a motive to fabricate arises. When several persons are complicit in a crime, each may seek to cooperate with the government in order to receive more lenient treatment. Typically, cooperation involves giving incriminating testimony against others. Does the motive to fabricate arise at the time of arrest? United States v. Trujillo, 376 F.3d 593, 611 (6th Cir. 2004) (it is not believable that "a day or two after [declarant-witnesses] were stopped with more than fifty kilograms of marijuana in their car and were subsequently arrested, they did not have a motive to lie, regarding the source of the marijuana, to get lenient treatment"). Or, not until discussions begin about what benefits, if any, are to be received in exchange for cooperation? Several Circuit Courts have refused to hold that a motive to fabricate always attaches upon arrest and require the trial court to make a finding about motive on the specific facts:

> [S]tatements made after arrest are not automatically and necessarily contaminated by a motive to fabricate in order to curry favor with the government. Indeed, we recognize that a variety of motives may drive a person's decision to disgorge the details of a crime he has committed . . .
>
> But given the complexity of the human psyche, we agree with the Fourth, Seventh, and Eighth Circuits that whether a witness had a motive to fabricate when prior consistent statements were made is plainly a question of fact to be resolved by the trial court based precisely on the particular circumstances of an individual case. Quite simply, the trial court is in the best position to make that determination and its determination deserves great deference. [United States v. Prieto, 232 F.3d 816, 820-821 (11th Cir. 2000).]

Do you think factfinding about the motives of the human psyche is possible? Would a bright-line legal rule about when a motive to fabricate will be held to have arisen in plea bargaining situations be preferable?

b. Justification for the FRE 801(d)(1)(B)(i) Limitation

At common law, it was clear that only consistent statements made *before* the motive to fabricate arose were admissible. Broader admissibility, it was thought, would create a risk of admitting manufactured consistent statements, and could unfairly surprise the opponent. The majority in *Tome* adopted this common law justification.

c. Beyond Motive: FRE 801(d)(1)(B)(ii)

As of December 1, 2014, subsection B(ii) allows a prior consistent statement of a testifying declarant "to rehabilitate the declarant's credibility as a witness when attacked on another ground." That is, when the attack on the declarant's credibility does not involve an express or implicit accusation of recent fabrication or a recently acquired motive to lie, his prior consistent statement, to the extent it is relevant, will be admissible as evidence for its truth.

d. Limits on Credibility-bolstering Statements Continue to Apply

Consistent statements may still be relevant to bolster credibility. As noted by the Advisory Committee, their admission for that purpose will be subject to "the traditional and well-accepted limits," which we discussed in Chapter Seven.

5. Explanation of FRE 801(d)(1)(C): Prior Statements of Identification

a. Preliminary Factfinding

In our lineup example, now assume that Joe identified Sam at the lineup as the perpetrator of the crime or tort and also identified Sam when testifying in court. Statements identifying a person are admitted under FRE 801(d)(1)(C) without any necessary predicate testimony from the declarant-witness that is consistent or inconsistent with the out-of-court identification. The foundational requirements are:

- the statement identifies a person; and
- the statement identifies that person as someone the declarant perceived earlier.

You can see that these foundation requirements are minimal. Joe's identification of either Sam or Peter at the lineup clearly qualifies. Indeed, the statement may be made in contexts other than lineups, and no oath is required. Thus, FRE 801(d)(1)(C) adds to what may be admitted under (A) and (B). A prior identification that is *consistent* with in-court testimony (Joe's identification of Sam) can be admitted without proof of any attack on Joe's sincerity. And it can be admitted even if Joe has forgotten the underlying event and cannot make an in-court identification at all. If a pretrial identification is *inconsistent* with in-court testimony (Joe's identification of Peter), it can be admitted even if not admissible under FRE 801(d)(1)(A) because not made under oath or at a hearing. The jury as factfinder determines the accuracy of the out-of-court identification. The inability or hesitancy of a witness to make an in-court identification, recantation of a prior identification, or discrepancies in the descriptions given of the person identified, are all "customary grist for the jury mill." Manson v. Braithwaite, 432 U.S. 98, 116 (1977).

The Statement Identifies a Person as Someone the Declarant Perceived Earlier. According to the Advisory Committee Note, FRE 801(d)(1)(C) was intended to include statements of identification made at traditional lineups and show-ups. The declarant would be reperceiving the person whom she had seen previously committing a crime or participating in some other disputed event. But the language used in the rule is not limited to *reperceptions at lineups*. Subsection (C) has been interpreted very broadly to include statements that identify a person seen after the disputed event in a chance encounter; that identify the photograph of the person; and that identify a police artist's sketch of the person. It has also been held to permit the admission of hearsay statements that identify people (for example, in surveillance photos) who are known to the declarant, but when the declarant did not perceive the underlying disputed event.

The Third Circuit has held that a statement to police, made on the day after a series of home invasions in a neighborhood, that the witness "had seen three of the defendants in the area of the crime during the time the homes were invaded" was admissible under FRE 802(d)(1)(C). United States v. Lopez, 271 F.3d 472, 485 (3d Cir. 2001). This statement was made without reperception of the defendants, and was acknowledged by the court to be simply "a person coming forward after a crime is committed and saying he saw particular persons at a certain place and time." This "Lopez rule" was rejected and, in our view, soundly criticized as contrary to the meaning of "identification" as had been used in Rule 801(d)(1)(C) prior to the restyling. United States v. Kaquatosh, 242 F. Supp. 2d 562, 566-567 (E.D. Wis. 2003) (statement of identification requires designation of a particular person (or photo) upon reperception as being the same as the person previously perceived). If reperception is not required, subsection (C) allows admission of out-of-court statements that identify perpetrators of crimes but are really nothing but accusations that have no particular indicia of reliability. Federal case law has not taken up the *Lopez/Kaquatosh* debate, but the majority of state courts that have cited it hold with the *Lopez* view that subsection (C) statements are not limited to those made at formal lineups, etc., and, if made by a person who knows the subject of the identification, can be made in police interviews without reperception. Commonwealth v. Adams, 941 N.E.2d 1127, 1130-1133 (Mass. 2011) (defendant's younger brother identified defendant as a shooter in two police interviews). The restyling of subsection (C)—that the statement "identifies a person as someone the declarant perceived earlier"—does not either explicitly support or reject the *Lopez* view.

A similar split in authority exists as to whether a physical description of a person given by the declarant to the police, also without any re-perception of the person, fits within FRE 801(d)(1)(C). United States v. Brink, 39 F.3d 419 (3d Cir. 1994) (admitting bank teller's statement to police, on the day following a bank robbery, that the robber had dark-colored eyes); Puryear v. State, 810 So. 2d 901 (Fla. 2002) (excluding robbery victim's statement to police that assailant was a black male, missing every other tooth, and had body odor). Case law in state courts continues to reflect this split.

Our concern is that statements of accusation and description are usually admitted under the hearsay exceptions for spontaneous and excited statements under FRE 803(1) and (2), which we discuss on pages 528-530, infra. If they are admitted instead under FRE 801(d)(1)(C), it is without any of the limits of timing and stressful circumstances that those exceptions impose, although subsection (C) does require that the declarant testify as a witness and be subject to cross-examination. Whether such statements are "testimonial" and whether they are subject to exclusion in criminal trials under the Confrontation Clause, as interpreted by Crawford v. Washington, is discussed in Section G, infra.

Identifies a Person.   As drafted, subsection (C) appears to be limited to statements about the physical characteristics of persons. Why should identifications of persons but not, for example, automobiles be admissible? If that seems too far an extension of the exemption, what about descriptions of the clothing worn by the person? The answer to how narrowly or broadly to construe the language of subsection (C) lies in the justification for the admission of prior statements identifying people. In gray areas, one should be able to state the reasons for the exemption and argue by analogy for exclusion or admission of a particular piece of evidence.

b. Justifications for the Admissibility of Prior Statements of Identification

Remember that the basic justification for the FRE 801(d)(1) exemptions is the opportunity to cross-examine the witness-declarant. But since *all* prior statements are not admitted, why are prior statements of identification included within the exemption?

Subsection (C) is justified by the *need* for prior identification testimony. Although it applies to both civil and criminal actions, this exemption is of primary benefit to prosecutors in criminal proceedings. The Advisory Committee Note describes identifications made in court as "unsatisfactory and inconclusive . . . as compared with those made at an earlier time under less suggestive conditions." In some cases, the prosecutor's use of the prior statement of identification for its truth may be essential to avoid a directed verdict of acquittal. Some witnesses may have genuinely lost the ability to make an in-court identification, as occurred in the *Owens* case discussed at page 491, supra. In this situation, neither a prior inconsistent nor a prior consistent statement would be admissible without subsection (C). There is also a risk that a prosecution witness may testify falsely at trial because of intimidation or threats to self or family members. The categorical approach to admission, however, does not permit such a case-by-case assessment of need. If the out-of-court statement satisfies the categorical requirements, it is admissible.

It is not clear that the reliability of the declarant's testimonial qualities is enhanced by the subsection (C) foundational requirements. The out-of-court statement may be more reliable because it was made closer in time to the event in which the person identified participated. On the other hand, an oath is not required, the setting may be quite informal, and no circumstance decreases the risk of improper motive for making the identification. Moreover, when the statement is made in the context of a police-arranged lineup, neither the witness nor even the police officers who arranged for the identification may have been aware of possible subtle suggestive factors that could have influenced it. Studies have demonstrated that individuals' memories fade quickly. For an excellent summary of the psychological data bearing on the reliability of eyewitness identification testimony, see Brian L. Cutler & Steven D. Penrod, Mistaken Identifications: The Eyewitness, Psychology, and the Law (1995). Thus, the argument for the admission of prior identifications is strongest with respect to identifications made soon after the perception of the person identified. Would it be desirable to amend subsection (C) to provide that the statement of identification must be made "soon" or "shortly" after the witness perceived the person identified?

c. Constitutional Dimension

In addition to the hearsay issue, there is a substantial body of case law that focuses on whether a prior identification violated a criminal defendant's constitutional right to counsel or due process of law. See, e.g., Gilbert v. California, 388 U.S. 263 (1967) (criminal defendant has right to counsel at postindictment confrontation between witness and defendant; denial of right to counsel requires exclusion of pretrial identification evidence); Manson v. Brathwaite, 432 U.S. 98, 105-06 (1977) (due process requires exclusion of suggestive pretrial identification in the presence of substantial likelihood of misidentification). Equally important, when police carry out an intentionally suggestive identification procedure that prompts the witness to identify the defendant as a perpetrator of the alleged crime, admitting the witness's identifying statement into evidence would violate due process. *Foster v. California*, 394 U.S. 440, 442-443 (1969). On the other hand, no due process violation is present when the police mishandle a lineup or other identification process by making it suggestive unintentionally and in good faith. *Perry v. New Hampshire*, 132 S. Ct. 716 (2012).

KEY POINTS

1. The prior out-of-court statement of a testifying witness may be admitted for the truth of the matter it asserts if it is (A) inconsistent with the witness's testimony and was given in a prior proceeding subject to penalties for perjury; (B) consistent with the witness's testimony and rebuts a charge of recent fabrication or improper influence or motive or responds to a different attack on the witness's credibility; or (C) a statement of identification of a person, made after perceiving that person.

2. The judge must be persuaded, pursuant to FRE 104(a), that the foundational requirements are satisfied prior to admitting any such statement.

3. The witness must be subject to cross-examination concerning the statement; the witness need not necessarily remember the underlying event or making the prior statement.

PROBLEMS

8.32. Esther Kingsley and Robert Roby were riding in a car that crossed the median strip on a two-lane highway and collided with a pickup truck driven by William Burditt. Esther was killed in the crash and the executor of her estate is suing Robert for wrongful death, alleging that he was driving the car and that his negligence caused the accident. Robert claims that Esther was driving and that the accident was her fault.

    (a) Several hours after the accident, William Burditt told a state trooper that "a man was driving." Two days later Burditt told a friend "the woman was not driving the car." Called by the plaintiff executor to testify at trial, Burditt testifies "I have a picture in my mind that the woman was behind the wheel. It seems when we hit, she was on the driver's side." Can the plaintiff use Burditt's prior statements to prove that Robert was driving? To impeach Burditt's credibility? If there is no other evidence that Robert was driving, will the judge grant a directed verdict against the plaintiff?

    (b) What if Burditt's deposition had been taken by plaintiff and Burditt said "a man was driving"—admissible? For what purpose?

    (c) What if there was no deposition but Burditt had previously submitted a sworn affidavit that said "a man was driving" in support of plaintiff's motion for summary judgment against Robert? Admissible? For what purpose?

    (d) Assume that the statements in (a) are admitted to impeach Burditt. Plaintiff also asks Burditt: "Isn't it true that Robert paid you for the extensive damage done to your truck in the collision, just a week before this trial?" Burditt answers "Yes." Relevant? Admissible?

(e) Assume that the evidence in (d) is admitted. Robert then offers the testimony of Burditt's coworker that, on the day before the trial started, Burditt said: "You know, I think that it was the woman driving." Relevant? Admissible?

(f) Assume that two *men*—Edwin and Robert—were in the car that collided with Burditt's truck. Edwin was killed in the crash and his estate sues Robert for wrongful death, claiming that Robert was driving. Robert says that Edwin was driving. Plaintiff offers testimony that Burditt said to a state trooper, just after the accident, "that man there was driving" and then pointed at Robert. Admissible? For what purpose?

(g) Same facts as (f). What if, several days after the accident, Burditt said to a friend, "It was the man with black hair and the blue jacket who was driving." (Robert has black hair and was wearing a blue jacket on the day of the accident.)

8.33 Return to Problem 3.3, United States v. Ray, at page 149, supra. At Ray's trial, in January of 2016, Beth Barker testifies for the prosecution on direct examination that she remembers June Jacobs giving her the March 14, 2015 memorandum written by the outside auditor Andrews. She further testifies that she placed it in Ray's "inbox" on that same day, March 14, and then removed it the next day, March 15, from his "out box." She also remembers that Ray's initials were on the memorandum.

(a) On cross-examination, defense counsel asks the following:

1 Q: Ms. Barker, you testified at a preliminary hearing on December 1, 2015,
2   in this case, did you not?
3 A: Yes.
4 Q: And I asked you some questions at that time, do you recall that?
5 A: Yes.
6 Q: Isn't it true that I asked you the following questions, and you gave the
7   following answers: [reading from transcript]
8   "Q: When did June Jacobs give you the auditor's memo?
9   A: I believe it was March 18."

Is Barker's answer from the preliminary hearing transcript admissible, over the prosecutor's hearsay objection, to prove that June Jacobs delivered the auditors' memo to Ray's office on March 18?

(b) Defense counsel next offers Exhibit B into evidence, an authenticated written affidavit signed by Beth Barker dated December 19, 2015, which states (in pertinent part):

I, Beth Barker, declare:

On March 18, 2015, June Jacobs personally handed me a copy of Andrews' auditor's memo and said "Mr. Ray needs to see this." I remember this incident because it was unusual for Ms. Jacobs to deliver a document for Mr. Ray personally.

I declare under penalty of perjury that the foregoing is true and correct to the best of my knowledge.

[signed] Beth Barker

Is this affidavit admissible, over the prosecutor's hearsay objection, to prove that June Jacobs delivered the auditors' memo to Ray's office on March 18?

(c) On cross examination, defense counsel asks Barker the following questions:

1 Q: Ms. Barker, on January 20, 2016, you were arrested for embezzling $250
2   from a petty cash fund, while employed at Rundown?
3 A: Yes.
4 Q: And that alleged embezzlement occurred on January 5, 2016, isn't that
5   so?
6 A: I believe so.
7 Q: Ms. Barker, isn't it a fact that you made up the testimony you gave today
8   about removing the March 14, 2015, auditor's memorandum, with Mr.
9   Ray's initials on it, from Mr. Ray's out box on March 15, 2015 in order to
10   get a deal from the prosecutor on your embezzlement charge?
11 A: No, that's not true.
12 *Defense Counsel*:   I have no further questions.

The prosecutor then calls an FBI agent who will testify that in June of 2015 he interviewed Beth Barker and she told him that she remembered removing a memorandum dated March 14, 2015, written by the outside auditor Andrews, from Mr. Ray's out box on March 15, 2015. She also told the agent that it had Mr. Ray's initials on it, and that she filed it. Is this testimony admissible over defense counsel's hearsay objection?

8.34. Ed Larson is being prosecuted for armed robbery of a bank. Terry Davis, an alleged accomplice, pleaded guilty to the same charge and is currently serving a 20-year sentence. Davis admitted that he was involved in the robbery, but he claimed that he could not remember whether he had a partner or, if he did have one, who the partner might have been. He also claimed not to remember ever having made a statement to anyone about having a partner. To prove that Larson committed the robbery with Davis the prosecutor offers (a) a transcript of Davis's grand jury testimony describing Larson's participation in the robbery and (b) the testimony of a police officer to the effect that following Davis's arrest several days after the robbery, he confessed to the crime and named Larson as his accomplice. The defendant has objected to both pieces of evidence. What result?

8.35. Larry Emerson is being tried for arson. The government's key witness, Alice Hastings, testified under a grant of immunity that she had cooperated with Larry in planning the arson, but then had withdrawn from the scheme. On cross-examination, defense counsel inquired about promises made to Hastings in return for her testimony and suggested that she was testifying against Emerson in order to shift responsibility for the crime from herself. The government then calls a police officer who was present at Hastings's arrest to testify that Hastings voluntarily began talking to the police; that she did not ask any questions about what benefits she might obtain; that another officer informed Hastings that her cooperation would be brought to the attention of the District Attorney; and that before any other statements about cooperation were made, Hastings identified Larry Emerson as the arsonist. Is this testimony admissible under FRE 801(d)(1) (B)?

8.36. A fight broke out between Defendant and Joe Williams in a nightclub. Williams lay collapsed on the floor and Defendant was ejected from the club. It is alleged that Defendant returned with a gun and shot Williams. Although the alleged murder weapon was never recovered, Defendant is charged in federal court with the crime of unlawful possession of a firearm and ammunition by a convicted felon. At trial, Holmes, a friend of Williams, testified that he witnessed the fight and the shooting committed by Defendant. Williams's girlfriend arrived at the club after the shooting, having been called by her nephew and told that Williams was lying on the floor after the fight. The girlfriend testifies that when she arrived at the club 30 minutes later, she met Holmes in the parking lot. She further testifies:

> I asked Holmes, "What happened, what happened?" Holmes said, "He shot him." I said, "Who shot him?" Holmes said, "Defendant shot him."

> Was it error for the trial court to admit this testimony under FRE 801(d)(1)(C)?

6. Explanation of FRE 801(d)(2): Party Admissions in General

Each subsection of FRE 801(d)(2) defines a specific type of out-of-court statement made by a declarant who is either a party in the case against whom the statement is being offered or has a specified affiliation with such a party. The foundational requirements of subsections (A)-(E) focus primarily on the relationship between the party and the declarant. The single common requirement for all the subsections is that the proponent must offer the declarant's statement *against* the opposing party. It is the proponent's choice whether or not to use an opposing party's own statements, or statements of affiliates, to prove the case *against that party* at trial.

Before we discuss each FRE 801(d)(2) subsection in detail, you should read through them all again briefly:

(d) *Statements That Are Not Hearsay.* A statement that meets the following conditions is not hearsay:

(2) *An Opposing Party's Statement.* The statement is offered against an opposing party and:

(A) was made by the party in an individual or representative capacity;

(B) is one the party manifested that it adopted or believed to be true;

(C) was made by a person whom the party authorized to make a statement on the subject;

(D) was made by the party's agent or employee on a matter within the scope of that relationship and while it existed; or

(E) was made by the party's co-conspirator during and in furtherance of the conspiracy.

The statement must be considered but does not by itself establish
the declarant's authority under (C); the existence or scope of the relationship under (D); or the existence of the conspiracy or participation
in it under (E).

We will use the following example to illustrate subsections (A)-(E):

Suppose that Day and Moore are partners in a business. They are being tried jointly for
preparing and filing a false partnership income tax return in 2014. The government's
evidence tends to show that Day and Moore diverted income from the partnership to
themselves by cashing checks made out to the partnership. The government claims
that Day and Moore did not account for the proceeds in either the partnership or
their own income tax returns. At trial, Moore testifies in his own defense and denies
all knowledge of and participation in such a scheme. The government then seeks to
introduce against both Day and Moore a properly authenticated tape recording of a
statement that Moore made, unbeknownst to Day, in an interview with an Internal
Revenue Service agent who was investigating the 2014 partnership return. Moore's
recorded statement implicates both Day and Moore in the income diversion and tax
evasion scheme. It was not made under oath, however, and would not be admissible as
a prior inconsistent statement under FRE 801(d)(1)(A).

Would Moore's recorded statement be admissible against Moore himself under FRE
801(d)(2)(A)? Would it be admissible against Day? Would the statement be admissible against Day under FRE 801(d)(2)(B), (C), (D), or (E)? If you can fit the statement
under (A) against Moore, or under (B), (C), (D), or (E) against Day, then although it
is offered for the truth of the matter it asserts—that Moore and Day both participated
in the illegal scheme to file a false tax return—it will be exempt from the definition of
hearsay and will be admissible as substantive evidence for its truth.

7. Explanation of FRE 801(d)(2)(A): A Party's Own Statements

a. Preliminary Factfinding

The foundational requirements for a party admission are:

- the statement is made by a party; and
- the statement is offered against that party.

This is perhaps the simplest foundation of all the hearsay exemptions and exceptions.
Moore's recorded statement easily satisfies it, so long as it is offered against Moore
himself. *Any* out-of-court statement made in *any* context by *any* party (whether plaintiff or defendant) to *any* action (whether civil or criminal) may be admissible—unless
excludable on other ground—when offered *against* that party.

The party's statement must of course be relevant and not subject to exclusion
under other rules of evidence. Guilty pleas, depositions, personal documents, and
prepared charts, as well as conversational oral statements, have all been admitted for

their truth under FRE 801(d)(2)(A). Trull v. Volkswagen of America, Inc., 187 F.3d
88, 98 (1st Cir. 1999) (plaintiffs' diagram from a prior lawsuit, showing a different
version of the collision in question, was admitted against them in their suit against
the manufacturer of their van). If a party's nonverbal conduct is hearsay under FRE
801(a) because it is intended as an assertion, it is a statement for the purposes of
this or any other hearsay exception or exemption. A nod of assent in response to an
incriminating question, for example, would be admissible as an admission against a
defendant in a subsequent prosecution.

If a proponent offers a Rule 801(d)(2)(A) statement *against* a party at trial, the
proponent must think that the statement is adverse to the interest of that party. For
this reason, party admissions are sometimes referred to as "admissions against interest." We strongly urge you to avoid the phrase "admission against interest." First, the
foundational requirements for the admissions exemption *do not require that the statement be "against interest" when it is made, nor that the person making the statement
think that it is.* Sometimes a party's statement attains its "against interest" significance
long after it is made. Second, as you will see, there is a completely distinct exception
to the hearsay rule for "declarations against interest." Getting used to referring to party
admissions simply as admissions should help to avoid confusion between declarations
against interest and admissions.

b. Individual and Representative Capacity

FRE 801(d)(2)(A) controls the admission of statements made by an individual person that are offered against that same individual person at trial. But a person can speak,
and can be a party, either as an individual or as a representative—a trustee, executor, or
guardian—of some other entity or individual. The rule provides for the admission of statements against the individual person even if those statements were made when the individual was speaking as a representative outside of court. In re Special Federal Grand Jury
Empanelled Oct. 31, 1985 Impounded, 819 F.2d 56, 59 (3d Cir. 1987) (statements made
to a grand jury solely in the declarant's capacity as an agent for a corporation is admissible
against him as an individual). And statements made outside of court by a person, whether
as an individual or as a representative, will be admissible against that person if he appears
as a party solely in a representative capacity. Estate of Shafer v. Commissioner, 749 F.2d
1216, 1219 (6th Cir. 1984) (letter written by son of a decedent admissible against him as
coexecutor of his father's estate, whether it was written by the son as an individual or in his
capacity as executor). When an entity such as a corporation is a party, the statements of its
representatives can be admitted against the entity under FRE 801(d)(2)(C) or (D), but not
pursuant to FRE 801(d)(2)(A), as we will discuss at pages 511-515, infra.

c. Admissions, Personal Knowledge, and Lay Opinions

The admissions exemption differs from other hearsay exemptions and exceptions in
two respects. First, there is *no* requirement that a party admission be based on firsthand
knowledge. This is in contrast to all other hearsay exceptions and Rule 801(d)(1) statements. The Advisory Committee Note to FRE 801(d)(2)(a) states that admissions of
a party-opponent are free from "the restrictive influences of the opinion rule and the

rule requiring first hand knowledge . . . ." McCormick offers the following justification for dispensing with the personal knowledge requirement for a party's own admissions:

> [T]he vast majority of admissions that become relevant in litigation concern some matter of substantial importance to declarants upon which they would likely have informed themselves. As a result, most admissions possess greater reliability than the general run of hearsay, even when not based on firsthand observation. Moreover, the possibility is substantial that the declarant may have significant information that the opponent cannot prove. [McCormick on Evidence, Vol. 2 §255, at 183 (Kenneth S. Broun, ed., 6th ed. 2006).]

Do you find this justification convincing? Is there some other justification for dispensing with the requirement? Would the proponent of the admission find it easy to prove what a party opponent knows about the facts of their dispute without using the party's out-of-court statements?

Second, courts have tended to be liberal in admitting statements of opinion if the evidence is an admission. Since the party against whom an admission is offered can take the witness stand and explain the basis for the opinion, suppressing the opinion rule in this context seems reasonable. Combining freedom from the personal knowledge requirement and from the opinion rule's limitations means that a party's admissions may be based on hearsay statements of others, or the party's inferences from circumstances.

8. FRE 801(d)(2)(A): Policies and Practical Applications

As you can see from the breadth of Rule 801(d)(2)(A), the justification for its admissibility cannot rest on a claim of enhanced reliability. There are no limitations in the rule concerning the content of the out-of-court statement or the circumstances in which it was made. We emphasize again that it need not have been "against interest" when made. Instead, all five of the subsections of FRE 801(d)(2) are justified by considerations relating to the adversarial system of trial and to values of freedom of choice and personal responsibility in our larger society. These considerations operate most powerfully as justifications for the admissibility of a party's own statements under subsection (A). A party confronted with his own out-of-court statement has no plausible complaint about his inability to cross-examine the declarant (himself). As we will see in succeeding sections of this chapter, these justifications become less powerful as the relationship between the party and the declarant becomes weaker. Then circumstances that may increase the need for or the reliability of the out-of-court statement are added to the foundational requirements of each subsection.

a. The Opportunity to Cross-examine and Explain

Hearsay is excluded primarily because the opponent lacks the opportunity to expose weaknesses in the declarant's narration, sincerity, perception, and memory through cross-examination. As we already mentioned, however, parties to an action cannot reasonably complain about the lack of an opportunity for cross-examining themselves. There is a viable alternative. If a party's hearsay statement has been admitted against

him, he can take the stand in rebuttal and have a full opportunity to explain any difficulties with the accuracy of the statement. In short, it seems absurd for a party who
is directly affected by the outcome in the case, and who is sitting in the courtroom,
to complain about not being able to cross-examine herself. These observations hold
true in civil cases and, subject to Fifth Amendment concerns, to which we now turn,
in criminal cases as well.

b. Fifth Amendment Concerns

When a criminal defendant's own admission is offered against him as inculpatory evidence, it must be voluntary under the Fifth Amendment. Miranda v. Arizona,
384 U.S. 436 (1966). This means that government agents cannot elicit a confession
by subjecting the defendant to threats, extortion, and violence, or by carrying out a
custodial interrogation without first informing the defendant about his right to remain
silent, about the fact that anything he says might subsequently be used as evidence
against him in a court of law, and about his right to be represented by his own attorney
or a public defender. Any such violation triggers the suppression of the defendant's
confession for being involuntary. Moreover, a defendant cannot be convicted on the
basis of her or his uncorroborated confession. To secure the defendant's conviction,
the prosecution must produce some independent confirmation for the defendant's
self-incriminating statement. Opper v. United States, 348 U.S. 84, 89 (1954). These
requirements substantially increase the reliability of criminal defendants' confessions.

Criminal trials still differ from civil cases in one important respect for purposes of
party-admission evidence. While it is true that a criminal defendant is as free as a civil
litigant to testify and rebut any out-of-court statement attributed to him, it is also true
that he has the Fifth Amendment right not to testify. Admitting a criminal defendant's
statement under FRE 801(d)(2)(A) thus puts some pressure on the defendant to abandon that right. Any number of factors, however, may make a defendant feel pressured
to testify, and only some of them raise constitutional problems. At one extreme, a
direct threat of punishment for refusing to testify would be regarded as a violation of
the Fifth Amendment right to remain silent. At the other extreme, the defendant may
feel pressure to testify simply because of the nature or strength of the prosecutor's case,
and this type of pressure raises no constitutional problems. The right to silence means
only that defendants deciding not to testify should suffer no repercussions in the form
of punishment or inferences of guilt. In Hohfeldian terms, this right is merely a "liberty" rather than a "claim right": it does not obligate the government to make it beneficial for defendants to remain silent. The FRE 801(d)(2)(A) exemption therefore
justifiably applies to criminal defendants and not just to civil litigants.

9. Further Elaboration of FRE 801(d)(2)(A)

a. Preliminary Factfinding on the Identity of the Declarant

The foundational requirements for all hearsay exceptions and exemptions are preliminary questions of fact subject to FRE 104, and are typically for the judge to decide

pursuant to FRE 104(a). These requirements are imposed by hearsay policy; they do not establish the relevance of the out-of-court statement. But consider a case in which relevancy and hearsay policy are determined by the same question of fact. Suppose that it is alleged that the defendant started a fight with a coworker. The defendant denies starting the fight. What if the coworker had previously received an unsigned letter expressing great animosity toward the coworker? The coworker claims that the defendant wrote this letter and that the animosity is relevant to prove that defendant started the fight. The defendant denies sending the letter and the coworker offers it for its truth. Since the letter is hearsay, the coworker offers it under FRE 801(d)(2)(A) against the defendant. Should FRE 104(a) or (b) control the judge's factfinding on whether the defendant wrote the letter?

In this case, this same fact is necessary both to the relevance (and authentication) of the letter under FRE 401 and to the admissibility of the hearsay statement under FRE 801(d)(2)(A). FRE 104(b) governs the relevance and the authentication questions; FRE 104(a) governs the hearsay policy question. Which should control? The difference between them would be that under FRE 104(b), the judge would have to admit the letter with less foundational evidence—only evidence sufficient to support a finding—that the defendant wrote it. Under FRE 104(a), the judge should admit the letter only if the judge is actually persuaded by a preponderance of the evidence that the defendant wrote it.

In this example, the letter *can only be relevant and harmful* to the defendant if the defendant in fact wrote it and meant what he said. If the defendant did not write the letter or intended it to be a prank, the animosity it expresses *could not* rationally be used in a way that is harmful to the defendant.

Arguably, since the Federal Rules of Evidence favor greater admissibility of relevant evidence, it would seem that the question should be decided under Rule 104(b) as a matter of relevance policy. It would be much easier for the coworker to meet the FRE 104(b) standard and to get the letter admitted than if FRE 104(a) were to apply. Of course, the defendant can still deny being the author and the jury will ultimately decide the question. The crucial point is that if the jury finds that it was not written by the defendant, we are fairly confident that the jury can disregard the letter as irrelevant. On the other hand, if the hearsay policy were to tighten the conditions under which hearsay statements become admissible, FRE 104(a) and its preponderance requirement should trump FRE 104(b).

b. Admissibility of Party Admissions in Multiparty Cases: The *Bruton* Problem

In some cases, there are multiple plaintiffs or defendants. One party's party admission is not admissible against anyone other than the party who made the statement. The potential for improper use against another party would be resolved under FRE 403. But in criminal cases, there is a potential violation of the Confrontation Clause.

In Bruton v. United States, 391 U.S. 123 (1968), Bruton and Evans were tried jointly for armed robbery. Evans did not testify but was in court. The prosecution introduced into evidence an earlier confession by Evans that implicated both Evans and Bruton. Since the confession was admissible as a party admission only against Evans, the trial court instructed the jury that it could consider the confession as evidence only against Evans. Because Evans did not testify, Bruton could not cross-examine him. The Supreme Court, relying in part on the probable inability of the jury to limit its consideration of the confession to Evans, held that introduction of the confession had violated Bruton's constitutional entitlement to confrontation and due process. Hence, when a defendant's out-of-court confession implicates his codefendant, *Bruton* deems this spillover incurable by a FRE 105 limiting instruction to the jury, as well as too prejudicial to the codefendant to leave it to the trial judge's discretion under FRE 403. Based on these assumptions, *Bruton* precludes the confession's admission unless the confessor can be cross-examined.

Another way to accommodate the *Bruton* rule is to sever the trials of the codefendants. This, however, is an expensive remedy and prosecutors have sought other solutions. If all specific references to the codefendant are redacted from the declarant-defendant's statement, it may then be offered against the declarant-defendant alone. Richardson v. Marsh, 481 U.S. 200 (1987). Confessions redacted by substituting a single codefendant's name with blank spaces or symbols have been held to be incriminating of the codefendant and inadmissible under *Bruton*. Gray v. Maryland, 523 U.S. 185 (1998). Correspondingly, in United States v. Jass, 569 F.3d 47, 62 (2d Cir. 2009), the court disapproved the following redaction of a codefendant's confession for being suggestive: "When I realized the guard had pulled the alarm, I turned and said to another person, 'Look, other person, we have to get out of here.'" Substitution of names with neutral pronouns such as "other guys" or "persons" has been held not to incriminate specific codefendants when there are several of them, and therefore not to violate *Bruton*. United States v. Molina, 407 F.3d 511 (1st Cir. 2005); United States v. Taylor, 745 F.3d 15, 28-30 (2d Cir. 2014) (explaining that redaction will satisfy *Bruton* when it prunes the names of actual people from the confessor's statement and uses instead "another person," "others," "other people" or similar non-suggestive terms that broaden the "choice of the implied identity"). But in United States v. Lujan, 529 F. Supp. 2d 1315 (D.N.M. 2007), the court held that the sheer magnitude of the incriminating statements (265 pages from two defendants other than Lujan), the difficulty of the redaction in statements referring to all three defendants, the risk of distorting certain statements that might be exculpatory to one defendant, and the confusion resulting from replacing names with pronouns, compelled the findings that redaction would not cure the confrontation problem and that the trials must consequently be severed.

10. Explanation of FRE 801(d)(2)(B): Adoptive Admissions

a. Preliminary Factfinding

The foundational requirements for an adoptive admission are:

* a statement has been made;
* the party has done something to manifest adoption of the statement or belief in its truth; and
* the statement is offered against the party.

Under FRE 801(d)(2)(B), there is no limitation on who may make the statement that is subsequently offered against a party. It is thus not an exemption based on a relationship between the declarant and the party. Rather, it is based on the party's own communicative conduct.

In the false partnership tax return example, for the government to use subsection (B) to secure the admission of Moore's recorded statement for its truth against Day, it would first have to prove that Day had heard Moore's statement or knew of it, and that he appeared to adopt it or to accept it as true. If the recording had been played to Day and he nodded "yes," or said, "That's right," the government could argue that these words satisfied the foundational requirements of subsection (B).

A party may manifest adoption of a statement in any number of ways, including through words, conduct, or silence. United States v. Jinadu, 98 F.3d 239 (6th Cir. 1996) (defendant answered "yes" during interrogation to question "you know that's China White heroin"); United States v. Pulido-Jacobo, 377 F.3d 1124, 1132 (10th Cir. 2004) (to prove truth of contents of a document, mere possession does not constitute adoption but "surrounding circumstances can tie the possessor and the document together in a meaningful way," e.g., by accepting the document and acting upon it); United States v. Joshi, 896 F.2d 1303, 1311 (11th Cir. 1990) (party nodded head after statement by another, and made a sound of agreement); Wagstaff v. Protective Apparel Corp., 760 F.2d 1074, 1078 (10th Cir. 1985) (party used for its own advantage a written statement prepared by another); Pillsbury Co. v. Cleaver-Brooks Div. of Aqua-Chem, Inc., 646 F.2d 1216, 1218 (8th Cir. 1981) (party signed statement prepared by another); United States v. Weaver, 565 F.2d 129, 135 (8th Cir. 1977) (party repeated statement of another); United States v. Safavian, 435 F. Supp. 2d 36, 43 (D.D.C. 2006) (party's words "manifested an adoption or belief" in the truth of the statements of other people as he forwarded their e-mails). If ambiguous, the meaning of a party's behavior is ultimately for the jury to assess after determination of this preliminary question by the judge. State v. Carlson, 808 P.2d 1002 (Or. 1991). However, courts appear to disagree as to whether these preliminary questions are decided pursuant to FRE 104(a) or 104(b). Id. at 1006-1009 (holding that Rule 104(a) applies after a thorough discussion of the precedent and policy).

b. Justification for the Admissibility of Adoptive Admissions

If a party has done something to manifest adoption or belief in the truth of an uncross-examined statement made by another, an inference can be drawn that the party knows that the contents of the statement are accurate, or thinks that the person speaking is reliable and knowledgeable. The party can still dispute these inferences, and the statement's accuracy, at trial. The party can explain why the statement was unreliable and why, at the time, the party did not repudiate the statement. If the party in fact knew nothing about what the statement asserted, then the party went along with it presumably to get some advantage, or induce some reliance. This makes it fair to admit the statement against the party at trial.

c. Adoption by Silence

A common type of adoptive admission is the admission by silence. In United States v. Duval, 496 F.3d 64 (1st Cir. 2007), Duval was convicted of possession of a firearm by a convicted felon. To prove possession, the prosecution offered the testimony of an undercover informant. The informant testified at trial that while Duval and his companion were staying at the informant's apartment, the companion stated that he and Duval wanted to sell firearms that were in their possession. The prosecution claimed that the companion's incriminating statement implicated Duval because he was present when the statement was made but did not attempt to disassociate himself from it. Another good illustration is United States v. Hoosier, 542 F.2d 687, 687-688 (6th Cir. 1976). In this case, the Sixth Circuit approved the admission of testimony describing the statement made to the witness by the robbery defendant's girlfriend while the defendant was present: "That ain't nothing, you should have seen the [sacks of] money we had in the hotel room." The Circuit reasoned that "[u]nder the total circumstances, we believe that probable human behavior would have been for appellant promptly to deny his girl friend's statement if it had not been true. . . ."

One problem with using nonresponsiveness or silence as the basis for an inference of a subsection (B) admission is the ambiguity of the party's conduct. What does it mean if someone fails to respond to another person's statement? To a letter? Or to the calculation of a bill? These ambiguities are resolved by preliminary factfinding on the question of whether the party's conduct "manifests" adoption or belief. "[T]he burden is on the proponent to convince the judge [under FRE 104(a)] that in the circumstances . . . a failure to respond is so unnatural that it supports the inference that the party acquiesced in the statement." Weston-Smith v. Cooley Dickinson Hospital, Inc., 282 F.3d 60, 67 (1st Cir. 2002). The judge considers the nature of the statement, the audience, and the surrounding circumstances. For example, in Weston-Smith, failure to respond to an accusatory statement made at a social occasion, when the party did not have information necessary to assess the accusation's truthfulness, was held not to be an adoptive admission. Id. at 68. The court's decision calls for an evaluation of probable human behavior. The party who opposes the admissibility of the statement can of course offer evidence on the preliminary fact questions as part of the judge's factfinding process. This evidence may be resubmitted to the jury to reduce the probative value of the statement, if it is admitted.

In United States v. Duval, supra, Duval contended that the facts described were insufficient to prove that he had *actually heard* the companion's statement, which was necessary to the prosecution's showing under FRE 801(d)(2)(B) that he could have adopted the statement or believed in its truth. Duval offered the testimony of a fourth person present who testified that he had not heard the statement himself. The appellate court upheld the finding of the district judge that, based on testimony that the conversation took place in a small room, and that Duval was in that room, the foundation was adequate to admit the companion's statement. This decision, alas, should have been made under FRE 104(a) and its preponderance requirement. Hearing the companion's statement amounted to a preliminary fact pursuant to hearsay policy rather than relevancy (indeed, evidence of the companion's statement would be relevant and harmful to Duval whether he heard it or not).

11. Explanation of FRE 801(d)(2)(C) and (D): Admissions by Agents, Servants, and Employees

a. Preliminary Factfinding

The foundational requirements for authorized admissions under subsection (C) are:

- the statement is on a subject;
- the statement was made by person whom a party authorized to make a statement on that subject; and
- the statement is offered against that party.

In the example of the false partnership tax return, Moore's recorded statement could only be admitted against Day under subsection (C) if the government had evidence showing that Day had given Moore authority to make the recorded statement on Day's behalf. FRE 801(d)(2) also states that the contents of the statement itself may be used to prove the issue of authority (if Moore stated on the tape that Day had asked him to speak with the government about their scheme, for example) but other independent evidence of authority (a "corroboration") is also required. The foundational requirements for admissions by agents and employees under subsection (D) focus on the existence of the agency or employee relationship and do not require any showing of authority, which is presupposed:

- the declarant is an agent or employee of a party;
- the statement was made while this relationship existed;
- the statement is on a matter within the scope of the agency or employment relationship; and
- the statement is offered against that party.

Under subsection (D), Moore's statement might be admitted against Day if a principal-agent or employer-employee relationship existed between them. Partners are treated as agents of the partnership; but are partners agents of each other? An agency relationship is typically defined by *control*; that is, the principal having "the right to control the manner and method in which the work is carried out by the alleged agent." Chemtool, Inc. v. Lubrication Technologies, Inc., 148 F.3d 742, 745 (7th Cir. 1998). But authorization, express or implied, will do, too: United States v. Saks, 964 F.2d 1514, 1523 (5th Cir. 1992) (The general rule is that the declarations of one partner about the partnership's affairs are admissible against the other partners.).

In addition, the proponent would need to prove that the statement was made during the relationship and that it was on a matter within Moore's duties as an agent of Day. The contents of the statement itself may be used to prove the fact of agency and the scope thereof, but the *statement alone is not sufficient* under FRE 801(d)(2). Gomez v. Rodriguez, 344 F.3d 103, 117 (1st Cir. 2003) (statement by mayor's wife that she was interviewing employment applicants for him and applying "political" criteria, held inadmissible as statement of an agent, since no independent evidence in the record supported the existence of the agency relationship).

Statements by Attorneys. Many of the cases involving authorized admissions offered under subsection (C) concern statements made by attorneys on behalf of their clients. When an attorney represents a party in litigation, statements of facts made in formal litigation documents—pleadings, answers to interrogatories, responses to requests for documents, briefs—and in opening and closing statements at trial may all be found to be within the scope of the attorney's authority even though there is no specific grant of authority to make the particular statement. In other settings, the scope of an attorney's representation of the party, and the specific tasks undertaken by the attorney or other agent, create *implied* authority to speak on the party's behalf. Whether or not such authority exists is a preliminary question for the judge to decide under FRE 104(a).

Other Specifically Authorized Statements. Some agents would ordinarily be viewed as having authority from a party to make statements that are necessary to the performance of their duties; for example, minutes taken by the secretary at a school board would be admissible as authorized statements under FRE 801(d)(2)(C) if offered against the board. Other employees of a party may be given specific authority to speak on a one-time basis, or to speak on a topic not within their normal relationship with the party. Subsection (C) may also apply to authorized statements made by persons in relationships with the party that are not within the definition of agency, such as employer-independent contractor, or parent-child.

Statements Made During the Relationship on a Matter Within the Scope of an Agent's Employment. Subsection (D) does not require that the declarant have specific authority to speak. Nor does it require that the statement be made on the job, that is, *within* the scope of the agent's duties. Rather, subsection (D) focuses on subject matter: The statement must be *on a matter* within the scope of the employment or agency relationship.

Prior to its restyling, subsection (D) required that the statement "concern" a matter within the scope of the employment or agency. The term "concern" was interpreted as meaning the statement must "relate to" the scope of employment or agency, or the subject matter of the statement must "match" the subject matter of the employee's or agent's job description. Because the restyling was not intended to change the substance of any rule, we assume that the term "on" will be given the same meaning as "concern."

Typical cases have involved agents speaking about their own job performance or about events that happened on the job that would be of legitimate concern to the speaker. For example, statements by superiors to company employees concerning the employee's standing in the company may be within subsection (D), depending on the superior's job, duties, and role in relation to the employee. In Carter v. University of Toledo, 349 F.3d 269, 271-272 (6th Cir. 2002), the plaintiff, an African American professor, sued the defendant for failure to renew her contract because of her race. The plaintiff sought to testify that the University's Vice-Provost had said to her that the Dean who had refused the renewal was "trying to whitewash the college of education" and "was trying to get rid of black professors." The appellate court held that while the

Vice-Provost was not a "direct decisionmaker" concerning the plaintiff's employment, he did have "oversight of the affirmative action process at the University" and thus his statements concerned a matter within his authority. On the other hand, statements have been excluded as not concerning a matter within the scope of the agency when the declarant acted as a bystander eyewitness who describes an event perceived at work that has no relation to her job. Wilkinson v. Carnival Cruise Lines, 920 F.2d 1560 (11th Cir. 1991) (statement by cabin steward about previous problems with sliding glass door in ship's swimming pool area did not concern a matter within scope of steward's employment since his job involved no responsibilities in the engineering department or for the swimming pool). Since the contents of the hearsay statement alone are not sufficient to prove the scope of authority, the proponent must present corroborating evidence. Mercado v. City of Orlando, 407 F.3d 1152, 1156 (11th Cir. 2005).

The proponent of a statement under subsection (D) must also provide evidence that the statement was made while the principal-agent relationship existed. This does not mean that the statement must be made "on the job" or during the performance of duties. Rule 801(d)(2)(D) abandons the common law requirement that agents must be *acting* within the scope of their authority when they make the statement. The exemption thus includes statements made away from the workplace to third parties uninvolved in the speaker's work. Kraus v. Sobel Corrugated Containers, Inc., 915 F.2d 227, 230-231 (6th Cir. 1990) (statement praising job performance of plaintiff shortly before her termination, made by a department manager during holiday dinner at the home of the plaintiff, would be admissible against the defendant in an age discrimination case).

Statements of employees are admitted not only against employer corporations but also against their corporate supervisors if direct supervision and control is proved. United States v. Agne, 214 F.3d 47, 55 (1st Cir. 2000) (statements admissible against the president of a corporation under FRE 801(d)(2)(D), because evidence showed that the declarant, an employee of the corporation's wholly-owned company, was directly responsible to the president and often acted for him).

b. Justification for the Admissibility of Statements Under FRE 801(d)(2)(C) and (D): Necessity, Fairness, and Reliability

Under both subsections (C) and (D), there is no guarantee that the declarant will be available to testify at trial. Thus, the principal rationale for admitting statements under subsections (A) and (B)—that the party can choose to explain the statement—may not apply. If the declarant is out of the country or otherwise unavailable, and the party had little or no knowledge of the statement when made, the justification that cross-examination is unnecessary because the party can explain the declarant's statement seems particularly weak.

Instead, other reasons justify these exemptions (and other exceptions) to the hearsay rule: necessity, fairness, and reliability. Necessity stems from the fact that individuals, corporations, and other institutional entities conduct their affairs through authorized representatives, agents, and employees. These persons constitute a primary source of information about corporate activities. Such information is necessary to impose liability on corporate and institutional entities. And, as a matter of substantive law, individual and corporate or institutional parties are legally responsible for the activities of their authorized representatives, employees, and agents. It is probably essential for the proper functioning of this liability scheme for these declarants' statements to be admissible against principals and employers.

Permitting the use of hearsay statements by these representatives, agents and employees can also be justified on grounds of fairness. If proponents cannot use this hearsay, they would either have to call the declarants as hostile witnesses or forgo the information altogether if the declarant has disappeared. Parties gain advantages by being able to conduct their business affairs through their representatives, agents, and employees. Moreover, third parties rely on statements of these people when doing business with the principal. The advantages obtained and the reliance incurred make it seem fair to place some burden of accountability for such out-of-court statements onto the principal. When an agent's hearsay is admitted under subsection (D), the principal is not irrevocably bound by it but does bear the burden of contesting its reliability, if the principal does not want the jury to use it. While it may be difficult for the principal to obtain the information necessary to explore weaknesses in the declarant's statement, the principal is probably better able to do so, and to do so more efficiently, than the proponent of the statement.

In addition, the foundational requirements of FRE 801(d)(2)(C) and (D) generate some inferences about the reliability of the declarants' testimonial qualities. To state the strongest case, if a statement is authorized, it may be reasonable to infer that the principal selected a trustworthy and reliable spokesperson. Second, if a statement is authorized or is about a matter central to the activities of the agent, the declarant may have a solid basis for making the statement, and if central, the statement would also be made carefully and accurately. Third, if the declarant is an agent at the time of the statement, it may be inferred that the declarant is loyal to the interests of the principal and would not lie to injure the principal and risk termination.

c. Personal Knowledge and Lay Opinions

Many courts dispense with the personal knowledge requirement and the lay opinion rule under FRE 801(C) and (D) as well as (A) and (B). It is thus possible to admit a representative's or agent's conclusory statement that is based only on hearsay and rumor. This puts the principal under a heavy burden of disproving the reliability of the statement. Abandoning the personal knowledge requirement for a party's own admissions under subsection (A) may be justified because parties can disprove their own out-of-court statements by establishing their own lack of firsthand knowledge. But the principal may not be so easily able to show lack of firsthand knowledge in an employee's statement, especially in a far-flung corporate context and particularly if the employee is not available. Again, necessity and fairness must justify abandoning the personal knowledge requirement. Abandoning the requirement means that more hearsay will be admitted and that corporate parties will bear the burden of attacking its reliability and suffer the consequences of being unable to do so. Do you think that this result strikes the proper balance between necessity and fairness?

d. Admissions by Government Employees

When can statements made by government employees be offered against the government in civil or criminal cases? Some courts adhere to the traditional common law position that the answer is never, based on the rationale that no individual can bind the sovereign. Courts adhere to this principle in criminal cases. United States v. Evans, 1990 WL 32581 (6th Cir. 1990) (excluding testimony about an out-of-court statement made by the assistant U.S. Attorney on the case to the effect that Evans did not have the requisite intent to be guilty of the crime charged); United States v. Yildiz, 355 F.3d 80, 82 (2d Cir. 2004) (out-of-court statements of a government informant are not admissible in a criminal trial under FRE 801(d)(2)(D)). But some courts have admitted statements of prosecutors made in court and in pleadings. United States v. Bakshinian, 65 F. Supp. 2d 1104, 1106 (C.D. Cal. 1999) (prosecutors have the power to bind the sovereign and are not disinterested in the outcome).

In civil cases, government manuals, sworn affidavits submitted to a judge, depositions and prior testimony given by government employees have been admitted under subsection (D). Timber Products Co. v. United States, 2010 U.S. Claims LEXIS 5 (Fed. Cl. 2010) (prior testimony by a litigation coordinator for the Forest Service concerning the Service's decisionmaking process admissible against the government under (D) in a suit for breach of contract by the Service). In C & H Commercial Contractors v. United States, 35 Fed. Cl. 246, 256 (1996), a highly relevant memorandum by a government contracting officer that recited damaging representations made by government officials to a private contractor was admitted under subsection (D) without hesitation.

12. Explanation of FRE 801(d)(2)(E): Co-conspirators' Admissions

a. Preliminary Factfinding

The foundational requirements for coconspirators' admissions are:

- the declarant and the party against whom the statement is offered were both members of the same conspiracy;
- the statement was made during the conspiracy; and
- the statement was made in furtherance of the conspiracy.

The typical coconspirator statement is offered by the government against a criminal defendant to prove that defendant's criminal conduct. The recorded statement by Moore in the false partnership tax return hypothetical would not be admissible against Day under subsection (E), even if the government had evidence that Moore and Day were co-conspirators. Statements made to tax investigators, after the tax return has been filed, would not be considered to be made *during* or *in furtherance of* a conspiracy.

Consider also the following example, which is a typical situation in which the government seeks to use subsection (E):

A government informer has infiltrated a drug-selling ring. He speaks and works only with a few people involved in the ring, and never sees or talks to the boss. The people he deals with, however, make many statements about the boss, such as "he gets the best stuff" or "he sold this for $100 per gram." These out-of-court statements, if true, are evidence of the boss's drug-selling activities.

If the boss is charged with selling drugs and with conspiracy to sell drugs, may the informant testify that the out-of-court statements about the boss were made by the various "small fry" in the drug ring?

Proof of Comembership.   First, the proponent of a co-conspirator's statement under FRE 801(d)(2)(E) must prove that a conspiracy existed and that both the declarant (the "small fry") and the party (the boss) were its members. Membership in a conspiracy requires a meeting of the minds to join an enterprise with others with the aim of accomplishing a specific criminal purpose, sometimes phrased as "specific intent to further a common objective . . . and knowing and voluntary participation." The conspirators do not have to have contact with, or ever know, all of the other conspirators, but "[n]o one can join a conspiracy without knowledge of its existence . . . [and] the aim to forward or assist" it. United States v. Garcia-Torres, 280 F.3d 1, 4 (1st Cir. 2002). A conspiracy can be "a joint venture for an illegal purpose, or for a legal purpose using illegal means." United States v. Gil, 604 F.2d 546, 549 (7th Cir. 1979). There does not have to be a formal charge of conspiracy for the co-conspirators' statements exception to apply. Indeed, the exception is not limited to use in criminal prosecutions. As a practical matter, however, the exception is most frequently invoked by prosecutors in criminal cases. Our discussion here reflects this common usage.

During the Course of the Conspiracy.   Statements made to the government informant in the drug ring example will satisfy this requirement if the conspiracy was ongoing when they were made. Statements made prior to a defendant's joining the conspiracy may not be used to prove the defendant's participation, but may be admissible to show the nature of the illegal enterprise and its preparations. United States v. Segura-Gallegos, 41 F.3d 1266 (9th Cir. 1994). And statements about events that occurred prior to the defendant's joining a conspiracy are admissible so long as these events were part of a "single, overarching" conspiracy and not multiple, independent conspiracies. United States v. Handlin, 366 F.3d 584, 591 (7th Cir. 2004). A defendant must affirmatively withdraw from a conspiracy for statements of co-conspirators no longer to be admissible against him. United States v. Robinson, 390 F.3d 853, 882 (6th Cir. 2004) (arrest or incarceration does not qualify as affirmative withdrawal).

The principal issue with respect to the *during* requirement is whether it extends to statements made in the so-called concealment phase of the conspiracy, after the objectives of the conspiracy have been either met or thwarted. If the conspiracy is terminated, it is usually by arrest or failure. United States v. Osorio-Soto, 139 F.3d 913 (10th Cir. 1998) (DEA's seizure of illegal drugs ended the conspiracy because it was no longer possible to achieve its objectives). If statements made during a police investigation or after an arrest cast blame on others, perhaps the declarant is lying in order to shift the blame away from him- or herself. There is a greater likelihood that each co-conspirator will be primarily concerned with self-protection. The majority position is that statements made during this phase are not within the scope of the exemption, as was true regarding Moore's recorded statement to the tax investigator. Osorio-Soto, id. (statements made to conceal criminal conduct after the conspiracy's objectives have either failed or been achieved are not admissible under the co-conspirator exception).

But if some activities of the conspiracy are still ongoing, and can be covered up, statements in furtherance of those concealment activities may be admissible. United States v. Gajo, 290 F.3d 922, 928 (7th Cir. 2002) ("concealment is . . . one of the main criminal objectives of an arson-for-profit scheme because it facilitates the primary objective of fraudulently acquiring insurance proceeds"); United States v. Urrego-Linares, 879 F.2d 1234, 1240 (4th Cir. 1989) (statements by co-conspirator on a monitored telephone call to the defendant who had already been arrested held to still be in the course of the conspiracy).

In Furtherance of the Conspiracy.   Statements that further the common objectives of the conspiracy, or set in motion transactions that are part of it, will satisfy the "in furtherance" requirement. Statements naming the drug ring boss in order to secure a sale, or to confirm lines of command, seem to further the goals of the illegal enterprise. "Idle chatter" and statements among conspirators that merely narrate past events have been held not to satisfy the requirement. United States v. Cornett, 195 F.3d 776, 783 (5th Cir. 1999). But statements that inform new conspirators, or keep co-conspirators informed, of significant events and problems have been held admissible, even though they do not actually further the enterprise. United States v. Jefferson, 215 F.3d 820, 823 (8th Cir. 2000) (conversations among three alleged co-conspirators concerning their botched attempt to murder their target by arson, and the resulting deaths of five others, admitted as "in furtherance"). Statements to customers, and to outsiders from whom the co-conspirator seeks help, may or may not further the conspiracy. In United States v. Urbanik, 801 F.2d 692 (4th Cir. 1986), casual conversation about weightlifting followed a drug purchase, during which the seller described the defendant to the buyer both as an excellent weightlifter and as the supplier of drugs. This was held not admissible against defendant because it was not in furtherance of the conspiracy. In United States v. Lee, 374 F.3d 637 (8th Cir. 2004), a co-conspirator's confession of murder to his brother (not a co-conspirator) to enlist his aid in selling weapons stolen from the murder victim was admitted as in furtherance of the conspiracy to use ill-gotten proceeds to fund a white supremacist group. Similarly, a co-conspirator's statement to a person not participating in the conspiracy was held admissible after it was shown to be instrumental to attaining the conspiracy's goal: United States v. Gupta, 747 F.3d 111, 125 (2d Cir. 2014). Moreover, a court's finding on a preponderance of the evidence that a statement was made in furtherance of the conspiracy will not be overturned on appeal unless it is clearly erroneous, which cannot be said about a statement that could be interpreted both ways. Id. at 124.

b. Justification for the Admissibility of Co-conspirators' Statements

One largely artificial rationale for the co-conspirator exemption is that each co-conspirator authorizes (or is deemed to have authorized) the statements of other co-conspirators.

A more practical rationale is necessity: Conspiracies tend to be secret enterprises. The criminal activities, particularly of the leadership, are very difficult to prove. Some of the best evidence—and perhaps essential evidence if a prosecutor is to prove a defendant's guilt beyond a reasonable doubt—will be statements about the conduct of other co-conspirators. Thus, it is arguably appropriate to burden a person who chooses to engage in a conspiracy or an ongoing criminal enterprise (particularly, as an organizer or leader) with the risk that false or inaccurate co-conspirators' statements will be used against him or her.

One should consider another, somewhat speculative, reliability rationale for the exception. Arguably, when the "*during*" and "*in furtherance*" requirements are taken seriously, co-conspirators' statements tend to be trustworthy because they advance the interest of the speaker in the success of the criminal enterprise.

13. Elaboration on FRE 801(d)(2)(E): Applying FRE 104 to the Co-conspirator Exemption

Since it is the co-conspirator relationship that justifies the admission of co-conspirator hearsay, much attention has been paid to the process of proving this relationship.

a. Bourjaily v. United States

In 1987, the Supreme Court held in Bourjaily v. United States, 483 U.S. 171 (1987), that all of the preliminary facts necessary to admit hearsay under FRE 801(d)(2)(E), including the co-conspirator relationship, are FRE 104(a) questions for the judge to decide by a preponderance of the evidence. The judge will *not* instruct the jury to decide the relationship issue as a necessary precondition to using the statement for its truth. This conclusion seems to be quite sound. The foundational question of co-membership in a conspiracy is a hearsay policy issue, not a relevance issue. Thus, *Bourjaily*'s adoption of the FRE 104(a) test for deciding this question appears desirable.

Bourjaily also held that it is appropriate for the judge to consider the content of the hearsay statement itself in deciding whether the foundational requirements have been satisfied:

> Rule 104(a) provides: "In making its [preliminary fact] determination [the court] is not bound by the rules of evidence except those with respect to privileges." Similarly, Rule 1101(d)(1) states that the Rules of Evidence (other than with respect to privileges) shall not apply to "[t]he determination of questions of fact preliminary to admissibility of evidence when the issue is to be determined by the court under rule 104." . . . The Rule on its face allows the trial judge to consider any evidence whatsoever, bound only by the rules of privilege . . . .

It is sufficient for today to hold that a court, in making a preliminary factual determination under Rule 801(d)(2)(E), may examine the hearsay statements sought to be admitted. As we have held in other cases concerning admissibility determinations, "the judge should receive the evidence and give it such weight as his judgment and experience counsel." [Id. at 178-81.]

Bourjaily's decision that the hearsay statement itself may "bootstrap" the statement's admissibility is reasonable and consistent with the terms of FRE 104(a). But since there may be reasons to distrust the reliability of alleged co-conspirators' statements, it may well be that it would be unwise to rely on *nothing* but the statement at issue to establish the foundational requirement of the party's membership in the conspiracy. Arguably, the statement must receive corroboration from other evidence, but the Court found it unnecessary to consider this argument in *Bourjaily*.

b. The Amendment to FRE 801(d)(2): The Requirement of Additional Evidence

Later on, the Supreme Court promulgated an amendment, effective in December 1997, that added the following language to FRE 801(d)(2):

The statement must be considered but does not by itself establish the declarant's authority under (C); the existence or scope of the relationship under (D); or the existence of the conspiracy or participation in it under (E).

This language does not specify what kind of additional proof is needed, nor how much. Most courts post-*Bourjaily* had required some additional evidence from a source *independent* of the co-conspirator's hearsay statement to corroborate the defendant's membership in the conspiracy. The Advisory Committee Note to the amendment, however, appears to contemplate that evidence of the identity of the speaker and the context in which statement was made, as well as corroboration, might suffice. As we have noted previously, the requirement of additional evidence also applies to the key foundational issues under subsections (C) and (D) as well.

Prior to this amendment, courts found the requirement of independent evidence to be satisfied by behavior of the defendant that established a connection to the conspiracy: the defendant's own statements or statements of others that the defendant adopts; presence at locations where the co-conspirator said the defendant would be; attempts to silence the victim of the conspiracy; frequent phone or other contact with co-conspirators; or presence at drug deliveries. "Mere association" was held to be insufficient evidence of membership, but repeated meetings that coincide with large-scale drug deliveries were held sufficient. United States v. Ammar, 714 F.2d 238, 250 (3d Cir. 1983).

Reported cases since the amendment have continued to enforce the requirement of evidence corroborating the defendant's participation in the conspiracy's activities. "The quantum of independent evidence needed to corroborate the existence of a conspiracy necessarily is dependent on the totality of circumstances, including the strength of the hearsay statements themselves." United States v. Abu-Jihaad, 531 F. Supp. 2d 289, 296 (D. Conn. 1998). Here, the court found no independent evidence of the formation of the conspiracy prior to the co-conspirator statements offered against the defendant and wrote: "[T]his case is precisely what [those] requirements are designed to catch." Id. at 289.

Examples of cases in which independent corroboration has been found include: United States v. Sudeen, 434 F.3d 385 (5th Cir. 2005) (co-conspirator received and deposited a check for defendant, received a commission from defendant, and explained delays to defendant's customers); United States v. Capelton, 350 F.3d 231 (1st Cir. 2003) (defendant possessed marked bills from drug transaction and was on the scene during the transaction); United States v. Stotts, 323 F.3d 520 (7th Cir. 2003) (defendant accompanied brother, who actually sold the drugs, to and from the sale, gestured for the buyer to follow him in her car, and nodded in agreement for her to inspect the drugs before paying).

c. Process for Admission of a Co-conspirator's Statement

It is well settled that the trial court has discretion to use the tool of conditional admissibility with respect to a co-conspirator's statements. "A court may conditionally admit a challenged statement subject to later proof to satisfy the co-conspirator rule and defer a final ruling on admissibility until after hearing the relevant evidence." United States v. Roach, 164 F.3d 403, 409 (8th Cir. 1998). Should the judge give any instruction to the jury when conditionally admitting the co-conspirator's statement? The judge could say something like, "I am provisionally admitting these hearsay statements pursuant to what is called the co-conspirator admission provision. If the prosecutor does not introduce sufficient independent evidence of the existence of a conspiracy, I may ask you later to disregard these hearsay statements." Would this be a good idea? What are the risks?

However, once a judge has conditionally admitted a co-conspirator's statement, the judge may be reluctant to find that the FRE 104(a) preliminary fact standard has not been satisfied. Such a finding would require the judge either to instruct the jury to disregard the co-conspirator's statement or to declare a mistrial. The instruction to disregard is not a realistic solution in many cases. Can the jury be expected to be able to obey it? And because the prosecutor will have presented all—or at least a substantial part—of the state's case before it becomes clear that the foundational requirements cannot be satisfied, the mistrial alternative will frequently be quite expensive. For these reasons, it may be wise for the judge to insist on proof of the foundational facts before proof of the co-conspirator's statement. United States v. Saneaux, 365 F. Supp. 2d 493, 502 (S.D.N.Y. 2005) (paucity of government's proof that statements were "in furtherance" at motion in limine held to preclude conditional admission; government should place before the jury all evidence it relies on to satisfy the required foundation before jury may hear the recorded co-conspirator statements).

KEY POINTS

1. Under FRE 801(d)(2)(A), any statement made out of court by a party may be used against that party to prove the truth of the matter it asserts, so long as it is relevant and not otherwise objectionable.

2. FRE 801(d)(2) also provides a hearsay exemption for: (B) statements about which the party manifests adoption or belief their truth; (C) statements authorized by the party; (D) certain statements made by an agent or employee of the party during the relationship on matters within the scope of the agent's employment; and (E) certain statements made by a co-conspirator of the party during and in furtherance of the conspiracy.

3. The judge must be persuaded, pursuant to FRE 104(a), that the foundational requirements for each of these exemptions are satisfied. The judge may use the statement itself in deciding the preliminary questions, but other evidence is necessary as well to find authority, the existence or scope of the agency or employment, and the existence of and participation in a conspiracy.

4. The primary justification for the FRE 801(d)(2) exemptions is that the party cannot fairly complain about the loss of cross-examination of the declarant because the party can explain the unreliability in the statement, or because it is necessary and fair to impose on the party the risk and burden of not being able to do so.

PROBLEMS

8.37. Return to Problem 3.3, United States v. Ray, at page 149. The prosecution offers the following evidence. Defense counsel objects to each piece of evidence as hearsay. How should the court rule?

(a) A Rundown V.P. to testify: "On March 15, 2015, Bernard Ray said to me that he had just read a memo from his auditor, Andrews, and Rundown stock was going to take a beating."

(b) A senior VP at Andrews's accounting firm to testify: "On March 16, 2015, I spoke with Bernard Ray at our club. I said, 'Bernard, I hear that Rundown is going to project big losses in a few days. I assume you've already dumped most of your holdings.' Then Bernard said, 'Don't worry about me—I'm all set.'"

(c) The prosecution offers an authenticated copy of the March 14, 2015 outside auditor's memo to prove that Andrews in fact projected Rundown losses for the second quarter of 2015.

8.38. Daniel Mahlandt has sued the Wild Canid Survival & Research Center, Inc. and its director of education, Kenneth Poos, for injuries sustained when Daniel was allegedly bitten by a wolf named Sophie. Sophie was owned by the Center but lived temporarily at the Poos home. She was enclosed in the yard by a five-foot chain link fence and was chained to the fence with a six-foot-long chain. Daniel, who was three-and-a-half years old at the time of the alleged biting, was found bleeding and hysterical inside the yard with Sophie. There were no eyewitnesses as to how Daniel got into the yard or whether Sophie bit him. One witness testified that she heard a child's screams and observed Daniel on the ground with Sophie straddling him. Sophie's face was near Daniel's, and Sophie was wailing. Kenneth Poos's son found Daniel and carried him into the house.

Kenneth Poos will testify that Sophie had been hand raised by humans since birth, has been very gentle, and that he takes her to various schools and institutions as part of his educational program for the Center. A defense witness, an expert on animal behavior, will testify that when a wolf licks a child's face, that is a sign of care; that a wolf's wail is a sign of compassion; and that Daniel's particular injuries were not consistent with a wolf attack.

Mr. Poos arrived at his home shortly after the incident. After seeing that Daniel was taken to a hospital, Mr. Poos talked to his son about what happened and then went to the Center to report the incident to the Center's president. The president was not in, so Mr. Poos left the following note on his door: "Please call me at home. Sophie bit a child that came into our backyard. All has been taken care of. I need to convey to you what happened. KP." Several weeks later there was a meeting of the Board of Directors of the Center. Mr. Poos was not present. The minutes of that meeting state that there was a "great deal of discussion about the incident of Sophie biting the child and its legal aspects." Plaintiff has offered into evidence against both Mr. Poos and against the Center (a) the note written by Mr. Poos and (b) the foregoing passage from the minutes of the board meeting. Both defendants have objected on hearsay grounds to the admission of both pieces of evidence. With respect to each defendant, what result?

8.39. Tom Hay went to the emergency room (ER) complaining of chest pains and excessive sweating. Standard ER tests were run by Dr. Gatwick. These tests ruled out a recent heart attack but did not rule out cardiovascular disease as the cause of his symptoms. Two weeks later Hay suffered a heart attack and died.

Plaintiff, Hay's wife Barbara, has filed suit against Dr. Gatwick for medical malpractice seeking damages for her loss of consortium and support. It is agreed that the prevailing standard of care is that Gatwick should have advised Hay, his patient, to agree to enter the hospital for observation and additional tests. There is evidence suggesting that Hay's heart disease might have been treatable had it been discovered by further tests that can be administered only to a hospitalized patient. Gatwick asserts that he gave the required advice, and that Hay left the hospital that day *against* medical advice.

At trial, Plaintiff testifies that she arrived at the ER as Hay was leaving, and that Hay said, "The doctor told me that I was lucky and could safely leave." She further testifies that Gatwick was standing close enough that, in her opinion, he could have heard Hay's statement. Is Plaintiff's testimony admissible?

8.40. The United States is suing the Sheriff of Paxton County, Virginia, for refusing to consider women for a deputy sheriff (patrol) position in violation of Title VII, 42 U.S.C. §§2000 et seq. The government offered the testimony of an equal opportunity employment investigator who was investigating complaints against the Sheriff. The investigator recited the contents of a conversation with Mr. Giana, the county attorney who was representing the Sheriff regarding the discrimination claim:

> Mr. Giana: "The sheriff wants big tall men for that job [patrolman], that could defend themselves and be somewhat imposing. Females don't have a chance in this position."

Are Mr. Giana's statements admissible against the Sheriff?

8.41. Return to Problem 4.5 on page 208. The prosecution wants to argue that Bonds authorized his trainer, Greg Anderson, to speak to the BALCO lab on his behalf. Recall that when Anderson delivered urine samples to BALCO, he allegedly told Valente that the samples were from Barry Bonds. The government concedes that it cannot prove that Bonds gave specific authority to Anderson, but that by allowing Anderson to have the samples tested, Bonds *impliedly* authorized Anderson to identify them to BALCO. What do you think of this argument? Could any section of FRE 801(d)(2) be used to admit Anderson's hearsay statements against Bonds?

8.42. Return to Problem 3.2, Pedroso v. Driver, on page 148. Paul's mother testifies for plaintiffs that Paul's teacher told her, several weeks after the accident, that Driver's supervisor had told the teacher that, in his opinion, Driver was not keeping a proper lookout before the accident. Defendants object on grounds of hearsay. Admissible?

8.43. Plaintiff, an African American employee of Johnson Welding, filed an EEOC complaint for hostile work environment on the job. After the complaint was filed, plaintiff contends, the company retaliated by intentionally isolating him from other employees, instructing them not to talk with him, and moving plaintiff's work station to the "back" of the welding facility. After trial, the jury awarded plaintiff both compensatory and punitive damages. On appeal, Johnson Welding claims error in the admission of testimony by one of plaintiff's witnesses, Alan Mason. Mason was a coworker of plaintiff at Johnson Welding. Mason testified as follows:

> At a barbecue at my home, my brother-in-law, David, made a statement to me. David works at Johnson also. David said that Tom (plaintiff's supervisor) told David that "some bad stuff is going to happen in the back" and that "David should tell Mason that he should stay out of it unless he wants to be fired."

Plaintiff claims this testimony was relevant to show Johnson Welding's vindictive state of mind toward him and that its treatment of him was retaliatory. Was it error to admit Mason's testimony?

8.44. Seven members of the Gangster Disciples (GD), a street gang (6,000 members) that operated a massive drug distribution business in the Chicago area, are being prosecuted for drug, weapons, and money-laundering offenses. The leader of the GD is known to be Larry Hoover, who for years ran the gang from inside of various prisons. His female partner owned a legitimate business called Save the Children Promotions. In an authorized IRS search of the Save the Children offices, agents found a document in a folder marked "L.H./Sr." The document was a list describing the hierarchical and territorial organization of the entire GD operation. In some taped conversations, Hoover had mentioned his desire to develop such a document to keep track of gang members and their payments to GD. All seven defendants are mentioned in the list. On what basis can they object to admission of the list against them at trial? What result?

8.45. In the prosecution of a wealthy show horse owner for insurance fraud, the government seeks to prove that the owner conspired to have one of his horses, Charisma, killed in order to collect insurance proceeds. The person who was hired to kill Charisma, Burns, was hired by Marty, the owner's horse trainer, and told that "the owner wanted it done on December 15 because he was in Asia, and because Charisma was scheduled to travel from New York to Florida on December 16." Marty paid Burns to do the job. Can the government use Burns's testimony about Marty's statements against the owner? Suppose that the government has independent proof that the owner was indeed in Asia on December 15, and that Charisma was scheduled to travel to Florida on December 16? What result? Suppose that the government can also prove that, after Charisma's death, the owner intentionally lied to the insurance company about who was allowed to ride Charisma, in order to avoid one of the insurance policy's exceptions?

D. HEARSAY EXCEPTIONS NOT REQUIRING THE UNAVAILABILITY OF THE DECLARANT

FRE 803 excepts 23 different types of hearsay statements from the general rule of exclusion. There is no requirement in this rule that the declarant be unavailable to testify as a witness. Thus, the justifications for admitting this much hearsay are especially important for your overall evaluation of the hearsay rule in practice. Some of the FRE 803 exceptions are legacies of almost 300 years of common law development and are rarely used in modern federal litigation. We will focus primarily on the exceptions that are most used today.

The premise of all FRE 803 exceptions is that these types of statements are reliable enough to be used in the jury's factfinding even without cross-examination of the declarant by the opponent. In the words of the Advisory Committee Note, these kinds of statements "possess circumstantial guarantees of trustworthiness sufficient to justify nonproduction of the declarant in person at the trial even though he may be available." This means that something about the hearsay statement—its content, its source, the circumstances in which it was made—reveals something "trustworthy" about the declarant's testimonial qualities. This is the "reliability approach" to the admission of hearsay that we already saw at work in FRE 801(a) and (c) and in the FRE 801(d) exemptions as well.

Nearly all of the Rule 803 exceptions are categorical. They each define a specific type of out-of-court statement that may be admitted for the truth of the matter it asserts, and they each identify preliminary facts that the proponent must satisfy pursuant to the process described above in Section B. Again, the preliminary facts required to establish the applicability of a hearsay exception (or an exception to the exception) are FRE 104(a) questions. They are facts upon which the application of an evidence exclusion rule depends, and the party asserting the rule (or exception) must convince the judge by a preponderance of the evidence that the required facts are probably true.

In this section, we will examine the required preliminary facts and the reliability rationales underlying the more important FRE 803 exceptions. Remember that even if a hearsay statement fits within a Rule 803 exception, other rules may operate to exclude it: the best evidence rule, the character evidence prohibitions, privilege, and, of course, FRE 403, may all have to be applied as well.

Two other general points apply to all Rule 803 (and Rule 804) exceptions. Because the declarant's statement is offered for its truth, the declarant is a source of knowledge for the jury, analogous to a witness testifying at trial. Therefore, the fundamental requirement that witnesses must speak from personal knowledge applies as well to hearsay declarants under most of the FRE 803 and FRE 804 hearsay exceptions. The Advisory Committee Note to Rule 803 makes this clear:

> In a hearsay situation, the declarant is, of course, a witness, and neither this rule nor Rule 804 dispenses with the requirement of firsthand knowledge. It may appear from his statement or be inferable from circumstances. See Rule 602.

In addition, the opponent to an item of hearsay can attack the credibility of hearsay declarants in most of the ways that witnesses can be attacked. FRE 806 makes this clear:

RULE 806. ATTACKING AND SUPPORTING THE DECLARANT'S CREDIBILITY

When a hearsay statement—or a statement described in Rule 801(d)(2)(C), (D), or (E)—has been admitted in evidence, the declarant's credibility may be attacked, and then supported, by any evidence that would be admissible for those purposes if the declarant had testified as a witness. The court may admit evidence of the declarant's inconsistent statement or conduct, regardless of when it occurred or whether the declarant had an opportunity to explain or deny it. If the party against whom the statement was admitted calls the declarant as a witness, the party may examine the declarant on the statement as if on cross-examination.

It is more difficult, of course, to impeach a hearsay declarant without the tool of cross-examination. Issues regarding impeachment under FRE 806 are discussed in Margaret Meriwether Cordray, Evidence Rule 806 and the Problem of Impeaching the Nontestifying Declarant, 56 Ohio St. L.J. 495 (1995).

1. FRE 803

RULE 803. EXCEPTIONS TO THE RULE AGAINST HEARSAY—REGARDLESS OF WHETHER THE DECLARANT IS AVAILABLE AS A WITNESS

The following are not excluded by the rule against hearsay, regardless of whether the declarant is available as a witness:

(1) *Present Sense Impression.* A statement describing or explaining an event or condition, made while or immediately after the declarant perceived it.

(2) *Excited Utterance.* A statement relating to a startling event or condition, made while the declarant was under the stress of excitement that it caused.

(3) *Then-Existing Mental, Emotional, or Physical Condition.* A statement of the declarant's then-existing state of mind (such as motive, intent, or plan)

or emotional, sensory, or physical condition (such as mental feeling, pain, or bodily health), but not including a statement of memory or belief to prove the fact remembered or believed unless it relates to the validity or terms of the declarant's will.

(4) *Statement Made for Medical Diagnosis or Treatment.* A statement that:

(A) is made for—and is reasonably pertinent to—medical diagnosis or treatment; and

(B) describes medical history; past or present symptoms or sensations; their inception; or their general cause.

(5) *Recorded Recollection.* A record that:

(A) is on a matter the witness once knew about but now cannot recall well enough to testify fully and accurately;

(B) was made or adopted by the witness when the matter was fresh in the witness's memory; and

(C) accurately reflects the witness's knowledge.

If admitted, the record may be read into evidence but may be received as an exhibit only if offered by an adverse party.

(6) *Records of a Regularly Conducted Activity.* A record of an act, event, condition, opinion, or diagnosis if:

(A) the record was made at or near the time by—or from information transmitted by—someone with knowledge;

(B) the record was kept in the course of a regularly conducted activity of a business, organization, occupation, or calling, whether or not for profit;

(C) making the record was a regular practice of that activity;

(D) all these conditions are shown by the testimony of the custodian or another qualified witness, or by a certification that complies with Rule 902(11) or (12) or with a statute permitting certification; and

(E) the opponent does not show that the source of information or the method or circumstances of preparation indicate a lack of trustworthiness.

(7) *Absence of a Record of a Regularly Conducted Activity.* Evidence that a matter is not included in a record described in paragraph (6) if:

(A) the evidence is admitted to prove that the matter did not occur or exist;

(B) a record was regularly kept for a matter of that kind; and

(C) the opponent does not show that the possible source of the information or other circumstances indicate a lack of trustworthiness.

(8) *Public Records.* A record or statement of a public office if:

(A) it sets out:

(i) the office's activities;

(ii) a matter observed while under a legal duty to report, but not including, in a criminal case, a matter observed by law-enforcement personnel; or

(iii) in a civil case or against the government in a criminal case, factual findings from a legally authorized investigation; and

(B) the opponent does not show that the source of information or other circumstances indicate a lack of trustworthiness.

(9) *Public Records of Vital Statistics.* A record of a birth, death, or marriage, if reported to a public office in accordance with a legal duty.

(10) *Absence of a Public Record.* Testimony—or a certification under Rule 902—that a diligent search failed to disclose a public record or statement if the testimony or certification is admitted to prove that:

(A) the record or statement does not exist; or

(B) a matter did not occur or exist, if a public office regularly kept a record or statement for a matter of that kind.

(11) *Records of Religious Organizations Concerning Personal or Family History.* A statement of birth, legitimacy, ancestry, marriage, divorce, death, relationship by blood or marriage, or similar facts of personal or family history, contained in a regularly kept record of a religious organization.

(12) *Certificates of Marriage, Baptism, and Similar Ceremonies.* A statement of fact contained in a certificate:

(A) made by a person who is authorized by a religious organization or by law to perform the act certified;

(B) attesting that the person performed a marriage or similar ceremony or administered a sacrament; and

(C) purporting to have been issued at the time of the act or within a reasonable time after it.

(13) *Family Records.* A statement of fact about personal or family history contained in a family record, such as a Bible, genealogy, chart, engraving on a ring, inscription on a portrait, or engraving on an urn or burial marker.

(14) *Records of Documents That Affect an Interest in Property.* The record of a document that purports to establish or affect an interest in property if:

(A) the record is admitted to prove the content of the original recorded document, along with its signing and its delivery by each person who purports to have signed it;

(B) the record is kept in a public office; and

(C) a statute authorizes recording documents of that kind in that office.

(15) *Statements in Documents That Affect an Interest in Property.* A statement contained in a document that purports to establish or affect an interest in property if the matter stated was relevant to the document's purpose—unless later dealings with the property are inconsistent with the truth of the statement or the purport of the document.

(16) *Statements in Ancient Documents.* A statement in a document that is at least 20 years old and whose authenticity is established.

(17) *Market Reports and Similar Commercial Publications.* Market quotations, lists, directories, or other compilations that are generally relied on by the public or by persons in particular occupations.

(18) *Statements in Learned Treatises, Periodicals, or Pamphlets.* A statement contained in a treatise, periodical, or pamphlet if:

(A) the statement is called to the attention of an expert witness on cross-examination or relied on by the expert on direct examination; and

(B) the publication is established as a reliable authority by the expert's admission or testimony, by another expert's testimony, or by judicial notice.

If admitted, the statement may be read into evidence but not received as an exhibit.

(19) *Reputation Concerning Personal or Family History.* A reputation among a person's family by blood, adoption, or marriage—or among a person's associates or in the community—concerning the person's birth, adoption, legitimacy, ancestry, marriage, divorce, death, relationship by blood, adoption, or marriage, or similar facts of personal or family history.

(20) *Reputation Concerning Boundaries or General History.* A reputation in a community—arising before the controversy—concerning boundaries of land in the community or customs that affect the land, or concerning general historical events important to that community, state, or nation.

(21) *Reputation Concerning Character.* A reputation among a person's associates or in the community concerning the person's character.

(22) *Judgment of a Previous Conviction.* Evidence of a final judgment of conviction if:

(A) the judgment was entered after a trial or guilty plea, but not a nolo contendere plea;

(B) the conviction was for a crime punishable by death or by imprisonment for more than a year;

(C) the evidence is admitted to prove any fact essential to the judgment; and

(D) when offered by the prosecutor in a criminal case for a purpose other than impeachment, the judgment was against the defendant.

The pendency of an appeal may be shown but does not affect admissibility.

(23) *Judgments Involving Personal, Family, or General History or a Boundary.* A judgment that is admitted to prove a matter of personal, family, or general history, or boundaries, if the matter:

(A) was essential to the judgment; and

(B) could be proved by evidence of reputation.

2. Explanation of FRE 803(1): Present Sense Impression

There are two exceptions that provide for the admission of two different kinds of spontaneous hearsay statements—present sense impressions and excited utterances. The categorical requirements for each are somewhat different. FRE 803(1) provides:

(1) *Present Sense Impression.* A statement describing or explaining an event or condition, made while or immediately after the declarant perceived it.

a. Preliminary Factfinding

The factual requirements for present sense impressions are:

- the occurrence of an event or condition;
- the contents of the statement describe or explain the event or condition; and
- the declarant made the statement while or immediately after perceiving the event or condition.

Think back to the first illustration of an out-of-court statement that we used in this chapter. We found that Sally's statement "the gray SUV ran the red light and hit a pedestrian" would be hearsay, if reported by George at trial. But Sally's statement might have been made to George either while Sally was seeing the SUV, or within seconds or minutes of seeing it. Thus, it might be admissible hearsay, if it qualifies as a present sense impression. The pedestrian, the proponent of the statement, must present evidence to show that it falls within the categorical terms of FRE 803(1). These are preliminary questions for the judge to determine pursuant to FRE 104(a). The court should be convinced by a preponderance of the evidence that there was an event occurring just before Sally's statement was made, and that Sally's statement describes it.

Many present sense impressions are presented in court through the testimony of witnesses who also perceived the event or condition themselves. If George saw the accident, he would be able to provide evidence showing that the event occurred and that Sally made the statement contemporaneously with it. The judge could then determine whether the statement describes or explains the event or condition from the contents of the statement itself.

b. Justification for the Admissibility of Present Sense Impressions

The primary justification for admitting present sense impressions is that the contemporaneity of the statement and the event it is offered to prove tends to ensure the declarant's sincerity. This rationale falls squarely within the reliability theory advanced for admitting trustworthy hearsay. It is based on the generalization that, with little or no time passing between statement and event, the statement is spontaneous rather than premeditated. If the statement is spontaneous, there is no time to develop the intent to fabricate. If there is no time or opportunity to fabricate, the statement is probably sincere. Additionally, the contemporaneity of the statement and the event virtually eliminates any memory problem.

3. Explanation of FRE 803(2): Excited Utterance

FRE 803(2) provides:

> (2) *Excited Utterance.* A statement relating to a startling event or condition, made while the declarant was under the stress of excitement that it caused.

a. Preliminary Factfinding

The factual requirements for excited utterances are:

* the occurrence of a startling event or condition;
* the statement relates to the startling event or condition;
* the statement was made by the declarant while under stress of excitement; and
* the stress of excitement was caused by the startling event or condition.

Sally's statement to George might also be an excited utterance. Again, the proponent must present evidence to satisfy the factual requirements, and the judge will decide the preliminary questions pursuant to FRE 104(a). The judge may conclude that an SUV running through a red light and hitting a pedestrian is a *startling* event. Again, George would be the witness to testify that the event occurred and that Sally was under stress of excitement when she made the statement. How might George describe Sally's behavior to prove that she was *under stress of excitement*? George might also establish that Sally's stress was caused by the startling event, if he said, "She was perfectly calm before the accident." In Boucher v. Grant, 74 F. Supp. 2d 444, 450 (D.N.J. 1999), the court held that declarant Grant's hearsay statement was admissible under the following analysis:

> An automobile accident and a contemporaneous statement by an individual involved in that accident concerning its cause undoubtedly satisfy the first three elements of the excited utterance hearsay exception. The question becomes, then, whether the hearsay statements meet the last condition of admissibility, namely, spontaneity. . . .
>
> Boucher testified that his exchange with Grant occurred "within a minute" of the accident . . . Grant himself testified that as a result of the crash, he was "scared . . . shaken up." . . . The brief lapse of time coupled with Grant's mental state cannot give rise to a finding of conscious reflection. Therefore, I conclude that the statement was made while Grant was still in an excited state and before he could reflect and fabricate.

Many factors are relevant to the question of whether the defendant was under stress of excitement from the startling event at the time the statement was made:

> [W]e consider . . . the lapse of time between the startling event and the statement, whether the statement was made in response to an inquiry, the age of the declarant, the physical and mental condition of the declarant, the characteristics of the event, and the subject matter of the statement. [United States v. Wilcox, 487 F.3d 1163, 1170 (8th Cir. 2007).]

b. Justification for the Admissibility of Excited Utterances

The justification for the exception is similar to the argument that present sense impressions are reliable. A statement made under the stress of a startling event or condition is likely to be spontaneous, and a person under stress is not likely to develop the intent to fabricate. If there is no opportunity to fabricate, the statement is likely to be sincere. Notice, however, that there is no requirement of "contemporaneity" between the event and the statement. Stress of excitement is the substitute for contemporaneity. A longer time lag will not defeat application of the FRE 803(2) exception if the declarant remains under stress. So long as stress is continuous from the moment of the startling event, there is assumed to be no opportunity to plan to make a false statement and thus the statement is likely to be sincere. United States v. DeMarce, 564 F.3d 989, 997 (8th Cir. 2009) ("The rationale of the excited utterance exception is that stress of nervous excitement or physical shock stills the reflective faculties, thus removing an impediment to truthfulness."). In *De Marce*, the plaintiff in an attempted sexual assault case initially fabricated a story about tripping in the hallway to explain why she had a bloody lip. Then she returned and told her mother about the attempted assault. The court held that her statements "demonstrate a level of reflection that prohibit their admission as an excited utterance."

Since the duration of the declarant's stress of excitement is likely to be relatively short, memory danger may also be lessened. However, as commentators have long recognized, the stress that decreases the sincerity danger may increase perception dangers and memory dangers, and perhaps even narration dangers as well. Consider the effects of seeing someone hit by a car—how carefully and accurately are you able to perceive and recount the details of such an event? Nonetheless, the exception is well established in the Federal Rules and in most jurisdictions.

Compare the concern for contemporaneity or spontaneity under FRE 803(1) and (2) with the lack of such requirements for statements identifying a person admitted under FRE 801(d)(1)(C). We noted there that application of this exemption to statements not made at lineups and other formal opportunities for reperception, but rather after a lapse of time and in the absence of stress, undermines the potential reliability of such statements.

4. FRE 803(1) and (2): Practical Effects of the Categorical Approach

a. The Categories Determine Admissibility

Do you agree that the probability of Sally's sincerity in making her statement about the gray SUV is increased by the fact that her statement was made contemporaneously with seeing the SUV? Or by the fact that it was made under stress of a startling event? Analyzing this question requires you to think in terms of generalizations about large groups of out-of-court declarants who share either the FRE 803(1) or the FRE 803(2) characteristic in common. How can we be sure that everyone within this large group does have enhanced sincerity? The answer is, we can't be sure. Even more troubling, how do we know that Sally has good eyesight and could perceive the SUV from the distance at which she was standing, or could perceive that the light was red? The answer is, we don't know. The only facts about Sally's testimonial qualities that FRE 803(1) and (2) require to be presented to the jury are the facts about spontaneity that satisfy the categorical requirements of the exceptions.

The effects of this categorical approach are twofold. First, if a statement clearly fits within the broad categorical generalizations of the specific exception, it must be admitted over a hearsay objection, without any case-specific inquiry into its reliability. Except for three specific exceptions that build in a case-by-case reliability inquiry (FRE 803(6), 803(8), and 804(b)(3)), there is no explicit judicial discretion to *exclude* a particular statement that fits within a categorical exception where the judge doubts the sincerity, perception, memory, or narration of the hearsay declarant. Second, and conversely, if a judge thinks that a hearsay statement seems to be particularly trustworthy but it is neither contemporaneous with an event (it was made a day later) nor made under the stress of excitement (it was made calmly), then the judge has no explicit discretion under FRE 803(1) or (2) to admit it. The categorical requirements of each exception determine admissibility. Only FRE 807 permits the *admission* of hearsay based on judicial determinations that it is trustworthy.

b. The Categorical Terms Require Judicial Interpretation

Although there is no explicit discretion in most of the hearsay exceptions, judges do have some leeway when they interpret and apply the categorical terms of the exceptions to particular statements. How long a time lag is permitted by the term "immediately thereafter" in FRE 803(1)? Just what is "stress" in FRE 803(2), and how long does it last? There are no clear-cut answers to these questions in the text of the rule or the case law. You will see in many of the Rule 803 and Rule 804 exceptions that there is considerable room for judicial interpretation. Since the categorical requirements are determinative of admissibility, judicial interpretation of these requirements is crucial to the administration of hearsay policy. These requirements are intended to ensure the trustworthiness of one or more of the declarant's testimonial qualities. It follows that judges should interpret and apply the doctrinal terms with the awareness that different interpretations can either increase or decrease the apparent trustworthiness of admitted hearsay statements.

Time Lapse Between Event and Statement.   Not all seemingly contemporaneous statements are really spontaneous. They might have been thought up in advance, if the declarant had any foreknowledge that the relevant event might occur. And a time lapse of more than a few minutes may be plenty of time to think up something self-serving to say. Particularly if a statement is obviously self-serving, one may doubt its spontaneity and, therefore, its sincerity. Rigorous application of the contemporaneity requirement of FRE 803(1) would reduce this problem. Many courts have interpreted "immediately after" in FRE 803(1) to mean within a matter of seconds, or as soon as is possible. United States v. Shoup, 476 F.3d 38, 42 (1st Cir. 2007) (911 phone call made "only one or two minutes . . . immediately following" event). Some courts, however, have stretched the interpretation of that doctrinal phrase to admit apparently spontaneous statements made 10 to 15 minutes after the event they describe or explain. See, e.g., United States v. Obayagbona, 627 F. Supp. 329 (E.D.N.Y. 1985) (statement made by undercover police officer about a drug transaction, made 14 minutes afterward, "was as spontaneous as possible" since it could not be made until after the arrest.) Courts also look to the context within which the statement was given, and any intervening events. United States v. Ramos, 397 Fed. App'x 767, 771 (3d Cir. 2010) (statement inadmissible when 20 minutes had elapsed between event and statement and declarant was securely detained within police car; requirement of "no time to fabricate or misrepresent" not satisfied).

FRE 803(2) places no specific time restraint on the scope of the exception. The temporal gap is therefore not dispositive, but is a relevant consideration in determining whether the statement is made while the declarant is still under stress. "Our cases do not demand a precise showing of the lapse of time . . . The exception may be based solely on '[t]estimony that the declarant still appeared nervous or distraught and that there was a reasonable basis for continuing [to be] emotional[ly] upset.'" United States v. Davis, 577 F.3d 660, 669 (6th Cir. 2009). Other relevant factors include the characteristics of the event; the subject matter of the statement; whether the statement was made in response to an inquiry; and the declarant's age, motive to lie, and physical and mental condition. In cases where the event is less startling, courts tend to require a shorter time lapse between event and statement.

Statements of young children about incidents of sexual abuse are frequently made hours or even days after the alleged incident occurred. Some courts admit these statements under FRE 803(2) citing various justifications—the "first real opportunity" to speak to an adult or caregiver, or fear and guilt causing child to delay reporting, or lack of capacity to fabricate—while other courts are suspicious of such lengthy delays. Reed v. Thalacker, 198 F.3d 1058, 1062 (8th Cir. 1999) ("distorted recollection . . . can occur through deliberate coaching, inadvertent suggestion, confusion of fact and fantasy, or a simple defect in memory").

Cases involving domestic violence may also justify courts in extending the period of time during which the declarant is under stress: "trauma and anxiety prompted by a spousal assault—which form the predicate for calling something an excited utterance—do not suddenly dissipate when the assailant leaves the scene." United States v. Green, 125 Fed. App'x 659, 662 (6th Cir. 2005). Excited utterances about criminal activity made to 911 operators and police present challenging issues under Crawford v. Washington's holding that the confrontation clause applies to "testimonial" statements. See Section G, infra.

Opportunity to Fabricate as an Interpretive Guide. The spontaneity of the statement under FRE 803(1) or (2)—that is, the apparent lack of the declarant's opportunity to fabricate—is an underlying rationale for these two hearsay exceptions. But the absence of an opportunity to fabricate is not an express factual element: Spontaneity implies a lack of opportunity to fabricate rather than the other way around. Nevertheless, sometimes the rationale can be offered in argument as a persuasive guide to a judge applying the rule in a given fact situation. For example, as noted above, some courts have used lack of an opportunity to fabricate to justify admitting present sense impressions despite longer time lapses.

With excited utterances, the stress of excitement is normally supposed to be continuous from the time of the exciting event to prevent the opportunity to fabricate. But at least one case has held that the stress of a startling event can be rekindled by events that remind the declarant of the startling event or generate additional anguish. United States v. Lossiah, 129 Fed. App'x 434 (10th Cir. 2005) (child under age of 12 saw defendant at her school and "ran to tell" her teacher "Don't let him check me out

. . . he raped me"; alleged attack had occurred two months before, but caused child to be fearful when she saw defendant at school). The reasoning here would seem to be that the rekindled stress was itself a new startling event.

An opportunity to fabricate occurs when a person has the time and mental space for reflection. In thinking about this issue, it should be borne in mind that the human mind can work very rapidly. In some circumstances, reflection could be almost instantaneous. Consider, for example, your process as a law student in taking class notes. Unless you are operating as a stenographer making a verbatim record, you are most likely exercising editorial judgment and discretion—deciding what statements are worth noting down, and often rephrasing them in your own words. While your process is near contemporaneous, it is also reflective. For this reason, your class notes and, more generally, note taking to memorialize meetings and conversations, are not good candidates for the FRE 803(1) exception. But see United States v. Ferber, 966 F. Supp. 90 (D. Mass. 1997) (handwritten notes reciting what someone said at a meeting fall within the exception).

Scope of the Statement. The FRE 803(1) requirement that the declaration be one *describing or explaining an event or condition* is intended to be a limitation on the scope or subject matter of the statement that is consistent with the exception's underlying rationale. But the Advisory Committee Note states that the language of FRE 803(2)—*relating to a startling even or condition*— "affords a broader scope of subject matter coverage." It is not intuitively obvious why a broader range of facts should be admissible under an FRE 803(2) excited utterance than under an FRE 803(1) present sense impression, but that is the significance of "relating to" as compared to "describing" and "explaining." Still, there are limits to how broadly the term "relating to" will be applied. *See, e.g.,* United States v. Alarcon-Simi, 300 F.3d 1172, 1176 (9th Cir. 2002) (defendant sought admission of his own exculpatory statement made just after the "traumatic incident" of being arrested for fraudulent check-cashing; statement that "he didn't know about [it]" held inadmissible as not "relating to" what "occurred *at the time of his arrest*," but to earlier events).

c. Use of the Statement Itself in Preliminary Factfinding

FRE 104(a) governs the judge's preliminary factfinding necessary to apply the categorical terms of the FRE 803 exceptions. FRE 104(a) permits the judge to consider inadmissible evidence, including the hearsay statement itself, in determining whether the preliminary facts for the exceptions have been shown to be probably true. This is the same "bootstrapping" issue that we discussed in the context of the Rule 801(d)(2)(C), (D) and (E) exemptions for agent, employee, and co-conspirator statements.

This issue becomes particularly important where there is limited information about the underlying event. Recall that that the occurrence of an event (or a startling event) is a factual element of the FRE 803(1) and (2) exceptions. In many cases, there is likely to be proof that the event occurred without relying on the hearsay statement itself. But sometimes, such independent evidence will not be available. For example, if Sally was speaking to George on her car phone when she said "a gray SUV just ran the red light and hit a pedestrian," George cannot provide independent evidence that the event described by Sally actually occurred. Statements admitted under FRE 803(1) and (2) can also be in writing, so there may be no other person present to verify either the event or when the written statement was made.

Strange as it may seem, the contents of the hearsay statement alone may satisfy the Rule 104(a) burden of proving that an event occurred, when it occurred, and what kind of an event it was. *See* United States v. Arnold, 486 F.3d 177, 180 (6th Cir. 2007) (to establish a startling event, court relied on declarant's statement during 911 call that defendant had just threatened her with a gun). Advisory Committee Note to FRE 803(2) ("an excited utterance may of itself be sufficient to establish the occurrence of the startling event"); but see Arnold, 486 F.3d at 208 (dissenting opinion) ("anyone could contrive a fact that—if real—would cause excitement, and state it in an exclamatory manner. To hold that such a statement, standing alone, is admissible for the truth of the matter asserted stands the hearsay rule on its head."). If the judge is persuaded that the FRE 803(1) or (2) elements have been shown in this circumstance, the statement is admitted into evidence and is, by necessary implication, sufficient to support a finding pursuant to FRE 104(b) or 901 that the event occurred. However, the judge's ruling admitting the hearsay evidence does not bind the jury to agree that the event occurred; the jury remains free to disbelieve the hearsay evidence.

d. Proof of Personal Knowledge

As we stated above, a hearsay declarant functions as a witness because her statement is offered to prove the truth of the facts it asserts—just as live witness testimony is offered to prove the truth of the facts asserted by the in-court witness. Consistent with this general principle, courts have held that the proponent of a present sense impression or excited utterance must show that "the declarant had personally perceived the event or condition about which the statement is made." United States v. Mitchell, 145 F.3d 572, 575 (3d Cir. 1998). The content of the statement, and the circumstances surrounding the making of it, may be sufficient, even when the declarant is unidentified. In Miller v. Keating, 754 F.2d 507 (3d Cir. 1985), an unidentified bystander ran up to the parties involved in an automobile collision and exclaimed that one car (the defendant's) had cut into the line of traffic, thus causing the accident. The appellate court reversed the trial court's admission of this statement:

> When there is no evidence of personal perception, apart from the declaration itself, courts have hesitated to allow the excited utterance to stand alone as evidence of the declarant's opportunity to observe . . . In some cases, however, the substance of the statement itself does contain words revealing perception. A statement such as, "I saw that blue truck run down the lady on the corner," might stand alone to show perception if the trial judge finds, from the particular circumstances, that he is satisfied by a preponderance that the declarant spoke from personal perception . . . [Id. at 511-512.]

The court in *Miller* found no evidence to support an inference that the declarant actually saw what had happened, that he could have seen it, or that he was excited. The court treated the issue of personal knowledge as an FRE 104(a) issue for the judge. Most other opinions on this point agree. Miller v. Crown Amusements, Inc., supra, 821 F. Supp. at 705-706 ("the Court finds by a preponderance of the evidence that the declarant observed the accident. The caller specifically stated, '[W]e *noticed* [the truck sideswipe a person]' thus indicating actual perception."). Since *Miller*, courts are no longer hesitant in admitting excited utterances made by unidentified bystanders. United States v. Montero-Camargo, 177 F.3d 1113, 1123 (9th Cir. 1999) ("[T]rustworthiness of the statement is bolstered by the declarant's status as a mere bystander with no apparent motivation for providing false information."); Miller v. Crown Amusements, Inc., 821 F. Supp. 703 (S.D. Ga. 1993) (unidentified 911 caller).

e. Criticism of FRE 803(1) and (2)

There is much to criticize about the purported reliability rationale of FRE 803(1) and (2). Judge Posner put the criticism cogently in a recent case:

> The rationale for the exception for a "present sense impression" is that if the event described and the statement describing it are near to each other in time, this "negate[s] the likelihood of deliberate or conscious misrepresentation." Advisory Committee Notes to 1972 Proposed Rules. I don't get it, especially when "immediacy" is interpreted to encompass periods as long as 23 minutes, as in United States v. Blakey, 607 F.2d 779, 785-786 (7th Cir. 1979), 16 minutes in United States v. Mejia-Velez, 855 F. Supp. 607, 614 (E.D.N.Y. 1994), and ten minutes in State v. Odom, 316 N.C. 306, 341 S.E.2d 332, 335-336 (N.C. 1986). Even real immediacy is not a guarantor of truthfulness. It's not true that people can't make up a lie in a short period of time. Most lies in fact are spontaneous. See, e.g., Monica T. Whitty et al., "Not All Lies Are Spontaneous: An Examination of Deception Across Different Modes of Communication," 63 J. Am. Society of Information Sci. & Technology 208, 208-209, 214 (2012). . . . Suppose I run into an acquaintance on the street and he has a new dog with him—a little yappy thing—and he asks me, "Isn't he beautiful"? I answer yes, though I'm a cat person and consider his dog hideous. . . .
>
> It is time the law awakened from its dogmatic slumber. The "present sense impression" exception never had any grounding in psychology. It entered American law in the nineteenth century, see Jon R. Waltz, "The Present Sense Impression Exception to the Rule Against Hearsay: Origins and Attributes," 66 Iowa L. Rev. 869, 871 (1981), long before there was a field of cognitive psychology; it has neither a theoretical nor an empirical basis; and it's not even common sense—it's not even good folk psychology.

As for FRE 803(2):

> . . . .While psychologists would probably concede that excitement minimizes the possibility of reflective self-interest influencing the declarant's statements, they have questioned whether this might be outweighed by the distorting effect of shock and excitement upon the declarant's observation and judgement. [United States v. Boyce, 742 F.3d 792, 800-802 (2014) (Posner, J., concurring) (quoting 2 McCormick on Evidence §272, p. 366 (7th ed. 2013))].

On the other hand, Judge Posner's criticism might not itself be above criticism. No hearsay exception is based on the idea that it is perfectly reliable, in some absolute sense. That people are capable of fabricating very quickly does not tell us much about the reliability of spontaneous statements *relative to* statements made after considerable time to fabricate. Compare a present sense impression to the admissible nonhearsay testimony of a witness who has had months to think about her testimony and perhaps also had coaching by lawyers. And Posner's critique does not tell us much about how to balance the unreliable aspects of spontaneous hearsay against the cost of losing the evidence by excluding it. Here, it is also worth noting that Posner does not actually advocate excluding spontaneous hearsay statements; ultimately, his critique winds up in a very debatable recommendation of admitting more hearsay statements of all kinds under an expanded residual exception. (See FRE 807, below.) We discuss this issue in the reflection section at the end of this chapter.

KEY POINTS

1. Present sense impressions, FRE 803(1), describe an event or occurrence while it is happening or very shortly thereafter, while excited utterances, FRE 803(2), relate to a startling event or occurrence and are made before the stress of excitement wears off.

2. Present sense impressions, FRE 803(1), and excited utterances, FRE 803(2) are considered reliable hearsay because the spontaneity, near-contemporaneous timing, and, under FRE 803(2), the stress of excitement suggest that the declarant lacks an opportunity to fabricate and perhaps is better able to remember what she describes. These factors may be pertinent to considering whether too much time has elapsed between the event and the statement. But these factors do not address reliability concerns stemming from perception and narration problems.

3. The scope of subject matter that can be included in an FRE 803(2) statement "*relating* to a startling event or condition" is deemed broader than the permissible scope of an FRE 803(1) statement "*describing or explaining* an event or condition."

4. The judge may use the statement—either in conjunction with other evidence, or by itself—to determine whether the factual elements of the hearsay exception have been met, including whether and when the event or condition occurred, and whether the declarant had firsthand knowledge of the event or condition. These issues will be decided by the judge pursuant to FRE 104(a).

PROBLEMS

8.46. In the case involving the pedestrian suing the driver of the SUV (pages 443, 529), George would testify to the following: (Each statement is an alternative, not cumulative.)

(a) Sally was standing right next to me on the street corner, and she said, "That gray SUV just ran a red light and hit a pedestrian." I looked up and saw the SUV stopped near a person lying on the street.

(b) I was at my desk when Sally came running into the office, out of breath and very agitated. She said, "You won't believe what I just saw. A gray SUV ran a red light and hit a pedestrian!"

(c) Sally came back to the office from lunch and calmly stated, "I was on my way back from lunch when I saw yet another SUV running a stoplight and knocking someone down. Go figure. I spoke with the police for 30 minutes."

8.47. Victor was arrested by a group of law enforcement officers who burst into the apartment, guns drawn, in which Victor was meeting with others. The officers shouted at the group to "show their hands"; asked, "Is this dope, is this dope?"; and pointed to money inside a car seat and asked, "Is that money? How much?" Victor responded, "I was buying a truck, man." Victor offers the officers' authenticated tape recording of his statement at his trial. Admissible?

8.48. Return to Problem 3.2, Pedroso v. Driver, at page 148. A teacher at Paul's school testifies for plaintiffs that Ann, who was on the school bus with Paul, was playing during recess in the schoolyard several days after the accident. Ann suddenly started to cry and exclaimed, "That's the bus driver who hit Paul on the side of the road" just as Denise Driver was walking by. Admissible?

8.49. Defendant Louis D'Onofrio is charged with illegal possession of a firearm as a convicted felon and two counts of brandishing a deadly weapon, one occurring on January 24 and one on January 26.

(a) A 911 call was made by Mrs. D'Onofrio from her home at 2:15 A.M. on January 26. She told the operator that her husband, Louis, was drunk and threatening to shoot her. The operator could hear Louis yelling loudly, but she heard no threats. The operator asked whether her husband had a weapon. Mrs. D'Onofrio said that he has a gun and is pointing it at her. Can the tape recording of this conversation be admitted at defendant's trial?

(b) Police officers arrived at the D'Onofrio home at 2:30 A.M. Louis D'Onofrio had just left the house with the gun, according to Mrs. D'Onofrio, who was upset and crying. She stated that she and Louis had been arguing on the evening of January 24; that he held the gun and threatened to kill her during the argument; that when she returned from work on January 25, Louis had the gun and killed the family cat; that he spent the evening of January 25 drinking and that she had called 911 at 2:15 A.M. when he began to make more threats. Mrs. D'Onofrio consented to a search for a gun, but none was found. Defendant had no gun in his possession when he was arrested. Mrs. D'Onofrio now refuses to testify, claiming spousal privilege, and there is no other evidence that defendant possessed a firearm. Can the officers testify about her statements at defendant's trial?

5. Explanation of FRE 803(3): Declarant's Statement of His Then-Existing State of Mind

FRE 803(3) provides:

(3) *Then-Existing Mental, Emotional, or Physical Condition.* A statement of the declarant's then-existing state of mind (such as motive, intent, or plan) or

emotional, sensory, or physical condition (such as mental feeling, pain, or bodily health), but not including a statement of memory or belief to prove the fact remembered or believed unless it relates to the validity or terms of the declarant's will.

a. Preliminary Factfinding

The factual requirements for statements of state of mind are:

- the contents of the statement express the declarant's state of mind that is currently existing at the time of the statement;
- state of mind may include motive, intent, plan; emotional, sensory, or physical condition; mental feeling, pain, or bodily health; and
- a state of mind of memory or belief may not be used to prove the fact remembered or believed unless it relates to the validity or terms of the declarant's will.

As with all exceptions that depend on content as a categorical requirement, the judge can determine content from proof of the statement itself. Thus, the statements "I like Harold the best of all my children" or "I am miserably unhappy at work" fall within the FRE 803(3) exception, and will be admissible for their truth, if those current feelings are relevant. No other preliminary facts concerning the declarant or the circumstances within which the statement was made are required.

Notice that Rule 803(3) defines *state of mind* broadly to include any sensation present in the mind of declarant. The state of mind of a party, or of any person who becomes involved in litigated events, may be relevant at trial: For example, a criminal defendant's state of mind of "love" or "hate" can be relevant to show motive for the crime; a civil defendant's state of mind of "knowledge" can be relevant to prove notice; and in any type of case, a witness's state of mind of "bias" or "malice" toward one of the parties can be relevant to impeach the witness's credibility. Statements of an official representative of a corporate or governmental entity are admissible under FRE 803(3) to prove the motives underlying the business decisions of the entity. Municipal Revenue Service, Inc. v. Xspand, Inc., 700 F. Supp. 2d 692, 705-706 (M.D. Pa. 2010).

But the scope of the FRE 803(3) exception is specifically limited. Statements of memory or belief may be used to prove a declarant's then-existing relevant state of mind, but may not be admitted to prove the fact remembered or believed (unless that fact relates to the terms or validity of the declarant's will). This exclusion of facts remembered or believed can be confusing at first and is sufficiently important to understanding the limits of the rule that we discuss it in detail in the next subsection.

b. Exclusion of "Facts Remembered or Believed"

FRE 803(3) provides that statements of memory or belief to prove the fact remembered or believed may not be admitted through the state-of-mind exception.[5] Why are such statements of memory and belief excluded from this hearsay exception?

---

5. There is a very narrow exception to this point, allowing statements of memory and belief concerning the declarant's will. We'll set that aside for now and briefly return to it later.

Consider the drafting problem involved. A person's subjective mental state (such as his intent, emotion, physical sensation) is very difficult to prove. In the absence of a statement by the person describing her own thought or feeling, we would be limited to circumstantial evidence. A person's own statement of his subjective mental state is thus potentially valuable, highly probative evidence, if that mental state is relevant to a case.

At the same time, the hearsay rule is designed to restrict the admissibility of facts asserted by persons who are not presented at trial as live witnesses. The problem is that the kinds of fact assertions that the hearsay rule is designed to exclude—events or conditions that occurred outside the mind of the hearsay declarant—are known to the hearsay declarant as thoughts in her mind. These thoughts take the form of beliefs or memories. Even recollections of one's own past subjective mental states can be problematic: How well do you remember you moods, feelings, or intentions of the past week, month, or year? Your current memory of your own past subjective mental states can be unreliable due to the limitations of human memory.

The intent of the state-of-mind exception is to admit statements of the declarant describing her subjective mental state at the moment of speaking or writing, but to exclude (1) current memories or beliefs about events or conditions outside of the declarant's mind, and (2) current memories or beliefs *about the declarant's own past mental states*. Such a rule is not easily written, but the FRE drafters did a good job in describing examples of current subjective mental states, while expressly excluding "statements of memory or belief to prove the fact remembered or believed."

c. Justification for the State-of-Mind Exception

A statement relevant to prove the declarant's current state of mind requires inferences about the declarant's sincerity and narration. The fact of consequence is what is going on inside the mind of the declarant, and the declarant's statement must sincerely and accurately express what that is. The declarant is not perceiving anything outside the declarant's own mind, so there is no traditional risk of misperception. And, since the statement expresses the *then-existing* mental state, there is no memory problem. Thus, the primary rationale for the state-of-mind exception is that there are no perception or memory dangers. Under the reliability rationale of the Rule 803 exceptions, the absence of these dangers provides circumstantial guarantees of trustworthiness, and thus diminishes the importance of cross-examining the declarant.

There is, however, a weakness in this trustworthiness justification. Although it has been said that statements that express a present state of mind are likely to be spontaneous and therefore sincere, there is no independent requirement of proving spontaneity and there is no limit to the circumstances in which such statements can be made. The rule thus offers no purported safeguards against sincerity and narration dangers. The statement "I love my spouse" may be spontaneous, or it may be calculated to mislead if the declarant has a reason to want to create the false impression of affection. There are no definitive means of proving that the declarant really has the mental state that is being spoken about. Thus, the sincerity risks in FRE 803(3) statements are substantial. If the statement is not spontaneous, then the declarant has the opportunity to fabricate.

The categorical approach to hearsay exceptions should in theory preclude courts from examining this latter issue: There is no element built into FRE 803(3) that requires spontaneity or otherwise addresses sincerity concerns. Nevertheless, some courts have taken it upon themselves to do so. See United States v. Secor, 73 Fed. App'x 554, 566-567 (4th Cir. 2003) (treating FRE 803(3) as a subset of FRE 803(1) and adding requirement that the declarant "must not have had time to reflect and to fabricate"). These cases usually involve offers by criminal defendants of their own statements made either long after the crime was committed, when their current states of mind may no longer be relevant, or after they suspect they are under investigation and have a clear motive to represent their current mental state of "innocence." But see United States v. DiMaria, 727 F.2d 265, 271-272 (2d Cir. 1984) (although an accused can easily fabricate a declaration of mental state, when the statement falls within the terms of FRE 803(3) "its truth or falsity was for the jury to determine").

Necessity may justify the admission of state-of-mind statements despite their sincerity risks. Mental states are a pervasive part of our substantive law and a person's own statements are a primary source of evidence about mental states. However, the state-of-mind exception is used beyond its necessity in proving essential elements, and people's conduct can be more probative than people's words in assessing mental states.

d. State-of-Mind Utterances Are Classified as Either Direct or Circumstantial

Some utterances directly assert the declarant's mental state. For example, to prove that a witness has a motive to lie in favor of plaintiff, the defendant could offer evidence that the witness once said, "I can't stand the defendant." This is a direct statement of the witness's feelings and state of mind. But what if the witness said, "The defendant is a vile person who has done me great harm"? This statement is not a direct assertion of a mental state, but it probably reflects a state of mind of intense dislike. Because the mental state is not directly asserted, courts and commentators call this type of statement "circumstantial evidence" of the witness's state of mind.

Utterances that are circumstantial evidence of the declarant's state of mind are not offered to prove the truth of the literal matters they assert. The witness's statement is not offered to prove that the defendant is vile, or that the defendant has done great harm to the witness. Thus, some courts and commentators have taken the position that such utterances are nonhearsay. But unlike the categories of nonhearsay that we discussed at pages 453-59, supra—*effect on listener* and *legally operative facts*—the relevance of state-of-mind utterances *does* involve potential sincerity and narration risks. If the witness in our hypothetical is lying or joking, and does not sincerely believe that the defendant is vile and has done wrong, then the witness's statement is not relevant to prove a motive to lie in favor of the plaintiff. Therefore, utterances that are circumstantial evidence of state of mind are not a true nonhearsay category.

FRE 803(3) provides such a broad hearsay exception for statements of a declarant's then-existing state of mind that labeling them as direct or circumstantial, hearsay or nonhearsay, is purely academic in terms of admissibility under the Federal Rules. United States v. Quinones, 511 F.3d 289, 312 (2d Cir. 2007) (under either theory, a state of mind can be proved circumstantially by statements that are not intended to assert the truth of the fact being proved).

6. FRE 803(3): Relevant Uses of State-of-Mind Evidence

a. Future and Past State of Mind of the Declarant

A declarant's current statement of state of mind may be just one step in the inferential process to establish some fact of consequence. Frequently, inferences both forward and backward in time are made from statements of currently existing mental states. For example, consider a case in which a criminal defendant wishes to establish that some third person had a motive for killing the victim and that the third person was in fact the killer. The third person's statement, "I hate the victim," made a week *before* the killing, is admissible under FRE 803(3) to prove that one week before the killing the third person hated the victim. From hatred at that time we infer a future state of mind—there was probably still hatred a week later, when the killing occurred. The inference is based on the generalization that strong emotional feelings about an individual are not likely to change over a relatively short period of time. Hatred a week later is relevant to show a motive to harm the victim, and from motive we infer the possibility that the third person killed the victim.

State of mind can also be used to prove a past state of mind without relying on the declarant's perception or memory. Consider in the preceding murder case that the third person said two days *after* the murder, "The thought of the victim fills me with rage." The present state of mind of "rage" would be relevant to prove that the declarant was probably also angry at the victim two days earlier, again because of a generalization about the stability of such states of mind. If angry two days earlier, the declarant may have had a motive to kill the victim at that time.

In these cases, the court will examine the circumstances to decide whether the inference of continuity of state of mind is reasonable.

> Some expressions of emotion last a lifetime, while others may be unlikely to persist long after their triggering events. Some professions of state of mind may be too vague or tenuous to support an inference of continuity, particularly where there is a significant lapse of time between the declaration and the *mens rea* at issue. Intervening events may also signal a possible change in the declarant's state of mind." [United States v. Farhane, 634 F.3d 127, 173 (2d Cir. 2011).]

Statements made months after the time at which the declarant's state of mind was relevant have been held too remote to be probative. United States v. Reyes, 239 F.3d 722, 743 (5th Cir. 2001).

b. Statements of Intent to Prove the Declarant's Subsequent Conduct

Mary's statement on Monday "I plan to leave on my vacation to Hawaii on Tuesday" may be relevant to prove that she in fact left on Tuesday, and that she went to Hawaii. We first must infer the truth of the matter she asserts—that on Monday,

Mary sincerely planned to leave on Tuesday for her vacation in Hawaii. Then, from this state of mind, we can infer that she probably had the same intent on Tuesday and, then, that she carried it out and did go to Hawaii.

The generalizations underlying the inference from Mary's state of mind to her future conduct concern the behavior of people; that people with intentions or plans of the type that Mary had generally do the things that they intend or plan to do. The probability of each inference from intent to future conduct will vary depending on the nature of the intended activity and the time lag involved. In some situations, intent may be stated so far in advance, or may be so contingent, that there is little probative force to the generalization that people act in conformity with intent. What is important is that the inferences from Mary's state of mind to her conduct do not require any further evaluation of Mary's testimonial qualities.

FRE 803(3) does not itself establish the relevance of statements of intent to prove the declarant's subsequent conduct. That relevance is a matter of common sense generalizations and FRE 401-402. But FRE 803(3) makes clear that such statements fit within the hearsay exception. FRE 803(3) can thus be used to overcome a hearsay objection against using Mary's statement of intent to show that she had that intent and acted on it later. Staelens ex rel. Estate of Staelens v. Staelens, 677 F. Supp. 2d 499, 503 (D. Mass. 2010) (decedent's statement that he continued to name his former wife as the beneficiary to his 401(k) account because he wanted to be sure she would be okay admissible to prove that naming her was not a mistake).

c. Distinguishing State of Mind from Past Facts

We've already discussed that FRE 803(3) creates an exception for presently existing, subjective mental states; but that it excludes past facts, whether facts external to the declarant that the declarant remembers or believes, or memories of the declarants' own past mental states. A problem arises when both the permitted mental states and the excluded past facts are contained in the same hearsay statement.

It is common that past facts are asserted in the context of state-of-mind evidence; but proof of the truth of the past facts is not an acceptable use of FRE 803(3). To show the bias of Emily, a witness against John, evidence is offered that Emily said outside of court, "I am angry at John because he stole all of my money last year." The statement about the theft is a statement of memory or belief. FRE 803(3) could not be used if the statement is offered to prove that John did in fact steal the money, the fact remembered or believed. Why? The past fact of theft is an event outside of Emily's mind. Her accurate perception and memory would be necessary to the statement's relevance. Since the justification for the FRE 803(3) exception is that these risks are nonexistent, the exception cannot be used when those risks are present. The same is true if Emily, the declarant, said, "I believe that John stole all my money last year." United States v. Cohen, 631 F.2d 1223 (5th Cir. 1980) (The exception "does not permit a declarant to relate . . . why he held the particular state of mind, or what he might have believed that would have induced the state of mind.").

It is possible that if the past fact of theft is not relevant to the litigation, then the declarant's entire statement might be admissible under FRE 803(3) simply to prove the relevant fact—Emily's anger at John. Theft would be a good reason to feel angry and it makes her statement all the more probative of her relevant state of mind of bias against John. Indeed, the past fact of theft need not even be true; if Emily believes it, her state of mind of anger is more probable. Finally, even if the theft is an issue in the case, it is possible that the judge could allow the entire statement and instruct the jury that the theft assertion is admissible only to the extent that it sheds light on the degree of Emily's anger, and not to prove any facts about an alleged theft.

FRE 403 might be the basis for objection if the statement about the theft raises dangers of unfair prejudice against a party or confusion of the issues. It is also possible that the court could decide to split the statement up—admitting "I am angry at John," but excluding "because he stole money from me." This would depend on FRE 403 considerations.

All statements about past facts contain an implicit "I remember," "I think," or "I believe." Admitting such statements as expressing a state of mind of "memory" or "belief" would swallow the hearsay prohibition. For that reason, as discussed, FRE 803(3) excludes statements of memory or belief to prove the fact remembered or believed. However, there may be circumstances where a statement seemingly about memory or belief is offered to prove a relevant mental state—and can thus be admitted over a hearsay objection under FRE 803(3). For example, the statement of belief, "I believe my brakes are bad," or the statement of memory, "I remember that my brakes squeaked yesterday," may be used to prove the declarant's current state of mind of knowledge (notice), *but not the fact that the brakes are bad.*

d. Statements About the Declarant's Will

FRE 803(3) carves out a single narrow exception to the exclusion of statements of memory or belief to prove the fact remembered or believed. The FRE 803(3) hearsay exception extends to, and thus admits over a hearsay objection, statements of fact about the declarant's will. "I have left my entire estate to Harold in my will" is admissible over a hearsay objection to prove *the terms of the declarant's will.*

Statements of memory or belief used to prove facts concerning the validity and terms of a declarant's will do require reliance on the declarant's memory and perception, as well as sincerity and narrative ability. Making a will is an external event that the declarant has perceived and remembers. But admission of these statements is justified by the likelihood that persons will speak carefully about their wills and the necessity that arises from the unavailability of the declarant.

e. The Hillmon Case: Using the Declarant's Statement of Intent to Prove the Conduct of Another

Prior to the Federal Rules of Evidence, some courts applied the state-of-mind exception more broadly (and some courts still do). One of the leading state-of-mind cases, Mutual Life Insurance Co. of New York v. Hillmon, 145 U.S. 285 (1892), presents a challenging interpretation of the exception. *Hillmon* was an action by Sallie Hillmon to recover the proceeds of life insurance policies on the life of her husband

John Hillmon, who, she alleged, died in Crooked Creek, Colorado, on March 17, 1879. The principal issue in the case was whether a body found in Crooked Creek was Hillmon's. The plaintiff contended that it was. The defendant insurance companies tried to establish that Hillmon was not dead. They alleged that a man named Walters had traveled to Crooked Creek with Hillmon and that the body was Walters's, not Hillmon's. Their evidence included the contents of a letter Walters had written to his sister:

> Dear sister and all: I now in my usual style drop you a few lines to let you know that I expect to leave Wichita on or about March the 5th, with a certain Mr. Hillmon, a sheeptrader, for Colorado or parts unknown to me. I expect to see the country now. News are of no interest to you, as you are not acquainted here. I will close with compliments to all inquiring friends. Love to all. I am truly your brother, Fred. Adolph Walters. [Id. at 288.]

The trial court excluded proof of this and a similar letter from Walters as hearsay, and the jury found in favor of Sallie Hillmon. In reversing this judgment, the Supreme Court explained why proof of the letters was admissible:

> The letters in question were competent, not as narratives of facts communicated to the writer by others, nor yet as proof that he actually went away from Wichita, but as evidence that, shortly before the time when other evidence tended to show that he went away, he had the intention of going, *and of going with Hillmon,* which made it more probable both that he did go *and that he went with Hillmon,* than if there had been no proof of such intention. In view of the mass of conflicting testimony introduced upon the question whether it was the body of Walters that was found in Hillmon's camp, this evidence might properly influence the jury in determining that question. [Id. at 295-296 (emphasis added).]

Walters's Future Conduct.   It is correct that Walters's statement in his letter is relevant to prove his own intent to leave Wichita and to go to Colorado. The Court held as much in the same paragraph — Walters's statement would be admissible to prove his own intent and his own future conduct.

Hillmon's Future Conduct.   Some courts, in apparent reliance on the italicized portions of the above quotation, have interpreted *Hillmon* to stand for the proposition that Walters's letters could also be used to show Hillmon's future conduct — that Hillmon went to Crooked Creek with Walters. As a result, these courts have used a declarant's statement about what a third person plans to do to prove what that third person in fact did, and they have justified admission of these statements under the state-of-mind exception. See United States v. Pheaster, 544 F.2d 353 (9th Cir. 1976) (statement of declarant's intent to meet Angelo to get drugs admissible to show that declarant did meet Angelo); People v. Alcalde, 148 P.2d 627 (Cal. 1944) (victim's statement of intent to go out with Frank admissible to prove that Frank went out with victim and thus had the opportunity to commit murder).

Such use of this exception is problematic, however, because the relevance of Walters' assertion about Hillmon is necessarily dependent on Walters's belief about *Hillmon's state of mind* to travel to Colorado and to travel with Walters. In other words, Walters's statement about Hillmon is a statement of memory or belief to prove the fact remembered or believed: what Hillmon's plans were. All the hearsay dangers are present in Walters's statement: His belief must be accurate, based on Walters's perception and memory of some past fact—something that Hillmon said or did to indicate that he was going to Colorado and wanted to travel with Walters. Otherwise, Walters's statement about leaving Wichita with Hillmon for Colorado is sheer specu- lation and cannot be relevant. If Walters's letter directly expressed the fact on which his knowledge of Hillmon's intent was based (e.g., Hillmon had invited Walters to go with him), such an additional statement would be a statement of memory or belief offered to prove the fact believed. FRE 803(3) may not be used to admit such a past fact, as we know.

In Walters's letter, past facts about Hillmon's past state of mind and conduct are implied, not expressed, by Walters's plan to travel "with Hillmon." Still, the relevance of Walters's own state of mind to prove the state of mind of another person (Hillmon's intent to travel) or the future conduct of another person (Hillmon did travel to Crooked Creek) depends on an inference about Walters's perception and memory of some past fact about that other person. Permitting the state-of-mind exception to admit statements for purposes that so clearly depend on the declarant's perception and memory of past facts would undermine the policies of the rule.[6]

Recent Interpretations of *Hillmon*.   A number of federal courts have held that FRE 803(3) does not support the use of a declarant's state-of-mind declaration to prove the conduct of a third person. The House Judiciary Committee approved the Rule 803(3) exception under the explicit assumption that the rule would limit the *Hillmon* doctrine to use of the declarant's state of mind to prove only the declarant's own future conduct. Other courts, however, have admitted declarants' statements of intent to travel with or to meet a third person against that third person, to prove that the declarant and that person *did in fact travel together or meet*. United States v. Barraza, 576 F.3d 798, 805 (8th Cir. 2010) (admitting statement in declarant's diary that she intended to travel to Mexico with Barraza); United States v. Johnson, 354 F. Supp. 2d 939, 962 (N.D. Iowa 2005) (discussing collected cases). Most of these decisions have required independent corroboration of the third person's conduct. See Joseph A. Devall, Jr., Comment, 78 Tul. L. Rev. 911 (2004) (surveying split in state court over *Hillmon* doctrine). The problem with these decisions is that if we commit to the trial judge's discretion the evaluation of the reliability of an inference from intent (or belief) backward to a third person's past act that caused the intent (or belief), we are abandoning FRE 803(3) as we know it in favor of judicial discretion.

Another possible scenario in cases like *Hillmon* is to rely on the declarant's intent to act *only* if a specific person acts as well. For example, would it be appropriate to infer that Walters planned to leave Wichita and travel *only* if he went with Hillmon?

---

6. The *Hillmon* case has fascinated evidence law specialists for years. But never has it aroused more interest than recently, due to the efforts of Professor Marianne Wesson to determine, once and for all, whose body was buried at Crooked Creek. Her history of the dispute over the proceeds of Hillmon's insur- ance policy is fascinating, as reported at: www.thehillmoncase.com/index.html.

If so, since Walters was not in Wichita, the inference could be made, without reliance on Walters's perception or memory, that Hillmon must have decided to leave and travel with Walters. Another ingenious solution to the problem of using state-of-mind statements to prove the conduct of third persons was upheld in United States v. Persico, 2011 WL 1661420, at *12-13 (2d Cir.). In a prosecution for murder, the court upheld the admission of testimony by the victim's wife that, on the day he disappeared, the victim telephoned her to say that he "was going to meet" the defendant Persico [the alleged murderer] later that day. This statement, the court held,

> was in no way offered to show that in fact "Persico met [the victim] at the Shore Road location". . . . rather, that statement was properly admitted to show [victim's] intent to meet Persico there and to support an inference that [victim] acted in furtherance of that intent, from which the jury could reasonably infer that [victim] had communicated to Persico that [victim] would be at Shore Road expecting to meet Persico there.

Which inference do you think is more likely? That Persico had engaged in some past act to lure his victim to Shore Road? Or that the unsuspecting victim set up the meeting on his own?

KEY POINTS

1. Statements expressing a declarant's current state of mind are admissible under FRE 803(3) to prove that state of mind, if it is relevant in the case. States of mind include physical or mental feelings or sensations, emotions, intentions, and motivations, among other things. The state of mind must have existed at the time the declarant expressed it.

2. State-of-mind statements admissible under FRE 803(3) do not include assertions of past facts of any kind, including past states of mind or things that caused a past or present state of mind. The state-of mind exception also excludes opinions, perceptions, beliefs, or memories about facts external to the declarant. If statements of state of mind were used to include these matters, this exception would swallow the hearsay rule.

3. Some statements mix an admissible state of mind statement with an assertion about a past fact or fact external to the declarant. In such instances, only the part of the statement dealing with the state of mind is admissible, assuming it is relevant by itself.

4. Statements of a person's intention to do something come within 803(3), and such statements are often relevant to prove that the person subsequently carried out his intention and did the thing. Some courts permit statements of a declarant's intent to be used to prove the future conduct of a third person, as well as the declarant's conduct, if there is corroboration.

5. Statements of past state of mind and past facts relating to the validity and terms of declarant's will may, however, be admitted under FRE 803(3).

PROBLEMS

8.50. William Winchell has just testified against Don Davis in a civil case brought by Paul Peterson. On cross examination, Davis' lawyer asks:

1   *Q:* Isn't it a fact that two years ago you told Don Davis that "you would get
2   even with him" for giving you bad investment advice?
3   *Counsel for Peterson:* Objection, relevance.
4   *Counsel for Davis:* It's relevant to show bias your honor, that this witness has
5   a motive to lie against my client.
6   *The Court:* Overruled.
7   *Counsel For Peterson:* Then I object that it's hearsay.
8   How should the court rule?

8.51. The United States has filed an interpleader action to determine the true owner of the boxing championship belts awarded to boxer Roberto Duran. Duran claims they were stolen from his house by his brother-in-law in 1993. The FBI recovered the belts in 2003 from businessman Louis Baez, who claimed that the belts were not stolen. To prove theft, Duran and a number of witnesses would testify that in 2000, the brother-in-law apologized to Duran for stealing the belts. Admissible? Would the statement of apology alone be admissible?

8.52. Lyons Partnership owns all of the intellectual property rights to the character "Barney," the well-stuffed Tyrannosaurus Rex with a green chest and stomach, green spots on its back, and yellow "toeballs." Barney is readily recognizable to young children. The *Barney and Friends* TV show is viewed weekly by 14 million children, and over 50 million copies of Barney-related videos have been sold. Lyons controls the "live" appearances of the Barney character played by adults in costume, and Lyons does not license Barney costumes.

Lyons filed suit against Nelson Costumes, alleging trademark infringement arising out of rental of Nelson's costume, "Duffy the Dragon," to the public. Lyons had to prove, under the Lanham Act, that the defendant is infringing its valid mark by creating consumer confusion. Proof of *actual confusion* is often paramount to the success of such a claim. Lyons offered three types of evidence of confusion at trial, all of which the district court excluded as "unreliable hearsay." Was this error? The evidence offered was as follows:

(a) Testimony from parents that when they rented the Duffy costume for their children's birthday parties, they were confused because the costume looked just like Barney.

(b) Testimony from a principal of an elementary school that when she wore the Duffy costume at a school rally, the children shouted, "Barney, Barney, Barney!"

(c) The results of a survey conducted by Lyons at several shopping malls. Shoppers were shown a photograph of the Duffy costume and asked whether they could identify the character. Fifty percent identified the character as Barney; 50 percent had no idea who the character was.

8.53. Return to Problem 3.2, Pedroso v. Driver, at page 148. Joan testifies for defendants that she also rode the same school bus as Paul and Tom, and that Paul and Tom always got off at the same stop. On the day of the accident, Tom said to Joan, "Paul and I are going to play tag when we get off the bus today." Admissible?

7. Explanation of FRE 803(4): Statements Made for Medical Diagnosis or Treatment

FRE 803(4) states:

> (4) *Statement Made for Medical Diagnosis or Treatment.* A statement that:
>   (A) is made for—and is reasonably pertinent to—medical diagnosis or treatment; and
>   (B) describes medical history; past or present symptoms or sensations; their inception; or their general cause.

a. Preliminary Factfinding

The factual requirements for FRE 803(4) statements are:

- the statement must be made for the purpose of medical diagnosis or treatment;
- the statement must describe medical history, past or present symptoms or sensations, or the inception or the general cause of the symptoms or sensations; and
- the statement is reasonably pertinent to diagnosis or treatment.

There is some overlap between this exception and statements of mental state admitted under FRE 803(3). A patient's description of currently existing sensation ("I feel dizzy") could fall within both. But FRE 803(4) also admits statements to prove current symptoms that exist outside the mind of the declarant ("The thermometer says I have a temperature of 102") and to prove past symptoms as well ("I had a runny nose yesterday, and I coughed a lot"). The relevance of these statements depends upon the accuracy of the declarant's perception and memory, as well as sincerity and narration. The perceived reliability of these hearsay statements is that the declarant's motive to obtain medical treatment provides a strong incentive to present truthful and accurate information, thus reducing sincerity risk.

FRE 803(4) does not specify that the declarant be the patient, relating the declarant's own medical history and symptoms. Family, friends, nurses, and other medical personnel may convey information for purposes of medical treatment that will be admitted under FRE 803(4). Campos v. MTD Products, Inc., 2009 WL 425012, at *12 (M.D. Tenn.) (statements by immediate family members included under this exception). Even an unidentified declarant speaking to an ambulance crew may qualify under the exception if the court is persuaded that the declarant spoke for purposes of securing medical care for the patient. Bucci v. Essex Ins. Co., 393 F.3d 285, 299 (1st Cir. 2005). And if the patient is speaking to an intermediary—a child to a parent, for example, so that the parent can relate the symptoms to a doctor—the terms of the exception could still apply so long as the purpose of seeking medical help exists. "[A]dmissibility . . . is based, not on the person to whom made, but on the purpose for which they are made, which gives rise to the presumption of reliability." Williams v. Virgin Islands, 271 F. Supp. 2d 696, 704-705 (D.V.I. 2003).

Courts have applied FRE 803(4) to statements made to psychotherapists, social workers, pharmacists, and other health care personnel, not just physicians and nurses. However, FRE 803(4) has been interpreted to apply only to statements by persons *seeking* care, not *giving* care. Thus, statements made by doctors to patients, by consulting physicians to treating physicians, are not within the FRE 803(4) exception. Field v. Trigg County Hosp., Inc., 386 F.3d 729, 735-736 (6th Cir. 2004).

b. Justification for the Admissibility of Statements for Medical Purposes

The justification for this exception rests on the declarant's "selfish motive to be truthful" in making the statement. The assumption is that a person seeking medical diagnosis and treatment is highly motivated to speak carefully and honestly about symptoms and conditions in order to receive effective medical care. Thus, even though the declaration may not be spontaneous, and even though there may be perception and memory risks when past conditions and causes are related, the statement bears less danger of insincerity and inaccuracy.

Can a motive to be truthful when speaking with a physician always be assumed? According to some surveys, between 13 and 32 percent of patients lie or stretch the truth to their doctor, in particular about smoking, risky sex, alcohol and drug use, and taking medications as prescribed http://www.newsweek.com/2009/01/07/little-white-coat-lies.html.

c. Statements About the Cause or External Source Must Be "Pertinent"

It is common for persons seeking medical treatment to describe how their injury occurred ("I was hit from behind while sitting in my car, and my neck aches terribly"). FRE 803(4) explicitly includes such hearsay statements to prove the truth of the matters they assert (the declarant was hit from behind in her car) if they are "reasonably pertinent to diagnosis or treatment." Sanders v. The Ritz-Carlton Hotel Co., 2008 WL 4155635, at *2 (S.D.N.Y.) (plaintiff statement in his medical records that he "tripped" rather than "slipped" when he injured his ankle describe the general cause of his injury).

But sometimes, patients' statements make more specific attributions of causation, naming specific persons or entities that caused them harm. Should these statements also be admitted by FRE 803(4)? In general, pertinence is determined from testimony of the medical professional as to the type of information reasonably relied on by a physician in treatment or diagnosis. If the declarant's statements are not medically pertinent, there is some reason to suspect the declarant's motivation in speaking and thus to suspect lack of sincerity. Thus, a statement such as "I was hit from behind by a red Mustang, with license plate number 445HCN, while I was sitting in my car" is not likely to fall within Rule 803(4).

The issue of pertinence frequently arises in cases of child abuse and molestation when the victim names the abuser to the health care professional. In United States v.

Tome, 61 F.3d 1446 (10th Cir. 1995), the child declarant's statements identifying her father as the abuser were held to fall within the "pertinence" requirement. Quoting its own precedent, the court reasoned that

> [a]ll victims of domestic sexual abuse suffer emotional and psychological injuries, the exact nature and extent of which depend on the identity of the abuser. The physician generally must know who the abuser was in order to render proper treatment because the physician's treatment will necessarily differ when the abuser is a member of the victim's family or household. In the domestic sexual abuse case, for example, the treating physician may recommend special therapy or counseling and instruct the victim to remove herself from the dangerous environment by leaving the home and seeking shelter elsewhere. [Id. at 1450.]

Statements made by adult victims of domestic violence have also been admitted by some courts when the identity of the abuser is stated to a treating physician. United States v. Hall, 419 F.3d 980 (9th Cir. 2005) (statements to doctor that live-in boyfriend caused patient's injuries admissible). Other past facts about causation of physical and mental problems are also subject to the dual test of "motivation" and "pertinence." Willingham v. Crooke, 412 F.3d 553, 561-562 (4th Cir. 2005) (plaintiff's description of her arrest, including a gun being pointed at her, was admissible for diagnosis and treatment of her emotional trauma and physical injuries); McCollum v. McDaniel, 32 Fed. App'x 49, 55 (4th Cir. 2002) (statement that injuries were caused by "assault" were admissible as statements relating to cause more than to fault).

It is important to distinguish the pertinence requirement from the statement's relevance in the case. FRE 803(4) is simply another categorical hearsay exception, based on the supposed reliability of this type of statement. Hearsay that qualifies for this exception can be admitted to prove any relevant matter—nothing in the rule restricts use of the statement to proving medical treatment issues. Suppose the declarant told the EMT worker that his leg was injured because he was hit by a car. If that fact is pertinent to diagnosis and treatment, then the statement is admissible under FRE 803(4) and can be used to prove causation. If there is other testimony in the case that the defendant's car was the only one seen at the time of the accident, it might also be relevant to show the identity of the defendant in a hit and run case, for example.

d. Requiring Proof of Medical Purpose

Courts are likely to assume that adults, and even teenagers, understand the purpose for which they are asked to give information to medical personnel. With young children being examined for sexual abuse, however, many courts have rejected this assumption and require that the child's treatment motive be established on the record. In the Eighth Circuit, identifications of abusers by child abuse victims are admissible only "where the physician makes clear to the victim that the inquiry into the identity of the abuser is important to diagnosis and treatment, and the victim manifests such an understanding." Olsen v. Class, 164 F.3d 1096, 1098 (8th Cir. 1999). Other courts have rejected the Eighth Circuit's requirement of such a specific showing.

8. FRE 803(4): Patients' Statements to Medical Expert Witnesses

FRE 803(4) is written in terms broad enough to encompass statements made by a party for the purpose of diagnosis in preparation for litigation. The sincerity rationale, of course, may not apply when a statement of physical condition is made for a litigation purposes. The treatment motive that tends to ensure sincerity is lacking. Moreover, the possibility of receiving a high damage award is an incentive to exaggerate present and past symptoms or suffering. For this reason, the common law physical condition exception did not apply to declarations made for the purpose of diagnosis in preparation for litigation. However, nothing in FRE 803(4) suggests an intention to preserve this common law limitation. Most courts have held that admission of statements made to physicians for the purpose of providing expert testimony is now permitted by the rule.

FRE 803(4)'s admission of statements made to testifying experts may not be justified by the reliability of such statements, but it is understandable when one considers this exception in conjunction with the rules regulating expert opinion testimony. When a person's physical condition is at issue, there frequently will be an expert witness to testify about the nature of the condition, likely based at least in part on the basis of what the person said outside of court about present and past symptoms. The common law restriction against use of self-serving hearsay statements of physical condition, combined with the common law requirement that expert witnesses had to base their opinions solely on admissible evidence, led to awkward evidence presentation. The patient had to testify about the physical condition at issue and then the treating physicians would have to testify (and be cross-examined) about the patient's treatment. The expert would then be asked to offer an opinion in response to a hypothetical question that incorporated the information already described in court.

Well aware of the problems with hypothetical questions, the drafters of the Federal Rules consciously sought to avoid them in providing for the presentation of expert information. See FRE 702, 703, and 705, discussed in Chapter Nine. A medical expert who has been consulted for diagnosis in preparation for litigation is almost certainly going to rely on the patient's statements about past and present symptoms and will want to recite these statements when explaining the diagnosis. FRE 803(4) takes full advantage of the information that medical experts can supply by making statements of physical condition fully admissible.

KEY POINTS

1. Statements describing medical history and symptoms are admissible under FRE 803(4). If they qualify for admission under the exception, they can be used as substantive proof on any relevant point; they are not restricted to proving the extent of the declarant's injuries.
2. The statements may be made by the patient or by others seeking care by providing medical information about the patient. They extend to statements made to medical professionals, or to intermediaries who are expected to convey the information to medical professionals.

3. If the statement contains information about the external cause or source of the medical condition, there must be evidence that such information is reasonably pertinent to treatment or diagnosis.
4. Statements made for purposes of medical diagnosis undertaken in preparation for litigation are included within the FRE 803(4) exception.

PROBLEMS

8.54. Consider whether the following declarations would be admissible in a personal injury action if made to the declarant's spouse, to the declarant's physician for treatment, or to a physician consulted for the purpose of giving expert testimony at trial:

(a) "I have a severe headache."
(b) "Yesterday, I had a severe headache."
(c) "I was hit in the head with a baseball bat."
(d) "John Jones hit me in the head with a baseball bat."

8.55. Return to Problem 8.4, Broadback v. Trapp, at page 454. Are any of the statements made to the ambulance driver admissible under FRE 803(4)?

8.56. Return to Problem 3.4, State v. Blair, at page 150. Norma's doctor would testify that during a routine medical examination in 2009, Norma explained some bruising on her ribs. She told the doctor that her boyfriend had hit her in the middle of an argument. The doctor then recommended a local counseling program for victims of domestic violence to her. Would the doctor's testimony be admissible? What if it is mandatory under state law for a doctor to report, to local law enforcement, injuries that are reasonably suspected to be related to domestic violence?

9. Explanation of FRE 803(5): Recorded Recollection

FRE 803(5) states:

> (5) *Recorded Recollection.* A record that:
> (A) is on a matter the witness once knew about but now cannot recall well enough to testify fully and accurately;
> (B) was made or adopted by the witness when the matter was fresh in the witness's memory; and
> (C) accurately reflects the witness's knowledge.

If admitted, the record may be read into evidence but may be received as an exhibit only if offered by an adverse party.

a. Preliminary Factfinding

The factual requirements for the recorded recollection exception are:

* the declarant is testifying as a witness;
* the statement is in the form of a record;
* the statement is on a matter about which the witness once had personal knowledge;
* the witness cannot remember the matter sufficiently to testify fully and accurately;
* the statement was made or adopted by the witness when the matter was fresh in the witness's memory; and
* the statement accurately reflects the witness's knowledge.

Written or recorded memoranda or notes about events are often a substitute for failed memory in our everyday lives. Try to remember the details of something you once knew but now are unable to remember fully—say, whether a particular case was assigned in your Torts class during your first year of law school. You kept notes of all your first year law school assignments. Or, when people pack their household belongings for a cross-country move, they often keep detailed lists of objects placed in particular moving boxes. These kinds of memory aids are potentially admissible over a hearsay objection under FRE 803(5).

Prior to the restyling, this rule was called "past recollection recorded." Since recollections are necessarily about past matters, that wording seemed redundant—hence, the style change in the new rule. You should be aware of the older terminology, however, since you may encounter it in older reported cases.

No Limits on Contents of the Statement. FRE 803(5) places no limit on the subject matter or contents of a statement admitted as a recorded recollection. The notes and lists discussed above could qualify. So could any form of record of any sort of event that later becomes relevant in litigation. United States v. Cash, 394 F.3d 560 (7th Cir. 2005) (record of a threatening phone call from a veteran written by a Veterans' Administration representative); United States v. Jones, 601 F.3d 1247 (11th Cir. 2010) (video recording of witness's interview with a police detective). Cases also include the use of diaries, police arrest and booking forms, and transcripts of wiretapped phone calls. If the record is a regular part of a business or governmental function, the exceptions for business and public records, FRE 803(6), (8), may also be available and the more onerous factual requirements of FRE 803(5) would not need to be satisfied.

The Declarant Must Be a Witness . . . with Incomplete Memory. FRE 803(5) is unique in the Rule 803 exceptions in that it requires the presence of the declarant in court, as a witness. In this respect, therefore, the exception is analogous to the Rule 801(d)(1) exemptions for prior statements of a witness. Under FRE 803(5), however, it is categorically required that the witness *have incomplete memory* of the underlying events that are the subject of the out-of-court statement, and that the statement must be in written or recorded form. Thus, in one sense the witness is only partially unavailable: She is on the witness stand and may remember some, but not all of the events recorded.

Statement Was Made with Personal Knowledge and Fresh Memory.   FRE 803(5) requires a showing that the witness "once knew" the matter recorded. Typically, if the witness remembers making the record, he will be able to testify that he knew the substance of the record and the circumstances of its creation. If the witness cannot remember making the written record, then the record's own contents, or the testimony of someone who saw the record being made, or other circumstantial evidence, would be used to satisfy the requirement of personal knowledge and fresh memory. See United States v. Cash, 394 F.3d at 561 (admitting memo of phone conversation by Veterans Administration representative based on her testimony of a habit of making such records).

The record can either be *made or adopted* by the witness. Thus, if the witness did not actually write or record the statement, but read over and signified agreement with or approval of the written statements made by another, the requirement can be satisfied. Plaza-Bonilla v. Cortazzo, 2009 WL 605909, at *2, n.4 (E.D. Pa.) (witness to an alleged incident of excessive force by police "provided the statement just a couple of hours after the incident took place . . . initialed each and every answer he provided, signed the bottom of every page, and subscribed the last page, on which he indicated that he had been given 'the chance to read, correct, and initial [his] statement' and that 'everything in this statement [was] true and correct.'"). That the contents of the record reflected what the witness knew from firsthand knowledge would still have to be shown.

Courts have not adopted a bright-line rule to determine whether the witness's memory was "fresh" when the record was made. Statements recorded years after the events described in them have been rejected. One court stated "it would seem difficult for a memorandum drafted by a witness either one month or three months after the fact" to be deemed "fresh." SEC v. Johnson, 534 F. Supp. 2d 63, 66 n.4 (D.D.C. 2008). Other courts are more generous. United States v. Green, 258 F.3d 683, 689 (7th Cir. 2001) ("the trial court may consider the lapse of time along with other circumstances that may be relevant in determining [whether] the witness had an accurate memory," citing cases where a three-year and 15-month delay were held not excessive under the circumstances); United States v. Lewis, 954 F.2d 1386, 1394 (7th Cir. 1992) (trial court is in the best position to gauge the significance of these difficulties, and this is why arbitrary time limitations are inappropriate). Additional evidence, such as clarity of statement, richness of detail, and making changes and corrections, can show that the witness's recollection was still sufficiently fresh.

The Record Reflects the Witness's Knowledge Accurately.   Some evidence that the statement is an accurate reflection of knowledge and memory — that is, both sincerely and accurately recorded — is required. A typical question asked is whether the contents are "true and accurate." United States v. Jones, supra, at 1262. But if the witness cannot adequately remember the events recorded, it may be impossible for the witness to testify truthfully that the record is an accurate reflection of what the witness knew when the record was made. What may often happen is that the witness-declarant simply answers "yes" to the typical question asked and the basis for the witness's ability to so testify is not probed. In some cases, there are circumstances from which accuracy can be inferred. Erasures and corrections in the list may indicate care about accuracy. Or a written statement signed by a suspect in criminal custody could contain the language, "This is an accurate statement to the best of my recollection." And, the witness can testify as to why the statement is *likely to have been accurate* at the time that it was made. As a law student, you could testify that you had strong motivation to record your Torts assignments accurately.

FRE 104(a) and 104(b).   These foregoing factual requirements are FRE 104(a) questions for the judge to decide. This is so even though these factual requirements seem to overlap considerably with the foundation for such a document under FRE 602, 901, and 104(b). Assuming the recorded recollection contains relevant information, satisfying the FRE 803(5) factual requirements will also necessarily satisfy any remaining foundation requirements. That's because if a judge is persuaded by a preponderance of the evidence that the document is an accurate statement of the witness's past firsthand knowledge made under circumstances supporting its accuracy, then a reasonable jury could also have been so persuaded. The jury remains free to determine what weight, if any, to give the recorded recollection once it is admitted.

"Read into Evidence."   FRE 803(5) specifically states that an offering party may have the contents of the recorded recollection "read into evidence." It may be read aloud by the witness or the attorney in the jury's presence into the trial record. But the record may not be received as an exhibit unless the opponent wants it to be. Thus, it may not be handed around by the jury or taken into the jury room for deliberations, "for fear that a factfinder would be unduly influenced by the document rather than the testimony." United States v. Cuesta, 2007 WL 2729853, at *19 (E.D. Cal.). (When testimony in a deposition is admitted into evidence, it is typically treated in the same manner: The contents of the deposition are read to the jury, but the deposition is not itself admitted as an exhibit, or at least is not allowed into the jury room, unlike other admissible documents or records.) If for some tactical reason of advantage the opponent wishes to have the FRE 803(5) record before the jury as a document, the opponent may offer it as an exhibit.

If there is a concern about jurors being "unduly influenced" by looking at a recorded recollection in written form, it may seem strange that courts have no problem in allowing audio or video recordings to be played for the jury when they qualify as recorded recollections under FRE 803(5). But that seems to be the general practice. See, e.g., United States v. Sollars, 979 F.2d 1294, 1298 (8th Cir. 1992); Pickett v. United States, 822 A.2d 404, 405 (D.C. 2003). However, as with written documents, the recordings are not admitted in evidence as exhibits and taken into the jury room, unless moved into evidence by the opponent. See United States v. Mayhew, 2011 U.S. Dist. LEXIS 13906, 2011 WL 601546 (D. Utah Feb. 11, 2011).

b. Justification for the Admissibility of Recorded Recollections

The limits of human memory, and the widespread use of memoranda to compensate, create a compelling practical need for the admission of recorded recollections. FRE 803(5) seeks to create conditions tending to increase the probability of the record's trustworthiness. Obviously, if the record was made when the matter was fresh in the witness's mind, memory problems may be minimized. The requirement of accuracy provides information concerning the witness's sincerity and care in recording the statement. The factual requirements do not address the accuracy of the witness's perception of the matter reported in the statement, but the witness's current availability for general cross-examination may furnish information pertinent to perception ability and opportunity. The opposing party's opportunity, through cross-examination, to probe the basis for a witness's testimony that a written memo is "true and accurate," provides additional guarantees that sincerity and narration dangers are decreased. These requirements are only effective, however, if trial courts apply them strictly.

c. Recorded Recollections Created by Multiple Declarants

Sometimes one person observes events and tells them to a second person who then makes a record based on what was said. When that occurs, there are two levels of hearsay contained in one document. For example, John might do the packing of his household goods and then call out what he puts into each box while a second person, Bob, makes the list. There are two declarants in this situation: the observer, John, who has observed the event (what item is packed where), and the recorder, Bob, who transfers information obtained from the observer into the record. If the observer-declarant does not check and adopt these lists, then the observer cannot later testify in court that the lists correctly reflect what he saw. Therefore, the observer-declarant alone cannot provide a complete Rule 803(5) foundation. There are many other possible examples of this scenario. Employers may make oral statements that are recorded and transcribed by secretarial staff; people make statements at group meetings where one of the group members takes notes.

FRE 803(5) does not specifically address the effect of multiple person involvement in making the record. The Advisory Committee Note to FRE 803(5) states, "Multiple person involvement in the process of observing and recording . . . is entirely consistent with the exception." A leading treatise states that "courts have held the written statement admissible if the person reporting the facts testifies to the correctness of the oral report (although at the time of the testimony, the detailed facts cannot be remembered) and the recorder of that statement testifies to faithfully transcribing that oral report." McCormick on Evidence, Vol. 2 §283, at 300 (Kenneth S. Broun ed., 6th ed. 2006).

The proponent of the cooperative report can satisfy all of the FRE 803(5) requirements only if both out-of-court declarants—the original observer of the information and the later recorder of the information—testify about the observing and recording process. This also gives the opposing party the opportunity to cross-examine both the observer and the recorder about their part in the creation of the record. Thus, if the proponent relies solely on Rule 803(5) to admit a record produced by multiple declarants, each declarant in the hearsay chain must be presented as a witness. United States v. Green, 258 F.3d at 689 ("both the witness and the one transcribing the statement must testify"). This can be a cumbersome process for the proponent, and some of the declarants may not be available.

There are other strategies to admit a cooperative report created by multiple declarants. It can be analyzed as a generic "hearsay within hearsay" or "statement within a statement" problem, of the sort identified by FRE 805. This means that any combination of hearsay exemptions, exceptions, or nonhearsay purposes can be used so long as the admissibility of each level of statement is established. (See the discussion of FRE 805, at pp. 485-86, supra.)

For example, suppose several friends help John pack up his household goods, and each one tells the recorder what is in each box. The recorder later compiles a list based on their hearsay statements. Even if the friends are unavailable to testify, their statements are probably present sense impressions within FRE 803(1). The combination of this exception for the observer-declarants (the friends) and the recorded recollection exception for the recorder-declarant who will testify in court will satisfy FRE 805 and overcome any multiple hearsay objection. Other combinations are also possible, if the record is made of an excited utterance or an admission by a party opponent, for example. United States v. Cuesta, 2007 WL 2729853, at *19 (ranger's citation that recorded defendant's date of birth from a driver's license was admitted under FRE 803(5); the date of birth on the license is an official record or adoptive admission).

If the recorder-declarant is not available as a witness, or has no memory of the accuracy of the particular recording, another exception might apply to the recorder, such as FRE 803(1) or the exception for business records, FRE 803(6). It is important in applying the recorded recollection exception that the recorder be truly recording, as opposed to interpreting or editing, what the witness was saying and has now forgotten. The absence of interpretation ensures that it is the observer's perception and memory, not the recorder's consciously altered version, that is recorded.

10. Refreshing Memory versus Recorded Recollection: FRE 612

a. Explanation of Refreshing Memory

The recorded recollection exception should not be confused with the process of refreshing the memory of a witness. (This process is sometimes referred to as "refreshing recollection" or "present recollection refreshed" to contrast with the former phrase "past recollection recorded"). When a witness initially cannot recall something, it may be possible to refresh the witness's memory by presenting that witness with a document or something else that the examiner thinks, or that the witness suggests, may cause the witness to regain memory of the relevant fact. John, for example, might remember actually packing the objects that he placed in a particular box if he looks briefly at a packing list.

The idea of refreshing memory is a matter of common experience. We've all had the experience of, for instance, a friend or family member referring to some past incident about which we can recall nothing. But perhaps by hearing a few details of the incident, or seeing a photo, it comes back to us. It is permissible to "jog the memory" of a witness in essentially the same ways.

Refreshing the memory of a witness is not a hearsay exception, but rather a witness examination technique. We bring it up here because of its overlap with recorded recollection—both deal with the problem of memory loss of a witness on the stand—and hence the possibility of confusing the two concepts. The primary conceptual difference is this: With refreshing memory, the witness has his memory refreshed and then testifies from his own present memory. The admissibility of the testimony is regarded no differently than if the witness did not have the memory lapse. With recorded recollection, the witness does not have a present memory of the past fact; the record is used in place of the witness's testimony on that point.

In addition to that fundamental conceptual difference between refreshing memory and recorded recollection, there are some rule differences between the two. First, a witness's memory can be refreshed only when the witness's memory is "exhausted"—that is, the witness has no memory on the fact(s) in question. In contrast, the recorded recollection exception is triggered when the witness's memory is merely incomplete: "[T]he witness. . . cannot recall well enough to testify fully and accurately." FRE 803(5).

Second, recorded recollection overcomes a hearsay objection to the use of a written or recorded memory aid—that document is admissible evidence, and it (or the relevant portion of it) is read to the jury. In contrast, the thing used to refresh a witness's memory is not evidence. If feasible, it is not shown to the jury. Once the witness's memory is refreshed, he must testify from his memory, and not by reading from or summarizing the document or thing used to refresh. If his memory is not sufficiently refreshed, the witness should be barred from attempting to provide the information.

Third, recorded recollections are limited to writings or recordings that meet the elaborate preliminary fact requirements of FRE 803(5). In contrast, counsel can attempt to refresh a witness's memory with anything, including inadmissible matter. As one court summarized a state-law version of the rule:

> In a more conventional mode, the process might proceed, "Your Honor, I am about to show the witness a written report, ask him to read it and then inquire if he can now testify from his own memory thus refreshed." In a far less conventional mode, the process could as well proceed, "Your Honor, I am pleased to present to the court Miss Rosa Ponselle who will now sing 'Celeste Aida' for the witness, for that is what was playing on the night the burglar came through the window."[7] Whether by conventional or unconventional means, precisely the same end is sought. One is looking for the effective elixir to revitalize dimming memory and make it live again in the service of the search for truth. [Baker v. State, 371 A.2d 699, 705-706 (Md. App. 1977).]

Thus, inadmissible matter, such as a hearsay document, can be used to refresh recollection. It is even permissible to use a suggestive question. In the same way that your memory of a past incident can be jogged with a suggested detail ("Your aunt and

---

7. [The court's little piece of cultural show-offery doesn't quite work. Rosa Ponselle (d. 1981) was a great soprano. "Celeste Aida" is sung by a male tenor. Perhaps she might have sung it in the shower?— EDS.]

uncle were there—do you remember now?"), such information can be provided by the questioner: "Would it refresh your recollection if I were to tell you that your aunt and uncle were present at the meeting?"

b. The Impact of FRE 612 on Refreshing Recollection

With a friendly witness, the process of refreshing memory might take place outside the courtroom while discussing and rehearsing the direct and anticipated cross-examination. If during this or any other preparation for courtroom or deposition testimony the witness uses a writing to refresh memory, the opposing party may be entitled to inspect the writing. This is because FRE 612 provides as follows:

#### RULE 612.	WRITING USED TO REFRESH A WITNESS'S MEMORY

(a) *Scope*. This rule gives an adverse party certain options when a witness uses a writing to refresh memory:
    (1) while testifying; or
    (2) before testifying, if the court decides that justice requires a party to have those options.

(b) *Adverse Party's Options; Deleting Unrelated Matter*. Unless 18 U.S.C. §3500 provides otherwise in a criminal case, an adverse party is entitled to have the writing produced at the hearing, to inspect it, to cross-examine the witness about it, and to introduce in evidence any portion that relates to the witness's testimony. If the producing party claims that the writing includes unrelated matter, the court must examine the writing in camera, delete any unrelated portion, and order that the rest be delivered to the adverse party. Any portion deleted over objection must be preserved for the record.

(c) *Failure to Produce or Deliver the Writing*. If a writing is not produced or is not delivered as ordered, the court may issue any appropriate order. But if the prosecution does not comply in a criminal case, the court must strike the witness's testimony or—if justice so requires—declare a mistrial.

FRE 612 is not merely a rule of admissibility; it is also a rule of discovery. One of the things it means is that any documents that a person looks at in preparing for a deposition may be discoverable by the opposing party—including perhaps documents that would otherwise be protected by the work-product doctrine or some privilege. Since many of you are likely to become involved in the process of taking depositions long before you are responsible for a trial, we urge you to find a special place in your memory for FRE 612.

c. Witness Memory Lapses in Practice: The Interplay of Recorded Recollection and Refreshing Memory

When a witness doesn't remember facts that you need to introduce in evidence, you thus have various options arising from the recorded recollection and refreshing memory rules, either used separately or in combination. You may know about the witness's memory issue before trial, in which case you can try to plan out your strategy, or the memory problem may arise in the course of questioning, in which case you will have to think quickly on your feet.

If the witness does not remember a point, and you have a document that may qualify as a recorded recollection, you have two options. If you prefer the document to the witness's testimony, you can have the witness testify to the preliminary facts for FRE 803(5) and then read the document into evidence.

But you might prefer the witness to testify to the facts in her own words, from her own memory—perhaps because the witness, with refreshed memory, would convey the facts more completely or persuasively. Or perhaps you don't have a document that qualifies for FRE 803(5); or perhaps you thought you had such a document, but the witness fails to deliver the testimony needed to show the 803(5) preliminary facts. In any of these cases, you will want to use the refreshing memory technique.

It's also possible that you prefer to refresh the witness's memory, but the document doesn't succeed in doing so. Or perhaps you're indifferent about how the evidence comes in. Here, a common way to satisfy the FRE 803(5) foundational requirement of insufficient current memory is to show the witness the record, ask if it refreshes the witness's memory, and offer it as a recorded recollection if the memory is not refreshed.

There are two important procedural points to bear in mind about all this. First, technically speaking, the preliminary fact of memory loss is stricter for refreshing recollection than it is for FRE 803(5) recorded recollection. Again, to refresh memory, the witness's memory must be exhausted; to trigger FRE 803(5), memory need only be incomplete. If opposing counsel or the judge are strict about this preliminary fact, you may have to switch grounds from incomplete memory to exhausted memory by getting the witness to "draw a blank." This can be done by narrowing the frame of reference of the fact in question. A witness may have a partial memory of a past event framed broadly: "I remember packing various household items, but I don't necessarily remember every individual item" is probably an incomplete memory for FRE 803(5), but probably not an exhausted memory for refreshing recollection. This problem can be solved by asking for specifics: "Do you remember packing the Tiffany desk lamp?" If the witness says "no," then you have exhausted memory on that point.

The second key point is that refreshed memory is refreshed memory, not a reading test. The witness with refreshed memory must testify from memory, not by verbally reproducing the item used to refresh. It is all too common, for instance, for a police officer on the witness stand to be handed an inadmissible police report to refresh her memory, only to have her say that her memory is refreshed, and then proceed to read aloud from the report. That is objectionable, of course. See United States v. Weller, 238 F.3d 1215 (10th Cir. 2001) (not error for trial court to prohibit witness's use of an appraisal list of objects to refresh recollection where the judge believed that the list would be the source of direct testimony). As opposing counsel in a refreshing recollection situation, you should be on guard for this improper use of a refreshing document, though it may be difficult to prevent it in specific situations.

If the object is a writing that refreshes the witness's memory, the opposing party is entitled to inspect the document, and also to introduce into evidence "those portions which relate to the testimony of the witness." FRE 612. If the writing has refreshed the witness's memory, however, it will probably contain information that corroborates what the witness has said. Thus, it is unlikely that the opposing party would want to introduce it into evidence. If the object does not revive the witness's memory, there will be no further occasion to refer to the object, unless the object happens to have some independent relevance to the lawsuit.

KEY POINTS

1. Written or recorded statements concerning any relevant matters may be admissible for their truth under FRE 803(5) if the declarant testifies as a witness and is not able to fully recollect those matters. The witness must have made or adopted the record when her memory was still fresh and have made an effort at accuracy in making the record.
2. If a statement is the product of reporting and recording by two or more out-of-court declarants, then all declarants must testify if FRE 803(5) is the sole hearsay exception relied on to admit the statement. FRE 803(5) can be used in combination with other exemptions and exceptions to admit statements containing multiple levels of hearsay.
3. Recorded recollection is distinguished from refreshing memory. The latter is not a hearsay exception, but a witness examination technique. The witness may be shown anything, including inadmissible matter, reasonably expected to jog the witness's memory. The witness then may only testify from her refreshed memory.

PROBLEMS

8.57. Plaintiff Rhoda Bolt, a CPA and Chief Auditor for Aquatic Marine Corp. (AMC), has filed suit against AMC for sexual harassment and wrongful discharge due to AMC's creation of a hostile work environment. She alleges that the harassment, consisting of overtly sexual and demeaning comments and behavior from other employees, began in July 2012; that the atmosphere in the Auditing Department was overtly hostile to her; that this affected her ability to perform her job; and that she was wrongfully discharged in 2015.

  (a) At trial, Plaintiff will offer notes that she wrote outlining many specific incidents of harassment that she cannot entirely recall. She testifies that she is not sure when she began taking notes on the incidents, but that it was some time in 2013; that she made the notes at home, usually but not always on the same day as the incident reported; and that the only reason she made the notes was to accurately record what happened and when. The notes terminate in 2015 when she was discharged by AMC. Are Bolt's notes admissible to prove a hostile work environment?

(b) Defendant AMC will offer the personal notes made by Leveritt Darnell, Chief Financial Officer of AMC and Bolt's supervisor. Darnell testifies that after Bolt made several complaints about the problems and hostile work environment in the Auditing Department, he became concerned about Bolt's job performance. He says he wrote these notes for his own reference for a period of several months in 2015, before he discharged Bolt. The notes describe Darnell's analysis of accounting mistakes made in accounting documents written by Bolt in her role as Chief Auditor, dating back as early as 2012. The notes were not shown to Bolt nor to anyone else, but were placed by Darnell into his file on Bolt. Are Darnell's notes admissible if Darnell has insufficient memory to testify fully and accurately?

8.58. While Andrew was crossing an intersection, he was hit by an automobile, which fled the scene of the accident. Sadie, Andrew's companion, rushed to his side, and asked, "Are you okay?" Andrew, who was still conscious, responded, "I don't know, but I got the license number of the car that hit me. It was 879-ACY. Write it down so we won't forget." Sadie had nothing to write on, so she kept repeating the license number to herself. When she got home, a few hours later, she wrote down the number. Andrew has brought an action for personal injuries against Roland Bowers, who is the registered owner of a green Plymouth with the license number 879-ACY. Neither Andrew nor Sadie remembers the license number now. Is Sadie's record of it admissible under any hearsay exceptions? Which ones?

8.59. Officer Kristi Curtis investigated the crime scene of a residential burglary, where she made numerous personal observations, such as footprints in the flower bed (that eventually matched the defendant's cowboy boots), a broken window latch, various drawers and cupboards that were left open, etc. She wrote up a detailed report later during the same work shift. On direct examination at trial a year later, Curtis seems to have forgotten many details. The prosecutor hands Curtis a copy of her police report and asks when she wrote it. The defense counsel objects that the police report is inadmissible under FRE 803(8)(A)(ii), and the objection is sustained. (You will read about that exception shortly. You don't need to know it to answer this question.) The prosecutor then asks if the report would refresh Curtis's recollection. Curtis says it would. The prosecutor then asks, "What did you observe?" Curtis responds, "Footprints were found in the flower bed, eventually matched to defendant's cowboy boots—." Defense counsel wants to object. What objection? What, if anything, can the prosecution do to get Officer Curtis' personal observations of the crime scene into evidence?

11. Explanation of FRE 803(6): Records of a Regularly Conducted Activity

FRE 803(6) provides:

(6) *Records of a Regularly Conducted Activity.* A record of an act, event, condition, opinion, or diagnosis if:

(A) the record was made at or near the time by—or from information transmitted by—someone with knowledge;

(B) the record was kept in the course of a regularly conducted activity of a business, organization, occupation, or calling, whether or not for profit;

(C) making the record was a regular practice of that activity;

(D) all these conditions are shown by the testimony of the custodian or another qualified witness, or by a certification that complies with Rule 902(11) or (12) or with a statute permitting certification; and

(E) the opponent does not show that the source of information or the method or circumstances of preparation indicate a lack of trustworthiness.

a. Preliminary Factfinding

The factual requirements for records of a regularly conducted activity are:

- the statement is a record;
- the record is of an act, event, condition, opinion, or diagnosis;
- the record was made at or near the time of the act, etc.;
- the record was made by someone with knowledge of the act, etc.; or
- the record was made from information transmitted by someone with knowledge;
- the record was kept in the course of a regularly conducted activity of a business, organization, occupation, or calling, whether or not for profit;
- it was a regular practice of that activity to make the record.

In addition to these requirements, FRE 803(6) also contains two unique features. It requires the proponent to produce a "custodian or other qualified witness" to testify about the factual requirements or to present a written declaration certifying such foundation facts pursuant to FRE 902(11) or (12). FRE 803(6)(E) also permits execlusion of a record that otherwise fits the exception, if the opponent shows that the record's source or method or circumstances of preparation are untrustworthy.

The Broad Scope of FRE 803(6)(B), "Regularly Conducted Activity." FRE 803(6) and its state law equivalents have long been known as the "business records exception." Prior to the restyling, FRE 803(6) used the term "business records" and defined "business" very broadly. That term continues in use, in part because the vast majority of records admitted under FRE 803(6) are in fact business records, even though the rule extends to activities defined more broadly than a for-profit business. The more than 30 years of existing case law that we draw on to interpret and apply the provisions of FRE 803(6) has focused primarily on the records of "businesses." Also "business records," at four syllables, is much easier to say than the 15-syllable "records of a regularly conducted activity." Courts and practitioners, and probably your professor, are likely to use the term "business records" for these reasons. We thus use the "business" terminology in the text below.

The important point is to remember, however, that the exception is not limited strictly to records of "businesses." In its present form FRE 803(6)(B) explicitly includes records of organizations, occupations, and callings, whether or not for profit. Thus, the records of groups that do not seem to be businesses, such as the expense records of a Scout Troop, or records of expenses kept by students working on a student law journal or other student organization, easily fall within Rule 803(6)(B). When record-keeping activity assumes a public role, or provides a function within an "organization," the terms of the exception apply.

FRE 803(6)(C): Making the Record Was a Regular Practice. The term *"record"* has been interpreted to include a broad range of documents—memoranda, reports, recordings, or data compilations. The distinguishing feature of the FRE 803(6) records is that information about acts and events, etc., has been stored somewhere outside of the human mind and can be recalled in some form other than oral testimony. The permissible contents of these records are likewise broad, and include acts, events, conditions, opinions, or diagnoses.

The principal limitation on what counts as a record has less to do with its contents, and more to do with the regularity with which the organization (or the participants in the "regularly conducted activity") made records of that type. Regularly recorded organizational matters are within the core of the rule. The business records exception requires a showing that it was a *regular* practice to make the record, meaning that making such a record, or records like it, happened systematically or repeatedly. Compare United States v. Skeddle, 981 F. Supp. 1069, 1072 (N.D. Ohio 1997) (customary for an accounting firm employee to take notes at client meetings, place them in the client files, and refer to them at a later time; therefore, notes were kept as part of the regular course of business) with AgriBioTech, Inc. v. Thomas, 2005 U.S. Dist. LEXIS 6465 (D. Nev. 2005) (document entitled "Trott conference" appears to be notes of a meeting but no evidence offered that employee regularly took notes at meetings, or that it was his practice to make such notes, or that he was under any "business" duty to report his notes of the events of the meeting). In United States v. Kaiser, 609 F.3d 556, 574 (2d Cir. 2010), a participant in the fraudulent business scheme charged against defendant made notes in his "business planner" concerning telephone calls during which defendant asked him to send letters confirming financial obligations that were false. Kaiser argued that the participant's note taking was too sporadic and selective to meet the standard of "regular practice," and that the participant stated on cross-examination that he only wrote down "highlights" and what he thought was important. The court overruled these objections, holding that "part of the participant's business was to sign these confirmations, and these are records of conversations he had in connection with that part of his business . . . [they are] unquestionably business records." Further,

> [t]he selectivity that Kaiser points out. . . is the nature of all note-taking. A business record need not be mechanically generated to be part of a "regular practice." . . . [The participant's] contact log is different in kind from the types of "miscellaneous jottings" that courts have found inadmissible under this exception, because it was maintained in a consistent way and was focused on a certain range of issues that were relevant to his business. *Cf.* United States v. Ramsey, 785 F.2d 184, 192 (7th Cir. 1986) ("Occasional desk calendars, in which entries may or may not appear at the whim of the writer, do not have the sort of regularity that supports a reliable inference.") [Id. at 575.]

What about records made by individuals, as opposed to organizations? The wording of FRE 803(6) does not rule out the records of individuals. Again, the determining factor is the regularity *of the activity for which* the records were kept, FRE 803(B), and the regularity with which the records were made. FRE 803(6)(C). Probably your notes as a student do not qualify as business records, nor would casual records you keep of your household expenses. But there are cases in which a person's own records of expenses, or income, kept for business reasons such as balancing bank accounts, maintaining a budget, or preparing tax returns can qualify under FRE 803(6), so long as they are "systematically checked and regularly and continually maintained." Keogh v. IRS, 713 F.2d 496, 499 (9th Cir. 1983). Your receipts and bills for goods and services that you purchase are business records of the seller or the credit card company, but they are not your business records. Courts do not treat people as being in the business of being a consumer.

FRE 803(6)(A): Personal Knowledge and Near Contemporaneity Are Required. The original source of a FRE 803(6) record is like the observer discussed in regard to FRE 803(5). This original source must have personal knowledge of a matter and must start the process of making a record of that matter. The source may make the written record, or may transmit information orally or in some written format to a series of other people who record the information in various formats. FRE 803(6) also requires that the original source start this process of record-keeping at or near the time that the source observed the matter.

An example will help to illustrate these requirements. In a suit for breach of contract, the purchaser claims that goods purchased from the seller were delivered in a damaged condition. To prove damaged condition, the purchaser offers a document entitled "Damage Report." It identifies the shipment of goods as coming from the seller and describes the damaged condition of the items. Joan, the purchaser's employee who wrote the report, has left the company and is unavailable to testify. Since the report is offered to prove the truth of the matters it asserts—that the boxes were labeled as coming from seller, and that the goods were damaged—it is hearsay. To fit within the business record exception, the proponent must prove that Joan had personal knowledge of the matters described and that she wrote the report or transmitted her knowledge close in time to her observation of the shipment.

It is important to identify the activity with which the record should be contemporaneous. In In Re WorldCom, Inc. Securities Litigation, 2005 U.S. Dist. LEXIS 2215, at *24-25 (S.D.N.Y. 2005), the consolidated securities class action arising out of the collapse of the telecommunications giant WorldCom, one of the defendants filed a motion in limine to exclude the Restatement of WorldCom's 2000 and 2001 financial statements. The Restatement, issued in 2004, revealed an overstatement of WorldCom's net income by $74 billion in those two years. In response to the claim that the Restatement was not contemporaneous with the financial events of 2000-2001, the court held that a financial statement is never created contemporaneously with the underlying business records, but is always "filed months after the end of the fiscal year[.]" As for the Restatement, that was "the result of a [regular] process of review . . . that reflects the accounting work done [by the reviewer] 'at or near the time' that the report was created." In other words, the Restatement was deemed sufficiently contemporaneous with the regular *review process*, as opposed to the actual financial events reflected in the earlier financial statements.

Made Pursuant to a "Business Duty."   The business record exception has long been interpreted to include a requirement that the persons making the business record—those who provide the initial information and those who transmit it within the organization—have a "business duty to report" the information. This normally means some sort of formal obligation stemming from the person's employment in the business, or assigned task or role in the organization or regularly conducted activity. FRE 803(6) does not expressly state such a factual requirement, but it has been inferred from the regularity requirements of FRE 803(6)(B) and (C). See United States v. Patrick, 959 F.2d 991 (D.C. Cir. 1992) (receipt with defendant's name and address on it was not an admissible business record because defendant had no business duty to supply name and address when purchasing a television).

The business duty to provide or report information is implicit in the business routine of generating the record, and is considered an element that guarantees accuracy. See MCC Mgmt. of Naples, Inc. v. Int'l Bancshares Corp., 468 F. App'x 816, 828-829 (10th Cir. 2012); United States v. Pazsint, 703 F.2d 420, 424-425 (9th Cir. 1983). Indeed, the Advisory Committee refers to the business duty to report as "a duty of accuracy." See Advisory Committee Note to FRE 803(6). Unlike the recorded recollection exception, FRE 803(6) does not require testimony as to the accuracy of the contents of the record. Instead, if "the supplier of the information does not act in the regular course [of business activity], an essential link is broken; the assurance of accuracy does not extend to the information itself[.]" Id.

The business duty requirement generally means that information supplied by outsiders to the business or activity cannot be admitted as part of the business record under FRE 803(6). Such an outsider statement within a business record raises a problem of hearsay within hearsay under FRE 805. If offered for its truth, the outsider's statement would have to qualify for a different hearsay exception or exemption. However, some courts have extended the idea of a business duty to report to persons or entities outside the business who have a contractual or agency relationship with the business that requires them to report accurately. See Peak v. Kubota Tractor Corp., 559 F. App'x 517, 523 (6th Cir. 2014) (employee of defendant's contractor "was a participant in the chain producing the record in the course of [defendant's] regular business activity).

Custodian or Other Qualified Witness.   Courts have interpreted the language in FRE 803(6)(D) to require that the custodian of the record or some other qualified witness be able to explain the record-keeping procedures of the organization. Personal knowledge of the specific records at issue is not required:

> Rule 803(6) does not require that the custodian personally gather, input, and compile the information memorialized in a business record. The custodian . . . need not be in control of or have individual knowledge of the particular corporate records, but need only be familiar with the company's recordkeeping practices. [Guillermety v. Secretary of Education, 341 F. Supp. 2d 682, 690 (E.D. Mich. 2003).]

The foundation witness need not be an employee of the organization, so long as there is a showing of the witness's familiarity with the record-keeping system. And the end custodian of data may testify as to the process by which the data was generated, and transmitted by, other entities. Houston v. Smith, 2010 U.S. Dist. LEXIS 118135 (W.D.

Pa.) (satellite data generated by a computer and processed by Qualcomm and then used and stored by defendant corporation was shown to be transmitted from the other entities in the regular course of business by the testimony of defendant's witness).

FRE 803(6), together with FRE 902(11) and (12), now permits the foundation for business records to be provided by a written declaration, rather than a live testifying witness. While the factual requirements for the hearsay exception should not be altered by the streamlined foundation procedure in FRE 902(11) and (12), some cases seem to accept written declarations that speak in wholly conclusory terms: "[T]he records were made and kept in the course of business by an employee who had personal knowledge of the facts recorded . . . This is sufficient." Spurlock v. Commissioner, T.C. Memo 2003-124 (U.S. Tax Ct. 2003). In such a case, neither the opponent nor the jury is provided with any detailed, context-specific information with which to evaluate the reliability of the record. The notice requirement is intended to give the opponent the opportunity to take discovery to test the adequacy of the foundation in the declaration, but this results in increasing the costs of the opponent's pretrial discovery. United States v. Klinzing, 315 F.3d 803 (7th Cir. 2003) (defendant had right to depose record keepers or call them to the stand for cross-examination).

b. Justification for the Admissibility of Records of Regularly Conducted Activities

No business or other organized entity can survive in today's world without keeping records of its activities. And there is very little civil litigation that does not use some type of record as evidence. As with many other exceptions, the admissibility of FRE 803(6) records is justified on the grounds of necessity and reliability. The necessity is twofold. First, there is frequently multiple person involvement in the production of these records. It would be time-consuming, inconvenient, and perhaps impossible to call each individual who had a part in generating the record as a witness. Second, even if the people who were responsible for making the record were on the witness stand, they might not have any present memory of matters contained in the record. With respect to routine matters recorded in the ordinary course of business, all they can testify about is their routine practice in making such a record. The record itself is the only accurate source of the substantive information.

The reliability rationale for the exception is based on several factors. The requirement that the record be made at or near the time of the matter recorded minimizes any memory problem. A person who makes a record in the regular course of activity has an incentive to be honest and accurate in order to advance both the purposes of the organization or business, and to be personally successful within the business or organization. The fact that the record is kept in the regular course suggests that it may be relied on or checked for accuracy, which provides an added guarantee of trustworthiness and an incentive for the record maker to be accurate in the first place. The routine nature of many records that are made and kept in the regular course of organized activity suggests that there is not likely to be an incentive to lie about routine matters. And finally, the regularity of the record-making process often gives the record maker some expertise in record-making that tends to ensure accuracy. Many of these generalizations might not apply to the kinds of personal records described above that may not qualify as FRE 803(6) records.

12. FRE 803(6): Practical Applications and Problems

Not all records that are made and kept in the regular course of business or organized activities are reliable. Consider, for example, records that are created for self-serving purposes, such as for promotion and public relations, or in preparation for litigation. You might think differently about the reliability of a discussion of the safety of an automobile braking system contained in a company's testing report, as opposed to a discussion in a report prepared to defend against a lawsuit. Or consider the difference between job site accident reports filed by injured employees or by an official public investigator.

a. Exclusion for Untrustworthiness

FRE 803(6)(E) permits the judge to exclude a record if "the source of information or the method or circumstances of preparation indicate a lack of trustworthiness." This exclusionary clause is based on a concern articulated by the Supreme Court in Palmer v. Hoffman, 318 U.S. 109 (1943). The plaintiff, who was injured in a railroad grade crossing accident, claimed that the railroad was negligent in that the engineer failed to ring a bell, blow a whistle, or have a light burning in the front of the train. The defendant offered into evidence as a business record an accident report made by the engineer, who died before the trial. The Supreme Court, interpreting the then-existing federal business record statute, upheld exclusion of the record as not made "in the regular course of business."

> [I]t is manifest that in this case those reports are not for the systematic conduct of the enterprise as a railroad business. Unlike payrolls, accounts receivable, accounts payable, bills of lading and the like, these reports are calculated for use essentially in the court, not in the business. Their primary utility is in litigating, not in railroading. [Id. at 113-114.]

Palmer v. Hoffman interprets what constitutes regular business conduct so as to eliminate documents prepared with a self-interested business or personal motivation. In our hypothetical, the Damage Report prepared by Joan about the damaged shipment, might be excluded under Palmer v. Hoffman. Yet it could be a regular practice of a company to prepare such reports, and it would serve a regular business interest to do so. The approach of FRE 803(6) is to permit the judge to deal with the risk of untrustworthiness on a case-by-case basis. However, Palmer v. Hoffman remains good law, and records whose "primary utility is in litigating" are likely to face at least a heavy presumption of unreliability under FRE 803(6)(E). As in *Palmer*, litigation-oriented reports prepared by insurance claims adjusters or investigators, whose business includes regular litigation, are nevertheless generally held untrustworthy. See Jordan v. Binns, 712 F.3d 1123, 1135 (7th Cir. 2013) (citing *Palmer*); Certain Underwriters at Lloyd's, London v. Sinkovich, 232 F.3d 200, 205 n.4 (4th Cir.2000) (same).

Burden of Persuasion.   FRE 803(6)(E) states, as the final element to the business records exception, that "the opponent does not show" circumstances indicating a lack of trustworthiness. Thus, an opponent to the proffered record has the burden of persuading the judge that it lacks trustworthiness. (Because a minority of judicial decisions had held otherwise, FRE 803(6)(E) was amended in 2014 to clarify that this burden falls on the party opposing admission of the business record. See Advisory Committee Note to 2014 Amendment.) Thus, the seller of the damaged goods would attack Joan's self-interest (on behalf of her employer) in writing the Damage Report, and could question her method of preparing it. That the custodian or other qualified witness does not know whether the records are complete, or completely accurate, does not establish untrustworthiness. The opponent must produce "specific and credible" evidence of untrustworthiness. Morris v. B.C. Olympiakos, SFP, 721 F. Supp. 2d 546 (S.D. Tex. 2010). Of course, the proponent of the record must be prepared to respond to the opponent's attack with facts that show trustworthiness.

Circumstances Indicating Lack of Trustworthiness.   The greatest concern about trustworthiness focuses on sincerity dangers, such as the motivation of the preparer. The purpose of the record is central; records specifically prepared for litigation are viewed as infused with a motive to distort the truth. Certain Underwriters at Lloyd's, London v. Sinkovich, 232 F.3d 200, 205 (4th Cir. 2000) (report of an insurance investigator hired by plaintiff Underwriters was inadmissible as prepared in anticipation of litigation, even though the investigator regularly prepared such reports in the regular course of his business; the primary motive was to prepare for litigation). Where accident reports are prepared pursuant to a statutory duty, or a regular business routine, some courts may find that they are not oriented toward litigation. Other motives may also affect trustworthiness. Opponents charged that the Restatement prepared in the *WorldCom* case was unreliable because the preparers were motivated to maximize the Restatement adjustments for tax purposes. The court held that this possible motive did not justify exclusion of the Restatement as untrustworthy, since it was required to comply with "generally accepted accounting principles" (GAAP); was under intense scrutiny from the courts, the SEC, and the parties; and was created by scores of people, making any plan of manipulation exceedingly difficult. In re WorldCom, Inc. Securities Litigation, 2005 U.S. Dist. LEXIS 2215, at *26-27. Where the original source of the information or the method of preparation of the record is unclear or unknown, courts may find untrustworthiness. Kay v. Lamar Advertising of South Dakota, Inc., 2009 WL 2731054 (D.S.D.) (in an personal injury case, speed of plaintiffs' motorcycle appearing in ambulance report untrustworthy; source of the statement not identified or explained; no evidence showing it was given in a routine, business manner). It has been held that when the author of the record is testifying as a witness, "the degree of reliability for admission is greatly reduced." United States v. Kaiser, 609 F.3d at 576.

b. Opinions and Diagnoses

FRE 803(6) states that opinions and diagnoses contained within records of regular activities are admissible. The potential subjectivity of opinions and diagnoses do not give rise to a categorical basis to object to their admission as business records, so long as the regularity, contemporaneity, and firsthand knowledge requirements of FRE 803(6)(A)-(C) have been met. Thus, business records may include medical and other expert opinions and conclusions. See In re WorldCom, Inc. Securities Litigation, 2005 U.S. Dist. LEXIS 2215, at *26 (financial statement is a business record even though it "reflects accounting judgments"). In this respect, FRE 803(6) is broader than some of its state-law counterparts. See Cal. Evid. Code §1271 (business records include only "an act, condition, or event").

The difficulty with admitting opinions and diagnoses is that there will not necessarily be an opportunity to cross-examine the person who made these statements. The opponent will be less able to explore the underlying factual bases for the opinion or diagnosis and, in the case of expert opinions, to explore the purported expert's degree of expertise. In some cases, information about the expert or about the factual support for the opinion may be available from the foundation witness or may be contained in the document itself. To the extent that such information is not available, the party against whom the evidence is offered can argue for exclusion under the expert witness rules: such as that the source has not been qualified as an expert (FRE 702), or that the bases for the expert opinion cannot be disclosed (FRE 703). Van der AA v. Commissioner, 2005 U.S. Tax Ct. LEXIS 21 (U.S. Tax Ct.) (the business record rule does not override the rules governing opinion testimony; court would not admit valuation report into evidence without the availability of the author for cross-examination). Some courts treat these issues as a question of lack of trustworthiness under FRE 803(6). Aumand v. Dartmouth Hitchcock Medical Center, 611 F. Supp. 2d 78, 86 (D.N.H. 2009) (rather than seek exclusion of an opinion in a medical report, the "adverse party bears the burden to show . . . lack of trustworthiness"). Others analyze the issue under FRE 403, asking whether the probative value of the evidence is substantially outweighed by the risk that, in the absence of critical evaluation, the jury will be misled and will give undue weight to the opinion. These concerns are particularly significant "if the opinion involves difficult matters of interpretation and a central dispute in the case, such as causation." McCormick on Evidence, Vol. 2 §293, at 322 (Kenneth S. Broun ed., 6th ed. 2006).

c. Records Containing Multiple Levels of Hearsay

If several people contribute to the creation of FRE 803(6) records, then there are multiple levels of hearsay in the document. Under FRE 805, each level must fit within a hearsay exception or exemption. If only FRE 803(6) is used to admit the entire document, then *all* declarants must be shown to satisfy *all* of its factual requirements. For example, in the case of the Damage Report just discussed, Joan may have inspected the damaged goods and written notes about them; then her assistant, Linda, may have entered the contents of the notes onto a company Damage Form; and Eileen, the manager of the division, may have actually written the Damage Report based on the Damage Form. Each of these declarants perceived something as part of their regular business duty: Joan perceived the damaged goods, Linda perceived the notes, and Eileen perceived the Damage Form. If the information is transmitted along this business chain with near contemporaneity, then its final incarnation as the Damage Report may fall within FRE 803(6). The actual maker of the record, Eileen, does not have to have personal knowledge of the damaged goods. Rather, it is sufficient, according to the language of the rule, that the record was made at or near the time by—or from information transmitted by—someone with knowledge. The custodian or other foundation witness would be required to testify (or submit a declaration) about the process by which the information was transmitted and the record was created.

Records containing multiple levels of hearsay are created in a wide variety of situations: A recording secretary may take notes on what happened at a board meeting and give those notes to a stenographer to transcribe; a doctor may orally recite her observations about a patient, which are then recorded by a medical assistant; an employee of a seller may report shipping information to an employee of a purchaser, who then records it. In testifying about how third-party cost estimates were incorporated into his own business records, a witness testified that he would receive outside estimates, incorporate them into his project file on his computer, do a scope comparison to see that the estimate was what he requested, check the reasonableness of the estimate, and look for mistakes or omissions. BP Amoco Chemical Co. v. Flint Hills Resources, LLC, 697 F. Supp. 2d 1001, 1021-1022 (N.D. Ill. 2010).

At each level, there is of course some risk that the declarants may fabricate, misunderstand, or incorrectly remember the events reported or recorded. It is the belief that, in general, routinely prepared records are accurate that justifies admission of the documents.

Sources of Information with No Business Duty.   What if the original source of the information recorded in a business record is not acting in the regular course of business—that is, has no business duty to report on the events observed? In the preceding hypothetical concerning the Damage Report, that Joan's Damage Report contains the following statement: "Just after delivery, Bystander reported to me that he had seen the seller's delivery truck in a rear-end collision on the highway an hour previously." If the Damage Report is offered to prove that the rear-end collision caused the damage to the delivered goods while in seller's custody, there is now an additional hearsay step in the record—from Bystander to Joan. It is the truth of Bystander's statement that the record is offered to prove. Bystander has no business duty to observe or report this accident, or to ensure the accuracy of Joan's record. Thus, the rationale for the business records exception is not applicable to Bystander's statement to Joan. Yet the record was made "from information transmitted by . . . a person [Bystander] with knowledge." FRE 803(6), if read literally, would appear to make the record admissible.

As we have seen, FRE 803(6) has been interpreted as imposing a requirement that the information in a business record be supplied by persons with a business duty to report. Nevertheless, courts have recognized an exception to this business duty requirement. "[I]nformation provided by an outsider can become a business record if it is shown that (1) the business has a policy of verifying the information provided to it, or (2) the business possesses a sufficient self-interest in the accuracy of the record to justify an inference of trustworthiness." MCC Mgmt. of Naples, Inc. v. Int'l Bancshares Corp., 468 F. App'x 816, 828-829 (10th Cir. 2012); see United States

v. Sokolow, 91 F.3d 396, 403 (3d Cir. 1996) (proof of claim forms submitted by insurance claimants were verified and audited before being incorporated into the insurance adjuster's records). Although FRE 803(6) has sometimes been used to apply to police reports, courts have not extended this verification principle to them. Law enforcement investigators have an interest in casting a wide net, and typically record all witness statements rather than recording only those which can be independently verified.

Use of Multiple Exceptions and Exemptions. The source of information in a FRE 803(6) record may be a declarant whose statement falls within *another hearsay exception or exemption.* If Bystander's statement to Joan had been, "I just saw that truck in a rear-end collision," it might have been admissible under FRE 803(1), the present sense impression exception. If so, combining that exception for Bystander's statement with FRE 803(6) for the other hearsay steps would make the entire record admissible, assuming that Joan has a duty to report that a Bystander's statement was made to her. What if a doctor's record describing a patient's symptoms includes the patient's statement, "My arm is broken because I was assaulted by Paul"? The patient's statements about the general cause of injury may fit within FRE 803(4), the exception for statements made for medical treatment. Naming the assailant, however, is not likely to be pertinent to diagnosis or treatment. Therefore, FRE 803(4) would probably not be available to admit the name of the alleged attacker. And the information about who is responsible for the patient's injury is arguably not pertinent to treatment; therefore the doctor may have no professional duty to record such information. Or the potential risks become a basis for arguing that the recording of the statement about Paul lacks trustworthiness.

Customer surveys are often taken by market research companies to generate a report about what customers believe about products or about their relationship with suppliers. The customers are not acting within a business duty when they respond to a survey, but their statements are usually admitted as "state of mind" under FRE 803(3) as long as they are not used to prove *facts* remembered or believed. DeBeans Cone Co., LLC v. Norse Dairy Systems, LLC, 678 F. Supp. 2d 883 (N.D. Iowa 2009) (categorizations of survey responses and conclusions in the report are within the regular business activity of the survey firm).

d. Computer Documents and Electronic Data

FRE 803(6) also permits reliance on computer, electronic and website documents. See the Advisory Committee Note to FRE 803:

> The form which the "record" may assume under the rule is described broadly . . . The expression "data compilation" is used as broadly descriptive of any means of storing information other than the conventional words and figures in written or documentary form. It includes, but is by no means limited to, electronic computer storage.

Some computer documents, such as accounting records, represent the storage and sorting of declarations of fact that are entered by persons into the system. The process by which the data were input and used must be pursuant to a regular duty in accordance with regular practice. Some courts have also insisted on evidence concerning procedures for input control, including tests to insure accuracy and reliability. United States v. Scholle, 553 F.2d 1109 (8th Cir. 1997). Other computer documents, such as telephone records, are automatically generated by the computerized system without any human input of underlying data. These records may not be hearsay at all because there is no human declarant making a statement, but the accuracy of the process by which they are produced is still necessary for authentication under FRE 901(b)(9). Houston v. Smith, 2010 U.S. Dist. LEXIS, at *10-12 (satellite tracking data processed through a computer authenticated by testimony of data recipient).

Many businesses and organizations publish internal information about their activities on websites. Every digital data entry is a record of such information, and provided that all of the requirements are satisfied, each printout of this information would be admitted under FRE 803(6). For both computer and website documents, if the data was collected and entered into the computer or onto the website in the regular course of business, then printing out a document for purposes of litigation does not trigger the untrustworthiness concerns of Palmer v. Hoffman. Documents culled from a business's data base by a query that selects a smaller subset of data is within the FRE 803(6) exception. Health Alliance Network, Inc. v. Continental Casualty Ins. Co., 245 F.R.D. 121 (S.D.N.Y. 2007).

E-mail documents may also qualify as FRE 803(6) records if it can be shown that it was the regular practice of employees to write and maintain such e-mails. An exchange of e-mails between people in different companies may also be admissible under FRE 803(6) if adequate declarations as to business duty are provided by both businesses. DirecTV v. Murray, 307 F. Supp. 2d 764 (D.S.C. 2004).

KEY POINTS

1. FRE 803(6) provides a hearsay exception for records of "regularly conducted activit[ies]," which includes business as well as other types of organizations, and even possibly individuals for activities sufficiently routinized and businesslike.
2. The records must be made and kept on a regular basis pursuant to the regularly conducted activity, and must be based on relatively recent information from firsthand sources with a business duty to provide the information. Such information can be passed from person to person within the organization without taking the record outside coverage of 803(6), so long as each person has a business duty to report.
3. The factual requirements to admit a business record may come either from a person with firsthand knowledge of the making and keeping of the record, or from a person familiar with the record-making and keeping practice of the organization. These factual requirements are likely to satisfy the FRE 901-902 foundation requirements at the same time, and can be supplied by an affidavit in place of a live witness.

4. The judge has discretion to exclude a business record if the opposing party demonstrates that the information source or circumstances of making the record indicate untrustworthiness. Records made for litigation purposes, even if routinely made, are given a presumption of untrustworthiness in the case law.

5. The record may contain opinions and diagnoses, in addition to other kinds of facts.

6. If the source of information is an outsider to the organization (with no business duty to report), FRE 803(6) will still cover the record if the organization makes it a routine practice to verify the outside information. Otherwise, an additional level of hearsay may be involved requiring combining the business record exception with another exception or exemption.

PROBLEMS

8.60. Return to Problem 8.57, at page 562. The notes written by Leveritt Darnell are offered as business records under FRE 803(6) because Darnell is unavailable to testify. Who might serve as the foundation witness for these notes? What questions should be asked to satisfy FRE 803(6)? Will they be admitted?

In addition, Defendant AMC will also offer a memorandum evaluating Bolt's job performance that was written by Darnell approximately five months after Bolt was terminated. Darnell based the memorandum on (1) his own notes in Problem 8.57(b), and (2) interviews that he conducted with employees in the Auditing Department who worked under Bolt. The employees told him that from 2012 to 2015, Bolt kept interfering in their assigned tasks, and that she refused to delegate appropriate tasks to them. In this memorandum, Darnell expresses his opinion that it was proper to discharge Bolt (1) because of her lack of expertise in accounting principles and (2) because she failed to manage her staff effectively. He admits that this document was written to "express management's perspective" in the face of an impending EEOC investigation of Bolt's complaint. Is this memorandum admissible as a business record under FRE 803(6)?

8.61. Joseph Reyes is charged with multiple counts of racketeering, murder, assault, firearms, and narcotics violations, as well as conspiracy charges, for the role he played as the head of a large drug distribution organization. At the time of these crimes, Reyes was confined in a state prison where he was visited by Ralph Vargas and others to receive instructions. Vargas became a cooperating witness and testified about his meetings with Reyes in prison and the orders he received to commit murders. To corroborate this testimony, the government offers the visitor logbook from the prison, which indicated that Vargas and other gang members visited Reyes on several occasions, including on days close in time to several murders. The coordinator of inmate records at the prison, who has overall responsibility for storing and maintaining the logbooks, testified that visitors must sign the logbooks in the prison lobby when they enter the building and that they are required to show identification to the lobby officer. The coordinator testified that she observed her own visitors sign the books; that she had no personal knowledge whether all visitors showed identification or whether the lobby officer checked the identification against the log entry, but that these were procedures that were supposed to be followed. The logbooks themselves reflect irregularities such as missing names, missing addresses, and different names in the same handwriting. Reyes also contends that visitors of inmates have an incentive to provide misinformation to avoid monitoring of their contacts.

What arguments would you make on behalf of Reyes to exclude the logbooks under FRE 803(6)? As the government, how would you respond? What result?

8.62. Jeffrey Stanwick is on trial for securities fraud. The prosecution seeks the admission of an e-mail sent by Stanwick's broker, Stephanie Lane, to her supervisor, recounting a telephone conversation that Lane had with Stanwick. The e-mail quotes or summarizes various statements made by Stanwick, which seem to show his guilty knowledge of a fraudulent scheme in which he allegedly engaged. Lane is prepared to testify that it was her regular practice to send such e-mails to coworkers after important telephone conversations with clients. The prosecution offers the e-mail as a business record. There is no evidence that Lane had any reason to believe something illegal was going on at the time of the phone conversation; she will testify that this e-mail was sent to her supervisor strictly as a matter of routine. But there is also no evidence that Lane's practice of sending out confirmatory e-mails was required of her by her employer; rather it was something she did on her own initiative. The defendant objects that Lane had no "business duty to report" and therefore that the e-mail is not a business record. How should the court rule?

13. Explanation of FRE 803(8): Public Records and Reports

Every jurisdiction permits certain public records and reports to be admitted into evidence for their truth. The exception for public records has common law origins, but there are also many statutes governing the admissibility of particular kinds of public records. FRE 803(8) provides for the admission of three types of records:

> (8) *Public Records*. A record or statement of a public office if: ˙
>   (A) it sets out:
>   (i) the office's activities;
>   (ii) a matter observed while under a legal duty to report, but not including, in a criminal case, a matter observed by law-enforcement personnel; or
>   (iii) in a civil case or against the government in a criminal case, factual findings from a legally authorized investigation; and
>   (B) the opponent does not show that the source of information or other circumstances indicate a lack of trustworthiness.

a. Preliminary Factfinding

The basic factual requirements for public records under FRE 803(8) are:

- the statement is in the form of a record or statement of a public office;
- the contents set out the following:
  - the activities of that office;
  - matters observed under a duty imposed by law to report, but not a matter observed by law enforcement in criminal cases; or
  - factual findings from a legally authorized investigation, if in a civil case or against the government in a criminal case.

Activities of the Office.   FRE 803(8)(A)(i) is generally interpreted to admit records pertaining to a public office's own internal "housekeeping" functions such as its own personnel records and budgetary information. It also includes records of official activities of the office that are necessary to the performance of its public duties independent of any specific investigation or litigation. Such records are likely to qualify as business records under FRE 803(6) as well as public records, but the FRE 803(8)(A)(i) preliminary fact showing is minimal compared to the factual requirements of FRE 803(6). In the *Johnson* case, the "C" file on defendant Johnson contained records of Johnson's movements into and out of the California Department of Corrections, which set out the official activities of the CDC—housing and transporting prisoners. This would probably have qualified as (A)(i) public records. See United States v. Clarke, 628 F. Supp. 2d 15, 19 (D.D.C. 2009) (certificate of naturalization sets out the activity of the INS, that is, a granting of a petition for naturalization by the Attorney General).

FRE 803(8)(A)(ii): Matters Observed Under a Legal Duty to Report.   Records that report what public employees have observed pursuant to their public duties are admitted under subsection (A)(ii) upon a minimal foundation. Consider the differences between these public reports and the records admitted under FRE 803(6). The factual elements for business and other records of regular activities require evidence of near contemporaneity and regularity—circumstances that increase the trustworthiness of the records. These indicia of reliability are not required by FRE 803(8)(A)(ii).

Observing and reporting matters under a legal duty to report rarely requires independent proof of the pertinent law establishing such a duty. Instead, a "legal duty" should be considered as roughly synonymous with job responsibility: The legal duty is presumed from the purpose of the public office itself and the scope of employment of the public employee. The "matters" covered by the rule extend to everything that might fall within the legal duty. Thus, (A)(ii) public records span many fields, and may include weather reports, police reports, records of border crossings, and accident scene investigations.

The legal duty to report creates a limitation on the contents of the public record that is closely analogous to the "business duty to report" requirement that, we saw, has been read into FRE 803(6). Many public records and reports are the product of multiple levels of hearsay, when one public employee observes and reports observations to a colleague or subordinate who is also a public employee, and who then records them. As long as each link in the chain bears a public duty, FRE 803(8)(A)(ii) encompasses the entire report. However, statements of third parties who are not employed by the public entity do not have a "legal duty to report." Therefore, their statements constitute an additional level of hearsay requiring an exception or exemption other than FRE 803(8). Thus, "[i]t is well established that entries in a police report which result from the officer's own observations and knowledge may be admitted but that statements made by third persons under no business duty to report may not." United Technologies Corp. v. Mazer, 556 F.3d 1260, 1278 (11th Cir. 2009). Moral or legal obligations to provide accurate information to law enforcement officials do not qualify as a "legal duty to report" within the meaning of this exception.

FRE 803(8)(A)(iii): Factual Findings in Investigative Reports.   Subsection (A)(iii) provides for admission of a wide range of government investigative reports in civil cases, and against the government in criminal cases. The phrase "factual findings from a legally authorized investigation" makes for a wide scope of admissible reports, including official misconduct, accident reports by police, or incident reports by specialized agencies, safety and diagnostic studies relating to public health issues, and reports and studies on housing and employment discrimination. Such reports are powerful evidentiary tools, both because of the allegedly neutral weight of government investigation behind them and because of the persuasive impact of their findings and conclusions.

FRE 803(8)(A)(iii) permits use of factual findings only in civil cases and against the government in criminal cases. The prohibition against use against criminal defendants is grounded on concern that multiple, potentially inadmissible hearsay sources in such reports could run afoul of the Sixth Amendment Confrontation Clause that protects a criminal accused's right to confront and cross-examine witnesses.

The term "factual findings" has been authoritatively construed to include evaluative opinions and conclusions contained in public investigative reports. "As long as the conclusion is based on a factual investigation and satisfies the Rule's trustworthiness requirement, it should be admissible along with other portions of the report." Beech Aircraft Corp. v. Rainey, 488 U.S. 153, 170 (1988) (government report concluding that pilot error caused naval air crash admissible as "factual finding" under FRE 803(8).) The analytic difficulty of drawing a line between "fact" and "opinion" and the opportunity for exclusion of opinions and conclusions that lack trustworthiness under the exclusionary clause of FRE 803(8) justified that interpretation. Id.

The scope of "factual finding" is not unlimited, however. The following cases illustrate types of reports excluded from FRE 803(8)(A)(iii) because not deemed factual findings. Roxbury-Smellie v. Florida Dept. of Corrections, 324 Fed. App'x 783 (11th Cir. 2009) (interview notes of statements of potential witnesses); Sullivan v. Dollar Tree Stores, Inc., 623 F.3d 770 (9th Cir. 2010) ("pure legal conclusion" that defendant was a "successor in interest"); Smith v. Isuzu Motors Ltd., 137 F.3d 859 (5th Cir. 1998) (preliminary or interim evaluative opinions and, interim reports).

FRE 803(8)(A)(ii): Exclusion for Criminal Cases.   Subsection (A)(ii) prohibits applying the public records exception to "a matter observed by law-enforcement personnel" "in a criminal case." Reports authored by police officers are readily identifiable as law enforcement. We will discuss at pages 580-82, infra, how courts have applied this term to other public employees involved in law enforcement activities. Despite the text of the rule, it has been held in most Circuits that criminal defendants may offer FRE 803(8)(A)(ii) records against the government. United States v. Carneglia, 256 F.R.D. 384 (E.D.N.Y. 2009). FRE 803(8)(A)(iii) plainly permits use of factual findings only in civil cases and against the government in criminal cases.

The prohibition against use of (A)(ii) observations and (A)(iii) findings against criminal defendants is grounded on concern that multiple, potentially inadmissible hearsay sources in such reports could run afoul of the Sixth Amendment Confrontation Clause. That clause protects a criminal accused's right to confront and cross-examine witnesses. The prohibition overlaps somewhat with the current definition of "testimonial hearsay," but extends to nontestimonial hearsay in such reports.

A criminal defendant is free to offer (A)(ii) observations and (A)(iii) findings in his defense, against the government. Once the record is admitted, the prosecution becomes free to use it against the defendant. If the defendant offers part of a public record under (A)(ii) or (A)(iii), the prosecution may be able to invoke FRE 106 to have the rest of the report admitted, if excluding parts of the report would be unfair or misleading.

Exclusion for Lack of Trustworthiness. FRE 803(8)(B) provides an exclusion from the public records exception for lack of trustworthiness. The exclusion for lack of trustworthiness applies to all three subsections of FRE 803(8)(A). As with the similarly worded untrustworthiness exclusion in FRE 803(6), the burden is on the opponent to persuade the judge that the public record is untrustworthy. As a practical matter, of course, the proponent should be prepared to respond by citing factors that show trustworthiness. Under FRE 803(B), the focus of most challenges is on the hearsay nature of the underlying sources and the circumstances surrounding the factual investigation. The Advisory Committee Note emphasizes the timeliness of the report; the skill, expertise, and motivation of the investigator; and the procedures followed in preparation of the record. Desrosiers v. Flight International of Florida, Inc., 156 F.3d 952, 962 (9th Cir. 1998) (JAG report containing opinions regarding the cause of an air crash was partially redacted as untrustworthy because the author was not shown to be an expert, had not attended accident reconstruction school, had no formal training in investigation of aircraft accidents, and had not previously written such reports). It has been held that the subsection (B) should be applied "in a common sense manner . . . in determining whether the hearsay document . . . has sufficient independent indicia of reliability to justify its admission." Hickson Corp. v. Norfolk Southern Railway Co., 124 Fed. App'x 336, 345 (6th Cir. 2005).

Preliminary Factfinding. In contrast with the relatively elaborate factual requirements for business records under FRE 803(6), the FRE 803(8) requirements are relatively simple, such that a records custodian is not required. Testimony by a police officer that she prepared a report may be enough to qualify it as a public record.

FRE 902(a)(1) and (2) provide that public records can be authenticated without a live witness, if they are certified and signed.

b. Justification for the Admissibility of Public Records

The rationale for the public records exception—at least with respect to routine matters—is virtually identical to the rationale for the FRE 803(6) records exception: The inconvenience of calling public officials to testify and the likelihood that public officials may not recall the information in the records create the need for the exception. United States v. Midwest Fireworks Mfg. Co., 248 F.3d 563, 567 (6th Cir. 2001) (the public records exception "is a practical necessity [for] . . . government officers who have made in the course of their duties thousands of similar written hearsay statements"). The public official's duty and the likelihood that public access to the records will reveal inaccuracies tend to ensure the records' reliability. As with all hearsay exceptions, there must be a sufficient showing of personal knowledge in subsection (A)(i) and (ii) records. There are no specific factual requirements, however, that the record be made at or near the time of the event or that it be a regular practice of the public agency to make the record. Opinions and conclusions admitted under subsection (A)(iii) may, as we shall see, rest on information outside the investigator's own firsthand knowledge. "It is the methodology of factual investigation which provides a threshold safeguard against untrustworthiness." Ariza v. City of New York, 139 F.3d 132, 133 (2d Cir. 1998).

14. FRE 803(8)(A)(ii) and (iii) in Practice

The most contentious issues with the public records exception tend to concern 803(8)(A)(ii) and (iii).

a. The Meaning of Law Enforcement Personnel

The phrase "law enforcement personnel" in 803(8)(A)(ii) requires interpretation, so that we know what kinds of government reports are excluded from criminal cases. Obviously, police officers fall within that term. The question is, who else?[8]

"Law enforcement personnel" was initially given a broad interpretation that has since been narrowed. An early Circuit court opinion, United States v. Oates, 560 F.2d 45 (2d Cir. 1977), was influential in the provision that is now 803(8)(A)(ii). On appeal from the defendant's conviction for possession of heroin with intent to distribute, the Second Circuit held that the reports of forensic chemists were hearsay

---

8. Prior to the restyling, subsection (B) of FRE 803(8) excluded matter observed by "police and law enforcement." The "police" has been dropped and "law enforcement personnel" stands on its own as the term of exclusion. We assume that all prior case law interpreting the "law enforcement" term still applies to subsection (A)(ii).

and were "factual findings" under FRE 803(8)(A)(iii), thus inadmissible against a criminal defendant. The court also considered whether the documents were admissible under FRE 803(8)(A)(ii) (then codified as 803(8)(B)). The court construed "law enforcement personnel" "to include, at the least, any officer or employee of a governmental agency which has law enforcement responsibilities" and then elaborated on the extensive role Customs Service chemists play in the development of evidence for criminal prosecutions. While this interpretation is sensible, most courts since *Oates* have interpreted "law enforcement" more narrowly, including the Second Circuit. See, e.g., United States v. James, 712 F.3d 79, 89 (2d Cir. 2013) (autopsy reports by state medical examiners were not observations by law enforcement personnel).

Prosecutorial Function. Courts have included within this exclusionary language public officers whose functions are similar to police officers. This includes public employees who perform a "prosecutorial" or investigative function in specific cases. In part, courts are responding to Congress's concern that it might violate a defendant's confrontation right to use a police report instead of the live testimony of a police officer, particularly when the report contained the police officer's eyewitness account of criminal conduct. The same concern would extend to other public officials who are investigating specific cases of criminal conduct, such as customs inspectors and border patrol agents. It also became clear that "law-enforcement," as interpreted by *Oates*, would exclude statements by those who are not responsible for enforcing the criminal law, who perform administrative duties in a regulatory scheme, make administrative decisions, or seek compliance with fines and citations. Since *Oates*, courts have upheld admission of the factual observations contained in autopsy reports from the medical examiner's office because the employees of the office had no responsibilities for enforcing the law. The conclusions in the report as to the manner and cause of death, however, would be excluded under FRE 803(8)(A)(iii). United States v. Rosa, 11 F.3d 315 (2d Cir. 1993).

In a more recent case, an interview conducted by an official of the Immigration and Naturalization Service (INS) resulted in the prosecution of the defendant for having entered into a fraudulent marriage and for lying on an immigration document. The Ninth Circuit in United States v. Orellana-Blanco, 294 F.3d 1143, 1150 (9th Cir. 2002), overturned the trial court's admission of defendant's statement, written by the official but signed by the defendant, under FRE 803(B), now (A)(ii):

> An interview such as the one in the exhibit is adversarial in nature. [Defendant] was separated from his wife, obviously so that they could not coordinate their stories as they told them, and put under oath. Numerous cases treat INS officers and agents as "law enforcement" personnel, which are covered by the exclusion to the hearsay exception. Though the interview might not have been used for law enforcement purposes had the INS officer been satisfied, it was in fact used for that purpose, and in the natural course would be, if the INS was unsatisfied. Because [defendant] was put under oath and then charged with lying under oath on the form, the interview itself, at the INS office, was the "scene of the crime," and Officer Kendall's notes were in fact his subjective recordation of his aural observations at the scene of the crime as it took place.

In criminal cases, the focus on admissibility of many types of public records now includes the question of whether such reports and records are "testimonial" statements of the declarant under the interpretation of the confrontation clause set forth in Crawford v. Washington. See Section G., infra.

Routine and Regular Activities. It is now well established that routine, bureaucratic and nonadversarial reports made by law enforcement personnel, and even by police officers, do not fall within the subsection (A)(ii) exclusion. Thus, courts have admitted records kept in an automated data base kept by the California Department of Justice of firearms purchases from information provided by firearms dealers; a federal Secret Service data base identifying counterfeit currency by denomination, serial number, and date and location of its seizure; a warrant of deportation, which records deportation of aliens; reports of the time and date of crimes, but not the facts and circumstances involved; a log of all 911 calls; stolen vehicle reports; and records relating to the regular maintenance checks of a breathalyzer unit. All of these records were considered reliable because they were routine and ministerial, that is, not made in an adversarial setting. Two recent cases appear to be somewhat more problematic in holding that records are not made by "law-enforcement" personnel: United States v. Dowdell, 595 F.3d 50 (1st Cir. 2010) (arrest booking sheets containing identifying information about the person arrested, including photograph and description of clothing later used in an identification by an eyewitness); United States v. Reyes, 2009 WL 3273896 (S.D. Fla.) (a Situation Report of the names of persons taken on board a Coast Guard cutter, according to standard practice, from a capsized ship smuggling illegal aliens into the United States). Again, even for routine reports, the question remains whether the statements made therein are "testimonial" under *Crawford*.

b. The Relationship Between FRE 803(8)(A)(ii) and (iii) and Other Exceptions

If a report is excluded as a matter observed by law enforcement personnel under FRE 803(8)(A)(ii), or a factual finding under FRE 803(8)(A)(iii), the report cannot be admitted under the public records exception. But could it be admitted under another hearsay exception?

The two most obvious candidates for other applicable hearsay exceptions to admit such government reports are business records under FRE 803(6) and recorded recollections under FRE 803(5). The court in *Oates* considered whether the two chemists' reports could have been admitted as business records pursuant to FRE 803(6):

> [T]he government argues . . . that the chemist's report and worksheet in the case at bar fall clearly within the literal terms of . . . FRE 803(6) . . . [W]e assume for purpose of argument here, that . . . the chemist's report and worksheet might fall within the literal language of FRE 803(6) . . . This would not be the first time that a court has encountered a situation pitting some literal language of a statute against a legislative intent that flies in the face of that literal language. Our function as an interpretive body is, of course, to construe legislative enactments in such a way that the intent of the legislature is carried out . . . .
>
> [P]olice and valuative reports not satisfying the standards of FRE 803(8)(B) and (C) [now restyled as (A)(ii) and (iii)] may not qualify for admission under FRE 803(6) or any of the other exceptions to the hearsay rule. . . . [560 F.2d at 73-77.]

Thus, under *Oates*, if a document is inadmissible under FRE 803(8) because of the specific exclusionary terms in subsections (A)(ii) and (iii), it would be a subversion of the legislative intent to permit the document to be used as an FRE 803(6) business record. That holding seems sound, because the justifications for admitting business and public records are very similar. Most courts to consider the issue have followed this aspect of *Oates*. See, e.g., United States v. Hoffman-Vaile, 568 F.3d 1335, 1341 (11th Cir. 2009) ("Statements inadmissible as public agency reports under Rule 803(8) may not be received merely because they satisfy Rule 803(6)."); United States v. King, 613 F.2d 670, 673 (7th Cir. 1980) (same); but see United States v. Roulette, 75 F.3d 418, 421 (8th Cir. 1999) (admitted lab reports of illegal drugs under FRE 803(6)). By the same token, it should not be permissible to circumvent the specific limitations on the scope of FRE 803(8) by resorting to the residual exception FRE 807.

The rationale for prohibiting use of FRE 803(6) "as a back door for evidence excluded by [FRE 803](8)," however, does not apply with the same force to FRE 803(5). Recall that that rule requires the attendance of the author of the public record as a witness, obviating much of the confrontation-related concern. Contrary to some dicta in *Oates*, if the police or law enforcement officer does testify and is available for cross-examination, courts seem willing to allow use of FRE 803(5) by the government in criminal cases, even though the recorded recollection also happens to be in a public record made by law enforcement personnel. United States v. Sawyer, 607 F.2d 1190 (7th Cir. 1979); see also Goy v. Jones, 72 P.3d 351, 353 (Ariz. Ct. App. 2003).

15. FRE 803(8): The Problem of Multiple Hearsay Sources Within Investigative Reports

a. Is the Report Itself Admissible?

Many investigations that result in factual findings are based on hearsay information. Factual findings might be based on interviews of witnesses conducted by the investigator or on research evaluating both public and private records. In the *Beech* case, for example, the investigator relied on eyewitness accounts of the plane crash and reports analyzing the condition of the aircraft after the crash. Subsection (A)(iii) clearly contemplates that the investigator may use those sources, evaluate them, and then reject them or rely on them in making factual findings. Thus, unlike records under FRE 803(6) and public records under FRE 803(8)(A)(ii), where all sources must be operating under a "business" or organizational or legal duty to conform to the requirement of the exceptions, sources relied on under FRE 803(8)(A)(iii) need not be operating under any sort of public duty in relaying information to the investigator. In re September 11 Litigation, 621 F. Supp. 2d 131, 156 (S.D.N.Y. 2009) ("relevant and appropriate findings made by the Commission are potentially trustworthy and admissible. . . . The Commission heard 160 witnesses, was free from bias, and conducted public hearings that were the adequate equivalent of cross-examination. . . .").

Some hearsay sources may fall within their own exception or exemption to the rule of exclusion—for example, excited utterances, statements of parties, or business records. This would satisfy FRE 805 and would also provide some circumstantial guarantees of trustworthiness. Weinstein v. Stevens, 2010 WL 4824952, at *5 (E.D. Mich. 2010) (third-party witness statements were defendants' employees, authorized to speak on the subject or speaking about matters within the scope of their employment, thus entirely admissible). If the underlying hearsay sources are not admissible, one safeguard may be the public agency's ability to evaluate such sources before it decides to rely on them. If the original source has personal knowledge and no reason to misrepresent the information to the public official, under the circumstances, then the public report may be admitted. In re Air Disaster at Lockerbie Scotland on December 21, 1988, 37 F.3d 804 (2d Cir. 1994) (investigation of air crash relied in part on computerized records of passenger baggage based on hearsay reports from passengers' and crew members' friends and relatives).

But if factual findings are based on hearsay sources that are unidentified or that the court finds to be unreliable, the report itself may be excluded as lacking in trustworthiness. Lang v. Cullen, 725 F. Supp. 2d 925, 959 (C.D. Cal. 2010) (presentence report inadmissible under FRE 803(8) because the sources are not subject to evidentiary standards and may also contain factual errors); Hickman v. Norfolk Southern Railway Co., 124 Fed. App'x at 346 (unknown source reporting a toxic leak, transmitted by multiple levels of hearsay through state agencies and resulting in an erroneous time of occurrence, lacked "the necessary indicia of reliability"); Miller v. Field, 35 F.3d 1088 (6th Cir. 1994) (judgment for defendants reversed on grounds of erroneous admission of official report disputing alleged inmate rape of plaintiff, since report was based on inadmissible hearsay statements of the assailants and the local prosecutor).

b. Are Otherwise Inadmissible Hearsay Sources Admissible?

FRE 803(A)(iii) does not admit otherwise inadmissible hearsay sources for the truth of the matters they assert, even if they are relied on by the author of the report. In re September 11 Litigation, 621 F. Supp. 2d at 157: "The statements of the terrorists, even though found in The 9/11 Report, cannot qualify as factual findings [and] . . . will be excluded." If inadmissible sources appear in the text of the public report, the jury might decide to use them anyway, in violation of the basic principle of the hearsay rule of exclusion. Thus, there is a conflict between admitting the investigator's entire report—including the substantive contents of *all* of its sources—and keeping inadmissible hearsay from the jury. A similar conflict exists when opinions of testifying expert witnesses are admitted together with all of the expert's underlying, potentially inadmissible sources, as will be discussed in Chapter Nine. FRE 703 now provides its own approach to this conflict, as we will discuss infra. It seems possible that the balancing test provided in Rule 703 could be applied to subsection (A)(iii) reports as well. The jury would be instructed that the underlying hearsay sources are admitted not for their truth but in order for the jury to evaluate the basis for the investigation's findings. Otherwise, the hearsay sources would be redacted from the report, or application of the untrustworthiness clause of Rule 803(8) could be used to exclude the report altogether.

c. Administrative Findings

It is well established that the findings and conclusions that result from judicial proceedings do not fall within FRE 803(8)(A)(iii). Nipper v. Snipes, 7 F.3d 415, 417 (4th Cir. 1993) ("a judge in a civil trial is not an investigator"). However, agency hearings within the executive branch, even those presided over by officials called Administrative Law Judges, do qualify as investigations. In a case involving a trial-type hearing, the presentations of witnesses, cross-examination and a review of records and tests, the ALJ issued a decision with detailed factual findings concerning the airworthiness of an airplane for purposes of suspending the aircraft's National Transportation Safety Board certificate of airworthiness. These findings and decision were later admitted in a trial for breach of contract against the company that had attempted to restore the aircraft to airworthy condition. Zeus Enterprises, Inc. v. Alphin Aircraft, Inc., 190 F.3d 238 (4th Cir. 1999). Such findings are not automatically admissible, however. The trial judge has discretion pursuant to FRE 403 to assess the probative value of such reports and findings, as well as their Rule 403 dangers:

> The party against whom such a determination is admitted must attempt to expose the weaknesses of the report . . . an effort that may well confuse or mislead the jury and result in an undue waste of time . . . We believe that the district court is in the best position to consider the quality of the report, its potential impact on the jury, and the likelihood that the trial will deteriorate into a protracted and unproductive struggle over how the evidence admitted at trial compared to the evidence considered by the agency. [Paolitto v. John Brown E.&C., Inc., 151 F.3d 60, 65 (2d Cir. 1998).]

PROBLEMS

8.63. Return to problem 8.59 at page 563. Suppose Officer Curtis's police report does not refresh her recollection in the burglary prosecution. Can she read passages of the report into evidence?

8.64. At the trial of a suit filed against Dolores Rio for causing an intersection collision because she failed to stop for a blinking red light, Dolores offers a police report written by the officer who came to the scene of the collision. The report states that Frank Chan, the plaintiff, was talking on a cell phone when he drove into the intersection. The officer testifies at trial to authenticate the report and states that he cannot recall whether the information that he wrote down came from the plaintiff, from someone accompanying the plaintiff, or from a third party who observed the accident. Is the police report admissible to prove the plaintiff's conduct?

8.65. Return to Problem 3.2, Pedroso v. Driver, on page 148. The defendants offer a police report filed on the day of the accident by Officer Rojas who arrived at the scene five minutes after the accident. The report describes the location and position of the school bus after the impact. It states that Driver said, "Paul ran out unexpectedly." It also states "Officer Nelson arrived at the scene a few minutes after I did. She interviewed children who had witnessed the incident. She reports that several of them claimed that the boy ran in front of the bus, and that although they were very distressed, they seemed to be reliable." In the space for "Conclusions," Officer Rojas wrote "No apparent violation." How much of the police report can the defendants introduce against plaintiffs? Must Officer Rojas testify as a witness in order to secure the report's admission?

8.66. John James, a New York City policeman, filed a civil rights suit against the city and the Police Department for unlawful retaliation taken against him because he made public statements criticizing some of the Department's controversial policies. He seeks admission of portions of a report written and circulated by the Department's Internal Affairs Bureau entitled "Police Corruption and Culture." He argues that the report should be admitted pursuant to FRE 803(8)(C) and that these portions of the report are relevant to prove the existence of an unofficial policy of retaliation against officers who speak out about the Department's problems in general. The report was the product of a project in which 23 groups of 12 to 15 officers each convened to participate in guided group discussions. The report then summarized the discussions, which included the unofficial retaliation James seeks to prove, and made generalized recommendations regarding future departmental behavior. Its stated purpose was "to identify and explore some of the prevailing attitudes, perceptions, and opinions of Police Officers toward a range of integrity-related issues." For the defendants, what objections would you make to the admission of this report? Are any other hearsay exceptions or exemptions available? What result?

16. Other Exceptions for Records Under FRE 803

In addition to the business and official records exceptions, FRE 803 contains a variety of exceptions for other types of records. You should read FRE 803(9), (11), (12), (13), (14), (15), (16), and (17) at least once. These exceptions for the most part are based on the notion that the records are likely to be reliable because of the nature of the entity preparing them, the routine nature of their preparation, and their subject matter. The scope and operation of these exceptions should be easily discernable from the language of the rule and the Advisory Committee Notes.

FRE 803(18) provides that a court can admit into evidence an excerpt from a treatise or periodical when it "is called to the attention of an expert witness on cross-examination or relied on by the expert on direct examination" and when "the publication is established as a reliable authority by the expert's admission or testimony, by another expert's testimony, or by judicial notice." For this hearsay exception to apply, the publication's proponent must show that it is authored by a "reliable authority." Ostensibly, any source identified by the expert witness as authoritative would satisfy this requirement. Recently, however, the Supreme Judicial Court of Massachusetts ruled that this is not the case and that organizations such as hospitals and even universities cannot satisfy the "reliable authority" requirement by their institutional credentials. This requirement—the Court explained – can only be satisfied by the person who authors the publication. Kace v. Liang,—N.E.3d—2015 WL 5253356 (Mass.

2015). We believe that this interpretation is too narrow. There is no good reason to exclude reputable institutional publications (e.g., Mayo Clinic web pages) verified by an expert witness. This interpretation also strengthens the pro-incumbent bias of academic and professional publishers, who tend to prefer reputable authors over young and not yet established academics and professionals. Those publishers now have an additional reason for acting upon that preference: it will make their publications admissible as evidence and increase sales.

FRE 803(7) and FRE 803(10) set forth hearsay exceptions for the *absence* of entries in business, organizational and public records, offered for the purpose of proving the nonoccurrence or nonexistence of a matter if that matter was of a kind that was regularly recorded if it occurred or existed. As the Advisory Committee noted, it is unlikely that the failure to make the entry is the result of a conscious intent to assert that an event did not occur. Thus, the failure to make an entry may not constitute a hearsay "statement" in the first place. The exceptions exist, according to the Advisory Committee, "[i]n order to set the question at rest in favor of admissibility. . . ." The search for public records must be diligent, and a showing must be made that the documents searched are proper FRE 803(6) or public records. The results of such a search have been held *not* to be excluded in criminal cases by the exclusionary clauses of subsections FRE 803(8)(a)(ii) and (iii). United States v. Mendez, 514 F.3d 1035, 1044-1045 (10th Cir. 2008) (search in U.S. Central Index System containing regularly reported data on legal entries into the United States did not disclose defendant's name, indicating he had not entered the country legally; absence of public record admissible pursuant to FRE 803(10) and not excluded as created with an eye toward litigation by FRE 803(8)(B), now (A)(ii)).

KEY POINTS

1. FRE 803(8) provides for the admission of (A)(i) records of the activities of public offices and agencies, (A)(ii) matters observed pursuant to public duty to report by employees of public offices, and (A)(iii) public investigative reports, including factual findings. The factual requirements are largely limited to identifying the document as coming from a "public office." The judge has discretion to exclude a public record if the opposing party demonstrates that the information source or "other circumstances" indicate untrustworthiness.

2. The information in a public record may go from person to person within the public office without taking the record outside coverage of 803(8), so long as each person has a "legal duty to report." The legal duty is one imposed due to employment by the public agency, and does not extend to outsiders, bystanders, etc. Where relevant information comes from such outside sources, an additional level of hearsay may be involved requiring combining the public record exception with another exception or exemption

3. In criminal cases, the prosecution may not use FRE 803(8)(A)(ii) to admit reports of matters observed by law enforcement officials against criminal

defendants. This limitation may not apply to matters observed by public officers not engaged in the investigation or prosecution of criminal cases. It plainly does not apply to FRE 803(A)(i) routine "housekeeping" records.

4. Under FRE 803(8)(A)(iii), factual findings include opinions and conclusions. Investigative reports and factual findings may not be used by the prosecutor against defendants in criminal cases. Multiple hearsay contained in such reports may be used as the basis for the findings, but unless it falls within an exemption or exception, is not admitted for its truth. Courts may also exclude factual findings as lacking trustworthiness because of reliance on inadmissible and unreliable hearsay.

17. Explanation of FRE 803(22): Judgment of Previous Conviction

A judgment on the merits in a criminal or civil action is relevant to prove the actual occurrence of the facts essential to support the judgment. The judgment is hearsay evidence of those facts. Indeed, it may be multiple hearsay. A defendant's plea of guilty is itself a hearsay statement, and a judge's or a jury's conclusions about the evidence presented in a trial or summary proceeding are offered to prove the truth of those conclusions.

FRE 803(22) provides for the use of criminal felony convictions:

(22) *Judgment of a Previous Conviction.* Evidence of a final judgment of conviction if:
(A) the judgment was entered after a trial or guilty plea, but not a nolo contendere plea;
(B) the judgment was for a crime punishable by death or by imprisonment for more than a year;
(C) the evidence is admitted to prove any fact essential to the judgment; and
(D) when offered by the prosecutor in a criminal case for a purpose other than impeachment, the judgment was against the defendant.
The pendency of an appeal may be shown but does not affect admissibility.

a. Preliminary Factfinding

The factual requirements for the use of a final judgment of conviction are as follows:

- the judgment must follow a criminal trial or guilty plea;
- the judgment must be for a crime punishable by death or more than one year's imprisonment;
- the judgment must be offered to prove any fact essential to the judgment; and
- a judgment offered against a criminal defendant must be a judgment entered against that defendant, unless it is offered only for impeachment.

The relevance of a judgment to prove underlying events requires a determination as to what "essential" facts were necessarily decided by the judge or jury. Also keep in mind that the judgment serves only as *some evidence* of those facts. The exception does not raise issues of the possible *binding* effect of a prior judgment—a matter to be resolved under principles of collateral estoppel or issue preclusion.

b. *Justification for the Admissibility of Criminal Judgment*

FRE 803(22) reflects confidence that a judgment of guilt in a criminal felony case is reliable proof of the facts essential to sustain the judgment. The high standard of proof—beyond a reasonable doubt—is probably the strongest argument in favor of reliability. The exclusion of judgments entered after a plea of nolo contendere is based on the fact that a nolo plea, which can be entered only with the leave of the court, is specifically designed to resolve a criminal matter without the expense of a trial or the defendant's acknowledgment of guilt. Evidence of judgments entered against persons other than the defendant are excluded from criminal trials, unless used for impeachment, because of concern about the defendant's right to confront and cross-examine those adverse witnesses whose testimony provided the basis for judgment. United States v. Austin, 786 F.2d 986 (10th Cir. 1986) (marijuana convictions reversed because government informed jury that ten co-conspirators had already been convicted for participating in the same alleged conspiracy). Confidence in the reliability of judgments in civil cases is not so deeply felt. When claims involve substantial monetary damages or important principles, it is reasonable to believe that the parties will put forth their best efforts in trying to vindicate their positions. Nevertheless, the standard of persuasion—a preponderance of the evidence—is significantly lower than in criminal cases. If the stakes are small, a litigant may not have a serious interest in devoting the resources that would be necessary to vindicate the litigant's position. Even if one wanted to include judgments from major civil cases, any attempt to define the difference between major and minor cases would probably seem quite arbitrary.

c. *The Admission of Misdemeanor Convictions for Impeachment*

The most frequent use of judgments is to impeach testifying witnesses pursuant to FRE 609. As we noted in Chapter Seven, courts invariably admit misdemeanor convictions for *crimen falsi* to impeach witnesses pursuant to FRE 609(a)(2), even though misdemeanors are not included within FRE 803(22).

E. HEARSAY EXCEPTIONS REQUIRING THE UNAVAILABILITY OF THE DECLARANT

FRE 804 provides five categorical hearsay exceptions that may be used only when the hearsay declarant is unavailable—former testimony, dying declarations, declarations against interest, statements of personal and family history, and statements offered against a party whose wrongdoing procured the unavailability of the declarant as a witness.

Why unavailability is a requirement for only these five categorical exceptions is by no means clear. The Advisory Committee Note to FRE 803 suggests that unavailability is not required for the FRE 803 exceptions because they are reliable hearsay and, therefore, as acceptable as live testimony. By contrast, according to the Advisory Committee, hearsay falling within an FRE 804 exception "is not equal in quality to testimony of the declarant on the stand. . . ." These hearsay statements are admissible only as a last resort; that is, only if the declarant is unavailable to testify in person.

We encourage you to think critically about whether there is a significant reliability difference between the Rule 803 and the Rule 804 exceptions. At the same time, we caution you against trying too hard to come up with an overarching theory to rationalize the existing law. The earliest common law exceptions—former testimony and dying declarations—were both premised in part on arguments of necessity because of death; dying declarations were also premised in part on religious beliefs. It is likely that historical precedent is the best explanation for the current state of the unavailability requirement.

1. FRE 804

RULE 804. EXCEPTIONS TO THE RULE AGAINST HEARSAY— WHEN THE DECLARANT IS UNAVAILABLE AS A WITNESS

(a) *Criteria for Being Unavailable.* A declarant is considered to be unavailable as a witness if the declarant:

(1) is exempted from testifying about the subject matter of the declarant's statement because the court rules that a privilege applies;

(2) refuses to testify about the subject matter despite a court order to do so;

(3) testifies to not remembering the subject matter;

(4) cannot be present or testify at the trial or hearing because of death or a then-existing infirmity, physical illness, or mental illness; or

(5) is absent from the trial or hearing and the statement's proponent has not been able, by process or other reasonable means, to procure:

(A) the declarant's attendance, in the case of a hearsay exception under Rule 804(b)(1) or (6); or

(B) the declarant's attendance or testimony, in the case of a hearsay exception under Rule 804(b)(2), (3), or (4).

But this subdivision (a) does not apply if the statement's proponent procured or wrongfully caused the declarant's unavailability as a witness in order to prevent the declarant from attending or testifying.

(b) *The Exceptions.* The following are not excluded by the rule against hearsay if the declarant is unavailable as a witness:

(1) *Former Testimony.* Testimony that:

    (A) was given as a witness at a trial, hearing, or lawful deposition, whether given during the current proceeding or a different one; and

    (B) is now offered against a party who had—or, in a civil case, whose predecessor in interest had—an opportunity and similar motive to develop it by direct, cross-, or redirect examination.

(2) *Statement Under the Belief of Imminent Death.* In a prosecution for homicide or in a civil case, a statement that the declarant, while believing the declarant's death to be imminent, made about its cause or circumstances.

(3) *Statement Against Interest. A statement that:*

    (A) a reasonable person in the declarant's position would have made only if the person believed it to be true because, when made, it was so contrary to the declarant's proprietary or pecuniary interest or had so great a tendency to invalidate the declarant's claim against someone else or to expose the declarant to civil or criminal liability; and

    (B) is supported by corroborating circumstances that clearly indicate its trustworthiness, if it is offered in a criminal case as one that tends to expose the declarant to criminal liability.

(4) *Statement of Personal or Family History.* A statement about:

    (A) the declarant's own birth, adoption, legitimacy, ancestry, marriage, divorce, relationship by blood, adoption, or marriage, or similar facts of personal or family history, even though the declarant had no way of acquiring personal knowledge about that fact; or

    (B) another person concerning any of these facts, as well as death, if the declarant was related to the person by blood, adoption, or marriage or was so intimately associated with the person's family that the declarant's information is likely to be accurate.

(5) [*Other Exceptions.*] [Transferred to Rule 807.]

(6) *Statement Offered Against a Party That Wrongfully Caused the Declarant's Unavailability.* A statement offered against a party that wrongfully caused—or acquiesced in wrongfully causing —the declarant's unavailability as a witness, and did so intending that result.

Our initial discussion focuses on FRE 804(a). We discuss the remainder of the rule later in the chapter.

2. Explanation of FRE 804(a): Grounds for a Finding of Unavailability

FRE 804(a) contains a broad, reasonable definition of unavailability that applies to the exceptions under FRE 804(b)(1)-(4), though not to FRE 804(b)(6). Before the adoption of the Federal Rules, what constituted unavailability would vary among jurisdictions and even among hearsay exceptions within a single jurisdiction. For some exceptions, a claim of privilege or absence from the jurisdiction or, occasionally, even absence from the courtroom would suffice. For dying declarations, death was the only acceptable type of unavailability. Now, any of the five subparts may be used for any of the 804(b)(1)-(4) exceptions.

Preliminary Factfinding.   As is generally true in applying the hearsay exceptions, these preliminary questions are to be decided by the judge pursuant to FRE 104(a). Statements of counsel to the court have been held sufficient to establish the absence or unavailability of a witness under FRE 804(a)(5), so long as good-faith efforts have been made to secure the witness, including requests for voluntary attendance and subpoenas. But when the issue is a witness's claim of privilege under FRE 804(a)(1), some courts hold that statements from counsel are insufficient to show that the witness *actually* will not testify. In other words, the witness must claim the privilege in court. Invocation of FRE 804(a)(2) requires the witness's presence in court and a court order directing the witness to testify; FRE 804(a)(3) requires testimony from the witness as to failed memory but not a court order. Evidence that a mental or physical infirmity (confined to home because of heart condition, unable to walk because of back condition, incapacitated by a stroke) will continue for some length of time is usually necessary under FRE 804(a)(4); otherwise, the court may seek a continuance in order to call a witness who is merely ill, if the testimony is significant. United States v. Amaya, 533 F.2d 188 (5th Cir. 1976) (FRE 804(a) requirement of unavailability satisfied by probability that the duration of illness or loss of memory will be long enough so that the trial cannot be postponed).

Preference for Former Testimony or Deposition.   FRE 804(a)(5) states a preference for former testimony that applies when the declarant is absent, but not deceased. The purpose of FRE 804(a)(5)(B) is to make clear that the proponent of an absent declarant's dying declaration, declaration against interest, or declaration of pedigree must first use the declarant's former testimony or deposition; if none exists, the proponent must make reasonable efforts to obtain the declarant's deposition testimony (and seek the declarant's attendance as a witness) as a precondition to the declarant being held to be unavailable. The preference for former testimony, and the requirement of an attempt to depose a declarant, may reflect even stronger suspicion about the reliability of FRE 804(b)(2), (3), and (4) exceptions. After studying these exceptions, you can decide whether this suspicion makes sense.

Unfortunately, this preference sometimes produces problematic results. Where the absent declarant has flatly denied wrongdoing in a deposition taken for a tort case, but has made inculpatory hearsay statements to various people that the defendant seeks to admit, it has been held that the deposition must be used pursuant to FRE 804(a)(5) and that the oral statements are inadmissible for their truth (though, presumably, they could be used to impeach). Campbell v. Coleman Co., 786 F.2d 892 (8th Cir. 1986).

Reasonable Means to Procure Attendance.   "Reasonable means" to procure the attendance of an absent witness under FRE 804(a)(5) requires a good-faith effort on the part of the proponent of hearsay, but not the doing of a futile act. At least one circuit has held that, when the government has the name and address of a foreign witness, some effort must be made to contact that witness in the witness's native country or else a finding of unavailability will be error. United States v. Pena-Gutierrez, 222 F.3d 1080, 1086 (9th Cir. 2000). Offers from the government to pay airfare, met with refusal by the foreign witness, has been held to be a reasonable effort. United States v. Siddiqui, 253 F.3d 1318, 1323-1324 (11th Cir. 2000). A decision by the government not to personally serve subpoenas on two allegedly unavailable witnesses until after the first day of trial was found not to be "reasonable" absent further extenuating facts. United States v. Pluta, 176 F.3d 43, 48 (2d Cir. 1999); compare United States v. Olafson, 213 F.3d 435 (9th Cir. 2000) (in a criminal case, district court has broad discretion under Fed. R. Crim. P. 15(a) in deciding whether to order a deposition, and it is not unreasonable to refuse to do so when conditions in Mexico make it unsafe for American prosecutors, and there is no indication that the unavailable witnesses would cooperate).

Unavailability Caused by the Proponent.   If a witness is unable to, or refuses to, testify *because of the conduct of the proponent* of the hearsay statement, FRE 804(a) directs that the witness not be found to be unavailable. Proof of threats made against a witness are not enough; there must be an actual finding of presumptive unavailability. United States v. Pizarro, 717 F.2d 336 (7th Cir. 1983). There must also be a finding of "purpose" underlying the proponent's conduct. The government's carelessness in losing custody of a witness, or an inability to keep track of a witness, may not qualify as causing "unavailability" of that witness under FRE 804(a). It has also been held that the government's refusal to grant immunity to a witness who exercises a Fifth Amendment right not to testify is neither "procurement" nor "wrongdoing" and does not negate the witness's status as "unavailable" under FRE 804(a)(1), so that prior testimony may be admissible. United States v. Dolah, 245 F.3d 98, 103 (2d Cir. 2001).

PROBLEM

8.67. Consider which of the following may be sufficient to constitute unavailability for the purposes of satisfying FRE 804(a). What other steps might the proponent have to take before unavailability is adequately proved?

   (a) A criminal defendant asserts the Fifth Amendment privilege not to testify at trial and the defense offers the defendant's own prior testimony.

   (b) A witness invokes the Fifth Amendment privilege against self-incrimination in court.

   (c) The party offering the hearsay evidence submits his or her attorney's affidavit stating that the declarant is in another state beyond the subpoena power of the court.

   (d) The party offering the hearsay evidence submits the declarant's affidavit stating that the declarant does not recall the events in question.

   (e) The hearsay declarant is on the witness stand and claims to have no current memory of the events in question, and the judge believes this testimony.

(f) The hearsay declarant is on the witness stand and claims to have no current memory of the events in question, and the judge does not believe this testimony.

3. Explanation of FRE 804(b)(1): Former Testimony

FRE 804(b)(1) states:

(b) *The Exceptions.* The following are not excluded by the rule against hearsay if the declarant is unavailable as a witness:

(1) *Former Testimony.* Testimony that:

(A) was given as a witness at a trial, hearing, or lawful deposition, whether given during the current proceeding or a different one; and

(B) is now offered against a party who had—or, in a civil case, whose predecessor in interest had—an opportunity and similar motive to develop it by direct, cross-, or redirect examination.

a. Preliminary Factfinding

The factual requirements for former testimony are:

* the statement must be in the form of testimony given at a hearing or in a "lawful" deposition;
* in a criminal case, the party against whom the statement is being offered must have had an opportunity and similar motive to develop the testimony at the prior hearing or deposition by direct, cross- or redirect examination; and
* in a civil case, either the party against whom the statement is being offered, or a predecessor in interest to that party, must have had an opportunity and similar motive to develop the testimony at the prior hearing or deposition by direct, cross- or redirect examination.

Trial, Hearing, or Lawful Deposition.   This phrase broadly includes transcripts or other recordings of sworn testimony given at a formal adversarial proceeding before a person authorized to administer oaths. It thus includes trials, evidentiary hearings in court, adversarial administrative hearings, and "lawful deposition[s]." This latter phrase simply means a deposition taken in conformity with a procedural code governing the resolution of disputes. See, e.g., Fed. R. Civ. P. 30. The former testimony need not have been given in the same case in which the former testimony is currently being offered. In other words, in the case at hand, a party could use FRE 804(b)(1) to offer a transcript of testimony from a prior trial or a deposition taken in a wholly different case. The former trial or deposition might even be from a case in a different court system (such as a state court).

Opportunity and Similar Motive to Develop the Testimony.   Any former testimony admitted under FRE 804(b)(1) must have been created in a proceeding in which the opposing party (against whom the testimony is now offered) had an opportunity and motive to examine the witness. Generally, this requires an adversarial proceeding. But testimony from an ex parte proceeding such as a grand jury hearing could be offered against the prosecution.

> For example:

> Paula has sued Drew for personal injuries caused in an automobile accident. Wilma, a passenger in Drew's car, testifies for Paula that Drew was drunk at the time and had been driving on the wrong side of the road. There is a judgment for Paula, but the judgment is reversed on appeal because of improper jury instructions and a new trial is ordered. Wilma dies before the retrial, so Paula offers a transcript of Wilma's testimony from the first trial.

Even though Wilma's former testimony is hearsay, it will be admissible against Drew in the retrial under FRE 804(b)(1). All of the factual requirements are satisfied. Wilma's statement was given at the first trial, obviously a *hearing*. Drew was the adverse party at that trial. Because exactly the same factual issues about which Wilma testified are disputed in the retrial, Drew's *motive* to develop the testimony fully was as great at the first trial as it is now. Moreover, Drew had an *opportunity* to develop the testimony through cross-examination. And it is clear that opportunity is enough, even if Drew did not take advantage of it. Nor is it necessary that the former testimony have been given in a trial or formal hearing: So long as the opportunity and similar motive requirements are satisfied, testimony taken in Wilma's deposition during discovery could be admitted under FRE 804(b)(1) as well.

The "similar motive" requirement is a recognition that not all opportunities to examine a witness are equal. The procedures may differ, and the former hearings may have raised different issues that did not require examining the witness on the now-relevant subject. For example, suppose a criminal defendant's alleged co-conspirator testifies at a hearing to suppress evidence of packages of cocaine found in the search of his car. If the only issue at the hearing is the legality of the search, the only relevant facts in the hearing may be whether the alleged co-conspirator consented to the search of the car. In such a case, the defendant would not have the motive to fully explore the nature of the alleged conspiratorial relationship. In United States v. Duenas, 691 F.3d 1070 (9th Cir. 2012), the Court held that a criminal defendant did not have a similar motive to develop a police officer witness's testimony at a suppression hearing as at trial: "The issue at trial was whether the evidence proved [the defendant's] guilt beyond a reasonable doubt, not the circumstances of his confession." Id. at 1090 (citations omitted).

At the same time, similar motive does not have to mean identical motive. Courts have identified several factors to be considered in determining whether a prior party, in a prior proceeding, had a sufficiently similar motive to develop the testimony of a witness. Most plainly, the questioner must be on the same side of the same issue at both proceedings, and must have a substantially similar interest in asserting and prevailing on the issue. United States v. DiNapoli, 8 F.3d 909, 912 (2d Cir. 1993). "Circumstances or factors which influence motive to develop testimony include (1) the type of proceeding in which the testimony was given, (2) trial strategy, (3) the potential penalties or financial stakes, and (4) the number of issues and parties." United States v. Reed, 227 F.3d 763, 768 (7th Cir. 2000).

Similarity between the factual issues in dispute in the first and second proceedings also influence a party's motive to develop the witness's testimony. Compare McKnight v. Johnson Controls, Inc., 36 F.3d 1396 (8th Cir. 1994) (defendant manufacturer had same interest in developing testimony of witness in previous personal injury case involving same type of accident), with Cordance Corp. v. Amazon.com, Inc., 639 F. Supp. 2d 406 (D. Del. 2009) with Schmidt v. Duo-Fast Corp., 1976 U.S. Dist. LEXIS 6106 (E.D. Pa. 1996) (defendant manufacturer did not have same interest in developing testimony of witness in previous personal injury case involving different kind of accident with the same equipment).

Although usually thought of as cross-examination, the requirement of an opportunity to develop testimony has a broader meaning:

> Wilma, called as a witness by Paula at the first trial, surprised Paula by testifying on direct examination that Paula had been speeding and that Paula drove across the center line and hit Drew's car. At the second trial, Drew offers this former testimony, and Paula objects on the ground that she did not have an opportunity to cross-examine Wilma.

Under FRE 804(b)(1), it does not matter that Paula did not have an opportunity to "cross-examine" Wilma. It is sufficient, in the language of the exception, that Paula had the opportunity and similar motive "to develop the testimony by *direct*, cross, or *redirect* examination" (emphasis added). FRE 804(b)(1) specifically permits a party to impeach the credibility of any witness, including a witness called by the party, under FRE 607. And, as we discussed in Chapter Two, FRE 611 sets forth general guidelines for the "mode and order" of presenting evidence and provides sufficient flexibility for Paula to develop fully and to explore weaknesses in Wilma's testimony. Thus, unless the trial judge unduly restricted Paula's direct and redirect examination, she has nothing to complain about.

No Opportunity.   In some proceedings where the former testimony was given, a party had no meaningful opportunity to examine the witness. In United States v. Deeb, 13 F.3d 1532 (11th Cir. 1994), defendant was a fugitive from justice, tried in absentia, and was not represented. Testimony taken against him was not admissible in a later proceeding under FRE 804(b)(1). If the former testimony is taken at a proceeding where, due to its nature or due to the conduct of the judge, a party was present but had no meaningful opportunity to develop testimony, courts have held that the prior testimony is inadmissible under FRE 804(b)(1). In re Paducah Towing Co., 692 F.2d 412 (6th Cir. 1982) (Coast Guard employee did not have necessary skills to test an expert witness's qualifications at the first hearing, and was not permitted to impeach the witness; held, no adequate opportunity to examine the witness).

No Requirement of "Offered on Same Issue."   Apart from ensuring that the motive to develop the testimony is the same, however, there is no reason to insist that the legal issue be precisely the same. Assume, for example, that the judgment in our Paula v. Drew hypothetical was reversed because the jury was instructed to apply a gross negligence rather than a negligence standard to the defendant's conduct. Wilma's former testimony should not be precluded at the second trial because the issue to which the testimony relates is now somewhat different. The testimony is undoubtedly still relevant, and it is difficult to believe that the motive of the parties to develop the testimony is any different because of the different legal standard against which the defendant's culpability will be measured. Before FRE 804(b)(1), some cases had articulated a requirement that the evidence had to be offered on the same *legal* issue. Appropriately, FRE 804(b)(1) makes no reference to an "offered on same legal issue" requirement.

Opportunity to Develop by Same Party or a Predecessor in Interest.   Former testimony of a witness who has become unavailable can be offered against a criminal defendant in the current case so long as that defendant is the one who had the earlier opportunity and similar motive to "develop" that former testimony. It does not matter whether the *former* proceeding in which the testimony was given was criminal or civil.

In contrast, where the former testimony of a now-unavailable witness is offered in a *current civil case*, the party against whom the former testimony is being offered need not be the same one who had the earlier opportunity and motive to develop the former testimony. It is permissible if a third-party "predecessor in interest" developed the former testimony. Again, that former testimony may have been given in either a civil or a criminal proceeding. Concern with a criminal defendant's personal opportunity to confront and cross-examine witnesses underlies FRE 804(b)(1)'s differing treatment of criminal and civil cases.

b. Justification for the Admissibility of Former Testimony

A principal justification for admitting former testimony under FRE 804(b)(1) is necessity. Since Wilma is dead, the choice is not between live testimony or hearsay, but rather hearsay or nothing. This all-or-nothing choice, of course, always exists when the hearsay declarant is unavailable (although there may sometimes be other relevant evidence on the same point, so the need for the hearsay will in fact vary from case to case). Although perhaps the law should be otherwise, the all-or-nothing choice is not itself enough to justify the admission of hearsay evidence. There must also be circumstantial guarantees of trustworthiness or some other reasons to justify the loss of the opportunity for live cross-examination.

The *prior* opportunity and motive to develop testimony are important justifications for the lack of present cross-examination. If Drew's cross-examination of Wilma had cast any doubt on the truth of what Wilma said, Drew could introduce relevant parts of the cross-examination at the retrial. In fact, given the oath, courtroom formalities and the prior opportunity to develop testimony, prior testimony seems far closer to live testimony than any of the Rule 803 exceptions.

Yet the reason for imposing an unavailability limitation on use of former testimony is readily apparent. Without such a limitation, parties could make wholesale substitutions of former trial transcripts for live testimony in cases retried after a hung jury, mistrial, or reversal on appeal. Indeed, depositions or preliminary hearing transcripts could be substituted wholesale for live witness testimony in the initial trial. Plainly, the drafters of the rule wished to avoid such eventualities.

Note. The former testimony exception helps explain the awkwardness of the definition of hearsay. It is common, and nicely succinct, to refer to hearsay as "out-of-court statements," but that description is not entirely accurate. As FRE 804(b)(1) makes clear (together with FRE 801(d)(1)(A), which contemplates use of former testimony that is inconsistent with the witness's trial testimony) hearsay includes former testimony given in court at prior proceedings. Hence, for accuracy and completeness, FRE 801(c)(1) defines a hearsay statement as one that "the declarant does not make while testifying at the current trial or hearing."

4. FRE 804(b)(1): Practical Problems and Applications

In this section, we look further at FRE 804(b)(1) problems that arise when testimony is offered by or against parties who were not party to the original action in which the testimony was given. We will also look at practical aspects of using former testimony.

a. Former Testimony Offered By or Against a Nonparty to the Original Action

Offered by a Nonparty. Under FRE 804(b)(1), there is no requirement that the party *offering the former testimony* must have been a party to the original proceeding in which the testimony was given. Indeed, FRE 804(b)(1) doesn't look at the status of the offering party at all: Rather, the rule focuses on the party against whom the testimony is now offered. The rule requires only that the party *against whom the evidence is offered* had an opportunity to develop the testimony. Returning to the preceding hypothetical: What if another party, not the original plaintiff Paula, offers Wilma's testimony against Drew at another proceeding?

> Rhoda, another passenger in Paula's car, has sued Drew for her own personal injuries. By the time Rhoda's case goes to trial, Wilma has died, and Rhoda offers Wilma's testimony from the first Paula v. Drew trial about Drew's being drunk and driving on the wrong side of the road.

Here, since Drew had an opportunity to develop the testimony, it does not matter that the person now offering the testimony is a second plaintiff, Rhoda, rather than the original plaintiff, Paula, as long as the "similar motive" requirement is also satisfied.

Offered Against a Nonparty ("Predecessor in Interest"). Suppose Paula offers Wilma's testimony against a new party—someone who was an outsider to the original Paula v. Drew trial. FRE 804(b)(1)(B) specifically provides that testimony from the original proceeding can be offered against someone who was not a party to that original proceeding, *if* the current proceeding is a civil case *and* the nonparty is a "predecessor in interest" to someone who had the motive and opportunity to develop the testimony in the original case.

> Paula now sues Barney to recover damages for her injuries in the accident with Drew. Barney is the owner of the tavern where Drew had been drinking before the accident.

> Wilma has died, and Paula offers Wilma's testimony from the first Paula v. Drew trial about Drew's being drunk and driving on the wrong side of the road.

Here, we have a civil case. Before admitting the testimony against Barney, we have to answer two questions affirmatively. First, did Drew have a motive and opportunity to develop Wilma's testimony? And second, is Drew a *predecessor in interest* to Barney? These questions may overlap to some degree.

"Predecessor in Interest" Analysis. Cases decided soon after the enactment of FRE 804(b)(1) interpreted the statutory language and legislative history in, broadly speaking, three different ways. Some interpreted the term *"predecessor in interest"* narrowly, to include only relationships in which individuals stand in privity to each other in some traditional property or contract law sense. Under this view, Drew would not be a predecessor in interest to Barney. Other courts expanded the notion of privity somewhat more broadly to include, for example, subsidiary and parent corporations, or coemployees such as a district attorney and a city solicitor. More recently, courts have adopted the more liberal approach of equating *interest* with *motive*, just as the rule was originally drafted: Any party to an earlier proceeding who had a similar motive to develop the testimony fully is a predecessor in interest. The narrow and broad "privity" approaches require facts about the relationship between Drew and Barney that may not be directly relevant to the litigation. The third, or "liberal" approach, essentially merges the "predecessor in interest" question into the "similar motive" question.

Under this third interpretation, since the same factual issues are in dispute in both the first and the second proceeding, and Drew and Barney are on the same side of those issues with the same interest in discrediting Wilma's opinion, Drew had a similar motive to develop Wilma's testimony as Barney would have had. Both Drew and Barney could fend off liability by showing that Drew was not drunk; hence, their motive to discredit Wilma's opinion is similar if not identical. To be sure, Barney might have other defenses even if Drew was drunk, so their legal position is not identical. But their orientation toward Wilma's testimony is probably similar enough that Drew would be considered a predecessor in interest to Barney.

Offering Wilma's testimony against Barney, even in a civil case, is somewhat troublesome. Here, Barney did not have an opportunity to develop Wilma's testimony when it was given, because he was not a party to that proceeding. By forcing Barney to rely on the prior cross-examination of Wilma from the first trial, Drew's selection of counsel is in effect imposed on Barney. If Drew was represented by a mediocre attorney who did not do a good job of cross-examining Wilma, Barney would be stuck with that result even though his attorney might have done a much better job of discrediting Wilma. But given the fact that the alternative is to forgo highly relevant evidence, whatever Drew's lawyer accomplished with the cross-examination of Wilma is arguably sufficient to permit admission of the evidence against Barney. Moreover, absent an objectively cognizable failure of competence (akin to an ineffective assistance of counsel claim in a post-conviction criminal proceeding), it would be unduly complicated to require judges to make detailed assessments of the relative skills of attorneys as a predicate to admitting former testimony.

b. Lack of Similar Motive Due to Differences in Procedural Context

In some procedural contexts, parties do not have the same motive to develop a witness's testimony that they will have later at a full trial on the merits. United States v. Powell, 894 F.2d 895 (7th Cir. 1990) (no error to exclude criminal defendant's offer of former testimony given by the witness at his guilty plea hearing; the government's motive to test the voluntariness of the plea, and its factual basis, is not the same as at a trial).

In United States v. Salerno, 505 U.S. 317 (1992), the Supreme Court considered the question whether grand jury testimony could be offered *by a criminal defendant*, against the government, when grand jury witnesses were unavailable due to an assertion of privilege. The witnesses DeMatteis and Bruno had been presented to the grand jury by a member of the prosecution team. Their grand jury testimony, however, tended to exculpate the defendant. The prosecutor, presumably, then had a motive to develop their testimony—that is, to impeach or challenge it. At trial, the defendant sought to use the former testimony of DeMatteis and Bruno in his own defense. The government admitted that it was the "same party," but contended that it had not had, and would indeed never have, a "similar motive" to develop testimony at a grand jury proceeding as it would at trial: "A prosecutor . . . must maintain secrecy during the investigatory stages of the criminal process and therefore may not desire to confront grand jury witnesses with contradictory evidence . . . [A] prosecutor may not know, prior to indictment, which issues will have importance at trial. . . ." Id. at 325. The Supreme Court held that this argument had to be addressed and remanded the case to the Second Circuit.

On remand, the court held en banc that the grand jury testimony should not have been admitted under FRE 804(b)(1):

> The proper approach . . . [to similarity of motive] must consider whether the party resisting the offered testimony at a pending proceeding has at a prior proceeding an interest of substantially similar intensity to prove (or disprove) the same side of a substantially similar issue. The nature of the two proceedings—both what is at stake and the applicable burden of proof—and, to a lesser extent, the cross-examination at the prior proceeding—both what was undertaken and what was foregone—will be relevant though not conclusive on the ultimate issue of similarity of motive. [United States v. DiNapoli, 8 F.3d 909 (2d Cir. 1993).]

The Second Circuit believed that the government had no motive to press these particular witnesses at the grand jury hearing because the defendants had already been indicted. Because the grand jury was already persuaded that a conspiracy existed, the government had little incentive to attack DeMatteis's and Bruno's exculpating testimony. The prosecutor did attack them somewhat, by accusing them of lying and confronting them with contradictory evidence. The court held that this was not full-blown cross-examination, and that the questions were carefully limited to matters already publicly disclosed. Thus, no secret information was used, as it might be at trial.

In light of the holdings in *Salerno* and *DiNapoli*, perhaps the admissibility of preliminary hearing testimony given by a government witness against a criminal defendant should be rethought. Traditionally, preliminary hearing testimony can be admitted under FRE 804(b)(1) against the defendant later at trial, despite the fact that the defendant had little actual motive to develop the testimony fully at the preliminary hearing. However,

> (1) the preliminary hearing is at such an early stage of the proceedings that the defendant may not have sufficient information to cross-examine the witness adequately; (2) like the prosecutor at the grand jury, the defendant at the preliminary hearing has no wish to "tip his hand" by aggressive cross-examination, and would much prefer to attack the witness at trial; and (3) because of the minimal standard of proof, it is often a foregone conclusion that the defendant will lose at the preliminary hearing, so that any attempted cross-examination or impeachment of inculpatory witnesses will be so much wasted effort at that point . . . [Stephen A. Saltzburg, Michael M. Martin & Daniel J. Capra, Federal Rules of Evidence Manual 1838 (7th ed. 1998).]

These concerns about the adequacy of opportunity to cross-examine will also affect the defendant's right to confrontation under *Crawford* if preliminary hearing testimony is offered at trial. See Section G, infra.

c. Using Former Testimony at the Current Proceeding

When former testimony is admissible, any witness with present knowledge of the content of the former testimony can relate what was said. In theory, this could be someone who heard the testimony in person at the former proceeding. However, by far the most common method of getting former testimony before the factfinder is to use a transcript of the testimony.

Technically speaking, use of a transcript for this purpose actually involves multiple hearsay. First, there is the statement of the now unavailable witness; second, there is the activity of the court reporter in making a verbatim shorthand record of what the witness says; and third, there is the activity of the court reporter in making a transcript of the testimony. FRE 804(b)(1) addresses only the first level of hearsay: the witness's statement. The court reporter's hearsay could probably be admitted as a present sense impression under FRE 803(1). The court reporter, both in taking down the testimony and transcribing her shorthand into a transcript, is describing an event or condition (first, the live testimony, and later, the shorthand notes) while perceiving it; her training and official oath to transcribe accurately, without editorial judgment, suggests a lack of opportunity to fabricate. Alternatively, the court reporter's regular record-making as part of her occupation, and the semi-official nature of her position (as a court official, or as a certified freelance reporter authorized to administer oaths) probably qualifies the transcripts for the business or official records exceptions of FRE 803(6) and (8). Whatever the rationale, courts and parties invariably overlook the court reporter's hearsay declarant role in admitting former testimony, in the absence of some genuine reason to doubt the authenticity of the transcript.

Courts generally allow counsel to use varying methods to introduce former testimony. If the former testimony was videotaped, the relevant portion of the video can simply be played for the jury. If the testimony is recorded only on a written transcript, the relevant portions are read to the jury. The reading can be done by the attorney for a short snippet of testimony. For longer passages, courts frequently permit a cocounsel, legal assistant, or even perhaps an actor to take the witness stand and role-play the witness in a responsive reading of the transcript between the lawyer and sit-in witness. (The jury would be informed, of course, that the person in the witness chair is merely reading former testimony.) The record of the former testimony is normally not admitted in evidence as an exhibit and therefore not taken into the jury room during its deliberations. (Nor for that matter does the jury have access to transcripts of the testimony it heard live.) Although the hard copy transcript is not admitted in evidence, the court is likely to require presentation of some foundation identifying the witness, the attorneys, and the date of testimony.

Regardless of what method is used to introduce former testimony, there is a possibility that particular questions and answers within the former testimony may be objectionable for some reason. For example, the former testimony may have been elicited in response to a leading question; it may have contained an impermissible lay opinion; it may have been privileged; or it may recite inadmissible hearsay statements, within the broader hearsay of the testimony itself. In these types of situations, the question arises whether objections can be made to exclude former testimony that meets all the requirements of the former testimony exception. The Federal Rules do not address this issue. While reported decisions vary, the majority view is that objections to the form of the lawyer's question in former testimony are waived if they were not made at the original hearing. Objections going to the inadmissibility of the witness's answer are not waived, even if they weren't made at the original hearing. They can be made for the first time at the current hearing, when the former testimony is offered. See the Trial Objection Cheat Sheet, Chapter 2, pages 120-22, for examples of the two types of objections.

KEY POINTS

1. Assuming unavailability, testimony given at a prior hearing (or deposition) may be admitted against a civil party or a criminal party if that party was present at the prior hearing, had a meaningful opportunity to examine the witness, and had a similar motive to examine the witness as at the current trial.

2. A judge may find that the party did not have a sufficiently similar motive at the prior hearing if different facts are at issue in the two proceedings, or if the procedural context in the prior hearing eliminated the party's incentive to fully examine the witness.

3. Testimony given at a prior hearing (or deposition) may also be admitted against a civil party if a predecessor in interest to that party—someone with the same motive because disputing the same factual issues—had the opportunity to examine the witness at the prior hearing.

PROBLEM

8.67. Alex and Brenda Dawson are suing the Delta Insurance Company for the loss they sustained when a warehouse they jointly owned was destroyed in a fire.

Delta has refused payment because a clause in the policy precludes recovery in the event that either owner is responsible for damage to the property. The insurance company claims that Alex arranged to have Eddy Hall burn the building. Eddy pleaded guilty to arson and testified against Alex at Alex's arson trial, which resulted in a hung jury. Eddy falls ill in prison and is not available to testify in the current action. Delta offers a properly authenticated transcript of Eddy's testimony at Alex's arson trial. Alex objects on the ground that he now has new evidence with which to impeach Eddy; Brenda objects on the ground that she did not have any opportunity to cross-examine Eddy. How should the court rule?

5. Explanation of FRE 804(b)(2): Dying Declarations

FRE 804(b)(2) provides:

(b) *The Exceptions.* The following are not excluded by the rule against hearsay if the declarant is unavailable as a witness:. . .

(2) *Statement Under the Belief of Imminent Death.* In a prosecution for homicide or in a civil case, a statement that the declarant, while believing the declarant's death to be imminent, made about its cause or circumstances.

a. Preliminary Factfinding

The factual requirements for dying declarations are:

* the statement concerns the cause or circumstances of what the declarant believes is impending death;
* the statement is made while the declarant believes death to be imminent; and
* the statement is offered in a homicide prosecution or a civil case.

Statements concerning the cause or circumstances of the declarant's death include identifications of the perpetrator and descriptions of accidents and of past events that led up to the mortal injury or disease. Even though the belief in imminent death may *generally* enhance a declarant's sincerity, contents other than the cause or circumstances of death are not included within the exception. Does the hearsay statement have to concern the cause of only the declarant's death, or could it extend to the cause of death of another? The language of FRE 804(b)(2) appears to be ambiguous on this point, but presumably it means the declarant's *own* death.

A belief in imminent death means the lack of hope of recovery—"a settled hopeless expectation that death is near at hand and what is said must have been spoken in the hush of its impending presence." Shepard v. United States, 290 U.S. 96, 100 (1933). This state of mind can be shown by the declarant's own statement, by circumstances such as the nature of the declarant's wound, by evidence that the declarant was told that death was imminent, or by the opinion of a physician. Vazquez v. National Car Rental System, Inc., 24 F. Supp. 2d 197 (D.P.R. 1998). Thus, the jury is not instructed that it must find the declarant's belief in imminent death before it may consider the statement, but evidence that tends to show that the declarant did not have this belief may be used by the opponent to argue to the jury that the statement is not reliable.

Note that the relevant inquiry is the declarant's subjective belief of imminent death: It need not be shown that the declarant in fact died. This is implicit in FRE 804(a)(5)(B), which contemplates situations in which a "dying declarant" is unavailable because "absent from the trial or hearing." That form of unavailability is distinguished from absence due to death or physical incapacity in FRE 804(a)(4).

Homicide defendants have invoked the dying declaration exception in homicide cases to show that some third person committed the murder. As a practical matter, however, it will usually be prosecutors who want to take advantage of the dying declaration exception.

b. Justification for the Admissibility of Dying Declarations

The dying declaration exception is one of the oldest common law exceptions to the rule excluding hearsay. It is also one of the most problematic in terms of the soundness of its underlying rationale. As usual, the unavailability of the declarant means that there may not be another means of obtaining the same or similar evidence. Reliability is said to inhere in the notion that people who realize that death is imminent will be especially likely to be sincere, since their condition obviates any motive to misstate the truth. Or, declarants may believe it is in their interest to "meet their maker" with clean hands, or least with hands that have not recently been soiled by falsehood. Finally, it might be argued that the exception acts as a deterrent to someone who might try to kill a potential adverse witness.

However, both the necessity justifications for this exception are questionable. It is not clear that the need for a dying declarant's statement about the cause or circumstances of death is any greater than the need for the statements of any unavailable witness. There may be an absence of available eyewitnesses to all sorts of events; and there may be alternative forms of evidence available to prove the cause of death in a homicide or civil case. And the forfeiture by wrongdoing exception is more closely tailored to the problem of killing a potential witness.

The notion that dying declarations are likely to be reliable is also suspect. The proposition that individuals who believe death is imminent are particularly likely to be sincere is sheer speculation. There is no requirement that dying declarants be shown to be religious, and no requirement of other circumstances that reduce a motive to misrepresent the cause of death. Furthermore, even if one assumes that dying declarants are likely to be sincere, the circumstances surrounding a dying declaration may exacerbate other hearsay dangers. If the declarant is the victim of a sudden attack, there is reason to question the accuracy of the victim's perceptions. Additionally, an individual who is suffering enough to believe that death is imminent may have somewhat reduced capacities for narration and memory.

There are additional indications of doubt about the justifications for the admission of dying declarations. In some jurisdictions the party against whom a dying declaration is admitted is entitled to a jury instruction that these statements are to be considered with caution. And the limitation to homicide cases was generated by the concern of the House Judiciary Committee: "The Committee did not consider dying declarations as among the most reliable forms of hearsay. Consequently, it amended the provision to limit their admissibility in criminal cases to homicide prosecutions, where exceptional need for the evidence is present." What this means, of course, is that we are willing to use evidence whose reliability we question in order to obtain criminal convictions that carry the most severe sanctions.

KEY POINT

Assuming unavailability, statements made by a declarant who believes that death is imminent are admissible in civil cases and in homicide cases so long as the contents of the statement concern the cause or circumstances of the declarant's impending death.

PROBLEM

8.68. Fueled by alcohol, rivalry, and the desire for the victim's new car, five men hatched a plot to carjack an acquaintance of theirs and murder him. Three of them carried out the plan. In his dying moments, the victim identified by name the three who attacked him. Unfortunately, he was wrong about two of them, which the government's own proof substantiates. The government nevertheless seeks to use the dying statement against the third attacker who, it claims, was accurately named. May this defendant prevent the admission of the dying declaration? On what grounds? May a fourth defendant, who the government claims did participate in the attack but who was not named by the victim, use the dying declaration at trial to show that he was not an attacker?

6. Explanation of FRE 804(b)(3): Declarations Against Interest

FRE 804(b)(3) states:

(b) *The Exceptions.* The following are not excluded by the rule against hearsay if the declarant is unavailable as a witness: . . .
(3) *Statement Against Interest.* A statement that:
(A) a reasonable person in the declarant's position would have made only if the person believed it to be true because, when made, it was so contrary to the declarant's proprietary or pecuniary interest or had so great a tendency to invalidate the declarant's claim against someone else or to expose the declarant to civil or criminal liability; and
(B) is supported by corroborating circumstances that clearly indicate its trustworthiness, if it is offered in a criminal case as one that tends to expose the declarant to criminal liability.

a. Preliminary Factfinding

The factual requirements for declarations against interest are:

- the content of the statement, at the time the statement was made, was
  - ◆ against the pecuniary or proprietary interest of the declarant;
  - ◆ could subject the declarant to civil or criminal liability; or
  - ◆ could render invalid a claim held by the declarant;
- the statement was against any of the above interests of the declarant to an extent great enough such that a reasonable person, in declarant's position, would not have made such a statement unless it was true; and
- if the statement exposes the declarant to criminal liability and is offered in a criminal case, evidence of corroborating circumstances that clearly indicate the trustworthiness of the statement must be offered.

Content Against Interest.   The focus of the *against-interest* requirement is usually on the content of the statement. This content must be contrary to one of the specific interests of the declarant identified in the rule when the statement is made. At trial, the statement is offered to prove the truth of those facts. Assume, for example, that Mark tells a friend that he owes a lot of money to Ryan. The fact of owing money is against Mark's *pecuniary* interest. We assume that people in general have an interest in maintaining ownership of their money as well as their possessions, so Mark's statement that he owes money should qualify as contrary to his proprietary interest as well. Suppose Mark told his friend that he had robbed a convenience store in order to pay the debt. This statement could subject Mark to criminal liability and thus would be against Mark's *penal* interest.

To be against a declarant's pecuniary, penal, or civil claim interests, a statement under FRE 804(b)(3) need not have been said in the face of immediate adverse consequences. For instance, the rule does not require that Mark's admission of robbing the store have been made to a police officer. Indeed, even if Mark reasonably believed that his friend would keep his statements confidential, that would not alter their against-interest quality. Courts typically focus and rely on the against-interest *content* of the facts disclosed. Thus, a better test is whether the statements would harm Mark's interest if disclosed publicly or to the relevant authorities.

Nevertheless, sometimes a statement that on its face appears to be against interest is not in fact against the declarant's interest because surrounding circumstances change the surface meaning of the contents of the statement into something neutral or self-serving. A statement by Mark that he owes Ryan $500 may not be against Mark's interest if Mark knows that Ryan claims that the debt is really $2,000. If the facts in the statement can no longer cause trouble for the declarant (e.g., he has been convicted of the crime whereof he speaks) then the against-interest element may not be satisfied. And in many situations, particularly those that involve bargaining between crime suspects and law enforcement officials, against-interest admissions can be made with powerful self-serving objectives. We discuss this problem further below.

Ascertaining the Declarant's Knowledge. The declarant's knowledge comes up in two different senses under FRE 804(b)(3). Like other FRE 803 and 804 exceptions, FRE 804(b)(3) requires a showing that the declarant (Mark) had personal knowledge of the against-interest fact when the statement was made. In addition, FRE 804(b)(3) applies only if Mark knows (or reasonably should know) that the fact is against his interest. If particular facts affect the declarant's assessment of what is against interest, then these facts will be taken into account. FRE 804(b)(3) calls for evaluation of the probable understanding of an individual by asking what a reasonable person in that individual's position would be thinking; and we typically apply "objective," reasonable person standards in light of the circumstances and facts known to the particular individual whose conduct or statement is at issue. In most cases, it will be relatively easy to determine that the declarant knows the statement is "against interest."

Distinct from Party Admission. It is important not to confuse FRE 801(d)(2)(A) admissions of a party with declarations against interest. You can see that FRE 804(b)(3) requires many more factual requirements. It also applies to statements made by anyone: The FRE 804(b)(3) declarant need not be a party, and typically is not. (The most common use against a party for this is the offer of one codefendant's against-interest statement against another codefendant, where the codefendant/declarant is unavailable due to the assertion of a privilege.) Parties are likely available as witnesses, whereas the FRE 804(b)(3) declarant must be unavailable. Moreover, where the declarant is a party, it is much easier to admit the statement as a statement of party opponent under FRE 801(d)(2)(A).

b. Justification for the Admissibility of Declarations Against Interest

The content of Mark's statement that he owes money reflects damage to his pecuniary interest. This against-interest factor is thought to give the statement a sufficient circumstantial guarantee of trustworthiness to warrant admissibility, at least if the alternative is forgoing the evidence altogether, which it is since the exception requires unavailability. The underlying theory of human behavior is that most people generally tell the truth in the absence of a motive to lie, and motivations to lie are nearly always self-serving: statements against interest, which are the opposite of self-serving by definition, are thus seen as reflecting an absence of a motive to lie. Such a statement is therefore likely to be reliable, even though oath and cross-examination are lacking. The other types of interests that are included within the exception—not being subjected to civil and criminal liability, possessing valid claims against others—are also assumed to be important enough that people should have no reason to lie if they say something that reflects badly on such interests. Some courts speak of a requirement to show that the declarant did not have a motive to lie, but this is not an independent requirement for the exception.

7. FRE 804(b)(3): Practical Applications and Problems

a. Doubts About the Underlying Rationale for the Exception

The most serious problem with the declaration against interest exception is its empirical assumptions. The first premise underlying the exception makes good common sense: People seldom intentionally state facts that truly reflect against their interest. But the next, converse, premise is more dubious: that against-interest statements, when made, are therefore likely to be trustworthy. The second premise is in tension with the first. It seems much more likely that a statement that appears to be against interest is in fact not against interest, but reflects an ulterior motive that may be difficult to discern.

Most statements that are characterized as declarations against interest are likely to fall into one of two categories:

Mixed Motive Statements. "Mixed motive" statements *appear* to be against interest but have a high risk of being unreliable due to a likely ulterior self-interested motive for making the statement. For example, a declarant might say he owes money in order to justify asking the listener for a loan; the declarant may "admit" robbing a convenience store or dealing drugs to impress the listener. An against-interest statement may be made to gain credibility in order to convince the listener to believe an accompanying falsehood. Numerous criminal cases involve statements to law enforcement officials made by declarants who both admit culpability while also blaming others in order to curry favor with the authorities, or to secure immunity from prosecution. See, e.g., United States v. Bobo, 994 F.2d 524 (8th Cir. 1993) (in a prosecution for possession of a firearm, no error to exclude the defendant's brother's statement that a gun was his, and not the defendant's; court distrusted the brother's motive and the timing of the statement just before trial); Donovan v. Crisostomo, 689 F.2d 869 (9th Cir. 1982) (statements of foreign employees that they did not work overtime were not declarations against their pecuniary interest, because they may have been motivated to make the statements to avoid being sent back to their country of origin).

Sometimes, however, there may not be much available information bearing on the real motivation of the declarant, and the court may fail to see that the declarant also had a self-serving reason to make the statement. If courts do not discern such mixed motives, untrustworthy statements may be admitted.

Statements Made with No Motive to Lie. The second type of statements admitted under FRE 804(b)(3) are reliable statements whose reliability has more to do with lack of motivation to lie and less to do with their against-interest characterization. Mark's statement that he owes money may be, to him, merely a neutral recitation of a fact. The fact that the statement may be characterized as being against interest may have nothing to do with its sincerity. In this respect the statement is no different from many other hearsay statements that do not fall within the declaration against interest (or any other hearsay) exception.

b. Statements That Inculpate Accomplices

Mixed motive statements raise special, recurring problems in criminal cases. Consider a case in which prosecutors have charged two defendants, Worrell and Holmes, with robbing a bank. Holmes makes a written confession to the crime at the police station and in the confession names Worrell as his accomplice. At Worrell's separate trial, Holmes successfully asserts his Fifth Amendment right not to testify and is therefore unavailable. The prosecutors offer Holmes's written confession against Worrell, arguing that it is a statement against the penal interest of the declarant, Holmes under FRE 804(b)(3).

A key question presented in cases of potential statements against penal interest that inculpate the defendant in addition to the hearsay declarant will be whether the statement constitutes "testimonial" hearsay under Crawford v. Washington. If it does, then the statement is barred by the confrontation clause, unless the defendant had a prior opportunity to cross-examine the now-unavailable declarant. Inadmissibility under the confrontation clause cuts off any inquiry into whether the statement qualifies for admission under FRE 804(b)(3). Any statement given under police questioning at the station house, whether a written confession as in the Worrell-Holmes hypothetical or tape recorded interview, as in *Crawford* itself, plainly falls within the core application of the *Crawford* definition.

Since *Crawford*, federal courts have continued to struggle with the contours of the "testimonial" definition, as will be discussed in Section G, infra. Suppose Holmes's statement implicating Worrell was made in circumstances that makes the statement "nontestimonial"? For example, suppose Holmes is arrested while trying to flee the scene of the bank robbery. The officers ask whether he has any accomplices and if they are armed. Holmes replies, "Yeah, Worrell robbed the bank with me. He's probably made it back to his place by now," and gives the officers Worrell's address. Such a statement is arguably nontestimonial under current doctrine, since the officers' inquiry was intended to address an ongoing emergency (a suspected and possibly armed bank robber still at large) rather than to establish investigative facts for a subsequent prosecution.

If the hearsay offered under FRE 804(b)(3) is held to be not testimonial, then it is necessary to analyze whether a mixed motive statement like Holmes's is truly against the declarant's interest. Pre-*Crawford* authorities analyzing this question in the context of statements made to law enforcement have held that FRE 804(b)(3) should not allow admission of statements that inculpate purported accomplices unless they also specifically self-inculpate the declarant as well. A broad narrative that is only generally self-inculpatory might not be found to be sufficiently against interest, while statements that intertwine self-inculpation could be genuinely against the interest of the declarant; for example, "I hid the gun in Joe's apartment" could show both self-incrimination and Joe's involvement. See Williamson v. United States, 512 U.S. 594 (1994); United States v. Smalls, 605 F.3d 765, 780-787 (10th Cir. 2010) (remanding case to district court to determine which parts of co-conspirator's extended, nontestimonial confession to confidential informant were sufficiently against penal interest); United States v. Westmoreland, 240 F.3d 618, 626 (7th Cir. 2001). The question is difficult and troubling, and context matters. In the above example, perhaps Holmes falsely named Worrell to cover the identity of the true accomplice; or perhaps he was trying start a process of cooperating with the police in order to mitigate his own punishment. If Holmes believed that he was caught red-handed in the course of a bank robbery, he may have felt that he was not giving anything away by conceding his own involvement.

c. Requirement of Corroboration for Inculpatory Statements in Criminal Cases

FRE 804(b)(3)(B) imposes special corroboration requirements on declarations against penal interest that are offered in criminal cases. In such cases, an out-of-court declarant has typically made a statement assuming criminal responsibility for the crime with which the defendant is charged. The requirement is framed in terms of "corroborating circumstances" that "clearly indicate the trustworthiness of the statement." Courts look to circumstances that corroborate either the content of the statement (other evidence that the facts that exculpate the defendant are true) or the trustworthiness of the declarant (voluntariness, lack of motive to curry favor, lack of subsequent inconsistent statements). Recantation of exculpatory statements, and assertions of the Fifth Amendment privilege have been held to weigh against trustworthiness. United States v. Davis, 2001 WL 524374 (D.C. Cir. 2001).

Background to Current Rule.   The history of this requirement is worth noting. FRE 804(b)(3) was amended to its present form in 2010. Prior to that, FRE 804(b)(3) was written to require corroboration only of exculpatory statements against interest offered by an accused. Classic examples would include purported admissions of guilt by declarants other than the defendant who had since died, disappeared, or asserted the privilege against self-incrimination. The drafters of the original version of the rule were undoubtedly concerned about the fabrication of exculpatory evidence in criminal cases. Since the rule applies only where the declarant is unavailable, the drafters were undoubtedly concerned about the ease with which a made-up confession could be attributed to a declarant known to be unavailable—perhaps one who has absconded or died. Courts have long been exceedingly focused on this possibility. See Advisory Committee Note to FRE 804(b)(3) ("[O]ne senses in the decisions a distrust of evidence of confessions by third persons offered to exculpate the accused arising from suspicions of fabrication either of the fact of the making of the confession or in its contents, enhanced in either instance by the required unavailability of the declarant."); see also State v. Higginbotham, 212 N.W.2d 881, 883 (Minn. 1973) ("[H]earsay statements tending to exculpate the accused must be regarded with suspicion.").

There were two objections to this corroboration requirement. First, the problem it purports to address is not a hearsay problem. The FRE 804(b)(3) statement must still be presented by a live witness in court. The witness whom the drafters fear will fabricate the against-interest statement of an unavailable declarant will thus himself be on the witness stand and subject to cross-examination. Second, critics argued that if against-penal interest statements are less reliable and require corroboration, there is no reason to limit the FRE 804(b)(3) corroboration requirement solely to statements offered to exculpate the defendant. Prosecution witnesses are at least as likely as defense witnesses, critics argue, to fabricate FRE 804(b)(3) statements against penal interest. Note that such statements would necessarily take the form of mixed motive statements by a declarant other than the accused, as described in the previous section. This is so because inculpatory admissions by an accused would be admissible as an opposing party's own statement under FRE 801(d)(2)(A). If such a mixed motive statement were found to have been made in an informal, spontaneous setting to someone unconnected with law enforcement, there is an argument that the statement is nontestimonial and thus falls outside *Crawford*. Again, this is not a hearsay problem, but rather a problem of a witness lying on the stand by fabricating someone else's purported statement. Nevertheless, rather than removing the nonhearsay concern from the exception, the rule was amended to conform to a "turnabout is fair play" principle. It now applies to FRE 804(b)(3) against-penal-interest statements whether offered by the prosecution or the defense.

Notwithstanding these concerns, and the corroboration requirement for the particular category of statements against interest, doubts about the credibility of the testifying witness should not be a factor in assessing the trustworthiness of the *declarant's* statement. United States v. Atkins, 558 F.2d 133 (3d Cir. 1977).

Ongoing Constitutional Difficulties.   Prior to its amendment in 2010, the corroboration requirement for exculpatory against-penal-interest statements was constitutionally questionable. It applied only to statements offered by the defense, with prosecutors being free to rely on any statement against penal interest, corroborated and uncorroborated. This evidentiary freedom was at odds with the Sixth Amendment confrontation requirement, as interpreted both before and after Crawford v. Washington, 541 U.S. 36 (2004). See Daniel J. Capra, Amending the Hearsay Exceptions for Declarations Against Penal Interest in the Wake of Crawford, 105 Colum. L. Rev. 2409, 2425-2427 (2005). The prosecutorial advantage under FRE 804(b)(3) was also constitutionally suspect for violating due process. Arguably, defendants should be able to rely on hearsay statements under the same, if not better, conditions than prosecutors. See Richard A. Nagareda, Reconceiving the Right to Present Witnesses, 97 Mich. L. Rev. 1063, 1146-1148 (1999).

But the 2010 amendment of FRE 804(b)(3) equalizing the corroboration requirement remains constitutionally suspect insofar as it prevents defendants from using uncorroborated third-party admissions of guilt as exculpatory evidence. An argument can be made that the Compulsory Process Clause should entitle defendants to present virtually any rational proof tending to make guilt less probable. This argument received some support from Holmes v. South Carolina, 547 U.S. 319 (2006), where the Court held that South Carolina's restrictions on the admissibility of third-party admissions of guilt as exculpatory evidence were unconstitutional. More recently, however, in Nevada v. Jackson, 133 S. Ct. 1990 (2013), the Supreme Court found that no established precedent forbade a state from excluding exculpatory hearsay evidence suggesting that the alleged rape victim made unfounded accusations against the defendant on several prior occasions. For recent analysis of the Court's compulsory process decisions, see Alex Stein, Inefficient Evidence, 66 Ala. L. Rev. 423, 460-469 (2015).

KEY POINTS

1. Assuming unavailability, statements that are against the declarant's pecuniary, proprietary, penal, or civil liability interest may be admissible. The statement must be so far against that interest that a reasonable person would not be lying when making that statement.
2. In order to determine whether the statement is against interest, the court should examine the situation and motives of the declarant. Mixed motive statements should be examined carefully to see whether the predominating motive is self-serving rather than against interest.
3. Statements of fact that inculpate others, made in the context of a self-inculpating statement, are admissible only if each specific statement is against the declarant's interest. Courts are divided as to whether such statements, made in custody, can be admitted as against the declarant's interest.
4. Statements against penal interest offered in a criminal case must be corroborated as to contents, the trustworthiness of the declarant, or both.

PROBLEMS

8.69. Hanna Mason has sued the Acme Rental Company for personal injuries that she sustained as a pedestrian when she was hit by an Acme truck driven by James Lowe, an Acme employee. Lowe was fired the day after the accident, and six months later moved to Acapulco. Just before leaving the country, Lowe told his friend, Andy Becker, that he had been drinking at the time of the accident and had failed to stop at a stop sign. Lowe also made the same statement in a deposition taken during the discovery phase of the current lawsuit. Lowe has refused to respond to plaintiff's letter requesting that he return to the United States to testify. At trial, Hanna calls Andy Becker to testify about Lowe's statement. Is the evidence admissible?

8.70. In the film *The Shawshank Redemption*, Andy DuFresne (Tim Robbins) is serving a life sentence at Shawshank Penitentiary for the murder of his wife and her lover. DuFresne always maintained his innocence. About 20 years into his sentence, DuFresne befriends a young convict named Tommy Williams, who has been sent to Shawshank on a burglary conviction. Eventually, Williams tells DuFresne that a former cellmate in a local jail, named Elmo Blatch, admitted to committing the murder of which DuFresne was convicted. According to Blatch, he killed the two victims (a golf pro and his girlfriend) in the course of an armed burglary/robbery; he later learned (to his amusement) that the murder was pinned on the woman's husband, "a banker" — DuFresne.

Andy DuFresne wants to seek a new trial of his murder charge based on this newly discovered evidence. He assumes the evidence could be introduced through the testimony of Tommy Williams. Can it?

Hint: Assume this is an evidentiary hearing pursuant to a writ of habeas corpus by DuFresne seeking a new trial based on the newly discovered evidence of

Blatch's statement to Tommy Williams. Assume also that Williams is alive and available to testify. (Spoiler alert: in the film, he is murdered by the warden.) The issue for this problem is whether Williams's testimony will be admissible at all as a statement against interest. Defense counsel should call whatever witnesses you deem necessary to establish the elements of this exception.

8.71. Joshua Thomas has been charged for his alleged role in arson and vandalism of an SUV dealership, destroying a number of Hummers and doing other property damage. Thomas denies any involvement in the act. A group called the Environmental Liberation Front (ELF) claimed responsibility for the act shortly after it occurred. The city newspaper reported that an anonymous source communicated with reporter Bob Adams, the author of the news story, in three e-mails and two telephone interviews, claiming to be responsible for the arson and vandalism, while indicating that Thomas is innocent. Consider whether defense counsel for Thomas, preparing his case for trial, can introduce this information as evidence. What form would this evidence take? What witnesses would the defense need to call? What objections would the prosecution make, and how would the defense respond? What further investigation would defense counsel have to undertake in order get this evidence in admissible form?

8. Explanation of FRE 804(b)(4): Statements of Personal or Family History

FRE 804(b)(4) provides:

(b) *The Exceptions.* The following are not excluded by the rule against hearsay if the declarant is unavailable as a witness: . . .
(4) *Statement of Personal or Family History.* A statement about:
(A) the declarant's own birth, adoption, legitimacy, ancestry, marriage, divorce, relationship by blood, adoption, or marriage, or similar facts of personal or family history, even though the declarant had no way of acquiring personal knowledge about that fact; or
(B) another person concerning any of these facts, as well as death, if the declarant was related to the person by blood, adoption, or marriage or was so intimately associated with the person's family that the declarant's information is likely to be accurate.

a. Preliminary Factfinding

The factual requirements for statements of personal or family history are:

- the content must concern the declarant's own personal or family history; or
- the statement concerns the personal or family history of one to whom the declarant is related or was intimately associated.

Personal Knowledge of One's Own Personal and Family History.   FRE 804(b)(4)(A), like the common law pedigree exception, does not require that the declarant have personal knowledge. Obviously, a declarant has no personal recollection of birth or place of birth. United States v. Hernandez, 105 F.3d 1330, 1832 (9th Cir. 1997) (statement that declarant was born in Mexico admissible without personal knowledge). However, any declarant meeting the requirements of subsection (A) is inevitably going to have knowledge of circumstantial evidence of personal and family relationships.

Statements of Relations and Intimate Associates.   The common law also required that a declarant speaking about the pedigree of another be related by blood or marriage to the person about whom the declaration is made. FRE 804(b)(4)(B) expands the common law pedigree exception to close family members and intimate associates so long as the relationship is such that the declarant would have accurate information about the family history. Do the reasons for eliminating the personal knowledge requirement in subsection (A) also apply to the declarants listed in subsection (B)? Independent evidence may be required that the declarant was a family member or so intimately associated with a family as to be knowledgeable.

Concerning Personal History.   The exception is limited to past facts and events of an objective, rather than subjective, nature. Statements as to motives or purpose for marriage are beyond the scope of FRE 804(b)(4). United States v. Carvalho, 742 F.2d 146 (4th Cir. 1984) (statements from former spouses as to the defendants' previous motives to marry in order to obtain citizenship were admitted in error).

b. Justification for the Admissibility of Statements of Personal or Family History

A justification for this exception is necessity. The kinds of details covered by FRE 804(b)(4) are likely to be difficult or impossible to prove through documentary evidence, and may be known through "family lore," statements of now-deceased relatives, and the like. The exception overlaps to a great degree with FRE 803(19), by extending beyond "reputation" evidence to include statements of facts that may be known only to the unavailable declarant. Statements about the declarant's own pedigree are assumed to be reliable enough to be admitted if the declarant is unavailable. No special assurances of reliability are required. The common law hearsay exception required that the declaration be made prior to the time of the controversy that is the subject of the litigation. The Advisory Committee Note to FRE 804(b)(4) explains the absence of this requirement on the ground that the timing of the statement has a "bearing more appropriately on weight than admissibility."

KEY POINTS

1. Assuming unavailability, a statement asserting the declarant's own family history may be admitted without a showing of personal knowledge.
2. A statement asserting the family history of another person may be admitted if the declarant had accurate knowledge as a result of being related to or intimately associated with the other person's family.

PROBLEMS

8.72. John Bowman has filed an action in probate court, claiming to be the closest kin—a nephew—of the wealthy decedent, George Bowman. George died
intestate and had no children or surviving spouse. To establish his claim, John
offers the affidavit of one Jacob Bowman, John's father, who John claims is
brother to George. Jacob is now deceased. In this affidavit, Jacob states that he
and George are brothers and that they emigrated to the United States together
from Germany in 1905. John offers no other evidence of a family relationship.
Another distant relative who claims the estate offers an authenticated letter from
Emily Bowman, deceased wife of Jacob. The letter states that her husband,
Jacob, was bribed by John to make the affidavit and that, to her knowledge,
George and Jacob were not brothers. Is Jacob's affidavit admissible? Is Emily's
letter admissible?

9. Explanation of FRE 804(b)(6): Forfeiture by Wrongdoing

FRE 804(b)(6) provides:

> (b) *The Exceptions.* The following are not excluded by the rule against
> hearsay if the declarant is unavailable as a witness: . . .
> (6) *Statement Offered Against a Party That Wrongfully Caused the
> Declarant's Unavailability.* A statement offered against a party that wrong-
> fully caused—or acquiesced in wrongfully causing—the declarant's
> unavailability as a witness, and did so intending that result.

This exception, added to the Federal Rules in 1997, codified a line of cases beginning
with United States v. Mastrangelo, 693 F.2d 269 (2d Cir. 1982), in which key prosecution witnesses would "suddenly" became unavailable due to violence or intimidation allegedly perpetrated against them by the defendants against whom they were
to testify. Admission of the unavailable witnesses' hearsay statements was justified on
a theory of waiver or forfeiture. *Mastrangelo* held that although a criminal defendant's Sixth Amendment right of confrontation "is an essential trial right, it may be
waived by the defendant's misconduct." United States v. Dhinsa, 243 F.3d 635, 651
(2d Cir. 2001). This waiver-by-misconduct rule permitted the admission of the hearsay statements of unavailable witnesses when the defendant had "wrongfully procured
the witnesses' silence through threats, actual violence or murder," id., despite the
lack of confrontation. The waiver principle was then extended to include the hearsay
rule—waiver of confrontation rights simultaneously waived "the right to object on
hearsay grounds to the admission of [the] out-of-court statements." United States v.
Houlihan, 92 F.3d 1271, 1281 (1st Cir. 1996). The Advisory Committee Note to FRE
804(b)(6) makes it clear that the new hearsay exception was intended to implement
Mastrangelo and its progeny.

a. Preliminary Factfinding

The factual requirements for forfeiture-by-wrongdoing statements are:

- the party engaged or acquiesced in wrongdoing;
- the wrongdoing was intended to procure the unavailability of the declarant as a witness against the party;
- the wrongdoing did render the declarant unavailable as a witness; and
- the declarant's statement is offered against the party.

The Declarant Was a Witness or a Potential Witness Against a Party. It is clear from the case law that the purpose of FRE 804(b)(6) is to secure the admission at trial of hearsay statements made by unavailable declarants who were serving as witnesses against a party, for example by giving grand jury testimony or by being scheduled to appear in an upcoming trial. If there was instead only an ongoing criminal investigation, declarants are *potential* witnesses if they are assisting in this investigation. Both prior to and after FRE 804(b)(6), courts have held that the forfeiture rule applies to wrongdoing against both actual and potential witnesses. United States v. Houlihan, 92 F.3d 1271, 1279 (1st Cir. 1996) ("We see no [difference] between a defendant who assassinates a witness on the eve of trial and a potential defendant who assassinates a potential witness before charges have officially been brought.").

The Party Engaged in Wrongdoing Procured the Unavailability of the Declarant. The party against whom the declarant's statements are offered must be shown to have "procured" the unavailability of the declarant by engaging in or acquiescing in "wrongdoing." The proponent of the statements show that the party did so act. In general, wrongdoing is defined broadly to mean threats, intimidation, kidnapping, hiding, acts of violence, and, ultimately, murder to secure the silence of the then-unavailable declarant. Engaging in wrongdoing means "he or she participated directly in planning or procuring the declarant's unavailability." United States v. Cherry, 217 F.3d 811, 820 (10th Cir. 2000) (defendant's obtaining the car used in the declarant's murder under false pretenses, and her apparent proximity to the actual murderer around the time of the murder, might be sufficient circumstantial evidence that she participated in the planning of the murder).

Evidence used to prove the party's engagement in wrongdoing may include the declarant's hearsay statements. As we know from the Supreme Court's opinion in *Bourjaily*, discussed on page 518-19, supra, FRE 104(a) permits the court to "bootstrap" a finding of a foundational fact by relying on the contested hearsay statement itself. Should courts impose a requirement, similar to the language in FRE 801(d)(2), that the contested hearsay statement may be used but is not sufficient to prove the party's wrongdoing?

Intent to Procure the Declarant's Unavailability as a Witness. To admit a statement under this exception, the trial court must find that the party acted with the specific intention of making the declarant unavailable as a witness, at least in criminal cases. In Giles v. California, 554 U.S. 353 (2008), the Supreme Court held that the confrontation clause requires this specific intent element for the forfeiture by wrongdoing exception to apply in criminal cases. On that ground, the Court rejected a state law rule that applied the state's hearsay forfeiture exception to admit statements made by a murder victim without requiring any finding that the defendant had killed the victim with a specific intent to make her unavailable as a witness; the fact that the defendant had made the witness unavailable by murdering her did not suffice to establish forfeiture in a manner that would satisfy the confrontation clause.

Does the intent to make the witness unavailable have to be the defendant's sole motivation to permit the use of the unavailable witness's statement? In *Giles*, for example, the defendant Giles had been convicted of first-degree murder of his girlfriend based on evidence that included hearsay testimony from the victim that Giles had beaten and threatened to kill her three weeks before the murder. The testimony had been offered to establish his intent to kill and to rebut Giles's claim of self-defense. The Supreme Court vacated the conviction and remanded the case to the state court to determine whether Giles intended to make the victim unavailable as a witness. According to the Court, the prior incident of domestic violence would be relevant to that inquiry:

> Acts of domestic violence often are intended to dissuade a victim from resorting to outside help, and include conduct designed to prevent testimony to police officers or cooperation in criminal prosecutions. Where such an abusive relationship culminates in murder, the evidence may support a finding that the crime expressed the intent to isolate the victim and to stop her from reporting abuse to the authorities or cooperating with a criminal prosecution—rendering her prior statements admissible under the forfeiture doctrine. [554 U.S. at 377.]

Lower courts, both before and after *Giles*, have held that it is *not* necessary "to show that the defendant's sole motivation was to procure the declarant's absence; rather, [the prosecution] need only show that the defendant was motivated *in part* by a desire to silence the witness." United States v. Dhinsa, 243 F.3d 635, 652 (2d Cir. 2001); accord United States v. Jackson, 706 F.3d 264; 267 (4th Cir. 2013) (rejecting defendant's claim that sole motivation must be shown).

At Which Trial Can the Statement Be Used?   In the classic forfeiture by wrongdoing case, the unavailable declarant's statements pertain to past events or offenses (such as racketeering or drug sales) that the declarant could have testified about at the time the declarant was silenced by the defendant's wrongdoing. The statements are then admitted against the defendant to prove these past offenses. Increasingly, however, the government also prosecutes the defendant for the act of wrongdoing—typically murder—that has made the declarant unavailable. The content of some of the declarant's hearsay statements may concern the murder itself, not the defendant's past offenses as to which the declarant would have been a witness or potential witness.

Defendants have argued that this is an improper extension of the forfeiture-by-wrongdoing principle since the declarant's status as "witness" is not related to any trial for his own murder. The above-quoted language from *Giles* seems contrary to this narrow view. See *Giles*, 554 U.S. at 377 (suggesting that "intent to isolate the victim and to stop her from reporting [ongoing domestic] abuse" could sustain a forfeiture finding in a prosecution the victim's death from the abuse). Lower courts, both before and after *Giles*, have unanimously declined to impose any such limit on the application of Rule 804(b)(6), holding that its broad terminology includes within its reach the admission of statements by the declarant when the murder of the declarant is the crime charged. See United States v. Stewart, 485 F.3d 666, 672 (2d Cir. 2007) ("The text of Rule 804(b)(6) requires only that the defendant intend to render the declarant unavailable 'as a witness.' The text does not require that the declarant would otherwise be a witness at any particular trial."); *Dhinsa*, 243 F.3d at 652 (same). United States v. Battle, 473 F. Supp. 2d 1185, 1195 (S.D. Fla. 2006) ("Rule 804(b)(6) places no limitation on the subject matter of a declarant's statement that can be offered against a defendant at trial."); State v. Miller, 234 Ariz. 31, 39, 316 P.3d 1219, 1227 (2013) cert. denied, 134 S. Ct. 2668, 189 L. Ed. 2d 216 (2014) ("Miller argues that this exception permits hearsay only in the trial for which the defendant silenced the witness — here, the arson case. But Rule 804(b)(6) contains no such limitation. Moreover, such a restriction would frustrate the rule's purpose of preventing a defendant from benefiting from his wrongdoing.").

b. Justification for the Admissibility of Forfeiture-by-Wrongdoing Statements

The justification for the admissibility of forfeiture-by-wrongdoing statements is straightforward: "[T]he law [will not] allow a person to take advantage of his own wrong." *Mastrangelo*, 693 F.2d at 272. An oft-quoted explication of this policy was stated in United States v. White, 116 F.3d 903, 911 (D.C. Cir. 1997):

> . . . It is hard to imagine a form of misconduct more extreme than the murder of a potential witness. Simple equity supports a forfeiture principle, as does a common sense attention to the need for fit incentives. The defendant who has removed an adverse witness is in a weak position to complain about losing the chance to cross-examine him. And where a defendant has silenced a witness through the use of threats, violence or murder, admission of the victim's prior statements at least partially offsets the perpetrator's rewards for his misconduct.

There is no reliability inquiry authorized by FRE 804(b)(6). The trial court need not look for indicia of trustworthiness under either the hearsay rule or the confrontation clause. Once the defendant has waived these rights, the court "is not required to assess independently the reliability of those statements." United States v. Dhinsa, 243 F.3d at 655.

c. Acquiescence in Wrongdoing

One of the principal concerns voiced to the Advisory Committee as it was considering the adoption of FRE 804(b)(6) was the breadth of the term "*acquiesced in wrongfully causing* . . . *the declarant's unavailability.*" The broadest application of the rule has been stated by the Tenth Circuit in United States v. Cherry, which applied the rule to statements offered against co-conspirators who did not plan or in any way participate in wrongdoing that caused the unavailability of the declarant.

> [T]he use of the words "engaged or acquiesced in wrongdoing" lends support to the government's assertion that, at least for purposes of the hearsay rules, waiver can be imputed under an agency theory of responsibility to a defendant who "acquiesced" in the wrongful procurement of a witness's unavailability but did not actually "engage" in wrongdoing apart from the conspiracy itself. [217 F.3d at 816.]

Cherry involved five defendants charged with a drug conspiracy. Much of the evidence against them came from a cooperating witness named Lurks, who was murdered by one of the five prior to trial. The district court rejected the use of FRE 804(b)(6) against three of the defendants, finding that there was "absolutely no evidence" that the three "had actual knowledge of, agreed to or participated in the murder of . . . Lurks." Id. at 820. The government took an interlocutory appeal, since exclusion of Lurks's statements against the three would destroy its case. The Court of Appeals reversed, applying the principles of conspiratorial liability enunciated in Pinkerton v. United States, 328 U.S. 640 (1946) to define "acquiescence":

> . . . A defendant may be deemed to have waived his or her Confrontation Clause rights (and, a fortiori, hearsay objections) if a preponderance of the evidence establishes . . . [that] the wrongful procurement [of the defendant's unavailability] was in furtherance, within the scope, and reasonably foreseeable as a necessary or natural consequence of an ongoing conspiracy . . . Actual knowledge is not required for conspiratorial waiver by misconduct if the[se] elements . . . are satisfied . . . We note that the scope of the conspiracy is not necessarily limited to a primary goal—such as bank robbery—but can also include secondary goals relevant to the evasion of apprehension and prosecution for that goal—such as escape, or, by analogy, obstruction of justice . . . We further reiterate that . . . a defendant is not responsible for the acts of co-conspirators if that defendant meets the burden of proving he or she took affirmative steps to withdraw from the conspiracy before those acts were committed. [217 F.3d at 820.]

If *Cherry* is correctly decided, the rule extends to active participants in the wrongdoing, as well as those who knew about it as members of a conspiracy and either agreed with it or simply failed to dissociate themselves from the conspiracy. *Cherry* extends acquiescence even further to include those without knowledge, as long as they were part of a conspiracy in which some members procured a witness's unavailability for the benefit of the conspirators. Perhaps the only category of person excluded from this concept of acquiescence is someone who merely benefited from the unavailability of the witness, and nothing more. To date, other circuits have tended to follow *Cherry*. United States v. Dinkins, 691 F.3d 358, 383-386 (4th Cir. 2012) (following *Cherry*); United States v. Martinez, 476 F.3d 961 (D.C. Cir. 2007) (FRE 804(b)(6) satisfied when defendant was "aware" that his co-conspirators were "willing to engage in murder to protect the conspiracy"); United States v. Thompson, 286 F.3d 950, 965 (7th Cir. 2002) ("[T]he waiver-by-misconduct of one conspirator may be imputed to another conspirator if the misconduct was within the scope and in furtherance of the conspiracy, and was reasonably foreseeable to him.").

Whether *Cherry* was correctly decided or not, it is important to undertake a careful analysis of "secondary goals" of the conspiracy. We have seen how a conspiracy to commit a crime might be deemed to end, for purposes of the co-conspirator hearsay exception, once the conspiracy has entered a "concealment phase." Whether concealment is analyzed as the same conspiracy as that formed to undertake the primary crime, or as a new conspiracy to cover it up, may be a fact-intensive inquiry not suitable to a broad legal rule.

d. Practical Applications

FRE 403.   Admission of the unavailable declarant's statements is not automatic, however, as the court must still perform the balancing test under FRE 403. Prior to the adoption of FRE 804(b)(6), this inquiry included evaluation of the reliability of the declarant's statement to avoid the admission of "facially unreliable hearsay." *Dhinsa*, 243 F.3d at 655. Now that the specific exception is in place, however, it would be highly unusual for the court to exclude a statement that falls within the categorical exception on the basis of "low probative value" based on the court's doubts about its reliability. However, since FRE 804(b)(6) is a categorical exception that requires absolutely no indicia of reliability, perhaps Rule 403's balancing test should take reliability into account. There also remains the danger of ambiguity, confusion, and undue prejudice from the inflammatory nature of the evidence or its context for the court to consider.

Is an FRE 104(d) Hearing Required?   Admission of the statement under FRE 804(b)(6) requires the government to prove by a preponderance of the evidence that the defendant procured the unavailability of the declarant by wrongdoing, and did intend to do so to prevent the declarant from being an actual or potential witness. Courts are divided about whether this hearing should, as a matter of course, be held outside the presence of the jury. Compare *Dhinsa*, 243 F.3d at 653 (hearing should be held outside presence of the jury), with United States v. Baskerville, 448 F. App'x 243, 249-250 (3d Cir. 2011) (district court retains discretion to admit 804(b)(6) statement conditionally "to avoid wasting judicial resources by conducting in effect a trial before the trial"); United States v. Emery, 186 F.3d 921, 926 (8th Cir. 1999) (same). See also United States v. Gray, 405 F.3d 227, 241 (4th Cir. 2005) ("The district court need not hold an independent evidentiary hearing if the requisite findings may be made based upon evidence presented in the course of the trial."). This will be more of an issue in cases where the defendant is being tried for the original underlying crime. Consider whether the jury could adhere to the admonition of the judge to ignore a conditionally admitted hearsay statement of a murder victim, where the government eventually fails to present sufficient evidence of admissibility under FRE 804(b)(6). Where the trial involves the defendant's participation in the murder of the witness, however, sufficient evidence to sustain the FRE804(b)(6) finding will be present if there is enough evidence for the jury to convict the defendant of the murder.

KEY POINTS

1. If a party has procured the unavailability of a hearsay declarant by wrongdoing, and intended to do so to prevent the declarant from being an actual or potential witness, then the declarant's statements are admissible against that party.
2. The party's conduct may have involved planning of, participation in, or acquiescence in the wrongdoing.

PROBLEMS

8.73. Return to Problem 3.4, State v. Blair, at page 150. Police investigation reveals that several weeks before the attack on Norma, she filed a complaint against Jimmy for assault and battery. A police officer then interviewed both Jimmy and Norma; Norma told the officer she wanted to drop the charges. Since the attack, Norma is still unable to remember anything about what happened that night, and she says she is unwilling to testify against Jimmy. The prosecutor wants to know whether, if Norma is called to the stand as a witness, all of the entries in her diary that describe Jimmy's violent temper and his beating of her over the past three years can be admitted under FRE 804(b)(6). What issues in the application of this exception are raised in this case? What would have to happen at trial for the diary to be admitted?

8.74. Returning to problem 8.70 at page 612, in *The Shawshank Redemption*, Andy DuFresne, in a state of great agitation, tells the warden of Shawshank, Mr. Norton, about Williams's potential testimony. Unfortunately for DuFresne, Warden Norton is running a corrupt business scheme out of the prison relying heavily on the assistance of DuFresne's accounting and banking expertise. He therefore wants to keep DuFresne locked up in Shawshank, and has Tommy Williams murdered by Byron Hadley, the captain of the guards, in what is made to look like an escape attempt by Williams.

DuFresne and several other inmates, including Red Redding (Morgan Freeman) heard Tommy Williams's account of the statement by Elmo Blatch. Could any of them testify about it if DuFresne were given a new trial?

8.75. In the film *Traffic*, Helena Ayala (Catherine Zeta Jones) hires a series of hit men to murder Eduardo Ruiz, a mid-level drug dealer who has reluctantly agreed to testify for the prosecution against Ayala's husband, Carlos, a drug kingpin who has been jailed while awaiting trial. After an unsuccessful car bomb attempt on Ruiz, he is murdered the morning he is due to testify by the delivery of a poisoned breakfast to the hotel room where he is being held in protective custody. In the movie, the prosecution voluntarily dismisses the case telling the judge that without Ruiz, they cannot meet their burden of proof.

Assume that no incriminating written or verbal messages have passed between Helena and Carlos during his pretrial detention. Did the prosecution have any alternatives under the rules of evidence?

F. THE RESIDUAL EXCEPTION

The Federal Rules of Evidence as originally promulgated by the Supreme Court provided a broad residual exception in both FRE 803 and FRE 804 for a "statement not specifically covered by any of the foregoing exceptions but having comparable circumstantial guarantees of trustworthiness." Effective December 1, 1997, the Rules were amended to eliminate the two subsections and to add a single, identical residual hearsay exception as FRE 807. This repositioning of the residual exceptions did not change the substance of the rule. Because of the continued validity of pre-1997 case law referring to the residuals under FRE 803(24) and 804(b)(5), and to avoid confusion, those section numbers have not been reassigned to other rules. They continue as placeholders that cross reference the reader to FRE 807.

1. FRE 807

RULE 807. RESIDUAL EXCEPTION

(a) *In General.* Under the following circumstances, a hearsay statement is not excluded by the rule against hearsay even if the statement is not specifically covered by a hearsay exception in Rule 803 or 804:

(1) the statement has equivalent circumstantial guarantees of trustworthiness;

(2) it is offered as evidence of a material fact;

(3) it is more probative on the point for which it is offered than any other evidence that the proponent can obtain through reasonable efforts; and

(4) admitting it will best serve the purposes of these rules and the interests of justice.

(b) *Notice.* The statement is admissible only if, before the trial or hearing, the proponent gives an adverse party reasonable notice of the intent to offer the statement and its particulars, including the declarant's name and address, so that the party has a fair opportunity to meet it.

2. Explanation of FRE 807

The factual requirements for FRE 807 are:

* the statement must have circumstantial guarantees of trustworthiness;
* these guarantees should be "equivalent" to the exceptions in Rules 803 and 804;
* the statement is offered to prove a material fact;
* the statement is more probative on the point for which it is offered than any other evidence that can be obtained through reasonable efforts;
* admission will serve the general purposes of the rules and the interests of justice; and
* notice is given to the opponent.

a. Principles and Policies Underlying the Residual Exception

Justification. The first thing to notice about FRE 807 is that it is not a categorical exception. There are no categorical requirements concerning the identity of the declarant, the content of the statement, or the circumstances in which the statement was made. There is no categorical requirement that the declarant be unavailable. Instead, the principal requirements for admission are that the statement has "circumstantial guarantees of trustworthiness" and that it is "more probative" than other reasonably available evidence—clearly individualized judgments to be made by the trial judge.

The residual exception is justified primarily on grounds of necessity. It envisions exceptional cases where the exclusion of hearsay evidence will result in an injustice, due to the combined weight of the proponent's need for the evidence and the presence of factors suggesting that the hearsay in question is reliable and comes close to qualifying for one of the categorical hearsay exceptions.

At the same time, the residual exception stands in significant tension with the system of categorical exceptions to the hearsay rule. Although there are many exceptions that allow hearsay statements to be admitted for their truth (and exemptions that allow many out-of-court statements to be admitted as technical nonhearsay), a great deal of hearsay is still excluded from evidence under the general principle of FRE 802. By maintaining a categorical approach, and adhering with reasonable strictness to the definitional facts that trigger the exceptions and exemptions, the continued vitality of the hearsay rule is preserved. Giving broad discretionary powers to judges to admit hearsay deemed "reliable" could undermine the hearsay rule.

Limitations on Use of the Exception.   The residual exception is quite plainly a discretionary power to admit hearsay deemed reliable. Is there a way to square this circle—to sustain a broad general hearsay exclusion with categorically limited exceptions and exemptions, while at the same time acknowledging a discretionary reliability exception? Perhaps so, but only by confining the Residual Exception to truly exceptional circumstances. It is probably fair to say that the intent of the Residual Exception is such that it should not be used at all in the majority of cases.

The Advisory Committee Note to the residual exception made this clear:

> It is intended that the residual hearsay exceptions will be used very rarely, and only in exceptional circumstances. The committee does not intend to establish a broad license for trial judges to admit hearsay statements that do not fall within one of the other exceptions contained in rules 803 and 804(b). The residual exceptions are not meant to authorize major judicial revisions of the hearsay rule, including its present exceptions. Such major revisions are best accomplished by legislative action.

Congress intended that Rule 807 "be used very rarely, and only in exceptional circumstances." Coyle v. Kristjan Palusalu Mar. Co., 83 F. Supp. 2d 535, 545 (E.D. Pa. 2000); accord United States v. Bailey, 581 F.2d 341, 347 (3d Cir.1978) (residual hearsay exception is "to be used only rarely, and in exceptional circumstances" and is meant to "apply only when certain exceptional guarantees of trustworthiness exist and when high degrees of probativeness and necessity are present").

b. Preliminary Factfinding

The following example illustrates some of the major preliminary factfinding issues in applying the residual exception:

Ed Barns has sued Acme Used Cars for injuries that he sustained when he and a friend were examining a used car at the Acme lot. The car would not start, so Fred Anders, an Acme mechanic, offered his assistance. Barns was pouring gasoline from a small can into the carburetor while his companion attempted to start the engine. The engine backfired and ignited the can, and Barns suffered severe burn injuries. At trial, Barns claimed that he was acting pursuant to Fred Anders's instructions to pour the gasoline directly into the carburetor. Acme claimed that, to the contrary, Anders warned Barns to stop what he was doing.

Anders died before the trial. Acme offers into evidence Exhibit B, an authenticated handwritten statement signed by Anders that describes the incident and states that he warned Barns not to pour the gasoline. Acme offers the foundational testimony of Anders's supervisor, Georgia Breen:

> I learned of the accident within several hours of its occurrence. I immediately instructed Fred Anders to go into a room, not to talk to anyone else, and to write down everything that happened. Anders obeyed my instruction and came back with a handwritten statement within 30 minutes. I recognized his handwriting and he signed the document in my presence. I recognize Exhibit B as that document.

Exhibit B does not fall within any of the categorical exceptions under FRE 803 and FRE 804. Should it be admitted into evidence under FRE 807?

c. FRE 807(a)(1): Circumstantial Guarantees of Trustworthiness

To admit Anders's statement under the residual exception, Acme would have to show by a preponderance of the evidence that the statement bears "circumstantial guarantees of trustworthiness." Case law has established two principal means of establishing trustworthiness.

Reliability of Testimonial Qualities.   The most common means of satisfying the trustworthiness requirement is to show that one or more of Anders's testimonial qualities appears to be reliable because of the circumstances within which it was made.

> [A]ll of the traditional hearsay exceptions minimize one or more of the four hearsay risks: (1) insincerity; (2) faulty perception; (3) faulty memory; and (4) faulty narration...the Court must determine the relative degree to which the [proffered item] is prone to the hearsay risks, and if any of the risks are minimized by circumstantial guarantees of trustworthiness. [United States v. Southern Indiana Gas and Electric Co., 258 F. Supp. 2d 884, 890 (S.D. Ind. 2003).]

Facts relating to the identity, knowledge, qualifications, and motivation of the declarant; the content of the statement; and the circumstances in which it was made are all considered for their effect on testimonial qualities. For example, in United States v. Tome, 61 F.3d 1446, 1453 (10th Cir.1995), the Tenth Circuit considered the admissibility under the residual exception of statements made by defendant's daughter concerning acts of alleged sexual abuse. Statements made to a social worker were considered to be trustworthy because the social worker was trained in interviewing children and used open-ended, nonleading questions (context promotes sincerity), and the declarant used childish language while describing the abuse with specificity and detail (content indicates sincerity and memory). Other circumstances, however, cast doubt on the statement's trustworthiness: The statement was not spontaneous because the declarant knew that she was taken to the social worker in order to say what the defendant had done to her (context provides opportunity for insincerity); it was made a year after the events described (context affects memory); and it was made when the declarant arguably had a motive to lie because she wanted to live with her mother, not her father (identity of declarant provides motive to lie). The court held that the statement did not qualify for the residual exception because of these equivocal circumstances. Other factors relevant to reliability would be the length of time between the incident and making the hearsay statement, and whether the child made the same statements consistently to adults.

Motive and incentive to lie commonly figure in evaluations of trustworthiness: United States v. Walker, 410 F.3d 754 (5th Cir. 2005) (interview at police station, not under oath, facing the threat of criminal charges); United States v. Wright, 363 F.3d 237 (3d Cir. 2004) (self-serving statements made when declarant knew he was under investigation); Land Grantors v. United States, 86 Fed. Cl. 35, 42 (Fed. Cl. 2009) (direct interest in mineral rich land indicated guarantees of trustworthiness were lacking). Other courts mention factors relating to perception and memory: New Colt Holding Corp. v. RJG Holdings of Fla., Inc., 312 F. Supp. 2d 195, 223 (D. Conn. 2004) ("A methodologically sound survey can reduce . . . the danger of insincerity and faulty narration [and] . . . a particular memory survey which . . . relates to events that were learned by direct perception and are unlikely to be forgotten, can . . . minimize all five of the classes of risk ordinarily associated with survey evidence."); In re Columbia Securities Litigation, 155 F.R.D. 466, 475 (S.D.N.Y. 1994) ("Unless their author is available for cross-examination, newspaper stories generally will present a blank face that gives little clue as to the reliability of the reporter's perception, memory, narration, or sincerity, and in addition facts to disclose how the article was changed in the editing process".).

In the hypothetical case against Acme Used Cars, what circumstances bear on the reliability of Anders's testimonial qualities? You should by now be able make arguments both for and against trustworthiness.

Independent Corroboration.   The second means of establishing trustworthiness is to show by way of independent corroborating evidence that the facts asserted in the particular hearsay statement are probably accurate. Larez v. City of Los Angeles, 946 F.2d 630, 643 & 643 n.6 (9th Cir. 1991) (news account of a specific quotation from the defendant met "circumstantial guarantees of trustworthiness" requirement when three independent newspapers attributed similar quotations to defendant). Testimony given before a grand jury was frequently admitted under the residual exception when its contents were corroborated. Under the Supreme Court opinion in Crawford v. Washington, however, grand jury testimony qualifies as a "testimonial" statement. Because the criminal defendant is not present during the grand jury proceeding and cannot cross-examine the witnesses there, the prosecution is prohibited from using grand jury testimony under the confrontation clause in criminal cases, unless the declarant also testifies. It is possible, however, that this testimony might still be admitted under the residual exception in a civil case.

d. FRE 807(a)(1) (continued): Equivalence

FRE 807(a)(1) also requires that the guarantees of trustworthiness be "equivalent," presumably to the guarantees in FRE 803 and FRE 804. Since the apparent trust-worthiness of the hearsay admitted under all 28 categorical exceptions varies widely in both kind and degree, it is impossible to identify a single standard, and a rigor-ous showing of "equivalence" is not required. But courts sometimes do analogize the hearsay sought to be admitted to the indicia of trustworthiness of some categori-cally admitted hearsay, such as spontaneity, against interest, or careful routine. United States v. Perez, 217 F.3d 323, 329 (5th Cir. 2000) (statements by illegal immigrants "bore . . . indicia of reliability equivalent to declarations against interest" because made to agency responsible for their deportation and possible prosecution; however, inadmissible because made not under oath and in an informal interview); Conoco, Inc. v. Department of Energy, 99 F.3d 387, 392 (Fed. Cir. 1997) (purchase summaries do not have same indicia of reliability as commercial publications).

The "near miss" doctrine. A "near miss" is said to occur when a hearsay statement almost, but not quite, fits within one of the categorical hearsay exceptions and would thus be inadmissible but for the residual exception. The majority of Circuits now agree that the language of FRE 807 — "not specifically covered by a hearsay exception in Rule 803 or 804" — means that statements found to be inadmissible under the Rule 803 and 804 categories may still be considered under Rule 807. That a statement "almost fits" into other hearsay exceptions can be held to favor admissibility under FRE 807, but that factor is not determinative and does not alone compel admission. United States v. Bonds, 608 F.3d 495, 501 (9th Cir. 2010). The "near miss" doctrine obviously stands in considerable tension with the categorical approach to the hearsay exceptions, which presumes that the absence of one of the elements tends to under-mine the reliability of the statement.

e. FRE 807(a)(2)-(4): Preventing Overuse of the Exception

FRE 807(a)(2)-(4) are best understood as limitations intended to prevent the resid-ual exception from being overused and thereby swallowing the hearsay rule. Looked at in isolation, subsections (a)(2) and (a)(4) don't seem particularly meaningful. Subsection (a)(2) requires that the proponent must show that the statement is offered as evidence of a "material" fact. On its face, this term means nothing more than that the statement must be relevant. Subsection (a)(4)'s requirement that admitting the hearsay should "best serve the purposes of these rules and the interests of justice" has been criticized as "so abstruse in formulation as to constitute little guidance for the court." In re Drake, 786 F. Supp. 229, 233 (E.D.N.Y. 1992).

Subsection (a)(3) seems somewhat more meaningful. It requires a showing of both great need for the evidence and that the proponent has been reasonably diligent in attempting to secure evidence in admissible form instead of placing undue reliance on using the residual exception. See United States v. Patrick, 248 F.3d 11, 25 (1st Cir. 2001) (affidavit inadmissible since officer who conducted the search described in the affidavit was available); Andrekus v. Board of Educ., 2004 U.S. Dist. LEXIS 19388, at *28 (N.D. Ill.) (affidavits and depositions rather than hearsay note are "better evidence" for summary judgment proceedings); Conoco Inc. v. Department of Energy, 99 F.3d 387, 393 (Fed. Cir. 1997) (original underlying records of purchases of crude oil were more probative than summaries, and DOE made no showing that reasonable efforts would not produce them). If the declarant is deceased and once had knowledge about a central fact that would be otherwise unavailable, courts weigh this need heavily in making the Rule 807 decision. Bohler-Udderholm Am., Inc. v. Ellwood Group, Inc., 247 F.3d 79 (3d Cir. 2001) (affidavit of deceased representative of plaintiff at a crucial board of directors' meeting was the only available source to contradict defendant's version of what was said at the meeting).

Subsections (a)(2) through (a)(4) are thus best understood in conjunction at getting at a single idea: The residual exception should be resorted to only when, despite diligent efforts to obtain admissible evidence, none is available to prove a crucial point other than the inadmissible, but reliable hearsay, whose exclusion from evidence would result in an injustice. Viewed in this way, subsections (a)(2) through (a)(4) signal to courts that the residual exception should be rarely used, and as a last resort on behalf of reasonably diligent parties. United States v. Libby, 475 F. Supp. 2d 73, 79 (D.D.C. 2007) (hearsay admitted under the residual exception must be "very important and very reliable such that it is the best evidence to prove the [offering party's] point and there is no other evidence available that would have the same influence."). See also United States v. Washington, 106 F.3d 983, 1001 (D.C.Cir.1997) (the residual exception is to be narrowly construed).

f. Notice

The proponent is required by FRE 807(b) to inform the opponent of the intent to use the residual exception, and of the particulars of the statement and location of the declarant. This enables the opponent to prepare in order to argue more effectively against admission. It also serves to prevent reliance on the residual exception as a spur-of-the-moment fallback argument for parties whose hearsay evidence has been excluded, and to stiffen the resolve of judges to resist lawyers' last-minute protestations of need.

The requirement that notice be given *before trial* is, however, far from absolute. Some courts have interpreted the requirement liberally, upholding admission if the hearsay statement was disclosed within sufficient time—even on the first day of trial—to permit the opponent to prepare to contest the use of the statement. A continuance may be granted to permit the opponent to meet the evidence. In United States v. Panzardi-Lespier, 918 F.2d 313, 316-318 (1st Cir. 1990), the court discussed the conflicting case law on the strict versus the flexible approach to pretrial notice. It held that even in a criminal case, notice on the first day of trial was sufficient where seven days elapsed before the statement was actually offered into evidence. There was no surprise to its content, and opposing party had ample time to review it and prepare its defense. And if the proponent could not have reasonably anticipated the need for the residual exception, the notice requirement may be excused altogether by the judge. There are limits, however, even to this flexible approach. In United States v. Coney, 51 F.3d 164 (8th Cir. 1995), it was held to be not an abuse of the trial court's discretion to refuse admission to a report offered by the defendant under the residual exception 45 minutes before she wanted to introduce it. If the opponent knows of the existence of the hearsay statement before trial, and of the proponent's intent to use it, courts have applied the notice requirement flexibly where there is no prejudice.

3. FRE 807 in Practice: How Much Hearsay Is Admitted Under the Residual Exception?

The trial judge's decision whether to admit Anders's statement under FRE 807 might be influenced by the general policy underlying the residual exception. Is the residual exception—which is, after all, a radical departure from the strict categorical approach of the common law—to be used frequently or rarely? Liberally or sparingly? According to the Senate Judiciary Committee:

> It is intended that the residual hearsay exceptions will be used very rarely, and only in exceptional circumstances. The committee does not intend to establish a broad license for trial judges to admit hearsay statements that do not fall within one of the other exceptions contained in rules 803 and 804(b). The residual exceptions are not meant to authorize major judicial revisions of the hearsay rule, including its present exceptions. Such major revisions are best accomplished by legislative action.

There is language in appellate opinions in most of the Circuits that FRE 807 was designed for "exceptional" circumstances, and Circuit courts have given district courts wide discretion in its application. In a study of reported decisions from 1975 through 1991, the following kinds of statements were most frequently admitted under the residual exceptions (also called "catchall" exceptions):

> Prosecutors attempted to introduce grand jury testimony in thirty-seven cases pursuant to the 804(b)(5) catchall exception. In twenty-nine of these cases, the court admitted the hearsay. Another hidden catchall category encompasses written and oral statements made to law enforcement officials which are prior consistent or inconsistent statements [of a testifying witness] not fitting the Rule 801 criteria. A growing number of cases appear to include statements to law enforcement officials by declarants not present at trial. Such declarants have ranged from accomplices to spouses, victims, and truly disinterested individuals. [Myrna S. Raeder, Commentary: A Response to Professor Swift, 76 Minn. L. Rev. 507, 514-516 (1992).]

Professor Raeder expressed concern that such decisions "permit the total erosion of the hearsay rule by judicial discretion." Id. at 517. We will see in Section G, infra, that the application of the confrontation clause following Crawford v. Washington will change these results in criminal cases. Grand jury testimony and statements made to law enforcement may be excluded, although all prior statements of a testifying witness would be admitted. Concern has also been expressed that undue focus on whether a statement is or is not a "near miss" has distracted courts from careful evaluation of the "equivalency" of the circumstantial guarantees of trustworthiness required by FRE 807. Elizabeth DeCoux, Textual Limits on the Residual Exception to the Hearsay Rule: The "Near Miss" Debate and Beyond, 35 S.U. L. Rev. 99 (2007).

Judge Richard Posner has recently proposed dramatically expanding the residual exception to "swallow" the hearsay rule. In Posner's conception, a simplified hearsay rule would simplify FRE 807 to admit hearsay "when it is reliable, when the jury can understand its strengths and limitations, and when it will materially enhance the likelihood of a correct outcome." United States v. Boyce, 742 F.3d 792, 802 (2014) (Posner, J., concurring)

KEY POINTS

1. Under FRE 807, the judge has discretion to admit hearsay statements that appear to be reliable; that is, they have circumstantial guarantees of trustworthiness either because the statement has circumstantial guarantees of trustworthiness similar to one or more of the categorical hearsay exceptions or exemptions, or because the contents of the statement are corroborated.

2. The offering party must have great need for the evidence, because of its importance to his case and his inability to obtain evidence on that point despite reasonable diligence. The proponent should have an argument that failure to admit the evidence under the residual exception could led to an unjust result.

3. The proponent of the statement must also notify the opponent of the intent to invoke the residual exception, preferably before trial. This requirement prevents reliance on the residual exception as an afterthought.

PROBLEMS

8.76. Return to Problem 8.49 at page 538. At 3:00 A.M. on January 26, Mrs. D'Onofrio was asked to complete and sign a complaint form by one of the police officers. She repeated, in writing, the statements she had made earlier concerning her husband's behavior on January 24, 25 and 26. She signed her name twice, acknowledging that the police officer was relying upon her allegations to establish probable cause to arrest Louis D'Onofrio for brandishing a weapon, and affirming that her statements were true. This form, as well as the hearsay statements in Problem 8.49, are the only proof that Louis D'Onofrio had a gun in his possession and threatened her with it. At trial, Mrs. D'Onofrio asserts her marital privilege, which prevents the government from calling her as a witness against her husband. Is the written statement admissible into evidence?

8.77. In preparing the prosecution of Barry Bonds, Problem 4.5 on page 208, the government contended that the statements made by Bonds's trainer Greg Anderson to James Valente at BALCO identifying the urine samples as coming from Bonds were admissible under FRE 807. The government based its argument on these statements "nearly missing" admissibility as statements against interest under FRE 804(b)(3), and being "exactly the type of scenario" FRE 807 was intended to remedy when Anderson refused to testify. Should Anderson's statements be admitted under the residual exception? Consider *all* of its terms in constructing your argument.

G. HEARSAY AND THE CONFRONTATION CLAUSE

The Confrontation Clause in the Sixth Amendment to the United States Constitution states: "In all criminal prosecutions, the accused shall enjoy the right . . . to be confronted with the Witnesses against him." The meaning of this terse phrase is far from clear: There is virtually no legislative history shedding light on the Framers' intent, and the words themselves are subject to a number of possible interpretations. When the prosecution presents a *witness* at trial, the Supreme Court's most frequently cited analysis is that the clause requires

> a personal examination and cross-examination of the witness in which the accused has the opportunity, not only of testing the recollection and sifting the conscience of the witness, but of compelling him to stand face to face with the jury in order that they may look at him, and judge by his demeanor upon the stand and the manner in which he gives his testimony whether he is worthy of belief. [Mattox v. United States, 156 U.S. 237, 242-243 (1895).]

As you know, most hearsay admitted through the exceptions and exemptions does not require the presence of the hearsay declarant as a witness in court. Thus, the admission of hearsay presents an immediate threat to the criminal defendant's confrontation right. A literal reading of the clause, however, might hold that it operates *only* when the prosecutor calls witnesses. *All* hearsay could be admitted without regard to confrontation rights. Or, "witnesses" might be interpreted more broadly to include all individuals who provide evidence against the defendant. *All* hearsay would then be within the reach of the clause and *no* hearsay could be admitted without confrontation and cross-examination.

In Crawford v. Washington, 541 U.S. 124 (2004), the U.S. Supreme Court provided a new interpretation of criminal defendants' confrontation right. In keeping with its own past opinions, the Court held that the Confrontation Clause bars the use of some, but not of all, hearsay against criminal defendants. It provided a new set standard to test when the confrontation right is violated. The *Crawford* opinion will concern us throughout this section. We begin our discussion with a brief analysis of the Court's interpretation of the confrontation clause prior to *Crawford*. The approach developed in Ohio v. Roberts, 448 U.S. 56 (1980), is important for understanding the Court's critique of *Roberts*, its new stance in *Crawford*, and its evolving development of the confrontation right.

1. Ohio v. Roberts

In *Roberts*, the Supreme Court had seemed to establish a two-pronged test—unavailability and reliability—for satisfying the accused's confrontation right when hearsay is admitted but the declarant does not testify:

> The Confrontation Clause operates in two separate ways to restrict the range of admissible hearsay. First, in conformity with the Framers' preference for face-to-face accusation, the Sixth Amendment establishes a rule of necessity. In the usual case (including

cases where prior cross-examination has occurred), the prosecution must either produce, or demonstrate the unavailability of, the declarant whose statement it wishes to use against the defendant . . . . The second aspect operates once a witness is shown to be unavailable. Reflecting its underlying purpose to augment accuracy in the factfinding process by ensuring the defendant an effective means to test adverse evidence, the Clause countenances only hearsay marked with such trustworthiness that "there is no material departure from the reason of the general rule." The Court has applied this "indicia of reliability" requirement principally by concluding that certain hearsay exceptions rest upon such solid foundations that admission of virtually any evidence within them comports with the "substances of the constitutional protection." [Mattox v. United States, 156 U.S. 237, 244 (1895).] . . . In sum, when a hearsay declarant is not present for cross-examination at trial, the Confrontation Clause normally requires a showing that he is unavailable. Even then, his statement is admissible only if it bears adequate "indicia of reliability." Reliability can be inferred without more in a case where the evidence falls within a firmly rooted hearsay exception. In other cases, the evidence must be excluded, at least absent a showing of particularized guarantees of trustworthiness. [448 U.S. at 65-66.]

Twelve years later, in White v. Illinois, 502 U.S. 346, 354 (1992), the Court virtually abandoned the unavailability requirement by limiting it to statements admitted as former testimony under FRE 804(b)(1).

Thus, for most hearsay, the confrontation clause under *Roberts* imposed only an inquiry whether the hearsay statement fits within a "firmly rooted" exception and, if it does not, whether there are "particularized guarantees" of the statement's trustworthiness.

a. "Firmly Rooted" Hearsay Exceptions

Many exceptions under FRE 803 and 804 were then found to be "firmly rooted." In *Roberts*, the Court stated that exceptions for business records, dying declarations, and public records are firmly rooted. Co-conspirator statements were found to be firmly rooted in Bourjaily v. United States 483 U.S. 171, 182 (1987) (with vigorous dissent); and statements falling within the traditional exceptions for present sense impression, excited utterances, statements of state of mind, and past recollection recorded survived challenge under the confrontation clause. This meant that the legislatively drawn categorical hearsay exceptions of the Federal Rules stood in for judicial analysis of the right to confrontation in most cases.

b. Not Firmly Rooted Exceptions Require "Particularized Guarantees of Trustworthiness"

A Supreme Court plurality in Lilly v. Virginia, 527 U.S. 116 (1999), held that statements against penal interest, admitted under FRE 804(b)(3), are not firmly rooted. The Court had previously discussed the "particularized guarantees of trustworthiness" test in Idaho v. Wright, 497 U.S. 805 (1990), when it held that the residual exception (now FRE 807) was not firmly rooted. In *Wright*, the Court characterized "particularized guarantees of trustworthiness" as the inherent trustworthiness of the declarant's statement, to be found in the circumstances that "surround the making of the statement." Id. at 821. The Court specifically prohibited the consideration of corroboration, that is, independent evidence that corroborates the contents of the statement itself. Courts had come to rely on corroboration to satisfy the residual exception's requirement of "circumstantial guarantees of trustworthiness," particularly in admitting statements of grand jury witnesses, which often bore few indicia of inherent trustworthiness. Under *Wright*, the use of corroboration was prohibited to satisfy the "particularized" trustworthiness standard for all not firmly rooted hearsay.

Also in Lilly v. Virginia, Justices Scalia and Thomas each wrote separately to state their views that the proper scope of the confrontation right was more limited than the Court's opinions in *Roberts*, *Wright*, and *Lilly* had held. That right, they asserted, "is implicated by extra judicial statements only insofar as they are contained in formalized testimonial material, such as affidavits, depositions, prior testimony or confessions." 527 U.S. at 365. Justice Breyer wrote in his separate concurrence that *Roberts*'s linkage of the confrontation right so closely to the "firmly rooted" provisions of the hearsay rule was both too broad and too narrow a standard, and that this linkage was an open question to be considered at another time. In *Crawford*, five years after *Lilly*, that time had come.

2. Crawford v. Washington

CRAWFORD v. WASHINGTON
541 U.S. 36 (2004)

Justice Scalia delivered the opinion of the Court, in which Stevens, Kennedy, Souter, Thomas, Ginsburg, and Breyer, JJ., joined. Rehnquist, C.J., filed an opinion concurring in the judgment, in which O'Connor, J., joined.

Petitioner Michael Crawford stabbed a man who allegedly tried to rape his wife, Sylvia. At his trial, the State played for the jury Sylvia's tape-recorded statement to the police describing the stabbing, even though he had no opportunity for cross-examination. The Washington Supreme Court upheld petitioner's conviction after determining that Sylvia's statement was reliable. The question presented is whether this procedure complied with the Sixth Amendment's guarantee that, "[i]n all criminal prosecutions, the accused shall enjoy the right . . . to be confronted with the witnesses against him."

I

On August 5, 1999, Kenneth Lee was stabbed at his apartment. Police arrested petitioner later that night. After giving petitioner and his wife *Miranda* warnings, detectives interrogated each of them twice.[9] Petitioner eventually confessed that he and

---

9. [Petitioner Michael Crawford's and his wife Sylvia's interrogations were tape recorded by the Olympia Police Department.—Eds.]

Sylvia had gone in search of Lee because he was upset over an earlier incident in which Lee had tried to rape her. The two had found Lee at his apartment, and a fight ensued in which Lee was stabbed in the torso and petitioner's hand was cut.

Petitioner gave the following account of the fight:

1 "Q. Okay. Did you ever see anything in [Lee's] hands?
2 "A. I think so, but I'm not positive.
3 "Q. Okay, when you think so, what do you mean by that?
4 "A. I coulda swore I seen him goin' for somethin' before, right before everything
5   happened. He was like reachin', fiddlin' around down here and stuff . . . and I
6   just . . . I don't know, I think, this is just a possibility, but I think, I think that he
7   pulled somethin' out and I grabbed for it and that's how I got cut . . . but I'm
8   not positive. I, I, my mind goes blank when things like this happen. I mean,
9   I just, I remember things wrong, I remember things that just doesn't, don't
10   make sense to me later." (punctuation added).

Sylvia generally corroborated petitioner's story about the events leading up to the fight, but her account of the fight itself was arguably different—particularly with respect to whether Lee had drawn a weapon before petitioner assaulted him:

11 "Q. Did Kenny do anything to fight back from this assault?
12 "A. (pausing) I know he reached into his pocket . . . or somethin' . . . I don't know
13   what.
14 "Q. After he was stabbed?
15 "A. He saw Michael coming up. He lifted his hand . . . his chest open, he might
16   [have] went to go strike his hand out or something and then (inaudible).
17 "Q. Okay, you, you gotta speak up.
18 "A. Okay, he lifted his hand over his head maybe to strike Michael's hand down or
19   something and then he put his hands in his . . . put his right hand in his right
20   pocket . . . took a step back . . . Michael proceeded to stab him . . . then his
21   hands were like . . . how do you explain this . . . open arms . . . with his hands
22   open and he fell down . . . and we ran (describing subject holding hands open,
23   palms toward assailant).
24 "Q. Okay, when he's standing there with his open hands, you're talking about
25   Kenny, correct?
26 "A. Yeah, after, after the fact, yes.
27 "Q. Did you see anything in his hands at that point?
28 "A. (pausing) um um (no)." (punctuation added).

The State charged petitioner with assault and attempted murder. At trial, he claimed self-defense. Sylvia did not testify because of the state marital privilege, which generally bars a spouse from testifying without the other spouse's consent. In Washington, this privilege does not extend to a spouse's out-of-court statements admissible under a hearsay exception, so the State sought to introduce Sylvia's tape-recorded statements to the police as evidence that the stabbing was not in self-defense. Noting that Sylvia had admitted she led petitioner to Lee's apartment and thus had facilitated the assault, the State invoked the hearsay exception for statements against penal interest, Wash. Rule Evid. 804(b)(3) (2003).

Petitioner countered that, state law notwithstanding, admitting the evidence would violate his federal constitutional right to be "confronted with the witnesses against him." Amdt. 6. According to our description of that right in Ohio v. Roberts, 448 U.S. 56 (1980), it does not bar admission of an unavailable witness's statement against a criminal defendant if the statement bears "adequate 'indicia of reliability.' " To meet that test, evidence must either fall within a "firmly rooted hearsay exception" or bear "particularized guarantees of trustworthiness." The trial court here admitted the statement on the latter ground, offering several reasons why it was trustworthy: Sylvia was not shifting blame but rather corroborating her husband's story that he acted in self-defense or "justified reprisal"; she had direct knowledge as an eyewitness; she was describing recent events; and she was being questioned by a "neutral" law enforcement officer. The prosecution played the tape for the jury and relied on it in closing, arguing that it was "damning evidence" that "completely refutes [petitioner's] claim of self-defense." The jury convicted petitioner of assault.

The Washington Court of Appeals reversed. It applied a nine-factor test to determine whether Sylvia's statement bore particularized guarantees of trustworthiness, and noted several reasons why it did not: The statement contradicted one she had previously given; it was made in response to specific questions; and at one point she admitted she had shut her eyes during the stabbing. The court considered and rejected the State's argument that Sylvia's statement was reliable because it coincided with petitioner's to such a degree that the two "interlocked." The court determined that, although the two statements agreed about the events leading up to the stabbing, they differed on the issue crucial to petitioner's self-defense claim: "[Petitioner's] version asserts that Lee may have had something in his hand when he stabbed him; but Sylvia's version has Lee grabbing for something only after he has been stabbed."

The Washington Supreme Court reinstated the conviction, unanimously concluding that, although Sylvia's statement did not fall under a firmly rooted hearsay exception, it bore guarantees of trustworthiness: " '[W]hen a codefendant's confession is virtually identical [to, i.e., interlocks with,] that of a defendant, it may be deemed reliable.' " The court explained:

> Although the Court of Appeals concluded that the statements were contradictory, upon closer inspection they appear to overlap . . . .
>
> [B]oth of the Crawfords' statements indicate that Lee was possibly grabbing for a weapon, but they are equally unsure when this event may have taken place. They are also equally unsure how Michael received the cut on his hand, leading the court to question when, if ever, Lee possessed a weapon. In this respect they overlap.
>
> [N]either Michael nor Sylvia clearly stated that Lee had a weapon in hand from which Michael was simply defending himself. And it is this omission by both that interlocks the statements and makes Sylvia's statement reliable.[10]

---

10. The court rejected the State's argument that guarantees of trustworthiness were unnecessary since petitioner waived his confrontation rights by invoking the marital privilege. It reasoned that "forcing the defendant to choose between the marital privilege and confronting his spouse presents an untenable Hobson's choice." The State has not challenged this holding here. The State also has not challenged the Court of Appeals' conclusion (not reached by the State Supreme Court) that the confrontation violation, if it occurred, was not harmless. We express no opinion on these matters.

We granted certiorari to determine whether the State's use of Sylvia's statement violated the Confrontation Clause.

II

The Sixth Amendment's Confrontation Clause provides that, "[i]n all criminal prosecutions, the accused shall enjoy the right . . . to be confronted with the witnesses against him." We have held that this bedrock procedural guarantee applies to both federal and state prosecutions. Pointer v. Texas, 380 U.S. 400 (1965). As noted above, *Roberts* says that an unavailable witness's out-of-court statement may be admitted so long as it has adequate indicia of reliability—*i.e.*, falls within a "firmly rooted hearsay exception" or bears "particularized guarantees of trustworthiness." Petitioner argues that this test strays from the original meaning of the Confrontation Clause and urges us to reconsider it.

A

The Constitution's text does not alone resolve this case. One could plausibly read "witnesses against" a defendant to mean those who actually testify at trial, those whose statements are offered at trial, see 3 J. Wigmore, Evidence §1397, p 104 (2d ed. 1923) (hereinafter Wigmore), or something in-between. We must therefore turn to the historical background of the Clause to understand its meaning.

The right to confront one's accusers is a concept that dates back to Roman times. The founding generation's immediate source of the concept, however, was the common law. English common law has long differed from continental civil law in regard to the manner in which witnesses give testimony in criminal trials. The common-law tradition is one of live testimony in court subject to adversarial testing, while the civil law condones examination in private by judicial officers. See 3 W. Blackstone, Commentaries on the Laws of England 373-374 (1768).

Nonetheless, England at times adopted elements of the civil-law practice. Justices of the peace or other officials examined suspects and witnesses before trial. These examinations were sometimes read in court in lieu of live testimony, a practice that "occasioned frequent demands by the prisoner to have his 'accusers,' *i.e.*, the witnesses against him, brought before him face to face." 1 J. Stephen, History of the Criminal Law of England 326 (1883). In some cases, these demands were refused. See 9 W. Holdsworth, History of English Law 216-217, 228 (3d ed. 1944); *e.g.*, Raleigh's Case, 2 How. St. Tr. 1, 15-16, 24 (1603).

Pretrial examinations became routine under two statutes passed during the reign of Queen Mary in the 16th century. These Marian bail and committal statutes required justices of the peace to examine suspects and witnesses in felony cases and to certify the results to the court. It is doubtful that the original purpose of the examinations was to produce evidence admissible at trial. Whatever the original purpose, however, they came to be used as evidence in some cases, see M. Hale, Pleas of the Crown 284 (1736), resulting in an adoption of continental procedure.

The most notorious instances of civil-law examination occurred in the great political trials of the 16th and 17th centuries. One such was the 1603 trial of Sir Walter Raleigh for treason. Lord Cobham, Raleigh's alleged accomplice, had implicated him in an examination before the Privy Council and in a letter. At Raleigh's trial, these were read to the jury. Raleigh argued that Cobham had lied to save himself: "Cobham is absolutely in the King's mercy; to excuse me cannot avail him; by accusing me he may hope for favour." 1 D. Jardine, Criminal Trials 435 (1832). Suspecting that Cobham would recant, Raleigh demanded that the judges call him to appear, arguing that "[t]he Proof of the Common Law is by witness and jury: let Cobham be here, let him speak it. Call my accuser before my face . . . ." The judges refused, and, despite Raleigh's protestations that he was being tried "by the Spanish Inquisition," the jury convicted, and Raleigh was sentenced to death.

One of Raleigh's trial judges later lamented that "'the justice of England has never been so degraded and injured as by the condemnation of Sir Walter Raleigh.'" Through a series of statutory and judicial reforms, English law developed a right of confrontation that limited these abuses. For example, treason statutes required witnesses to confront the accused "face to face" at his arraignment. Courts, meanwhile, developed relatively strict rules of unavailability, admitting examinations only if the witness was demonstrably unable to testify in person. Several authorities also stated that a suspect's confession could be admitted only against himself, and not against others he implicated.

One recurring question was whether the admissibility of an unavailable witness's pretrial examination depended on whether the defendant had had an opportunity to cross-examine him. In 1696, the Court of King's Bench answered this question in the affirmative, in the widely reported misdemeanor libel case of King v. Paine. The court ruled that, even though a witness was dead, his examination was not admissible where "the defendant not being present when [it was] taken before the mayor . . . had lost the benefit of a cross-examination."

Paine had settled the rule requiring a prior opportunity for cross-examination as a matter of common law, but some doubts remained over whether the Marian statutes prescribed an exception to it in felony cases. The statutes did not identify the circumstances under which examinations were admissible, and some inferred that no prior opportunity for cross-examination was required . . . .

B

Controversial examination practices were also used in the Colonies. Early in the 18th century, for example, the Virginia Council protested against the Governor for having "privately issued several commissions to examine witnesses against particular men *ex parte*," complaining that "the person accused is not admitted to be confronted with, or defend himself against his defamers." A decade before the Revolution, England gave jurisdiction over Stamp Act offenses to the admiralty courts, which followed civil-law rather than common-law procedures and thus routinely took testimony by deposition or private judicial examination. Colonial representatives protested that the Act subverted their rights "by extending the jurisdiction of the courts of admiralty beyond its ancient limits." Resolutions of the Stamp Act Congress §8th (Oct. 19, 1765). John Adams, defending a merchant in a high-profile admiralty case, argued: "Examinations of witnesses upon Interrogatories, are only by the Civil Law. Interrogatories are unknown at common Law, and Englishmen and common Lawyers have an aversion to them if not an Abhorrence of them." Draft of Argument in Sewall v. Hancock (1768-1769).

Many declarations of rights adopted around the time of the Revolution guaranteed a right of confrontation. The proposed Federal Constitution, however, did not. At the Massachusetts ratifying convention, Abraham Holmes objected to this omission precisely on the ground that it would lead to civil-law practices: "The mode of trial is altogether indetermined; . . . whether [the defendant] is to be allowed to confront the witnesses, and have the advantage of cross-examination, we are not yet told . . . . [W]e shall find Congress possessed of powers enabling them to institute judicatories little less inauspicious than a certain tribunal in Spain, . . . the *Inquisition.*" 2 Debates on the Federal Constitution 110-111 (J. Elliot 2d ed. 1863). Similarly, a prominent Antifederalist writing under the pseudonym Federal Farmer criticized the use of "written evidence" while objecting to the omission of a vicinage right: "Nothing can be more essential than the cross examining [of] witnesses, and generally before the triers of the facts in question. . . . [W]ritten evidence . . . [is] almost useless; it must be frequently taken ex parte, and but very seldom leads to the proper discovery of truth." R. Lee, Letter IV by the Federal Farmer (Oct. 15, 1787). The First Congress responded by including the Confrontation Clause in the proposal that became the Sixth Amendment . . . .

III

This history supports two inferences about the meaning of the Sixth Amendment.

A

First, the principal evil at which the Confrontation Clause was directed was the civil-law mode of criminal procedure, and particularly its use of *ex parte* examinations as evidence against the accused. It was these practices that the Crown deployed in notorious treason cases like Raleigh's; that the Marian statutes invited; that English law's assertion of a right to confrontation was meant to prohibit; and that the founding-era rhetoric decried. The Sixth Amendment must be interpreted with this focus in mind.

Accordingly, we once again reject the view that the Confrontation Clause applies of its own force only to in-court testimony, and that its application to out-of-court statements introduced at trial depends upon "the law of Evidence for the time being." 3 Wigmore §1397, at 101; accord, Dutton v. Evans, 400 U.S. 74, 94 (Harlan, J., concurring in result). Leaving the regulation of out-of-court statements to the law of evidence would render the Confrontation Clause powerless to prevent even the most flagrant inquisitorial practices. Raleigh was, after all, perfectly free to confront those who read Cobham's confession in court.

This focus also suggests that not all hearsay implicates the Sixth Amendment's core concerns. An off-hand, overheard remark might be unreliable evidence and thus a good candidate for exclusion under hearsay rules, but it bears little resemblance to the civil-law abuses the Confrontation Clause targeted. On the other hand, *ex parte* examinations might sometimes be admissible under modern hearsay rules, but the Framers certainly would not have condoned them.

The text of the Confrontation Clause reflects this focus. It applies to "witnesses" against the accused—in other words, those who "bear testimony." 1 N. Webster, An American Dictionary of the English Language (1828). "Testimony," in turn, is typically "[a] solemn declaration or affirmation made for the purpose of establishing or proving some fact." *Ibid.* An accuser who makes a formal statement to government officers bears testimony in a sense that a person who makes a casual remark to an acquaintance does not. The constitutional text, like the history underlying the common-law right of confrontation, thus reflects an especially acute concern with a specific type of out-of-court statement.

Various formulations of this core class of "testimonial" statements exist: "*ex parte* in-court testimony or its functional equivalent—that is, material such as affidavits, custodial examinations, prior testimony that the defendant was unable to cross-examine, or similar pretrial statements that declarants would reasonably expect to be used prosecutorially," Brief for Petitioner 23; "extrajudicial statements . . . contained in formalized testimonial materials, such as affidavits, depositions, prior testimony, or confessions," White v. Illinois, 502 U.S. 346 (1992) (Thomas, J., joined by Scalia, J., concurring in part and concurring in judgment); "statements that were made under circumstances which would lead an objective witness reasonably to believe that the statement would be available for use at a later trial," Brief for National Association of Criminal Defense Lawyers et al. as *Amici Curiae* 3. These formulations all share a common nucleus and then define the Clause's coverage at various levels of abstraction around it. Regardless of the precise articulation, some statements qualify under any definition—for example, *ex parte* testimony at a preliminary hearing.

Statements taken by police officers in the course of interrogations are also testimonial under even a narrow standard. Police interrogations bear a striking resemblance to examinations by justices of the peace in England. The statements are not *sworn* testimony, but the absence of oath was not dispositive. Cobham's examination was unsworn, see 1 Jardine, Criminal Trials, at 430, yet Raleigh's trial has long been thought a paradigmatic confrontation violation. Under the Marian statutes, witnesses were typically put on oath, but suspects were not. Yet Hawkins and others went out of their way to caution that such unsworn confessions were not admissible against anyone but the confessor.

That interrogators are police officers rather than magistrates does not change the picture either. Justices of the peace conducting examinations under the Marian statutes were not magistrates as we understand that office today, but had an essentially investigative and prosecutorial function. England did not have a professional police force until the 19th century, so it is not surprising that other government officers performed the investigative functions now associated primarily with the police. The involvement of government officers in the production of testimonial evidence presents the same risk, whether the officers are police or justices of the peace.

In sum, even if the Sixth Amendment is not solely concerned with testimonial hearsay, that is its primary object, and interrogations by law enforcement officers fall squarely within that class.[11]

---

11. We use the term "interrogation" in its colloquial, rather than any technical legal, sense. Cf. Rhode Island v. Innis, 446 U.S. 291, 300-301 (1980). Just as various definitions of "testimonial" exist, one can imagine various definitions of "interrogation," and we need not select among them in this case. Sylvia's recorded statement, knowingly given in response to structured police questioning, qualifies under any conceivable definition.

B

The historical record also supports a second proposition: that the Framers would not have allowed admission of testimonial statements of a witness who did not appear at trial unless he was unavailable to testify, and the defendant had had a prior opportunity for cross-examination. The text of the Sixth Amendment does not suggest any open-ended exceptions from the confrontation requirement to be developed by the courts. Rather, the "right . . . to be confronted with the witnesses against him," Amdt. 6, is most naturally read as a reference to the right of confrontation at common law, admitting only those exceptions established at the time of the founding. As the English authorities above reveal, the common law in 1791 conditioned admissibility of an absent witness's examination on unavailability and a prior opportunity to cross-examine. The Sixth Amendment therefore incorporates those limitations. The numerous early state decisions applying the same test confirm that these principles were received as part of the common law in this country.[12]

[This] is not to deny, as the Chief Justice notes, that "[t]here were always exceptions to the general rule of exclusion" of hearsay evidence. Several had become well established by 1791. See 3 Wigmore §1397, at 101. But there is scant evidence that exceptions were invoked to admit *testimonial* statements against the accused in a *criminal* case.[13] Most of the hearsay exceptions covered statements that by their nature were not testimonial-for example, business records or statements in furtherance of a conspiracy. We do not infer from these that the Framers thought exceptions would apply even to prior testimony. Cf. Lilly v. Virginia, 527 U.S. 116 (1999) (plurality opinion) ("[A]ccomplices' confessions that inculpate a criminal defendant are not within a firmly rooted exception to the hearsay rule.").[14]

IV

. . .

Our cases have . . . remained faithful to the Framers' understanding: Testimonial statements of witnesses absent from trial have been admitted only where the declarant is unavailable, and only where the defendant has had a prior opportunity to cross-examine.[15]

---

12. The Chief Justice claims that English law's treatment of testimonial statements was inconsistent at the time of the framing, but the examples he cites relate to examinations under the Marian statutes. As we have explained, to the extent Marian examinations were admissible, it was only because the statutes *derogated* from the common law[.]

13. The one deviation we have found involves dying declarations[.] Although many dying declarations may not be testimonial, there is authority for admitting even those that clearly are. We need not decide in this case whether the Sixth Amendment incorporates an exception for testimonial dying declarations. If this exception must be accepted on historical grounds, it is *sui generis*.

14. []Involvement of government officers in the production of testimony with an eye toward trial presents unique potential for prosecutorial abuse—a fact borne out time and again throughout a history with which the Framers were keenly familiar. This consideration does not evaporate when testimony happens to fall within some broad, modern hearsay exception, even if that exception might be justifiable in other circumstances.

15. [W]e reiterate that, when the declarant appears for cross-examination at trial, the Confrontation Clause places no constraints at all on the use of his prior testimonial statements. See California v. Green, 399 U.S. 149 (1970). The Clause does not bar admission of a statement so long as the declarant is present at trial to defend or explain it. (The Clause also does not bar the use of testimonial statements for purposes other than establishing the truth of the matter asserted.)

V

Although the results of our decisions have generally been faithful to the original meaning of the Confrontation Clause, the same cannot be said of our rationales. *Roberts* conditions the admissibility of all hearsay evidence on whether it falls under a "firmly rooted hearsay exception" or bears "particularized guarantees of trustworthiness." 448 U.S., at 66. This test departs from the historical principles identified above in two respects. First, it is too broad: It applies the same mode of analysis whether or not the hearsay consists of *ex parte* testimony. This often results in close constitutional scrutiny in cases that are far removed from the core concerns of the Clause. At the same time, however, the test is too narrow: It admits statements that *do* consist of *ex parte* testimony upon a mere finding of reliability. This malleable standard often fails to protect against paradigmatic confrontation violations.

Members of this Court and academics have suggested that we revise our doctrine to reflect more accurately the original understanding of the Clause. They offer two proposals: First, that we apply the Confrontation Clause only to testimonial statements, leaving the remainder to regulation by hearsay law—thus eliminating the overbreadth referred to above. Second, that we impose an absolute bar to statements that are testimonial, absent a prior opportunity to cross-examine—thus eliminating the excessive narrowness referred to above.

In *White*, we considered the first proposal and rejected it. Although our analysis in this case casts doubt on that holding, we need not definitively resolve whether it survives our decision today, because Sylvia Crawford's statement is testimonial under any definition. This case does, however, squarely implicate the second proposal.

A

Where testimonial statements are involved, we do not think the Framers meant to leave the Sixth Amendment's protection to the vagaries of the rules of evidence, much less to amorphous notions of "reliability." Certainly none of the authorities discussed above acknowledges any general reliability exception to the common-law rule. Admitting statements deemed reliable by a judge is fundamentally at odds with the right of confrontation. To be sure, the Clause's ultimate goal is to ensure reliability of evidence, but it is a procedural rather than a substantive guarantee. It commands, not that evidence be reliable, but that reliability be assessed in a particular manner: by testing in the crucible of cross-examination. The Clause thus reflects a judgment, not only about the desirability of reliable evidence (a point on which there could be little dissent), but about how reliability can best be determined. Cf. 3 Blackstone, Commentaries, at 373 ("This open examination of witnesses . . . is much more conducive to the clearing up of truth"); M. Hale, History and Analysis of the Common Law of England 258 (1713) (adversarial testing "beats and bolts out the Truth much better").

The *Roberts* test allows a jury to hear evidence, untested by the adversary process, based on a mere judicial determination of reliability. It thus replaces the constitutionally prescribed method of assessing reliability with a wholly foreign one. In this respect, it is very different from exceptions to the Confrontation Clause that make no claim to be a surrogate means of assessing reliability. For example, the rule of forfeiture by wrongdoing (which we accept) extinguishes confrontation claims on essentially equitable grounds; it does not purport to be an alternative means of determining reliability. See Reynolds v. United States, 98 U.S. 145, 158-159.

The Raleigh trial itself involved the very sorts of reliability determinations that *Roberts* authorizes. In the face of Raleigh's repeated demands for confrontation, the prosecution responded with many of the arguments a court applying *Roberts* might invoke today: that Cobham's statements were self-inculpatory, that they were not made in the heat of passion, and that they were not "extracted from [him] upon any hopes or promise of Pardon." It is not plausible that the Framers' only objection to the trial was that Raleigh's judges did not properly weigh these factors before sentencing him to death. Rather, the problem was that the judges refused to allow Raleigh to confront Cobham in court, where he could cross-examine him and try to expose his accusation as a lie.

Dispensing with confrontation because testimony is obviously reliable is akin to dispensing with jury trial because a defendant is obviously guilty. This is not what the Sixth Amendment prescribes.

B

The legacy of *Roberts* in other courts vindicates the Framers' wisdom in rejecting a general reliability exception. The framework is so unpredictable that it fails to provide meaningful protection from even core confrontation violations. Reliability is an amorphous, if not entirely subjective, concept.

. . .

The unpardonable vice of the *Roberts* test, however, is not its unpredictability, but its demonstrated capacity to admit core testimonial statements that the Confrontation Clause plainly meant to exclude. Despite the plurality's speculation in *Lilly*, 527 U.S., at 137, that it was "highly unlikely" that accomplice confessions implicating the accused could survive *Roberts*, courts continue routinely to admit them. One recent study found that, after *Lilly*, appellate courts admitted accomplice statements to the authorities in 25 out of 70 cases — more than one-third of the time. Kirst, Appellate Court Answers to the Confrontation Questions in *Lilly v. Virginia*, 53 Syracuse L. Rev. 87, 105 (2003). Courts have invoked *Roberts* to admit other sorts of plainly testimonial statements despite the absence of any opportunity to cross-examine. See[, e.g.,] United States v. Aguilar, 295 F.3d 1018, 1021-1023 (CA9 2002) (plea allocution showing existence of a conspiracy); United States v. Papajohn, 212 F.3d 1112, 1118-1120 (CA8 2000) (grand jury testimony).

To add insult to injury, some of the courts that admit untested testimonial statements find reliability in the very factors that *make* the statements testimonial. As noted earlier, one court relied on the fact that the witness's statement was made to police while in custody on pending charges — the theory being that this made the statement more clearly against penal interest and thus more reliable. Other courts routinely rely on the fact that a prior statement is given under oath in judicial proceedings, [e.g., plea allocution, grand jury testimony]. That inculpating statements are given in a testimonial setting is not an antidote to the confrontation problem, but rather the trigger that makes the Clause's demands most urgent. It is not enough to point out that most of the usual safeguards of the adversary process attend the statement, when the single safeguard missing is the one the Confrontation Clause demands.

C

Roberts' failings were on full display in the proceedings below. [The Court recounted the lower courts' reliance on conflicting factors indicating that Sylvia Crawford's recorded statement was both seemingly unreliable and reliable as an example of *Roberts*'s "unpredictable and inconsistent application."]

. . .

We readily concede that we could resolve this case by simply reweighing the "reliability factors" under *Roberts* and finding that Sylvia Crawford's statement falls short. But we view this as one of those rare cases in which the result below is so improbable that it reveals a fundamental failure on our part to interpret the Constitution in a way that secures its intended constraint on judicial discretion. Moreover, to reverse the Washington Supreme Court's decision after conducting our own reliability analysis would perpetuate, not avoid, what the Sixth Amendment condemns. The Constitution prescribes a procedure for determining the reliability of testimony in criminal trials, and we, no less than the state courts, lack authority to replace it with one of our own devising.

We have no doubt that the courts below were acting in utmost good faith when they found reliability. The Framers, however, would not have been content to indulge this assumption. They knew that judges, like other government officers, could not always be trusted to safeguard the rights of the people; the likes of the dread Lord Jeffreys were not yet too distant a memory. They were loath to leave too much discretion in judicial hands. Cf. U.S. Const., Amdt. 6 (criminal jury trial); Amdt. 7 (civil jury trial). By replacing categorical constitutional guarantees with open-ended balancing tests, we do violence to their design. Vague standards are manipulable, and, while that might be a small concern in run-of-the-mill assault prosecutions like this one, the Framers had an eye toward politically charged cases like Raleigh's—great state trials where the impartiality of even those at the highest levels of the judiciary might not be so clear. It is difficult to imagine *Roberts* providing any meaningful protection in those circumstances.

. . .

Where nontestimonial hearsay is at issue, it is wholly consistent with the Framers' design to afford the States flexibility in their development of hearsay law—as does *Roberts*, and as would an approach that exempted such statements from Confrontation Clause scrutiny altogether. Where testimonial evidence is at issue, however, the Sixth Amendment demands what the common law required: unavailability and a prior opportunity for cross-examination. We leave for another day any effort to spell out a comprehensive definition of "testimonial." Whatever else the term covers, it applies at a minimum to prior testimony at a preliminary hearing, before a grand jury, or at a former trial; and to police interrogations. These are the modern practices with closest kinship to the abuses at which the Confrontation Clause was directed.

In this case, the State admitted Sylvia's testimonial statement against petitioner, despite the fact that he had no opportunity to cross-examine her. That alone is sufficient to make out a violation of the Sixth Amendment. *Roberts* notwithstanding, we decline to mine the record in search of indicia of reliability. Where testimonial statements are at issue, the only indicium of reliability sufficient to satisfy constitutional demands is the one the Constitution actually prescribes: confrontation.

The judgment of the Washington Supreme Court is reversed, and the case is remanded for further proceedings not inconsistent with this opinion.

It is so ordered.

Chief Justice REHNQUIST, with whom Justice O'CONNOR joins, concurring in the judgment.

I dissent from the Court's decision to overrule Ohio v. Roberts[. . . .] It is a change of course not in the least necessary to reverse the judgment of the Supreme Court of Washington in this case. The result the Court reaches follows inexorably from *Roberts* and its progeny without any need for overruling that line of cases. In Idaho v. Wright, 497 U.S. 805, 820-824 (1990), we held that an out-of-court statement was not admissible simply because the truthfulness of that statement was corroborated by other evidence at trial. [T]he Supreme Court of Washington gave decisive weight to the "interlocking nature of the two statements." No re-weighing of the "reliability factors," which is hypothesized by the Court, is required to reverse the judgment here. A citation to Idaho v. Wright, *supra*, would suffice.

KEY POINTS

1. In *Crawford*, the Supreme Court held that the Confrontation Clause of the Sixth Amendment applies to the government's use of "testimonial" hearsay statements against a criminal defendant. The Court based its holding on what it considered to be the core value of the Clause, which is to protect the criminal defendant's right to cross-examination.

2. The Court did not establish a single definition of "testimonial," but stated three possible definitions. At its core, according to the Court, "testimonial" means a statement made when the declarant is acting like a witness who "bears testimony," further defined as a "solemn declaration or affirmation made for the purpose of establishing or proving some fact."

3. Testimonial hearsay statements may be admitted at trial against a criminal defendant only if the declarant is unavailable and the defendant has had a prior opportunity to cross-examine the declarant. In addition, the government's use of all hearsay statements made by a testifying witness does not violate the defendant's confrontation right. And, admission of nontestimonial hearsay against the defendant does not violate that right.

PROBLEMS

8.78. Return to Problem 3.3, State v. Blair, at page 149. The prosecutor seeks to admit the following out-of-court statements by Norma. The court cites three different doctrinal definitions of "testimonial" statements from three different sources. How do they differ in application to Norma's statements? Do the different tests identify different concerns about "testimonial" statements?

  (a) A friend of Norma's says that a month before the attack, Norma told the friend, "Last week I told Jimmy that I was going to break up with him and leave the Bay Area soon. Jimmy was furious."

  (b) Inside the locked drawer in which police found photographs of Norma showing severe bruising and date-stamped July 25, 2009, a handwritten diary was also found. On the page dated July 21, 2009, it stated: "Jimmy beat me after an argument."

  (c) On August 1, 2009, Norma filed a formal complaint against Blair for assault and battery at the local police station. A week later she withdrew the complaint.

8.79. Return to Problem 8.49 on page 538. Are Mrs. D'Onofrio's statements during the 911 call "testimonial" under *Crawford*? Are her subsequent statements to the police officers "testimonial" under *Crawford*? (Assume that both sets of statements would be admissible under the hearsay rule.)

NOTES

1. The *Crawford* opinion suggests that statements falling within the hearsay exceptions for dying declarations and the doctrine of forfeiture by wrongdoing might be excepted from the ban on testimonial statements due to their historical pedigree. Both exceptions are discussed in Section 7 starting on page 678, infra.

2. In *dicta*, the Court also indicates that certain types of hearsay are not testimonial, including business records and co-conspirators' statements. Unless "testimonial" is given the most narrow definition of formalized testimonial materials, this seems plainly wrong. Both types of statements could certainly fit within the "reasonable expectations" test. Government business records are often created just for that purpose, as courts have had to acknowledge. See page 666, infra.

3. Note that the Supreme Court did not review the holding below that Sylvia Crawford was unavailable due to the defendant's invocation of the state marital privilege. Doesn't it seem a bit peculiar to think of Mrs. Crawford as constitutionally unavailable for cross-examination by her husband when it is her husband's choice to keep her off the stand?

4. The new approach to confrontation announced in *Crawford* was applied to cases that were currently pending in both federal and state courts. In Whorton v. Bockting, 549 U.S. 406 (2007), the Supreme Court decided that *Crawford* was not

a "watershed" holding that applies retroactively, meaning that it is not applicable to pre-*Crawford* convictions under habeas corpus review in federal courts. State courts, however, may choose to give broader effect to new rules of constitutional criminal procedure. See Danforth v. Minnesota, 552 U.S. 264 (2008).

5. The Supreme Court held in its next major Confrontation Clause opinion, Davis v. Washington, 547 U.S. 813 (2006), that if a statement is nontestimonial, the confrontation clause has no bearing on its admissibility. Id. at 824.

6. One of the definitions of "testimonial" offered by the Supreme Court was that proposed by Justices Scalia and Thomas in White v. Illinois—"extrajudicial statements . . . contained in formalized testimonial materials, such as affidavits, depositions, prior testimony, or confessions," 502 U.S. at 346. And in *Crawford* itself, the majority concluded its opinion by stating that, at a minimum, "testimonial" applies to "prior testimony at a preliminary hearing, before a grand jury, or at a former trial; and to police interrogations." 541 U.S. at 68. Courts have readily adopted these categories. United States v. Bruno, 383 F.3d 65, 78 (2d Cir. 2004) (plea allocution transcripts and grand jury testimony of unavailable witnesses are testimonial). The Court itself applied the "formalized testimonial materials" standard in Melendez-Diaz v. Massachusetts, 557 U.S. 305 (2009). See page 662, infra.

7. Another of the definitions of testimonial statements mentioned, but not explicitly adopted, in *Crawford* was statements "made under circumstances which would lead an objective witness reasonably to believe that the statement would be available for use at a later trial." After *Crawford*, lower courts started to apply a similar definition, usually using "reasonable expectations" terminology to exclude statements they found to be testimonial. United States v. Cromer, 389 F.3d 662, 674-678 (6th Cir. 2004) (statements given by confidential informants to police that implicated others in criminal activities); United States v. Summers, 414 F.3d 1287, 1302 (10th Cir. 2005) (statement by declarant in custody but not during interrogation); United States v. Hinton, 423 F.3d 355, 360 (3d Cir. 2005) (victim made identification while riding in police car).

3. The Definition of "Testimonial" Statements After *Crawford*: Statements Made During Questioning by Police

Many police interrogations are like that of Mrs. Crawford. They are formal, recorded, consist of structured questions, and have a law enforcement purpose. Such interrogations lie at the core of concern about a defendant's confrontation right. But a difference of opinion quickly emerged after *Crawford* as to how broadly this core concern extends. Some courts defined "interrogation" to include most statements made in response to police questions. Other courts held that responses to initial police inquiries at a crime scene are typically not testimonial. In 2006, the Supreme Court addressed this split of opinion in two companion cases, Davis v. Washington and Hammon v. Indiana.

a. The "Primary Purpose" Test: Davis v. Washington

DAVIS v. WASHINGTON, HAMMON v. INDIANA
547 U.S. 813 (2006)

Justice SCALIA delivered the opinion of the Court, in which ROBERTS, C.J., STEVENS, KENNEDY, SOUTER, GINSBURG, BREYER, and ALITO, JJ., joined. THOMAS, J., filed an opinion concurring in the judgment in part and dissenting in part.

These cases require us to determine when statements made to law enforcement personnel during a 911 call or at a crime scene are "testimonial" and thus subject to the requirements of the Sixth Amendment's Confrontation Clause.

I

A

The relevant statements in Davis v. Washington, No. 05-5224, were made to a 911 emergency operator on February 1, 2001. When the operator answered the initial call, the connection terminated before anyone spoke. She reversed the call, and Michelle McCottry answered. In the ensuing conversation, the operator ascertained that McCottry was involved in a domestic disturbance with her former boyfriend Adrian Davis, the petitioner in this case:

1	"911 Operator:	Hello.
2	"Complainant:	Hello.
3	"911 Operator:	What's going on?
4	"Complainant:	He's here jumpin' on me again.
5	"911 Operator:	Okay. Listen to me carefully. Are you in a house or an
6		apartment?
7	"Complainant:	I'm in a house.
8	"911 Operator:	Are there any weapons?
9	"Complainant:	No. He's usin' his fists.
10	"911 Operator:	Okay. Has he been drinking?
11	"Complainant:	No.
12	"911 Operator:	Okay, sweetie. I've got help started. Stay on the line with
13		me, okay?
14	"Complainant:	I'm on the line.
15	"911 Operator:	Listen to me carefully. Do you know his last name?
16	"Complainant:	It's Davis.
17	"911 Operator:	Davis? Okay, what's his first name?
18	"Complainant:	Adran.
19	"911 Operator:	What is it?
20	"Complainant:	Adrian.
21	"911 Operator:	Adrian?
22	"Complainant:	Yeah.
23	"911 Operator:	Okay. What's his middle initial?
24	"Complainant:	Martell. He's runnin' now."

As the conversation continued, the operator learned that Davis had "just run out the door" after hitting McCottry, and that he was leaving in a car with someone else.

McCottry started talking, but the operator cut her off, saying, "Stop talking and answer my questions." She then gathered more information about Davis (including his birthday), and learned that Davis had told McCottry that his purpose in coming to the house was "to get his stuff," since McCottry was moving. McCottry described the context of the assault, after which the operator told her that the police were on their way. "They're gonna check the area for him first," the operator said, "and then they're gonna come talk to you."

The police arrived within four minutes of the 911 call and observed McCottry's shaken state, the "fresh injuries on her forearm and her face," and her "frantic efforts to gather her belongings and her children so that they could leave the residence."

The State charged Davis with felony violation of a domestic no-contact order. "The State's only witnesses were the two police officers who responded to the 911 call. Both officers testified that McCottry exhibited injuries that appeared to be recent, but neither officer could testify as to the cause of the injuries." McCottry presumably could have testified as to whether Davis was her assailant, but she did not appear. Over Davis's objection, based on the Confrontation Clause of the Sixth Amendment, the trial court admitted the recording of her exchange with the 911 operator, and the jury convicted him. The Washington Court of Appeals affirmed. The Supreme Court of Washington, with one dissenting justice, also affirmed, concluding that the portion of the 911 conversation in which McCottry identified Davis was not testimonial, and that if other portions of the conversation were testimonial, admitting them was harmless beyond a reasonable doubt.

In Hammon v. Indiana, No. 05-5705, police responded late on the night of February 26, 2003, to a "reported domestic disturbance" at the home of Hershel and Amy Hammon. They found Amy alone on the front porch, appearing "'somewhat frightened,'" but she told them that "'nothing was the matter.'" She gave them permission to enter the house, where an officer saw "a gas heating unit in the corner of the living room" that had "flames coming out of the . . . partial glass front. There were pieces of glass on the ground in front of it and there was flame emitting from the front of the heating unit."

Hershel, meanwhile, was in the kitchen. He told the police "that he and his wife had 'been in an argument' but 'everything was fine now' and the argument 'never became physical.'" By this point Amy had come back inside. One of the officers remained with Hershel; the other went to the living room to talk with Amy, and "again asked [her] what had occurred." Hershel made several attempts to participate in Amy's conversation with the police, but was rebuffed. The officer later testified that Hershel "became angry when I insisted that [he] stay separated from Mrs. Hammon so that we can investigate what had happened." After hearing Amy's account, the officer "had her fill out and sign a battery affidavit." Amy handwrote the following: "Broke our Furnace & shoved me down on the floor into the broken glass. Hit me in the chest and threw me down. Broke our lamps & phone. Tore up my van where I couldn't leave the house. Attacked my daughter."

The State charged Hershel with domestic battery and with violating his probation. Amy was subpoenaed, but she did not appear at his subsequent bench trial. The State called the officer who had questioned Amy, and asked him to recount what Amy told him and to authenticate the affidavit. Hershel's counsel repeatedly objected to the admission of this evidence. At one point, after hearing the prosecutor defend the affidavit because it was made "under oath," defense counsel said, "That doesn't give us the opportunity to cross examine [the] person who allegedly drafted it. Makes me mad." Nonetheless, the trial court admitted the affidavit as a "present sense impression," and Amy's statements as "excited utterances" that "are expressly permitted in these kinds of cases even if the declarant is not available to testify." The officer thus testified that Amy

> "informed me that she and Hershel had been in an argument. That he became irrate [sic] over the fact of their daughter going to a boyfriend's house. The argument became . . . physical after being verbal and she informed me that Mr. Hammon, during the verbal part of the argument was breaking things in the living room and I believe she stated he broke the phone, broke the lamp, broke the front of the heater. When it became physical he threw her down into the glass of the heater. . . . She informed me Mr. Hammon had pushed her onto the ground, had shoved her head into the broken glass of the heater and that he had punched her in the chest twice I believe."

The trial judge found Hershel guilty on both charges, and the Indiana Court of Appeals affirmed in relevant part. The Indiana Supreme Court also affirmed, concluding that Amy's statement was admissible for state-law purposes as an excited utterance; that "a 'testimonial' statement is one given or taken in significant part for purposes of preserving it for potential future use in legal proceedings," where "the motivations of the questioner and declarant are the central concerns"; and that Amy's oral statement was not "testimonial" under these standards. It also concluded that, although the affidavit was testimonial and thus wrongly admitted, it was harmless beyond a reasonable doubt, largely because the trial was to the bench. We granted certiorari.

II

The Confrontation Clause of the Sixth Amendment provides: "In all criminal prosecutions, the accused shall enjoy the right . . . to be confronted with the witnesses against him." In Crawford v. Washington, we held that this provision bars "admission of testimonial statements of a witness who did not appear at trial unless he was unavailable to testify, and the defendant had had a prior opportunity for cross-examination." A critical portion of this holding, and the portion central to resolution of the two cases now before us, is the phrase "testimonial statements. . . ."

Our opinion in *Crawford* set forth "various formulations" of the core class of "'testimonial'" statements. . . . Among those, we said, were "statements taken by police officers in the course of interrogations." The questioning that generated the deponent's statement in *Crawford*—which was made and recorded while she was in police custody, after having been given *Miranda* warnings as a possible suspect herself—"qualifies under any conceivable definition" of an "interrogation." We therefore did not define that term, except to say that "we use [it] . . . in its colloquial, rather than any technical legal, sense," and that "one can imagine various definitions . . . , and we need not select among them in this case." The character of the statements in the present cases is not as clear, and these cases require us to determine more precisely which police interrogations produce testimony.

Without attempting to produce an exhaustive classification of all conceivable statements—or even all conceivable statements in response to police interrogation—as either testimonial or nontestimonial, it suffices to decide the present cases to hold as follows: Statements are nontestimonial when made in the course of police interrogation under circumstances objectively indicating that the primary purpose of the interrogation is to enable police assistance to meet an ongoing emergency. They are testimonial when the circumstances objectively indicate that there is no such ongoing emergency, and that the primary purpose of the interrogation is to establish or prove past events potentially relevant to later criminal prosecution.[16]

III

A

. . .

The question before us in *Davis*, then, is whether, objectively considered, the interrogation that took place in the course of the 911 call produced testimonial statements. When we said in *Crawford*, that "interrogations by law enforcement officers fall squarely within [the] class" of testimonial hearsay, we had immediately in mind (for that was the case before us) interrogations solely directed at establishing the facts of a past crime, in order to identify (or provide evidence to convict) the perpetrator. . . . A 911 call, on the other hand, and at least the initial interrogation conducted in connection with a 911 call, is ordinarily not designed primarily to "establish or prove" some past fact, but to describe current circumstances requiring police assistance.

The difference between the interrogation in *Davis* and the one in *Crawford* is apparent on the face of things. In *Davis*, McCottry was speaking about events *as they were actually happening*, rather than "describing past events." Sylvia Crawford's interrogation, on the other hand, took place hours after the events she described had occurred. Moreover, any reasonable listener would recognize that McCottry (unlike Sylvia Crawford) was facing an ongoing emergency. Although one *might* call 911 to provide a narrative report of a crime absent any imminent danger, McCottry's call was plainly a call for help against a bona fide physical threat. Third, the nature of what was asked and answered in *Davis*, again viewed objectively, was such that the elicited statements were necessary to be able to *resolve* the present emergency, rather than simply to learn (as in *Crawford*) what had happened in the past. That is true even of the operator's effort to establish the identity of the assailant, so that the dispatched officers might know whether they would be encountering a violent felon. And finally, the difference in the level of formality between the two interviews is striking. Crawford was responding calmly, at the station house, to a series of questions, with the officer-interrogator taping and making notes of her answers; McCottry's frantic answers were

---

16. This is not to imply, however, that statements made in the absence of any interrogation are necessarily nontestimonial. The Framers were no more willing to exempt from cross-examination volunteered testimony or answers to open-ended questions than they were to exempt answers to detailed interrogation. . . . And of course even when interrogation exists, it is in the final analysis the declarant's statements, not the interrogator's questions, that the Confrontation Clause requires us to evaluate.

provided over the phone, in an environment that was not tranquil, or even (as far as any reasonable 911 operator could make out) safe.

We conclude from all this that the circumstances of McCottry's interrogation objectively indicate its primary purpose was to enable police assistance to meet an ongoing emergency. She simply was not acting as a *witness*; she was not *testifying*. What she said was not "a weaker substitute for live testimony" at trial, like Lord Cobham's statements in *Raleigh's Case* . . . , or Sylvia Crawford's statement in *Crawford*. In each of those cases, the *ex parte* actors and the evidentiary products of the *ex parte* communication aligned perfectly with their courtroom analogues. McCottry's emergency statement does not. No "witness" goes into court to proclaim an emergency and seek help.

. . .

This is not to say that a conversation which begins as an interrogation to determine the need for emergency assistance cannot, as the Indiana Supreme Court put it, "evolve into testimonial statements," once that purpose has been achieved. In this case, for example, after the operator gained the information needed to address the exigency of the moment, the emergency appears to have ended (when Davis drove away from the premises). The operator then told McCottry to be quiet, and proceeded to pose a battery of questions. It could readily be maintained that, from that point on, McCottry's statements were testimonial, not unlike the "structured police questioning" that occurred in *Crawford*. This presents no great problem . . . . [T]rial courts will recognize the point at which, for Sixth Amendment purposes, statements in response to interrogations become testimonial. Through *in limine* procedure, they should redact or exclude the portions of any statement that have become testimonial, as they do, for example, with unduly prejudicial portions of otherwise admissible evidence. Davis's jury did not hear the *complete* 911 call, although it may well have heard some testimonial portions. We were asked to classify only McCottry's early statements identifying Davis as her assailant, and we agree with the Washington Supreme Court that they were not testimonial. That court also concluded that, even if later parts of the call were testimonial, their admission was harmless beyond a reasonable doubt. Davis does not challenge that holding, and we therefore assume it to be correct.

B

Determining the testimonial or nontestimonial character of the statements that were the product of the interrogation in *Hammon* is a much easier task, since they were not much different from the statements we found to be testimonial in *Crawford*. It is entirely clear from the circumstances that the interrogation was part of an investigation into possibly criminal past conduct—as, indeed, the testifying officer expressly acknowledged. There was no emergency in progress; the interrogating officer testified that he had heard no arguments or crashing and saw no one throw or break anything. When the officers first arrived, Amy told them that things were fine, and there was no immediate threat to her person. When the officer questioned Amy for the second time, and elicited the challenged statements, he was not seeking to determine (as in *Davis*) "what is happening," but rather "what happened." Objectively viewed, the primary, if not indeed the sole, purpose of the interrogation was to investigate a possible crime—which is, of course, precisely what the officer *should* have done.

G. Hearsay and the Confrontation Clause

It is true that the *Crawford* interrogation was more formal. It followed a *Miranda* warning, was tape-recorded, and took place at the station house. While these features certainly strengthened the statements' testimonial aspect—made it more objectively apparent, that is, that the purpose of the exercise was to nail down the truth about past criminal events—none was essential to the point. It was formal enough that Amy's interrogation was conducted in a separate room, away from her husband (who tried to intervene), with the officer receiving her replies for use in his "investigation." What we called the "striking resemblance" of the *Crawford* statement to civil-law *ex parte* examinations, is shared by Amy's statement here. Both declarants were actively separated from the defendant—officers forcibly prevented Hershel from participating in the interrogation. Both statements deliberately recounted, in response to police questioning, how potentially criminal past events began and progressed. And both took place some time after the events described were over. Such statements under official interrogation are an obvious substitute for live testimony, because they do precisely *what a witness does* on direct examination; they are inherently testimonial.

Both Indiana and the United States as *amicus curiae* argue that this case should be resolved much like *Davis*. For the reasons we find the comparison to *Crawford* compelling, we find the comparison to *Davis* unpersuasive. The statements in *Davis* were taken when McCottry was alone, not only unprotected by police (as Amy Hammon was protected), but apparently in immediate danger from *Davis*. She was seeking aid, not telling a story about the past. McCottry's present-tense statements showed immediacy; Amy's narrative of past events was delivered at some remove in time from the danger she described. And after Amy answered the officer's questions, he had her execute an affidavit, in order, he testified, "to establish events that have occurred previously."

Although we necessarily reject the Indiana Supreme Court's implication that virtually any "initial inquiries" at the crime scene will not be testimonial, we do not hold the opposite—that *no* questions at the scene will yield nontestimonial answers. We have already observed of domestic disputes that "officers called to investigate . . . need to know whom they are dealing with in order to assess the situation, the threat to their own safety, and possible danger to the potential victim. Such exigencies may *often* mean that "initial inquiries" produce nontestimonial statements. But in cases like this one, where Amy's statements were neither a cry for help nor the provision of information enabling officers immediately to end a threatening situation, the fact that they were given at an alleged crime scene and were "initial inquiries" is immaterial.[17]

---

17. Police investigations themselves are, of course, in no way impugned by our characterization of their fruits as testimonial. Investigations of past crimes prevent future harms and lead to necessary arrests. While prosecutors may hope that inculpatory "nontestimonial" evidence is gathered, this is essentially beyond police control. Their saying that an emergency exists cannot make it be so. The Confrontation Clause in no way governs police conduct, because it is the trial *use* of, not the investigatory *collection* of, *ex parte* testimonial statements which offends that provision. But neither can police conduct govern the Confrontation Clause; testimonial statements are what they are.

IV

Respondents in both cases, joined by a number of their *amici*, contend that the nature of the offenses charged in these two cases—domestic violence—requires greater flexibility in the use of testimonial evidence. This particular type of crime is notoriously susceptible to intimidation or coercion of the victim to ensure that she does not testify at trial. When this occurs, the Confrontation Clause gives the criminal a windfall. We may not, however, vitiate constitutional guarantees when they have the effect of allowing the guilty to go free. But when defendants seek to undermine the judicial process by procuring or coercing silence from witnesses and victims, the Sixth Amendment does not require courts to acquiesce. While defendants have no duty to assist the State in proving their guilt, they *do* have the duty to refrain from acting in ways that destroy the integrity of the criminal-trial system. We reiterate what we said in *Crawford:* that "the rule of forfeiture by wrongdoing . . . extinguishes confrontation claims on essentially equitable grounds. That is, one who obtains the absence of a witness by wrongdoing forfeits the constitutional right to confrontation."

We have determined that, absent a finding of forfeiture by wrongdoing, the Sixth Amendment operates to exclude Amy Hammon's affidavit. The Indiana courts may (if they are asked) determine on remand whether such a claim of forfeiture is properly raised and, if so, whether it is meritorious.

. . .

We affirm the judgment of the Supreme Court of Washington in No. 05-5224. We reverse the judgment of the Supreme Court of Indiana in No. 05-5705, and remand the case to that Court for proceedings not inconsistent with this opinion.

It is so ordered.

Justice THOMAS, concurring in the judgment in part and dissenting in part.

In Crawford v. Washington, we abandoned the general reliability inquiry we had long employed to judge the admissibility of hearsay evidence under the Confrontation Clause, describing that inquiry as "*inherently,* and therefore *permanently,* unpredictable." Today, a mere two years after the Court decided *Crawford*, it adopts an equally unpredictable test, under which district courts are charged with divining the "primary purpose" of police interrogations. Besides being difficult for courts to apply, this test characterizes as "testimonial," and therefore inadmissible, evidence that bears little resemblance to what we have recognized as the evidence targeted by the Confrontation Clause . . . . [T]he plain terms of the "testimony" definition we endorsed necessarily require some degree of solemnity before a statement can be deemed "testimonial."

This requirement of solemnity supports my view that the statements regulated by the Confrontation Clause must include "extrajudicial statements . . . contained in formalized testimonial materials, such as affidavits, depositions, prior testimony, or confessions." Affidavits, depositions, and prior testimony are, by their very nature, taken through a formalized process. Likewise, confessions, when extracted by police in a formal manner, carry sufficient indicia of solemnity to constitute formalized statements and, accordingly, bear a "striking resemblance," to the examinations of the accused and accusers under the Marian statutes. . . . In *Crawford*, for example, the interrogation was custodial, taken after warnings given pursuant to Miranda v. Arizona. *Miranda* warnings, by their terms, inform a prospective defendant that "'anything he says can be used against him in a court of law.'" This imports a solemnity to the process that is not present in a mere conversation between a witness or suspect and a police officer.

. . .

B

. . .

The Court's determination that the evidence against Hammon must be excluded extends the Confrontation Clause far beyond the abuses it was intended to prevent. When combined with the Court's holding that the evidence against Davis is perfectly admissible, however, the Court's *Hammon* holding also reveals the difficulty of applying the Court's requirement that courts investigate the "primary purposes" of the investigation. . . . [T]he fact that the officer in *Hammon* was investigating Mr. Hammon's past conduct does not foreclose the possibility that the primary purpose of his inquiry was to assess whether Mr. Hammon constituted a continuing danger to his wife, requiring further police presence or action. It is hardly remarkable that Hammon did not act abusively towards his wife in the presence of the officers, and his good judgment to refrain from criminal behavior in the presence of police sheds little, if any, light on whether his violence would have resumed had the police left without further questioning, transforming what the Court dismisses as "past conduct" back into an "ongoing emergency." Nor does the mere fact that McCottry needed emergency aid shed light on whether the "primary purpose" of gathering, for example, the name of her assailant was to protect the police, to protect the victim, or to gather information for prosecution. In both of the cases before the Court, like many similar cases, pronouncement of the "primary" motive behind the interrogation calls for nothing more than a guess by courts.

II

Because the standard adopted by the Court today is neither workable nor a targeted attempt to reach the abuses forbidden by the Clause, I concur only in the judgment in Davis v. Washington, and respectfully dissent from the Court's resolution of Hammon v. Indiana.

KEY POINTS

1. In cases involving statements made during the course of police questioning, a key issue is whether the statement is made in which the circumstances, viewed objectively, indicate that the primary purpose of the questioning is to enable police assistance to meet an ongoing emergency. Such statements are nontestimonial. Statements are testimonial when circumstances objectively indicate that there is no ongoing emergency or that the primary purpose of

the questioning is to find or prove past facts potentially relevant to subsequent criminal prosecution.

2. Several factors bear on this objective inquiry: Is the declarant speaking about events as they are actually happening or describing past events? Is the declarant facing an ongoing emergency? Is the content of the questions and answers necessary to resolve a present emergency or simply to learn what happened in the past? Does the extent of or level of formality in the questioning indicate an emergency or a structured interrogation?

PROBLEM

8.80. H.D. was convicted by a jury of possession of a firearm by a felon pursuant to 18 U.S.C. §922(g)(1). It is undisputed that H.D. is a "felon" under this statute. Officer Carlton testified at trial for the prosecution as follows:

> I observed the defendant on Elm Street pushing another man in a wheelchair. I exited my squad car and headed in defendant's direction. Defendant looked at me, took a gun from his waistband, and fled on foot. I chased him on foot and I observed a gun in his right hand. I ran at him full speed, crashed into him, subdued him on the ground and seized the gun. The gun was not fired.

H.D. made no objection to this testimony. However, H.D. denies that he possessed a gun and claims that Officer Carlton lied about the gun during his testimony. It is undisputed that H.D. was the person chased and knocked down by Officer Carlton. The gun that Officer Carlton said he seized from H.D.'s possession was not offered into evidence at trial because it could not be located. H.D. did not testify.

The court permitted Officer Carlton to testify as follows just prior to his statements quoted above. Does admission of this testimony violate the confrontation clause?

> I answered the phone at the police station. The caller refused to identify herself. She spoke in a calm and quiet voice. She said: "The neighborhood bully is just walking by on Elm Street, pushing a man in a wheelchair." I asked her what the problem was. She said: "I see a gun stuck into his pants." Then she hung up. I immediately left the station and drove my squad car to Elm Street. We have been unable to determine who this caller was.

NOTES AND QUESTIONS

1. Does the "primary purpose" test respond to hearsay risks generated by the conduct of police interrogators, the mental state of the declarant, or both? Does the Court explicitly hold whose "primary purpose" is dispositive of the status of the statement—the interrogator's or the declarant's?

2. Is the distinction between statements made for the purpose "to enable police assistance in an ongoing emergency" versus "to establish or prove past events potentially relevant to later criminal prosecution" a bright-line rule? Is it easy to apply or are there difficult line-drawing questions? What about the police asking a crime victim who is lying, bleeding, on the ground, "Who did this?" versus "Is the person who did this still around?" What about a frightened and emotional statement made by a woman to her best friend telling the friend that she was violently assaulted the day before by her boyfriend? What is her purpose in making this statement? To seek emotional support or to create a record should anything happen to her? Courts seem to be fairly consistent in their analysis of fact patterns that are easily analogized to the facts in *Davis/Hammon* fact patterns, whereas they are decidedly more varied when considering fact patterns far outside the scope of 911 calls or emergency situations involving police.

3. Although the Court's opinion contained no factual basis for inferring that either of the defendants in *Davis* and *Hammon* had induced the hearsay declarants not to testify in their respective cases, the Court nevertheless closed Part IV with a discussion of the doctrine of forfeiture by wrongdoing. This Court returned to this issue in Giles v. California, 554 U.S. 353 (2008), as will be discussed on page 680, infra.

4. Lower court decisions, both state and federal, have indicated a growing consensus that statements establishing the identity of a perpetrator when made in informal settings during the immediate aftermath of a crime can be nontestimonial if the court finds that an "ongoing emergency" exists. See, e.g., State v. Calhoun, 657 S.E.2d 424 (N.C. App. 2008) (finding that in an interrogation with the primary purpose of enabling police assistance to deal with an ongoing emergency, permissible questions may "'establish the identity of the assailant, so that the dispatched officers might know whether they would be encountering a violent felon'") (quoting *Davis*); State v. Slater, 939 A.2d 1105 (Conn. 2008) (holding that a rape victim's statements to bystanders who inquired about her distress were nontestimonial because the victim "clearly was seeking aid" and the men responded with "no indication that their primary purpose was to do anything but aid her").

b. The "Primary Purpose" Test: Michigan v. Bryant

In 2011, the Supreme Court decided its second case involving statements made during police questioning. In Michigan v. Bryant, 562 U.S. 344 (2011), the Court applied the primary purpose test in a context very different from the domestic violence situations in *Davis* and *Hammon*. In *Bryant*,

> Around 3:25 a.m. on April 29, 2001, Detroit, Michigan police officers responded to a radio dispatch indicating that a man had been shot. At the scene, they found the victim, Anthony Covington, lying on the ground next to his car in a gas station parking lot. Covington had a gunshot wound to his abdomen, appeared to be in great pain, and spoke with difficulty.
>
> The police asked him what had happened, who had shot him, and where the shooting had occurred. . . . Covington stated that "Rick" shot him at around 3 a.m. . . . He also indicated that he had a conversation with Bryant, whom he recognized based

on his voice, through the back door of Bryant's house. Covington explained that when he turned to leave, he was shot through the door and then drove to the gas station, where police found him.

Covington's conversation with the police ended within 5 to 10 minutes when emergency medical services arrived. Covington was transported to a hospital and died within hours. The police left the gas station after speaking with Covington, called for backup, and traveled to Bryant's house. They did not find Bryant there but did find blood and a bullet on the back porch and an apparent bullet hole in the back door. Police also found Covington's wallet and identification outside the house. [Id. at 349-50.]

Covington's statements were admitted against the defendant Bryant at his trial on charges of second degree murder. Bryant was convicted, and the Michigan Court of Appeals upheld the trial court's determination that these statements were nontestimonial, made for the purpose of resolving an ongoing emergency. The Michigan Supreme Court reversed, applying the *Davis* factors and holding that Covington's statements were testimonial and thus, Bryant's confrontation right had been violated:

> These statements related solely to events that had occurred in the past and at a different location. None of these statements referred to events occurring at the time the statements were made, none alleged any ongoing threat, and none asserted the possible presence of the alleged perpetrator. The circumstances, in our judgment, clearly indicate that the "primary purpose" of the questioning was to establish the facts of an event that had already occurred; the "primary purpose" was not to enable police assistance to meet an ongoing emergency. . . . The police asked the victim what had happened in the past, not what was currently happening. That is, the "primary purpose" of the questions asked, and the answers given, was to enable the police to identify, locate, and apprehend the perpetrator. [People v. Bryant, 768 N.W.2d 65 (Mich. 2009).]

The Supreme Court granted certiorari, and a five-Justice majority held as follows:

> [T]he circumstances of the interaction between Covington and the police objectively indicate that the "primary purpose of the interrogation" was "to enable police assistance to meet an ongoing emergency." *Davis*, 547 U.S., at 822. Therefore, Covington's identification and description of the shooter and the location of the shooting were not testimonial statements, and their admission at Bryant's trial did not violate the Confrontation Clause.

The majority opinion was written by Justice Sotomayor, joined by Chief Justice Roberts, and Justices Kennedy, Breyer, and Alito. Justice Thomas's concurrence was grounded on the same position he had asserted in *Davis*, that questioning by police lacked sufficient formality and solemnity for Covington's statements to be considered to be testimonial. Justices Scalia and Ginsburg filed dissenting opinions, discussed below, and Justice Kagan took no part in the consideration of the case. The effect of the majority view is, of course, to permit the conviction of Bryant to stand, grounded as it was on the hearsay statements of the deceased victim of the crime who was never cross-examined by the defendant.

The majority opinion reviewed the Court's confrontation jurisprudence starting with *Crawford* and continuing through *Davis*, citing the factors that the *Davis*

Court had developed to determine the primary purpose of statements made during police questioning. Justice Sotomayor took issue with the Michigan Supreme Court's finding of no ongoing emergency. The opinion found that the Michigan court had focused too narrowly on whether there was an emergency because of an ongoing threat to the victim, and it had ignored the ongoing threat that an unknown shooter with a gun posed both to the police themselves and to the public. This emergency, the Justice wrote, "stretches more broadly" than those in *Davis* and *Hammon*. The majority opinion continued:

> We reiterate, moreover, that the existence *vel non* of an ongoing emergency is not the touchstone of the testimonial inquiry; rather, the ultimate inquiry is whether the "primary purpose of the interrogation [was] to enable police assistance to meet [the] ongoing emergency." *Davis*, 547 U.S., at 822. We turn now to that inquiry, as informed by the circumstances of the ongoing emergency just described. The circumstances of the encounter provide important context for understanding Covington's statements to the police. When the police arrived at Covington's side, their first question to him was "What happened?" Covington's response was either "Rick shot me" or "I was shot," followed very quickly by an identification of "Rick" as the shooter. In response to further questions, Covington explained that the shooting occurred through the back door of Bryant's house and provided a physical description of the shooter. When he made the statements, Covington was lying in a gas station parking lot bleeding from a mortal gunshot wound to his abdomen. His answers to the police officers' questions were punctuated with questions about when emergency medical services would arrive. He was obviously in considerable pain and had difficulty breathing and talking. From this description of his condition and report of his statements, we cannot say that a person in Covington's situation would have had a "primary purpose" "to establish or prove past events potentially relevant to later criminal prosecution."
>
> For their part, the police responded to a call that a man had been shot. As discussed above, they did not know why, where, or when the shooting had occurred. Nor did they know the location of the shooter or anything else about the circumstances in which the crime occurred. The questions they asked—"what had happened, who had shot him, and where the shooting occurred,"—were the exact type of questions necessary to allow the police to "'assess the situation, the threat to their own safety, and possible danger to the potential victim'"[18] and to the public, including to allow them to ascertain "whether they would be encountering a violent felon," In other words, they solicited the information necessary to enable them "to meet an ongoing emergency."
>
> Nothing in Covington's responses indicated to the police that, contrary to their expectation upon responding to a call reporting a shooting, there was no emergency or that a prior emergency had ended. Covington did indicate that he had been shot at another location about 25 minutes earlier, but he did not know the location of the shooter at the time the police arrived and, as far as we can tell from the record, he gave no indication that the shooter, having shot at him twice, would be satisfied that

---

18. [References to the *Davis/Hammon* opinion and other cases are omitted.—Eds.]

Covington was only wounded. In fact, Covington did not indicate any possible motive for the shooting, and thereby gave no reason to think that the shooter would not shoot again if he arrived on the scene. As we noted in *Davis*, "initial inquiries" may "*often . . .* produce nontestimonial statements." The initial inquiries in this case resulted in the type of nontestimonial statements we contemplated in *Davis*.

Finally, we consider the informality of the situation and the interrogation. This situation is more similar, though not identical, to the informal, harried 911 call in *Davis* than to the structured, station-house interview in *Crawford*. As the officers' trial testimony reflects, the situation was fluid and somewhat confused: the officers arrived at different times; apparently each, upon arrival, asked Covington "what happened?"; and, contrary to the dissent's portrayal, (opinion of Scalia, J.), they did not conduct a structured interrogation.

. . .

> Because the circumstances of the encounter as well as the statements and actions of Covington and the police objectively indicate that the "primary purpose of the interrogation" was "to enable police assistance to meet an ongoing emergency," Covington's identification and description of the shooter and the location of the shooting were not testimonial hearsay. The Confrontation Clause did not bar their admission at Bryant's trial. [Id. at 374-78.]

The method of the majority deserves some further comment. The majority employed what the opinion calls a "combined" approach to determining the primary purpose of the police interrogation. That is, in applying the factors outlined in *Davis*, a court must look to the circumstances in which an encounter between police and declarant occurs; the statements and actions of both the declarant and the interrogators; the nature (content) of what was asked and answered; acknowledge the possibility of mixed motives on the part of both police and declarant; and not look for "purpose" by looking solely at one participant. In short, a court must arrive at an objective determination of the primary purpose of "the interrogation" itself by examining its contents and the combined circumstances of the participants.

More startling is the majority's explicit reference to the "reliability" of statements, such as Covington's, made during ongoing emergencies:

> The existence of an ongoing emergency is relevant to determining the primary purpose of the interrogation because an emergency focuses the participants on something other than "prov[ing] past events potentially relevant to later criminal prosecution." *Davis*, 547 U.S., at 822. Rather, it focuses them on "end[ing] a threatening situation." *Id.*, at 832. Implicit in *Davis* is the idea that because the prospect of fabrication in statements given for the primary purpose of resolving that emergency is presumably significantly diminished, the Confrontation Clause does not require such statements to be subject to the crucible of cross-examination.

> This logic is not unlike that justifying the excited utterance exception in hearsay law. Statements "relating to a startling event or condition made while the declarant was under the stress of excitement caused by the event or condition," Fed. Rule Evid. 803(2); see also Mich. Rule Evid. 803(2) (2010), are considered reliable because the declarant, in the excitement, presumably cannot form a falsehood. See Idaho v. Wright, 497 U.S. 805, 820 (1990) ("The basis for the 'excited utterance' exception . . . is that such statements are given under circumstances that eliminate the possibility of

fabrication, coaching, or confabulation . . . . An ongoing emergency has a similar effect of focusing an individual's attention on responding to the emergency").[19] [Id. at 361.]

This departure from the philosophy and methodology of *Crawford*, and its seeming invitation to return to the reliability rationale of *Roberts*, was received with scathing criticism from Justice Scalia in dissent:

> The Court attempts to fit its resurrected interest in reliability into the *Crawford* framework, but the result is incoherent. Reliability, the Court tells us, is a good indicator of whether "a statement is . . . an out-of-court substitute for trial testimony." That is patently false. Reliability tells us *nothing* about whether a statement is testimonial. Testimonial and nontestimonial statements alike come in varying degrees of reliability. An eyewitness's statements to the police after a fender-bender, for example, are both reliable and testimonial. Statements to the police from one driver attempting to blame the other would be similarly testimonial but rarely reliable. [Id. at 392.]

Justice Scalia's dissenting opinion finds that Covington's statements were testimonial, and in this conclusion he was joined by Justice Ginsburg. In *Davis*, the majority opinion, written by Justice Scalia, has refused to give primacy to any one of the factors it considered in finding "primary purpose," including whether the purpose of the police or the declarant counted for more. In *Bryant*, Justice Scalia made clear that he believes that it is the declarant's intent and understanding that counts:

> *Crawford* and *Davis* did not address whose perspective matters—the declarant's, the interrogator's, or both—when assessing "the primary purpose of [an] interrogation." In those cases the statements were testimonial from any perspective. I think the same is true here, but because the Court picks a perspective so will I: The declarant's intent is what counts. In-court testimony is more than a narrative of past events; it is a solemn declaration made in the course of a criminal trial. For an out-of-court statement to qualify as testimonial, the declarant must intend the statement to be a solemn declaration rather than an unconsidered or offhand remark; and he must make the statement with the understanding that it may be used to invoke the coercive machinery of the State against the accused. See Friedman, Grappling with the Meaning of "Testimonial," 71 Brooklyn L. Rev. 241, 259 (2005). That is what distinguishes a narrative told to a friend over dinner from a statement to the police. The hidden purpose of an interrogator cannot substitute for the declarant's intentional solemnity or his understanding of how his words may be used.
>
> A declarant-focused inquiry is also the only inquiry that would work in every fact pattern implicating the Confrontation Clause. The Clause applies to volunteered testimony as well as statements solicited through police interrogation. An inquiry into an officer's purposes would make no sense when a declarant blurts out "Rick shot me" as soon as the officer arrives on the scene. I see no reason to adopt a different test—one

---

19. Many other exceptions to the hearsay rules similarly rest on the belief that certain statements are, by their nature, made for a purpose other than use in a prosecution and therefore should not be barred by hearsay prohibitions. See, *e.g.*, Fed. Rule Evid. 801(d)(2)(E) (statement by a co-conspirator during and in furtherance of the conspiracy); 803(4) (Statements for Purposes of Medical Diagnosis or Treatment); 803(6) (Records of Regularly Conducted Activity); 803(8) (Public Records and Reports); 803(9) (Records of Vital Statistics); 803(11) (Records of Religious Organizations); 803(12) (Marriage, Baptismal, and Similar Certificates); 803(13) (Family Records); 804(b)(3) (Statement Against Interest).

that accounts for an officer's intent—when the officer asks "what happened" before the declarant makes his accusation. (This does not mean the interrogator is irrelevant. The identity of an interrogator, and the content and tenor of his questions, can bear upon whether a declarant intends to make a solemn statement, and envisions its use at a criminal trial. But none of this means that the interrogator's purpose matters.) [Id. at 381-82.]

Justice Scalia is certainly correct that the majority opinion requires judges to conduct an open-ended inquiry into the totality of the circumstances surrounding a police interrogation in order to determine its "primary purpose." This inquiry would still be framed by the factors outlined in *Davis*. If conflicting purposes are inferred, some type of "balancing test" might have to be applied to determine primacy. To what extent "reliability" will seep into that determination remains to be seen.

PROBLEMS

8.81. Father is charged with the crime of aggravated assault and battery on his 15-year-old son, Joe, who suffered a slash wound on his cheek and neck. The prosecution claims that Father and Joe got into an argument at home; Father pushed Joe; Joe fell onto a glass coffee table and smashed the glass top; Father grabbed a very sharp piece of glass from the coffee table and deliberately cut Joe. Father's defense is that Joe accidentally fell over the glass coffee table and cut his face on the shattered glass.

Immediately after he was injured, Joe ran out of the house. A neighbor had heard the father and son yelling and had called 911 to report a domestic disturbance. Police Officer Mullin went to Father's home, saw blood on the floor, and saw Father cleaning up broken glass from the smashed coffee table top. Father told Mullin that Joe had fallen onto the table and cut himself, but that Joe was OK. The neighbor who called 911 told Mullin that Joe and his father were always fighting.

One hour later, Mullin was sent to a location a mile away where a male youth was sitting on a curb, his face slashed. Mullin asked the youth for his name, and learned that he was Father's son, Joe. Mullin called for emergency medical personnel to take Joe to a hospital. Mullin then asked Joe, "What happened between you and your father?" Joe said: "I got into an argument with my father; he pushed me and I fell over the coffee table. The glass top broke. My father picked up a piece of glass and cut me." The emergency medical team arrived and Mullin asked no further questions.

Joe has disappeared. If Joe is not available to testify at Father's trial, Officer Mullin would testify as to what Joe said in response to his question. Officer Mullin would also testify that his own primary purpose in his questioning of Joe was to assess whether there was an ongoing emergency in Joe's home. Would Joe's statement to Mullin about the cause of his injury be admissible under the Confrontation Clause?

8.82. Hannah owns a small accessories store on a busy shopping street. She was robbed at gunpoint as she stood behind the counter of her store. The robber took cash from the cash box and her purse. Immediately after the robber left her store, Hannah ran outside and asked a bystander to observe the license plate number of the car that she had seen the robber get into and start to drive away. The bystander did so, and wrote the license number on a piece of paper. He gave the paper to Hannah, who gave it to the investigating police officer. The license number was registered to a car owned by defendant. The bystander is not available to testify at defendant's trial for the robbery of Hannah's store, and the bystander was never cross-examined by the defendant. May the piece of paper be admitted against the defendant? Consider all possible objections.

NOTES AND QUESTIONS

1. The split of opinions in *Bryant* reveals that Justice Scalia has lost his ability to control the implementation of the "testimonial" standard, at least insofar as the "primary purpose" test is concerned. It would seem that application of the multifactor "combined approach" of the majority could lead to future differences in outcomes as well. Remember that in *Crawford* the Court roundly criticized the prior "reliability" approach to the confrontation right in Ohio v. Roberts as amorphous, indeterminate, and unpredictable. In *Bryant*, hasn't the testimonial standard revealed the same weaknesses? Justice Scalia criticizes the combined approach of the majority on those grounds:

> The only virtue of the Court's approach (if it can be misnamed a virtue) is that it leaves judges free to reach the "fairest" result under the totality of the circumstances. If the dastardly police trick a declarant into giving an incriminating statement against a sympathetic defendant, a court can focus on the police's intent and declare the statement testimonial. If the defendant "deserves" to go to jail, then a court can focus on whatever perspective is necessary to declare damning hearsay nontestimonial. And when all else fails, a court can mix-and-match perspectives to reach its desired outcome. Unfortunately, under this malleable approach "the guarantee of confrontation is no guarantee at all." [Id. at 1170.]

2. How realistic is it to search for a "primary" purpose of police questioning of victims at or near a potential crime scene? When asked, police officers will tell you that they have two equally powerful motives—to define and resolve any emergency situation and to gather evidence for future prosecution. Is it sensible for a legal doctrine to require courts to struggle so hard to construct an alternate reality?

4. The Definition of "Testimonial" Statements After *Crawford*: Government Forensic Reports

Application of the confrontation clause to routine governmental reports, prepared by public employees who are not directly involved in crime investigation and law enforcement, has presented a dilemma for courts making the transition from the "reliability" theory of Ohio v. Roberts to the "testimonial statement" theory of *Crawford*. Under *Roberts*, routine noninvestigative factual reports were often treated as business or public records, thus admissible under "firmly rooted" hearsay exceptions. In addition, after *Roberts*, many states enacted special legislation providing that official reports of standardized chemical tests analyzing narcotics and other drugs, prepared and submitted under oath by the proper governmental analyst, were admissible as prima facie evidence of the chemical composition of the tested substance without the testimony of the analyst in court. See, e.g., Mass. Gen. Laws, ch. 111, §13. Routine and regularized data collection, and the application of standardized tests, were held to provide sufficient reliability to dispel the need for confrontation and cross-examination of both types of documents.

After *Crawford*, some courts still held that government documents that were routine and objective cataloging of unambiguous factual matters, not made in anticipation of litigation, were nontestimonial. Examples include a certificate of no record (CNR), reporting that a diligent search of appropriate records indicated no license to carry a weapon issued to a defendant; a warrant of deportation recording that a deportee actually left the country; raw data generated by diagnostic machines; and even the conclusion drawn from a standardized laboratory test despite the author's knowledge that the report would be used by the prosecution. In June 2009, the Supreme Court decided Melendez-Diaz v. Massachusetts, 557 U.S. 305 (2009), a case that impacted the admissibility of many types of these governmental forensic reports.

a. Melendez-Diaz v. Massachusetts

Defendant Melendez-Diaz was charged with distributing and trafficking in cocaine. At issue was the admissibility of three "certificates of analysis," which stated that the substance in the bags found in defendant's possession was cocaine. These certificates had been prepared pursuant to the special Massachusetts statute cited above (Mass. Gen. Laws, ch. 111, §13), and their admission into evidence at defendant's trial had been upheld.

Justice Scalia, writing for a five-Justice majority that included Justices Stevens, Thomas, Souter, and Ginsburg, found these certificates to be testimonial and held that their admission against Melendez-Diaz was error, thus requiring reversal and remand of the judgment against him. On this point, the majority opinion was brief.

> The Sixth Amendment to the United States Constitution, made applicable to the States via the Fourteenth Amendment, Pointer v. Texas, 380 U.S. 400, 403 (1965), provides that "[i]n all criminal prosecutions, the accused shall enjoy the right . . . to be confronted with the witnesses against him." In *Crawford*, after reviewing the Clause's historical underpinnings, we held that it guarantees a defendant's right to confront those "who 'bear testimony'" against him. 541 U.S., at 51. A witness's testimony against a defendant is thus inadmissible unless the witness appears at trial or, if the witness is unavailable, the defendant had a prior opportunity for cross-examination. *Id.*, at 54.
>
> Our opinion described the class of testimonial statements covered by the Confrontation Clause as follows:
>
>> "Various formulations of this core class of testimonial statements exist: *ex parte* in-court testimony or its functional equivalent—that is, material such as affidavits, custodial

examinations, prior testimony that the defendant was unable to cross-examine, or similar pretrial statements that declarants would reasonably expect to be used prosecutorially; extrajudicial statements . . . contained in formalized testimonial materials, such as affidavits, depositions, prior testimony, or confessions; statements that were made under circumstances which would lead an objective witness reasonably to believe that the statement would be available for use at a later trial." *Id.*, at 51-52 (internal quotation marks and citations omitted).

There is little doubt that the documents at issue in this case fall within the "core class of testimonial statements" thus described. Our description of that category mentions affidavits twice. See also White v. Illinois, 502 U.S. 346, 365, (1992) (Thomas, J., concurring in part and concurring in judgment) ("[T]he Confrontation Clause is implicated by extrajudicial statements only insofar as they are contained in formalized testimonial materials, such as affidavits, depositions, prior testimony, or confessions"). The documents at issue here, while denominated by Massachusetts law "certificates," are quite plainly affidavits: "declaration[s] of facts written down and sworn to by the declarant before an officer authorized to administer oaths." Black's Law Dictionary 62 (8th ed. 2004). They are incontrovertibly a "'solemn declaration or affirmation made for the purpose of establishing or proving some fact.'" *Crawford, supra,* at 51 (quoting 2 N. Webster, An American Dictionary of the English Language (1828)). The fact in question is that the substance found in the possession of Melendez-Diaz and his codefendants was, as the prosecution claimed, cocaine — the precise testimony the analysts would be expected to provide if called at trial. The "certificates" are functionally identical to live, in-court testimony, doing "precisely what a witness does on direct examination." Davis v. Washington, 547 U.S. 813, 830 (2006) (emphasis deleted).

Here, moreover, not only were the affidavits "'made under circumstances which would lead an objective witness reasonably to believe that the statement would be available for use at a later trial,'" *Crawford, supra,* at 52, but under Massachusetts law the *sole purpose* of the affidavits was to provide "prima facie evidence of the composition, quality, and the net weight" of the analyzed substance, Mass. Gen. Laws, ch. 111, §13. We can safely assume that the analysts were aware of the affidavits' evidentiary purpose, since that purpose — as stated in the relevant state-law provision — was reprinted on the affidavits themselves.

In short, under our decision in *Crawford* the analysts' affidavits were testimonial statements, and the analysts were "witnesses" for purposes of the Sixth Amendment. Absent a showing that the analysts were unavailable to testify at trial *and* that petitioner had a prior opportunity to cross-examine them, petitioner was entitled to "'be confronted with'" the analysts at trial. *Crawford, supra,* at 54. [557 U.S. at 309-311.]

Justice Thomas, once again, filed a short concurrence to note that his position, advanced in his opinions since 1992, is that "the Confrontation Clause is implicated by extrajudicial statements only insofar as they are contained in formalized testimonial materials, such as affidavits, depositions, prior testimony, or confessions." He joined the majority opinion because, in his words, the "documents at issue in this case 'are quite plainly affidavits'. . . [that] 'fall within the core class of testimonial statements' governed by the Confrontation Clause." 557 U.S. at 330.

In the following excerpt from the dissent, Justice Kennedy, joined by Justices Breyer and Alito and Chief Justice Roberts, leveled a direct attack on Justice Scalia's formal approach to defining "testimonial statements" in *Crawford, Davis,* and now *Melendez-Diaz,* as well as on the majority's holding in the case, and makes a series of attacks on the outcome of the majority opinion as well.

II

The Court's fundamental mistake is to read the Confrontation Clause as referring to a kind of out-of-court statement—namely, a testimonial statement—that must be excluded from evidence. The Clause does not refer to kinds of statements. Nor does the Clause contain the word "testimonial." The text, instead, refers to kinds of persons, namely, to "witnesses against" the defendant. Laboratory analysts are not "witnesses against" the defendant as those words would have been understood at the framing. There is simply no authority for this position.

Instead, the Clause refers to a conventional "witness"—meaning one who witnesses (that is, perceives) an event that gives him or her personal knowledge of some aspect of the defendant's guilt. Both *Crawford* and *Davis* concerned just this kind of ordinary witness—and nothing in the Confrontation Clause's text, history, or precedent justifies the Court's decision to expand those cases.

A

The Clause states: "In all criminal prosecutions, the accused shall enjoy the right . . . to be confronted with the witnesses against him." U.S. Const., Amdt. 6. Though there is "virtually no evidence of what the drafters of the Confrontation Clause intended it to mean,". . .it is certain the Framers did not contemplate that an analyst who conducts a scientific test far removed from the crime would be considered a "witnes[s] against" the defendant.

The Framers were concerned with a typical witness—one who perceived an event that gave rise to a personal belief in some aspect of the defendant's guilt. There is no evidence that the Framers understood the Clause to extend to unconventional witnesses. As discussed below, there is significant evidence to the contrary. . . . In these circumstances, the historical evidence in support of the Court's position is "'too meager . . . to form a solid basis in history, preceding and contemporaneous with the framing of the Constitution.'" . . . The Court goes dangerously wrong when it bases its constitutional interpretation upon historical guesswork.

The infamous treason trial of Sir Walter Raleigh provides excellent examples of the kinds of witnesses to whom the Confrontation Clause refers . . . see *Crawford*, 541 U.S., at 44-45 (Raleigh's trial informs our understanding of the Clause because it was, at the time of the framing, one of the "most notorious instances" of the abuse of witnesses' out-of-court statements); *ante*, at 9 (same). Raleigh's accusers claimed to have heard Raleigh speak treason, so they were witnesses in the conventional sense. We should limit the Confrontation Clause to witnesses like those in Raleigh's trial.

The Court today expands the Clause to include laboratory analysts, but analysts differ from ordinary witnesses in at least three significant ways. First, a conventional witness recalls events observed in the past, while an analyst's report contains near-contemporaneous observations of the test. An observation recorded at the time it is made is unlike the usual act of testifying. A typical witness must recall a previous event that he or she perceived just once, and thus may have misperceived or misremembered. But an analyst making a contemporaneous observation need not rely on memory; he or she instead reports the observations at the time they are made. We gave this consideration substantial weight in *Davis*. There, the "primary purpose" of the victim's 911 call was "to enable police assistance to meet an ongoing emergency," rather than "to establish or prove past events potentially relevant to later criminal prosecution." 547 U.S., at 822,

827 . . . . The Court cites no authority for its holding that an observation recorded at the time it is made is an act of "witness[ing]" for purposes of the Confrontation Clause.

Second, an analyst observes neither the crime nor any human action related to it. Often, the analyst does not know the defendant's identity, much less have personal knowledge of an aspect of the defendant's guilt. The analyst's distance from the crime and the defendant, in both space and time, suggests the analyst is not a witness against the defendant in the conventional sense.

Third, a conventional witness responds to questions under interrogation. But laboratory tests are conducted according to scientific protocols; they are not dependent upon or controlled by interrogation of any sort. Put differently, out-of-court statements should only "require confrontation if they are produced by, or with the involvement of, adversarial government officials responsible for investigating and prosecuting crime.". . . There is no indication that the analysts here—who work for the State Laboratory Institute, a division of the Massachusetts Department of Public Health— were adversarial to petitioner. Nor is there any evidence that adversarial officials played a role in formulating the analysts' certificates.

Rather than acknowledge that it expands the Confrontation Clause beyond conventional witnesses, the Court relies on our recent opinions in *Crawford* and *Davis*. . . . The Court assumes, with little analysis, that *Crawford* and *Davis* extended the Clause to any person who makes a "testimonial" statement. But the Court's confident tone cannot disguise the thinness of these two reeds. Neither *Crawford* nor *Davis* considered whether the Clause extends to persons far removed from the crime who have no connection to the defendant. Instead, those cases concerned conventional witnesses. *Davis, supra*, at 826-830 (witnesses were victims of defendants' assaults); *Crawford, supra*, at 38 (witness saw defendant stab victim).

It is true that *Crawford* and *Davis* employed the term "testimonial," and thereby suggested that any testimonial statement, by any person, no matter how distant from the defendant and the crime, is subject to the Confrontation Clause. But that suggestion was not part of the holding of *Crawford* or *Davis*. Those opinions used the adjective "testimonial" to avoid the awkward phrasing required by reusing the noun "witness." The Court today transforms that turn of phrase into a new and sweeping legal rule, by holding that anyone who makes a formal statement for the purpose of later prosecution—no matter how removed from the crime—must be considered a "witness against" the defendant. The Court cites no authority to justify this expansive new interpretation.

NOTES

1. The dissent contended that confrontation and cross-examination are not effective ways to detect errors in scientific tests. Instead, the dissent suggested that new tests should be conducted, or the defendant may call his own expert "to explain to the jury the test's flaws and the dangers of relying on it . . . ," or the defendant may subpoena the government's analyst himself. Moreover, according to the dissent, defendants' objections to the results of the laboratory tests will be "formalistic and pointless" since there are rarely (as evidenced by the *Melendez-Diaz* case itself) any significant challenges made to the accuracy of such standardized, routine procedures.

The majority replied by pronouncing its view of the core concept of the Confrontation Clause:

> Converting the prosecution's duty under the Confrontation Clause into the defendant's privilege under state law or the Compulsory Process Clause shifts the consequences of adverse-witness no-shows from the State to the accused. More fundamentally, the Confrontation Clause imposes a burden on the prosecution to present its witnesses, not on the defendant to bring those adverse witnesses into court. Its value to the defendant is not replaced by a system in which the prosecution presents its evidence via *ex parte* affidavits and waits for the defendant to subpoena the affiants if he chooses. [557 U.S. at 324-25.]

2. Several types of government reports found to be nontestimonial under *Crawford* have been reclassified by courts applying *Melendez-Diaz*. Many certificates of no result (CNRs) have been found testimonial when they "are not routinely produced in the course of government business but are generated exclusively for use at trial." United States v. Martinez-Rios, 595 F.3d 581 (5th Cir. 2010). Other more routine and objective governmental reports have been found to be nontestimonial. United States v. Caraballo, 595 F.3d 1214 (11th Cir. 2010) (INS forms that record biographical information required of every entrant are nontestimonial); United States v. Mashek, 606 F.3d 922 (8th Cir. 2010) (records from local pharmacies that defendant had made frequent pseudoephedrine purchases, purportedly used to manufacture methamphetamine, are not testimonial).

3. Forensic reports other than drug analyses have been found testimonial, which requires the prosecution to produce the author of the report. Wood v. State, 299 S.W.2d 200 (Tex. Ct. App. 2009) (autopsy report); State v. Locklear, 681 S.E.2d 293 (N.C. 2009) (reports of nontestifying forensic pathologist and forensic dentist identifying the remains of the victim); State v. Dilboy, 2010 WL 1541447 (N.H. 2010) (blood and urine tests); Government of Virgin Islands v. Vicars, 340 Fed. App'x 807 (3d Cir. 2009) (physician's report of a rape examination); Commonwealth v. Loadholt, 923 N.E.2d 1037 (Mass. 2010) (ballistics certificate stating that a weapon was a "firearm" and that bullets were "ammunition").

b. Bullcoming v. New Mexico

Adhering closely to *Melendez-Diaz*, a new five-Justice majority of the Supreme Court held in Bullcoming v. New Mexico, 131 S. Ct. 2705 (2011), that a forensic report stating a defendant's blood alcohol content was the testimonial statement of the analyst who had run the underlying test and signed the report. As such, its use at trial without the appearance of the analyst as a witness violated Bullcoming's confrontation right. The New Mexico Supreme Court had acknowledged that the report was testimonial, but had held that in-court testimony from a knowledgeable laboratory official provided the defendant with an adequate opportunity for cross-examination in satisfaction of the *Melendez-Diaz* and *Crawford* standards.

The majority opinion, written by Justice Ginsburg and joined in its significant holdings by Justices Scalia, Thomas, Sotomayor, and Kagan, expressed no doubt that the analyst's certification of the test results, written for the purpose of proving a particular fact in court, was testimonial. That Justice Thomas agreed indicates that his "solemnity" and "formality" tests were passed despite the fact that the certification was not a sworn affidavit, as the report in *Melendez-Diaz* had been. The majority noted that the report also contained statements of the analyst about the procedures he had followed, and that the operation of the gas chromatograph machine generates at least some risk of human error. In footnote 6, which Justice Thomas did not join, the opinion applied the "primary purpose" test of *Davis*: "To rank as 'testimonial,' a statement must have a 'primary purpose' of 'establish[ing] or prov[ing] past events potentially relevant to later criminal prosecution.'"

The majority further held that the testimony of the surrogate witness could not fulfill the defendant's confrontation right for two reasons. First, the surrogate had not supervised or observed any of the testing involved in this case and could not have answered any questions on cross-examination about the particular test of Bullcoming's blood alcohol content; the surrogate could not be cross-examined on why the missing analyst was on "unpaid leave" from his job and was not himself testifying; and the surrogate did not assert his own independent opinion concerning the alcohol content of Bullcoming's blood. More importantly, the majority held, the Sixth Amendment does not itself suggest such an open-ended exception to its terms, nor should a court create such an exception because it believes that the underlying "values" of the confrontation clause are fulfilled:

> [T]he Clause does not tolerate dispensing with confrontation simply because the court believes that questioning one witness about another's testimonial statements provides a fair enough opportunity for cross-examination. [Id. at 2716.]

The *Bullcoming* opinion thus puts an end to speculation about whether the majority that followed Justice Scalia in *Melendez-Diaz* would survive the retirement of Justices Stevens and Souter. The dissenters in *Melendez-Diaz* dissented again, making the argument that the analyst in this case was even less of a "witness" against the defendant and played even less of a role in the generation of the inculpating evidence against him than had the analysts in *Melendez-Diaz*. Given the testimony of the surrogate witness concerning all of the laboratory's protocols and procedures, the dissenters rejected the majority's insistence that the analyst be available for cross-examination as a "hollow formality."

PROBLEM

8.83. Prosecution of Jones for unlawful possession of a firearm by a convicted felon. The prosecution offers a firearm, in a plastic bag with a tag attached to it, into evidence as an exhibit. To admit the exhibit, the prosecution must produce evidence sufficient to support a finding that the firearm was in the possession of Jones.

For the prosecution, Police Officer Green testifies as follows:

> On January 10, 2011, I arrested Jones in his apartment. I seized a firearm from his jacket pocket and placed it in a plastic evidence bag with a label that I wrote

identifying it as the firearm seized from Jones. Later that day, I took the firearm to the evidence storage room in the Police Department. I gave the plastic bag containing the firearm that I seized from Jones to the custodian of the storage room. The custodian wrote on a tag, and attached the tag on the plastic bag with the firearm in it. It is the regular and customary practice of the evidence custodian to fill out a property receipt for any type of evidence that is stored in the storage room and to state the source of the evidence.

Officer Green further testifies that she cannot identify the firearm offered by the prosecution as the weapon she seized from Jones. She acknowledges that the plastic bag does not have any label on it that she wrote. However, she recognizes the handwriting on the tag as the handwriting of the custodian. The custodian is now deceased.

The tag on the firearm reads:

PROPERTY RECEIPT:

Firearm received from Office Green.

DATE: January 10, 2010

SIGNED: A. Adams, Custodian

Is the receipt admissible to prove that the firearm offered by the prosecution is the firearm that Officer Green seized from Jones? Consider all possible objections.

8.84. Prosecution of defendant for murder. The state offers a qualified expert witness to testify to all of the following:

(1) The expert is employed by the state forensic laboratory. She herself obtained a sample of defendant's saliva for purposes of DNA testing. After performing the proper test procedures (extraction, amplification, detection of genetic type), the expert obtained a DNA profile of the defendant.

(2) The expert then performed the same proper test procedures on a blood sample, and obtained a DNA profile of the blood sample.

(3) According to Report A, written by a police forensic specialist, the specialist had retrieved this blood sample from the clothes of the murder victim and had delivered it to the state forensic laboratory for testing.

(4) The expert then compared the DNA profile of the blood sample to the defendant's DNA profile and declared that they match.

Would the expert's testimony be admissible under the Confrontation Clause? Would the police forensic specialist have to testify? What if the DNA profile of the blood sample had been obtained after testing at Cellmark Laboratory, a private testing lab? Could the expert rely on the profile obtained by Cellmark to declare a match?

NOTES

1. The dissent in *Bullcoming* also takes aim at the overall methodology of the Court's confrontation opinions since *Crawford*. The dissent noted the "weaving in and out" of concerns for reliability and for solemnity; the elusive distinction between a primary purpose of proving past facts and resolving an emergency; the failure to state a clear rule on what witnesses were required to render a scientific report admissible; the failure to command a clear set of common principles in applying *Crawford*; and in particular, the "amorphous" and "highly context-dependent" "combined approach" of *Bryant*, a majority opinion in which, it must be noted, all of the *Bullcoming* dissenters had joined.

The inability of the seven Justices in the *Crawford* majority to agree on a single definition of "testimonial" has led to the current state of doctrinal complexity and disarray. Perhaps the four dissenters are indicating that they have had enough of the definitionless limbo into which *Crawford* plunged the Court. The dissenters express some nostalgia for returning to the "basic purpose" of the confrontation clause: "to bar admission of out-of-court statements obtained through formal interrogation in preparation for trial" which may be unreliable, are untested, might not have been uttered at all, and might not have been true—a purpose that they believe did not apply to the lab report in this case.

2. The majority and dissent also engaged in a dispute over whether requiring the test analyst to appear in court was having disastrous practical consequences for governments' ability to prosecute. Both opinions cite data presented to the Court in *amicus* briefs, and in Part IV of the majority opinion, joined only by Justice Scalia, Justice Ginsburg takes note of a variety of ways in which the burden on prosecutors is and can be reduced. 131 S. Ct. at 2717-2719.

c. *Williams v. Illinois*

Several days after the release of the *Bullcoming* opinion, the Supreme Court granted certiorari in Illinois v. Williams, 939 N.E.2d 268 (Ill. 2010). Defendant Williams had been tried and convicted of rape in a bench trial, and the Illinois Supreme Court had upheld the conviction against a confrontation challenge. At trial, an expert witness testified for the prosecution, stating her opinion that there was a match between a DNA profile obtained from vaginal swabs retrieved from the victim of the sexual assault and a DNA profile from a blood sample previously obtained from the defendant Williams. The expert witness based her opinion on in-court testimony from the state forensic analyst who had obtained the DNA profile from the defendant's blood sample, and on the work that a private Cellmark lab had done in deducing a male DNA profile from the vaginal swabs.

The Cellmark lab report was not itself offered or admitted into evidence, presumably because it would have been found inadmissible under the Confrontation Clause holdings of *Melendez-Diaz* and *Bullcoming*. As stated above, Rule 703 can permit an expert to rely on inadmissible evidence as a matter of policy regarding the proper basis for an expert opinion. But other state supreme courts have rejected this strategy as a violation of the defendant's confrontation right if the testifying expert refers to the results of a missing analyst's tests. Commonwealth v. Bizanowicz, 945 N.E.2d 356, 365 (Mass. 2011).

Five Justices voted to uphold the ruling of the Illinois Supreme Court that the testimony of the prosecution's expert witness did not violate Williams' right to confrontation. Williams v. Illinois, 132 S. Ct. 2221 (2012). However, there was no majority agreement on the grounds for this result.

The Plurality Opinion in *Williams*. Justice Alito, joined by Chief Justice Roberts and Justices Kennedy and Breyer, found that although the prosecution's expert witness referred to the DNA profile obtained by Cellmark, this reference did not violate the confrontation standard established under *Crawford* and its progeny. Two grounds of analysis were relied on for this holding.

First, the plurality posed the question as set forth by Justice Sotomayor in *Bullcoming*: whether an expert witness could discuss the out-of-court statements of others if those statements themselves were not admitted as evidence. The plurality held as follows:

> When an expert testifies for the prosecution in a criminal case, the defendant has the opportunity to cross-examine the expert about any statements that are offered for their truth. Out-of-court statements that are related by the expert solely for the purpose of explaining the assumptions on which that opinion rests are not offered for their truth and thus fall outside the scope of the Confrontation Clause. Applying this rule to the present case, we conclude that the expert's testimony did not violate the Sixth Amendment. [132 S. Ct. at 2228.]

Justice Alito premised this holding on both common law practice and Rule 703, which permit expert witnesses to rely on facts about which they lack personal knowledge in forming their opinions. In addition, the Justice wrote, the Illinois and Federal Rules place no restriction on revealing such information to the judge in a bench trial. Most importantly, the plurality opinion justified this result by stating that the information revealed by the prosecution's witness — that "the matching DNA profile was 'found in semen from the vaginal swabs'" — was not admissible for the truth of the matter asserted but for a nonhearsay purpose.

> [T]hat fact was a mere premise of the prosecutor's question, and [the expert] simply assumed that premise to be true when she gave her answer indicating . . . a match between the two DNA profiles. There is no reason to think that the trier of fact took [the expert's] answer as substantive evidence to establish where the DNA profiles came from. [132 S. Ct. at 2236.]

Justice Alito also insisted that the expert's reference to the Cellmark report was offered

> not to prove the truth of the matter asserted in the report, i.e., that the report contained an *accurate* profile of the perpetrator's DNA, but only to establish that the report contained a DNA profile that matched the DNA profile deduced from petitioner's blood. [132 S. Ct. at 2240, emphasis added.]

These nonhearsay purposes, the plurality insisted, differentiated the expert's reliance on the Cellmark results from the use to which the reports admitted into evidence in *Melendez-Diaz* and *Bullcoming* had been put—to prove the truth of what they asserted. *Crawford*, the plurality stated, had held that the "Confrontation Clause applies only to out-of-court statements 'use[d] to establish[h] the truth of the matter asserted.'" 132 S. Ct. at 2240.

The second ground for the plurality's holding was that the Cellmark report was itself not a testimonial statement under the "primary purpose" test established in Davis v. Washington and applied in *Melendez-Diaz* and Michigan v. Bryant.

> It plainly was not prepared for the primary purpose of accusing a targeted individual. In identifying the primary purpose of an out-of-court statement, we apply an objective test. . . . We look for the primary purpose that a reasonable person would have ascribed to the statement, taking into account all of the surrounding circumstances.
>
> Here, the primary purpose of the Cellmark report, viewed objectively, was not to accuse petitioner or to create evidence for use at trial. When the ISP lab sent the sample to Cellmark, its primary purpose was to catch a dangerous rapist who was still at large, not to obtain evidence for use against petitioner, who was neither in custody nor under suspicion at that time. Similarly, no one at Cellmark could have possibly known that the profile that it produced would turn out to inculpate petitioner—or for that matter, anyone else whose DNA profile was in a law enforcement database. Under these circumstances, there was no "prospect of fabrication" and no incentive to produce anything other than a scientifically sound and reliable profile. [132 S. Ct. at 2243-2244.]

The plurality opinion then engaged in an almost explicit analysis of the risk of unreliability in such lab reports, both private and governmental, finding that risk to be very low. It further harked back to two losing arguments in *Melendez-Diaz*: First, that "if DNA profiles could not be introduced without calling the technicians who participated in the preparation of the profile, economic pressures would encourage prosecutors to forgo DNA testing and rely instead on older forms of evidence, such as eyewitness identification, that are less reliable" 132 S. Ct. 2228; Second, it opined that its holding "will not prejudice any defendant who really wishes to probe the reliability of the DNA testing done in a particular case because those who participated in the testing may always be subpoenaed by the defense and questioned at trial." Id.

Justice Thomas's Concurrence in the Judgment.   Justice Thomas concurred in the judgment of the plurality and its holding that there had been no confrontation violation in Williams's trial. But Justice Thomas decried the plurality's "flawed analysis" and adhered to his own particular definition of testimonial statements.

Justice Thomas explicitly disagreed with the plurality's nonhearsay theory concerning the expert's reference to the Cellmark report.

> In my view . . . there was no plausible reason for the introduction of Cellmark's statements other than to establish their truth. . . . There is no meaningful distinction between disclosing an out-of-court statement so that the factfinder may evaluate the expert's opinion and disclosing that statement for its truth. "To use the inadmissible information in evaluating the expert's testimony, the jury must make a preliminary judgment about whether this information is true." D. Kaye, D. Bernstein, & J. Mnookin, The New Wigmore: A Treatise on Evidence: Expert Evidence §4.10.1, p. 196 (2d ed. 2011) . . . [132 S. Ct. at 2256-2257.]

He also explicitly rejected the plurality's "new" primary purpose test requiring "'the primary purpose of accusing a targeted individual of engaging in criminal conduct.' . . . That test lacks any grounding in constitutional text, in history, or in logic." 132 S. Ct. at 2262. However, he then found no confrontation violation because "Cellmark's statements lacked the requisite 'formality and solemnity' to be considered 'testimonial.'" 132 S. Ct. at 2256. The Cellmark report differed from the reports in *Melendez-Diaz* and *Bullcoming*, he wrote, because they were neither attested to by the reporting analyst nor denoted as a "certificate." This distinction is "constitutionally significant," Justice Thomas believes, because "the scope of the confrontation right is properly limited to extrajudicial statements similar in solemnity to the Marian examination practices that the Confrontation Clause was designed to prevent." 132 S. Ct. 2260.

Justice Thomas, therefore, continues to insist that confrontation analysis be limited to identifying those out-of-court statements that are "functionally identical to live, in-court testimony, doing precisely what a witness does on direct examination." 132 S. Ct. at 2261, citing *Melendez-Diaz*.

Justice Kagan's Dissent.   Joined by Justices Scalia, Ginsburg, and Sotomayor, Justice Kagan argued in dissent that, without cross-examination of the Cellmark analyst who generated the DNA profile relied on by the prosecution's expert witness, the confrontation violation is "an open-and-shut case" under the Court's precedents. 132 S. Ct. at 2265.

The dissent first characterized the Cellmark report as identical to the report in *Bullcoming*

> was made to establish "some fact" in a criminal proceeding; . . . the results of forensic testing on evidence gathered by police; .. comparable title; similarly describes the relevant samples, test methodology and results; and likewise includes the signatures of laboratory officials. . . . So under this Court's prior analysis, the substance of the report could come into evidence only if Williams had a chance to cross-examine the responsible analyst. [132 S.Ct. at 2266-2267.]

And then Justice Kagan rejected the plurality's "nonhearsay" analysis of the use made of the Cellmark report:

> [F]ive Justices agree, in two opinions reciting the same reasons, that this argument has no merit: [The expert witness's] statements about Cellmark's report went to its truth, and the State could not rely on her status as an expert to circumvent the Confrontation Clause's requirements . . . [T]o determine the validity of the witness's conclusion, the factfinder must assess the truth of the out-of-court statement on which it relies. That is why the principal modern treatise on evidence variously calls the idea that such "basis evidence" comes in not for its truth, but only to help the factfinder evaluate an expert's opinion "very weak," "factually implausible," "nonsense," and "sheer fiction" . . . "to pretend that it is not being introduced for the truth of its contents strains credibility." [132 S. Ct. at 2268-2269.]

Justice Kagan also rejected the plurality's conclusion that the Cellmark report was not testimonial because its primary purpose was not focused on a "targeted individual."

> We have previously asked whether a statement was made for the primary purpose of establishing "past events potentially relevant to later criminal prosecution. . . ." None of our cases has ever suggested that, in addition, the statement must be meant to accuse a previously identified individual. [132 S. Ct. at 2274.]
>
> The expert witness at trial had acknowledged that all reports in this case were prepared for criminal investigation and eventual litigation. The plurality's attempt to characterize the Cellmark report as a response to an ongoing emergency (a rapist on the loose) was belied by the fact that the swabs were not sent to Cellmark until nine months following the attack.

Finally, Justice Kagan also explained why there is no good reason for such a "targeted individual" requirement: "[The] typical problem with laboratory analyses — and the typical focus of cross-examination — has to do with careless or incompetent work, rather than personal vendettas." 132 S. Ct. at 2274. The majority in *Melendez-Diaz* had also rejected a reliability justification for the admission of technical reports, noting serious deficiencies in forensic evidence used in criminal trials.

NOTES

1. What does the split of opinions in *Williams* mean for the future of the Confrontation Clause? The four plurality Justices dissented in *Melendez-Diaz* (in which they hinted at their readiness to overturn *Crawford*) and seem to be committed to evading the "testimonial" standard by all possible means. Justices Kagan and Sotomayor are aligned with Justices Scalia and Ginsburg in adhering to *Crawford*. One possibility is that Justice Thomas's views about the scope of the Confrontation Clause (endorsed by no other Justice) will control future outcomes, at least in cases before the Supreme Court. In other words, Justice Thomas will join with the *Williams* dissenters when he thinks there is sufficient formality or solemnity and with the plurality when he thinks there is not. Another possibility is that *Williams* provides no useful holding for lower courts beyond the particular facts of the case. This interpretation has been adopted by the Second Circuit. Noting that "[n]o single rationale disposing of the *Williams* case enjoys the support of a majority of the Justices," the court explained that the opinion does not "yield a single, useful holding to the case before us." United States v. James, 712 F.3d 79, 95 (2d Cir. 2013). Accordingly, the Court explained that it must therefore rely on pre-*Williams* precedent, including *Melendenz-Diaz* and *Bullcoming*.

2. Courts have reached different results on whether to characterize autopsy reports as testimonial. Compare United States v. James, supra (holding autopsy reports are non-testimonial) with United States v. Ignasiak, 667 F.3d 1217, 1231-1232 (11th Cir. 2011) (holding autopsy reports are testimonial).

5. The Definition of "Testimonial" Statements after *Crawford*: Statements Not Made to Law Enforcement

In *Crawford* and subsequent cases, the Supreme Court left open a question that had caused considerable confusion among lowers courts: whether, and under what circumstances, statements made to persons other than law enforcement personnel can be testimonial. The Court addressed that issue in Ohio v. Clark, 135 S. Ct. 2173 (2015).

a. Child Statements: Ohio v. Clark

Clark involved statements by a three-year-old boy to preschool teachers. After being questioned by a teacher about his injuries, the boy (L.P.) made statements identifying his mother's boyfriend (the defendant) as his abuser. The child did not testify at the defendant's trial, after being declared incompetent to do so. The child's statements to his teachers were admitted as evidence at trial, and the defendant was convicted. The Ohio Supreme Court concluded that introducing the child's statements at trial violated the Confrontation Clause, in part, because Ohio law required mandatory reporting of such statements to law enforcement. The United States Supreme Court reversed, with every Justice concluding that the statements are not testimonial. Justice Alito wrote the majority opinion for the Court. Justice Scalia (joined by Justice Ginsburg) and Justice Thomas concurred in the result and each wrote separate opinions.

According to the Court, statements made to persons other than law enforcement may still be testimonial. Applying the "primary purpose" test to the facts of this case, however, the Court held that the child's statements are not testimonial. Justice Alito explained:

> We are therefore presented with the question we have repeatedly reserved: whether statements to persons other than law enforcement officers are subject to the Confrontation Clause. Because at least some statements to individuals who are not law enforcement officers could conceivably raise confrontation concerns, we decline to adopt a categorical rule excluding them from the Sixth Amendment's reach. Nevertheless, such statements are much less likely to be testimonial than statements to law enforcement officers. And considering all the relevant circumstances here, L. P.'s statements clearly were not made with the primary purpose of creating evidence for Clark's prosecution. Thus, their introduction at trial did not violate the Confrontation Clause.
>
> L. P.'s statements occurred in the context of an ongoing emergency involving suspected child abuse. When L. P.'s teachers noticed his injuries, they rightly became worried that the 3-year-old was the victim of serious violence. Because the teachers needed to know whether it was safe to release L. P. to his guardian at the end of the day, they needed to determine who might be abusing the child. . . .
>
> There is no indication that the primary purpose of the conversation was to gather evidence for Clark's prosecution. On the contrary, it is clear that the first objective was to protect L. P. At no point did the teachers inform L. P. that his answers would be used to arrest or punish his abuser. L. P. never hinted that he intended his statements to be used by the police or prosecutors. And the conversation between L. P. and his teachers was informal and spontaneous. The teachers asked L. P. about his injuries immediately upon discovering them, in the informal setting of a preschool lunchroom and classroom, and they did so precisely as any concerned citizen would talk to a child who might be the victim of abuse. This was nothing like the formalized station-house questioning in *Crawford* or the police interrogation and battery affidavit in *Hammon*.

> L. P.'s age fortifies our conclusion that the statements in question were not testimo-
> nial. Statements by very young children will rarely, if ever, implicate the Confrontation
> Clause. [Id. at 2181-2182.]

Justice Alito's opinion also explained that historical practices may be relevant for
determining whether a particular type of statement falls outside the scope of the
Confrontation Clause:

> As a historical matter, moreover, there is strong evidence that statements made in cir-
> cumstances similar to those facing L. P. and his teachers were admissible at common
> law. See Lyon & LaMagna, The History of Children's Hearsay: From Old Bailey to
> Post-Davis, 82 Ind. L. J. 1029, 1030 (2007); see also id., at 1041-1044 (examining child
> rape cases from 1687 to 1788); J. Langbein, The Origins of Adversary Criminal Trial
> 239 (2003) ("The Old Bailey" court in 18th-century London "tolerated flagrant hearsay
> in rape prosecutions involving a child victim who was not competent to testify because
> she was too young to appreciate the significance of her oath."). And when 18th-century
> courts excluded statements of this sort, see, e.g., King v. Brasier, 1 Leach 199, 168 Eng.
> Rep. 202 (K. B. 1779), they appeared to do so because the child should have been
> ruled competent to testify, not because the statements were otherwise inadmissible.
> See Lyon & LaMagna, supra, at 1053-1054. It is thus highly doubtful that statements
> like L. P.'s ever would have been understood to raise Confrontation Clause concerns.
> [Id. at 2182.]

In his concurrence, Justice Scalia argued that, with regard to historical practices, the
burden is on the prosecution to demonstrate that a particular type of hearsay was
historically admitted without cross-examination. In his concurrence, Justice Thomas
continued to adhere to his conception of testimonial statements as requiring sufficient
formality or solemnity.

NOTES

1. In *Clark*, the majority stated that statements by small children will "rarely, if
ever, implicate the Confrontation Clause." This will be true in situations similar to
the circumstances in *Clark*, and it may also be true if one focuses solely on the declarant's perspective. If one focuses on the perspective of the questioner, however, the
primary purpose of the questioning may be to generate evidence for use in a criminal
prosecution. See Paul F. Rothstein, Ambiguous-Purpose Statements of Children and
Other Victims of Abuse Under the Confrontation Clause, 44 Sw. U. L. Rev. (2015).

2. The Court in *Clark* rejected the idea that the teachers' mandatory duty to
report abuse made the statements testimonial: "It is irrelevant that the teachers' questions and their duty to report the matter had the natural tendency to result in Clark's
conviction. The statements at issue in *Davis* and *Bryant* supported the defendants'
convictions, and the police always have an obligation to ask questions to resolve an
ongoing emergency." What do you think of this analogy?

3. When children do testify at trial they may do so by closed circuit television,
pursuant to the narrow exception established in Maryland v. Craig, 497 U.S. 836
(1990), to protect the physical and psychological well-being of the child. When they

do so testify, this counts as an in-court appearance for purposes of admitting their other hearsay statements, so long as the specific finding of necessity mandated in *Craig* is satisfied. United States v. Turning Bear, 357 F.3d 730, 738 (8th Cir. 2004).

b. Medical Interviews and Examinations

Statements made to medical personnel also raise difficult questions regarding the scope of the Confrontation Clause. When medical interviews and examinations involve nongovernment employees, courts have engaged in a fact-intensive analysis to determine whether the questioning is the "functional equivalent of a police interrogation." See Hernandez v. State, 946 So. 2d, 1284-1285 (Fla. App. 2007) (court applied a four-factor test that included (1) the legal status of the examining entity as an arm of law enforcement, (2) the involvement of law enforcement in the production of the statements, (3) the purpose of the exam conducted by the nurse, and (4) the absence of any ongoing emergency). In *Hernandez*, the court focused on the purpose of the examiner in conducting the interview:

> Ms. Shulman regularly appeared in court to give testimony about the results of the examinations that she performed on children. She told the jury that she had been qualified as an expert in the area of child assault medical examinations "[w]ell over a hundred times" and had testified as an expert witness in Hillsborough, Pinellas, Pasco, and Dade counties. Based on Ms. Shulman's background and her focus on forensic issues, there is no doubt that Ms. Shulman reasonably expected that she would be appearing in court to testify against Mr. Hernandez about the results of her examination and the statements made by the child and her parents during the course of the examination.

See also United States v. Bordeaux, 400 F.3d 548, 556 (8th Cir. 2005) ("The purpose of the interview (and by extension, the purpose of the statements) is disputed, but the evidence requires the conclusion that the purpose was to collect information for law enforcement."). Other courts have focused on the declarant's knowledge and purpose. See, e.g., Blount v. Hardy, 337 Fed. App'x 271 (4th Cir. 2009) (holding that admission at trial of out-of-court statements made by a three-year-old victim to therapists, where the victim did not know or have reason to know that her statements would be used against the defendant at trial, did not violate defendant's Confrontation Clause rights). Courts have also recognized that statements may have multiple purposes. In State ex rel. Juvenile Dept. of Multnomah County v. S.P., 215 P.3d 847 (Or. 2009), the court found that an organization whose purpose was the diagnosis and treatment of child abuse served as a "proxy" for police, a fact that weighed in favor of finding that the victim's statements were testimonial. Other courts have found that statements made during medical examinations that result in immediate treatment, without the involvement of police, are for the primary purpose of treatment and are nontestimonial. See, e.g., People v. Cage, 155 P.3d 205, 218-220 (Cal. 2007).

c. Other Types of Nontestimonial Hearsay

The Supreme Court asserted in *Crawford* that there are certain types of hearsay statements, corresponding to specific hearsay exceptions, that are simply not testimonial "by their nature" and thus not within the scope of the Confrontation Clause. 541 U.S. at 1367. The Court repeated this assertion in *Bryant*, 562 U.S. at 362 n.9 ("Many other exceptions to the hearsay rules . . . rest on the belief that certain statements are, by their nature, made for a purpose other than use in a prosecution."). Courts have relied on this seeming "categorical" approach. For example, statements not intended as assertions (such as questions) may escape the definition of hearsay and thus the reach of the confrontation clause. Other such types mentioned in *Crawford* and *Bryant* include casual remarks to acquaintances, some business and public records, and co-conspirator statements in furtherance of a conspiracy.

Some lower courts have adopted a categorical approach. See, e.g., Doan v. Carter, 548 F.3d 449 (6th Cir. 2008) (statements of victim about abuse to friends and family were nontestimonial); United States v. King, 541 F.3d 1143 (5th Cir. 2008) (co-conspirator statements made in furtherance of a conspiracy not testimonial).

6. Testimonial Statements That Satisfy the Confrontation Right

Under *Crawford*, testimonial statements can satisfy the confrontation right in two ways: (1) if the declarant testifies as a witness at trial and thus is available for cross-examination by the defendant, and (2) if the declarant is unavailable at trial but the defendant has previously had the opportunity to cross-examine the declarant. Existing case law has established the parameters of these requirements, and the Court in *Crawford* gave no indication that their meaning was to change.

a. The Declarant Testifies

The Supreme Court stated in *Crawford* that

[w]hen the declarant appears for cross-examination at trial, the Confrontation Clause places no constraints at all on the use of his prior testimonial statements. See California v. Green, 399 U.S. 149 (1970). The Clause does not bar admission of a statement so long as the declarant is present at trial to defend or explain it. [541 U.S. at 59, n.9.]

The prior statements must, of course, fall within a hearsay exception; the confrontation right may not coincide precisely with the hearsay rule.

The issue of the adequacy of cross-examination of the declarant, such as when the declarant is unable to recall the events that are the subject of the hearsay statement, appears to be well settled under United States v. Owens, 484 U.S. 554 (1988), as discussed on pages 489-90, supra. United States v. Ghilarducci, 480 F.3d 542, 549 (7th Cir. 2007) (declarant did not claim a "total loss of memory regarding the events"); United States v. Harty, 476 F. Supp. 2d 17, 25 (D. Mass. 2007) (witness's lack of recollection of reasons why he had selected defendant's photograph did not violate confrontation clause); Yanez v. Minnesota, 562 F.3d 958, 963 (8th Cir. 2009) (holding that a child witness's faulty memory did not deprive defendant of the ability to cross-examine where the defendant could remind the jury of the witness's "inability to recall the abuse or any details related to the criminal acts and thus call into question her reliability.").

b. Unavailability and Prior Opportunity for Cross-examination

The Court in *Crawford* stated that the Framers would not have permitted the admission of testimonial statements *unless* the declarant "was unavailable to testify and the defendant had had a prior opportunity for cross-examination." 541 U.S. at 57. Prior cross-examination can thus satisfy the confrontation right, if the declarant is unavailable at trial.

Unavailability. Typically, the federal or state requirements of "unavailability" under the hearsay rule, such as FRE 804(a), will be used to determine unavailability for Confrontation Clause purposes as well, with one addition. In Barber v. Page, 390 U.S. 719 (1968), the Supreme Court held that the Sixth Amendment requires the prosecution to demonstrate in court that it had made a good-faith effort to produce the hearsay declarant, even if its effort was unsuccessful. There is also Supreme Court precedent that does not permit the prosecution to offer a testimonial statement when the unavailability of the declarant was caused by the prosecution's own negligence. Motes v. United States, 178 U.S. 458, 474 (1900). The *Crawford* opinion does not mention *Barber* or *Motes*, although in the circumstances of Crawford's exercise of his spousal privilege, there was no need to do so. State courts have help that prior standards of good faith and reasonable diligence are still applicable after *Crawford*. United States v. Tirado-Tirado, 563 F.3d 117, 120 (5th Cir. 2009).

Prior Opportunity for Cross-examination. Where the defendant had strong motive and a full opportunity to cross-examine the declarant at a prior trial, the requirements of *Crawford* have been found to be satisfied. Romans v. Berghuis, 2007 U.S. Dist. LEXIS 88905 (E.D. Mich. 2007).

In Ohio v. Roberts, the Supreme Court approved the admission of statements made by the declarant at a preliminary hearing when the defendant's counsel had engaged in cross-examination. However, as we stated on page 600, a criminal defendant may lack motivation to cross-examine witnesses vigorously at preliminary hearings, due to an inability to prepare adequately and a reluctance to reveal strategy. There are also states in which preliminary hearings are truncated proceedings, and cross-examination is fruitless because the court will not weigh the credibility of witnesses. See People v. Fry, 92 P.3d 970 (Colo. 2004). See also Beasley v. State, 258 S.W.3d 728, 731-735 (Ark. 2007) (exclusion of testimony at bond reduction hearing where defendant did not have strong motive to cross-examine the witness). The Court left open the question of whether opportunity alone, or merely cursory questioning, would satisfy the confrontation requirement. The Court in *Crawford* wrote in terms of "opportunity" but did not discuss the issue fully.

7. Exceptions to the Requirement of Confrontation

The *Crawford* opinion mentioned two possible exceptions to the confrontation requirement under which testimonial statements could be admitted. The first is an exception for dying declarations, grounded on the historical admission of such statements during the time when the right to confrontation was developed. 541 U.S. at 56, n.6. The second is an exception based on a defendant's "forfeiture" of the right to confrontation based on wrongful conduct that has made the declarant unavailable to testify. 541 U.S. at 62. In *Clark*, the Court also reaffirmed that historical evidence indicating that a type of statement was typically admitted without cross-examination might create further exceptions to the confrontation requirement. 135 S. Ct. at 2180 ("the Confrontation Clause does not prohibit the introduction of out-of-court statements that would have been admissible in a criminal case at the time of the founding.").

a. Dying Declarations

In *Crawford*, *Giles*, and *Bryant*, the Supreme Court has suggested that dying declarations, even if testimonial, may be admitted as an historically incorporated exception to the requirement of confrontation. Michigan v. Bryant, 131 S. Ct. at 1151, n.1. State supreme courts and other lower courts have admitted dying declarations as non-testimonial. People v. D'Arcy, 226 P.3d 040, 971-973 (Cal. 2010); Commonwealth v. Nesbitt, 829 N.E.2d 299, 309-312 (Mass. 2008); Gilmore v. Lafler, 2010 U.S. Dist. LEXIS 59488, at *26-31 (E.D. Mich. 2010) (on habeas review, held that admitting a dying declaration is not contrary to Supreme Court precedent).

b. Forfeiture by Wrongdoing

As explained on page 615, supra, a theory of "forfeiture" of a defendant's confrontation right developed from the holding in United States v. Mastrangelo, 693 F.2d 269 (2d Cir. 1982), that this right may be waived by the defendant's misconduct in making the hearsay declarant unavailable. The Supreme Court accepted this doctrine explicitly in *Crawford*:

> The rule of forfeiture by wrongdoing (which we accept) extinguishes confrontation claims on essentially equitable grounds; it does not purport to be an alternative means of determining reliability. [541 U.S. at 62.]

And again in *Davis*, the Court explicitly approved the use of this doctrine against defendants who act "in ways that destroy the integrity of the criminal-trial system." See page 652, supra.

A key issue in forfeiture doctrine, however, is whether the *purpose* of the defendant's wrongdoing must be *to prevent the declarant from testifying against the defendant*. This requirement is explicit in the hearsay exception for forfeiture, FRE 804(b)(6). But immediately following *Crawford*, several courts held such a purpose was not necessary to justify forfeiture of the constitutional right to confrontation. See, e.g., United States v. Garcia-Meza, 403 F.3d 364, 370-371 (6th Cir. 2005) (holding that the motive for the defendant's wrongdoing is irrelevant, since "the forfeiture doctrine's equitable basis, as enunciated in *Crawford*, prevent[s] the defendant from benefiting in any way from his wrongdoing . . .").

Dispensing with the "purpose" requirement expanded forfeiture doctrine considerably. The expanded doctrine was frequently applied in cases involving domestic violence, such as in *Garcia-Meza* where the defendant was charged with the murder of his wife. The court upheld admission of the wife's statements to police, made after being assaulted by her husband five months previously, that her husband was becoming violent toward her because she had spoken to a former boyfriend. Since many victim statements in domestic violence and child abuse cases are found to be "testimonial" and would have been excluded under *Crawford*, the forfeiture exception became an important component of these prosecutions.

However, in Giles v. California, 554 U.S. 353 (2008), the Supreme Court rejected this broadened interpretation of constitutional forfeiture doctrine. In that case, Dwayne Giles was charged and tried for the murder of his ex-girlfriend Brenda Avie. Giles claimed self-defense, asserting that Avie was jealous and violent. On the day of her death, she threatened him and charged at him, causing him to close his eyes and shoot to defend himself. At trial, the prosecution introduced statements that Avie had made to a police officer responding to a domestic violence report three weeks earlier. Avie had accused Giles of choking her, punching her, and threatening to kill her with a knife if she ever cheated on him. These statements describing threats of physical injury were admissible hearsay under a California statute. Giles was convicted of first degree murder. On appeal, the California Supreme Court upheld Giles's conviction. The court assumed that Avie's statements were testimonial but held that they did not violate the Confrontation Clause because *Crawford* had recognized a doctrine of forfeiture, and that Giles's intentional act had made Avie unavailable to testify.

The Majority Opinion in *Giles*.   The Supreme Court granted Giles's petition for *certiorari* to determine whether this broadened scope of constitutional forfeiture doctrine was legitimate: "We held in *Crawford* that the Confrontation Clause is 'most naturally read as a reference to the right of confrontation at common law, admitting only those exceptions established at the time of the founding . . . .' We therefore ask whether the theory of forfeiture by wrongdoing accepted by the California Supreme Court is a founding-era exception to the confrontation right." 554 U.S. at 358. The majority opinion, authored by Justice Scalia, thus focused on whether the early common law forfeiture doctrine had required proof that the defendant's purpose in making a declarant unavailable was to prevent the declarant from testifying.

The Court concluded that forfeiture doctrine required at common law, and thus must require today, that defendant's purpose in making a declarant unavailable was to prevent his testimony.

> In sum, our interpretation of the common-law forfeiture rule is supported by (1) the most natural reading of the language used at common law; (2) the absence of common-law cases *admitting* prior statements on a forfeiture theory when the defendant had not engaged in conduct designed to prevent a witness from testifying; (3) the common law's uniform exclusion of unconfronted inculpatory testimony by murder victims (except testimony given with awareness of impending death) in the innumerable cases in which the defendant was on trial for killing the victim, but was not shown to have done so for the purpose of preventing testimony; (4) a subsequent history in which the dissent's broad forfeiture theory has not been applied. The first two and the last are highly persuasive; the third is in our view conclusive. [Id. at 368.]

Six Justices joined in this conclusion as to the proper scope of forfeiture doctrine. The Court vacated the judgment of the California Supreme Court and remanded the case for further proceedings on the question whether defendant had the requisite intent to prevent Avie from reporting abuse or cooperating with authorities when he killed her.

The Concurring Opinion of Justices Souter and Ginsburg. Justices Souter and Ginsburg joined in a separate concurrence[20] that agreed that the majority opinion was right about the scope of the confrontation right at the time of the Framing and ratification of the Sixth Amendment:

> [It] was subject to exception on equitable grounds for an absent witness's prior relevant, testimonial statement, when the defendant brought about the absence with intent to prevent testimony. It was, and is, reasonable to place the risk of untruth in an unconfronted, out-of-court statement on a defendant who meant to preclude the testing that confrontation provides. [Id. at 379.]

But for Justices Souter and Ginsburg, the equitable, rather than the historical, basis for forfeiture doctrine was primary. It was the defendant's intent to prevent testimony that made it fair to place this risk of unconfronted hearsay on the defendant through forfeiture of the confrontation right. Otherwise, they seemed to say, admitting a victim's statement in a murder trial to prove the murder solely on the ground that the defendant probably committed the killing was too close to "question begging":

> The only thing saving admissibility and liability determinations from question begging would be (in a jury case) the distinct functions of judge and jury: judges would find by a preponderance of evidence that the defendant killed (and so would admit the testimonial statement), while the jury could so find only on proof beyond a reasonable doubt. Equity demands something more than this near circularity before the right to confrontation is forfeited, and more is supplied by showing intent to prevent the witness from testifying. [Id.]

The Dissenting Opinion in *Giles*. Three dissenters, Justices Breyer, Stevens, and Kennedy, argued against the majority's conclusion on the historical record. They claimed that "the language that courts have used in setting forth the exception is broad enough to cover the wrongdoing in the present case (murder) and much else besides" and that the basic equitable "purposes and objectives" of forfeiture doctrine—to prevent the defendant from gaining an advantage from his own evil practices—applied to Giles. Their principle dispute with the majority focused on the element of "intent" that had been found against Giles, which they considered sufficient to prove that it was fair to require forfeiture of his confrontation right. Justice Breyer's dissent strongly objected to the majority opinion's seeming substitution of *purpose* or *motive* for the element of intent.

As to the historical record found in seventeenth-, eighteenth-, and nineteenth-century evidence law, the dissent claimed that

---

20. Justices Thomas and Alito also wrote brief concurrences stating their doubts that Avie's statements to the police were "testimonial" at all, but acknowledging that this issue was not before the Court.

a review of the cases set forth [by the majority] makes clear that no case limits forfeiture to instances where the defendant's *purpose* or *motivation* is to keep the witness
away. . . . Rather . . . , the relevant cases suggest that the forfeiture rule would apply
where the witness' absence was the *known consequence* of the defendant's intentional
wrongful act. [Id. at 389-392.]

NOTES AND QUESTIONS

1. Only by reading the full majority and dissenting opinions can one appreciate the difficulty of analyzing the historical record in order to determine the precise
scope of forfeiture doctrine "at the time of the Framing and the adoption of the Sixth
Amendment." When the historical record is in doubt, the Justices must turn to constitutional, evidentiary, and common law policies to interpret the confrontation right.

2. The *Giles* opinions acknowledge that *Crawford* has a special impact on cases
involving vulnerable victims who will not or cannot testify, or who cannot be effective
as witnesses. Some commentators believe that police practices will change to accommodate the change in law, in particular by creating more informal questioning opportunities that do not cry out "interrogation"; by creating more opportunities for pretrial
cross-examination in hearings or depositions; and by working closely with fearful witnesses to enable them to testify. Articles on the effects of *Crawford* on these types
of cases include Rothstein, supra, David A. Sklansky, Hearsay's Last Hurrah, 2009
Sup. Ct. Rev. 1 (2010); Robert P. Mosteller, Crawford v. Washington: Encouraging
and Ensuring the Confrontation of Witnesses, 39 U. Rich. L. Rev. 511 (2005); Tom
Lininger, Prosecuting Batterers After *Crawford*, 91 Va. L. Rev. 747 (2005); Celeste E.
Byrom, The Use of the Excited Utterance Hearsay Exception in the Prosecution of
Domestic Violence Cases After Crawford v. Washington, 23 Rev. Litig. 409 (2005).

H. REFLECTION ON THE HEARSAY RULE

Critics of the hearsay rule are plentiful. Their criticisms focus primarily on the complexity of the categorical structure of the exemptions and exceptions and on whether
such an elaborate structure is necessary to fulfill hearsay policy. This, in turn, raises the
deeper question of what hearsay policy should be in the context of modern litigation.

1. The Traditional Goals of Hearsay Policy

We presented the traditional formulation of the policy excluding hearsay in Section
A of this chapter: A witness's oath, demeanor, and cross-examination are thought to
reduce testimonial dangers and make in-court testimony *more* reliable than out-of-
court statements. A somewhat stronger version of this policy would state that hearsay is inherently weak evidence, that juries cannot properly evaluate it, that verdicts

should not be based on hearsay, and that excluding hearsay protects against fraudulent evidence. A thorough analysis and critique of this traditional policy can be found in Paul S. Milich, Hearsay Antinomies: The Case for Abolishing the Rule and Starting Over, 71 Or. L. Rev. 723 (1992).

Based on this view of the weaknesses of hearsay evidence, the two primary justifications for admitting it through categorical exceptions and exemptions are *reliability* and *necessity*: The goal of traditional hearsay policy is to admit hearsay that is more reliable than run-of-the-mill hearsay, or that seems necessary to the rational resolution of litigated disputes. This "reliability theory" of the hearsay exceptions presumes that reliable hearsay can be identified in advance by identifying those circumstances that may reduce some risks of insincerity, to a lesser extent risk of loss of memory, and only occasionally a risk of inaccurate perception.

2. The Reliability Theory Does Not Work

It is easy to criticize the reliability theory of the traditional hearsay rule. We have done so implicitly throughout this chapter by pointing out where the factual requirements of the categorical exceptions and exemptions fail to fulfill their goal. Much seemingly unreliable hearsay is admitted, and it may be that much that seems reliable is excluded. Even the Advisory Committee's Introductory Note to Article VIII of the Federal Rules of Evidence acknowledges these criticisms:

> The solution evolved by the common law has been a general rule excluding hearsay but subject to the numerous exceptions under circumstances supposed to furnish guarantees of trustworthiness. Criticisms of this scheme are that it is bulky and complex, fails to screen good from bad hearsay realistically, and inhibits the growth of the law of evidence.

A similar critique is found in Michael Seigel, Rationalizing Hearsay: A Proposal for a Best Evidence Hearsay Rule, 72 B.U. L. Rev. 893, 912-913 (1992):

> Sadly, our current system employs the *least rational* means of evaluating the reliability of hearsay evidence: preconceived categories. Each categorical exception is theoretically supported by an initial inductive hypothesis about human behavior that, if true, reduces the probability that an out-of-court statement falling within the category suffers from one of the hearsay dangers. Accordingly, any such statement is deemed reliable and, therefore, admissible. However, even assuming the accuracy of the categories' foundation hypotheses, an out-of-court statement's reliability is simply not measurable through what is, in effect, an unidimensional test. A statement may be grossly unreliable despite the fact that it falls within the bounds of a categorical exception, in light of other information in the case. This more specific information may demonstrate that the category's behavioral assumption is inapplicable to the particular statement at issue; or the statement may present a danger not accounted for by the assumption underlying the specific exception; or other more definitive evidence might make the accuracy of the hearsay suspect. At the same time, the categorical exceptions are not comprehensively inclusive; the facts surrounding excluded hearsay may indicate that it is reliable even though it fails to meet the strictures of any given exception.

The trouble is, there is not much agreement on an alternative approach to determining the reliability of the hearsay that should be admitted.

3. A Rule of Discretion

One option is to change the rule to a Rule 403-type of balancing test, whereby the trial judge would be given discretion to admit hearsay that the judge thinks is more probative because it is more credible, and to exclude hearsay that is less probative because less credible. Under the categorical approach, the credibility of hearsay evidence is not to be weighed by the judge. The advantages of a discretionary rule were forcefully argued in Jack B. Weinstein, The Probative Force of Hearsay, 46 Iowa L. Rev. 331 (1961). A discretionary approach was also described, but rejected, in the Advisory Committee's Introductory Note:

> Admissibility would be determined by weighing the probative force of the evidence against the possibility of prejudice, waste of time, and the availability of more satisfactory evidence. The bases of the traditional hearsay exceptions would be helpful in assessing probative force. . . . Procedural safeguards would consist of notice of intention to use hearsay, free comment by the judge on the weight of the evidence, and a greater measure of authority in both trial and appellate judges to deal with evidence on the basis of weight. The Advisory Committee has rejected this approach to hearsay as involving too great a measure of judicial discretion, minimizing the predictability of rulings, enhancing the difficulties of preparing for trial, adding a further element to the already over-complicated congeries of pretrial procedures, and requiring substantially different rules for civil and criminal cases.

According to Professor Seigel, a discretionary rule would vest considerably more authority over the outcomes of trials in the judge:

> Simply put, the power to exclude evidence is the power to determine the outcome of cases. If truly discretionary—in other words, if not subject to appellate review—this power is too great to vest in individual trial judges. Moreover, absent clear guidelines defining reliable hearsay, the exclusionary process would be akin to a game of roulette. On the other hand, imposing clear guidelines and enforcing them through appellate review would cause the standard of reliability to evolve slowly into a set of rules. The final outcome would be the recreation of what existed prior to codification of the rules of evidence: an ad hoc common law hearsay regime. [Seigel, 72 B.U. L. Rev. at 914.]

Another option has been suggested by Judge Richard Posner, in a recent concurring opinion:

> What I would like to see is Rule 807 ("Residual Exception") swallow much of Rules 801 through 806 and thus many of the exclusions from evidence, exceptions to the exclusions, and notes of the Advisory Committee. The "hearsay rule" is too complex, as well as being archaic. Trials would go better with a simpler rule, the core of which would be the proposition (essentially a simplification of Rule 807) that hearsay evidence should be admissible when it is reliable, when the jury can understand its strengths and limitations, and when it will materially enhance the likelihood of a correct outcome. [United States v. Boyce, 742 F.3d 792, 802 (2014) (Posner, J., concurring).]

4. Abolition

The more extreme option would be to abandon the search for reliability and abolish the rule of exclusion altogether. The admission of hearsay would be governed only by its relevance under FRE 401 and its risks of FRE 403 dangers, which should not include concerns about the credibility of the declarant. Under a truly *abolitionist* regime, exclusion would depend solely on the judge's estimation of Rule 403 dangers that might negatively affect the jury's ability to evaluate the credibility of hearsay.

What might be the consequences of an abolitionist regime? An article by Professor Eleanor Swift, Abolishing the Hearsay Rule, 75 Cal. L. Rev. 495 (1987), predicted that potentially admissible hearsay would raise three kinds of problems: (1) statements by unidentified persons about whom very little is known, so that the jury has little factual basis on which to apply its own general knowledge and experience; (2) statements that bear obvious risks, in particular a declarant's motive to misrepresent, requiring the jury to make hard choices between conflicting inferences; and (3) statements presented in documentary form without any witness to supply information about them, thus permitting the proponent to avoid presenting either the declarant or a foundation witness for cross-examination.

The Advisory Committee rejected an abolitionist regime on grounds that it "has been unconvinced of the wisdom of abandoning the traditional requirement of some particular assurance of credibility as a condition precedent to admitting the hearsay declaration of an unavailable declarant."

5. Reformulating Hearsay Policy

a. Is There a Need for a Hearsay Rule in Modern Civil Litigation?

In his article, The Evolution of the Hearsay Rule to a Rule of Admission, 76 Minn. L. Rev. 797, 797-801 (1992), Professor Ronald Allen describes why the hearsay rule of exclusion is no longer important in civil litigation due to prevalent use of discovery depositions, party admissions, and the numerous exceptions and exemptions. His concern is that its continued existence imposes too great a cost:

> My instinct is that . . . [g]iven all the inroads into the rule, it no longer can seriously be contended that the rule contributes in any robust way to substantial justice.[21] To be sure, an occasional case will turn on hearsay, and occasionally justice might be done because of exclusion for reason of hearsay, but against this must be balanced the probability that without a hearsay rule the evidence would have been excluded under some other rule, most likely relevancy. Further to be considered in the balance are cases of injustice resulting from the exclusion of hearsay as well as the astounding cost of maintaining the rule.

---

21. I put aside Confrontation Clause questions in criminal cases.

The cost of maintaining the rule is not just a function of its contribution to justice. It also includes the time spent on litigating the rule. And of course that is not just a cost voluntarily borne by the parties, for in our system virtually all the cost of the court—salaries, administrative costs, and capital costs—are borne by the public. As expensive as litigation is for the parties, it is supported by an enormous public subsidy. Each time a hearsay question is litigated, the public pays. The rule imposes other costs as well.

Enormous time is spent teaching and writing about the hearsay rule, which are both costly enterprises. In some law schools, students spend over half their time in evidence classes learning the intricacies of the hearsay rule, and . . . enormous academic resources are expended on the rule.

Like other social practices, the hearsay rule should be required to pull its own freight; only if its costs are justified should it be maintained.

b. Regulation Premised on the Excesses of the Adversary System

One justification for regulating the admission of hearsay derives from the excesses of the adversary system of proof.

> Consider for instance, the possibility that a hearsay declarant might be a bad witness, or . . . might be shown incredible on cross-examination. A party might prefer to offer the [hearsay statement] rather than to call the declarant to the stand. In effect, such a choice would be a deliberate choice to mislead the factfinder, because the hearsay would not be accompanied by information that would enable the jury to evaluate the evidence properly. [Craig R. Callen, Foreword to the First Virtual Forum: Wallace Stevens, Blackbirds and the Hearsay Rule, 16 Miss. Col. L. Rev. 1, 10 (1995).]

Hearsay policy could be premised on mitigating this adversarial tactic. Professor Seigel proposes a principle for admitting hearsay only when it is the "best evidence" available from a particular declarant source. Seigel, 72 B.U. L. Rev. at 930-938. Professor Swift proposes that admission of hearsay be based on the production of a foundation witness who would be able to present information that the jury needs to evaluate the hearsay statement. Eleanor Swift, A Foundation Fact Approach to Hearsay, 75 Cal. L. Rev. 1339 (1987).

c. Notice-based Admission in Civil Cases: Reliance on the Adversary System

Several proposals have been made to admit hearsay more freely in civil cases, premised on sufficient notice to the opponent. Professor Roger Park recommends a notice-based residual exception that makes no provision for reliability screening by judges in: A Subject Matter Approach to Hearsay Reform, 86 Mich. L. Rev. 51 (1987). The proponent of hearsay would state whether the declarant is available or unavailable. Then, the opponent could demand that the declarant be produced and examined by the proponent and be available for cross-examination. In certain circumstances, the trial judge would be authorized to shift costs of production to the opponent. In the view of Professor Milich, all that is needed is notice of an intent to offer information from a source *not* to be called to testify at trial. The notice would include the name and location of the source so that the opponent could interview, depose, or produce the source if desired. Milich, 71 Or. L. Rev. at 774-776.

d. Why Hearsay Should Be Treated Differently in Criminal Cases

The confrontation clause does place a constraint on hearsay reform in criminal cases. Most legislators, courts, attorneys, and commentators agree that the criminal defendant's interest in personal liberty does weigh more heavily in favor of a require- ment that the prosecution's use of hearsay be limited. Eileen A. Scallen, Constitutional Dimensions of Hearsay Reform: Toward a Three-Dimensional Confrontation Clause, 76 Minn. L. Rev. 623 (1992). The approach in *Crawford* is to identify what might be thought of as the most *unreliable* categories of hearsay—testimonial statements—and to exclude them unless confrontation is or has been provided. These same risks of unreliability were identified previously by Professor Park in recommending that a cat- egorical approach to admitting hearsay in criminal cases be maintained:

> Generally, out-of-court statements relevant to criminal cases are made, in the broadest sense, with a view to litigation, or at least with knowledge that the legal process may be brought to bear on the matter being described. . . . Moreover, many of the declar- ants' statements are taken by police, often under interrogation—a process essential in producing investigative leads but not calculated to elicit spontaneous statements that spring from a spirit of candor. [Park, A Subject Matter Approach to Hearsay, 86 Mich. L. Rev. at 94-97, 99.]

Under *Crawford*, prosecutors will remain constrained in their use of hearsay even should the hearsay rule itself be changed and further liberalized.

6. A Rebuttal

Many of the hearsay rule's critics seem to focus on the logical and conceptual messi- ness of the hearsay exceptions and exemptions. The world of trials they seem to envi- sion would be largely the same with a reformed or abolished hearsay rule. Hearsay statements would continue to represent only bits and pieces of the overall mass of evi- dence offered in a trial, and the only change is that more of them would be admitted. But consider the following question. The hearsay rule goes hand-in-hand with FRE 602, the firsthand knowledge requirement. How do you enforce a firsthand knowl- edge requirement without a hearsay rule? Viewed this way, the problem is not one of admitting more of the sort of hearsay statements currently offered in trials, but rather of replacing firsthand witnesses with hearsay declarants on a routine basis—perhaps going so far as to entirely replace live witnesses with paper submissions. Finding and presenting firsthand witnesses is one of the "costs" of litigating under the hearsay rule, and parties have strong incentives to avoid that cost.

Try to imagine on what principle you could still implement a preference for first- hand witness testimony without a hearsay rule. You might try to do so with some vari- ation of the best evidence rule: A witness with personal knowledge must be presented instead of hearsay if that witness is reasonably available. Or rather than categorically preferring firsthand testimony, judges could require the most probative available evidence, again under a variant of the best evidence rule or under FRE 401/403 to enforce a broad policy of requiring the most probative evidence. See Dale A. Nance, The Best Evidence Principle, 73 Iowa L. Rev. 227 (1988) (advocating such a principle). Or, as Judge Posner has proposed, FRE 807 could be used to "swallow much of Rules 801 through 806," to allow "reliable" hearsay on a case-by-case basis. But then you would see parties constantly litigating the meaning of "availability," or "reliability," converting questions that might have had clear enough answers under the hearsay rules into occasions for more extended litigation. The additional litigation, in turn, would likely create tremendous pressure to create a new set of various categorical convenience-and-reliability-based exceptions—just as has happened with the hearsay rule itself.

Arguably, all exclusionary evidence rules could be replaced by FRE 403-type discretion, not just hearsay. The problem with such ad hoc, case-by-case approaches to admissibility is that they lack any semblance of the regularity and predictability that the law usually demands. Is it any less conceptually messy to bury the arguable inconsistencies of the hearsay exceptions under the purely discretionary approach of FRE 403? The most predictable result of such an approach would be the reemergence of codified or common law rules to the effect that FRE 403 requires exclusion of certain types of evidence. (Arguably, FRE 404 is an example of this.) Perhaps too few, or too simple, rules generate as much litigation as too complex or too many rules: As long as there are cases and lawyers, there will be arguments that this case is different from the one contemplated by the general rule.

7. Conclusion

This debate over hearsay reform should convince you of at least one thing: The general rule excluding hearsay evidence creates significant tensions with some important values that underlie our system of trial proof: reliance on the inferential reasoning of lay factfinders, adversarial control of proof, and relaxed judicial control. The hearsay rule and its exceptions are far from perfectly calibrated to admit the most and exclude the least reliable and probative hearsay statements. Despite the liberalization of proof under the Federal Rules of Evidence, hearsay is treated with suspicion and remains subject to judicial regulation.

At the same time, none of the commentators discussed above favors total abolition of the general rule against hearsay offered against criminal defendants, suggesting that the hearsay rule also serves fundamental values. While the right to confront adverse witnesses is stronger in criminal cases, and gets express constitutional protection there, a premise of the confrontation principle is that the presentation of live witnesses, and the ability to cross examine them, is a fundamental part of due process of law. Consider the difference between a witness swearing out an affidavit, putting his signature (even under penalty of perjury) at the bottom of a document written by a lawyer; and that same witness showing up in court, swearing to tell the truth in the solemnity of the courtroom in front of the judge and jury, testifying in his own words, and then being tested by cross-examination. It is certainly possible as an empirical matter that more accurate modes of factfinding are possible; but arguably reformers bear a heavy burden of persuasion to demonstrate that significant alteration of the hearsay rule would serve better.

ASSESSMENTS

A-8.1. FRE 801(a)-(c).   The most accurate definition of hearsay is:
- A   a statement made out of court by a person not testifying in court.
- B   an assertion made out of court by which its proponent purports to prove the truth of the matter asserted.
- C   a person's out-of-court communication—verbal and nonverbal, explicit or implied—aiming to prove the truth of the matter that the person intended to communicate.
- D   none of the above.

A-8.2. FRE 801(a)-(c).   Witness W testified in a criminal trial that, on May 1, 2015, she saw the defendant parking his car in a garage featuring a sign "The Main Street Garage." This testimony is offered to prove that the defendant was in the Main Street Garage on May 1, 2015. Not hearsay.

A-8.3. FRE 801(a)-(c).   To prove that D had a motive to kill V, P calls D's friend to testify that she heard V threatening to ruin D's business and reported to D about this threat. This testimony is not hearsay.

A-8.4. FRE 801(a)-(c).   A traveler contracts pneumonia after a three-hour bus trip through upstate New York in January. He sues the bus company for the cost of his hospitalization, claiming that he got sick because the driver failed to keep the bus adequately heated. The driver testifies that two passengers took off their sweaters midway through the trip. This testimony is hearsay.

A-8.5. FRE 801(a)-(c).   To defend himself against robbery charges on the grounds of duress, D testifies that an anonymous caller threatened to kill him if he refuses "to do the job" with the bank robbers. D's testimony about the caller's threat is admissible hearsay.

A-8.6. FRE 801(d).   To prove that Donald conspired with Edgar to kidnap Victor and demand ransom from Victor's family, the prosecution produces a wiretapped note allegedly e-mailed by Edgar to his girlfriend. This e-mail reads as follows: "Donald and I will soon get Victor. Don't forget to open the bank account I told you about. E." To make this e-mail admissible, the prosecution only needs to properly authenticate it.

A-8.7. FRE 801(a)-(c) and the Sixth Amendment to the U.S. Constitution. In a murder trial in which D and E appear as codefendants, the prosecution introduces E's confession that also implicates *D*. This evidence is admissible against *E* alone, and the judge must instruct the jury to ignore it in deciding whether to convict *D*.

A-8.8. FRE 803(1) & (2). Defendant Jack Jordan is being tried for arson as a result of a fire that destroyed his clothing store and the apartments above it. The prosecution claims that Jack employed his brother Mark and friend Thomas Telford to commit the deed and gave them a key to the store, which had not been broken into. The fire was ablaze by 11:00 P.M. and, apparently, Telford remained at the scene. He was told by tenants exiting the building that there might be other people trapped inside. At 2:00 A.M., Telford knocked on the window of his friend Larry's apartment, appeared "all hyped up" and "nervous" according to Larry, and told Larry that "Mark and I lit a building for Jack." The prosecution offers Telford's statement in evidence, and Jordan's counsel objects that it is hearsay. The objection should be:

   A. Overruled, because Telford is describing an event, the arson, while perceiving it.
   B. Overruled, because Telford was probably "hyped up" and "nervous" due to a startling event—having unintentionally probably injured or killed people in the arson fire—and is likely still under the stress of excitement.
   C. Sustained, because Telford is expressing remorse about unintentionally injuring or killing people in the arson fire, and remorse suggests reflection, which undercuts the inference that he was continuously under the stress of excitement.
   D. Sustained, because Telford's statement does not relate to the startling event.

A-8.9. FRE 803(3). In a breach of contract case, in order to prove a lack of mutual assent, the defendant David D'Amico calls a witness to testify: "As soon as he finished reading the contract, David turned to me and said, 'I don't understand a word of this legal jargon.'" The plaintiff's counsel objects that the statement is hearsay. The objection should be:

   A. Overruled, because the statement is not offered for the truth of the matter asserted.
   B. Overruled, because it is a statement of state of mind, relevant to show a lack of agreement to the terms of the contract.
   C. Sustained, because the statement is one of belief offered to prove the fact believed, that the contract was filled with jargon.
   D. Sustained, because the statement is offered to prove the truth of the contents of the written document.

A-8.10. FRE 803(4). Paul Preston is suing National Motor Corporation ("NMC") for personal injuries arising out of an auto accident in which his "Bounder" sports utility vehicle rolled over while making a tight turn on a highway entrance ramp. Preston claims that a design defect in the Bounder makes it prone to rollover accidents. To prove his injuries, and rebut the defendant's anticipated contention that he was intoxicated at the time he was driving, Preston offers into evidence his medical records from the emergency room where he was treated immediately after the accident. The records state, "Patient reports nausea, dizziness, and intermittent loss of

consciousness. Patient states that he has consumed no alcohol in the past 24 hours."
Do the records fit within FRE 803(4)?

A. No, because we don't know who took down the information.
B. No, because the relevant portion is the statement about alcohol consumption,
   which is unreliable, since anyone involved in a car accident will know he has
   an incentive to claim that he has not consumed alcohol.
C. Yes, but only the symptoms, and not the statement about alcohol consumption.
D. Yes, because the entire statement was probably made for, and reasonably pertinent to, diagnosis and treatment.

A-8.11. FRE 803(5).   Mark Whitman, an executive of Pharmacorp, worked as
an government informant during the FBI's investigation of Pharmacorp for violation of antitrust laws in pricing its drug, Vimmex. At the FBI's direction, Whitman
kept a written diary in which he made notes of events and conversations relating to
Pharmacorp's pricing of Vimmex. At trial, Whitman testifies that he faithfully made
the diary entries at the end of each day while the events and conversations were fresh
in his mind, and that he tried to be as accurate as possible. From time to time on the
witness stand, when Whitman testifies that he "can't remember" or "can't recall all
the details," the prosecutor asks him to read pertinent portions of the diary aloud, to
the jury. The defense objects to this reading from the diary. The objection should be:

A. overruled, because the witness's memory can be refreshed with anything, including inadmissible matter.
B. overruled, because the diary qualifies as a recorded recollection and is properly admitted by reading it into the record.
C. sustained, because there has been no showing the Whitman's memory is exhausted, and indeed he remembers some things.
D. sustained, because Whitman was a government informant when he made diary entries, making them inherently untrustworthy.

A-8.12. FRE 803(6).   Mary Martina is suing Jan Johnson for personal injuries
resulting from an automobile accident. As part of her case, Mary calls Frank Williams,
a bystander who observed the accident. He testifies that Jan ran a red light and collided with Mary. As part of her defense, Jan offers a properly authenticated police
report, which contains the following statement: "Bystander Frank Williams stated
that Mary ran red light." Which of the following are the best grounds for refusing to
admit Williams's statement through the police report?

A. Police accident reports are not made as a regular practice by the police organi-
   zation.
B. Police reports are made for purposes of litigation.
C. Williams does not have a business duty to report.
D. All of the above are equally strong grounds for denying admission as a business
   record.

A-8.13. FRE 803(8).   In the *Johnson* case, each correctional officer prepared a
CDC 115 Report of his own observations of the incident involving inmate Johnson.

These reports may lead to officer or inmate discipline. Suppose that a state law rule identical to FRE 803(8) applies. The prosecution offers Walker's CDC 115 Report to prove Walker's version of the incident. Does the report qualify for admission under the public records exception?

   A. No, because Walker should be classified as "law enforcement personnel" for purposes of the 803(8)(A)(ii) exclusion.
   B. No, because the CDC report deals with Walker's own conduct and could be used to discipline him; because he is an interested party, his report should be excluded as untrustworthy.
   C. Yes, because CDC 115 reports are routine housekeeping matters under FRE 803(8)(A)(i).
   D. A and B are arguably correct, but C is not.

A-8.14. FRE 804(b)(1).   David Bond and his parents have sued David's treating physicians and their practice group for medical malpractice in failing to diagnose David's extremely rare form of encephalitis. Defendants noticed a deposition of plaintiffs' expert witness, Dr. Lakeman, whose test of David's cerebral spinal fluid was positive for this disease whereas defendants' test, administered one day previously, was negative. At trial, Dr. Lakeman is unavailable and plaintiffs seek the admission of his deposition pursuant to FRE 804(b)(1). Defendants object that the deposition is inadmissible hearsay. The objection should be:

   A. Sustained, because the defendants did not have a "similar motive" to develop Lakeman's testimony during pretrial discovery as they have at trial.
   B. Sustained, because the deposition was not an adversarial proceeding.
   C. Overruled, because the defendants had an opportunity and similar motive to discredit Lakeman's opinion at the deposition.
   D. Overruled, because defendants initiated the deposition process, and so the resulting testimony can be used against them.

A-8.15. FRE 804(b)(3).   Cosimo Demasi sued the Whitney Trust & Savings Bank for $6,500 dollars that the plaintiff claimed the bank held in a joint savings account that he maintained with his wife. The bank defended on the ground that all but $700 had been withdrawn by the plaintiff's daughter with the consent of Mr. or Mrs. Demasi. A judgment for the defendant was reversed on appeal, and before the new trial Mrs. Demasi sought to withdraw the $700 that the bank conceded remained in the account. In order to receive the money, the bank required that Mrs. Demasi sign an affidavit indicating that she had consented to the prior withdrawals. Mrs. Demasi signed the affidavit, withdrew the $700, and died before the second trial began. At the retrial, the bank offers her affidavit.

TRUE or FALSE: The statement should be admitted under FRE 804(b)(3).

A-8.16. FRE 804(b)(3).   Raymond Ochoa is charged with conspiracy to commit mail fraud for filing a false insurance claim on his automobile, which he falsely reported as stolen. The prosecution learned that Ochoa's former tenant, Dave McLaughlin, had put Ochoa in touch with a "chop shop," which would help him dispose of his allegedly stolen car. McLaughlin was approached by an FBI agent who told McLaughlin that he would benefit from talking to the FBI. McLaughlin made statements to the agent describing his role in the conspiracy and implicating Ochoa in the plan to dispose of the car and make the false claim. On the very next day, when the FBI attempted to serve McLaughlin with a subpoena, the agents were told by McLaughlin's current landlord that he had left town "for Maryland" with all his belongings.

TRUE or **FALSE**:   The statement should be admitted under FRE 804(b)(3).

A-8.17. FRE 804(b)(6).   Return to problem A-8.16. The FBI agent also visited McLaughlin's employer looking for him. He learned that McLaughlin had stopped coming to work but was owed his last paycheck. On the day after the FBI's visit, McLaughlin actually called the employer to ask for his paycheck. When he hung up, the employer used caller ID and determined that the call was made from Ochoa's home phone number. Phone records later revealed that seven phone calls were made from Ochoa's phone number to McLaughlin's employer during the next two days. McLaughlin then apparently disappeared and was never found, despite good-faith efforts by the government. May the government use McLaughlin's hearsay statements against Ochoa pursuant to FRE 804(b)(6)?

A. Yes, because Ochoa probably helped McLaughlin disappear.
B. Yes, because McLaughlin is unavailable and the government made good faith efforts to find him.
C. No, because there is no evidence that Ochoa knew McLaughlin was going to try to disappear or helped him do so.
D. No, because the government is relying entirely on hearsay statements of Ochoa's employer.

A-8.18. FRE 807.   David Dixon has been charged with conspiracy to sell and with selling heroin. Two alleged co-conspirators, Brown and Green, were granted immunity and were prepared to testify against Dixon. Since Green had a long history of involvement with drugs and several drug-related convictions, the prosecution planned to make Brown the star witness. Brown, however, died of a heart attack several days before the trial. At Dixon's trial the prosecution authenticates and offers into evidence a letter from Brown to his mother, telling her that he is feeling sick, that he thinks he is about to die, and that he wants to confess to her. The letter then describes his drug dealings with Dixon. The prosecution offers this letter in evidence.

TRUE or **FALSE**: The court should exclude the letter.

ANSWERS

A-8.1 The best answer is **C**. A is false because it omits the critical part of the hearsay definition: To be considered hearsay, an out-of-court statement must be offered to establish its truth. Furthermore, A also fails to acknowledge that intentionally assertive conduct can be hearsay as well. B is better than A, but it still fails to include intentionally assertive conduct in the definition of hearsay. Answer C, on the other hand, offers a definition that includes every aspect of hearsay. For that reason, C is the best answer, and D is false.

A-8.2. True. "The Main Street Garage" is an out-of-court statement of the garage owners. This statement, however, is not offered to prove the garage's location on Main Street. Rather, it is offered to prove the name of the business, and for that reason isn't hearsay. Other parts of W's testimony implicate no out-of-court statements and thus can't be considered hearsay as well.

A-8.3. True. V's out-of-court statement threatening to ruin D's business is offered to show its effect on the listener (D) rather than its truth. Hence, it isn't hearsay.

A-8.4. False. The passengers' conduct indicated that the bus was heated, but they took their sweaters off in order to feel cooler rather than to communicate to someone that the bus was heated. This conduct was not intentionally assertive and it isn't hearsay for that reason.

A-8.5. False. D's testimony is admissible *nonhearsay* because it cites an out-of-court statement containing a threat to prove the statement's effect on D as part of his defense of duress (as in the classic British case, Subramaniam v. Public Prosecutor [1956] 1 W.L.R. 965).

A-8.6. False. Here, Edgar's statement is offered to prove its truth about the facts of the parties' conspiracy to kidnap Victor and demand ransom from his family. Hence, it is hearsay. The statement is potentially admissible under the co-conspirator exception to the hearsay rule, FRE 801d(2)(E). To make it admissible, however, it would not be enough to authenticate Edgar's e-mail pursuant to FRE 901(a). Edgar's statement could only be admitted if the prosecutor offers independent evidence to confirm "the existence of the conspiracy or participation in it," as required by FRE 801d(2).

A-8.7. False. In a regular "multiple purpose" situation, evidence admissible for one purpose but not for another goes in subject to the court's limiting instruction pursuant to FRE 105. Here, however, E's confession—admissible against E alone—has a strong and potentially unconstitutional spillover effect on D, who cannot cross-examine E, in violation of Due Process and D's Sixth Amendment right to confront witnesses. For that reason, the Supreme Court held that such confessions cannot be admitted into evidence as a matter of constitutional law. Bruton v. United States, 391 U.S. 123 (1968).

A-8.8. FRE 803(1) & (2). The best answer is probably **B**, but C is also a very good answer. Starting with the wrong answers: A is wrong because the three-hour passage of time is probably too long for the contemporaneity requirement of FRE 803(1)'s present sense impression, and it's arguable that his statement is not describing an event, but rather reporting historical (here causal) facts about it. D is wrong because the statement clearly "relates to" the startling event. B is a good answer because learning that there were people in the building was a startling event, and it is easily imaginable that a person could be under stress from that event continuously for at least three hours. But C is a good answer for the reasons stated in the answer. The problem is based on United States v. Tocco, 135 F.3d 116 (2d Cir. 1998), where the court had no trouble in admitting this statement as an excited utterance. There must also be sufficient proof of Telford's personal knowledge that the job was done "for Jack." The circumstantial facts that the defendant's brother was also involved (proved by the contents of the statement) and that the two arsonists had a key to the premises were deemed sufficient to indicate the probable involvement of "Jack," the store's owner.

A-8.9. FRE 803(3). The best answer is **B**, for the reasons stated. David's lack of understanding is a relevant mental state experienced at the moment of making the statement. Answer A is incorrect, because the statement asserts a fact—David's lack of understanding—that has to be true to be relevant. C is incorrect, because whether the contract contains jargon is not the relevant point: What matters is whether David understood it. D is wrong because the point of the statement is to prove David's state of mind of understanding the document: The contents of the document are relevant here for the nonhearsay purpose of effect on the listener. (And in the case overall, the contract is relevant as a legally operative fact, another nonhearsay purpose.)

A-8.10. FRE 803(4). The best answer is **D**. The relevant statement is the one about lack of alcohol consumption, which is pertinent to diagnosis and treatment of most conditions, especially with symptoms like those reported here. Therefore, C is wrong. A is not a good answer, because the rule does not specify proof of the identity of the medical professional or her particular job description. Obviously some medical professional put it in the hospital record. B is wrong because reliability is not an independent criterion of admissibility: Like all the categorical exceptions, reliability is built into the other factual requirements, which are satisfied here.

A-8.11. FRE 803(5). The best answer is **B**. The problem provides a complete foundation for a recorded recollection, 803(5), which can be read into the record where, as here, the witness testifies and his memory is incomplete. A is wrong because there is no indication that the refreshing memory technique is being used, and a witness cannot read from the document used to refresh, but must testify from his refreshed memory. C is wrong because, unlike the refreshing recollection technique, FRE 803(5) requires only that the witness's memory be less than full and accurate. D is not the best answer because there is no trustworthiness exclusion to recorded recollection, and courts routinely allow notes made in anticipation of litigation as recorded recollections.

A-8.12. FRE 803(6). The best answer is **C**. Numerous cases have held that bystanders do not have a business duty to report under FRE 803(6) (or even a legal duty to report, under FRE 803(8)). Police departments tend not to make it a routine practice to verify witness statements before recording them; on the contrary, standard practice is to take down all witness statements, and evaluate their veracity later. A is wrong, however, because making police reports is a routine practice. B is arguable, but not the best answer, because the presumption of untrustworthiness applies to records made by parties with an interest in the litigation; presumably, the police would be neutral as between parties to an accident. (B would be a stronger argument in a criminal case, however.) Because A is wrong, and B is a weaker answer than C, D cannot be correct.

A-8.13. FRE 803(8). The best answer is **D**. A and B both offer solid reasons for excluding the report. Although there is some debate about how far the definition of "law enforcement" extends, it is clear in the *Johnson* case that the guards were acting as police officers within the prison, with power to arrest and to report misconduct leading to punishment. Therefore, A is probably correct. B is also correct for the reason stated. C is not a good answer: Reporting on misconduct, crimes, accidents, and the like is not a matter of "routine housekeeping." FRE 803(A)(i) includes things like time cards and payroll records.

A-8.14. FRE 804(b)(1). The best answer is **C**. The purposes of taking an adverse witness deposition are to discover facts, preserve testimony, and discredit adverse testimony. Parties are generally on notice that depositions may be used where witnesses become unavailable. And a tactical decision to save cross-examination material for trial is a calculated risk that should not be held against the opposing party. A devastating cross-examination of an expert witness in particular can undermine the opposing party's case—so the defendant's motive was there. Thus A is wrong. B is wrong because depositions are adversarial proceedings—both parties are represented, and may question the witness. D is nonsensical; there is no hearsay exception allowing statements to be used against the party who discovered them in pretrial proceedings.

A-8.15. FRE 804(b)(3). **FALSE**. The statement appears against Demasi's pecuniary interest only if taken out of context. The facts make clear that signing the statement was in her short-term pecuniary interest in getting the money. Although it was arguably against her long-term interest, the motive was clearly mixed, and Demasi judged the benefits of taking the smaller sum now as outweighing the cost of giving up the uncertain larger sum in the future. The fact that we might have weighed the cost-benefit differently does not make the statement against interest.

A-8.16. FRE 804(b)(3). **FALSE**. To begin with, there is insufficient evidence to find McLaughlin unavailable. The landlord's mere say-so is not enough to establish that McLaughlin has left the state, and even if he had, there must be some effort to locate him and attempt to obtain his voluntary compliance or to take his deposition where he is. Even if McLaughlin were unavailable, it is far from clear that his statement is against interest. Since he himself was involved in the criminal activity, McLaughlin's cooperation was currying favor. His mixed motive statement arguably had a predominant self-serving motive.

A-8.17. FRE 804(b)(6). The best answer is **C**. The rule requires the government to show by a preponderance of the evidence that Ochoa procured or acquiesced in McLaughlin's unavailability. While circumstantial evidence is permissible, the mere fact that Ochoa housed McLaughlin is probably not enough—there is not even any evidence that Ochoa was "hiding" McLaughlin at his place. Thus, A is not a good answer. B is not a good answer; while unavailability is a required element, B neglects the "procured or acquiesced in" element. The government's diligence goes to unavailability, not to "procured or acquiesced in." D is wrong because hearsay evidence is permissible under 104(a), which is the governing standard for the factual elements of this and all other hearsay exceptions.

A-8.18. FRE 807. We believe "**TRUE**" is the better answer. First, the circumstantial guarantees of trustworthiness of this letter stem from its "near miss" to the dying declaration and statement against interest exceptions. But those exceptions offer some of the most dubious reliability guarantees of all the hearsay exceptions, for the reasons discussed in the text. It is just as likely that Brown would want to minimize his bad conduct in "confessing" to his mother by shifting blame onto Dixon, as that he would speak truthfully. Not only is his motive mixed, but his illness might affect the accuracy of his memory. Second, the need for the evidence and interests of justice do not strongly favor use of FRE 807 here. The purpose of the rule is not to allow the offering party to sanitize its case or present evidence that is more persuasive. "More probative" should be understood to mean a stronger logical connection to the facts, rather than less subject to impeachment. Furthermore, a court should always prefer live witness testimony to hearsay on the same point where, as here, admissibility comes down to a comparison between the two.

CHAPTER NINE

LAY OPINIONS AND EXPERT WITNESSES

Considering the emphasis in trials of presenting "facts," you may be surprised by the amount of testimony that can be categorized as "opinion." In this chapter, we examine the various issues involved in offering opinions as evidence. Ordinary fact witnesses offering firsthand knowledge under FRE 602 are permitted to offer opinions under certain circumstances. The term "lay" witness is used in the context of opinion testimony to refer to a so-called layman, a person who lacks specialized knowledge and relies on commonsense reasoning. The term is roughly equivalent to a "percipient" witness. We examine FRE 701, which addresses opinions by lay witnesses, in Section A of this chapter.

A person who testifies on the basis of specialized knowledge is identified as an expert by the law of evidence. In the remaining sections of this chapter, we examine FRE 702-706, the rules covering expert witnesses. The most significant part of the testimony by an expert witness is categorized as opinion testimony.

A. LAY OPINIONS

1. FRE 701

RULE 701.   OPINION TESTIMONY BY LAY WITNESSES

If a witness is not testifying as an expert, testimony in the form of an opinion is limited to one that is:

(a) rationally based on the witness's perception;

(b) helpful to clearly understanding the witness's testimony or to determining a fact in issue; and

(c) not based on scientific, technical, or other specialized knowledge within the scope of Rule 702.

2. Explanation of FRE 701

FRE 701 makes clear that opinion testimony by lay witnesses is admissible. Superficially, and in the traditional language of the common law, lay witnesses were expected to testify to what they observed (i.e., "facts") rather than to any inferences, summaries, or conclusions about facts. Such inferences, summaries, and conclusions were grouped together as "opinions." Despite its surface presentation as limiting opinion testimony, FRE 701 in effect relaxes a common law tendency to disfavor opinion testimony. The rule recognizes that opinions are unavoidable features of how people conceptualize and describe perceived facts, and thus generally allows lay opinion testimony, subject to three sensible qualifications.

Rationally Based on Perception.   FRE 701(a)'s requirement that a lay opinion must be "rationally based on the witness's perception" simply expresses the idea that FRE 602 still applies to the lay witness testimony. Allowing opinion testimony does not authorize lay/percipient witnesses to depart from the requirement of personal knowledge. This requirement prevents unfounded opinions, and ensures that an opinion stems from firsthand knowledge of case-specific facts rather than speculation or free-floating generalizations about the world.

Helpful to the Trier of Fact.   FRE 701(b) requires that the opinion be helpful to the factfinder in "clearly understanding the witness's testimony or to determining a fact in issue." This rule is designed to prevent witnesses from usurping the jury's function by drawing inferences or conclusions that the jury can and should draw on its own. It also tends to force witnesses to stick to the facts to the extent possible.

Not Based on Expert Knowledge.   FRE 701(c) draws the boundary between lay and expert opinion. Lay opinions must be based on common knowledge. If an opinion requires "scientific, technical or other specialized knowledge" it can't be given by a lay witness. Only a witness qualified as an expert can give such opinions, as we discuss further in the expert witness sections. For now, note that "other specialized knowledge" is an extremely broad catchall, that refers to anything outside common knowledge.

3. FRE 701: Practical Applications

Consider the following two items of testimony. (1) The defendant grinned when he signed the contract. (2) The defendant was happy when he signed the contract. Both statements could be characterized as an opinion. After all, what is a grin? It is a facial expression involving the contraction of certain muscles in the face, in which the corners of the mouth turn up, the lips part, the corners of the eyes crinkle, etc. The word "grin" is a conclusion or summary of those details, together with several others not mentioned, and thus is an opinion of sorts.

But you can see the problem. If a judge were to conclude that "grin" was an impermissible opinion and direct the witness to specify the underlying facts, it would tax the narrative abilities of the witness to an excessive degree. And there might be a corresponding loss of information: The detailed description of a grin given in the previous paragraph is probably less informative than the well-understood word "grin." The opinion, if it is an opinion, is helpful to the jury both directly and indirectly by allowing witnesses to testify in natural speech. Contrast the statement that the witness was "happy." Here it is easier to imagine the witness supplying more underlying detail. (He smiled, pumped his fist in the air, and shouted "woo-hoo!") The underlying detail is more informative and vivid, and the conclusion (if relevant) is left to the jury. For reasons that we'll explore further, a court is much more likely to disallow the "happy" opinion than the "grin" opinion, and indeed, the "grin" testimony might not be deemed an opinion at all.

The difference between an opinion that a court will decide to analyze under FRE 701 and a fact that will not be deemed to trigger FRE 701 is a matter of . . . well . . . opinion. In the following subsections, we'll start with a sort of "field guide" to recognizing opinions, and then drill down analytically to provide you with tools to distinguish fact and opinion, and to determine when opinions are likely to be held inadmissible.

a. Recognizing Opinions

It may be useful to identify three broad categories of opinions. These categories are not spelled out in the evidence rules or case law, but may be useful in thinking analytically about opinion testimony. Also the three categories should not be deemed rigidly distinct, since they may tend to overlap somewhat.

Estimates. A witness might estimate the speed a car is going, the duration of time of an event, or a distance between two points. You might also think of estimates as including verbal approximations of sense perceptions: for instance, "it smelled like something was burning." Courts frequently deem such estimates to be admissible opinions, provided that there is ESSF of a firsthand opportunity to observe.

Summaries. An opinion might take the form of a summary of a number of more detailed items of data. In the example above, characterizing a facial expression as a "grin" can be understood as a summary of many composite facts, even if those composite facts are difficult to articulate. FRE 405(a) and 406 allow testimony of character and habit in the form an "opinion." As used there, "opinion" refers to the witness's summary of his own firsthand observations about the person's behavior. In the *Johnson* trial, when one of the guards described Johnson's behavior as "combative," he was offering an (objectionable) opinion that in effect summarized a number of specific behaviors under a single label. Likewise, describing someone as drunk is a summary label applied to specific observations—slurred his speech, walked unsteadily, reeked of alcohol, spoke loudly and offensively, etc.

Inferences. An opinion might be classified as an inference when it plausibly fills in a missing fact, adds an extra fact, or draws a conclusion from more detailed facts. Inferences also go beyond merely labeling a set of facts and take them a step further to imply or explain causes or motivations. For example, calling a set of facial expressions a "grin" is a summary; concluding that the grinning person is "happy" is an inference: It adds a plausible extra fact.

A Fourth Category: Subjective Feelings or Judgments Are Not FRE 701 Opinions. A person's subjective likes, dislikes, tastes, preferences, and feelings about things or persons are called "opinions" in common parlance. Ironically, these types of "opinion" will not be categorized as FRE 701 opinions at all. They may well be relevant as motivations for relevant conduct, or to show the bias of a witness, but their subjectivity takes them out of the purview of FRE 701. A witness's estimate, summary, or inference that another person has a particular subjective feeling, or about the extent of such a feeling, may trigger FRE 701, however.

b. Fact versus Opinion

By its terms, FRE 701 governs testimony by lay witnesses "in the form of an opinion," as opposed to a fact. Thus, the core problem in deciding whether FRE 701 applies to an item of testimony is the difficulty in distinguishing a "fact" from an "opinion. All facts are "opinions" at some level, because any assertion of fact requires an estimate, summary, or inference.

Consider the chair you're probably sitting on right now. (If you're standing, or lying down, or riding an exercycle, then humor us and picture a chair.) To assert that "this is a chair" seems like a straightforward example of a fact: It's simple, clear, objective, not fairly debatable. Yet labeling that thing a "chair" is certainly the result of a summary of the discrete characteristics of chairs. You could break down the chair's description into more specific facts: It is a piece of furniture with four legs, a back, and a surface for sitting on.

Undoubtedly, in most cases, a witness would be allowed to testify about the chair without triggering FRE 701. A witness to a bar fight might testify that the defendant "threw a chair at" the plaintiff. But imagine, instead, a civil suit for breach of contract by a client against a furniture designer. The client contracted for a set of dining room chairs, and paid a large sum of money to the designer. The client received a set of beautiful objects, each with a very narrow seat and back, and so delicate that one of them broke under the weight of a 200-pound dinner guest. As plaintiff, the client argues that what was delivered was not a chair. In this example, the case turns on disputed opinions about what a chair is.

This example gives you a significant insight into the fact/opinion distinction. There is no clear analytical distinction or definitional line between the two. Instead, the fact/opinion distinction is a pragmatic or functional one that depends on the application of two sliding scales. First, how specific is the assertion? The more specific the assertion, the more likely it is to be characterized as a fact. Second, how close is the assertion to a disputed issue? An assertion stated at a relatively high level of generality is more likely to be characterized as an opinion when the assertion involves a disputed issue. Both of these factors will be in play in determining whether an item of testimony will be deemed a fact or opinion.

c. Rationally Based on the Perception of the Witness

The lay opinion rule does not excuse or substitute for the requirement of firsthand knowledge. On the contrary, FRE 701(a) restates the firsthand knowledge requirement. The rule merely allows firsthand knowledge to be expressed in the form of an opinion—as an estimate, summary, or inference, in the terms we suggested. What does it mean for an opinion to be *not* rationally based on a witness's perception? Most likely, one of the following:

Hidden Hearsay. An opinion might be based on secondhand information—hearsay. The hearsay could be masked by the fact that the assertion takes the form of an opinion. Suppose a police officer was called to a car accident scene following the accident and interviews several eyewitnesses. At trial, she may be asked, "Officer Curtis, what in your opinion happened?" She responds, "The blue Honda SUV ran the red light and collided with the Subaru." On the surface, Officer Curtis was asked for an opinion, and gave what sounds like a fact. She answered the question truthfully without reference to any hearsay. But the opinion is based on hearsay: She wasn't there to see the car running a red light and is no doubt relying on eyewitness accounts. When a lay witness is asked for an opinion, it is important to be on the alert for hidden hearsay: The unanswered question is, "How does the witness know that?"—the FRE 602 foundation question.

Speculation. A second common form of unfounded opinion—one not rationally based on the witness's perception—involves speculation. The witness doesn't have all the facts, but fills them in more or less plausibly and reaches a conclusion—and states it as an opinion. Such speculative opinions often arise when a witness offers to characterize the mental state of another person.

Unfounded Inferences or Overgeneralizations. Opinions might be deemed not rationally based on the witness's perception when a witness states an opinion involving too large an inferential leap based on too few case-specific facts. Similarly, the opinion might be largely or entirely based on generalizations about the world rather than case-specific facts. For example, in a reverse sex-discrimination case, a witness for the male plaintiff testifies that the female applicant "must have gotten the job because of affirmative action," but without any specific knowledge of that applicant's qualifications or the specific employer's practices. What's the basis for the opinion? "Because that's how employers are these days." Such an opinion would fail the personal knowledge requirement of FRE 701(a).

· In any of the above examples of unfounded opinions, a clever lawyer might argue, "but Your Honor, a witness always has firsthand knowledge of his own opinion!" True. But an opinion not rationally based on case-specific facts is irrelevant, and should be excluded under both FRE 401/402 and 701.

d. Helpful to the Trier of Fact

Opinions must be helpful to the trier of fact. As FRE 701(b) puts it, an admissible opinion must be "helpful to clearly understanding the witness's testimony or to determining a fact in issue." At this point, let's assume that we have determined that the testimony in question is an opinion, rather than a "fact," that FRE 701 has been invoked, and that FRE 701(a) has been satisfied. Thus, we are assuming that the witness is giving an estimate, summary, or inference based on more specific facts. We can also assume that those facts are within the witness's personal knowledge, or else the opinion testimony would have been barred by FRE 701(a). The question now is whether the witness will be allowed to give the opinion, or instead will have to provide the more specific facts.

Availability of More Detailed Facts. In deciding whether an opinion is helpful to the trier of fact, the court will primarily consider two factors: (1) the availability of the more detailed facts, and (2) the proximity of the opinion to an important disputed issue in the case. The availability of more detailed facts comes down to a problem of narration. In some instances, it will be easy to break a fact down into its component parts, but in others it could be quite difficult. In the example given above, a "grin" is very difficult to break down into specific component facts, compared to the conclusion that the witness was "happy." It's also possible that seeking more specificity could result in a loss of information. A summary opinion that the defendant "approached me in a threatening manner" might ultimately be more informative than pressing for details from a witness who is not a talented storyteller with an eye for minute detail. Such a witness might not be able to manage more than, "I don't know, he was just threatening." Even high-level generalizations might not be amenable to detailed breakdowns: "He was well-liked by his coworkers," for instance.

Perhaps a good practical test for this is to imagine posing such questions as: "Can you be more specific?" or "Can you explain what you mean [by 'threatening']?" If you can easily imagine a satisfactory response to that question, you are more likely to have an opinion that would be more helpfully replaced by detail. This question is highly context-specific, so that case law will seemingly come out in different ways. Compare, e.g., Alexis v. McDonald's Restaurants of Mass., Inc., 67 F.3d 341 (1st Cir. 1995) (rejecting opinion testimony that rudeness to customer was racially motivated due to lack of supporting detail), with Bohannon v. Pegelow, 652 F.2d 729 (7th Cir. 1981) (permitting testimony that assault was racially motivated, despite lack of supporting detail).

Proximity to a Disputed Issue. The second factor, proximity to a disputed issue, primarily concerns the extent to which an opinion substitutes the judgment of the witness for that of the jury. "[T]he closer the subject of the opinion gets to critical issues, the likelier the judge is to require the witness to be more concrete." United States v. Allen, 10 F.3d 405, 414 (7th Cir. 1993). The factfinder is the one charged to draw inferences; the witnesses are supposed to relate factual observations, leaving to the factfinder the inferences to be drawn. "Lay opinions are not helpful when the jury can readily draw the necessary inferences and conclusions without the aid of the opinion." Lynch v. City of Boston, 180 F.3d 1, 16 (1st Cir. 1999) (in an employment discrimination case, the court excluded an opinion that plaintiff was responsible for the success and growth of the program, having already admitted much specific detail praising her job performance). There is no hard and fast rule barring lay opinions on "ultimate issues." Cf. FRE 704 (permitting expert opinion on most ultimate issues). However, where courts believe that a jury is as capable of drawing conclusions from specific evidence as the witness, they are likely to find a witness's ultimate conclusion to be unhelpful.

e. Not Based on Specialized Knowledge

FRE 701(c) provides that lay opinion cannot be "based on scientific, technical, or other specialized knowledge within the scope of Rule 702." The rule draws a clear line between lay and expert testimony. Lay opinions must be on matters of common knowledge, whereas opinions based on specialized knowledge must conform to the more rigorous requirements of the expert opinion rules.

FRE 701(c) was added as an amendment to the FRE in 2000 to close a perceived loophole through which, it was believed, "the reliability requirements set forth in Rule 702 [were being] evaded through the simple expedient of proffering an expert in lay witness clothing." Advisory Committee Note to FRE 701. "[T]the amendment also ensures that a party will not evade the expert witness disclosure requirements set forth in Fed. R. Civ. P. 26 and Fed. R. Crim. P. 16." Id. Even prior to the revision to Rule 701(c), many courts recognized a rigid division between expert and lay testimony. See, e.g., Certain Underwriter's at Lloyd's, London v. Synkovich, 232 F.3d 200 (4th Cir. 2000) ("This rule . . . generally does not permit a lay witness to express an opinion as to matters which are beyond the realm of common experience and which require the special skill and knowledge of an expert witness."). This amendment allows judges much discretion to tailor a ruling on the admissibility of testimony to the qualifications and the extent of firsthand knowledge of an individual witness. See, e.g., United States v. Ayala-Pizarro, 407 F.3d 25 (1st Cir. 2005) (law enforcement agent allowed to testify about nature of drug distribution points and what occurs there without being qualified as expert, because knowledge of points was gained through firsthand observation). Rules 701 and 702 distinguish between expert and lay testimony rather than expert and lay witnesses, making it possible for the same witness to provide both lay and expert testimony in a single case. See, e.g., United States v. Figueroa-López, 125 F.3d 1241, 1246 (9th Cir. 1997) (law enforcement agents allowed to testify that the defendant was acting suspiciously, without being qualified as experts; however, the rules on experts were applicable where the agents testified on the basis of extensive experience that the defendant was using code words to refer to drug quantities and prices). This allows judges to faithfully follow the letter and spirit of Rule 702 and yet not be forced into formulaic exclusions of testimony.

Older cases tried to draw a few categorical lines distinguishing lay and expert testimony, some of which remain good law. For example, many courts allow lay opinion to the effect that another person was drunk. It is also common for courts to allow lay witnesses to estimate the speed of a motor vehicle. These, and a handful of others, have been generally allowed even though, in theory, they might have been categorized as requiring specialized knowledge.

f. Opinion Testimony: Practice Pointers

Objecting to Lay Opinion Testimony.   The grounds to object to improper lay opinion should be fairly apparent from the foregoing discussion. Where the witness's opinion is not "rationally based" on firsthand knowledge, the opinion lacks foundation, or may be irrelevant, or both. It may also be based on hidden hearsay, in which case a hearsay objection is appropriate. The opinion could be objected to as unhelpful to the jury where it can and should be broken down more specifically, or where it usurps the jury's function of drawing inferences. And finally, the opinion may be objectionable because it asks a lay witness for expert opinion. As with all objections, no magic words are required. "Improper lay opinion" should suffice to cover any of the above objections.

Foundation for Lay Opinion.   The danger of improper lay opinion is offset by self-correcting incentives of lawyers presenting the testimony. Juries will almost always find details more persuasive than naked opinions. If an opinion is admitted, it will still be more persuasive if its basis is explained. Suppose your witness on direct examination offers an opinion, which is admitted without objection. The best follow-up question is likely to be, "Why do you think so?" or "Can you explain why you say that?" Those questions elicit the basis for the opinion, and make for more persuasive testimony.

Conversely, for the same reasons, it may be smart tactics to decline to object if your opponent offers unsupported lay opinion testimony. Even if your objection is sustained, you may simply succeed in prompting your opponent to get the witness to provide more persuasive detail. Tactically, you should object only if you have reason to believe that the witness lacks the firsthand knowledge (or perhaps the narrative ability) to explain the underlying details of the opinion.

Lay Opinion on Questions of Law.   Courts traditionally prohibited opinions on questions of law. If by "questions of law" one means questions that are for the judge rather than the jury to decide, it is obviously appropriate that jurors not hear evidence on the issue in any form. The evidence from their perspective would be irrelevant. On the other hand, if the issue is one for the jury to decide, there would appear to be no sound reason to prohibit an opinion merely because one can characterize the issue as embodying "law" or a "legal concept." Indeed, to have a rule that prohibits opinions on jury issues that are characterized as questions of law—or, as some courts have said, "mixed questions of law and fact"—and, at the same time, to permit opinions about ultimate issues of "fact" (see FRE 704) may lead to an abstract, unresolvable debate about whether the issue is one of "fact" or "law." There may, of course, be times when an opinion embracing a legal concept would be confusing (e.g., if the witness were using the term differently from the manner in which the law used it), not very helpful (e.g., if it were a substitute for the underlying facts), or a matter of expertise.

A witness's opinion about law may actually itself be a relevant fact in a case. Consider, for example, a civil rights case in which the plaintiff is suing a municipality on the theory that it has failed to train its officers properly in the use of reasonable force. It would be relevant, and not an improper "legal conclusion," to ask a police officer employed by that municipality, "What is your understanding of when the law allows you to use deadly force?"

Courts can deal adequately with these problems on a case-by-case basis, just as they can deal adequately on a case-by-case basis with opinions on ultimate issues of "fact." Regardless of how one characterizes the issue to which the opinion is directed, the critical question should be whether the opinion will be helpful to the jury.

KEY POINTS

1. Lay witnesses can offer opinion testimony (estimates, summaries, conclusions) so long as the opinion is rationally based on the witness's firsthand knowledge, is helpful to the jury, and is not based on specialized knowledge.

2. Limitations on lay opinion testimony are based on concerns that such testimony may be based on hearsay or otherwise lack foundation, that it may sometimes deprive the jury of important factual detail, or that it may usurp the jury's role of drawing inferences and conclusions, especially on ultimate facts.

3. The distinction between opinions, which fall within FRE 701, and facts, which don't, can't be determined by definition. Instead, the distinction is a function of the level of specificity of the fact assertion and its proximity to a disputed issue in the case. Opinions tend to be stated at a higher level of generality, and courts are more likely to exclude opinions on important contested issues where facts can be described in greater detail.

PROBLEMS

9.1. Cindy Wilton sued her former employer, Store Mart, for sexual harassment by her manager, Donald Clay. One of the elements of the claim under the substantive law is that the sexual advances or conduct were "unwanted" by the plaintiff. One element of an affirmative defense asserted by Store Mart is that the company has good policies, procedures, and training in place to prevent harassment.

(a) One of Cindy's coworkers is prepared to testify, "I saw Donald Clay wink at Cindy several times a day, and on three occasions, I saw him grope her. Clay's actions were unwanted by Cindy. She was definitely turned off by them." Store Mart objects that this entire testimony is inadmissible lay opinion.

(b) Later, in cross-examining Clay, plaintiff's counsel asks, "Mr. Clay, can it be sexual harassment for an employee of Store Mart to repeatedly touch the body of a coworker?" Store Mart objects that this question seeks "an impermissible legal opinion, in violation of Rule 701."

What arguments should be made for and against admission under FRE 701?

9.2. Review the following excerpts from People v. Johnson and consider whether any objections could have been made, and would have been sustained, on the ground that improper opinion testimony was being sought or offered. (Ignore objections to questions as "leading" – assume that a non-leading question had been asked.)

(a) page 15, lines 6-17;

(b) page 25, line 28;

(c) page 31, lines 30-35;

(d) page 51, lines 20-27;

(e) page 62, lines 14-15.

9.3. A police officer investigating a murder found a hatchet near the scene of the crime. In the trial of the accused, should the officer be allowed to testify to his estimation of how long the hatchet had rested in that spot? Or, should the officer be required to describe that the area where he found the hatchet contained old, brown, moist grass in the late stages of decomposition, and that when he retrieved the hatchet, its face was caked with moist, decomposing grass? Or both?

B. ADMISSIBILITY OF EXPERT TESTIMONY

Expert witnesses present evidence based on specialized knowledge acquired through training, study, or experience. Specialized knowledge refers to a degree and focus of knowledge beyond common knowledge. With expert witnesses, the fact-opinion distinction discussed in the context of lay witnesses is frequently inapplicable. In some circumstances, an expert happens also to have been a firsthand observer of the underlying events, and may testify to those to the same extent as a percipient witness. In all other respects, the law of evidence considers expert testimony to be "opinion" testimony by definition. This is a somewhat peculiar definition of "opinion," reflecting that expert witnesses usually give opinion testimony that is not based on their own firsthand perception of litigated events, but are applying specialized knowledge to the firsthand testimony of others to help the jury draw conclusions. Experts usually receive the case-specific background facts from the parties who hire them. The validity of experts' opinions consequently may depend upon independent proof of those facts.

For our analytical purposes, it is useful to think of expert "opinions" as comprising two types.

(1) **Case-specific Facts or Conclusions.** Experts can provide case-specific facts that can't be discerned by direct observation of witnesses based on common knowledge. For example, a chemist analyzes a substance to determine that it is cocaine. Some case-specific facts take the form of inferences and conclusions on ultimate issues that can be determinative of the case's outcome. For example, a scientist might testify that the defendant's pharmaceutical caused the plaintiff's illness.

(2) **Generalizations**. As discussed in the Relevance and Foundation chapters, factfinders rely on generalizations about the world to connect evidentiary facts to essential elements (FOC(EE)s). What if the generalizations are outside common knowledge? Those must be supplied by experts. For example, in a toxic tort case, an expert may have to testify about the effects of a chemical on the human body.

An expert witness may offer an opinion of either type or both. Everything the expert witness says on the stand will consist of opinions of one or both of these types, as well as information relating to the reliability of his opinions: his methodology, the facts and data he considered, or his possible biases. The cluster of rules we will study, FRE 702-705, all deal in one way or another with the above aspects of expert testimony: the qualifications of an expert witness, the reliability of the opinion, the kinds of facts that may be used, the kinds of opinions that may be offered, and the ways that opinions may be expressed. Although most experts by far are retained and presented by the parties, FRE 706 authorizes the court itself to appoint an expert witness.

The fundamental problem posed by the expert witness rules is this. Many, perhaps the majority, of cases involve one or more important facts that can't be perceived or fully understood by applying common knowledge to direct sense perception. Experts are needed to perceive such facts, or to explain generalizations needed to understand them. Often, a party will be unable to meet its burden of proof without such expert testimony. This raises a conundrum:

> We call expert witnesses to testify about matters that are beyond the ordinary understanding of lay people (that is both the major practical justification and a formal legal requirement for expert testimony), and then we ask lay judges and jurors to judge their testimony. [Samuel Gross, *Expert Evidence*, 1991 Wis. L. Rev. 1113, 1182.]

FRE 702 and the case law applying it place a great deal of emphasis on the judge's "gatekeeping" role. This role stems from a concern that jurors can be overawed by experts' opinions, and are likely to have difficulty distinguishing valid from "junk" expertise. The judge keeps the gate by evaluating the reliability of the expert opinion as an FRE 104(a) factfinding matter before admitting it. While it is probably true that the average judge has more formal education than the average juror, the above quotation makes a good point: There is no guarantee that the judge will know enough to evaluate the reliability of an expert in nonlegal areas of specialization. As we study the specific evidence rules dealing with experts, we should consider how well the rules deal with that problem.

1. FRE 702

RULE 702. TESTIMONY BY EXPERT WITNESSES

A witness who is qualified as an expert by knowledge, skill, experience, training, or education may testify in the form of an opinion or otherwise if:

(a) the expert's scientific, technical, or other specialized knowledge will help the trier of fact to understand the evidence or to determine a fact in issue;

(b) the testimony is based on sufficient facts or data;

(c) the testimony is the product of reliable principles and methods; and

(d) the expert has reliably applied the principles and methods to the facts of the case.

2. Explanation of FRE 702(a)

a. Scientific, Technical, or Other Specialized Knowledge

Taken together, FRE 702's introductory sentence and subpart (a) make admissible a broad array of expert testimony. While experts traditionally testified about scientific, technical, and medical issues, the pragmatic phrase "other specialized knowledge" is intended to cover any matter outside common knowledge. In addition, while expert credentials traditionally involved advanced degrees in primarily the "hard" sciences (chemistry, biology, medicine, etc.), FRE 702 is written to include all potential fields of expert knowledge that might be gained from any type of background:

> The rule is broadly phrased. The fields of knowledge which may be drawn upon are not limited merely to the "scientific" and "technical" but extend to all "specialized" knowledge. Similarly, the expert is viewed, not in a narrow sense, but as a person qualified by "knowledge, skill, experience, training, or education." Thus within the scope of the rule are not only experts in the strictest sense of the word, e.g. physicians, physicists, and architects, but also the large group sometimes called "skilled" witnesses, such as bankers or landowners testifying to land values. [Advisory Committee Note to FRE 702.]

Any knowledge that is not likely to be possessed by the factfinder—i.e., that is not common knowledge—qualifies for admission under this rule, no matter how the knowledge is obtained. A person possessing a "skill" can testify to it and its implications, even if the skill was gained through experience rather than formal study.

b. Help the Trier of Fact

FRE 702(a) permits only that expert testimony that will "help the trier of fact to understand the evidence or to determine a fact in issue[.]" This concept of helpfulness has several aspects.

Knowledge Is Relative to the Factfinder. The knowledge that qualifies for admission is relative to the factfinder. When a potential expert witness possesses knowledge that the factfinder is not likely to possess, even though some other factfinder somewhere else might, the testimony is admissible. For example, if the qualities of nitrogen fertilizer are relevant to a case in New York City, a farmer from Iowa knowledgeable of the matter through years of experience would qualify as an expert, even though the farmer had never formally studied the matter. If the trial were held in an Iowa farming community, quite possibly no expert testimony would be admissible because the factfinder's common knowledge and experience might very well extend to the relevant issues. It is these two factors—(1) specialized knowledge relative to the factfinder (2) gained by experience—that explain the court's decision in *Johnson* permitting Officer Huston to give an expert opinion about tray collection from inmates.

Fact in Issue Cannot Be Determined by Common Knowledge.   Where a fact in issue can't be determined as a matter of common knowledge applied to firsthand perception, expert opinion is automatically helpful. (Whether it is sufficiently reliable to be admitted into evidence is a separate question.) Some facts simply can't be perceived by lay witnesses at all. Consider a toxic tort case in which the plaintiff alleges that chemicals dumped by the defendant entered the municipal water supply. No percipient witness can testify that he saw the chemicals leach through the soil and into an underground aquifer before making their way into the city's drinking-water wells. Testimony of an expert in geology and groundwater flow will be helpful—indeed necessary—to prove this fact. Similarly, expert testimony may be necessary to supply a crucial generalization to allow the jury to make an inference necessary to a party's burden of proof. Suppose the plaintiff in a product liability case suffers a skin rash that appeared several days after using defendant's household cleanser. To link the rash to the chemicals in the cleanser may require an expert to testify, at least as a general matter, about the likely effects of that chemical on human skin.

Expert Testimony Sheds Light on Facts in Issue.   The helpfulness requirement can also be met in an instance where there is a gray area between common and specialized knowledge. This sort of gray area occurs in many cases, particularly where the specialized knowledge arises from social science or from experience with repeated observations of everyday life. For example, juries are asked to determine whether a police officer used excessive force in a police brutality case. This is considered by the law as a matter of reasonableness based on common sense, and expert testimony is not required. At the same time, courts are likely to allow expert testimony on police use of force on the theory that such events are sufficiently unusual that expert testimony can shed additional light on the question.

Helpfulness Requirement as a Limitation on Experts Usurping Jury's Function. The helpfulness requirement provides a useful limitation on expert testimony that purports to offer conclusions that the jury is capable of reaching. This aspect of the helpfulness requirement is more or less the same as that discussed in connection with FRE 701. Juries are asked to draw conclusions about whether evidentiary facts prove an essential element of the party's case. Where that can be done as a matter of common sense and experience, an expert opinion based on the same logical thought process expected from the jury is properly deemed unhelpful. For example, a police detective might testify that he has investigated over 1,000 criminal cases; that 100 of those cases went to trial; that his judgment about the defendant's guilt or innocence was correct in 99 of those cases; and that, in his opinion, the defendant is guilty in the current case. While the detective is no doubt an expert in criminal investigations, it is inconceivable that this testimony would be allowed. The most likely explanation is that it usurps the jury's role, and is therefore unhelpful. While there is no absolute bar to an expert testifying on an ultimate issue in most circumstances (see FRE 704, discussed below), the helpfulness requirement will frequently be used to bar such conclusions from experts. The key question is whether the jury is capable of drawing the ultimate conclusions from the evidence on its own.

c. A Witness Qualified as an Expert

If specialized information will help the trier of fact, the trial judge must then determine whether the person offered to present the information is qualified to do so. As noted above, the qualifications need not include formal education in the subject matter. Rather, as FRE 702 provides, one can be qualified as an expert based on "knowledge, skill, experience, [or] training," as well as education. As a result, courts admit an extremely wide variety of testimony on this basis. FBI agents have been permitted to testify to the structure of various criminal schemes based on their law enforcement experience. Farmers have testified to the likely value of their ruined crops, and so on. The crucial questions are whether the proposed witness has specialized knowledge, however obtained, and whether it would be helpful to the jury.

d. Burden of Proof

FRE 702 should be understood as setting out criteria for the admission of expert testimony. It is an admission rule rather than an exclusion rule, meaning that the party seeking admission of the testimony bears the burden of proof that the FRE 702 requirements have been met. In theory, this might be viewed as an FRE 104(b) foundation requirement (expert testimony is not relevant unless a qualified expert offers reliable testimony). But FRE 104(a) includes "any preliminary question about whether a witness is qualified," and this would seem to apply to expert witness qualifications. The Supreme Court has confirmed that the admissibility of expert testimony should be decided under FRE 104(a). See Daubert v. Merrell Dow Pharmaceuticals, 509 U.S. 579 (1993). In other words, the party offering expert testimony has the burden to persuade the trial judge that the expert is qualified and that the expert's opinions are reliable.

3. Explanation of FRE 702(b)-(d): the Reliability Requirement

Often, the need for expert testimony and the qualifications of the expert will be sufficiently apparent to shift the focus of dispute from FRE 702(a) to FRE 702(b), (c), and (d). These rules work together as an authorization for the judge to determine whether the expert's testimony is sufficiently reliable to be admitted. The language of FRE 702(b)-(d) appears to be fairly clear and self-explanatory. For expert testimony to be sufficiently reliable to be admitted in evidence, the testimony must show that the expert has applied reliable analytical methods to sufficient facts or data.

The reliability of live witness testimony is normally an FRE 104(b) question, which the judge screens for evidence sufficient to support a finding. Like 104(b) questions, the reliability of testimony is a fact on which its relevance depends: If an expert's testimony is unreliable, it should be disregarded. In theory, then, the reliability of expert testimony could be screened for evidence sufficient to support a finding: Could a reasonable jury find the testimony reliable? Some courts seem to analyze the question in these terms.

Nevertheless, the black letter doctrine makes clear that the reliability of expert testimony must be treated as an FRE 104(a) question for the judge to decide based on a preponderance of the evidence. Perhaps this approach makes sense, for two reasons. First, as noted above, there are significant risks that the jury may be overawed by expertise; arguably, the judge is likely to be at least slightly better positioned to make threshold reliability determinations. Second, as we will see, FRE 703 allows expert testimony to rely on hearsay and other inadmissible information. Therefore, a jury might not be in a good position to consider the reliability of the "facts and data" used by the expert. Whether you agree with these justifications or not, FRE 702's reliability requirement should be viewed as an exception to the general rule that the prima facie reliability of testimony is an FRE 104(b) question.

Despite the apparent clarity of this rule, numerous questions arise as to its application to certain types of experts. The most significant case law developments regarding expert witnesses have concerned the test that should be applied by courts to determine this reliability. Moreover, these case law developments have a history that, as a practitioner, you need to know to fully understand how courts approach the question. We therefore present this material in more traditional casebook style, using the case method.

4. Development of the FRE 702 Reliability Requirement: *Daubert* and Its Progeny

a. The Frye Test

Prior to the adoption of the FRE, federal courts nearly all applied a test articulated in Frye v. United States, 293 F. 1013 (D.C. Cir. 1923). In *Frye*, the D.C. Circuit upheld the trial court's exclusion of expert testimony based on the use of the results of an early type of lie detection device—a systolic blood pressure test. The key language in the opinion stated that "while courts will go a long way in admitting expert testimony deduced from well-recognized scientific principle or discovery, the thing from which the deduction is made must be sufficiently established to have gained general acceptance in the particular field in which it belongs." Id. at 1014. The *Frye* opinion is unclear about whether "the thing" that must have gained "general acceptance" is the relationship between truth telling and blood pressure, or the ability of an expert to measure and interpret the changes in blood pressure, or both. Despite this ambiguity and despite the court's failure to explain further or to cite precedent for its holding, most federal circuits adopted the "general acceptance" test, commonly referred to as the "*Frye* test."

After the adoption of the Federal Rules, the Frye test continued to be applied in federal courts, even though FRE 702 made no reference to the "general acceptance" standard. As originally drafted, FRE 702 stated:

> If scientific, technical, or other specialized knowledge will assist the trier of fact to
> understand the evidence or to determine a fact in issue, a witness qualified as an expert
> by knowledge, skill, experience, training, or education, may testify thereto in the form
> of an opinion or otherwise.

Given the language of FRE 702, some commentators took the position that the Federal Rules rejected the *Frye* test. Lower courts divided on the issue. The Supreme Court addressed the *Frye* test and the reliability criteria in the *Daubert* case.

b. Daubert

If you plan to use expert witnesses in your law practice, or even to take part in an informed discussion about the law of expert witnesses, you have to know the *Daubert* case. *Daubert*, decided in 1993, has been clarified by subsequent cases and an amendment to FRE 702. Quite arguably, the extent of those clarifications and amendments are such that *Daubert* has been superseded. Nevertheless, courts and commentators invariably speak as though *Daubert* were a complete statement of the controlling legal standard and the source of expert witness law. At a minimum, *Daubert* represents a watershed in the history of FRE 702. So you must read it.

DAUBERT v. MERRELL DOW PHARMACEUTICALS, INC.
509 U.S. 579 (1993)

Justice BLACKMUN delivered the opinion of the Court.

In this case we are called upon to determine the standard for admitting expert scientific testimony in a federal trial.

I

Petitioners Jason Daubert and Eric Schuller are minor children born with serious birth defects. They and their parents sued respondent in California state court, alleging that the birth defects had been caused by the mothers' ingestion of Bendectin, a prescription anti-nausea drug marketed by respondent. Respondent removed the suits to federal court on diversity grounds.

After extensive discovery, respondent moved for summary judgment, contending that Bendectin does not cause birth defects in humans and that petitioners would be unable to come forward with any admissible evidence that it does. In support of its motion, respondent submitted an affidavit of Steven H. Lamm, physician and epidemiologist, who is a well-credentialed expert on the risks from exposure to various chemical substances.[1] Doctor Lamm stated that he had reviewed all the literature on Bendectin and human birth defects—more than 30 published stud-

---

1. Doctor Lamm received his master's and doctor of medicine degrees from the University of Southern California. He has served as a consultant in birth-defect epidemiology for the National Center for Health Statistics and has published numerous articles on the magnitude of risk from exposure to various chemical and biological substances.

ies involving over 130,000 patients. No study had found Bendectin to be a human teratogen (i.e., a substance capable of causing malformations in fetuses). On the basis of this review, Doctor Lamm concluded that maternal use of Bendectin during the first trimester of pregnancy has not been shown to be a risk factor for human birth defects.

Petitioners . . . responded to respondent's motion with the testimony of eight experts of their own, each of whom also possessed impressive credentials.[2] These experts had concluded that Bendectin can cause birth defects. Their conclusions were based upon "in vitro" (test tube) and "in vivo" (live) animal studies that found a link between Bendectin and malformations; pharmacological studies of the chemical structure of Bendectin that purported to show similarities between the structure of the drug and that of other substances known to cause birth defects; and the "reanalysis" of previously published epidemiological (human statistical) studies.

The District Court granted respondent's motion for summary judgment. . . . The court concluded that petitioners' evidence did not meet [the *Frye*] standard. Given the vast body of epidemiological data concerning Bendectin, the court held, expert opinion which is not based on epidemiological evidence is not admissible to establish causation. Thus, the animal-cell studies, live-animal studies, and chemical-structure analyses on which petitioners had relied could not raise by themselves a reasonably disputable jury issue regarding causation. Petitioners' epidemiological analyses, based as they were on recalculations of data in previously published studies that had found no causal link between the drug and birth defects, were ruled to be inadmissible because they had not been published or subjected to peer review.

The United States Court of Appeals for the Ninth Circuit affirmed. Citing Frye v. United States, the court stated that . . . based on a methodology that diverges "significantly from the procedures accepted by recognized authorities in the field . . . cannot be shown to be generally accepted as a reliable technique." . . . Contending that reanalysis is generally accepted by the scientific community only when it is subjected to verification and scrutiny by others in the field, the Court of Appeals rejected petitioners' reanalyses as "unpublished, not subjected to the normal peer review process and generated solely for use in litigation." The court concluded that petitioners' evidence provided an insufficient foundation to allow admission of expert testimony that Bendectin caused their injuries and, accordingly, that petitioners could not satisfy their burden of proving causation at trial.

. We granted certiorari in light of sharp divisions among the courts regarding the proper standard for the admission of expert testimony.

---

2. For example, Shanna Helen Swan, who received a master's degree in biostatics from Columbia University and a doctorate in statistics from the University of California at Berkeley, is chief of the section of the California Department of Health and Services that determines causes of birth defects, and has served as a consultant to the World Health Organization, the Food and Drug Administration, and the National Institutes of Health. Stewart A. Newman, who received his master's and a doctorate in chemistry from Columbia University and the University of Chicago, respectively, is a professor at New York Medical College and has spent over a decade studying the effect of chemicals on limb development. The credentials of the others are similarly impressive.

II

A

In the 70 years since its formulation in the *Frye* case, the "general acceptance" test has been the dominant standard for determining the admissibility of novel scientific evidence at trial. . . . The *Frye* test has its origin in a short and citation-free 1923 decision concerning the admissibility of evidence derived from a systolic blood pressure deception test, a crude precursor to the polygraph machine. In what has become a famous (perhaps infamous) passage, the then Court of Appeals for the District of Columbia described the device and its operation and declared:

> Just when a scientific principle or discovery crosses the line between the experimental and demonstrable stages is difficult to define. Somewhere in this twilight zone the evidential force of the principle must be recognized, and while courts will go a long way in admitting expert testimony deduced from a well-recognized scientific principle or discovery, the thing from which the deduction is made must be sufficiently established to have gained general acceptance in the particular field in which it belongs.

Because the deception test had "not yet gained such standing and scientific recognition among physiological and psychological authorities as would justify the courts in admitting expert testimony deduced from the discovery, development, and experiments thus far made," evidence of its results was ruled inadmissible.

[Petitioners] . . . contend that the *Frye* test was superseded by the adoption of the Federal Rules of Evidence. We agree. . . .

Here there is a specific Rule that speaks to the contested issue. Rule 702, governing expert testimony, provides:

> If scientific, technical, or other specialized knowledge will assist the trier of fact to understand the evidence or to determine a fact in issue, a witness qualified as an expert by knowledge, skill, experience, training, or education, may testify thereto in the form of an opinion or otherwise.*

Nothing in the text of this Rule establishes "general acceptance" as an absolute prerequisite to admissibility. . . . The drafting history makes no mention of *Frye*, and a rigid "general acceptance" requirement would be at odds with the "liberal thrust" of the Federal Rules and their general approach of relaxing the traditional barriers to "opinion" testimony. . . . [*Frye's*] austere standard, absent from and incompatible with the Federal Rules of Evidence, should not be applied in federal trials.

B

That the *Frye* test was displaced by the Rules of Evidence does not mean, however, that the Rules themselves place no limits on the admissibility of purportedly scientific evidence. Nor is the trial judge disabled from screening such evidence. To the contrary, under the Rules the trial judge must ensure that any and all scientific testimony or evidence admitted is not only relevant, but reliable.

---

*[Again, this is FRE 702 prior to its 2000 amendments. — EDS.]

. . . [Rule 702] clearly contemplates some degree of regulation of the subjects and theories about which an expert may testify. . . . The subject of an expert's testimony must be "scientific . . . knowledge." The adjective "scientific" implies a grounding in the methods and procedures of science. Similarly, the word "knowledge" connotes more than subjective belief or unsupported speculation. The term "applies to any body of known facts or to any body of ideas inferred from such facts or accepted as truths on good grounds." Webster's Third New International Dictionary 1252 (1986). Of course, it would be unreasonable to conclude that the subject of scientific testimony must be "known" to a certainty; arguably, there are no certainties in science. But, in order to qualify as "scientific knowledge," an inference or assertion must be derived by the scientific method. Proposed testimony must be supported by appropriate validation—i.e., "good grounds," based on what is known. In short, the requirement that an expert's testimony pertain to "scientific knowledge" establishes a standard of evidentiary reliability.[3]

Rule 702 further requires that the evidence or testimony "assist the trier of fact to understand the evidence or to determine a fact in issue." This condition goes primarily to relevance. . . . The consideration has been aptly described . . . as one of "fit." "Fit" is not always obvious, and scientific validity for one purpose is not necessarily scientific validity for other, unrelated purposes. . . . The study of the phases of the moon, for example, may provide valid scientific "knowledge" about whether a certain night was dark, and if darkness is a fact in issue, the knowledge will assist the trier of fact. However (absent creditable grounds supporting such a link), evidence that the moon was full on a certain night will not assist the trier of fact in determining whether an individual was unusually likely to have behaved irrationally on that night. Rule 702's "helpfulness" standard requires a valid scientific connection to the pertinent inquiry as a precondition to admissibility.

That these requirements are embodied in Rule 702 is not surprising. Unlike an ordinary witness, see Rule 701, an expert is permitted wide latitude to offer opinions, including those that are not based on first-hand knowledge or observation. See Rules 702 and 703. Presumably, this relaxation of the usual requirement of first-hand knowledge—a rule which represents "a 'most pervasive manifestation' " of the common law insistence upon 'the most reliable sources of information,' " Advisory Committee's Notes on Fed. Rule Evid. 602—is premised on an assumption that the expert's opinion will have a reliable basis in the knowledge and experience of his discipline.

---

3. We note that scientists typically distinguish between "validity" (does the principle support what it purports to show?) and "reliability" (does application of the principle produce consistent results?). See Black, A Unified Theory of Scientific Evidence, 56 Ford. L. Rev. 595, 599 (1988). Although "the difference between accuracy, validity, and reliability may be such that each is distinct from the other by no more than a hen's kick," Starrs, Frye v. United States Restructured and Revitalized: A Proposal to Amend Federal Evidence Rule 702, 26 Jurimetrics J. 249, 256 (1986). Our reference here is to evidentiary reliability—that is, trustworthiness. Cf., e.g., Advisory Committee's Notes on Fed. Rule Evid. 602 (" '[T]he rule requiring that a witness who testifies to a fact which can be perceived by the senses must have had an opportunity to observe, and must have actually observed the fact' is a 'most pervasive manifestation' of the common law insistence upon 'the most reliable sources of information;' " (citation omitted)): Advisory Committee's Notes on Art. VIII of the Rules of Evidence (hearsay exceptions will be recognized only "under circumstances supposed to furnish guarantees of trustworthiness"). In a case involving scientific evidence, evidentiary reliability will be based upon scientific validity.

C

Faced with a proffer of expert scientific testimony, then, the trial judge must [make] a preliminary assessment of whether the reasoning or methodology underlying the testimony is scientifically valid and of whether that reasoning or methodology properly can be applied to the facts in issue. We are confident that federal judges possess the capacity to undertake this review. Many factors will bear on the inquiry, and we do not presume to set out a definitive checklist or test. But some general observations are appropriate.

Ordinarily, a key question to be answered in determining whether a theory or technique is scientific knowledge that will assist the trier of fact will be whether it can be (and has been) tested. K. Popper, Conjectures and Refutations: The Growth of Scientific Knowledge 37 (5th ed. 1989) ("[T]he criterion of the scientific status of a theory is its falsifiability, or refutability, or testability").

Another pertinent consideration is whether the theory or technique has been subjected to peer review and publication. Publication (which is but one element of peer review) is not a sine qua non of admissibility; it does not necessarily correlate with reliability, see S. Jasanoff, The Fifth Branch: Science Advisors as Policymakers 61-76 (1990), and in some instances well-grounded but innovative theories will not have been published, see Horrobin, The Philosophical Basis of Peer Review and the Suppression of Innovation, 263 J. Am. Med. Assn. 1438 (1990). Some propositions, moreover, are too particular, too new, or of too limited interest to be published. But submission to the scrutiny of the scientific community is a component of "good science," in part because it increases the likelihood that substantive flaws in methodology will be detected. The fact of publication (or lack thereof) in a peer-reviewed journal thus will be a relevant, though not dispositive, consideration in assessing the scientific validity of a particular technique or methodology on which an opinion is premised.

Additionally, in the case of a particular scientific technique, the court ordinarily should consider the known or potential rate of error, and the existence and maintenance of standards controlling the technique's operation.

Finally, "general acceptance" can yet have a bearing on the inquiry. A "reliability assessment does not require, although it does permit, explicit identification of a relevant scientific community and an express determination of a particular degree of acceptance within that community." United States v. Downing, 753 F.2d, at 1238. Widespread acceptance can be an important factor in ruling particular evidence admissible, and "a known technique that has been able to attract only minimal support within the community," Downing, supra, may properly be viewed with skepticism.

The inquiry envisioned by Rule 702 is, we emphasize, a flexible one. Its overarching subject is the scientific validity—and thus the evidentiary relevance and reliability—of the principles that underlie a proposed submission. The focus, of course, must be solely on principles and methodology, not on the conclusions that they generate.

Throughout, a judge assessing a proffer of expert scientific testimony under Rule 702 should also be mindful of other applicable rules. Rule 703 provides that expert opinions based on otherwise inadmissible hearsay are to be admitted only if the facts or data are "of a type reasonably relied upon by experts in the particular field in forming opinions or inferences upon the subject." Rule 706 allows the court at its discretion to procure the assistance of an expert of its own choosing. Finally, Rule 403 permits the exclusion of relevant evidence "if its probative value is substantially outweighed by the danger of unfair prejudice, confusion of the issues, or misleading the jury . . . ." Judge Weinstein has explained: "Expert evidence can be both powerful and quite misleading because of the difficulty in evaluating it. Because of this risk, the judge in weighing possible prejudice against probative force under Rule 403 of the present rules exercises more control over experts than over lay witnesses."

III

We conclude by briefly addressing what appear to be two underlying concerns of the parties and amici in this case. Respondent expresses apprehension that abandonment of "general acceptance" as the exclusive requirement for admission will result in a "free-for-all" in which befuddled juries are confounded by absurd and irrational pseudoscientific assertions. In this regard respondent seems to us to be overly pessimistic about the capabilities of the jury, and of the adversary system generally. Vigorous cross-examination, presentation of contrary evidence, and careful instruction on the burden of proof are the traditional and appropriate means of attacking shaky but admissible evidence. Additionally, in the event the trial court concludes that the scintilla of evidence presented supporting a position is insufficient to allow a reasonable juror to conclude that the position more likely than not is true, the court remains free to direct a judgment, Fed. Rule Civ. Proc. 50(a), and likewise to grant summary judgment, Fed. Rule Civ. Proc. 56. These conventional devices, rather than wholesale exclusion under an uncompromising "general acceptance" test, are the appropriate safeguards where the basis of scientific testimony meets the standards of Rule 702.

Petitioners and, to a greater extent, their amici exhibit a different concern. They suggest that recognition of a screening role for the judge that allows for the exclusion of "invalid" evidence will sanction a stifling and repressive scientific orthodoxy and will be inimical to the search for truth. It is true that open debate is an essential part of both legal and scientific analyses. Yet there are important differences between the quest for truth in the courtroom and the quest for truth in the laboratory. Scientific conclusions are subject to perpetual revision. Law, on the other hand, must resolve disputes finally and quickly. The scientific project is advanced by broad and wide-ranging consideration of a multitude of hypotheses, for those that are incorrect will eventually be shown to be so, and that in itself is an advance. Conjectures that are probably wrong are of little use, however, in the project of reaching a quick, final, and binding legal judgment—often of great consequence—about a particular set of events in the past. We recognize that in practice, a gatekeeping role for the judge, no matter how flexible, inevitably on occasion will prevent the jury from learning of authentic insights and innovations. That, nevertheless, is the balance that is struck by Rules of Evidence designed not for the exhaustive search for cosmic understanding but for the particularized resolution of legal disputes.

IV

To summarize: "general acceptance" is not a necessary precondition to the admissibility of scientific evidence under the Federal Rules of Evidence, but the Rules of

Evidence—especially Rule 702—do assign to the trial judge the task of ensuring that an expert's testimony both rests on a reliable foundation and is relevant to the task at hand. Pertinent evidence based on scientifically valid principles will satisfy those demands.

The inquiries of the District Court and the Court of Appeals focused almost exclusively on "general acceptance," as gauged by publication and the decisions of other courts. Accordingly, the judgment of the Court of Appeals is vacated and the case is remanded for further proceedings consistent with this opinion.

It is so ordered.

Chief Justice REHNQUIST, with whom Justice STEVENS joins, concurring in part and dissenting in part. . . .

[I] defer to no one in my confidence in federal judges; but I am at a loss to know what is meant when it is said that the scientific status of a theory depends on its "falsifiability," and I suspect some of them will be, too. I do not doubt that Rule 702 confides to the judge some gatekeeping responsibility in deciding questions of the admissibility of proffered expert testimony. But I do not think it imposes on them either the obligation or the authority to become amateur scientists in order to perform that role. I think the Court would be far better advised in this case . . . to leave the further development of this important area of the law to future cases.

NOTES AND QUESTIONS

1. *Daubert* was decided under a pre-2000 version of Rule 702. In 2000, the rule was amended "in response to *Daubert*," and consistently with it, though without intending "to codify" *Daubert*. See Advisory Committee Notes on 2000 Amendment to Fed. R. Evid. 702. The new rule, and excerpts from the Advisory Committee Notes, are presented following the *Kumho Tire* case, below.

2. Does it make sense to apply the four *Daubert* factors to expert testimony that is not based on "science"?

3. What would be the consequences of using the *Frye* rule in tort cases claiming that chemical exposures caused diseases or cellular-level physical injuries?

4. Is the *Daubert* rule more "liberal" toward admission of expert testimony than the *Frye* rule? Note that "general acceptance" is retained as one of the four *Daubert* factors. The immediate reaction to *Daubert* was that it loosened the standards of admissibility for expert testimony, but at least some lower federal courts have tended to interpret *Daubert* as justification to take long, hard looks at expert witnesses being proffered. Some commentators detected a trend in reported cases suggesting that courts have increasingly declined to admit the testimony. But see Advisory Committee Note to FRE 702—2000 Amendment ("A review of the caselaw after *Daubert* shows that the rejection of expert testimony is the exception rather than the rule. *Daubert* did not work a sea change over federal evidence law."). The post–Supreme Court history of the *Daubert* litigation itself is instructive. On remand, the Ninth Circuit, now applying *Daubert*, reached the same conclusion it had previously that the evidence was inadmissible. Daubert v. Merrell Dow Pharmaceuticals, Inc., 43 F.3d 1311 (9th

Cir. 1995). In reaching that conclusion, however, the court also considered a number of factors in addition to the Supreme Court's list. One was whether the expert was testifying on the basis of research conducted independently of the litigation. How important is this criterion? Consider how much research is now conducted for hire in one way or another. See also Edward K. Cheng & Albert H. Yoon, Does *Frye* or *Daubert* Matter? A Study of Scientific Admissibility Standards, 91 Virginia L. Rev. 471 (2005) (using a jurisdiction-removal criterion for ascertaining tort defendants' revealed preferences to show that the shift from *Frye* to *Daubert* was operationally insignificant).

   5. The actual holding in *Frye* excluding the result of lie detector tests became for a time the universal rule in this country. This rule began to slowly change in the mid-1990s with several decisions allowing polygraph evidence coming in the wake of *Daubert.* A number of jurisdictions began admitting the evidence, probably because a per se rule of exclusion seemed contradictory to the new statement of the standard which was enunciated in *Daubert.* For an influential, pre-*Daubert* decision, see, e.g., United States v. Piccinonna, 885 F.2d 1529 (11th Cir. 1989). *Piccinonna* held that polygraph results would be admissible to impeach or corroborate testimony if three conditions were met: (1) notice of intent to use the evidence must be given to the opposition; (2) the opposing side must be given an opportunity to administer its own test; and (3) admissibility of the evidence is to be governed by the normal rules for the admissibility of corroboration and impeachment evidence, so that, for example, corroborating evidence would not be admissible until a witness's character for truthfulness has been attacked under FRE 608. The 11th Circuit has continued to adhere to these three conditions post-*Daubert.* See United States v. Henderson, 409 F.3d 1293 (11th Cir. 2005) (stating that Piccinonna's ruling is still valid post-*Daubert*). In United States v. Posado, 57 F.3d 428 (5th Cir. 1995), the court held that the results of polygraph examinations may be admissible in certain criminal cases regardless of stipulations (here one was offered but rejected). The court read *Daubert* as liberalizing the admission of scientific evidence, and concluded that the 70 percent to 90 percent accuracy rate now achieved with polygraphs exceeded the level of reliability of much evidence presently admitted. The court expressed concern about the prejudicial effect of such evidence, but found it not to be a problem here because the issue was who to believe, the state or the defendants, at a suppression hearing where dramatically different stories were being told and where other evidence cast doubt on the state's version of events. Despite these decisions, courts in some jurisdictions are still regularly excluding polygraph evidence. See United States v. Gill, 513 F.3d 836 (8th Cir. 2008) ("polygraph evidence is disfavored"); United States v. Prince-Oyibo, 320 F.3d 494 (4th Cir. 2003) (adhering to per se inadmissibility standard for polygraph results); United States v. Thomas, 167 F.3d 299, 308 (6th Cir. 1999) (polygraph evidence "generally disfavor[ed]"). See also D. Michael Risinger, Navigating Expert Reliability: Are Criminal Standards of Certainty Being Left on the Dock?, 64 Alb. L. Rev. 99 (2000); David C. Raskin, et al., The Scientific Status of Research on Polygraph Techniques: The Case for Polygraph Tests, 19-2.0, in 1 Modern Science Evidence: The Law and Science of Expert Testimony (David L. Faigman, David H. Kaye, Michael J. Saks & Joseph Sanders eds., 2002 & Supp. 2003).

6. *Daubert* stimulated, and continues to stimulate, an avalanche of academic writing on the topic of scientific evidence. See, e.g., David E. Bernstein, The Misbegotten Judicial Resistance to the *Daubert* Revolution, 89 Notre Dame L. Rev. 27, 30, 67 (2013); Ronald J. Allen & Esfand Nafisi, *Daubert* and Its Discontents, 76 Brook. L. Rev. 131 (2010); Cheng & Yoon, supra; Jennifer L. Groscup et al., The Effects of *Daubert* on the Admissibility of Expert Testimony in State and Federal Criminal Cases, 8 Psy. Pub. Poly. & L. 339 (2002); Joseph Sanders et al., Legal Perceptions of Science and Expert Knowledge, 8 Psy. Pub. Poly. & L. 139 (2002); Jeffrey L. Harrison, Reconceptualizing the Expert Witness: Social Cost, Current Controls and Proposed Responses, 18 Yale J. on Reg. 253 (2001); Brandon L. Jensen, Litigating the Crossroads Between *Sweet Home* and *Daubert*, 24 Va. L. Rev. 169 (2000); Derek L. Mogck, Are We There Yet? Refining the Test for Expert Testimony Through *Daubert, Kumho Tire* and Proposed Federal Rule of Evidence 702, 33 Conn. L. Rev. 303 (2000).

c. Joiner

Chief Justice Rehnquist dissented in *Daubert* from the idea that judges could adequately act as gatekeepers for expert testimony, but within just a few years, he seems to have accommodated himself to the idea in the next major Supreme Court decision on expert witnesses, General Electric Co. v. Joiner. Use the following questions to focus your reading of the case:

1. What is the central legal principle articulated by the *Joiner* decision?
2. What does it mean to say that the district court did not "abuse its discretion" in *Joiner*? Does that mean that the district court's ruling excluding plaintiff's expert was "correct"?
3. How does *Daubert* apply to this case? Does it help explain what was wrong with the expert's opinion?

GENERAL ELECTRIC CO. v. JOINER
522 U.S. 136 (1997)

Chief Justice Rehnquist delivered the opinion of the Court.

[Respondent Robert Joiner worked as an electrician in the Water & Light Department of Thomasville, Georgia (City) for several years, during which his work exposed him to repeated contact with chemicals containing polychlorinated biphenyls (PCBs). After being diagnosed with lung cancer in 1991, Joiner, a smoker, sued various manufacturers of the chemicals in Georgia state court, claiming that his exposure to PCBs contributed to his cancer. Petitioners (the defendants) removed the case to federal court. The district court granted summary judgment for the defendants because the testimony of Joiner's experts had failed to show that there was a link between exposure to PCBs and lung cancer. The court believed that the testimony of respondent's experts to the contrary did not rise above "subjective belief or unsupported speculation," and was therefore inadmissible.

The Court of Appeals for the Eleventh Circuit reversed. It held that "[b]ecause the Federal Rules of Evidence governing expert testimony display a preference for admissibility, we apply a particularly stringent standard of review to the trial judge's exclusion of expert testimony." Applying that standard, the Court of Appeals held that the District Court had erred in excluding the testimony of Joiner's expert witnesses, because a district court should limit its role to determining the "legal reliability of proffered expert testimony, leaving the jury to decide the correctness of competing expert opinions."]

We have held that abuse of discretion is the proper standard of review of a district court's evidentiary rulings.. . . [The] Court of Appeals erred in its review of the exclusion of Joiner's experts' testimony. In applying an overly "stringent" review to that ruling, it failed to give the trial court the deference that is the hallmark of abuse-of-discretion review. . . .

III

. . . [A] proper application of the correct standard of review here indicates that the District Court did not abuse its discretion. Joiner's theory of liability was that his exposure to PCBs and their derivatives "promoted" his development of small-cell lung cancer. In support of that theory he proffered the deposition testimony of expert witnesses. Dr. Arnold Schecter testified that he believed it "more likely than not that Mr. Joiner's lung cancer was causally linked to cigarette smoking and PCB exposure." Dr. Daniel Teitelbaum testified that Joiner's "lung cancer was caused by or contributed to in a significant degree by the materials with which he worked."

Petitioners contended that the statements of Joiner's experts regarding causation were nothing more than speculation. Petitioners criticized the testimony of the experts in that it was "not supported by epidemiological studies . . . [and was] based exclusively on isolated studies of laboratory animals." Joiner responded by claiming that his experts had identified "relevant animal studies which support their opinions." He also directed the court's attention to four epidemiological studies on which his experts had relied. [Epidemiological studies examine the pattern of disease in human populations.]

The District Court agreed with petitioners that the animal studies on which respondent's experts relied did not support his contention that exposure to PCBs had contributed to his cancer. The studies involved infant mice that had developed cancer after being exposed to PCB's. The infant mice in the studies had had massive doses of PCBs injected directly into their peritoneums or stomachs. Joiner was an adult human being whose alleged exposure to PCB's was far less than the exposure in the animal studies. The PCBs were injected into the mice in a highly concentrated form. The fluid with which Joiner had come into contact generally had a much smaller PCB concentration of between 0-to-500 parts per million. The cancer that these mice developed was alveologenic adenomas; Joiner had developed small-cell carcinomas. No study demonstrated that adult mice developed cancer after being exposed to PCBs. One of the experts admitted that no study had demonstrated that PCBs lead to cancer in any other species.

Respondent failed to reply to this criticism. Rather than explaining how and why the experts could have extrapolated their opinions from these seemingly far-removed animal studies, respondent chose "to proceed as if the only issue [was] whether animal studies can ever be a proper foundation for an expert's opinion." Of course, whether animal studies can ever be a proper foundation for an expert's opinion was not the issue. The issue was whether these experts' opinions were sufficiently supported by the animal studies on which they purported to rely. The studies were so dissimilar to the facts presented in this litigation that it was not an abuse of discretion for the District Court to have rejected the experts' reliance on them.

The District Court also concluded that the four epidemiological studies on which respondent relied were not a sufficient basis for the experts' opinions. The first such study involved workers at an Italian capacitor plant who had been exposed to PCBs. The authors noted that lung cancer deaths among ex-employees at the plant were higher than might have been expected, but concluded that "there were apparently no grounds for associating lung cancer deaths (although increased above expectations) and exposure in the plant." Given that [the study was] unwilling to say that PCB exposure had caused cancer among the workers they examined, their study did not support the experts' conclusion that Joiner's exposure to PCBs caused his cancer.

The second study . . . . found that the incidence of lung cancer deaths among [the subjects] was somewhat higher than would ordinarily be expected. The increase, however, was not statistically significant and the authors of the study did not suggest a link between the increase in lung cancer deaths and the exposure to PCBs. The third and fourth studies were likewise of no help. . . .

Respondent points to *Daubert*'s language that the "focus, of course, must be solely on principles and methodology, not on the conclusions that they generate." He claims that because the District Court's disagreement was with the conclusion that the experts drew from the studies, the District Court committed legal error and was properly reversed by the Court of Appeals. But conclusions and methodology are not entirely distinct from one another. Trained experts commonly extrapolate from existing data. But nothing in either *Daubert* or the Federal Rules of Evidence requires a district court to admit opinion evidence that is connected to existing data only by the ipse dixit[4] of the expert. A court may conclude that there is simply too great an analytical gap between the data and the opinion proffered. That is what the District Court did here, and we hold that it did not abuse its discretion in so doing. . . .

. . . Whether Joiner was exposed to furans and dioxins, and whether if there was such exposure, the opinions of Joiner's experts would then be admissible, remain open questions. We accordingly reverse the judgment of the Court of Appeals and remand this case for proceedings consistent with this opinion.

NOTES AND QUESTIONS

1. A central issue in appellate procedure is the applicable "standard of review." This refers to the degree of scrutiny or deference that an appellate court will apply when reviewing the decision of the trial court. Nondeferential review (called "de

---

4. [Latin for "the mere say-so." – EDS.]

novo" review in the federal system, meaning "from scratch" or "anew") means that the appellate court will redecide the question without giving any weight to the lower court's decision: It will substitute its judgment for that of the district court. Deferential review means that the appellate court will give latitude to the lower court's decision, and ask whether it was reasonable: that is, within a range in which reasonable minds could disagree. A reasonable decision will be upheld on appeal under such a standard even if the appellate judges would themselves have decided the matter differently had they been the trial judge. Which standard was applied in *Joiner*?

2. The last two sentences of the "ipse dixit" paragraph are a crucial aspect of *Joiner*. Try to articulate in your own words what the Court meant.

3. Does *Joiner* stand for the proposition that PCBs do not cause lung cancer, and that the opinion of any expert who claims otherwise will be excluded from evidence in federal courts?

d. *Kumho Tire*

Daubert explicitly dealt only with scientific evidence. Immediately following the case, the circuits split on how, or whether, *Daubert* applied to "technical or other specialized knowledge." The Court addressed this issue in the following case involving a tire blowout. Consider the following questions to focus your reading of the case:

1. What is the central legal principle articulated by *Kumho Tire*?
2. Does *Daubert* apply to cases that do not involve "scientific" knowledge? If so, how? Do the four *Daubert* factors apply or not?
3. What is the trial judge's role in evaluating expert testimony?

KUMHO TIRE COMPANY, LTD. *v.* CARMICHAEL
526 U.S. 137 (1999)

Justice BREYER delivered the opinion of the Court.

. . . [This] case requires us to decide how *Daubert* applies to the testimony of engineers and other experts who are not scientists. We conclude that *Daubert*'s general holding—setting forth the trial judge's general "gatekeeping" obligation—applies not only to testimony based on "scientific" knowledge, but also to testimony based on "technical" and "other specialized" knowledge. See Fed. Rule Evid. 702. We also conclude that a trial court may consider one or more of the more specific factors that *Daubert* mentioned when doing so will help determine that testimony's reliability. But, as the Court stated in *Daubert*, the test of reliability is "flexible," and *Daubert*'s list of specific factors neither necessarily nor exclusively applies to all experts or in every case. Rather, the law grants a district court the same broad latitude when it decides how to determine reliability as it enjoys in respect to its ultimate reliability determination. Applying these standards, we determine that the District Court's decision in this case—not to admit certain expert testimony—was within its discretion and therefore lawful.

I

[The Carmichaels brought a diversity suit against the manufacturer and distributor of a tire that blew out while the Carmichaels were driving their minivan, causing the death of one passenger and severe injuries to other passengers. The plaintiff's claim that the tire was defective rested in significant part on the testimony of their tire failure analysis expert, Dennis Carlson. It was undisputed that the blowout was caused by a separation of the tire tread from the inner steel-belted "carcass" of the tire. However, the defendants disputed Carlson's conclusion that a defect caused the separation. This conclusion was based on Carlson's belief that a design or manufacturing defect is probably the cause of such a separation whenever the blown-out tire in question has fewer than two of the following four physical signs of "overdeflection" (essentially, car-owner misuse) of the tire: (a) tread wear on the tire's shoulder that is greater than the tread wear along the tire's center; (b) signs of a "bead groove," where the beads have been pushed too hard against the bead seat on the inside of the tire's rim; (c) sidewalls of the tire with physical signs of deterioration, such as discoloration; and/or (d) marks on the tire's rim flange.]

Carlson added that he had inspected the tire in question. He conceded that the tire to a limited degree showed greater wear on the shoulder than in the center, some signs of "bead groove," some discoloration, a few marks on the rim flange, and inadequately filled puncture holes (which can also cause heat that might lead to separation). But, in each instance, he testified that the symptoms were not significant, and he explained why he believed that they did not reveal overdeflection. For example, the extra shoulder wear, he said, appeared primarily on one shoulder, whereas an overdeflected tire would reveal equally abnormal wear on both shoulders. Carlson concluded that the tire did not bear at least two of the four overdeflection symptoms, nor was there any less obvious cause of separation; and since neither overdeflection nor the punctures caused the blowout, a defect must have done so.

[Kumho Tire moved for summary judgment, arguing that Carlson's testimony should be excluded from evidence because his methodology failed Rule 702's reliability requirement; and without Carlson's testimony, plaintiff would be unable to prove that a manufacturing or design defect caused the blow-out and the injuries. The district court agreed, excluded Carlson's testimony, and dismissed the case. The Eleventh Circuit reversed, holding that Carlson's testimony, which it viewed as relying on experience rather than scientific methodology, "falls outside the scope of *Daubert*," that "the district court erred as a matter of law by applying *Daubert* in this case," and that the case must be remanded for further (non-*Daubert*-type) consideration under Rule 702.]

...We granted certiorari in light of uncertainty among the lower courts about whether, or how, *Daubert* applies to expert testimony that might be characterized as based not upon "scientific" knowledge, but rather upon "technical" or "other specialized."

II

A

In *Daubert*, this Court held that Federal Rule of Evidence 702 imposes a special obligation upon a trial judge to "ensure that any and all scientific testimony . . . is not only relevant, but reliable." The initial question before us is whether this basic gate-keeping obligation applies only to "scientific" testimony or to all expert testimony. We, like the parties, believe that it applies to all expert testimony.

For one thing, Rule 702 itself says:

> If scientific, technical, or other specialized knowledge will assist the trier of fact to understand the evidence or to determine a fact in issue, a witness qualified as an expert by knowledge, skill, experience, training, or education, may testify thereto in the form of an opinion or otherwise.

This language makes no relevant distinction between "scientific" knowledge and "technical" or "other specialized" knowledge. It makes clear that any such knowledge might become the subject of expert testimony. In *Daubert*, the Court . . . referred only to "scientific" knowledge . . . [but only] "because that was the nature of the expertise" at issue.

Neither is the evidentiary rationale that underlay the Court's basic *Daubert* "gate-keeping" determination limited to "scientific" knowledge. *Daubert* pointed out that Federal Rules 702 and 703 grant expert witnesses testimonial latitude unavailable to other witnesses on the "assumption that the expert's opinion will have a reliable basis in the knowledge and experience of his discipline." The Rules grant that latitude to all experts, not just to "scientific" ones.

Finally, it would prove difficult, if not impossible, for judges to administer evidentiary rules under which a gatekeeping obligation depended upon a distinction between "scientific" knowledge and "technical" or "other specialized" knowledge. There is no clear line that divides the one from the others. . . . Neither is there a convincing need to make such distinctions. Experts of all kinds tie observations to conclusions through the use of what Judge Learned Hand called "general truths derived from . . . specialized experience." And whether the specific expert testimony focuses upon specialized observations, the specialized translation of those observations into theory, a specialized theory itself, or the application of such a theory in a particular case, the expert's testimony often will rest "upon an experience confessedly foreign in kind to [the jury's] own." The trial judge's effort to assure that the specialized testimony is reliable and relevant can help the jury evaluate that foreign experience, whether the testimony reflects scientific, technical, or other specialized knowledge.

We conclude that *Daubert*'s general principles apply to the expert matters described in Rule 702. The Rule, in respect to all such matters, "establishes a standard of evidentiary reliability." It "requires a valid . . . connection to the pertinent inquiry as a precondition to admissibility." Id., at 592, 113 S. Ct. 2786. And where such testimony's factual basis, data, principles, methods, or their application are called sufficiently into question, see Part III, infra, the trial judge must determine whether the testimony has "a reliable basis in the knowledge and experience of [the relevant] discipline." 509 U.S. at 592, 113 S. Ct. 2786.

B

Petitioners ask more specifically whether a trial judge determining the "admissibility of an engineering expert's testimony" may consider several more specific factors that Daubert said might "bear on" a judge's gatekeeping determination. These factors include:

— Whether a "theory or technique . . . can be (and has been) tested";
— Whether it "has been subjected to peer review and publication";
— Whether, in respect to a particular technique, there is a high "known or potential rate of error" and whether there are "standards controlling the technique's operation"; and
— Whether the theory or technique enjoys "general acceptance" within a "relevant scientific community."

Emphasizing the word "may" in the question, we answer that question yes.

Engineering testimony rests upon scientific foundations, the reliability of which will be at issue in some cases. In other cases, the relevant reliability concerns may focus upon personal knowledge or experience. As the Solicitor General points out, there are many different kinds of experts, and many different kinds of expertise. See Brief for United States as Amicus Curiae 18–19, and n.5 (citing cases involving experts in drug terms, handwriting analysis, criminal modus operandi, land valuation, agricultural practices, railroad procedures, attorney's fee valuation, and others). Our emphasis on the word "may" thus reflects *Daubert*'s description of the Rule 702 inquiry as "a flexible one." *Daubert* makes clear that the factors it mentions do not constitute a "definitive checklist or test." And *Daubert* adds that the gatekeeping inquiry must be "'tied to the facts'" of a particular "case." We agree with the Solicitor General that "[t]he factors identified in *Daubert* may or may not be pertinent in assessing reliability, depending on the nature of the issue, the expert's particular expertise, and the subject of his testimony." The conclusion, in our view, is that we can neither rule out, nor rule in, for all cases and for all time the applicability of the factors mentioned in *Daubert*, nor can we now do so for subsets of cases categorized by category of expert or by kind of evidence. Too much depends upon the particular circumstances of the particular case at issue. . . .

At the same time, and contrary to the Court of Appeals' view, some of *Daubert*'s questions can help to evaluate the reliability even of experience-based testimony. In certain cases, it will be appropriate for the trial judge to ask, for example, how often an engineering expert's experience-based methodology has produced erroneous results, or whether such a method is generally accepted in the relevant engineering community. Likewise, it will at times be useful to ask even of a witness whose expertise is based purely on experience, say, a perfume tester able to distinguish among odors at a sniff, whether his preparation is of a kind that others in the field would recognize as acceptable.

We must therefore disagree with the Eleventh Circuit's holding that a trial judge may ask questions of the sort *Daubert* mentioned only where an expert "relies on the application of scientific principles," but not where an expert relies "on skill- or experience-based observation." We do not believe that Rule 702 creates a schematism that segregates expertise by type while mapping certain kinds of questions to certain kinds of experts. Life and the legal cases that it generates are too complex to warrant so definitive a match.

To say this is not to deny the importance of *Daubert*'s gatekeeping requirement. The objective of that requirement is to ensure the reliability and relevancy of expert testimony. It is to make certain that an expert, whether basing testimony upon professional studies or personal experience, employs in the courtroom the same level of intellectual rigor that characterizes the practice of an expert in the relevant field. Nor do we deny that, as stated in *Daubert*, the particular questions that it mentioned will often be appropriate for use in determining the reliability of challenged expert testimony. Rather, we conclude that the trial judge must have considerable leeway in deciding in a particular case how to go about determining whether particular expert testimony is reliable. That is to say, a trial court should consider the specific factors identified in Daubert where they are reasonable measures of the reliability of expert testimony.

[Our] opinion in *Joiner* makes clear that a court of appeals is to apply an abuse-of-discretion standard when it "review[s] a trial court's decision to admit or exclude expert testimony." That standard applies as much to the trial court's decisions about how to determine reliability as to its ultimate conclusion. Otherwise, the trial judge would lack the discretionary authority needed both to avoid unnecessary "reliability" proceedings in ordinary cases where the reliability of an expert's methods is properly taken for granted, and to require appropriate proceedings in the less usual or more complex cases where cause for questioning the expert's reliability arises. . . .

III

We further explain the way in which a trial judge "may" consider *Daubert*'s factors by applying these considerations to the case at hand, a matter that has been briefed exhaustively by the parties and their 19 amici. The District Court did not doubt Carlson's qualifications, which included a masters degree in mechanical engineering, ten years' work at Michelin America, Inc., and testimony as a tire failure consultant in other tort cases. Rather, it excluded the testimony because, despite those qualifications, it initially doubted, and then found unreliable, "the methodology employed by the expert in analyzing the data obtained in the visual inspection, and the scientific basis, if any, for such an analysis." . . . It fell outside the range where experts might reasonably differ, and where the jury must decide among the conflicting views of different experts, even though the evidence is "shaky." In our view, the doubts that triggered the District Court's initial inquiry here were reasonable, as was the court's ultimate conclusion.

[The] specific issue before the court was not the reasonableness in general of a tire expert's use of a visual and tactile inspection to determine whether overdeflection had caused the tire's tread to separate from its steel-belted carcass. Rather, it was the reasonableness of using such an approach, along with Carlson's particular method of analyzing the data thereby obtained, ... could reliably determine the cause of this tire's separation. . . .

[The] transcripts of Carlson's depositions support both the trial court's initial uncertainty and its final conclusion. Those transcripts cast considerable doubt upon the reliability of both the explicit theory (about the need for two signs of abuse) and the implicit proposition (about the significance of visual inspection in this case).

Among other things, the expert could not say whether the tire had traveled more than 10, or 20, or 30, or 40, or 50 thousand miles, adding that 6,000 miles was "about how far" he could "say with any certainty." The court could reasonably have wondered about the reliability of a method of visual and tactile inspection sufficiently precise to ascertain with some certainty the abuse-related significance of minute shoulder/center relative tread wear differences, but insufficiently precise to tell "with any certainty" from the tread wear whether a tire had traveled less than 10,000 or more than 50,000 miles. And these concerns might have been augmented by Carlson's repeated reliance on the "subjective[ness]" of his mode of analysis in response to questions seeking specific information regarding how he could differentiate between a tire that actually had been overdeflected and a tire that merely looked as though it had been. They would have been further augmented by the fact that Carlson said he had inspected the tire itself for the first time the morning of his first deposition, and then only for a few hours. (His initial conclusions were based on photographs.)

Moreover, prior to his first deposition, Carlson had issued a signed report in which he concluded that the tire had "not been . . . overloaded or underinflated," not because of the absence of "two of four" signs of abuse, but simply because "the rim flange impressions . . . were normal." That report also said that the "tread depth remaining was 3/32 inch," id., at 336, though the opposing expert's (apparently undisputed) measurements indicate that the tread depth taken at various positions around the tire actually ranged from .5/32 of an inch to 4/32 of an inch, with the tire apparently showing greater wear along both shoulders than along the center.

Further, in respect to one sign of abuse, bead grooving, the expert seemed to deny the sufficiency of his own simple visual-inspection methodology. He testified that most tires have some bead groove pattern, that where there is reason to suspect an abnormal bead groove he would ideally "look at a lot of [similar] tires" to know the grooving's significance, and that he had not looked at many tires similar to the one at issue.

Finally, the court, after looking for a defense of Carlson's methodology as applied in these circumstances, found no convincing defense. Rather, it found (1) that "none" of the *Daubert* factors, including that of "general acceptance" in the relevant expert community, indicated that Carlson's testimony was reliable; (2) that its own analysis "revealed no countervailing factors operating in favor of admissibility which could outweigh those identified in *Daubert*"; and (3) that the "parties identified no such factors in their briefs." For these three reasons taken together, it concluded that Carlson's testimony was unreliable.

[No] one denies that an expert might draw a conclusion from a set of observations based on extensive and specialized experience. Nor does anyone deny that, as a general matter, tire abuse may often be identified by qualified experts through visual or tactile inspection of the tire. See Affidavit of H.R. Baumgardner 1–2, cited in Brief for National Academy of Forensic Engineers as Amicus Curiae 16 (Tire engineers rely on visual examination and process of elimination to analyze experimental test tires). . . .

The particular issue in this case concerned the use of Carlson's two-factor test and his related use of visual/tactile inspection to draw conclusions on the basis of what seemed small observational differences. We have found no indication in the record that other experts in the industry use Carlson's two-factor test or that tire experts such as Carlson normally make the very fine distinctions about, say, the symmetry of comparatively greater shoulder tread wear that were necessary, on Carlson's own theory, to support his conclusions. Nor, despite the prevalence of tire testing, does anyone refer to any articles or papers that validate Carlson's approach. Indeed, no one has argued that Carlson himself, were he still working for Michelin, would have concluded in a report to his employer that a similar tire was similarly defective on grounds identical to those upon which he rested his conclusion here. Of course, Carlson himself claimed that his method was accurate, but, as we pointed out in *Joiner*, "nothing in either *Daubert* or the Federal Rules of Evidence requires a district court to admit opinion evidence that is connected to existing data only by the ipse dixit of the expert."

Respondents additionally argue that the District Court too rigidly applied *Daubert's* criteria. They read its opinion to hold that a failure to satisfy any one of those criteria automatically renders expert testimony inadmissible. . . . [However, the court] explicitly recognized that the relevant reliability inquiry "should be 'flexible,'" that its "'overarching subject [should be] . . . validity' and reliability," and that "*Daubert* was intended neither to be exhaustive nor to apply in every case." And the court ultimately based its decision upon Carlson's failure to satisfy either *Daubert's* factors or any other set of reasonable reliability criteria. In light of the record as developed by the parties, that conclusion was within the District Court's lawful discretion.

In sum, Rule 702 grants the district judge the discretionary authority, reviewable for its abuse, to determine reliability in light of the particular facts and circumstances of the particular case. The District Court did not abuse its discretionary authority in this case. Hence, the judgment of the Court of Appeals is reversed.

NOTES AND QUESTIONS

1. Note that in all three cases on experts and FRE 702, *Daubert, Joiner*, and *Kumho Tire*, the issue arose in the context of a motion for summary judgment. The moving party in a summary judgment motion must meet its burden of production with admissible evidence. (Why?) Why do you think a summary judgment motion could turn on an evidence objection under FRE 702?

2. We have now heard a few times that the trial judge (the district court judge) is the "gatekeeper" when it comes to admitting expert testimony. What does this mean?

3. Would the district court have abused its discretion if it had admitted Carlson's testimony?

4. Suppose the Eleventh Circuit had reversed the district court, as here, but had done so by applying *Daubert* and concluding that Carlson's testimony met one of the *Daubert* factors. Would the Supreme Court have affirmed the Eleventh Circuit?

5. It is widely assumed that *Daubert* establishes the basic standard for admitting expert testimony. Does that mean that at least one prong of the four-part *Daubert* test must be met in order to admit expert testimony? What does *Kumho* say about this?

5. The 2000 Amendments to FRE 702

In 2000, FRE 702 was amended to its current form, replacing the original language that was quoted in the previous section of the textbook. Judges and practitioners now find themselves in the unenviable position of having to quote three sources of authority that, while generally consistent, adopt varying language (and arguably slightly varied approaches) to expert witness reliability. *Daubert* sets out its four-factor test, noting that not all of them will apply in all cases. *Kumho Tire* purports to reaffirm *Daubert* and extend it beyond the traditional "laboratory" sciences, but notes that in some cases, it may be appropriate to apply *none* of the four *Daubert* factors:

> [t]he factors identified in *Daubert* may or may not be pertinent in assessing reliability, depending on the nature of the issue, the expert's particular expertise, and the subject of his testimony. The conclusion, in our view, is that we can neither rule out, nor rule in, for all cases and for all time the applicability of the factors mentioned in *Daubert*[.] [*Kumho Tire*, 526 U.S. at 150 (internal quotations omitted).]

Finally, in 2000, FRE 702 was amended to specify three reliability factors in subsections (b)-(d). For convenience, we repeat them here:

(b) the testimony is based on sufficient facts or data;
(c) the testimony is the product of reliable principles and methods; and
(d) the expert has reliably applied the principles and methods to the facts of the case.

As the Advisory Committee explained, these factors were added "in *response* to *Daubert*," but "no attempt has been made to 'codify' the specific factors" stated in *Daubert*. Advisory Committee Notes to FRE 702—2000 Amendment (emphasis added). *Daubert* is thus one of the stranger controlling precedents you will encounter: Everyone claims to be following it, but its factors need not be adhered to, either in whole or in part. The one doctrinal point we know for sure is that trial judges have broad discretion to rule on the reliability of expert testimony, and their rulings will be reviewed deferentially on appeal—subject to reversal only for an abuse of discretion.

The Advisory Committee Note to the 2000 Amendment to FRE 702 provides a particularly comprehensive and well-reasoned explanation of the reliability requirement, and its application to various types of expert testimony. It is worth reading in its entirety. Here, we break it down to emphasize its most important points.

Daubert Not Codified in Rule 702.   The Advisory Committee begins by making clear that amended FRE 702 is not a codification of *Daubert*.

> Rule 702 has been amended in response to Daubert v. Merrell Dow Pharmaceuticals, Inc., 509 U.S. 579 (1993), and to the many cases applying *Daubert*, including Kumho Tire Co. v. Carmichael, 119 S. Ct. 1167 (1999). In *Daubert* the Court charged trial judges with the responsibility of acting as gatekeepers to exclude unreliable expert testimony, and the Court in *Kumho* clarified that this gatekeeper function applies to all expert testimony, not just testimony based in science. The amendment affirms the trial court's role as gatekeeper and provides some general standards that the trial court must

use to assess the reliability and helpfulness of proffered expert testimony. Consistently with *Kumho*, the Rule as amended provides that all types of expert testimony present questions of admissibility for the trial court in deciding whether the evidence is reliable and helpful. . . . [T]he proponent [of the expert testimony] has the burden of establishing that the pertinent admissibility requirements are met by a preponderance of the evidence.

Daubert set forth a non-exclusive checklist for trial courts to use in assessing the reliability of scientific expert testimony. . . . The Court in *Kumho* held that these factors might also be applicable in assessing the reliability of nonscientific expert testimony, depending upon "the particular circumstances of the particular case at issue." 119 S. Ct. at 1175.

No attempt has been made to "codify" these specific factors. *Daubert* itself emphasized that the factors were neither exclusive nor dispositive. Other cases have recognized that not all of the specific *Daubert* factors can apply to every type of expert testimony. . . . The standards set forth in the amendment are broad enough to require consideration of any or all of the specific *Daubert* factors where appropriate.

Other Factors Relevant. The Advisory Committee proceeds to outline its own list of reliability factors.

Courts both before and after *Daubert* have found other factors relevant in determining whether expert testimony is sufficiently reliable to be considered by the trier of fact. These factors include:

(1) Whether experts are "proposing to testify about matters growing naturally and directly out of research they have conducted independent of the litigation, or whether they have developed their opinions expressly for purposes of testifying." Daubert v. Merrell Dow Pharmaceuticals, Inc., 43 F.3d 1311, 1317 (9th Cir. 1995).

(2) Whether the expert has unjustifiably extrapolated from an accepted premise to an unfounded conclusion. See General Elec. Co. v. Joiner, 522 U.S. 136, 146 (1997) (noting that in some cases a trial court "may conclude that there is simply too great an analytical gap between the data and the opinion proffered").

(3) Whether the expert has adequately accounted for obvious alternative explanations.

(4) Whether the expert "is being as careful as he would be in his regular professional work outside his paid litigation consulting." See Kumho Tire Co. v. Carmichael, 119 S. Ct. 1167, 1176 (1999) (*Daubert* requires the trial court to assure itself that the expert "employs in the courtroom the same level of intellectual rigor that characterizes the practice of an expert in the relevant field").

(5) Whether the field of expertise claimed by the expert is known to reach reliable results for the type of opinion the expert would give.

[Other] factors may also be relevant. See *Kumho*, 119 S. Ct. 1167, 1176 ("[W]e conclude that the trial judge must have considerable leeway in deciding in a particular case how to go about determining whether particular expert testimony is reliable."). Yet no single factor is necessarily dispositive of the reliability of a particular expert's testimony.

***Daubert* Did Not Raise the Bar for Admitting Expert Testimony.**   The Advisory Committee stated "A review of the case law after *Daubert* shows that the rejection of expert testimony is the exception rather than the rule. *Daubert* did not work a 'sea change over federal evidence law,' and 'the trial court's role as gatekeeper is not intended to serve as a replacement for the adversary system.'"

Contradictory Expert Testimony Not Per Se Unreliable.   Parties frequently present experts who contest one another's testimony. It is perfectly logical for a court to admit both as reliable, and allow the jury to decide between them.

> When a trial court, applying this amendment, rules that an expert's testimony is reliable, this does not necessarily mean that contradictory expert testimony is unreliable. The amendment is broad enough to permit testimony that is the product of competing principles or methods in the same field of expertise. As the court stated in In re Paoli R.R. Yard PCB Litigation, 35 F.3d 717, 744 (3d Cir. 1994), proponents "do not have to demonstrate to the judge by a preponderance of the evidence that the assessments of their experts are correct, they only have to demonstrate by a preponderance of evidence that their opinions are reliable. . . . The evidentiary requirement of reliability is lower than the merits standard of correctness.". . .

Reliability Inquiry May Extend to Conclusions.   The Advisory Committee observed that a focus on the reliability of methodology does not insulate conclusions from inquiry:

> The Court in *Daubert* declared that the "focus, of course, must be solely on principles and methodology, not on the conclusions they generate." 509 U.S. at 595. Yet as the Court later recognized, "conclusions and methodology are not entirely distinct from one another." General Elec. Co. v. Joiner, 522 U.S. 136, 146 (1997). Under the amendment, as under *Daubert*, when an expert purports to apply principles and methods in accordance with professional standards, and yet reaches a conclusion that other experts in the field would not reach, the trial court may fairly suspect that the principles and methods have not been faithfully applied. The amendment specifically provides that the trial court must scrutinize not only the principles and methods used by the expert, but also whether those principles and methods have been properly applied to the facts of the case. . . .

Reliability Inquiry Applies to All Expert Testimony.   The Advisory Committee emphasized *Kumho Tire*'s holding that reliability is a question for all expert testimony, not just scientific experts.

> As stated earlier, the amendment does not distinguish between scientific and other forms of expert testimony. The trial court's gatekeeping function applies to testimony by any expert. While the relevant factors for determining reliability will vary from expertise to expertise, the amendment rejects the premise that an expert's testimony should be treated more permissively simply because it is outside the realm of science. An opinion from an expert who is not a scientist should receive the same degree of scrutiny for reliability as an opinion from an expert who purports to be a scientist.

Some types of expert testimony will be more objectively verifiable, and subject to the expectations of falsifiability, peer review, and publication, than others. Some types of expert testimony will not rely on anything like a scientific method, and so will have to be evaluated by reference to other standard principles attendant to the particular area of expertise. The trial judge in all cases of proffered expert testimony must find that it is properly grounded, well-reasoned, and not speculative before it can be admitted. The expert's testimony must be grounded in an accepted body of learning or experience in the expert's field, and the expert must explain how the conclusion is so grounded. . . .

The amendment requires that the testimony must be the product of reliable principles and methods that are reliably applied to the facts of the case. While the terms "principles" and "methods" may convey a certain impression when applied to scientific knowledge, they remain relevant when applied to testimony based on technical or other specialized knowledge. For example, when a law enforcement agent testifies regarding the use of code words in a drug transaction, the principle used by the agent is that participants in such transactions regularly use code words to conceal the nature of their activities. The method used by the agent is the application of extensive experience to analyze the meaning of the conversations. So long as the principles and methods are reliable and applied reliably to the facts of the case, this type of testimony should be admitted.

Demonstrating Reliability of Nonscientific Expert Testimony.   The Advisory Committee attempted to fill in an important gap in the *Kumho Tire* opinion: How can experts outside the science and technology fields demonstrate reliability, in the absence of peer publications, error rates, and testing?

Nothing in this amendment is intended to suggest that experience alone—or experience in conjunction with other knowledge, skill, training or education—may not provide a sufficient foundation for expert testimony. To the contrary, the text of Rule 702 expressly contemplates that an expert may be qualified on the basis of experience. In certain fields, experience is the predominant, if not sole, basis for a great deal of reliable expert testimony.

If the witness is relying solely or primarily on experience, then the witness must explain how that experience leads to the conclusion reached, why that experience is a sufficient basis for the opinion, and how that experience is reliably applied to the facts. The trial court's gatekeeping function requires more than simply "taking the expert's word for it." The more subjective and controversial the expert's inquiry, the more likely the testimony should be excluded as unreliable. . . .

The Rule Does Not Forbid Hypothetical Opinions.   Prior to the FRE, experts were not allowed to testify about case-specific facts. Instead, they framed their testimony in the form of opinions on hypothetical questions designed to track the facts in the case. Such hypotheticals were often extremely cumbersome and elaborate, and resulted in making expert testimony even harder to follow than it is today. Although the rules no longer require such expert hypotheticals, neither do they forbid them. The Advisory Committee states that "the language 'facts or data' is broad enough to allow an expert to rely on hypothetical facts that are supported by the evidence."

Courts May Not Resolve Underlying Factual Disputes in Ruling on Admissibility of Expert Testimony. Under FRE 104(a), a court may have to resolve factual disputes going to the reliability of the expert's qualifications and methodology, and the reliability of the "facts or data." The problem here is that at least some of the "facts or data" used by the expert will include reliance on the offering party's version of disputed underlying case facts. As the Advisory Committee states, "When facts are in dispute, experts sometimes reach different conclusions based on competing versions of the facts. The emphasis in the amendment on 'sufficient facts or data' is not intended to authorize a trial court to exclude an expert's testimony on the ground that the court believes one [party's] version of the facts and not the other." Thus, the court can't use its ruling on the admissibility of expert testimony as an occasion to resolve disputed "what happened" facts that are for the jury to decide.

KEY POINTS

1. FRE 702 permits expert opinion testimony based on specialized knowledge that is helpful to the jury to understanding a fact in issue. Specialized knowledge includes scientific, technical, or any other kind of knowledge outside common knowledge. Expertise can be gained through study, training, skill, or experience.

2. Expert opinion is automatically deemed helpful to the trier of fact where a case-specific fact or generalization necessary to a party's case either can't be known or can't be understood as a matter of common knowledge. Expert opinion may be helpful to the trier of fact where expert information sheds additional light on matters that fall within a gray area of common and expert knowledge.

3. FRE 702(b)-(d) require that expert testimony be based on applying reliable methods to sufficient facts or data. The trial judge has broad discretion to determine reliability, as an FRE 104(a) question, which will be reviewed deferentially on appeal.

4. The reliability inquiry, requiring use of "reliable principles and methods," applies to all expert testimony, whether scientific or not. The original *Daubert* factors may be applicable in certain cases, but are not controlling in cases where they are not pertinent to the expert opinion in question.

PROBLEMS

9.4. In United States v. Cross, defendant Steven Cross is charged with possession with intent to sell cocaine and conspiracy to sell cocaine. Cross had driven a car to a motel parking lot, where he met Tony Genovese, a government informant. Genovese said, "Let's open the trunk." When the automatic trunk latch didn't work, Cross got out and the two men went to the back of the car. Cross opened the trunk with the car key, revealing ten 16-oz. packages of Gold Label brand granulated sugar. Cross was arrested in the parking lot by waiting FBI agents. It is undisputed that the packages contained cocaine. But Cross testifies that he thought he was merely dropping off the car at the request of his friend Barry Styles, who was loaning the car to Genovese. The prosecution wants to call Drug Enforcement Agency (DEA) Agent Barbara Cousins to testify as follows:

> I have been involved in the investigation and prosecution of over 500 cases of narcotics dealing over the course of 15 years with the DEA. I have trained state and federal law enforcement agents in investigating drug crimes for the past five years. I have investigated at least 100 cases in which a defendant making a drug delivery has claimed that he was unaware that he was carrying drugs in the luggage or car trunk, but merely believed he was delivering something for a friend. That claim has never been true in any of those cases, not even once. It is a standard lie told by drug couriers.

What arguments can be made for admission or exclusion of this testimony under FRE 702?

9.5. In a personal injury suit against a grocery store, Maxine Black sought to introduce the testimony of Dr. Reyna, her algologist (a doctor who treats persistent pain). Ms. Black developed fibromyalgia (a nonspecific, chronic-pain illness) after a slip-and-fall accident. At trial, Dr. Reyna testified that she fully apprised herself of Ms. Black's prior medical history before the accident, that she determined that no post-accident incident was an intervening cause for the onset of Ms. Black's fibromyalgia, and that no other factors—based upon her review of tests performed prior to accepting Ms. Black as a patient, as well as those tests which Dr. Reyna, herself, directed to be made—contributed to Ms. Black's fibromyalgia. Reyna acknowledged that fibromyalgia has no known etiology (i.e., medical science does not know whether the cause of the condition is muscle, nerve, or hormone damage); but she was willing to testify that the fall contributed to the development of Ms. Black's condition. Should Dr. Reyna be allowed to testify?

9.6. As part of a conspiracy trial, the government called a handwriting analyst to testify to the identity of persons who had addressed an envelope containing illegal drugs. The analyst, Dr. Learned, had attended courses and seminars on handwriting identification, was employed by the secret service as a handwriting expert, and had testified in over 100 court cases. Handwriting analysis essentially involves comparing a known sample of a person's writing with the writing on the document sought to be identified. The analyst compares the characteristics of the writing, including the slant of the writing, the height and shape of the letters, and the spacing between letters and words. After the court ruled that Dr. Learned's testimony was admissible, the defense tried to call Lou Bowden, a law professor who had no formal training in handwriting analysis and who lacked practical experience in the field. Bowden nevertheless had published an article in a well-respected law review, criticizing the field of handwriting analysis and its use in litigation. Bowden's main critique of this type of analysis was that it lacked standards to guide experts in weighing the match or nonmatch of particular handwriting characteristics. The prosecution objects that Bowden is not a handwriting analysis expert, and therefore his testimony is irrelevant and inadmissible. What are the arguments for and against admissibility?

C. FACTUAL BASIS FOR EXPERT OPINION

FRE 702(b)-(d) tell us that an admissible expert opinion must be based on "sufficient facts or data" (or "facts of the case") to which "reliable principles and methods" have been "reliably applied." The judge will have access to these underlying "facts or data" in determining whether the expert meets FRE 702's test for reliability. But if knowing the underlying facts is important to assessing the reliability of an expert's opinion, doesn't it stand to reason that the jury should learn those facts too?

Of course it does. But the problem is that expert analysis outside the courtroom is not limited to the rules of evidence: Experts consider hearsay and other sorts of inadmissible evidence all the time. Requiring experts to conform to courtroom evidence rules risks unduly interfering with the reliability of their analytical work or hampering their explanation of it in their testimony, or both. But freeing expert witnesses from evidence rules risks presenting inadmissible evidence to the jury through the testimony of the expert. Prior to the adoption of the FRE, common law evidence rules tended to opt for the first (restrictive) approach. The FRE has shifted somewhat in the other direction, loosening the restrictions on experts while still trying to limit the amount of inadmissible evidence that may come in. FRE 703 and 705 attempt to deal with these issues.

1. FRE 703

RULE 703.   BASES OF AN EXPERT'S OPINION TESTIMONY

An expert may base an opinion on facts or data in the case that the expert has been made aware of or personally observed. If experts in the particular field would reasonably rely on those kinds of facts or data in forming an opinion on the subject, they need not be admissible for the opinion to be admitted. But if the facts or data would otherwise be inadmissible, the proponent of the opinion may disclose them to the jury only if their probative value in helping the jury evaluate the opinion substantially outweighs their prejudicial effect.

2. Explanation of FRE 703

FRE 703's three sentences make three basic points about the "facts or data" an expert witness can rely on in offering an admissible opinion.

"Made aware of or personally observed."   An expert witness can be given case facts through hearsay. Prior to trial, the attorney may simply summarize case facts for the expert with a written or verbal summary, or give the expert copies of evidentiary documents, depositions, and other discovery materials to review. These are the most typical ways that expert witnesses are "made aware of" case facts or data.

In some instances, an expert may have personally observed litigated events as they occurred. The most common example is a treating physician or other medical staff, who may have observed a victim's or plaintiff's injuries very shortly after they occurred. Such a witness may be asked both to explain what happened, as a percipient witness with firsthand knowledge under FRE 602, and to give an expert diagnosis or opinion under FRE 702.

What about a forensic chemist who tests a substance weeks after it was seized from the defendant, and identifies it as cocaine—is that a personal observation, or a fact of which the chemist was "made aware"? You could argue for either, but the distinction is academic here. The point is that the chemist could present his observations in expert testimony either way.

"Reasonably rely on." The second sentence makes clear that an expert witness may base an opinion on facts that would be inadmissible as courtroom evidence "[i]f experts in the particular field would reasonably rely on those kinds of facts or data in forming an opinion on the subject." The opinion does not become inadmissible because the underlying facts on which it is based are inadmissible.

An example of this would be an opinion based on hearsay. Most experts practice their disciplines outside the litigation system without using the hearsay rule. In medicine, for example, the hospital night nurse informs the day nurse who informs the doctor that the patient had a high fever, and the doctor prescribes action in part on the basis of that report. Given the reasonableness of reliance on hearsay to make medical diagnoses, FRE 703 allows medical experts to base their opinions on hearsay in litigated cases. Note that the hearsay provided to an expert does not necessarily have to take the exact form and manner it would have take in "the real world": As an attorney, you don't have to provide hearsay to your retained medical expert by having a nurse make entries on a hospital chart. The point is that doctors reasonably rely on hearsay reports of symptoms and other medical facts; therefore, you can provide such hearsay information to the doctor you have retained as your expert witness.

Hearsay is not the only example, of course. A psychiatrist or social worker may reasonably rely on character evidence that would be inadmissible in litigation. A building contractor might reasonably rely on a verbal summary of information from a blueprint, rather than always looking at the original blueprint herself (violating the best evidence rule). FRE 703 allows you as an attorney to provide your expert witness any information that, though inadmissible as evidence in court, is of a general type or form that that an expert in that field would use when practicing her expertise outside the litigation system.

Whether an expert in a particular field "reasonably relies on" a certain type of inadmissible matter is a fact question that the judge would decide under FRE 104(a). Sometimes, it is easily disposed of as a matter of common sense. Where reasonable reliance is disputed, the question is likely to overlap with disputes over the reliability of the opinion, or the scope of the witness's expertise. Compare Sphere Drake

Insurance PLC v. Trisko, 226 F.3d 951 (8th Cir. 2000) (in insurance coverage dispute over stolen jewelry, police detective allowed to testify as expert about *modi operandi* of jewel thieves based in part on conversations with informants), with Redman v. John D. Brush & Co., 111 F.3d 1174 (4th Cir. 1997) (in products liability case for allegedly defective store safe, design expert on materials and assembly of safes did not reasonably rely on conversations with store personnel to identify a standard of burglary protection capacity).

Finally, it is important to remember that the "reasonably rely on" limitation applies only to inadmissible matter that the expert relies on for his testimony. Experts may rely on any admissible evidence in forming an opinion, whether or not that evidence is of a type the expert usually encounters and relies on outside of the litigation setting.

Reverse 403 Test for Inadmissible Facts. As noted above, logic dictates that a jury be informed about the factual basis for an expert's opinion. FRE 702 sensibly states that the reliability of the factual basis is a key logical factor in the judge's assessment of the reliability of an expert opinion. And what's logic for the judge is logic for the jury. The problem, however, is that if all the facts and data made known to an expert were passed on to the jury, the expert witness could become a conduit for getting all kinds of inadmissible evidence in front of the jury. Expert testimony could thereby become an exception that swallows the entire body of exclusionary evidence rules.

FRE 703 tries to strike a balance between these two goals — protecting the policies underlying the various evidence exclusion rules, and allowing the jury a meaningful opportunity to assess the reliability of expert testimony. The rule does so by imposing a "reverse FRE 403" balancing test. Inadmissible facts relied on by the expert can be disclosed to the jury "only if their probative value in helping the jury evaluate the opinion substantially outweighs their prejudicial effect."

3. FRE 703: Policies, Problems, and Applications

a. Historical Background.

When faced with a conflict between the legal requirements concerning evidence, such as the hearsay rule, and the conventions of other disciplines, such as the reliance on hearsay accounts in a hospital setting, the common law tended to demand that witnesses from other disciplines conform their practice to ours. Experts were permitted to testify only on the basis of evidence that was admissible under the rules. Further, experts could not themselves present facts that had not been presented to the jury — that would, in effect, be hearsay testimony. Thus, an expert could only refer to facts that had been admitted in evidence at that point in the trial that the expert heard while sitting in the courtroom. But if the expert had not sat through the trial, or the relevant evidence had not yet been presented, the expert could not be deemed to know the case facts because he could not be supplied the facts through hearsay (such as a lawyer's summary of the evidence). See Williams v. Illinois, 132 S. Ct. 2221, 2257 (2012) (Thomas, J., concurring in the judgment). To work around this limitation, experts typically were asked long and involved hypothetical questions. The examiner would summarize the evidence presented to that point, and expected to be presented, in the form of hypothetical factual assumptions. The expert then offered an opinion based on the assumed facts. Use of the hypothetical question approach ensured that the premises of an opinion had been the subject of earlier testimony or admissible testimony forthcoming from other witnesses. But it also created a significant artificiality in trials. The hypothetical questions were extremely awkward, the expert's testimony would be made harder to follow, and advocates often felt compelled to put their experts on the stand at the end of their case, by which time admissibility questions would have been resolved.

The drafters of the Federal Rules rejected this aspect of the common law in FRE 703, providing that experts can testify on the basis of data that would be legally inadmissible, so long as "experts in the particular field would reasonably rely on those kinds of facts or data in forming an opinion on the subject." Thus, under FRE 703 experts no longer must conform their practices to the law's conventions, but rather the law bends to accommodate the practices of the other disciplines. The rule change also resolved a conundrum in common law treatment of expert testimony. What makes an expert an expert in many instances is a heavy dose of book learning. To the extent that an expert relies on academic study (books and treatises and the like) or on conversations with others such as occur during "rounds" at teaching hospitals, the expertise is based on hearsay, much of which would be inadmissible or too costly to produce at trial. The common law courts overlooked this point. Thus, even though the common law courts "purported" to require a basis of admissible evidence for an expert's opinion, opinions remained admissible even though they relied heavily on knowledge gained through a form of inadmissible, or at least unadmitted, hearsay. Under FRE 703, this is not a problem.

b. The Jury's Use of Inadmissible Facts Underlying Expert Opinion (Inadmissible "Basis Evidence")

The biggest problem presented by FRE 703 has always been the extent to which the rule permits the jury to be informed of inadmissible evidence relied on by the expert to form an opinion, when that opinion has itself been admitted in evidence. Does FRE 703 take precedence over various specific exclusionary rules by allowing the expert to divulge various items of inadmissible evidence, or does it restrict the expert to expressing and explaining the opinion, without divulging the inadmissible evidence? Can an expert witness in effect become a conduit for presenting inadmissible evidence to the jury?

FRE 703's Restrictive Approach to Inadmissible Basis Evidence. The original version of FRE 703 did not address this issue at all. For 25 years following the adoption of the federal rules, courts took inconsistent approaches to this question. Some liberally allowed experts to describe what has come to be called "basis evidence," referring to the facts (whether admissible or not) on which the expert reasonably based her opinion. See, e.g., Williams v. Illinois, 132 S. Ct. at 2239 (using the term "basis evidence"). Others approached such basis evidence with varying degrees of restrictiveness. In 2000, FRE 703 was amended to add the last sentence of the rule: The proponent of the opinion may not present the jury with inadmissible basis evidence unless a reverse FRE 403 standard is met: "probative value . . . substantially outweighs . . . prejudicial effect." There is an unavoidable cost to this resolution of the controversy: In some, perhaps many cases, the jury will not know all the facts the expert considered, and therefore will not be in a position to give a full evaluation to the expert's opinion. But the alternative is costly too: With no restriction, FRE 703 would make expert witnesses a conduit for much, if not all, the inadmissible evidence otherwise excluded in the case.

Limited Use of Otherwise Inadmissible Basis Evidence. The addition of the reverse 403 balancing test clears up only part of the controversy over the rule's meaning. Basis evidence will still be disclosed to the jury where the reverse 403 test is met. In such a case, is it admissible only to help the factfinder understand the opinion that is based on it? Or may the factfinder rely on the inadmissible basis evidence to draw inferences concerning the material propositions in the case?

The answer is clear: The factfinder may use the otherwise inadmissible basis evidence only to evaluate the expert's opinion, and not as substantive proof of other issues in the case. The rule apparently codifies what had been the majority approach to basis evidence even before the 2000 amendment. The reverse 403 balancing test in FRE 703 weighs the inadmissible fact's "probative value in helping the jury evaluate the opinion." Thus, the rule allows disclosure of otherwise inadmissible facts for the express purpose of evaluating the expert's opinion. To be sure, this language does not unambiguously imply the converse—disallowing jurors from considering the evidence for other purposes, namely as substantive proof of other issues in the case. But courts interpret it as restricting the use of otherwise inadmissible facts to evaluating the expert opinion. As the Supreme Court recently stated, FRE 703 "in appropriate cases, permits an expert to explain the facts on which his or her opinion is based without testifying to the truth of those facts." Williams v. Illinois, 132 S. Ct. 2221, 2228 (2012) (plurality opinion).

The Limiting Instruction Problem. There remains a problem, however. Where inadmissible basis evidence is relevant to prove a contested point outside the expert's testimony, it becomes necessary to give a puzzling limiting instruction to the jury—to consider the basis evidence only to the extent that it bears on the reliability of expert's opinion. In some cases, such an instruction can appear illogical. The expert's reliance on a fact necessarily implies that the expert believed it to be true and accurate. And if the jury believes that the expert opinion is reliable, then it too will believe that the disclosed basis facts are true and accurate. How can it be reasonable for an expert to rely on inadmissible basis facts, but not a jury to do so?

This problem was pointedly raised in an influential nonfederal appellate case operating under rules analogous to FRE 703. See In re Melton, 597 A.2d 892 (D.C. 1991). In *Melton*, a civil commitment hearing tried before a jury, the key issue was whether the respondent, Melton, was a danger to himself or others. Called as experts by the prosecution, two psychiatrists characterized Melton as schizophrenic and dangerous, citing secondhand accounts of Melton's violent or antisocial behavior. The trial court instructed the jury that the hearsay reported in the experts' testimony was to be considered only "for the purpose of evaluating the reasonableness and correctness of the doctors' conclusions," and not "to establish the truth of the matters asserted by [the declarants]." But as the appellate court cogently observed:

> The problem raised by Melton cannot, however, be avoided simply by calling the evidence expert testimony rather than hearsay. Labels cannot perform juridical alchemy. By resort[ing] to expert testimony, the District was able to bring to the jury's attention matters that could obviously prejudice Melton, including, e.g., reports that he had punched his mother, and that on an earlier occasion he had threatened his sister with a screwdriver. Melton was never able to cross-examine those who accused him of these anti-social acts.

The trial judge in Melton had tried to address this problem by giving a jury instruction fairly typical of what most federal courts do in allowing disclosure of otherwise inadmissible basis evidence.

> [T]hese statements are admitted only to demonstrate the information relied upon by the doctors in forming their conclusion. They are to be considered by you only for the purpose of evaluating the reasonableness and correctness of the doctors' conclusions. They are not to be considered by you as actual proof of the incidents described. They are hearsay and as such are not admissible to establish the truth of the matters asserted by them.

Critics observe that limiting instructions are unlikely to be followed by juries when they require jurors to ignore relevant evidence. Likewise, jurors may be unable to make subtle or sophisticated distinctions to avoid using evidence for a relevant, but impermissible purpose. But in a case like *Melton*, the problem is worse: The jury is being asked, not to make a sophisticated distinction, but *an illogical one*. The problem with the reasoning underlying the *Melton* trial court instruction is that, as the *Melton* appellate court so aptly put it, "you cannot believe that the testimony about the punch tends to show that Melton is dangerous unless you first believe that he actually punched his mother." 597 A.2d at 907. A jury cannot accept an opinion as true without accepting its factual basis as true. If the basis evidence is inadmissible hearsay, then logically it is offered for its truth, to substantiate and explain an expert opinion offered as valid.

The logical problem is not present in every case. For example, suppose the issue in *Melton* had been not the broad and rather all-inclusive question of "dangerousness," but rather whether he had committed an armed robbery. Suppose further that the psychiatrists were testifying about the validity of an insanity defense offered by Melton. Here, the apparent conundrum of accepting the truth of the hearsay about Melton punching his mother, but disregarding it for the substantive question of whether he committed the armed robbery, is not really different from admitting any other specific acts evidence for a limited purpose. Juries are routinely instructed to consider a prior bad act as relevant to "motive, intent, opportunity," etc., but not to consider it as showing a propensity to commit crime. Here, the problem seems no different.

However, where the inadmissible basis evidence gives rise to the same inference in the expert's testimony as it would when disclosed directly to the jury, such a limiting instruction seems much more problematic. This will almost invariably be the case where the basis evidence is inadmissible hearsay. Consider an arson case where the defendant contends that the fire was an accident. An arson investigator testifies for the prosecution that, in his expert opinion, the fire was set intentionally. The basis for his conclusion is that the remnants of a can of a flammable accelerant were found on the premises. Although such an accelerant is a common item found stored in people's basements, he believes this can was brought to the building the day before the fire, supporting his conclusion of arson. How does he know that? Because a witness interviewed by police stated that he saw the defendant bringing the can of accelerant to the building the day before the fire. In this hypothetical, the witness's statement is inadmissible testimonial hearsay, but is reasonably relied on by the inspector in investigating the cause of the fire—and in forming an opinion as an expert witness. But because the inspector uses the hearsay to draw the same conclusion that the jury would draw, the limiting instruction doesn't work. The jury can't consider the hearsay true for the expert's reasoning without considering it true for its own independent reasoning on the same point: that the defendant is more likely guilty of arson because he brought a can of accelerant to the building the day before the fire.

FRE 703's Compromise Solution.   FRE 703, as amended, attempts to deal with the problem of the illogical jury instruction by a sort of compromise. By limiting the number of cases in which inadmissible basis evidence will be disclosed to the jury, the restrictive reverse 403 balancing test in effect limits the number of cases in which the troublesome jury instruction will be needed. Where inadmissible basis evidence passes the reverse 403 test, and is thus disclosed to the jury, federal courts seem committed to the idea that a jury instruction will address the problem of the jury using the basis evidence for an inadmissible purpose. See Sphere Drake Insurance PLC v. Trisko, 226 F.3d 951 (8th Cir. 2000) (affirming the jury instruction to "give no weight to the statements of [the informants] in the consideration of the issues in this case. You are to consider that testimony only in developing what [the expert witness] did in the course of his investigation."); United States v. Madrid, 673 F.2d 1114 (10th Cir. 1982) ("I have instructed you as to opinions by experts and that they may state their reasons for such opinions. You are not to consider such evidence for any other purpose than in evaluating the expert testimony."). If you find the jury instruction unsatisfactory, consider how this problem would occur more frequently without the restrictive reverse-403 balancing test.

FRE 703 Basis Evidence and the Confrontation Clause.   A new wrinkle is added to the implications of FRE 703 by way of *Crawford* and *Melendez-Diaz*, which have been discussed at greater length in Chapter Eight, Section G. The question becomes whether inadmissible matter reasonably relied on by an expert is testimonial hearsay. If it is, does it violate the confrontation clause to disclose it to the jury under the FRE 703's reverse 403 balancing test? Courts and commentators have struggled with this question. Compare United States v. Mejia, 545 F.3d 179 (2d Cir. 2008) (expert on gang culture barred from describing gang procedures because the information was gathered through custodial interrogations with informants, and was therefore testimonial hearsay), with United States v. Ayala, 601 F.3d 256 (4th Cir. 2010) ("the question when applying *Crawford* to expert testimony is whether the expert is, in essence, giving an independent judgment or merely acting as a transmitter for testimonial hearsay."); United States v. Henry, 472 F.3d 910 (D.C. Cir. 2007) (*Crawford* "did not alter an expert witness's ability to rely on (without repeating to the jury) otherwise inadmissible evidence"); United States v. Forstell, 656 F. Supp. 2d 578 (E.D. Va. 2009) (holding *Melendez-Diaz* does not apply to every person involved in establishing chain of custody or accuracy of testing devices). See also Julie A. Seaman, Triangular Testimonial Hearsay: The Constitutional Boundaries of Expert Opinion Testimony, 96 Geo. L.J. 827 (2008).

The Supreme Court addressed the FRE 703 issue somewhat obliquely, and not definitively, in Williams v. Illinois, 132 S. Ct. 2221 (2012). In a bench trial for rape, the prosecution called a forensic laboratory specialist, Sandra Lambatos, to testify that she compared the DNA profile of a blood sample taken from the defendant with the DNA profile of a semen sample taken from a vaginal swab of the victim, and found a match between the two samples. While the blood sample was authenticated through live testimony of another state forensic analyst, the semen sample was analyzed by a private forensic lab, Cellmark. The only evidence of the Cellmark analysis was a lab report. The defendant objected that the Cellmark lab report was inadmissible testimonial evidence barred by the Confrontation Clause, so that it could not be disclosed to the trier of fact under FRE 703 or used substantively to prove the necessary forensic link between the victim and the defendant.

Five justices agreed that the evidence was admissible, but without a majority opinion. The Court's Confrontation Clause analysis has been discussed in Chapter Eight. The implications of the case for FRE 703 is unclear. A four-justice plurality suggested both that a hearsay statement can be admitted under FRE 703's reverse balancing test, because the fact finder can disregard the evidence as substantive proof "for its truth," and consider it only as it bears on the expert's testimony. See 132 S. Ct. at 2234 n.2. The bulk of the plurality's argument seems to be that expert basis evidence is a nonhearsay purpose, which implies that hearsay statements in basis evidence are in fact admissible in the same manner as any hearsay statement that is relevant for both a nonhearsay and hearsay purpose. That would be strange as a general proposition: It would have the effect of taking all hearsay statements used as basis evidence out of FRE 703 entirely, because it would be admissible nonhearsay evidence, without any need to apply a reverse 403 test. Fortunately for the future of FRE 703, five justices disagreed with this conclusion:

> [W]hen a witness, expert or otherwise, repeats an out-of-court statement as the basis for a conclusion, . . . the statement's utility is then dependent on its truth. If the statement is true, then the conclusion based on it is probably true; if not, not. So to determine the validity of the witness's conclusion, the factfinder must assess the truth of the out-of-court statement on which it relies. That is why the principal modern treatise on evidence variously calls the idea that such "basis evidence" comes in not for its truth, but only to help the factfinder evaluate an expert's opinion "very weak," "factually implausible," "nonsense," and "sheer fiction." D. Kaye, D. Bernstein, & J. Mnookin, The New Wigmore: Expert Evidence §4.10.1, pp. 196-197 (2d ed. 2011); id., §4.11.6, at 24 (Supp. 2012). "One can sympathize," notes that treatise, "with a court's desire to

permit the disclosure of basis evidence that is quite probably reliable, such as a routine analysis of a drug, but to pretend that it is not being introduced for the truth of its contents strains credibility." Id., §4.10.1, at 198 (2d ed. 2011).

132 S. Ct. at 2268-2269 (Kagan, J., joined by Scalia, Ginsburg and Sotomayor, JJ, dissenting); accord 132 S. Ct. at 2257 (Thomas, J., concurring in the judgment) ("statements introduced to explain the basis of an expert's opinion are not introduced for a plausible nonhearsay purpose"). Even the plurality seemed somewhat queasy about admitting this type of evidence. The plurality relied heavily on the fact that the case involved a bench trial, and that therefore the Justices "must assume" that the trial judge could carefully distinguish between using the basis evidence to assess the expert's opinion and using it as substantive proof of its hearsay assertion. Had the case involved a jury trial, "[t]he dissent's argument would have force" and "[a]bsent an evaluation of the risk of juror confusion and careful jury instructions, the testimony could not have gone to the jury[.]" 132 S. Ct. at 2236 (plurality opinion).

4. FRE 705

RULE 705. DISCLOSURE OF THE FACTS OR DATA UNDERLYING AN EXPERT'S OPINION

Unless the court orders otherwise, an expert may state an opinion—and give the reasons for it—without first testifying to the underlying facts or data. But the expert may be required to disclose those facts or data on cross-examination.

5. Explanation of FRE 705

FRE 705 gives the direct examiner the flexibility to elicit the opinion or conclusion before developing all the details that support it, unless ordered by the judge to present the underlying basis first. The rule goes on to imply that the direct examiner need not present the jury with the underlying facts and data at all—otherwise, the last sentence would not be meaningful. The cross-examiner has the option to bring out any facts underlying the expert's opinion that have not been disclosed on direct examination.

"And give the reasons for it."   The phrase set off in dashes—"and give the reasons for it"—is distinguished from "underlying facts or data." Presumably, then, "reasons" refers to methodology. This suggests that FRE 705 does not permit an expert to give a bare conclusion without explaining her methodology. But that explanation can follow the opinion.

Facts and Data Must Be Presented to the Judge.   Significantly, FRE 705 is a rule of trial practice, not a rule of admissibility. Admissibility is determined under FRE 702, under which experts are not permitted to offer opinion testimony unless and until the offering party has persuaded the court that the requirements of FRE 702 have been met. Thus, FRE 705 manifestly does not permit parties to offer conclusory expert opinions without at least ensuring the judge that a reliable methodology has been applied to reliable underlying facts or data. See FRE 702(c), (d). Whether those facts or data must thereafter be presented *to the jury* is discretionary with the judge under FRE 703 and 705.

6. FRE 705: Practical Applications

FRE 705, in conjunction with FRE 703, implicitly eliminates the common law requirement that experts testify in the form of responses to hypothetical questions. The advantage to FRE 705's approach is that it permits the proponent of the evidence to structure her case in the manner she deems most effective. The proponent of the expert testimony might be concerned that jurors will get lost in the details, or will not pay careful attention to them, if they haven't first heard the summarizing opinion of the expert. FRE 705 permits that concern to be addressed by introducing the opinion early in the expert's testimony. On the other hand, if the proponent prefers to lay the foundation first and then bring out the opinion, that approach is also permissible.

Since presenting a bare opinion without explaining the underlying factual basis generally makes for an unpersuasive presentation, few practitioners are likely to avail themselves of the right under FRE 705 to forgo presenting the underlying data. But rather than ensuring in every case that direct examination will reveal the basis for an opinion, FRE 705 leaves these matters to the proponents' incentives and to cross-examination. In some cases, the information revealed on cross-examination can be quite damaging to the party that offered the expert witness, either because it weakens the expert's credibility or because it muddles the story the jury hears. By clarifying the cross-examiner's right to bring out undisclosed facts, the rule tends to discourage cherry-picking by the direct examiner (that is, presenting only favorable facts and trying to ignore unfavorable ones).

If there is reason to suspect that the information on which the expert bases the opinion is so unreliable that it may be appropriate to exclude the opinion altogether, the opponent will often want to test that suspicion before rather than after the jury hears the opinion. By explicitly giving the judge authority to require that the basis for an opinion be brought out before the opinion is given, FRE 705 provides a reasonable means for solving this type of problem. See, e.g., United States v. Brien, 59 F.3d 274 (1st Cir. 1995) (holding that the defense was not entitled to offer expert testimony without disclosing the underlying data; rather the data must be supplied to the judge upon demand and may be used in making a preliminary ruling on admissibility). This is more of an issue in criminal cases, since in civil cases, the discovery process usually results in a relatively full pretrial disclosure of the expert opinion and its grounds. Neither the rule nor the Advisory Committee Note suggests any criteria for the judge to apply in deciding whether to require that the basis evidence precede the opinion. This is a matter that could not easily be reduced to rules, and thus is best left to the discretion of the trial judge.

The Advisory Committee explained the role of cross-examination as follows:

> If the objection is made that leaving it to the cross-examiner to bring out the supporting data is essentially unfair, the answer is that he is under no compulsion to bring out any facts or data except those unfavorable to the opinion. *The answer assumes that the cross-examiner has the advance knowledge which is essential for effective cross-examination.* This advance knowledge has been afforded, though imperfectly, by the traditional foundation requirement. *Rule 26(b)(4) of the Rules of Civil Procedure, as revised, provides for substantial discovery in this area, obviating in large measure the obstacles which have been raised in some instances to discovery of findings, underlying data, and even the identity of the experts.* [Emphasis added.]

The Advisory Committee's answer to bringing out supporting data may be sufficient for civil cases. In criminal cases, where discovery traditionally has been more limited, the cross-examiner may be at a serious disadvantage if the underlying facts and data are not revealed on direct examination. In such a case it would be appropriate for the trial judge to require that the bases for the opinion be elicited on direct examination.

KEY POINTS

1. Under FRE 703, an expert may give opinion testimony on the basis of admissible evidence "made known to" her by the offering party's attorneys or by reviewing the evidence and litigation documents. Under FRE 703 and 705, an expert is no longer required to base her testimony on assumed facts posed in hypothetical questions.
2. FRE 703 allows expert witnesses to base their opinions on reasonably reliable but otherwise inadmissible facts or data. If inadmissible, these facts must be of the sort that experts in that field normally rely on. The underlying inadmissible facts will normally not be disclosed to the jury.
3. Under FRE 703, inadmissible evidence reasonably relied on by the expert will be disclosed to the jury only on a showing that the probative value in helping the jury evaluate the opinion substantially outweighs its prejudicial effect.
4. FRE 705 allows the offering party to have the expert testify to her opinion before—or without—explaining its underlying factual basis to the jury.

PROBLEMS

9.7. Return to problem 9.4, at page 736, United States v. Cross. What arguments can be made for admitting and excluding evidence of some of the 100 other cases under FRE 703?
9.8. Wally Daniels is charged with murder and arson. The prosecution's theory is that Wally killed his wife and then, at about 7:00 P.M., set fire to the house in order to make the death look like an accident. Wally claims that he was not near the house at the relevant times and that the fire was the result of bad electrical wiring. The prosecutor's expert, a fire marshal, offers to testify that in his opinion the

fire was the result of arson. The fire marshal is prepared to testify about the bases for his opinion, which include, inter alia, the following:

(a) interviews with next door neighbors, John and Wilma Smith, who say they saw Wally running from the house at about 7:00 P.M. shortly before they noticed the fire;

(b) a written police report prepared by Officer June Adkins, stating that she was patrolling the area shortly before the fire was discovered and that she observed an adult male running from the defendant's house at about 7:00 P.M.; and

(c) the fact that Wally had twice previously been convicted of arson.

Wally has objected to all of this evidence. To support the objection, he offers to prove that John Smith is an alcoholic who almost daily is in an alcohol-induced stupor from 3:00 P.M. until midnight. What result?

9.9. In a criminal trial, the defendant pleaded not guilty by reason of insanity. The prosecution called a psychiatrist as an expert witness to testify to an opinion that the defendant was sane at the time he committed the criminal act. During direct examination, the witness was asked how confident he was in his opinion. He responded: "Very confident. Indeed, I called Dr. Smith, the world's leading expert in this particular area. I explained the case and my diagnosis to him, and he concurred in my conclusions." The defense counsel objected and moved to strike this answer. Should it be stricken?

D. OPINIONS ON AN ULTIMATE ISSUE

In the most radical rejection of the common law dealing with opinion testimony, the Federal Rules explicitly permit opinion on ultimate issues in all save one situation.

1. FRE 704

RULE 704.   OPINION ON AN ULTIMATE ISSUE

(a) *In General—Not Automatically Objectionable.* An opinion is not objectionable just because it embraces an ultimate issue.

(b) *Exception.* In a criminal case, an expert witness must not state an opinion about whether the defendant did or did not have a mental state or condition that constitutes an element of the crime charged or of a defense.

2. Explanation of FRE 704(a)

FRE 704(a) makes clear that opinion testimony by a witness on an "ultimate issue" in the case is not per se inadmissible. The one exception to this rule, stated in subsection (b), is that experts can't opine that a criminal defendant has or lacks a mental state that constitutes an element of the crime or defense.

Nothing in FRE 704(a) limits its application to expert opinions. The rule covers both lay and expert testimony. The FRE 704(b) exclusion applies only to expert witnesses, and only in criminal cases. See United States v. Goodman, 633 F.3d 963 (10th Cir. 2011) ("there is no [express] prohibition against allowing lay witnesses to give their opinions as to the mental states of others"); Advisory Committee Note to FRE 704.

An "ultimate issue" is not defined in the rule, but that term is best thought of as synonymous with an essential element expressed in case-specific terms. In other words, it is the case-specific factual conclusion or inference that establishes one of the elements of the claim or defense required by the substantive law—what we have been identifying as FOC (EE) in the diagrams. An opinion on an ultimate issue, in effect, makes the last inference that a jury must make in order to find that an FOC (EE) has been proven.

While FRE 704(a) does not require exclusion of ultimate issue opinions, it does not require their admission either. An opinion on an ultimate issue will often be relevant, but the risk of usurping the role of the jury by providing the last needed inference remains a concern. Instead of automatically excluding such opinions, their admission will depend on a judge's determination that the opinion is helpful to the jury. Note that both FRE 701 (lay opinions) and 702 (expert opinions) have a helpfulness-to-the-jury requirement as a condition of admitting the opinion testimony.

3. FRE 704: Policy, Problems, and Applications

FRE 704(a). FRE 704 abolishes a previous common law rule that lay and expert witnesses could not offer opinions on an ultimate issue in a case. The typical rationale for this rule was that such an opinion would invade the province of the jury. As Wigmore pointed out, it is not clear how or why an opinion on an ultimate issue "invades the province of the jury." 7 John Henry Wigmore, Evidence §1920 at 18 (James Chadbourn rev. 1978). The rule drafters took the view that this policy was better served by discretionary application of the helpfulness requirements of FRE 701 and 702, together with FRE 403. "The basic approach to opinions, lay and expert, in these rules is to admit them when helpful to the trier of fact. In order to render this approach fully effective and to allay any doubt on the subject, the so-called 'ultimate issue' rule is specifically abolished by the instant rule." Advisory Committee Note to FRE 704. Further, according to the Advisory Committee, the rule against opinions on ultimate issues

> generally served only to deprive the trier of fact of useful information. . . . Efforts to meet the felt needs of particular situations led to odd verbal circumlocutions which were said not to violate the rule. . . . [In] cases of medical causation, witnesses were sometimes required to couch their opinions in cautious phrases of "might or could," rather than "did," though the result was to deprive many opinions of the positiveness to which they were entitled, accompanied by the hazard of a ruling of insufficiency to

support a verdict. In other instances the rule was simply disregarded, and, as concessions to need, opinions were allowed upon such matters as intoxication, speed, handwriting, and value, although more precise coincidence with an ultimate issue would scarcely be possible.

FRE 704(b). Subsection (b) was added by amendment to the original version of FRE 704, which simply abolished the categorical "ultimate issue" exclusion. The legislative impetus for the change arose out of John Hinckley's acquittal on insanity grounds of the attempt to assassinate President Reagan, which led to substantial public controversy over the insanity defense. Congress enacted legislation that for the first time provided a federal statutory definition for insanity and that made insanity an affirmative defense that must be proved by the defendant. As part of that legislation, Congress amended FRE 704 to add FRE 704(b).

According to the Report of the House Judiciary Committee (quoting an earlier Senate Judiciary Committee Report):

> The purpose of this amendment is to eliminate the confusing spectacle of competing expert witnesses testifying to directly contradictory conclusions as to the ultimate legal issue to be found by the trier of fact. Under this proposal, expert psychiatric testimony would be limited to presenting and explaining their diagnoses, such as whether the defendant had a severe mental disease or defect and what the characteristics of such a disease or defect, if any, may have been. . . .
>
> Moreover, the rationale for precluding ultimate opinion psychiatric testimony extends beyond the insanity defense to any ultimate mental state of the defendant that is relevant to the legal conclusion sought to be proven. The Committee has fashioned its Rule 704 provision to reach all such "ultimate" issues, e.g., premeditation in a homicide case, or lack of predisposition in entrapment.

What Is an Ultimate Issue? The question of what constitutes an opinion on an ultimate issue would be academic, but for FRE 704(b). Whether a lay opinion under FRE 701(a) "embraces an ultimate issue" need not be determined precisely, because there the only question is whether the opinion helps the jury. But because ultimate opinions by experts on a defendant's mental state are excluded under FRE 704(b), it becomes important to draw the distinction with clarity only in those instances where expert testimony touches on a criminal defendant's mental state.

Deciding what constitutes an opinion on an ultimate issue can raise a challenging analytical problem. Consider a case in which the defendant is charged with possessing cocaine with the intent to sell. To prove intent to sell, the prosecution calls a narcotics investigator who is prepared to offer the following expert testimony:

(1) A typical user or addict possesses X amount of cocaine for personal use at any one time.
(2) The defendant possessed Y amount of cocaine, which is much more than X, the amount a typical user or addict possesses for personal use at any one time.
(3) The defendant possessed Y amount of cocaine, which is an amount that usually suggests that the person intends to sell it.
(4) In my opinion, because the defendant possessed Y amount of cocaine, he intended to sell it.

We've defined an opinion on the ultimate issue as the last factual inference to be made in concluding that an essential element has been proven. If that definition is right (and we think it is), then statement (1) seems clearly permissible under FRE 704(b)'s ultimate mental state opinion prohibition and statement (4) is impermissible. But those are easy cases.

Statements (2) and (3) are much harder. Statement (3) is a bit closer to the ultimate issue than statement (2). Both can be said to require one inference more to reach the ultimate issue that the defendant intended to sell cocaine. But it could be said that the argument to exclude them under FRE 704(b) is that the "one inference more" is trivially small, so that statement (3) and perhaps even statement (2) are mere circumlocutions of statement (4). If either of these statements were admitted, it could be argued, the prohibition against opinions on an ultimate issue would appear to be more one of form than of substance.

It could also be argued that statements (2) and (3) should be admitted over an FRE 704(b) objection. The expert has not specifically asserted that the jury should conclude that the defendant intended to sell. The jury's finding of the defendant's intent may be influenced by the presence or absence of other evidence on intent aside from the amount in possession. Putting it another way, the jury can accept the truth of statements (2) and (3) while, at the same time, logically concluding that the defendant did not intend to sell. So long as that is the case, arguably there remains one substantial inference between the expert's opinion and the ultimate issue.

The best test we can articulate for defining an ultimate issue is admittedly imperfect, but serviceable: An opinion does *not* "embrace the ultimate issue" so long as the opinion can be accepted as true without logically compelling the conclusion that the defendant had or lacked the mental state in question. Statements (2) and (3) probably pass this test, and our sense is that the majority of courts would permit statements (2) and (3).

FRE 704(b) Policies and Problems.   The above cocaine prosecution example illustrates both the benefit and one of the potential problems with opinions about matters that are, or are closely related to, ultimate issues in a lawsuit. Jurors unfamiliar with the use of drugs may not know what quantities of a particular drug individuals are likely to possess for personal use. Thus, the narcotics officer's testimony can be helpful—indeed, perhaps critical—to the jury's evaluation of the defendant's intent. The narcotics officer's testimony would be most helpful if the jury were assured of learning the basis for the officer's opinion, for example, how much of the particular drug a person can be expected to use in a given period of time and the habits of drug users with respect to stockpiling. Yet the prosecutor may fail to bring out all of the underlying data on direct examination for fear of running afoul of the "ultimate opinion" rule, and defense counsel may be reluctant to explore the matter on cross-examination for fear of bolstering the officer's testimony. If the subject matter of the opinion testimony is not critical to the resolution of the lawsuit, the failure to develop the underlying facts may not be a problem of major concern. It is particularly important, however, that jurors have as much detailed factual information as possible on the ultimate issues in a lawsuit, for the resolution of those issues is their primary responsibility.

There are important countervailing policies in support of FRE 704(b). First, even if jurors have all of the underlying facts and data and are fully capable of resolving the ultimate issues, the mere fact that they hear witnesses express opinions on those issues may mislead them into believing that they should give some special deference to the opinions. Why else would the evidence be presented to them? Second, if an opinion on an ultimate issue embraces a legal concept or conclusion, there may be uncertainty about whether the expert is using that concept in the same manner in which the law uses it.

In support of its 1984 amendment adding subsection (b), the House Judiciary Committee quoted from the American Psychiatric Association's Statement on the Insanity Defense (1982):

> [I]t is clear that psychiatrists are experts in medicine, not the law. As such, it is clear that the psychiatrist's first obligation and expertise in the courtroom is to "do psychiatry," i.e., to present medical information and opinion about the defendant's mental state and motivation and to explain in detail the reason for his medical-psychiatric conclusions. When, however, "ultimate issue" questions are formulated by the law and put to the expert witness who must then say "yea" or "nay," then the expert witness is required to make a leap in logic. He no longer addresses himself to medical concepts but instead must infer or intuit what is in fact unspeakable, namely, the probable relationship between medical concepts and legal or moral constructs such as free will. These impermissible leaps in logic made by expert witnesses confuse the jury. Juries thus find themselves listening to conclusory psychiatric testimony that defendants are either "sane" or "insane" or that they do or do not meet the relevant legal test for insanity. This state of affairs does considerable injustice to psychiatry and, we believe, possibly to criminal defendants. In fact, in many criminal insanity trials both prosecution and defense psychiatrists do agree about the nature and even the extent of mental disorder exhibited by the defendant at the time of the act.
>
> Psychiatrists, of course, must be permitted to testify fully about the defendant's diagnosis, mental state and motivation (in clinical and common sense terms) at the time of the alleged act so as to permit the jury or judge to reach the ultimate conclusion about which they and only they are expert. Determining whether a criminal defendant was legally insane is a matter for legal factfinders, not for experts.

Do you think that jurors may sometimes have difficulty relating a psychiatrist's diagnosis to the legal standard for insanity without some expert assistance? If so, does the problem lie with the amendment to FRE 704 or with the legal definition of insanity or both?

Even if a witness cannot offer an opinion about a defendant's "sanity," "premeditation," "predisposition," or other mental state, is it likely that jurors will be unaware of what the witness feels about such an issue? If not, of what practical benefit is the amendment to FRE 704? Keeping in mind that FRE 403, 701, 702, and 705 are available to regulate opinion testimony about ultimate issues, do you believe that the amendment to FRE 704 improved the Federal Rules of Evidence? Notably, the Supreme Court has held that a state-law equivalent of FRE 704(b) comports with due process. See Clark v. Arizona, 548 U.S. 735 (2006) (rejecting due process challenge to Arizona 704(b) equivalent that excluded testimony of psychological experts as to whether the defendant had the requisite mens rea for the crime on trial, while allowing experts to opine on whether the defendant was mentally ill and give observational testimony about the defendant's behavioral traits).

KEY POINTS

1. FRE 704(a) permits an opinion by a lay or expert witness on an ultimate issue, so long as the opinion is helpful to the jury. An "ultimate issue" is the case-specific factual conclusion or inference that establishes one of the elements of the claim or defense (an "FOC (EE)").
2. FRE 704(b) prohibits expert testimony on the ultimate issue where that issue is whether a criminal defendant did or did not have a mental state that constitutes an element of the crime or defense.

PROBLEMS

9.10. Return to problem 9.4, at page 736, United States v. Cross. What arguments can be made for admitting and excluding the opinion under FRE 704?

9.11. Corey Boyd was convicted by a jury in the United States District Court for the District of Columbia for possession with intent to distribute crack cocaine. Boyd was arrested after police officers briefly spotted him on the street holding a plastic bag between himself and another individual. The officers observed the two men for only a couple of seconds, so they could not see precisely what Boyd and his compatriot were doing, nor could they tell who controlled the plastic bag that was between them. Neither Boyd nor his compatriot was heard to say anything, nor seen to do anything (other than look into the plastic bag), and no money or drug paraphernalia was seen or found. Both men ran upon being spotted by the police, Boyd with the plastic bag still in hand. While being chased, he threw the bag under a truck, and it was recovered by the police. During his trial, the government introduced the expert testimony of Officer Stroud, who testified that, on the basis of a "hypothetical situation" exactly mirroring the facts of Boyd's arrest, in his opinion, the hypothetical facts showed possession with intent to distribute. Is there a problem with, or an appropriate objection to, this testimony?

9.12. Edward Santos is being tried for threatening to kill President Bill Clinton. In its attempts to prove the mental element of the crime, the prosecution elicits testimony from a psychiatric expert that Santos's efforts to "throw people off his trail" indicate that he "knew what he was doing was wrong." As an attorney for the defense, make an objection. Do you think you will be able to persuade the judge that the statements should be stricken from the record?

E. FRE 702–705: PRACTICAL APPLICATIONS

In this section, we present various practice issues and practical applications of FRE 702 through 705.

1. Defining the Scope of Expertise

There is no such thing as an expert on everything. FRE 702 states that a person "qualified as an expert by knowledge, skill, experience, training, or education" may offer opinion testimony to the extent that "the expert's scientific, technical, or other specialized knowledge will help the trier of fact." FRE 702 & subd. (a). Two key points follow from the joint requirement of specialized knowledge to qualify as an expert, and the need for this expert knowledge to assist the factfinder "to determine a fact in issue." (1) The expert's field of specialization must be identified. And (2) the expert's opinion testimony must stay within the field. The expert is a "specialist" — not a free-ranging know-it-all who can opine on all matters outside of common knowledge. This requires that the party offering the testimony and the party opposing it pay careful attention to the scope of the expert's opinion.

In practice, it's typical for the offering party to state the subject matter on which the expert will testify. This may be done in very specific or more general terms. Opposing counsel must be alert to whether the expert's qualifications reasonably support the claim of expertise on the proposed subject matter of the testimony, and, then, whether the testimony stays within the specified topics. Going outside the scope of a witness's expertise can be properly objected to as "improper opinion" or "beyond the scope of the witness's expertise."

Consider, for example, an orthopedic surgeon who testifies for the plaintiff in a personal injury case. Plaintiff's counsel states that the orthopedic surgeon will "give opinions regarding the extent of plaintiff's broken leg, his prognosis for healing, and the physical after-affects of the plaintiff's broken leg." Suppose the expert then offers the following opinions:

(1) The bone will never completely fuse and will, therefore, be permanently weaker than before the break.

(2) The plaintiff will be unable to run and will walk with a permanent limp.

(3) The plaintiff will be unable to carry more than 40 pounds of weight, or to run more than 20 yards without risk of re-injury to the leg.

(4) The plaintiff will likely experience pain from standing in excess of two hours at a time.

(5) The plaintiff will be unable to perform jobs that require running, standing more than two hours at a time, or lifting more than 40 pounds of weight.

(6) The plaintiff will be precluded from resuming his former work in the construction field.

(7) The plaintiff is unlikely to find new work that will match his former income as a construction worker.

As a matter of common sense, Opinions 1 and 2 fit fairly within the designated subject matter and expertise. Arguments might reasonably begin with Opinions 3 and 4: defense counsel might argue that these are outside the surgeon's field, and fall within another area of specialization (e.g., the relatively new field of physical medicine and rehabilitation). Yet that argument might be said to take a very restrictive view of the expert's field. Opinion 5, while still within the designated subject matter, is probably in a gray area at the margin of the witness's expertise — the argument that the expert is not qualified to give that opinion is stronger than the argument against Opinion 4. Opinion 6 is something of a stretch for both the subject matter and the expertise. If the surgeon can testify to having a lot of experience in follow-up care with construction workers, perhaps the subject matter could be redescribed to include this opinion. Opinion 7 is clearly outside the designated subject matter expertise of an orthopedic surgeon. An occupational therapist or some other specialist would be needed for this issue.

2. Types of Expert Opinions

Generalizations Versus Case-specific Assertions.   The most common form of expert opinion is rendered as a case-specific fact. A physician testifies, "In my medical opinion, the plaintiff's son suffered leukemia as a result of ingesting the chemical trichlorethylene in his drinking water over a period of years." This opinion goes to the specific fact of causation in a specific toxic tort case.

But expert opinions can also take the form of generalizations. Consider this example, from the *Johnson* trial. Johnson's cellmate Butler testified that, after Johnson's initial refusal to hand over the tray, the guards who returned to the cell door to retrieve Johnson's tray were wearing gloves. The relevance argument was that by putting on work gloves, the guards outwardly revealed an intent to beat up Johnson. The following diagram illustrates:

Diagram 7-1

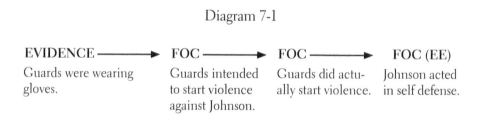

If the prosecution wanted to object to this evidence as irrelevant, its argument would necessarily focus on the debatable generalization in the first inferential step. Could a reasonable jury believe, in general, that guards put on work gloves right before going to an inmate's cell because they probably intend to beat up the inmate? Again, if the judge doubts this generalization, he could require that it be replaced with case-specific evidence: Perhaps there is testimony that one of the guards said, "Let's put on the boxing gloves!" But suppose there is no such case-specific evidence, and that Johnson's relevance argument relies entirely on inference from the generalization to supply the missing fact (why did the guards put on gloves?). Here, the judge might ask: Is the glove-wearing behavior of prison guards a matter of common sense and common knowledge of jurors?

If the answer to that question is "no," the judge might require the opinion of an expert witness. Expert witnesses testify about matters outside the common knowledge of jurors. Johnson would need someone who, through experience, training, or study, has acquired specialized knowledge about prison guard behavior to offer an expert opinion to help the jury determine the significance of the gloves. Indeed, Butler might qualify as an expert based on sufficiently long experience with prison culture, or with Pelican Bay's prison culture, as an inmate.

An increasingly common example of expert opinions in the form of generalizations occurs in eyewitness identification cases. The expert opinions typically take the form of a generalization about cognitive biases and other perception problems that can reduce the accuracy of eyewitness identifications. The jury is asked to consider those "facts about the world" in deciding how much weight to give the testimony of an eyewitness who identifies the defendant. Indeed, while courts increasingly admit such testimony, most expressly prohibit the expert from rendering a case-specific opinion on the accuracy of the eyewitness identification in the case at hand. (These are discussed further at the end of this chapter, at pp. 793-94.)

For present purposes, the point is to understand that expert testimony can be used to supply a missing generalization that establishes the relevance of an important piece of evidence. FRE 702 requires that expert testimony must "help the trier of fact to understand the evidence or to determine a fact in issue." Generalizations can meet this test in the appropriate circumstances. There is no requirement that admissible expert opinions always express case-specific conclusions.

Ultimate and Subsidiary Opinions.   An expert's testimony will usually consist of one or a small number of ultimate opinions. But these might depend on a number of subsidiary, more specific opinions. For example, a plaintiff's expert in a police excessive-force case might offer the following overarching or ultimate opinion: "In my opinion, the use of deadly force by officer Smith in this case was excessive." In explaining this opinion, the expert might say, "Officer Smith could have gotten Mr. Jones [the plaintiff's decedent] under control by kicking Mr. Jones's legs out from under him, putting him down on the ground, and handcuffing him." Further, "Mr. Jones was not threatening serious bodily harm."

Note that the two assertions offered in support of the ultimate conclusion, that Smith could have gotten control over Jones without deadly force and that Jones was not threatening serious bodily harm, could be characterized as "facts" or "opinions." As we discussed in the context of lay opinions under FRE 701, the fact/opinion distinction is indefinite, and often based on contextual or functional considerations. Here, a court is more likely to consider the assertions as opinions, since they are disputed, close to the dispositive issue, and can be broken down into further detail. But note, too, that the fact/opinion distinction here is academic. There is no requirement in FRE 702 that opinions be stated at the highest level of generality or that an expert can offer only an "ultimate opinion," nor does any language in the FRE suggest that subsidiary, more specific opinions are inadmissible. At the same time, opinions can be based on "facts or data." So the underlying assertions in this example are allowable whether characterized as "fact" or "opinion."

Opinions on Questions of Law. A common law rule barred opinion testimony on questions of law, deeming them to be either "purely legal" matters for the judge rather than the jury to decide, or else "mixed questions of law and fact" that were ultimate issues for the jury. As noted above in our discussion of lay opinions (see page 706), questions for the judge to decide should not be the subject of evidence presented to the trier of fact in any event. But opinion testimony going to the factfinder's duty to apply facts to the legal elements of a claim—"ultimate issues" in former parlance—should not be objectionable as calling for "a legal conclusion." Such opinion testimony is properly viewed as coming within the scope of FRE 704, and should be disallowed only if it is unhelpful to the jury. You still may encounter courts sustaining objections to questions calling for "a legal conclusion" when what they really mean is that it is an ultimate issue opinion that is unhelpful to the trier of fact.

Indeed, it is not unknown (and certainly not forbidden) in litigation in highly specialized areas of the law, such as antitrust or intellectual property matters, to present opinion testimony from legal experts on ultimate issue questions involving interpretations of complex statutes and legal doctrines.

3. Types of Experts

Experts can play various roles in a litigated case. Procedure and evidence rules may vary somewhat, depending on whether the expert witness was hired ("retained") for the express purpose of testifying in the case, or was instead actually involved in the litigated events. A second distinction is drawn among hired experts between those hired to give opinion testimony, and those who consult behind the scenes to help the attorneys prepare the case.

a. Retained Versus Percipient Experts

"Retained" experts are hired for the purposes of rendering expert testimony or consultation in the litigation. But experts may have been involved in the underlying litigated events. A physician who treated a person injured in a crime or tort can be a percipient witness to relevant events when that case is litigated. Investigating law enforcement officers, accountants, engineers, or experts of all sorts may have played some role in litigated events. We refer to such experts here as "percipient experts," to reflect the fact that they may have relevant information both as lay witnesses testifying from direct perception under FRE 602 and as witnesses whose expert opinions about what they saw or heard are relevant to the case. Although the Federal Rules of Evidence do not distinguish between these two types of experts, the distinction between them matters for certain evidence-related purposes.

Disclosure in Civil Cases. The formal distinction between retained and percipient experts can be found in the Federal Rules of Civil Procedure. Rule 26(a)(2)(B) refers to an expert witness who is "retained or specially employed to provide expert testimony in the case or one whose duties as the party's employee regularly involve giving expert testimony." All experts, whether retained or percipient, must be disclosed under F. R. Civ. P. 26(a)(2)(A): "[A] party must disclose to the other parties the identity of any witness it may use at trial to present evidence under Federal Rule of Evidence 702, 703, or 705." Typically, this must be done 90 days before trial.[5] But retained experts are subject to special disclosure requirements: Their disclosure must include a detailed packet of information. This so-called expert report must include "a complete statement of all opinions the witness will express and the basis and reasons for them," including supporting facts, data, and exhibits. The report must be accompanied by a statement of the witness's expert qualifications (typically, a résumé or curriculum vita ("CV")), a list of other cases in which the witness testified as an expert going back four years, and a statement of the witness's compensation. F. R. Civ. P. 26(a)(2)(B). Disclosure of nonretained experts must meet the 90-day advance disclosure requirement, but need only contain a description of the subject matter and "a summary of the facts and opinions" about which the witness will present expert testimony.

The purpose of these disclosures is to allow the other side to conduct discovery relating to the expert's testimony. Primarily, discovery of expert testimony is conducted through the deposition of the expert, which can be taken on relatively short notice. There is insufficient time to serve written party discovery on the expert witness (interrogatories, document requests), since expert witness disclosures are normally made very close to the "discovery cutoff"—the date set by the court in which to "complete discovery" under Rule 16(b)(2). However, since the expert report must be detailed and must include supporting exhibits, the need for document requests is obviated.

The practical difference here is that the opposing party will receive considerable information to use in deposing and cross-examining a retained, but not a percipient, expert prior to taking the expert's deposition.

Disclosure in Criminal Cases.   Under the Federal Rules of Criminal Procedure, Rule 16(a)(1)(G), the prosecution must give the defendant, on request, a written summary of any expert testimony it intends to use during its case-in-chief at trial. The defense's disclosure obligation is not symmetrical: It must disclose a written summary of any expert testimony it plans to use at trial if either (1) the prosecution has complied with the defense request, above; or (2) the defense has given notice of an intent to present expert testimony on the defendant's mental condition. See F. R. Crim. P. 16(b)(1)(c). There is no provision for pretrial depositions or further discovery into the expert opinion, as there is in civil cases.

---

5. This disclosure must be made at the time designated by the court or by stipulation, or else "at least 90 days before the date set for trial or for the case to be ready for trial." F. R. Civ. P. 26(a)(2)(D)(i). Experts whose testimony "is intended solely to contradict or rebut evidence on the same subject matter" covered by the opposing expert may be disclosed "within 30 days after the other party's disclosure." Id., at (ii). The idea of this latter provision is to give a party time to obtain a rebuttal expert.

Qualifying Experts "On the Fly."   Consider the following testimony from the *Johnson* trial:

1 *Prosecutor, Mr. Cummings:*   At that point in time did somebody order the door
2   be opened?
3 *Correctional Officer Huston:*   Yes. Officer Smith.
4 Q: And is that an appropriate method to get back the trays?
5 A: Yes.
6 *Mr. Deemer:*   Excuse me. A, lack of qualifications; B, lack of foundation; and, C,
7   it's leading.
8 *The Court:*   Are you asking for an expert opinion, Mr. Cummings?
9 Q. by Mr. Cummings: Officer Huston, you stated that you have worked as a cor-
10   rectional officer at Pelican Bay for six years?
11 A: Yes.
12 Q: And during those six years, did you receive special education and training for
13   your job?
14 A: Yes.
15 Q: What was that?
16 A: There are training manuals, and training courses for correctional officers on-
17   site and throughout the state that we attend.
18 Q: And does this training include the handling of specific problems that inmates
19   sometimes cause?
20 A: Yes it does.
21 Q: And based on this training, do you have an opinion on the proper means to
22   handle situations like inmate Johnson's, that is, on whether it is appropriate to
23   open the cell door? Just tell us whether you have an opinion.
24 A: Yes I do.
25 *Mr. Cummings:*   I would offer Officer Huston's opinion now based on his special
26   experiences and training at Pelican Bay.
27 *The Court:*   You may answer.
28 Q. by Mr. Cummings: Is opening the cell door an appropriate way to get back
29   the food trays?
30 A: Yes, on the General Population side it is. [He proceeds to elaborate.]

In the foregoing example, the prosecutor asked a percipient witness for what was arguably considered an expert opinion. The answer required specialized knowledge beyond ordinary common knowledge, based on training and experience. You can also see that the prosecutor had not planned to qualify Officer Huston as an expert in anything. But following the objection and the court's question, prosecutor Cummings spontaneously asked a few voir dire questions to establish Huston's expertise in prison procedures. The court allowed this rather informal qualification of Huston as an expert.

Given the comparatively lax rules about disclosure of experts in criminal cases, perhaps this was technically proper. On the other hand, in a civil case, such ad hoc, "on the fly" attempts to qualify an expert witness would seem to violate the disclosure rules of F. R. Civ. P. 26(a)(2)(C). That would provide a ground to object to such expert testimony.

In practice, however, courts may not always be strict about this even in civil cases. The problem is that there are too many situations in too many cases where ordinary people gain a limited amount of specialized knowledge not known outside a particular workplace or other specialized community. Is a clerical worker an "expert" in his employer's particular intra-office procedures for assigning e-mail addresses? At what point does training become sufficiently specialized to qualify for expert treatment under FRE 702? Courts are unlikely to have frequent occasion to answer such imponderables, because they arise only where (1) the matter is characterized as an "opinion" rather than a fact observed firsthand, and (2) the opinion is reasonably claimed to be one involving specialized knowledge. In borderline cases, a court is likely to allow the testimony by characterizing it as fact, or lay opinion, or perhaps by allowing an "on the fly" qualification of the witness as an expert, as in the *Johnson* excerpt, above.

Nevertheless, a significant potential problem remains. There can sometimes be a strong incentive on the part of attorneys to try to frame what really should be expert opinions as lay opinions. Doing so can avoid the strictures of FRE 702, and the procedural notice requirements cross-referenced to it. As a practitioner, you should be on guard against this.

b. Consultants versus Testifying Experts

Not all retained experts give testimony. Experts might also be hired to assist lawyers in fact investigation, trial strategy, and other trial preparation. Consider a complex business lawsuit involving sophisticated accounting issues. The lawyers handling the case may not be able to understand the basic case facts without assistance from an accountant. Similarly, in Anderson v. Cryovac, the toxic tort case portrayed in the nonfiction book *A Civil Action* (and portrayed more loosely in the 2000 film by the same title), plaintiffs' attorney Jan Schlictmann retained a geological expert during the prefiling investigation of the case to help him determine whether chemicals dumped by nearby industries could have leached into the ground and reached the city's drinking-water wells. Schlictmann hired different experts to provide trial testimony on this point.

The key evidence implication of this distinction between testifying and nontestifying experts stems from differences in what those experts are required to disclose. No disclosures need be made regarding nontestifying consulting experts. Work performed by nontestifying experts has always been deemed "trial preparation material" subject to the qualified work product privilege. See F. R. Civ. P. 26(b)(4)(D). A party might even claim work product protection for the identity of such consultants and even the fact that they were hired.

The scope of discovery of testifying experts is notably broader. The opposing party is entitled to inquire into all the facts considered by the expert, as well as the full details of the methodology employed by the expert in reaching a conclusion. But as amended in 2010, F. R. Civ. P. 26(b)(4)(B) and (C) place restrictions on what was formerly discoverable from experts. Prior to the 2010 amendment, it was generally assumed that anything said or shown to the testifying expert by the attorney was discoverable—subject to mandatory disclosure to the opponent through the civil discovery process. Practitioners sometimes said that when talking to your expert, you should act as if there is a microphone in the room transmitting directly to opposing counsel. This former rule was based on the fiction that expert witnesses were completely objective and independent analysts of the facts. The former rule made it exceedingly difficult to prepare experts for their deposition and trial testimony, and virtually impossible to consult with them about trial strategy and tactics. Under the current rule, communications between the expert and the attorneys retaining her, as well as preliminary drafts of expert reports, are protected as attorney work product to the same degree as other "trial preparation materials" under Rule 26(b)(3). The older "microphone-in-the-room" rule may still be operative under some state practice codes.

With the rule change limiting discovery of testifying experts' preliminary work, the utility of nontestifying experts seems to be somewhat diminished. Nevertheless, Rule 26(b)(4)(D) specifically provides that discovery cannot be made into the opinions of nontestifying experts absent a showing of exceptional need. The nontestifying expert still provides a much surer and safer avenue to expert consultation on case strategy without fear of disclosure.

4. Working with Experts

When Do You Need an Expert Witness?   In some cases experts are necessary, in other cases optional. Where a party cannot prove an essential element of the case based on commonsense inferences from facts perceived by witnesses with personal knowledge, an expert is required. In *Daubert*, for example, no percipient witness could observe firsthand the effect of the drug Bendectin on a human fetus. In Anderson v. Cryovac, described above, no percipient witness could observe firsthand the leaching of chemicals from the defendants' manufacturing plants into the ground water and their flow into the city's wells. Circumstantial evidence of firsthand witnesses would undoubtedly be held insufficient by a court to meet the burden of production on causation. A witness could say, "I saw the chemical dumped on the ground. A few months later, the drinking water tasted funny." The plaintiff in *Daubert* could testify to taking Bendectin during pregnancy and to the appearance of her newborn baby. But these examples would fall far short of what a court would accept as proof of causation: Too many other things could have happened to allow a causation inference to be drawn from these remote before-and-after stories.

In sum, expert testimony is required when a fact necessary to a party's theory of the case can't be directly perceived, or reasonably inferred from circumstantial facts that were perceived by witnesses with firsthand knowledge. As noted above, where a generalization needed to connect two facts perceived firsthand falls outside common knowledge, expert testimony will be required there, too. In addition, where complex calculations have to be made, even on the basis of evidence that is not itself complex, experts are usually required. A common example involves calculations of money damages where past losses include compound interest, or future losses must be reduced to present value.[6] A forensic economist is typically called to provide such testimony.

6. "Present value" is the amount of money that would have to be paid in a lump sum today in order to equal one or more payments of money expected in the future. The key variable in present value calculations is the interest rate. If you were owed $10 at the end of one year, a $9 payment today would be the equivalent if you could invest it at an interest rate of 11%. The law regarding damage awards generally requires that future income streams—such as lost future wages—be "reduced" to present value, i.e., a lump sum.

Expert testimony is optional where the necessary inferences or conclusions are deemed to be matters of common sense and common knowledge, but are also subjects of expert study, training, or experience that can improve the jury's understanding of the facts. These are, in essence, gray areas at the border between common and expert knowledge, and there are many of them. Whether a person is intoxicated, whether a person acted in reasonable self defense, whether a police officer used excessive force, whether a certain type of injury would produce emotional distress in the victim are just a few examples. The list is as unlimited as are the plausible areas of expertise about everyday occurrences and conditions. In such matters, whether to call an expert witness is a strategic decision, not a legal requirement.

Sometimes percipient witnesses can present more compelling testimony than experts, as the following actual case illustrates. A developmentally disabled man who was unable to speak, was briefly employed as a janitor by a national pizza restaurant chain. He sued for disability discrimination after he was fired from his job just three weeks after he had started work. A visiting district manager made statements suggesting an aversion to the plaintiff's disability, and ordered the plaintiff fired. A number of former employees of the restaurant, who quit in protest of the plaintiff's firing, testified to these revealing comments by the district manager. On the issue of damages, the employer presented testimony by an expert witness, a psychiatrist, who opined that it was unlikely that the plaintiff suffered any emotional distress, primarily because the plaintiff had held the job only a short time and because his inability to use language suggested a lack of emotional sensitivity to such an incident. Rather than calling an expert to rebut this testimony, the plaintiff introduced testimony of family members and coworkers that the plaintiff woke up early every morning to go to work, and that he frequently smiled on the job; whereas, after his firing, he lost weight, became withdrawn, and stopped shaving. The jury found the employer liable and awarded $13 million in damages—obviously rejecting the expert testimony. (Under the damages caps of the Americans with Disabilities Act, this award was reduced to $300,000.) See David Callendar, Jury awards disabled man $13 million, The Capital Times (Madison, Wis., Nov. 6, 1999).

Finding Subject Matter Experts.   It can be challenging to find an expert witness for your case. As a lawyer, your professional colleagues are likely to be other lawyers, so your network of acquaintances may not include physicians, accountants, or scientists who are interested in testifying in a court case.

To find an expert witness, the first thing you need to do is think about the issues on which expert testimony is needed, and use your own knowledge about the world to try to identify the appropriate field of specialization. From there your research is likely to differ from standard legal research. Using more general research techniques, you might be able to refine the field of specialization (e.g., "geriatric oncology" as opposed to "general oncology" or "general medicine"). Consulting with colleagues in your firm or outside it, you may get some leads about experts other lawyers have used (or opposed) in litigation. Some legal research databases have expert witness directories and transcripts of expert witness testimony. Once you start getting names, you can start a winnowing-down interview process. In a brief conversation with a potential expert, you might learn more about relevant subspecialties. After describing the facts of your case in a general way, perhaps the expert says, "This isn't exactly my field; what you need is a ___."

When you have narrowed down your list of candidates, you have to start considering more practical issues. Are the expert's qualifications sound and impressive? Can the expert, in good faith, offer a reliable opinion that meets the needs of your case? Does the expert seem as though she will make a convincing, appealing witness before a jury? Are her rates affordable given the economics of the case and your client's ability to pay?

5. Direct and Cross Examination of Experts

Direct Examination.   The rules of direct examination apply to expert witnesses with certain modifications. Traditionally, it was required to start the expert examination with "voir dire" (not to be confused with jury voir dire discussed in Chapter Two), in which the direct examiner would elicit the expert's qualifications. When the direct examiner believed he had done enough, he would offer the witness as an expert on a stated subject matter. The court would then signal acceptance of the expert.

Federal court and many state courts now dispense with these formalities. The "offer" was deemed awkward since it might convey to the jury the judge's approval of the persuasiveness of the expert's opinion, rather than simply its reliability and admissibility. As for the qualifications, it is likely in contemporary trials for the expert to have been prescreened by the judge during summary judgment or a pretrial conference; or the opposing counsel may be willing to "stipulate" (agree) that the expert is qualified in order to dispense with the voir dire. As the party offering the expert, it is a mistake to dispense with voir dire. The jury needs to hear the expert's qualifications to properly assess the reliability of the testimony, both as a matter of persuasion and logical relevance. And you need to be absolutely certain that the witness's qualifications are somewhere in the record for appeal purposes. Under current practice in most courts, you will complete your voir dire—usually a series of questions to have the expert present their résumé in an abbreviated, verbal form. You'll then go straight into the substance of the testimony without "offering" the witness.

FRE 705, as noted above, permits you next to go straight to the witness's ultimate opinion, if you choose. It is probably required to have the witness explain the methodology, and you will want the expert to explain as much as possible of the underlying facts considered to show the thoroughness of the expert's analysis. This is subject to the limits of FRE 703, discussed above.

As a matter of tactics and of the requirements of FRE 611, you will conduct your examination primarily with nonleading questions. FRE 611 generally requires nonleading questions on direct, and you want as much as possible for the jury to be persuaded that the expert knows what she is talking about. If you supply the answer with leading questions, you diminish this impression. That being said, FRE 611 allows the judge latitude to allow leading questions on direct to facilitate a clear presentation of evidence. Where the expert's testimony is lengthy and complicated, filled with technical terms, or (heaven forbid) confusing, courts will often allow the direct examiner leeway to pose a leading "sum-up" question, in layman's terms if possible: "So, what you're saying is ___."

While evidence law usually permits practical communication rather than magic words, with expert testimony, there are sometimes magic words required by case law to meet an applicable burden of proof with expert testimony. For example, some federal or state courts require a medical expert to couch the opinion as having "a reasonable degree of medical certainty." Where the expert testimony is your sole proof of an essential element (like causation), the expert's degree of certainty needs to meet or exceed your burden of persuasion. In the Ninth Circuit decision in *Daubert* after remand from the Supreme Court ("*Daubert II*"), the Court of Appeals reaffirmed its earlier decision to exclude the plaintiff's medical experts. Some of those experts were excluded because they testified that it was merely "possible" that Bendectin caused the birth defects. The court observed that, even if believed, this testimony could not support the necessary jury finding that the drug probably (more likely than not) caused the plaintiff's injuries. In *Daubert II*, it may have been reasonable for the court to conclude that the experts' hedging on probability did indeed fail to meet the burden of proof. In other cases, the requirement of specific language to express probability (e.g., "reasonable degree of medical certainty") might seem to elevate form over substance. Either way, you must carefully research the question of how your expert's testimony has to be framed to meet your burden of proof.

Cross-examination.   Cross-examination of experts is challenging because, as the questioning lawyer, you are likely dealing with someone who knows her subject matter better than you do. FRE 702 implies various avenues to discredit the expert's opinion. You can try to attack the expert's qualifications, though unless your opponent has done a poor job by retaining an obviously unqualified expert, this is unlikely to be fruitful. A slightly better option might be to show that the expert is a biased "hired gun"—perhaps because the expert's résumé shows that he has always testified on one side of the kind of case in question, or because expert testimony is his main source of income, or because he makes frequent presentations at trade shows to drum up business. But juries often resent personal attacks on witnesses, so the utility of this approach, too, may be limited to extreme cases.

FRE 702(b)-(d) tell us that a reliable opinion must be based on sufficient facts and data, reliable methodology, and reliable application of that methodology to the facts and data. This suggests three further avenues of attack. Attacking the witness's methodology in general (subdivision (c)) is the most difficult, because this is where the expert usually holds the greatest knowledge advantage over the lawyer. Unless the expert is an obvious quack, in which case he is unlikely to have gotten past a screening for qualifications, you are likely to need assistance of your own expert to help you see any methodological problems. The same goes for the application of methodology in subdivision (d), with one exception. You can always score a few points by showing what the expert *didn't do* in analyzing the case. Unless your adversary has an unlimited expert budget, and the expert has a lot of time to spend, the expert witness is likely to have economized somewhere in working up his analysis. "You didn't read the deposition of [key witness X]" or "You have an opinion of my client's emotional state, but you've never actually spoken with him," will give the jury something to think about in considering how much weight to give the expert testimony.

The most promising avenue of cross-examination is often to attack the validity of the underlying facts and data. Even the most reliable methodology will produce an incorrect result when applied to incorrect facts. ("Garbage in, garbage out" in accounting and computer lingo.) It is very common for expert witnesses to base their opinions on the disputed version of key facts asserted by the party calling the expert. You can sometimes get the expert to admit that if *your* side's version of events were true, the ultimate opinion would be different. "You have testified that Officer Smith's use of force was excessive because the plaintiff was unarmed. But if the plaintiff had been armed, your conclusion would be different?"

When cross-examining experts, it is particularly important to be disciplined about asking leading rather than open-ended questions. Expert witnesses are disposed by their educative role to speak at great length, so asking any nonleading question—most particularly, "Why?" or "Can you explain?"—almost guarantees a long, self-serving answer. You have to try your best to control the expert with short, leading questions, and avoid as much as possible trying to get the witness to agree with your major arguments. The expert is likely to argue back. At the same time, because the expert purports to have superior knowledge of his subject in contrast to a lay witness, the judge is likely to be less protective of expert witnesses, giving you more latitude to argue with the witness or cut off a long-winded answer with your next question.

KEY POINTS

1. Expert witnesses must confine their opinions to the scope of their qualifications and to the subject matter on which they're called to testify. This boundary is not always completely clear.

2. Experts testifying in civil cases must be disclosed at least 90 days before trial under the Federal Rules of Civil Procedure. As part of this disclosure, those hired for the express purpose of testifying, or whose job duties include regular expert testimony, must provide detailed background information on their qualifications and on their opinions in the case. Experts who are also percipient witnesses need not provide such information, but must still be identified 90 days before trial.

3. Experts hired to consult for trial preparation and strategy, but not testimony, need not be disclosed. Their work is protected by the attorney work product doctrine.

4. Expert testimony must be used to prove an essential element of the case where that element can't be proved by commonsense inferences from facts perceived by witnesses with personal knowledge. Expert testimony is optional where the necessary inferences or conclusions are deemed to be matters of common sense and common knowledge, but are also subjects of expert study, training, or experience. Where common and expert knowledge overlap, the expert testimony will be admissible, and may be desirable, if it can improve the jury's understanding of the facts.

PROBLEMS

9.13. Return to one of the expert witness problems, above, and try to outline a brief direct and cross-examination of the expert witness in question. We recommend problems 9.4, 9.6, or 9.8 as particularly well suited to this exercise.

9.14. Scott Michaels is a professor of law at the Wisconsin State University Law School. His area of research specialization is community policing, which includes the building of ties between a police department and its local community, including its high-crime areas, as well as community-based alternatives to reliance on a strong police presence as a deterrent to crime. Prior to becoming a professor, Michaels was a police officer in Green Bay, Wisconsin (a city of approximately 105,000 people) for ten years, rising through the ranks from a patrol officer to the rank of lieutenant. He then attended law school, and after graduating, was hired as chief of police of La Cross, Wisconsin, a city of approximate 52,000 people. He served in that job for four years before being hired onto the law faculty at Wisconsin State.

Michaels has been retained as an expert witness in a federal civil rights suit arising out of an alleged excessive force incident in Kansas City, Kansas, in which an allegedly nonresisting suspect was shot and wounded. The plaintiff claims that the use of deadly force was unreasonable and excessive. He has sued the individual officer, Darrell Spear, for using excessive force, and has sued Kansas City for inadequately training its officers in the use of force. Michaels has been offered as an expert on "the appropriate use of force by police officers in arrest situations." His opinions will include the following assertions:

(1) Deadly force was unreasonably used in this case; therefore, force was excessive.

(2) Defendant Darrell Spear was inadequately trained.

(3) Kansas City improperly trains its officers in the use of deadly force, because Spear should have been fired based on a previous incident in which he hit a handcuffed suspect with his flashlight.

Prepare a direct and cross-examination of Professor Michaels. Consider all possible objections to his testimony and responses to those objections.

F. REFLECTIONS ON EXPERT TESTIMONY

1. Data on the Use of Experts in Litigation

The following studies are now several years old, but there is no more recent research indicating that the extent of expert usage has significantly diminished. They thus provide a useful snapshot of the usage of experts in federal court.

SAMUEL GROSS, EXPERT EVIDENCE

1991 Wis. L. Rev. 1113, 1118-1120

There is next to nothing to be learned from published data on the use of experts in American litigation. A few patchy studies report that experts are used in a sizeable minority of felony prosecutions, and that they are more likely to be called by the prosecution. There are no systematic studies of the use of experts in civil cases. The data described here will begin to fill that gap. They are based on reports on 529 civil trials that led to jury verdicts in California State Superior Courts in 1985 and 1986 . . . .

1. *The frequency of expert testimony.* Experts testified in 86 percent of these civil jury trials. Overall, there were an average of 3.3 experts per trial; in the trials in which any experts appeared, there were an average of 3.8. Most trials with experts had two, three, four or five of them. Plaintiffs called more expert witnesses than defendants—about 64% of the total.

2. *The specialties of expert witnesses.* Half of the experts in our data were medical doctors, and an additional 9 percent were other medical professionals—clinical psychologists, rehabilitation specialists, dentists, etc. Engineers, scientists and related experts made up the next largest category, nearly 20 percent of the total. The only other sizeable categories were experts on various aspects of business and finance (11%), and experts in reconstruction and investigation (8%).

3. *The cases in which experts appear.* Over 70 percent of these trials concerned claims of wrongful death or personal injury. As a group, these trials involved more experts than the remainder. There were expert appearances in nearly 95 percent of the personal injury or death trials, an average of 3.8 witnesses per case. Looking at smaller categories, the highest rates of use were in: (i) medical malpractice cases (97% of trials, an average of five witnesses per trial), where almost all the witnesses were medical experts and (ii) products liability cases (100% of trials, an average of 4.7 witnesses per trial), where an unusually high proportion of the witnesses (1.8 per trial) were engineers, scientists and the like.

4. *Conflicts between opposing experts.* In nearly three-quarters of the trials in which experts testified (or 63% of all trials) there were experts on both sides. In two-thirds of the trials with expert testimony (57% of all trials) there were opposing experts in the same general area of expertise—most often, opposing medical experts. Similarly, for over two-thirds of the appearances by expert witnesses, there were opposing experts in the same general area. Again, such conflicts were particularly common for medical witnesses—their testimony was opposed by other medical witnesses 78 percent of the time. In sum, most expert witnesses were disputed by similar experts for the opposing side, and most juries had to resolve such disputes.

5. *The testimonial experience of expert witnesses.* Most expert testimony is given by repeat players. Nearly 60 percent of the appearances by expert witnesses in California Superior Court civil jury trials were by witnesses who testified in such cases at least two times over a six-year period. For a particular appearance before a jury, the average number of times the same expert testified over a six-year period was 9.4; the median was 2.2. It is important to note that these numbers greatly underrepresent the experts' total experience in litigation. They do not, for instance, include testimony in criminal

trials or in civil trials in courts other than California State Superior Courts. More important, the numbers do not catch the many cases in which the same experts were consulted, wrote reports, or even testified in depositions, but failed to testify in court because the cases were settled or dismissed before trial.

One way to put the trial experience of witnesses in perspective is to compare it to that of trial lawyers. Judging from the 1985-1986 cases, when an attorney examines an expert witness in a civil jury trial in California, the expert is twice as likely to have testified in another such case in the preceding six months as the attorney is to have tried one (42% to 21%).

CAROL KRAFKA ET AL., JUDGE AND ATTORNEY EXPERIENCES, PRACTICES, AND CONCERNS REGARDING EXPERT TESTIMONY IN FEDERAL CIVIL TRIALS

Federal Judicial Center (2002)

Questions that remain about expert evidence far outnumber those that research has begun to address. . . . What types of cases, for instance, are most likely to involve expert testimony? What types of experts testify, how frequently do they appear, and on whose behalf are they testifying? What issues do the experts address? . . . The research we report here involved [three] surveys of judges and attorneys. Data sources included a 1998 survey of [303 U.S. district court] judges, a 1991 survey of [335 U.S. district court] judges, and a 1999 survey of [302] attorneys [involved in district court cases presided over by the aforementioned judges]. The most frequent types of [federal] trials involving experts—45 percent of the 299 trials reported—were tort cases, primarily those involving personal injury or medical malpractice. Tort cases were followed in frequency by civil rights cases (23%); contract cases (11%); intellectual property cases, primarily patent cases (10%); labor cases (2%); prisoner cases (2%); and other civil cases (8%).

To gauge whether expert testimony is differentially associated with certain case types, we compared the distribution of sample cases to the distribution of all federal civil cases terminating during or after a bench or jury trial in the year before and year of our survey. Compared to all civil trials, experts were overrepresented in tort cases (which constituted only 26% of all civil trials) and intellectual property cases (3% of all civil trials). Experts were underrepresented in contract cases (14% of all civil trials); labor cases (4% of all civil trials); general (nonprisoner) civil rights cases (31% of all civil trials); and prisoner cases, nearly all of which are civil rights actions (14% of all civil trials). In cases classified as "other" civil trials, experts were represented in equal proportion to the general case type (8%).

Ninety-two percent of reported trials involved expert testimony by plaintiffs, and 79 percent of trials involved expert testimony by defendants. Seventy-three percent of the trials had experts testifying for both plaintiffs and defendants. These figures are comparable to statistics from 1991, when 95 percent of trials involved expert testimony for the plaintiff, 81% involved expert testimony for the defendant, and 76 percent had experts testifying on both plaintiff and defendant side. Seventy-seven percent of the civil trials we surveyed in 1998 were conducted before juries. . . . The jury trial rate for cases with expert evidence is somewhat higher than for cases as a whole—in 1998 jury trials accounted for 64 percent of all civil trials—suggesting that experts appear with somewhat disproportionate frequency in jury trials.

The average number of experts testifying for plaintiffs was 2.47, compared to 1.85 for defendants. Tort cases had the highest mean number of testifying experts—an average of 3.11 experts testified for plaintiffs, with 2.28 testifying for defendants. Civil rights cases averaged 1.81 experts for the plaintiff and 1.24 experts for the defense; case types that fell into the "other" category averaged 2.70 and 2.00 experts, respectively. . . . The mean number of testifying experts in 1998 was 4.31 per trial. This figure is somewhat lower than in 1991, when cases averaged 4.80 experts per trial. . . .

In both the judge and attorney surveys, respondents were asked to describe the types of experts who testified and the issues addressed by their testimony . . . Medical and mental health specialists were the most frequently presented category of experts, accounting for more than 40 percent of the experts presented overall. The medical profession, representing many types of specialists, collectively accounted for about one-third of all testifying experts. This showing is not surprising, given that 45 percent of the survey trials were tort cases. Specialists from business, law, and financial worlds accounted for another 25 percent of experts. This category includes the most frequently heard professional, the economist, representing almost 12 percent of all experts. Engineers and other safety, or process, specialists registered close behind experts from the business/ law/ financial sector. These professionals accounted for about 22 percent of all experts. Individuals representing scientific fields such as chemistry, ballistics, toxicology, and metallurgy accounted for only a small percentage, less than 8 percent, of testifying experts.

* * *

2. Scientific Evidence and the *Daubert* Case

a. Introduction

Trials in the Anglo-American tradition originally gathered together individuals with knowledge of local affairs to decide notorious disputes. Jurors were expected to have, and use, specific knowledge of the case. As times changed, the self-informing aspect of juries was supplemented with the testimony of other members of the community. Eventually, litigated matters became more complex, and the gap of knowledge separating the factfinders from the witnesses increased. More and more frequently what witnesses said had to be explained to make it understandable. As such cases became more common, the traditional model of factfinding was largely followed. The parties were merely obligated to explain a little bit more, to put the juror in a position to understand what the witnesses were saying, and thus to decide the case in an intelligent fashion.

Are there any cases that cannot be accommodated within the traditional model? Do some cases present issues for decision that defy the ability of factfinders to understand them? The answer is surely no. Judges and jurors lack knowledge about various branches of human inquiry, as we all do, but there is little reason to believe that, with instruction, they could not adequately master the relevant fields. Ironically, and again counterintuitively, jurors, because they sit on juries, are possibly better able to master the relevant subjects than judges. The issue is not whether every single juror understands adequately every single issue, but whether the jury, collectively, adequately understands. With the wealth of talent almost always contained in even a randomly selected group of six to 12 individuals, it would be a remarkable case that truly defied their collective cognitive abilities. The need for expert witnesses does not disprove this point. Experts may very well develop skills that could not be imparted to a jury. But the knowledge acquired by those skills surely can. If deciding a case is actually reduced to a choice between the hunches of experts that cannot be further explained, perhaps it does not belong in the courts.

The real objection to the argument for educating juries is not that it is wrong, but that it would be too costly. In some cases, undoubtedly that is true. At the same time, some case require months of what amounts to educating the jury on extensive case facts that do not require expert explanation. Traditional white-collar criminal cases and complex conspiracy cases may be tried without experts. In these cases we do not permit juror deference to juridical outsiders such as experts; we require the parties to connect the case through evidence to the experience of the jurors.

Why, then, do we flirt with, and perhaps adopt, a more deferential mode when something comes into court labeled "expert testimony"? The cognitive questions are highly similar, even if not identical, in both sets of cases. The social costs of the resources devoted to litigation are largely identical. Perhaps the difference between complex conventional cases and cases that call for expert testimony is that the latter demand expertise that is missing from the former. People do possess specialized non-conventional knowledge about mathematics, economics, toxicology, oncology, and so on. Perhaps no one possesses expertise about complex conventional cases such as bank fraud or criminal conspiracies. Perhaps so, but this argues not for our current system of presenting competing versions of expertise at trial, but instead for a form of judicial notice (see FRE 201, discussed in Chapter Eleven, infra).

If expertise exists and can be identified with the certainty that the existence of Lake Michigan bordering the city of Chicago can be, trials should not pause over it. Its lessons should be taken as true, and the factfinder so constricted. Whether in any particular case there is expertise in this sense should be easy to determine by judges or legislatures, and its implications mined for what they are worth. We would defer to such knowledge just as we defer to the indisputable knowledge that Lake Michigan borders Chicago. We would not litigate whether Lake Michigan does; that would simply waste resources. If expertise does exist, we waste resources each time (at least beyond the first or unless conditions have changed) that we litigate the issue.

We not only waste time when we litigate the existence of expertise; we also deliberately engage in nonsensical activity. One of the reasons to litigate the existence of expertise is to provide opinions to which jurors can defer. This is the opposite of education, of course. Jurors are not expected to understand the relevant fields of inquiry; they are simply to decide which expert to believe. How is this to be done intelligently without understanding the relevant fields? This question, which reverberates over the increasing use of expertise at trial, has no satisfactory answer, precisely because the two points cannot be reconciled. Though it is true that juries routinely evaluate the credibility of witnesses and the veracity of their statements, the senses and instincts useful in judging the testimony of an eyewitness are useless when contrasting the credentials of two experts or the scientific likelihood of the theories they propound. It is painfully obvious that jurors (and judges) who do not know enough about the relevant fields of knowledge to decide intelligently cannot decide intelligently which expert to believe among those providing competing versions of that field. Consequently, even if our view of the cognitive capacity of juries is rejected, the present system still is nonrational, and the central problem remains. Obversely, if jurors can decide intelligently about which expert to believe, they can with a little more education reason intelligently about the matters in issue, so that deference to the expert is not necessary.

Deference and education are not analytically distinct entities; they are opposite points on a spectrum. Jurors will virtually never see true "raw" data at trial. Deference occurs to some extent whenever a jury decides whether a witness has testified truthfully.

Still, the extent of deference, or of education, is a variable; one can have more of one and less of the other. This is particularly obvious when one considers a case involving not just reporting of sensory experience ("the light was red") but the drawing of inferences ("in light of these studies, I am of the opinion that Bendectin causes birth defects"). In the typical case, the jury is supposed to be able to understand the reasoning process that led the witness from observation to conclusion. Understanding may bring either acceptance or rejection, of course, and the decision will be made by the jury's own lights. Often with experts there is no expectation that the reasoning process can be understood. Acceptance or rejection cannot occur by the jury's own lights, and thus we see a much larger dose of deference. How well a witness's analytical process can be understood is again clearly a variable. Some can be understood completely, some partially, and some not at all. The legal question is the significance of this variable.

b. Three Models of Expert Testimony

The Normal, Educational Approach. Expert testimony can be treated just like any other testimony, which means for it to be relevant it must be understandable by the factfinder. To make an expert's testimony understandable will require the jury to be educated about the relevant matters, and thus the "normal approach" collapses into adopting an education model. The difficulty is cost, especially the fact that cost may skew decision toward those with greater resources. The more impecunious a party, the less able the party will be to provide the necessary educative function or to respond to an opponent's case. The latter point is another detrimental aspect of our system's failure to make parties bear the true cost of their cases, which includes the opponent's cost of responding. Without cost shifting, a wealthier party can make the cost of suit too high for the opponent. Adopting the normal approach to expert testimony would exacerbate this problem by tending to make cases involving expertise more protracted. Offsetting this factor in part is that higher costs are a laudable disincentive to sue or an equally laudable incentive to agree to resolution in other, less costly forums.

The Deference Model. Factfinders can be required to defer to established expertise, as occurs whenever experts are required to testify in hypothetical question format. The advantages are obvious. Those with the ability to decide rationally make the decision, costs are reduced, and consistency in decision is advanced. If the decisions about expertise are correct, accuracy in decision should be advanced as well. The disadvantage is the resultant extension of official orthodoxy, which removes decision from the jury and trial judge to some higher level court or legislature. Also, if the decision about expertise is incorrect, consistency of decision will remain, but the decisions will be consistently wrong.

The Adversary Model. Parties can choose either to educate the jury with the assistance of expert testimony or to convince the jury to defer to an expert's opinion. This leaves the whole matter up to the parties, save only for the admissibility decision of judges. That admissibility decision, in turn, would have to be made in anticipation of either education or a request for deference. Again, the advantages are obvious. The parties know their dispute and their resources better than anyone else, and are in the best position to make choices that optimize their interests. The difficulties are that the cost of education will tend to make deference more attractive and that deference cannot occur rationally with any great frequency. The reduction in the likelihood of rationality is at odds with the essence of the common law mode of trial, that is, the pursuit of factual accuracy through rational deliberation. Indeed, there is a high irony here: In a case in which the parties employ a deference mode, the mere admission by the trial judge of competing expert views without requiring full explanation of those views, including instruction on the underlying field of inquiry, ensures that a decision will be nonrational if not irrational. Only if a juror could see clearly that one side was right and the other wrong would nonrationality be avoided; but if that were so, the judge would admit only the one version and exclude the other. If reasonable people could rationally disagree about which expert is right, they in addition would be able to understand the underlying dispute, and thus deference would not be needed. Note also what a dramatic qualification of the normal rules of relevancy deference entails. Normally, a party must explain the relevance of evidence by adequately connecting the evidence to the factfinder's understanding. With experts in a deferential model, one party can shift that cost of explanation to the opponent by producing an unexplained opinion.

As this brief presentation demonstrates, the use of expert testimony poses fundamental challenges to the common law system of adjudication. Experts are often expert because of years of specialized training, and thus there often will be formidable barriers to educating the fact finder about the relevant issues at trial. Hence, pressure arises to defer to the expertise of experts as a means of keeping trials to a manageable length, but the pressure to defer constitutes a challenge to the core concept of trials, and puts into issue our basic commitment to decisions based on rational deliberation on the evidence. This explains in part the remarkable controversy over expert testimony even as expert testimony is becoming ever more prevalent at trial, for lurking here is the fundamental question of the nature of litigation: To what extent is rational deliberation the hallmark of adjudication?

The *Daubert* case presented these issues to the Court, but its opinion did not address them. The opinion offered no recognition that what was at stake was not just a technical rule of evidence but a conception of trial, and thus the implications of its decision for rational deliberation were not addressed. The Court focused on two other matters that formed the basis of the lower court's ruling in favor of the defendants: First, that the general acceptance standard of *Frye* governed the admissibility of expert testimony in federal court, and second that the standard could not be met with evidence of reanalyses of data that had not previously been published and subjected to peer review. The deep conceptual issue of the defining characteristics of litigation was overlooked in the Court's unenlightening, but thankfully not positively harmful, discussion of the general acceptance standard.

The Court's failure to deal with the core issues presented to it in *Daubert* is all the more unfortunate because still operating are the pressures that over time have resulted in modification of the litigation process to permit large amounts of deference to experts. First is the added cost of educating fact finders so that they may follow the reasoning of the expert in the same way the factfinders can follow the reasoning of a lay witness (thus essentially converting an expert into a lay witness). There is in addition the lottery effect. If reasons for opinions need not be given in detail, one has an increased chance of a lottery-effect jury verdict if the trial judge qualifies a witness as an expert. One effect of *Daubert* has been to transmute the mechanical invocation of the *Frye* test by the trials courts into a more ostensibly subtle but in fact largely identical process of qualification of expert witnesses. What else can they do? The Supreme Court did not take its opportunity to tell trial judges to admit purported expertise only if the basis of the expertise were understandable, as it could and should have done. Trial judges will thus continue to look for a justification to defer to expertise, and they will continue to find it in the general acceptance of that expertise in generally accepted bodies of knowledge.

Telling the lower courts not to invoke mechanically "general acceptance" may prove marginally helpful, but none of the important questions in the case were addressed. In particular, the conflict between the demands of education and deference was ignored. Indeed, if anything the dichotomy between deference and education was reinforced by the Court's opinion. The list of criteria provided by the Court is only relevant to a system willing to defer; by providing the list, the Court, although surely unintentionally, gave sustenance to deference. This is also why the Court's limitation of its discussion to "scientific" evidence is not problematic. The other kinds of information listed in Rule 702 are unlikely to require deference; information of those types can be explained. A car mechanic can qualify as an expert under the rule, but few would claim that such expertise would defy the cognitive capacity of factfinders. As you saw in *Kumho*, however, the Court has proved even more willing to perpetuate the tendency to allow deference than some critics initially thought.

The most regrettable aspect of *Daubert* is that the Court seemed quite unaware of the implications of admitting data without a basis for believing that the data can be understood. By doing so, it seems to be putting its stamp of approval on undeliberative and nonrational legal decisionmaking, which are the antitheses of the law's aspirations. Jurors or judges who cannot understand the reasoning of a witness can only accept or reject the witness's conclusions, but neither acceptance nor rejection will occur rationally. The choice will not be made because a factfinder understands the reasoning and sees either its cogency or its flaws; it will be made for some other reason. And the set of "some other reasons" is, from the point of view of the law's aspirations, filled with unsavory characters.

Yet another interesting aspect of the expert evidence area that may remain undisturbed by *Daubert* is the special treatment that expert testimony gets with regard to the distinction between sufficiency and admissibility. Often trial courts seem to make a sufficiency determination in the guise of an admissibility determination. The explanation, we think, is that trial judges are admitting evidence that they know they and jurors cannot be expected to understand. Such evidence should not be admitted unless the trial judge is willing to let a verdict rest on it, and so the admissibility decision becomes a sufficiency decision. This all confirms the entrenchment of a deference mode of decision at the trial court level.

Perhaps there is no feasible alternative. Perhaps the cost of truly educating the factfinders would be too high in some cases, or perhaps our skepticism about the point does not dispose of concerns about the cognitive capacity of factfinders. If either is true, the answer again is obvious: Unless we are also wrong that the core aspiration of litigation is decision through rational deliberation, the common law form of decisionmaking should not be employed for those cases.

3. Court Appointed Experts

One possible response to some of the problems discussed in the previous section is an increased use of court-appointed experts. The FRE provides for this.

a. FRE 706

RULE 706.   COURT APPOINTED EXPERT WITNESSES

(a) *Appointment Process*. On a party's motion or on its own, the court may order the parties to show cause why expert witnesses should not be appointed and may ask the parties to submit nominations. The court may appoint any expert witness that the parties agree on and any of its own choosing. But the court may only appoint someone who consents to act.

(b) *Expert's Role*. The court must inform the expert of the expert's duties. The Court may do so in writing and have a copy filed with the clerk or may do so orally at a conference in which the parties have an opportunity to participate. The expert:

(1) must advise the parties of any findings the expert makes;

(2) may be deposed by any party;

(3) may be called to testify by the court or any party; and

(4) may be cross-examined by any party, including the party that called the expert.

(c) *Compensation*. The expert is entitled to reasonable compensation, as set by the court. The compensation is payable as follows:

(1) in a criminal case or in a civil case involving just compensation under the Fifth Amendment, from any funds that are provided by law; and

(2) in any other civil case, by the parties in the proportion and at the time that the court directs—and the compensation is then charged like other costs.

(d) *Disclosing the Appointment to the Jury*. The court may authorize disclosure to the jury that the court appointed the expert.

(e) *Parties' Choice of Their Own Experts*. This rule does not limit a party in calling its own experts.

b. Is FRE 706 Underutilized?

FRE 706 permits courts to appoint their own experts. The advantage in doing so is the securing of disinterested, objective testimony concerning the issues in the case. This can provide a factfinder with important information when the adversarial system fails to bring the two sides of an issue to light. See, e.g., Grove v. Principle Mutual Life Insurance Co., 200 F.R.D. 434 (S.D. Iowa 2001) (appointing two experts to assist the court where both parties in a class action suit supported a settlement agreement but what was missing was someone to play the "devil's advocate"). As one circuit court observed, a neutral expert in a Fair Debt Collection Case could have been a "possible alternative to the often unedifying spectacle of a battle of party-appointed experts," and suggested that, at least in such cases, "[d]istrict judges may want to consider exercising the clearly authorized but rarely exercised option of appointing their own expert." DeKoven v. Plaza Associates, the Seventh Circuit pointed out that 599 F.3d 578 (7th Cir. 2010).

There are certain disadvantages to employing FRE 706. First, is cost. In criminal and civil "just compensation" cases (i.e., cases involving condemnation or other takings of property), the funding to pay the expert must come from a statutory source, perhaps the court's own budget. In other civil cases, the expert fees are charged to the parties, who are likely to resist the appointment. Second, is the disconnect between the procedure and the adversarial norm. A court-appointed expert is likely to have a significant impact on factfinding, but is not party directed. Many judges and may simply be uncomfortable with interjecting "neutral" evidence presentation into the process, and lawyers are likely to resent what they will perceive as interference with the presentation of their cases.

A third problem is that many disciplines have internal disputes so that any expert selected by the court might not be fully "objective." Instead he or she might have an axe to grind within the discipline, and would be testifying from the perspective of one whose view of the field is not universally shared. A good example of this is psychiatry. Freudian psychiatrists are called as expert witnesses, yet very little within the field has been empirically verified. As a consequence, psychiatry as a field is moving away from Freudian concepts, yet Freudian concepts still have their adherents. The choice of an "expert" in psychiatry must thus resolve the contested issue of the validity of these concepts. In contrast, adversarial presentation of experts could counteract what might otherwise be a tendency toward the creation of an official orthodoxy in litigated cases.

Whether animated by these concerns or others, courts have essentially refused to take advantage of the power given them by this rule, leaving it a functional dead letter, and leaving it to the parties to fight out among themselves basic disciplinary disputes when necessary for the adjudication of a case.

An illustration of how Rule 706 can work in practice arose from the nationwide litigation of silicone breast implant tort claims. U.S. District Judge Robert E. Jones, while he was overseeing all federal breast implant litigation in Oregon, noted that "litigation over the ability of silicone gel breast implants to cause disease in women has been chaotic in its results" and thus appointed a panel of independent experts to review all of the scientific evidence supporting the plaintiffs' claim that breast implants have caused serious diseases in women. See Hall v. Baxter Healthcare Corp., 947 F. Supp. 1387 (1996). In this decision, however, Judge Jones made the interesting decision to appoint the panel under FRE 104 (Preliminary Questions) rather than under FRE 706. He appointed a panel of "technical advisors," representing the fields of epidemiology, rheumatology, immunology, toxicology, and polymer chemistry, but refrained from designating them as court appointed experts "[t]o keep the advisors independent of any ongoing proceedings." Faced with the daunting task of evaluating extensive scientific evidence in silicone breast implant cases, other courts followed suit. U.S. District Judges Jack Weinstein and Harold Baer, Jr., who managed all breast implants cases in the U.S. District Courts for the Eastern and Southern Districts of New York respectively, came up with a similar plan but named a team of three special masters to help determine the types of expertise that would be needed in a Rule 706 panel. See Mark Hansen, Panel to Examine Implant Evidence: Unusual Move by Two New York Federal Judges Could be Copied Elsewhere, A.B.A. J., June 1996, at 34.

The most far-reaching order was issued by Judge Samuel Pointer of the U.S. District Court for the Northern District of Alabama, who was at the time coordinating about 21,000 cases on a pretrial basis. In a two-step plan, Judge Pointer appointed a "Selection Panel" whose duty it would be to recommend to the court the names of "neutral, impartial persons," qualified to sit on the "Science Panel" and "review, critique, and evaluate exiting scientific literature, research, and publications—addressing such matters as the meaning, utility, significance, and limitations of such studies—on topics as, from time to time, may be identified by the Court as relevant in breast-implant litigation, particularly on issues of 'general causation.'" Order No. 31 (May 31, 1996). As Judge Pointer envisioned it, the appointments would be made on a national basis "for potential use in all federal courts and as permitted in state courts." Though both the attorneys for the plaintiffs and for the defendants expressed some trepidation about the process, Rule 706 preserves a party's right to call its own expert witnesses and to cross-examine the court appointed experts. The four member panel of scientists eventually appointed by Judge Pointer, issued a report in December of 1998, after two years of investigation, concluding that the evidence had not yet shown that silicone breast implants caused disease, though the connection might still be established in the future. By all accounts, the report was very damaging to plaintiffs, who now found themselves in a disadvantaged position for settlement and with diminished prospects for success at trial. In the years since the report was issued, judges from many jurisdictions have cited the panel's findings as support for exclusion of expert testimony intended to prove a causal link between implants and disease. See, e.g., Pozefsky v. Baxter Healthcare Corp., 2001 U.S. Dist. LEXIS 11813 (N.D.N.Y. Aug. 16, 2001); Havard v. Baxter International Inc., 2000 U.S. Dist. LEXIS 21316 (N.D. Ohio, July 21, 2000); Toledo v. Medical Engineering Corp., 50 Pa. D. & C.4th 129 (C.P. Ct. Phila. Cnty., Dec. 29, 2000). Though the courts succeeded in adopting a more efficient system of hearing expert testimony, do you think that one court should be able to exercise so great an influence over the success of cases in so many jurisdictions?

4. Summary Witnesses

Summary witnesses represent a blurring of the line between who qualifies as an "expert witness" and who remains a "lay witness." In some trials, usually those involving large amounts of evidence or extraordinarily complicated evidence, a lay witness will be permitted to testify as to what the aggregate of the evidence shows—in other words, to summarize the evidence. Because the witness is simply serving as a human "tape recorder," the witness need not be qualified as an expert to provide this summary. However, if the witness draws conclusions from this evidentiary summation for the purposes of assisting the jury, it is probable that the witness should be certified as an expert. See, e.g., United States v. Pree, 408 F.3d 855, 869 (7th Cir. 2005) (admission of summary witness testimony regarding the tax consequences of a series of complicated stock sales in a fraud case). For more on summary witnesses, see D. Michael Risinger, Preliminary Thoughts on a Functional Taxonomy of Expertise for the Post-Kumho World, 31 Seton Hall L. Rev. 508 (2000).

5. Problems in Forensic Science: Overview

Different kinds of scientific evidence and expert testimony have, for one reason or another, caused difficulties for the courts. Interestingly, it was only recently that DNA evidence was regularly questioned by defendants and courts. Now, while it seems that the acceptance of most DNA evidence is firmly rooted in the judicial system, more traditional methods of forensic science are causing controversy because they lack the theoretical scientific basis of DNA.

The concerns about the dearth of detailed analysis outside of DNA led Congress to authorize a study of forensic sciences. In 2009, under the supervision of the National Academy of Sciences (NAS), members of the forensic community, including crime laboratories, legal experts, and medical examiners, published a report on the serious problems present in the traditional forensic science fields as well as recommendations on how best to solve them. Selected excerpts from the report follow.[7]

---

7. Hereinafter NAS Report 2009.

THE NATIONAL ACADEMIES, STRENGTHENING FORENSIC SCIENCE IN THE UNITED STATES: A PATH FORWARD

(2009)

CHALLENGES FACING THE FORENSIC SCIENCE COMMUNITY

For decades, the forensic science disciplines have produced valuable evidence that has contributed to the successful prosecution and conviction of criminals as well as to the exoneration of innocent people. Over the last two decades, advances in some forensic science disciplines, especially the use of DNA technology, have demonstrated that some areas of forensic science have great additional potential to help law enforcement identify criminals. Many crimes that may have gone unsolved are now being solved because forensic science is helping to identify the perpetrators.

Those advances, however, also have revealed that, in some cases, substantive information and testimony based on faulty forensic science analyses may have contributed to wrongful convictions of innocent people. This fact has demonstrated the potential danger of giving undue weight to evidence and testimony derived from imperfect testing and analysis. Moreover, imprecise or exaggerated expert testimony has sometimes contributed to the admission of erroneous or misleading evidence.

Further advances in the forensic science disciplines will serve three important purposes. First, further improvements will assist law enforcement officials in the course of their investigations to identify perpetrators with higher reliability. Second, further improvements in forensic science practices should reduce the occurrence of wrongful convictions, which reduces the risk that true offenders continue to commit crimes while innocent persons inappropriately serve time. Third, any improvements in the forensic science disciplines will undoubtedly enhance the Nation's ability to address the needs of homeland security.

. . .

PROBLEMS RELATING TO THE INTERPRETATION OF FORENSIC EVIDENCE

Often in criminal prosecutions and civil litigation, forensic evidence is offered to support conclusions about "individualization" (sometimes referred to as "matching" a specimen to a particular individual or other source) or about classification of the source of the specimen into one of several categories. With the exception of nuclear DNA analysis, however, no forensic method has been rigorously shown to have the capacity to consistently, and with a high degree of certainty, demonstrate a connection between evidence and a specific individual or source. In terms of scientific basis, the analytically based disciplines generally hold a notable edge over disciplines based on expert interpretation. But there are important variations among the disciplines relying on expert interpretation. For example, there are more established protocols and available research for fingerprint analysis than for the analysis of bite marks. There also are significant variations within each discipline. For example, not all fingerprint evidence is equally good, because the true value of the evidence is determined by the quality of the latent fingerprint image. These disparities between and within the forensic science disciplines highlight a major problem in the forensic science community: The simple reality is that the interpretation of forensic evidence is not always based on scientific studies to determine its validity. This is a serious problem. Although research has been done in some disciplines, there is a notable dearth of peer-reviewed, published studies establishing the scientific bases and validity of many forensic methods.

. . .

THE ADMISSION OF FORENSIC SCIENCE EVIDENCE IN LITIGATION

Forensic science experts and evidence are used routinely in the service of the criminal justice system. DNA testing may be used to determine whether sperm found on a rape victim came from an accused party; a latent fingerprint found on a gun may be used to determine whether a defendant handled the weapon; drug analysis may be used to determine whether pills found in a person's possession were illicit; and an autopsy may be used to determine the cause and manner of death of a murder victim. In order for qualified forensic science experts to testify competently about forensic evidence, they must first find the evidence in a usable state and properly preserve it. A latent fingerprint that is badly smudged when found cannot be usefully saved, analyzed, or explained. An inadequate drug sample may be insufficient to allow for proper analysis. And, DNA tests performed on a contaminated or otherwise compromised sample cannot be used reliably to identify or eliminate an individual as the perpetrator of a crime. These are important matters involving the proper processing of forensic evidence. The law's greatest dilemma in its heavy reliance on forensic evidence, however, concerns the question of whether—and to what extent—there is science in any given forensic science discipline.

Two very important questions should underlie the law's admission of and reliance upon forensic evidence in criminal trials: (1) the extent to which a particular forensic discipline is founded on a reliable scientific methodology that gives it the capacity to accurately analyze evidence and report findings and (2) the extent to which practitioners in a particular forensic discipline rely on human interpretation that could be tainted by error, the threat of bias, or the absence of sound operational procedures and robust performance standards. These questions are significant. Thus, it matters a great deal whether an expert is qualified to testify about forensic evidence and whether the evidence is sufficiently reliable to merit a factfinder's reliance on the truth that it purports to support. Unfortunately, these important questions do not always produce satisfactory answers in judicial decisions pertaining to the admissibility of forensic science evidence proffered in criminal trials.

In 1993, in Daubert v. Merrell Dow Pharmaceuticals, Inc.,[8] the Supreme Court ruled that, under Rule 702 of the Federal Rules of Evidence (which covers both civil trials and criminal prosecutions in the federal courts), a "trial judge must ensure that any and all scientific testimony or evidence admitted is not only relevant, but reliable."[9] The Court indicated that the subject of an expert's testimony should be scientific knowledge, so that "evidentiary reliability will be based upon scientific validity."[10] The Court also emphasized that, in considering the admissibility of evidence, a trial judge should focus "solely" on the expert's "principles and methodology," and "not on

---

8. 509 U.S. 579 (1993).
9. Ibid., p. 589.
10. Ibid., pp. 590 and 591 n.9 (emphasis omitted).

the conclusions that they generate."[11] In sum, *Daubert*'s requirement that an expert's testimony pertain to "scientific knowledge" established a standard of "evidentiary reliability."[12]

In explaining this evidentiary standard, the *Daubert* Court pointed to several factors that might be considered by a trial judge: (1) whether a theory or technique can be (and has been) tested; (2) whether the theory or technique has been subjected to peer review and publication; (3) the known or potential rate of error of a particular scientific technique; (4) the existence and maintenance of standards controlling the technique's operation; and (5) a scientific technique's degree of acceptance within a relevant scientific community.[13] In the end, however, the Court emphasized that the inquiry under Rule 702 is "a flexible one."[14] The Court expressed confidence in the adversarial system, noting that "[v]igorous cross-examination, presentation of contrary evidence, and careful instruction on the burden of proof are the traditional and appropriate means of attacking shaky but admissible evidence."[15] The Supreme Court has made it clear that trial judges have great discretion in deciding on the admissibility of evidence under Rule 702, and that appeals from *Daubert* rulings are subject to a very narrow abuse-of-discretion standard of review.[16] Most importantly, in Kumho Tire Co., Ltd. v. Carmichael, the Court stated that "whether *Daubert*'s specific factors are, or are not, reasonable measures of reliability in a particular case is a matter that the law grants the trial judge broad latitude to determine."[17]

Daubert and its progeny have engendered confusion and controversy. In particular, judicial dispositions of *Daubert*-type questions in criminal cases have been criticized by some lawyers and scholars who thought that the Supreme Court's decision would be applied more rigorously.[18] If one focuses solely on reported federal appellate decisions, the picture is not appealing to those who have preferred a more rigorous application of *Daubert*. Federal appellate courts have not with any consistency or clarity imposed standards ensuring the application of scientifically valid reasoning and reliable methodology in criminal cases involving *Daubert* questions. This is not really surprising, however. The Supreme Court itself described the *Daubert* standard as "flexible." This means that, beyond questions of relevance, *Daubert* offers appellate courts no clear substantive standard by which to review decisions by trial courts. As a result, trial judges exercise great discretion in deciding whether to admit or exclude expert testimony, and their judgments are subject only to a highly deferential "abuse of discretion" standard of review. Although it is difficult to get a clear picture of how trial courts handle

---

11. Ibid., p. 595. In General Electric Co. v. Joiner, 522 U.S. 136, 146 (1997), the Court added: "[C]onclusions and methodology are not entirely distinct from one another. Trained experts commonly extrapolate from existing data. But nothing in *Daubert* or the Federal Rules of Evidence requires a district court to admit opinion evidence that is connected to existing data only by the ipse dixit of the expert."

12. *Daubert*, 509 U.S. at 589, 590 n.9, 595.

13. Ibid., pp. 593-94.

14. Ibid., p. 594. In Kumho Tire Co., Ltd. v. Carmichael, 526 U.S. 137 (1999), the Court confirmed that the *Daubert* factors do not constitute a definitive checklist or test. *Kumho Tire* importantly held that Rule 702 applies to both scientific and nonscientific expert testimony; the Court also indicated that the *Daubert* factors might be applicable in a trial judge's assessment of the reliability of nonscientific expert testimony, depending upon "the particular circumstances of the particular case at issue." Ibid., at 150.

15. *Daubert*, 509 U.S. at 596.

16. See Gen. Elec. Co. v. Joiner, 522 U.S. 136, 142-143 (1997).

17. *Kumho Tire*, 526 U.S. at 153.

18. See, e.g., P. J. Neufeld. 2005. The (Near) Irrelevance of *Daubert* to Criminal Justice: And Some Suggestions for Reform. American Journal of Public Health 95(Supp.1): S107.

Daubert challenges, because many evidentiary rulings are issued without a published opinion and without an appeal, the vast majority of the reported opinions in criminal cases indicate that trial judges rarely exclude or restrict expert testimony offered by prosecutors; most reported opinions also indicate that appellate courts routinely deny appeals contesting trial court decisions admitting forensic evidence against criminal defendants.[19] But the reported opinions do not offer in any way a complete sample of federal trial court dispositions of *Daubert*-type questions in criminal cases.

The situation appears to be very different in civil cases. Plaintiffs and defendants, equally, are more likely to have access to expert witnesses in civil cases, while prosecutors usually have an advantage over most defendants in offering expert testimony in criminal cases. And, ironically, the appellate courts appear to be more willing to second-guess trial court judgments on the admissibility of purported scientific evidence in civil cases than in criminal cases.[20]

Prophetically, the *Daubert* decision observed that "there are important differences between the quest for truth in the courtroom and the quest for truth in the laboratory. Scientific conclusions are subject to perpetual revision. Law, on the other hand, must resolve disputes finally and quickly."[21] But because accused parties in criminal cases are convicted on the basis of testimony from forensic science experts, much depends upon whether the evidence offered is reliable. Furthermore, in addition to protecting innocent persons from being convicted of crimes that they did not commit, we are also seeking to protect society from persons who have committed criminal acts. Law enforcement officials and the members of society they serve need to be assured that forensic techniques are *reliable*. Therefore, we must limit the risk of having the reliability of certain forensic science methodologies judicially certified before the techniques have been properly studied and their accuracy verified by the forensic science community. "[T]here is no evident reason why ['rigorous, systematic'] research would be infeasible."[22] However, some courts appear to be loath to insist on such research as a condition of admitting forensic science evidence in criminal cases, perhaps because to do so would likely "demand more by way of validation than the disciplines can presently offer."[23]

The adversarial process relating to the admission and exclusion of scientific evidence is not suited to the task of finding "scientific truth." The judicial system is encumbered by, among other things, judges and lawyers who generally lack the scientific expertise necessary to comprehend and evaluate forensic evidence in an informed manner, trial

---

19. Ibid., p. S109.

20. See, e.g., McClain v. Metabolife Int'l, Inc., 401 F.3d 1233 (11th Cir. 2005); Chapman v. Maytag Corp., 297 F.3d 682 (7th Cir. 2002); Goebel v. Denver & Rio Grande W. R.R. Co., 215 F.3d 1083 (10th Cir. 2000); Smith v. Ford Motor Co., 215 F.3d 713 (7th Cir. 2000); Walker v. Soo Line R.R. Co., 208 F.3d 581 (7th Cir. 2000); 1 D.L. Faigman, M.J. Saks, J. Sanders, & E.K. Cheng. 2007-2008. Modern Scientific Evidence: The Law and Science of Expert Testimony. Eagan, MN: Thomson/West, §1.35, p. 105 (discussing studies suggesting that courts "employ *Daubert* more lackadaisically in criminal trials—especially in regard to prosecution evidence—than in civil cases—especially in regard to plaintiff evidence").

21. *Daubert*, 509 U.S. at 596-597.

22. J. Griffin & D.J. LaMagna. 2002. *Daubert* Challenges to Forensic Evidence: Ballistics Next on the Firing Line. The Champion, September-October:20, 21 (quoting P. Giannelli and E. Imwinkelried. 2000. Scientific Evidence: The fallout from Supreme Court's Decision in *Kumho Tire*. Criminal Justice Magazine 14(4):12, 40).

23. Ibid. See, e.g., United States v. Crisp, 324 F.3d 261, 270 (4th Cir. 2003) (noting "that while further research into fingerprint analysis would be welcome, to postpone present in-court utilization of this bedrock forensic identifier pending such research would be to make the best the enemy of the good." (internal quotation marks omitted)).

judges (sitting alone) who must decide evidentiary issues without the benefit of judicial colleagues and often with little time for extensive research and reflection, and the highly deferential nature of the appellate review afforded trial courts' *Daubert* rulings. Given these realities, there is a tremendous need for the forensic science community to improve. Judicial review, by itself, will not cure the infirmities of the forensic science community.[24] The development of scientific research, training, technology, and databases associated with DNA analysis have resulted from substantial and steady federal support for both academic research and programs employing techniques for DNA analysis. Similar support must be given to all credible forensic science disciplines if they are to achieve the degrees of reliability needed to serve the goals of justice. With more and better educational programs, accredited laboratories, certified forensic practitioners, sound operational principles and procedures, and serious research to establish the limits and measures of performance in each discipline, forensic science experts will be better able to analyze evidence and coherently report their findings in the courts. The current situation, however, is seriously wanting, both because of the limitations of the judicial system and because of the many problems faced by the forensic science community.

The NAS report is thoroughly discussed in Symposium: Forensic Science for the 21st Century, 50 Jurimetrics J. 1-146 (2009). For additional research on issues arising out of this report, see, e.g., Jessica D. Gabel, Realizing Reliability in Forensic Science from the Ground Up, 104 J. Crim. L. & Criminology 283 (2014); Paul C. Giannelli, *Daubert* and Forensic Science: The Pitfalls of Law Enforcement Control of Scientific Research, 2011 U. Ill. L. Rev. 53.

* * *

6. Problems in Forensic Science: Some Specific Controversies

In part because *Daubert* has given trial judges such broad discretion in their role as "gatekeepers," inconsistent rulings on admissibility are not uncommon when a new type of "scientific" evidence first begins appearing in court. There is often significant disagreement even between experts within a field, thus making it almost impossible for a factfinder using the deference model to reach a rational conclusion. We have already mentioned the ongoing debates surrounding polygraph testing, see note 5, page 721. The following discussion highlights a few more of these topics.

a. Recent Debates in DNA Testing

Courts and commentators are currently debating the extent to which trawling DNA databases to find a match to a sample taken at a crime scene could result in a

---

24. See J. L. Mnookin, Expert Evidence, Partisanship, and Epistemic Competence. 73 Brook. L. Rev. 1009, 1033 (2008) ("[S]o long as we have our adversarial system in much its present form, we are inevitably going to be stuck with approaches to expert evidence that are imperfect, conceptually unsatisfying, and awkward. It may well be that the real lesson is this: those who believe that we might ever fully resolve—rather than imperfectly manage—the deep structural tensions surrounding both partisanship and epistemic competence that permeate the use of scientific evidence within our legal system are almost certainly destined for disappointment.").

false match. The likelihood of a false match is highly contested, and defendants prosecuted based on these matches have argued that the lack of an agreement in the scientific community should prevent courts from admitting the evidence. Nonetheless, courts faced with the question have allowed the DNA evidence to be admitted, and as governments and various organizations establish DNA databases, law enforcement officials are increasingly able to solve both old and new cases after finding a DNA match in a database. For more information on the current debate and an argument courts should continue to allow the DNA evidence, see David H. Kaye, Rounding Up the Usual Suspects: A Legal and Logical Analysis of DNA Trawling Cases, 87 N.C. L. Rev. 425 (2009).

b. Psychological and Behavioral Sciences

Following some widely publicized convictions based on syndrome evidence and repressed memory, courts recognize that such "scientific evidence," if misused, can be a dangerous tool. "Syndromes" are collections of symptoms that occur together and characterize a particular abnormality. Experts frequently are offered at trial for information and opinions about syndromes of various kinds. In medical science, the term tends to be used to refer to a set of symptoms whose underling etiology was not fully understood at the time the syndrome was identified, as is the case, for example, with Down Syndrome. The knowledge of experts in the relevant medical areas frequently is based on carefully controlled studies (Down's Syndrome is again a good example), and can be valuable in litigation. In a medical malpractice suit alleging a mistake involving amniocentesis leading to the birth of a seriously disabled child, medical testimony concerning Down's Syndrome and its detectability through amniocentesis will be crucial.

Over the last few decades, syndrome evidence of a different kind has emerged. Battered woman syndrome, posttraumatic stress disorder, post-Vietnam syndrome, rape trauma syndrome, and child sexual abuse accommodation syndrome, are just a few. As the diagnosis of these syndromes began producing therapeutic successes and thus respectability, experts were permitted to testify that a person has suffered some legally cognizable harm, such as child or sex abuse, based on various symptoms that the alleged victim possesses.[25] These claims were often coupled with testimony that the victim repressed memory of the traumatic event for a considerable period of time, in many instances stretching into decades.

When a therapist diagnoses a patient with a psychological syndrome, the therapist is making a decision to use certain methods of treatment that have been beneficial to patients with like symptoms. The diagnostic process may not reveal any of the causes of the patient's symptoms and a therapist's speculative opinions about such causes may be highly prejudicial. Though syndrome evidence is usually inadequate for proof of causation, it can be effectively and appropriately used as rebuttal evidence. An example is in rape prosecutions where the victim has delayed reporting the crime. The defense may present this fact as an indication of a false charge. It may be helpful

---

25. See Robert Rosenthal, State of New Jersey v. Margaret Kelly Michaels: An Overview, 1 Psychol., Pub. Poly. & L. 246 (1995) for a description of the prosecution of Margaret Kelly Michaels for child abuse on the basis of repressed memory.

to the factfinder in such a case to be educated about the frequency of delayed reports among rape victims. See, e.g., United States v. Simmons, 470 F.3d 1115 (5th Cir. 2006) (finding no error in admitting such evidence even though not all *Daubert* factors were satisfied); People v. Hampton, 746 P.2d 947 (Colo. 1987) (admitting such evidence). For a more detailed examination of the controversy surrounding this and other types of psychological and behavioral evidence, see Henry F. Fradella et al., The Impact of *Daubert* on the Admissibility of Behavioral Science Testimony, 30 Pepp. L. Rev. 403 (2003) (studying *Daubert*'s application to psychological expert testimony); Christopher Slobogin, Doubts About *Daubert*: Psychiatric Anecdata as a Case Study, 57 Wash. & Lee L. Rev. 919 (2000) (arguing that opinion testimony from psychologists and psychiatrists concerning past mental state and proffered by criminal defendants, should be admissible under *Daubert-Kumho* though it may be considered "unreliable"); Rosemary L. Flint, Child Sexual Abuse Accommodation Syndrome: Admissibility Requirements, 23 Am. J. Crim. L. 171 (1995).

c. Toxic Tort Causation

A toxic tort . . . is a cause of action that arises when a plaintiff has developed a disease following long-term exposure to a physical agent—either a chemical or a form of energy such as electromagnetic fields (EMFs). Typically, the defendant's economic activity resulted in the plaintiff's exposure to the agent. Courts essentially must determine whether the plaintiff's exposure and subsequent disease are causally related, as that relationship is defined by the applicable law, or whether the exposure and disease are associated merely by chance. For example, did the asbestos inhaled by the plaintiff cause his lung cancer? Did the radar gun used by the traffic control officer cause his testicular cancer? Did the Bendectin taken by the plaintiff cause the birth defects that occurred thereafter? Traumatic injury occurs instantaneously, but disease develops over a period of time. The cause of disease, therefore, cannot be the direct object of the senses and can only be inferred. [Andrew A. Marino and Lawrence E. Marino, The Scientific Basis of Causality in Toxic Tort Cases, 21 Dayton L. Rev. 1, 2 (1995).]

You will recall that *Daubert* addressed the admissibility of expert testimony in a case in which a family alleged that their children's birth defects had been caused by the mothers' ingestion of Bendectin during pregnancy. The defendant, Merrell Dow Pharmaceuticals, Inc., argued that the plaintiffs could not prove that the prescription antinausea drug had caused the defects.[26] It is not surprising that such a seminal case should grow out of a dispute about toxic tort causation. As a central element of all toxic tort claims and one about which most fact finders know little, proving causation can be extremely difficult and often requires the plaintiff to call numerous expert witnesses.

The expert in a toxic tort case must rationalize an assertion that the plaintiff's disease and the dosage of the toxin received were causally related and not merely a chance association. For example, in the case of a traffic control officer who used a radar gun and developed cancer, the plaintiff's exposure to electromagnetic fields and his disease

---

26. For a thorough look at the steady stream of Bendectin cases that began in 1977, see Joseph Sanders, Bendectin on Trial: A Study of Mass Tort Litigation (Ann Arbor: The University of Michigan Press, 1998).

occurred in the context of many factors, among others: the plaintiff ate peanuts; smoked cigarettes; wore blue socks; drove a motorcycle; lifted weights; collected coins; lived near a superhighway; and had arthritic knees. The question arises, therefore, why the expert singled out electromagnetic fields as the causative agent, as opposed to myriad other co-existing circumstances. [Andrew A. Marino & Lawrence E. Marino, The Scientific Basis of Causality in Toxic Tort Cases, 21 Dayton L. Rev. 1, 21 (Fall, 1995).]

Since it is unlikely that the mechanism by which an agent causes a disease will be known in a toxic tort case, to be able to opine that the agent "caused" the disease, the expert will have to express why this explanation is more likely than other possible explanations. It may be that this logical gap, inherent in evidence of a toxic tort, creates a certain uneasiness among trial courts and leads them to decide cases one at a time, making it difficult for observers to predict the outcomes.

In Wright v. Willamette Industries, Inc., 91 F.3d 1105 (8th Cir. 1996), the appellate court asked whether sufficient evidence had been offered at trial to support the plaintiffs' claim that the formaldehyde emitted by the defendant's fiberboard manufacturing plant had caused the plaintiffs' headaches, sore throats, watery eyes, running noses, dizziness, and shortness of breath. The jury found for the plaintiffs and awarded compensatory damages of $226,250.00. The court reversed, explaining that, although the plaintiffs had proved their exposure to the defendant's emissions, they had failed to prove that their level of exposure was hazardous and that the defendant's emissions probably caused their particular ailments. The court characterized the expert testimony that had been offered in the following way:

> Their experts' information on this subject was simply insufficient. Dr. Fred Fowler, an industrial hygienist, and Dr. Jimmie Valentine, a pharmacologist, did offer testimony about the levels of gaseous formaldehyde that might be expected to cause symptoms like the ones that plaintiffs claim to have experienced. But the Wrights do not claim to have been injured from breathing gaseous formaldehyde, and they make no reference to any studies that reveal the levels of exposure to wood fibers impregnated with formaldehyde that are likely to produce adverse consequences. It is true that Dr. Frank Peretti, after a great deal of prodding, testified that the Wrights' complaints were more probably than not related to exposure to formaldehyde, but that opinion was not based on any knowledge about what amounts of wood fibers impregnated with formaldehyde involve an appreciable risk of harm to human beings who breathe them. The trial court should therefore have excluded Dr. Peretti's testimony, as Willamette requested it to do, because it was not based on scientific knowledge. See Daubert v. Merrell Dow Pharmaceuticals, Inc., 509 U.S. 579, 589-91 (1993); Fed. R. Evid. 702; Federal Judicial Center, Reference Manual on Scientific Evidence 47-48 (1994). Dr. Peretti's testimony regarding the probable cause of the Wrights' claimed injuries was simply speculation. [Wright v. Willamette Industries, Inc., 91 F.3d 1105, 1107-1108 (8th Cir. 1996).]

Thus, the court accepted scientific testimony that "gaseous formaldehyde" could cause the types of ailments suffered by the plaintiffs but it distrusted the experts' opinion that formaldehyde carried by particulate matter could have the same effect. For a critique of Wright, see Erica Beecher-Monas, The Heuristics of Intellectual Due Process: A Primer for Triers of Science, 75 N.Y.U. L. Rev. 1563 (2000).

In Zuchowicz v. United States, 140 F.3d 381 (2d Cir. 1998), the United States appealed an unfavorable decision in which the district court held that the plaintiff's wife's fatal lung condition was the result of the government's negligence in prescribing an overdose of the drug Danocrine. There was no question that the government had erred in its prescription or that the plaintiff's wife died from primary pulmonary hypertension (PPH). The only question before the trial court had been whether the one had caused the other. The trial court found that Danocrine had been extensively studied and prescribed for many years and that even though the Food and Drug Administration had approved it for use in dosages not exceeding 800 mg/day, the plaintiff's wife was accidentally instructed to take 1,600 mg/day. At the time of the trial, there had been no formal studies of effects of such high doses of Danocrine and it was thought that very few women had ever taken so much. Despite the plaintiff's inability to close this gap, his experts were permitted to testify that, although all of the other possible causes of the plaintiff's wife's PPH could not be excluded, the experts were "confident to a reasonable medical certainty that the Danocrine caused Mrs. Zuchowicz's PPH." There are many more examples of courts being more or less demanding of a plaintiff's experts in toxic tort litigation. With the great discretion accorded to trial judges within this area, it will take some time for courts to begin reaching more consistent conclusions. But cf. Plourde v. Gladstone, 190 F. Supp. 2d 708, 721 (D. Vt. 2002) (discussing some factors considered in admissibility of expert testimony in toxic tort cases); see also Williams v. Utica College, 453 F.3d 112 (2d Cir. 2006) (distinguishes *Zuchowicz* based on factors, found in *Zuchowicz* but absent in the present case, that make the causal inference reliable).

d. Traditional Law Enforcement Investigative Tools

Recently, several types of evidence that have been used for years in U.S. courtrooms have been questioned anew. The renewed scrutiny of handwriting identification, fingerprint identification, and comprehensive bullet lead analysis (CBLA) may be attributed to a belated recognition that "new" scientific techniques are not the only ones that should be subject to a *Daubert* analysis. As a result, the use of each of these techniques, though not novel, is less settled now than ten or even five years ago.

Handwriting Identification.   According to the thorough history provided in D. Michael Risinger, Mike P. Denbeaux & Michael J. Saks, Exorcism of Ignorance as a Proxy for Rational Knowledge: The Lessons of Handwriting Identification "Expertise," 137 U. Pa. L. Rev. 731, 762 (1988), by 1925 all but five jurisdictions in the United States had declared handwriting expertise permissible. Despite its early and continued[27] recognition, some courts can still be persuaded to exclude handwriting identification

---

27. Many courts continue to allow handwriting identification evidence. See D. Michael Risinger, Navigating Expert Reliability: Are Criminal Standards of Certainty Being Left on the Dock?, 64 Alb. L. Rev. 99, 140 n.161 (2000) for an extensive list which includes: United States v. Battle, No. 98-3246, 188 F.3d 519 (10th Cir. Aug. 6, 1999) (rejecting the defendant's challenge to the testimony of a qualified document examiner who testified that the defendant had forged the signature of another individual); United States v. Paul, 175 F.3d 906, 911 (11th Cir. 1999) (affirming the trial court's decision to allow an FBI document examiner to testify that the defendant authored an extortion note); United States v. Jones, 107 F.3d 1147, 1161 (6th Cir. 1997) (upholding the admissibility of a United States Postal Service forensic document analyst's testimony that the defendant's signature was on various documents related to a stolen credit card).

evidence. In *United States v. Saelee*, 162 F. Supp. 2d 1097 (D. Alaska 2001), the defendant, charged with three counts of importing opium in violation of federal drug laws, sought to exclude the testimony of John W. Cawley, III, a forensic document analyst with the U.S. Postal Service. After concluding that the 2000 amendments to FRE 702 required a *Daubert* hearing on the admission of Mr. Cawley's testimony, as it was based on "technical or other specialized knowledge," the court concluded that testimony on handwriting identification was unreliable for several reasons:

> [Reliability in this case may be determined by asking] whether the theories and techniques of handwriting comparison have been tested, whether they have been subjected to peer review, the known or potential error rate of forensic document examiners, the existence of standards in making comparisons between known writings and questioned documents, and the general acceptance by the forensic evidence community [of handwriting analysis]. [*United States v. Saelee*, 162 F. Supp. 2d 1097, 1101 (D. Alaska 2001).]

After concluding that the field of handwriting analysis failed to meet the first four of these requirements, the court examined the fifth and ultimately excluded the evidence, stating:

> Finally, the evidence does indicate that there is general acceptance of the theories and techniques involved in the field of handwriting analysis among the closed universe of forensic document examiners. This proves nothing. Testimony from these experts has, until recently, been uncritically accepted as reliable in the courts. Having previously testified somewhere as an expert document examiner was usually sufficient qualification. "Courts have long received handwriting analysis testimony as admissible evidence." *United States v. Paul*, 175 F.3d 906, 910 n.2 (11th Cir. 1999). However, the fact that this type of evidence has been generally accepted in the past by courts does not mean that it should be generally accepted now, after *Daubert* and *Kumho*. [*United States v. Saelee*, 162 F. Supp. 2d 1097, 1104-1105 (D. Alaska 2001).]

Nonetheless, one commentator points out: "Even when the most vulnerable forensic sciences—[including] handwriting—are attacked, the courts routinely affirm admissibility citing earlier decisions rather than facts established at a hearing. Defense lawyers generally fail to build a challenge with appropriate witnesses and new data. Thus, even if inclined to mount a *Daubert* challenge, they lack the requisite knowledge and skills, as well as the funds, to succeed."[28] The NAS Committee Report agrees that "[t]he scientific basis for handwriting comparisons needs to be strengthened." However, while concerned that research to quantify the "reliability and replicability" of handwriting analysis is limited, the Committee acknowledged that "recent studies have increased [the scientific community's] understanding of handwriting," and that "there may be a scientific basis for handwriting comparison."[29]

Fingerprint Identification. The *Saelee* court's statement to the fact that handwriting analysis evidence "has been generally accepted in the past . . . does not mean that it should be generally accepted now" might just as well be applied to a recent

28. NAS Report 2009, citing P. J. Neufeld. 2005. The (near) irrelevance of *Daubert* to criminal justice: And some suggestions for reform. American Journal of Public Health 95 (Supp. 1): S107, S110.
29. NAS Report 2009 (internal citations omitted).

decision on fingerprint analysis, which seemed to be well-settled evidence until United States v. Plaza, 179 F. Supp. 2d 492 (E.D. Pa. 2002), *vacated*, 188 F. Supp. 2d 549 (E.D. Pa. 2002). In *Plaza*, the defendant moved to exclude testimony on FBI fingerprint analysis (ACE-V) for failure to meet the criteria set forth in *Daubert* and *Kumho*. After a lengthy consideration of the history of the use of fingerprint evidence in U.S. courts and the science behind such evidence, the court ruled that "no expert witness for any party will be permitted to testify that, in the opinion of the witness, a particular latent print is—or is not—the print of a particular person." *Plaza*, 179 F. Supp. 2d at 518. The reasoning for the ruling was stated as follows:

> The court finds that ACE-V does not adequately satisfy the "scientific" criterion of testing (the first *Daubert* factor) or the "scientific" criterion of peer review (the second *Daubert* factor). Further, the court finds that the information of record is unpersuasive, one way or another, as to ACE-V's "scientific" rate of error (the first aspect of *Daubert*'s third factor), and that, at the critical evaluation stage, ACE-V does not operate under uniformly accepted "scientific" standards (the second aspect of *Daubert*'s third factor). [United States v. Plaza, 179 F. Supp. 2d 492, 517 (E.D. Pa. 2002).]

Though the court later reversed its decision in light of new evidence on the reliability of the ACE-V methodology, the *Plaza* case marked the first time that fingerprint evidence had been rejected under a *Daubert* analysis. Subsequent cases have generally admitted testimony on fingerprint identification. See, e.g., United States v. Mitchell, 365 F.3d 215 (3d Cir. 2004) (admitting fingerprint identification testimony after extensive *Daubert* hearing); United States v. Crisp, 324 F.3d 261 (4th Cir. 2003), *cert. denied*, 540 U.S. 888 (2003); United States v. George, 363 F.3d 666 (7th Cir. 2004); United States v. Janis, 387 F.3d 682 (8th Cir. 2004); United States v. Abreu, 406 F.3d 1304 (11th Cir. 2005). However, after *Plaza*, exclusion of fingerprint evidence is now at the district court's discretion in at least one jurisdiction. See Jacobs v. Virgin Islands, 53 Fed. App'x. 651 (3d Cir. 2002) (affirming exclusion of fingerprint evidence as within district court's discretion).

For current views on the issue, it is once again useful to turn to the NAS Committee Report:

> Over the years, the courts have admitted fingerprint evidence, even though this evidence has "made its way into the courtroom without empirical validation of the underlying theory and/or its particular application."[30] The courts sometimes appear to assume that fingerprint evidence is irrefutable. For example, in United States v. Crisp, the court noted that "[w]hile the principles underlying fingerprint identification have not attained the status of scientific law, they nonetheless bear the imprimatur of a strong general acceptance, not only in the expert community, but in the courts as well."[31] The court went on to say:
>
> > [E]ven if we had a more concrete cause for concern as to the reliability of fingerprint identification, the Supreme Court emphasized in *Daubert* that "[v]igorous cross-examination, presentation of contrary evidence, and careful instruction on the burden of proof are the traditional and appropriate means of attacking shaky but admissible evidence." *Daubert*, 509

---

30. M. A. Berger, Procedural Paradigms for Applying the *Daubert* test. 78 Minn. L. Rev. 1345, 1354 (1994).
31. 324 F.3d 261, 268 (4th Cir. 2003).

U.S. at 596. Ultimately, we conclude that while further research into fingerprint analysis would be welcome, "to postpone present in-court utilization of this bedrock forensic identifier pending such research would be to make the best the enemy of the good."[32]

Opinions of this sort have drawn sharp criticism:

> [M]any fingerprint decisions of recent years . . . display a remarkable lack of understanding of certain basic principles of the scientific method. Court after court, for example, [has] repeated the statement that fingerprinting met the *Daubert* testing criterion by virtue of having been tested by the adversarial process over the last one-hundred years. This silly statement is a product of courts' perception of the incomprehensibility of actually limiting or excluding fingerprint evidence. Such a prospect stilled their critical faculties. It also transformed their admissibility standard into a *Daubert*-permissive one, at least for that subcategory of expertise.[33]

This is a telling critique, especially when one compares the judicial decisions that have pursued rigorous scrutiny of DNA typing with the decisions that have applied less stringent standards of review in cases involving fingerprint evidence.

In holding that fingerprint evidence satisfied *Daubert*'s reliability and relevancy standards for admissibility, the Fourth Circuit's decision in *Crisp* noted approvingly that "the Seventh Circuit [in United States v. Havvard, 260 F.3d 597 (7th Cir. 2001)] determined that *Daubert*'s 'known error rate' factor was satisfied because the expert in *Havvard* had testified that the error rate for fingerprint comparison was 'essentially zero.' "[34] This statement appears to overstate the expert's testimony in *Havvard*, and gives fuel to the misconception that the forensic discipline of fingerprinting is infallible. The *Havvard* opinion actually described the expert's testimony as follows:

> [The expert] testified that the error rate for fingerprint comparison is essentially zero. Though conceding that a small margin of error exists because of differences in individual examiners, he opined that this risk is minimized because print identifications are typically confirmed through peer review. [The expert] did acknowledge that fingerprint examiners have not adopted a single standard for determining when a fragmentary latent fingerprint is sufficient to permit a comparison, but he suggested that the unique nature of fingerprints is counterintuitive to the establishment of such a standard and that through experience each examiner develops a comfort level for deciding how much of a fragmentary print is necessary to permit a comparison.[35]

This description of the expert's equivocal testimony calls into question any claim that fingerprint evidence is infallible.

The decision in *Crisp* also pointed out that "[f]ingerprint identification has been admissible as reliable evidence in criminal trials in this country since at least 1911."[36] The court, however, pointed to no studies supporting the reliability of fingerprint evidence. When forensic DNA first appeared, it was sometimes called "DNA fingerprinting" to suggest that it was as reliable as fingerprinting, which was then viewed as the premier identification science and one that consistently produced irrefutable results. During the effort to validate DNA evidence for courtroom use, however, it became

---

32. Ibid., pp. 269-270 (second alteration in original) (other internal citation omitted).

33. 1 Faigman et al., op. cit., §1:1, p. 4; see also J. J. Koehler, Fingerprint Error Rates and Proficiency Tests: What They Are and Why They Matter. 59 Hastings L.J. 1077 (2008).

34. 324 F.3d at 269 (quoting *Havvard*, 260 F.3d at 599).

35. *Havvard*, 260 F.3d at 599. The *Havvard* decision is sharply criticized by 1 Faigman et al., op. cit., §1:30, pp. 86-89.

36. *Crisp*, 324 F.3d at 266. The decision cites a number of other legal references, including, *inter alia*: People v. Jennings, 96 N.E. 1077 (1911); J. L. Mnookin, Fingerprint Evidence in an Age of DNA Profiling. 67 Brook. L. Rev. 13 (2001) (discussing history of fingerprint identification evidence).

apparent that assumptions about fingerprint evidence had been reached without the scientific scrutiny being accorded DNA. When the Supreme Court decided *Daubert* in 1993, with its emphasis on validation, legal commentators turned their attention to fingerprinting and began questioning whether experts could match and attribute fingerprints with a zero error rate as the FBI expert claimed in *Havvard*, and whether experts should be allowed to testify and make these claims in the absence of confirmatory studies. As noted above, most of these challenges have thus far failed, but the questions persist.

The 2004 Brandon Mayfield case refueled the debate over fingerprint evidence. The chronology of events in the Mayfield case is as follows:

> March 11, 2004: Terrorists detonate bombs on a number of trains in Madrid, Spain, killing approximately 191 people, and injuring thousands more, including a number of United States citizens.
>
> May 6, 2004: Brandon Bieri Mayfield, a 37-year-old civil and immigration lawyer, practicing in Portland, Oregon, is arrested as a material witness with respect to a federal grand jury's investigation into that bombing. An affidavit signed by FBI Special Agent Richard K. Werder, submitted in support of the government's application for the material witness arrest warrant, [avers] that Mayfield's fingerprint has been found on a bag in Spain containing detonation devices similar to those used in the bombings, and that he has to be detained so that he cannot flee before the grand jury has a chance to obtain his testimony.
>
> May 24, 2004: The government announces that the FBI has erred in its identification of Mayfield and moves to dismiss the material witness proceeding.[37]

In March 2006, the Office of the Inspector General of the U.S. Department of Justice issued a comprehensive analysis of how the misidentification occurred.[38] And in November 2006, the federal government agreed to pay Mayfield $2 million for his wrongful jailing in connection with the 2004 terrorist bombings in Madrid.[39] The Mayfield case and the resulting report from the Inspector General surely signal caution against simple, and unverified, assumptions about the reliability of fingerprint evidence.

In Maryland v. Rose, a Maryland State trial court judge found that the Analysis, Comparison, Evaluation, and Verification (ACE-V) process of latent print identification does not rest on a reliable factual foundation.[40] The opinion went into considerable detail about the lack of error rates, lack of research, and potential for bias.

The judge ruled that the State could not offer testimony that any latent fingerprint matched the prints of the defendant. The judge also noted that, because the case

---

37. S. T. Wax and C. J. Schatz. 2004, A Multitude of Errors: The Brandon Mayfield Case. The Champion. September-October, p. 6. The facts of the case and Mayfield's legal claims against the government are fully reported in Mayfield v. United States, 504 F. Supp. 2d 1023 (D. Or. 2007).

38. Office of the Inspector General, Oversight and Review Division, U.S. Department of Justice. 2006. A Review of the FBI's Handling of the Brandon Mayfield Case. Available at: www.usdoj.gov/oig/special/s0601/exec.pdf.

39. E. Lichtblau. 2006. U.S. Will Pay $2 Million To Lawyer Wrongly Jailed. New York Times. November 30, at A18.

40. Maryland v. Rose, Case No. K06-0545, mem. op. at 31 (Balt. Cnty. Cir. Ct. Oct. 19, 2007) (holding that the ACE-V methodology of latent fingerprint identification was "a subjective, untested, unverifiable identification procedure that purports to be infallible" and therefore ruling that fingerprint evidence was inadmissible). The ACE-V process is described in Chapter Five.

involved the possibility of the death penalty, the reliability of the evidence offered against the defendant was critically important.[41]

Compositional Analysis of Bullet Lead. Another previously well-settled area of expert testimony that has been largely discredited is Compositional Analysis of Bullet Lead (CABL or CBLA), a method by which bullets used in the commission of a crime are compared with bullets found in the possession of a suspect. In such an analysis, metal from the bullets at the scene is compared on a molecular level with metal from bullets possessed by the suspect; if the bullets are sufficiently similar in composition, the bullets are deemed to be from the same lot and the suspect may be charged accordingly. This method of analysis has been used by law enforcement since the 1960s.[42] Courts have traditionally admitted CABL. However, in the wake of a number of recent reports calling into question the reliability of CABL as a methodology,[43] courts subject the method to increased scrutiny and, in some cases, exclude expert testimony on CABL for failure to meet *Daubert* criteria. In United States v. Mikos, 2003 U.S. Dist. LEXIS 22069 (N.D. Ill. Dec. 5, 2003), the defendant moved to exclude CABL expert testimony that a bullet recovered from the body of a murder victim matched bullets found in the defendant's possession. The reasoning of the court in that case reflects the skepticism in CABL as a scientific technique:

> We understand that the FBI Laboratory has performed comparative bullet lead analysis (CBLA) for many years. Furthermore, we understand that persons from the FBI

---

41. Professor Jennifer Mnookin has also highlighted an important concern over "the rhetorical dimensions of the testimony . . . provide[d] in court" by members of the fingerprint community:

> At present, fingerprint examiners typically testify in the language of absolute certainty. Both the conceptual foundations and the professional norms of latent fingerprinting prohibit experts from testifying to identification unless they believe themselves certain that they have made a correct match. Experts therefore make only what they term "positive" or "absolute" identifications — essentially making the claim that they have matched the latent print to the one and only person in the entire world whose fingertip could have produced it. In fact, if a fingerprint examiner testifies on her own initiative that a match is merely "likely" or "possible" or "credible," rather than certain, she could possibly be subject to disciplinary sanction! Given the general lack of validity testing for fingerprinting; the relative dearth of difficult proficiency tests; the lack of a statistically valid model of fingerprinting; and the lack of validated standards for declaring a match, such claims of absolute, certain confidence in identification are unjustified, the product of hubris more than established knowledge. Therefore, in order to pass scrutiny under *Daubert*, fingerprint identification experts should exhibit a greater degree of epistemological humility. Claims of "absolute" and "positive" identification should be replaced by more modest claims about the meaning and significance of a "match."

J. L. Mnookin, The Validity of Latent Fingerprint Identification: Confessions of a Fingerprinting Moderate. Law, Probability and Risk 7(2):127 (2008); see also Koehler, supra note 33.

42. See Committee on Scientific Assessment of Bullet Lead Elemental Composition Comparison, National Research Council: Forensic Analysis: Weighing Bullet Lead Evidence (2004).

43. See, e.g., Michael O. Finkelstein & Bruce Levin, Compositional Analysis of Bullet Lead as Forensic Evidence, 13 J.L. & Poly. 119 (2005); William A. Tobin, Comparative Bullet Lead Analysis: A Case Study In Flawed Forensics, 28 Champ. 12 (July 2004); Edward J. Imwinkelried and William A. Tobin, Comparative Bullet Lead Analysis (CBLA) Evidence: Valid Inference or Ipse Dixit?, 28 Okla. City U. L. Rev. 43 (2003); William A. Tobin and Wayne Duerfeldt, How Probative Is Comparative Bullet Lead Analysis?, 17 Crim. Just. 26 (2002); Robert D. Koons and Diana M. Grant, Compositional Variation in Bullet Lead Manufacture, 47 J. Foren. Sci. 950 (2002); Erik Randich et al., A Metallurgical Review of the Interpretation of Bullet Lead Compositional Analysis, 127 Foren. Sci. Intl. 174 (2000).

Laboratory . . . have for years been allowed to testify at trials as to their opinions regarding the source of tested bullets based on CBLA. In our opinion, however, the required standard of scientific reliability is met only as to the proposed opinion testimony that the elements composition of the bullets recovered from the body is indistinguishable from the composition of the bullets found in the Defendant's car. There is no body of data to corroborate the government's expert's further opinion that from this finding it follows that the bullets must or even likely came from the same batch or melt. The motion to exclude the expert testimony . . . relating to comparative bullet lead analysis is therefore granted. [United States v. Mikos, 2003 U.S. Dist. LEXIS 22069, at *18 (N.D. Ill. Dec. 5, 2003).]

In contrast to fingerprint evidence, which is still generally believed to be reliable despite recent findings to the contrary, CABL evidence is beginning to be viewed with disfavor in many jurisdictions, to the point that some courts have reversed previous convictions that were based on CABL evidence. See, e.g., State v. Behn, 375 N.J. Super. 409 (N.J. Super. Ct. App. Div. 2005) (reversing conviction and remanding for new trial where defendant was convicted on the basis of unreliable CABL testimony). See also Ragland v. Commonwealth, 191 S.W.3d 569 (Ky. 2006) (disallowing CABL evidence and describing scholarship that criticizes CABL).

Perhaps most pertinently, in 2004, at the request of the FBI, the National Academies of Science completed a study on the reliability of CABL as a technique, concluding:

> The available data do not support any statement that a crime bullet came from a particular box of ammunition. In particular, references to "boxes" of ammunition in any form should be avoided as misleading under Federal Rule of Evidence 403.
>
> Compositional analysis of bullet lead data alone also does not permit any definitive statement concerning the date of bullet manufacture.
>
> Detailed patterns of the distribution of ammunition are unknown, and as a result, experts should not testify as to the probability that the crime scene bullet came from the defendant. Geographic distribution data on bullets and ammunition are needed before such testimony can be given.
>
> It is the conclusion of the committee that, in many cases, CABL is a reasonably accurate way of determining whether two bullets could have come from the same compositionally indistinguishable volume of lead. It may thus in appropriate cases provide additional evidence that ties a suspect to a crime, or in some cases evidence that tends to exonerate a suspect. CABL does not, however, have the unique specificity of techniques such as DNA typing to be used as standalone evidence. It is important that criminal justice professionals and juries understand the capabilities as well as the significant limitations of this forensic technique.

Eyewitness Identifications. Courts historically were reluctant to admit expert testimony on the limits of eyewitness identifications. At first, courts tended to deem this evidence as highly reliable while distrusting the contrary expert testimony. Later, courts tended to assume that the expert opinions were matters of common sense already known to the jury.. If the jurors already are appropriately skeptical of eyewitness identifications, putting an expert on the stand to discourage the jury from believing eyewitness testimony may result in an erroneous verdict through increasing the already appropriate level of skepticism of the jurors. See, e.g., United States v.

Smith, 122 F.3d 1355 (11th Cir. 1997) (holding expert testimony on the reliability of eyewitness identification inadmissible, because not helpful to jury); United States v. Hall, 165 F.3d 1095 (7th Cir. 1998) (". . . expert testimony relating to eyewitness identification is strongly disfavored."). To be confident that such testimony is "helpful," one must know the reliability of the information presented and how it is likely to affect the factfinder, which includes knowing the baseline from which the factfinder is presently operating. This judicial attitude is changing, however, as most courts find that such evidence is admissible in certain circumstances. See, e.g., United States v. Rodriguez-Berrios, 573 F.3d 55 (1st Cir. 2009) (affirming that admission of expert testimony on the flaws inherent in eyewitness identification "is a matter of case-by-case discretion"); United States v. Brownlee, 454 F.3d 131 (3d Cir. 2006) (holding that expert testimony on eyewitness identification would have been helpful to trier of fact and exclusion of expert was reversible error); United States v. Smithers, 212 F.3d 306 (6th Cir. 2000) (exclusion of expert on eyewitness identification reversible error); United States v. Brien, 59 F.3d 274 (1st Cir. 1995) (holding the exclusion of such evidence discretionary, not per se inadmissible); United States v. Rodrigues-Felix, 450 F.3d 1117 (10th Cir. 2006) (collecting cases).

Admissibility of such testimony has gained credence with the growth of what are collectively called "social framework" research. This refers to cognitive biases that can affect perception and belief arising out of racial and other social differences. This research has influenced scholars who favor admission of expert testimony raising doubts about eyewitness identifications. See Harvey Gee, Eyewitness Testimony and Cross-Racial Identification, 35 New Eng. L. Rev. 835 (2001) (reviewing Elizabeth Loftus, Eyewitness Testimony (1996)); Jennifer L. Devenport, Steven D. Penrod, and Brian L. Cutler, Eyewitness Identification Evidence: Evaluating Commonsense Evaluations, 3 Psy. Pub. Poly. & L. 338 (1997); Michael R. Leippe, The Case for Expert Testimony About Eyewitness Memory, 1 Psy. Pub. Poly. & L. 909 (1995). In any event, the person offering an expert witness must be prepared to qualify the witness as having knowledge that the jury lacks that would be helpful to its decision.

QUESTION

The above discussion touches only a few of the more controversial types of scientific evidence. Debates also surround statistics, survey research, horizontal gaze nystagmus (the observation of eye tremors as a method for gauging intoxication), the estimation of economic losses in damages awards, identification through bite marks, modus operandi, and the outer reaches of medical testimony. Though each type of scientific evidence raises unique questions, can you articulate a systematic approach for determining whether a given piece of expert testimony will be admissible under the Federal Rules and *Daubert/Kumho*? Do you have a sense of the concerns, either enunciated by judges or not, that will lead courts to exclude probative evidence?

7. A Law and Economics Perspective on Experts

RICHARD A. POSNER, THE LAW AND ECONOMICS
OF THE ECONOMIC EXPERT WITNESS
13 J. Econ. Perspectives 91 (1999)

There are several recurrent criticisms of the use of expert witnesses. They are made with reference to expert witnesses in general, but they do not exclude economists. All these criticisms belong to the genre of economic theory known as "agency costs." The court corresponds to the principal in an ordinary principal-agent relation, and the expert witness to the agent. The parties have asymmetric information. The agent knows more; the principal knows this and takes steps to try to align the agent's incentives with those of the principal.

The first criticism is that expert witnesses paid by the respective parties are bound to be partisans ("hired guns") rather than being disinterested, and hence presumptively truthful, or at least honest, witnesses. This factor alone does not distinguish expert witnesses sharply from a number of other common types of witnesses, notably the parties themselves; but the difference, and the second criticism, is that expert witnesses, it is feared, can mislead judges and juries more readily than lay witnesses can because they are more difficult to pick apart on cross-examination—they can hide behind an impenetrable wall of esoteric knowledge. Even if an expert witness is demolished on cross-examination by a lawyer who has been carefully prepped by another expert, the jury may not understand the questions and answers given on cross-examination well enough to realize that the expert has been demolished.

The concern with tilt and the concern with the "bounded rationality" of the trier of fact interact. The expert has both motive and means of slanting the truth in favor of the client.

Third, and related to both preceding points, it is believed that opposing experts often cancel each other out; the jury cannot choose between them, so it ignores them and decides the case on the basis of the nonexpert evidence. In such a case the expert evidence is wasted.

The first concern (excessive partisanship) does not seem to me very grave with respect to economic witnesses when they are testifying in areas in which there is a substantial professional consensus (a vital qualification, however, as we'll see). There are four reasons for my conclusion.

1) Because most expert witnesses, including most economic expert witnesses, are repeat players (unlike most lay witnesses), they have, like other potentially disloyal agents, a financial interest in creating and preserving a reputation for being honest and competent. Any public judicial criticism of a witness—in an opinion, whether or not formally published, or even in the transcript of a trial or other hearing—is apt to impair the witness's career as a witness, sometimes fatally, because the criticism is likely to be mentioned in the cross-examination of the witness in any future case. Furthermore, many economic expert witnesses are employed by consulting firms, which have a corporate reputation that can be damaged by the errors of their employees. There is a danger that judicial criticism of an expert may be uninformed. But,

if so, the negative impact on the expert's reputation will be less, since the next time the expert testifies will offer an opportunity to rebut the criticism if confronted with it during cross-examination.

The foregoing is not a complete answer to the criticism, because it is the repeat player who also has an incentive to please clients so as to be rehired in the future. The one-time expert witness presumably has nothing to lose or gain from testifying in a partisan manner, given the impermissibility of contingent fees for expert witnesses.

2) An expert witness who has a record of academic publication will be "kept honest" by the fact that any attempt to repudiate his academic work on the stand will invite devastating cross-examination. This implies that a warning flag should go up whenever the expert witness either has no record of academic publication or is testifying about matters on which he has never published. Not only is such an economist less likely to testify truthfully, but the lawyer's choice of that person as an expert implies that the lawyer was unable to find a knowledgeable economist willing to testify in support of the client's position.

3) Because of the adversarial character of the American system of litigation, and the requirement that the expert disclose evidence during the pretrial discovery process and thus before the trial begins (and in machine-readable form), expert evidence is subject to intense critical scrutiny, which should deter irresponsible expert testimony. In the case of economics, where the tradition of replicating previous academic studies is weaker than in the natural sciences, a study conducted for purposes of litigation is likely to receive more intense scrutiny than an academic study, even one published in a refereed journal.

4) An expert witness's evidence is inadmissible if it does not satisfy the methodological standards in the expert's field—something that is easier for the judge to determine than whether the analysis is correct. This rule acts as a screen against "junk science." The mesh of the screen may actually be too fine, especially for economic expert evidence, much of which is statistical. There is some judicial reluctance to admit into evidence statistical studies that do not pass the 5 percent test of statistical significance. . . .

The second concern with the use of expert witnesses—the concern with intelligibility once the evidence has been admitted—has undoubted merit, but is easily overstated because it ignores the lawyer's incentive to call persuasive witnesses. If a witness cannot communicate in a way that the court understands, the testimony is unlikely to be persuasive. This is a particularly important consideration in jury trials, because jurors give less weight to credentials than to clarity, and leads me to predict that jurors may understand expert testimony as well as judges do; that is, the lawyer will adjust the complexity of expert testimony to the comprehension of the audience.

The third concern about expert testimony—that opposing experts often cancel each other out—would be alleviated if, instead of testifying, they selected a neutral expert. Even when there is no neutral, it might seem that whenever the opposing experts canceled each other out the parties would agree not to call them as witnesses, to reduce the expense of litigation. This happens occasionally, but not often, maybe because a lawyer who suggested that neither side should call expert witnesses would be understood to be signaling that the available experts on one side would actually be weaker than the opposing experts.

Note that if market or other incentives kept experts fully honest, defendants' lawyers would often not introduce expert testimony at all, because they would find it difficult to locate a reputable expert who would contradict the plaintiff's expert. So we should expect both sides in a lawsuit to present expert witnesses more often the "softer" the science related to the case. Where the use of economic experts is most problematic is in the areas of economics in which there is no professional consensus. This used to be, and to some extent still is, the situation with regard to antitrust economics. A perfectly respectable economist might be an antitrust "hawk," another equally respectable economist a "dove." Each might have a long list of reputable academic publications fully consistent with systematically pro-plaintiff or pro-defendant testimony, and so a judge or jury would have little basis for choosing between them. There might be no available neutrals, in which event a court-appointed expert would perforce be a partisan.

ASSESSMENTS

A-9.1. FRE 701. Defendant crashed into Plaintiff's car at an intersection. Plaintiff alleges that Defendant was driving over the speed limit, was intoxicated, and ran a red light. To establish these facts, Plaintiff wants to call Walter Wheeler, who was at the scene and will testify that Defendant, when he exited his car, was wobbly and looked like he was drunk, that the smell of alcohol was detectable, and that he slurred his speech and acted belligerently toward bystanders who offered to help him. What is the best argument against admitting that portion of Wheeler's testimony that the defendant "looked like he was drunk"?

A. The opinion is not rationally based on the witness's perception.
B. The opinion is not helpful to the jury, because the witness can describe the underlying facts in greater detail and let the jury reach the conclusion about whether the witness was drunk, a key issue in the case.
C. The opinion requires application of "scientific. . . or other specialized knowledge" that can only be offered by an expert witness.
D. The opinion lacks foundation.

A-9.2. FRE 702-705. Donald Downs is being prosecuted for armed bank robbery. His defense is mistaken identity: The perpetrator was someone other than himself. As its final witness, the prosecution calls FBI agent Eugene Columbo, who investigated the case, as an expert witness. He will testify that he is a specialist in bank robbery investigations, with over 15 years of field investigative experience; that he teaches bank robbery investigation and criminal profiling techniques at the FBI training academy; and that he has been invited as a guest instructor in bank robbery investigations by over 20 police departments around the country. Based on his investigation, which includes reviewing all of the evidence offered by the prosecution in the case, plus certain inadmissible evidence from the case file that has not been disclosed to the jury, Columbo is prepared to testify that he is certain that Downs robbed the bank in question in this case. The best argument for the defense to exclude this testimony is:

    A. The opinion usurps the jury's role and is therefore unhelpful, because the jury should be able to reach this conclusion on its own from the admissible evidence.

    B. FRE 704 bars Columbo's testimony, because it embraces the ultimate issue in a criminal case.

    C. FRE 703 bars Columbo's testimony, because an expert witness cannot base his opinion on inadmissible matter.

    D. Columbo is not qualified to give an expert opinion on this subject.

A-9.3. FRE 702-705. Brent Nemerov is being prosecuted for possession of marijuana with intent to distribute. The FBI agent who arrested Nemerov is on the witness stand, and will testify as follows, in the absence of any objection: "On April 19, 2015, I executed a search warrant of Nemerov's home and discovered 30 plants in his growing room. Government's Exhibit 1 is a photograph taken by a forensic photographer (whose name I forget) which accurately depicts Nemerov's growing room. Under my personal supervision, the plants were removed from Nemerov's house by evidence technicians and taken to the FBI evidence storage facility." Defense counsel objects to the term "growing room" as an "improper conclusion or opinion." The objection should be:

    A. Overruled, because growing room is a fact perceived by the witness with his senses, and not an opinion.

    B. Overruled, because the defense counsel stated no valid ground or evidence rule.

    C. Sustained, because growing room is an opinion.

    D. Sustained, because growing room is an expert opinion, and the Agent must be qualified as an expert before giving it.

A-9.4. FRE 702-705. A jury found that ABC Radio breached its contract with Children's Radio and misappropriated trade secrets. During the trial, the judge allowed economist Stephen Willis to testify that, absent ABC's damaging conduct, Children's Radio would have been valued at $30 million. The expert stated that any or all of the defendant's allegedly wrongful acts would have caused the same amount of damages. On defendant's post-trial motion, the judge ruled that Willis's testimony should not have been admitted because, although he applied an "uncontroversial accounting method," his ultimate opinions were dubious. On appeal, Children's Radio argued that, under *Daubert*, a court can review only the methodology of the expert, not his or her conclusions.

    TRUE or FALSE: The trial judge's post-trial motion excluding the expert testimony is within the trial court's discretion, because the trial court can decide that the ultimate opinion is dubious even if the methodology is reliable.

A-9.5. FRE 702-705. James Boyd was terminated from his job when, after he missed five weeks of work for claimed mental health reasons, the company's psychologists reported that his leave was not medically required. Boyd brought suit under the Family Medical Leave Act (FMLA). On a motion for summary judgment the employer offered the depositions of the company's psychologists, neither of whom supported Boyd's claim that his absence, purportedly due to the stress and anxiety of his job, constituted protected leave under the FMLA. Boyd responded with the affidavit testimony of his expert witness, Dr. Emory. The affidavit consisted of three paragraphs detailing Dr. Emory's expert credentials. The one paragraph dealing specifically with Boyd's case stated as follows, in its entirety:

> Based upon my review of the records and my examination of Mr. Boyd, it is my professional opinion that Mr. Boyd's health condition rendered him unable to perform his job, and in fact left him disabled. Continued work would have increased his health problems and, in my professional opinion, the only solution to Mr. Boyd's medical condition would have been a leave of absence. At a minimum, Mr. Boyd required a leave of absence to obtain treatment for his condition.

The defendant moves for summary judgment, claiming that the Emory affidavit should be excluded and that, without it, Boyd raises no genuine issue as to whether he suffered a serious health condition under FMLA. Boyd argues that Dr. Emory's affidavit should not be excluded because Rule 705 permits Dr. Emory to give his opinion without prior disclosure of the underlying facts and data.

TRUE or FALSE: The affidavit should be excluded.

A-9.6. FRE 702. The CEO of a company suspected of bribery and kickbacks allegedly deleted documents from the company's computer. The government's specialist electronically searched the computer for deleted files, using special software, and came to court to testify about the findings. This testimony must satisfy FRE 702 in order to be admissible. TRUE or FALSE?

A-9.7. FRE 702. TRUE or FALSE: When a scientific expert's testimony contradicts scientific consensus, the trial judge must exclude it.

ANSWERS

A-9.1. FRE 701. The best answer is **B**, for the reasons stated. See FRE 701(b). A is not the best answer, because the witness has firsthand knowledge of facts from looking at the defendant that might support the opinion. D is a restatement of A, and is not the best answer for the same reason. C is not the best answer, because most courts deem observing drunkenness to be a matter of ordinary experience of most people.

A-9.2. FRE 702-705. The best answer is **A**. The expert opinion, to be admissible, must "assist the trier of fact to understand the evidence." Here, because the opinion goes to the ultimate issue in the case, there is a risk that it will intrude on the factfinders' job. Columbo has made inferences based on circumstantial evidence in his investigation and concluded that Douglas is guilty. But making inferences based on nontechnical, circumstantial evidence to determine guilt or innocence is exactly what we rely upon juries to do. If that were viewed as requiring special expertise, there would be no point in having a lay jury sit as the factfinder. Finally, the opinion is unhelpful to the jury because it goes without saying that the government believes Douglas is guilty—otherwise, they should not be prosecuting him. The jury system is supposed to be an independent review of the government's decision; this type of opinion would turn it into a rubber stamp. B is wrong because FRE 704 bars ultimate issue opinions only when they purport to state whether or not a criminal defendant has the mental state constituting an element of the crime charged or an element of a defense. Any policy concern about ultimate issue opinion testimony here folds back into answer A. D is wrong, because Columbo would undoubtedly qualify as an expert under FRE 702 based on his specialized knowledge arising from his extensive skill, experience, and training.

C is not a good answer, if your ground for making it is the mere fact of reliance on inadmissible matter. FRE 703 permits an expert to rely on inadmissible evidence so long as such evidence is of a type "reasonably relied upon by experts in the particular field." FRE 703. However, C could be built into a good argument—perhaps as strong as A—based on the concern that Columbo is suggesting there is evidence of guilt available to him but not the jury. This raises a significant issue of unfair prejudice. Moreover, it is far from clear that inadmissible evidence should be considered by experts in criminal investigations, at least in reaching conclusions about whether to bring a case to trial. To the extent that investigation methodology properly relies on inadmissible evidence, that methodology seems directly to conflict with the policy of trying criminal defendants on admissible evidence.

A-9.3. FRE 702-705. The best answer is **D**, for the reasons stated. Characterizing the room as a "growing room" suggests a conclusion about how the room is being used based on various specific facts, only some of which have been provided. Undoubtedly, the opinion is not a matter of common knowledge; the Agent could probably be qualified as an expert without great difficulty, however. For this reason, A is not a good answer. The fact/opinion distinction is relative, but here the level of generality and closeness to a central, disputed issue make "growing room" highly likely to be found an opinion. B is wrong, because no magic words are required for an objection; counsel used enough language to make clear that he was invoking FRE 701 and 702. C is not the best answer, because it is incomplete—not all opinion testimony is objectionable.

A-9.4. FRE 702-705. TRUE:

> This assertion [by Willis] that any or all of the alleged wrongful acts would have caused the same outcome is dubious. Children's argues that, under *Daubert*, a court can review only the methodology of the expert, not his or her conclusions. "But nothing in ... *Daubert* ... requires a district court to admit opinion evidence that is connected to existing data only by the ipse dixit of the expert. A court may conclude that there is simply too great an analytical gap between the data and the opinion proffered." General Elec. Co. v. Joiner, 522 U.S. 136, 146 (1997).

Children's Broadcasting Corp. v. Walt Disney Co., 245 F.3d 1008, (8th Cir. 2001).

A-9.5. FRE 702-705. TRUE. FRE 705 is intended to permit the expert to state his opinion first, before explaining the methodology. But FRE 705 does not dispense with the need to explain methodology to the trier of fact. Moreover, FRE 705 governs only how the evidence will be presented at trial, and does not trump FRE 702(b)'s requirement that admissibility depends on a showing of "sufficient facts or data." Here, the expert gives only a bare conclusion. Again, as *Joiner* makes clear, a district court has discretion to exclude such opinions—and probably should, in the absence of the FRE 702 showing. An important practice point here is that, in a summary judgment affidavit, expert conclusions should be affirmatively supported by the showings required under FRE 702(b)-(d) for admissible expert testimony.

A-9.6. TRUE.   This testimony relies on technical or, at the very least, "other specialized" knowledge as to how the government's software works to detect deleted computer files. Hence, it falls under FRE 702. The government's specialist testifies as an expert, rather than percipient, witness. United States v. Ganier, 468 F.3d 920 (6th Cir. 2006) (categorizing government's witness as an expert on similar facts).

A-9.7. FALSE.   FRE 702 and the *Daubert* multifactor test have rejected the consensus rule of *Frye* and given trial judges broad discretion in the matter.

THE PROCESS OF PROOF IN CIVIL AND CRIMINAL CASES:
Burdens of Proof, Judicial Summary and Comment, and Presumptions

We have studied in great detail the proof process at the level of individual elements and items of evidence. We turn now to aspects of the process of proof that affect the structure of trials and the sufficiency of evidence as a whole. The roles of the judge and the jury and their relationship to each other continue to be a central focus of our inquiry.

Even if all the evidence each party wishes to produce is admitted into evidence, the role of the trial judge is not at an end. Just as the trial judge must make a preliminary determination concerning the logical force and legal admissibility of any offered evidence, she must also make a preliminary determination of the overall strength of each party's case. The judge is empowered to issue rulings that terminate the litigation at various stages in the proceedings based in large measure on her assessment as to how reasonable people would analyze the evidence offered at trial. In civil cases, judges may issue a summary judgment before trial, Fed. R. Civ. P. 56, or a judgment as a matter of law at or after trial, Fed. R. Civ. P. 50, if no reasonable jury could find for the party against whom the judgment is issued (usually, the plaintiff). Similarly, courts may dismiss a criminal case, Fed. R. Crim. P. 29, or overturn a criminal conviction, Jackson v. Virginia, 443 U.S. 307 (1979), if no reasonable jury could find guilt beyond a reasonable doubt. Judges must also instruct juries about what standard of proof to apply in assessing the evidence as a whole.

In addition to evaluating the sufficiency of the evidence and instructing the jury about the standard of proof, the trial judge has various means to influence the jury's deliberations. We have already encountered one indirect instance of such power. By ruling on the admissibility of specific proffers, the judge can dramatically influence the jury's perspective. For example, if a judge finds that a proposed witness lacks personal knowledge and thus cannot be placed on the stand, the jury will not have before it that witness's testimony. Suppose that the witness would have contradicted an important witness of the adversary. By excluding the testimony, the judge affects the proof process by constraining the jury's perspective. Thus, the judge, by deciding questions of the admissibility of evidence, has significant power to influence the deliberative process. As we will see, the judge may also influence the deliberative process by summarizing or commenting on the evidence.

We first discuss the process of proof in civil cases and then discuss the process of proof in criminal cases. We treat them separately because of the different standards and constitutional issues that arise in criminal cases. First understanding how the various evidentiary devices operate in civil cases will allow you to better understand the additional complexities that arise in criminal cases. Although our primary focus will be on jury trials, many of the same principles, issues, and devices arise in bench trials as well.

A. THE PROCESS OF PROOF IN CIVIL CASES

In this section, we discuss three related aspects of the process of proof in civil cases: the burdens of proof, judicial summary and comment on the evidence, and evidentiary presumptions.

1. The Burdens of Proof in Civil Cases

A critical part of evaluating the parties' evidence is the application of rules governing the burden of proof. There are two aspects to the burden of proof—the burden of persuasion and the burden of production. For the burden of persuasion, there are decision rules that the jury must apply in evaluating the evidence. For most civil cases the decision rule is a "preponderance of the evidence." For example, a plaintiff in a negligence action must persuade the jury by a preponderance of the evidence that the defendant negligently injured the plaintiff. In some special civil actions, the standard is "clear and convincing evidence." The second aspect of the burden of proof is the production burden or the burden of producing evidence. For the burden of production, the judge applies rules to determine whether a party has produced enough evidence to create a factual issue before the jury and avoid an adverse judgment on that issue. If a party fails to meet its production burden prior to trial, the judge will issue a summary judgment for the other side. Fed. R. Civ. P. 56. If a party fails to meet a production burden at trial, the judge will issue a judgment as a matter of law for the other side. Fed. R. Civ. P. 50. We first discuss the burden of production and then the burden of persuasion.

a. The Burden of Production

The Role of and Rationale for Production Burdens. Our system of civil litigation does not give each party the automatic right to proceed through the entire trial process and have the jury resolve the case on the basis of whatever evidence the parties choose to introduce. Rather, in order to proceed to that stage a party must produce evidence that satisfies a burden of production.

Each issue to be litigated, whether it is an element or an affirmative defense, has a burden of production associated with it that requires one party or the other to produce evidence relevant to the particular issue. If the party with a burden of production fails to produce sufficient evidence on a particular issue, the judge will not permit the issue to go to the jury. Thus, the burden of production informs the parties how issues will be decided if no evidence is produced.

How, though, is one to know when a party with a burden of production has produced sufficient evidence to avoid a ruling that would decide an issue for the other side? A burden of production is satisfied when the underlying purpose of the requirement is met. In civil cases, the primary purpose of a burden of production is to ensure that there are issues in the case that need to be resolved by the jury. Issues need to be resolved by juries whenever there could be reasonable disagreement as to which party should prevail. If there could be no reasonable disagreement, there is no reason to go to the expense and trouble of a trial, or to risk the possibility that the jury will render an unsubstantiated verdict. In such a case, the judge should, and will, render a judgment for the appropriate party. Thus, the failure to satisfy a burden of production will result in the adversary's prevailing on that particular issue. For this reason, the burden of production is sometimes referred to as the *risk of nonproduction*.

The Relationship Between Production Burdens and Persuasion Burdens.   To decide if there could be reasonable disagreement about which party should prevail, the judge must consider the burden of persuasion. Assume, for example, that the plaintiff must prove a particular fact by a preponderance of the evidence, a standard commonly understood to mean that the disputed fact is "more likely true than not." The plaintiff will satisfy the burden of production by presenting enough evidence to create a jury issue regarding that fact. In other words, the plaintiff must produce enough evidence so that a jury could find that the fact is "more likely true than not." If no reasonable person could conclude that the plaintiff has satisfied the relevant burden of persuasion, then there is no reason to prolong the proceedings on that issue. The judge should terminate the proceedings with respect to the fact in favor of the defendant. Similarly, if the plaintiff's evidence is so overwhelming that any reasonable jury would find the fact more likely true than not, and the defendant does not challenge or rebut the plaintiff's evidence, the judge should terminate the proceedings with respect to that fact in favor of the plaintiff. In short, the burden of production is a function of the burden of persuasion. John T. McNaughton, Burden of Production of Evidence: A Function of a Burden of Persuasion, 68 Harv. L. Rev. 1382 (1955). Whether a burden of production has been met depends on whether, in light of the evidence, there could be reasonable disagreement over which party should win. When there is room for such disagreement, a jury question has been generated and the case should proceed to trial.

The Relationship Between the Two Burdens Illustrated.   The relationship between burdens of production and burdens of persuasion may be understood in more detail by reflecting on the burdens in terms of probabilities. Jurors evaluate evidence by making rough estimates of the likelihood that facts are true. In other words, although jurors may not articulate or even tacitly assign specific quantified degrees of probability to their conclusions, they make factual assessments that may be expressed as probabilities. We may also express burdens of persuasion in terms of probabilities — for example, the preponderance standard could be taken to mean "more than 50 percent likely." For purposes of illustration only, assume that jurors do think in roughly probabilistic terms and that a preponderance of the evidence means more than a 50 percent chance of the relevant fact being true.

Under these assumptions, one may diagram the evidentiary process in such a way as to highlight the relationship between burdens of production and burdens of persuasion. Assume that the party with a burden of production produces some evidence. That evidence will indicate that there is a certain chance that the relevant facts are true. However, the evidence is likely to be not perfectly clear as to what probability it generates. Looking at that evidence, reasonable people could disagree about the probability to which the evidence establishes some necessary fact. Does that mean that every time evidence is produced a jury issue is generated because there always will be reasonable disagreement about its implications? No; a jury issue will be generated only when there is disagreement about which party should win, and that requires referring to the burden of persuasion. Consider now the three possibilities charted in Diagram 10-1:

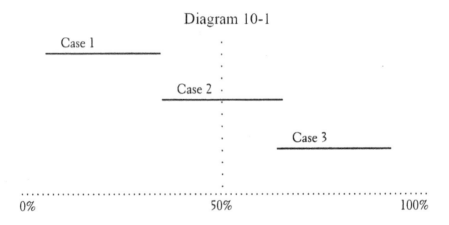

Diagram 10-1

After a party produces evidence on an issue, this chart reflects the three relevant possibilities in terms of the implications of the evidence. First, the evidence produced may not be very convincing. A reasonable person looking at it may conclude that it has some persuasive force, but not very much. That possibility is represented by Case 1. It indicates that, given the evidence, the probability of the relevant fact being true ranges from about 10 to 35 percent (we could have drawn that line segment anywhere between 0 and 50%, just so long as it did not exceed 50%). In this case, the burden of production has not been satisfied. Since no reasonable person could conclude that the party producing the evidence should win, there is no reason to send this issue to the jury. In Case 2, the evidence has generated a jury issue. The evidence indicates a range of reasonable persuasiveness from about 40 to 60 percent (here we could have drawn the line segment in any fashion so long as it ranged over 50%). Since reasonable people could disagree about the implications of the evidence in this case, the issue will be sent to the jury. Case 3 is similar to Case 1 in that again no reasonable disagreement could exist as to the implications of the evidence. The evidence indicates somewhere between a 65 and 90 percent chance of the relevant fact being true (here the line could be drawn anywhere to the right of 50%).

Case 3 is different from Case 1 in one respect. We have been assuming that the party with the burden of production has produced evidence. In Case 1, the burden has not been met, and thus there is no reason to proceed further. In Case 2, the burden of production has been met, and the case will proceed. In Case 3, the burden has not only been met, but exceeded. No reasonable person could disagree about who should win. This conclusion, though, is based solely on the evidence produced by one party. Case 3 differs from Case 1 in that rather than the judge disposing of the issue, Case 3 requires that the adversary be given a chance to produce contrary evidence in order to demonstrate that there is a reasonable dispute about the relevant fact. In Case 1, there is no reason to have the adversary proceed because the party's evidence itself indicates that the relevant fact cannot be established. Having the adversary produce still more information substantiating that conclusion would be a waste of time and other resources. In Case 3, however, the adversary has not yet been heard and may be in possession of information that would affect the analysis of how likely the relevant fact is, given all the evidence (including the adversary's). Accordingly, in Case 3, the judge will not dispose of the relevant issue. The party with the initial burden of production cannot prevail before the adversary has an opportunity to respond. After the adversary responds—and each side has had a chance to rebut evidence submitted by the other side—one or both parties may ask the judge to rule on the sufficiency of the evidence.

Procedural Mechanisms for Enforcing Burdens of Production. The manner in which a party asks a judge to determine whether the opponent has met a production burden depends on the time at which the judge is asked to make such a ruling, and here we see the interaction between the rules of evidence and civil procedure. One possibility is that before any evidence is produced a party can move for summary judgment. Fed. R. Civ. P. 56. The judge will grant the motion if it can be determined from the pleadings and any supporting documentation that there are no issues in need of judicial resolution in the case. Such a decision, however, is equivalent to saying that either Case 1 or Case 3 in the Diagram 10-1 is present—evidence presented by the party with the production burden is either manifestly insufficient (Case 1) or overwhelmingly strong (Case 3). If Case 2 is present, the judge will deny the motion for summary judgment (by either party) and the litigation will proceed.

Another possibility is that, if a case goes to trial, the judge may be asked to test the strength of the evidence by a motion for judgment as a matter of law at the end of a party's case. Fed. R. Civ. P. 50. The analysis is similar to the analysis of summary judgment. For both summary judgment and judgment as a matter of law, the judge's decision will rest on the ability of a party to meet its burden of persuasion and the adversary's ability to respond with sufficient evidence to justify taking the issue to a jury. As the Supreme Court observed in Anderson v. Liberty Lobby, Inc., 477 U.S. 242, 252 (1986):

> [T]he inquiry involved in a ruling on a motion for a summary judgment . . . necessarily implicates the substantive evidence standard of proof that would apply at trial on the merits. . . . The judge's inquiry, therefore, invariably asks whether reasonable jurors could find by a preponderance of the evidence that the plaintiff is entitled to a verdict.

See also Reeves v. Sanderson Plumbing Prods., Inc., 530 U.S. 133, 150 (2000) (explaining that the standard for judgment as a matter of law "mirrors" the standard for summary judgment). In short, the burden of production and the motions for summary judgment and judgment as a matter of law are functions of the burden of persuasion. For further discussion of the relationships between these procedural devices and the proof process, see Michael S. Pardo, Pleadings, Proof, and Judgment: A Unified Theory of Civil Litigation, 51 B.C. L. Rev. 1451 (2010).

The Allocation of Burdens of Production.   Typically, the pleading or moving party bears both the burden of pleading and the burden of production. In general, whoever is asking the court to modify the status quo, which is either the plaintiff or a party who filed a motion for some sort of relief, must introduce sufficient evidence of the relevant factual claims to justify a finding of fact consistent with those claims. Thus, who bears the burden of production will normally be a function of the position of the parties. If X sues Y for a breach of contract, X will bear the burden of production on most factual issues. If, by contrast, Y sues X in a declaratory judgment action asking the court to certify that no breach had occurred, Y will bear the burden of production on most of the identical factual issues. In most instances there will be a well-established precedent allocating the burden of production. If there is no such precedent, however, there is "no satisfactory test" for allocating the burden of production. Fleming James Jr., Burdens of Proof, 47 Va. L. Rev. 58, 58 (1961). We should note in this connection that the Supreme Court's introduction of "plausibility" requirements for pleadings (Ashcroft v. Iqbal, 556 U.S. 662 (2009); Bell Atlantic Corp. v. Twombly, 550 U.S. 544 (2007)) did not change the allocation of the burdens of proof. See Littlejohn v. City of New York, 795 F.3d 297, 307-311 (2d Cir. 2015).

KEY POINTS

1. Every factual element of a claim or a defense has a production burden associated with it.
2. The purpose of the production burden is to require the party who has it to present enough evidence to create a jury question.
3. The failure to satisfy the burden of production will result in a judgment against the party with the burden.
4. The party with the burden of pleading a matter typically has the burden of production with respect to that matter.

b. The Burden of Persuasion

The skeptic will say that we can know nothing with certainty (although one might ask how the skeptic knows that). Even if there are matters that we can know with certainty, disputes at trial typically do not fall into that category. Indeed, without some uncertainty cases would not make it to trial in the first place. Jurors (or judges in bench trials) will usually be less than certain about the determinations they are called upon to make. There may be credible, conflicting accounts about what happened; there may be uncertainty about how much weight to give scientific evidence; or there may be conflicting views about how much weight to give a circumstantial inference. For example, in the *Johnson* case, to what extent does evidence of Officer Walker's character for violence suggest that he may have been the first aggressor?

Burdens of Persuasion Are Decision Rules That Manage Uncertainty. A burden of persuasion is a rule of decision that informs the jury how to decide a case in light of the uncertainties that inevitably will accompany the presentation of evidence. For example, one possible rule of decision is that a plaintiff should prevail only if the evidence establishes the plaintiff's case to a 95 percent certainty. This rule would require a verdict for the defendant if there were more than a slight doubt about the truth of the facts that the plaintiff must establish.

Such a rule may initially seem to have an intuitive appeal—people (defendants) should not be required to pay unless they have done something wrong. Notwithstanding this intuitive appeal, it is not the rule generally found in civil litigation because it would put plaintiffs at a serious disadvantage. Requiring plaintiffs to meet such a high burden, it is believed, would result in a disproportionate number of wrongful verdicts for defendants at the expense of deserving plaintiffs. The opposite rule—requiring defendants to show to a 95 percent certainty that they should not be held liable— would have the opposite effect. Rather than adopt either of these two extremes, the virtually uniform practice in civil litigation is to define the burden of persuasion as a preponderance of the evidence. Plaintiffs must prove each of their necessary factual claims to a preponderance of the evidence, and defendants must establish affirmative defenses by the same standard. Accordingly, judges instruct juries in civil cases to analyze the evidence and render a verdict for the party in whose favor the evidence "preponderates." As we noted earlier, preponderance is usually defined as meaning "more likely true than not." Thus, the task for juries is to determine whether the evidence makes the plaintiff's story appear more likely true than not with respect to the factual elements of a cause of action and to determine whether the evidence makes the defendant's story appear more likely true than not with respect to affirmative defenses.

The Premises Underlying the Preponderance Rule. The preponderance rule incorporates an underlying assumption concerning the participants in litigation: Plaintiffs as a class and defendants as a class generally ought to be treated as equals. The reason behind this assumption is twofold. First, the legal system must be unbiased and evenhanded: Granted that mistakes in adjudicative decisions are inevitable, money or property that a plaintiff loses undeservedly should be considered to be as regrettable as a similar undeserved loss suffered by the defendant. With the loss factor being equal for both sides, the party with better—that is, preponderating—evidence should prevail. Second, before a case is resolved, one cannot know who should win; hence, it is as likely that the defendant should win as the plaintiff. (Probability theorists call this assumption the "principle of indifference" or the "principle of insufficient reason.") Assume that the plaintiff is suing the defendant for $200 allegedly owed under a contract. Before the parties to this dispute produce evidence relevant to its resolution, how should we conceptualize the case—as one in which the plaintiff is trying to get $200 of the defendant's money, as a case in which the defendant is wrongfully refusing to pay, or as a case in which two individuals are contesting whose $200 it is? The last view is intuitively most compelling. Without knowing the facts, it seems just as likely that the defendant is refusing to pay what is owed as that the plaintiff is attempting to obtain an undeserved benefit.

One implication of the equivalency notion is that there should be roughly the same number of errors made for plaintiffs as for defendants. The preponderance standard may implement this result if certain conditions exist. First, assume that in the set of all cases going to trial there are approximately as many deserving plaintiffs as deserving defendants. To cast it in terms of the famous Priest-Klein hypothesis, when a civil dispute goes to trial, it is generally safe to assume that the plaintiff's and the defendant's chances to prevail are more or less equal. Had this not been the case, the parties would have cheaply settled their dispute out of court instead of litigating it expensively. George L. Priest & Benjamin Klein, The Selection of Disputes for Litigation, 13 J. Legal Stud. 1 (1984).

Second, assume further that the jury will make a rough probability assessment of the strength of each case presented by the parties. Presumably, those probability assessments will range from 0.0 to 1.0. Now compare the set of cases in which plaintiffs deserve to win to the set of cases in which defendants deserve to win. For each set, it is reasonable to suppose that evidence will reflect the merits of the case. That is, in most of the cases in which plaintiffs deserve to win the facts will support that conclusion, thus creating a probability assessment of more than .5, which will result in a verdict for the plaintiff. Only in the minority of cases in which the probability assessment is .5 or less will there be wrongful verdicts for defendants. By the same token, in most cases that defendants deserve to win evidence will demonstrate that the defendant deserves to win, thus creating a probability assessment of .5 or less for the plaintiff's claim. Only in the minority of cases in which the probability assessment is more than .5 will there be wrongful verdicts for plaintiffs. If one assumes that the probability assessments for these two sets are in a normal distribution over the range of 0.0 to 1.0, then the number of errors made for plaintiffs will approximate the number of errors made for defendants, and the preponderance of the evidence standard will have done its job. Moreover, the number of factually correct jury verdicts will be greater than the number of verdicts that are factually incorrect.

Diagram 10-2 demonstrates this proposition geometrically.[1] The horizontal axis is the probability that juries assign to cases, and the vertical axis is the number of

---

1. We are indebted for what follows, including the graphs, to Richard S. Bell, Decision Theory and Due Process: A Critique of the Supreme Court's Lawmaking for Burdens of Proof, 78 J. Crim. L. & Criminology 557 (1987).

Diagram 10-2

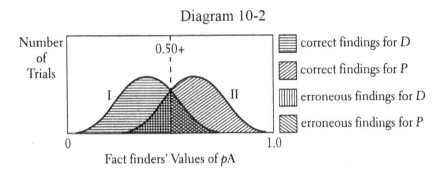

cases assigned a particular probability. Graph I is the set of cases in which defendants deserve to win (which means if we knew all the facts to certainty, the defendant would win). Graph II is the set of cases in which plaintiffs deserve to win.

In Graph I, all of those cases to the right of the .5 level, which is the heavily shaded area, are errors. In Graph II, all of the cases to the left of the .5 level, which is again the heavily shaded area, are errors. The larger the heavily shaded areas are, the more errors there are; the smaller the heavily shaded areas are, the fewer errors there are. So long as the heavily shaded areas under the two graphs are of approximately equal size, then the preponderance standard will have done its appointed task of equalizing errors among plaintiffs and defendants. Note, however, that this equalization will occur only if three conditions are met: The relevant areas under the two graphs are roughly the same size; evidence presented in the cases is generally a good indicator of which party deserves to win; and the juries make no systematic errors in assessing the evidence. If any of these conditions are not met, errors may not be allocated equally and the jurors' verdicts might not be predominantly correct.

Higher Burdens of Persuasion. We can use these same graphs to demonstrate why alternative, higher burdens of persuasion are occasionally relied upon in civil cases. Courts use these burdens when the parties' stakes in the dispute are unequal. For example, many jurisdictions require allegations in civil cases of fraud or of activity that would be criminal to be proven by clear and convincing evidence. See also Addington v. Texas, 411 U.S. 418 (1979) (civil commitment requires clear-and-convincing proof as a matter of constitutional Due Process). Because of the gravity of such allegations for one party, the chosen allocation of errors should favor that party (which also explains the higher burden of persuasion in criminal cases). Making the same assumptions as we did above, we illustrate the effect of raising the burden of persuasion from a preponderance to "clear and convincing" evidence in Diagram 10-3. The shaded area again represents errors, and the effect of raising the burden of proof is obvious. Errors favoring defendants increase and errors favoring plaintiffs decrease, which is precisely the effect that the higher burden of persuasion is designed to accomplish. Again, though, bear in mind that the actual distribution of errors will depend on the accuracy of the assumptions we are making.

Diagram 10-3

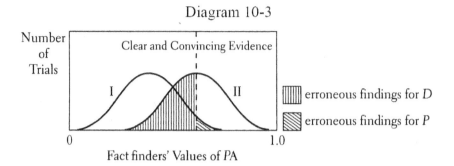

Fact finders' Values of PA

Although our primary concern here is civil cases, note that Diagram 10-3 can also explicate the proof beyond reasonable doubt requirement for criminal cases: Assume that the horizontal and vertical axes retain the same significance and simply move somewhat to the right the vertical line representing the burden of persuasion standard. This will show that the criminal proof standard allows many guilty criminals to go free to avoid a mistaken conviction of a single innocent defendant. This societal preference is understandable and likely justified, but it is not as straightforward as many people believe. See Larry Laudan, Truth, Error and Criminal Law: An Essay in Legal Epistemology 55-61 (2006).

The Meaning of "Preponderance of the Evidence" in Practice.   Burdens of persuasion, or at least the preponderance burden, may not operate as they are intended to. In an interesting study, Professors Rita James Simon and Linda Mahan obtained data indicating that jurors may understand "preponderance of the evidence" to mean a probability somewhere between .7 and .8, while judges consistently indicate that it means slightly more than .5. Rita James Simon and Linda Mahan, Quantifying Burdens of Proof, 5 Law & Soc'y Rev. 319 (1971). In this study, jurors were asked to translate the phrase *preponderance of the evidence* into a probability assessment rather than being informed that the phrase means "50 percent plus." When so informed, however, there is data indicating that individuals can follow such instructions. Dorothy K. Kagehiro & W. Clark Stanton, Legal v. Quantified Definitions of Standards of Proof, 9 Law & Hum. Behav. 159 (1985). When factfinders base their decisions on the "relative plausibility" criterion, discussed in Chapter Two, they must choose the best explanation for the evidence and adopt the factual scenario that is more comprehensive, more coherent, and better evidenced than its rivals. This system allows a plaintiff to prevail only when her evidence clearly outscores the defendant's evidence. See Ronald J. Allen & Alex Stein, Evidence, Probability, and the Burden of Proof, 55 Ariz. L. Rev. 557, 574 (2013).

As also discussed in Chapter Two, there is empirical evidence that jurors decide cases by constructing and evaluating overarching stories or theories of what happened, often selecting among one of the two presented by the parties. See pages 89-91, supra. Thus, in practice, the preponderance standard will often be implemented by selecting which version of what happened jurors find to be more plausible, rather than by making explicit probability assessments. See Michael S. Pardo, Second-Order Proof Rules, 61 Fla. L. Rev. 1083 (2009).

The Relative Nature of the Burden of Persuasion. From the standpoint of the parties to an action, any burden of persuasion is relative. If the plaintiff has a greater than 50 percent burden of persuasion, the defendant will lose unless the jury can be convinced by at least a 50 percent probability that the plaintiff's version of the facts is untrue. If the defendant does not carry that burden, the inevitable logical result will be that the jury believes that the plaintiff's version of the facts is more than 50 percent likely to be true. Thus, to say that the plaintiff has a greater than 50 percent burden of persuasion is to say that the defendant has a 50 percent burden of persuasion. Similarly, to say that a plaintiff has a 70 percent burden of persuasion is to say that a defendant has a greater than 30 percent burden of persuasion.

The Allocation of the Burden of Persuasion. As is true of production burdens, a burden of persuasion for each necessary element of a cause of action must be allocated to one party or the other. Usually, the law is clear on which party has the burden of persuasion. Plaintiffs typically bear the burden to prove by a preponderance all of the elements of their claims, and defendants bear the burden of persuasion for the elements of "affirmative defenses." If the law is not clear on this issue, however, there is no very helpful formula or litmus test for determining who should have the burden. Courts may consider a variety of factors, including (1) which party has better access to evidence; (2) "the extent to which a party's contention departs from what would be expected in light of ordinary human experience"; (3) "a feeling that a charge of wrongdoing should in fairness be proven by the party making it"; and (4) "real or supposed reasons of policy [for which] the law sometimes disfavors claims or defenses which it nevertheless allows." Fleming James Jr., Burdens of Proof, 47 Va. L. Rev. 58-59 (1961).

As far as constitutional law is concerned, states are free to allocate burdens of proof in civil cases virtually any way they like. Lavine v. Milne, 424 U.S. 577, 585 (1976) ("Outside the criminal area, where special concerns attend, the locus of the burden of persuasion is normally not an issue of federal constitutional concern."); Cruzan v. Dir., Mo. Dep't of Health, 497 U.S. 261, 280 (1990) (due process does not forbid states from requiring clear and convincing evidence as a proof of patient's wish for the withdrawal of life-sustaining treatment). For example, a state may require one party to bear a burden of production on an issue and the other party to bear the burden of persuasion on that issue. States on occasion exercise the power to allocate the burdens of proof in interesting ways. Consider the following case.

SCHECHTER v. KLANFER

321 N.Y.S.2d 99, 28 N.Y.2d 228, 269 N.E.2d 812 (1971)

BREITEL, Judge.

In this negligence action for personal injuries, the issue is whether the jury should have been instructed to hold plaintiff, who had by amnesia lost his memory of the events causing his injury, to a lesser degree of proof than a plaintiff who could have testified to the events.

Upon the trial, a verdict in favor of defendants was returned. The trial court initially instructed the jury to hold plaintiff to a lesser degree of proof if it found his amnesia to be genuine. Upon defendants' objection, however, the charge was withdrawn, plaintiff taking exception.

There should be a reversal and a new trial in order that the jury may consider whether plaintiff should be held to a lesser degree of proof.

Robert Schechter and his companion, Alice Stone, were involved in a motorboat collision on the night of August 25, 1964. Both were then 14 years old. They had left a party at a lakeshore home and, with Robert operating his father's boat, had begun motoring across the lake. Alice sat in the front seat, to the left of Robert. Alice testified that the night was clear and moonlit, that the boat's lights were on, and that Robert was taking a straight course at about four miles an hour. They had not gone far, Alice continued, when she looked to her right and saw a motorboat some 50 feet distant heading towards them, its bow out of water. About one second later, she estimated, the other boat, operated by defendant Robert Klanfer, struck the Schechter boat near the driver's seat. Alice estimated that the Klanfer boat was traveling at 30 miles an hour. The nighttime speed limit on the lake was 10 miles an hour. The defendants disputed Alice's testimony as to the speed of their boat and the lighting of the Schechter boat. Robert testified but not as to the accident, claiming that, as a result of the collision, he had no memory of the events. He had sustained a fractured skull, fractured arm, fractured jaw, and other physical injuries. He had been comatose for several days. Plaintiff's medical expert testified that Robert had suffered severe emotional shock and psychiatric change, including amnesia, due to brain damage.

The rule providing when a plaintiff may prevail on a lesser degree of proof was best crystallized in Noseworthy v. City of New York, 80 N.E.2d 744. The court there held that "in a death case a plaintiff is not held to as high a degree of proof of the cause of action as where an injured plaintiff can himself describe the occurrence." Moreover, despite some contrary notions, the rule has been applied in wrongful death cases where the plaintiff has called an eyewitness. . . .

The Committee on Pattern Jury Instruction of the Association of Supreme Court Justices recommends, in a pattern instruction, that the amnesiac plaintiff be held to a lesser degree of proof if the jury is satisfied from medical and other evidence that plaintiff is suffering from loss of memory and that the injuries plaintiff incurred were a substantial factor in causing plaintiff's loss of memory (PJI 1:62).[2] In a thoughtful and well-documented comment to the instruction, the committee explains: "The limitation that the accident must have been a substantial factor in causing the loss of memory is predicated on the rationale of the Noseworthy case, which is not merely plaintiff's inability to present proof, but the unfairness of allowing the defendant, who has knowledge of the facts, to benefit by standing mute when plaintiff's inability results from defendant's acts." (1 N.Y. PJI 36, emphasis in original).

---

2. "If, however, you are satisfied from the medical and other evidence presented that plaintiff is suffering from a loss of memory that makes it impossible for him to recall events at or about the time of the accident and that the injuries plaintiff incurred in the accident were a substantial factor in causing his loss of memory, the plaintiff is not held to as high a degree of proof as would be a plaintiff who can himself describe the occurrence."

Of course, an amnesiac plaintiff can no more "describe the occurrence" that produced his injury than can a plaintiff's decedent, a toddler or an imbecile. Other States, faced with an analogous choice of extending to amnesiac plaintiffs a "presumption of due care" normally accorded plaintiffs' decedents, have reasoned that the amnesiac's inability to testify entitles him to the preferential rule.

The rule even as applied to amnesiacs does not, however, shift the burden of proof or eliminate the need for plaintiffs to introduce evidence of a *prima facie* case. The jury must rest its findings on some evidence to establish negligence and also the absence of contributory negligence. In this case, however, plaintiff did introduce evidence to make out a *prima facie* case, so that there was an opportunity to apply the lesser burden of persuasion. If the jury had been told to apply a lesser burden of persuasion, it could have and, therefore, might have found plaintiff free from contributory negligence. The circumstances testified to by Alice Stone that Robert drove the boat in a straight line, at a speed of four miles an hour, and with the boat lights on, were relevant on the issue of contributory negligence. It also could have found defendants negligent upon Alice's testimony of the speed and course of the Klanfer boat.

The danger is, of course, that amnesia is easily feigned. The dangers may be ameliorated. Plaintiff has the burden of proof on the issue of amnesia as on other issues. A jury should be instructed that before the lesser burden of persuasion is applied, because of the danger of shamming, they must be satisfied that the evidence of amnesia is clear and convincing, supported by the objective nature and extent of any other physical injuries sustained, and that the amnesia was clearly a result of the accident.

The above is undoubtedly a more severe test than that suggested by the Pattern Jury Instructions. Yet it would seem a small price to pay for a liberal rule treating amnesiac plaintiffs on a par with the representatives of decedents in death actions. The reasons for so treating amnesiacs are similar to those advanced for representatives of persons silenced in fatal accidents, but the risk and ease of shamming are measurably greater.

Accordingly, the order of the Appellate Division should be reversed and a new trial ordered, with costs to abide the event.

Order reversed, etc.

NOTES AND QUESTIONS

1. According to the *Schechter* court, the plaintiff must present a prima facie case of negligence in order to be in a position to get the benefit of the reduced burden of proof rule. What is a prima facie case? The *Schechter* court does not tell us, but usually courts use that term to describe the production burden that a party must meet. If that is what the court means here, and it seems likely that it is, the plaintiff must introduce enough evidence of the defendant's negligence to raise a jury issue. In other words, in holding that the plaintiff had presented a prima facie case, the court, in effect, was saying that the evidence of the defendant's negligence resembled Case 2 in Diagram 10-1 on page 806, supra.

2. Could or should the *Schechter* court have been more precise in articulating how amnesia could affect the plaintiff's burden of proof? The court stated that in the case of amnesia caused by the defendant the plaintiff "is not held to as a high a degree of proof as would be a plaintiff who can himself describe the occurrence," and the court also stated that "the rule even as applied to amnesiacs does not . . . shift the burden of proof." If the plaintiff's ordinary burden of persuasion is just slightly greater than 50 percent, and if that burden is lessened, how is the burden of persuasion not shifted to the defendant?

3. What justification is there for giving a reduced burden of persuasion to a plaintiff with amnesia?

4. If burdens of persuasion operate as they are intended to operate, precisely what cases would come out differently under a rule that allocated the preponderance burden of persuasion to one party instead of the other? Is not the answer only those cases in which the jury is in equipoise and is unable to say whether the burden of persuasion is met or not? How large a class of cases do you think that is likely to be? Changing a burden of persuasion from preponderance to clear and convincing evidence, by contrast, is more likely to affect the results in cases, again assuming burdens of persuasion operate roughly as intended.

Consider the implication of these observations in the context of *Schechter*. If holding the plaintiff with amnesia to a lower standard of persuasion than other plaintiffs means that the plaintiff's burden is reduced slightly from the preponderance standard, the effect is to make the plaintiff's burden something less than 50-plus percent—say, 49 percent. This is the equivalent of saying that the burden of persuasion shifts to the defendant to persuade the jury by a 51-plus percent preponderance that the defendant is not negligent. Thus, contrary to the court's assertion, the amnesia rule does shift the burden of proof to the defendant (unless, of the course, the fact finder understands preponderance to mean more than 50-plus percent). Such a shift, however, is unlikely to affect many cases. The practical impact of the amnesia rule lies not in the question whether there is a shifting of the preponderance burden but rather in how much of a shift the amnesia rule creates.

5. In Santosky v. Kramer, 455 U.S. 745, 768-770 (1982), the Supreme Court decided that misconduct justifying the termination of a person's parental rights must be proven by clear and convincing evidence. The Court also explained that the applicable standard of proof will depend on the general type of case at issue, and is not something to be allocated on a case-by-case basis, because "litigants and the factfinder must know at the outset of a given proceeding how the risk of error will be allocated." Id. at 757. Is *Schechter* consistent with this principle?

6. There are statements in many cases that the "burden of proof never shifts; it always rests with the party to whom it was originally allocated." For the most part this statement is true, but it is more misleading than helpful. Factfinders generally tend to give a party's evidence more credence when her opponent provides no counterevidence. As a practical matter at least, this means that the opponent bears the burden of countering the proponent's evidence. This informal burden is often identified as "tactical." Also reconsider Diagram 10-1, page 806, supra. When a party has demonstrated such a strong case that no reasonable person could disagree that the party deserves on the evidence so far produced to win, a judgment will be entered unless the adversary produces more evidence that lowers the probabilities to a point where reasonable people could disagree. In such a case, the adversary bears a functional burden of production; the adversary can produce evidence or lose. In this sense, the "burden of production" can shift numerous times during the course of a trial.

7. There are various policies that could be pursued through different choices concerning burdens of persuasion. We have mentioned some, such as error equalization over parties. Others include the reduction of erroneous determinations of liability, reduction of total dollars wrongfully allocated as a result of trial, and the minimization of large mistakes. Different burden of proof rules may serve these various policies better than others. Alex Stein, Foundations of Evidence Law 143-153 (2005).

KEY POINTS

1. Burden of persuasion is a rule of decision that requires a party to persuade the factfinder of a proposition to a specified degree of certainty.
2. The usual burden of persuasion in civil cases is a "preponderance of the evidence," which is generally understood as meaning "more likely true than not"; in some special categories of civil cases, the burden of persuasion is "clear and convincing evidence."
3. From the perspective of the parties to the action, the burden of persuasion is relative: To say that the plaintiff must prove some proposition to be true by greater than 50 percent in order to win is to say that the defendant must prove that proposition to be false by no less than 50 percent.
4. Each party must plead and prove her own case. The plaintiff must plead and subsequently prove all the facts underlying her cause of action, as defined by substantive law. The defendant, in turn, must plead and subsequently prove all the facts underlying his affirmative defenses, as defined by substantive law. Hence, the burden of persuasion usually tracks the burdens of pleading and production: The party who has the burdens of pleading and production on the matter bears the burden of persuasion as well.

2. Judicial Summary and Comment in Civil Cases

At common law, trial judges had the power to sum up the evidence at the close of the trial and to comment on its implications. The power to sum up the evidence allows the judge to review for the jury all the evidence that the parties presented. The value of summary is that it gives the jury an impartial review of the evidence. The power to comment on the evidence goes considerably further, though. It permits the court to express its own views on the implications of the evidence, thus injecting the judge's personal opinion into the litigation. Many states therefore have outlawed the summary and comment practice by statute or on constitutional grounds.

a. *The Advantages and Disadvantages of Permitting Judicial Summary and Comment*

The attractiveness of comment and summary is that it may inject into the trial process a disinterested element that is valuable to the jury in its appraisal of the evidence. To the extent one believes that there is such a thing as a "disinterested observer," and to the extent one distinguishes the "evidence" presented at trial from "inferences" one draws from the evidence, one may be convinced that summary and comment are laudable features of trials. Both of these points have another side to them, however.

Trial judges certainly are disinterested in some respects, but they, like the rest of us, have their own way of looking at things that undoubtedly affects both what they observe and retain as well as what inferences they draw from evidence. Reconsider the discussion of relevancy in Chapter Three. Factfinders evaluate evidence in the context of their belief systems—the way they look at the world. Suppose, for example, that a person returns home one night and before entering the house wonders if her husband is at home. She notices that the evening paper is not on the doorstep and that the deadbolt on the front door is unlocked. Moreover, she knows from prior experience that when her husband returns home he invariably picks up the paper and leaves the deadbolt unlocked after entering the house. She also knows that she has a reliable paper delivery service. By comparing what she observes—no newspaper and deadbolt unlocked—she can infer that her spouse has already arrived home.

Of course, the inference she has drawn may be erroneous. It is possible, for example, that the paper blew away or was not delivered that day and that she or her husband inadvertently left the deadbolt unlocked in the morning. These matters, too, might be considered in light of observations made at the time, which would also be compared to previous experience. Is it a windy day? What happens to the paper on such a day? How often is the deadbolt inadvertently unlocked? The process of inference, in short, requires that evidence be compared to previous experience. That is what jurors do collectively when they consider evidence, and indeed it explains in large measure why we cherish the jury system. In deciding the facts of a case, we want a representative mix of the population to bring their differing views to bear on the question of what inferences may be drawn from evidence and what generalizations about the world can and cannot go into factfinding.

This inevitable reliance on personal experience in factfinding explains in large measure the resistance to judicial comment on the evidence, and to some extent summary as well. Judges commenting on the implications of evidence are, in a very real sense, commenting on their previous experience, and the injection of their previous experience into the factfinding process may have an undesirable influence. Trial judges, like all of us, have individual biases and prejudices that may affect how they summarize or comment on the evidence. In addition, there may be a kind of group bias stemming from the common, not particularly diverse backgrounds that judges to a substantial extent still share. Judges as a class tend to be well educated, educated in a similar manner, economically comfortable, and accustomed to respect in the community. In addition, judges still tend to be predominantly white and male and from middle- or upper-class backgrounds. Any small and cohesive group—such as trial judges were, and probably still are—tends to share beliefs and attitudes that may affect how they perceive evidence as well as what inferences they draw from that evidence. Allowing judges to summarize and comment on the evidence permits their beliefs and attitudes to creep into the factfinding process, skewing it in favor of the interests of this particular elite group. See Dan M. Kahan et. al, Whose Eyes Are You Going to Believe? Scott v. Harris and the Perils of Cognitive Illiberalism, 122 Harv. L. Rev. 837 (2009).

b. The Criteria for Evaluating Judicial Summary and Comment

In federal courts, summary and comment are appropriate "to assist [the jury] in arriving at a just conclusion." Vicksburg & M.R.R. v. Putnam, 118 U.S. 545, 553 (1886). The difficulty is that the criteria for determining what properly assists a jury—and what goes too far—are not clear.

Consider Nunley v. Pettway Oil Co., 346 F.2d 95 (6th Cir. 1965), where the jury was unable to decide if the plaintiff had been an invitee or a licensee. In order to encourage the jury to break the impasse, the judge gave the jury the following instruction during a break from deliberations:

> Now, the jury of course is the sole and exclusive judge of the facts in this lawsuit. It is appropriate that the court in an effort to be possibly of some help to the jury may comment upon the evidence. I refrain from doing that and have refrained until this time from doing it in this case. However, in an effort to be of some possible assistance to you I think that I should under these circumstances make some comment upon the evidence upon this issue of invitee-licensee. I want you to understand, however, that in making these comments that you are not in any degree, in any respect, obligated to receive or accept or agree with what I may say. It is your duty to accept what I say with regard to the law in the case, but it is not your duty to accept any comment that I may make or any evaluation that I make or conclusion that I might reach on the evidence. That is solely your responsibility and solely your duty. But, with that understanding, it is the opinion of the court in this case that, from all the evidence upon the issue of invitee or licensee, that the evidence will establish that at the time and place of the accident the plaintiff was a licensee and not an invitee. Now, I say that just for the purpose, as I say, of possibly being of some help to you, but I want you to understand that making that comment you are not obligated whatsoever to accept that comment as your comment or as your opinion in the case, because it is your job and your responsibility to resolve that issue. I only make that with the thought and the hope that it may be of some possible assistance to you. At any rate, I want to ask you once again to retire and consider your verdict and see if you cannot come to some agreement, some verdict that will reflect the views of all of the jurors. Have respect for the views of your fellow jurors. If you find there are jurors that have different views from you, don't hesitate to change your mind if you should be persuaded by reason and logic to accept a different view. Attempt if you can in good conscience to arrive at a unanimous verdict. After you have considered the views of all others you shouldn't give up a firm conviction that you have just for the purpose of arriving at a unanimous verdict, but see if you cannot resolve this issue. Make one more effort, please. [Id. at 98.]

In reversing a judgment for the defendant, the court of appeals said that "the trial judge's opinion on the licensee-invitee issue was an opinion on an ultimate fact question peculiarly for jury consideration and amounted to an instructed verdict as to defendant. . . ." Id. Do you agree?

c. Standardized Comments

Perhaps in response to restraints on the power to summarize and comment, a practice of providing "standardized inferences" has developed. These are instructions that inform the jury that proof of one fact gives rise to an inference of another fact. Such instructions come in a variety of forms. For examples, see Longenecker v. General Motors, 594 F.2d 1283 (9th Cir. 1979) (inference of a defect from a product failure); Ina Aviation Corp. v. United States, 468 F. Supp. 695 (E.D.N.Y.), aff'd, 610 F.2d 806 (1st Cir. 1979) (inference that evidence in a party's control but not produced at trial would have been unfavorable to that party). For a discussion, see 2 McCormick on Evidence §342, at 496-497 n.9, 497-498 (Kenneth S. Broun ed., 6th ed. 2006).

The sources of a standardized inference can be statutory or common law based. When the source is the common law, the standardized inference is, in essence, a summary of collected judicial wisdom with respect to a certain matter. Such a standardized inference may be preferable to a normal comment on the evidence because the personal views of the trial judge are relegated to a lesser role. To some extent the same is true of standardized inferences that are authorized by statute, except that the source of the inference is legislative rather than judicial wisdom. On the other hand, because instructions on standardized inferences typically do not incorporate references to specific evidence in the case and because they sometimes contain excessive legal jargon, they may not convey information to the jury as well as individualized comments. Charles T. McCormick, Charges on Presumptions and Burdens of Proof, 5 N.C. L. Rev. 291, 299-301 (1972).

d. The Relationship Between Comments on the Evidence and the Burden of Persuasion

By commenting on the evidence, the judge puts her thumb on the scales. When her comment has its intended effect on the jury, it inevitably has the consequence of shifting the burdens of persuasion of the parties in the case. Consider, for example, a comment that is favorable to the plaintiff, who has the persuasion burden of proving fact X by a preponderance of the evidence. If there were no comment, the plaintiff in order to prevail would have to introduce enough evidence to convince the jury that fact X is 50-plus percent likely to be true; the defendant in order to prevail would have to convince the jury that there was at least a 50-50 chance that fact X is untrue. With a comment favorable to the plaintiff, the plaintiff will have to do less to persuade the jury that fact X is true, and the defendant will have to do more to persuade the jury that fact X is untrue. For example, the plaintiff's evidence standing alone may convince the jury that there is only a 45 percent probability that X is true, but the evidence along with the comment may convince the jury by a greater than 50 percent probability that X is true. In such a case, the effect of the comment is to permit the plaintiff to prevail even though the plaintiff has introduced evidence to satisfy only a

45 percent persuasion burden. The defendant, in order to prevail in the case, would have had to introduce enough evidence to convince the jury by a 55-plus percent probability that X was untrue.

KEY POINTS

1. Judicial summary of and comment on the evidence are permissible in federal courts, but many states prohibit judicial comment or summary or both.
2. If summary or comment is permissible, an important criterion for evaluating the propriety of a particular summary or comment should be its accuracy.
3. Unless a summary or comment merely states the obvious to the jury, the summary or comment will inevitably be helpful to one party and harmful to the other, thereby shifting the parties' relative burdens of persuasion.

NOTES AND QUESTIONS

1. Reconsider the *Schechter* case at page 813, supra. Try to formulate a comment on the evidence that would have roughly the equivalent effect of the burden-reducing amnesia instruction that the court approved.

2. Would a comment of the type contemplated in Note 1 be permissible? If the answer is yes, which device—the comment or the explicit burden-reducing instruction—is preferable? If the answer is no, why should it be permissible to reduce the plaintiff's burden of persuasion in one way but not the other?

3. Presumptions in Civil Cases

Presumption is a term that courts and commentators use to describe rules that regulate the process of proof by creating a special *legal* relationship between one fact, A, a proven basic fact that gives rise to the presumption, and another fact, B, the presumed fact. For example, many jurisdictions have a rule that on proof of the fact that a person has been missing for seven years (fact A), there is a presumption that the person is dead (fact B). Typically, this rule or presumption means that proof of fact A (e.g., that a person has not been heard from in seven years) *requires* a finding of fact B (e.g., that the person is dead) unless the party against whom the presumption operates adequately rebuts fact B.

There almost always will be some *inferential* relationship between a presumed fact and the fact that gives rise to the presumption, the basic fact. For example, under the presumption-of-death, proof of fact A (not heard from in seven years) provides some inferential support for fact B (death). Indeed, in some cases a reasonable fact-finder may be warranted in finding fact B on proof only of fact A even if there were no presumption. The significance of saying that proof of fact A gives rise to a presumption of fact B is that the presumption connotes some special *legal* relationship

Chapter Ten. The Process of Proof in Civil and Criminal Cases

between the two facts. There is, however, no unique evidentiary device or concept referred to by the term *"presumption."* Rather, *presumption* is a label that courts, legislatures, and commentators attach to a variety of devices that manipulate the process of proof. It would be possible to describe those manipulations specifically and directly and to eliminate the term *presumption* from legal discourse. Morejon v. Rais Constr. Co., 851 N.E.2d 1143 (N.Y. 2006) ("The dizzying array of formulations (from mandatory inferences to permissive presumptions), however, suggests that things would be far less complicated if we viewed [the issue] without undue emphasis on labels and pigeonholes."). Indeed, as the materials throughout this section imply, such a reform would be desirable.

Presumptions come in different shapes and forms. Some are irrebuttable or conclusive, and some are rebuttable. Some rebuttable presumptions affect only the burden of production, and some affect the burden of persuasion. Some rebuttable presumptions are mandatory, in the sense that they require a finding of the presumed fact in the absence of sufficient rebuttal. Other rebuttable presumptions are permissive inferences. They permit but do not require a finding of the presumed fact even if there is no rebuttal. The use of the term *"presumption"* is therefore often ambiguous, and when it is not clear from the context which type is being referred to this ambiguity creates confusion.

As we will explain, presumptions fall into four main types or categories: (1) conclusive presumptions, (2) production-burden presumptions, (3) persuasion-burden presumptions, and (4) permissive presumptions. After discussing examples of these four types of presumptions, we will explore some further complexities in presumption analysis. We will then consider and critique the approach to presumptions in the Federal Rules of Evidence.

As we begin the consideration of presumptions, you should keep in mind two issues that affect the operation of presumptions.

First, who has what burden of persuasion with respect to the basic facts? In other words, in order for the aforementioned presumption of death (fact B) to come into play, who has what burden of persuasion with respect to proof that the individual has not been heard from in seven years (fact A)? The *"Who?"* part of this question is not controversial: The person who wishes to take advantage of the presumption has the burden of establishing the basic facts that give rise to the presumption. The answer to the *"What?"* part of the question is likely to be a preponderance of the evidence, which is the common, although seldom articulated, standard of proof for basic facts. There may be instances, however, in which a court sets forth a higher standard. Cf. Schechter v. Klanfer at page 813, supra (to get advantage of reduced burden of proof plaintiff must prove amnesia by clear and convincing evidence).

Second, who decides whether the party wishing to take advantage of a presumption has satisfied the appropriate burden of persuasion with respect to the basic facts? Assume, for example, that a woman wishes to take advantage of the presumption of death (fact B) with respect to her husband. If there is conflicting evidence about whether he has been heard from within seven years (fact A), does the judge decide or does the jury decide that question? We will elaborate on this issue in the context of our discussion of the different types of presumptions.

a. Irrebuttable or Conclusive Presumptions

Some presumptions are conclusive or irrebuttable. In other words, once there is proof of fact A, the fact giving rise to the presumption, fact B, the presumed fact, is conclusively established. The party against whom the presumption operates is not even allowed to present evidence of non-B. The Federal Coal Mine Health and Safety Act of 1969, which entitles totally disabled coal miners to compensation, creates such an irrebuttable or conclusive presumption. Upon proof by X-ray or other clinical evidence that a miner has complicated pneumoconiosis (fact A), the law conclusively presumes that the miner is totally disabled (fact B) and, therefore, entitled to compensation. 30 U.S.C. §921(c) (1994). In other words, when the miner establishes fact A, the miner becomes entitled to compensation; the mine owner is not permitted to try to prove that the miner may not in fact be totally disabled (fact B).

A conclusive presumption is nothing more than a somewhat awkwardly worded substantive rule of law: If the law states that a plaintiff must prove fact B to prevail and if, on proof of fact A, fact B is conclusively presumed to exist, the rule of law really is that the plaintiff will prevail by proving *either* fact A *or* fact B. Usery v. Turner Elkhorn Mining Co., 428 U.S. 1 (1976); Wiehe v. Kissick Constr. Co., 232 P.3d 866 (Kan. App. 2010) (irrebuttable presumption of impairment under workers' compensation statute if employee tests above a specified level for alcohol or drugs).

As long as the classification created by a conclusive presumption is not so arbitrary or irrational that it raises due process or equal protection concerns, there is no valid basis for objecting to it. For example, if, as the Court held in *Usery*, Congress could have enacted a statute specifically providing that the two categories of miners were entitled to compensation, there should be no reason to object to the statute merely because Congress utilized presumption jargon to accomplish this objective. On the other hand, if a court were to conclude that a legislative classification is so arbitrary or irrational that it is unconstitutional, the classification should be unconstitutional regardless of whether the legislature used presumption language to create the categories. In re Adoption of Doe, 2008 WL 5070056 (Fla. Cir. Ct. Aug. 29, 2008) (irrebuttable presumption that "it is never in the best interest of any adoptee to be adopted by a homosexual" held unconstitutional). In short, what should matter is not the manner in which the legislature chooses to formulate its categories, but rather whether the categories themselves present constitutional issues.

Because a conclusive presumption is nothing more than a substantive rule of law, the question whether the facts giving rise to a conclusive presumption exist is, as it should be, one for the jury to decide. To put the matter somewhat differently, a conclusive presumption is nothing more than a somewhat awkward way of stating that identical legal ramifications follow from two classifications (fact B, which may be proved without regard to the presumption, and fact A, which by virtue of the conclusive presumption is legally indistinguishable from fact B). If the jury is the decision maker with respect to fact B, the jury should also be the decision maker with respect to fact A.

KEY POINTS

1. A conclusive presumption is a somewhat awkward way of drafting a substantive rule of law.
2. As long as it is constitutionally permissible to attribute the same legal consequences to the presumed fact and the fact giving rise to the conclusive presumption, there should be no reason for objecting to a conclusive presumption.

PROBLEMS

10.1. Casanova, a life beneficiary, and Linus and Lucy, two remaindermen of a testamentary trust, seek to accelerate and thereby terminate the trust. They argue that the class of remaindermen who are the issue of Casanova has been effectively closed by reason of a vasectomy performed on Casanova, which rendered him sterile. The Trustee defends on the ground that there is in this jurisdiction an irrebuttable presumption that a man or woman irrespective of his or her age or physical capacity is conclusively presumed to be capable of producing children. Moreover, the Trustee argues the vasectomy may be reversible. The Trustee moves for a directed verdict. Should it be granted?

10.2. Husband is being sued by Wife for support for a child born to Wife during the marriage to Husband. The marriage has since ended in divorce, and Husband defends on the ground that he and his wife had not had sexual relations for two years before the birth of the child. Wife asks the trial judge to instruct the jury on the irrebuttable presumption that a child born during wedlock is presumed to belong to the husband. Should such an instruction be given, assuming that the law is as Wife asserts? Would it make any difference if Husband could prove beyond any doubt, based on blood test for example, that he is not the father of the child?

b. *Mandatory Rebuttable Presumptions*

Mandatory rebuttable presumptions create special burden of proof rules for designated situations. The particular rationale for a special burden of proof rule—like the rationales for general allocations of production and persuasion burdens—is often elusive. Nonetheless, it is fair to say that in general the purpose for creating special burden of proof rules is to fine-tune the process of proof in order to advance the goal of rational and accurate factfinding or other goals related to the allocation of burdens of proof. See Notes 4 and 7 at pages 816-817. Because of the complexity and confusion in the analysis of presumptions, however, the use of presumptions often detracts from rather than advances these goals.

Mandatory Rebuttable Presumptions That Shift a Burden of Production. Some presumptions create a mandatory relationship between fact A, the basic fact, and fact B, the presumed fact, that affects only the burden of producing evidence.

Once a party establishes fact A, there *must* be finding of fact B unless the party against whom the presumption operates produces evidence of non-B. In other words, if the party against whom the presumption operates fails to produce evidence of the presumed fact, the party will lose on that fact. If the party meets the production burden, the presumption has no further impact on the case. Courts and commentators, following the lead of Professor James Bradley Thayer, commonly refer to this type of presumption as a "bursting bubble" presumption. Once the party against whom the presumption operates produces sufficient evidence, the presumption—the bubble—disappears or bursts. See James B. Thayer, A Preliminary Treatise on Evidence at Common Law 336-337 (1898).

Consider a case in which, in the absence of any presumption, the plaintiff would have to establish that the defendant received a letter in order to prevail. Assume that there is a mandatory production burden presumption that on proof of mailing (fact A) receipt of the letter (fact B) is presumed. In re Yoder Co., 758 F.2d 1114 (6th Cir. 1985); City & County of Denver v. East Jefferson County Sanitation District, 771 P.2d 16 (Colo. App. 1988); Winkfield v. American Continental Insurance Co., 110 Ill. App. 2d 156, 249 N.E.2d 174 (1969) (all dealing with the presumption of receipt on proof of mailing). In order to take advantage of the presumption, the person in whose favor the presumption operates must establish that the basic facts exist. Thus, in our example, to take advantage of the presumption the plaintiff must establish that the letter was mailed. If the plaintiff fails to do so and if there is no other evidence of receipt, the plaintiff will lose. If the plaintiff establishes that the letter was mailed (fact A) and if the defendant produces no evidence of nonreceipt (non-B), the court will direct a verdict in favor of the plaintiff on the receipt issue regardless of the strength or weakness of inference of receipt in the particular case; the presumption mandates that result. On the other hand, if the defendant presents counterproof that meets the production burden, the presumption disappears and the case will proceed without inferential mandates. Typically, this means that the judge will send the case to the jury with the instruction that the plaintiff, in order to prevail, must convince the jury by a preponderance of the evidence that the defendant received the letter (fact B). In any particular instance, however, whether the judge should send the matter to the jury or issue a judgment as a matter of law for one of the parties should depend on which Case in Diagram 10-1 at page 806, supra, accurately represents the totality of the evidence. In re Estate of Wood, 374 Mich. 278, 132 N.W.2d 35 (1965).

As the preceding discussion demonstrates, a mandatory production burden presumption is in effect a specialized judgment-as-a-matter-of-law rule. As such, it has two consequences. First, establishing the basic facts will require the court to render a judgment as a matter of law on the presumed fact against an opposing party who fails to meet the production burden mandated by the presumption. Second, establishing the basic facts protects the party in whose favor the presumption operates from a judgment as a matter of law, at least until the opposing party produces counterproof. Since proof of fact A requires a finding of fact B in the absence of rebuttal, it would be improper, before rebuttal, to issue a judgment against the person invoking the mandatory presumption regardless of how weak the inference from fact A to fact B may be.

NOTES AND QUESTIONS

1. Courts rarely focus in detail on how much evidence a party must produce to burst the bubble of a mandatory production burden presumption. Courts use phrases like "some evidence" or "any evidence" or "credible evidence" to describe what the presumption demands, but whether a party's evidence meets the articulated standard is seldom an issue. As a general matter, evidence necessary to rebut a production burden presumption should be no different from the evidence required to satisfy other production burdens. The question should be whether the party who has the production burden has produced enough evidence to create a jury issue on the nonexistence of the presumed fact. See Diagram 10-1 and accompanying discussion at pages 806-808, supra.

2. Even if there are instances in which special production burden rules seem appropriate, it is important to note that there is no need to resort to the rhetoric of presumption to accomplish the desired end. One can simply and directly allocate the production burden.

KEY POINTS

1. A mandatory production burden presumption is the equivalent of a specialized judgment-as-a-matter-of-law rule.
2. Once a party establishes facts giving rise to a mandatory production burden presumption, the presumption requires a finding of the presumed fact in the absence of any rebuttal of that fact.
3. Establishing the facts that give rise to a mandatory production burden presumption also protects a party in whose favor the presumption works from an opponent's request for a judgment as a matter of law—at least before any rebuttal of the presumed fact.

Mandatory Rebuttable Presumptions That Shift the Burden of Persuasion. Some mandatory rebuttable presumptions shift the burden of persuasion to the party against whom they operate. Consider, for example, a case in which the plaintiff wishes to establish that the defendant, her former husband, is the father of her child. Normally, the plaintiff as the moving party would have both the burden of producing sufficient evidence of paternity and the burden of persuading the factfinder that the defendant was the father. Assume, though, that there is a mandatory rebuttable presumption in the jurisdiction that a child born or conceived during a valid marriage relationship is the child of the husband. Assume further that this presumption shifts the burden of persuasion to the person against whom it operates. Cal. Fam. Code §7611. To take advantage of the presumption the plaintiff will have to establish that she was legally married (fact A-1) to the defendant (fact A-2) at the time of the child's conception or birth (fact A-3). If the plaintiff can establish these basic facts, the factfinder must find that the defendant is the father (fact B) unless the defendant rebuts the presumption. One possible strategy for the defendant in this case is to attack one or more of the basic facts: A-1, A-2, or A-3. If the plaintiff cannot establish by the requisite degree of proof—probably a preponderance of the evidence—that they exist, there is no presumption in the case, and the plaintiff retains the burden of persuading the factfinder that the defendant is the father of the child. (Even if there were doubts about whether the child was born or conceived during the marriage relationship, the plaintiff may be able to establish with a DNA test or other evidence that the defendant is probably the father.) Another, not mutually exclusive, strategy for the defendant is to attack the presumed fact, paternity, directly. For example, the defendant might present witnesses to testify that he was out of the country during the possible time of conception and, therefore, could not be the father. If the plaintiff can establish facts A-1, A-2, and A-3, the reasonable inference of paternity that one can draw from these facts is sufficiently strong, without regard to the presumption, to permit the factfinder to find paternity. Regardless of the strength of this inference, however, the mandatory persuasion burden presumption means, at a minimum, that the defendant must persuade the jury by a preponderance of the evidence that he is not the father of the child.

A persuasion burden presumption has the same effect as an *affirmative defense*, the term used to describe the direct placement of a persuasion burden on a defendant. Fed. R. Civ. P. 8(c) (listing a number of affirmative defenses that must be proven by defendants). Consider, for example, the persuasion burden presumption of paternity that arises on proof of conception during a valid marriage. To say that there is a "presumption of paternity that allocates or shifts the burden of persuasion" to the defendant and that there is an "affirmative defense of nonpaternity" that requires the defendant to prove that fact is to make functionally identical statements. There is nothing in the concept of a presumption as such that facilitates the allocation of a burden of persuasion. Rather, presumptions that shift the burden of persuasion are simply affirmative defenses created for the same reasons of policy that generally inform the lawmaker's decision to allocate burdens of persuasion.

NOTES AND QUESTIONS

1. What is the justification for allocating the burden of persuasion to a (former) husband in a paternity action?

2. As we pointed out in our initial discussion of burdens of persuasion, shifting the preponderance burden from one party to another may not have an impact on very many cases.

KEY POINTS

1. A mandatory persuasion-burden presumption requires the party against whom the presumption operates to carry the burden of persuasion on the issue.
2. A mandatory persuasion-burden presumption is the functional equivalent of an affirmative defense.

Decisionmaking with Respect to the Facts Giving Rise to Mandatory Presumptions. Despite the functional equivalence of mandatory rebuttable presumptions and direct allocations of burdens of proof, courts tend to implement the two sets of rules differently. If there is a question about who has the "normal" burden of proof with respect to an issue, there is general agreement that the question is one for the court or legislature to determine. This question is categorized as a "question of law." By contrast, when the burden of proof rule depends on proof of some particular fact, which is of course always the situation with presumptions, the question whether that basic fact exists typically is one for the jury.

Revisit our "mailing and receipt" example. If the defendant produces sufficient evidence of nonreceipt to satisfy the production burden created by the presumption, there is no need to deal further with the presumption; the bubble has burst. Indeed, it is not necessary even to consider whether the presumption arose in the first place. When the defendant offers no evidence of nonreceipt, however, it is necessary to determine whether the plaintiff should have the benefit of the presumption. In any such case, the jury typically decides whether the plaintiff has established the basic fact of mailing (fact A), which gives rise to the presumption of receipt (fact B). Subsequently, absent evidence of receipt other than the plaintiff's proof of mailing, the court would instruct the jury that it must find for the plaintiff if it finds that the plaintiff mailed the letter.

KEY POINT

Typically, the jury decides whether the facts giving rise to a mandatory rebuttable presumption exist.

PROBLEMS

10.3. Plaintiff sues Defendant and one element of Plaintiff's claim is fact B. In the absence of any presumption, Plaintiff would have to prove fact B by a preponderance of the evidence. There is a presumption in the jurisdiction that if fact A is proven, fact B is presumed to exist. It is a mandatory *production* burden presumption.

Assume that Plaintiff introduces no direct evidence of fact B, but that Plaintiff introduces sufficient evidence of fact A to create a jury issue over whether fact A exists. Assume further that the inference from fact A to fact B is sufficiently strong that if fact A exists, a reasonable juror could find that fact B exists, too. Finally, assume that there is nothing in the evidence or common experience that would permit a finding of fact B in the absence of fact A.

(a) At the close of Plaintiff's case, both parties move for judgment as a matter of law. What result?

(b) Assume that there is no motion for judgment as a matter of law at the close of Plaintiff's case and that Defendant rests without presenting any evidence.

Now both parties move for judgment as a matter of law. Should either party's motion be granted? If not, what should the judge tell the jury about how to decide the case? In answering this question assume alternatively (1) that Plaintiff's evidence of fact A is so overwhelming that no reasonable person could disbelieve it and (2) that reasonable people could disagree about the existence of fact A.

(c) Assume that Defendant introduces evidence of only non-A before resting and that reasonable people viewing all of the evidence could disagree about the truth of both fact A and fact B. What should the judge tell the jury about how to decide the case?

(d) Assume that Defendant introduces evidence of only non-B before resting and that reasonable people could disagree about the truth of both fact A and fact B. What should the judge tell the jury about how to decide the case?

(e) Assume that Defendant introduces evidence of both non-A and non-B before resting and that reasonable people could disagree about the truth of both fact A and fact B. What should the judge tell the jury about how to decide the case?

10.4. Assume the same facts and alternative possibilities as in Problem 10.3 except now the mandatory rebuttable presumption is one that places the burden of *persuasion* on the party against whom it operates.

c. Permissive or "Weak" Presumptions

Sometimes the law creates a special relationship between two facts—fact A, the basic fact, and fact B, the presumed fact—but makes that relationship discretionary for the jury to find out, rather than mandatory. In other words, upon proof of fact A the factfinder may, but is not required to, find fact B even when the opponent makes no effort to rebut fact B. Courts and commentators refer to these permissive relationships variously as "permissive presumptions," "weak presumptions," or "permissive inferences."

The most common permissive presumption is res ipsa loquitur. Although the content and effect of res ipsa loquitur vary somewhat among the jurisdictions, a fair statement of the doctrine is this: If the plaintiff proves that she was injured in an event that normally does not occur without negligence (fact A-1), that the defendant was in exclusive control of the instrumentality that caused the plaintiff's injury (fact A-2), and that the plaintiff was not contributorily negligent (fact A-3), the factfinder may (but is not required to) find that the defendant negligently caused the plaintiff's injury (fact B). Although facts A-1, A-2, and A-3 standing alone create a fairly strong inference of fact B without regard to the res ipsa doctrine, the significance of res ipsa is twofold. First, the judge will tell the jury that they may, but are not obligated to, deduce the defendant's negligence from facts A-1, A-2, and A-3 if they find that the plaintiff proved these facts by a preponderance of the evidence. The res ipsa presumption thus creates a standardized judicial comment on the plaintiff's circumstantial evidence of negligence. Second, and perhaps more important, the res ipsa presumption helps the plaintiff's suit survive the defendant's motion to dismiss it summarily. When the plaintiff makes a prima facie showing that facts A-1, A-2, and A-3 are present, the judge must move the case to the jury. See Ariel Porat & Alex Stein, Tort Liability Under Uncertainty 84-100 (2001).

KEY POINTS

1. Permissive presumptions—sometimes referred to as "weak" presumptions or permissive inferences—are the equivalent of standardized comments on the evidence.
2. Permissive presumptions also help the plaintiff make a prima facie case against the defendant, thus obligating the judge to move the case to the jury rather than dismiss it summarily.

NOTES AND QUESTIONS

1. The Supreme Court has recognized that legislatures have wide latitude in allocating civil burdens of proof as they like. Lavine v. Milne, 424 U.S. 577, 585 (1976). Thus, one would think that the use of a presumption to allocate a burden of production or burden of persuasion should present no special difficulty. Nonetheless, in dealing with rebuttable presumptions, the Supreme Court has stressed the need for a rational relationship between the basic fact that gives rise to a presumption and the presumed fact. Consider, for example, Usery v. Turner Elkhorn Mining Co., 428 U.S. 1 (1976), where the Court upheld several production burden presumptions set forth in the Federal Coal Mine Health and Safety Act of 1969. One of the presumptions provided that upon proof that a coal miner with ten years of employment in the mines had pneumoconiosis, it was presumed that the miner contracted the disease from employment. According to the Court:

> We have consistently tested presumptions arising in civil statutes such as this, involving matters of economic regulation, against the standard articulated in Mobile, J. & K.C.R. Co. v. Turnipseed, 219 U.S. 35, 43 (1910):
>
> > That a legislative presumption of one fact from evidence of another may not constitute a denial of due process of law or a denial of the equal protection of the law it is only essential that there shall be some rational connection between the fact proved and the ultimate fact presumed, and that the inference of one fact from proof of another shall not be so unreasonable as to be a purely arbitrary mandate.
>
> Moreover, as we have recognized:
>
> > The process of making the determination of rationality is, by its nature, highly empirical, and in matters not within specialized judicial competence or completely commonplace, significant weight should be accorded the capacity of Congress to amass the stuff of actual experience and cull conclusions from it. United States v. Gainey, 380 U.S. 63, 67 (1965).
>
> Judged by these standards the . . . [presumption is] constitutionality valid . . . . [I]t is agreed here that pneumoconiosis is caused by breathing coal dust, and that the likelihood of a miner's developing the disease rests upon both the concentration of dust to

which he was exposed and the duration of his exposure. Against this scientific background, it was not beyond Congress' authority to refer to exposure factors in establishing a presumption that throws the burden of going forward on the operators. And in view of the medical evidence before Congress indicating the noticeable incidence of pneumoconiosis in cases of miners with ten years' employment in the mines, we cannot say that it was "purely arbitrary" for Congress to select the ten-year figure as a point of reference for these presumptions. No greater mathematical precision is required. [428 U.S. at 28-29.]

Perhaps an allocation of a burden of proof—whether by way of presumption or otherwise—could be so arbitrary or unreasonable as to raise a constitutional issue. See, for example, Western & A.R. Co. v. Henderson, 279 U.S. 639, 642-644 (1929) (holding Georgia Civil Code provision "A railroad company shall be liable for any damages done to persons, stock, or other property by the running of the locomotives, or cars, or other machinery of such company, or for damage done by any person in the employment and service of such company, unless the company shall make it appear that their agents have exercised all ordinary and reasonable care and diligence, the presumption in all cases being against the company" unreasonable and arbitrary contrary to the Due Process Clause of the Fourteenth Amendment).

If the implications of *Lavine* are correct, however, Congress seemingly could enact—without regard to any medical evidence—a compensation scheme for coal miners that did not mention presumptions that placed on coal mine operators the burden of coming forward with evidence that a miner's pneumoconiosis was not contracted during employment. If that is correct, why is the Court concerned, as it was in *Usery*, about the empirical relationship between the proven and presumed facts when Congress uses presumption language to allocate the burden of production?

2. Compare *Usery* with the following passage from *Lavine*, supra. In *Lavine*, the Court considered the constitutionality of a statute that "deemed" persons applying for welfare within 75 days after voluntarily terminating their employment or reducing their earning capacity to have done so "for the purpose of qualifying for such assistance or a larger amount thereof, in the absence of evidence to the contrary. . . . N.Y. Soc. Serv. Law §131(11)":

Although the District Court found this [provision] to be an unconstitutional "rebuttable presumption," the sole purpose of the provision is to indicate that, as with other eligibility requirements, the applicant rather than the State must establish that he did not leave employment for the purpose of qualifying for benefits. The provision carries with it no procedural consequence; it shifts to the applicant neither the burden of going forward nor the burden of proof, for he appears to carry the burden from the outset.

The offending sentence could be interpreted as a rather circumlocutory direction to welfare authorities to employ a standardized inference that if the Home Relief applicant supplies no information on the issue, he will be presumed to have quit his job to obtain welfare benefits. However, such an instruction would be superfluous for the obvious reason that the failure of an applicant to prove an essential element of eligibility will always result in a nonsuit. The only "rebuttable presumption"—if, indeed, it can be so called—at work here is the normal assumption that an applicant is not entitled to benefits unless and until he proves his eligibility.

Despite the rebuttable presumption aura that the second sentence of §131(11) radiates, it merely makes absolutely clear the fact that the applicant bears the burden of proof on this issue, as he does on all others. And since appellees do not object to the substantive requirement that Home Relief applicants must be free of the impermissible benefit-seeking motive, their underlying complaint may be that the burden of proof on this issue has been unfairly placed on welfare applicants rather than on the State [a complaint that the Court rejected]. 424 U.S. at 583-85.

Note that the Court said that there was no "procedural consequence," as though it is one thing to structure burdens of proof before any evidence is heard, and another to provide for burdens of proof to shift after evidence is heard. Can you make any sense out of that distinction?

3. In St. Mary's Honor Center v. Hicks, 509 U.S. 502 (1993), a racial discrimination case brought under Title VII of the Federal Civil Rights Act of 1964, the Supreme Court elaborated on the nature of a rebuttable presumption that it had created to help resolve discrimination claims. The *Hicks* Court began with a description of the prior law:

With the goal of "progressively . . . sharpening the inquiry into the elusive factual question of intentional discrimination," Texas Dept. of Community Affairs v. Burdine, 450 U.S. 248, 255 n.8 (1981), our opinion in McDonnell Douglas Corp. v. Green, 411 U.S. 792 (1973), established an allocation of the burden of production and an order for the presentation of proof in Title VII discriminatory-treatment cases. The plaintiff in such case, we said, must first establish, by a preponderance of the evidence, a "prima facie" case of racial discrimination . . . .

. . . "[E]stablishment of the prima facie case in effect creates a presumption that the employer unlawfully discriminated against the employee." To establish a "presumption" is to say that a finding of the predicate fact (here, the prima facie case) produces "a required conclusion in the absence of explanation" (here, the finding of unlawful discrimination). Thus, the *McDonnell Douglas* presumption places upon the defendant the burden of producing an explanation to rebut the prima facie case—i.e., the burden of "producing evidence" that the adverse employment actions were taken "for a legitimate, nondiscriminatory reason." 509 U.S. at 506-507.

There was no dispute in *Hicks* that the defendant had established a prima facie case by proving "(1) that he is black, (2) that he was qualified for the position of shift commander, (3) that he was demoted from that position and ultimately discharged, and (4) that the position remained open and was ultimately filled by a white man." Id. at 506. There was also no dispute that upon adequate rebuttal the plaintiff retained the burden of persuasion. The issue involved the adequacy of the defendant's rebuttal:

The District Court, acting as trier of fact in this bench trial, found that the reasons petitioners gave [severity and accumulation of rule violations] were not the real reasons for respondent's demotion and discharge. . . . It nonetheless held that respondent had failed to carry his ultimate burden of proving that his race was the determining factor in petitioners' decision first to demote and then to dismiss him. In short, the District Court concluded that "although [respondent] has proven the existence of a crusade to terminate him, he has not proven that the crusade was racially rather than personally motivated." The Court of Appeals set this determination aside on the ground that "once [respondent] proved all of [petitioners'] proffered reasons for the adverse employment actions to be pretextual, [respondent] was entitled to a judgment as a matter of law. Id. at 508.

A majority of the Supreme Court, in an opinion by Justice Scalia, agreed with the district court and reversed the judgment of the court of appeals. Justice Souter, in a dissent joined by Justices White, Blackmun, and Stevens, agreed with the court of appeals.

4. Neither opinion in *Hicks* is right or wrong as far as presumptions in the abstract are concerned. *Presumption*, after all, is only a term used to describe various rules that modify or fine-tune general burden of proof rules. Once the plaintiff establishes a prima facie case, it is analytically coherent, as the majority holds, to have a burden of proof rule that merely requires the defendant to come forward with some evidence of nondiscrimination and that has no other impact on the case. Similarly, it is analytically coherent to have a burden of proof rule that, on proof of a prima facie case, treats the defendant's rejected reasons as the equivalent of failing to produce evidence. This latter approach, as the *Hicks* dissent points out, has the effect of focusing the inquiry on the legitimacy of the defendant's reasons. The plaintiff's burden of persuasion, once the prima facie case is established, is to show the falsity of the defendant's proffered reasons. The ultimate question should be which burden of proof rule better serves the objectives of Title VII of the Civil Rights Act.

5. In defense of his position that offering disbelieved reasons was adequate to rebut the presumption in *Hicks* Justice Scalia wrote:

> We have no authority to impose liability upon an employer for alleged discriminatory employment practices unless an appropriate factfinder determines, according to proper procedures, that the employer has unlawfully discriminated. We may, according to traditional practice, establish certain modes and orders of proof, including an initial rebuttable presumption of the sort . . . [that we hold applies in this case]. But nothing in law would permit us to substitute for the required finding that the employer's action was the product of unlawful discrimination, the much different (and much lesser) finding that the employer's explanation of its action was not believable. Id. at 514-515.

If the Court can, as the *Hicks* majority conceded, hold the nonresponding employer liable regardless of how weakly the plaintiff's prima facie case may suggest discrimination, why should the Court not be able to require that the employer's explanation be believable? Indeed, is it not true, as the dissent maintained, that the majority's approach substantially undermines the purpose for placing a production burden on the employer in the first place?

6. In Reeves v. Sanderson Plumbing Prods, Inc., 530 U.S. 133 (2000), the Supreme Court again addressed the relationship between production burdens and the burden of persuasion in Title VII cases. The jury returned a verdict in favor of the plaintiff on his age discrimination claim after the plaintiff proved a prima facie case and offered sufficient evidence that explanations the defendant produced in response were "pretextual" (i.e., not the real reasons for its conduct toward the plaintiff). The defendant argued that this was insufficient evidence to get to a jury and that it was entitled to judgment as a matter of law. In other words, the defendant argued that the plaintiff— who bore the burden of persuasion—needed additional evidence to meet its burden of production. The Supreme Court disagreed. While noting that the plaintiff did have additional evidence, the Court explained that in Title VII cases proof of a prima facie case, along with disproving the defendant's proffered explanations, may be sufficient evidence from which a reasonable jury could find for the plaintiff.

d. The Federal Rules Approach to Presumptions

Congress attempted to deal with the problem of presumptions in FRE 301, which provides that the effect of a presumption is to place a burden of production on the party against whom the presumption operates:

> In a civil case, unless a federal statute or these rules provide otherwise, the party against whom a presumption is directed has the burden of producing evidence to rebut the presumption. But this rule does not shift the burden of persuasion, which remains on the party who had it originally.

The exception for what is otherwise provided in "these rules" is an apparent cross-reference to FRE 302:

> In a civil case, state law governs the effect of a presumption regarding a claim or defense for which state law supplies the rule of decision.

For similar deferrals to state law, see FRE 501 (privileges) and FRE 601 (competency). These deferrals originate from the *Erie* doctrine, which holds that in diversity cases procedures will be governed by federal law, but issues that are substantive (privileges and competency) or outcome-determinative (presumptions and burdens of proof) will be decided by applicable state law. Erie Railroad Co. v. Tompkins, 304 U.S. 64 (1938).

Despite the seemingly straightforward language of FRE 301, the rule is fraught with difficulties. We touch briefly on two of them here. For a more comprehensive analysis of FRE 301's deficiencies, see Ronald J. Allen, Presumptions, Inferences and Burdens of Proof in Federal Civil Actions—An Anatomy of Unnecessary Ambiguity and a Proposal for Reform, 76 Nw. U. L. Rev. 892 (1982).

The "Federal Statute" Exception. What are the criteria for determining whether a federal statute "provide[s] otherwise"? Nothing in the rule or its legislative history specifically addresses this question. As a result, it is not clear whether, for example, this category includes presumptions that do not directly shift the burden of persuasion but that have been interpreted as doing so. Similarly, it is not clear whether the language extends to all of the variations of language that Congress has chosen to employ in formulating evidentiary burdens created by statute. Poncy v. Johnson & Johnson, 460 F. Supp. 795, 803 (D.N.J. 1978) (FRE 301 applies to federal statute containing provision for a prima facie case).

If FRE 301 does not apply to a wide variety of statutes and is limited only to those that clearly allocate burdens of production, then it is superfluous. If, by contrast, it has a wider application, then Congress has significantly changed federal law in the form of a simple rule of evidence. Courts that have wanted a presumption to have a greater effect than merely shifting a production burden have not found FRE 301 to be a constraint. Hood v. Knappton Corp., 986 F.2d 329 (9th Cir. 1993); American Coal Co. Benefits Review Board, 738 F.2d 387 (10th Cir. 1984).

The Relationship Between FRE 301 Presumptions and Other Means of Allocating Burdens of Proof.   FRE 301 does not address presumptions and their relationships to a judge's authority to allocate burdens of production and persuasion, to instruct the jury on inferences, or to comment on the evidence. Yet, as we have seen, the word *presumption* is merely a label applied to various manipulations of these other judicial prerogatives. Any attempt to define the scope of presumptions without dealing with these related areas was thus doomed to fail. The dominant judicial response to FRE 301 with regard to these issues has been to ignore it. The Supreme Court has noted the impotency of FRE 301 in this context. In National Labor Relations Board v. Transportation Management Corp., 462 U.S. 393 (1983), the Court reviewed a change in NLRB rules that required employers to bear the burden of persuasion on the issue whether discharge of an employee was for a permissible reason. The employer argued that this shift in the burden of persuasion was in contravention of FRE 301. The Court concluded to the contrary, but in such a way that demonstrates the insignificance of FRE 301: "The Rule merely defines the term 'presumption.' It in no way restricts the authority of a court or an agency to change the customary burdens of persuasion in a manner that otherwise would be permissible." Id. at 403 n.7.

KEY POINTS

1. FRE 301 purports to make federal presumptions production-burden presumptions unless Congress has otherwise provided.
2. Because of the uncertain scope of the "provide otherwise" clause, and because FRE 301 fails to address devices other than statutory presumptions that allocate burdens of proof, FRE 301 provides little guidance for or constraint on judicial decision-making.

B. THE PROCESS OF PROOF IN CRIMINAL CASES

The process of proof in criminal cases is similar but not identical to the process of proof in civil cases. As in civil cases, the law determines what facts need to be proven in order to establish that a crime has occurred. The criminal law also possesses virtually the same rules for the allocation of burdens of proof as in civil cases. The "plaintiff," which is the state, must plead and prove the elements of the crime, and in many jurisdictions there are affirmative defenses with respect to which defendants bear the burden of production or persuasion. The primary differences between the civil and criminal arenas are that the burden of persuasion in criminal cases is proof beyond reasonable doubt and that as a result of In re Winship, 397 U.S. 358 (1970), the prosecution always carries that burden with respect to the necessary elements of the offense.

In this section, as with the process of proof in civil cases, we first discuss the burdens of proof and then discuss comments on the evidence and presumptions.

1. The Burdens of Proof in Criminal Cases

a. *The Burden of Persuasion: In re Winship's Mandate of Proof Beyond a Reasonable Doubt*

Because the proof beyond a reasonable doubt rule has been so uniformly accepted as the standard of proof for criminal cases, the Supreme Court did not have occasion specifically to address the question whether due process required that standard of proof until 1975 in *In re Winship*. Even then, the immediate issue for the Court was not whether a criminal defendant was entitled to have guilt proven beyond a reasonable doubt. Rather, *Winship* was a challenge to the New York rule utilizing the preponderance standard in juvenile delinquency cases. The Court affirmed its prior dictum that due process required the proof beyond a reasonable doubt standard in adult criminal prosecutions and went on to hold that due process required the same standard in delinquency adjudications based on conduct that would be criminal if committed by an adult. According to the Court:

> The requirement that guilt of a criminal charge be established beyond a reasonable doubt dates at least from our early years as a Nation. The "demand for a higher degree of persuasion in criminal cases was recurrently expressed from ancient times, [though] its crystallization into the formula 'beyond a reasonable doubt' seems to have occurred as late as 1789. It is now accepted in common law jurisdictions as the measure of persuasion by which the prosecution must convince the trier of all the essential elements of guilt." Although virtually unanimous adherence to the reasonable-doubt standard in common-law jurisdictions may not conclusively establish it as a requirement of due process, such adherence does "reflect a profound judgment about the way in which law should be enforced and justice administered." . . .
>
> The reasonable-doubt standard plays a vital role in the American scheme of criminal procedure. It is a prime instrument for reducing the risk of convictions resting on factual error. The standard provides concrete substance for the presumption of innocence—that bedrock "axiomatic and elementary" principle whose "enforcement lies at the foundation of the administration of our criminal law." . . .
>
> The requirement of proof beyond a reasonable doubt has this vital role in our criminal procedure for cogent reasons. The accused during a criminal prosecution has at stake interests of immense importance, both because of the possibility that he may lose his liberty upon conviction and because of the certainty that he would be stigmatized by the conviction. Accordingly, a society that values the good name and freedom of every individual should not condemn a man for commission of a crime when there is reasonable doubt about his guilt. As we said in Speiser v. Randall [357 U.S. 513, 525-26 (1958)]: "There is always in litigation a margin of error, representing error in factfinding, which both parties must take into account. Where one party has at stake an interest of transcending value—as a criminal defendant his liberty—this margin of error is reduced as to him by the process of placing on the other party the burden of . . . persuading the factfinder at the conclusion of the trial of his guilt beyond a reasonable doubt. Due process commands that no man shall lose his liberty unless the Government has borne the burden of . . . convincing the factfinder of his guilt." To this end, the reasonable-doubt standard is indispensable, for it "impresses on the trier of fact the necessity of reaching a subjective state of certitude of the facts in issue." Dorsen & Reznick, In re Gault and the Future of Juvenile Law, 1 Family Law Quarterly, No. 4,

pp. 1, 26 (1976).

Moreover, use of the reasonable-doubt standard is indispensable to command the respect and confidence of the community in applications of the criminal law. It is critical that the moral force of the criminal law not be diluted by a standard of proof that leaves people in doubt whether innocent men are being condemned. It is also important in our free society that every individual going about his ordinary affairs have confidence that his government cannot adjudge him guilty of a criminal offense without convincing a proper factfinder of his guilt with utmost certainty.

Lest there remain any doubt about the constitutional stature of the reasonable-doubt standard, we explicitly hold that the Due Process Clause protects the accused against conviction except upon *proof beyond a reasonable doubt of every fact necessary to constitute the crime with which he is charged.* [397 U.S. at 362-364 (emphasis added)].

NOTES AND QUESTIONS

1. Despite the wide acceptance and the familiarity of the reasonable doubt standard, its precise meaning remains elusive. Although the due process clause requires courts to apply the beyond a reasonable doubt standard, "the Constitution neither prohibits trial courts from defining reasonable doubt nor requires them to do so as a matter of course." Victor v. Nebraska, 511 U.S. 1, 8 (1994). Consider the following three attempts to define proof beyond a reasonable doubt:

(a) A reasonable doubt is one that is founded upon a real tangible substantial basis and not upon mere caprice and conjecture. It must be such doubt as would give rise to a grave uncertainty, raised in your mind by reasons of the unsatisfactory character of the evidence or lack thereof. A reasonable doubt is not a mere possible doubt. It is an actual substantial doubt. It is a doubt that a reasonable man can seriously entertain. What is required is not an absolute or mathematical certainty, but a moral certainty.

(b) A defendant in a criminal action is presumed to be innocent until the contrary is proved, and in case of a reasonable doubt whether his guilt is satisfactorily shown, he is entitled to a verdict of not guilty. This presumption places upon the State the burden of proving him guilty beyond a reasonable doubt.

Reasonable doubt is defined as follows: It is not a mere possible doubt; because everything relating to human affairs, and depending on moral evidence, is open to some possible or imaginary doubt. It is that state of the case which, after the entire comparison and consideration of all the evidence, leaves the minds of the jurors in that condition that they cannot say they feel an abiding conviction, to a moral certainty, of the truth of the charge.

(c) The burden is always on the state to prove beyond a reasonable doubt all of the material elements of the crime charged, and this burden never shifts.

"Reasonable doubt" is such a doubt as would cause a reasonable and prudent person, in one of the graver and more important transactions of life, to pause and hesitate before taking the represented facts as true and relying and acting thereon.

It is such a doubt as will not permit you, after full, fair, and impartial consideration of all the evidence, to have an abiding conviction, to a moral certainty, of the guilt of the accused. At the same time, absolute or mathematical certainty is not required. You may be convinced of the truth of a fact beyond a reasonable doubt and yet be fully aware that possibly you may be mistaken. You may find an accused guilty upon the strong probabilities of the case, provided such probabilities are strong enough to exclude any doubt of his guilt that is reasonable. A reasonable doubt is an actual and substantial doubt arising from the evidence, from the facts or circumstances shown by the evidence, or from the lack of evidence on the part of the state, as distinguished from a doubt arising from mere possibility, from bare imagination or from fanciful conjecture.

In Cage v. Louisiana, 498 U.S. 39 (1990) (per curiam), the Supreme Court held that instruction (a) above violated the defendant's right to due process. The Court concluded that "a reasonable juror could have interpreted the instruction to allow a finding of guilt based on a degree of proof below that required by the Due Process Clause." Id. at 41. Instructions (b) and (c) were before the Court in Victor v. Nebraska, supra. The *Victor* Court distinguished *Cage* and held that the instructions were constitutional. What precisely is there in instructions (b) and (c) that suggests the requirement of a higher degree of proof than the first instruction? Are any of the instructions likely to be helpful to the jury? Or is that question impossible to answer until we have clearer guidance as to what the legal meaning of "beyond a reasonable doubt" in fact is?

2. Is the notion of reasonable doubt sufficiently difficult to define that we would be better off not trying to define it for jurors? No, according to Justice Ginsburg in her separate opinion in *Victor*:

> Because the trial judges in fact defined reasonable doubt in both jury charges we review, we need not decide whether the Constitution required them to do so. Whether or not the Constitution so requires, however, the argument for defining the concept is strong. While judges and lawyers are familiar with the reasonable doubt standard, the words "beyond a reasonable doubt" are not self-defining for jurors. Several studies of jury behavior have concluded that "jurors are often confused about the meaning of reasonable doubt," when that term is left undefined. Note, Defining Reasonable Doubt, 90 Colum. L. Rev. 1716, 1723 (1990) (citing studies). Thus, even if definitions of reasonable doubt are necessarily imperfect, the alternative—refusing to define the concept at all—is not obviously preferable. Cf. Newman, Beyond "Reasonable Doubt," 68 N.Y.U. L. Rev. 979, 984 (1993) ("I find it rather unsettling that we are using a formulation that we believe will become less clear the more we explain it.") [511 U.S. at 43].

Justice Ginsburg then endorsed the following reasonable doubt instruction:

> The government has the burden of proving the defendant guilty beyond a reasonable doubt. Some of you may have served as jurors in civil cases, where you were told that it is only necessary to prove that a fact is more likely true than not true. In criminal cases, the government's proof must be more powerful than that. It must be beyond a reasonable doubt.
>
> Proof beyond a reasonable doubt is proof that leaves you firmly convinced of the defendant's guilt. There are very few things in this world that we know with absolute

certainty, and in criminal cases the law does not require proof that overcomes every possible doubt. If, based on your consideration of the evidence, you are firmly convinced that the defendant is guilty of the crime charged, you must find him guilty. If on the other hand, you think there is a real possibility that he is not guilty, you must give him the benefit of the doubt and find him not guilty. [Id. at 44, quoting Federal Judicial Center, Pattern Criminal Jury Instructions 17-18 (1987) (instruction 21)]

3. Commentators have also lamented the lack of clarity surrounding "beyond a reasonable doubt." See Larry Laudan, Truth, Error, and Criminal Law: An Essay in Legal Epistemology 31 (2006) ("The most earnest jury, packed with twelve people desirous of doing the right thing and eager to see that justice is done, are left dangling with respect to how powerful a case is required before they are entitled to affirm that they believe the guilt of the defendant beyond a reasonable doubt. In such circumstances, simply muddling on is not an attractive prospect.").

4. The criminal proof standard is sometimes explained and justified based on the idea that it is designed to produce a certain ratio of false acquittals to false convictions. The common source cited for this idea is William Blackstone's adage that it is better for ten guilty men to go free than for one innocent man to be convicted, although several other sources and ratios may be found. See Alexander Volokh, Guilty Men, 146 U. Pa. L. Rev. 173 (1997). This idea may be more misleading than it is enlightening, however. A ratio of ten to one, for example, would be satisfied by a decision rule that in 100 cases produced (1) 90 false acquittals; (2) nine false convictions; and (3) one accurate verdict. We obviously care about accurate verdicts—acquittals and convictions—as much as we care about errors. For further discussion, see Ronald J. Allen & Larry Laudan, Deadly Dilemmas, 41 Tex. Tech. L. Rev. 65 (2008).

KEY POINT

In a criminal prosecution, due process requires proof beyond a reasonable doubt of every fact necessary to constitute the crime charged.

b. The Scope of Winship: Explicit Shifts in the Burden of Persuasion and Other Matters

The *Mullaney* Decision.   Mullaney v. Wilbur, 421 U.S. 684 (1975), involved a homicide defendant who claimed that he killed his victim in the heat of passion provoked by a homosexual assault. The issue was the applicability of Winship to a Maine homicide statute that defined murder as requiring "malice aforethought" on top of a simple intent to kill a person and placed the burden of persuasion on the defendant to prove that the killing was "in the heat of passion on sudden provocation" in order to reduce the crime from murder to manslaughter. The Supreme Court affirmed the granting of a writ of habeas corpus to the defendant:

After reading the statutory definitions of both offenses [murder and manslaughter], the court charged that "malice aforethought is an essential and indispensable element of the crime of murder," without which the homicide would be manslaughter. The jury was further instructed, however, that if the prosecution established that the homicide was both intentional and unlawful, malice aforethought was to be conclusively implied unless the defendant proved by a fair preponderance of the evidence that he acted in the heat of passion on sudden provocation. The court emphasized that "malice aforethought and heat of passion on sudden provocation are two inconsistent things"; thus, by proving the latter the defendant would negate the former and reduce the homicide from murder to manslaughter. . . .

. . . Felonious homicide is punished as murder—i.e., by life imprisonment—unless the defendant proves by a fair preponderance of the evidence that it was committed in the heat of passion on sudden provocation, in which case it is punished as manslaughter—i.e., by a fine not to exceed $10,000 or by imprisonment not to exceed 20 years. . . .

[T]he fact at issue here—the presence or absence of the heat of passion on sudden provocation—has been, almost from the inception of the common law of homicide, the single most important factor in determining the degree of culpability attaching to an unlawful homicide. And . . . the clear trend has been toward requiring the prosecution to bear the ultimate burden of proving this fact. . . .

Petitioners . . . note that as a formal matter the absence of the heat of passion on sudden provocation is not a "fact necessary to constitute the crime" of felonious homicide in Maine. This distinction is relevant, according to petitioners, because in *Winship* the facts at issue were essential to establish criminality in the first instance . . . . [H]ere . . . , petitioners maintain, the defendant's critical interests in liberty and reputation are no longer of paramount concern since, irrespective of the presence or absence of the heat of passion on sudden provocation, he is likely to lose his liberty and certain to be stigmatized. . . .

Maine has chosen to distinguish those who kill in the heat of passion from those who kill in the absence of this factor. Because the former are less "blameworth[y]," they are subject to substantially less severe penalties. By drawing this distinction, while refusing to require the prosecution to establish beyond a reasonable doubt the fact upon which it turns, Maine denigrates the interests found critical in *Winship*.

. . . [W]hen viewed in terms of the potential difference in restrictions of personal liberty attendant to each conviction, the distinction established by Maine between murder and manslaughter may be of greater importance than the difference between guilt or innocence for many lesser crimes.

Moreover, if *Winship* were limited to those facts that constitute a crime as defined by state law, a State could undermine many of the interests that decision sought to protect without effecting any substantive change in its law. It would only be necessary to redefine the elements that constitute different crimes, characterizing them as factors that bear solely on the extent of punishment. Id. at 696-98.

Mullaney, which was a unanimous decision, generated considerable litigation challenging state rules placing burdens of persuasion on the defendant. The Court revisited the issue two years later in Patterson v. New York, 432 U.S. 197 (1977). Although the *Patterson* Court purported to distinguish *Mullaney*, *Patterson* in fact overrules *Mullaney* in all but the most formalistic sense. As you will see, however, that formalistic sense retains considerable importance.

The *Patterson* Decision.   Patterson was convicted of murdering the partner of his estranged wife. The killing took place after the defendant had "observed his wife through a window in a state of semiundress" with the victim. The New York homicide statute defined the elements of murder as an "intent to cause the death of another person" and "causing the death of such person." The statute required no "malice aforethought" nor premeditation. New York also recognized as an affirmative defense acting "under the influence of extreme emotional disturbance for which there was a reasonable explanation or excuse." Extreme emotional distress reduced murder to manslaughter, and the burden of persuasion with respect to this affirmative defense rested with the defendant.

In rejecting Patterson's contention that placing the burden of proof with respect to extreme emotional distress on him was unconstitutional the Court observed that

1. "dealing with crime is much more the business of the States than it is of the Federal Government";
2. the New York "extreme emotional distress" defense is "a considerably expanded version of the common-law defense of heat of passion on sudden provocation";
3. subsequent to *Mullaney*, the Court in Rivera v. Delaware, 429 U.S. 877 (1976), reaffirmed its previous ruing in Leland v. Oregon, 343 U.S. 790 (1952), that placing the burden of proof with respect to insanity on the defendant did not violate due process; and
4. states may be reluctant to create or expand affirmative defenses if they have to disprove them beyond a reasonable doubt.

Mullaney, according to the Court, was not controlling for the following reasons:

> The crime of murder [in New York] is defined by statute . . . as causing the death of another person with intent to do so. The death, the intent to kill, and causation are the facts that the State is required to prove beyond a reasonable doubt if a person is to be convicted of murder. No further facts are either presumed or inferred in order to constitute the crime. The statute does provide an affirmative defense [of extreme emotional disturbance] . . . which, if proved by a preponderance of the evidence would reduce the crime to manslaughter, an offense defined in a separate section of the statute. It is plain enough that if the intentional killing is shown, the State intends to deal with the defendant as a murderer unless he demonstrates the mitigating circumstances. . . .

> In *Mullaney* . . . the Maine statute defined [murder] as the unlawful killing of a human being "with malice aforethought, either express or implied." The trial court instructed the jury that the words *malice aforethought* were most important because "malice aforethought is an essential and indispensable element of the crime of murder." . . . The instructions emphasized that "malice aforethought and 'heat of passion on sudden provocation are two inconsistent things.'" . . .

> The Maine Supreme Judicial Court held that murder and manslaughter were varying degrees of the crime of felonious homicide and that the presumption of malice arising from the unlawful killing was a mere policy presumption operating to cast on the defendant the burden of proving provocation if he was to be found guilty of manslaughter rather than murder. . . .

> This Court . . . unanimously agreed with the Court of Appeals [in *Mullaney*] that [the defendant's] due process rights had been invaded by the presumption casting upon him the burden of proving by a preponderance of the evidence that he had acted in the heat of passion upon sudden provocation.

Mullaney's holding, it is argued, is that the State may not permit the blameworthiness of an act or the severity of punishment authorized for its commission to depend on the presence or absence of an identified fact without assuming the burden of proving the presence or absence of that fact, as the case may be, beyond a reasonable doubt. In our view, the Mullaney holding should not be so broadly read. . . .

Mullaney surely held that a State must prove every ingredient of an offense beyond a reasonable doubt, and that it may not shift the burden of proof to the defendant by presuming that ingredient upon proof of the other elements of the offense. . . . Such shifting of the burden of persuasion with respect to a fact which the State deems so important that it must be either proved or presumed is impermissible under the Due Process Clause.

It was unnecessary to go further in *Mullaney*. . . . [A] killing became murder in Maine when it resulted from a deliberate, cruel act committed by one person against another, "suddenly without any, or without a considerable provocation." . . . [M]alice, in the sense of absence of provocation, was part of the definition of that crime. Yet malice, i.e., lack of provocation, was presumed and could be rebutted by the defendant only by proving by a preponderance of the evidence that he acted with heat of passion upon sudden provocation. . . .

As we have explained, nothing was presumed or implied against Patterson. 432 U.S. at 205-206, 212-216.

The Functional Equivalence of *Mullaney* and *Patterson*.   Except for the fact that New York's "extreme emotional distress" defense is somewhat broader than the Maine "heat of passion" defense, *Mullaney* and *Patterson* are functionally identical. In both cases to obtain a murder conviction the state had to prove an intentional killing beyond a reasonable doubt, and in both cases proof of provocation made a killing, that would otherwise be murder, manslaughter. The only difference between the two cases is in the language that the state legislatures used to achieve this gradation in homicide crimes. Maine defined the critical element of murder as "malice aforethought," a concept that encompassed the absence of provocation and cold-blooded killing. Maine then created a rule that proof of intent gave rise to a presumption or mandatory finding of malice unless the defendant proved provocation by a preponderance of the evidence. New York defined murder initially as requiring only proof that the defendant intentionally killed a person and then defined provocation as an affirmative defense for the defendant to prove by a preponderance of the evidence. This means that in New York, too, a person becomes guilty of murder only when he kills another human being with malice aforethought. Technically, however, "malice aforethought" was not written into the definition of murder as one of its elements, and this technical detail was the only factor that separated *Patterson* from *Mullaney*.

Evaluating *Mullaney* and *Patterson*: The Theory That the Greater Includes the Lesser.   Our preceding discussion does not necessarily lead to the conclusion that *Patterson* rather than *Mullaney* was the correct decision. Whenever a defendant fails to establish an affirmative defense, the possibility is presented that, had the prosecution been required to disprove the defense beyond a reasonable doubt, the trier of fact would have either convicted the defendant of a lesser offense or acquitted altogether.

Such verdicts would expose the defendant to a lesser punishment or no punishment at all. Thus, affirmative defenses undeniably affect the interests articulated in *Winship*. Yet one cannot jump from this fact alone to the conclusion that requiring the prosecutor to disprove affirmative defenses beyond a reasonable doubt serves the due process interest. Assuming that the punishment for the higher offense is constitutionally acceptable, *given that the prosecution must prove its elements beyond a reasonable doubt,* the allocation of the persuasion burden for the mitigating factor has no bearing on whether the defendant suffers unconstitutional punishment.

An example may help to clarify this point. Consider a state with an intentional homicide statute that punishes every intentional homicide with 30 years of imprisonment; if the state proves that the defendant intentionally killed the victim, then a flat sentence of 30 years is imposed regardless of the presence of any mitigating factor. *Assume* that such a statute is constitutional. Now consider how the constitutionality of that statute is affected if we simply add to it a provision that no more than 20 years of imprisonment may be imposed when defendants prove by a preponderance of the evidence that they acted under the influence of extreme emotional disturbance. If the constitutional interest in the reasonable doubt standard centers on liberty deprivation, the addition of a chance to mitigate a constitutionally valid punishment cannot invalidate the statute. To put it another way, if a state may constitutionally imprison all intentional killers for 30 years by proving beyond a reasonable doubt only intent and causation, then whatever liberty interest defendants constitutionally possess in the context of homicide prosecutions surely is fully accommodated by such a statute. The addition of a mitigating circumstance in the form of an affirmative defense that reduces punishment as a matter of concession to human frailty, as some describe it, cannot violate the already fully accommodated interest.

According to this theory—sometimes referred to as "the greater includes the lesser" theory — the analysis of the constitutionality of an affirmative defense must proceed to another level. One must ask whether the greater punishment—the punishment authorized in the event the defendant fails to establish the affirmative defense— is constitutional. In other words, one must ask how to give content to *Winship*'s command that the state "prove beyond a reasonable doubt every fact necessary to constitute the crime." To state the matter in terms of the issue in *Mullaney* and *Patterson*: Is it constitutionally permissible for Maine or New York to impose its penalty for intentional killings perpetrated in cold blood on individuals whose homicidal actions are the result of extreme provocation or extreme emotional distress? In the next subsection, we discuss several possible tests for resolving this issue.

Giving Content to *Winship*: Tests for Assessing the Validity of Affirmative Defenses.

(1) The Elements Test. Pursuant to the technical "elements" test adopted by *Patterson*, the state must prove beyond reasonable doubt whatever factual issues it labels as elements of the offense. A component of this test is the "physical location" rule, a rule of statutory construction providing that a particular factual issue is an element of an offense only if it is incorporated into the text of the basic statute formulating the offense.

At various points throughout the *Patterson* opinion, the Court alluded to that test, most explicitly in the statement that it "will not disturb the balance struck in previous cases holding that the Due Process Clause requires the prosecution to prove beyond reasonable doubt all of the elements included in the definition of the offense of which the defendant is charged." 432 U.S. at 210. Furthermore, the Court emphasized that the emotional upheaval defense raised by Mr. Patterson was extraneous to that definition: It did "not serve to negative any facts of the crime which the State is to prove in order to convict of murder." Id. at 207. Both examples given by the Court of unconstitutional burden shifts also tend to support this view. The Court noted that the legislature cannot declare an individual guilty or presumptively guilty, nor can it declare that the filing of an indictment or proof of the identity of the accused shall create a presumption of the existence of all the facts essential to guilt. These are situations in which no elements are included within the definition of "crime," which may suggest that any affirmative defense will be sustained so long as the legislature does not drain all substantive content from a crime's definition.

It is difficult to see what constitutional interest is served by the elements test. The physical location rule is obviously an arbitrary means of determining the "definition" of an offense. The legislature may wish to "define" an offense in one way but determine the elements of the prosecution's case in another, and either could be considered the "definition" of the crime. There is no reason why the validity of a state statute placing the burden of proving provocation on the defendant should depend on whether the state "defines" murder (1) as intent, causation, and no provocation in one statute and in another places the burden of proving provocation on the defendant, or simply (2) as intent and causation with another statute authorizing provocation as an affirmative defense.

(2) Federalism and the Political Compromise Test. A second standard that has been proposed for judging the validity of an affirmative defense, while somewhat more sophisticated than the elements test, is no more persuasive. This is the "political compromise" test, which permits affirmative defenses that result from the compromise of competing forces in state legislatures. This test responds to the fear that states may be unwilling to provide certain affirmative defenses if they cannot place on the defendant the burden of proof for the factual issue created. The *Patterson* decision mentioned this fear as well. Id. at 209-210. Commentators have often pointed out that a decision like *Mullaney*, if followed, would likely inhibit states' experimentation with new affirmative defenses and undermine their self-government in the field of criminal law. To avoid that harsh irony, the political compromise test looks to whether the legislature would have refused to adopt the defense but for the provision imposing the burden of proof on the defendant.

This test suffers from an inner paradox: If the only justification for legitimizing burden-shifting affirmative defenses is that otherwise the legislature would be forced to choose between two diametrically opposed but constitutional alternatives, then the argument implicitly assumes the unconstitutionality of those defenses. The real point, in other words, is that burden-shifting affirmative defenses are unconstitutional, but because this constitutional truth triggers bad legislative choices, it is socially preferable to vindicate those defenses as constitutional.

(3) **The Proportionality Test.** Within the last century, the Cruel and Unusual Punishment clause of the Eighth Amendment[3] has been interpreted to require a rough proportionality between the culpability of an offense and the punishment imposed on the offense's perpetrator. This requirement of proportionality provides the method of testing the constitutionality of affirmative defenses, and it also provides the means of delineating the extent of the federal interest in the reasonable doubt standard. Reconsider the intentional homicide hypothetical in subsection 1.b.5, supra. If the courts conclude that a given punishment (30 years in the hypothetical) is not disproportional to what the state has proved beyond reasonable doubt (intentional killing), notwithstanding the presence or absence of any mitigating factors, then a defendant's liberty interest would obviously be satisfied by a statute that required proof of only those elements and that imposed that particular punishment. Accordingly, the mere addition to that statute of an affirmative defense, which after all could constitutionally be ignored, should be equally satisfactory. The import of the proportionality principle is, then, that the state should be required to prove enough to justify the imposition of the maximum sentence permissible under the statute. Once that is accomplished, the accused has been fully protected against an unwarranted deprivation of liberty, and the state should be permitted to elaborate on the basic statute as it sees fit.

The thesis that due process requires proof beyond a reasonable doubt only with respect to those elements of the offense that are "essential" by virtue of the Eighth Amendment concretely expresses the role of the reasonable doubt standard. Due process and the Eighth Amendment protect criminal defendants from unwarranted deprivations of liberty by requiring the state to establish sufficient factual elements to justify the allotted punishment and by requiring the state, in establishing those elements, to minimize the risk of error adverse to the defendant. Once the overriding constitutional command is satisfied, however, the need for the protective procedure is likewise satisfied, and the traditional state power should reassert itself, permitting the states to allocate burdens of proof as they desire.

The theoretical appeal of the proportionality test, in our view, is compelling. The inherent vagueness of the notion of proportionality, however, may lead courts to impinge on legislative judgments about affirmative defenses. Alternatively, the vagueness may lead courts to defer to legislative judgments except in the most extreme cases. Indeed, the Supreme Court, particularly in recent years, has upheld against proportionality challenges quite severe penalties for relatively minor misconduct. Hutto v. Davis, 454 U.S. 370 (1982) (upholding 40-year prison term for possession and distribution of approximately nine ounces of marijuana); Rummell v. Estelle, 445 U.S. 263 (1980) (upholding constitutionality of a recidivist statute under which defendant received mandatory life sentence for three crimes of fraud that netted a total sum of less than $230). But see Solem v. Helm, 463 U.S. 277 (1983) (striking down life sentence for uttering "no-account" check for less than $100). In the civil context, however, the Supreme Court has been more willing to impose constitutional proportionality

---

3. U.S. Const. amend. VIII ("Excessive bail shall not be required, nor excessive fines imposed, or cruel and unusual punishment inflicted.").

limits in cases involving punitive damages. See State Farm v. Campbell, 538 U.S. 408 (2003); BMW v. Gore, 517 U.S. 559 (1996).

(4) Justice Powell's Two-Part Test.   In his *Patterson* dissent, Justice Powell suggested a two-part test for determining whether it is unconstitutional to place the burden of persuasion on the defendant. First, the facts must make "a substantial difference in punishment of the offender and in the stigma associated with the conviction." Second, in the Anglo-American legal tradition the facts must historically have had "that level of importance." If, but only if, both of these things are true—as Justice Powell argued they were with respect to extreme emotional distress, it is unconstitutional to place the burden of proof on the defendant.

Affirmative Defenses After *Patterson*.   *Patterson* did not adopt either the proportionality test or Justice Powell's two-part test for determining what the state must prove beyond a reasonable doubt. *Patterson*, however, did acknowledge, as *Mullaney* pointed out earlier, that reliance solely on the elements test creates the possibility that states can undermine *Winship* by making most factors critical to the imposition or degree of punishment 'affirmative defenses'. Moreover, the *Patterson* Court stated that "there are obviously constitutional limits beyond which the States may not go in this regard." What might those limits be?

Singling Out Excusatory Defenses.   Arguably, it is both constitutional and morally justified to require defendants relying on excusatory defenses to prove these defenses by a preponderance of the evidence. Excusatory defenses—insanity, diminished responsibility, duress, and several others—relate to the personal traits and circumstances of the defendant and have nothing to do with the general and impersonal characteristics of his criminal act. These defenses are granted as a matter of leniency and concession to human frailty and not because the defendant's act was not criminal or less criminal. The *Winship* mandate therefore does not extend and should not extend to these defenses. See Alex Stein, Foundations of Evidence Law 180-183 (2005). Do you agree with this argument and its underlying act-actor distinction?

MARTIN v. OHIO

480 U.S. 228 (1987)

Justice WHITE delivered the opinion of the Court.

The Ohio Code provides that "(e)very person accused of an offense is presumed innocent until proven guilty beyond a reasonable doubt, and the burden of proof for all elements of the offense is upon the prosecution. The burden of going forward with the evidence of an affirmative defense, and the burden of proof by a preponderance of the evidence, for an affirmative defense, is upon the accused." Ohio Rev. Code Ann. §2901.05(A) (1982). An affirmative defense is one involving "an excuse or justification peculiarly within the knowledge of the accused, on which he can fairly be required to adduce supporting evidence." Ohio Rev. Code Ann. §2901.05(C)(2) (1982). The

Ohio courts have "long determined that self-defense is an affirmative defense," and that the defendant has the burden of proving it as required by §2901.05(A).

As defined by the trial court in its instructions in this case, the elements of self-defense that the defendant must prove are (1) that the defendant was not at fault in creating the situation giving rise to the argument; (2) the defendant had an honest belief that she was in imminent danger of death or great bodily harm and that her only means of escape from such danger was in the use of such force; and (3) the defendant must not have violated any duty to retreat or avoid danger. The question before us is whether the Due Process Clause of the Fourteenth Amendment forbids placing the burden of proving self-defense on the defendant when she is charged by the State of Ohio with committing the crime of aggravated murder, which, as relevant to this case, is defined by the Revised Code of Ohio as "purposely, and with prior calculation and design, caus[ing] the death of another." Ohio Rev. Code Ann. §2903.01 (1982).

The facts of the case, taken from the opinions of the courts below, may be succinctly stated. On July 21, 1983, petitioner Earline Martin and her husband, Walter Martin, argued over grocery money. Petitioner claimed that her husband struck her in the head during the argument. Petitioner's version of what then transpired was that she went upstairs, put on a robe, and later came back down with her husband's gun which she intended to dispose of. Her husband saw something in her hand and questioned her about it. He came at her, she lost her head and fired the gun at him. Five or six shots were fired, three of them striking and killing Mr. Martin. She was charged with and tried for aggravated murder. She pleaded self-defense and testified in her own defense. The judge charged the jury with respect to the elements of the crime and of self-defense and rejected petitioner's Due Process Clause challenge to the charge placing on her the burden of proving self-defense. The jury found her guilty.

Both the Ohio Court of Appeals and the Supreme Court of Ohio affirmed the conviction. . . . We granted certiorari, and affirm the decision of the Supreme Court of Ohio.

In re Winship declared that the Due Process Clause "protects the accused against conviction except upon proof beyond a reasonable doubt of every fact necessary to constitute the crime with which he is charged." A few years later, we held that *Winship*'s mandate was fully satisfied where the State of New York had proved beyond reasonable doubt, each of the elements of murder, but placed on the defendant the burden of proving the affirmative defense of extreme emotional disturbance, which, if proved, would have reduced the crime from murder to manslaughter. Patterson v. New York[, 432 U.S. 197 (1977)]. . . . Referring to Leland v. Oregon, 343 U.S. 790, and Rivera v. Delaware, 429 U.S. 877, we added that New York did no more than *Leland* and *Rivera* permitted it to do without violating the Due Process Clause and declined to reconsider those cases. It was also observed that "the fact that a majority of the States have now assumed the burden of disproving affirmative defenses—for whatever reasons—[does not] mean that those States that strike a different balance are in violation of the Constitution." As in *Patterson*, the jury was here instructed that to convict it must find, in light of all the evidence, that each of the elements of the crime of aggravated murder must be proved by the State beyond reasonable doubt and that the burden of proof with respect to these elements did not shift. To find guilt, the jury had to be convinced that none of the evidence, whether offered by the State or by Martin in connection with her plea of self-defense, raised a reasonable doubt that Martin had killed her husband, that she had the specific purpose and intent to cause his death, or that she had done so with prior calculation and design. It was also told, however, that it could acquit if it found by a preponderance of the evidence that Martin had not precipitated the confrontation, that she had an honest belief that she was in imminent danger of death or great bodily harm, and that she had satisfied any duty to retreat or avoid danger. The jury convicted Martin.

We agree with the State and its Supreme Court that this conviction did not violate the Due Process Clause. The State did not exceed its authority in defining the crime of murder as purposely causing the death of another with prior calculation or design. It did not seek to shift to Martin the burden of proving any of those elements, and the jury's verdict reflects that none of her self-defense evidence raised a reasonable doubt about the state's proof that she purposefully killed with prior calculation and design. She nevertheless had the opportunity under state law and the instructions given to justify the killing and show herself to be blameless by proving that she acted in self-defense. The jury thought she had failed to do so, and Ohio is as entitled to punish Martin as one guilty of murder as New York was to punish Patterson.

It would be quite different if the jury had been instructed that self-defense evidence could not be considered in determining whether there was a reasonable doubt about the state's case, i.e., that self-defense evidence must be put aside for all purposes unless it satisfied the preponderance standard. Such instruction would relieve the state of its burden and plainly run afoul of *Winship*'s mandate. The instructions in this case could be clearer in this respect, but when read as a whole, we think they are adequate to convey to the jury that all of the evidence, including the evidence going to self-defense, must be considered in deciding whether there was a reasonable doubt about the sufficiency of the state's proof of the elements of the crime.

We are thus not moved by assertions that the elements of aggravated murder and self-defense overlap in the sense that evidence to prove the latter will often tend to negate the former. It may be that most encounters in which self-defense is claimed arise suddenly and involve no prior plan or specific purpose to take life. In those cases, evidence offered to support the defense may negate a purposeful killing by prior calculation and design, but Ohio does not shift to the defendant the burden of disproving any element of the state's case. When the prosecution has made out a *prima facie* case and survives a motion to acquit, the jury may nevertheless not convict if the evidence offered by the defendant raises any reasonable doubt about the existence of any fact necessary for the finding of guilt. Evidence creating a reasonable doubt could easily fall far short of proving self-defense by a preponderance of the evidence. Of course, if such doubt is not raised in the jury's mind and each juror is convinced that the defendant purposely and with prior calculation and design took life, the killing will still be excused if the elements of the defense are satisfactorily established. We note here, but need not rely on it, the observation of the Supreme Court of Ohio that "Appellant did not dispute the existence of [the elements of aggravated murder], but rather sought to justify her actions on grounds she acted in self-defense." Petitioner submits that there can be no conviction under Ohio law unless the defendant's conduct is unlawful and

that because self-defense renders lawful what would otherwise be a crime, unlawfulness is an element of the offense that the state must prove by disproving self-defense.
This argument founders on state law, for it has been rejected by the Ohio Supreme
Court and by the Court of Appeals for the Sixth Circuit. White v. Arn, 788 F.2d 338,
346-347 (6th Cir. 1986); State v. Morris, 8 Ohio App. 3d 12, 18-19, 455 N.E.2d 1352,
1359-1360 (1982). It is true that unlawfulness is essential for conviction, but the Ohio
courts hold that the unlawfulness in cases like this is the conduct satisfying the elements of aggravated murder—an interpretation of state law that we are not in a position to dispute. The same is true of the claim that it is necessary to prove a "criminal"
intent to convict for serious crimes, which cannot occur if self-defense is shown: the
necessary mental state for aggravated murder under Ohio law is the specific purpose
to take life pursuant to prior calculation and design.

As we noted in *Patterson*, the common law rule was that affirmative defenses,
including self-defense, were matters for the defendant to prove. "This was the rule
when the Fifth Amendment was adopted, and it was the American rule when the
Fourteenth Amendment was ratified." Indeed, well into this century, a number of
States followed the common law rule and required a defendant to shoulder the burden of proving that he acted in self-defense. We are aware that all but two of the
States, Ohio and South Carolina, have abandoned the common law rule and require
the prosecution to prove the absence of self-defense when it is properly raised by
the defendant. But the question remains whether those States are in violation of the
Constitution; and, as we observed in *Patterson*, that question is not answered by cataloging the practices of other States. We are no more convinced that the Ohio practice
of requiring self-defense to be proved by the defendant is unconstitutional than we are
that the Constitution requires the prosecution to prove the sanity of a defendant who
pleads not guilty by reason of insanity. We have had the opportunity to depart from
Leland v. Oregon but have refused to do so. Rivera v. Delaware, 429 U.S. 877 (1976).
These cases were important to the *Patterson* decision and they, along with *Patterson*,
are authority for our decision today.

The judgment of the Ohio Supreme Court is accordingly affirmed.

NOTES AND QUESTIONS ON MARTIN

1. Consider carefully the relationship between self-defense and the "prior calculation and design" element of aggravated murder. In a dissenting opinion, Justice
Powell argued that "prior calculation" and self-defense were mutually exclusive. Thus,
he regarded self-defense as negating one of the elements of murder. The defendant,
however, pursued a different line of argument. As the majority pointed out, she did
not dispute the existence of the elements of aggravated murder.

To the extent that Justice Powell's characterization of the relationship between
"prior calculation" and self-defense is correct, the principal problem with *Martin*,
as Justice Powell pointed out, is a potentially confusing jury instruction: "It makes
no sense to say that the prosecution has the burden of proving an element beyond
a reasonable doubt and that the defense has the burden of proving the contrary by a

preponderance of the evidence." On the other hand, if the mens rea for aggravated murder is not inconsistent with self-defense, *Martin* is a much more troubling decision. Assume for the sake of argument that "prior calculation and design" means no more forethought than would typically go into a decision to kill in self-defense or under extreme emotional distress. Now compare a killing allegedly committed under extreme emotional distress with a killing allegedly committed in self-defense. Reasonable people may differ about whether extreme emotional distress is sufficiently mitigating that the defendant should not be punished as a *murderer* unless the prosecution disproves the extreme emotional distress claim beyond a reasonable doubt. The defendant who kills under the influence of extreme emotional distress will be punished, however. The killing is a culpable, criminal act; the extreme emotional distress mitigates the crime but does not justify or excuse it. By contrast, the person who kills in self-defense has not committed a crime; the killing is justified. Thus, when the central issue in a case is self-defense, the entire question whether there was culpable criminal conduct turns on a resolution of that issue. To convict a person claiming self-defense of aggravated murder—a capital offense in Ohio—without requiring the prosecution to disprove self-defense beyond a reasonable doubt is to convict someone for whom there has been no proof beyond a reasonable doubt of culpable conduct!

2. Unfortunately, the broad, troublesome implications of *Martin* appear to be the correct ones. The *Martin* majority's superficial analysis did not move beyond the fact that Ohio proved beyond a reasonable doubt the elements that it had included in its murder statute. Moreover, White v. Arn, 788 F.2d 338 (6th Cir. 1986), one of the cases setting forth constitutional interpretations of Ohio law that the *Martin* majority was "not in a position to dispute," involved self-defense and nonaggravated murder. In that case, there was no plausible inconsistency between having the mental state defined in the murder statute (purposefulness) and having the mental state required for self-defense. In other words, there could be a purposeful killing in self-defense. Indeed, *White* specifically relied on this lack of inconsistency to hold that proof of self-defense does not negate purposefulness and, therefore, that it was not unconstitutional to place the burden of proof with respect to self-defense on the defendant. Id. at 346.

3. After *Martin*, is it still true, as the *Patterson* majority claimed, that "there are obviously constitutional limits beyond which the States may not go"? Could a state constitutionally define murder simply as "causing the death of another human being"? How would that statute differ from what the Court approved in *Martin*?

4. Consider now a different line of argument that seemingly vindicates the *Martin* decision. To the extent Ms. Martin relied on self-defense as an affirmative defense, then, as per Ohio law, she had to prove it by a preponderance of the evidence. But she could—and, arguably, did—rely on the underlying facts of self-defense, along with the evidence supporting her self-defense claim, to negate the "prior calculation and design" element of aggravated murder. To the extent she pursued this line of defense, she benefited from the *Winship* protection as the prosecution had to disprove these facts beyond a reasonable doubt. Does this argument vindicate the *Martin* decision? Cf. Leland v. Oregon, 343 U.S. 790 (1952) (upholding the constitutionality of Oregon law requiring defendants to prove the insanity defense beyond a reasonable doubt (!)

while allowing the defendant to use any evidence of his insanity to negate mens rea); Clark v. Arizona, 548 U.S. 735 (2006) (holding that states can constitutionally require defendants to prove the insanity defense by clear and convincing evidence, while emphasizing that the defendant could—and did—use the facts underlying his mental illness, save for conclusory psychiatric opinions banned by Arizona law, to raise a reasonable doubt as to his intent to kill the victim); Dixon v. United States, 548 U.S. 1, 10-11, 15-17 (2006) (holding that defendants accused of federal crimes must prove duress by a preponderance of the evidence, but when the alleged offense includes malice, the defendant may use her evidence of duress to raise a reasonable doubt as to whether her actions were malicious).

KEY POINTS

1. Courts interpret the *Winship* mandate as a requirement that the prosecution prove beyond a reasonable doubt each fact listed in the statutory definition of the crime.
2. It is permissible to place the burden of persuasion on the defendant with respect to affirmative defenses such as extreme emotional distress or self-defense, as long as the state categorizes them as affirmative defenses rather than elements of the crime.
3. When a defendant's affirmative defense overlaps an element of the alleged crime, the defendant can—and will do well to—use the evidence underlying that defense to raise a reasonable doubt as to the presence of the requisite element. By pursuing this line of defense, the defendant will avail himself of the *Winship* protection.
4. There are some unspecified limits beyond which the states may not go in creating affirmative defenses that limit the *Winship* proof beyond a reasonable doubt mandate.

NOTES AND QUESTIONS ON THE APPLICATION OF *WINSHIP* IN OTHER CONTEXTS

1. *Winship* and Sentencing. In Apprendi v. New Jersey, 530 U.S. 466 (2000), the defendant was convicted of weapons offenses as a result of his shooting a gun into the home of an African-American family that had recently moved into a previously all-white neighborhood. The maximum sentence for Apprendi's offenses was ten years, but a separate New Jersey statute—a "hate crimes" statute—permitted adding up to ten additional years to the sentence if the judge found by a preponderance of the evidence that the crime was racially motivated. At Apprendi's sentencing, the judge made the requisite finding and sentenced Apprendi to 12 years imprisonment. The Supreme Court held that the sentencing violated Apprendi's constitutional rights. According to the Court, any fact increasing the penalty beyond the prescribed statutory maximum (here ten years), other than the fact of a prior conviction, must be submitted to the jury and proven beyond a reasonable doubt.

Apprendi, like Mullaney v. Wilbur, page 839, supra, unleashed a flood of litigation. Would *Apprendi* apply if, for example, (a) the hate-crime provision had been part of the same statute that was the basis for Apprendi's conviction, (b) the judge did not exceed the statutory maximum but gave an unusually harsh sentence on the basis of facts found by a preponderance of the evidence at sentencing, or (c) the judge relied on sentencing guidelines to increase a defendant's sentence? In the last case, would it matter if the guidelines were mandatory or discretionary?

Patterson v. New York, page 840, supra, resolved many of the uncertainties created by *Mullaney* with its adoption of the "elements" test for determining what the prosecution must prove beyond a reasonable doubt. Similarly, United States v. Booker, 543 U.S. 220 (2005), appears to have resolved many of the constitutional uncertainties created by *Apprendi*.

Booker was convicted of possessing with the intent to distribute over 50 grams of cocaine. The statutory penalty for the offense was ten years to life imprisonment. The Federal Sentencing Guidelines, however, required a sentence of between 17 and 22 years in the absence of any aggravating or mitigating factors. The sentencing judge found by a preponderance of the evidence that Booker had obstructed justice and had possessed an additional 566 grams of cocaine. With these aggravating factors, the Federal Sentencing Guidelines mandated a sentence of between 30 years and life. The judge imposed a 30-year sentence—12 years longer than the sentence that could have been imposed on the basis of facts found by the jury beyond a reasonable doubt.

The same five-Justice majority that had upheld Apprendi's claim (Stevens, Souter, Scalia, Thomas, and Ginsburg) held that *Apprendi* applied to mandatory sentencing guidelines: The judge cannot impose a sentence that exceeds the maximum authorized by the jury's finding or a guilty plea, regardless of whether the maximum was created by statute or sentencing guideline. All nine Justices agreed that in the absence of statutory or guideline mandates, there would be no constitutional problem. In other words, if there had been no mandatory guidelines alongside the statutory penalty of ten years to life, the trial judge could have given Booker any sentence within the statutory range—even if the judge chose a relatively high sentence on the basis of a preponderance finding that Booker obstructed justice and possessed additional amounts of cocaine! In short, the *Booker* "solution" to the *Apprendi* problem is as formalistic and artificial as is the *Patterson* solution to the *Mullaney* problem. In one case it is a matter of statutory "elements," and in the other it is a matter of mandatory sentencing limits.

In one important respect, though, *Booker* is quite different from *Patterson*. *Patterson*'s elements test has the effect of deferring to legislative judgments about how to define crimes. By contrast, *Booker* interferes with legislative judgments about how to regulate sentencing: Mandatory sentencing guideline systems, which a number of jurisdictions had adopted to regulate sentencing disparity, are now unconstitutional. Unregulated sentence discretion, on the other hand, is alive and well. What values protected by the *Winship* reasonable doubt requirement and the Sixth Amendment jury trial right justify Booker's interference with legislative judgments?

2. *Winship* problems may arise when a state permits the jury to convict the defendant of a single crime without necessarily agreeing on the facts that support the conviction or when a jury convicts a defendant of a greater crime (for which there is reasonable doubt) because they were not given the option of convicting for a lesser crime (for which there is proof beyond a reasonable doubt). See Schad v. Arizona, 501 U.S. 624 (1991) (upholding first degree murder conviction under jury instructions that did not require jury to distinguish between felony-murder and premeditated murder); Beck v. Alabama, 477 U.S. 625 (1980) (holding unconstitutional a statute that prohibited instructions for lesser included offenses in criminal cases).

3. In Montana v. Egelhoff, 518 U.S. 37 (1996), a murder prosecution, the Supreme Court upheld a Montana statute that made evidence of voluntary intoxication inadmissible "in determining the existence of a mental state which was an element of the offense." According to Justice Scalia's plurality opinion, this restriction on the right to introduce evidence did not violate a " 'fundamental principle of justice.' " Id. at 42.

The defendant had argued, inter alia, that the statute had the effect of reducing the state's burden of proof on the mens rea element in violation of *Winship*. The Montana Supreme Court had agreed, relying on the following passage from Martin v. Ohio:

> It would be quite different if the jury had been instructed that self-defense evidence could not be considered in determining whether there was a reasonable doubt about the State's case, i.e., that self-defense evidence must be put aside for all purposes unless it satisfied the preponderance standard. Such instruction would relieve the State of its burden and plainly run afoul of *Winship*'s mandate. The instructions in this case . . . are adequate to convey to the jury that all of the evidence, including the evidence going to self-defense, must be considered in deciding whether there was a reasonable doubt about the sufficiency of the State's proof of the elements of the crime. 480 U.S. at 233-234.

Justice Scalia's response to the *Winship-Martin* argument was as follows:

> This passage can be explained in various ways—e.g., as an assertion that the right to have a jury consider self-defense evidence (unlike the right to have a jury consider evidence of voluntary intoxication), is fundamental, a proposition that the historical record may support. But the only explanation needed for present purposes is the one given in Kokkonen v. Guardian Life Ins. Co., 511 U.S. 375, 379 (1994): "It is to the holdings of our cases, rather than dicta, that we must attend." [518 U.S. at 56.]

What do you think of the defendant's *Winship* argument? Of Justice Scalia's response?

Justice Ginsburg, concurring in the judgment, maintained that the Montana statute should be understood as redefining mens rea, not as restricting evidence:

> Beneath the labels (rule excluding evidence or redefinition of the offense) lies the essential question: Can a State, without offense to the Federal Constitution, make the judgment that two people are equally culpable where one commits an act stone sober, and the other engages in the same conduct after his voluntary intoxication has reduced his capacity for self-control? Id. at 57.

What do you think of Justice Ginsburg's formulation of the issue? Of her affirmative answer? See Ronald J. Allen, Forward: Montana v. Egelhoff—Reflections on the Limits of Legislative Imagination and Judicial Authority, 87 J. Crim. L. & Criminology 633 (1997).

Chapter Ten. The Process of Proof in Civil and Criminal Cases

4. In Clark v. Arizona, 548 U.S. 735 (2006), the Supreme Court upheld Arizona's statute and common law that limited a defendant's psychiatric expert testimony about his mental illness to the affirmative defense of insanity—an issue the defendant needed to prove by clear and convincing evidence—and excluded the expert's opinion on the issue of mens rea that went beyond factual observations about the defendant's tendency to think in a certain way and his behavioral characteristics. The defendant, who was convicted of first degree murder for intentionally killing a police officer, argued that expert testimony about his schizophrenia showed that he was acting out of delusions caused by his mental illness and not with the requisite intent. By upholding the state law limiting the use of this evidence, is the Court in effect saying that it is constitutional to make defendants prove lack of mens rea when they wish to introduce expert testimony on the issue? Consider in this context FRE 704(b), according to which, "In a criminal case, an expert witness must not state an opinion about whether the defendant did or did not have a mental state or condition that constitutes an element of the crime charged or of a defense. Those matters are for the trier of fact alone."

If states may shift the burden of persuasion on the issue of mens rea (at least with regard to mentally ill defendants), we ask once again: What are the constitutional limits on what states may do? For further discussions of *Clark*, see Ronald J. Allen, Clark v. Arizona: Much (Confused) Ado About Nothing, 4 Ohio St. J. Crim. L. 135 (2006); Peter Westen, The Supreme Court's Bout with Insanity: Clark v. Arizona, 4 Ohio St. J. Crim. L. 143 (2006); Alex Stein, Constitutional Evidence Law, 61 Vand. L. Rev. 65, 120-121 (2008).

5. Federal criminal law, both statutory and judge made, routinely requires defendants to prove affirmative defenses by a preponderance and even by clear and convincing evidence. See Dixon v. United States, 548 U.S. 1, 15-17 (2006) (requiring defendants relying on duress as an affirmative defense to prove it by a preponderance of the evidence). See also 18 U.S.C. §17 (b) ("The defendant has the burden of proving the defense of insanity by clear and convincing evidence.").

c. The Burden of Production in Criminal Cases

As we discussed in Section A, at pages 804-807, supra, the primary significance of a production burden is that the failure to meet it will preclude the party who has that burden from presenting the matter to the jury. The court will resolve the issue against the party with the production burden. For example, if the prosecution fails to present sufficient evidence to permit a finding beyond a reasonable doubt of each element of the crime, the court will direct a verdict of acquittal for the defendant.

It is frequently said that because of a criminal defendant's constitutional right to a jury trial, it is impermissible to direct a verdict against a criminal defendant. In fact, however, courts commonly engage in activity that is the equivalent of directing verdicts against criminal defendants. Consider, for example, the refusal of a judge to instruct the jury on a particular defense or lesser included offense on the grounds that insufficient evidence of that defense has been produced—a practice approved by the Supreme Court in United States v. Bailey, 444 U.S. 394 (1980).

Bailey involved defendants' challenges to their convictions for escaping from a federal institution. In upholding the convictions, the Court rejected claims that the trial court erred in failing to instruct the jury on the common law defenses of duress and necessity. The defendants testified that their actions were motivated by death threats, and they requested an instruction on duress or necessity. The Court concluded that even if Congress intended to allow such defenses—a point left undecided until the defenses were recognized in Dixon v. United States, 548 U.S. 1 (2006)—the defendants failed to make a sufficient showing of duress or necessity to justify a jury instruction. The defendants, in other words, failed to meet a burden of production, and the district court practically directed a verdict on their defenses by refusing to instruct on them.

NOTES AND QUESTIONS

1. What the *Bailey* Court did not do, unless it did so implicitly, was to inquire into the constitutional necessity of establishing the fact in issue—in this case, whether or not the defendants had acted under duress or necessity. Without that inquiry, the Court's analysis is incomplete. If the fact in issue was one that must be established in order to justify the potential sanction, then permitting the district court to remove that issue from the case resulted in a conviction when one essential fact had not been proven beyond reasonable doubt to the jury's satisfaction, which is inconsistent with *Winship*. But see Dixon v. United States, 548 U.S. 1 (2006) (holding that duress and necessity are available as affirmative defenses under federal law, but only when the defendant proves the underlying facts by a preponderance of the evidence).

2. If the fact in issue does not need to be established beyond a reasonable doubt, then *Bailey* provides an acceptable, if not ideal, analysis of burdens of production on nonessential elements. The analysis is not ideal because of the majority's position that personal testimony of the defendants did not justify a jury instruction. 444 U.S. at 415. The Court is playing the role of factfinder with such a test and concluding that the defendants' testimony is incredible. As a matter of policy, such questions should be left to the jury even on nonessential issues. Indeed, pursuant to the *Dixon* precedent, it is up to the jury to decide whether the defendant proved duress or necessity by a preponderance of the evidence.

KEY POINTS

1. Courts typically refuse to give instructions on defenses and lesser included offenses when they find that the defendant has produced insufficient evidence to warrant such instructions. These rulings are the equivalent of directed verdicts against criminal defendants.
2. Although the Supreme Court has not addressed the issue, refusing to give such an instruction has the potential for undermining *Winship*.

2. Judicial Summary and Comment on the Evidence in Criminal Cases

In the criminal context, courts apply a similar standard for evaluating summary and comment as in civil cases. See our discussion of summary and comment in civil cases in Section A.2, supra. For example, in Quercia v. United States, 289 U.S. 466, 468-469 (1933), the trial judge instructed the jury in the following manner:

> And now I am going to tell you what I think of the defendant's testimony. You may have noticed, Mr. Foreman and gentlemen, that he wiped his hands during his testimony. It is rather a curious thing, but that is almost always an indication of lying. Why it should be so we don't know, but that is the fact. I think that every single word that man said, except when he agreed with the Government's testimony, was a lie.
>
> Now, that opinion is an opinion of evidence and is not binding on you, and if you don't agree with it, it is your duty to find him not guilty.

In reversing the ensuing conviction, the Supreme Court stated:

> This privilege of the judge to comment on the facts has its inherent limitations. His discretion is not arbitrary and uncontrolled, but judicial, to be exercised in conformity with the standards governing the judicial office. In commenting upon testimony he may not assume the role of a witness. He may analyze and dissect the evidence, but he may not either distort it or add to it. His privilege of comment in order to give appropriate assistance to the jury is too important to be left without safeguards against abuses. . . .
>
> Nor do we think that the error was cured by the statement of the trial judge that his opinion of the evidence was not binding on the jury and that if they did not agree with it they should find the defendant not guilty. His definite and concrete assertion of fact, which he had made with all the persuasiveness of judicial utterance, as to the basis of his opinion, was not withdrawn. Id. at 469, 472.

NOTES AND QUESTIONS

1. Courts regularly cite and quote from *Quercia* in cases involving challenges to judicial summary and comment. In most of these cases, the judge's statements to the jury are not as extreme as the remarks in *Quercia*. United States v. Maguire, 918 F.2d 254, 268-269 (1st Cir. 1990) (instruction summarizing government's theory of the case proper); United States v. Paiva, 892 F.2d 148, 159 (1st Cir. 1989) (judge's explanation of what a field test for cocaine is went beyond proper bounds of judicial comment absent testimony about what a field test involved, but error was harmless).

2. Is the standard implicit in *Quercia* inherently inconsistent? How can one "analyze and dissect the evidence" without "adding to it"? For a discussion, see Ronald J. Allen, More on Constitutional Process-of-Proof Problems, 94 Harv. L. Rev. 1795 (1981); and Charles R. Nesson, Rationality, Presumptions, and Judicial Comment: A Response to Professor Allen, 94 Harv. L. Rev. 1574, 1589-1590 (1981).

3. A judicial comment will either be obvious or not obvious to the jury. If it is obvious, the reiteration of the obvious by the trial judge should not be grounds for reversal. If the judge's comment is not obvious, a critical question should be whether the comment is accurate:

> Consider a murder trial where the defendant has injected the "defense" of alibi. Assume that on the basis of the evidence adduced without judicial comment, a well-informed, rational jury would conclude that there is a 15 percent chance that the facts of the alibi story are true. The verdict would be not guilty, since a 15 percent chance of error surely is a "reasonable doubt." First, take the case in which the trial judge comments on the evidence tending to prove or disprove the alibi and assume that the comment is factually inaccurate. Assume further that as a result of the inaccurate comment, the same jury would conclude that there is only a very small chance that the alibi is true. The verdict, then, all other things remaining the same, would be guilty. In order to escape the guilty verdict, and the effect of the trial judge's comments, the defendant would unfairly be forced to produce stronger, more persuasive evidence of the alibi. In effect, his burden of persuasion has been increased beyond that of merely raising a reasonable doubt.
>
> Now consider the case where the judge's comments on the evidence are accurate. Assume again that the comments caused the jury to discredit the alibi sufficiently to render a guilty verdict. Once again, the defendant's burden of persuasion has been increased—he would have to present stronger evidence to gain an acquittal—but this time the defendant has no constitutional grounds to complain. By altering the jury's factual matrix to one more in accordance with reality, the judicial comment has enabled the jury to perceive that guilt was indeed proven beyond a reasonable doubt.
>
> The example illustrates that inaccurate judicial comment detrimental to the defendant, on an issue that constitutionally must be included in a state's definition of a crime, violates the mandate of In re Winship by effectively lowering the state's burden of proving guilt beyond a reasonable doubt. . . . Accurate comment, on the other hand, can prevent an erroneous verdict when the jury is unable to appreciate the implications of certain facts proven at trial. Ronald J. Allen, Structuring Jury Decisionmaking in Criminal Cases: A Unified Constitutional Approach to Evidentiary Devices, 94 Harv. L. Rev. 321, 348-349 (1980).

3. Presumptions in Criminal Cases: The Impact of *Winship*

Review the discussion of *Mullaney* and *Patterson* at pages 839-840, supra. A presumption that explicitly shifts the burden of persuasion to the defendant is obviously unconstitutional if the presumed fact is one that the prosecution must prove beyond a reasonable doubt. For example, the Court in *Mullaney*, beginning with the premise that the prosecution must establish malice aforethought beyond a reasonable doubt, held unconstitutional the "conclusive inference" of malice from proof of an unlawful, intentional killing. This "conclusive inference," which *Patterson* characterized as a presumption, was indeed a traditional mandatory persuasion burden presumption.

Patterson, of course, called into question the underlying premise that the state had to prove malice (i.e., the absence of provocation) beyond a reasonable doubt. As we suggested in Section B, however, the Supreme Court has relied primarily on how a state chooses to define a crime as the basis for determining what the state must prove beyond a reasonable doubt. Thus, *Mullaney* stands for the proposition that once a state includes a fact as part of the definition of a crime, the state cannot create a presumption that shifts the burden of persuasion on that fact. Similarly, the state cannot create a conclusive or irrebuttable presumption that an element of a crime exists. Sandstrom v. Montana, 442 U.S. 510 (1979). *Unless we state otherwise, we will assume in the ensuing discussion that we are dealing with facts that the state has defined as elements of offenses and that must, therefore, be proven beyond a reasonable doubt.*

In order to avoid a *Mullaney*-type conflict with *Winship*, presumptions in criminal cases are typically permissive rather than mandatory: If the factfinder believes the facts giving rise to the presumption, the factfinder may, but is not required to, find the presumed fact. The factfinder must be convinced of the presumed fact beyond a reasonable doubt. Merely making the presumption permissive, however, does not altogether eliminate *Winship*-related problems.

To determine whether a jury instruction about a presumption violates *Winship*, it is important to focus on the language of the instruction itself. If jurors could reasonably understand the instruction as permitting proof of the presumed fact by less than beyond a reasonable doubt, the instruction is unconstitutional. Sandstrom v. Montana, 442 U.S. at 510. According to County Court of Ulster County v. Allen, 442 U.S. 140 (1979), a permissive presumption instruction with respect to an element of an offense is constitutional (1) if the instruction as a whole makes it clear that the jury must be convinced of each element of the crime beyond a reasonable doubt; (2) if there is a rational connection between the basic facts—that need to be proved beyond a reasonable doubt—and the presumed facts; and (3) if the presumed facts are more likely than not to flow from the basic facts. In deciding whether the crucial "more likely than not" relationship exists, the primary focus is on the evidence in the case, not on whether the relationship exists in the abstract. In Ulster County, the Court upheld the constitutionality of a permissive presumption that allowed jurors to find any person occupying an automobile to be in possession of a firearm that is found in the automobile except when the firearm is found upon the person of another occupier of the same car. The Court ruled that it was "more likely than not" that the defendants possessed the handguns recovered from their vehicle, which established the requisite nexus between the basic and the presumed facts and authorized jurors to find the fact of possession on the totality of the evidence.

A production burden presumption—that is, a presumption instructing the jury that the presumed fact is present unless the defendant produces evidence to rebut it—is constitutionally suspect. According to a dictum in *Ulster County*, if jurors could reasonably understand the instruction as requiring them to find the presumed fact unless the defendant produces a certain amount of evidence, the instruction would likely be unconstitutional. In essence, it recommends jurors to convict the defendant because of his failure to come forward with evidence, regardless of whether the jury is convinced beyond a reasonable doubt that the defendant committed the crime. On the other hand, if the instruction makes it clear that the defendant's obligation is minimal while underscoring *Winship's* beyond-a-reasonable-doubt mandate, it may be tantamount to a permissive presumption. Such an instruction would likely be constitutional when the presumption meets the "more likely than not" requirement for the case-specific connection between the basic and the presumed facts.

NOTES AND QUESTIONS

1. In criminal cases prior to *Ulster County*, the Supreme Court had assessed the constitutionality of presumptions primarily in terms of the empirical relationship between the presumed facts and the facts giving rise to the presumption. The recurring issue was whether the relationship had to exist beyond a reasonable doubt or whether a more-likely-than-not relationship was sufficient. Barnes v. United States, 412 U.S. 837 (1973); Turner v. United States, 396 U.S. 398 (1970). *Ulster County* resolved the issue for permissive presumptions by settling on the more-likely-than-not standard. In addition, dictum in *Ulster County* suggests that a presumption shifting the burden of persuasion to the defendant may be constitutional if the general (as opposed to case-specific) relationship between the basic and the presumed facts exists beyond a reasonable doubt. 442 U.S. at 157-159 and nn.16-17. Sandstrom v. Montana, however, makes no reference to this dictum in holding unconstitutional a presumption instruction that could have been understood as shifting the burden of persuasion to the defendant.

2. Why should the empirical relationship between the basic and the presumed facts matter?

For a discussion of the criteria that should be used in evaluating presumptions in criminal cases, see Ronald J. Allen, Structuring Jury Decisionmaking in Criminal Cases: A Unified Constitutional Approach to Evidentiary Devices, 94 Harv. L. Rev. 321 (1980).

KEY POINTS

1. In assessing the constitutionality of a presumption instruction, it is important to focus precisely on what the court tells the jury. If the jury could understand the instruction in a manner that violates *Winship*, the presumption is unconstitutional.
2. Presumptions that conclusively deem elements of crimes present are unconstitutional.
3. Presumptions that shift the burden of persuasion to the defendant with respect to elements of offenses are unconstitutional as well (subject to the above-mentioned dictum in the *Ulster County* case, not followed in Sandstrom v. Montana).
4. Permissive presumptions are constitutional if the relationship between the basic facts—that must be proven beyond a reasonable doubt—and the presumed facts meets the "more likely than not" standard in light of the evidence in the case.

PROBLEMS

10.5. Defendant Morgan was convicted of driving under the influence of intoxicating beverages. Some 90 minutes after Morgan drove his vehicle off the road and through a fence, an officer interviewed him at a friend's home. According to the officer, Morgan appeared unsteady and smelled of alcohol, but Morgan claimed that he had not consumed any alcohol since the accident. A breathalyzer test at the time of the interview indicated that Morgan had a blood alcohol level of .14 percent. Morgan is 19 years old, 5 feet 10 inches tall, and weighs 190 pounds. In the instructions to the jury, the judge stated that Morgan was to be found guilty "if, and only if, you believe from all the evidence beyond a reasonable doubt (a) that the defendant was driving a motor vehicle and (b) that while doing so he was under the influence of alcohol." The judge also read verbatim to the jury the following statutory language and told the jury to "consider this as evidence in the case":

(a) In any criminal prosecution in which the defendant is charged with having operated a vehicle while under the influence of intoxicating beverages, the amount of alcohol in the defendant's blood as determined at the time of making an analysis of his blood, urine, breath, or other bodily substance, shall give rise to the following presumptions: (i) If there was .05 percent or less by weight of alcohol in such blood, it shall be presumed that the defendant was not under the influence of intoxicating beverages; (ii) If there was more than .05 percent but less than .10 percent by weight of alcohol in such blood, such fact shall not constitute a presumption that the defendant either was or was not under the influence of intoxicating beverages, but such fact may be considered together with other competent evidence, in determining the guilt or innocence of the defendant; (iii) If there was .10 percent or more by weight of alcohol in such blood, it shall be presumed that the defendant was under the influence of intoxicating beverages.

(b) The provisions of subsection (a) of this section shall not be construed as limiting the introduction of any other competent evidence bearing on the question whether the defendant was under the influence of intoxicating beverages.

Did the instruction violate the defendant's constitutional rights?

10.6. Davis, a union official, was convicted of lying to the grand jury. The allegedly false statement was his denial that he had accepted campaign contributions from an employer. The trial judge's jury instructions included the following:

> Under federal law, it is improper for a union official to accept any union campaign contributions from any employer. Specifically, federal law provides that "no moneys of an employer shall be contributed or applied to promote the candidacy of any person in any election." This law applied even where the contribution may have been minimal.
>
> I want to caution you that the defendant is not charged in this indictment with receiving improper payments of union campaign expenses. I want to instruct you that you may only consider this instruction in determining the defendant's intent and state of mind in answering questions before the grand jury.

The purpose of the instruction, according to the prosecution, was to suggest to the jury that Davis had a motive to lie to the grand jury: Because receiving such funds is illegal and because Davis presumably knew it was illegal, he had a motive to lie about whether he had received the funds. Davis, on the other hand, points out that the only sanction for receiving such funds would have been his removal from office for the one remaining month of his term. Avoiding such a minor sanction, he suggests, is not worth the risk of a possible criminal conviction for lying to the grand jury. He claims that the instruction was unconstitutional because it created for the jury either an irrational permissive inference or a mandatory presumption. What result?

10.7. Libby was convicted of murder for stabbing his victim to death in a fight. There were no eyewitnesses to the stabbing, but witnesses did testify that Libby had been seen carrying a knife before the stabbing, that he had been seen running away from the site of the fight with blood on his clothes, that he was seen holding a knife shortly after the stabbing, that he admitted having stabbed the victim, and that he threatened anyone who might "snitch" on him. There was also testimony that he stabbed the victim because he thought the victim was about to jump him from behind and because he believed the victim was beating up a third person. The trial judge instructed the jury with respect to murder and voluntary manslaughter. The murder instruction included the following:

> Murder is the killing of a human being without legal justification or without excuse or without such extenuating circumstances as may reduce the crime to manslaughter; but with what is called in the law malice aforethought.
>
> Any intentional killing of a human being without legal justification or excuse and with no extenuating circumstances sufficient in law to reduce the crime to manslaughter is malicious.
>
> If the wicked intent to do injury to another person precedes the act by which the injury was done, it is malice aforethought. If the homicide is committed without legal justification or, that is to say, without due authority of law and not in self defense, and there is no issue here of self defense, nor in the heat of passion on great provocation, but with the specific intent to take the life of the one killed, or an unlawful act, the natural consequence of which would be to deprive another person of life, it is murder.
>
> Malice is implied in every deliberate cruel act by one against another.

The judge then gave the manslaughter instruction explaining that a killing under the influence of extreme emotional distress was manslaughter and that if there were evidence of extreme emotional distress, the jury could convict the defendant only of manslaughter unless the prosecution proved beyond a reasonable doubt that the killing was not done under the influence of extreme emotional distress. The judge told the jury to consider first whether the defendant was guilty of murder and then to consider the manslaughter charge unless the jury agreed that the defendant was guilty of murder. The judge also told the jury that to find the defendant guilty of any crime the prosecution had to prove each element beyond a reasonable doubt.

What constitutional challenges can the defendant make to these instructions?

ASSESSMENTS

A-10.1. Proof Beyond a Reasonable Doubt. New State's statute requires criminal defendants who raise the defense of duress to prove that defense by clear and convincing evidence. This requirement violates constitutional due process. True or False?

A-10.2. Proof Beyond a Reasonable Doubt. Under New State's Criminal Code, a person will be guilty of aggravated assault if he "maliciously inflicts grievous bodily harm on another person." The Code also provides that the defendant will be acquitted of aggravated assault charges if he proves self-defense by a preponderance of the evidence. This proof requirement is unconstitutional. True or False?

A-10.3. Presumptions in Criminal Cases. Permissive presumptions can be used by the prosecution in criminal trials so long as they satisfy the preponderance standard in connecting basic to presumed facts and make it clear to the jury that it should acquit the defendant when it has a reasonable doubt as to one of the elements of the alleged crime. True or False?

A-10.4. Presumptions in Criminal Cases. The New State's Patterned Jury Instructions authorize judges to instruct jurors that they can, but are not obligated, to presume that a person intends to bring about the ordinary consequences of his actions and to illustrate this presumption by a person who fires a gun at another human being.
  Using this presumption in murder cases would be:

  A   Unconstitutional because it would reduce the prosecution's burden of proving criminal intent.
  B   Unconstitutional because the instruction would imply without evidence that a person who shoots another human being normally intends to kill him.
  C   Unconstitutional because the jury might think that they have to follow the presumption when the defendant produces no evidence to the contrary.
  D   Perfectly constitutional if the judge also tells the jury that it is the prosecution's burden to prove the defendant's intent to kill beyond a reasonable doubt.

A-10.5 Presumptions in Civil Cases. Under West Virginia Law, a plaintiff suing a car manufacturer in products liability needs to prove by a preponderance of the evidence that the alleged car defect "was a factor in causing some aspect of the plaintiff's harm." This showing activates a permissive presumption of causation that allows the jury to find the defendant responsible for the entire damage suffered by the plaintiff even when there is no evidence linking that damage to the car defect.
  This presumption is:

  A   Constitutional.
  B   Unconstitutional because it violates due process.
  C   Unconstitutional because it discriminates against defendants and thereby violates equal protection.
  D   Constitutionally suspect and may be voided on constitutional grounds following a thorough judicial inquiry into its motives and implications.

A-10.6. Presumptions in Civil Cases. Res ipsa loquitur is:

A   A mandatory presumption that shifts the burden of persuasion to the defendant on the issue of negligence.

B   A permissive presumption that allows the plaintiff to move her case to the jury on the issue of negligence and have the judge instruct the jury that it is allowed, but not obligated, to find the defendant negligent when the basic facts are proven by a preponderance of the evidence.

C   Merely a judicial comment on the plaintiff's circumstantial evidence that identifies the defendant as prima facie negligent.

D   None of the above.

A-10.7. Affirmative Defenses. You are defending a company sued for a breach of contract. The company could not carry out its contractual obligations because of unexpected military activities in the Middle East that blocked its access to oil supplies. This development made two equally plausible arguments available: (1) Under the contract's proper interpretation, the company's nonperformance did not amount to a breach; (2) the company's nonperformance was completely excused by the impossibility and frustration of purpose defenses.

Your best trial strategy is:

A   To assert and subsequently try to prove both arguments.

B   To assert and subsequently try to prove Argument (2) only.

C   To assert and subsequently try to prove Argument (1) only.

D   To find more information in the hopes to improve the choice between the two arguments.

ANSWERS

A-10.1. FALSE. Duress is an affirmative defense, which the defendant can be constitutionally required to prove. Dixon v. United States, 548 U.S. 1, 10-11 (2006).

A-10.2. TRUE. Here, there is a complete overlap between "malice" as an element of the crime and lack of self-defense. Put differently, self-defense negates malice as a matter of the crime's definition. Hence, requiring a defendant to prove self-defense by a preponderance of the evidence is similar to requiring him to prove by a preponderance of the evidence that he acted without malice. This requirement violates due process, as interpreted in *Mullaney*, see supra at pages 839-840, because "malice" is an element of the crime that the prosecution must prove beyond a reasonable doubt.

A-10.3. TRUE. As per Sandstrom v. Montana, 442 U.S. 510 (1979), and County Court of Ulster County v. Allen, 442 U.S. 140 (1979).

A-10.4. The best answer is **D**, as per Sandstrom v. Montana, 442 U.S. 510 (1979).

A-10.5. The best answer is **A**. States are free to allocate burdens of proof in civil cases as they deem fit. Lavine v. Milne, 424 U.S. 577, 585 (1976).

A-10.6. The best answer is **B**, as explained in our discussion of the res ipsa presumption. See supra at page 829.

A-10.7. The best answer is **C**. Argument (1) will negate the plaintiff's breach allegation, which the plaintiff needs to prove by a preponderance of the evidence. If factfinders remain undecided about that allegation, the defendant will win the case. Argument (2), on the other hand, raises an affirmative defense that the defendant would have to prove by a preponderance of the evidence. Raising and trying to prove both arguments would not be a good strategy. Here is why: When the defendant fails to convince factfinders that Argument (1) is as likely as not, it would also fail to prove Argument (2) that requires preponderance of the evidence. From the defendant's perspective, therefore, pursuing Argument (2) is either bad or superfluous (given that Argument (1) is equally plausible). Because Argument (2) is never a good strategy, Answer D ("more information needed") is false as well.

CHAPTER ELEVEN

JUDICIAL NOTICE

Consider a case in which a large-scale livestock operation is being sued for allowing agricultural wastes to run off the animal lot into nearby waterways. Suppose the plaintiff is required to establish, as part of its case, the amount of rainfall that fell in the area during the preceding year. It seems as though there should be a clear, undisputed answer to the rainfall question; yet for the plaintiff to prove the rainfall amount using the kinds of evidence you have studied thus far might be difficult or exceedingly costly. There is no percipient witness who could give precise eyewitness testimony about how many inches of rainfall occurred. The plaintiff might have to go to the trouble of retaining an expert simply to establish an undisputable fact.

Fortunately, the Federal Rules provide a procedure that might simplify proof in this situation, known as "judicial notice." *Judicial notice* encompasses a range of situations in which judges take official cognizance of propositions of fact and of law. FRE 201, discussed in Section A, deals with judicial notice in the strict sense of a formal judicial determination that a particular "adjudicative" fact is "not subject to reasonable dispute." However, the term *judicial notice* is also often used more loosely to refer to other forms of judicial factfinding not addressed by the Federal Rules of Evidence. These are discussed in Sections B and C, infra.

A. JUDICIAL NOTICE OF ADJUDICATIVE FACTS

1. FRE 201

RULE 201. JUDICIAL NOTICE OF ADJUDICATIVE FACTS

(a) *Scope.* This rule governs judicial notice of an adjudicative fact only, not a legislative fact.

(b) *Kinds of Facts That May Be Judicially Noticed.* The court may judicially notice a fact that is not subject to reasonable dispute because it:

(1) is generally known within the trial court's territorial jurisdiction; or

(2) can be accurately and readily determined from sources whose accuracy cannot reasonably be questioned.

(c) *Taking Notice*. The court:

(1) may take judicial notice on its own; or

(2) must take judicial notice if a party requests it and the court is supplied with the necessary information.

(d) *Timing*. The court may take judicial notice at any stage of the proceeding.

(e) *Opportunity to Be Heard*. On timely request, a party is entitled to be heard on the propriety of taking judicial notice and the nature of the fact to be noticed. If the court takes judicial notice before notifying a party, the party, on request, is still entitled to be heard.

(f) Instructing the Jury. In a civil case, the court must instruct the jury to accept the noticed fact as conclusive. In a criminal case, the court must instruct the jury that it may or may not accept the noticed fact as conclusive.

2. Explanation of FRE 201(a) and (b)

FRE 201 authorizes, and in some circumstances requires, the judge to instruct the jury to accept certain facts as true, if those facts are "not subject to reasonable dispute." The judge may make such a ruling whether requested or not, but must make such a ruling on request of a party who properly demonstrates the undisputable quality of the fact. In criminal cases, the judge must qualify the instruction by advising the jury that it "may," but need not, accept the fact as true.

a. Types of Adjudicative Facts That Are Frequently Noticed

In theory, a court could take judicial notice of any evidentiary facts or propositions of background knowledge that meet the high standards of certainty required by FRE 201(b). In practice, the kinds of facts judicially noticed under this rule tend to fall into a predictable set of broad categories: business or government custom; calendar dates and time limits; product characteristics in copyright, patent, and trademark litigation; current events; general principles of economics and economic information; fees and salaries; geography; historical information; judicial records and proceedings; medical information; official records; scientific facts and principles, and performance of scientific equipment; and weather.

The rise of the Internet as a research tool has provided judges and lawyers with quick and easy access to a wealth of judicially noticeable facts, which might otherwise have required time-consuming research. Courts frequently rely on government and corporate websites, online news sources, and tools such as Google Maps to take judicial notice of facts that meet the criteria of FRE 201. See, e.g., Benavidez v. City of Irving, 638 F. Supp. 2d 709, 721 (N.D. Tex 2009) (census data from government website); Sprint Nextel Corp. v. AT&T Inc. 821 F. Supp. 2d 308, 325 n.29 (D.D.C.

2011) (news reports); Rindfleisch v. Gentiva Health Sys., Inc., 752 F. Supp. 2d 246, 259 n.13 (E.D.N.Y. 2010) ("Courts commonly use internet mapping tools to take judicial notice of distance and geography."). Indeed, in some circumstances it may be an abuse of discretion not to take judicial notice of such facts. See, e.g., O'Toole v. Northrop Grumman Corp., 499 F.3d 1218, 1225 (10th Cir. 2007) (abuse of discretion in failing to take judicial notice of earnings-history data available on the Internet); but see Lodge v. Kondauer Capital Corp., 750 F.3d 1263 (8th Cir. 2014) (no abuse of discretion in declining to take judicial notice when plaintiff failed to provide necessary information to do so). Whether such facts otherwise meet the criteria of FRE 201—in particular, whether the source's "accuracy cannot reasonably be questioned"—will depend on the particular website or source and the facts of the case. See generally Jeffrey Bellin & Andrew Guthrie Ferguson, Trial by Google: Judicial Notice in the Information Age, 108 Nw. U. L. Rev. 1137 (2014).

b. The Scope of FRE 201(a): What Are Adjudicative Facts?

FRE 201(a) states that the rule applies only to those situations in which judges take official cognizance of "adjudicative facts," but the rule itself does not define that term. Adjudicative facts are those facts that the jury typically decides at trial. Adjudicative facts may be either the alleged facts of consequence that are the essential elements of a dispute under the substantive law or the evidentiary facts that are relevant to prove those facts of consequence. As described by the Advisory Committee Note to FRE 201(a):

> Adjudicative facts are simply the facts of the particular case . . . . [T]he adjudicative facts are those to which the law is applied in the process of adjudication. They are the facts that normally go to the jury in a jury case. They relate to the parties, their activities, their properties, their businesses. [2 Kenneth Davis, Administrative Law Treatise 353 (1958).]

You know by now from your study of evidence how broad this concept of adjudicative facts really is—potentially any fact relevant to a dispute under FRE 401 would be an adjudicative fact and *could be* subject to FRE 201. The real limits to the scope of this rule come from FRE 201(b).

c. The Scope of FRE 201(b): The Required State of Knowledge of Adjudicative Facts That May Be Judicially Noticed

If a party requests the court to take judicial notice of an adjudicative fact pursuant to FRE 201, the party must persuade the court that the fact satisfies the standards of FRE 201(b). The fact must be indisputable as defined by the rule; it must not be subject to "reasonable dispute." That indisputability can be established through either of two means. First, the fact may be the kind of fact that is "generally known within the territorial jurisdiction of the trial court." For example, in Goldblatt v. Fed. Deposit Ins. Corp., 105 F.3d 1325, 1329 n.3 (9th Cir. 1999), the court took judicial notice of the interest bearing nature of money market accounts. By contrast, in Carley v. Wheeled

Coach, 991 F.2d 1117, 1126 (3d Cir. 1993), the appellate court concluded that the trial court had erred in taking judicial notice of the "well known rollover propensities of vehicles having a high center of gravity." According to the court, "[m]ost people probably know little, if anything, about how high centers of gravity cause vehicular accidents." The parties thus had to produce evidence on this issue, and the jury would ultimately decide it.

The second way to establish indisputability is by reference to "sources whose accuracy cannot reasonably be questioned." For example, in United States v. Pozsgai, 999 F.2d 719, 731 (3d Cir. 1993), the appellate court held that the trial court had properly taken judicial notice of the fact that the Pennsylvania Canal was or could be used in interstate commerce. The status of the Canal in interstate commerce was established by two scholarly history books and a U.S. Army Corps of Engineers report. As a result, the parties needed to produce no evidence on this issue, and the jury was instructed as to its truth. If indisputability cannot be established under either of these standards, the factual issue is subject to proof at trial.

These two criteria significantly narrow the scope of facts subject to judicial notice from FRE 201(a)'s broad reference to "adjudicative facts." Facts that are "generally known" or that are established by "unquestionably accurate" sources tend to be what we would think of as "background information." Such facts may be highly relevant and indeed essential to a party's claim or defense, but they are probably not unique to the case.

3. An Application of FRE 201(a) and (b)

IN RE THIRTYACRE

154 B.R. 497 (Bankr. C.D. Ill. 1993)

WILLIAM V. ALTENBERGER, Bankruptcy Judge.

[In a bench trial, a judgment creditor sought a finding from the Bankruptcy Court that the debt was nondischargeable as a willful and malicious injury, because it was based on a state court judgment that the debtor Thirtyacre had assaulted the creditor. The debtor Thirtyacre's defense was that his mental capacity to form an intent to act in a willful and malicious manner was impaired because he had been taking the drug Pamelor and drinking alcohol at the time of the assault. Thirtyacre asked the court to take judicial notice of the effects of Pamelor.] . . .

The first evidentiary issue is whether this Court should take judicial notice of the drug manufacturer's pamphlet for the drug Pamelor. This pamphlet contains sections entitled: Description, Actions, Indications, Contraindications, Warnings, Precautions, Adverse Reactions, Dosage and Administration, and How Supplied. The Defendant [Mr. Thirtyacre] asked this Court to take judicial notice of the definition of Pamelor. In effect he was asking this Court to take judicial notice of the matters in the pamphlet, including that the drug when taken with an excessive consumption of alcohol may have adverse consequences.

Rule 201 of the Federal Rules of Evidence governs judicial notice of adjudicative facts . . . .

Clearly the pamphlet does not fall within the scope of the rule . . . .It cannot be said that the effects of Pamelor when taken with an excessive consumption of alcohol are generally known within the jurisdiction of this Court. As stated in McCormick on Evidence:

> [T]he more reflective opinions speak in terms of the knowledge of "most men," or of "what well-informed persons generally know," or "the knowledge that every intelligent person has."

The information contained in the pamphlet does not fall within those standards.

Nor can it be said that the effect of the drug when taken with an excessive consumption of alcohol can be accurately or readily determined by resorting to the pamphlet. It is appropriate to take judicial notice of a proposition of science, but the Defendant's request does not fall within that category. Rather, the Defendant asks this Court to take judicial notice from the pamphlet of the effect on the Defendant of his using the drug while drinking. It does not follow from the pamphlet what the specific effect of the Defendant's use while drinking might be.

As the court stated in Clark v. South Central Bell Tel. Co. . . . :

> F.R.E. 201 states that facts may be noticed if they are "capable of accurate and ready determination by resort to sources whose accuracy cannot reasonably be questioned." For a Court to notice facts judicially, if they are not matters of general knowledge, the sources of those facts must be placed before the Court. If a party places the source before the Court and requests judicial notice, the Court must take it if the facts are susceptible of judicial notice.

This standard of "indisputability" was discussed in Louisell & Mueller, Federal Evidence, §57, Rule 201, p.437:

> Facts may be indisputable within the meaning of Rule 201 because (even though not generally known) they can be verified by resort to sources whose accuracy cannot reasonably be questioned. At one time courts indulged in the obvious fiction of consulting sources to refresh recollection, but it is clear enough that courts in reality simply inform themselves of facts which nobody is likely to carry around in his head from whatever sources the trial judge deems to be unquestionably accurate. Almanacs, encyclopedias, calendars, historical works and charts tabulating information deduced from the application of the laws of physics form only a part of what must be a list too long to be worth enumerating of sources to which a court may in proper circumstances resort for the purpose of deriving judicially noticeable information.

If the Defendant had submitted information regarding Pamelor that had been obtained from the FDA or a medical dictionary (as he represented it was), then perhaps it would have been admissible. But for this Court to find that the manufacturer's own representations regarding the drug are "sources whose accuracy cannot reasonably be questioned" within the meaning of FRE 201(b) goes far beyond any reported application of that rule. There is no element of objectivity with such an application. In United States v. Houston, . . . the court held that judicial notice could be taken of a two-page publication setting out information pertaining to the background, pharmacological information, pattern of use, and subjective effects of the drug phen-cyclidine, finding that the information was factual and could be readily obtained from the National Institute of Drug Abuse. The court in that case was willing to go beyond the record and do its own independent verification. In this Court's view, the burden is on the party seeking to have the court take judicial notice of the fact to put the sources before the court and establish their complete accuracy.

NOTES AND QUESTIONS

1. As Thirtyacre's lawyer, how would you state the proposition of fact that you would ask the court to judicially notice? Why is this an adjudicative fact?

2. If you sought judicial notice of this fact on behalf of Thirtyacre, what kind of information might you have attempted to present to satisfy FRE 201(b)? What kind of instruction, in a jury trial, would you request from the court if you were able to satisfy FRE 201? And what would you do if the court refused to take judicial notice of this fact?

3. The *Thirtyacre* opinion lists the kinds of sources of information that judges typically use to satisfy the "general knowledge" and "accurate and ready determina-tion" standards of FRE 201(b). The more specifically the facts concern the individual litigant, the more difficult it is to satisfy these standards. Storm Plastics, Inc. v. United States, 770 F.2d 148, 155 (10th Cir. 1985) (trial judge improperly took judicial notice of the quality of plaintiff's fishing lures, as this fact was not generally known in the community nor one capable of accurate determination by plainly accurate sources). If sources are used to establish propositions of generalized background knowledge, then they must be well recognized. United States v. Simon, 842 F.2d 552, 555 (1st Cir. 1988) (trial judge not required to take judicial notice of the fact that Rastafarians use marijuana as part of their religion because this fact is not generally known and the offered sources—a 1967 dissertation and a 1960 research paper—were "hardly sources whose accuracy cannot reasonably be questioned"). And if judges take judicial notice of adjudicative facts on the basis of their own personal experience, they are likely to be reversed. United States v. Lewis, 833 F.2d 1380, 1384 (9th Cir. 1987) (judge erred in finding a confession to be involuntary by taking judicial notice of the effects of general anesthetic following an operation, relying on his own personal experience).

4. Explanation of FRE 201(c) and (e)

Subsection (c) of FRE 201 provides that a court *may* take judicial notice of a fact on its own initiative; the court may determine that a fact should be noticed, and it may obtain information from its own investigation to determine whether the standards of FRE 201(b) are met. The judge in *Thirtyacre* refused to engage in his own search for information concerning the indisputability of the Pamelor pamphlet. He held instead that "the burden is on the party seeking to have the court take judicial notice of the fact to put the sources before the court and establish their complete accuracy." This holding is consistent with FRE 201(c)(1) and (2), which plainly imply that a court is not required to take judicial notice on its own initiative. Under subsection (c)(2), the court *must* take judicial notice of an adjudicative fact *only* when the party seeking notice has provided the information necessary to satisfy FRE 201(b).

FRE 201 contains only minimal direction for the court on the process to be followed before notice of an adjudicative fact is taken. Because of the close connection of these facts to the matters in dispute, they will usually have an immediate impact on the litigants' case. Therefore FRE 201(e) provides that a party, upon timely request, has the right to be heard on the "propriety of taking judicial notice and the nature of the fact to be noticed." For example, if defendant Thirtyacre had produced scientific literature concerning the effects of taking Pamelor with alcohol, the plaintiff could have requested the opportunity to attack the accuracy of defendant's sources or to produce other contradictory information. This opportunity must be given upon the party's request whether the judicial notice was initiated by the opposing party under subsection (c)(1) or the judge under (c)(2). The "opportunity to be heard" does not necessarily mean the right to a formal hearing, but simply the right to object to judicial notice. See American Stores v. Commission of Internal Revenue Service, 170 F.3d 1267 (10th Cir. 1999).

5. Explanation of FRE 201(d) and (f)

a. Judicial Notice of Adjudicative Facts in Civil Cases: Mini Directed Verdicts

Judicial notice of adjudicative facts has two major effects on the civil trial process: (1) It simplifies the jury's factfinding role because it removes a fact from dispute and (2) it relieves a party both from the burden of producing evidence of the noticed fact to the jury and from the threat of having the jury hear contradictory evidence from the opponent. Remember that the party must present evidence *to the judge* that satisfies the standards of FRE 201(b). Under the first sentence of FRE 201(f), once the judge decides that these standards are satisfied, the jury will be instructed that it must accept the noticed fact. The party's evidence need not be presented to the jury; the opponent may present no contradictory evidence; no closing argument need be made in support of the fact; and no argument can be made against it. In effect, the court is directing a verdict on the judicially noticed fact.

b. Judicial Notice of Adjudicative Facts in Criminal Cases: Judicial Comments

Judicial notice in criminal cases poses somewhat different problems from judicial notice in civil cases. The second sentence of FRE 201(f) provides: "In a criminal case, the court must instruct the jury that it *may or may not* accept the noticed fact as conclusive." (Emphasis added.) It may seem contradictory to tell the jury that it "may" accept a fact that has been judicially noticed. After all, judicial notice is supposed to dispose of issues. The explanation for this apparent incongruity is that juries are given greater deference in criminal cases than in civil. Indeed, it is frequently said that there are no directed verdicts against criminal defendants, and as we have just observed, to take binding judicial notice of a fact is to direct a verdict on that fact. Thus, treating judicial notice as binding would seem to conflict with the conventional view of the role of jurors in criminal cases. United States v. Mentz, 840 F.2d 315, 318 (6th Cir. 1988) (a conclusive instruction to the jury on a noticed fact in a criminal case is an error of constitutional magnitude). If the judge takes judicial notice in a criminal case, she will call the noticed fact to the jury's attention in something like the following terms:

> You may accept the court's declaration as evidence and regard as proved the fact or event which has been judicially noticed. You are not required to do so, however, since you are the sole judges of the facts.

United States v. Chapel, 41 F.3d 1338, 1339 (9th Cir. 1994). Such an instruction allows the judge, in effect, to make a nonbinding comment that the judicially noticed fact is obvious, generally known, or indisputable.

c. Timing of Judicial Notice

Pursuant to FRE 201(d), judicial notice may be taken at any time in the proceeding. This means that adjudicative facts may be noticed during pretrial proceedings, such as in motions to dismiss, to narrow the scope of discovery, or for summary judgment. See, e.g., Milo & Gabby, LLC v. Amazon.com, Inc., 12 F. Supp. 3d 1341 (W.D. Wash. 2014) (explaining that district courts may use FRE 201(b) to take judicial notice of documents mentioned in pleadings "when there is no factual dispute about the documents' authenticity or enforceability.") In a jury trial, facts are usually noticed before the court gives its instructions so that the proper instructions may be given. In a bench trial, notice can be taken or refused at any time during the judge's deliberations, as was done in the *Thirtyacre* case.

Judicial Notice to Preserve Civil Verdicts.   At least in civil cases, courts may also take judicial notice after a case has been submitted to the jury, after the jury's verdict has been rendered, or on appeal, even if not requested during the trial. When there is a gap in a winning party's proof, judicial notice of that fact could be taken by either the trial court or the appellate court in order to protect the jury's verdict. If the gap in proof is discovered after a party moves for a judgment as a matter of law, the trial court might be persuaded to take judicial notice of the missing fact by the nonmoving party as a way to fend off the judgment as a matter of law. FRE 201(d) has even been construed to allow an appellate court to take judicial notice where the other criteria for judicial notice are satisfied. See, e.g., Gustafson v. Cornelius Co., 724 F.2d 75, 79 (8th Cir. 1983) (appellate court took judicial notice of an unfair labor practice charge for the purpose of determining date at which a cause of action accrued); Havens Steel Co. v. Randolph Eng'g Co., 813 F.2d 186 (8th Cir. 1987) (appellate court took judicial notice of the average annual prime interest rate in rejecting the defendant's claim that the proof of damages at trial had been too imprecise); but see Colonial Leasing

Co. v. Logistics Control Group Int'l, 762 F.2d 454, 461, *modified*, 770 F.2d 479 (5th Cir. 1985) (taking judicial notice after trial would raise due process concerns).

Judicial Notice to Preserve Criminal Verdicts. Some courts have taken the same verdict-saving approach in criminal cases in which prosecutors have failed to prove the facts necessary for federal jurisdiction. United States v. Lavender, 602 F.2d 639 (4th Cir. 1979) (court took judicial notice that the Blue Ridge Parkway was located in federal territory); United States v. Piggie, 622 F.2d 486, 487-488 (10th Cir. 1980). Proponents of this approach argue that it is consistent with the spirit of judicial notice to promote judicial efficiency by obviating the need for evidentiary proof of irrefutable facts.

But such an approach seems to violate the clear intent of the second sentence of subsection (f), which prohibits binding judicial notice in criminal cases in order to preserve the jury's role to decide all issues of fact in criminal cases. See United States v. Dior, 671 F.2d 351, 358 n.11 (9th Cir. 1982); United States v. Jones, 580 F.2d 219 (6th Cir. 1978).

KEY POINTS

1. FRE 201 provides that courts may take judicial notice of adjudicative facts. Adjudicative facts are those facts that are usually decided by the jury.
2. Facts judicially noticed pursuant to FRE 201(b) must be established as certain beyond reasonable dispute, and this standard of certainty must be satisfied on the basis of general knowledge within the jurisdiction or from sources whose accuracy cannot reasonably be questioned.
3. In civil cases, the judge will instruct the jury that it must accept a judicially noticed fact as true. In criminal cases, the judge will instruct the jury that it may, but need not, accept the noticed fact as true.
4. Facts may be judicially noticed at any time, but if the winning party has failed to prove an essential element at trial, the taking of judicial notice to preserve the winning party's jury verdict may violate the constitutional rights of the opponent in both criminal and civil cases.

NOTES AND QUESTIONS

1. Although the second sentence of FRE 201(f) applies to criminal cases generally, the underlying concern is the supposed tension between binding judicial notice and a *criminal defendant's* right to jury trial. Compare FRE 201(f) with Md. R. Evid. 5-201(g), which makes judicial notice nonbinding only when the noticed fact is "adverse to the defendant."

2. Particularly in light of the fact that courts regularly direct verdicts against criminal defendants by not instructing juries on defenses for which there is insufficient evidence, why is it arguably unconstitutional for courts to take binding judicial notice in criminal

cases? Should it matter whether the noticed fact is a jurisdictional matter (e.g., the location of the crime) or a substantive element (e.g., the value of stolen goods)?

3. Even if binding judicial notice adverse to criminal defendants is not unconstitutional, one may for prudential reasons want to avoid restricting the scope of the jury's factfinding role. If so, would it be preferable to ban any form of "judicial notice" that is adverse to criminal defendants? Consider whether a nonbinding judicial notice instruction like the one quoted at page 872, supra, is likely to contribute to the jury's rational decisionmaking.

4. Since the last sentence of FRE 201(f) calls for what is in effect judicial comment, does FRE 201 imply that all judicial comment in criminal prosecutions must satisfy the certainty requirements of FRE 201(b)?

PROBLEMS

11.1. Review the agricultural waste runoff hypothetical at the beginning of this chapter. What sources might the plaintiff rely upon to request that the court take judicial notice of the amount of rainfall that occurred in the region the year preceding the runoff event? Can the defendant object to judicial notice without having a reasonable basis to dispute the amount of rainfall asserted in plaintiff's request for judicial notice?

11.2. The ship S.S. *Norton* broke from its moorings and ran aground, releasing 200,000 barrels of crude oil into the ocean near Guam. The owner, Kramden, sued the captain and the charterers for negligence, arguing that mooring the ship in Guam during the month of November—the peak of the typhoon season—posed a great danger to both the cargo of oil and the environment. At trial, the judge is asked to take notice that Guam is seriously vulnerable to typhoons, and that the month of November is the peak of the typhoon season. Objection? What kind of sources might be found that would satisfy FRE 201(b)?

11.3. In imposing sanctions against an extremely litigious inmate and issuing an injunction against further filings without paying full filing fees, the trial judge made a finding of fact that the inmate had access to considerable sums of money. That finding was based in part on the judge's judicial notice of a local newspaper article describing the inmate as extremely wealthy and quoting him as saying that he had made thousands of dollars from his extortion activities in prison. Was taking judicial notice proper?

11.4. In an age discrimination suit against Acme Aircraft Corp., defendant claims that the reason plaintiff lost his job was inadequate performance and reduction in the workforce. To support the latter claim, the defendant presents the court with a newspaper article describing widespread layoffs at Acme and asks the court to take judicial notice of the contents of the article. What result?

11.5. In a suit against tobacco companies for injuries related to smoking, the defendants request that the court take judicial notice that since the late 1960s (when plaintiffs began smoking) the health hazards and the addictive nature of smoking have been common knowledge. Are these proper matters for judicial notice?

11.6. The United States brought a civil action against Dr. Jones to recover federal student loans that Jones had received from the National Health Service Corps. Dr. Jones allegedly breached his mandatory four-year contract of employment with a community health center. The issue at trial was whether Dr. Jones left the health center because of a salary dispute or whether he was terminated because of attendance and other problems, which would trigger an obligation to pay back his loans. The district court granted summary judgment in favor of the government by taking judicial notice of factual findings that Jones was terminated for attendance and other problems. These findings had been made in an order entered by another district court in a suit by Jones against the health center. Dr. Jones contests this result on appeal. What result?

11.7. Defendant is charged with assault within federal territory. After proof at trial that Raybrook Federal Prison was owned by the federal government, the district court gave the following instruction that removed the federal jurisdictional element from defendant's assault charge:

> The Government must prove the alleged assault took place within the special maritime and territorial jurisdiction of the United States. This simply means that the alleged assault must have occurred in any lands reserved or acquired for the use of the United States and under the exclusive or concurrent jurisdiction thereof. I charge you now that [Raybrook] is a place that falls within the territorial jurisdiction of the United States. Therefore, if you find beyond a reasonable doubt that the acted [sic] alleged occurred at [Raybrook], the sixth element of the offense has been met.

On appeal, defendant contends that this instruction violated FRE 201(f) and his constitutional right to be convicted by the jury on proof beyond a reasonable doubt. What result?

11.8. Plaintiff has sued defendants alleging that they participated in a scheme to defraud him through the fictitious sale of Nigerian crude oil. Plaintiff asks the trial court to take judicial notice of the following: (1) that at all times pertinent to the lawsuit, there were Nigerian fraud scams perpetrated on people in the United States and other countries in the world, and (2) that the fraud scams involved, among other things, oil deals that never materialized. To support this request for judicial notice plaintiff has provided the trial judge with a congressional report dated December 12, 1995, a Senate committee report, at least two newspaper articles, a videotape from the television news magazine "20/20," a videotape from the television news magazine "60 Minutes," and a videotape from the British Broadcasting Corporation. What result?

B. JUDICIAL NOTICE AS PART OF JUDICIAL DECISIONMAKING

In performing their judicial function, judges must take official account of propositions of law, of generalized knowledge, and of specific facts in many different contexts.

Although the types of propositions, the sources from which they are established, and the uses to which they are put in judicial decisionmaking vary enormously, all of these judicial behaviors are sometimes called "taking judicial notice," even though FRE 201 does not—and often, as a practical matter, could not—apply. For example, if preliminary facts necessary to make admissibility decisions had to meet the certainty standard of FRE 201(b), much currently admissible evidence would be inadmissible. Similarly, if the factual premises underlying a court's interpretation of law had to meet the FRE 201(b) standard, it would be virtually impossible for courts to engage in the process of law interpretation. This section briefly discusses some of the contexts in which judges take official account of facts and of law—sometimes, but not always, under the guise of taking "judicial notice"—without the necessity of complying with FRE 201. As you can imagine, this loose and inconsistent usage of the term *judicial notice* occasionally creates confusion.

A caveat is in order about the materials that follow. Outside the area of adjudicative facts, the term *judicial notice* is most commonly associated with "legislative facts," which we discuss in subsection 2, infra. Keep in mind, though, that (1) there is nothing analytically significant about the use of the term judicial notice for any of the factfinding that we discuss here and (2) there is nothing analytically significant about the distinct categories of judicial fact finding that we describe here. Rather, the controlling and only analytically significant issue should be whether the judge is making a factual finding that would normally be made by a jury or whether the judge is making the finding for some other purpose. In the former situation FRE 201 applies; in the latter, it does not. If there is uncertainty about whether the finding is an adjudicative fact—that is, a "jury issue"—the uncertainty has nothing to do with judicial notice. Rather, the uncertainty is about application of the criteria for allocating fact finding generally between judge and jury.

For the leading scholarly critique of the limited scope of FRE 201 in light of these broader notions of "judicial notice," see Kenneth C. Davis, Judicial Notice, 1969 Law and the Soc. Order 513 (1969); and Dennis J. Turner, Judicial Notice and Federal Rule of Evidence 201—A Rule Ready for Change, 45 U. Pitt. L. Rev. 181 (1983).

1. Judicial Cognizance of Common Knowledge Without Formal Judicial Notice

a. The Jury's General Background Knowledge

We know that when juries decide questions of fact they must rely on their own generalized knowledge and experience to make the inferences necessary to jury reasoning. The jury's background knowledge and experience are largely unexamined by the judicial system. In a few contexts, however, judges do consider what common generalized knowledge the jury can be assumed to have. This is sometimes called taking judicial notice of such common knowledge, although FRE 201 does not apply and the propositions relied on could not possibly satisfy the rule's standards of certainty.

For example, when judges rule on questions of relevance in admitting evidence, they will occasionally articulate the generalized background knowledge that they assume the jurors can use to make the necessary inferences. And when there is a gap in proof to sustain a verdict, the court may find that, based on all the evidence, the jury's background knowledge could fill the gap. In United States v. Luckenbill, 421 F.2d 849 (9th Cir. 1970), the defendant was charged with forcing an accomplice to forge an endorsement on a government check in Spokane, Washington. No evidence was presented that the crime occurred in Spokane, which was necessary for venue. However, references in testimony to areas called "Nine Mile" and "Seven Mile" (areas known to be close to Spokane) were sufficient, the court held, to justify the jury in finding that the crime took place in Spokane.

Consider also the problem of jurors relying on unique personal knowledge or their independent investigatory information. If such independently obtained information is not general or common enough for the judge to assume that reasonable jurors already share it, then its injection into the jury room may violate the principles of public, adversarial proof-taking. In Thomas v. Kansas Power & Light Co., 340 P.2d 379 (Kan. 1959), for example, the court granted a new trial when it discovered that a juror had borrowed a book on electricity and had shared information on the arcing characteristics of electricity with other jurors.

b. Judges' Own Background Knowledge

When judges decide questions of fact, they must draw inferences on the basis of their own generalized knowledge and experience. Commentators sometimes refer to the process of using such background knowledge and experience as judicial notice:

> When the judge or jury use their pre-existing knowledge, they are said to be taking "judicial notice" of the facts thus utilized. Probably 99% of the judicial notice taken could be called "tacit" or "unconscious" judicial notice; that is, the process goes on without anyone being aware that reliance is being placed on extra-record facts. [21 Charles A. Wright & Kenneth W. Graham Jr., Federal Practice and Procedure §5102, at 460 (1990).]

As the Advisory Committee Note to FRE 201(a) makes clear, the rigors of FRE 201 do not apply: "It is apparent that this use of non-evidence facts in evaluating the adjudicative facts of the case is not an appropriate subject for a formalized judicial notice treatment." Unlike juries, however, judges must account for their decisions. Frequently, judges will articulate in their judicial opinions the background generalizations that they have used in their factfinding. Since FRE 201 does not apply, these generalizations are reviewed on appeal for their reasonableness. If reasonable, appellate courts will defer to the trial court's use of them under the deferential standard of "abuse of discretion." But what if a judge's background or experience is relatively unusual, giving the judge a unique factual perspective on the case? Should it be sufficient that the judge's factfinding is reasonable, or should any unique factual assumptions have to satisfy the certainty criteria of FRE 201(b)? Some of these issues are raised in the following case.

IN RE MARRIAGE OF TRESNAK

297 N.W.2d 109 (Iowa 1980)

McCormick, Justice.

This appeal involves a parental dispute over custody of two sons, Rick, age eleven, and Ryan, age nine. The parents are Emil James Tresnak (Jim) and Linda Lou Tresnak (Linda) who were married in 1965. In the August 1979 decree dissolving the marriage, the trial court awarded custody of the children to Jim. Linda appeals. We reverse and remand . . . .

In awarding custody of the children to Jim, the trial court said:

> The Petitioner at this time in life now desires to continue her education by attending law school at the University of Iowa. Although this is commendable insofar as her ambition for a career is concerned, in the opinion of the Court, it is not necessarily for the best interest and welfare of her minor children, who are now ten and eight years of age. Anyone who has attained a legal education can well appreciate the time that studies consume. Although the Petitioner, during her undergraduate work, was able to care for the children while attending the Northeast Missouri University at Kirksville by studying after the children were placed in bed, the study of law is somewhat different in that it usually requires library study, where reference material is required. Also, other than time in class during the day, there will be study periods during the day in the library necessary, as well as in the evening, and which would necessarily require the children being in the hands of a babysitter for many hours a day when not attending school. The weekends are usually occupied by study periods, and although the Petitioner has a high academic ability, she will find that by reason thereof there will be additional activities bestowed upon her, such as becoming a member of a law review, which is time-consuming. Although the Petitioner may believe that she would not have to engage in such, she by not doing so would be interfering with her own achievements for her own benefit and welfare in future years.

In challenging the trial court's reasoning, Linda contends no evidentiary support existed for the court's assumptions about law school and the children's activities. She also contends the assumed facts are not a proper subject of judicial notice. . . .

The only evidence about the demands of law school appeared in Linda's testimony. She acknowledged on cross-examination that law school would require many hours of study. However, she also said she did not expect to leave the children with babysitters often, she would take them to the library with her if necessary, and she did not believe her studies would interfere with her care of the children. Thus, while the record supports the trial court's inference that law school studies would occupy much of Linda's time, it does not lend much support to the court's statements about the necessity of library work away from the children, the likelihood of her involvement in extracurricular activities, or the effect of such factors on her care of the children.

Nor are these matters subject to judicial notice. "To be capable of being judicially noticed a matter must be of common knowledge or capable of certain verification." Motor Club of Iowa v. Department of Transportation, 251 N.W.2d 510, 517 (Iowa 1977). Courts are permitted to dispense with formal proof of matters which everyone knows. In this case, in overruling Linda's motion for new trial, the trial court defended its findings by asserting a "personal acquaintanceship with the studies of law school." However, judicial notice "is limited to what a judge may properly know in his judicial capacity, and he is not authorized to make his (personal) knowledge of a fact not generally or professionally known the basis of his action." Bervid v. Iowa State Tax Commission, 78 N.W.2d 812, 816 (1956). It is common knowledge in the legal profession that law school studies are demanding and time-consuming, but the requirements of a specific law school curriculum are not generally or professionally known.

The trial court's statements about the necessity of extensive library study and likelihood of Linda's work on the law review at the University of Iowa law school are not matters of common knowledge or capable of certain verification within the meaning of the judicial notice principle. Because the statements have only tenuous support in the evidence, they are entitled to little weight in evaluating the merits of the custody dispute. In saying this, however, we do not suggest the court could not consider the demands of law school which were shown in the evidence. . . .

Because either parent would be a good custodian of the children, the decision on the merits is difficult. Linda and Jim are stable and responsible persons who love their children and are capable of giving them adequate care. . . .

It is common knowledge that in many homes today both parents have demanding out-of-home activities, whether in employment, school or community affairs. Neither should necessarily be penalized in child custody cases for engaging in such activities. In this case, Linda seeks a legal education for self-fulfillment and as a means of achieving financial independence. These goals are not inimical to the children's best interests. Because the record shows she is capable of continuing to provide the children with the same high quality of care she has given them in the past, her attendance at law school should not disqualify her from having their custody. We perceive no reason for believing she will not give the children excellent care during her law school years and thereafter.

. . . We believe the long-range best interests of the children will be better served if Linda has their custody. Therefore we reverse the trial court and remand to permit the court to enter appropriate orders relating to child support and visitation.

Reversed and remanded.

NOTES AND QUESTIONS

The appellate court's reliance in *Tresnak* on "common knowledge" seems somewhat ironic, given its discussion of the trial court's decision. What kind of facts had the trial court judicially noticed? Can you tell, based on the appellate opinion, whether FRE 201 should have applied if the action were in federal court? Or was the court taking cognizance of propositions of fact that were not adjudicative facts? Would you say that the real lesson of cases like *Tresnak* is that trial judges should not explain the basis of their reasoning if they wish to avoid being reversed? Is that a disturbing commentary on the legal system?

2. Judicial Cognizance of Legislative Facts

Courts must make factual assumptions to decide law. Thus, judges take cognizance of propositions of fact when they interpret statutes (facts about legislative history or policy, or about how the statute affects the population) and when they develop principles of common law (facts about changed societal or economic conditions that justify a new legal rule). As an example, the Advisory Committee Note to FRE 201(a) cites the Supreme Court case of Hawkins v. United States, 358 U.S. 74 (1958), in which the Court relied on the following proposition to uphold the spousal testimonial privilege: If spouses testify against each other this would "be likely to destroy almost any marriage." Id. at 78. Another frequently cited example is the social science research, showing that segregation creates a feeling of inferiority, relied on in Brown v. Board of Education, 347 U.S. 483, 494 n.11 (1954), to hold that segregated schools are inherently unequal. These propositions are rarely indisputable, and they are necessary for judges to make sense of most questions of legal policy. It is clear from the text of the rule, and from the Advisory Committee Note, that FRE 201 does not apply to judges' use of such facts; and even the rules of evidence do not limit the materials that courts can use to resolve disputed issues of legislative fact.

Judges obtain information about these empirical propositions from their own research and from the parties, either at trial or in briefs to the court. Thus, the parties often do have the opportunity to debate the propriety of the court's reliance on certain legislative facts. However, not all facts necessary to creating law or policy can be put "into a party-prepared record of evidence. Judges . . . cannot confine their thoughts to facts that parties have prepared in a formal record. . . ." 2 Kenneth C. Davis & Richard J. Pierce Jr., Administrative Law Treatise §10.5, at 142 (3d ed. 1994). When judicial use of disputable legislative facts is based on the judges' own independent research, the parties may be excluded from the decisionmaking process. Some commentators have found this to be troublesome:

> We do not claim that Judges cannot rely on a broad range of facts to force the law forward. We suggest only that the parties should be permitted to participate in the march. . . . If a fact or set of facts is likely to be critical to a decision on the law to be applied to parties, there is every reason to want the parties to be heard on the factual question. Evidence need not always be taken. Briefs may work better in many situations. But some chance for the parties to be heard on decisive legislative facts is desirable. [1 Stephen A. Saltzberg, Michael M. Martin & Daniel J. Capra, Federal Rules of Evidence Manual 125 (7th ed. 1998).]

Although the Federal Rules do not expressly authorize judicial notice of legislative facts, the reality that courts must make factual assumptions to decide legal questions—under the rubric of "legislative fact"—has been recognized in numerous judicial decisions. Therefore the distinction between "adjudicative" and "legislative" facts can have significant practical impact on whether and how a party meets its burden of proof. Consider United States v. Gould, 536 F.2d 216 (8th Cir. 1976), in which the prosecution's expert failed to provide testimony that the cocaine hydrochloride found in defendants' possession was a derivative of coca leaves, as required to establish a violation of the drug laws then in force. The appellate court affirmed the conviction on the ground that the trial judge had permissibly taken judicial notice of a legislative fact. Not only did this obviate the need for expert testimony linking cocaine hydrochloride to cocaine, but the court could simply issue a jury instruction permitting the jury to so find without going through the formalities of FRE 201, which apply only to adjudicative facts:

> The precise line of demarcation between adjudicative facts and legislative facts is not always easily identified[.] "Legislative facts . . . do not relate specifically to the activities or characteristics of the litigants. . . ." Legislative facts are established truths, facts or pronouncements that do not change from case to case but apply universally, while adjudicative facts are those developed in a particular case.
>
> . . . When a court attempts to ascertain the governing law in a case for the purpose of instructing the jury, it must necessarily rely upon facts which are unrelated to the activities of the immediate parties. These extraneous, yet necessary, facts fit within the definition of legislative facts and are an indispensable tool used by judges when discerning the applicable law through interpretation. The District Court, therefore, was judicially noticing such a legislative fact when it recognized that cocaine hydrochloride is derived from coca leaves. . . . [536 F.2d at 219-220.]

NOTES AND QUESTIONS

1. Was the result in *Gould* correct, or was the court struggling to resolve the tension created when indisputable facts are essential elements in criminal cases? How does one determine whether a fact is legislative or adjudicative? Should the result in *Gould* depend upon the generality or universality of the fact that cocaine hydrochloride is a derivative of coca leaves, the incongruity of giving a nonbinding judicial notice instruction, the intent of congress, or something else?

2. Reconsider the instruction given in Problem 11.7 at page 875. Is this instruction a violation of FRE 201(f)? Is the federal status of Raybrook prison an adjudicative or a legislative fact?

3. In United States v. Dior, 671 F.2d 351 (9th Cir. 1982), the court considered whether the American-Canadian exchange rate could be classified as a legislative fact. Should it be under Gould? If not, then could the jurors be permitted to find that the illegally imported goods (worth $13,690 in Canadian dollars) were worth $5,000 or more in U.S. currency, based on their own generalized knowledge? The dissent in *Dior* suggested they could:

> [T]he only issue is whether the jurors could find beyond a reasonable doubt that $13,690 Canadian dollars equaled $5,000 American dollars at the time of the theft.
>
> Seattle, the place of trial, is approximately 100 miles from the long Canadian border. The two countries share a long history of cultural, personal and trade relations sustained and encouraged by easy and warm reciprocal travel on many levels. They interconnect by multi-lane superhighways. Out of this proximity and close relationship the jurors, as people of both countries everywhere, could easily have possessed the elementary and practical knowledge of the worth of Canadian currency. [671 F.2d at 359.]

4. What if a frustrated juror deciding the *Dior* case looked up the American-Canadian exchange rate for the date of the alleged crime and reported this fact to the rest of the jury during deliberations? If Dior is convicted, is the juror's conduct grounds for a new trial? Would your answer be the same if the trial judge in a bench trial had looked up the exchange rate?

3. Judicial Notice of Substantive Law

A court may "judicially notice," or is "presumed to know," the law of its own jurisdiction, which governs the cases before it. Obviously the judge investigates such law through traditional legal research. Questions of sister state and foreign law, however, have proved more troublesome. Common law rules required parties to plead and prove the content of such law. This requirement has been eliminated in the federal courts by Fed. R. Civ. P. 44.1 and Fed. R. Crim. P. 26.1, which commit the question of foreign law to the judge, whose "determination shall be treated as a ruling on a question of law," but many states still possess the common law rule.

KEY POINT

Courts use propositions of generalized knowledge in their own factfinding. Courts also use propositions of specific or general fact when interpreting legal standards and applying and developing rules of law. FRE 201 does not apply to judicial use of facts in these contexts.

PROBLEMS

11.9. To establish the unavailability for the purpose of offering testimony pursuant to the declaration against interest exception to the hearsay rule, the defendant offers affidavits of several individuals who state that the declarant is living someplace in Milan. In ruling that the hearsay testimony is admissible the trial judge states, "On the basis of the uncontested affidavits I find that the declarant is living in Milan, and I take judicial notice of the fact that Milan is in Italy, far beyond the jurisdiction of this court." Following a verdict for the defendant, the plaintiff appeals on the ground that the trial judge's taking of judicial notice was improper. According to the plaintiff, the declarant's unavailability is subject to reasonable dispute because "Milan" could refer to the small farming community of Milan (pronounced MY-lan), which is only several miles away. Assuming that the hearsay testimony is critical to the defendant's defense, what result?

11.10. The local M&P Grocery Store has sued Harold Hays for food purchased on credit by his estranged wife, Stella. M&P bases its claim on a state statute that makes husbands liable for all "necessaries" purchased by their wives. It is clear from the statute that food falls within the category of necessaries. At trial M&P

establishes that Stella did in fact make the purchases and that she was married to Harold at the time. Harold establishes that he did not authorize or benefit from any of the purchases. The judge takes the matter under advisement and eventually issues the following opinion:

> The statute was enacted at a time when husbands were the primary breadwinners; its purpose was to ensure that merchants would not deny wives the necessities of life. Today, we live in a much different world. I take judicial notice that the statute in question actually perpetuates the stereotypical notions of women as second class citizens. As a result I declare the statute unconstitutional under the state constitution's due process and equal protection provisions.

On appeal the plaintiff claims that the judicial notice was improper because the matter noticed does satisfy the certainty criteria in FRE 201(b). Plaintiff further claims that because there was no mention of the statute's possible unconstitutionality or the judicially notice fact at trial, plaintiff was denied the FRE 201(e) opportunity to be heard. What result?

11.11. Reconsider Problem 11.8 at page 875, where the plaintiff asked the court to take judicial notice of Nigerian fraud scams throughout the world. The problem is based on Qualley v. Clo-Tex Int'l, Inc., 212 F.3d 1123 (8th Cir. 2000). The trial judge granted the judicial notice request, and the jury returned a verdict for the plaintiff. The court of appeals, relying on *Gould* and quoting a portion of the excerpted passage, supra, held that the facts were legislative facts:

> The facts of which the trial court took judicial notice did not specifically concern the parties before the court. The trial court acknowledged that the evidence underlying the noticed facts "[had] to do with the pretty much universal publicity that was out about what Nigeria was doing. . . ." The videotapes contained nothing involving anyone with whom [plaintiff] had communicated. Nor were the other exhibits considered "specific to . . . others [involved in the scheme . . .]." . . . Thus . . . [the facts] were "legislative" rather than "adjudicative," and were therefore outside the scope of [FRE 201]. [212 F.3d at 1128.]

The court of appeals then concluded that the trial judge's action was prejudicial error:

> [B]oth during the trial and in the final instructions, the trial court instructed the jury pursuant to Federal Rule of Evidence 201[(f)] that it must accept the judicially noticed facts as proven. Thus, the trial court injected legislative facts—facts not within the jury's factfinding province—into the jury's deliberations by telling the jury that they must treat those facts as conclusively proven. [Id. at 1132.]

What do you think of the court's reasoning? The result?

11.12. Perez, an illegal alien, is seeking review of his denial of political asylum. The asylum request is based on his claim that if he is returned to his native country, he will be persecuted because of his religious affiliation. He claims to be a Jehovah's Witness. The immigration judge rejected Perez's asylum request on the ground that Perez had failed to establish the sincerity of his claim to religion and membership in the Jehovah's Witnesses. The judge's decision rested in part on the following: "In this proceeding Perez took the standard oath to testify truthfully. I take judicial notice that Jehovah's Witnesses are prohibited from swearing under oath." The judge went on to explain that "many Jehovah's Witnesses who have appeared before this court have declined to take the oath and have indicated that it is prohibited by their religion to swear under God or swear under oath." Was the judge's action proper?

11.13. In United States v. Jakobetz, 955 F.2d 786, 799-800 (2d Cir. 1992), the district court had conducted an extended hearing on the admissibility of DNA evidence against the defendant. The court heard nine experts, five for the government and four for the defense. The appellate court held:

> Given the findings made by the district court, and after careful consideration and review by this court, it appears that in future cases with a similar evidentiary issue, a court could properly take judicial notice of the general acceptability of the general theory and the use of these specific [laboratory] techniques. . . . Beyond such judicial notice, the threshold for admissibility should require only a preliminary showing of reliability of the particular data to be offered. . . .

Is this a proper application of FRE 201? Is the "general acceptance" (under *Frye*) or the "validity" (under *Daubert*) of the basic scientific theory and techniques underlying DNA profiling an adjudicative fact?

11.13. Lewis was convicted of carjacking in the Virgin Islands. The statute is applicable only to motor vehicles that have been "transported, shipped, or received in interstate or foreign commerce." To establish this element the prosecution relied on the testimony of Edgar Ames. Ames described himself as a police officer and lifelong resident of the Virgin Islands. He testified that no motor vehicles are manufactured in the Virgin Islands that all motor vehicles have to be shipped to the islands. On appeal Lewis claims that there is insufficient evidence of interstate or foreign commerce. He argues that Ames was not qualified to testify to this element merely because he was a lifelong resident of the Virgin Islands and that no foundation was laid for his testimony. In affirming the conviction, the court of appeals stated:

> We take judicial notice of the fact that the United States Virgin Islands consist of three main islands, which are closely grouped and have an area of only 136 square miles. We further take judicial notice of the fact that a police officer and life long resident of a place of this size has a sufficient basis to testify as to whether any motor vehicle manufacturing facilities are located there.

Was the court's action proper?

ASSESSMENTS

A-11.1 FRE 201. In deciding a motion to transfer venue in a civil case, a district court used Google Maps to estimate the distance and driving times for potential witnesses. Which statement is the most accurate?

    A. This was a proper use of judicial notice only if the parties were given an opportunity to be heard on the issue if requested in a timely manner.

    B. This was a proper use of judicial notice even if the parties were never given an opportunity to be heard because the accuracy of the information could not reasonably be doubted.

    C. This was an improper use of judicial notice because it took place before trial.

    D. This was an improper use of judicial notice because neither party requested it.

A-11.2 FRE 201. Defendant is on trial for illegally manufacturing methamphetamine. At trial, Defendant denied any involvement and testified that he has no knowledge of how to manufacture the drug and no knowledge of how to obtain the necessary equipment. The prosecution requested that the court take judicial notice of the fact that recipes and instructions for manufacturing the drug are readily available on the Internet, as are websites offering to sell the necessary equipment. The court took judicial notice of these facts and instructed the jury that it must accept these facts as proven. Which statement is the most accurate?

    A. The trial court abused its discretion in taking judicial notice of these facts.

    B. The trial court abused its discretion in instructing the jury.

    C. Judicial notice and the instruction were proper.

    D. Judicial notice was improper because this was a criminal case.

A-11.3 FRE 201. TRUE or FALSE: In civil cases, judicial notice is mandatory if a party requests it and supplies the court with the information necessary for determining the accuracy of the facts at issue.

ANSWERS

A-11.1. The best answer is **A**. Under FRE 201, the court may take judicial notice at any stage of the proceeding and may do so on its own. Therefore, C and D are incorrect. However, the court must allow the parties to be heard on the issue, if they make a timely request. Therefore, B is incorrect.

A-11.2. The best answer is **B**. Judicial notice is permissible in criminal cases, if the other criteria in FRE 201 are satisfied. However, the court must instruct the jury that it may or may not accept the judicially noticed fact as conclusive. A is incorrect because the judge could accurately and readily determine whether such websites exist. C is incorrect because the instruction was erroneous. D is incorrect because courts may take judicial notice in criminal cases.

A-11.3. TRUE. Courts must take judicial notice if requested and supplied with the necessary information. FRE 201(c)(2).

CHAPTER TWELVE

PRIVILEGES

A. THE LAW OF PRIVILEGE

1. A General Introduction

Most rules of evidence are designed to facilitate the factfinding process, but rules creating evidentiary privilege are different. For the most part, they exclude relevant evidence in order to promote extrinsic policies unrelated to accurate factfinding. Their primary aim is to protect certain relationships and interests in the world outside the courtroom that are deemed of sufficient importance to justify the costs imposed on the judicial process through the loss of useful evidence. Lawmakers also set up privileges to encourage socially beneficial activities that otherwise would not take place.

The scope of privilege law is quite broad. Some privileges have a direct constitutional basis: examples are the Fifth Amendment privilege against self-incrimination (the Fourth Amendment exclusionary rule for evidence obtained as the result of an illegal search and seizure has aspects of a privilege) and the executive privilege claimed on various occasions by presidents of the United States. These rules typically are studied in criminal procedure and constitutional law courses and they will be addressed in this chapter only where they intersect with privileges that have no constitutional pedigree. Our main focus will be on evidentiary privileges originating from common law and statutes. Many of these privileges are designed to protect confidential communications, thereby encouraging the free flow of information in certain relationships. This group includes the most prevalent privileges: the attorney-client, physician-patient, psychotherapist-patient, priest-penitent, and marital communications privilege. Still other privileges are intended to prevent interference with certain favored relationships, such as the marital testimonial privilege. Finally, privileges also exist to protect against the disclosure of specific types of information, such as privileges for the identity of news reporters' sources, diplomatic secrets, and other sensitive government information (the identity of police informants is an example).

The traditional justification for rules of privilege is the utilitarian argument espoused by John Henry Wigmore. This argument has been most commonly advanced in support of the confidential communication privileges. It is based on an underlying, untested empirical assumption: The benefit derived from recognizing a privilege—such as candid communication between attorney and client or between spouses—outweighs the cost of barring relevant evidence. The argument rests on an empirical assumption about how the existence of the privilege affects individual behavior. Without the protection of the privilege, Wigmore argued, communication will be impeded and certain relationships, such as attorney-client and physician-patient, will be jeopardized. This justification has been widely accepted by the courts and has greatly influenced the development of the law of privilege. Wigmore's conditions for the establishment of a privilege flow directly from his justification for privileges: (1) the communications must originate in a *confidence* that they will not be disclosed; (2) the element of *confidentiality must be essential* to the full and satisfactory maintenance of the relation between the parties; (3) the *relation* must be one that in the opinion of the community ought to be *sedulously fostered*; and (4) the injury that would inure to the relation by the disclosure of the communications must be *greater than the benefit* thereby gained for the correct disposal of the litigation. 8 John Henry Wigmore, Evidence §2285, at 527 (John T. McNaughton ed., rev. ed. 1961).

Another justification for privileges originates from the economics of rational choice. This justification is theoretical, rather than empirical: It presupposes that rational actors always try to generate evidence that might help them in future litigation and to avoid disclosure of unfavorable evidence. See Gideon Parchomovsky & Alex Stein, The Distortionary Effect of Evidence on Primary Behavior, 124 Harv. L. Rev. 518 (2010). A rational self-interested actor would disclose unfavorable information while interacting with his attorney, spouse, psychotherapist, or another professional only when his benefit from disclosure is greater than the loss. When the loss is greater than the benefit, the actor will keep the information to himself, and it is here where privileges come in handy. By granting the actor confidentiality protection, they incentivize him to engage in a beneficial exchange of information that otherwise would not take place. Such privileges therefore operate at a zero cost to factfinding because they suppress the same information that they bring into existence.

A distinct privacy-based rationale has also emerged for certain privileges. Rather than focus on the inducement of conduct in certain relationships, the privacy argument emphasizes the protection that privileges afford to individual privacy. According to this rationale, the confidentiality of communications is a privacy interest that itself acts as a legitimate constraint on the truth-finding function of trial. An advocate of the privacy rationale would argue, for example, that the existence of a marital communications privilege may have little, if any, impact on the extent to which spouses engage in confidential communications; nonetheless, the privilege is socially desirable because it provides recognition of and protection for the privacy of intimate aspects of the marital relationship. For an argument reconciling the traditional utilitarian justification and the privacy rationale, see Developments in the Law—Privileged

Communications, 98 Harv. L. Rev. 1450, 1481-1486 (1985).[1] The existence and scope of privileges vary from jurisdiction to jurisdiction. Under FRE 501 (reproduced in subsection 3, infra), federal common law governs the privileges applicable in federal question and criminal cases, while state law determines the privileges applicable in diversity actions and other suits decided by state law, for example, suits filed pursuant to the Federal Tort Claims Act of 1946. In state courts and in federal cases applying state law, the law of privilege is a varied collection of rules, created mostly by the state legislatures.

2. The Unique Operation of Privilege Rules

Regardless of the particular justification, rules of privilege operate differently from other rules of evidence in at least two and sometimes three respects. First, since the objective of the privilege would be frustrated by forced disclosure of privileged information at any time, the rules of privilege apply to all stages of judicial proceedings. Other rules of evidence are designed primarily to enhance the accuracy of factfinding, particularly in jury trials, and they therefore do not apply to various preliminary or relatively informal aspects of the adjudicatory process. For example, FRE 1101 provides that the rules of evidence, other than those relating to privileges, do not apply to FRE 104(a) preliminary fact determinations, grand jury proceedings, and other specified, relatively informal proceedings.

Second, the person who can claim or invoke a rule of privilege to exclude evidence will not necessarily be one of the litigants. Because the rules of evidence other than the rules of privilege are designed to enhance the factfinding process, they exist for the benefit of and may be invoked only by the parties to the dispute. By contrast, rules of privilege exist for the benefit of the persons whose communications or actions are covered by a privilege. Only these intended beneficiaries of a privilege (or persons acting on their behalf), who need not be parties to the action, can claim or forgo a privilege.

The third way in which rules of privilege sometimes differ—and perhaps should always differ—from other evidentiary rules relates to the impact on appeal of an erroneous trial court decision regarding admissibility of allegedly privileged information. If the trial judge erroneously excludes the evidence, the party who would have benefited from the evidence will be able to raise the improper exclusion on appeal. As is true whenever a judge erroneously excludes relevant evidence, the exclusion deprives the factfinder of information that would have enhanced the likelihood of a factually accurate result; this type of error, if serious enough, can be cured on appeal by reversal and retrial. And if a trial judge erroneously admits evidence, inflammatory character evidence, for example, the result often is to interject prejudicial or misleading information into the trial.

---

1. In Chapter Six, we noted that similar utilitarian and nonutilitarian justifications provide partial support for some of the relevance rules. See pages 360, 364, 367 supra.

By contrast, a trial judge's erroneous admission of privileged information results in the jurors having before them more relevant, helpful information than they would otherwise have had. The only impact of such an error is to enhance the likelihood of a factually accurate result. Thus, even if the person entitled to invoke the privilege happens to be one of the litigants, the injury from the erroneous admission of the evidence does not adversely affect the person's underlying substantive entitlement or liability. Moreover, the injury caused by the wrongful denial of the privilege is complete at the time the privileged information is presented to the factfinder. Reversal on appeal cannot un-ring the bell. Unless there is reason to believe that the possibility of reversal on appeal is a desirable way to make litigants and trial judges more sensitive to and more prone to accept claims of privilege, the error should not be grounds for reversal. And if the erroneous denial of a privilege claim is recognized as a possible ground for reversal on appeal, it should make no difference whether the person entitled to claim the privilege happens to be one of the litigants. Nonetheless, appellate courts do entertain such grounds for reversal, particularly in situations in which the appellant is also the primary beneficiary of the privilege, but they typically do not analyze carefully what interests are being vindicated.

A similar question relates to the timing of an appeal. In Mohawk Industry Inc. v. Carpenter, the District Court found that Mohawk had waived the attorney-client privilege, and Mohawk sought to appeal that decision through a collateral order before proceeding with the remainder of the trial. After dismissal at the appellate level, the Supreme Court addressed whether an allegedly erroneous admission of evidence, specifically when adverse to the attorney-client privilege, "qualifies for immediate appeal under the collateral order doctrine." 558 U.S. 100 (2009). Justice Sotomayor wrote that "[It does] not. Postjudgment appeals, together with other review mechanisms, suffice to protect the rights of litigants and preserve the vitality of the attorney-client privilege." The Court did not address the effect its decision would have on litigants and trial judges, but instead focused on the effects delayed review would have on the privilege versus the cost of allowing immediate appeal. In denying review, the Court reasoned that *ex ante* incentives for clients to have open conversations with counsel are not reduced by deferring review until final judgment, while the cost on the system of allowing immediate appeal would be significant. Note, however, that immediate appeal can still be available when a witness holding the allegedly privileged information disobeys the court's order and is held in contempt: The witness can then appeal the contempt order. In re Grand Jury, 705 F.3d 133, 137 (3d Cir. 2012).

3. Historical Background and Current Status of Privilege Rules

The earliest recognized privileges, the attorney-client, priest-penitent, and marital privileges, were judge made.[2] The attorney-client privilege, which has Roman law roots, finds its first expressions in the common law in the sixteenth century. The

---

2. For a more comprehensive historical analysis, see 21 Charles A. Wright & Kenneth W. Graham Jr., Federal Practice and Procedure: Evidence §5001-5005 (1977 & Supp. 2001), and Lawrence Meir Friedman, A History of American Law 134-137 (1973).

priest-penitent privilege was recognized by English courts before the Reformation and possibly after the Reformation as well. Robert John Araujo, S.J., International Tribunals and Rules of Evidence: The Case for Respecting and Preserving the "Priest-Penitent" Privilege Under International Law, 15 Am. U. Int'l L. Rev. 639, 648-649 (2000). The privilege of a witness spouse not to testify against a party spouse, which we will refer to as the marital testimonial privilege, also dates back to the sixteenth century. The origins of this privilege are obscure, although the privilege is frequently associated with the general common law rule of competency that prevented interested parties from testifying as witnesses. By contrast, the privilege for confidential communications between spouses received wide recognition in the later part of the nineteenth century, and it is frequently said to have common law origins. The privilege, however, received substantial support and recognition through legislative action both in this country and in England. We discuss these two privileges in Section D.

During the last half of the nineteenth century, courts became increasingly reluctant to expand existing privileges or to create new ones. Since that time the fashioning of privileges has become primarily—but not exclusively—a legislative matter. For example, the physician-patient privilege is a creature of the legislature, not the common law. As a result of such statutory revision of evidence law, privilege law varies widely from state to state.

Significantly, a detailed law of privileges has not been codified by the Federal Rules of Evidence. As drafted by the Advisory Committee and proposed by the Supreme Court, the Proposed Federal Rules of Evidence set forth nine discrete privileges governing: (i) required reports; (ii) attorney-client confidential communications; (iii) psychotherapist-patient confidential communications; (iv) prevention of spousal testimony; (v) clergy-communicant confidential communications; (vi) political vote; (vii) trade secrets; (viii) state secrets and other official information; and (ix) the identity of an informer.[3] Noticeably absent were the physician-patient, marital confidential communication, and journalist's privileges. Moreover, Proposed FRE 501 made it clear that, in the absence of a constitutional mandate, courts were not at liberty to alter the list.

Once submitted to Congress, the proposed rules excited considerable controversy and criticism, culminating in a congressional decision to delete the proposed rules relating to privilege. In its place, Congress enacted one general privilege rule, FRE 501, updated in 2009 to read:

The common law—as interpreted by United States courts in the light of reason and experience—governs a claim of privilege unless any of the following provides otherwise:

- the United States Constitution;
- a federal statute; or
- rules prescribed by the Supreme Court.

But in a civil case, state law governs privilege regarding a claim or defense for which state law supplies the rule of decision.

3. See Proposed FRE 502-510 and Advisory Committee Notes, 51 F.R.D. 360-380 (1971).

At the same time, Congress revoked the Supreme Court's rule-making power with respect to rules of privilege. This new Enabling Act stated that "[a]ny . . . amendment creating, abolishing, or modifying a privilege shall have no force or effect unless it shall be approved by act of Congress." 28 U.S.C. §2076 (1976). Note that this provision applies only to statutory amendments of privileges and that the Supreme Court still has the power to devise *common law* rules of evidence for federal courts, pursuant to Article III §1 of the Constitution, as interpreted in McNabb v. United States, 318 U.S. 332, 340-347 (1943), and Johnson v. United States, 318 U.S. 189, 198-199 (1943). Under FRE 501, the Supreme Court's power to create and develop evidentiary privileges as a matter of federal common law has become crucial.

In contrast to the proposed rules, FRE 501 provides for fluidity in the federal law of privilege. FRE 501's reference to "principles of the common law . . . interpreted . . . in light of reason and experience" grants courts discretion both to modify common law privileges and to create new ones:

> In rejecting the proposed rules and enacting Rule 501, Congress manifested an affirmative intention not to freeze the law of privilege. Its purpose rather was to "provide the courts with the flexibility to develop rules of privilege on a case-by-case basis" and to leave the door open to change. Trammel v. United States, 445 U.S. 40, 47 (1980), quoting Statement by Representative Hungate, 120 Cong. Rec. 40,891 (1974).

In accordance with this mandate, the Supreme Court, as we shall see shortly, has substantially narrowed the scope of one common law privilege.[4] The Supreme Court, and lower courts as well, have also recognized new privileges.[5] Although courts have referred to the proposed rules in deciding privilege questions, such rules have not controlled the development of the federal law of privileges. Although most states, 42 to date, have adopted rules of evidence modeled after the Federal Rules, the failure of Congress to enact specific rules of privilege has contributed to less uniformity among the states in this area of evidence law. Approximately one-third of the states that have promulgated rules of evidence since the adoption of the Federal Rules have followed their lead and omitted specific privilege provisions. In these states, the preexisting statutory and common law rules of privilege govern. Most of the remaining states have tended to use as models the Proposed Federal Rules relating to privilege or the privilege provisions in the Revised Uniform Rules of Evidence (1974) (a variation from the'Proposed Federal Rules[6]). States using either model have not been reluctant

---

4. See Trammel v. United States, page 962, infra.
5. See, e.g., Jaffee v. Redmond, 518 U.S. 1 (1996) (recognizing psychotherapist-patient privilege—*Jaffee* is reproduced at page 972, infra); In re Grand Jury Investigation, 918 F.2d 374 (3d Cir. 1990) (recognizing clergy-communicant privilege; Cusumano v. Microsoft Corp., 162 F.3d 708 (1st Cir. 1998) (acknowledging similarity of academic research and work product of journalists, thus recognizing limited scholar's privilege); In re Zuniga, 714 F.2d 632 (6th Cir. 1983) (acknowledging but not applying psychotherapist-patient privilege); In re Agosto, 553 F. Supp. 1298 (D. Nev. 1983) (recognizing parent-child privilege).
6. See generally 3 Jack B. Weinstein & Margaret A. Berger, Weinstein's Federal Evidence §§501.02-501.04 (Joseph M. McLaughlin ed., 2d ed. 1997).

to deviate from it.[7] Within the fluid, bifurcated, system of privilege rules, new privileges can spread among jurisdictions, gradually gaining or losing recognition over time. An interesting example of a privilege not recognized at common law, but slowly gaining acceptance, is the parent-child privilege. Under Wigmore's utilitarian test and the privacy-based rationale discussed above, this privilege has obvious appeal. There is currently no federal parent-child privilege, but a few states recognize some form of the privilege and it seems to be gaining support with federal legislators. See Section G at page 999, infra, for a discussion of the evolution of the parent-child privilege.

As we already mentioned, FRE 501 created a bifurcated system of privilege rules. In the situations in which state law supplies the rule of decision, such as diversity cases, state rules of privilege apply even though the case is in federal district court. In the situations in which federal law governs, the common law determines the applicable rules of privilege. This system is designed to protect state policies concerning privilege, but it does so only to a degree. If a case is not based on state law, state privileges do not apply, and information that a state would immunize from disclosure will be disclosed unless there is a corresponding federal privilege (which often there is not). For an example, see United States v. Schoenheinz, 548 F.2d 1389 (9th Cir. 1977) (holding that an employer-stenographer privilege available under Oregon law did not apply to a proceeding to enforce an IRS summons). Cases involving supplemental jurisdiction (pendent and ancillary jurisdiction) can pose particular problems, because the same case will have both federal and state claims. The typical resolution is to apply federal privilege law to all claims. See Hancock v. Hobbs, 967 F.2d 462 (11th Cir. 1992).

B. GENERAL STRUCTURE OF PRIVILEGES

1. Holder of the Privilege

A critically important concept in dealing with rules of privilege is that of the "holder" of a privilege—the person to whom in a sense the privilege "belongs." Since the attorney-client relationship exists for the benefit of the client, for example, the client is the holder of the privilege. The holder is entitled to claim the privilege and only the holder may waive a privilege. Once the holder has waived a privilege, no other person can invoke it.

The person who holds a privilege will not necessarily be one of the litigants. Nonparty witnesses may hold privileges that allow them to withhold evidence. Jurisdictions sometimes differ as to who holds a given privilege. Within the marital privilege, for example, the holder may be the spouses jointly, the communicating spouse, the witness spouse, or the party spouse. Section D at page 956, infra, discusses some of the reasons behind, and the implications of, locating the marital privilege with one or both spouses.

---

7. See generally 1 Gregory P. Joseph & Stephen A. Saltzburg, Evidence in America: The Federal Rules in the States, Ch. 23-24 (1987).

2. Invocation

A person other than the holder may be able to invoke the privilege on the holder's behalf. For example, a nonparty eyewitness to the event that is the subject of litigation may have made a confidential communication to his or her attorney for the purpose of obtaining legal advice about the event. The out-of-court communication of some historical fact, of course, is hearsay, but the communication may fall within a hearsay exception. Assume, for example, that the declaration is an excited utterance, or that the declarant is presently unavailable and the communication is a declaration against interest. The nonparty declarant may invoke the privilege; and in the absence of the declarant, the declarant's attorney may invoke the privilege *on behalf of* the declarant. If the declarant has expressed a desire not to claim the privilege, however, nobody can invoke the privilege.

Typically, if the holder of a privilege is unavailable to claim the privilege, individuals acting on behalf of the holder or the holder's estate, such as the holder's conservator or guardian, may claim the privilege. In the case of privileges covering conversations between a patient or client and a professional, the professional may claim the privilege on behalf of the patient or client. For example, in the physician-patient relationship, if the patient-holder has not specifically waived the privilege, the doctor may be able to claim the privilege on the patient's behalf. In some instances, as in the attorney-client relationship, the professional is obligated by rules of professional conduct to maintain confidentiality where the client has not expressed an intent to waive his privilege. In addition, there is precedent permitting the trial judge to invoke a privilege on behalf of an absent holder.[8] Interesting questions sometimes arise when the holder of the privilege is an entity, such as a corporation or governmental agency, rather than an individual. In Nixon v. Administrator of General Services, 433 U.S. 425 (1977), the former President sought to invoke the executive privilege "against the very Executive Branch in whose name the privilege is invoked." The Presidential Recordings and Materials Preservation Act required the former President to deliver presidential papers and tape recordings to an archivist of the Executive Branch to be screened and cataloged. Nixon resisted turning the materials over and invoked the presidential privilege. The Supreme Court held that the "privilege survives the individual President's tenure" but that the expectation of the confidentiality of executive communications is "subject to erosion over time after an administration leaves office." Though the Court allowed Nixon to invoke the privilege on behalf of the government, it upheld the Act as facially constitutional because the screening by the archivist would be but a "limited intrusion by personnel in the Executive Branch sensitive to executive concerns." It is unclear whether the former President would have been allowed to invoke the privilege if the Office of the President had attempted to waive it.

---

8. See, e.g., Coles v. Harsch, 129 Or. 11, 30-31, 276 P.2d 248, 255 (1929). Judge Weinstein and Professor Berger have suggested that this is an inherent judicial power that is not abrogated by the failure of a rule specifically to mention the authority of the judge to act on the holder's behalf. 3 Jack B. Weinstein & Margaret A. Berger, Weinstein's Federal Evidence §503.20[3] (Joseph M. McLaughlin ed., 2d ed. 1997).

In the corporate setting, some courts have struggled with whether an attorney may invoke the attorney-client privilege on behalf of the client-corporation when shareholders seek disclosure of communications between corporate officers and corporate attorneys. In Fausek v. White, 965 F.2d 126 (6th Cir. 1992), the defendant and majority shareholder of the corporation, Robert E. White, appealed from a district court judgment denying his claim of attorney-client privilege in an action alleging securities violations. The plaintiffs, former shareholders, brought suit against White alleging that he had abused his position to their financial detriment. The plaintiffs subpoenaed the corporation's attorney to testify about communications he had had with White but the attorney resisted, asserting the attorney-client privilege on behalf of the corporation. The appellate court affirmed the lower court, holding that the corporation could not claim the attorney-client privilege because it owed fiduciary duties to the plaintiffs and the latter had shown "good cause" for not permitting defendant to rely on the privilege.

The court provided a long list of factors for determining whether there is "good cause" to recognize an exception to the attorney-client privilege, including the

> number of shareholders and the percentage of stock they represent; . . . the nature of the shareholders' claim and whether it is obviously colorable; the apparent necessity or desirability of the shareholders having the information and the availability of it from other sources; . . . the extent to which the communication is identified versus the extent to which the shareholders are blindly fishing; the risk of revelation of trade secrets or other information in whose confidentiality the corporation has an interest for independent reasons.

The Fifth Circuit took a similar approach in Garner v. Wolfinbarger, 430 F.2d 1093 (5th Cir. 1970), and Ward v. Succession of Freeman, 854 F.2d 780 (5th Cir. 1988), but the Ninth Circuit drew a distinction between derivative suits brought by current shareholders and class actions brought by past shareholders and refused to recognize the exception in Weil v. Investment/Indicators, Research & Management, 647 F.2d 18 (9th Cir. 1981). For further discussion, see Keith W. Johnson, Fausek v. White: The Sixth Circuit Garners Support for a Good Cause Exception to the Attorney-Client Privilege, 18 Dayton L. Rev. 313 (1993). For more discussion on the derivative suit distinction, see Paul R. Rice, Attorney-Client Privilege in the U.S., Cause to Overcome Privilege—Limitations on Applicability of Garner—Must the Action Be Derivative for Garner Rule to Apply? ACPRIV-FED §8:20 (2010).

Another related subtlety of privileges is the ability of third parties to invoke them after the holder's death. Though confidential communications privileges are generally thought to survive the death of a holder, they may not always be invoked. The personal representative of the deceased, for example, may choose not to invoke the privilege; or an attorney may be deprived of the opportunity to invoke a privilege by the commonly recognized exception to the attorney-client privilege for communications "relevant to an issue between parties who claim through the same deceased client." Proposed FRE 503(d)(3).

The Supreme Court acknowledged the importance of maintaining the attorney-client privilege after a client's death in Swidler & Berlin v. United States, 524 U.S. 399 (1998). The Court allowed Deputy White House Counsel Vince Foster's attorney to invoke the attorney-client privilege on Foster's behalf after Foster committed suicide. The government sought to obtain notes from Foster's attorney that were taken in a meeting between the two, nine days before Foster's death. The Court held that an attorney's notes from his meeting with his client are privileged and immune to a federal grand jury subpoena. The dissent agreed that attorney-client privilege ordinarily survives the death of the client, but emphasized that the common law also dictates that privileges should be construed narrowly. In this criminal investigation into wrongdoings in the White House, the dissent stated, the "paramount value" of our criminal justice system—the protection of an innocent defendant—should "outweigh a deceased client's interest in preserving confidence."

3. Scope and Limits

Each privilege has a particularized scope; it covers some things but not others. The confidential communications privileges, for example, extend only to confidential communications. If an unnecessary third party is present during a conversation between lawyer and client or husband and wife, the conversation will not be privileged. Another example: The attorney-client privilege extends only to communications for purposes of obtaining legal advice. If a person who happens to be, or who becomes, a client communicates with a lawyer for some other purpose, the communication is not privileged. Similarly, conversations between clergy and their flock are only privileged if in a confessional, or perhaps counseling, situation.

Privileges may also be limited by the potential benefit and harm to the litigants. While most of the confidential communications privileges are immune to claims of need by the opposing party, privileges to protect disclosure of specific types of information are often less secure. When considering whether to protect the identity of an informant, for example, a court may balance the importance to the defendant of the informant's testimony against the government's interest in resisting disclosure. See United States v. Fischer, 531 F.2d 783 (5th Cir. 1976). Similarly, academic researchers enjoy a privilege limited by a party's non-frivolous claim of need and inability to otherwise obtain the information. See Cusumano v. Microsoft Corp., 162 F.3d 708 (1st Cir. 1998).[9]

4. Waiver

The holder of a privilege may waive the privilege in at least four different ways. First, the holder may indicate through words or conduct a desire to forgo the privilege. Second, if the holder refrains from invoking the privilege, the failure to assert the privilege typically will be regarded as a waiver. However, newly enacted FRE 502, discussed infra on pages 905-912, addresses the effects of waiver when communication

---

9. See also Nixon v. United States, 418 U.S. 683 (1974) (claim of absolute executive privilege for presidential communications will not prevail over demonstrated need for particular evidence); Dellwood Farms v. Cargill, Inc., 128 F.3d 1122 (7th Cir. 1997) (law enforcement investigatory privilege not absolute, rather surmountable by strong showing of need).

or information protected by the attorney-client privilege and the work-product doctrine is inadvertently disclosed; the rule generally limits the effect of such disclosure. Third, voluntary disclosure of a communication protected by those privileges, such as a client discussing legal advice he received from his attorney with a third person, will constitute a waiver. Voluntary disclosure of a confidential communication in the context of another privileged communication will not result in waiver, however. For instance, if a person, in the presence of his spouse, made a confidential statement to his attorney that was covered under the attorney-client privilege, the marital communication privilege would preclude the waiver of the attorney-client privilege. Proposed FRE 511 captured well this aspect of the common law:

> A person upon whom these rules confer a privilege against disclosure of the confidential matter or communication waives the privilege if he or his predecessor while holder of the privilege voluntarily discloses or consents to disclosure of any significant part of the matter or communication. This rule does not apply if the disclosure is itself a privileged communication.

With respect to waiver by disclosure, it is important to note that the voluntary disclosure must be a disclosure of *the confidential communication itself.* A voluntary statement—either as a witness or in a casual conversation—of facts that were the subject of the communication is not a waiver of the privilege. The privilege protects solely the confidential communication, not the facts for which any witness with knowledge can be subpoenaed.

Fourth, waiver may also occur through asserting a claim based on privileged information. "Waiver by claim assertion" of privileged materials has been generally recognized as requiring disclosure when a party "asserts a claim that in fairness requires examination of protected communications." United States v. Bilzerian, 926 F.2d 1285, 1292 (2d Cir. 1991). For example, in In re Grand Jury Proceedings, 350 F.3d 299, 305 (2d Cir. 2003), the Second Circuit held that where a letter was sent by a corporation to a U.S. attorney explaining that it had been told by federal agents that its actions were legal, there was no unfairness to the government and thus the company did not waive its privilege as a result of placing its claims at issue. In contrast, a party who asserts that action was taken on the advice of counsel waives the attorney-client privilege with respect to those communications. For example, in United States v. Cohn, 303 F. Supp. 2d 672, 681 (D. Md. 2003), the court held that an investment company indicted for mail and wire fraud waived its attorney-client privilege after its general counsel raised an advice of counsel defense in his opening statement at trial. The same principle applies to actions for damages caused by an attorney's malpractice. By filing such an action, the client waives the privilege with respect to all of her relevant communications with the defendant attorney. See, e.g., Christenbury v. Locke Lord Bissell & Lidell, LLP, 285 F.R.D. 675, 681-684 (N.D. Ga. 2012) (applying the principle and discussing supporting case law). By the same token, in a habeas suit claiming ineffective assistance of counsel, the defendant seeking to vacate his conviction must specify his allegations against the former attorney, which implicitly waives the privilege with respect to the required information. United States v. Pinson, 584 F.3d 972 (10th Cir. 2009).

5. Exceptions

Each privilege has a set of exceptions that are derived from the underlying policies the particular privilege is created to serve. For example, the attorney-client privilege does not extend to communications in furtherance of a crime or fraud. The purpose of the privilege is to facilitate the giving of legal advice with respect to presently existing legal problems and to assist a client in conforming to the dictates of the law; its purpose is not to facilitate transgressions of the law. Similarly, the marital privileges do not apply in cases of alleged spousal abuse and the priest-penitent privilege cannot be relied upon to cover up ongoing child abuse. Again, these privileges are designed to preserve relationships, not to encourage assaultive behavior.

6. Drawing Adverse Inferences from Invoking a Privilege

In Griffin v. California, 380 U.S. 609 (1965), the Supreme Court held that allowing comment on the defendant's decision not to testify violated his Fifth Amendment privilege against self-incrimination "by making its assertion costly." Proposed FRE 513 applied the *Griffin* rationale to the law of privileges generally:

> (a) *Comment or inference not permitted.* The claim of a privilege, whether in the present proceeding or upon a prior occasion, is not a proper subject of comment by judge or counsel. No inference may be drawn therefrom.
>
> (b) *Claiming privilege without knowledge of jury.* In jury cases, proceedings shall be conducted, to the extent practicable, so as to facilitate the making of claims of privilege without knowledge of the jury.
>
> (c) *Jury instructions.* Upon request, any party against whom the jury might draw an adverse inference from a claim of privilege is entitled to an instruction that no inference may be drawn therefrom.

Presently, there appears to be no general *constitutional* rule barring comment on a party's invocation of a confidential communications privilege, and the case law is divided[10] as to the propriety of comment about invoking privileges outside the *Griffin* context.[11] Cases allowing comment frequently draw an analogy to the long-established practice of permitting comments on and drawing adverse inferences from the destruction of evidence or the failure to produce available witnesses or documents. In contrast, cases barring comment echo *Griffin's* concern that comment or adverse inferences undermine the privilege.

---

10. See 3 Jack B. Weinstein & Margaret A. Berger, Weinstein's Federal Evidence §513.04 (Joseph M. McLaughlin ed., 2d ed. 1997).

11. *Griffin* itself applies only to comments regarding a criminal defendant's invocation of the privilege in a criminal prosecution: Adverse inferences from silence in a noncriminal trial are not unconstitutional even when a criminal defendant or suspect exercises the privilege against self-incrimination. See Baxter v. Palmigiano, 425 U.S. 308 (1976); Brink's, Inc. v. City of New York, 717 F.2d 700 (2d Cir. 1983).

7. Constitutional Limitations on Privileges

The Due Process Clause of the Fourteenth Amendment and the Sixth Amendment Compulsory Process Clause set constitutional limits for privileges in criminal prosecutions. When a privilege is claimed by a witness from whom a criminal defendant seeks to elicit relevant testimony or documents, it directly conflicts with the defendant's rights under these constitutional provisions, and in appropriate cases with the Confrontation Clause as well. The Constitution resolves such conflicts in the defendant's favor, a principle succinctly explained by Judge Learned Hand: "The government must choose; either it must leave the transactions in the obscurity from which a trial will draw them, or it must expose them fully." United States v. Andolschek, 142 F.2d 503, 506 (2nd Cir. 1944). See also Jencks v. United States, 353 U.S. 657, 671-672 (1957) (holding that government cannot withhold potentially exculpatory information by alluding to state secrecy); Davis v. Alaska, 415 U.S. 308 (1974) (defendant's right to confront and cross-examine key prosecution witness includes right to bring out witness's juvenile record despite state statute privileging those records); Pennsylvania v. Ritchie, 480 U.S. 39, 58-59 (1987) (defendant accused of sexual offenses against minor victim was entitled to have Pennsylvania Children and Youth Services file reviewed by trial court to determine whether it contained potentially exculpatory information, but he had no right to access that file by himself); Matter of Farber, 394 A.2d 330 (N.J. 1978) (holding statutory privilege protecting confidentiality of media informant's identity unconstitutional to the extent it limited criminal defendants' access to potentially exonerating information); Alex Stein, Constitutional Evidence Law, 61 Vand. L. Rev. 65, 77 (2008) (explaining that a criminal defendant is entitled to receive from the government all potentially exonerating information so long as it presses the charges and that the government cannot hide such information by communicating it to its attorney and claiming the attorney-client privilege, and citing relevant cases).

Another line of decisions imposes limits upon privileges that impede governmental investigation. Such privileges may be held unconstitutional as well. Courts also may refuse to recognize them as a matter of the common law development of privileges. See, e.g., Nixon v. United States, 418 U.S. 683 (1974) (sweeping claim of absolute executive privilege for general presidential communications will not prevail over demonstrated need for specific evidence).

C. THE ATTORNEY-CLIENT PRIVILEGE

1. Elements of the Privilege

A good statement of the modern attorney-client privilege is contained in Proposed FRE 503:

    (a) *Definitions.* As used in this rule:

        (1) A "client" is a person, public officer, or corporation, association, or other organization or entity, either public or private, who is rendered

professional legal services by a lawyer, or who consults a lawyer with a view to obtaining professional legal services from him.

(2) A "lawyer" is a person authorized, or reasonably believed by the client to be authorized, to practice law in any state or nation.

(3) A "representative of the lawyer" is one employed to assist the lawyer in the rendition of professional legal services.

(4) A communication is "confidential" if not intended to be disclosed to third persons other than those to whom disclosure is in furtherance of the rendition of professional legal services to the client or those reasonably necessary for the transmission of the communication.

(b) *General Rule of Privilege.* A client has a privilege to refuse to disclose and to prevent any other person from disclosing confidential communications made for the purpose of facilitating the rendition of professional legal services to the client,

(1) between himself or his representative and his lawyer or his lawyer's representative, or

(2) between his lawyer and the lawyer's representative, or

(3) by him or his lawyer to a lawyer representing another in a matter of common interest, or

(4) between representatives of the client or between the client and a representative of the client, or

(5) between lawyers representing the client.

(c) *Who May Claim the Privilege.* The privilege may be claimed by the client, his guardian or conservator, the personal representative of a deceased client, or the successor, trustee, or similar representative of a corporation, association, or other organization, whether or not in existence. The person who was the lawyer at the time of the communication may claim the privilege but only on behalf of the client. His authority to do so is presumed in the absence of evidence to the contrary.

(d) *Exceptions.* There is no privilege under this rule:

(1) *Furtherance of crime or fraud.* If the services of the lawyer were sought or obtained to enable or aid anyone to commit or plan to commit what the client knew or reasonably should have known to be a crime or fraud; or

(2) *Claimants through same deceased client.* As to a communication relevant to an issue between parties who claim through the same deceased client, regardless of whether the claims are by testate or intestate succession or by *inter vivos* transaction; or

(3) *Breach of duty by lawyer or client.* As to a communication relevant to an issue of breach of duty by the lawyer to his client or by the client to his lawyer; or

(4) *Document attested by lawyer.* As to a communication relevant to an issue concerning an attested document to which the lawyer is an attesting witness; or

(5) *Joint clients.* As to a communication relevant to a matter of common interest between two or more clients if the communication was made

> by any of them to a lawyer retained or consulted in common, when offered
> in an action between any of the clients.

As Proposed FRE 503 suggests, much of the law governing the attorney-client privilege is quite straightforward. The attorney-client privilege originally was based on the theory that it would be unprofessional for the lawyer to reveal confidential communications from the client. Thus, the lawyer was the holder of the privilege. Today, jurisdictions uniformly recognize that the attorney-client privilege exists for the benefit of the client, who is thus now the holder of the privilege. The privilege may be claimed on the client's behalf by various individuals representing the client. If the client waives the privilege, the attorney cannot refuse to reveal the confidential communications. Although Proposed FRE 503 does not treat the matter, the client alone may waive the privilege by disclosing the information, and Proposed FRE 503(d) lists the standard exceptions to the attorney-client privilege.

The primary difficulty here is determining the scope of the privilege. The following sections discuss which communications are and which are not covered by the attorney-client privilege.

a. Communications with a Lawyer or Representative of a Lawyer

The attorney-client privilege applies to any communication between client and lawyer made for the purpose of securing legal advice. If a person approaches someone reasonably believed to be an attorney for the purpose of obtaining legal advice, confidential communications between the two are privileged even if the person is mistaken in the belief, unless one of the exceptions applies. The privilege also attaches to preliminary discussions with an attorney, even if the attorney is not ultimately retained. Moreover, the presence of third parties who are necessary or useful to the objective of rendering legal advice, such as translators, does not destroy confidentiality. The attorney-client privilege applies not only to communications between the attorney and the client but also to communications between the client and a representative of the attorney, which is defined as a person who is "employed to assist the lawyer in the rendition of professional services." Proposed FRE 503(a)(3). But how far does the privilege extend over employees of a law firm who are not attorneys? In United States v. Kovel, 296 F.2d 918 (2d Cir. 1961), Judge Friendly wrote an influential opinion discussing the issue. In *Kovel*, an accountant was employed by a law firm specializing in tax law. Id. at 919. Although Kovel was not an attorney, he met with clients to discuss complex tax issues. Id. The suit involved Kovel's refusal to reveal communications with one of his clients when subpoenaed by a grand jury, invoking the attorney-client privilege. Id. The court held that the attorney-client privilege extends to nonlawyer employees of a law firm so long as the communications relate to legal advice. Id. at 922. The court justified extending the privilege as follows:

> [T]he complexities of modern existence prevent attorneys from effectively handling clients' affairs without the help of others. . . . "The assistance of these agents being indispensable to his work and the communications of the client being often necessarily committed to them by the attorney or by the client himself, the privilege must include all the persons who act as the attorney's agents." 8 Wigmore, Evidence, §2301. [Id. at 921.]

The court in *Kovel* further stated that the privilege exists if the lawyer has directed the client to tell his story to an accountant in order to provide better advice. Id. at 922.

The notorious prosecution of Martha Stewart for obstructing justice raised an interesting twist on the *Kovel* situation. In re Grand Jury Subpoenas Dated March 24, 2003, 265 F. Supp. 2d 321 (S.D.N.Y. 2003), dealt with "the troublesome question whether and to what extent the attorney-client privilege and the protection afforded to work product extend to communications between and among a prospective defendant in a criminal case, her lawyers, and a public relations firm hired by the lawyers to aid in avoiding an indictment." Martha Stewart and her lawyers had hired a public relations firm, and the grand jury subpoenaed communications between Stewart, the lawyers, and the firm. Discovery was resisted on the ground that the public relations firm had been hired as part of Stewart's legal defense. In particular, Stewart claimed that the "unbalanced and often inaccurate press reports about Target created a clear risk that the prosecutors and regulators conducting the various investigations would feel public pressure to bring some kind of charge against her," and the public relations firm was hired to help redress the purported imbalance in the media. In an interesting opinion that relied heavily on *Kovel*, the court concluded that:

> This Court is persuaded that the ability of lawyers to perform some of their most fundamental client functions—such as (a) advising the client of the legal risks of speaking publicly and of the likely legal impact of possible alternative expressions, (b) seeking to avoid or narrow charges brought against the client, and (c) zealously seeking acquittal or vindication—would be undermined seriously if lawyers were not able to engage in frank discussions of facts and strategies with the lawyers' public relations consultants. For example, lawyers may need skilled advice as to whether and how possible statements to the press—ranging from "no comment" to detailed factual presentations—likely would be reported in order to advise a client as to whether the making of particular statements would be in the client's legal interest. And there simply is no practical way for such discussions to occur with the public relations consultants if the lawyers were not able to inform the consultants of at least some non-public facts, as well as the lawyers' defense strategies and tactics, free of the fear that the consultants could be forced to disclose those discussions. In consequence, this Court holds that (1) confidential communications (2) between lawyers and public relations consultants (3) hired by the lawyers to assist them in dealing with the media in cases such as this (4) that are made for the purpose of giving or receiving advice (5) directed at handling the client's legal problems are protected by the attorney-client privilege.

The court did note that, notwithstanding the formalism of it all, had Stewart hired the public relations firm herself, the privilege would not apply, and further that any communications for purposes other than legal advice would not be covered by the privilege.

A difficult question is whether the privilege covers communications between a criminal defendant and psychiatric experts retained by defense counsel, where the defendant asserts an insanity defense. The rule noted above that the attorney-client privilege applies to communications between a client and agents retained by defense counsel usually is extended to include psychiatrists. See Ballew v. State, 640 S.W.2d 237 (Tex. Crim. App. 1982); United States v. Talley, 790 F.2d 1468, 1470-1471 (9th

Cir. 1986) (recognizing "attorney-psychotherapist-client privilege" based in common law); but see Colo. Rev. Stat. §13-90-107(3) (scope of attorney-client privilege does not cover communications between a psychiatrist and a criminal defendant who asserts an insanity defense). However, some jurisdictions consider an insanity defense a waiver of the privilege through the assertion of a claim based on privileged information. This "waiver by claim assertion" of privileged materials has been generally recognized as requiring disclosure when a party "asserts a claim that in fairness requires examination of protected communications." United States v. Bilzerian, 926 F.2d 1285, 1292 (2d Cir. 1991). Compare Gray v. District Court, 884 P.2d 286, 292 (Colo. 1994) (holding that a defendant waives the right to claim the attorney-client and psychiatrist-patient privileges if mental condition is an issue), with People v. Knuckles, 165 Ill. 2d 125, 140, 650 N.E.2d 974, 981 (1995) (holding that there was no waiver of the attorney-client privilege with respect to communications between a defendant who raises an insanity defense and a psychiatrist employed by defense counsel to aid in the preparation of the defense). Also, Sixth Amendment challenges may arise from a state's limiting of the scope of the attorney-client privilege with respect to defense psychiatrists. However, the majority rule is that the Sixth Amendment is not violated by denying the privilege. See, e.g., Lange v. Young, 869 F.2d 1008, 1013 (7th Cir. 1989), aff'g State v. Lange, 126 Wis. 2d 513, 376 N.W.2d 868 (1985).

b. Communications for the Purpose of Legal Service

The person invoking the privilege bears the burden of proof to show that the attorney was contacted for a legal professional purpose. If the attorney was contacted for some other purpose, the privilege does not apply. For example, if the client solicits business or financial advice, or sees a lawyer about an accounting issue rather than legal matters, any communications between them are not protected by the privilege. See, e.g., In re Grand Jury Testimony of Attorney X, 621 F. Supp. 590, 592 (E.D.N.Y. 1985) ("where attorney is a mere 'conduit' the client may not invoke the privilege"); United States v. Woodruff, 383 F. Supp. 696, 698 (E.D. Pa. 1974) (attorney-client communication regarding time of trial not privileged). It can be a challenge to distinguish a "legal" purpose from another purpose, such as business or financial advice. In Georgia-Pacific Corp. v. GAF Roofing Manufacturing Corp., 1996 U.S. Dist. LEXIS 671 (S.D.N.Y. Jan. 24, 1996), GAF's in-house counsel, Scott, was asked to review certain environmental provisions of a proposed asset purchase agreement. He then negotiated the provisions of the agreement, and after execution of the agreement, he negotiated related matters. After the agreement was terminated, his testimony was needed to determine whether GAF agreed to assume certain environmental risks. Scott asserted the attorney-client privilege to avoid disclosure, stating that he had merely provided legal advice to management. The court held that, as a negotiator for GAF, Scott was acting in a business capacity, and with no litigation in sight, he was not giving legal advice. Therefore, no attorney-client privilege applied.

Proposed FRE 503(d)(5) implies that in a joint client situation, communications between an attorney and either of his joint clients are privileged against outsiders, which is the standard rule. Where two different parties have different representation, courts typically extend the privilege to cover what is called "common interest" or "joint defense" situations, as again Proposed FRE 503(b)(3) indicates. United States v. Schwimmer, 892 F.2d 237 (2d Cir. 1989). Problems arise when the joint defense breaks down and the previous cooperating parties become adversaries. Some courts take the position that in such circumstances a lawyer may not use against the now adverse party any confidences disclosed while the parties were cooperating, at least if their agreement so specifies. See, e.g., United States v. Anderson, 790 F. Supp. 231 (W.D. Wash. 1992).

c. The Scope of Confidential Communications Included in Privilege

Confidential conversations between an attorney and client are covered, so long as the conversations relate to legal advice. However, what about non-verbal communications, or documents exchanged between an attorney and client? In In re Navarro, 93 Cal. App. 3d 325, 155 Cal. Rptr. 522 (1979), the court considered whether an attorney's act of handing a police report to his client was a "communication" within the attorney-client privilege. In Navarro, an attorney was subpoenaed and refused to answer whether or not she showed a police report to her client, invoking the privilege. The court stated that the privilege covers "information transmitted between a client and his lawyer," and thus even turning over to the client a public document, such as the police report in question, if given as part of her legal advice or strategy, is covered by the privilege. Id. at 327.

Some courts have extended the privilege beyond mere communications. In State v. Meeks, 666 N.W.2d 859 (Wis. 2003), the Wisconsin Supreme Court held that an attorney's opinions and impressions of a former client's competence were protected by the attorney-client privilege. Although the attorney's opinion is not a communication, the court stated that "a lawyer's opinion about a client's competence or state of mind is inextricably mixed with the client's private communications." Id. at 870. However, a majority of courts have held that the attorney-client privilege does not protect an attorney's perceptions of a former client's mental competency unless relating the perceptions would reveal the substance of a confidential communication. See Darrow v. Gunn, 594 F.2d 767 (9th Cir. 1979).

For the privilege to attach, not only must the communication be confidential, but also clients must take "reasonable precautions" to ensure confidentiality. See, e.g., Suburban Sew 'N Sweep v. Swiss-Bernina, 91 F.R.D. 254 (N.D. Ill. 1981) (client who placed confidential documents in dumpster failed to take adequate precautions and lost protection of the privilege). Eavesdroppers present special problems for the privilege. The modern trend is to allow the claim of privilege to prevent testimony by the eavesdropper as long as the setting of the conversation suggests that the speakers intended the conversation to be confidential. Communicating in a public setting, for example, would tend to negate the claim that the participants intended the conversation to be confidential. Still, location is not dispositive. If the parties were speaking in hushed tones and thus not likely to be overheard, that their meeting took place in a public place would not automatically negate a claim of confidentiality. See, e.g., In re Sealed Case, 737 F.2d 94, 101-102 (D.C. Cir. 1984).

d. *Limitations on Waiver of the Privilege*

What if confidential material is inadvertently disclosed, perhaps as a result of a clerical error during discovery? Whether inadvertent disclosure of privileged lawyer-client communications and attorney work product should operate as a waiver of the protected material is a question that has plagued courts for decades. The problem has grown exponentially worse since e-discovery has become prevalent in most major civil litigation. As vast amounts of electronic documents are exchanged, it is increasingly easy to disclose inadvertently protected materials.

Outdated legal precedents added uncertainty as to the results of such disclosure. Most courts provided some protection where inadvertent waivers have occurred in modern, document-intensive litigation if the party holding the privilege could show that it had not been careless with the privileged materials. See, e.g., Gray v. Bicknell, 86 F.3d 1472, 1484 (8th Cir. 1996). Some courts, however, continued to strictly find waiver in cases of inadvertent disclosure. See, e.g., Wichita Land & Cattle Co. v. American Federal Bank, F.S.B., 148 F.R.D. 456 (D.D.C. 1992) ("Disclosure of other-wise-privileged materials, even where the disclosure was inadvertent, serves as waiver of the privilege."). Inadvertent waiver could be particularly harsh when conjoined with what is sometimes called subject matter waiver. Some courts held that disclosure of any aspect of privileged material resulted in a waiver of all privileged material related to the topic. For an excellent discussion of the general area of waiver, see Richard L. Marcus, The Perils of Privilege: Waiver and the Litigator, 84 Mich. L. Rev. 1605 (1986). As a result, large amounts of resources were dedicated to document reviews, and costs were frequently grossly disproportionate to the stakes of the litigation. Further, the in-depth review process itself impeded the efficient processing of cases through the system.[12]

Federal Rule 502, the first new rule concerning privileges since 1975, has been adopted to deal with this problem, among other issues.

RULE 502. ATTORNEY-CLIENT PRIVILEGE AND WORK PRODUCT; LIMITATIONS ON WAIVER

The following provisions apply, in the circumstances set out, to disclosure of a communication or information covered by the attorney-client privilege or work-product protection.

(a) *Disclosure Made in a Federal Proceeding or to a Federal Office or Agency; Scope of a Waiver*

When the disclosure is made in a federal proceeding or to a federal office or agency and waives the attorney-client privilege or work-product protection, the waiver extends to an undisclosed communication or information in a federal or state proceeding only if:

   (1) the waiver is intentional;

   (2) the disclosed and undisclosed communications or information concern the same subject matter; and

---

12. See Remarks made to the House of Representatives by Congresswoman Jackson-Lee of Texas; H7818 Congressional Record—House September 8, 2008.

(3) they ought in fairness to be considered together.

(b) *Inadvertent disclosure*

When made in a federal proceeding or to a federal office or agency, the disclosure does not operate as a waiver in a federal or state proceeding if:

(1) the disclosure is inadvertent;

(2) the holder of the privilege or protection took reasonable steps to prevent disclosure; and

(3) the holder promptly took reasonable steps to rectify the error, including (if applicable) following Federal Rule of Civil Procedure 26(b)(5)(B).

(c) *Disclosure Made in a State Proceeding*

When the disclosure is made in a State proceeding and is not the subject of a state-court order concerning waiver, the disclosure does not operate as a waiver in a federal proceeding if the disclosure:

(1) would not be a waiver under this rule if it had been made in a federal proceeding; or

(2) is not a waiver under the law of the state where the disclosure occurred.

(d) *Controlling Effect of a Court Order*

A federal court may order that the privilege or protection is not waived by disclosure connected with the litigation pending before the court—in which event the disclosure is also not a waiver in any other federal or state proceeding.

(e) *Controlling Effect of a Party Agreement*

An agreement on the effect of disclosure in a federal proceeding is binding only on the parties to the agreement, unless it is incorporated into a court order.

(f) *Controlling Effect of this Rule*

Notwithstanding Rules 101 and 1101, this rule applies to state proceedings and to federal court-annexed and federal court-mandated arbitration proceedings, in the circumstances set out in the rule. And notwithstanding Rule 501, this rule applies even if state law provides the rule of decision.

(g) *Definitions*

In this rule:

(1) "attorney-client privilege" means the protection that applicable law provides for confidential attorney-client communications; and

(2) "work-product protection" means the protection that applicable law provides for tangible material (or its intangible equivalent) prepared in anticipation of litigation or for trial."

e. Explanation of FRE 502

As the Advisory Committee Notes explain, this new rule serves two major purposes:

1) It resolves some longstanding disputes in the courts about the effect of certain disclosures of communications or information protected by the attorney-client privilege or as work product—specifically, disputes involving disclosure of privileged information

and whether it constitutes a comprehensive subject-matter (or transactional) waiver, as opposed to a waiver limited to the information actually disclosed.

2) It responds to the widespread complaint that litigation costs necessary to protect against waiver of attorney-client privilege or work product have become prohibitive due to the concern that any disclosure (however inadvertent or minimal) will operate as a subject matter waiver of all protected communications or information.

FRE 502 seeks to provide a predictable, uniform set of rules that determine the consequences of a disclosure of a communication or information covered by the attorney-client privilege or work-product protection. Parties to litigation need to know what happens when they disclose privileged information intentionally or by mistake. Parties also need to have an assurance that if they exchange privileged information pursuant to a confidentiality order, the court's order will be enforceable. Moreover, if a federal court's confidentiality order is not enforceable in a state court, then the burdensome costs of privilege review and retention are unlikely to be reduced.[13]

The new rule does not alter federal and state law governing whether information is protected under the attorney-client privilege or the work-product doctrine. This rule only determines the consequences of disclosing information protected by the attorney-client privilege. The effect of disclosure of information protected by other evidentiary privileges continues to be a question of federal common law.[14] The rule also does not displace applicable waiver doctrines. Rather, it limits the consequences of those doctrines in a uniform way.

f. Applying FRE 502: Practical Issues

Scope of Waiver Under FRE 502(a) and Subject Matter Waiver.   Inadvertent disclosure of privileged information will never result in a subject matter waiver. Rather, the waiver will only extend to the information actually disclosed. Similarly, when intentional disclosure of privileged information is found to waive the protection, the waiver will not extend beyond the disclosed information. The important exception to this rule is when protected information is intentionally disclosed in a selective or misleading manner to disadvantage the adversary. Under such circumstances, a judge may find that fairness requires further disclosure of related, protected information, i.e., a subject matter waiver. Note the similarity of the language to Rule 106. The principle behind the "ought in fairness" language is the same under both rules. According to the Committee, "Under both Rules, a party that makes a selective, misleading presentation that is unfair to the adversary opens itself to a more complete and accurate presentation."[15]

Appleton Papers, Inc. v. E.P.A., 702 F.3d 1018 (7th Cir. 2012) provides an excellent example of FRE 502(a) in operation. The government accused Appleton Papers Inc. ("API") and seven other companies of contaminating the Fox River near Green

---

13. Explanatory Note on Evidence Rule 502 Prepared by the Judicial Conference Advisory Committee on Evidence Rules (Revised 11/28/2007).

14. See Advisory Committee Notes.

15. See Advisory Committee Notes.

Bay, Wisconsin, and causing a $1 billion damage. The government then hired a consultant that prepared reports on the companies' responsibility for the contamination. The government disclosed some of those reports to obtain a consent decree that established another company's liability. Following that disclosure, API claimed that the government must now show it all of the reports, otherwise protected by the "work product" doctrine. The Seventh Circuit disagreed. "Federal Rule of Evidence 502," it explained, governs such situations where a party unfairly discloses only a portion of privileged material. This Rule "abolished the dreaded subject-matter waiver, i.e., that any disclosure of privileged matter worked a forfeiture of any other privileged information that pertained to the same subject matter." (citing Trustees of Elec. Workers Local No. 26 Pension Trust Fund v. Trust Fund Advisors, Inc., 266 F.R.D. 1, 11 (D.D.C. 2010). The circuit court then went on to determine that there is no indication of unfairness on the part of the government and that "to the extent API . . . fears that the government will use the newer numbers against it in future litigation, Rule 26 requires disclosure before trial." Id. at 1026.

Subsection (a) also stipulates that a waiver made under FRE 502 "extends to an undisclosed communication or information in a federal or state proceeding." Thus, when the effect of a party's waiver of the attorney-client privilege is determined by federal law—FRE 502—it will not be changed in a subsequent state court proceeding. State law, no matter what it says, cannot modify the nature and consequences of a waiver that took place in a federal proceeding.

When Does an Inadvertent Disclosure Waive Protection Under FRE 502(b)? FRE 502(b) is about inadvertent disclosure. Under this rule, the privilege is waived only when its holder does not take reasonable steps to prevent disclosure and does not take reasonable steps to rectify his error (e.g., by demanding the return of the mistakenly disclosed documents pursuant to Fed. R. Civ. P. 26(b)(5)(B), when applicable). Previously, some courts ruled that inadvertent disclosure of information waives the privilege automatically, while others decided that it did not. FRE 502(b) "opts for the middle ground." Reasonableness of the steps taken by the holder of the privilege will be decided on the particular facts of each case. The Advisory Committee Notes clarify that factors previously employed by the courts to determine the reasonableness of disclosure can still be persuasive. Specifically, the Notes state that:

> [Various cases] set out a multifactor test for determining whether inadvertent disclosure is a waiver. The stated factors (none of which is dispositive) are the reasonableness of precautions taken, the time taken to rectify the error, the scope of discovery, the extent of disclosure and the overriding issue of fairness. The rule does not explicitly codify that test, because it is really a set of non-determinative guidelines that vary from case to case. The rule is flexible enough to accommodate any of those listed factors. Other considerations bearing on the reasonableness of a producing party's efforts include the number of documents to be reviewed and the time constraints for production. Depending on the circumstances, a party that uses advanced analytical software applications and linguistic tools in screening for privilege and work product may be found to have taken "reasonable steps" to prevent inadvertent disclosure. The implementation of an efficient system of records management before litigation may also be relevant.

FRE 502(b) does not require the producing party to engage in a post-production review to determine whether any protected communication or information has been produced by mistake. But the rule does require the producing party to follow up on any obvious indications that a protected communication or information has been produced inadvertently.

If Disclosure Is Made in a State Proceeding, the More Protective Law Will Apply Under FRE 502(c). FRE 502(c) addresses the problems that arise when disclosure is made in a state proceeding and the same information or communication is offered as evidence in a subsequent federal proceeding. When the state and federal laws are inconsistent, the federal court will apply the law most protective of the privilege. The reason for this rule is laid out in the Advisory Committee Notes:

> If the state law is more protective (such as where the state law is that an inadvertent disclosure can never be a waiver), the holder of the privilege or protection may well have relied on that law when making the disclosure in the state proceeding. Moreover, applying a more restrictive federal law of waiver could impair the state objective of preserving the privilege or work-product protection for disclosures made in state proceedings. On the other hand, if the federal law is more protective, applying the state law of waiver to determine admissibility in federal court is likely to undermine the federal objective of limiting the costs of production.

Note that this rule is not intended to change the effect of a state court order concerning waiver. The Advisory Committee Notes point out that under existing law (28 U.S.C. §1738) and principles of federalism and comity, a state court order continues to be generally enforceable in a subsequent federal proceeding. However, this enforceability is "not absolute." See Tucker v. Ohtsu Tire & Rubber Co., 191 F.R.D. 495, 499 (D. Md. 2000). Under certain circumstances, federal courts will modify or circumvent a state court order. Thus, it may be the case that after FRE 502 federal court orders will have greater consequences in state courts than state court orders have in federal courts.

Controlling Effect of a Court Order Under FRE 502(d). This subsection authorizes a federal court to "order that the privilege or protection is not waived by disclosure connected with the litigation pending before the court—in which event the disclosure is also not a waiver in any other federal or state proceeding." This authorization allows a party to condition her disclosure of a document or other information that she claims to be privileged upon "opting out" from the default provisions set by FRE 502(a) and (b). That is, a party can argue that the information in question is privileged, but she would be willing to disclose it if she gets full protection against disclosure of further information by the court's order. Then, if the court issues the protective order, it would be effective in any subsequent court proceeding, state or federal. Moreover, the order would be effective against all parties (in rem) and not only against the parties to the proceeding in which it was given. Such orders can be issued with or without the parties' agreement.

FRE 502(d) recognizes that confidentiality orders are needed to reduce the cost of document review for purposes of discovery. Confidentiality orders can reduce those costs effectively only when they provide protection in subsequent suits and against third parties. Without such protection, parties will carry out an extensive and costly document review and will claim the attorney-client privilege whenever they can plausibly do so.

Controlling Effect of a Party Agreement Under FRE 502(e).   This subsection codifies the well-established practice of using party agreements to limit the effect of waiver by disclosure. It is important because of its relationship to FRE 502(d). An agreement under this subsection applies only to the documents exchanged between and among the parties and binds only the parties to the agreement. Unlike court orders, such agreements have no in rem effect. The Advisory Committee Notes make clear that parties who seek protection against nonparties must make the agreement pursuant to a court order under FRE 502(d). As a practical matter, parties can ask the court to issue the agreed-upon protective order to enable them to disclose specific documents without claiming the privilege.

Controlling Effect of FRE 502.   According to the Advisory Committee Notes, subsection (f) clarifies that (1) FRE 502 protection against waiver must be applicable in subsequent state proceedings, and that (2) FRE 502 "applies to state law causes of action brought in federal courts." The first part reiterates subsection (d) and implies that privileged communication or information disclosed in a federal proceeding, and not waived due to application of FRE 502, cannot be used in a subsequent state proceeding. The second part dictates that FRE 502 will be followed even if state law provides the rule of decision. Federal law thus always determines the consequences of a waiver that took place in a federal proceeding. Additionally, subsection (f) makes clear that FRE 502 should not be limited by FRE 101 and FRE 1101, which could otherwise be seen as in tension with this rule.

g. Potential Problems with FRE 502

The Rule Does Not Eliminate the Need to Review Documents Prior to Disclosure.   As noted above, the rule applies only to information and communication protected by the attorney-client privilege or the work-product doctrine. However, documents are reviewed during discovery for various reasons other than fear of waiving these protections. For example, rules of professional conduct, privacy laws, or confidentiality agreements may prohibit lawyers from breaching confidentiality or waiving the attorney-client privilege. Failure to review documents during discovery will also potentially produce documents protected by other privilege doctrines (e.g., settlement negotiations and self-evaluative documents). FRE 502 does not extinguish an attorney's responsibilities under the lawyer's code of conduct or other legal standards, nor does it protect information and communication protected by other privileges.

Furthermore, disclosure of protected information has the potential to severely prejudice a case, even if the information cannot be used directly by the receiving party. Once a receiving party has read privileged information, the court can only prohibit its use in trial; it cannot force the attorney to unlearn the information. The document itself may reveal strategy or thinking about the case. It may contain business-sensitive documents, such as trade secrets or processes that should not be revealed to a competitor. The document may expose the client to additional unrelated claims, or allow the receiving attorney to formulate further discovery requests that will target critical information. For all these reasons, attorneys and their clients may find that extensive document review is necessary, notwithstanding FRE 502.

The Constitutionality of the Rule's Application to State Court Proceedings. Constitutional concerns arise because FRE 502, a federally created rule, directs state courts on how to handle potential evidence. As Henry Noyes points out, FRE 502 may face a constitutional challenge because it is a federal action that causes a "direct loss of state control over the operation of the state courts." Henry S. Noyes, Federal Rule of Evidence 502: Stirring the State Law of Privilege and Professional Responsibility with a Federal Stick, 66 Wash. & Lee L. Rev. 673, 727 (2009). A possible response to this argument is that it was within Congress's power to determine both the scope of the attorney-client privilege for federal proceedings and the effects of federal litigation behavior (waiver of the attorney-client privilege in a federal proceeding). Also, FRE 502 was passed under Congress's power to regulate activity that substantially affects interstate commerce. However, the rule regulates all attorney-client or work-product material; it is not limited to information that relates to interstate commerce. Cf. Pierce Country v. Guillen, 537 U.S. 129 (2003) (holding a federal statute, protecting information relating to highway safety from discovery in state courts, constitutional under Congress's commerce clause power, because it addressed the channels and instrumentalities of interstate commerce). Further, while Congress passed FRE 502 to make the discovery process more efficient and cost-effective, there are no findings about the burden and cost of privilege review on interstate commerce.

The Rule May Not Significantly Reduce the Cost of Discovery. One of the admitted goals of FRE 502 is to reduce the cost of discovery. The theory is that limiting the necessity for pre-disclosure review will significantly reduce cost. However, under FRE 502(b), pre-disclosure review must be "reasonable" to prevent waiver; without further elaboration of this requirement, attorneys may continue to impose extensive reviews to ensure the process is considered reasonable. There are two additional problems with this contention. First, as discussed above, there are numerous reasons why parties will continue to engage in intensive pre-disclosure review. Second, if the parties are not concerned with negative implications of disclosing documents, the new rule may encourage parties to turn over too much information. These "data dumps" shift the cost of discovery from the disclosing party to the receiving party. Importantly, the overall cost likely increases as well, because the receiving party is likely to be less efficient at sorting through the documents.

The Rule May Jeopardize the Attorney-Client Privilege. As mentioned above, an FRE 502 order can be initiated by a judge without the consent of the parties. A short time-frame imposed on discovery requests combined with a mandated FRE 502 order may effectively force attorneys to hand over confidential information. However, the attorney-client privilege exists for the benefit of the client and is beneficial because it creates incentives for the client to disclose information to her attorney. If FRE 502 damages the confidentiality of the relationship, it may have significant, counter-productive, long-term consequences.

KEY POINTS

1. The attorney-client privilege extends to confidential communications between an attorney and client made for the purpose of obtaining legal advice. The privilege does not cover communications made to a lawyer for the purpose of obtaining any other kind of advice, such as business or tax advice. Determining which is which is not always easy.
2. The client is the holder of the privilege, but the privilege may be claimed on behalf of the client by the attorney and other individuals responsible for the client's interests.
3. The privilege extends over communications between joint clients and their attorney, and also covers "common interest" or "joint defense" cases, in which multiple parties and multiple attorneys are involved.
4. A communication does not necessarily have to be verbal. However, reasonable precautions must be taken by the parties to ensure confidentiality for the privilege to attach.
5. The privilege is not waived due to inadvertent disclosure in a federal proceeding if reasonable steps were taken to prevent disclosure.

NOTES AND QUESTIONS

1. The fact that FRE 502 is limited to attorney-client and work-product-protected information may have a significant impact on the effectiveness of the rule. Do you understand why a protective order under FRE 502 may not entice lawyers to forgo pre-disclosure document review?

2. Under FRE 502(a), a party that intentionally produces a privileged document may face a subject matter waiver. However, a party that unintentionally produces a privileged document will never face a subject matter waiver and will only be found to waive the privilege as to the disclosed document if the steps taken to protect the document and to rectify the error were unreasonable. Thus, FRE 502(b) requires courts to determine whether disclosure was "inadvertent" and whether "reasonable steps" were taken. How much room does this leave for courts to determine the definition of "inadvertent"? See Silverstein v. Federal Bureau of Prisons, 2009 U.S. Dist. LEXIS 121753 (D. Colo. Dec. 14, 2009) (finding that 502(b) covers "unintended, rather than mistaken, disclosure," and disclosure was not inadvertent when document was mislabeled). Similarly, after reading the Advisory Committee Notes for subsection (b), are you confident that you can employ "reasonable steps" to prevent waiving

the privilege through unintentional disclosure? What does it mean to take "reasonable steps"? How much is still left to the discretion of the judge? See Amobi v. D.C. Dept. of Corr., 262 F.R.D. 45 (D.D.C. 2009) (finding that reasonable steps were not taken when procedures were not described to the court and there was "no indication of what specific efforts were taken to prevent disclosure"); Rhoads Industries, Inc. v. Building Materials Corp., 254 F.R.D. 216 (E.D. Pa. 2008) (finding steps taken to prevent disclosure were not reasonable after reviewing multiple factors and specifically concerned that party claiming privilege did not prepare for discovery sufficiently far in advance). Do you think that a judge's definition of "reasonable" or "inadvertent" may be affected by the old waiver rules in his or her Circuit?

3. FRE 502 frequently refers to "subsequent state and federal proceedings," specifically indicating that the federal ruling governs subsequent determinations on the scope of a waiver. The Advisory Committee Notes indicate that this is necessary "to assure protection and predictability." Why is this so? Does it help if you know that plaintiff groups frequently share documents that are produced during a lawsuit? Would the rule be effective if protective orders ceased at the end of trial? How much confidence would an FRE 502 order give defendants if it was not enforceable in subsequent procedures and against third parties?

4. As a defense attorney, do you want the judge to unilaterally impose an FRE 502 order?

PROBLEMS

12.1. Brent Carson and Gloria Green were charged with importing cocaine, and retained separate counsel. At a meeting involving Brent, Gloria, and Gloria's attorney, Gloria supposedly said that Brent did not know anything about the plan to import cocaine. Gloria subsequently fled the jurisdiction, and Brent is now on trial. He calls Gloria's attorney to testify about her statement that he was not involved in the cocaine scheme. The prosecutor has objected to this testimony and asserted the attorney-client privilege on behalf of Gloria. How should the court rule?

12.2. Metro Display Advertising, Inc. (MDA) was in the business of buying and selling advertising space on bus stop shelters before it was forced to declare bankruptcy in the aftermath of an SEC investigation. The government has charged Munoz, one of MDA's independent sales agents, with mail fraud and has subpoenaed Sherron to testify against him. Sherron was once Munoz's attorney in an unrelated matter prior to either's employment with MDA. Subsequently, Sherron was retained by MDA. Munoz communicated to Sherron about the current charges against him, mistakenly believing that Sherron was representing him as well as MDA. Munoz now seeks to prevent Sherron from testifying about his damaging statements by invoking his attorney-client privilege. Should the court allow Sherron's testimony?

12.3. Dunlap was the director of the Lincoln Challenge Project, a betterment program for teenaged high school dropouts. In 1994, he hired Peters to teach in the program, requiring him to consent to criminal and educational background checks as a condition of his employment. When Peters sought to have his contract renewed in 1996, Dunlap informed him that he would be required to sign a much broader release consenting to, among other things, the full and complete disclosure of the records of attorneys, whether representing him or another person, in any case in which Peters has had an interest. Peters refused to sign the release and his employment contract was not renewed. Peters sued Dunlap. Can an employer require an employee to waive all attorney-client privileges as a condition of employment? Could any constitutional argument(s) be made by Peters to protect the privileged information?

12.4. Suburban Sew 'N Sweep is a retail store selling sewing machines manufactured and distributed by Fritz, Inc. A few years ago Suburban began suspecting that Fritz was engaging in unlawful price discrimination and conspiring to restrain trade in violation of the Clayton Act and the Sherman Antitrust Act. To confirm its suspicions, Suburban began regularly searching the Dumpster behind Fritz's office. Over the course of two years, Suburban found hundreds of relevant documents, many of which were confidential correspondences between Fritz's officers and Fritz's corporate counsel. It is uncontested that the documents were intended to be confidential and would be protected by attorney-client privilege if they had not been discovered by Suburban. Are these documents privileged?

12.5. Habs Brewing Company brought suit against Blue Jay Importers, alleging patent and trademark infringement resulting from Blue Jay's marketing of "dry" beer. Blue Jay motioned the court to compel production of certain documents, which Habs claims are protected by the attorney-client privilege. The 15 documents for which the plaintiffs are asserting the privilege were initiated by or received by Beardsley. Beardsley is a member of the legal department of Habs, and serves as their Intellectual Property Officer. Although not an attorney, Beardsley is registered as a patent agent before the U.S. Patent and Trademark Office. The Patent office allows nonlawyer patent agents to perform certain legal tasks before it, such as giving patent advice and preparing patent applications. Patent agents do not have any corresponding authorization to practice trademark law. Can Habs successfully assert the attorney-client privilege with respect to the communications by and to Beardsley? Does it make a difference whether such communications involved patent or trademark law?

NOTE ON THE ATTORNEY-CLIENT PRIVILEGE, THE WORK-PRODUCT DOCTRINE, AND THE ETHICAL DUTY OF CONFIDENTIALITY

Three sources protect confidentiality in the attorney-client relationship: the attorney-client privilege, the work-product doctrine, and the ethical duty of confidentiality. While the attorney-client privilege and work-product doctrine find their source in the law of evidence, the duty of confidentiality is grounded in the code of professional ethics.

The work-product doctrine often overlaps or supplements the attorney-client privilege. Protection for the "work product" of an attorney or party has been codified under Fed. R. Civ. P. 26(b)(3). Under Rule 26(b)(3), a party may obtain discovery of documents and tangible things prepared "in anticipation of litigation" by an attorney or representative of the opposing party only on a showing of "substantial need" and on a showing that the party seeking discovery is unable, without undue hardship, to obtain the substantial equivalent from alternative means. Furthermore, even if the required showing is put forth, the court must protect against disclosure of "the mental impressions, conclusions, opinions, or legal theories of an attorney or other representative of a party concerning the litigation." While both the attorney-client privilege and work-product doctrine act as a bar to discovery, there exist some crucial distinctions between the two. First, the work-product doctrine recognizes a qualified privilege, while the attorney-client privilege is usually considered absolute, although this is slowly beginning to change. See, for example, Greater Newburyport Clamshell Alliance v. Public Service Co. of N.H., 838 F.2d 13, 19 (1st Cir. 1988) (in civil damages action, "fairness requires that the privilege holder surrender the privilege to the extent that it will weaken, in a meaningful way, the defendant's ability to defend"); In re Grand Jury Proc., Des Moines, Iowa, 568 F.2d 555, 557 (8th Cir. 1977) (opponent's need relevant to a determination of privilege). At least with respect to discovery of "documents and tangible things," as opposed to "mental impressions, conclusions, opinions, or legal theories of an attorney," work-product protection is subject to a substantial need test. By contrast, if the attorney-client privilege is applicable, a showing of need will typically not overcome the privilege.

Second, whereas the work-product doctrine applies only to information prepared "in anticipation of litigation," the attorney-client privilege protects confidential communications, regardless of whether litigation is expected. Although the scope of work-product protection may seem unduly limited by the litigation requirement, in reality the work-product doctrine covers a much larger category of material than the attorney-client privilege. The work-product doctrine applies to all information collected by the attorney or the agent of the client insofar as it is gathered in anticipation of litigation. Most Circuits hold that a document is prepared in "anticipation of litigation" if the document is prepared "because of" the upcoming litigation. See United States v. Adlman, 134 F.3d 1194 (2d Cir. 1998). However, the Fifth Circuit applies a narrower "primary purpose" test—protecting a document only if the primary purpose of the document is to prepare for litigation. United States v. El Paso Co., 682 F.2d 530 (5th Cir. 1982). Under both standards, the protection applies not only to information passing from client to attorney, but to information from outside sources as well, such as a statement of a nonparty witness to an attorney as well as work compiled by an investigator, without the attorney's participation. In contrast, the attorney-client privilege applies solely to confidential communications between attorney and client, or representatives on either party's behalf.

A third source for the protection of confidentiality in attorney-client relations is the ethical duty of a lawyer to keep confidential matters about a client's affairs. The American Bar Association's Model Rules of Professional Conduct set forth this obligation in Rule 1.6, which as amended in 2005 now states:

(a) A lawyer shall not reveal information relating to the representation of a client unless the client gives informed consent, the disclosure is impliedly authorized in order to carry out the representation or the disclosure is permitted by paragraph (b).

(b) A lawyer may reveal information relating to the representation of a client to the extent the lawyer reasonably believes necessary:

(1) to prevent reasonably certain death or substantial bodily harm;

(2) to prevent the client from committing a crime or fraud that is reasonably certain to result in substantial injury to the financial interests or property of another and in furtherance of which the client has used or is using the lawyer's services;

(3) to prevent, mitigate or rectify substantial injury to the financial interests or property of another that is reasonably certain to result or has resulted from the client's commission of a crime or fraud in furtherance of which the client has used the lawyer's services;

(4) to secure legal advice about the lawyer's compliance with these Rules;

(5) to establish a claim or defense on behalf of the lawyer in a controversy between the lawyer and the client, to establish a defense to a criminal charge or civil claim against the lawyer based upon conduct in which the client was involved, or to respond to allegations in any proceeding concerning the lawyer's representation of the client; or

(6) to comply with other law or a court order.

Comment Two accompanying Model Rule 1.6 provides the rationale behind the ethical obligation.

> A fundamental principle in the client-lawyer relationship is that, in the absence of the client's informed consent, the lawyer must not reveal information relating to the representation. . . . This contributes to the trust that is the hallmark of the client-lawyer relationship. The client is thereby encouraged to seek legal assistance and to communicate fully and frankly with the lawyer even as to embarrassing or legally damaging subject matter. The lawyer needs this information to represent the client effectively and, if necessary, to advise the client to refrain from wrongful conduct. . . .

The duty of confidentiality is an important mechanism by which the rules of ethics protect these interests. The rule was relaxed slightly in the 2005 update, now allowing the lawyer to breach confidentiality to prevent any reasonably certain bodily harm, no longer limited to harm caused by a client's criminal act. Further, in the wake of financial scandals such as Enron, the updated rule allows for a breach of confidentiality to prevent a client's crime or fraud from causing harm to financial interests or property. Despite these few exceptions, the ethical duty of confidentiality remains essential to the protection of the client-lawyer relationship. Violation of Rule 1.6 may lead to professional censure and possible suspension or loss of license.

Comment Three to Rule 1.6 clarifies the distinction between evidentiary privileges and the ethical duty of confidentiality:

The principle of client-lawyer confidentiality is given effect by related bodies of law: the attorney-client privilege, the work product doctrine and the rule of confidentiality established in professional ethics. The attorney-client privilege and work-product doctrine apply in judicial and other proceedings in which a lawyer may be called as a witness or otherwise required to produce evidence concerning a client. The rule of client-lawyer confidentiality applies in situations other than those where evidence is sought from the lawyer through compulsion of law. The confidentiality rule, for example, applies not only to matters communicated in confidence by the client but also to all information relating to the representation, whatever its source. A lawyer may not disclose such information except as authorized or required by the Rules of Professional Conduct or other law. . . .

The duty of confidentiality covers much more than the privilege—it covers all communications between a client and an attorney, including those that are not specifically tied to seeking legal advice, and those that are not meant to be confidential. The duty of confidentiality also covers more than just verbal communications, unlike the attorney-client privilege. However, a lawyer can still be called on to testify regarding these communications, so the protection afforded by the duty of confidentiality may not be as great as that afforded by the privilege.

An interesting empirical question is whether the lawyer's ethical obligation to maintain confidentiality is sufficiently analogous to the privilege to encourage communications between client and attorney. If clients can be encouraged by the attorney's ethical obligation not to disclose information, then the attorney-client privilege may not be needed. See, in this regard, ABA Code of Professional Responsibility, Ethical Consideration 4-1:

> A lawyer should be fully informed of all the facts of the matter he is handling in order for his client to obtain the full advantage of our legal system. It is for the lawyer in the exercise of his independent professional judgment to separate the relevant and important from the irrelevant and unimportant. The observance of the ethical obligation of a lawyer to hold inviolate the confidences and secrets of his client not only facilitates the full development of facts essential to proper representation of the client but also encourages laymen to seek early legal assistance.

NOTES AND QUESTIONS

1. How absolute should the protection be for a client's confidential communications or a lawyer's thought processes and other creative efforts? Even if the existence of rules of confidentiality produce benefits, isn't it conceivable in a particular case that their costs would exceed their benefits? What should happen in such cases? In thinking about this issue, do not neglect the costs of deciding on a case-by-case basis if the costs of confidentiality exceed the benefits. If a witness uses a document protected by the attorney-client privilege or the work-product doctrine to refresh the witness's memory before testifying, should the judge be able to order production of the document pursuant to FRE 612?

2. The American Bar Association's Model Code of Professional Responsibility, the predecessor to the Model Rules of Professional Conduct, included a similar confidentiality provision. ABA Model Code of Professional Responsibility Disciplinary Rule 4-101. The exception for contemplated criminal conduct by a client, however, extended to *all* crimes, and there was also an exception permitting a lawyer to reveal confidences "when required by law or court order." With respect to the omission of this latter exception in the Model Rules, the Comment accompanying Rule 1.6 states: "Whether another provision of law supersedes Rule 1.6 is a matter of interpretation beyond the scope of these Rules, but a presumption should exist against such a supersession." How compelling a case for confidentiality does the Comment to Rule 1.6 make? Do the rule and commentary deal adequately with the relationship between the ethical obligation of confidentiality and the attorney-client privilege? Is Rule 1.6's permission for a lawyer to disclose a client's contemplated criminal conduct too narrow? Why should there be a "presumption" that provisions of law mandating disclosure do not supersede Rule 1.6's obligation of confidentiality?

3. There is one situation in which the Model Rules of Professional Conduct specifically provide that the rule of confidentiality is superseded. See Model Rule 3.3:

(a) A lawyer shall not knowingly:

(1) make a false statement of material fact or law to a tribunal;

(2) fail to disclose a material fact to a tribunal when disclosure is necessary to avoid assisting a criminal or fraudulent act by the client;

(3) fail to disclose to the tribunal legal authority in the controlling jurisdiction known to the lawyer to be directly adverse to the position of the client and not disclosed by opposing counsel; or

(4) offer evidence that the lawyer knows to be false. If a lawyer has offered material evidence and comes to know of its falsity, the lawyer shall take reasonable remedial measures.

(b) The duties stated in paragraph (a) continue to the conclusion of the proceeding, and apply even if compliance requires disclosure of information otherwise protected by Rule 1.6.

(c) A lawyer may refuse to offer evidence that the lawyer reasonably believes is false.

PROBLEMS

12.6. Al Driver, who is suspected of bank robbery, tells his attorney, George Shippers, where to locate the mask and gun used in the robbery. Shippers retrieves the mask and gun and places them in the office safe. Has Shippers acted unethically? What disclosures about the gun and mask is he now permitted or required to make?

What if it had been Shippers's secretary who had, without Shippers's permission, retrieved the mask and gun? In either case, should it matter (a) whether the police or some third person would have been likely to find the mask and gun or (b) whether the initial information about the mask and gun came from some person other than the client?

After Shippers first learned about the mask and gun, what would have been the appropriate course of action for him to take?

12.7. Sarah Johnson, an attorney, represents Oscar Rivers, who has been charged with murder. Rivers and his girlfriend, Elsie Lewis, are both prepared to testify that they were together at Elsie's apartment at the time of the killing. Oscar has consistently told Sarah this alibi story; Elsie, however, has confided in Sarah that she was not with Oscar at the time of the killing and that Oscar admitted to her that he was the murderer. The only eyewitness to the killing, Elvira Dugan, is an elderly woman with failing eyesight.

What should Sarah do if both Oscar and Elsie are adamant about testifying that they were together at Elsie's apartment when the murder was committed? Does your answer depend on whether Sarah believes Oscar or Elsie?

Sarah is convinced that she can neutralize Elvira Dugan's eyewitness testimony during cross-examination. Is there any problem with her doing so if she is convinced that Oscar is guilty and that Elvira's identification is in fact accurate?

2. The Corporate Client

The attorney-client privilege extends not only to individual clients but also to corporate and other organizational clients. Application of the privilege in this context has proved troublesome because an organization can make confidential communications only through individual members. Thus, the question necessarily arises: Who can speak for the organization for the purposes of the attorney-client privilege? Or to phrase the issue in terms of the language of Proposed FRE 503: Who is a "representative of the client"?

Courts are divided as to the extent of the privilege in the corporate context. As the law has evolved on the subject, three approaches can be discerned. Under the early decisions, any officer, employee, or member of an organization was a representative of the organization. See, e.g., United States v. United Shoe Mach. Corp., 89 F. Supp. 357 (D. Mass. 1950). Although this definition had the advantage of ease in application, it was widely criticized for being too broad.

A second approach to defining representative of the client was the "control group" test. See City of Philadelphia v. Westinghouse Elec. Corp., 210 F. Supp. 483 (E.D. Pa. 1962). According to this test an employee's communication is privileged only if the employee "is in a position to control or even to take a substantial part in a decision about any action which the corporation may take upon the advice of the attorney." Although widely adopted, the control group test was subject to criticism on two grounds. First, it was unclear precisely to whom the privilege would apply, and this lack of certainty would inhibit candid communication. Second, because the control group test tended to limit the attorney-client privilege to communications by upper level management, the test did not go far enough in protecting communications of employees who might have information that would be critical in order for the attorney to give sound legal advice to the organization.

A third approach to defining representative of the client was the "subject matter" test. See Harper & Row Publishers, Inc. v. Decker, 423 F.2d 487 (7th Cir. 1970), *aff'd mem.*, 400 U.S. 955 (1971). Under this test an employee's communication is privileged if the employee "makes the communication at the direction of his superiors" and the subject matter of the communication "is the performance by the employee of the duties of his employment." This test avoids both the problem of bringing within the scope of the privilege communications by any and all employees and the problem of limiting the privilege to communications from members of the control group. But is the subject matter test itself too broad? Would the first prong of the test be satisfied if every employee were routinely directed to channel all business reports through corporate counsel? See Note, Evidence—Privileged Communications—The Attorney-Client Privilege in the Corporate Setting: A Suggested Approach, 69 Mich. L. Rev. 360 (1970). Would the first prong be satisfied if *any* superior for *any* reason directed the employee to communicate with the attorney?

The drafters of the Federal Rules chose not to define "representative of the client." Without elaboration, the Advisory Committee concluded that the matter was "too hot to handle" and "better left to resolution on a case-by-case basis."[16] The Supreme Court addressed the issue in *Upjohn.*

UPJOHN CO. v. UNITED STATES

449 U.S. 383 (1981)

Justice REHNQUIST delivered the opinion of the Court.

We granted certiorari in this case to address important questions concerning the scope of the attorney-client privilege in the corporate context and the applicability of the work-product doctrine in proceedings to enforce tax summonses. . . . We . . . conclude that the attorney-client privilege protects the communications involved in this case from compelled disclosure and that the work-product doctrine does apply in tax summons enforcement proceedings.

I

Petitioner Upjohn Co. manufactures and sells pharmaceuticals here and abroad. In January 1976 independent accountants conducting an audit of one of Upjohn's foreign subsidiaries discovered that the subsidiary made payments to or for the benefit

---

16. See Hearings on Proposed Rules of Evidence Before the Special Subcommittee on Reform of Federal Criminal Laws of the House Committee on the Judiciary, 93d Cong., 1st Sess. 524 (1973) (testimony by Professor Cleary). In earlier drafts the Advisory Committee had included a version of the control group test in the definition section of Proposed FRE 503. Prior to the final draft, however, the Supreme Court affirmed by an equally divided vote the decision that had announced the subject matter test. Harper & Row Publishers v. Decker, 400 U.S. 348 (1970). As Weinstein and Berger noted: The Advisory Committee recognized that lack of consensus in the Supreme Court precluded the possibility of drafting a rule satisfactory to a majority of the justices. Consequently, the Committee eliminated the definition of "representative of the client" in subdivision (a) of the rule. [3 Jack B. Weinstein & Margaret A. Berger, Weinstein's Federal Evidence §503 App.01[2] (Joseph M. McLaughlin ed., 2d ed. 1997).]

of foreign government officials in order to secure government business. The accountants so informed petitioner Mr. Gerard Thomas, Upjohn's Vice President, Secretary, and General Counsel. Thomas is a member of the Michigan and New York Bars, and has been Upjohn's General Counsel for 20 years. He consulted with outside counsel and R. T. Parfet, Jr., Upjohn's Chairman of the Board. It was decided that the company would conduct an internal investigation of what were termed "questionable payments." As part of this investigation the attorneys prepared a letter containing a questionnaire which was sent to "All Foreign General and Area Managers" over the Chairman's signature. The letter began by noting recent disclosures that several American companies made "possibly illegal" payments to foreign government officials and emphasized that the management needed full information concerning any such payments made by Upjohn. The letter indicated that the Chairman had asked Thomas, identified as "the company's General Counsel," "to conduct an investigation for the purpose of determining the nature and magnitude of any payments made by the Upjohn Company or any of its subsidiaries to any employee or official of a foreign government." The questionnaire sought detailed information concerning such payments. Managers were instructed to treat the investigation as "highly confidential" and not to discuss it with anyone other than Upjohn employees who might be helpful in providing the requested information. Responses were to be sent directly to Thomas. Thomas and outside counsel also interviewed the recipients of the questionnaire and some 33 other Upjohn officers or employees as part of the investigation.

On March 26, 1976, the company voluntarily submitted a preliminary report to the Securities and Exchange Commission on Form 8-K disclosing certain questionable payments. A copy of the report was simultaneously submitted to the Internal Revenue Service, which immediately began an investigation to determine the tax consequences of the payments. Special agents conducting the investigation were given lists by Upjohn of all those interviewed and all who had responded to the questionnaire. On November 23, 1976, the Service issued a summons pursuant to 26 U.S.C. sec. 7602 demanding production of:

> All files relative to the investigation conducted under the supervision of Gerard Thomas to identify payments to employees of foreign governments and any political contributions made by the Upjohn Company or any of its affiliates since January 1, 1971 and to determine whether any funds of the Upjohn Company had been improperly accounted for on the corporate books during the same period.
>
> The records should include but not be limited to written questionnaires sent to managers of the Upjohn Company's foreign affiliates, and memorandums or notes of the interviews conducted in the United States and abroad with officers and employees of the Upjohn Company and its subsidiaries. . . .

The company declined to produce the documents specified in the second paragraph on the grounds that they were protected from disclosure by the attorney-client privilege and constituted the work product of attorneys prepared in anticipation of litigation. . . . [T]he United States filed a petition seeking enforcement of the summons . . . in the United States District Court for the Western District of Michigan. That court adopted the recommendation of a Magistrate who concluded that the summons should be enforced. Petitioners appealed to the Court of Appeals for the Sixth Circuit which rejected the Magistrate's finding of a waiver of the attorney-client privilege, . . . but agreed that the privilege did not apply "[t]o the extent that the communications were made by officers and agents not responsible for directing Upjohn's actions in response to legal advice . . . for the simple reason that the communications were not the client's." . . . The court reasoned that accepting petitioners' claim for a broader application of the privilege would encourage upper-echelon management to ignore unpleasant facts and create too broad a "zone of silence." Noting that Upjohn's counsel had interviewed officials such as the Chairman and President, the Court of Appeals remanded to the District Court so that a determination of who was within the "control group" could be made. In a concluding footnote the court stated that the work-product doctrine "is not applicable to administrative summonses issued under 26 U.S.C. sec. 7602." . . .

II

. . . The attorney-client privilege is the oldest of the privileges for confidential communications known to the common law. . . . Its purpose is to encourage full and frank communication between attorneys and their clients and thereby promote broader public interests in the observance of law and administration of justice. The privilege recognizes that sound legal advice or advocacy serves public ends and that such advice or advocacy depends upon the lawyer's being fully informed by the client. [I]n Fisher v. United States, 425 U.S. 391, 403 (1976), we recognized the purpose of the privilege to be "to encourage clients to make full disclosure to their attorneys." This rationale for the privilege has long been recognized by the Court. . . . Admittedly complications in the application of the privilege arise when the client is a corporation, which in theory is an artificial creature of the law, and not an individual; but this Court has assumed that the privilege applies when the client is a corporation, . . . and the Government does not contest the general proposition.

The Court of Appeals, however, considered the application of the privilege in the corporate context to present a "different problem," since the client was an inanimate entity and "only the senior management, guiding and integrating the several operations, . . . can be said to possess an identity analogous to the corporation as a whole." . . . The first case to articulate the so-called "control group test" adopted by the court below, Philadelphia v. Westinghouse Electric Corp., 210 F. Supp. 483, 485 (ED Pa.), *petition for mandamus and prohibition denied sub nom.* General Electric Co. v. Kirkpatrick, 312 F.2d 742 (CA3 1962), *cert. denied*, 372 U.S. 943 (1963), reflected a similar conceptual approach:

> Keeping in mind that the question is, Is it the corporation which is seeking the lawyer's advice when the asserted privileged communication is made?, the most satisfactory solution, I think, is that if the employee making the communication, of whatever rank he may be, is in a position to control or even to take a substantial part in a decision about any action which the corporation may take upon the advice of the attorney, . . . then, in effect, *he is (or personifies) the corporation* when he makes his disclosure to the lawyer and the privilege would apply. (Emphasis supplied [by the Court].)

Such a view, we think, overlooks the fact that the privilege exists to protect not only the giving of professional advice to those who can act on it but also the giving of information to the lawyer to enable them to give sound and informed advice. The first step in the resolution of any legal problem is ascertaining the factual background and sifting through the facts with an eye to the legally relevant. See ABA Code of Professional Responsibility, Ethical Consideration 4-1:

> A lawyer should be fully informed of all the facts of the matter he is handling in order for his client to obtain the full advantage of our legal system. It is for the lawyer in the exercise of his independent professional judgment to separate the relevant and important from the irrelevant and unimportant. The observance of the ethical obligation of a lawyer to hold inviolate the confidences and secrets of his client not only facilitates the full development of facts essential to proper representation of the client but also encourages laymen to seek early legal assistance.

. . . In the case of the individual client the provider of information and the person who acts on the lawyer's advice are one and the same. In the corporate context, however, it will frequently be employees beyond the control group as defined by the court below—"officers and agents . . . responsible for directing [the company's] actions in response to legal advice"—who will possess the information needed by the corporation's lawyers. Middle-level—and indeed lower-level—employees can, by actions within the scope of their employment, embroil the corporation in serious legal difficulties, and it is only natural that these employees would have the relevant information needed by corporate counsel if he is adequately to advise the client with respect to such actual or potential difficulties. . . .

The control group test adopted by the court below thus frustrates the very purpose of the privilege by discouraging the communication of relevant information by employees of the client to attorneys seeking to render legal advice to the client corporation. The attorney's advice will also frequently be more significant to noncontrol group members than to those who officially sanction the advice, and the control group test makes it more difficult to convey full and frank legal advice to the employees who will put into effect the client corporation's policy. See, e.g., Duplan Corp. v. Deering Milliken, Inc., 397 F. Supp. 1146, 1164 (S.C. 1974) ("After the lawyer forms his or her opinion, it is of no immediate benefit to the Chairman of the Board or the President. It must be given to the corporate personnel who will apply it").

The narrow scope given the attorney-client privilege by the court below not only makes it difficult for corporate attorneys to formulate sound advice when their client is faced with a specific legal problem but also threatens to limit the valuable efforts of corporate counsel to ensure their client's compliance with the law. In light of the vast and complicated array of regulatory legislation confronting the modern corporation, corporations, unlike most individuals, "constantly go to lawyers to find out how to obey the law," Burnham, The Attorney-Client Privilege in the Corporate Arena, 24 Bus. Law. 901, 913 (1969), particularly since compliance with the law in this area is hardly an instinctive matter, see, e.g., United States v. United States Gypsum Co., 438 U.S. 422, 440-441 (1978) ("the behavior proscribed by the [Sherman] Act is often difficult to distinguish from the gray zone of socially acceptable and economically justifiable business conduct").[17] The test adopted by the court below is difficult to apply in practice, though no abstractly formulated and unvarying "test" will necessarily enable courts to decide questions such as this with mathematical precision. But if the purpose of the attorney-client privilege is to be served, the attorney and client must be able to predict with some degree of certainty whether particular discussions will be protected. An uncertain privilege, or one which purports to be certain but results in widely varying applications by the courts, is little better than no privilege at all. The very terms of the test adopted by the court below suggest the unpredictability of its application. The test restricts the availability of the privilege to those officers who play a "substantial role" in deciding and directing a corporation's legal response. Disparate decisions in cases applying this test illustrate its unpredictability. Compare, e.g., Hogan v. Zletz, 43 F.R.D. 308, 315-316 (N.D. Okla. 1967), aff'd in part sub nom. Natta v. Hogan, 392 F.2d 686 (CA10 1968) (control group includes managers and assistant managers of patent division and research and development department), with Congoleum Industries, Inc. v. GAF Corp., 49 F.R.D. 82, 83-85 (E.D. Pa. 1969), aff'd, 478 F.2d 1398 (CA3 1973) (control group includes only division and corporate vice presidents, and not two directors of research and vice president for production and research).

The communications at issue were made by Upjohn employees[18] to counsel for Upjohn acting as such, at the direction of corporate superiors in order to secure legal advice from counsel. As the Magistrate found, "Mr. Thomas consulted with the Chairman of the Board and outside counsel and thereafter conducted a factual investigation to determine the nature and extent of the questionable payments *and to be in a position to give legal advice to the company with respect to the payments.*" (Emphasis supplied [by the Court].). . . . Information, not available from upper-echelon management, was needed to supply a basis for legal advice concerning compliance with securities and tax laws, foreign laws, currency regulations, duties to shareholders, and potential litigation in each of these areas. The communications concerned matters within the scope of the employees' corporate duties, and the employees themselves were sufficiently aware that they were being questioned in order that the corporation could obtain legal advice. The questionnaire identified Thomas as "the company's General Counsel" and referred in its opening sentence to the possible illegality of payments such as the ones on which information was sought. . . . A statement of policy accompanying the questionnaire clearly indicated the legal implications of the investigation. The policy statement was issued "in order that there be no uncertainty

17. The Government argues that the risk of civil or criminal liability suffices to ensure that corporations will seek legal advice in the absence of the protection of the privilege. This response ignores the fact that the depth and quality of any investigations to ensure compliance with the law would suffer, even were they undertaken. The response also proves too much, since it applies to all communications covered by the privilege: an individual trying to comply with the law or faced with a legal problem also has strong incentive to disclose information to his lawyer, yet the common law has recognized the value of the privilege in further facilitating communications.

18. Seven of the eighty-six employees interviewed by counsel had terminated their employment with Upjohn at the time of the interview. . . . Petitioners argue that the privilege should nonetheless apply to communications by these former employees concerning activities during their period of employment. Neither the District Court nor the Court of Appeals had occasion to address this issue, and we decline to decide it without the benefit of treatment below.

in the future as to the policy with respect to the practices which are the subject of this investigation." It began "Upjohn will comply with all laws and regulations," and stated that commissions or payments "will not be used as a subterfuge for bribes or illegal payments" and that all payments must be "proper and legal." Any future agreements with foreign distributors or agents were to be approved "by a company attorney" and any questions concerning the policy were to be referred "to the company's general Counsel." . . . This statement was issued to Upjohn employees worldwide, so that even those interviewees not receiving a questionnaire were aware of the legal implications of the interviews. Pursuant to explicit instructions from the Chairman of the Board, the communications were considered "highly confidential" when made, . . . and have been kept confidential by the company. Consistent with the underlying purposes of the attorney-client privilege, these communications must be protected against compelled disclosure.

The Court of Appeals declined to extend the attorney-client privilege beyond the limits of the control group test for fear that doing so would entail severe burdens on discovery and create a broad "zone of silence" over corporate affairs. Application of the attorney-client privilege to communications such as those involved here, however, puts the adversary in no worse position than if the communications had never taken place. The privilege only protects disclosure of communications; it does not protect disclosure of the underlying facts by those who communicated with the attorney. . . . Here the Government was free to question the employees who communicated with Thomas and outside counsel. Upjohn has provided the IRS with a list of such employees, and the IRS has already interviewed some 25 of them. While it would probably be more convenient for the Government to secure the results of petitioner's internal investigation by simply subpoenaing the questionnaires and notes taken by petitioner's attorneys, such considerations of convenience do not overcome the policies served by the attorney-client privilege. . . .

Needless to say, we decide only the case before us, and do not undertake to draft a set of rules which should govern challenge to investigatory subpoenas. Any such approach would violate the spirit of Federal Rule of Evidence 501. See S. Rep. No. 93-1277, p.13 (1974) ("the recognition of a privilege based on a confidential relationship . . . should be determined on a case-by-case basis"). . . . While such a "case-by-case" basis may to some slight extent undermine desirable certainty in the boundaries of the attorney-client privilege, it obeys the spirit of the Rules. At the same time we conclude that the narrow "control group test" sanctioned by the Court of Appeals in this case cannot, consistent with "the principles of the common law as . . . interpreted . . . in the light of reason and experience," Fed. Rule Evid. 501, govern the development of the law in this area.

III

Our decision that the communications by Upjohn employees to counsel are covered by the attorney-client privilege disposes of the case so far as the responses to the questionnaires and any notes reflecting responses to interview questions are concerned. The summons reaches further, however, and Thomas has testified that his notes and memoranda of interviews go beyond recording responses to his questions. . . . To the extent that the material subject to the summons is not protected by the attorney-client privilege as disclosing communications between an employee and counsel, we must reach the ruling by the Court of Appeals that the work-product doctrine does not apply to summonses issued under 26 U.S.C. sec. 7602.[19] The Government concedes, wisely, that the Court of Appeals erred and that the work-product doctrine does apply to IRS summonses. . . . This doctrine was announced by the Court over 30 years ago in Hickman v. Taylor, 329 U.S. 495 (1947). In that case the Court rejected "an attempt, without purported necessity or justification, to secure written statements, private memoranda and personal recollections prepared or formed by an adverse party's counsel in the course of his legal duties." Id., at 510. The Court noted that "it is essential that a lawyer work with a certain degree of privacy" and reasoned that if discovery of the material sought were permitted

> much of what is now put down in writing would remain unwritten. An attorney's thoughts, heretofore inviolate, would not be his own. Inefficiency, unfairness and sharp practices would inevitably develop in the giving of legal advice and in the preparation of cases for trial. The effect on the legal profession would be demoralizing. And the interests of the clients and the cause of justice would be poorly served. [Id., at 511.]

The "strong public policy" underlying the work-product doctrine was reaffirmed in United States v. Nobles, 422 U.S. 225, 236-240 (1975), and has been substantially incorporated in Federal Rule of Civil Procedure 26(b)(3).[20]

. . . While conceding the applicability of the work-product doctrine, the Government asserts that it has made a sufficient showing of necessity to overcome its protections. The Magistrate apparently so found. . . . The Government relies on the following language in *Hickman*:

> We do not mean to say that all written materials obtained or prepared by an adversary's counsel with an eye toward litigation are necessarily free from discovery in all cases. Where relevant and nonprivileged facts remain hidden in an attorney's file and where production of those facts is essential to the preparation of one's case, discovery may properly be had. . . . And production might be justified where the witnesses are no longer available or can be reached only with difficulty. [*Hickman*, 329 U.S., at 511.]

The Government stresses that interviewees are scattered across the globe and that Upjohn has forbidden its employees to answer questions it considers irrelevant. The

---

19. The following discussion will also be relevant to counsel's notes and memoranda of interviews with the seven former employees should it be determined that the attorney-client privilege does not apply to them. See n.[23], supra.

20. This provides, in pertinent part:

> [A] party may obtain discovery of documents and tangible things otherwise discoverable under subdivision (b)(1) of this rule and prepared in anticipation of litigation or for trial by or for another party or by or for that other party's representative (including his attorney, consultant, surety, indemnitor, insurer, or agent) only upon a showing that the party seeking discovery has substantial need of the materials in the preparation of his case and that he is unable without undue hardship to obtain the substantial equivalent of the materials by other means. In ordering discovery of such materials when the required showing has been made, the court shall protect against disclosure of the mental impressions, conclusions, opinions, or legal theories of an attorney or other representative of a party concerning the litigation.

above-quoted language from *Hickman*, however, did not apply to "oral statements made by witnesses . . . whether presently in the form of [the attorney's] mental impressions or memoranda." Id., at 512. As to such material the Court did "not believe that any showing of necessity can be made under the circumstances of this case so as to justify production. . . . If there should be a rare situation justifying production of these matters, petitioner's case is not of that type." Id., at 512-513. . . . Forcing an attorney to disclose notes and memoranda of witnesses' oral statements is particularly disfavored because it tends to reveal the attorney's mental processes, 329 U.S., at 513 ("what he saw fit to write down regarding witnesses' remarks"); id., at 516-517 ("the statement would be his [the attorney's] language, permeated with his inferences") (Jackson, J., concurring).[21] Rule 26 accords special protection to work product revealing the attorney's mental processes. The Rule permits disclosure of documents and tangible things constituting attorney work product upon a showing of substantial need and inability to obtain the equivalent without undue hardship. This was the standard applied by the Magistrate. . . . Rule 26 goes on, however, to state that "[i]n ordering discovery of such materials when the required showing has been made, the court shall protect against disclosure of the mental impressions, conclusions, opinions or legal theories of an attorney or other representative of a party concerning the litigation." Although this language does not specifically refer to memoranda based on oral statements of witnesses the *Hickman* court stressed the danger that compelled disclosure of such memoranda would reveal the attorney's mental processes. It is clear that this is the sort of material the draftsmen of the Rule had in mind as deserving special protection. See Notes of Advisory Committee on 1970 Amendment to Rules, 28, U.S.C. App., p.442 ("The subdivision . . . goes on to protect against disclosure the mental impressions, conclusions, opinions, or legal theories . . . of an attorney or other representative of a party. The *Hickman* opinion drew special attention to the need for protecting an attorney against discovery of memoranda prepared from recollection of oral interviews. The courts have steadfastly safeguarded against disclosure of lawyers' mental impressions and legal theories. . . .").

Based on the foregoing, some courts have concluded that *no* showing of necessity can overcome protection of work product which is based on oral statements from witnesses. . . . Those courts declining to adopt an absolute rule have nonetheless recognized that such material is entitled to special protection. . . .

We do not decide the issue at this time. It is clear that the Magistrate applied the wrong standard when he concluded that the Government had made a sufficient showing of necessity to overcome the protections of the work-product doctrine. The Magistrate applied the "substantial need" and "without undue hardship" standard articulated in the first part of Rule 26(b)(3). The notes and memoranda sought by the Government here, however, are work product based on oral statements. If they reveal communications, they are, in this case, protected by the attorney-client privilege. To

---

21. Thomas described his notes of the interviews as containing "what I considered to be the important questions, the substance of the responses to them, my beliefs, as to the importance of these, my beliefs as to how they related to the inquiry, my thoughts as to how they related to other questions. In some instances they might even suggest other questions that I would have to ask or things that I needed to find elsewhere." . . .

the extent they do not reveal communications, they reveal the attorneys' mental processes in evaluating the communications. As Rule 26 and *Hickman* make clear, such work product cannot be disclosed simply on a showing of substantial need and inability to obtain the equivalent without undue hardship.

While we are not prepared at this juncture to say that such material is always protected by the work-product rule, we think a far stronger showing of necessity and unavailability by other means than was made by the Government or applied by the Magistrate in this case would be necessary to compel disclosure. . . . [W]e . . . reverse the judgment of the Court of Appeals for the Sixth Circuit and remand the case to it for such further proceedings in connection with the work-product claim as are consistent with this opinion. . . .

Chief Justice BURGER, concurring in part and concurring in the judgment.

I join in Parts I and III of the opinion of the Court and in the judgment. As to Part II, I agree fully with the Court's rejection of the so-called "control group" test, its reasons for doing so, and its ultimate holding that the communications at issue are privileged. As the Court states, however, "if the purpose of the attorney-client privilege is to be served, the attorney and client must be able to predict with some degree of certainty whether particular discussions will be protected." . . . For this very reason, I believe that we should articulate a standard that will govern similar cases and afford guidance to corporations, counsel advising them, and federal courts.

The Court properly relies on a variety of factors in concluding that the communications now before us are privileged. . . . Because of the great importance of the issue, in my view the Court should make clear now that, as a general rule, a communication is privileged at least when, as here, an employee or former employee speaks at the direction of the management with an attorney regarding conduct or proposed conduct within the scope of employment. The attorney must be one authorized by the management to inquire into the subject and must be seeking information to assist counsel in performing any of the following functions: (a) evaluating whether the employee's conduct has bound or would bind the corporation; (b) assessing the legal consequences, if any, of that conduct; or (c) formulating appropriate legal responses to actions that have been or may be taken by others with regard to that conduct. . . . Other communications between employees and corporate counsel may indeed be privileged . . . but the need for certainty does not compel us now to prescribe all the details of the privilege in this case.

Nevertheless, to say we should not reach all facets of the privilege does not mean that we should neglect our duty to provide guidance in a case that squarely presents the question in a traditional adversary context. Indeed, because Federal Rule of Evidence 501 provides that the law of privileges "shall be governed by the principles of the common law as they may be interpreted by the courts of the United States in the light of reason and experience," this Court has a special duty to clarify aspects of the law of privileges properly before us. Simply asserting that this failure "may to some slight extent undermine desirable certainty" . . . neither minimizes the consequences of continuing uncertainty and confusion nor harmonizes the inherent dissonance of acknowledging that uncertainty while declining to clarify it within the frame of issues presented.

KEY POINTS

1. The attorney-client privilege extends to corporations, but there is not a simple test to determine whether a communication is covered by the privilege. If an employee makes a communication to a lawyer at the direction of a superior for the purpose of obtaining legal advice for the corporation about a matter relevant to the scope of the employee's corporate duties, the communication is likely to be privileged.
2. Privileging the communication to the attorney does not privilege the underlying facts. The employee may be deposed and must answer truthfully and fully about the relevant matter, but may not be asked "What did you say to corporate counsel?"

NOTES AND QUESTIONS

1. *Upjohn* involved application of the work-product doctrine in addition to the attorney-client privilege. The Supreme Court initially announced the doctrine, now codified in Fed. R. Civ. P. 26(b)(3), in Hickman v. Taylor, 329 U.S. 495, 511 (1947):

> Proper preparation of a client's case demands that [the lawyer] assemble information, sift what he considers to be the relevant from the irrelevant facts, prepare his legal theories and plan his strategy without undue and needless interference. . . .
>
> . . . This work is reflected, of course, in interviews, statements, memoranda, correspondence, briefs, mental impressions, personal beliefs, and the countless other tangible and intangible ways—aptly though roughly termed by the Circuit Court of Appeals in this case as the "work product of the lawyer." Were such materials open to opposing counsel on mere demand, much of what is now put down in writing would remain unwritten. An attorney's thought, heretofore inviolate, would not be his own. Inefficiency, unfairness and sharp practices would inevitably develop in the giving of legal advice and in preparation of cases for trial. The effect on the legal profession would be demoralizing. And the interests of the clients and the cause of justice would be poorly served.

Although the Court's rhetoric may be a bit extreme, this language suggests a rationale for the work-product doctrine that is similar to that often suggested for the attorney-client privilege.

2. Should corporations possess an attorney-client privilege? How do they differ in relevant respects from individuals? In thinking about this, is it pertinent that corporations cannot claim the Fifth Amendment privilege against self-incrimination? Is it sensible to speak of a corporation's "expectation of privacy"?

3. What are the consequences of permitting assertion of the privilege in *Upjohn*? What would have been the consequences of forbidding it? How costly would discovery have been? How costly do you think the litigation trying to avoid discovery was? How do these costs relate to the policies of the privilege?

4. Where does the law stand in the aftermath of *Upjohn*? The Court rejected the control group test, but refused to replace it with a new test, electing instead to

determine on a case-by-case basis whether the privilege exists. How clear is the Court's opinion? Could it have been clearer? Should it have been? Where does the subject matter test stand in the wake of *Upjohn*?

5. When new management take over a corporation, they, not the previous management, are the holders of the corporation's privilege, and may decide whether to assert or waive it, even with respect to statements made by previous management. Commodity Futures Trading Comm'n v. Weintraub, 470 U.S. 1026 (1985).

6. One issue that often arises is whether a corporation waives its attorney client privilege when it conducts an internal investigation of corporate wrongdoing. In In re Woolworth Corp. Securities Class Action Litig., 1996 U.S. Dist. LEXIS 7773 (S.D.N.Y. June 6, 1996), the court held that an internal investigative report prepared jointly by attorneys and accountants was protected by the attorney-client privilege. Relying on *Upjohn*, the court stated that where counsel had been retained by upper management to conduct an internal investigation, notes and memoranda reflecting communications between a corporation's employees and counsel were protected by the attorney-client privilege. The court also stated that strong public policy considerations militated against a broad finding of waiver with regard to the investigator's underlying notes and memoranda, when the investigative report was given to the SEC and released to the public: "A finding that publication of an internal investigative report constitutes waiver might well discourage corporations from taking the responsible step of employing outside counsel to conduct an investigation when wrongdoing is suspected." In contrast, in In re Kidder Peabody Securities Litigation, 168 F.R.D. 459 (S.D.N.Y. 1996), the court held that a securities firm waived the attorney-client privilege by publicly releasing an internal investigative report and by attempting to use the favorable report as a "sword" in litigation. The securities firm had invoked the privilege with respect to notes from interviews of individuals who were employed by the firm at the time of the interview. Relying on In re von Bulow, 828 F.2d 94, 100-103 (2d Cir. 1987), the court said that the scope of any waiver by virtue of disclosure was to be defined by the so-called fairness doctrine, which turns on the circumstances of the disclosure. The court said that disclosure in a "judicial" setting does trigger a waiver by implication for related and otherwise privileged materials. It held that, under the particular facts of the case, Kidder had waived its privilege by repeated injection of the substance of the investigative report into "this and other litigations" and into related litigation contexts. The offer of the Kidder report to the SEC was said to represent Kidder's continuing effort to influence the outcome of pending or anticipated litigations and agency investigations. It is not clear how this case would be treated under the new FRE 502; however, if the disclosure was intentional, the "ought in fairness" language of FRE 502(a) would likely lead the court to similar results. In re Omnicom Group Securities Litigation, 233 F.R.D. 400, 406-409 (S.D.N.Y. 2006), has a lengthy discussion of relatively current views on the matter.

7. Some critics express concern that privilege challenges and crime-fraud proceedings are undermining the ability of corporate defendants to protect legitimate claims of privilege, especially in highly regulated industries where product liability litigation has been significant. In one example, the State of Minnesota and Blue Cross and Blue Shield of Minnesota brought suit against 11 tobacco manufacturers for reimbursement of Medicaid costs related to the treatment of smoking-related illnesses in State by Humphrey v. Philip Morris, Inc., 1998 Minn. App. LEXIS 431 (Minn. Ct. App. Mar. 17, 1998), *stay denied*, 523 U.S. 1056 (1998). The plaintiffs used broad allegations of fraud and conspiracy in its production requests, which ultimately resulted in the production of more than 33 million pages and privilege logs identifying more than 200,000 privileged documents. The Minnesota district court found that an *in camera* review of the privileged documents was required after the plaintiff's prima facie showing of crime-fraud.

To facilitate the massive task of reviewing the documents, the court instituted a system of random review or spot checking. The defendants were ordered to separate the privileged documents into 16 categories. To determine where there was privilege, the special master reviewed documents from each category. He eventually reviewed approximately 800 of the 200,000 documents and made his recommendation based on this "illustrative" sample. The court held that four categories of documents were not privileged, releasing approximately 39,000 documents to the plaintiffs. Privilege challenges, it has been argued, are becoming a more common trial strategy for plaintiffs who are unburdened by massive production requests that drain the resources of corporate defendants. For an in-depth discussion of the problem, see John J. Mulderig, Leslie Wharton & Cynthia S. Cecil, Tobacco Cases May Be Only the Tip of the Iceberg for Assaults on Privilege, 67 Def. Counsel J. 16 (2000); David J. Fried, Too High a Price for Truth: The Exception to the Attorney-Client Privilege for Contemplated Crimes and Frauds, 64 N.C. L. Rev. 443 (1986). The privilege as it relates to crime-fraud proceedings is discussed more fully in the section "Exceptions to the Privilege," beginning on page 934, infra. It is mentioned here to sensitize you to one of the problems with the attorney-client privilege that occurs within the corporate context.

PROBLEMS

12.8. Defendant Admiral Insurance Co. has filed a petition for writ of mandamus directing the district court to vacate its order compelling production of communications secured by Admiral's counsel in anticipation of a securities fraud suit. In June 1987, counsel for Admiral had interviewed the two Admiral executives who were most informed about Admiral's allegedly fraudulent transactions in Arizona properties. The two executives resigned soon after the interviews. When plaintiffs, individuals injured by the transactions, scheduled the former executives for deposition, counsel for the two executives responded that they would invoke the Fifth Amendment. Plaintiffs seek production of the statements on the basis that the information is unavailable from any other source. Admiral argues that these statements are protected from disclosure by the attorney-corporate client privilege. How should the court rule?

12.9. Plaintiffs have moved to compel the production of a diary written by Jeanette Curry while she was an employee of defendant Dayco Corporation. Jeanette compiled the diary at the direction of outside counsel to her employer. The diary chronicled events that form the basis for part of the present securities litigation. Plaintiffs contend that any privilege that might protect the contents of the diary has been waived since a newspaper reporter obtained a copy of the diary from an unidentified source. The defendants (Dayco and Jeanette) argue that the contents are protected by the attorney-corporate client privilege and work-product doctrine. They argue that since Jeanette did not authorize disclosure, there has been no waiver. What result?

12.10. Employees of several Chemical Bank branches under the supervision of Demauro were investigated for violation of the Bank Secrecy Act, which makes "laundering" money (exchanging large denomination bills for small ones) illegal. Demauro gave false testimony to a grand jury about his knowledge of the violations and has been charged with perjury. To establish that he knowingly made false statements to the grand jury, the prosecution seeks to introduce the testimony of Chemical Bank's attorney, Martin. When Chemical Bank became aware of the criminal investigation, it asked Martin to conduct an internal investigation into employee wrongdoing. In the course of the investigation, Martin interviewed Demauro in his capacity as Vice President in charge of 23 branches. Demauro insists that his communications with Martin are protected by attorney-client privilege. Should the judge allow Martin's testimony?

12.11. Chicago Police Officer Rehling was injured and had part of one leg amputated after an automobile ran him down several years ago. Rehling finished a long period of medical leave and then requested reassignment on a limited duty basis to District 16, his former assignment. He worked for a few months processing citations at District 16 before he was transferred to the Alternative Response Unit, where officers handle incoming requests for the dispatch of squad cars. Rehling was unhappy with the transfer and sued the city under the American's with Disabilities Act, claiming discrimination against him due to his disability and failure to provide him with a reasonable accommodation. The City made a motion in limine to bar the testimony of Zoufal, General Counsel to the Superintendent of Police, based on their attorney-client privilege. Zoufal had allegedly stated that the Chicago Police Department could not have a "cripple" in a position where he would interact with the public because of the likelihood of the negative reaction it would draw. Rehling has argued that Zoufal, in his "business capacity as a decisionmaker," decided to have him transferred out of District 16. The city has countered by asserting that Zoufal was giving legal advice when he encouraged ranking members of the Police Department to order the transfer. Is Zoufal's testimony privileged?

3. The Government Client

The attorney-client privilege extends to entity clients other than corporations. Federal courts generally agree that the government, as client, should be afforded the protection of the attorney-client privilege. Some of the same difficulties that arise in regards to corporate clients are also present when the client is the government: Who exactly is the client? Who may invoke and waive the privilege? What is required to maintain a privilege's requirement of confidentiality? And, what constitutes a waiver? Since there has been no equivalent to *Upjohn* to define the parameters of the governmental attorney-client privilege, courts have tended to follow the law of corporate privilege. See, e.g., Galarza v. United States, 179 F.R.D. 291 (S.D. Cal. 1998).

In In re Grand Jury Subpeona Duces Tecum, 112 F.3d 910 (8th Cir. 1997), *cert. denied sub nom.* Office of the President v. Office of the Independent Counsel, 521 U.S. 1105 (1997), the court held that the White House may not use a governmental attorney-client privilege to withhold potentially relevant information from a federal grand jury. The strong public interest in honest government and in exposing wrongdoing by public officials, it said, would be ill-served by the use of a governmental attorney-client privilege in criminal proceedings.

In so deciding, the court highlighted two important distinctions between corporate and governmental clients. The White House, unlike private corporations, is not subject to any criminal liability and all government agents have a public duty to report wrongdoing. There seems to be an intuitive problem, the court said, with allowing the government to conceal evidence from a court, especially in criminal cases.

Only a year later, the Independent Counsel moved to compel the grand jury testimony of Deputy White House Counsel Bruce Lindsey after he declined to answer certain questions based on the governmental attorney-client privilege in In re Lindsey (Grand Jury Testimony), 158 F.3d 1263 (D.C. Cir. 1998). Like the Eighth Circuit, the court abrogated the governmental attorney-client privilege in criminal grand jury proceedings. Both cases clearly rejected the privilege in criminal proceedings only, leaving the governmental attorney-client privilege intact in civil cases. The Seventh Circuit also has rejected the privilege. In re Witness Before the Special Grand Jury 2000-2, 288 F.3d 289 (7th Cir. 2002) (holding that no attorney-client privilege existed between a state officer and government lawyer in context of federal criminal investigation).

However, the Second Circuit declined to follow *Lindsey*, in In re Grand Jury Investigation, 399 F.3d 527 (2d Cir. 2005), holding that the privilege exists and is enforceable in criminal proceedings as well. The court held that the Connecticut governor's office could invoke the attorney-client privilege against federal grand jury inquiries into conversations with former legal counsel, which were sought in connection with a federal bribery investigation. Id. at 536. The court reasoned that "[u]pholding the privilege furthers a culture in which consultation with government lawyers is accepted as a normal, desirable, and even indispensable part of conducting public business." Id. at 534. Although federal law applied in the case, the court gave weight to the fact that Connecticut had enacted a statute granting the privilege, noting that "the people of Connecticut, acting through their representatives, concluded that the public interest is advanced by upholding a governmental privilege even in the face of a criminal investigation." Id.

The Second Circuit took a similarly expansive view of the scope of privilege in civil cases. In In re County of Erie, 473 F.3d 413 (2d Cir. 2007), the court addressed whether the attorney-client privilege protects e-mails passed between a government lawyer and a public official, when the e-mails assessed "the legality of a policy and propose[d] alternative policies in that light." While the trial judge had denied protection of the e-mails because they went "beyond rendering legal advice," the court of appeals relied on In re Grand Jury Investigation, 399 F.3d 527 (2d Cir. 2005), and applied the attorney-client privilege. Specifically, the court emphasized that legal considerations should play a role in government policymaking and when a lawyer is assessing compliance with legal requirements "the lawyer's recommendation of a policy that complies (or better complies) with the legal obligation . . . is legal advice." Id. at 422.

4. Exceptions to the Privilege

There are four main exceptions to the attorney-client privilege:

a. Breach of Duty by a Lawyer or Client

The first exception applies to controversy between attorney and client. As we already mentioned, if a client sues for damages for the attorney's negligence or the attorney sues for fees due, the client may not invoke the privilege to bar admission of relevant evidence. Though the attorney-client communications remain protected against disclosure to outsiders, as between attorney and client the privilege is inapplicable. McCormick argues that the exception is premised on the "practical necessity that if effective legal service is to be encouraged the privilege must not stand in the way of the lawyer's just enforcement of his rights to be paid a fee and to protect his reputation." Kenneth S. Broun et al., McCormick on Evidence §91, at 143 (5th ed. 1999). Is that persuasive to you? Why is "encouraging effective legal service" important enough to pierce the veil of confidentiality, but determining, say, who committed a murder is not?

b. Document Attested by a Lawyer

A second exception concerns the attorney who acts as attesting witness on a document executed by the client. The exception is most commonly applied in will contests between the heirs or personal representatives of the deceased client. Although the privilege generally survives the death of a client, if an attorney acts as attesting witness to his client's will, the attorney is permitted to testify regarding the validity or interpretation of the will.

c. Identity of Client, Fee Information, and Related Matters

The third exception, which is the subject of increasing controversy in the courts, denies the privilege for certain fundamental information about the attorney-client relationship, such as the identity of the client, the client's address and occupation, and the attorney's fee arrangement. The exception is supported by some courts on the ground that such information does not involve a confidential communication. See In the Matter of Witnesses Before the Special March 1980 Grand Jury Appeal of United States, 729 F.2d 489 (7th Cir. 1984). Other courts have argued that such matters are not privileged because they are "preliminary, by their nature, establishing only the existence of the relation between client and counsel." In re Grand Jury Subpoenas (United States v. Hirsch), 803 F.2d 493, 496 (9th Cir. 1986).

Notwithstanding such arguments, courts have created three exceptions to the traditional rule that attorney's fees and client identity are not privileged. The first exception, known as the "legal advice" exception, holds that such information is protected by the privilege where there is a strong likelihood that disclosure would implicate the client in the very matter for which legal advice was sought. See In re Grand Jury Proceedings (Twist), 689 F.2d 1351, 1352 (11th Cir. 1982). The second exception, known as the "communication rationale" exception, holds that identity and fee information are privileged if disclosure would connect the client with a previously disclosed and independently privileged communication. See In re Shargel, 742 F.2d 61, 64 (2d Cir. 1984). The third exception privileges identity and fee information if it provides the "last link" in a chain of incriminating evidence that could result in criminal prosecution of the client. See In re Grand Jury Proceedings (Pavlick), 680 F.2d 1026, 1027 (5th Cir. 1982) (en banc), rev'g 663 F.2d 1057 (5th Cir. 1981); Baird v. Koerner, 279 F.2d 623, 633 (9th Cir. 1960) (attorney made payment to IRS of back taxes for client but refused to reveal name of client). These exceptions have not been uniformly approved by the courts. In fact, after a small burst of enthusiasm for them following the seminal decision in Baird v. Koerner, the courts have become disenchanted. For example, the Ninth Circuit, which decided *Baird*, now takes the position that only the "communications rationale" exception remains good law. Tornay v. United States, 840 F.2d 1424 (9th Cir. 1988). Much more typical of the current judicial attitude toward these matters is In re Grand Jury Investigation 83-2-35 (Durant), 723 F.2d 447 (6th Cir. 1983). In *Durant*, checks had been stolen from IBM and deposited in various bank accounts. Durant, an attorney, had been paid for legal services out of one of these accounts. Thus, identifying the client who had paid him would probably identify a person involved with the thefts. Durant was required to disclose that information. For an argument that exceptions to the privilege should focus exclusively on the client's intent, see Developments in the Law—Privileged Communications, 98 Harv. L. Rev. 1501 (1985).

d. Communication in Furtherance of a Crime or Fraud

Though communications regarding a past crime or fraud are privileged, communications in furtherance of an ongoing or future illegality are not. The rationale behind the exception is that where a client seeks advice to aid a future or ongoing crime or fraud, the client does not retain an attorney in his professional capacity. In order to defeat the privilege, the party seeking disclosure bears the burden of bringing the communication within the crime-fraud exception.

In applying the crime-fraud exception, many courts follow the intent-based test announced in Clark v. United States, 289 U.S. 1 (1933). Under this test, the party invoking the exception must make a prima facie showing that the attorney-client communications were made for the purpose of furthering the commission of a future or present crime or fraud. The test focuses strictly on the client's intent. Thus, even if the attorney acted in good faith and was unaware of the wrongdoing, the privilege may be lost. For an example, see In re Grand Jury Proceedings No. 96-55344, 87 F.3d 377 (9th Cir. 1996). The Second Circuit has referred to the burden in terms of a probable cause showing to believe that the client consulted the attorney for the purpose of furthering wrongful conduct. See In re Grand Jury Subpoena Duces Tecum Dated Sept. 15, 1983, 731 F.2d 1032, 1039 (2d Cir. 1984). Other courts have defined the evidentiary standard differently. For example, in In re Grand Jury Investigation, 842 F.2d 1223 (11th Cir. 1987), the court used a two-part test to decide whether the crime-fraud exception applied to an attorney-client communication, not only requiring the prima facie showing of crime-fraud purpose, but also "showing that the attorney's assistance was obtained in furtherance of the criminal or fraudulent activity or was closely related to it." Id. at 1226. The correct answer should be that the finding is governed by FRE 104(a), and thus that its necessary conditions must be found by a preponderance of the evidence.

Note that the crime-fraud exception only applies to attorney-client communications that promote a crime or a fraud, as opposed to other misconduct. See, e.g., In re Spalding Sports Worldwide, Inc., 203 F.3d 800, 806–807 (Fed. Cir. 2000) (inequitable conduct not amounting to crime or fraud does not vitiate the attorney-client privilege). For example, discussions of a possible breach of contract by the client will remain privileged because breach of contract is neither a crime nor a fraud, and is not even considered misconduct from an economic standpoint. See, e.g., Barry E. Adler, Efficient Breach Theory Through the Looking Glass, 83 N.Y.U. L. Rev. 1679, 1688-1689 (2008).

Remember that privileges do apply in preliminary factfinding, FRE 104(a). Under what circumstances, then, may allegedly privileged material be consulted to determine if it is privileged? This was the question facing the Court in United States v. Zolin, 491 U.S. 554 (1989). The Court held that before engaging in in camera review of the allegedly privileged material to decide the privilege question, the trial court "should require a factual basis adequate to support a good faith belief by a reasonable person" that in camera review would establish that the crime-fraud exception applies and that the communication would be admitted. Id. at 572. The court concluded that the evidentiary threshold could be satisfied by any relevant evidence, whether or not it was independent of the allegedly privileged communication. Id. at 574.

The crime-fraud exception applies both to the attorney-client privilege and to the attorney's ethical duty of confidentiality. See Rules 1.2(d) and 1.6(b) in the ABA's Model Rules of Professional Conduct (2005) for provisions dealing with a client's illegal conduct. Is an attorney ethically obligated to report future crimes on the part of a client? What about past crimes? Compare ABA Model Rules of Professional Conduct, Rule 1.6(b), with ABA Model Code of Professional Responsibility, DR 4-101(C).

The crime-fraud exception has also been applied to the work-product privilege. In In re Murphy, 560 F.2d 326, 328 (8th Cir. 1977), the court applied a two-part test to determine which work-product documents would be admitted into evidence. Under the test, the party must (1) make a prima facie showing of crime or fraud; and (2) show a relationship between the illegal conduct and the attorney's work product. This test has been criticized on the ground that it disregards the client's intent. See, e.g., In re International Sys. & Controls Corp Sec. Litig., 693 F.2d 1235, 1243 (5th Cir. 1982).

PROBLEMS

12.12. A federal grand jury indicted Edwin Lewis and three others with conspiring to violate federal immigration laws. The indictment alleged that Lewis had falsely held himself out to be an attorney, and had filed fraudulent amnesty applications with the Immigration and Naturalization Service (INS) on behalf of over 100 clients. A search warrant allowed the government to seize client files from Lewis's office. The files contained four types of documents: (1) completed INS forms; (2) forms prepared in house by the law firm (forms designed to elicit information for the applications); (3) materials designed to corroborate the information contained in the INS forms; and (4) notes apparently prepared by agents of the law firm. Some of the other items seized from the offices included blank boarding passes; blank stationery from airlines and blank stationery from various Consulates General, presumably used to create false evidence of foreign travel; and blank pay receipts from various businesses, presumably used to create false evidence of employment.

Some of Lewis's clients had filed for amnesty with the INS, while others had sought his legal advice regarding amnesty but had not filed applications at the time Lewis was arrested. The only way the government can find out the identity of these latter clients is by looking at Lewis's files. What arguments can the government make that they are entitled to all of the evidence seized from Lewis's office? Are there any special problems they might run into regarding the anonymous clients?

12.13. The government obtained a warrant and seized files and materials from a law firm that is the subject of a criminal proceeding. The files are currently sealed by court order, pending a decision as to whether the files should be protected by the attorney-client privilege. The government concedes that the firm has the right to invoke the privilege on behalf of its clients but contends that the crime-fraud exception removes these materials from the scope of the privilege. Should the crime-fraud exception apply where the alleged criminality being investigated is solely that of the law firm? If so, the government will be given access to the confidential files of innocent clients. If not, the law firm will be able to hinder an investigation of its own alleged criminal conduct by asserting a privilege designed to protect clients. Should the court allow the files to be unsealed?

12.14. Ralls was paid by a client/fee-payer to defend Bonnette against criminal charges connected to Bonnette's attempt to transport 300 pounds of cocaine from Arizona to California. The government sought to discover the name of the person who hired Ralls and the amount and method of payment. Ralls moved to quash the government's grand jury subpoena on the basis of attorney-client privilege. The district court ordered Ralls to testify as to the client's identity and the fee arrangements but held that the conversations between Ralls and the client were privileged. Should an appellate court affirm this decision?

12.15. Elsa and Arlen were in the midst of a messy divorce. During a custody fight over their two sons, Lars and Herbie, Elsa met with her attorney, Friedman. Elsa was convinced that Arlen had been sexually abusing the children. Friedman invited Elsa's friend, Margie, to be present in order to have a "cool head" in the room. While in front of Friedman, Elsa and Margie began discussing ways of killing Arlen or hurting the children and framing Arlen for it. Friedman, afraid that Elsa and Margie might be serious, informed a judge. The judge announced the substance of Friedman's disclosure at the custody hearing, and Arlen was granted custody, while Friedman's appearance as Elsa's counsel was stricken. Margie later broke into Arlen's house carrying a gun, found him asleep in his bed, and fired two shots, hitting him once in the leg. Margie was arrested and pled guilty to a series of assault related crimes. Elsa is now on trial for conspiracy to commit murder and conspiracy to commit assault. The prosecution has called Friedman to testify to the conspiracy related communications that he witnessed between Elsa and Margie in his office, but Elsa has asserted the attorney-client privilege to bar his testimony. What result?

5. Reflection on the Attorney-Client Privilege

The attorney-client privilege is the oldest of the confidential communication privileges. Still, debate has continued over why the privilege should exist. Such debate has often focused on the costs that the privilege entails. One argument, employing a micro-economic perspective, has been made that the attorney-client privilege has benefits that justify its costs. The following excerpt discusses these and other related matters:

RONALD J. ALLEN, MARK F. GRADY, DANIEL D. POLSBY, AND MICHAEL S. YASHKO, A POSITIVE THEORY OF THE ATTORNEY-CLIENT PRIVILEGE AND THE WORK PRODUCT DOCTRINE

19 J. Legal Stud. 359 (1990)

I. INTRODUCTION

Protecting the confidentiality of legal information is an odd goal in a judicial system that values openness as highly as ours does. In some litigation settings we make a fetish out of free access to all information. Modern discovery rules can require parties to exchange boxcars of records with one another, and attorneys are under an obligation to disclose cases that run against the arguments that they make. The argument for openness is in principle strong. When there are no surprises at trial, the parties more likely will join issue on the real questions of fact and law—those that properly should determine case outcomes.

Why, then, do the confidentiality doctrines remain? The conventional response quickly runs up against an insoluble dilemma. It accepts the aspirations of modern discovery systems, including the one forbidding counsel from participating in perjurious efforts; it posits costless rules of confidentiality that have no effect on the opponent's ability to obtain information; and then it asserts that these supposedly costless rules nonetheless create incentives for clients to disclose information to counsel.[22] How can this be? If confidentiality rules do not increase the cost of obtaining information once it is in the lawyer's possession, and if the lawyer must rigorously police the client's responses to the opponent to ensure no prevarication or sleight of hand, then the client will have no incentive to disclose unfavorable information to the lawyer.

Because of the tension between the conventional view of the confidentiality rules and their purported consequences, some scholars have recognized that the justifications for the rules are insubstantial,[23] but they have not examined the assumption that confidentiality rules are costless.[24] This failure may be a testament to the strength of the commitment to openness in the legal process. To admit that the rules of confidentiality are costly requires one to recognize that they do indeed constrain openness. If confidentiality rules impose costs, and we assert that they do, the effect is to increase the cost to the opponent of securing the relevant information, whatever it may be. Because of the confidentiality rules, for example, rather than simply asking the attorney to turn over the entire case file, the opponent must secure that information in other ways, such as deposing the client. That in itself may increase costs, and in addition the client will have the aid of counsel before and at the deposition, which may make the opponent's task of extracting the information more difficult and thus more costly still. After all, merely having to ask two questions instead of one to get the requested information increases costs. Under our theory, however, the costs of confidentiality are not regrettable; rather, they are the conditions that create incentives to disclose to the lawyer: the more costly an opponent's efforts to obtain information disclosed to the lawyer, the less likely the opponent will secure that information, and the greater the corresponding incentive to disclose it to the lawyer. Once the information is in the lawyer's possession, the lawyer may guide the litigation in directions unanticipated by the client, and here lie the benefits of the confidentiality rules that justify their costs.

---

22. See, for example, Stephen A. Saltzburg, Corporate and Related Attorney-Client Privilege Claims: A Suggested Approach, 12 Hofstra L. Rev. 279, 283-284 (1984).

23. It is this recognition that makes explaining such matters as waiver under the privilege so difficult. See, for example, Richard Marcus, The Perils of Privilege: Waiver and the Litigator, 84 Mich. L. Rev. 1605, 1619-1622 (1986).

24. Yet other scholars, convinced that the rules of confidentiality impose greater costs than they secure benefits, argue for eliminating some or all of the rules. See, for example, Marvin Frankel, Partisan Justice (1980). For a discussion, see Albert Alschuler, The Preservation of a Client's Confidences: One Value Among Many or a Categorical Imperative?, 52 Colo. L. Rev. 349 (1981).

We develop these points here and propose a positive theory that explains the confidentiality rules. Two doctrines authorize or mandate lawyers to preserve the confidentiality of their clients' legal affairs. The attorney-client privilege exempts from discovery and production at trial confidential communications from client to lawyer, and confidential communications from lawyer to client that may expose a client's confidential communication, if made for the purpose of securing legal advice.[25] The work product doctrine exempts from production material generated by the attorney in anticipation of litigation.[26] These doctrines affect decisionmaking on two margins. The expectation of confidentiality can affect a client's decision concerning how much unfavorable information to divulge to a lawyer and, at a limit, whether to go to a lawyer at all. Without legal protection, a client might otherwise anticipate that divulging information to a lawyer would reduce an opponent's cost of acquiring it. Thus, contrary to the conventional theory of the privilege, one of effects of the privilege must be to raise—or at least not lower—the cost of obtaining useful information once it is in the hands of the attorney. Confidentiality can also affect the amount of information produced by the lawyer. When lawyers cannot produce favorable information without also producing unfavorable information, lack of confidentiality would reduce the amount of favorable information that lawyers would produce.[27] In brief, our argument is that the attorney-client privilege and the work product doctrine offer two perspectives on a larger goal, which is to increase the amount of information available to courts about disputes and to work against the disincentives to the production of that information which would otherwise exist. In our legal system, lawyers are both conduits of information from their clients to the courts and independent producers of information for the same audience. The attorney-client privilege takes the client's perspective and establishes the level of confidentiality needed to get the client to consult a lawyer and to divulge the optimum amount of information to him. The work product doctrine then takes the attorney's perspective and provides the level of confidentiality needed to induce the attorney to perform the optimal amount of legal investigation. . . .

---

25. John Henry Wigmore, 4 Evidence §§2285-2292 (1905). We are relying on the 1905 edition of Wigmore because we are more interested in his views than his subsequent compilers. See also Developments in the Law: Privileged Communications, 98 Harv. L. Rev. 1450, 1501 (1985).

26. Hickman v. Taylor, 329 U.S. 495 (1947); Fed. Rule Civil Proc. 26(b)(3).

27. Ethical rules also comprise a form of legally mandated confidentiality. The lawyer's ethical obligations pose the problem of how to prevent the agent from expropriating the principal—the lawyer could threaten to inform on his client and thereby get a payment from him. The other two rules—the attorney-client privilege and the work product doctrine—address a different problem: how much information about legal disputes will clients and lawyers produce. Accordingly, the ethical obligations of lawyers are beyond the scope of this Article. . . .

We also put aside the question of the implications of the privilege for nonlitigation oriented activity. The problem there, again, does not center on the production of legal information. Instead, it centers on providing the optimum incentives to ensure compliance with the law. For a preliminary exploration of that issue, see Ronald J. Allen & Cynthia M. Hazelwood, Preserving the Confidentiality of Internal Corporate Investigations, 12 J. Corp. L. 355 (1987).

II. THE ATTORNEY-CLIENT PRIVILEGE AND THE CONTINGENT CLAIM THEORY . . .

A. Theories About the Attorney-Client Theory

1. *The Contingent Claim Theory*

In contrast to some contemporary theories of the privilege, ours assumes that it must impose some costs upon the adversary. If a person believes that disclosure of an unfavorable fact to an attorney could reduce the other side's costs to discover it, this belief may deter the party from divulging the fact to his lawyer. And without a privilege, a party may very well believe that disclosure to an attorney would reduce his opponent's cost of discovery. The attorney is a repeat player in the legal system, and so is likely to co-operate with other repeat players. Moreover, the attorney is ethically bound to respect the system's rules. Accordingly, a client reasonably could believe that in the absence of a privilege an attorney would truthfully answer the question: "What has your client told you?" A client left entirely to his own, by contrast, may feel that he has more room to maneuver. Thus, one might expect a client to conclude that, absent a privilege, divulging information to a lawyer will reduce his opponent's costs of discovering information.

The existence of a privilege changes things. The privilege at a minimum does not decrease the adversary's costs in obtaining information, and in fact it may increase them. There is no decrease because the adversary must still obtain information from the client, just as he would have been required to do had the client never consulted an attorney. Costs may increase because the lawyer may give the client guidance in how to respond honestly but craftily to an interrogatory, thus making the adversary's task of obtaining complete information more difficult. In any event, if the privilege does not increase the other side's discovery costs, there is no conceivable reason for it, a point that Kaplow and Shavell have made before us.[28] Moreover, there is evidence suggesting that the privilege does increase discovery costs. The most telling datum may be the continuing existence of attorney-client privilege cases. If opponents could acquire information just as cheaply by alternative means, there would be little reason for them to litigate whether that same information is protected by the privilege. In addition, studies indicate that lawyers often assert after trial that the other side did not acquire all the relevant unfavorable facts. Some of these unfavorable facts must be privileged under the current rules, which is one reason they never see the light.

Moreover, notwithstanding the ostensible dedication of the legal system to open discovery, the attorney is not in fact expected to act as a policeman regulating in detail the forthrightness of the client's responses to an opponent. Perjury is a limit, but there is a large gap between absolute candor and perjury. As the activity of the client moves towards the perjurious pole, the chances increase that a court will hold there to be no privilege, but there nonetheless remains a large area within which clients and

---

28. Louis Kaplow & Steven Shavell, Legal Advice About Information to Present in Litigation: Its Effects and Social Desirability, 102 Harv. L. Rev. 565, 570 (1989).

attorneys may maneuver while blanketed with the protections of the privilege.[29] It is here that the actual incentives created by the privilege become clear, and they entail the possibility that the privilege will detract from, rather than just be neutral with respect to, the objective of openness in the system.

Given that the privilege must entail costs—and the enormous volume of litigation over the privilege could hardly be explained unless it were pretty clear that the privilege did impede full discovery—it is necessary to understand the benefits it provides. Existing theories of the privilege do not answer this question. In fact, two benefits result. First, the privilege facilitates the examination of contingent claims and in so doing furthers the values served by those claims. Second, it reduces perjury in the system as a whole. We discuss these points in turn.

Many legal claims depend on facts that may appear to the lay person as unfavorable to the party asserting the legal claim. For example, a party's defense of contributory negligence often entails the concession of his own negligence. Similarly, for a party to claim that he was incompetent to enter a contract often involves conceding that an agreement was reached.

This contingent structure of the law may be the most visible remnant of the old system of special pleading.[30] Under common law pleading requirements, the parties pleaded against each other until they joined issue on a question of law or fact. Each time one party pleaded, the other would have an opportunity either to demur, or to deny the truth of his opponent's allegations, or to introduce new matter and thus to confess and avoid it.[31] In the earliest days of the common law, unlike our modern era, the two were strict alternatives. The common law's nurturance of special pleas made contingent claims common. Parties could and frequently did confess and avoid the pleas of their opponents. Thus, if a party pleaded the making of a contract, his opponent could specially plead that he was incompetent to contract because of age or some other reason. If a party pleaded that the defendant struck him, his opponent could specially plead that he was acting in self defense. A special plea (confession and avoidance) by the defendant would open the door to further special pleading by the plaintiff, for instance, that the defendant used more force than was necessary to defend himself. Ultimately special pleading made lawsuits depend on narrow issues of fact or law, a result that seems alien to our civil procedure. Nonetheless, the hierarchical imprint and doctrinal structure both remain.

---

29. The formal rules of confidentiality actually protect a certain amount of evasion by the attorney. For example, the Model Rules of Professional Conduct, in a Comment to rules on "Candor Toward the Tribunal," state that "An advocate . . . is usually not required to have personal knowledge of matters asserted in [pleadings and other litigation documents], for litigation documents ordinarily present assertions by the client, or by someone on the client's behalf, and not assertions by the lawyer." Rule 3.3, Comment, Representations by a Lawyer [2] (1984). Creating a distinction between the client's and the lawyer's knowledge encourages lawyers to learn of the client's information without fully "knowing" it for purposes of the ethical rules.

30. See Richard A. Epstein, A Theory of Strict Liability, 2 J. Legal Stud. 151 (1973); Richard A. Epstein, Defenses and Subsequent Pleas in a System of Strict Liability, 3 J. Legal Stud. 165 (1974).

31. See Thomas Chitty, Treatise on Pleading with Precedents and Forms (13th ed. 1859); James Fitzjames Stephen, A Treatise on the Principles of Pleading in Civil Actions (Tyler ed. 1882); Joseph H. Koffler and Alison Reppy, Common Law Pleading 433-531 (1969); Richard A. Epstein, Pleadings and Presumptions, 40 U. Chi. L. Rev. 556 (1973).

Our theory proceeds on the assumption that a modern litigant, like his common law ancestors, still has two main strategies for defeating an adverse claim. He can deny the claim in its own terms or defeat it with an affirmative defense, or some similar contingent claim. In the driver-pedestrian example, the driver can deny he was negligent or prove that the pedestrian was contributorily negligent. However, and this is the heart of the matter, a potential client ignorant of the law has one option and not two. He must deny the claim against him in its own terms. Of course if potential clients were always honest, they would never deceitfully deny claims. We assume that individuals will sometimes be dishonest in pursuit of their self-interest. However—and this is the second crucial component of our argument—a legal regime that reduces the costs of information about contingent claims should facilitate their examination and consequently reduce the amount of perjury. Reducing the cost of litigating contingent claims gives potential clients an incentive to substitute away from dishonest denials. Even a client inclined to commit perjury about whether he was in the intersection against the light will have less reason to do so if he can easily learn from his lawyer that the plaintiff's claim can be defeated honestly—by proving that the plaintiff was contributorily negligent in jumping out into the intersection so soon after the light changed, and without looking for opposing traffic.

In sum, by increasing the adversary's costs of obtaining information about communications between lawyers and clients, the privilege facilitates inquiry into legal claims beyond the ken of lay persons. By doing so, the values that underlie contingent claims are furthered, and contingent claims, no less than others, produce real benefits. For instance, if contributory negligence were less often interposed as a defense, it would reduce the incentives of potential victims to use the proper amount of precaution.[32] This praiseworthy result is also accompanied by a decrease in fraud in the system, which occurs each time an individual who otherwise would have committed fraud in litigation is channeled to litigate a truthful contingent claim. Under our theory, then, the ultimate justification for the privilege lies in the improvements in behavior that result from the increased availability of contingent claims.

The foregoing discussion has emphasized how "No, I didn't" and "Yes, but" can be substituting strategies for defendants. What about plaintiffs' claims, though? A plaintiff's original claim may appear to be uncontingent, depending only on facts favorable to it, but even plaintiffs' claims can become contingent when defendants oppose them. For instance, a plaintiff's claim that he lent the defendant money, which the defendant never repaid, begins life in an entirely uncontingent form, as every prima facie showing does. Nonetheless, if the defendant maintains that he was underage at the time he borrowed, the plaintiff's claim changes character, because it can then depend on whether he made the loan so that the defendant could purchase "necessities." Similarly a plaintiff who originally pleads that the defendant was negligent may find that his ultimate claim depends on whether he or the defendant had the last clear chance.

---

32. See for example Richard Posner, A Theory of Negligence, 1 J. Legal Stud. 29 (1973); John Prather Brown, Toward An Economic Theory of Liability, 2 J. Legal Stud. 323 (1973); Mark Grady, Common Law Control of Strategic Behavior: Railroad Sparks and the Farmer, 17 J. Legal Stud. 15 (1988).

Contingent claims are not strictly affirmative defenses. Suppose that someone has promised that he will put X's first born daughter through college. Making his communication with his lawyer confidential would increase the odds that he would truthfully claim that there was no consideration and reduce the odds that he would falsely claim that he never said it. So long as there is any set of facts more favorable to the party than those which a typical lay person would think necessary to secure a claim or defense, the contingent claim theory would predict a privilege. To give a different example, a plaintiff in a contracts case may think that all contracts have to be in writing to be enforceable, and thus is willing to assert falsely that a writing has been destroyed in order to win a case in which there was an oral promise in front of a witness. Encouraging the plaintiff to be truthful with the lawyer will lead the lawyer to direct the litigation toward the enforceable oral contract. Similarly, if a plaintiff is unaware of the nature of executory contracts, he may falsely assert reliance; but if he fully discloses to counsel, the litigation can be channeled in the proper direction.

Because both plaintiffs' and defendants' claims are or can become contingent in the litigation process, we would expect that the privilege would apply to both types. If by contrast defendants simply denied claims made against them in precisely the same form originally used by plaintiffs, or if plaintiffs' claims were not or could not become contingent, we would not predict a privilege, even though we would predict that clients would still hire lawyers. . . .

The legal system might, but does not, make confidentiality depend on whether the client's communication actually bore on a denial or a contingent claim. It would be difficult, even after litigation, to sort communications so strictly; so much more while litigation is still in progress. Moreover, a strict privilege would neglect the fact that the critical incentives must exist at a time when the reluctant client is still ill-informed about the law. Thus, if a hypothetical client would assess some nontrivial probability that a communication would be helpful in devising a contingent claim, we would expect that the communication would be privileged (unless the opponent's costs of self-production by other means are very high). If the privilege were narrower, some contingent claims would be lost. Our theory thus predicts a broad privilege, but not an unlimited one. When the lawyer could not possibly use information to develop a contingent claim, and even a relatively ignorant client would know it, our theory predicts that the client's communication would not be privileged. Many cases bear out this hypothesis.

Our theory also predicts that the privilege does not reduce the cost of making a dishonest contingent claim.[33] We will return to this point when we examine the cases, because it is critical to our theory. Nonetheless, even if the privilege did to some extent reduce the cost of dishonest contingent claims, there would still be the question of which effect dominates: whether the privilege prevents more dishonest denials or induces more dishonest contingent claims.

In sum, the real question raised by the attorney-client privilege is virtually the opposite of the one posed by the many scholars who have criticized it. The question

---

33. This prediction is confirmed in cases such as Nix v. Whiteside, 475 U.S. 157 (1986), in which the Supreme Court held that the attorney acted properly in refusing to permit the client to testify falsely about a claim of self-defense.

is not whether the privilege increases perjury, but whether the increased costs created by the privilege can be justified by the *reduced* perjury that the privilege brings about and the greater number of contingent claims that it allows to be litigated, with their beneficial real-world effects.

This perspective also provides a powerful ordering principle for the privilege. As a result of failing properly to perceive the incentive structure that underlies the privilege, traditional theorists such as Wigmore have promulgated a general "absolute" rule followed by a welter of apparently ad hoc case law exceptions. Under our theory, the appropriate question would always remain the same: Would providing a privilege advance the exploration of contingent claims at trial? Cases finding no privilege can best be understood as expressing conclusions to the contrary.[34]

Numerous critics have charged that the attorney-client privilege encourages perjury and reduces the deterrent power of the law. We think these theories are wrong, and examine the best known ones here.

2. The Morgan Theory

Edmund Morgan's argument against the privilege was that its only practical consequence is to protect perjurers. Morgan thought that the complexity of modern law cases oblige lay persons to seek legal counsel.[35] Such persons could choose either to reveal all their facts to their lawyer or to suppress some. Called as a witness at the subsequent trial, the client would be positioned thus:

> If he told his lawyer the truth, he must now tell the same thing from the witness box. If he told his lawyer a lie and sticks to it, he will tell the same story at the trial or hearing. If he told his lawyer the truth and now tells a lie, why should he be protected from exposure? Is the privilege retained in order to protect perjurers? How can that either directly or indirectly further the administration of justice?[36]

Morgan's primary error was to use the average case to discredit the marginal one. When the marginal case is considered, it becomes evident that instead of increasing perjury, the attorney-client privilege reduces it. Typically, a client will be motivated to commit perjury when someone has made a claim against him. Even if Morgan was correct that people with legal problems will usually consult lawyers, it does not follow that therefore a client will necessarily disclose to his lawyer all unfavorable facts about himself. On the margin, he will be less likely to do so as the costs associated

---

34. The prediction of the contingent claim theory that the privilege is best understood as a qualified rather than an absolute bar to discovery is beginning to be explicitly expressed in the cases. See, for example, Greater Newburyport Clamshell Alliance et al. v. Public Service Co. of N.H., 838 F.2d 13, 19 (1st Cir. 1988); In re Grand Jury Proc., Des Moines, Iowa, 568 F.2d 555, 557 (8th Cir. 1977) (opponent's need relevant to a determination of privilege).

35. Edmund M. Morgan, Forward to the American Law Institute's Model Code of Evidence 25 (1942).

36. Id. at 26-27. Morgan's theory was foreshadowed by Whiting v. Barney, 30 N.Y. 330, 332 (1864), in which Judge Selden stated that the original purpose of the privilege came from the ancient rule of procedure that parties could not be compelled to testify. As the rules of litigation became more complex, lawyers became necessary, but "as parties were not then obliged to testify in their own cases, and could not be compelled to disclose facts known only to themselves, they would hesitate to employ professional men, and make the necessary disclosures to them, if the facts thus communicated were thus within the reach of their opponent." Id. at 333. Judge Selden then wondered whether legislation placing parties under obligations to testify had removed the reason for the privilege. Id. at 342.

with disclosure increase. The defendant who is unaware of the defense of contributory negligence is that much less likely to admit his own negligence.

Morgan thought, mistakenly, that the law can reduce perjury only by using sticks; he did not think of carrots. But it makes perfect sense to conceive of confidentiality as a carrot to induce people to refrain from lying; when the attorney-client privilege reduces the cost of contingent claims, it should also reduce the amount of perjury.

3. The Bentham-Kaplow-Shavell Theory

Jeremy Bentham's argument against the attorney-client privilege has been taken up and extended by Professors Louis Kaplow and Steven Shavell. According to Bentham, the attorney-client privilege reduces the deterrent effect of the law by giving lawbreakers the hope that the unfavorable information that they reveal to their attorneys would never be presented against them in a court of law. With his characteristic flair, he wrote,

> "A counselor, solicitor, or attorney, cannot conduct the cause of his client," (it has been observed) "if he is not fully instructed in the circumstances attending it; but the client" (it is added) "could not give the instructions with safety, if the facts confided to his advocate were to be disclosed." Not with safety? So much the better. To what object is the whole system of penal law directed, if it be not that no man shall have it in his power to flatter himself with the hope of safety, in the event of his engaging in the commission of an act which the law, on account of its supposed mischievousness, has thought fit to prohibit? The argument employed as a reason against the compelling such disclosure, is the very argument that pleads in favour of it. . . .
>
> [T]o the man who, having no guilt to disclose, has disclosed none to his lawyer, nothing could be of greater advantage than that this should appear; as it naturally would if the lawyer were subject to examination.[37]

Kaplow and Shavell make the same point, albeit with a much more elaborate model.[38] Kaplow and Shavell posit that lawyers act as filters for the information that triers of fact ultimately receive. When the lawyer is effective, the trier of fact receives less unfavorable information and more favorable information about the client and so is more likely to decide in his favor. According to this theory, the primary effect of the privilege is to reduce the expected sanction that a party faces for a possibly unlawful act. Hence, the privilege ought to be regarded as counterproductive whenever the client is factually liable, excepting only the case where the sanctions for the individual's act are too high. Deterrence would therefore increase, and that would be undesirable only in cases in which the law had established excessive sanctions in the first place. In such a case, the proper reform would be to correct the sanction rather than extend a privilege to suppress evidence.

Although superficially attractive, the Bentham-Kaplow-Shavell theory proves too much. By the same reasoning, for example, people should not be allowed to have

---

37. Jeremy Bentham, 7 The Rationale of Evidence, b. 9, 4, ch. 5 at 474 et seq. (Bowring ed. 1827).
38. Kaplow & Shavell, supra [note 33]. The basic model employed by Kaplow and Shavell in large measure is an elaboration of a model first proposed by B. Peter Pashigian, Regulation, Preventive Law, and the Duties of Attorneys, 21-25, in William J. Carney, ed., The Changing Role of the Corporate Attorney (1982).

lawyers at all. Kaplow and Shavell give no account of the good that the privilege might do, other than acknowledging that the privilege makes it easier for the innocent to escape liability. Under a normative interpretation of their theory, the privilege should be available only to individuals who have been mistakenly (or maliciously) accused of wrongdoing; or, put differently, that people charged with wrongdoing should not be able to consult lawyers unless they are in fact innocent. But of course if we knew how cases ought to be decided, there would be little reason to have a legal process, or indeed to have lawyers.[39] Kaplow and Shavell's argument is deficient because it ignores the useful role lawyers play in helping clients to develop contingent claims. . . . When clients are deterred from asserting contingent claims, because they are reluctant to reveal the bad facts upon which such claims may depend, society loses the benefit of whatever interest the contingent claim is supposed to serve. Kaplow-Shavell miss this effect, as did Bentham before them.

4. The Wigmore Theory

John Henry Wigmore defended the theory of the privilege against Bentham's attack, declaring: "In order to promote freedom of consultation of legal advisers by clients, the apprehension of compelled disclosure by the legal advisers must be removed; and hence the law must prohibit such disclosure by the legal advisers except on the client's consent.[40] Bentham's argument was that the privilege operates as a mere filter that would encourage unlawful acts. As Wigmore pointed out, this argument erroneously assumed that "all the acts and facts on one side have been wholly right and lawful and all of those on the other wholly wrong and unlawful."[41] But in a large proportion of cases, each party would have something to fear. Without a privilege, "a person who has a partly good cause would often be deterred from consultation by virtue of the bad part or of the part that might possibly (to his notion) be bad."[42] Wigmore's idea that the privilege is needed to ensure full disclosure—still the dominant theme in the literature—adumbrates the contingent claim theory by recognizing that the facts and law will not uniformly favor either party. Nevertheless, this idea is too simple to explain the cases. This is particularly evident in the famous Wigmore gloss upon the privilege. According to Wigmore, the conditions for the privilege are:

> Where legal advice of any kind is sought (2) from a professional legal adviser in his capacity as such, (3) the communications relevant to that purpose, (4) made in confidence (5) by the client, (6) are at his instance permanently protected (7) from disclosure by himself or by the legal adviser, (8) except the client waives the protection.[43]

The critical ingredient missing from his exegesis, which has exposed it to the contemporary attack, is any recognition of the relevance of behavioral incentives. Even if

---

39. It is unclear precisely of what the Kaplow/Shavell theory of the attorney-client privilege consists. Theories are generally tested by their predictive power. The only prediction that seems to emerge from the Kaplow/Shavell theory is that lawyers should only be provided for innocent individuals, if sanctions are set at the appropriate levels. This prediction is falsified by the facts.

40. Wigmore, supra note [25], §2991, at 3196.

41. Id. at 3202.

42. Id.

43. Wigmore, supra note [25], §2292, at 3204.

each of Wigmore's conditions is met, it would be senseless to provide confidentiality if the privilege would not advance the exploration of contingent claims. Courts have intuited this point, and have often refused to recognize a privilege, even when the Wigmore conditions have clearly been met, where doing so would not advance the exploration of contingent claims. Of course, courts have not formulated the issue in this way, but have simply engrafted upon Wigmore a long list of ad hoc exceptions. The contingent claim theory explains the cases more parsimoniously than Wigmore's ideas do because it focuses explicitly on the relevant incentives, and it gives a more satisfactory account of the beneficial purposes that the privilege seeks to advance.

5. *Rights-Based Theories*

Several commentators have proposed that under some circumstances it would be wrong—immoral—for the legal system to force the disclosure of attorney-client communications. David Louisell, for example, has urged that respect for privacy could adequately explain the privilege.[44] Charles Fried, on another tack, has defended the privilege as necessary to allow people in legal scrapes to discover what their rights are.[45] Neither of these theories adequately explains the privilege.

(a) *Privacy*

Louisell's notion that the privilege is founded on privacy leaves one to ponder: what is privacy founded upon? The legal system has routinely sacrificed the privacy of litigants to the interests of justice. A litigant can be obliged to reveal the most sordid and intimate details of his marriage or even to pull his pants down in front of the jury. Of course one could say that the system respects privacy, not absolutely, but only to the extent that it respects privacy. Surely a useful theory requires a deeper tread.

(b) *Adjective Right*

According to Fried, the attorney-client privilege is rooted in the sense of personal autonomy that legal systems must respect.[46] "[I]t is immoral for society to limit [a person's] liberty other than according to the rule of law," and is therefore "immoral for society to constrain anyone from discovering what the limits of its power over him are." Similarly, it is "immoral for society to constrain anyone from informing another [about] those limits. . . ."[47] Supposing that certain attorney-client communications would be less likely to occur in the absence of the privilege, Fried must explain why

---

44. Louisell has written:

> [T]here are things more important to human liberty than accurate adjudication. One of them is the right to be left by the state unmolested in certain human relations. . . . It is the historic judgment of the common law . . . that whatever handicapping of the adjudicatory process is caused by recognition of the privilege, it is not too great a price to pay for secrecy in certain communicative relations. . . .

David Louisell, Confidentiality, Conformity and Confusion: Privileges in Federal Court Today, 31 Tul. L. Rev. 101, 110 (1956).

45. Charles Fried, Correspondence, 86 Yale L.J. 573, 586 (1977).
46. Id. at 586.
47. Id.

refusing to recognize the privilege ought to count as a morally unacceptable "constraint." Not every change in the world that makes a certain end state more or less likely qualifies as a "constraint." When government subsidizes a certain activity (or refuses to subsidize it) it makes the activity more or less likely to occur without "constraining" that result. But even if denial of the privilege is a constraint, the question of justification must be addressed by more than mere assertion. Again some inquiry into the particular consequences and their desirability is required.[48] . . .

III. THE WORK PRODUCT DOCTRINE AND THE JOINT PRODUCTION THEORY

A. INTRODUCTION

The work product doctrine has proven to be as puzzling as the attorney-client privilege. The doctrine was first articulated in 1947, in Hickman v. Taylor,[49] where the Supreme Court held that there is a qualified immunity from discovery for attorney work product prepared in anticipation of litigation. The plaintiff had brought suit to recover for the death of a seaman in the sinking of the defendants' tug. The defendants' attorney had interviewed all of the survivors of the sinking and taken statements from them. The plaintiff sought copies of these statements in discovery, and the district court held the attorney in contempt for failing to provide them. The Supreme Court reversed, holding that the statements that the plaintiff sought were protected from discovery as attorney's work product. In so holding, the Court did not rely upon the Federal Rules of Civil Procedure—though after the Hickman case an explicit work product provision was added[50]—but instead found an analogy in the English practice of protecting from discovery "all documents prepared by or for counsel with a view to litigation." Two opinions were filed in the case, that of the Court, authored by Justice Murphy, and a concurring opinion by Justice Jackson (in which Justice Frankfurter joined). The Murphy opinion stressed that the plaintiff's attorney could have acquired similar statements directly from the witnesses themselves, since they were all still alive, and asserted that the purpose of the doctrine is to protect the privacy of the lawyer's thoughts. He worried that, if the plaintiff won, lawyers would be deterred from writing down their thoughts. He also predicted that "Inefficiency, unfairness and sharp practices would inevitably develop in the giving of legal advice and in the preparation of cases for trial," presumably because in the absence of a work product doctrine lawyers would seek other ways to keep the relevant material out of

---

48. Some commentators have justified the privilege on the grounds that individuals in trouble with the law are in need of a friend. Albert Alschuler, The Preservation of a Client's Confidences: One Value Among Many or a Categorical Imperative?, 52 Colo. L. Rev. 349 (1981). The cases do not support such a theory. See for example U.S. v. Tedder, 801 F.2d 1437 (4th Cir. 1986). Indeed, in Morris v. Slappy, 461 U.S. 1 (1983), the Supreme Court held that the sixth amendment does not guarantee a "meaningful relationship" between attorney and client. Nor are people in trouble with the law the only ones in need of friends. The point, in short, has little explanatory power.
49. 329 U.S. 495 (1947).
50. See Fed. Rule Civil Proc. 26.

the hands of their opponents.[51] The Jackson approach had a different emphasis: that discovery of work product would be inconsistent with the adversary system and would allow a lawyer to live on "wits borrowed from the adversary."[52] Modern scholars have disagreed on both the merits of the doctrine and its justification.[53] The best explanatory account now available is Judge Easterbrook's. He argues that the work product doctrine operates in much the same way as other rights restricting the use of intellectual property.[54] Just as too few songs would be written if there were no copyrights, too little legal information would be produced in the absence of the work product doctrine.[55] Although we rely on Easterbrook's argument that the work product doctrine is essentially a property-right system in some ways similar to copyright,[56] we think he missed the essential idea that makes it important for the law to enforce these property rights. Easterbrook suggests that the doctrine protects and nurtures lawyer creativity; we think that it mainly protects and encourages something different but just as important—lawyer perseverance.

B. Theories About the Work Product Doctrine

1. The Joint Production Theory

Most litigation activity involves a form of "joint production," whereby the lawyer cannot get information helpful to his side of the case without also producing information helpful to the other side. In order to get helpful information (of which more is preferred to less), he has to take harmful information (of which less is preferred to more). Both a trial lawyer's factual investigations and the resulting legal theorizing are subject to joint production. It is difficult to generate helpful legal theories and useful "facts" without also generating theories and facts more helpful to the other side. In many factual investigations, the same conditions apply. It is often impossible to interview witnesses to find facts helpful to one's own side without discovering facts helpful

---

51. *Hickman*, 329 U.S. at 511. Murphy wrote: "[T]he general policy against invading the privacy of an attorney's course of preparation is so well recognized and so essential to an orderly working of our system of legal procedure that a burden rests on the one who would invade that privacy to establish adequate reasons to justify production through a subpoena or court order." *Hickman*, 329 U.S. at 512.

52. Id. at 516. Jackson also worried that a contrary decision would allow witnesses to be impeached with opposing counsel's summaries of their pre-trial statements and that in many cases opposing counsel himself would have to be called as a witness.

53. As even those who provide the justifications acknowledge. See, for example, Kevin Clermont, Surveying Work Product, 68 Corn. L. Rev. 755 (1983): "As proof of [the] difficulty [of the work product doctrine], I note—without insult by citation—the serious shortcomings of almost all of that commentary."

54. Frank Easterbrook, Insider Trading, Secret Agents, Evidentiary Privileges, and the Production of Information, 1981 Sup. Ct. Rev. 309. See also Richard Posner, The Economics of Justice 244 (1983) ("the attorney-work product doctrine is, I think, best understood as the use of secrecy to protect the lawyer's (and hence client's) investment in research and analysis of a case").

55. See generally Edmund Kitch, The Law and Economics of Rights in Valuable Information, 9 J. Legal Stud. 683 (1980); Edmund Kitch, The Nature and Function of the Patent System, 20 J. L. and Econ. 265 (1977).

56. The first suggestion of this idea in the literature is in Richard Posner, Privacy, Secrecy, and Reputation, 28 Buff. L. Rev. 1, 11 (1979), although the idea is not developed.

to the other side.[57] A lawyer will normally want to consider carefully the strongest positions that could be asserted by an opponent, and this may oblige an attorney to think about a case from the opponent's point of view.

As Gordon Tullock has pointed out, the private and social value of the investment in lawyering activity may be significantly out of line with each other.[58] Tullock hypothesized that the net benefits from litigation would often appear higher to private litigants than they would to society, giving private parties an incentive to overinvest. In the context of much of lawyering activity, however, the reverse may be true. If a legal investigation is subject to joint production, it can be quite easy for the expected private value of the information generated to be zero, even when its expected social value is large. In such a case, there would be inadequate private incentive to undertake such investigations even when they are socially valuable. To the extent this is true, the concern is the opposite of Tullock's; it is not that too much will be invested in the resolution of "private" disputes but rather too little. The work product rule is a solution to this problem. Under this doctrine, attorneys are allowed to hold the detrimental results of their joint production investigations in confidence from the other side, thus lowering the private costs of the lawyering effort.[59] This strategy has social costs, however, which we predict are reflected in the rules themselves. The principal one is the duplication of production. An optimal rule of confidentiality would seek to maximize the private incentive to undertake socially valuable joint production investigation subject to the constraint of duplication. Formally stated, a party should be able to suppress disclosure up to the point where the value of the increased information produced is equal to the increased cost of duplicative effort. In addition, under our theory no valuable incentive is lost by requiring a party to disclose information favorable to his case, so we would expect that such information would be discoverable even when it was produced under conditions of joint production. It is coerced disclosure of unfavorable information and ambiguously favorable information (for example, early drafts of legal briefs) that would reduce the private incentive for joint production, so it is here that the courts should be especially protective if they are deciding cases in a way explained by our theory.

---

57. Wigmore writes, "Men do not gather grapes of thorns, nor figs of thistles; yet they may enter one and the same field and find diverse fruits." Wigmore, supra note [25], §2295, at 3212. He makes little of this insight however.

It should be noted that whether evidence is helpful or not is a function of at least two variables: its absolute value, that is, does it tend to confirm or deny the party's allegations, and its relative value, that is, its value given the evidence already known. Indeed, there are further complexities, for the attorney must make at least two different assessments: 1.) what probability range will the jury assign to the evidence; 2.) what is the probability that further investigation will turn up information that will affect the probability range the jury would assign. These matters are beyond the scope of the present article.

58. Gordon Tullock, Trial on Trial: The Pure Theory of Legal Procedure 154-158 (1980).

59. The typical criticism of the work product doctrine is to the effect that lawyers will investigate and prepare their cases even in the absence of the doctrine. See for example Kathleen Waits, Work Product Protection for Witness Statements: Time for Abolition, 1985 Wisc. L. Rev. 305, 331 ("Because preparation increases the chances of a favorable outcome, it is its own reward. This remains true even if some of the preparatory documents must be shared with the other side. We therefore should not fear that abolition of work product would cause parties to abandon all investigative efforts."). This is another lump-up argument. The concern is not whether all investigative efforts will be abandoned but rather with the scale of the efforts that are undertaken. Disincentives to such efforts are likely to reduce their scale.

We do not claim that courts have adopted the joint production theory in their opinions, but only that this theory gives a better account of their actual results in work product cases than their stated theories. The privacy theory that Murphy emphasized in Hickman is both too broad and too narrow when measured against the subsequent case results that define the doctrine, including the Court's own. Nonetheless, it is probably no accident that the Court found the Hickman facts to be an especially appealing basis for the doctrine. In terms of our theory, the documents that the plaintiff sought were the quintessential result of joint production. When the defendants' attorney interviewed the accident survivors, no one knew the cause of the tug's sinking. Ex ante, the lawyer would have predicted that the interviews would reveal both favorable and unfavorable information about why the tug sank. In this situation, if the defendants' lawyer knew that he would have to disclose to his opponent all the information that he acquired, he would have less incentive to conduct the interviews in the first place. The consequence would be a reduction in the amount and quality of information available at trial.

Indeed, Murphy's opinion may be read to suggest the joint production theory, although one almost needs a microscope to find it. Recall that Murphy predicted that without the doctrine lawyers would not write things down and "inefficiency, unfairness and sharp practices" would result. Perhaps what he meant was that in the absence of the work product doctrine lawyers would still be reluctant to disclose the unfavorable information yielded by their joint production activities. Hence, lawyers would be reluctant to record this unfavorable information, because this would make it more accessible to their opponents. By extension, if lawyers had to constantly cull their records to ensure that they contained nothing unfavorable to their side, it would certainly be inefficient, and for lawyers to suppress unfavorable information (in the absence of the doctrine's protection) may be the sharp practice that Murphy envisioned. Hence, what the Court wrote in Hickman is consistent with the joint production theory.

2. The Easterbrook Theory

Frank Easterbrook stresses that our legal system relies on the attorney's self-interest to stimulate the production of legal goods or "lawyering." If such goods are to be produced, it will be necessary to allow the producer to profit from the production or otherwise to subsidize the production of such goods. If producers cannot derive any special benefits from their creation, if nonproducers are welcome to use them without having to pay for or contribute to their creation, there is a substantial risk that not enough of the good will be produced. Under Easterbrook's theory, the work product doctrine is analogous to copyright protection. Just as the creative efforts of artists must be protected in order to induce the optimal scale of them, so must be the creative efforts of lawyers.

The copyright theory of the work product doctrine places the wrong stress on the legal production process. The work product doctrine protects not so much legal inspiration, but legal perspiration. Thomas Edison would maintain that the two are related, and so do we. Nonetheless, instead of merely protecting the lawyer's creative inspirations as such, the work product doctrine protects a broader class of information: the results of investigations that can yield both favorable and unfavorable information. Of course, even legal inspiration may be produced under joint production conditions. In simply thinking about the theory of a case, a lawyer may produce insights more helpful to the other side than to his own. In this situation, both our theory and Easterbrook's predict that the unfavorable insight would be protected by the work product doctrine.

The joint production theory includes legal creativity as a subset. When lawyer-produced information involves no legal creativity, we would predict that the work product doctrine would nonetheless protect it if the information is produced under joint conditions. Thus, interviewing witnesses in an accident case certainly involves little legal creativity—indeed, the lawyer may often delegate the task to an investigator for this reason—but the results of the interviews should nonetheless be protected, at least if courts accept the joint production theory. The reason is simple: interviewing witnesses can just as easily yield unfavorable as favorable information.

We have one further disagreement with Judge Easterbrook's analysis. Easterbrook, elaborating on a model first suggested by Tullock, suggests that litigation is often a "fight over spilt milk" where the outcome of the case may have little influence on how the parties behave in the future. If litigation has only a stakes dividing function, it is socially desirable to restrict as much as possible the expenditure of resources resolving the dispute. Thus, any incentives to expend resources on such an effort—such as those created by the work product doctrine—would be, as Tullock points out, socially perverse. The error in this argument is that it overlooks the intimate relationship between accurate stakes dividing and rule enforcement. If cases are not accurately decided, the underlying rules will not be implemented, with a corresponding loss in the deterrent function of those rules. Thus, by offsetting disincentives to the production of legal information, the work product doctrine advances rather than retards the social interest, which explains its persistence in the cases.

In any event, whether the better account of the doctrine is Easterbrook's theory or our own is something that ultimately must be determined by looking at the cases.

NOTES AND QUESTIONS

1. One of the many interesting facets of the attorney-client privilege is that even its friends have serious doubts about it. Among the strongest advocates of the privilege, Dean Wigmore stated:

> [T]he privilege remains an exception to the general duty to disclose. Its benefits are all indirect and speculative; its obstruction is plain and concrete. . . . It is worth preserving for the sake of a general policy, but is nonetheless an obstacle to the investigation of the truth. It ought to be strictly confined within the narrowest possible limits consistent with the logic of its principle. [8 John Henry Wigmore, Evidence §2291, at 554 (1905).]

Similarly, in United States v. Nixon, 418 U.S. 683 (1974), the Supreme Court addressed the scope of privileges generally, specifically referring to the attorney-client privilege:

> [T]he public . . . has a right to every man's evidence, except for those persons protected by a constitutional, common-law, or statutory privilege, [citing precedents]. . . . And, generally, an attorney . . . may not be required to disclose what has been revealed in professional confidence. . . . [P]rivileges against forced disclosure . . . [a]s exceptions to the demand for every man's evidence are not lightly created nor expansively construed, for they are in derogation of the search for truth. [Id. at 709-710.]

Thus, the Supreme Court seems to be in accord with the view that the privilege should be narrowly construed. The reason for this is that the costs of privilege are obvious, while the benefits obscure. Do the contingent claim and joint production theories redress this imbalance? Are they persuasive? Plausible?

2. Recall that the Supreme Court in *Upjohn* took a somewhat different view of the privilege than that expressed in *Nixon*. There the Court said: "Application of the attorney-client privilege to communications such as those involved here, however, puts the adversary in no worse position than if the communication had never taken place. The privilege only protects disclosure of communications; it does not protect disclosure of the underlying facts by those who communicated with the attorney." Is this correct? In large measure it depends on what the baseline is, doesn't it? If the baseline is the cost of securing information from the opposing client, the Court might be right, but why is that the correct baseline? Why isn't it instead the cheapest cost of obtaining the information, which obviously is from the attorney, once the attorney is in possession of the relevant information? Rather than depose the client, the adversary need merely ask the attorney for copies of the attorney's files. So, we are back to the same question: What justifies the increased cost of obtaining the relevant information? In addition, do you believe that putting the information in the hands of the attorney will not increase the adversary's costs of obtaining that information from the client? Isn't it obvious that part of what counsel will do is advise how to answer discovery requests in a legal, but as unhelpful as possible, manner?

Last, don't arguments like the Court's in *Upjohn* suggest that counsel will not engage in behavior that raises the costs of their adversary? But what exactly does that mean? Suppose a client says X to its lawyer, but Y at a deposition. Must the lawyer correct this misimpression? If so, as the conventional arguments for the privilege implicitly suggest, isn't it obvious that the privilege provides no incentive to disclose? Isn't it thus obvious that we do not expect attorneys to police their clients in this fashion? Isn't it thus obvious that one thing that must be explained is why such tactics are tolerated, and that naive statements such as the Court's in *Upjohn* dramatically miss the point of what is going on? Again, how do the contingent claim and joint production theories measure up here?

3. In thinking about the contingent claim theory, remember that its predictions and Wigmore's are largely consistent. The difference lies in Wigmore's need to create numerous ad hoc exceptions. The central argument of the contingent claim theory is that it captures the essence of what the cases do without the need for exceptions.

4. In the Allen et al. article from which the preceding excerpt is taken, the authors proceed to discuss numerous cases in an effort to show that their theories better explain the cases than any of the alternatives. We cannot reproduce the detailed arguments here, but urge you to consult that discussion. To whet your appetite, consider two matters:

(a) The contingent claim theory predicts that the privilege will become qualified rather than absolute. This is a somewhat bold prediction, but in fact cases are beginning to adopt this view. See, e.g., Greater Newburyport Clamshell Alliance v. Public Service Co. of N.H., 838 F.2d 13, 20 (1st Cir. 1988) (in civil damages action, "fairness requires that the privilege holder surrender the privilege to the extent that it will weaken, in a meaningful way, the defendant's ability to defend"); In re Grand Jury Proceedings, Des Moines, Iowa, 568 F.2d 555, 557 (8th Cir. 1977) (opponent's need relevant to a determination of privilege).

(b) Also, consider the following from the same article:

> The theory has a number of other predictions that are borne out by the cases. First, when a client consults a lawyer to perform some function that could not possibly lead to a contingent claim, the client's communications ought not to be privileged. In this type of case, the client's expectation that he would be conveying unfavorable information to the lawyer could not deter him from obtaining the lawyer's advice about a contingent claim, since that is not his purpose. Accordingly, we find in the cases that the privilege does not apply when the attorney has been retained as an agent to procure a loan, when the attorney is asked to witness a deposition, and in similar cases.
>
> Our core proposition is that the purpose of the privilege is to encourage clients to divulge unfavorable information to their attorneys upon which contingent claims might rest. It follows that there is no need for the privilege when a regulatory agency or some other binding authority has obliged the client to hire an attorney and divulge unfavorable information to him. The cases bear out this prediction.
>
> An Eighth Circuit case, Simon v. G.D. Searle & Co., 816 F. 2d 397 (8th Cir. 1987), provides yet another demonstration of the explanatory power of the contingent claim theory. The case involved litigation over Searle's intrauterine contraceptive device. During discovery, Searle refused to turn over certain documents prepared by its risk management department. This department monitors the company's products liability litigation and analyzes its litigation reserves. In doing so, the department utilizes individual case reserves determined by the assessment of the company's legal staff. Relying on various arguments of Wigmore, the court held that the attorney-client privilege did not protect the documents prepared by the risk management department. The court asserted that these documents did not embody communications relevant to obtaining legal advice and that the documents related to business rather than legal matters.
>
> In dissent, Judge Gibson politely noted the court's opinion verged on the incoherent: "Only by concluding that Searle is in the business of litigation can the court convert these litigation-oriented documents into business planning documents." Judge Gibson's lament is correct, but so too is the majority's result. No contingent claim could conceivably rest upon the information collected and utilized by the risk management department and the company's lawyers. The result reached, then, is perfectly in accord with the predictions of the contingent claim theory, even though, as Judge Gibson rightly says, the court's opinion is virtual nonsense if analyzed from the perspective of the conventional explanations of the privilege. [Allen et al. supra, 19 J. Legal Stud. at 382-383.]

5. If Allen et al. are correct, and the work-product doctrine protects and encourages lawyer perseverance, how expansively should the doctrine be interpreted? While the doctrine only protects documents that are prepared "in anticipation of litigation," courts are divided as to the proper definition of the term. In a case heard en banc by the First Circuit, the court found that notes and memoranda drafted by in-house tax attorneys were not protected by the doctrine. The majority believed the documents were independently required by the IRS and would not be used in litigation, thus denying protection. The dissent, pointing out that the documents would not have been prepared if litigation was not anticipated, vigorously argued that the documents should have been protected. See United States v. Textron, 577 F.3d 21 (1st Cir. 2009), *petition for cert. filed*, 2009 WL 5115221 (U.S. Dec. 24, 2009) (No. 09-750). Which side is correct? Given the reason for the work-product doctrine, should dual purpose documents—documents that analyze future litigation possibilities, but are used primarily to make a business or tax decision—be protected? Should "in anticipation of litigation" be interpreted to mean prepared "because of" litigation or prepared for the "primary purpose of" litigation? See also G.D. Searle & Co, supra Note 4, finding that the risk management documents were not prepared for purposes of litigation, and thus not protected by the work-product doctrine, but noting that the documents "may be protected from discovery to the extent that they disclose the individual case reserves calculated by Searle's attorneys, [because such] figures reveal the mental impressions, thoughts, and conclusions of an attorney in evaluating a legal claim." Id. at 401.

D. THE MARITAL PRIVILEGES

There are two distinct marital privileges, the marital communications privilege and the marital testimonial privilege: The *marital communications privilege* protects confidential communications between spouses; the *marital testimonial privilege*, applicable predominantly in criminal trials, prevents an accused's spouse from testifying against the accused. A particular jurisdiction may have either or both privileges. In drafting the Proposed Federal Rules on privilege, the Advisory Committee included only the marital testimonial privilege. Subsequently, the Supreme Court in Trammel v. United States, 445 U.S. 40, 51 (1980), indicated in dictum that it would continue to apply the marital confidential communications privilege as well. *Trammel* is reproduced in Subsection 2, infra. Federal courts recognized the two privileges both prior to and after the adoption of the Federal Rules of Evidence.

1. The Marital Communications Privilege

a. Elements of the Privilege and Its Justifications

The marital communications privilege has three requirements: (1) the privilege extends only to words or acts that are communications to the other spouse, (2) the communication must have been made during a valid marriage, and (3) the communication must have been made with the intent that it remain confidential. See United States v. Marashi, 913 F.2d 724, 729 (9th Cir. 1990). The party asserting the privilege has the burden of proving that disclosure would reveal words or acts "intended as communications." The party also has the burden of proving that the communication was made during a valid marriage. If these two elements are established, then the final element of confidentiality is presumed. See United States v. Hamilton, 19 F.3d 350, 354 (7th Cir. 1994). The party opposing the privilege can overcome this presumption by showing that the communication in question was not intended to be confidential.

Similar to the justifications that have been offered for the attorney-client privilege, two justifications are commonly offered for the marital communication privilege: (1) to encourage open and frank discussions between spouses and (2) regardless of the privilege's encouraging effect, to protect the privacy of intimate spousal communications. Consistent with both these rationales, the marital communications privilege applies to communications that take place during the marriage relationship, and the privilege does not end with the termination of the marriage.

b. Holder

Jurisdictions differ as to who holds this privilege. The holder may be the spouses jointly, the communicating spouse, the witness spouse who heard the communication, or the spouse who is also a party. Most federal courts have held that the privilege is held by both spouses and that each can invoke the privilege to prevent the other from testifying about spousal communications. See United States v. 281 Syosset Woodbury Rd., 71 F.3d 1067 (2d Cir. 1995). In criminal cases, some courts have held that the exclusive holder of the privilege is the defendant. See, e.g., United States v. Acker, 52 F.3d 509 (4th Cir. 1995). This permits the defendant to compel the spouse to testify about spousal communications, if such evidence can exculpate the defendant. In cases where both spouses are holders of the privilege, one but not the other may have waived it. Can a non-waiving witness or party subsequently claim the privilege? The cases have been split on this issue.

c. Scope of the Privilege

As with all privileges, the marital communications privilege is limited by judicial interpretation of its requirements.

Valid Marriage. The party who asserts the privilege must prove that a valid marriage existed at the time the communication was made. If the parties were separated, the privilege technically still applies, but many courts refuse to uphold the privilege in such circumstances. Some courts adopt a categorical rule rejecting the privilege in such circumstances. United States v. Fulk, 816 F.2d 1202 (7th Cir. 1987). More commonly, courts use a balancing test to determining whether upholding the privilege will serve the purpose of promoting full communication between spouses. In United States v. Roberson, 859 F.2d 1376 (9th Cir. 1988), the court upheld the district court's ruling that the privilege did not apply because the couple was "irreconcilably" separated at the time of their confidential communications. In future cases, the court said, judges should consider whether, at the time of the communication, a divorce action had been filed, as well as other relevant evidence: for example, whether there were statements by either party regarding irreconcilability; or whether there were allegations of gross misconduct or grievances stretching back over a period of years. Such evidence "may distinguish the failed marriage from the occasional disharmony that sometimes accompanies these relationships." Id. at 1380. How well suited do you think courts are to make these kinds of determinations? The *Roberson* court also said that the inquiry should address the interest society has in preserving the confidentiality of marriages generally, not the confidentiality of the couple before the court. Does a categorical rule better achieve this purpose?

For the most part, courts construe the marriage requirement very narrowly. For instance, neither federal nor state courts have extended the protection of the privilege to unmarried opposite-sex couples who cohabitate. United States v. Acker, 52 F.3d 509 (4th Cir. 1995) (finding no valid marriage where the heterosexual couple involved had been living together for 25 years in two states that did not recognize common law marriage). But see In re Grand Jury Proceedings Witness Ms. X, 562 F. Supp. 486 (N.D. Cal. 1983) (stating in dicta that it might be appropriate to allow unmarried opposite-sex partners to invoke the marital communication privilege). The reason for this refusal to recognize unmarried partnerships rests on two grounds. First, courts point to the benefits of a bright-line rule that does not require an inquiry into the details of the relationship. United States v. Acker, 52 F.3d at 515 (discussing the administrative difficulty of determining what relationships would qualify as "de facto" marriages). Second, some courts also have stated that the privilege should not extend to unmarried cohabitants because they have not assumed the responsibilities of marriage. Id.

In the case of same-sex couples, the idea that couples are intentionally avoiding the responsibilities of marriage does not hold true, as until recently such individuals were legally prevented from obtaining valid marriages in many states. Same-sex couples consequently had a stronger case for claiming the privileges as unmarried cohabitants. The recent Supreme Court's decision in Obergefell v. Hodges, 135 S. Ct. 2584 (2015), has changed things dramatically by obligating every state to recognize and license same-sex marriage. From now on, therefore, the marital privileges will likely attach only to same-sex couples who formalized their relationship through marriage.

Confidentiality. It is a near universal rule that all marital communications will be treated as confidential unless the party seeking to introduce the evidence shows that the communication was not intended to be, or should not be, considered confidential. The presence of third persons is an almost certain indication that the requisite intent of confidentiality is lacking. Wolfle v. United States, 291 U.S. 7, 16 (1934) (use of stenographer destroyed the privilege). If a child is old enough to comprehend what is being said, spousal statements made in the presence of the child—at the dinner table, for example, or on a drive in the family automobile—will typically not be privileged. Chamberlain v. State, 348 P.2d 280, 286 (Wyo. 1960). Sometimes courts will find that a third party is constructively present if the spouse made the same communication to a third party on another occasion. People v. Burton, 286 N.E.2d 792, 798 (Ill. Ct. App. 1972). The location in which the communication is made also is probative as to whether the spouse intended a confidential communication. State of Maine v. Smith, 384 A.2d 687, 691 (1978) (finding that communicating in a public location does not necessarily mean that the communication was not confidential; rather, the inquiry should focus on the spouse's reasonable expectation of confidentiality).

What Is a "Communication"?   An issue that often arises in cases involving the marital communications privilege is whether conduct—acts and gestures—is protected by the privilege. Courts are required to distinguish between non-communicative behavior and conduct that has communicative content. For example, testimony from a wife identifying a pair of pants as being the style and size worn by her husband was admitted as involving no communication at all. United States v. Bolzer, 556 F.2d 948 (9th Cir. 1977); similarly, in United States v. Lefkowitz, 618 F.2d 1313 (9th Cir. 1980), testimony concerning the fraudulent nature of documents turned over to the IRS, and the location of other records, was found to be based on the personal observations of the wife, not on any communicative conduct of the husband. Other acts observed by spouses, however, have been found by some courts to be communicative and thus privileged:

> [W]hen the defendant revealed the stolen objects [a gun and camera] to his wife he was imparting a confidence as clearly as if he had told his wife, "I have stolen a gun and a camera." . . . Where as here conduct by a spouse can be reasonably interpreted as intending to convey a message to the other spouse, a marital communication has occurred. [State v. Smith, 384 A.2d 687, 690 (Me. 1978).]

The "intent to communicate" test as to whether spousal conduct should be privileged replicates the test provided under FRE 801(a)(2) to determine whether conduct is hearsay or not. Some courts, however, adopt a broader test. In People v. Daghita, 299 N.Y. 194, 86 N.E.2d 172 (N.Y. 1949), the court held that it was a violation of the confidential communications privilege to admit a wife's testimony that her husband hid proceeds of a theft under the bed:

> [T]he term communication . . . includes knowledge derived from the observance of disclosive acts done in the presence or view of one spouse . . . because of the confidence existing between them by reason of the marital relation. . . . [The husband] was, in a word, confiding in her the information disclosed by his conduct. [Id. at 198-199.]

Contrast *Daghita* with the holding in United States v. Estes, 793 F.2d 465, 467 (2d Cir. 1986), that "counting, hiding and laundering of the money conveyed no confidential message. . . . Acts do not become privileged communications simply because they are performed in the presence of the actor's spouse." Which do you think is the better result?

Consider the testimony of a rape defendant's ex wife: "I drove the defendant in my car. He was sitting in the passenger seat reading a newspaper. I heard like water, I heard a tear drop hit the paper and I looked over and the defendant was crying. He was looking at the composite sketch of the rape victim's assailant as he wept." The North Carolina Court of Appeals decided that this information was not privileged. See State v. Matsoake, 777 S.E.2d 810 (N.C. App. 2015). Do you agree?

d. Exceptions

Like the attorney-client privilege, there is an exception to the marital communications privilege that permits the admission—by a willing spousal witness—of statements made in the course of, or concerning, ongoing criminal activity between the spouses. In *Estes*, the first communications from the husband to the wife that first disclosed his crime to her were privileged; only those communications made after she became an accessory were excepted from the privilege. Id. at 466.

At common law, the privilege did not apply to spousal communications in specific kinds of litigation. Although there is variation from state to state, the privilege is most frequently inapplicable in prosecutions for crimes committed by one spouse against the other or against children of either, and in actions by one spouse against the other, typically divorce. McCormick on Evidence, Vol. 1, §84, 131 (5th ed. 1999).

The Supreme Court of Pennsylvania has held that a defendant's communications to his spouse were not subject to the spousal communication privilege where the statements were intended to create or further marital discord. Commonwealth v. Spetzer, 572 Pa. 17, 813 A.2d 707 (Pa. 2002). In *Spetzer*, the defendant admitted to his wife that he had raped his stepdaughter, detailed plans for future abuse, and attempted to intimidate his wife. 572 Pa. at 39. The court noted that the communications were not of the "marital harmony-inspiring" type envisioned by the common law or the Pennsylvania General Assembly:

> Certainly the persistent and sadistic statements at issue here, concerning a husband's actual and contemplated crimes against his wife and her children, cannot rationally be excluded on the pretext that "considerations of domestic peace and harmony of the marital relation forbid their disclosure." *Seitz*. It would be perverse, indeed, to indulge a fiction of marital harmony to shield statements which prove the declarant spouse's utter contempt for, and abuse of, the marital union. Accordingly, we hold that here, as in Seitz, the challenged communications "did not arise from the confidence existing between the parties, but from the want of it," *id.*, and, as such, the communications were admissible. 572 Pa. at 40.

PROBLEMS

12.16. Randy Dwayne Hurley was charged and convicted of armed robbery, felony murder, and first degree murder. On appeal, the defendant objects to the trial court's admission of letters containing incriminating information that were written from him to his wife on the ground that the letters should have been protected by the marital confidential communications privilege. Hurley, who had married his wife after the arrest but prior to trial, had written the letters to his wife from jail. At the time of the trial, however, the two were separated. The wife was a willing witness. What result?

12.17. Jim Montague and his sister Mary O'Connell are charged with conspiracy to commit mail fraud and several counts of mail fraud for mishandling reservations of rentals by their property management company and sidetracking money from the owners of the units by not reporting reservations. Jim's wife, Louise, also was an owner but agreed to cooperate with the government and to testify against Jim and Mary. The prosecution is seeking to present as evidence a letter that Louise wrote Jim and left for him on the kitchen counter in their home. The letter discussed Mary's fraudulent activities and stated that Louise wanted Jim to confront Mary. Louise testified that she did not intend the information in the letter to remain private, as she hoped that Jim would communicate it to Mary. Jim and Louise had children residing in the house at the time the letter was left on the kitchen counter. Jim has asserted the spousal communication privilege to prevent the letter, or testimony about its contents, from being used in the trial. Was the communication privileged? If so, can Louise waive the privilege?

12.18. Craig Klaxon is charged with mail fraud and wire fraud for filing a fraudulent insurance claim for a $4,000 silver tray that he listed as having been stolen. Klaxon's wife, Connie, is prepared to testify that she and her husband never owned a silver tray and that she refused, when her husband had asked her (when both Klaxon and the insurance agent were on the phone) to sign the insurance claim. Would this testimony be excluded by the marital communications privilege?

12.19. Chester Newman is being prosecuted for arson, burglary, and theft. An investigation had uncovered that a fire at the Good Times Club was a result of arson and that stereo equipment owned by the club was missing. Defendant's wife, Catherine Newman, is prepared to testify about certain events involving her husband on the night of the fire. Catherine will testify that on the night in question her husband returned home from the Good Times Club with a set of expensive stereo equipment. She then accompanied her husband to sell the stereo equipment to John Palmer, a potential purchaser. Communications concerning the source of the equipment—that it had been "snatched" from the Club—took place during the negotiation and sale of the equipment. Defendant filed a motion to suppress his wife's testimony on the ground that such conversations constituted privileged confidential communications. Should this testimony be admissible over Chester's objection?

2. The Marital Testimonial Privilege

a. Elements of the Privilege and Its Justifications

The modern justification for the marital testimonial privilege is that it exists to promote harmony in an ongoing marriage relationship; without the privilege, one spouse could be required to testify against the other in a criminal proceeding, bringing disharmony to the marriage. Consistent with this rationale, the privilege is not limited to testimony about confidential communications, and for the privilege to apply the witness and the party must be married at the time the privilege is invoked. See United States v. Bolzer, 556 F.2d 948 (9th Cir. 1977).

Unlike the marital communications privilege, the marital testimonial privilege predominantly applies in criminal, as distinguished from civil, cases. In federal courts, it is also well established that the testifying spouse holds the privilege and may waive it in order to testify. The Supreme Court addressed this issue, and the scope of the privilege, in the following case:

TRAMMEL v. UNITED STATES

445 U.S. 40 (1980)

Mr. Chief Justice B<small>URGER</small> delivered the opinion of the Court. . . .

I

On March 10, 1976, petitioner Otis Trammel was indicted with two others, Edwin Lee Roberts and Joseph Freeman, for importing heroin into the United States from Thailand and the Philippine Islands and for conspiracy to import heroin in violation of 21 U.S.C. sec. 952(a), 962(a), and 963. The indictment also named six unindicted co-conspirators, including petitioner's wife Elizabeth Ann Trammel.

According to the indictment, petitioner and his wife flew from the Philippines to California in August 1975, carrying with them a quantity of heroin. Freeman and Roberts assisted them in its distribution. Elizabeth Trammel then traveled to Thailand where she purchased another supply of the drug. On November 3, 1975, with four ounces of heroin on her person, she boarded a plane for the United States. During a routine customs search in Hawaii, she was searched, the heroin was discovered, and she was arrested. After discussions with Drug Enforcement Administration agents, she agreed to cooperate with the Government.

Prior to trial on this indictment, petitioner moved to sever his case from that of Roberts and Freeman. He advised the court that the Government intended to call his wife as an adverse witness and asserted his claim to a privilege to prevent her from testifying against him. At a hearing on the motion, Mrs. Trammel was called as a Government witness under a grant of use immunity. She testified that she and petitioner were married in May 1975 and that they remained married.[60] She explained that her cooperation with the Government was based on assurances that she would be given lenient treatment.[61] She then described, in considerable detail, her role and that of her husband in the heroin distribution conspiracy.

After hearing this testimony, the District Court ruled that Mrs. Trammel could testify in support of the Government's case to any act she observed during the marriage and to any communication "made in the presence of a third person"; however, confidential communications between petitioner and his wife were held to be privileged and inadmissible. The motion to sever was denied.

At trial, Elizabeth Trammel testified within the limits of the court's pretrial ruling; her testimony, as the Government concedes, constituted virtually its entire case against petitioner. He was found guilty on both the substantive and conspiracy charges and sentenced to an indeterminate term of years pursuant to the Federal Youth Corrections Act, 18 U.S.C. sec. 5010(b). . . . [The Court of Appeals affirmed the conviction.]

---

60. In response to the question whether divorce was contemplated, Mrs. Trammel testified that her husband had said that "I would go my way and he would go his."

61. The Government represents to the Court that Elizabeth Trammel has not been prosecuted for her role in the conspiracy.

II

The privilege claimed by petitioner has ancient roots. Writing in 1628, Lord Coke observed that "it hath been resolved by the Justices that a wife cannot be produced either against or for her husband." 1 E. Coke, A Commentarie upon Littleton 6b (1628). See, generally, 8 J. Wigmore, Evidence sec. 2227 (McNaughton rev. 1961). This spousal disqualification sprang from two canons of medieval jurisprudence: first, the rule that an accused was not permitted to testify in his own behalf because of his interest in the proceeding; second, the concept that husband and wife were one, and that since the woman had no recognized separate legal existence, the husband was that one. From those two now long-abandoned doctrines, it followed that what was inadmissible from the lips of the defendant-husband was also inadmissible from his wife.

Despite its medieval origins, this rule of spousal disqualification remained intact in most common-law jurisdictions well into the 19th century. . . . Indeed, it was not until 1933, in Funk v. United States, 290 U.S. 371, that this Court abolished the testimonial disqualification in the federal courts, so as to permit the spouse of a defendant to testify in the defendant's behalf. *Funk*, however, left undisturbed the rule that either spouse could prevent the other from giving adverse testimony. Id., at 373. The rule thus evolved into one of privilege rather than one of absolute disqualification. . . .

The modern justification for this privilege against adverse spousal testimony is its perceived role in fostering the harmony and sanctity of the marriage relationship. Notwithstanding this benign purpose, the rule was sharply criticized. Professor Wigmore termed it "the merest anachronism in legal theory and an indefensible obstruction to truth in practice." 8 Wigmore §2228, at 221. The Committee on Improvements in the Law of Evidence of the American Bar Association called for its abolition. 63 American Bar Association Reports 594-595 (1938). In its place, Wigmore and others suggested a privilege protecting only private marital communications, modeled on the privilege between priest and penitent, attorney and client, and physician and patient. See 8 Wigmore §2332 et seq.[62] . . .

In Hawkins v. United States, 358 U.S. 74 (1958), this Court considered the continued vitality of the privilege against adverse spousal testimony in the federal courts. There the District Court had permitted petitioner's wife, over his objection, to testify against him. With one questioning concurring opinion, the Court held the wife's testimony inadmissible; it took note of the critical comments that the common-law rule had engendered, . . . but chose not to abandon it. Also rejected was the Government's suggestion that the Court modify the privilege by vesting it in the witness-spouse, with freedom to testify or not independent of the defendant's control. The Court viewed this proposed modification as antithetical to the widespread belief, evidenced in the rules then in effect in a majority of the States and in England, "that the law should

---

62. This Court recognized just such a confidential marital communications privilege in Wolfle v. United States, 291 U.S. 7 (1934), and in Blau v. United States, 340 U.S. 332 (1951). In neither case, however, did the Court adopt the Wigmore view that the communications privilege be substituted *in place of* the privilege against adverse spousal testimony. The privilege as to confidential marital communications is not at issue in the instant case; accordingly, our holding today does not disturb *Wolfle* and *Blau*.

not force or encourage testimony which might alienate husband and wife, or further inflame existing domestic differences." Id., at 79.

Hawkins, then, left the federal privilege for adverse spousal testimony where it found it, continuing "a rule which bars the testimony of one spouse against the other unless both consent." Id., at 78. . . . However, in so doing, the Court made clear that its decision was not meant to "foreclose whatever changes in the rule may eventually be dictated by 'reason and experience.'" [Id.], at 79.

III

. . . The Federal Rules of Evidence acknowledge the authority of the federal courts to continue the evolutionary development of testimonial privileges in federal criminal trials "governed by the principles of the common law as they may be interpreted . . . in the light of reason and experience." Fed. Rule Evid. 501. . . .

Although Rule 501 confirms the authority of the federal courts to reconsider the continued validity of the *Hawkins* rule, the long history of the privilege suggests that it ought not to be casually cast aside. That the privilege is one affecting marriage, home, and family relationships—already subject to much erosion in our day—also counsels caution. At the same time, we cannot escape the reality that the law on occasion adheres to doctrinal concepts long after experience suggests the need for change. . . .

Since 1958, when *Hawkins* was decided, support for the privilege against adverse spousal testimony has been eroded further. Thirty-one jurisdictions, including Alaska and Hawaii, then allowed an accused a privilege to prevent adverse spousal testimony. . . . The number has now declined to 24. In 1974, the National Conference on Uniform State Laws revised its Uniform Rules of Evidence, but again rejected the *Hawkins* rule in favor of a limited privilege for confidential communications. See Uniform Rules of Evidence, Rule 504. That proposed rule has been enacted in Arkansas, North Dakota, and Oklahoma—each of which in 1958 permitted an accused to exclude adverse spousal testimony.[63] The trend in state law toward divesting the accused of the privilege to bar adverse spousal testimony has special relevance because the laws of marriage and domestic relations are concerns traditionally reserved to the states. . . .

Testimonial exclusionary rules and privileges contravene the fundamental principle that " 'the public . . . has a right to every man's evidence.' " United States v. Bryan, 339 U.S. 323, 331 (1950). As such, they must be strictly construed and accepted "only to the very limited extent that permitting a refusal to testify or excluding relevant evidence has a public good transcending the normally predominant principle of

---

63. In 1965, California took the privilege from the defendant-spouse and vested it in the witness-spouse, accepting a study commission recommendation that the "latter [was] more likely than the former to determine whether or not to claim the privilege on the basis of the probable effect on the marital relationship." See Cal. Evid. Code Ann. §970-973 (West 1966 and Supp. 1979) and 1 California Law Revision Commission, Recommendation and Study relating to The Marital "For and Against" Testimonial Privilege, at F-5 (1956). See also 6 California Law Revision Commission, Tentative Privileges Recommendation—Rule 27.5, pp.243-244 (1964).

Support for the common-law rule has also diminished in England. In 1972, a study group there proposed giving the privilege to the witness-spouse, on the ground that "if [the wife] is willing to give evidence . . . the law would be showing excessive concern for the preservation of marital harmony if it were to say that she must not do so." Crim. L. Rev. Comm., 11. R., Evid. (General) 93.

utilizing all rational means for ascertaining truth." Elkins v. United States, 364 U.S. 206, 234 (1960) (Frankfurter, J., dissenting). . . . Here we must decide whether the privilege against adverse spousal testimony promotes sufficiently important interests to outweigh the need for probative evidence in the administration of criminal justice.

It is essential to remember that the *Hawkins* privilege is not needed to protect information privately disclosed between husband and wife in the confidence of the marital relationship. . . . Those confidences are privileged under the independent rule protecting confidential marital communications. . . . The *Hawkins* privilege is invoked, not to exclude private marital communications, but rather to exclude evidence of criminal acts and of communications made in the presence of third persons.

No other testimonial privilege sweeps so broadly. The privileges between priest and penitent, attorney and client, and physician and patient limit protection to private communications. These privileges are rooted in the imperative need for confidence and trust. The priest-penitent privilege recognizes the human need to disclose to a spiritual counselor, in total and absolute confidence, what are believed to be flawed acts or thoughts and to receive priestly consolation and guidance in return. The lawyer-client privilege rests on the need for the advocate and counselor to know all that relates to the client's reasons for seeking representation if the professional mission is to be carried out. Similarly, the physician must know all that a patient can articulate in order to identify and to treat disease; barriers to full disclosure would impair diagnosis and treatment.

The *Hawkins* rule stands in marked contrast to these three privileges. Its protection is not limited to confidential communications; rather it permits an accused to exclude all adverse spousal testimony. As Jeremy Bentham observed more than a century and a half ago, such a privilege goes far beyond making "every man's house his castle," and permits a person to convert his house into "a den of thieves." 5 Rationale of Judicial Evidence 340 (1827). It "secures, to every man, one safe and unquestionable and ever ready accomplice for every imaginable crime." Id., at 338.

The ancient foundations for so sweeping a privilege have long since disappeared. Nowhere in the common-law world—indeed in any modern society—is a woman regarded as chattel or demeaned by denial of a separate legal identity and the dignity associated with recognition as a whole human being. Chip by chip, over the years those archaic notions have been cast aside so that "[n]o longer is the female destined solely for the home and the rearing of the family, and only the male for the marketplace and the world of ideas." Stanton v. Stanton, 421 U.S. 7, 14-15 (1975).

The contemporary justification for affording an accused such a privilege is also unpersuasive. When one spouse is willing to testify against the other in a criminal proceeding—whatever the motivation—their relationship is almost certainly in disrepair; there is probably little in the way of marital harmony for the privilege to preserve. In these circumstances, a rule of evidence that permits an accused to prevent adverse spousal testimony seems far more likely to frustrate justice than to foster family peace.[64] Indeed, there is reason to believe that vesting the privilege in the accused

---

64. It is argued that abolishing the privilege will permit the Government to come between husband and wife, pitting one against the other. That, too, misses the mark. Neither *Hawkins* nor any other privilege prevents the Government from enlisting one spouse to give information concerning the other to aid in the other's apprehension. It is only the spouse's testimony in the courtroom that is prohibited.

could actually undermine the marital relationship. For example, in a case such as this, the Government is unlikely to offer a wife immunity and lenient treatment if it knows that her husband can prevent her from giving adverse testimony. If the Government is dissuaded from making such an offer, the privilege can have the untoward effect of permitting one spouse to escape justice at the expense of the other. It hardly seems conducive to the preservation of the marital relation to place a wife in jeopardy solely by virtue of her husband's control over her testimony.

IV

Our consideration of the foundations for the privilege and its history satisfy us that "reason and experience" no longer justify so sweeping a rule as that found acceptable by the Court in *Hawkins*. Accordingly, we conclude that the existing rule should be modified so that the witness-spouse alone has a privilege to refuse to testify adversely; the witness may be neither compelled to testify nor foreclosed from testifying. This modification—vesting the privilege in the witness-spouse—furthers the important public interest in marital harmony without unduly burdening legitimate law enforcement needs.

Here, petitioner's spouse chose to testify against him. That she did so after a grant of immunity and assurances of lenient treatment does not render her testimony involuntary. . . . Accordingly, the District Court and the Court of Appeals were correct in rejecting petitioner's claim of privilege, and the judgment of the Court of Appeals is affirmed.

[The concurring opinion of Justice Stewart is omitted.]

NOTES AND QUESTIONS

1. Consider carefully the last footnote in *Trammel*. As the Court acknowledged early in its opinion, Mrs. Trammel was heavily involved in drug trafficking and thus faced the possibility of serious criminal penalties. Thus, the government's offer of immunity to her was a substantial incentive for her to testify against her husband. Perhaps the Trammels' marriage was likely to end regardless of the immunity, and perhaps she would have been willing to testify against her husband in any event. If it were clear that she would have testified without a grant of immunity, however, it seems unlikely that the prosecutor would have offered her immunity. In any event, if we are serious about trying to preserve marital harmony—as recognizing the testimonial privilege suggests we are—why should we formulate the privilege in a way that encourages prosecutors to pressure one spouse into testifying against the other? If the accused spouse could claim the privilege, the government, as the Court recognized, would have no incentive to try to drive a wedge between the husband and wife with an offer of leniency or immunity in cases where the spouses were cohorts in crime or by trying to pit an innocent spouse against the charged spouse. On the other hand, in states where the accused spouse holds the privilege, prosecutors may not be able to compel testimony from the victim spouse in domestic violence cases. Malinda L.

Seymore, Isn't It a Crime: Feminist Perspectives on Spousal Immunity and Spousal Violence, 90 Nw. U. L. Rev. 1032, 1036 (1996).

2. The privilege may not apply if the marriage relationship is no longer viable at the time the testimony is sought. Should courts focus on whether the marriage is in a state of "disrepair" when the testimonial privilege is claimed? In United States v. Brown, 605 F.2d 389 (8th Cir. 1979), the Eighth Circuit reversed its prior approach and premised its rejection of the privilege primarily upon its opinion of the health of the marriage. Noting that the husband and wife had not seen each other for eight months, the court stated that is was "difficult to visualize" how protection of the marital bond "would have required the total exclusion of Mrs. Clincy from the witness stand." Should courts have the discretion to make such judgments? Some don't think so. See United States v. Lilley, 581 F.2d 182 (8th Cir. 1978).

3. Like the marital communications privilege, the testimonial privilege is construed narrowly to prevent fraud. Courts are reluctant to apply the privilege when it appears that the marriage was entered into solely for the purpose of preventing testimony. As stated by the Supreme Court in Lutwak v. United States, 344 U.S. 604, 614-615 (1953):

> When the good faith of the marital relation is pertinent and it is made to appear . . . that the relationship was entered into with no intention of the parties to live together as husband and wife but only for the purpose of using the marriage ceremony in a scheme to defraud, the ostensible spouses are competent to testify against each other.

However, the "sham marriage" doctrine is not easy to apply. See, for example, In re Grand Jury Subpoena, 884 F. Supp. 188 (D. Md. 1995) (holding that, while the marriage may have been primarily intended to prevent adverse testimony from one spouse against the other, there was evidence to suggest the marriage was in fact genuine); and Glover v. State, 816 N.E.2d 1197 (Ind. App. 2004) (refusing to recognize fraudulent marriage exception, as state's statutory scheme does not permit the exception).

Most federal courts hold that the privilege applies only to testimony by the spouse and does not block admission of out-of court statements when such statements are admissible under the hearsay rule. In United States v. Chapman, 866 F.2d 1326 (11th Cir. 1986), a bank robbery case, the out-of-court statements made by the defendant's spouse were held to be admissible hearsay. The requirement of unavailability was met because the out-of-court declarant was unavailable in that she refused, on the basis of her marital privilege, to give any substantive testimony. The court also held that the out-of-court statements bore sufficient indicia of reliability to be admissible. In holding the marital testimonial privilege to be inapplicable, the court relied on the Supreme Court's statement in *Trammel* that nothing in the law of privileges "prevents the Government from enlisting one spouse to give information concerning the other or to aid in the other's apprehension. It is only the spouse's testimony in the courtroom that is prohibited." Id. at 1333. In United States v. James, 128 F. Supp. 2d 291 (D. Md. 2001), the district court upheld the admissibility of the defendant's wife's call to the 911 operator, stating that her husband had assaulted her, as an excited utterance.

State courts, however, are split on whether the privilege prevents admission of out-of-court statements. The Ohio Supreme Court found that a recording between a criminal defendant and his or her spouse is admissible despite the testimonial privilege, because the statute establishing the privilege precludes only "spouse's tes-timony," not "communication through other means." Ohio v. Perez, 920 N.E.2d 104 (Ohio 2009). Michigan, Minnesota, Nevada, North Dakota, and Arkansas follow the same general approach, while Illinois and North Carolina have extended the privilege to outside recordings.

4. The marital privileges may attach to common law marriages, provided that the law of the domicile state recognizes them and that the marriage itself is legally valid under state law. See United States v. Lustig, 555 F.2d 737, 747-748 (9th Cir. 1978), (both of the marital privileges were lost because Alaska did not recognize common law marriages). However, neither federal nor state courts have extended the protec-tion of the privilege to unmarried cohabitants. See, e.g., United States v. Acker, 52 F.3d 509 (4th Cir. 1995) (finding no valid marriage where the heterosexual couple involved had been living together for 25 years in states that do not recognize common law marriage).

b. Exceptions

It is well established that the marital testimonial privilege does not apply when one spouse is prosecuted for a crime against the person or property of the other. Some states extend this exception to charges of crimes committed against family members or cohabitants. For example, Cal. Evid. Code §972(e)(1) (West 1995) provides:

> A married person does not have a privilege under this article in: (e) A criminal proceed-ing in which one spouse is charged with: (1) A crime against the person or property of the other spouse or of a child, parent, relative, or cohabitant of either, whether com-mitted before or during marriage.

In People v. Bogle, 41 Cal. App. 4th 770, 782 (1995), the court said that "cohabitant" should be interpreted broadly, because "individuals are uniquely vulnerable in their domestic environment." In *Bogle*, the court applied this exception to the privilege and upheld the wife's ability to testify against her husband in his trial for murder of the wealthy couple with whom he lived as a boarder, even though he was not related to them. More commonly, of course, the exception is applied where the defendant is charged with a crime against his spouse or against their children. If the crime is one of domestic violence, then the witness spouse can be compelled to testify despite her assertion of the privilege. But even where this exception exists, "married women [are left] unprotected by the legal system because of very narrow and uninformed views of what constitutes spousal violence." Malinda L. Seymore, Isn't It a Crime: Feminist Perspectives on Spousal Immunity and Spousal Violence, 90 Nw. U. L. Rev. 1032, 1036 (1996).

There is a split among federal circuits as to whether there is a "joint participants in crime" exception to the testimonial privilege. Subject to the Fifth Amendment privilege against self-incrimination, some courts require the witness spouse to tes-tify when the spouses have engaged in joint illegal behavior. United States v. Clark, 712 F.2d 299 (7th Cir. 1983). Others still apply the privilege, reasoning that the pol-icy of *Trammel* to protect the marriage is not outweighed and that compelled testi-mony would "undermine the marriage precisely in the manner that the privilege is designed to prevent." Appeal of Malfitano, 633 F.2d 276, 279 (3d Cir. 1980). See also In re Grand Jury Subpoena United States, 755 F.2d 1022 (2d Cir. 1985), *vacated on other grounds sub nom.* United States v. Koecher, 475 U.S. 133 (1986) ("In light of [the testimonial privilege's] existence since the early days of the common law and of the importance of the interests which the marital privilege serves, we would leave the creation of exceptions to the Supreme Court or to Congress."); United States v. Ramos-Oseguera, 120 F.3d 1028 (9th Cir. 1997) (citing language in *Trammel* to find no exception, despite acknowledging an exception to the marital communication privilege when the communication relates to present or future crimes in which both spouses are participants).

The marital testimonial privilege also does not apply to prosecutions under the Mann Act, where a wife is transported across state lines by her husband for the purpose of prostitution. Wyatt v. United States, 362 U.S. 525, 530 (1960).

KEY POINTS

1. Two privileges relate to the marital relationship. One immunizes confidential communications made during the marriage from disclosure; it applies both in civil and criminal cases. The other permits a spouse not to testify (or permits the accused spouse from stopping the other spouse from testifying) against the accused spouse in a criminal case.
2. The confidential communications privilege survives the marriage; the testimonial privilege does not.
3. Neither privilege applies in litigation between the spouses, or involving accusations of criminal acts of one spouse against the other.

PROBLEMS

12.20. Ellen Graves has been subpoenaed to provide a handwriting exemplar and fingerprints to the grand jury, which is investigating the filing of false joint income tax returns by Ms. Graves and her husband. Ms. Graves moves to quash the subpoena on the ground that compliance would violate her privilege not to testify against her husband. What result?

12.21. Ms. Witness's husband is the target of a grand jury investigation into illegal drug trafficking. Ms. Witness has been summoned to appear before the grand jury to testify about her own bank accounts and financial history both before and after they were married. The government's purpose is to determine whether her accounts were used for money laundering from illegal drug sales. Ms. Witness refuses to testify and seeks to invoke the marital testimonial privilege. Should she be compelled to testify? What if the government asserts that since its questions are about her personal financial history, they should be asked, answered, and examined on a question-by-question basis to determine whether the information elicited is "adverse" to the husband?

E. THE PHYSICIAN-PATIENT AND PSYCHOTHERAPIST-PATIENT PRIVILEGES

Neither the physician-patient privilege nor the psychotherapist-patient privilege existed at common law. The physician-patient privilege was first recognized in the United States by an 1828 New York statute that granted a testimonial privilege to physician-patient communications. In contrast, the psychotherapeutic privileges did not gain approval until the 1950s, when the fields of psychology and psychotherapy were first accorded professional recognition. The traditional justification for both privileges is the standard utilitarian argument that the privilege is necessary to encourage the patient to disclose information for the proper diagnosis and treatment of illness. By protecting the patient from the disclosure of potentially incriminating or liability-related information in court, the privilege helps to ensure the provision of effective medical or therapeutic treatment.

The utilitarian justification for the physician-patient privilege has been roundly criticized on the ground that patients will communicate all information that may aid in proper diagnosis and treatment whether or not a privilege exists. In contrast, the psychotherapist-patient privilege has received approval by both courts and commentators. Advocates argue that some form of protection is necessary in the psychotherapist-patient context because the communications usually involve matters that a patient regards as extremely personal.

We examine these two privileges in the next two subsections.

1. The Physician-Patient Privilege

The Proposed Federal Rules of Evidence did not recognize a physician-patient privilege. The Advisory Committee's Note to Proposed FRE 504 observed:

> While many states have by statute created the [physician-patient] privilege, the exceptions which have been found necessary in order to obtain information required by the public interest or to avoid fraud are so numerous as to leave little if any basis for the privilege. . . . California, for example, excepts cases in which the patient puts his condition in issue, all criminal proceedings, will and similar contests, malpractice cases, and disciplinary proceedings. . . . [Cal. Evid. Code §§990-1007.]

To this should be added the point noted above that the behavioral incentives typically are not needed in this context. For both reasons, most federal courts have rejected a physician-patient privilege. See United States v. Bercier, 848 F.2d 917, 920 (8th Cir. 1988) ("[b]ecause no physician privilege existed at common law . . . federal courts do not recognize the physician-patient privilege" . . . under federal common law); Patterson v. Caterpillar, 70 F.3d 503, 506 (7th Cir. 1995) (stating unequivocally that federal common law does not recognize this privilege).

Over three-quarters of the states have enacted statutes recognizing a physician-patient privilege. Most state statutes refer generally to "physicians" or "physicians or surgeons" to denote the type of health care providers covered by the statute. The Arizona physician-patient privilege statute is typical:

> In a civil action a physician or surgeon shall not, without the consent of his patient . . . be examined as to any communication made by his patient with reference to any physical or mental disease or disorder . . . or as to any such knowledge obtained by personal examination of the patient. [Ariz. Rev. Stat. Ann. §12-2235 (West 2003).]

Some state statutes, however, are more expansive, such as the Minnesota privilege statute which includes "dentists, chiropractors, and registered nurses" within the protection of the privilege. Minn. Stat. Ann. §§595.02(1)(d), (g) (West 2000).

Typically, the patient is the holder, and the privilege covers confidential communications made for the purpose of, or in connection with, obtaining medical assistance or advice. Such information could be obtained through conversation with the patient or through the physician's physical examination. The privilege is also sometimes extended to "[a] record of identity, diagnosis, evaluation, or treatment of a patient by a physician that is created or maintained by a physician." Tex. Occ. Code §159.002(b) (Vernon 2004). Similar to the attorney-client privilege, the facts that a patient has consulted a physician, has been treated by him, and the number and dates of the visits, are not covered by the privilege. In some states, the physician-patient privilege applies only to judicial proceedings and does not prohibit defense counsel from engaging in ex parte communications with plaintiff's physicians. Steinberg v. Jensen, 534 N.W.2d 361, 370 (Wis. 1995).

Waiver occurs in the normal manner through disclosure or putting physical condition into issue in litigation. Carson v. Fine, 867 P.2d 610 (Wash. 1994) (privilege waived as to fact and opinion information held by all physicians when plaintiff filed malpractice action). A patient may expressly waive his privilege by authorizing the release of medical information. A patient may also impliedly waive the privilege by either voluntarily disclosing such medical information to an outside party or through partial disclosure in a judicial proceeding. In Ziegler v. Department of Fire, 426 So. 2d 311, 313 (La. Ct. App. 1983), a patient's failure to assert the privilege in objection to a physician's testimony at trial resulted in a waiver for all later trials.

The presence of third persons may destroy the required confidentiality of a physician-patient communication. However, if the third person is a necessary participant to the consultation, such as a nurse acting under the direction of the physician, the privilege may remain intact. Sims v. Charlotte Liberty Mut. Ins. Co., 125 S.E.2d 326, 331 (N.C. 1962) (records made by "nurses, technicians, and others" may be included under the privilege statute if they are acting under a physician or surgeon).

In addition, state statutes commonly require physicians to report certain information related to public health and safety, such as information regarding child abuse, venereal disease, and gunshot injury. In the absence of the statutes, this information would generally be protected by the privilege. In most instances, the reporting systems expressly prohibit public release of the information obtained.

The Health Insurance Portability and Accountability Act (HIPAA) has created a uniform, but defeasible, doctor-patient privilege that applies nationwide. Under the regulations issued by the Secretary of Health and Human Services pursuant to HIPAA, holders of patient-related medical information are prohibited from disclosing it. 45 C.F.R. §160.103. This prohibition is subject to an exception that permits disclosure of protected information "in the course of any judicial or administrative proceeding." 45 C.F.R. §164.512(e)(1). Such disclosure can take place only pursuant to a court order and its conditions. 45 C.F.R. §164.512(e)(1)(i)-(ii). This order should protect the information against unnecessary disclosure. While exercising their gate-keeping role, courts should also juxtapose the information's value against the harm to the patient's privacy interest. For a recent decision explaining this statutory frame-work, see Caldwell v. Chauvin, 464 S.W.3d 139, (Ky. 2015). This framework sets up minimal protection for patients' medical information. State statutes and common law rules can expand that protection but not diminish it. 45 C.F.R. §160.203(b).

2. The Psychotherapist-Patient Privilege

a. Jaffee v. Redmond

In 1996, the U.S. Supreme Court established the psychotherapist-patient privilege under FRE 501 in the case of Jaffee v. Redmond, 518 U.S. 1 (1996). This privilege had been included as Rule 504 in the Proposed Federal Rules of Evidence, and each state has a version of the privilege. The existence of this privilege is thus well estab-lished, but it is by no means free from controversy; nor is its scope entirely clear. Our study of this privilege begins with *Jaffee*, which thoroughly canvasses the then-existing law and the relevant policy considerations.

JAFFEE v. REDMOND

518 U.S. 1 (1996)

Justice STEVENS delivered the opinion of the Court.

After a traumatic incident in which she shot and killed a man, a police officer received extensive counseling from a licensed clinical social worker. The question we address is whether statements the officer made to her therapist during the counseling sessions are protected from compelled disclosure in a federal civil action brought by the family of the deceased. Stated otherwise, the question is whether it is appropriate for federal courts to recognize a "psychotherapist privilege" under Rule 501 of the Federal Rules of Evidence.

I

Petitioner is the administrator of the estate of Ricky Allen. Respondents are Mary Lu Redmond, a former police officer, and the Village of Hoffman Estates, Illinois, her employer during the time that she served on the police force. Petitioner com-menced this action against respondents after Redmond shot and killed Allen while on patrol duty. On June 27, 1991, Redmond was the first officer to respond to a "fight in progress" call at an apartment complex. As she arrived at the scene, two of Allen's sisters ran toward her squad car, waving their arms and shouting that there had been a stabbing in one of the apartments. Redmond testified at trial that she relayed this information to her dispatcher and requested an ambulance. She then exited her car and walked toward the apartment building. Before Redmond reached the building, several men ran out, one waving a pipe. When the men ignored her order to get on the ground, Redmond drew her service revolver. Two other men then burst out of the building, one, Ricky Allen, chasing the other. According to Redmond, Allen was brandishing a butcher knife and disregarded her repeated commands to drop the weapon. Redmond shot Allen when she believed he was about to stab the man he was chasing. Allen died at the scene. Redmond testified that before other officers arrived to provide support, "people came pouring out of the buildings," and a threatening confrontation between her and the crowd ensued.

Petitioner filed suit in Federal District Court alleging that Redmond had violated Allen's constitutional rights by using excessive force during the encounter at the apartment complex. At trial, petitioner presented testimony from members of Allen's family that conflicted with Redmond's version of the incident in several important respects. They testified, for example, that Redmond drew her gun before exiting her squad car and that Allen was unarmed when he emerged from the apartment building. During pretrial discovery petitioner learned that after the shooting Redmond had participated in about 50 counseling sessions with Karen Beyer, a clinical social worker licensed by the State of Illinois and employed at that time by the Village of Hoffman Estates. Petitioner sought access to Beyer's notes concerning the sessions for use in cross-examining Redmond. Respondents vigorously resisted the discovery. They asserted that the contents of the conversations between Beyer and Redmond were protected against involuntary disclosure by a psychotherapist-patient privilege. The district judge rejected this argument. Neither Beyer nor Redmond, however, complied with his order to disclose the contents of Beyer's notes. At depositions and on the witness stand both either refused to answer certain questions or professed an inability to recall details of their conversations. In his instructions at the end of the trial, the judge advised the jury that the refusal to turn over Beyer's notes had no "legal justification" and that the jury could therefore presume that the contents of the notes would have been unfavorable to respondents. The jury awarded petitioner $45,000 on the federal claim and $500,000 on her state-law claim. The Court of Appeals for the Seventh Circuit reversed and remanded for a new trial. Addressing the issue for the first time, the court concluded that "reason and experience," the touchstones for acceptance of a privilege under Rule 501 of the Federal Rules of Evidence, compelled recognition of a psychotherapist-patient privilege. . . .

The Court of Appeals qualified its recognition of the privilege by stating that it would not apply if "in the interests of justice, the evidentiary need for the disclosure of the contents of a patient's counseling sessions outweighs that patient's privacy interests." . . . [T]he court concluded that the trial court had erred by refusing to afford protection to the confidential communications between Redmond and Beyer.

The United States courts of appeals do not uniformly agree that the federal courts should recognize a psychotherapist privilege under Rule 501.

II

. . . The common-law principles underlying the recognition of testimonial privileges can be stated simply. " 'For more than three centuries it has now been recognized as a fundamental maxim that the public . . . has a right to every man's evidence. When we come to examine the various claims of exemption, we start with the primary assumption that there is a general duty to give what testimony one is capable of giving, and that any exemptions which may exist are distinctly exceptional, being so many derogations from a positive general rule.'" United States v. Bryan, 339 U. S. 323, 331 (1950) (quoting 8 J. Wigmore, Evidence §2192, p. 64 (3d ed. 1940)).[65] See also United States v. Nixon, 418 U. S. 683, 709 (1974). Exceptions from the general rule disfavoring testimonial privileges may be justified, however, by a " 'public good transcending the normally predominant principle of utilizing all rational means for ascertaining the truth.'" Trammel, 445 U.S., at 50.

Guided by these principles, the question we address today is whether a privilege protecting confidential communications between a psychotherapist and her patient "promotes sufficiently important interests to outweigh the need for probative evidence. . . ." Both "reason and experience" persuade us that it does.

III

Like the spousal and attorney-client privileges, the psychotherapist-patient privilege is "rooted in the imperative need for confidence and trust." Trammel, 445 U.S., at 51. Treatment by a physician for physical ailments can often proceed successfully on the basis of a physical examination, objective information supplied by the patient, and the results of diagnostic tests. Effective psychotherapy, by contrast, depends upon an atmosphere of confidence and trust in which the patient is willing to make a frank and complete disclosure of facts, emotions, memories, and fears. Because of the sensitive nature of the problems for which individuals consult psychotherapists, disclosure of confidential communications made during counseling sessions may cause embarrassment or disgrace. For this reason, the mere possibility of disclosure may impede development of the confidential relationship necessary for successful treatment.[66] As the Judicial Conference Advisory Committee observed in 1972 when it recommended that Congress recognize a psychotherapist privilege as part of the Proposed Federal Rules of Evidence, a psychiatrist's ability to help her patients:

> "is completely dependent upon [the patients'] willingness and ability to talk freely. This makes it difficult if not impossible for [a psychiatrist] to function without being able to assure . . . patients of confidentiality and, indeed, privileged communication. Where there may be exceptions to this general rule . . . , there is wide agreement that confidentiality is a sine qua non for successful psychiatric treatment." Advisory Committee's Notes to Proposed Rules, 56 F.R.D. 183, 242 (1972) (quoting Group for Advancement of Psychiatry, Report No. 45, Confidentiality and Privileged Communication in the Practice of Psychiatry 92 (June 1960)).

---

65. The familiar expression "every man's evidence" was a well-known phrase as early as the mid-18th century. Both the Duke of Argyll and Lord Chancellor Hardwicke invoked the maxim during the May 25, 1742, debate in the House of Lords concerning a bill to grant immunity to witnesses who would give evidence against Sir Robert Walpole, first Earl of Orford. 12 T. Hansard, Parliamentary History of England 643, 675, 693, 697 (1812). The bill was defeated soundly. Id., at 711.

66. See studies and authorities cited in the Brief for American Psychiatric Association et al. as Amici Curiae 14-17, and the Brief for American Psychological Association as Amicus Curiae 12-17.

By protecting confidential communications between a psychotherapist and her patient from involuntary disclosure, the proposed privilege thus serves important private interests.

Our cases make clear that an asserted privilege must also "serve public ends." . . . The psychotherapist privilege serves the public interest by facilitating the provision of appropriate treatment for individuals suffering the effects of a mental or emotional problem. The mental health of our citizenry, no less than its physical health, is a public good of transcendent importance.[67] In contrast to the significant public and private interests supporting recognition of the privilege, the likely evidentiary benefit that would result from the denial of the privilege is modest. If the privilege were rejected, confidential conversations between psychotherapists and their patients would surely be chilled, particularly when it is obvious that the circumstances that give rise to the need for treatment will probably result in litigation. Without a privilege, much of the desirable evidence to which litigants such as petitioner seek access—for example, admissions against interest by a party—is unlikely to come into being. This unspoken "evidence" will therefore serve no greater truth-seeking function than if it had been spoken and privileged.

That it is appropriate for the federal courts to recognize a psychotherapist privilege under Rule 501 is confirmed by the fact that all 50 States and the District of Columbia have enacted into law some form of psychotherapist privilege. We have previously observed that the policy decisions of the States bear on the question whether federal courts should recognize a new privilege or amend the coverage of an existing one. See *Trammel*, 445 U.S., at 48-50. . . . Because state legislatures are fully aware of the need to protect the integrity of the factfinding functions of their courts, the existence of a consensus among the States indicates that "reason and experience" support recognition of the privilege. In addition, given the importance of the patient's understanding that her communications with her therapist will not be publicly disclosed, any State's promise of confidentiality would have little value if the patient were aware that the privilege would not be honored in a federal court.[68] Denial of the federal privilege therefore would frustrate the purposes of the state legislation that was enacted to foster these confidential communications.

It is of no consequence that recognition of the privilege in the vast majority of States is the product of legislative action rather than judicial decision. Although common-law rulings may once have been the primary source of new developments in federal privilege law, that is no longer the case. In Funk v. United States, 290 U.S. 371 (1933), we recognized that it is appropriate to treat a consistent body of policy determinations

---

67. This case amply demonstrates the importance of allowing individuals to receive confidential counseling. Police officers engaged in the dangerous and difficult tasks associated with protecting the safety of our communities not only confront the risk of physical harm but also face stressful circumstances that may give rise to anxiety, depression, fear, or anger. The entire community may suffer if police officers are not able to receive effective counseling and treatment after traumatic incidents, either because trained officers leave the profession prematurely or because those in need of treatment remain on the job.

68. At the outset of their relationship, the ethical therapist must disclose to the patient "the relevant limits on confidentiality." See American Psychological Association, Ethical Principles of Psychologists and Code of Conduct, Standard 5.01 (Dec. 1992). See also National Federation of Societies for Clinical Social Work, Code of Ethics V(a) (May 1988); American Counseling Association, Code of Ethics and Standards of Practice a.3. (effective July 1995).

by state legislatures as reflecting both "reason" and "experience." That rule is properly respectful of the States and at the same time reflects the fact that once a state legislature has enacted a privilege there is no longer an opportunity for common-law creation of the protection. . . .[69] The uniform judgment of the States is reinforced by the fact that a psychotherapist privilege was among the nine specific privileges recommended by the Advisory Committee in its proposed privilege rules. . . . In rejecting the proposed draft that had specifically identified each privilege rule and substituting the present more open-ended Rule 501, the Senate Judiciary Committee explicitly stated that its action "should not be understood as disapproving any recognition of a psychiatrist-patient . . . privilege contained in the [proposed] rules." Because we agree with the judgment of the state legislatures and the Advisory Committee that a psychotherapist-patient privilege will serve a "public good transcending the normally predominant principle of utilizing all rational means for ascertaining truth," *Trammel,* 445 U.S., at 50, we hold that confidential communications between a licensed psychotherapist and her patients in the course of diagnosis or treatment are protected from compelled disclosure under Rule 501 of the Federal Rules of Evidence.[70]

IV

All agree that a psychotherapist privilege covers confidential communications made to licensed psychiatrists and psychologists. We have no hesitation in concluding in this case that the federal privilege should also extend to confidential communications made to licensed social workers in the course of psychotherapy. The reasons for recognizing a privilege for treatment by psychiatrists and psychologists apply with equal force to treatment by a clinical social worker such as Karen Beyer.[71] Today, social workers provide a significant amount of mental health treatment. Their clients often include the poor and those of modest means who could not afford the assistance of

---

69. Petitioner acknowledges that all 50 state legislatures favor a psychotherapist privilege. She nevertheless discounts the relevance of the state privilege statutes by pointing to divergence among the States concerning the types of therapy relationships protected and the exceptions recognized. A small number of state statutes, for example, grant the privilege only to psychiatrists and psychologists, while most apply the protection more broadly. Compare Haw. Rules Evid. 504, 504.1 and N.D. Rule Evid. 503 (privilege extends to physicians and psychotherapists), with Ariz. Rev. Stat. Ann. §32-3283 (1992) (privilege covers "behavioral health professionals"); Tex. Rule Civ. Evid. 510(a)(1) (privilege extends to persons "licensed or certified by the State of Texas in the diagnosis, evaluation or treatment of any mental or emotional disorder" or "involved in the treatment or examination of drug abusers"); Utah Rule Evid. 506 (privilege protects confidential communications made to marriage and family therapists, professional counselors, and psychiatric mental health nurse specialists). The range of exceptions recognized by the States is similarly varied. Compare Ark. Code Ann. §17-46-107 (1987) (narrow exceptions); Haw. Rules Evid. 504, 504.1 (same), with Cal. Evid. Code Ann. §§1016-1027 (West 1995) (broad exceptions); R.I. Gen. Laws §5-37.3-4 (1956) (same). These variations in the scope of the protection are too limited to undermine the force of the States' unanimous judgment that some form of psychotherapist privilege is appropriate.

70. Like other testimonial privileges, the patient may of course waive the protection.

71. If petitioner had filed her complaint in an Illinois state court, respondents' claim of privilege would surely have been upheld, at least with respect to the state wrongful death action. An Illinois statute provides that conversations between a therapist and her patients are privileged from compelled disclosure in any civil or criminal proceeding. Ill. Comp. Stat., ch. 740, §110/10 (1994). The term "therapist" is broadly defined to encompass a number of licensed professionals including social workers. Ch. 740, §110/2. Karen Beyer, having satisfied the strict standards for licensure, qualifies as a clinical social worker in Illinois. . . .

a psychiatrist or psychologist, but whose counseling sessions serve the same public goals. Perhaps in recognition of these circumstances, the vast majority of States explicitly extend a testimonial privilege to licensed social workers. We therefore agree with the Court of Appeals that "drawing a distinction between the counseling provided by costly psychotherapists and the counseling provided by more readily accessible social workers serves no discernible public purpose." We part company with the Court of Appeals on a separate point. We reject the balancing component of the privilege implemented by that court and a small number of States. Making the promise of confidentiality contingent upon a trial judge's later evaluation of the relative importance of the patient's interest in privacy and the evidentiary need for disclosure would eviscerate the effectiveness of the privilege. As we explained in *Upjohn*, if the purpose of the privilege is to be served, the participants in the confidential conversation "must be able to predict with some degree of certainty whether particular discussions will be protected. An uncertain privilege, or one which purports to be certain but results in widely varying applications by the courts, is little better than no privilege at all." These considerations are all that is necessary for decision of this case. A rule that authorizes the recognition of new privileges on a case-by-case basis makes it appropriate to define the details of new privileges in a like manner. Because this is the first case in which we have recognized a psychotherapist privilege, it is neither necessary nor feasible to delineate its full contours in a way that would "govern all conceivable future questions in this area."[72]

V

The conversations between Officer Redmond and Karen Beyer and the notes taken during their counseling sessions are protected from compelled disclosure under Rule 501 of the Federal Rules of Evidence. The judgment of the Court of Appeals is affirmed.

It is so ordered.

Justice SCALIA, with whom THE CHIEF JUSTICE joins as to Part III, dissenting.

The Court has discussed at some length the benefit that will be purchased by creation of the evidentiary privilege in this case: the encouragement of psychoanalytic counseling. It has not mentioned the purchase price: occasional injustice. That is the cost of every rule which excludes reliable and probative evidence — or at least every one categorical enough to achieve its announced policy objective. In the case of some of these rules, such as the one excluding confessions that have not been properly "Mirandized," see Miranda v. Arizona, 384 U.S. 436 (1966), the victim of the injustice is always the impersonal State or the faceless "public at large." For the rule proposed here, the victim is more likely to be some individual who is prevented from proving a valid claim — or (worse still) prevented from establishing a valid defense. The latter is particularly unpalatable for those who love justice, because it causes the courts of law not merely to let stand a wrong, but to become themselves the instruments of wrong.

---

72. Although it would be premature to speculate about most future developments in the federal psychotherapist privilege, we do not doubt that there are situations in which the privilege must give way, for example, if a serious threat of harm to the patient or to others can be averted only by means of a disclosure by the therapist.

In the past, this Court has well understood that the particular value the courts are distinctively charged with preserving—justice—is severely harmed by contravention of "the fundamental principle that "the public . . . has a right to every man's evidence." . . . The Court today ignores this traditional judicial preference for the truth, and ends up creating a privilege that is new, vast, and ill-defined. I respectfully dissent.

I

The case before us involves confidential communications made by a police officer to a state-licensed clinical social worker in the course of psychotherapeutic counseling. Before proceeding to a legal analysis of the case, I must observe that the Court makes its task deceptively simple by the manner in which it proceeds. It begins by characterizing the issue as "whether it is appropriate for federal courts to recognize a 'psychotherapist privilege,'" and devotes almost all of its opinion to that question. Having answered that question (to its satisfaction) in the affirmative, it then devotes less than a page of text to answering in the affirmative the small remaining question whether "the federal privilege should also extend to confidential communications made to licensed social workers in the course of psychotherapy." Of course the prototypical evidentiary privilege analogous to the one asserted here—the lawyer-client privilege—is not identified by the broad area of advice-giving practiced by the person to whom the privileged communication is given, but rather by the professional status of that person. Hence, it seems a long step from a lawyer-client privilege to a tax advisor-client or accountant-client privilege. But if one recharacterizes it as a "legal advisor" privilege, the extension seems like the most natural thing in the world. That is the illusion the Court has produced here: It first frames an overly general question ("Should there be a psychotherapist privilege?") that can be answered in the negative only by excluding from protection office consultations with professional psychiatrists (i.e., doctors) and clinical psychologists. And then, having answered that in the affirmative, it comes to the only question that the facts of this case present ("Should there be a social worker-client privilege with regard to psychotherapeutic counseling?") with the answer seemingly a foregone conclusion. At that point, to conclude against the privilege one must subscribe to the difficult proposition, "Yes, there is a psychotherapist privilege, but not if the psychotherapist is a social worker." Relegating the question actually posed by this case to an afterthought makes the impossible possible in a number of wonderful ways. For example, it enables the Court to treat the Proposed Federal Rules of Evidence developed in 1972 by the Judicial Conference Advisory Committee as strong support for its holding, whereas they in fact counsel clearly and directly against it. The Committee did indeed recommend a "psychotherapist privilege" of sorts; but more precisely, and more relevantly, it recommended a privilege for psychotherapy conducted by "a person authorized to practice medicine" or "a person licensed or certified as a psychologist," Proposed Rule of Evidence 504, 56 F.R.D. 183, 240 (1972), which is to say that it recommended against the privilege at issue here. That condemnation is obscured, and even converted into an endorsement, by pushing a "psychotherapist privilege" into the center ring. The Proposed Rule figures prominently in the Court's explanation of why that privilege deserves recognition, and is ignored in the single page devoted to the sideshow which happens to be the issue presented for decision.

This is the most egregious and readily explainable example of how the Court's misdirection of its analysis makes the difficult seem easy; others will become apparent when I give the social-worker question the fuller consideration it deserves. My initial point, however, is that the Court's very methodology—giving serious consideration only to the more general, and much easier, question—is in violation of our duty to proceed cautiously when erecting barriers between us and the truth.

II

To say that the Court devotes the bulk of its opinion to the much easier question of psychotherapist-patient privilege is not to say that its answer to that question is convincing. At bottom, the Court's decision to recognize such a privilege is based on its view that "successful [psychotherapeutic] treatment" serves "important private interests" (namely those of patients undergoing psychotherapy) as well as the "public good" of "the mental health of our citizenry." I have no quarrel with these premises. Effective psychotherapy undoubtedly is beneficial to individuals with mental problems, and surely serves some larger social interest in maintaining a mentally stable society. But merely mentioning these values does not answer the critical question: are they of such importance, and is the contribution of psychotherapy to them so distinctive, and is the application of normal evidentiary rules so destructive to psychotherapy, as to justify making our federal courts occasional instruments of injustice? On that central question I find the Court's analysis insufficiently convincing to satisfy the high standard we have set for rules that are in derogation of the search for truth.

When is it, one must wonder, that the psychotherapist came to play such an indispensable role in the maintenance of the citizenry's mental health? For most of history, men and women have worked out their difficulties by talking to, inter alios, parents, siblings, best friends and bartenders—none of whom was awarded a privilege against testifying in court. Ask the average citizen: Would your mental health be more significantly impaired by preventing you from seeing a psychotherapist, or by preventing you from getting advice from your mom? I have little doubt what the answer would be. Yet there is no mother-child privilege. How likely is it that a person will be deterred from seeking psychological counseling, or from being completely truthful in the course of such counseling, because of fear of later disclosure in litigation? And even more pertinent to today's decision, to what extent will the evidentiary privilege reduce that deterrent? The Court does not try to answer the first of these questions; and it cannot possibly have any notion of what the answer is to the second, since that depends entirely upon the scope of the privilege, which the Court amazingly finds it "neither necessary nor feasible to delineate," If, for example, the psychotherapist can give the patient no more assurance than "a court will not be able to make me disclose what you tell me, unless you tell me about a harmful act," I doubt whether there would be much benefit from the privilege at all. That is not a fanciful example, at least with respect to extension of the psychotherapist privilege to social workers.

Even where it is certain that absence of the psychotherapist privilege will inhibit disclosure of the information, it is not clear to me that that is an unacceptable state of affairs. Let us assume the very worst in the circumstances of the present case: that to be truthful about what was troubling her, the police officer who sought counseling would have to confess that she shot without reason, and wounded an innocent man. If (again to assume the worst) such an act constituted the crime of negligent wounding under Illinois law, the officer would of course have the absolute right not to admit that she shot without reason in criminal court. But I see no reason why she should be enabled both not to admit it in criminal court (as a good citizen should), and to get the benefits of psychotherapy by admitting it to a therapist who cannot tell anyone else. And even less reason why she should be enabled to deny her guilt in the criminal trial—or in a civil trial for negligence—while yet obtaining the benefits of psychotherapy by confessing guilt to a social worker who cannot testify. It seems to me entirely fair to say that if she wishes the benefits of telling the truth she must also accept the adverse consequences. To be sure, in most cases the statements to the psychotherapist will be only marginally relevant, and one of the purposes of the privilege (though not one relied upon by the Court) may be simply to spare patients needless intrusion upon their privacy, and to spare psychotherapists needless expenditure of their time in deposition and trial. But surely this can be achieved by means short of excluding even evidence that is of the most direct and conclusive effect. . . .

The Court suggests one last policy justification: since psychotherapist privilege statutes exist in all the States, the failure to recognize a privilege in federal courts "would frustrate the purposes of the state legislation that was enacted to foster these confidential communications." . . . Since, as I shall discuss, state policies regarding the psychotherapist privilege vary considerably from State to State, no uniform federal policy can possibly honor most of them. If furtherance of state policies is the name of the game, rules of privilege in federal courts should vary from State to State, a la *Erie*.

The Court's failure to put forward a convincing justification of its own could perhaps be excused if it were relying upon the unanimous conclusion of state courts in the reasoned development of their common law. It cannot do that, since no State has such a privilege apart from legislation. . . . The Court concedes that there is "divergence among the States concerning the types of therapy relationships protected and the exceptions recognized." To rest a newly announced federal common-law psychotherapist privilege, assertable from this day forward in all federal courts, upon "the States' unanimous judgment that some form of psychotherapist privilege is appropriate," is rather like announcing a new, immediately applicable, federal common law of torts, based upon the States' "unanimous judgment" that some form of tort law is appropriate. In the one case as in the other, the state laws vary to such a degree that the parties and lower federal judges confronted by the new "common law" have barely a clue as to what its content might be.

III

Turning from the general question that was not involved in this case to the specific one that is: The Court's conclusion that a social-worker psychotherapeutic privilege deserves recognition is even less persuasive. In approaching this question, the fact that five of the state legislatures that have seen fit to enact "some form" of psychotherapist privilege have elected not to extend any form of privilege to social workers, ought to give one pause. So should the fact that the Judicial Conference Advisory Committee was similarly discriminating in its conferral of the proposed Rule 504 privilege. The Court, however, has "no hesitation in concluding . . . that the federal privilege should also extend" to social workers—and goes on to prove that by polishing off the reasoned analysis with a topic sentence and two sentences of discussion, as follows (omitting citations and nongermane footnote):

> "The reasons for recognizing a privilege for treatment by psychiatrists and psychologists apply with equal force to treatment by a clinical social worker such as Karen Beyer.
>
> Today, social workers provide a significant amount of mental health treatment. Their clients often include the poor and those of modest means who could not afford the assistance of a psychiatrist or psychologist, but whose counseling sessions serve the same public goals."

So much for the rule that privileges are to be narrowly construed.

Of course this brief analysis—like the earlier, more extensive, discussion of the general psychotherapist privilege—contains no explanation of why the psychotherapy provided by social workers is a public good of such transcendent importance as to be purchased at the price of occasional injustice. Moreover, it considers only the respects in which social workers providing therapeutic services are similar to licensed psychiatrists and psychologists; not a word about the respects in which they are different. A licensed psychiatrist or psychologist is an expert in psychotherapy—and that may suffice (though I think it not so clear that this Court should make the judgment) to justify the use of extraordinary means to encourage counseling with him, as opposed to counseling with one's rabbi, minister, family or friends. One must presume that a social worker does not bring this greatly heightened degree of skill to bear, which is alone a reason for not encouraging that consultation as generously. Does a social worker bring to bear at least a significantly heightened degree of skill—more than a minister or rabbi, for example? I have no idea, and neither does the Court. The social worker in the present case, Karen Beyer, was a "licensed clinical social worker" in Illinois, a job title whose training requirements consist of "master's degree in social work from an approved program," and "3,000 hours of satisfactory, supervised clinical professional experience." . . . But the rule the Court announces today—like the Illinois evidentiary privilege which that rule purports to respect,—is not limited to "licensed clinical social workers," but includes all "licensed social workers." "Licensed social workers" may also provide "mental health services" as described in §20/3(5), so long as it is done under supervision of a licensed clinical social worker. And the training requirement for a "licensed social worker" consists of either (a) "a degree from a graduate program of social work" approved by the State, or (b) "a degree in social work from an undergraduate program" approved by the State, plus "3 years of supervised professional experience." With due respect, it does not seem to me that any of this training is comparable in its rigor (or indeed in the precision of its subject) to the training of the other experts (lawyers) to whom this Court has accorded a privilege, or even of the experts (psychiatrists and psychologists) to whom the Advisory Committee and this Court proposed extension of a privilege in 1972. Of course these are only Illinois' requirements for "social workers." Those of other States, for all we know, may be even less demanding. Indeed, I am not even sure there is a nationally accepted definition of "social worker," as there is of psychiatrist and psychologist. It seems to me quite irresponsible to extend the so-called "psychotherapist privilege" to all licensed social workers, nationwide, without exploring these issues.

Another critical distinction between psychiatrists and psychologists, on the one hand, and social workers, on the other, is that the former professionals, in their consultations with patients, do nothing but psychotherapy. Social workers, on the other hand, interview people for a multitude of reasons. The Illinois definition of "licensed social worker," for example, is as follows:

> "Licensed social worker" means a person who holds a license authorizing the practice of social work, which includes social services to individuals, groups or communities in any one or more of the fields of social casework, social group work, community organization for social welfare, social work research, social welfare administration or social work education.

Thus, in applying the "social worker" variant of the "psychotherapist" privilege, it will be necessary to determine whether the information provided to the social worker was provided to him in his capacity as a psychotherapist, or in his capacity as an administrator of social welfare, a community organizer, etc. Worse still, if the privilege is to have its desired effect (and is not to mislead the client), it will presumably be necessary for the social caseworker to advise, as the conversation with his welfare client proceeds, which portions are privileged and which are not.

Having concluded its three sentences of reasoned analysis, the Court then invokes, as it did when considering the psychotherapist privilege, the "experience" of the States—once again an experience I consider irrelevant (if not counter-indicative) because it consists entirely of legislation rather than common-law decision. It says that "the vast majority of States explicitly extend a testimonial privilege to licensed social workers." There are two elements of this impressive statistic, however, that the Court does not reveal.

First—and utterly conclusive of the irrelevance of this supposed consensus to the question before us—the majority of the States that accord a privilege to social workers do not do so as a subpart of a "psychotherapist" privilege. The privilege applies to all confidences imparted to social workers, and not just those provided in the course of psychotherapy. . . .

Second, the Court does not reveal the enormous degree of disagreement among the States as to the scope of the privilege. . . . In Illinois and Wisconsin, the social-worker privilege does not apply when the confidential information pertains to homicide, and in the District of Columbia when it pertains to any crime "inflicting injuries" upon persons. In Missouri, the privilege is suspended as to information that pertains to a criminal act, and in Texas when the information is sought in any criminal prosecution. In Kansas and Oklahoma, the privilege yields when the information pertains to "violations of any law," in Indiana, when it reveals a "serious harmful act," and in Delaware and Idaho, when it pertains to any "harmful act." In Oregon, a state-employed social worker like Karen Beyer loses the privilege where her supervisor determines that her testimony "is necessary in the performance of the duty of the social worker as a public employee." In South Carolina, a social worker is forced to disclose confidences "when required by statutory law or by court order for good cause shown to the extent that the patient's care and treatment or the nature and extent of his mental illness or emotional condition are reasonably at issue in a proceeding." The majority of social-worker-privilege States declare the privilege inapplicable to information relating to child abuse. And the States that do not fall into any of the above categories provide exceptions for commitment proceedings, for proceedings in which the patient relies on his mental or emotional condition as an element of his claim or defense, or for communications made in the course of a court-ordered examination of the mental or emotional condition of the patient.

Thus, although the Court is technically correct that "the vast majority of States explicitly extend a testimonial privilege to licensed social workers," that uniformity exists only at the most superficial level. No State has adopted the privilege without restriction; the nature of the restrictions varies enormously from jurisdiction to jurisdiction; and ten States, I reiterate, effectively reject the privilege entirely. It is fair to say that there is scant national consensus even as to the propriety of a social-worker psychotherapist privilege, and none whatever as to its appropriate scope. In other words, the state laws to which the Court appeals for support demonstrate most convincingly that adoption of a social-worker psychotherapist privilege is a job for Congress. . . .

The question before us today is not whether there should be an evidentiary privilege for social workers providing therapeutic services. Perhaps there should. But the question before us is whether (1) the need for that privilege is so clear, and (2) the desirable contours of that privilege are so evident, that it is appropriate for this Court to craft it in common-law fashion, under Rule 501. Even if we were writing on a clean slate, I think the answer to that question would be clear. But given our extensive precedent to the effect that new privileges "in derogation of the search for truth" "are not lightly created," United States v. Nixon, 418 U.S., at 710, the answer the Court gives today is inexplicable.

In its consideration of this case, the Court was the beneficiary of no fewer than 14 amicus briefs supporting respondents, most of which came from such organizations as the American Psychiatric Association, the American Psychoanalytic Association, the American Association of State Social Work Boards, the Employee Assistance Professionals Association, Inc., the American Counseling Association, and the National Association of Social Workers. Not a single amicus brief was filed in support of petitioner. That is no surprise. There is no self-interested organization out there devoted to pursuit of the truth in the federal courts. The expectation is, however, that this Court will have that interest prominently—indeed, primarily—in mind. Today we have failed that expectation, and that responsibility. It is no small matter to say that, in some cases, our federal courts will be the tools of injustice rather than unearth the truth where it is available to be found. The common law has identified a few instances where that is tolerable. Perhaps Congress may conclude that it is also tolerable for the purpose of encouraging psychotherapy by social workers. But that conclusion assuredly does not burst upon the mind with such clarity that a judgment in favor of suppressing the truth ought to be pronounced by this honorable Court. I respectfully dissent.

NOTES AND QUESTIONS

1. Who has the better of the argument, the majority or the dissent? Could you have written a more persuasive majority opinion? Could you have responded more effectively to the dissent?

2. One of the concerns is that embarrassing revelations are frequently made in therapeutic sessions, and the Court is certainly correct that the possibility of exposing such matters will be a disincentive to their creation. Still, is the patient's knowledge that there is a privilege necessary to effective mental health counseling? To support the argument of necessity, the majority relied heavily on amicus briefs filed by various organizations that promote psychotherapy. Careful analysis of the studies relied on in these briefs, however, shows that they "do not substantiate the empirical claim that the typical patient is so concerned about the prospect of litigation that the . . . privilege will significantly affect his or her willingness to seek treatment or make necessary revelations to a therapist." Edward Imwinkelried, The Rivalry Between Truth and Privilege: The Weakness of the Supreme Court's Reasoning in Jaffee v. Redmond, 518 U.S. 1 (1996), 49 Hastings L.J. 969, 980 (1998). Should courts require that the utilitarian justification for privileges be empirically valid? How can courts, as opposed to legislatures, obtain empirical data?

3. Is the majority's policy analysis satisfactory? Reflect back on the contingent claim theory about the attorney-client privilege. Like there, isn't the question here the marginal gains and losses under two different regimes: one with a privilege and one without a privilege? And if that data is not available in some form (including judicial experience), should a court create a privilege? In this respect, is the legislative process fundamentally different from the judicial process?

4. The majority purports to establish an absolute privilege in *Jaffee*; that is, it rejected the balancing component that the Seventh Circuit Court of Appeals believed necessary to evaluate the patient's interest in autonomy and privacy versus the evidentiary need for disclosure. Yet, in its final footnote, the majority acknowledges that "there are situations in which the privilege must give way" and cites as an example the situation in which disclosure is the only means to protect the patient or others from the serious threat of harm by the patient. See page 977 n.72, supra. We discuss below the circumstances under which federal courts have found that the privilege must "give way." See generally Christopher B. Mueller, The Federal Psychotherapist-Patient Privilege After *Jaffee*: Truth and Other Values in a Therapeutic Age, 49 Hastings L.J. 945 (1998).

b. Scope of the Privilege After Jaffee

In the years since *Jaffee* was decided, the scope of the psychotherapist privilege has been tested in federal litigation. The privilege has developed on a case-by-case basis, since the Court did not spell out its full contours.

Who Is a Psychotherapist?   The psychotherapist-patient privilege in Proposed FRE 504 includes "a person authorized to practice medicine" — in other words, all physicians—and "a person licensed or certified as a psychologist" within the definition of psychotherapist. Since *Jaffee*, courts have also included licensed social workers and other mental health workers within the privilege. For example, rape crisis counselors who are not licensed but who have undergone special training and work under the direct control and supervision of social workers or psychotherapists were included in United States v. Lowe, 948 F. Supp. 97, 99 (D. Mass. 1996), citing the fact that a majority of states have a privilege for rape counseling communications. But see Jane Student 1 v. Williams, 206 F.R.D. 306 (S.D. Ala. 2002) (holding that the psychotherapist-patient privilege does not extend to unlicensed professional counselors).

In Oleszko v. State Compensation Insurance Fund, 243 F.3d 1154, 1158 (9th Cir. 2001), the Ninth Circuit extended the privilege to unlicensed counselors employed by an Employee Assistance Program, which provides worksite assistance, including mental health counseling. The court cited *Jaffee* in noting:

> [T]he provision of mental health services has significantly changed in the last quarter century. EAPs embody what may be viewed as a team approach to providing mental health services. Thus, although EAP personnel do not engage in psychotherapy themselves, they serve as a primary link between the troubled employee and psychotherapeutic treatment. [Id.]

Some courts are also willing to consider licensed marriage, family and child counselors as within the privilege. Speaker v. County of San Bernadino, 82 F. Supp. 2d 1105, 1109 (C.D. Cal. 2000). In Carman v. McDonnell Douglas Corp., 114 F.3d 790, 793 (8th Cir. 1997), however, the Eighth Circuit held that communications to an ombudsman employed to resolve workplace disputes without litigation were not protected by the psychotherapist privilege because the assistance was limited to dealing with workplace disputes, not mental health problems.

Communications. Communications falling within the privilege must be made in the course of or for the purpose of obtaining mental health services. For example, Proposed FRE 504 limits the psychotherapist-patient privilege to confidential communications "made [by the patient] for the purpose of diagnosis or treatment of his mental or emotional condition, including drug addiction." See Doe v. Ensey, 220 F.R.D. 422, 425 (M.D. Pa. 2004). California's psychotherapist-patient privilege is unusual in that it extends the privilege to communications made "for the purpose of scientific research on mental or emotional problems." Cal. Evid. Code §1011. Information that does not reveal the client's confidential communications—such as identity of therapist and client, occurrence of psychotherapy and dates of treatment—are not privileged. See, e.g., Vinson v. Humana, Inc., 190 F.R.D. 624, 626-627 (M.D. Fla. 1999); and Merrill v. Waffle House, Inc., 2005 WL 928602 (N.D. Tex. Feb. 5, 2005).

In situations where employees, such as police officers, are required to undergo psychological evaluations regarding fitness for duty and the results are disclosed to employers, it has been held that a psychotherapist privilege is not established because there is no treatment involved and there is no expectation of confidentiality. Kemper v. Gray, 182 F.R.D. 597, 599 (E.D. Mo. 1998). But where only a general conclusion is disclosed to the employer and the employee has been assured of confidentiality, the privilege has attached and prevents disclosure. See, e.g., Caver v. City of Trenton, 192 F.R.D. 154, 162 (D.N.J. 2000).

Waiver. As with the physician-patient privilege, the patient is the holder of the psychotherapist-patient privilege. Thus, the privilege may be waived only by the patient or an authorized representative on the patient's behalf. Parents can assert or waive the privilege on behalf of their minor children. But courts may find that invocation of the privilege may not be in the "best interests" of the child, for example in custody disputes where there are allegations of child abuse. Ellison v. Ellison, 919 P.2d 1, 8 (Okla. 1996).

Taking a broad view of waiver, some courts have held that a patient impliedly waives the psychotherapist privilege by raising the patient's mental condition as an element of the claim or defense; generally, by making any claims for mental and emotional distress. See, e.g., Maday v. Public Libraries of Saginaw, 480 F.3d 815 (6th Cir. 2007) ("[W]hen [plaintiff] put her emotional state at issue in the case, she waived [the psychotherapist-patient privilege], and the records may come in, subject to what appears to have been reasonable Rule 403 balancing by the district judge."); Doe v. Oberweis Dairy, 456 F.3d 704 (7th Cir. 2006) (seeking damages for emotional distress places psychological state in issue and waives privilege); Schoffstall v. Henderson, 223 F.3d 818 (8th Cir. 2000) (same); Utah v. Worthen, 222 P.3d 1144 (Utah 2009) (hatred toward defendant was emotional condition, represented an element of defense's theory, and triggered exception in psychotherapist-patient privilege). A more restrictive view of waiver, however, has been taken by other courts. This narrower view requires that the privilege holder make an affirmative use of the privileged material by calling the therapist as a witness or putting specific communications at issue. See, e.g., Fitzgerald v. Cassil, 216 F.R.D. 632 (N.D. Cal. 2003) (arguing that a narrow exception is more consistent with *Jaffee* and a broad approach is not necessary to achieve fairness for defendant); Vanderbilt v. Town of Chilmark, 174 F.R.D. 225, 230 (D. Mass. 1997) (noting that privilege is waived when substance of privileged communication is used by the party invoking the privilege); United States v. Sturman, 1998 U.S. Dist. LEXIS 3488 (S.D.N.Y. Mar. 9, 1998) (a criminal defendant's intention to use psychiatric testimony to negate the government's proof of specific intent does not waive the privilege prior to trial; defendant bears no burden on the issue of intent and does not put his mental condition "at issue" until he uses the testimony at trial).

A useful summary of this split in federal court opinions is contained in Fritsch v. City of Chula Vista, 187 F.R.D. 614 (S.D. Cal. 1999). The Supreme Court in *Jaffee* gave no guidance on this point. Indeed, the Supreme Court rejected the balancing test proposed by the Seventh Circuit Court of Appeals, but acknowledged that there would be circumstances in which the privilege must give way. See page 977, n.72, supra. Thus, both sides of this split of opinion are able to rely on policies discussed in *Jaffee* to justify their positions. The narrow view, requiring what amounts to actual waiver, protects the patient's imperative need for confidentiality and prevents post hoc balancing of the importance of privacy versus the evidentiary need for disclosure. Id. at 630. The broader view has been justified by the need for a fair discovery process when a patient "desires the jury to compensate for damage to her emotional condition . . . defendant is entitled to explore the circumstance [that] caused that injury." Id. at 569.

Many decisions regarding the waiver of the privilege are made during the discovery phase of trial when one party seeks to compel production of medical records or to depose a psychotherapist. Some courts require the party seeking discovery to show cause why the "intrusion into the therapeutic relationship is the only possible means to obtain relevant information" and to narrowly tailor discovery requests to information directly relevant to the lawsuit. Vasconcellos v. Cybex International, Inc., 962 F. Supp. 701, 709 (D. Md. 1997).

Due to the prevalence of group counseling sessions, several courts have held that the psychotherapist-patient privilege is not waived when statements are made by patients in the presence of others in the group. The rationale is that the joint therapy comprises part of the treatment. See, e.g., State v. Andring, 342 N.W.2d 128, 133-134 (Minn. 1984). However, the statements are not privileged in joint litigation between the patients. Redding v. Virginia Mason Medical Ctr., 878 P.2d 483 (Wash. Ct. App. 1994).

c. Exceptions to the Privilege

Although the Court in *Jaffee* rejected an outright balancing test, there are several exceptions to the privilege where the need for probative evidence is great or the interests underlying the privilege are nonexistent.

Constitutional Limits.   Doe v. Diamond, 964 F.2d 1325 (2d Cir. 1992), decided prior to *Jaffee*, involved a criminal defendant's request for the psychiatric records of a victim, Doe, who had initiated the criminal charges, and who would be a witness against him. Consider the following excerpt from the opinion, and pay close attention to the significance of the confrontation clause to the analysis. The confrontation clause may often mandate discovery regardless of the parameters of a privilege:

> Although appellant's [Doe's] psychiatric files do contain material that squarely implicates his privacy interests, the balance in this case weighs overwhelmingly in favor of allowing an inquiry into his history of mental illness. Appellant is not only the person who initiated the criminal investigation against Diamond [the criminal defendant] but also a witness whose credibility will be the central issue at trial. He has a long history of emotional illness, and there is expert psychiatric opinion in the record that this history is relevant to his credibility. That opinion includes the observation that appellant's "interpretation of reality" might have been affected during times in which he was undergoing psychiatric treatment, as he was at the time of the events about which he is to testify. We agree with Chief Judge Platt that a preclusion of any inquiry into appellant's psychiatric history would violate the Confrontation Clause and vitiate any resulting conviction of Diamond.
>
> Appellant poses for us various hypotheticals concerning the disclosure of communications made to psychotherapists thirty years ago, destruction of the privacy interests of a third party, and the violation of the professional obligations of the psychotherapists involved. These matters are not before us, however. The questions that appellant declined to answer concerned times at which he received psychiatric treatment and

the names of particular psychotherapists. They also concerned his refusal to consent to those psychotherapists being interviewed by counsel under the protective order. The hearing held by Chief Judge Platt was in camera, and appellant's answers to the questions and counsel's interviews of appellant's psychotherapists would have been subject to a protective order sufficient to prevent public revelation of confidential matters. His answers to the questions and consenting to the interests as an important factor to be weighed in the interviews would not, therefore, have resulted in the public disclosure of confidential matters. [Id. at 1329.]

In cases since *Jaffee*, courts have adhered to the reasoning in *Doe* and have held that a criminal defendant's Sixth Amendment rights to information that establishes an element of defense or impeaches a witness can justify discovery of a victim and/or witness's mental health records. United States v. Alperin, 128 F. Supp. 2d 1251, 1254 (N.D. Cal. 2001). But see United States v. Doyle, 1 F. Supp. 2d 1187 (D. Or. 1999) (victim's mental health records, relevant only to sentencing enhancement, need not be disclosed to already convicted defendant).

The psychotherapist-patient privilege can arise in criminal cases involving alleged child sexual abuse. If the child accuser confides his or her memories of abuse to a psychiatrist, the child may then assert the privilege when the accused attempts to discover the communications. See, e.g., Goldsmith v. State, 651 A.2d 866 (Md. 1995); State v. Speese, 545 N.W.2d 510 (Wis. 1996). The majority of courts hold that the defendant can have access to the psychiatric records of his accuser if the psychiatrist testifies at trial. Other concerns raised by these cases are whether courts should appoint counsel or guardians ad litem to assist minors in determining whether to assert or waive the privilege, whether the privilege should apply during discovery, and whether a person's refusal to waive the privilege should preclude that person from testifying at trial. Id. at 517.

Compelled Disclosures.   Statutory law typically abolishes the psychotherapist-patient privilege in proceedings to hospitalize the patient for mental illness, if the psychotherapist has determined that the patient is in need of hospitalization. And if a judge orders an examination of the mental or emotional condition of the patient, communications made in the course of the examination are not privileged with respect to the particular purpose for which the examination is ordered unless the judge orders otherwise. In many states, mental health professionals are also required to report their reasonable suspicions that children whom they treat have been abused, and some states create an exception to the privilege where child abuse is known or suspected.

Dangerous Patient.   In its concluding footnote, the majority opinion in *Jaffee* noted that "there are situations in which the privilege must give way, for example, if a serious threat of harm to the patient or to others can be averted only by means of a disclosure by the therapist." See page 977–72, supra. This footnote has generated some case law on whether threats made during therapy sessions can form the basis of prosecutions for violation of federal laws that define such threats as criminal conduct. In such instances, the therapist's testimony about the threats—in violation of the psychotherapist privilege—is the only evidence that the prosecutor has. Thus, the government has sought judicial recognition of a so-called dangerous patient exception. So far, federal courts have split on the question of whether the exception exists. The

Sixth and Ninth Circuits have declined to adopt the dangerous patient exception. See United States v. Hayes, 227 F.3d 578 (6th Cir. 2000); and United States v. Chase, 340 F.3d 978 (9th Cir. 2003). Recognizing that psychotherapists have professional and ethical duties to protect potential victims when threats are made during therapy, the court in *Hayes* stated that these duties "may require, among other things, disclosure to third parties or testimony at an involuntary hospitalization proceeding." *Hayes*, 227 F.3d at 585. The court held, however, that "compliance with the professional duty to protect does not imply a duty to testify against a patient in criminal proceedings or in civil proceedings other than directly related to the patient's involuntary hospitalization, and such testimony is privileged and inadmissible if a patient properly asserts the psychotherapist/patient privilege." Id. The court reasoned that once the appropriate warning had been given, or proceedings initiated, it would be highly unlikely that the therapist's testimony in a criminal prosecution would be the only means of avoiding harm to others, which was the standard adverted to in *Jaffee*. Thus, the court in *Hayes* concluded the *Jaffee* footnote was no more than an aside

> to the effect that the federal psychotherapist/patient privilege will not operate to impede a psychotherapist's compliance with the professional duty to protect identifiable third parties from serious threats of harm. We think the *Jaffee* footnote was referring to the fact that psychotherapists will sometimes need to testify in court proceedings, such as those for the involuntary commitment of a patient, to comply with their "duty to protect" the patient or identifiable third parties. [Id. at 584.]

However, the Fifth Circuit found, in United States v. Auster, 517 F.3d 312, 319 (5th Cir. 2008), that when the psychiatrist had warned the patient that his professional duties would require him to report any threatening communication, the "patient [had] no reasonable expectation of confidentiality." While the court implied that an expectation that a psychiatrist will reveal threatening communication would generally lead "the cost-benefit scales [to] favor disclosure," it held that any threatening communication made with *actual knowledge* that it would not be kept confidential was not privileged. Id. In United States v. Glass, 133 F.3d 1356, 1360 (10th Cir. 1998), the Tenth Circuit stated that if the threat of harm was serious and could be averted only by disclosure, compelled disclosure may be warranted.

Crime-Fraud Exception. In re Grand Jury Proceedings (Gregory P. Violette), 183 F.3d 71 (1st Cir. 1999), held that a "crime-fraud exception" applies to the psychotherapist patient privilege. The defendant was the target of a federal grand jury investigation focused on possible bank fraud crimes involving false claims of his disabilities. By analogy to the attorney-client privilege, the court found that the rationale for the privilege diminishes when communications made in therapy are in furtherance of crime. The exception will only apply, however, when the patient's purpose in making a communication is not therapy, but to promote a particular crime or fraud. It would not apply, for example, to a career criminal's confessions to his therapist even though the therapy may generally increase the patient's professional productivity. When the evidence indicates that defendant's communications to the therapists were made as part of a scheme to defraud lenders and/or disability insurers, the key ingredients of the crime-fraud exception are established.

KEY POINTS

1. Federal law recognizes a psychotherapist-patient privilege and, to a more limited extent, a physician-patient privilege as well. Most states recognize both privileges.

2. The federal psychotherapist-patient privilege has been extended to all physicians, psychologists, licensed social workers, and a variety of other mental health workers, when communications for the purpose of diagnosis or treatment of a mental or emotional condition are made with the reasonable expectation of confidence.

3. The privilege may be set aside when disclosure of the communication is necessary to protect the Compulsory Process and Confrontation rights of criminal defendants; when the patient has placed his emotional or mental condition at issue in litigation; and when the communications are intended to promote a crime or fraud.

4. The courts are in disagreement over the existence of a dangerous patient exception.

PROBLEMS

12.22. At Alice Draper's prosecution for murder of a federal official, the prosecution offers to introduce the following evidence: Shortly after the victim's death, an individual called an Alcoholics Anonymous hotline manned by volunteers and asked to speak with a doctor. When the volunteer who had answered the phone asked what the problem was, the caller responded, "Murder. I just killed a man. I need help." Another volunteer called the police, and the police traced the telephone call to a telephone booth, where they found and arrested Draper. Draper has objected to evidence of what she said to the AA volunteer on the ground that her statements fall within the psychotherapist-patient privilege. What result? What additional facts might affect the outcome?

12.23. Plaintiff Peters brought an action in federal court against his employer for unlawful discrimination and violation of the Family Medical Leave Act due to his termination from employment on the basis of his mental illness. The defendant employer seeks discovery of a journal that Peters started keeping after losing his job, but which he has not shown to the doctor who is providing psychological counseling. The journal concerns the events that surrounded Peters's termination. Peters claims that the journal should be protected pursuant to the psychotherapist-patient privilege because he started keeping the journal when his doctor suggested that "writing down what happened can help you understand some of the situation." Is the journal privileged?

12.24. Plaintiff Salter has filed an action under the American with Disabilities Act (ADA) against her employer for unlawful discharge and failure to make reasonable accommodation for her clinical depression, which, she claims, required medication that caused her difficulty in waking up and chronic tardiness at work. The ADA requires the plaintiff to make a prima facie case of discrimination, which includes that she is a member of a protected category, which means a person with physical or mental impairment; a person with a record of such impairment; or a person being regarded as having such impairment. May plaintiff protect the release of her medical records of her treating psychiatrist pursuant to the psychotherapist-patient privilege?

12.25. Walter and Sarah Wong have sued Walter's tax preparer H&R Block, Inc. for breach of contract for its unauthorized disclosure in 1998 of Walter's tax return information, a disclosure that led to a criminal investigation and civil audits by the IRS. Plaintiffs allege that they incurred actual damages in the form of legal fees and "severe emotional distress, including physical mental suffering, shame, and humiliation." In 1998, prior to their marriage but after the conduct alleged in this suit, Walter and Sarah attended joint counseling sessions with a licensed social worker to help with the health of their relationship. In 1999, Sarah went for an initial consultation to a licensed psychologist. Defendant H&R Block has filed notices of taking depositions of both the social worker and psychologist. Defendant asserts that any psychotherapist-patient privilege was waived (1) by plaintiffs alleging serious claims for emotional distress and (2) through the revelation in their own depositions of the identities of their mental health providers, as well as the dates and costs of the sessions, and the purpose of the visits to the social worker. Plaintiffs contend that they have not waived the privilege because they have not alleged psychic injury or disease nor psychiatric injury or disease or disorder, and that no psychological testimony will be offered at trial. What result?

F. THE CLERGY-COMMUNICANT PRIVILEGE

The priest-penitent privilege—now more commonly referred to as the clergy-communicant privilege—is accepted as legitimate by scholars and courts, at least to some degree. Indeed, every state has legislatively enacted some version of this privilege, and Proposed Federal Rule 506 specifically recognized a privilege protecting "confidential communication[s] by [a] person to a clergyman in his professional character as spiritual advisor." Pursuant to FRE 501, federal courts have recognized the existence of a clergy-communicant privilege as a matter of federal common law. See In re Grand Jury Investigation, 918 F.2d 374 (3d Cir. 1990); United States v. Dube, 820 F.2d 886 (7th Cir. 1987); United States v. Gordon, 655 F.2d 478 (2d Cir. 1981). See generally Lennard K. Whittaker, The Priest-Penitent Privilege: Its Constitutionality and Doctrine, 13 Regent U. L. Rev. 145 (2000-2001). The privilege is accepted in some form by all 50 states, but in the wake of the many high-profile cases involving child sexual abuse by clergy members in recent years, 40 states now require clergy members to report instances of child abuse as part of those states' mandatory reporting statutes (with some exceptions for communications within the scope of the privilege). See, e.g., Ga. Code Ann., §19-7-5 (providing that ". . . a member of the clergy shall not be required to report child abuse reported solely within the context of confession or other similar communication required to be kept confidential under church doctrine or practice. When a clergy member receives information about child abuse from any other source, the clergy member shall comply with the reporting requirements of this Code section, even though the clergy member may have also received a report of child abuse from the confession of the perpetrator."); 1 David M. Greenwald et al., Testimonial Privileges §6:14 (Trial Practice Series, 3d ed. 2005).

1. The Privilege and Its Justifications

The clergy-communicant privilege generally applies "to protect communications made (1) to a clergy person (2) in his or her spiritual and professional capacity (3) with a reasonable expectation of confidentiality." In re Grand Jury Investigation, 918 F.2d 374, 384 (3d Cir. 1990).

The privilege has been justified in four ways: (1) The traditional utilitarian justification, that the privilege is necessary to preserve the confidential relationship between clergy person and communicant, is often given. In this respect the privilege is similar to the attorney-client, physician-patient, psychotherapist-patient, and marital communications privileges.

(2) Another justification is constitutional in origin, based upon the Free Exercise Clause of the First Amendment. According to this argument, the clause prevents courts from compelling a priest to reveal confidential communications, where such disclosure would contradict their religious practice. Although the privilege is probably not mandated by the Constitution, the principle of religious freedom has historically offered compelling support for the privilege. See 1 Kent Greenawalt, Religion and the Constitution: Free Exercise and Fairness 246-260 (2006). See also 7 Jeremy Bentham, Works of Jeremy Bentham 366-367 (1843) (justifying the privilege by the principle of religious toleration).

(3) The privacy rationale, emphasizing the private nature of religious worship, is occasionally invoked as well. By creating a zone of privacy and protecting spiritual counseling from disclosure, the privilege accords respect for the intimacy of the communicant's relationship to clergy. According to this rationale, confidentiality is a privacy interest that itself acts as a legitimate constraint on the truth-finding function of trial.

(4) Last, the privilege is said to protect the credibility of our judicial system by preventing controversial clashes between court and clergy. Advocates of this rationale contend that "the spectacle of courts imprisoning members of the clergy for refusing to violate confidences entrusted to them might tend to subvert public faith in the judicial process." Developments in the Law—Privileged Communications, 98 Harv. L. Rev. 1450, 1562 (1985). In this sense, the privilege accords respect to the separation between church and state.

2. Scope of the Privilege

The most important issues in the interpretation of the clergy-communicant privilege are who counts as a clergy person, what kinds of communications are protected, and when does the presence of third persons waive the privilege. In most jurisdictions the holder of the privilege is the communicant, but a small minority of states grant the privilege and the decision to disclose communications to the clergy. Most state statutes, however, explicitly prohibit clergy from disclosing confidential communications without the communicant's consent. In a well-publicized case in New York, a priest revealed the confessional statement of a deceased parishioner, made 11 or 12 years earlier, that helped to exculpate two men wrongly convicted of the murder to which the deceased parishioner confessed. Such breach of confidence was proper, according to the priest and the Archdiocese of New York, because the confessional statement was not a formal confession within Catholic practice. Had the confession been formal, the priest would never have been able to reveal it, even after the parishioner's death. Morales v. Portuondo, 154 F. Supp. 2d 706, 714 (S.D.N.Y. 2001).

Even if the clergy person does not hold the privilege, the clergy have their own interests in protecting the privacy of their religious counseling. In Mockaitis v. Harcleroad, 104 F.3d 1522 (9th Cir. 1997), the court held that a tape-recorded conversation between a priest and a jail inmate—which the inmate knew was being taped by the state—was not privileged, but that disclosure would violate the priest's Fourth Amendment expectation of privacy and the federal Religious Freedom Restoration Act.

a. Definition of Clergy

Proposed FRE 506(a)(1) defined a member of the clergy as "a minister, priest, rabbi, or other similar functionary of a religious organization, or an individual reasonably believed so to be by the person consulting him." This definition was adopted by the Third Circuit in In re Grand Jury Investigation, 918 F.2d 374, 384-385 (3d Cir. 1990). The "reasonably believed to be" a clergy person clause serves to protect the reasonable expectations of the individual. Some state statutes fail to provide any definition other than "clergyman or priest," while others provide very broad language in defining the individuals covered. See, e.g., 735 Ill. Comp. Stat. 5/8-803 (2002) (referring to "a clergyman or practitioner of any religious denomination accredited by the religious body to which he or she belongs"). Georgia explicitly delineates which members of the clergy are included, confining the privilege to "any Protestant minister of the Gospel, and any priest of the Roman Catholic faith, any priest of the Greek Orthodox Catholic faith, any Jewish rabbi, or to any Christian or Jewish minister, by whatever name called." Ga. Code Ann. §24-9-22 (West 2003).

One issue that often arises is whether the privilege extends to situations in which communicants receive spiritual advice from individuals who are not officially ordained members of the clergy. The Third Circuit foresaw this problem and stated, in dicta, that its adoption of the broad definition of clergy in Proposed Rule 506 did not imply "that the privilege should be interpreted to comprehend communications to and among members of sects that denominate each and every member as clergy." In re Grand Jury Investigation, 918 F.2d at 384 n.13. The burden is on the party asserting the privilege to show that the person to whom communications were made is regularly engaged in activities which conform generally to the conduct of Catholic priests, Jewish rabbis, or Protestant ministers. United States v. Napolean, 46 M.J. 279, 284-285 (Ct. App. A.F. 1997) (citing 2 S. Saltzburg and M. Martin, Federal Rules of Evidence Manual 601-602 (5th ed. 1990)). In In re Verplank, 329 F. Supp. 433, 435-436 (C.D. Cal. 1971), the court protected confidential communications made to nonordained counselors from disclosure, because the counselors' services sufficiently resembled acts performed by the ordained minister who supervised them. The complexity of this issue can be seen in Cox v. Miller, 154 F. Supp. 2d 787 (S.D.N.Y. 2001), where the district court dramatically expanded the privilege to include statements made at Alcoholics Anonymous (AA) meetings. In *Cox*, the defendant's confession to two murders, made to his fellow AA members, were covered by the privilege, as the court noted that the Second Circuit had held that AA *was a religion*, by reason of the religious nature of its "Twelve Steps of Recovery." Although the decision was subsequently reversed by the Second Circuit in Cox v. Miller, 296 F.3d 89 (2d Cir. 2002), the case indicates how the clergy-communicant privilege can be susceptible to a quite broad interpretation.

b. Nature of the Communication

The clergy-communicant privilege applies only to communications made to a clergy person in that person's spiritual or professional capacity. Courts have interpreted this to mean that the communication is "related to a religious function. . . . [T]he communication must be essentially for an ecclesiastical and religious purpose." Ellis v. United States, 922 F. Supp. 539, 542 (D. Utah 1996). Such communications are to be distinguished from communications that simply advise clergy about events, as in *Ellis* (witness to a tragic accident at a church-sponsored outing informed church officials about the event for secular purposes), or that are made for emotional support and consolation rather than guidance and forgiveness as a formal act of religion or as a matter of conscience. United States v. Napolean, 46 M.J. at 285. A narrower view of the privilege—to apply only to acts of "confession"—could raise serious first amendment and equal protection concerns by limiting the privilege to certain religions.

c. Expectation of Confidentiality

As is the case with the attorney-client privilege, the presence of third parties, if essential to and in furtherance of the communication, should not void the privilege. For example, transmission of the communications within a church hierarchy may remain privileged. In Scott v. Hammock, 133 F.R.D. 610 (D. Utah 1990), the court applied Utah law to hold that communications from the communicant to a clergy person, and then passed vertically from one religious authority up to another within the church hierarchy, were privileged because such communication was necessary to the carrying out of church discipline. If communications among the church officers themselves could be discovered, then the privilege would be destroyed and the communicant's confidence abridged.

In In re Grand Jury Investigation, the government sought to compel the disclosure of communications among several family members and their pastor on the grounds that a nonfamily member had also been present. The Third Circuit reasoned as follows:

> In essence, the government claims that persons who are not related by blood or by marriage cannot, under federal law, engage together in protected communications with a member of the clergy acting in a spiritual or professional capacity. . . .
>
> The government is correct in observing that the traditional clergy-communicant privilege protected a penitential relationship in which a person privately confessed his or her sins to a priest, in order to receive some form of church sanctioned discipline or absolution. Neither family nor other types of group counseling fit neatly within this "one-to-one" model of the privilege. We have explained, however, that the modern view of the privilege is more expansive than the traditional one. We discern nothing in modern clergy-communicant privilege doctrine, as it finds expression in either proposed Rule 506 or the cases recognizing the privilege, that would limit the privilege's application solely to group discussions involving family members related by blood or marriage. Modern clergy-communicant privilege doctrine focuses, rather, on whether the presence of a third party is essential to or in furtherance of a communication to a member of the clergy. We think, consistent with the general constructional rule that evidentiary privileges should be narrowly construed, that recognition of the clergy-communicant privilege in this circumstance depends upon whether the third party's presence is essential to and in furtherance of a communication to a member of the clergy. As is the case with consultations between attorneys and clients, the presence of multiple parties, unrelated by blood or marriage, during discussions with a member of the clergy may, but will not necessarily, defeat the condition that communications be made with a reasonable expectation of confidentiality in order for the privilege to attach. 918 F.2d at 386.

However, the appellate court also found that the district court had not developed adequate facts upon which to make the necessary finding that the family members reasonably expected that their communications to their pastor were confidential. It remanded the case to the district court "to determine whether the [family members] communicated with Pastor Knoche in his spiritual or professional capacity and with a reasonable expectation of confidentiality. . . ." Id. at 387. This might require an inquiry "into the nature of the communicants' relationship as well as the pastoral counseling practices of the relevant synod of the Lutheran church . . . whether the parties shared a commonality of interest at the time of the communication and, if so, in what respect . . . [and] a fuller record . . . as to [the third person's] role in the counseling session. In order to ascertain whether her presence worked to vitiate or to waive the privilege, the court will have to inquire into whether the other group members, who apparently are subjects of the grand jury investigation, reasonably required her presence at the counseling session, either in furtherance of their communications to the pastor or to protect their interests." Id. at 387-388. And the appellate court was well aware that such an inquiry might require some degree of disclosure from the pastor as to what was discussed in the group meeting. It left to the discretion of the district court how to ascertain this information; whether to use *in camera* hearings; whether or not parties and/or counsel should be present; and how to accommodate "delicate first amendment issues." Id. at 388.

d. Exceptions

The main exception to the clergy-communicant privilege in state statutes involves a clash between the privilege and state mandatory reporting statutes in the area of child abuse. Due to clergy child sex abuse scandals, public outrage has spurred state legislatures to act. "Every state has passed a statute requiring mandatory reporting of child abuse." 1 Greenwald et al., Testimonial Privileges §6:14. Some states have amended these mandatory reporting statutes by including clergy members in the list of groups required to report instances of child abuse. See, e.g., Mass. Gen. Laws Ann. ch. 119, §51A (West 2002); Ala. Code §26-14-3 (1992 & Supp. 2004). Currently, the mandatory reporting statutes of approximately 40 states require clergy to disclose known or suspected incidents of child abuse, either by specifically listing clergy members within the list of applicable groups, or by the use of a catchall phrase, such as "any person." Greenwald, et al. §6:4. However, the majority of the states that require clergy to report child abuse still maintain an exception in the case of the clergy-communicant privilege, protecting such communications from the mandatory reporting requirements. Id. For example, although Massachusetts has amended its mandatory reporting statute to include clergy members, the statute still provides the following exception:

> [A] . . . clergy member . . . shall report all cases of abuse under this section, but need not report information solely gained in a confession or similarly confidential communication in other religious faiths. Nothing in the general laws shall modify or limit the duty of a . . . clergy member . . . to report a reasonable cause that a child is being injured as set forth in this section when the . . . clergy member . . . is acting in some other capacity that would otherwise make him a reporter. Mass. Ann. Laws ch. 119 §51A.

Essentially, this means that, in many states, a clergy member is required to report suspected or known child abuse so long as doing so would not reveal the substance of a confession or an otherwise confidential communication with a penitent. See, e.g., Ga. Code Ann., §19-7-5. A few states do the opposite, by specifically denying the privilege in their mandatory reporting statutes, see, e.g., Tex. Fam. Code Ann. §261.101 (Vernon 2002); N.H. Rev. Stat. Ann. §169-C:29 (2001), while others that require mandatory reporting do not mention its effect on the privilege. See, e.g., Ind. Code Ann. §31-33-5-1 (West 1999). For further discussion, see Norman Abrams, Addressing the Tension Between the Clergy-Communicant Privilege and the Duty to Report Child Abuse in State Statutes, 44 B.C. L. Rev. 1127 (2003); Christopher R. Pudelski, The Constitutional Fate of Mandatory Reporting Statutes and the Clergy-Penitent Privilege in a Post-*Smith* World, 98 Nw. U. L. Rev. 703, 706-707 (2004).

KEY POINTS

1. A clergy-communicant privilege has been recognized under federal law and in all state jurisdictions, though exceptions exist in several states for mandatory reporting of known or suspected child abuse.
2. Courts extend the privilege to communications made to ordained clergy or to people performing the same activities. The communications must be relevant to a religious function.
3. Communications made in the presence of third persons can be privileged if the third person's presence was essential to and in furtherance of the communication to the clergy.

PROBLEMS

12.26. Darlene is being tried for the crime of making threats through the U.S. mail. Darlene raises an insanity defense. The clergy person who leads Darlene's religious congregation testifies that during the time of Darlene's conduct, Darlene did "know right from wrong." The clergy person further states that this opinion is based on knowing Darlene, on observations of Darlene, and on speaking with Darlene during this period. Does this testimony violate the clergy-communicant privilege?

12.27. Jim Jones joined a mail order church for a fee of $100, which entitled him to the status of lay minister. The tenets of the church included a vow of poverty and the belief that personal income of ministers was not taxable by the federal government. Jones stopped paying income taxes and is now prosecuted for failure to file income tax returns from 1996 to 2000. In 1999, Jones also joined an established church and had several conversations with the minister concerning his beliefs about taxation. The government plans to call the minister who would testify that he advised Jones that his income was not exempt from taxation. Can Jones enforce the clergy-communicant privilege?

12.28. Sam Evans is being prosecuted for sexually assaulting his 12-year-old stepdaughter. Shortly after the incident that is the subject of the prosecution, Sam and his wife were separated. Sam began seeing his minister for spiritual guidance. At one session, which concerned marriage counseling, Sam's wife was also present. At this session, Sam admitted that he had sexually assaulted the stepdaughter, and he said that he had told his wife this the night before. The prosecution plans to call Sam's wife, who is willing to testify about both of Sam's admissions. The prosecution also plans to call the minister and ask him about what Sam said at the counseling session. The minister, however, has expressed an unwillingness to testify about these matters, and the minister is disturbed that Sam's wife is willing to testify. Does the minister have any personal right not to testify or to prevent Sam's wife from testifying? What objections can Sam make to the testimony of his wife and the minister? What additional facts might be needed to answer these questions? How would they be determined?

G. OTHER PRIVILEGES

1. Other Professional-Client Relationships

Privileges are occasionally recognized for confidential communications to other professionals, such as accountants, teachers, family and marriage counselors, social workers, lay advocates, and private detectives who counsel, advise, or act on behalf of their clients. Statutes enacting such privileges have been passed in a minority of states. For example, an accountant-client privilege exists in approximately one-third of the states. One interesting issue relating to the accountant-client privilege is whether the privilege is waived for the underlying information that is used to develop a publicly disclosed financial report, such as an Annual Report prepared by independent auditors that is required by the SEC for public companies. If a state's law does not create an exception for the privilege in such a situation, then it is likely that the privilege will still be available for the underlying information. See, e.g., In re Hillsborough Holdings Corp., 176 B.R. 223, 237 (M.D. Fla. 1994). However, according to case law, there is neither a privilege nor work-product protection for accountants in federal court. See United States v. Arthur Young & Co., 465 U.S. 805 (1984); Couch v. United States, 409 U.S. 322 (1973). In 1998, 26 U.S.C. §7525 extended the attorney-client privilege to "a federally authorized tax practitioner," who is a nonlawyer authorized to practice before the Internal Revenue Service. Though work product is still not protected, the new privilege provides that "the same common law protections of confidentiality which apply to a communication between a taxpayer and an attorney shall also apply to a communication between a taxpayer and a federally authorized tax practitioner to the extent the communications would be considered a privileged communication if it were between a taxpayer and an attorney." §7525(a)(1).

Another example is that privileges for various counseling professionals may be recognized under a state's psychotherapist-patient privilege. *Psychotherapist* may be defined to include professionals other than psychiatrists, psychologists, and psychotherapists, such as social workers; psychiatric nurses; counselors of rape victims, battered women, and drug and alcohol abusers; as well as school, family, and marriage counselors whose functions are analogous to those of a psychotherapist. See Catharina J. H. Dubbleday, Comment, The Psychotherapist-Client Testimonial Privilege: Defining the Professional Involved, 34 Emory L.J. 777 (1985). Another "counseling privilege" that some states recognize is a sexual assault victim-counselor privilege. See, e.g., Cal. Evid. Code §1035-1036.2 (West 1995 & Supp. 2005); 735 Ill. Comp. Stat. 5/8-802.1 (2002); 42 Pa. Cons. Stat. Ann. §5945.1(b) (West 2000 & Supp. 2005) ("[n]o sexual assault counselor may, without the written consent of the victim, disclose the victim's confidential oral or written communications to the counselor nor consent to be examined in any court or criminal proceeding"). Some states, such as Massachusetts, provide for an absolute privilege, while others, such as California, have enacted a qualified privilege permitting disclosure under certain circumstances. For further discussion, see Euphemia B. Warren, She's Gotta Have It Now: A Qualified Rape Crisis Counselor-Victim Privilege, 17 Cardozo L. Rev. 141 (1995).

2. Parent-Child Privilege

A privilege for parent-child communications was not recognized at common law. Presently, five states, Colorado, Idaho, Massachusetts, Minnesota, and Washington, have enacted legislation adopting a parent-child confidential communications privilege, although in Colorado and Washington the privilege is limited to communications made to an attorney by a child while in the presence of a parent. In contrast, the majority of states have refused to adopt the privilege. See, e.g., People v. Dixon, 161 Mich. App. 388, 393, 411 N.W.2d 760, 763 (1987); In re Gail D., 217 N.J. Super. 226, 232, 525 A.2d 337, 340 (1987). A New York court recognized a parent-child privilege based on the constitutional right to privacy. People v. Fitzgerald, 101 Misc. 2d 712, 422 N.Y.S.2d 309 (Westchester County Ct. 1979). However, *Fitzgerald* has not been followed by any New York court decision, and has since been limited by People v. Harrell, 87 A.D. 2d 21, 450 N.Y.S.2d 501, 504 (1982) and criticized in People v. Hilligas, 175 Misc. 2d 842, 670 N.Y.S.2d 744 (Erie County Ct. 1998), for its inappropriate extension of the privilege to adult children.

Prior to the passage of Washington's parent-child privilege statute, the Washington Supreme Court refused to adopt a general privilege. State v. Maxon, 110 Wash. 2d 564, 574, 756 P.2d 1297, 1302 (1988). As noted above, the Washington statute creates only a limited privilege, and as such the decision denying a general parent-child privilege in *Maxon* remains in effect, narrowing the scope of the privilege in Washington.

Addressing the constitutional claim for the privilege, the Washington Supreme Court stated:

> The Constitution does not mandate recognition of a parent-child privilege. The right of privacy line of cases gives no indication that the interest in confidential communications between parent and child qualifies as a fundamental right for the purpose of substantive due process analysis. Any infringement of this interest caused by nonrecognition of a parent-child privilege is indirect and incidental.

Maxon, supra, 756 P.2d at 1301 (quoting Donald Cofer, Comment, Parent-Child Privilege: Constitutional Right or Specious Analogy?, 3 U. Puget Sound L. Rev. 177, 210-211 (1979)).

In the absence of congressional action, federal courts have generally refused to recognize a parent-child privilege. See, e.g., Under Seal v. United States, 755 F.3d 213, 217-222 (4th Cir. 2014) (refusing to recognize a parent-child privilege for policy reasons that run against the creation of new privileges and after surveying court decisions that predominantly declined invitations to establish such a privilege under both state and federal law); In re Grand Jury Proceedings, 103 F.3d 1140, 1146-47 (3d Cir. 1997) (noting that the vast majority of federal and state courts do not recognize a parent-child privilege and refusing to recognize this privilege).

An interesting issue raised by many courts presented with a claim of the privilege has been whether the privilege would apply solely to communications from child to parent or to communications from parent to child as well. Commentators argue that the privilege should apply solely to conversations from child to parent since the policy behind the privilege is to encourage the child to confide in the parent.

Though parent-child privileges have not gained widespread acceptance, their supporters often refer to what has been called the "cruel trilemma" that witnesses face. The first option for a testifying parent or child is to choose to commit perjury in order to protect a family member. Rather than implicate his father, a son in United States v. Ismail, 756 F.2d 1253 (6th Cir. 1985), perjured himself at a grand jury hearing. The son later broke down on the witness stand, admitting that he had lied to the grand jury and had considered suicide to avoid testifying against his father. The second option for a witness in this position is to tell the truth and face what damage may be done to the relationship and the guilt that will come from having hurt a loved one. Terry Nichols was convicted for his involvement in the 1995 Oklahoma City bombing after his son Josh, 13, was forced to testify before a grand jury. Josh's mother told reporters that her son suffered from nightmares as a result of testifying.[73] The third option is to refuse to testify and be found in contempt of court. In State v. DeLong, 456 A.2d 877 (Me. 1983), a 15-year-old girl who had been sexually abused by her adoptive father was sentenced to jail for refusing to testify against him.

Because of the difficulty of choosing to testify truthfully against a family member, many judges and prosecutors worry about the veracity of a parent's or child's testimony. Furthermore, the appeal of family privacy can make the support of a parent-child privilege politically attractive. The issue came under national scrutiny in February 1998 when Independent Counsel Kenneth Starr subpoenaed Marcia Lewis, mother of Monica Lewinsky, to testify before a grand jury about her daughter's relationship with President Clinton. In the 1998 and 1999 congressional sessions, the spectacle inspired three bills in the U.S. House of Representatives and one in the Senate,[74] each of which proposed the creation of a federal parent-child privilege. The "Confidence in the Family Act," 105 H.R. 3577 (1998), was rejected by the House Judiciary Committee for many reasons, including concern that the broad scope of the bill might cover natural parents as well a stepparents and grandparents, adult as well as minor children, and criminal as well as civil cases.[75] The three remaining bills did not emerge from the House and Senate Judiciary Committees. Representative Andrews, a Democrat from New Jersey, has repeatedly attempted to obtain legislative approval for a parent-child privilege statute (see, e.g., the Parent-Child Privilege Act of 2005, 109 H.R. 3443 (2005)), though each attempt has been unsuccessful.

---

73. See Lance Gay, Lewinsky's Mother Torn Between Law and Loyalty, *Times Union*, Feb. 14, 1998, at A1.

74. See Confidence in the Family Act, 105 H.R. 3577 (1998) (amending Federal Rules of Evidence to include parent-child adverse testimonial privilege and confidential communications privilege in federal civil and criminal proceedings); Parent-Child Privilege Acts of 1998 and 1999, 105 H.R. 4286 (1998), 106 H.R. 522 (1999) (amending Federal Rules of Evidence establishing a parent-child privilege); Attorney General Guidelines for Familial Privacy, 105 S. 1721 (directing the Attorney General of the United States to develop guidelines for Federal prosecutors to protect familial privacy and communications between parents and children).

75. The bill was ultimately rejected by a vote of 162 to 256. See 144 Cong. Rec. H2278 (daily ed. Apr. 23, 1998).

3. Communications Made in Settlement Negotiations

One emerging area of privilege law is that of settlement negotiations. As discussed in Chapter Six, FRE 408 precludes communications made in settlement negotiations from being used at trial as evidence of liability. However, "[t]he court may admit [such] evidence for another purpose, such as proving a witness's bias or prejudice, negating a contention of undue delay, or proving an effort to obstruct a criminal investigation or prosecution." Fed. R. Evid. 408. A question remains as to whether FRE 408 applies only to admissibility of evidence at trial, or whether it implies that a privilege should exist to protect settlement communications from discovery. The primary justification for the privilege is the desire to promote settlements and the need for open discussion in settlement negotiations, including adopting hypothetical positions that may not be entirely self-interested in order to compromise effectively. If the statements made in settlement negotiations are not privileged, despite FRE 408 as a barrier to the use of the communications as evidence at trial, the statements could be subject to discovery, which could create a disincentive to open discussions during settlement negotiations.

The Sixth Circuit Court of Appeals held that a privilege does exist for communications made in furtherance of settlement negotiations, protecting them from third-party discovery. Goodyear Tire & Rubber Co. v. Chiles Power Supply, Inc., 332 F.3d 976 (6th Cir. 2003). In *Goodyear*, after the case was concluded, Chiles gave an interview in which settlement communications were improperly disclosed. Id. at 978. After learning about the communications, the plaintiffs in a separate lawsuit against both Goodyear and Chiles joined the suit and petitioned the district court to permit discovery of statements made in settlement negotiations. Id. at 979.

The Sixth Circuit relied heavily on the Supreme Court's decision in Jaffee v. Redmond, 518 U.S. 1 (1996), in discussing the parameters of a privilege. Id. at 979-980. The Sixth Circuit found a strong public policy interest in recognizing the privilege, as well as noting the tradition of confidentiality in settlement communications. Id. at 980. The court further concluded that information discovered from settlement negotiations was unlikely to be relevant:

> There exists a strong public interest in favor of secrecy of matters discussed by parties during settlement negotiations. This is true whether settlement negotiations are done under the auspices of the court or informally between the parties. The ability to negotiate and settle a case without trial fosters a more efficient, more cost-effective, and significantly less burdened judicial system. In order for settlement talks to be effective, parties must feel uninhibited in their communications. Parties are unlikely to propose the types of compromises that most effectively lead to settlement unless they are confident that their proposed solutions cannot be used on cross examination, under the ruse of "impeachment evidence," by some future third party. Parties must be able to abandon their adversarial tendencies to some degree. They must be able to make hypothetical concessions, offer creative quid pro quos, and generally make statements that would otherwise belie their litigation efforts. Without a privilege, parties would more often forego negotiations for the relative formality of trial. Then, the entire negotiation process collapses upon itself, and the judicial efficiency it fosters is lost. Id. at 980.

Although the Sixth Circuit has adopted the privilege, the issue has not yet been decided in other circuits. However, at least one district court has declined to follow the Sixth Circuit. In In re Subpoena Issued to Commodity Futures Trading Commission, 370 F. Supp. 2d 201 (D.D.C. 2005), the District Court for the District of Columbia held that it would not recognize a new settlement privilege to protect documents from third-party discovery. The court discussed several factors that the Supreme Court considers in assessing a potential privilege in reaching its decision. Id. at 208. The court noted that there is no broad consensus in federal courts, as few federal courts recognize the privilege, nor is there a consensus in state law supporting the privilege. Id. at 208-209. The court also reasoned that by enacting FRE 408, Congress chose to limit the admissibility of settlement matter rather than discoverability. Id. Last, the court opined that the proponents of the privilege had not made an adequate showing that the privilege would effectively advance a public good. Id. at 212.

Another similar privilege is the mediation communications privilege. The mediation privilege protects from discovery communication and documentation related to mediation negotiations between parties. The mediation privilege was not recognized in common law, but every state has enacted some statutory form of the privilege. By passing the Alternative Dispute Resolution (ADR) Act in 1998, 28 U.S.C. §651, Congress requires federal district courts to authorize by local rule ADR programs for all civil litigation. The ADR Act requires ADR proceedings to be confidential and requires district courts to develop safeguards to protect the confidentiality of communications within these ADR proceedings. Id. at §652(d). Although the ADR Act did not actually create a privilege, some federal courts have adopted the privilege to protect the confidentiality of such mediation communications. See, e.g., Folb v. Motion Picture Industry Pension & Health Plans, 16 F. Supp. 2d 1164 (C.D. Cal. 1998); Sheldone v. Pennsylvania Turnpike Commission 104 F. Supp. 2d 511 (W.D. Pa. 2000). However, other federal courts have declined to adopt such a privilege without a clearer mandate from Congress. See FDIC. v. White, 76 F. Supp. 2d 736, 738 (N.D. Tex. 1999) ("[t]he [c]ourt does not read the ADR [Act] or its sparse legislative history as creating an evidentiary privilege"). For further discussion of the mediation privilege, see Ellen E. Deason, Predictable Mediation Confidentiality in the U.S. Federal System, 17 Ohio St. J. on Disp. Resol. 239 (2002).

4. Privileges Protecting Outside Sources of Information

A unique category of privileges exists to protect confidential sources of information. Three privileges of this type are the government informant's privilege, the journalist's privilege, and the scholar's privilege. These privileges can be distinguished from the confidential communications privileges, for rather than focusing on the communication's content, these privileges mainly focus on the protection of the source's identity. The common justification is that absent protection, the mere possibility of disclosure would disrupt the future flow of information and thereby "harm the public by impeding law enforcement efforts, the dissemination of news, or the advancement of knowledge." Developments in the Law—Privileged Communications, 98 Harv. L. Rev. 1592, 1594 (1985).

a. Government Informant's Privilege

The government informant's privilege protects the identities of individuals who provide the government with information regarding crimes or other suspect activity. Though the privilege was once recognized as absolute, it has been curtailed due to concern for the constitutional rights of criminal defendants. In Roviaro v. United States, 353 U.S. 53, 62 (1957), the Supreme Court announced a test that "balanc[ed] the public interest in protecting the flow of information against the individual's right to prepare his defense." The informant's privilege arises most frequently in cases where a criminal defendant alleges that an informant's testimony is critical to his defense. In such circumstances, courts freely conduct *in camera* hearings with an informant to determine how the *Roviaro* balance should be struck. See, e.g., United States v. Anderson, 509 F.2d 724, 730 (9th Cir. 1974); United States v. Fischer, 531 F.2d 783 (5th Cir. 1976). As a general matter, the defendant's constitutional right to develop a defense will override the privilege. See Jencks v. United States, 353 U.S. 657, 671-672 (1957).

The informant privilege is also frequently invoked in the context of a defendant's challenge to a search in which the government claims that the informant provided the basis for probable cause. The privilege has been applied in civil cases as well. In applying the *Roviaro* balancing test, some civil courts maintain that the "strength of the privilege is greater in civil litigation than in criminal," In re United States, 565 F.2d 19, 22 (2d Cir. 1978), while others adhere to the standard used in criminal cases, see, e.g., Hodgson v. Charles Martin Inspector of Petroleum, Inc., 459 F.2d 303, 305 (5th Cir. 1972).

b. Journalist's Privilege

A privilege to protect journalists against the disclosure of the identities of their news sources has been consistently advocated by members of media organizations. Proponents assert a twofold justification for the privilege: (1) the privilege is necessary to encourage the flow of confidential information from external sources; and (2) the privilege protects the First Amendment guarantee of a free press. The constitutional argument was rejected by the Supreme Court in the 5 to 4 decision of Branzburg v. Hayes, 408 U.S. 665 (1972), which analyzed the privilege claim in the grand jury setting. Noting "the limited nature of the Court's holding," Justice Powell in his concurrence proposed a balancing test to determine journalist privilege claims. In line with Justice Powell's concurrence, many lower federal courts have recognized a qualified journalist's privilege based on the First Amendment. See, e.g., Continental Cablevision, Inc. v. Stores Broadcasting Co., 583 F. Supp. 427 (E.D. Mo. 1984); United States v. Burke, 700 F.2d 70 (2d Cir. 1983). But see Herbert v. Lando, 441 U.S. 153 (1979) (declining to recognize an editorial process privilege). The D.C. Circuit reiterated *Branzburg* in rejecting a First Amendment challenge to a federal grand jury subpoena. In re Grand Jury Subpoena, Judith Miller, 397 F.3d 964 (D.C. Cir. 2005). In *Miller*, two reporters and Time, Inc., the parent company of Time Magazine, were subpoenaed to testify about sources used in their articles to a federal grand jury investigating the alleged leak of a CIA agent's identity by government officials. Id. at 966-968. The court held that the First Amendment does not grant journalists a right to refuse to divulge information about sources in the context of a grand jury subpoena, and further held that, even if there is a common law journalist privilege, which was not determined, the privilege would be qualified, and the government overcame any qualification. Id. at 972-973.

At least one federal court has specifically held that the reporter's privilege does not apply in grand jury proceedings. In re Grand Jury Proceedings (Scarce), 5 F.3d 397, 403 (9th Cir. 1993).

Efforts to enact a federal statutory privilege have not succeeded. However, most states have enacted shield laws that vary in levels of protection. When a reporter's sources are confidential, normally the plaintiff must make a more substantial showing of need in order to overcome the privilege. Mark v. Shoen, 48 F.3d 412 (9th Cir. 1995). New York law states that in order to overcome the privilege, the party seeking disclosure must make "a clear and specific showing that the news: (i) is highly material and relevant; (ii) is critical or necessary to the maintenance of a party's claim, defense or proof of an issue material thereto; and (iii) is not obtainable from any alternative source." N.Y. Civ. Rights Law §79-h(c) (McKinney 1992). See also In re Application to Quash Subpoena to National Broadcasting Co., Inc., 79 F.3d 346, 351 (2d Cir. 1996), where the court held that in order to find unpublished news to be critical or necessary, there must be a finding that the claim for which the information is to be used "virtually rises or falls with the admission or exclusion of the proffered evidence." In contrast, the test is much less stringent where the material is not confidential:

> [W]here information sought is not confidential, a civil litigant is entitled to requested discovery notwithstanding a valid assertion of the journalist's privilege by a nonparty only upon a showing the requested material is: (1) unavailable despite reasonable alternative sources; (2) noncumulative; and (3) clearly relevant to an important issue in the case. [Mark v. Shoen, 48 F.3d at 416.]

The application of this privilege in libel and slander cases has been limited. In Desai v. Hersh, 954 F.2d 1408 (7th Cir. 1992), the court held that the privilege could not be invoked by a libel defendant, because the plaintiff had the burden of proving actual malice on the part of the reporter. Proof of actual malice under New York Times v. Sullivan, 376 U.S. 254 (1964), depends on knowing the identity of a reporter's source, since a libel plaintiff needs to demonstrate that the source was unreliable or that the reporter failed to take sufficient steps to verify the factual accuracy of the story. Because of this, the general rule is that in defamation actions in which a plaintiff must establish actual malice the reporter's privilege must give way to disclosure. Miller v. Transamerican Press, Inc., 621 F.2d 721, 725-726 (5th Cir. 1980). But see Condit v. National Enquirer, Inc., 289 F. Supp. 2d 1175 (E.D. Cal. 2003) (wife of former Congressman Gary Condit sued tabloid for libel; court upheld privilege protecting confidential source, concluding that plaintiff did not investigate all reasonable alternative information sources).

In criminal cases, the defendant's constitutional right to develop a defense will override the journalist's privilege even when the statute establishing that privilege made it absolute. See Matter of Farber, 394 A.2d 330 (N.J. 1978).

c. Scholar's (Academic Researcher's) Privilege

Academic researchers have advocated a privilege to protect the confidentiality of their research and the identity of their research subjects. Proponents advance two arguments to support their claim of the privilege. First, the scholar's privilege can arguably fall within the ambit of the more widely recognized journalist's privilege, particularly if the scholarly research is to result in publication. Second, proponents argue that academic freedom is a special concern of the First Amendment and that the privilege is necessary to protect the research process and encourage the flow of information from research subjects. In Cusumano v. Microsoft Corporation, 162 F.3d 708 (1st Cir. 1998), the court considered whether academic researchers who had interviewed over 40 current and former Netscape employees in preparation for a book could maintain the confidentiality of the interview notes, tapes, transcripts, and recordings. Microsoft moved to compel the surrender of the research materials after the researchers resisted a subpoena. The court held that academic researchers are analogous to journalists and that the First Amendment interest of preventing the "chilling effect on speech" mandates the protection of the scholar's sources as well as the journalist's. Without such a privilege, the court wrote, "an academician, stripped of sources, would be able to provide fewer, less cogent analyses" and thus would be less able to disseminate information to the public. The court found that Microsoft's need was not compelling when balanced against the First Amendment protection.

Other asserted bases for the privilege are that interference with ongoing research, especially scientific research, could occur if data were forced to be disclosed, and the potential for publishing research in peer reviewed or other scholarly publications could be harmed. This last asserted rationale has met with little success in the courts. See Burka v. United States Department of Health and Human Services, 87 F.3d 508 (D.C. Cir. 1996) (stating that there is not an established or well-settled practice of protecting research data on the ground that disclosure would harm a researcher's publication prospects).

Several federal and state statutes protect research and sources of academic researchers, although in limited areas, such as drug research. See, e.g., 21 U.S.C. §872(c) (2000) (drug research); Cal. Health & Safety Code §11603 (West 1991) (drug research); N.Y. Pub. Health Law §3371 (McKinney 2002, Supp. 2005) (drug research). Courts have generally been reluctant to recognize a scholar's privilege. See In re Grand Jury Subpoena, 750 F.2d 223 (2d Cir. 1984) (refusing to recognize scholar's privilege); In re Grand Jury Proceedings (Scarce), 5 F.3d 397 (9th Cir. 1993); United States v. Doe, 460 F.2d 328 (1st Cir. 1972). But see Richards of Rockford, Inc. v. Pacific Gas and Elec. Co., 71 F.R.D. 388 (N.D. Cal. 1976).

5. Peer Review Privilege

A peer review privilege has been claimed by both academic institutions and hospitals to protect the confidentiality of the peer review process, a process that ultimately determines which candidates receive academic tenure and hospital privileges. The justification for the privilege is the standard argument that compelled disclosure of peer review evaluations would obstruct the free flow of information that is essential to the integrity of the peer review process. Without protection against disclosure, the quality of the critiques would decline and less qualified candidates would be promoted, with a resultant impact on the quality of our universities and hospitals.

Notwithstanding such arguments, in University of Pennsylvania v. EEOC, 493 U.S. 182 (1990), the Supreme Court refused to recognize a federal privilege protecting the confidentiality of academic peer review materials from disclosure. The claim arose out of a race and sex discrimination suit brought by an associate professor of the University of Pennsylvania. The Court held that the privilege would not be recognized under either common law or First Amendment grounds. The Court was "especially reluctant to recognize a [common law] privilege" in an area where Congress, under Title VII, has balanced the problem of "invidious" discrimination in educational institutions against the interest of academic autonomy "but has not provided the privilege itself." The Court refused to expand the protection of the First Amendment right of academic freedom to embrace confidential peer review materials. Before the decision, a majority of federal courts of appeals had recognized a qualified peer review privilege in the academic setting.

In the hospital setting, federal and state courts have generally declined invitations to establish a peer review privilege judicially. See Memorial Hosp. v. Shadur, 664 F.2d 1058 (7th Cir. 1981); Robinson v. Magovern, 83 F.R.D. 79 (W.D. Pa. 1979). Several states have enacted statutes that accord protection to the hospital peer review process. See, e.g., Mich. Comp. Laws Ann. §333.21515 (West 2001). Some states have included an exception to provide for disclosure in the area of discrimination suits. See, e.g., Cal. Evid. Code §1157(c) (West 1995). Even though some courts recognize the privilege, it has been narrowly construed to allow plaintiffs to uncover evidence of wrongdoing. In Moretti v. Lowe, 592 A.2d 855, 857 (R.I. 1991), the court held that while the internal communications and deliberative processes of a peer review committee were privileged, the effect of those proceedings was not. Thus, the plaintiff in a medical malpractice action could discover whether a particular nurse had been disciplined by her hospital review committee. The court in Moretti also said that the privilege did not protect the identity of persons who might serve on peer review committees or who have given information to such committees.

The privilege also does not protect pre-existing documents that have been turned over to the peer-review committee. Roach v. Springfield Clinic, 157 Ill. 2d 29, 40-42, 623 N.E.2d 246, 251 (1993). In Roach, the court stated:

> If the simple act of furnishing a committee with earlier acquired information were sufficient to cloak that information with the statutory privilege, a hospital could effectively insulate from disclosure virtually all adverse facts known to its medical staff, with the exception of those matters actually contained in a patient's records.

On the other hand, the medical peer review privilege covers every exchange of information taking place during peer review, which includes communication of objective facts. See Krusac v. Covenant Medical Center, Inc., 865 N.W.2d 908 (Mich. 2015). To prove any such fact, a party needs to call a direct witness and would not be able to compel disclosure of the privileged communication. Communications taking place as part of a peer review proceeding receive full protection and are generally not disclosable. See Allred v. Saunders, 342 P.3d 204 (Utah 2014).

For a decision upholding the privilege under difficult circumstances, see Jackson v. Scott, 667 A.2d 1365 (D.C. Ct. App. 1995). In this case, the defendant hospital's review of deaths during cardiac surgery revealed evidence of gross negligence. A confidential informant, who "had to [have been] in the operating room" during the surgery performed on the plaintiff's wife, revealed that the surgery was "very mismanaged," resulting in the patient's death. The court upheld the hospital's claim of privilege regarding its internal investigation of the death. Relying on the District of Columbia's Health Care Peer Review Act of 1992, D.C. Code §§32-501 et seq., the court stated that the privilege was unqualified. Defense witnesses testified, without mentioning the internal report, that the hospital was not negligent in the patient's death. The court nevertheless held that, under a plain reading of the statute, the report could not be used for impeachment purposes.

6. Self-evaluative Privilege

A privilege similar to the peer review privilege, the "self-critical analysis privilege" has been asserted in the corporate context. The privilege is often asserted by companies with affirmative action policies, to protect against disclosure of intracorporate communications made during the employee review process and against disclosure of compliance investigations done by the corporation. The asserted justification for the privilege is that forcing disclosure of these communications will have a chilling effect on compliance with equal employment opportunity laws. In Aramburu v. Boeing Co., 885 F. Supp. 1434 (D. Kan. 1995), the court refused to recognize the privilege in a Title VII case. Relying on University of Pennsylvania v. EEOC, the court stated that it was reluctant to recognize such a privilege when it appeared that Congress had considered the issue but had failed to provide for the privilege. 885 F. Supp. at 1440. Similarly, the court in Roberts v. Hunt, 187 F.R.D. 71 (W.D.N.Y. 1999), found that the Supreme Court, in rejecting a "peer review" privilege in University of Pennsylvania, implicitly rejected the rationale for a self-evaluation privilege and thus left the privilege unavailable under federal law.

However, some lower federal courts have recognized this privilege. See, e.g., Troupin v. Metropolitan Life Insurance Company, 169 F.R.D. 546 (S.D.N.Y. 1996) (recognizing the privilege where "an intrusion into the self-evaluative analyses of an institution would have an adverse effect on the [evaluative] process, with a net detriment to a cognizable public interest"); Reichhold Chemicals, Inc. v. Textron, Inc., 157 F.R.D. 522 (N.D. Fla. 1994) (collecting cases recognizing self-critical analysis privilege); Banks v. Lockheed-Georgia Co., 53 F.R.D. 283 (N.D. Ga. 1971) (recognizing privilege in employment discrimination case). For a discussion, see Ronald J. Allen and Cynthia M. Hazelwood, Preserving the Confidentiality of Internal Corporate Investigations, 12 J. Corp. L. 355 (1987).

Congress has created a privilege for state and local governments, similar to the self-evaluative privilege, in the context of highway safety. In order to promote highway safety, in 1973 Congress created a hazard elimination program for public roadways, providing federal funds for states to identify, study, and eliminate hazardous conditions on the nation's roads. 23 U.S.C. §152. The program required the states to conduct surveys and collect data on accident statistics in order to identify potentially hazardous sites. Id. Although the program provided a mechanism to enhance highway safety, the information collected by the states became a potential liability, due to the threat of discovery in lawsuits against the states. In response to these threats and in the interest of obtaining the best possible information from the states to enhance highway safety, Congress enacted a statutory privilege similar to the self-evaluative privilege, protecting information collected by states for enhancing safety and improving hazardous roadways. 23 U.S.C. §409 (1995). The statute provides as follows:

> [R]eports, surveys, schedules, lists, or data compiled or collected for the purpose of identifying evaluating, or planning the safety enhancement of potential accident sites, hazardous roadway conditions, or railway-highway crossings, pursuant to sections 130, 144, and 152 of this title [23 U.S.C.S. §130, 144, and 152] or for the purpose of developing any highway safety construction improvement project which may be implemented utilizing Federal-aid highway funds shall not be subject to discovery or admitted into evidence in a Federal or State court proceeding or considered for other purposes in any action for damages arising from any occurrence at a location mentioned or addressed in such reports, surveys, schedules, lists, or data. 23 U.S.C. §409.

Although the statute establishes a federal privilege, the statute was challenged in the case of Pierce County v. Guillen, 537 U.S. 129 (2003). In *Guillen*, a widower filed a negligence suit against a county government and sought discovery of information obtained by the county relating to the intersection where his wife had been killed in an automobile accident. Id. The Supreme Court held that the statute was within the scope of Congress's power under the Commerce Clause, and that "§409 protects all . . . data actually compiled or collected for §152 purposes, but does not protect information that was originally compiled or collected for purposes unrelated to §152 and that is currently held by the agencies that compiled or collected it, even if the information was at some point 'collected' by another agency for §152 purposes." Id. at 144. Under this interpretation, an accident report collected only for law enforcement purposes and held by the county sheriff would not be protected under §409 in the hands of the county sheriff, even though that same report would be protected in the hands of the Public Works Department, so long as the department first obtained the report for §152 purposes. Id. This interpretation confined the privilege to road-improving activities funded by the federal government and minimized Congress's incursion into state rules of evidence. See Alex Stein, Constitutional Evidence Law, 61 Vand. L. Rev. 65, 102-103 (2008).

Although the development of a general self-evaluative privilege in the cases has been spotty, numerous statutes protecting discrete interests have been passed, particularly in the states. A good example is Oregon's environmental audit privilege for reports prepared as a result of voluntary environmental audits designed to assure compliance with the state's environmental laws. The privilege is thorough, protecting virtually all materials created for and during the audit. It protects the information from both private and governmental parties, even when filing a report is mandatory, and courts may not make case-by-case determinations whether disclosure would best serve the public interest. Similar, but sometimes less expansive, statutes have been passed in ten other states. For a discussion, see Peter Gish, The Self-critical Analysis Privilege and Environmental Audit Reports, 25 Envtl. L. 73 (1995).

7. Government Privileges—Executive Privilege

The Executive Branch has been the focus of most of the discussion of whether evidentiary privileges should be created to protect confidential communications within the government. But see United States v. Gillock, 445 U.S. 360 (1980) (holding that there is no privilege for state legislator in federal prosecution). The term *executive privilege* includes several different categories of privileges for governmental secrets. First, the state secrets privilege protects military, diplomatic, or sensitive national security secrets. Second, the qualified presidential communications privilege protects confidential conversations between the president and the president's advisers (e.g., the members of the cabinet). Last, there are privileges to protect a wide range of official information, such as law enforcement files and governmental agency deliberations.

a. State Secrets Privilege

The state secrets privilege protects against the disclosure of highly secret military and diplomatic information. Here the concern is that the release of such information might endanger the public or harm the nation. The privilege has protected such information as FBI activities, see In re United States, 872 F.2d 472 (D.C. Cir.), *cert. dismissed sub nom.* United States v. Albertson, 493 U.S. 960 (1989); missile technology, see Bentzlin v. Hughes Aircraft Co., 833 F. Supp. 1486 (C.D. Cal. 1993); radar system capabilities, see Zuckerbraun v. General Dynamics Corp., 935 F.2d 544 (2d Cir. 1991); and diplomatic conversations, see Attorney Gen. v. Irish People, Inc., 502 F. Supp. 63, 64-65 (D.D.C. 1980).

In United States v. Reynolds, 345 U.S. 1 (1953), the Supreme Court provided a thorough examination of the state secrets privilege. According to the court, the government is the exclusive holder of the privilege. The privilege must be formally invoked by the head of the government department concerned, after "actual personal consideration" by that executive official. In deciding on a claim of the privilege, the standard to be applied is whether there is a reasonable danger that disclosure will harm national security. If the reasonable danger standard is met, the privilege is absolute. The court noted that "even the most compelling necessity cannot overcome the claim of privilege if the court is ultimately satisfied that military secrets are at stake." In Black v. United States, 62 F.3d 1115 (8th Cir. 1995), the court dismissed a harassment suit against federal intelligence agencies where litigation would necessarily breach the state secrets privilege. Black was an electrical engineer who had government security clearance to work on defense projects with various contractors. After a Soviet mathematician at a lecture in Zurich allegedly asked him suspiciously intrusive questions, Black reported the contact to the U.S. Consulate and soon thereafter his security clearance was "unplugged." He claimed that he was the victim of harassment and psychological attack and sued the United States for the actions of the CIA, FBI, and Department of State. R. James Woolsey, Director of the CIA, formally invoked the state secret privilege and asserted that litigation of the claim would result in the disclosure of highly sensitive names, dates, and locations of U.S. counterintelligence operations. The lower court reviewed the documents *in camera* and dismissed all of the claims. The Court of Appeals affirmed the decision, according the "utmost deference" to the executive's determination of the impact of disclosure.

Whether the privilege is claimed in a criminal or civil proceeding, the denial of discovery will dramatically affect the opposing party's preparation of the case. In both criminal and civil proceedings, the court may order dismissal as it did in *Black* or other less drastic relief, such as striking particular testimony of a witness or finding against the government on a particular issue.

The Supreme Court's decision in General Dynamics Corp. v. United States, 563 U.S. 478 (2011), provides a vivid illustration for how the state secrets privilege works. After General Dynamics fell behind the agreed-upon schedule for developing a stealth aircraft for the Navy, the government rescinded the agreement that promised the company $4.8 billion and demanded the return of approximately $1.35 billion it paid the company for work it never accepted. The company argued that the government failed to share with it its "superior knowledge" about how to design the aircraft. The government for its part refused to disclose relevant information because it was a top military secret. As a result, the trial court was unable to adjudicate the company's facially plausible affirmative defense of "superior knowledge." The Supreme Court decided that neither party should be granted relief. The company should receive no further payments under its $4.8 billion contract with the government, and the government should not recover from the company $1.35 billion in restitution. As Justice Scalia explained, "Neither the question whether [the company was] in default nor the question whether performance of the entire contract would have left [it] with a loss can be judicially determined because of the valid assertion of the state-secret privilege." For that reason, "We leave the parties where they are."

The Classified Information Procedures Act (CIPA), 18 U.S.C. app. §§1-16 (2013), grants statutory recognition to the state secrets privilege in the area of criminal proceedings. The Act sets forth detailed procedures governing a criminal defendant's efforts to reveal or to obtain discovery of classified information and was passed by Congress in 1980 to address the defense tactic known as "graymail." The defendant who threatens to disclose classified information creates a dilemma for the government. It must either dismiss the charges against the defendant or allow the disclosure of sensitive information. The goal of CIPA is to provide pretrial procedures for the resolution of discovery and admissibility issues.

CIPA primarily functions in two ways. Section 5 requires defendants to notify the government of its intention to disclose classified information in the course of presenting a defense. Pretrial hearings on discovery and admissibility of evidence are governed by §§4 and 6. Section 4 expands on Federal Rule of Criminal Procedure 16 and permits courts to authorize the United States to delete specific classified information from documents, to substitute a summary of the information, or to substitute a statement admitting relevant facts that the classified information would tend to prove. Section 6 provides a pretrial hearing to determine relevance, §6(a), and a pretrial hearing to determine whether the substitutions offered in lieu of the classified documents provide the defendant with "substantially the same ability to make his defense as would disclosure of the specific classified information," §6(c).

"Graymail" may not be just a sneaky defense tactic but may be the result of legitimate efforts to prepare a criminal defense. Several high-profile defendants have raised the question of the constitutionality of CIPA because of the limitations it places on defendants' ability to launch effective defenses. In United States v. North, 708 F. Supp. 399 (D.D.C. 1988), the defendant, Oliver North, filed a written statement of relevant and material testimony he expected to disclose during the course of the trial for the court to consider in a pretrial hearing. North later objected to the fulfillment of the CIPA provision requiring the disclosure of the statement to the Independent Counsel on the grounds that it would violate his Fifth and Sixth Amendment rights. The court held that the Fifth Amendment due process claim was meritless because modern litigation involves extensive pretrial discovery and additionally, North had been given access to much of the government's information and witnesses. Similarly, the Sixth Amendment right to effective assistance of counsel argument was found by the court to be unpersuasive because North would still be able to call or not to call witnesses, and the tactical disadvantage of minimizing surprise would be "slight." The court held CIPA to be facially constitutional.

Since *North*, courts have consistently upheld the constitutionality of CIPA against arguments asserting the violation of due process, the Fifth Amendment privilege against self-incrimination and the right to remain silent unless and until one decides to testify, the Fifth and Sixth Amendment rights to testify in one's own defense, and the Sixth Amendment right to cross-examine witnesses. See United States v. McVeigh, 923 F. Supp. 1310 (D. Colo. 1996) (finding it unnecessary to reach the issue of the constitutionality of CIPA); United States v. Wen Ho Lee, 90 F. Supp. 2d 1324 (D.N.M. 2000) (denying the defendant's motion to find §§5 and 6 of CIPA unconstitutional); United States v. Bin Laden, 2001 U.S. Dist. LEXIS 719 (S.D.N.Y. Mar. 20, 2001) (denying the defendant's motion to find CIPA unconstitutional as it applies to him). For contemporary discussions of the privilege and empirical data regarding its use, see Daniel R. Cassman, Note, Keep it Secret, Keep it Safe: An Empirical Analysis of the State Secrets Doctrine, 67 Stan. L. Rev. 1173 (2015) (finding that post 9/11 the state secrets privilege has been invoked more frequently than before, but courts continued to uphold and deny it at roughly the same rate); Laura K. Donohue, The Shadow of State Secrets, 159 U. Pa. L. Rev. 77 (2010) (identifying and analyzing new graymail strategies followed by companies litigating against the government).

b. Presidential Communications Privilege

President Jefferson first sought to maintain the confidentiality of presidential communications in United States v. Burr, 25 F. Cas. 187 (C.C. Dist. Va. 1807) when Chief Justice Marshall issued two subpoenas for letters written by General Wilkinson to the President. Jefferson asserted an exclusive right to the papers and resisted the subpoenas. Since that time, several presidents have invoked the privilege but United States v. Nixon provided the first clear description of its parameters.

In United States v. Nixon, 418 U.S. 683 (1974), the Supreme Court addressed whether a privilege exists to protect confidential communications between the president and the president's close advisors. President Nixon raised three claims: that the separation of powers doctrine precludes judicial review of a President's claim of privilege; that the Constitution provides an absolute privilege of confidentiality for all presidential communications; and alternatively, that the "presumptive" privilege for presidential communications should prevail over the subpoena in question. The Court, quoting Marbury v. Madison, reaffirmed that "it is the providence of this Court 'to say what the law is' with respect to the claim of privilege presented in this case," thus asserting the appropriateness of judicial review. The Court went on to recognize a constitutionally based privilege derived from the separation of powers, but noted that the presidential communications privilege is a qualified one. The Court stated that the privilege "must yield to the demonstrated, specific, need for evidence in a pending criminal trial."[76] In recognizing the qualified privilege, the Court noted that the presidential need for confidentiality justified a presumptive privilege for presidential communications. The burden rests with the person seeking discovery of the information to rebut the presumption of privilege. Moreover, in conducting an *in camera* inspection, the trial court must use "scrupulous protection" to ensure that presidential communications that are not relevant or admissible are not disclosed. The privilege may be stronger in civil proceedings. In Cheney v. U.S. Dist. Court for Dist. of Columbia, 542 U.S. 367 (2004), a case involving the assertion of executive privilege to prevent disclosure of the names of certain de facto members of the National Energy Policy Development Group, the court stated that "[t]he need for information for use in civil cases, while far from negligible, does not share the urgency or significance of the criminal subpoena requests in Nixon." Id. at 2589. See Mark J. Rozell, Symposium: Executive Privilege and the Clinton Presidency, 8 Wm. & Mary Bill of Rts. J. 541 (2000) (arguing that presidents should use the power only for the most compelling reasons and not to protect information that is merely embarrassing or politically damaging, and proposing that each administration adopt guidelines for its members with formal procedures for handling and resolving executive privilege issues).

---

76. Three years later the Court again declined to permit the executive privilege to prevent the release of information where an ex-president sought to invoke the privilege "against the very Executive Branch in whose name the privilege is invoked." Nixon v. Administrator of General Services, 433 U.S. 425 (1977) (former president directed to deliver presidential papers and tape recordings to an official of the Executive Branch for the creation of public access under the Presidential Recordings and Materials Preservation Act, held to be facially constitutional and not violative of the presidential privilege doctrine).

In re Sealed Case, 121 F.3d 729 (D.C. Cir. 1997), provided the District of Columbia Court of Appeals with the opportunity to determine how far beyond direct communications with the President the presidential communications privilege might reach. As part of a grand jury investigation of former Secretary of Agriculture Mike Espy, the Office of the Independent Counsel tried to compel performance of a subpoena *duces tecum* issued by the grand jury and served on the Counsel to the President. The White House provided many of the requested documents but withheld 84 as privileged. The court held that the presidential privilege extends "down the line" from the President to his aides and advisors whenever they are in the "course of preparing advice" for the President even when they are not communicating directly with the President. The court found that all of the 84 documents—authored by White House Counsel, Deputy and Associate White House Counsel, legal externs to the White House Counsel's office, the Chief of Staff, the Press Secretary, and even three "no authored" documents—were privileged. The Office of the Independent Counsel, however, was given the opportunity on remand to demonstrate "sufficient need" in order to overcome the presidential communications privilege. The court sought to strike the "appropriate balance between openness and informed presidential deliberation."[77] In In re Sealed Case, 148 F.3d 1073 (D.C. Cir. 1998), *cert. denied sub nom.* Rubin v. United States 525 U.S. 990 (1998), the Government sought to extend the executive privilege to create a "protective function privilege" that would shield Secret Service agents from testifying. The Secret Service resisted the Independent Counsel's subpoena of 33 Secret Service officers to testify about their knowledge of President Clinton's affair with White House intern Monica Lewinsky. The Secret Service proposed an "absolute privilege that would preclude the OIC from compelling any testimony regarding information learned by Secret Service agents and officers while performing protective functions in physical proximity to the President where the information would tend to reveal the President's contemporaneous activities."[78] The court considered the three factors detailed by the Supreme Court in *Jaffee* (page 972, supra). It found that the privilege is not based in federal law[79] and Secret Service officers have testified previously;[80] the privilege is not supported by state precedents though the same need would presumably exist for state governors; and while there is a strong public policy interest in ensuring the safety of the President, the President will not resist the closeness of his protectors because of his own interest in his safety and

77. See Recent Case, 111 Harv. L. Rev. 861 (1998) (arguing that the court failed to recognize the difference in the privilege for the President and his advisors and disregarded other protections, such as the deliberative process privilege and statutory exceptions to the Freedom of Information Act, which would preserve the effectiveness of the executive branch).

78. In re Grand Jury Proceedings, 1998 WL 272884 (D.D.C. May 22, 1998).

79. There has been discussion in the Judiciary Committees of both the United States House of Representatives and the Senate about a potential protective function privilege. Senator Leahy introduced the Secret Service Protective Privilege Act of 1999, 106 S. 1360, which would prohibit testimony by Secret Service personnel or former personnel that was acquired during the performance of the protective function in physical proximity to the protectee. It was referred to the Senate Committee on the Judiciary but a report has not yet been issued.

80. See In re Grand Jury Proceedings, 1998 WL 272884, at *3 (D.D.C. May 22, 1998) discussing President Nixon's taping system and John Hinckley's attempted assassination of President Reagan where the Secret Service did not assert a protective function privilege.

because he is required by law to accept protection.[81] The court held that the absence of federal and state precedents and the Secret Service's failure to establish the need for the protective function privilege prevented its creation by the judiciary at this time.

c. Official Information (Deliberative Process) Privilege

The official information privilege exists to protect government deliberative processes and provides a limited executive privilege for executive officers other than the President. Not surprisingly, the rationale is that compelled disclosure of such communications would inhibit the exchange of opinions and advice among executive officials, and thereby impair the decisionmaking process. A related justification for the privilege is that the judiciary is not authorized to probe the mental processes of an executive or administrative officer. In re Franklin National Bank Securities Litig., 478 F. Supp. 577, 580-581 (E.D.N.Y. 1979). The privilege is the government's. Examples are government agency policy deliberations and law enforcement investigatory files. Both Proposed FRE 509 and the exemption provisions of the Freedom of Information Act, 5 U.S.C. §552 (1994), address the need for protection of such official information.

A qualified privilege protecting official information has been widely accepted by the federal courts. See, e.g., Kelly v. City of San Jose, 114 F.R.D. 653 (N.D. Cal. 1987); United States v. Board of Educ. of City of Chicago, 610 F. Supp. 695 (N.D. Ill. 1985); Kinoy v. Mitchell, 67 F.R.D. 1 (S.D.N.Y. 1975). In In re "Agent Orange" Product Liability Litig., 97 F.R.D. 427, 434 (E.D.N.Y. 1983), the court described the limited scope of the privilege:

> [The privilege] applies only to material reflecting [the] deliberative process—evaluations, expressions of opinions, and recommendations on policy matters. . . . Raw data and factual findings do not fall within the scope of the privilege because disclosures of facts, as opposed to opinions, would not hinder candor among government officials.

The D.C. Court of Appeals in In re Sealed Case, 121 F.3d 729 (1997), reiterated this requirement that the material be "deliberative" and not merely factual and also emphasized that it must be "predecisional." Furthermore, the court noted that the privilege is not absolute and may be overcome by a showing that the need for evidence in the specific case outweighs the harm that would result from disclosure. Quoting In re Subpoena Served Upon the Comptroller of the Currency, 967 F.2d 630 (D.C. Cir. 1992), the court described the appropriate test:

> "Each time [the deliberative process privilege] is asserted the district court must undertake a fresh balancing of the competing interests," taking into account factors such as "the relevance of the evidence," "the availability of other evidence," "the seriousness of the litigation," "the role of the government," and the "possibility of future timidity by government employees."

In Dellwood Farms v. Cargill, Inc., 128 F.3d 1122 (7th Cir. 1997), private civil plaintiffs sought materials gathered by the Department of Justice for use in criminal investigations. The FBI had been investigating charges of price fixing by Archer Daniels

---

81. 18 U.S.C. §3056(a) mandates the protection of the President.

Midland and other agricultural producers. The FBI recorded more than 150 hours of conversations within ADM and between ADM and its competitors. The government, without seeking any confidentiality agreement, played some of the recordings to the law firm representing ADM's outside directors to induce ADM to plead guilty to the criminal antitrust offenses. The plaintiffs in this civil case subpoenaed the tapes in the hope that they contained evidence of illegal conspiracy. The Department of Justice attempted to block the subpoena with the law enforcement investigatory privilege. The court held that the subpoena should be quashed because, though the privilege is not absolute and can be overridden through a showing of need, there ought to be a "pretty strong presumption" against lifting the privilege. It reasoned that crime investigation is the duty of the Executive Branch and it is inappropriate for the courts to be "thrust too deeply" into the process. Since the Freedom of Information Act would make the information available after the criminal trial is over, the court said, the civil suit could be postponed to await its release.

The plaintiffs additionally raised the issue of waiver since the Department of Justice had voluntarily played the recordings for ADM's lawyers. The court found that there had been a mere "selective waiver," described as the situation where, "having voluntarily disclosed privileged information to one person, the party who made the disclosure asserts the privilege against another person who wants the information." The court acknowledged that the government should have been more careful and obtained a protective order against further disclosure, as is normally required in selective disclosure cases. This error, however, the court said, should not be punished too harshly because there was no deliberate waiver of the privilege; to withhold the tapes from the plaintiffs and interference with criminal investigation would be an "excessive punishment."

The Supreme Court finally addressed the relationship between the official government information privilege and the Freedom of Information Act in United States v. Weber Aircraft Corp., 465 U.S. 792 (1984). The engine of an Air Force aircraft had failed, and the pilot was severely injured when he was ejected from the plane. He sued several entities responsible for the design and manufacture of his plane's ejection equipment. After the crash, the Air Force conducted both a "collateral investigation," designed to preserve evidence for use in whatever claims may ensue, and a "safety investigation," designed solely to permit corrective action to be taken in order to reduce the risk of similar occurrences. During safety investigations, witnesses are not sworn and are promised complete confidentiality. Lower courts had previously held the results of such investigations to be privileged from discovery, a holding the Supreme Court embraced. The plaintiff thus attempted to obtain the same information through a FOIA request, to which the Court responded:

> [R]espondents' contention that they can obtain through the FOIA material that is normally privileged would create an anomaly in that the FOIA could be used to supplement civil discovery. We have consistently rejected such a construction of the FOIA. We do not think that Congress could have intended that the weighty policies underlying discovery privileges could be so easily circumvented. [Id. at 801-802.]

After the passage of the Freedom of Information Act in 1967, many private litigants sought to use the new act rather than the normal rules of discovery to obtain information from the government in judicial proceedings. In NLRB v. Sears, Roebuck & Co., 421 U.S. 132 (1975), however, the Court examined the relationship between Exemption 5 of the FOIA and governmental privileges. The Court expressly found that Exception 5 contains a deliberative process privilege and a work product privilege and implied that a governmental attorney-client privilege should be recognized as well.

The Freedom of Information Act lists what each governmental agency must make available to the public and how the information is to be made accessible. There are several exceptions that allow agencies to maintain the confidentiality of some materials including those containing: matters of national defense or foreign policy, internal personnel rules, privileged or confidential trade secrets or financial information, geological or geophysical information and data concerning wells, and records or information compiled for law enforcement purposes to the extent that disclosure would interfere with enforcement, deprive a person of the right to a fair trial, constitute an unwarranted invasion of personal privacy, reveal the identity of a confidential source, endanger the life or physical safety of any individual, or disclose techniques and procedures for law enforcement investigations or prosecutions.

Exception 5 to the FOIA, which excludes inter-agency or intra-agency communications, has allowed agencies to resist disclosure of information by claiming the deliberative process privilege. The Supreme Court defined the deliberative process as covering documents "reflecting advisory opinions, recommendations and deliberations comprising part of a process by which governmental decisions and policies are formulated." NLRB v. Sears, Roebuck & Co., 421 U.S. 132, 150 (1975) (quoting Carl Zeiss Stiftung v. V.E.B. Carl Zeiss, Jena, 40 F.R.D. 318, 324 (D.C. 1966)).

In Department of the Interior and Bureau of Indian Affairs v. Klamath Water Users Protective Association, 532 U.S. 1 (2001), the Supreme Court addressed for the first time the question of whether the deliberative process privilege could be extended to cover communications between government agencies and "outsiders." The Klamath Water Users, an association of water users in the Klamath River Basin, filed requests under the FOIA for communications between the Bureau of Indian Affairs and the Native American Tribes of the area, regarding the allocation of water. The Bureau had consulted with the Tribes on the proposed Klamath Project Operation Plan in efforts to assess the likely impact of the plan. The Bureau sought to invoke the deliberative process privilege of Exception 5 to resist the plaintiffs' request for information. The Court acknowledged that courts have extended the privilege to communications between governmental agencies and outside consultants[82] but rejected the Bureau's portrayal of the Tribes as filling this sort of role. The Tribes, the Court found, had communicated with the Bureau with their own interests in mind and had acted as "self-advocates at the expense of others seeking benefits inadequate to satisfy everyone."

---

82. See, e.g., Hoover v. Dept. of Interior, 611 F.2d 1132, 1138 (5th Cir. 1980) ("the government may deem it necessary to seek the objective opinion of outside experts rather than rely solely on the opinions of government appraisers"); Lead Industries Assn. v. OSHA, 610 F.2d 70, 83 (2d Cir. 1979) (applying Exemption 5 to cover draft reports "prepared by outside consultants who had testified on behalf of the agency rather than agency staff"); Government Land Bank v. GSA, 671 F.2d 663, 665 (5th Cir. 1982) ("Both parties agree that a property appraisal, performed under contract by an independent professional, is an 'intra-agency' document for purposes of the exemption").

The Court thus rejected the intra-agency nature of the communications and held that they could not be exempted from discovery under Exception 5.

In the states, the extent of the protection afforded depends on the type of official information at issue. For example, in the context of government agency deliberations, a majority of states have recognized a qualified privilege based on the federal rule. In the context of law enforcement records, some states have enacted statutory privileges to protect the information, while others have conferred some level of protection through the more general "classified" official information statutes. Where a disclosure statute such as a state Freedom of Information Act is in effect, the statute takes precedence in determining the scope of protection.

In order to prevail on a claim of the official information privilege, the agency official asserting the privilege typically must specifically identify what government interest or privacy interest would be threatened by disclosure and describe how disclosure, even if made under a protective order, would create a substantial risk of harm. Chism v. County of San Bernadino, 159 F.R.D. 531, 534 (C.D. Cal. 1994). In *Chism*, the court held that a deputy sheriff's declaration failed to show that documents produced during an internal review of an allegedly unjustified shooting were protected by the official information privilege. The court said that a general assertion that the police department's internal investigatory system would be harmed by disclosure of its documents was insufficient. This information was presumptively discoverable because information in police files is often developed closer in time to the events in question, and therefore substantially comparable evidence is not available from other sources.

The official information privilege often arises in cases involving alleged violations of civil rights by police officers under 42 U.S.C. §1983 where plaintiffs want to discover the personnel records of police officer defendants. Despite the fact that many states have statutes protecting the confidentiality of these records, see, e.g., Kansas Open Records Act, Kan. Stat. Ann. §45-221(4) (2000); Cal. Penal Code §§832.7, 832.8 (Supp. 2005), and despite the fact that there are comparable confidentiality provisions for federal officers, 5 U.S.C. §552(b)(6) and (b)(7)(c), federal courts have been reluctant to recognize a privilege for police officer personnel records in §1983 cases. See, e.g., Mason v. Stock, 869 F. Supp. 828 (D. Kan. 1994); see also Welsh v. City and County of San Francisco, 887 F. Supp. 1293 (N.D. Cal. 1995).

8. Miscellaneous Privileges

While the material above has covered the major privileges, there are in fact numerous other privileges found in case law and state statutes. This means that lawyers have to research, and research carefully, to see what privileges apply in their jurisdiction or that may be idiosyncratic to their case. Some state statutes affect the breadth of the otherwise general privileges discussed above. For example, statutes passed by some states to address domestic abuse victims effectively reduce the scope of the marital communication and physician-patient privileges that would otherwise be applicable. See, e.g., C.R.S. 18-6-401.1 (2009) ("The statutory privilege between the victim-patient and his physician and between the husband and the wife shall not be available for excluding or refusing testimony in any prosecution of an act of child abuse."). Other statutes are passed to reach discrete areas that may not otherwise be covered by general privileges. For example, Illinois protects information disclosed to a licensed genetic counselor, 225 Ill. Comp. Stat. 135/90 (2010); Delaware recognizes a specific type of self-evaluative privilege for hospitals, 16 Del. C. §1010A (2010); Connecticut privileges information gathered by mediators in labor disputes, Conn. Gen. Stat. §31-96 (2010); and Georgia does not require information gathered during the licensing stage of blasting operations to be turned over, Ga. Code Ann. §25-8-11 (2010). Case law similarly affects the privileges available in any jurisdiction. Two examples that have been accepted in some jurisdictions, and of which lawyers should be aware, are the common-interest or joint-defense privilege—protecting communications focused on creating a defense strategy with others who are similarly situated—and the absolute privilege protecting information disclosed in judicial proceedings. Many more privileges are potentially available in any litigation; an attorney is well advised to check local statutes and case law before disclosing any document.

PROBLEMS

12.29. Michael McKinley is being prosecuted in Ireland for directing terrorism. He has asked the district court for an order to produce a tape recording that he believes will help him in cross-examining David Rogers, a key prosecution witness. The tape recordings are held by journalists who conducted interviews with Rogers for a contracted biography that they are writing. Rogers has not objected to the discovery, but the journalists have challenged, asserting the journalist's privilege. What result?

12.30. Ryan has lived with his grandmother for 15 years, all but a few months of his life, and she has always supported him financially and otherwise. Ryan has been charged with a crime and the prosecution is seeking to elicit the testimony of his grandmother about his statements to her following the alleged crime. Ryan's defense attorney objects on the ground that such statements were confidential and should be protected from disclosure under the parent-child privilege that is recognized in the state. Should the court permit testimony relative to statements made by Ryan to his grandmother?

12.31. All 230 persons aboard TWA flight 800 were killed when it exploded over the Atlantic Ocean on July 17th, 1996. The United States salvaged much of the wreckage and secured it in a building in Calverton, New York, to be used in the investigation of the accident. Sanders, an investigative journalist, pursued the hypothesis that a missile had caused the explosion and spoke with Captain Terrell, a senior 747 pilot with TWA who was involved in the investigation. Captain Terrell told Sanders that a "reddish" substance had been found on some of the seats that might be residue from an explosive. He later provided Sanders with a small portion of the substance that had been removed from the wreckage. Sanders wrote a book entitled The Downing of TWA Flight 800 in which he reported that this "reddish" substance tested consistent with the presence of solid rocket fuel. The FBI began investigating Sanders for violation of 49 U.S.C. §1155(b), which bans the unauthorized removal of "a part of a civilian aircraft involved in an accident." The government offered Sanders a nonprosecution agreement in exchange for the name of his confidential source but Sanders refused. After the government discovered his identity through other sources, Captain Terrell testified against Sanders in return for a reduction of his offense to a misdemeanor. Sanders argues that the journalist's privilege bars government coercion to disclose news sources and thus urges the court to use a balancing test weighing "the governmental interest served by prosecution" against "the detrimental impact of permitting such a prosecution to be used as a means of coercing disclosure of a journalist's source." Should the court hold that the journalist's privilege prevents prosecution from being used in this way?

12.32. Dr. Tambone has filed a complaint against Memorial Hospital for restraint of trade in violation of federal and state antitrust laws. He alleges that the physicians of Memorial Hospital have used the peer review and disciplinary process to exclude him from its medical staff, effectively destroying his practice. Dr. Tambone claims that he was the victim of a sham disciplinary proceeding that was used as a means of implementing the alleged restraint of trade. To prove this allegation he has sought discovery regarding the hospital's treatment of other doctors in comparable disciplinary proceedings. Can the hospital resist disclosure of the information under a peer review privilege?

12.33. The Federal Death Penalty Act of 1994 authorizes the death penalty for more than 40 crimes and sets the procedure for seeking the death penalty in federal cases. An Attorney General's Death Penalty Committee (DPC) reviews each case and conducts a meeting where the defendant's attorney may try to persuade the government not to seek the death penalty. The DPC then assists in advising the Attorney General as to the ultimate decision whether to pursue the death penalty. Defendant Jacobo is considered by the government to be a member of the "Mexican Mafia" and has been charged with murder in the furtherance of racketeering, an offence covered by the Federal Death Penalty Act. Jacobo has sought to discover information that might tend to mitigate the sentence in his case, including information from the DPC meetings and its completed "death penalty evaluation form." The government objects to the discovery request based on the deliberative process privilege. Should the court allow it to withhold this information from Jacobo?

12.34. USAID is a federal agency that oversees development projects under the government's foreign assistance program. USAID was involved in building a water treatment facility in Egypt, financing the project to be carried out by an Egyptian government agency. USAID hired a U.S. engineering firm, CDM, to design the project, while the construction contract was awarded to a joint venture (JV) between two companies. Under the contract, the builders deal directly with the host country, but USAID retains approval rights for significant changes and additional compensation.

The JV requested additional funds, but USAID refused after CDM assessed that the request should be much lower, and the parties have not been able to agree. USAID urged CDM to hire a consultant to evaluate the challenges to settlement. CDM hired Richard J. Roy, providing that a report of his findings was to be given only to USAID and the Egyptian government agency, without disclosure to other parties.

A Freedom of Information Act (FOIA) request was filed with USAID on behalf of the JV members for documents related to the dispute, including the Roy Report, which USAID refused to provide, arguing that the report was attorney work-product and was privileged under the attorney-client privilege. A FOIA lawsuit was filed in federal court alleging that USAID unlawfully withheld the report. What result?

ASSESSMENTS

A-12.1. Attorney-Client Privilege, FRE 502.   Pharmaceutical company Safe-Med (SM) defends against a products liability suit in a New State court. During discovery, SM agreed to give the plaintiff a copy of a letter from the company's general counsel. This letter urges the company to discontinue the production of a certain drug. In a parallel diversity suit before federal court, other plaintiffs demand the discovery of all letters and memos with regard to the drug's production forwarded to SM by its general counsel. The plaintiffs base this request on SM's waver of the attorney-client privilege under New State law. The federal court should deny this request. TRUE or FALSE?

A-12.2. Attorney-Client Privilege.   Attorney A represents client C in a tax fraud case. A asks a certified public accountant, CPA, to prepare a report about C's financial activities and their implications for the trial. Subsequently, the prosecution subpoenas CPA and demands the production of the report. The prosecution also demands that CPA testify about her conversations with A. All this information is privileged. TRUE or FALSE?

A-12.3. Attorney-Client Privilege.   By suing an attorney for malpractice, the attorney's client waives the attorney-client privilege with respect to all of her relevant communications with the attorney. TRUE or FALSE?

A-12.4. Attorney-Client Privilege.   When a convicted defendant files a habeas petition alleging ineffective assistance of counsel, he can keep the conversations he had with his trial attorney fully confidential. TRUE or FALSE?

A-12.5. Physician-Patient Privilege.   Federal law recognizes a qualified physician-patient privilege. Communications between a physician and his patient are privileged in principle, but the court can remove the privilege and order disclosure if the interests of justice so require. TRUE or FALSE?

A-12.6. Attorney-Client Privilege.   Shortly after a meeting with his attorney on a corporate matter, Jim was arrested for driving while intoxicated. At his trial, the prosecutor calls Jim's attorney to the stand and asks her whether Jim appeared drunk during the meeting. Jim objects to this question.

This objection should be:

A   sustained on irrelevancy grounds.
B   sustained, based on the attorney-client privilege.
C   sustained for another reason.
D   overruled.

A-12.7. Spousal Privileges.   Steve stands trial for drug dealing. The prosecution subpoenas Steve's wife, Mary, to testify that (1) She saw Steve hiding large quantities of cocaine at the spouses' house; and that (2) Steve asked her to deliver the cocaine to Fred, and she did so. Steve objects to Mary's testimony.

This objection should –

A   succeed as to (1), but fail as to (2).
B   succeed as to (2), but fail as to (1).
C   succeed on both counts.
D   fail on both counts.

A-12.8. Spousal Privileges. David Doe is tried for armed robbery of the Consolidated Mutual Funds Bank (CMFB). He pleaded not guilty. His former wife, Wanda, testifies for the prosecution that at the time that she and David were still married to each other, David told her about his intention to rob CMFB.

Wanda's testimony is:

A   admissible, but privileged.
B   not privileged and admissible.
C   both privileged and inadmissible.
D   not privileged, but inadmissible.

A-12.9. Attorney-Client Privilege.   Same facts as in A-12.9. David's former attorney, Axel, testifies that at the time that he still represented David in connection with the case, David advanced part of his fee, $9,000, with $100 bills. Axel also testifies that he kept those bills and identified them in front of the judge and the jury. The bills were admitted into evidence over David's objection after the prosecutors told the judge that they will adduce evidence showing that the bills belonged to CMFB.

Axel's testimony is:

A   admissible, but privileged.
B   not privileged and admissible.
C   both privileged and inadmissible.
D   not privileged, but inadmissible.

A-12.10. Mental Therapist-Patient Privilege.   Bystander B was caught in crossfire between FBI officers and drug dealers. By mistake, officer Doe fired at and killed B. B's widow, W, files a wrongful death action against the United States pursuant to the Federal Tort Claims Act. She discovers that officer Doe had several meetings with C, FBI's psychological therapist. Subsequently, officer Doe was killed in another FBI operation. W calls C to testify about those meetings. C and the United States contend that the meetings are privileged.

A   the meetings are privileged, and the court has no power to remove the privilege.

B   in principle, the meetings are privileged, but the court can remove the privilege in the interests of justice.

C   after Doe's death, the meetings are not privileged.

D   the meetings are not and have never been privileged.

A-12.11. State Secrets Privilege. Orr files a $12 million suit against the United States. The suit is based on a written agreement that promises Orr $15 million in exchange for certain spying activities in a foreign country hostile to the United States. The United States argues that Orr is not entitled to any payment pursuant to the agreement because he failed to deliver the promised information to the government. The United States also files a counterclaim against Orr demanding that he return $3 million it paid him upfront. Subsequently, the government invokes the state secrets privilege with respect to the information that Orr was supposed to deliver.

A   The government was not entitled to invoke the privilege after filing its counterclaim.

B   The government was entitled to invoke the privilege, but the court can set it aside at its discretion.

C   The government was entitled to invoke the privilege, but the court might draw adverse inferences against it in deciding whether Orr breached the agreement.

D   The court must dismiss both Orr's suit and the government counterclaim.

ANSWERS

A.12.1. TRUE. FRE 502(c) prescribes for circumstances like these that the rule most protective of the attorney-client privilege will apply and that disclosure of a single privileged document will not be interpreted as a comprehensive transactional waiver of the privilege. Because the waiver was document specific, and because it was made to the benefit of a different party in a different proceeding, the plaintiffs will not be able to successfully claim, pursuant to FRE 502(a)(1), (2), and (3), that they are entitled to see the entire correspondence between SM and its attorney.

A.12.2. TRUE. CPA's information is protected by the work-product doctrine.

A.12.3. TRUE. This is one of the instances of an implicit waiver of the attorney-client privilege with regard to all information pertaining to the quality of the attorney's work for the client.

A.12.4. FALSE. This is one of the instances of an implicit waiver of the attorney-client privilege. By raising an ineffective-assistance claim, the defendant waives the privilege with regard to all information pertaining to how effectively he was represented by his counsel during trial. The defendant cannot claim ineffective assistance while hiding behind the privilege.

A-12.5. TRUE. This qualified privilege exists under the Health Insurance Portability and Accountability Act, see page 971.

A-12.6. The best answer is **D.** The defendant's attorney was requested to testify about her client's appearance without revealing any communication between the two. A client's appearance is not protected by the attorney-client privilege. Hence, answer B is wrong. Answer A is wrong, too, because the attorney's testimony was relevant to the charges. Answer C alludes to the possibility that the defendant's attorney was asked to provide inadmissible opinion evidence. But testifying about whether a person you saw appeared drunk only requires common sense, and so the attorney's testimony was admissible under FRE 701. She was a regular percipient witness, and for that reason Answer C is false as well.

A-12.7. The best answer is **D.** A criminal defendant's spouse is entitled not to testify against him, but under federal law, this privilege does not belong to the defendant. Instead, it belongs to the testifying spouse who has the unilateral power to decide whether s/he will testify or not. In the case at bar, Steve's wife, Mary, chose to testify against him, and Steve has no say on that matter. He can still invoke the marital communications privilege that protects all confidential communications between married spouses. This privilege belongs to both spouses, each of whom can veto the other spouse's testimony. Here, however, the first part of Mary's testimony was about her observations, rather than communications with Steve. As for the testimony's second part, Steve's and Mary's confidential communication promoted a joint criminal goal, which triggers the "joint criminal enterprise" exception to the privilege. Also, Mary was entitled not to testify on the self-incrimination privilege grounds, but that privilege was hers, not Steve's, and so she could waive it. For these reasons, Steve's objection fails on both counts.

A-12.8. The best answer is **A.** Wanda's testimony about David's incriminating statement was admissible under the party-admission exception to the hearsay rule, FRE 801(d)(2)(A). However, this testimony falls under the marital confidential communications privilege, which can be invoked by any of the spouses. The "joint criminal enterprise" exception to that privilege does not apply here because Wanda didn't join David's criminal enterprise. Her testimony, therefore, is admissible but privileged.

A-12.9. The best answer is **B.** Axel's fee and the bills he received from David are not protected by the attorney-client privilege because they are neither a communication between an attorney and his client nor an attorney's work-product. The bills also constitute evidence, which the privilege doesn't protect. Because those bills are relevant to the accusations and Axel properly identified them pursuant to FRE 901(A), they are admissible.

A-12.10. The best answer is **A.** The Supreme Court made the mental therapist-patient privilege absolute: see Jaffee v. Redmond, 518 U.S. 1 (1996); page 972.

Hence, as under the attorney-client privilege, the "once privileged, always privileged" principle applies here as well.

A-12.11. The best answer is **D.** This question is modeled on the Supreme Court's decision, General Dynamics Corp. v. United States, 563 U.S. 478 (2011), discussed supra on page 1010, that dismissed the government's and the contractor's mutual claims. The government's rightful invocation of the state secrets privilege hides crucial evidence and renders the parties' dispute nonjusticiable.

TABLE OF CASES

Principal cases are indicated by italics.

TABLE OF AUTHORITIES

INDEX